THE
AMERICANA
ANNUAL

1994

GROLIER

AN ENCYCLOPEDIA OF THE EVENTS OF 1993

YEARBOOK OF THE ENCYCLOPEDIA AMERICANA

This annual has been prepared as a yearbook for general encyclopedias.
It is also published as *Encyclopedia Year Book.*

Contents

Feature Articles of the Year

© Christopher Morris/Black Star

© Wally McNamee/Sygma

© AP/Wide World

© Paul Morse/LGI Photo Agency

© Robert Pearcy/Animals Animals

The Alphabetical Section

Entries on the continents, major nations of the world, U.S. states, Canadian provinces, and chief cities will be found under their own alphabetical headings.

A Review of the Year 1993

© AP/Wide World

© Carol Rosegg/Martha Swope

No matter what historians say about 1993, no account of the year will be complete without mention of Nelson Mandela, the president of the African National Congress, and South Africa's President F. W. de Klerk *(at left and right, respectively, top photo, page 6)*; Israeli Prime Minister Yitzhak Rabin; and Palestine Liberation Organization Chairman Yasir Arafat. The former two political opponents will be remembered for winning the 1993 Nobel Peace Prize for their "efforts in dismantling" South Africa's apartheid system. The latter two foes will be recalled for a handshake on the White House lawn as an agreement on interim Palestinian self-rule was signed. Other major 1993 headliners included former Arkansas Gov. Bill Clinton, who probably discovered that running for the U.S. presidency was easier than being the nation's chief executive; Ruth Bader Ginsburg, who became the second woman to join the U.S. Supreme Court; Michael Jordan, who left the basketball court at the height of his career; Toni Morrison, who was the first black woman to be awarded the Nobel Prize in literature; and Norodom Sihanouk *(below)*, who again assumed the throne of Cambodia.

© Jason Bleibtreu/Sygma

The year also witnessed severe fighting in the former Yugoslavia for a third consecutive year; the unsuccessful efforts of UN peacekeepers to capture a Somali warlord, as well as unsuccessful international efforts to restore Jean-Bertrand Aristide to the presidency of Haiti; and the Great Flood of '93 that devastated nine Midwestern U.S. states. In February terrorism struck the United States, with New York City's World Trade Center as the lunchtime target; and in late winter and early spring, U.S. attention turned to Waco, TX, as a 51-day standoff developed between officials and members of the Branch Davidians, led by David Koresh. In Russia, Boris Yeltsin continued to move his country toward capitalism, and a violent struggle developed between forces loyal to the president and those supporting antireform parliamentarians. By year's end, ultranationalists had shown unexpected strength at the polls, while a Yeltsin-backed constitution was endorsed by the electorate. Canada's Liberal Party was returned to power. Also during 1993, the North American Free Trade Agreement (NAFTA) gained approval, and the Maastricht Treaty on European unity became effective. In the United States, First Lady Hillary Rodham Clinton led the Clinton administration's effort to reform the health-care system.

The U.S. Congress passed a deficit-reduction bill and the long-debated Brady gun-control bill. Britain and Ireland signed a pact on Northern Ireland. Unemployment was high in Germany. Japan gained a new princess. The stabbing of tennis star Monica Seles disturbed the sports world. The U.S. Holocaust Museum opened in Washington. The Hubble Space Telescope underwent repair. TV shopping and children's merchandise with a dinosaur theme were new trends. Financially troubled IBM hired a new chairman. Moviegoers were treated to *The Age of Innocence,* and a new version of *My Fair Lady*—starring Richard Chamberlain and Melissa Errico *(page 6)*—arrived on Broadway. Israel and the Vatican established diplomatic relations at year's end.

January

1   Czechoslovakia divides into two separate nations, the Czech Republic and Slovakia.

3   In Moscow, Russia's President Boris Yeltsin and U.S. President George Bush sign START II (the second Strategic Arms Reduction Treaty). The agreement calls for both nations to reduce their long-range nuclear arsenals to about one third of current levels within ten years and entirely eliminates land-based missiles.

© Strong/Sipa

In front of the Capitol's West Front before a crowd of some 250,000 on Jan. 20, 1993, former Arkansas Gov. William Jefferson Clinton was sworn in as 42d president of the United States by Chief Justice William H. Rehnquist, right. *The new chief executive then delivered one of the shorter inaugural addresses in U.S. history. Later, President and Mrs. Clinton,* below, *attended 11 inaugural balls.*

© Larry Downing/Sygma

© P.J. Griffiths/Magnum

5   The first session of the 103d U.S. Congress convenes.

The U.S.-owned oil tanker *Braer* is driven aground by a storm at the tip of the Shetland Islands in the North Sea. A major oil spill results.

6   Rudolf Nureyev, the Russian-born ballet dancer, dies in Paris.

Representatives of the National Football League (NFL) owners and players agree on a new seven-year labor contract that would introduce unrestricted free agency for the players.

8   U.S. President-elect Bill Clinton and Mexico's President Carlos Salinas de Gortari discuss the North American Free Trade Agreement (NAFTA) during a 90-minute meeting in Austin, TX.

13   In response to Iraq's violations of UN Security Council resolutions and allied peacekeeping endeavors, more than 100 U.S., British, and French warplanes attack Iraqi missile batteries and radar stations.

The U.S. Supreme Court rules 6-3 that federal courts cannot invoke a 122-year-old civil-rights law to prohibit antiabortion protesters from blocking access to abortion clinics.

A U.S. Senate select committee on prisoners of war missing in Indochina issues its final report, stating that there is "no compelling evidence" that U.S. prisoners of war still are being held in Indochina.

20   William Jefferson Clinton is inaugurated as 42d president of the United States. Former U.S. Sen. Albert Gore of Tennessee takes the oath as vice-president.

22   The Croatian army undertakes a ground offensive against a Serbian-held enclave near the coast of the Adriatic Sea, ending a year-old UN-supervised cease-fire.

President Clinton agrees to withdraw the nomination of Zoe Baird to be U.S. attorney general. Baird had come under fire for employing two illegal immigrants.

24   Thurgood Marshall, the first black to serve as a justice of the U.S. Supreme Court (1967-91), dies in Bethesda, MD.

25   President Clinton names his wife, Hillary Rodham Clinton, as chair of the President's Task Force on National Health Reform.

In Denmark, Poul Nyrup Rasmussen, a 49-year-old Social Democrat, forms a new government. He succeeds Premier Poul Schlüter, who resigned earlier in the month.

31   The Dallas Cowboys defeat the Buffalo Bills, 52-17, in professional football's Super Bowl XXVII.

February

1   U.S. Secretary of State Warren Christopher announces that he and UN Secretary-General Boutros Boutros-Ghali have agreed that a UN peacekeeping force should replace U.S. forces in Somalia "in the relatively near future."

2   Václav Havel, former president of Czechoslovakia, is inaugurated as president of the Czech Republic.

5   President Clinton signs into law a bill requiring large companies to provide employees with up to 12 weeks of unpaid leave for family and medical purposes.

10   Pope John Paul II concludes an eight-day tour of three African nations—Benin, Uganda, and Sudan.

12   The South African government and the African National Congress (ANC) agree on a transitional "government of national unity" in which both sides would be partners for five years.

© Renato Rotolo/Gamma-Liaison

The World Trade Center, a 16-acre (6.5-ha) complex in lower New York City, was damaged severely and left without electricity after a massive bomb exploded in one of the site's garages on February 26. Six persons were killed and some 1,000 were injured in the terrorist attack; some 50,000 workers and tourists had to be evacuated from the complex.

14 In Cyprus, Glafcos Clerides defeats President George Vassiliou in a runoff presidential election.

15 In Lithuania, Algirdas Brazauskas is declared the winner of the February 14 presidential election.

Michal Kovac, a 62-year-old economist, is chosen president of Slovakia.

17 President Clinton presents his economic program, including tax increases and spending reductions that would total $493 billion over four years, to a joint session of Congress.

Some 275 persons are confirmed dead as an overcrowded ferry sinks west of Port-au-Prince, Haiti.

22 The UN Security Council unanimously approves the formation of an international court to try war crimes that may have been committed in the former Yugoslavia.

24 Canada's Prime Minister Brian Mulroney announces his resignation as leader of the Conservative Party and, as a result, as head of government.

British Prime Minister John Major concludes two days of talks with President Clinton at the White House.

26 Six persons are killed as a massive bomb explodes in a garage below the World Trade Center in New York City.

28 U.S. Air Force planes begin to parachute relief supplies to Muslim towns under siege by Serbian forces in Bosnia-Herzegovina.

March

7 Leaders of eight rival factions in Afghanistan announce a peace agreement intended to end months of fighting for control of Kabul, the capital, and other areas.

Swiss voters approve a referendum to permit casino gambling.

11 Indonesia's President Suharto takes the oath for a sixth consecutive five-year term.

12 Janet Reno, 54-year-old Florida state attorney, is sworn in as attorney general of the United States.

13 A special four-day session of Russia's Congress of People's Deputies, which sought to curtail the powers of President Yeltsin, ends in Moscow.

The Australian Labor Party, headed by Prime Minister Paul Keating, is reelected for a fifth consecutive three-year term.

17 Actress Helen Hayes dies in Nyack, NY.

24 The Israeli parliament elects Ezer Weizman, a former military officer, to the largely ceremonial office of president.

26 The UN Security Council approves a resolution to send a peacekeeping force to Somalia. It would assume the duties—helping to deliver relief supplies and pacifying the war-torn nation—of the U.S.-led coalition in Somalia since December 1992.

28 A vote in Russia's Congress of People's Deputies to impeach President Yeltsin narrowly fails.

29 France's President François Mitterrand, a Socialist, names Edouard Balladur, a member of the neo-Gaullist Rally for the Republic party that scored a major win in general elections on March 21 and March 28, as prime minister.

At the annual Academy Awards presentations, *Unforgiven* is judged best picture.

31 In China the National People's Congress concludes its annual session. During the meeting, Li Peng was chosen for a second five-year term as the nation's premier and Communist Party General Secretary Jiang Zemin was selected as president.

Percival J. Patterson, who had succeeded Michael Manley as prime minister of Jamaica in March 1992, is elected to a full term.

A snowstorm called one of the most powerful of the 20th century struck the East Coast of the United States, including New York City, above, in mid-March. The storm, with its hurricane-force winds, caused tornadoes in the southern states.

April

1 Twenty-three years of military rule in the African nation of Lesotho ends as Ntsu Mokhehle is sworn in as prime minister.

2 In Portland, OR, President Clinton convenes a one-day meeting to discuss the dispute that arose from the suspension of timber cutting on federal lands to protect the endangered northern spotted owl.

4 Concluding a two-day summit with President Yeltsin, President Clinton promises $1.6 billion in U.S. aid to Russia.

5 The University of North Carolina wins the National Collegiate Athletic Association's Division I basketball championship, defeating the University of Michigan, 77-71.

8 Macedonia, a former Yugoslav republic, is admitted as the 181st member of the United Nations.

U.S. singer Marian Anderson, the first black to perform at New York City's Metropolitan Opera, dies at the age of 96.

9 U.S. planes and Iraqi antiaircraft batteries exchange fire in the UN-imposed "no-fly zone" in northern Iraq.

Laura D'Andrea Tyson (seated at left), *chairman of the U.S. Council of Economic Advisers, and Treasury Secretary Lloyd Bentsen listened as Leon Panetta, director of the White House Office of Management and Budget, presented the Clinton administration's budget for fiscal year 1994 on April 8.*

10 Chris Hani, the secretary-general of the South African Communist Party and a leader of the African National Congress (ANC), is assassinated in a Johannesburg suburb.

11 Germany's Bernhard Langer wins the Masters golf tournament in Augusta, GA.

16 President Clinton and Japan's Prime Minister Kiichi Miyazawa discuss trade issues in Washington, DC.

17 In Los Angeles, CA, a federal jury convicts two police officers and acquits two others of charges of violating the civil rights of Rodney King, a black motorist who was beaten in a videotaped incident in March 1991.

19 In Waco, TX, the compound of the Branch Davidians, who had been in a standoff with law-enforcement officials for 51 days, burns to the ground in what is described by the Federal Bureau of Investigation as a mass suicide.

22 With Italy facing a growing political-corruption scandal, Prime Minister Giuliano Amato announces his resignation. Italian voters had approved a series of government-reform measures on April 18-19.

Guy Hunt resigns as governor of Alabama immediately after being convicted of diverting money for his personal use from a fund established to finance his 1987 gubernatorial inauguration.

The U.S. Holocaust Memorial Museum is dedicated in Washington, DC.

25 In Russia some 58% of the voters taking part in a country-wide referendum indicate their support of President Yeltsin.

Pope John Paul II makes a one-day visit to Albania.

A march in support of civil rights and freedom from discrimination for homosexuals is held in Washington, DC.

26 In Italy central bank governor Carlo Azeglio Ciampi is named premier.

27 In Washington, Arab and Israeli delegations resume Middle East peace talks, which had been suspended for some four months.

The Republic of Yemen holds its first parliamentary elections since the unification of North Yemen and South Yemen in 1990.

© Georges deKeerle/Sygma

In a countrywide referendum on April 25, some 58% of Russian voters joined the woman at left in backing the policies of Boris Yeltsin. The president had called the referendum to garner support in a struggle with parliament.

29   Heads of organizations representing the governments of China and Taiwan sign four agreements calling for cooperation between the two nations.

30   Tennis star Monica Seles is hospitalized after being stabbed in the back during a break in a tennis match in Hamburg, Germany.

May

1   Sri Lanka's President Ranasinghe Premadasa is assassinated by a suicide bomb in Colombo, the nation's capital.

9   In Paraguay's first multiparty direct elections for a civilian head of state, Juan Carlos Wasmosy of the ruling Colorado Party is chosen president.

14   Nine of the ten former Soviet republics of the Commonwealth of Independent States agree to establish an economic union.

© Carlos Carrion/Sygma

Paraguayan voters showed their support for Juan Carlos Wasmosy of the ruling Colorado Party. The 54-year-old businessman was elected president of the Latin American nation in a three-man race on May 9.

© Noboru Hashimoto/Sygma

United Nations officials checked the credentials of voters in Cambodia as the Southeast Asian nation held its first multiparty elections since 1972 in May. A new 120-member constituent assembly was to draft a constitution and form a permanent government.

16   Turkey's Parliament elects Suleyman Demirel, the current premier, as president. He is to succeed Turgut Özal, who died on April 17.

18   In a referendum in Denmark, voters ratify the European Community's Treaty on European Union (the Maastricht Treaty). Danish voters had rejected the pact in June 1992.

19   The United States grants diplomatic recognition to the government of the southern African nation of Angola.

24   The Ethiopian province of Eritrea formally declares itself an independent nation. Voters in the province had approved a referendum favoring independence from Ethiopia on April 23-25.

25   Five of the seven persons who were dismissed on May 19 from the White House travel office on possible charges of financial mismanagement and political corruption are reinstated partially, after suggestions emerge that the firings resulted from the activities of friends and relatives of President Clinton who were eager for a part of the White House travel business.

27   Britain's Prime Minister John Major shuffles his cabinet. Kenneth Clarke, formerly home secretary, is named to succeed Norman Lamont as chancellor of the exchequer.

28   The European principality of Monaco and the new African nation of Eritrea are admitted to the United Nations.

President Clinton signs an executive order extending for one year most-favored-nation trade status to China. The president conditioned the renewal on China making "overall, significant progress" on human-rights issues.

29   One day after the German parliament gave final approval to constitutional changes limiting the guaranteed right of foreigners to seek asylum in Germany, five members of a Turkish family die in a firebomb attack on their home in Solingen in western Germany.

David R. Gergen, a magazine editor and television commentator and former adviser to President Ronald Reagan, is named counselor to President Clinton.

30   Brazil's Emerson Fittipaldi wins the 77th Indianapolis 500 auto race.

June

2   Melchior Ndadaye, representing the majority Hutu tribe, is elected president of Burundi.

3   Cambodia's Prince Norodom Sihanouk installs himself as head of state without forming a transitional government. UN-supervised elections ended in Cambodia on May 28.

President Clinton withdraws the nomination of Lani Guinier, a black law professor, to head the civil-rights division of the U.S. Justice Department. In withdrawing the nomination, which had caused controversy, the president admits that he had not read Guinier's contested articles until that day and that he found them "antidemocratic [and] difficult to defend."

Twenty-three UN peacekeepers are slain in attacks in Mogadishu, Somalia.

5   Texas state Treasurer Kay Bailey Hutchinson (R) is elected to the U.S. Senate, filling the seat vacated by Lloyd M. Bentsen, the secretary of the treasury.

Venezuela's bicameral legislature selects Ramon José Velasquez Mujica as interim president, succeeding Carlos Andrés Pérez, who in

May was suspended from office in view of charges of misappropriating government funds.

6   In Spain the Socialist Workers Party (PSOE) of Premier Felipe González emerges as the leading vote-getter in national elections, but fails to retain its parliamentary majority.

Guatemala's human-rights ombudsman Ramiro de Leon Carpio takes the oath as president, ending a leadership crisis following the ouster of President Jorge Serrano Elías on June 1.

Latvia concludes its first parliamentary elections since independence in 1991.

In Mongolia's first direct presidential elections, President Punsalmaagiyn Ochirbat is returned to power.

9   Opposition candidate Gonzalo Sanchez de Lozada is declared the winner of Bolivia's June 6 presidential election.

Japan's Crown Prince Naruhito marries Masako Owada, a 29-year-old former trade negotiator in Japan's foreign service.

The Montreal Canadiens win ice hockey's Stanley Cup.

11   The ninth International Conference on AIDS concludes in Berlin.

Iran's President Ali Akbar Hashemi Rafsanjani is reelected to a second four-year term.

14   President Clinton names Ruth Bader Ginsburg, a 60-year-old judge on the U.S. Court of Appeals for the District of Columbia, to the U.S. Supreme Court, succeeding Justice Byron White, who is retiring.

U.S. and allied forces conclude several days of attacks against Gen. Mohammed Farah Aidid, a Somalian warlord.

18   Japan's lower house of parliament is dissolved and elections are scheduled for July 18 after legislation approving a no-confidence motion against Prime Minister Kiichi Miyazawa is passed.

20   The Chicago Bulls capture their third consecutive National Basketball Association (NBA) crown.

21   The U.S. Supreme Court rules that the U.S. policy of forcing Haitian refugees headed for the United States on the high seas to return to Haiti without asylum hearings does not violate U.S. or international law.

23   Nigeria's military leader Gen. Ibrahim Babangida voids the results of presidential elections held on June 12 and announces he will not leave office on August 27 as planned.

24   The U.S. Federal Bureau of Investigation arrests eight men on charges of plotting a series of terrorist attacks against various sites in New York City.

25   In Canada, Kim Campbell, who was elected leader of the Progressive Conservative Party on June 13, succeeds Brian Mulroney as the nation's prime minister.

The World Conference on Human Rights concludes in Vienna, Austria. Representatives of 171 nations had attended the gathering, which opened on June 14.

26   The United States launches a missile attack against Iraq's intelligence headquarters in Baghdad. The attack is in response to reported evidence that the Iraqi government had sponsored a plot to assassinate former U.S. President George Bush during his April visit to Kuwait.

28   In a five-to-four decision, the U.S. Supreme Court rules that the constitutionality of the practice of organizing state legislative districts to increase minority representation can be challenged.

The White House Conference on AIDS disbands following four years of work. On June 25, President Clinton had designated Kristine N. Gebbie, a 49-year-old former nurse, as the government's first AIDS policy coordinator.

© Donna Bagby/Saba

In Texas on June 5, state Treasurer Kay Bailey Hutchinson was elected to the U.S. Senate seat vacated by the resignation of Treasury Secretary Lloyd Bentsen. The 49-year-old Republican would be the state's first woman senator.

Kim Campbell, 46, took the oath as Canada's 19th—and first woman—prime minister on June 25. The defense minister had been chosen to succeed Brian Mulroney as leader of the ruling Progressive Conservative Party on June 13.

© Norm Betts/Canada Wide/Sygma

July

2   Visiting the United States, South Africa's President F. W. de Klerk and African National Congress (ANC) President Nelson Mandela announce that an election in which blacks will vote for the first time will be held on April 27, 1994.

3   President Clinton extends until Oct. 1, 1994, a U.S. congressional moratorium on the testing of nuclear weapons. On July 1, President Yeltsin had declared that Russia would extend its ban on such testing.

4   Pete Sampras of the United States wins the men's singles tennis title at Wimbledon. Germany's Steffi Graf had taken the women's singles crown on July 3.

5   Tansu Ciller, 47-year-old former professor and economics minister, becomes the first woman to be installed as premier of Turkey.

9   The leaders of the Group of Seven—the world's seven leading industrial nations—conclude their annual summit in Tokyo. Multilateral trade was a prime topic of the meeting.

10   President Clinton addresses the South Korean parliament.

12   A strong earthquake strikes northern Japan, killing at least 200 people.

18   The president and prime minister of Pakistan resign amid a five-month political dispute between the two leaders. National elections are scheduled for October 6.

19   President Clinton eases the ban on homosexuals serving in the U.S. military. Under the new policy, homosexuals can serve in the military so long as they are discreet regarding their sexual orientation and do not engage in homosexual acts.

Robert V. Rota, the postmaster of the U.S. House of Representatives (1972-92), pleads guilty to charges of conspiracy and embezzlement, admitting that he had assisted House members in obtaining illegal funds from the House Post Office during his tenure.

The heads of government from the Group of Seven, the seven leading industrial nations (left to right)—Italy's Carlo Azeglio Ciampi, Germany's Helmut Kohl, France's François Mitterrand, the United States' Bill Clinton, Japan's Kiichi Miyazawa, Canada's Kim Campbell, and Britain's John Major—joined representatives of the European Community (EC) for the group's 19th annual summit in Tokyo. The July 7-9 conference focused on trade issues.

© Pool/Wagner/Saba

20 President Clinton names U.S. District Judge Louis J. Freeh as director of the Federal Bureau of Investigation (FBI). On July 19 the president had dismissed William S. Sessions from the post in view of ethical charges against him.

Vincent W. Foster, Jr., deputy White House counsel and a close friend of President and Mrs. Clinton, is found dead in northern Virginia—an apparent suicide.

22 Japan's Premier Kiichi Miyazawa resigns after the ruling Liberal Democratic Party (LDP) failed to capture a majority in elections for the lower house of the Diet (parliament) on July 18.

30 In Geneva, Switzerland, representatives of the Croats, Muslims, and Serbs in Bosnia-Herzegovina agree in principle to allow the division of their nation into ethnic republics in an effort to end 16 months of warfare among the groups.

31 Israel ends seven days of air raids and artillery strikes against suspected guerrilla bases in southern Lebanon. The military action had been in retaliation for rocket attacks by the pro-Iranian guerrilla group Hezbollah.

August

2 The British government officially ratifies the Treaty on European Union (the Maastricht Treaty).

4 A federal judge sentences Stacey Koon and Laurence Powell to two and one-half years in prison. The two Los Angeles policemen had been found guilty in April 1993 on charges of violating Rodney King's civil rights.

6 Japan's Diet elects Morihiro Hosokawa, 55-year-old founder and leader of the Japan New Party, as premier.

8 In Mogadishu, Somalia, four U.S. soldiers serving in the UN peace-keeping force are killed by a land mine.

9 U.S. Secretary of the Interior Bruce Babbitt announces changes in federal policy regarding the use of federally owned range lands. Increases in grazing fees and environmental-protection requirements for ranchers who use public lands are included in the changes.

In Belgium, Prince Albert of Liège is sworn in as King Albert, succeeding his brother King Baudouin, who died on July 31.

10 President Clinton signs the 1993 Omnibus Budget Reconciliation bill into law.

Ruth Bader Ginsburg takes the oath as an associate justice of the U.S. Supreme Court.

12 President Clinton signs legislation providing $6.2 billion in federal relief for victims of the flood that struck the U.S. Midwest for two months.

President Clinton welcomes Pope John Paul II to the United States. The pontiff is in the United States to attend the World Youth Day festival in Denver, CO.

14 In district court in New York City, Robert A. Altman is acquitted of charges in connection with the BCCI (Bank of Credit and Commerce International) case.

15 In North Carolina two 18-year-old boys are charged with the murder of James Jordan, the father of basketball great Michael Jordan.

19 In one of what the U.S. Defense Department calls the "most serious" military engagements since the end of the Persian Gulf war, U.S. jets bomb an Iraqi site after the installation fires on U.S. planes.

Prince Albert of Liège, 59, took the oath as king of Belgium in the national parliament in Brussels on August 9. The new monarch, who succeeded his brother the late King Baudouin, promised to continue to try to keep Belgium together despite long-standing linguistic controversies.

© Ches/Char/Face/Job/Sipa

On August 10, U.S. Chief Justice William H. Rehnquist (right) administered the oath of office to the Supreme Court's newest associate justice, Ruth Bader Ginsburg. Her husband and President Clinton were on hand for the ceremony.

25 After determining that China had sold missile components to Pakistan in violation of an international agreement, the United States imposes trade sanctions on the two nations.

26 In Nigeria, Gen. Ibrahim Babangida resigns as president and military leader and designates Ernest Shonekan as head of an interim government.

UN Secretary-General Boutros Boutros-Ghali initiates a plan to reduce UN costs.

In Prague, Czech Republic, and in Bratislava, Slovakia, Russia's President Boris Yeltsin signs friendship treaties with the leaders of the two nations.

29 Israel's Supreme Court overturns the conviction of John Demjanjuk, a Lithuanian native who had been sentenced to death in 1988 for war crimes during World War II.

30 Robert Malval is installed as premier of Haiti. The 50-year-old publisher was the nominee of ousted President Jean-Bertrand Aristide.

31 Russia completes its military withdrawal from Lithuania as its remaining 2,500 troops leave the Baltic nation.

September

2 After losing contact with command centers on Earth, the Mars Observer, a U.S. spacecraft, is presumed to be lost.

The United States and Russia sign agreements to design and construct jointly an international space station.

7 The white government of South Africa agrees to share power with a multiparty transition committee during the months preceding the nation's first universal election.

The Clinton administration unveils its plan for "reinventing government" so as to improve government efficiency and reduce costs.

9   In Mogadishu, some 100 Somali gunmen are killed when U.S. and Pakistani peacekeeping troops fire on Somalis whom U.S. officials claim were shooting at the troops.

12   Pete Sampras wins the men's singles tennis title at the U.S. Open. Steffi Graf had taken the women's crown on September 11.

13   Representatives of Israel and the Palestine Liberation Organization (PLO) sign a declaration of principles for interim Palestinian self-rule. Earlier the PLO had reaffirmed its recognition of Israel's right to exist and Israel recognized the PLO as the sole representative of the Palestinian people.

In general elections in Norway, the ruling Labor Party increases its number of parliamentary seats.

14   Quebec's Premier Robert Bourassa announces that he will retire from politics early in 1994.

At the White House, President Clinton signs three supplemental agreements to the proposed North American Free Trade Agreement (NAFTA).

China announces that it has released Wei Jingsheng, a prominent dissident, from prison.

21   After Russia's President Yeltsin dissolves parliament and calls elections for the lower chamber of a bicameral legislature for Dec. 11-12, 1993, the current parliament votes to depose him and installs Vice-President Aleksandr V. Rutskoi as acting president.

The 48th session of the UN General Assembly opens in New York.

22   In a speech before a joint session of Congress, President Clinton unveils his program for reforming the nation's health-care system.

An Amtrak train plunges off a bridge and into a bayou, about 10 mi (16 km) north of Mobile, AL, killing 47 persons.

24   After taking the royal oath as king of Cambodia, Norodom Sihanouk announces that his son, Prince Norodom Ranariddh, would be the nation's first premier and Hun Sen, the outgoing premier, would be second premier.

30   A devastating earthquake strikes central India, killing nearly 10,000 people.

At a September 13 White House ceremony to mark a new Middle East peace accord, two longtime enemies—Israel's Prime Minister Yitzhak Rabin and PLO Chairman Yasir Arafat—shook hands. Some 3,000 guests attended the historic festivities on the South Lawn.

© Rick Bloom/Saba

October

1 Separatists expel government troops from the Abkhazia region in the republic of Georgia.

3 President Clinton signs a $13 billion foreign-aid appropriations bill.

4 Russian troops crush an armed uprising by rebellious members of Parliament and their supporters against President Yeltsin. More than 125 persons are killed in the clashes.

Hosni Mubarak is reelected president of Egypt.

5 Authorities in India report that nearly 10,000 persons were killed in a powerful earthquake in central India on September 30.

Pope John Paul II issues an encyclical on moral theology.

6 Israel's Prime Minister Yitzhak Rabin and Palestine Liberation Organization Chairman Yasir Arafat meet in Cairo, Egypt, to coordinate negotiations regarding the implementation of the agreement on Palestinian self-rule.

7 President Clinton orders that 15,000 reinforcements be sent to Somalia after at least 12 U.S. soldiers are killed October 3-4 in Mogadishu, the capital of Somalia, in a 15-hour battle with supporters of Gen. Mohammed Farah Aidid. The president also sets March 31, 1994, as the target date for the withdrawal of most U.S. forces from the African nation.

10 The Panhellenic Socialist Movement (PASOK), led by former Prime Minister Andreas Papandreou, captures a parliamentary majority in general elections.

Geidar A. Aliyev takes office as president of Azerbaijan.

13 Russia's President Yeltsin concludes an official visit to Japan.

Researchers at the George Washington University Medical Center report that they have cloned human embryos, successfully splitting single embryos into identical twins or triplets.

14 Lech Walesa names Waldemar Pawlak, 34-year-old leader of the Polish Peasant Party (PSL), as premier.

15 South Africa's President F. W. de Klerk and African National Congress President Nelson Mandela are named winners of the 1993 Nobel Peace Prize for their efforts in dismantling the apartheid system.

19 In an effort to return the exiled Jean-Bertrand Aristide as president of Haiti, a United Nations oil and arms embargo against Haiti is reimposed.

Benazir Bhutto of the Pakistan People's Party (PPP) is elected prime minister of Pakistan. The PPP had won the most seats in October 6 parliamentary elections.

20 In Los Angeles County Superior Court two black men are acquitted of attempted murder in the videotaped beating of Reginald Denny, a white truck driver, during the 1992 Los Angeles riots.

Georgia's President Eduard Shevardnadze signs a decree by which his nation is to join the Commonwealth of Independent States.

23 The Toronto Blue Jays win baseball's World Series for a second consecutive time.

24 The death of Burundi's President Melchior Ndadaye in a military coup is confirmed. Burundi had been experiencing long-standing violence between the minority Tutsis and the Hutus, who comprise 85% of the population.

25 Canada's Liberal Party regains power as the ruling Progressive Conservative Party is overwhelmed in parliamentary elections. The separatist Bloc Québécois and the Reform Party score major gains, winning 54 and 52 parliamentary seats, respectively.

27 President Clinton and First Lady Hillary Rodham Clinton present the administration's plan for health-care reform to Congress at a ceremony at the Capitol.

28 A U.S. budget deficit of $254.9 billion is reported for fiscal year 1993.

30 The UN Security Council condemns Haiti's military leaders for preventing the return of exiled President Jean-Bertrand Aristide.

31 Voters in Peru narrowly approve a new constitution, increasing the power of the presidency.

Six counties in southern California were struck by a series of fires—considered the worst to hit the state in more than a decade—in late October and early November. Authorities believed arson was responsible for about half of the fires. Dry, brush-covered areas contributed to their spread. More than 1,000 homes were destroyed.

November

1 The European Community's treaty on European unity takes effect.

Hans Blix, the head of the International Atomic Energy Agency (IAEA), informs the UN General Assembly that North Korea continues to resist the IAEA's efforts to inspect that nation's nuclear-development sites.

The *Columbia* completes a 14-day flight, the longest mission in U.S. space-shuttle history.

2 Two Republicans—Christine Todd Whitman and George F. Allen—are elected governors of New Jersey and Virginia, respectively. In New York City's mayoralty race, Rudolph W. Giuliani (R) defeats incumbent David N. Dinkins (D).

In municipal elections in Israel, Ehud Olmert of the Likud Party defeats Jerusalem's incumbent mayor, Teddy Kollek.

4 In Canada, Liberal Party leader Jean Chrétien is sworn in as prime minister.

6 The ruling New Zealand National Party wins a one-seat majority in general elections.

© Liz Gilbert/Sygma

On November 16 the United Nations Security Council voted to conclude its unsuccessful attempt to arrest Somali warlord Gen. Mohammed Farah Aidid (above). His capture had been a major objective of UN forces in Mogadishu, Somalia, since June. Earlier in November, Aidid had called the UN the "biggest obstacle to peace" in Somalia.

8   Parliamentary elections are held in Jordan.

13   In Pakistan, Foreign Minister Farooq Leghari is chosen president.

14   In China the Communist Party's Central Committee issues a report on the economy calling on China to "speed up the process of establishing a socialist market economic system and bring about a sustained, swift, and sound development of the national economy."

In a referendum, residents of Puerto Rico vote in favor of continuing their U.S. commonwealth status.

17   In Nigeria, Defense Minister Gen. Sani Abacha announces that he has dissolved the government of interim President Ernest Shonekan and declares himself as the nation's ruler.

18   In South Africa the ruling National Party and leaders of some 20 other parties representing blacks and whites approve a new national constitution that provides fundamental rights to blacks.

20   Leaders from the Asia-Pacific Economic Cooperation group conclude the organization's first major summit in Seattle, WA. Prior to the summit's opening, President Clinton conferred with China's President Jiang Zemin.

22   Mexico's Senate approves the North American Free Trade Agreement (NAFTA), linking Canada, Mexico, and the United States. Both houses of the U.S. Congress had approved legislation implementing the treaty earlier in the month.

The 21,000-member Association of Professional Flight Attendants at American Airlines calls off a strike that had begun November 18.

23   President Clinton signs legislation repealing U.S. sanctions against South Africa.

25   The U.S. House of Representatives adjourns for 1993. The U.S. Senate had adjourned on November 24 after passing the Brady bill establishing a waiting period for handgun purchases.

28   In Honduras, Carlos Roberto Reina of the center-right Liberal Party is elected president.

December

2   Colombian drug trafficker Pablo Emilio Escobar Gaviria is killed in a shoot-out with police and soldiers in the Colombian city of Medellín.

3   The U.S. Labor Department reports that the national unemployment rate dropped to 6.4% in November from 6.8% in October.

5   Rafael Caldera Rodriguez is elected president of Venezuela.

Germany wins tennis' Davis Cup.

7   U.S. Secretary of Energy Hazel O'Leary reveals that the United States had conducted 204 underground nuclear tests from 1963 to 1990 without informing the public.

A gunman opens fire in a crowded Long Island [NY] Rail Road commuter train, killing several persons.

Felix Houphouët-Boigny, the president of Ivory Coast, dies.

11   Parliamentary elections are held in Russia.

Eduardo Frei Ruiz-Tagle of the ruling center-left Coalition of Parties for Democracy wins Chile's presidential election.

Leaders of the European Union (Community) conclude their semiannual summit in Brussels, Belgium.

13   In Canada, Kim Campbell resigns as leader of the Progressive Conservative Party.

© Blanche/Ribiero/Gamma-Liaison

© East News/Saba

The U.S. space shuttle *Endeavour* completes a 12-day mission to repair the Hubble Space Telescope.

14 Members of the United Mine Workers union ratify a new five-year contract, ending a seven-month strike.

15 British Prime Minister John Major and Ireland's Prime Minister Albert Reynolds issue a "framework for lasting peace" in Northern Ireland.

The Uruguay Round of the General Agreement on Tariffs and Trade concludes with agreement on new global-trade regulations.

16 President Clinton names Bobby Ray Inman to succeed Les Aspin as secretary of defense. Aspin had announced his resignation from the post on December 15, effective Jan. 20, 1994.

17 In a White House ceremony, President Clinton acknowledges the $500 million gift of philanthropist Walter Annenberg to public-education reform. The donation is to be awarded in matching grants over a five-year period.

18 Vice-President Al Gore completes a tour of three Commonwealth of Independent States countries—Kazakhstan, Kyrgyzstan, and Russia—during which he signed a series of agreements.

20 In Serbia, President Slobodan Milosevic's governing Socialist Party claims victory in December 19 parliamentary elections.

21 Hungary's parliament endorses the nomination of Peter Boross as premier, succeeding Jozsef Antall, who died in office on December 12.

22 The board of directors of Paramount Communications endorses the company's merge with QVC Network Inc.

The daughter of Cuba's Prime Minister Fidel Castro is granted political asylum in the United States.

23 President Clinton announces that he will instruct his lawyers to give investigators all documents relating to an investment that he and Mrs. Clinton made in the Whitewater Land Corporation before he became president.

26 Members of China's Communist Party gather in Beijing to commemorate the 100th anniversary of the birth of Mao Zedong.

28 U.S. Secretary of State Warren Christopher announces the appointment of Strobe Talbott, a former journalist and an authority on Russia and the former Soviet Union, as deputy secretary of state. Clifton R. Wharton, Jr., had submitted his resignation from the post on November 8.

30 Israel and the Vatican sign an agreement to establish diplomatic relations.

Some 55% of the eligible voters cast ballots in Russia's parliamentary elections December 11. The strong showing of the Liberal Democratic Party, headed by Vladimir V. Zhirinovsky (above), an ultranationalist lawyer, shocked Russia's reformers and caused international concern. A new constitution, backed by President Yeltsin, was approved by about 57% of those who voted.

Special Features

T he year 1993 saw one of the worst floods in U.S. history strike the Midwest; continued war, suffering, and devastation in the lands that were Yugoslavia, *page 25, top right;* and country music—with such stars as multiple award-winner Vince Gill, *page 25, bottom right*—enhance its position as "America's Music." At the same time, the working relationship between Bill Clinton and Al Gore (shown, *page 25, top left,* unveiling a plan to streamline the federal government) led to a fresh look at the office of U.S. vice-president, and proposals to reform the U.S. health-care system were unfolding. Accordingly, the following pages offer special coverage of those five topics. A discussion of the role of cults in U.S. society, including a synopsis of the Branch Davidians-Waco, TX, story; a look at the beautiful paintings of the Barnes Collection; and an update on people's preoccupation with their pets complete the Feature Section.

© Jeffrey Markowitz/Sygma

© Gary Knight/Saba

© Clark Jones/Impact Visuals

© Lowry/"Nashville Banner"/Liaison

THE YUGOSLAV WARS OF SECESSION

About the Author. Robin Alison Remington, professor of political science at the University of Missouri—Columbia, visited Yugoslavia during the summer of 1991 at the time of Croatian and Slovenian declarations of independence. The recipient of Fulbright and the American Council of Learned Societies grants, Professor Remington has written extensively on Yugoslavia's domestic developments and foreign policy since the 1970s. She frequently lectures on the Yugoslav wars of secession and has been interviewed by *The Christian Science Monitor, Newsweek,* The Voice of America, and CNN.

by Robin Alison Remington

In 1992 the Yugoslav state established in 1918 to unite the South Slav peoples had disappeared, and its remnants were torn apart by fratricidal wars. As these Yugoslav Wars of Secession entered their second winter in 1992-93, military campaigns in Bosnia and Herzegovina were exacting a steadily rising death toll and were the focus of international attention. The fighting followed recognition by the international community of an independent Bosnia and Herzegovina—the third breakaway republic of the former Yugoslavia. The condition of more than 2 million refugees made homeless by the misfortunes of war and by genocidal "ethnic cleansing" on all sides became more desperate as snow blanketed the killing fields. Meanwhile, the threat of starvation and the danger of death from exposure reached beyond the besieged cities, towns, and villages of Bosnia and Herzegovina to the rump Yugoslavia—the two

© A. Boulet/Sipa

remaining federal republics, Serbia and Montenegro—where those supporting and opposing the war alike struggled to survive in economies ruined by trade sanctions. By midsummer the death toll on all sides had reached 200,000, mostly civilians.

The carnage continued throughout the year, and U.S. State Department officials estimated in the fall that 4.2 million people were "at risk" as the war's third winter approached, including 700,000 refugees in Croatia, 647,000 in the rump Yugoslavia (565,000 in Serbia and 82,000 in Montenegro), 45,000 in Slovenia, and 27,000 in Macedonia. These estimates apparently did not include Serbs and Montenegrins placed at risk by the sky-rocketing cost of medicine, food, and heat in an economic climate of hyperinflation that, according to the Yugoslav Federal Statistics Office, was 18.7% per day by the beginning of December—an annual rate of 286 billion percent.

Battle Lines in Bosnia and Herzegovina. On the military front, the Bosnian Serb army led by Gen. Ratko Mladic controlled roughly 70% of the stillborn state throughout the year. Despite revolving cease-fires, Serbian and Bosnian Muslim fighting continued in eastern Bosnia. Ravaged by 20 months of siege, Sarajevo, the capital, although not entirely cut off from supplies, was pounded intermittently by Serbian gunfire, harassed by Serbian and Muslim snipers, and victimized by Bosnian Muslim gangs that by year's end Prime Minister Haris Silajdzic had had some success in combating.

The most serious battles, however, were between Bosnian Muslim troops and their former Croatian allies in central

Despite numerous peace initiatives, fighting continued in the land that once was Yugoslavia in 1993. Hostilities escalated in Bosnia and Herzegovina after the international community recognized the independence of that republic. Not only was the loss of life high, but a major landmark— the Old Bridge (above) in the Bosnian city of Mostar—was a tragic casualty. The bridge opened in 1566 and was a prime example of Ottoman architecture.

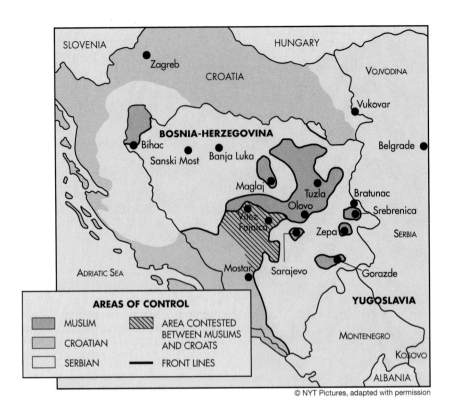

Bosnia, reportedly aided by some 65,000 regular Croatian troops deployed across the border. There mutual atrocities mingled with shifting battle lines that as the year closed appeared to have tilted in the Bosnian Muslims' favor. Despite their gains and reports of increasing supplies of men and arms from Islamic allies in the Middle East, the Bosnian Muslims faced yet another threat—a split within Muslim ranks created when the Bihac enclave in northwestern Bosnia declared its independence in September. Bihac was protesting the strategy of the Bosnian Muslim parliament, which refused to endorse the proposed tripartite peace plan put forward by the Geneva Permanent Peace Conference on the former Yugoslavia, cochaired by British Lord David Owen for the European Community (EC) and former Norwegian Foreign Minister Thorvald Stoltenberg for the United Nations (UN).

The situation on the ground at year's end, then, was as follows: The Bosnian Serbs had consolidated military victories that were certain to be cut back substantially in any settlement. The Bosnian Croats were in deep trouble and could be expected to require more military reinforcements from Croatian President Franjo Tudjman's Zagreb government. Bosnian Muslim forces were gaining against the Croats, but had made no significant headway against the Serbs, and were faced with a potential civil war if they insisted on trying to recover the Bihac region—whose leader, Fikret Abdic, already had signed separate agreements with Bosnia's Serbs and Croats to keep the enclave out of the war.

Sarajevo, a symbol of civilization abandoned that for artists and writers all over the world increasingly recalled Guernica in

the Spanish civil war, had been joined by Mostar, a Balkan Barcelona. Like historic monuments in the ancient walled city of Dubrovnik on the Croatian coast, the four-century-old Mostar Bridge—which had survived World War I and World War II—was destroyed in the autumn in the name of strategic advantage. But this time the destroyers were Croatian forces intent on keeping the Muslim half of the city hostage.

Confederal Bosnia: The Vance–Owen Peace Plan. The year began with three parties committed to preserving Bosnia and Herzegovina as a multiethnic state within its recognized boundaries—the Bosnian government headed by Muslim President Alija Izetbegovic, EC-UN negotiators associated with the permanent peace conference on Yugoslavia, and the Bill Clinton administration in Washington. This translated into the Vance-Owen plan (named for former U.S. Secretary of State Cyrus Vance, Stoltenberg's predecessor, as well as Lord Owen), envisioning ten autonomous districts under a loose federal umbrella.

Croatia was the clear winner according to this plan. Bosnian Croat cantons are adjacent to independent Croatia. Herzeg-Bosnia, a self-declared autonomous region governed by the Bosnian Croats, had adopted Croatian currency and already was becoming a de facto part of Croatia. Not surprisingly, then, the Croatian leaders in both Bosnia and Croatia were the first to sign on to the plan. Indeed, the strategy of international negotiators was to use this acceptance to bring the Bosnian government on board and then apply maximum international pressure on the Serbs. As a part of this campaign, Washington began

As with all wars, nothing was spared by the hostilities. Numerous housing complexes and cultural institutions, including Sarajevo's beautiful library, below right, were turned to ruins.

In October 1993 some 1,000 prisoners of war were released in an exchange negotiated by the Red Cross. The exchange began on October 19 but was suspended three days later.

seeking the support of North American Treaty Organization (NATO) allies for a policy of "strike and lift"—that is, striking Bosnian Serb artillery positions around Sarajevo and lifting the arms embargo on the Bosnian Muslims.

The Bosnian government was decidedly less enthusiastic, but under international pressure its negotiators signed, undoubtedly counting on the Bosnian Serbs to hold out. If so, Muslim doubters were not disappointed. Whatever his personal feelings, the pain of sanctions had convinced Serbian President Slobodan Milosevic to speak to the Bosnian Serb parliament in favor of the plan. Bosnian Serb leader Radovan Karadzic (of the Serb Democratic Party in Bosnia) still more reluctantly endorsed it. However, the commander of the Bosnian Serb army, Gen. Ratko Mladic, soundly attacked the plan as a sellout. And the general won that round. The Bosnian Serb parliament rejected the plan, and General Mladic then actively campaigned to make sure that the subsequent referendum of Bosnian Serbs did so as well.

Notwithstanding Lord Owen's November 25 accusation that the Vance-Owen plan died because Washington refused to commit troops to defend it, the passionate rejection by the Bosnian Serbs already had reduced the plan to a scrap of paper. Given the perverse logic of the situation, Bosnian Serb leader Radovan Karadzic was right: To succeed, any plan had to be equally unacceptable to all parties.

Divided Bosnia: The Owen-Stoltenberg Plan. With the plan for a confederal Bosnia and Herzegovina—that is, a de facto UN protectorate—dead, discussion returned to the idea of a tripartite division. Such a plan had been on the table in February 1992 when Serb, Croat, and Bosnian Muslim leaders met in Portugal, attempting to fend off the collapse into civil war. All three signed the resulting Lisbon Agreement. Then Bosnian President Izetbegovic—perhaps under the mistaken impression that he

had an assurance of U.S. support if the shooting started—followed the advice of Warren Zimmerman, U.S. ambassador to the former Yugoslavia, to withdraw if he was not satisfied. In retrospect, as Zimmerman acknowledged in August, the Lisbon Agreement did not look so bad. If one accepted the principle of ministates, Bosnian Muslims were clearly the winners in terms of territory—44%, equal to their percentage of the population but more than actually was owned by Muslims at that time—with only 18% of the Muslim population outside Muslim administrative control.

Renegotiated in summer 1993 as the Owen-Stoltenberg plan, the Lisbon formula appeared to represent the best agreement that could be had: After 17 months of war and devastation, some 30% of the region would be for Bosnian Muslims, 18% for Bosnian Croats, and roughly 52% for Bosnian Serbs. The Bosnian Muslim parliament accepted the plan in principle, but rejected the map on September 29. This shifted the negotiations away from concern with a confederal versus a divided Bosnia to the question of the viability of the proposed Bosnian Muslim state.

Plan Three: Sanctions for Land. The sticking points for Bosnian Muslim negotiators appeared to be roughly 3.5% of Serbian-held territory and sovereignty over their access to the sea rather than a leasing arrangement with Croatia. To get the peace process moving again the warring parties were pressed into discussing yet another peace plan in Geneva in November. The plan built on the rejected Owen-Stoltenberg plan and incorporated a German-French sanctions-for-land suggestion.

This "carrot-and-stick" strategy for dealing with the Serbs in Serbia and Bosnia was part of an ambitious new initiative. It called for negotiators to return to London in the new year, and it widened their task to include settlement of the relationship of the self-proclaimed Serbian autonomous region of Krajina with the Croatian government and the volatile question of the 90% Albanian Serbian province of Kosovo. In short, as described at the end of 1993 when the 1994 Peace Conference on Yugoslavia

Opposing Sides: A Bosnian soldier waits for the latest Croatian attack, and a Croatian soldier killed in battle receives a hero's funeral.

© Haviv/Saba

© Gary Knight/Saba

On July 12, 1993, French Lt. Gen. Philippe Morillon, 57, relinquished command of UN forces in Bosnia. In March he had conducted a fact-finding tour of Srebrenica (above left) and sought to negotiate the evacuation of wounded civilians from besieged Muslim towns. During the summer, U.S. troops under UN auspices (above right) were deployed to The Former Yugoslav Republic of Macedonia to help deter the ethnic factions fighting in Bosnia from spreading their conflicts to other regions.

was reconvening, it would attempt to deal not only with the partition of Bosnia and Herzegovina but with the implications of that decision for remaining Greater Serbia, Greater Croatia, and Greater Albania national/irredentist campaigns under way as well. The plan was a long shot.

• *Serbia and Serbs in Bosnia and Croatia.* The "carrot-and-stick" strategy asked Serbs in Bosnia and Herzegovina to trade territory in order to get sanctions lifted in Serbia proper. It assumed equal willingness on the parts of both Serbian President Milosevic and Bosnian Serb President Karadzic to cut such a deal—not altogether likely. A corollary assumption that the Bosnian Serb president could get the Bosnian Serb commander, General Mladic, to go along was still less likely, although Mladic did not reject the Owen-Stoltenberg plan for ministates out of hand.

With respect to the territorial conflict between Zagreb and the Republic of Serb Krajina, the carrot of lifting sanctions assumed that Milosevic could deliver Krajina, as he did in January 1992 when some 14,000 UN peacekeeping forces (UNPRO-FOR) went in to stabilize the region. This assumption was particularly problematical. While there was some evidence to support the idea of a coincidence of interests of Bosnian Serbs and Serbs in Serbia, there was none to suggest such an identity of goals binding Serbs in Krajina and Serbs in either Serbia or Bosnia. On the contrary, reports in October that Croatian troops burned 11 Serbian villages in the Medak region of Krajina and subsequent media accounts of the destruction of the homes of Serbs and of Croat opponents of the government alike made a deal in which Krajina Serbs would disarm simply for a promise of autonomy from Zagreb slim indeed.

• *Croatia.* This strategy implied that either Croatia accept demands for sovereign access to the sea for Bosnian Muslims and return to stalled negotiations with Krajina Serbs in Norway, or that it join Serbia on the target list of international sanctions. The credibility of this threat, however, was undercut at the out-

set by Zagreb's demonstrated ability to get away with open Croatian military support of Bosnian Croats throughout 1993, to dismiss UN reports of Croatian atrocities, and to maintain the siege of Muslim-controlled Mostar—all without suffering sanctions or warnings of air strikes against Croatian heavy artillery. Rather, despite a UN report of deliberate Croatian scorched-earth policy in the Medak region, President Tudjman's own threat in November not to renew the mandate of UNPROFOR forces led to extending the conditions for lifting sanctions on Serbia—originally tied to Serbian cooperation in ending the war in Bosnia and Herzegovina—to the Croatian front.

Moreover, assuming the Serbian stick failed to deliver the Krajina Serbs, there probably would be no Croatian carrot. The strategy both ignored the weakening of President Tudjman's position as a result of Croatian losses in Central Bosnia and assumed those losses would make him more willing to settle. Neither outcome was likely. While the strategy might work with respect to Bosnia, the Croatian delegation was not budging on the question of handing over to the Bosnian government access to a Dalmatian coast port. Furthermore, even if this diplomatic impasse could be broken by a deal with Belgrade that would allow Bosnia's Muslims access to the Adriatic Sea through the Prevlaka Peninsula—a demilitarized zone controlled by UN peacekeeping forces—Croatian concessions on the Bosnia and Herzegovina front would make it less, rather than more, likely that President Tudjman could afford to write off a third of Croatian territory and recognize the Republic of Serb Krajina.

• *The Bosnian Government.* Given the military balance, the Bosnian government had some reason to settle on a map with the Bosnian Serbs if additional territorial concessions could be arranged. However, unless Bosnian Muslim troops should start losing to Croatian forces in Central Bosnia, the Bosnian government had little incentive to agree to a Muslim-Croatian settlement, whether or not Zagreb became more accommodating.

• *Local Warlords.* Finally, with respect to the warring parties themselves, even if all official governments and armies could be persuaded to sign on, there was no evidence that the paramilitaries and local warlords would stop shooting.

• *International Diplomatic Positions.* From the start, Washington was equivocal, officially neither accepting nor rejecting the new Geneva Peace Conference initiative. Notwithstanding solid support from Russia's President Boris Yeltsin in other arenas prior to the December 12 Russian parliamentary elections, U.S. and British objections blocked Moscow's attempt to get the UN Sanctions Committee to allow 130 million cubic meters of natural gas per month to flow to Belgrade for heating homes, hospitals, and schools—although those objections were eased on December 10 to allow 20,000 tons of fuel to

Residents of Belgrade, Serbia, scrambled for free milk being distributed by an antigovernment party. International sanctions and hyperinflation contributed to a shortage of basic food products.

© Reuters/Bettmann

be imported by the UN High Commissioner for Refugees for refugee programs and 7,000 tons for orphanages and mental hospitals.

With respect to the European Community (later the European Union), conflict broke out in December 1992 over German pressure for EC recognition of The Former Yugoslav Republic of Macedonia before Greece replaced Belgium as community president for six months in January 1994. (The republic was admitted to membership in the UN on April 7, 1993.) There also was open nervousness that Greece was too pro-Serbian in the view of some community members. In short, while the UN increasingly lacked credibility, the EC continued to be divided, and the United States pulled back from involvement. In these circumstances, there was reason to doubt that those international negotiators who proved incapable of containing the war in Croatia, or of protecting the Bosnia and Herzegovina accepted to UN membership on May 22, 1992, would succeed by expanding the peace conference's agenda radically.

Throughout 1993 international diplomacy came half-circle, moving from insistence on a multiethnic Bosnia within the borders of the former federal republic to acceptance of a solution acknowledging the likelihood that Bosnian Serb and Bosnian Croat ministates eventually would join their neighboring motherlands. As those motherlands reasonably could be expected to pay a price, there was diplomatic logic to pressing Serbia and Croatia alike to apply the same principles to Serbs in Croatia and Albanians in Kosovo that they had demanded for Serbs and Croats in Bosnia and Herzegovina. This was undoubtedly the basis of unsubstantiated rumors of a Cyprus solution—that is, the partition of Kosovo.

Kosovo: The Albanian/Macedonian Question. The tormented region of Kosovo is the cradle of Serbian history and the birthplace of modern Albanian nationalism. There the battle of Kosovo Polje was fought in 1389. The Serbs were defeated by the Turks, and the Serbian empire disappeared from the map of Europe. There the Serbian Orthodox Church was founded. Kosovar Albanians would retort that Albanians fought side by side with Serbs against the Turks only to become second-class citizens in their own land. Most importantly, 90% of the people living in Kosovo in 1993 were Albanians.

Kosovar Albanians requested recognition of their independence by the same Dec. 23, 1991, deadline the EC set for Bosnia and Herzegovina. They were turned down. Kosovo was under de facto Serbian martial law. Yet Kosovar Albanians, led by Ibrahim Rugova—a pacifist leader who had succeeded in neutralizing his more militant rivals for the time being—ignored Serbian authority; boycotted Serbian elections; and even had established alternative government structures, schools, and civil society.

Rugova vowed to seek political solutions short of expanding the Yugoslav Wars of Secession. As tensions between the Macedonian majority and an Albanian minority (estimated at 20%-40% of the population, depending on whose figures are used) rose across the border in Macedonia, so did the danger that

After Vuk Draskovic, the chief critic of Serbia's President Slobodan Milosevic, and his wife were imprisoned following an antigovernment demonstration on June 1, 1993, a pro-Draskovic rally was held in Belgrade on June 19, below. Milosevic ordered the Draskovics released from jail on July 9 in light of growing international pressure.

© Art Zamur/Gamma-Liaison

Kosovo would be set aflame not by Serbian radicals but by Albanian militants in Macedonia or Albanian gun- and drug-runners stockpiling for guerrilla warfare.

Greek passions on the issue of Macedonia made it likely that Greece would not be unhappy to see the Macedonian republic divided and weakened. At the same time, Greece would have mixed feelings about a "greater Albania," while Germany—which was to become the EU president at the end of June 1994—could be expected to have its own agendas.

As 1993 ended, conflicts with the European Union offered little hope that a "let Europe handle it" policy could prevent a wider Balkan war if the danger was along the Albanian-Macedonian fault line. Presidents George Bush and Bill Clinton had committed the United States to possible unilateral action should war spread to Kosovo. Some 300 U.S. peacekeepers were stationed in Macedonia in the summer. In October the United States signed an agreement of military cooperation with Albania. In short, if the Yugoslav wars of secession spread from Skopje to Pristina to Tiranë and Belgrade, the U.S. military, willingly or unwillingly, may be dragged into a Balkan quagmire. When it comes to Kosovo, seeking opportunities for U.S.-Russian cooperation in a resolution of the Balkan conflict might be a promising alternative. The strong showing of Vladimir Zhirinovsky's nationalist party in the December 12 Russian parliamentary elections added to the urgency of exploring such options with Russian President Boris Yeltsin.

Although Zhirinovsky was thrown out of Bulgaria, his suggestion that Bulgarian territory should include Macedonia could incite Bulgarian extremists. To whatever degree extremist visions of a "greater Bulgaria" destabilize an independent Macedonia, the "Albanian question" in Macedonia and Kosovo becomes harder to answer peacefully.

Serbian Elections. The good news from the December 19 Serbian parliamentary elections was that Zeljko Raznatovic, the head of the paramilitary Tigers who is known as Arkan, lost his seat and his parliamentary immunity. Indeed, notwithstanding his Party of Serb Unity (SSJ) investment of $3 million, the party did not win a single seat. Vojislav Seselj's Serbian Radical Party (SRS)—openly supporting the war in Bosnia and advocating ethnic cleansing in Kosovo—dropped from 73 seats to 39. The bad news was that with Milosevic's Socialist Party of Serbia (SPS) taking 123 seats to 45 for the Democratic Movement of Serbia (DEPOS), there was—according to *The New York Times'* December 22 report of the Central Intelligence Agency (CIA) election postmortem—"no good and politically viable alternative." A question remained, however: Where would Milosevic find the additional three votes for a majority?

With regard to Serbia, there was a need for more carrot and less stick. Tightening the screws of international sanctions was too blunt an instrument to resolve Serbian parliamentary gridlock. To do so, as Croatian President Tudjman threatens direct intervention to aid the faltering forces of Bosnian Croats against Bosnian Muslims, only could weaken the prospects for U.S.-Russian cooperation regarding Kosovo.

Before the United Nations, which sought to bring peace to the devastated regions of the former Yugoslavia, Franco Tudjman (top) and Alija Izetbegovic (below) presented the Croatian and the Bosnian Muslim viewpoints, respectively.

Photos, © Alain Morvan/Gamma-Liaison

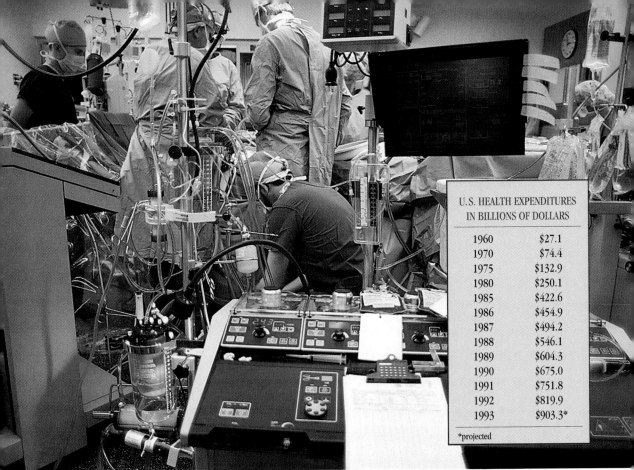

U.S. HEALTH EXPENDITURES IN BILLIONS OF DOLLARS	
1960	$27.1
1970	$74.4
1975	$132.9
1980	$250.1
1985	$422.6
1986	$454.9
1987	$494.2
1988	$546.1
1989	$604.3
1990	$675.0
1991	$751.8
1992	$819.9
1993	$903.3*

*projected

© Patrick Pfister/Medical Images, Inc; source for chart data: Health Care Financing Administration, U.S. Department of Health and Human Services

U.S. HEALTH CARE

Confronting the Crisis

By Julie Rovner

With the annual U.S. health-care bill approaching the trillion-dollar level and having a severe effect on the growing federal deficit, calls for reform of the system were widespread in 1993. Recent advances in medical technology were only one factor contributing to the escalating costs.

Legislation to reform the U.S. health-care system did not become law in 1993, but it was the year the issue moved to the front burner—and the front pages—for both average Americans and their elected representatives. By the end of the year the numbers involved were nearly as familiar to most Americans as their multiplication tables: 39 million people were without health insurance and another 25 million had inadequate health coverage. At the same time the nation's health bill was nearing the trillion-dollar-per-year mark, consuming one seventh of the nation's entire economic output (*see* chart above). In addition, Americans spent more than 30% more of their incomes on health care than any other nation, and an estimated 100,000 Americans lost their health insurance every month.

President Bill Clinton proved unable to keep his campaign pledge to see health-reform legislation enacted during his first year in office. But he did advance the debate further than had any president since Lyndon Johnson oversaw the creation of Medicare and Medicaid in 1965. And he found a valuable ally, salesperson, and ambassador in First Lady Hillary Rodham Clinton, whom he put in charge of the health-reform effort less than a week after his inauguration in January. Indeed, through the relentless salesmanship of the first couple—it often appeared that they still were on the campaign trail—it seemed clear that the Congress was poised to pass some major legislation to reshape the nation's health-care system in 1994. What was less clear was what form that change would take.

Perhaps little illustrated the sheer complexity of the health issue better than the delays in the launching of the president's own plan (*see* SIDEBAR/THE PRESIDENT'S PLAN). Clinton originally promised to deliver his plan to Congress within his first 100 days in office. But the 500 experts assembled by the task force headed by the first lady got mired in the details, while the cabinet members who served on the group could not agree on the plan's financing. The deadline for the public unveiling slipped from April to May to June, then the plan became entwined in the fight over the president's economic program. Congressional leaders asked the president to hold off on the health plan until they finished the budget bill, which did not happen until August.

About the Author. Julie Rovner has spent much of the last decade covering health policy in Washington, DC. For seven years she wrote regularly on health and human services for the *Congressional Quarterly Weekly Report*, and in 1993 she began covering health reform on television for the Medical News Network. She has written for a wide variety of publications, including *The Washington Post, USA Today*, and the British medical journal, *The Lancet*.

© Wally McNamee/Sygma

© Bettmann

In a televised speech before a joint session of the U.S. Congress on Sept. 22, 1993, President Bill Clinton presented his plan for health-care reform. Under the president's plan, "every American would receive a health-care security card [inset] that will guarantee a comprehensive package of benefits over the course of an entire lifetime, roughly comparable to the benefit package offered by most 'Fortune 500' companies."

The President's Plan

At more than 1,300 pages, President Bill Clinton's health-care plan, the Health Security Act, was nearly as complex as the health system it sought to reshape. But at its core it sought to accomplish two relatively simple goals: ensuring that all Americans obtained health insurance and curbing the spiraling growth of the nation's health-care bill.

Ensuring Coverage. The heart of the Clinton plan sought to establish "universal coverage," providing every American with health insurance "that can never be taken away," in the words of the plan, regardless of whether an individual was employed or unemployed, whether he or she had a preexisting health condition, or whether he or she was too poor to pay the premiums.

The primary means for ensuring coverage was an "employer mandate" requiring all businesses to offer insurance to workers and their families. Generally, employers would have to pay 80% of the costs of insurance, with workers picking up the remaining 20%. The federal government, however, was to provide subsidies— the administration called them "discounts"—to

Hillary Rodham Clinton, chair of the President's Task Force on National Health Reform, presented the administration's call for health-care reform to the American Medical Association in June 1993.

© Robert F. Kusel/Sygma

low-wage workers, those without jobs, small businesses, and those businesses with low-wage workers who would be affected adversely by the new requirements.

The plan called for reforms of the insurance industry to prohibit such practices as denying coverage or charging much higher rates for those most likely to need care, as well as trying to entice only the youngest and healthiest individuals. These changes were intended to eliminate "joblock," a situation in which workers who otherwise wanted to change jobs did not for fear of being unable to get new insurance coverage.

At the same time, the plan sought to make insurance more affordable by requiring all but the largest businesses to join state-run "health alliances," which would act as giant purchasing cooperatives to improve consumer bargaining power. Individual consumers could purchase more or less expensive plans, although every plan would be required to offer at least a minimum package of benefits laid out in the legislation.

Containing Costs. The Clinton plan sought to control health-care costs by combining two concepts from opposite ends of the ideological spectrum. Conservatives had been touting a proposal known as "managed competition," whereby the government would set rules for insurance companies—such as forbidding companies to deny coverage to people who had medical problems in the past—and help businesses who buy insurance for their workers to band together into purchasing groups to give them a stronger bargaining position. The theory, untested on any large scale, was that such competition on a level playing field would create the pressure needed to hold costs down.

Liberals not as opposed to government intervention preferred a more regulated system, in which the government either set prices—as it did for hospital and physician fees under Medicare—or else imposed "global budgets" that would set overall spending targets, but allow providers of health care to bargain with purchasers about how to meet the limits. The Clinton plan eschewed actual price controls and a firm global budget, but it included what its architects described as a "backstop" mechanism if managed competition failed to slow costs fast enough. The limits were in the form of "premium caps," which limited how much premiums for individual insurance plans could rise each year. That shifted pressure to keep costs down from the federal government to state governments and individual insurance companies.

JULIE ROVNER

Other Plans

While the Clinton administration was working to write its health-care plan, factions in Congress were not just sitting around waiting. By the time the president's plan reached Capitol Hill in late October, at least a half dozen other major bills had been introduced. They included:

Single Payer. Backed by liberal Democrats in the House and Senate, so-called "single payer" plans would have the government replace the health-insurance industry and pay all of the nation's health bills. Such a plan indeed would guarantee every American health coverage. It would not nationalize the health system, nor would it make doctors federal employees. Such a plan, however, would give the federal government total power to determine prices and would require a large tax increase to pay for the services.

Senate Republican Plan. A group of moderate Senate Republicans, led by John S. Chafee (RI), who had been meeting weekly for more than two years, was developing a health-care package of its own. Similar in many ways to the Clinton proposal, the Republican plan lacked such controversial elements as an employer mandate and budget caps. It, however, did seek to ensure universal coverage through an "individual mandate" that required each individual to purchase coverage if it was not provided by an employer; government subsidies for the poor were included in this plan.

Conservative Democratic Plan. Well before candidate Clinton embraced managed competition, a group of about 60 moderate-to-conservative Democrats had unveiled its own version of a plan to implement the concept, dreamed up by academics and health-industry executives. In 1993 the Democrats were joined by several Republicans in offering the plan, which like the Senate Republican plan lacked an employer mandate and cost controls, which they argued would interfere with the market forces they said managed competition would unleash.

Tax-Based. While most members of Congress—and most of the public—agreed that the nation's health system needed major repair, that opinion was far from unanimous. Many conservative Republicans, led by Sen. Phil Gramm (TX), argued that the U.S. medical system was the best in the world and needed only minor fixes. Their prescription for change was to place more responsibility and power directly in the hands of individual consumers, giving them a personal stake in holding down their own and, thus, the nation's health costs. Among their proposals were new tax credits to help those with low incomes purchase insurance, and special tax-preferred savings accounts from which all consumers could pay their own medical bills. Insurance would be saved for only "catastrophic" costs.

JULIE ROVNER

The plan actually made an unofficial debut in early September, when a draft marked "privileged and confidential" was leaked to the media from the offices of members of Congress who had been asked to review it. President Clinton presented the outlines in a nationally televised speech to a joint session of Congress on September 22, but even then the bill was not yet finished. It was not until October 27—more than another month later—after many more drafts and several more changes that the president and Mrs. Clinton hand carried their 1,342-page bill, the Health Security Act, to the congressional leadership.

For all the time and effort that went into the president's plan, its core was not changed much from the rough outline candidate Clinton proposed during the 1992 fall election campaign. Like much of the president's agenda, it sought to bridge the gap between liberals and conservatives. On one side, the plan embraced the idea being pushed by Republicans and conservative Democrats that market forces and competition could help curb rising health-care costs. But should those forces fail, it also included a "backup" mechanism of budget caps to keep costs in line. For liberals, the plan embraced the concept that every American should have health insurance, with the government

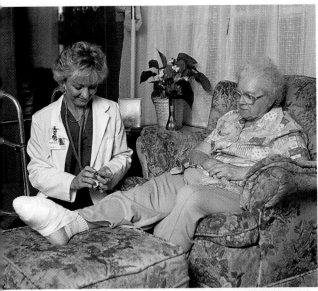

© Dan Reynolds/Medical Images, Inc.

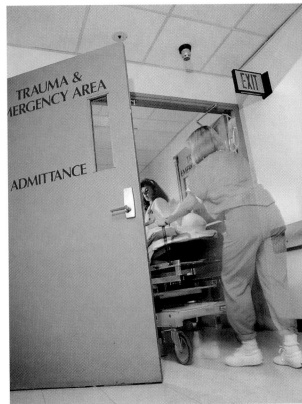

© Yoav Levy/Phototake

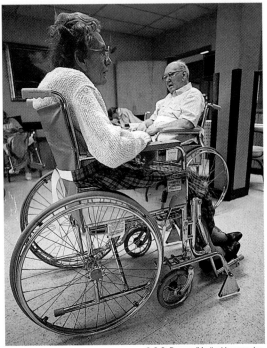

© C.C. Duncan/Medical Images, Inc.

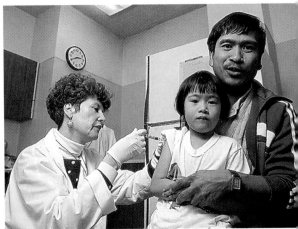

© David Maung/Impact Visuals

Care for the elderly, emergency care, and the lack of proper preventive care add special strains on the health-care system. Whether it be at home, top left, or in a nursing home, bottom left, the care of the elderly is extremely expensive. Even the uninsured receive emergency care, and at the expense of the insured. The fact that many of the nation's poor cannot afford preventive health care—including proper immunization, bottom right—increases the nation's health-care bill in the long run.

helping pay the bill for those who could not afford it otherwise. This concept was known as universal coverage. But like many of the plans introduced before it—dating back to President Richard Nixon's in 1971—the Clinton plan opted to build on the existing health system. Since most Americans obtained health insurance through their employers, the bill simply required that such coverage be offered, and that employers pay most of the costs.

This "mandate," as the requirement was called, was by far the most controversial part of the Clinton plan, and it was opposed vehemently by business groups, particularly groups representing small businesses. That was because small business-

The amount of paperwork that health-care providers are required to do is enormous and very costly. In presenting his reform proposal to Congress, President Clinton noted that it would reduce the "paperwork by simplifying the forms that have to be dealt with by doctors, by hospitals, by people with insurance." The president also said, "everyone can agree on at least this: that the paperwork in this system costs at least a dime on the dollar."

es were least likely to offer insurance, and many complained that such a requirement could push them into bankruptcy. The plan had detractors in Congress, too, many of whom introduced their own bills. Liberal Democrats backed "single payer" proposals similar to the system used in Canada, which would have the government—not insurance companies—pay all of the nation's health bills. At the other end of the spectrum, conservative Republicans insisted that there was little wrong with the system and proposed tax-credit plans that would help consumers pay for their own care. Still other proposals fell between those two extremes. (*See* SIDEBAR/OTHER PLANS.)

History. Efforts to reshape the way the nation delivers and pays for health services date back to Theodore Roosevelt in the early 1900s. In 1945, Harry S. Truman proposed a national health-insurance scheme to finish the work of Franklin Delano Roosevelt's New Deal. But it died in Congress, in part due to the vehement opposition of the American Medical Association (AMA), which denounced the plan as "socialized medicine."

Indeed, it was over the objections of the AMA that Congress in 1965 enacted Medicare and Medicaid, the former a federal health-insurance program for the elderly and disabled and the latter a joint federal-state health program for the poor. But while many in Congress thought Medicare and Medicaid merely would be precursors to a larger system-wide reform shortly thereafter, it was not to be. During the 1970s the cause of national health insurance continued to be championed by organized labor—and opposed by organized medicine. Among the most active on the issue then and into the 1990s was Sen. Edward M. Kennedy (D-MA). Indeed, it was in response to Kennedy's national health-insurance bill that President Nixon in 1971 offered legislation calling for the same sort of employer mandate Clinton embraced.

Congress next addressed the health issue in a major way in 1988, when it passed the Medicare Catastrophic Coverage Act.

CONSUMER PRICES *Medical Care* 1982 - 1984 = 100	
1983	100.6
1984	106.8
1985	113.5
1986	122.0
1987	130.1
1988	138.6
1989	149.3
1990	162.8
1991	177.0
1992	190.1
1993	202.9*

*August

All urban consumers; seasonally adjusted.

Source of data: U.S. Bureau of Labor Statistics.

The law was intended to fill many of the holes in Medicare coverage, most notably the fact that Medicare stopped paying for those who were the sickest. But in an era of tight federal budgets, Congress opted for a novel new financing scheme that required the wealthy to pay more for the new benefits than those with less means. The elderly rebelled, and Congress was forced to repeal the law in 1989, less than a year and a half after it was signed into law.

With no money and a public seemingly unwilling to pay more, the health issue languished during the administration of President George Bush. But Clinton reenergized it on the campaign trail, making health security a cornerstone of his campaign. The public responded, and during 1993 nearly every elected official agreed that the system needed substantial change.

Developing the Plan. President Clinton knew exactly what he wanted from a health-reform plan. "Let me just make clear to you the central element of this plan that is most important to me," the president told the congressional leadership the day he delivered the bill to the Capitol. "It guarantees every single American a comprehensive package of health benefits, and that to me is the most important thing—a comprehensive package of health-care benefits that are always there and that can never be taken away. This is the bill I want to sign, that is my bottom line. I will not support or sign a bill that does not meet that criteria."

But translating that simple concept into legislative language proved far more daunting a task than Clinton ever dreamed. The president's health-care task force officially began work on January 25, when Clinton formally named his wife to head the effort. But the day-to-day operation was overseen by Ira Magaziner, a self-made millionaire and former classmate of the president's at Oxford. Magaziner set up an elaborate system to devise the perfect plan, bringing together some 500 academics

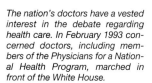

The nation's doctors have a vested interest in the debate regarding health care. In February 1993 concerned doctors, including members of the Physicians for a National Health Program, marched in front of the White House.

" TAKE TWO ASPIRINS AND CALL *HILLARY* IN THE MORNING! "

As overseer of the Clinton adminis-tration health-care-reform effort, Hillary Rodham Clinton traveled widely, met with experts in the field, and became the third first lady in U.S. history to testify before a committee of the U.S. Congress.

and other experts, both from around the country and from Capitol Hill and various federal agencies. Working under a news blackout in the Old Executive Office Building adjacent to the White House, the task-force staff often worked around the clock in hallways and overcrowded offices to meet incremental deadlines, dubbed "tollgates" by Magaziner. At these "tollgate" meetings, Magaziner and other senior officials would attempt to punch holes in various proposals and analyses, in order to make them as strong as possible.

After such a public buildup on the health issue, the news blackout—the White House press operation initially refused even to release the names of the 500 staff members—rankled much of official Washington. Not only did the media have to rely on questionable leaks from inside the task force, interest groups with a major financial stake in changing the system felt shut out—which was in part the administration's intent. Three interest groups even filed a lawsuit against the administration, charging that because Hillary Rodham Clinton was not techni-cally a federal employee, all of the task force's work must be public. Although the judge in the case sided substantially with the administration, the lawsuit did prompt the proceedings to become slightly more public.

In the end the biggest fight within the administration was not over what should be in the plan, but how to pay for it. As the summer's budget fight unfolded, it became clear to every-one that neither Congress nor the voters would support broad new taxes. But guaranteeing universal coverage was an expen-sive undertaking, and reconciling those two imperatives was what caused most of the delays. In the end, the administration opted to rely on a 75-cent-per-pack increase in the cigarette tax, as well as cuts in Medicare and Medicaid, to help find the funds to pay for the plan. Many in Congress doubted that the adminis-tration's financing was adequate for the job, but that was clearly a fight that would not be engaged in the nation and the halls of Congress until 1994.

THE GREAT FLOOD OF '93

By Lane Beauchamp

Record spring and summer rains led to severe flooding in the U.S. Midwest in 1993. Nine states were declared disaster areas as millions of acres of farmland were covered or completely flooded with water. More than 50 persons were killed.

About the Author. Lane Beauchamp is a staff writer for *The Kansas City Star,* assigned to the newspaper's Mid-America/National news desk in Springfield, MO. In covering the Great Flood of '93, he traveled to dozens of flooded areas and followed the rising waters of the Mississippi River from St. Paul, MN, to Ste. Genevieve, MO.

The dirty-brown line stretched along the sides of brick houses and the plaster walls of businesses, across the wooden billboards of a minor-league ballpark, and up steps leading to St. Louis' Gateway Arch. Anywhere, everywhere you looked across the heartland of the United States, "the line" symbolized the level of destruction—how high the water rose; how deep the devastation. Like a rampaging cancer with no cure, the relentlessly rising floodwaters of summer 1993 swallowed capital cities and small towns, family farms, and revitalized business districts, lingering with each bite and reveling in the ruin.

The "Great Flood of '93" left its mark across nine Midwestern U.S. states and on millions of lives. More than 50 persons died and property damage estimates reached beyond $17 billion. More than 20 million acres (8 million ha) of prime farmland and their crops were lost. Put simply, it was one of the worst natural disasters in the nation's history.

Heavy rains pounded the country's midsection and pushed nearly every river from its banks. The Mississippi, the Missouri, the Illinois, the Kansas all spread farther than ever before. The water saturated so much land that some called Iowa the sixth

Great Lake. Frightened residents fled for higher ground, leaving behind, when they had time, walls of sandbags to protect homes and history. In at least three cities, most notably Des Moines, the supply of tap water was cut off. Roads and bridges were knocked out, stranding commuters and isolating communities. Business along the rivers came to a standstill. "Our whole life floated away," said Linda Combs of Elwood, KS, whose convenience store was hit hard by the Missouri River floodwaters.

The federal government offered some assistance. In August, President Bill Clinton signed legislation providing $6.2 billion in aid for farmers, small-business loans, and other programs. Clinton also enacted a policy to repay states 90% of their costs to repair public facilities. And while the unremitting weather scarred the psyche of generations, the summerlong floods also will be remembered for a resurgence in the old-fashioned neighborly spirit. Strangers from coast to coast—even some from foreign countries—joined in the efforts of townsfolk across the Midwest. They filled burlap bags with sand and built makeshift levees. They donated clothes and cooked meals at relief shelters. Some celebrities joined in to hand out drinking water and lead telethon fund-raising efforts. In tiny Ste. Genevieve, MO, hundreds of volunteers labored day and night for weeks to save one of the oldest European settlements west of the Mississippi. As the mighty river toyed with everyone in town, Mayor Bill Anderson hardly could contain his emotions. "This outpouring of help is the most gratifying feeling in the world."

The First Warning Signs. The 1993 flood actually started in 1992 as exceptionally higher-than-normal amounts of rain and

© Joshua Roberts/Sipa

Bill Clinton joined local officials for firsthand inspections of the floodwaters. On August 12 the president signed legislation providing for $6.2 billion in federal relief aid for victims of the disaster.

© Alan Hawes/Sygma

In the eastern Iowa city of Davenport, right, on the Mississippi River, the business district as well as the sports stadium were consumed completely by water. The local minor-league baseball team—the Quad Cities River Bandits—was forced to play all of its late-season games away from home.

snow fell, especially in the upper river basins of the Midwest. By spring, a five-year drought in the region was all but forgotten as the rain continued to fall. As early as February, meteorologists had noted that the ground was near saturation and the flood potential for the Mississippi was high, specifically during the traditional snowmelt.

For the northern rivers of the United States, spring floods are normal. But in 1993 the spring floods arrived and never left. While the waters were high, more rain came and then more rain. Omaha, NE, for example, recorded more than twice as much rain as normal during the floods, sending weather experts back to 1875 to find comparable numbers. The saturated lands could not absorb any more water. Rivers and streams took as much as they could, then began their invasion toward land. It was the start of what many would call the 500-year flood.

So why did it rain so much and for so long? The intangible jet stream takes most of the blame. Weather experts explained that for some—as yet unknown—reason, the west-to-east-blowing jet stream remained locked over the United States, instead of making its usual retreat back into Canada. On opposing sides of the strong current of wind, warm and cold air fought for control, creating instability and thus the rain.

The Result. A flood is like no other natural disaster. Earthquakes and tornadoes strike suddenly and quickly, lingering never longer than a few moments. Even the hard-to-predict hurricane dies a speedy death once it hits land. But a flood loiters. It ambles downriver. It gains strength and it seeks out the weakest chinks in the armor of protection. While high-tech computers can warn of a flood, additional rain or a breached levee can throw off even the best predictions.

And so it was in 1993. At times, it seemed river-crest prognostications and weather forecasts changed hourly. The fickle

46

rivers occasionally forced police to demand the midnight evacuations of residents from their homes, only for the all clear to be sounded by the time morning arrived. The lingering disaster brought death across the Midwest. Most died in flash flooding when they drove into high water or slipped while fishing in strong river currents. In perhaps the single worst accident, two adult counselors and four children from a private home for troubled youths in St. Louis perished when flash floods stormed through a cave they had been exploring.

By Mother's Day, small towns along the streams and rivers of southern Minnesota began feeling the first wave of the Flood of '93. Within weeks, the water was rising to record levels. In Mankato, MN, the Minnesota River, which feeds the Mississippi, rose 12.5 ft (3.8 m) over flood stage. In historic Prairie du Chien, WI, the high waters covered a neighborhood that had been wiped out by the 1965 flood. Water there lapped at the sandbag wall protecting an 1870 Victorian mansion built by the state's first millionaire. By the fourth of July, the Mississippi River was above flood stage as far south as St. Louis, about 800 mi (1 287 km) from the Mississippi headwaters. The river, an interstate for much of the nation's farm product, was closed to all traffic north of St. Louis.

© P. Jones Griffiths/Magnum

Throughout the summer, Americans of all ages and from various locales formed chains to pile sandbags in an effort to hold off the Great Flood of '93.

At the same time, trouble had been brewing along the nation's other big river, the Missouri, and its tributaries. Thunderstorms in mid-June in Nebraska, Iowa, and northeast Missouri sparked flash flooding that would not diminish for weeks. On July 7 officials shut down the Missouri River to barge traffic. Three days later, the skies dumped 10 inches (25 cm) of rain on the Kansas City area, bringing it fully into the wrath of the 1993 floods.

For many Midwesterners, July would become a blur of disasters. Every day, it seemed, a story of destruction would emerge somewhere in the nation's heartland. On July 7 the focus was on the rural community of Keithsburg, IL. The town's levee along the Mississippi held firm, but the hostile floodwaters found a weak spot a few blocks into town along a creek that fed the river. The water broke through and flooded the town through its back door. "We could hear the water gurgling under our floors," resident Joe Gluba remembered. "It took only two hours from the time the levee broke for the water to show up on our doorstep." Weeks after the break, Gluba still did not know how bad the damage was in his ranch-style home because 8 ft (2.4 m) of water filled his basement.

On July 11 the focus shifted to Des Moines, some 150 mi (241 km) from the Mississippi but at the confluence of two of its tributaries, the Des Moines and Raccoon rivers. Rising floodwaters inundated the city's water-treatment plant and polluted its 810 mi (1 304 km) of water mains and pipes. For nearly two weeks, Des Moines residents suffered through having too much of the wrong kind of water. Residents had to wait in line for bottled water at elementary schools, and for portable toilets at grocery stores and fast-food restaurants.

As the floodwaters moved south, they grew stronger. On July 16 all eyes were on West Quincy, MO, where a suspicious

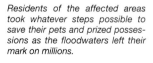

Residents of the affected areas took whatever steps possible to save their pets and prized possessions as the floodwaters left their mark on millions.

In St. Paul, MN, left, where the Mississippi crested in June, barge traffic was halted for awhile and a downtown airport which was inundated by water was forced to close temporarily.

© Pugliano/Gamma-Liaison

levee break flooded 15,000 acres (6 073 ha) of farmland and submerged the town. The break also closed the only bridge over the Mississippi open for 212 mi (341 km). The bridge remained impassable for more than two months. (Authorities in early October charged an Illinois man—23-year-old James R. Scott— with sabotaging the levee. If convicted, Scott faced up to life in prison for causing a catastrophe.)

Residents in nearly every town along a Midwestern waterway felt the fear of the flood. Pick a place and you find flood stories. Some residents, like those in Rock Island, IL, simply watched the high waters pass them by, praying their flood wall would hold. It did. Others, like those in Davenport, IA, across the Mississippi from Rock Island, watched as the river consumed a riverfront park, downtown businesses, and the picturesque home of the Quad Cities River Bandits minor-league baseball team. In Manhattan, KS, an estimated 5,000 residents fled their homes as officials released water from the dangerously overfull Tuttle Creek Lake. In St. Joseph, MO, the hungry Missouri River flooded that city's water plant, leaving residents in the same predicament faced just a few days earlier by those in Des Moines. Even the dead were not immune from nature's anger. The Missouri River flooded a 180-year-old cemetery near the central Missouri community of Hardin. Nearly 1,000 caskets and vaults were unearthed and left floating in the swollen waters.

As the miserable month of July came to a close, many people along the Midwest's rivers finally were watching the water recede. But as August approached, Missouri residents still braced for the worst as the Missouri and Mississippi rivers moved toward a potentially catastrophic convergence just north

© Les Stone/Sygma

Estimates of total property damage from the catastrophe exceeded $17 billion. By fall, the process of cleaning up and attempting to return to normalcy was under way. Many soggy towns were seeking to relocate to higher ground.

of St. Louis. Officials predicted record crests of the two rivers to occur almost simultaneously. The warnings came as St. Louis area levees weakened or gave way. In south St. Louis, the usually dry River Des Peres, essentially a storm sewer, was filled to the brim and threatened hundreds of homes and businesses. A levee in the suburb of Chesterfield, MO, was not as strong. The Missouri River broke through and flooded 4,400 acres (1 781 ha) of prosperous commercial businesses, causing an estimated $200 million in damage in that area alone. Among those hardest hit was the Spirit of St. Louis Airport, the second busiest airport in the state, which was not expected to reopen until late fall. Still, as the Mississippi River crested in St. Louis at a record 49.58 ft (15 m)—nearly 20 ft, or 6 m, above flood stage—most of the city dodged a bullet and escaped serious damage.

Then, just in case Midwesterners did not get Mother Nature's message from the spring and summer floods, she struck again in the fall. Heavy rains caused flash flooding from northeast Oklahoma to eastern Kansas, and from southwest Missouri north into Iowa. Families who just had moved back home were forced out by rising water. Towns like Springfield, MO, which were not hit during the summer, saw how much destruction a flood can bring. Preliminary damage estimates from a weekend of rain and flooding in Springfield reached $8 million, reminding everyone that man is not necessarily in control. Experts warned the Midwest that come spring, the floods could return; the farmlands may not be ready for planting, and history could repeat itself.

The Heroes and Humor. So many people survived the floods both physically and emotionally because of the help of strangers. Women, men, children answered the cries for help. For example: As water swirled around Denise Marie Harsche, a maid from Mandan, ND, she climbed through a window, dove under the water, and finagled her way to a man trapped in his basement apartment. And there was the effort to save Prairie du Rocher, IL, where officials exploded one end of a levee and intentionally flooded some farmland to divert the power of the Mississippi. Then volunteers, led—as in dozens of other efforts—by members of the National Guard, became a human

chain to shore up the settlement's levee. It worked, and Prairie du Rocher escaped essentially unharmed.

Through it all, flood victims somehow kept a sense of humor. Residents unofficially changed the Iowa state motto from "A Place to Grow" to "Iowa—A Place to Row." And a restaurant's sign advertising for a cocktail server noted: All applicants "must be good swimmers."

The Recovery. When the water finally started receding, the reach of the calamity grew clearer. The flood left homes in disrepair and forced businesses to start over. It left behind inches of mud and muck to be shoveled and washed away. Dead fish and raw sewage mixed with fertilizer and trash to stain walls and floors and ceilings. It would take weeks, perhaps months or longer, to scour clean what could be restored. The rest got tossed out. Skip Anderson stood outside his riverfront restaurant in Davenport, IA, where tables, chairs, carpeting—just about everything—was piled in a heap. "There was nothing we could do," Anderson said. "By the time they realized how high the water was eventually going to get, it had already surrounded us. All we could do was watch."

And with the physical recovery came the emotional release. Weeks of sensations, often choked back by endless efforts to save people and property, poured out. Teams of counselors, social workers, and nurses followed the floodwaters into stricken areas to help residents through a wide range of emotions— shock, fear, hostility, despair—all of it normal. Flood victim support groups formed at churches and relief shelters, opening avenues for people to talk about what they had been through.

As rivers slowly returned to their banks, some raised questions about man's effort to control nature. Some public-interest groups argued that levees damaged by the 1993 flood should not be rebuilt and instead should be converted to wetlands. They argued that levees contributed to the flood damage because they kept rivers from expanding into their natural floodplain.

The Memories. For those who did not watch the rising waters from their front porch or shovel filth from a neighbor's basement, the Flood of '93 will be remembered by the dramatic images seen in newspapers and magazines and on television. The sights included: human chains furiously stacking sandbags to save some small river town; weary men and women wading in chest-high water and covered in mud, carrying the last of their belongings to a waiting rescue boat; rain-soaked dogs being plucked from rooftops; and deer fleeing into the wilderness for drier ground.

Another remarkable sight was that of the farmhouse of Virgil Gummersheimer near Columbia, IL, on an August Sunday morning as a television helicopter hovered overhead, capturing the Mississippi River breaking through a levee and beginning its assault on the Gummersheimer family home. The two-story frame house, which had stood since 1907, grew weak. The river flexed its muscle. It ripped the home from its foundation, twirled it around, then devoured it. "We didn't have enough sandbags and enough men," a teary-eyed Gummersheimer would say later. "Old Man River won this time."

"It's as if another Great Lake has been added to the map of the United States."

Al Gore
U.S. Vice-President
Arnold, MO, July 1993

"I think the country as a whole has come to realize from the flood we can't control the environment. People have to understand we have to plan in harmony with this physical system that unites us."

David Lanegran
Macalester College
St. Paul, MN

© Alon Reininger/Contact

THE COUNTRY-MUSIC BOOM

By Alanna Nash

The new popularity of country has caused dance clubs featuring the music to spring up nationwide from Kentucky to California. The hottest trend at such clubs—like Denim & Diamonds of Santa Monica, CA, above—is line dancing to the latest hits.

By 1993, country music, long considered the entertainment choice of the hopelessly unsophisticated, had gained a new respectability across the United States, as well as unheard-of sales. With its mainstream breakthrough in 1991, country—with its emphasis on melody, lyric, and story—was suddenly the most popular U.S. music format, as much at home on a university campus as at a rattlesnake roundup. Billy Ray Cyrus' *Some Gave All*, which had sold 7 million copies by mid-1993, was the fastest-climbing debut album by any performer in history—including Elvis Presley and the Beatles. And Garth Brooks had emerged as the top-selling artist in any music format.

According to the Recording Industry Association of America (RIAA), country's slice of the pie of U.S. record sales grew from 8.8% in 1990 to 12.5% in 1991, the most significant growth of all genres. That figure, based on a 1991 consumer profile, amounted to a whopping $979 million, and it just kept growing. By 1993 country was estimated to be a $3-billion-per-year business.

© Paul Morse/LGI Photo Agency

© Adele Starr/LGI Photo Agency

Back in 1985, however, things were not looking so sunny. Country music was more than just sick—it was down on its side gasping for breath, a death rattle poised in its throat. The pop-influenced *Urban Cowboy* boom of 1980, with Kenny Rogers in the lead, finally had moved on, leaving a trail of dreadful country-pop schlock and plummeting record sales. Grave diggers were at the ready. How did such a dramatic turnaround occur in a relatively short period of time?

A sign of country music's move into the mainstream was the choice of Garth Brooks—country's most prominent performer—to sing the U.S. national anthem at pro football's 1993 Super Bowl (above left). Brooks' public appearances draw crowds of a size usually seen only for major rock-music stars.

The New Generation of Performers. By the mid-1980s, the cry had gone out for a new traditionalist—someone who would revive the back-to-basics, no-frills, hard-country sound and give the genre a much-needed resurgence in popularity. Ricky Skaggs did his best to return the city-slickered music to its roots instrumentation (acoustic guitar, dobro, mandolin, fiddle, and upright bass), as did Willie Nelson, George Strait, and—to some extent—the Judds, who played a joyful and highly melodic brand of classic and contemporary country music that sparked sales outside country's typical blue-collar audience.

But it was Randy Travis, with his glass-rattling baritone, his gift for emotional resonance, and his three big signature songs—"Forever and Ever, Amen," "Diggin' Up Bones," and "On the Other Hand"—who caught the public's fancy as traditional country's new savior, the man who would carry on the hard-country styles of George Jones and Merle Haggard and become the new standard-bearer. With his first album, *Storms of Life* (1986), Travis opened the floodgate for the long-awaited new traditionalism. In so doing, he made room for a host of competitors, among them Garth Brooks and Clint Black, both of whom immediately began to surpass him at award shows and in record stores. Brooks and Black, by occasionally adding pop inflections to traditional sounds, succeeded admirably in drawing new fans to country.

About the Author. Alanna Nash is a free-lance writer with a special interest in country music. She has written several books, including *Dolly* (1978), *Behind Closed Doors: Talking with the Legends of Country Music* (1988), and *Golden Girl: The Story of Jessica Savitch* (1988). Her work appears regularly in *Stereo Review* and *Entertainment Weekly*.

Music awards given specifically for the country genre, like those of the Academy of Country Music, have received growing publicity in recent years. Among country's rising stars are 1993 award winners Kix Brooks and Ronnie Dunn (top), Tracy Lawrence (near right), and Michelle Wright (far right).

The new stars, however, often came from very different backgrounds than the old-style country performers. "You got to have smelt a lot of mule manure before you can sing like a hillbilly," Hank Williams, country's patron saint, once said, describing what it takes to be a real country singer. But Brooks, the man who would eclipse Williams as country's greatest star, did nothing of the kind growing up in small-town Yukon, OK, the son of an oil-company worker.

Garth Brooks, the singer's 1989 debut album, was certified quadruple platinum, meaning that more than 4 million copies were sold. His follow-up record, *No Fences* (1990), fared even better, with sales at 10 million copies. But Brooks made truly head-turning history in 1991, when his third album, *Ropin' the Wind,* became the first country album to debut at Number 1 on *Billboard* magazine's *pop* chart, with almost 3 million copies sold in the first week of release. He was also the first performer

to have three albums in the top five on the country chart, and the first to have three country albums in pop's top 50. All that occurred despite the fact that *Ropin' the Wind* was the first country album to carry a new, higher price tag. By mid-1993, sales of *Ropin' the Wind* stood at 9 million, while 5 million units of his fourth album, *The Chase* (1992), had passed the cash register. *In Pieces*, released in late August 1993, debuted at the top of *Billboard*'s country and pop charts, representing the biggest first week yet for a Brooks album.

That is the kind of acceptance that early country stars such as Roy Acuff, Ernest Tubb, and Kitty Wells—who counted their following exclusively among rural Americans or displaced Southerners working in the industrial North—could fathom only in their wildest fantasies. "The secret to Garth's success," says his manager, Pam Lewis, "is that people can relate to him. He's an Everyman. He's chubby, he's round-faced, he's balding, the rest of his hair is starting to go gray, and sometimes his grammar's not the best, even though he's this close to a master's degree. He's very human."

Yet the popular-music field was ripe for somebody like Brooks. He ambled along in 1989 and played, mostly, the same kind of neotraditional music as Travis and Black—a fellow newcomer with whom Brooks at first was compared and confused. But then Brooks and his producer, Allen Reynolds, decided to reveal another side of the singer's personality, broadening his appeal with the release of a single called "The Dance," a mini-essay on the meaning of life and death. That song, along with its sentimental and powerful video that summoned the ghost of John Fitzgerald Kennedy, spoke to the same baby-boomer audience that revered Brooks' mainstream influences from the 1970s—country-tinged singer-songwriters Dan Fogelberg and

The Grand Ole Opry (below) in Nashville, TN, is felt by many to be synonymous with country music. Despite the wide media exposure attained by the new stars, an appearance on the Opry still is a sign that a performer has reached the pinnacle of success. Although Branson, MO, has thrived as a country mecca, Nashville still is a dream destination for most country-music fans.

© Mary Powell/LGI Photo Agency

Clint Black

Clint Black, 31, burst onto the country scene in 1989. His first two albums, *Killin' Time* (1989) and *Put Yourself in My Shoes* (1990), sold 5 million copies each, and his third, *The Hard Way* (1992), debuted near the top of *both* the pop and country charts. His 1993 album, *No Time to Kill*, also proved to be a hit.

© Michael Tackett/LGI Photo Agency

Wynonna Judd

Wynonna Judd, 29, a native of Ashland, KY, went solo in 1992 when her mother, Naomi, retired. The two, as The Judds, had been a successful country duo. Judd's self-titled first album, featuring rock-, blues-, and gospel-flavored country, sold 1 million copies in its first week. Her follow-up, *Tell Me Why* (1993), also was a success.

© Bill Schwab/Retna

Lorrie Morgan

Loretta Lynn (Lorrie) Morgan, 33, is steeped in country roots. The daughter of Grand Ole Opry star George Morgan, she made her first Opry appearance at 13 and toured with her father until he died in 1975; she later toured for two years with George Jones. Her 1993 album, *Watch Me,* climbed into the top 20 of the Billboard charts.

© William Campbell/Sygma

Trisha Yearwood

Trisha Yearwood, 29, a native of Monticello, GA, has business savvy as well as musical talent. She did not begin singing professionally until after college (where she majored in business administration). Nevertheless, her self-titled debut album went platinum within months of its 1991 release, and her first single hit Number 1.

© Beth Gwinn/Retna

Randy Travis

Randy Travis concentrates on a traditional country sound. In 1987, at 28, he became the youngest member ever of the Grand Ole Opry. Born in Marshville, NC, Travis conquered drug and alcohol problems before hitting it big. His first three albums (*Storms of Life*, 1986; *Always & Forever*, 1987; *Old 8 x 10*, 1988) all went platinum.

© Adele Starr/LGI Photo Agency

Kathy Mattea

Kathy Mattea often is called one of country's most adventurous performers. After dropping out of college, she moved to Nashville to be a songwriter, but soon branched into singing as well. Her song "Eighteen Wheels and A Dozen Roses" won the 1988 Country Music Association Single of the Year award.

James Taylor—and to the musical fence-sitters, who, like Brooks, wore a cowboy hat with their turtleneck shirts.

Suddenly, country music had a hero who seemed to speak for today's generation—a big change, since country traditionally had appealed to an older audience. Of course, Brooks also knew what his audience wanted to hear. As a marketing major in college, he set his sights on making music a vehicle for both his creative and his financial ambitions. And other commercially savvy stars have followed in his footsteps. Says Lisa Rebecca Gubernick, the author of *Get Hot or Go Home/Trisha Yearwood: The Making of a Nashville Star,* "These are people who view it as a profession. It's not a bunch of hillbillies."

© Beth Gwinn/Retna

Travis Tritt

Travis Tritt calls his music "country music with a rock 'n' roll attitude." Inspired as a youth by such groups as the Allman Brothers and the Eagles, Tritt adds various popular influences to a traditional country sound. His best-known song, "Here's a Quarter (Call Someone Who Cares)," has become something of a modern country classic.

© UPI/Bettmann

Reba McEntire

Reba McEntire is an established star of the "new country" music. She studied classical violin and piano in college while majoring in education. Picked four times by the Country Music Association as best female vocalist, in 1993 she released *It's Your Call*, which was expected to go double platinum, as did her previous album.

© William Campbell/Sygma

Mary-Chapin Carpenter

Mary-Chapin Carpenter, 35, was born in New Jersey, lived in Japan for a time as a child, and has a B.A. from Brown University. Carpenter won the Academy of Country Music's Top New Female Vocalist Award in 1990, has won two Grammy awards, and received the top female vocalist award from the Country Music Association in 1992 and 1993.

That awareness of the modern world spills over to country's new fans. What this means, says singer Mary-Chapin Carpenter, who earned a degree from Brown University, is that "the typical country fan doesn't adhere to a stereotype any longer. Many people who seek this music out today consider themselves urban dwellers and educated people. Just as the artists have changed in the last five years, the audience has, too."

The success of Brooks, Carpenter, and their like made country music "hip" in a way it never had been before. But while these new stars doubtless brought new fans to the fold and helped change audience demographics, the genre always has enjoyed a substantial number of closet fans. In 1991, when the bible of the music industry, *Billboard* magazine, adopted the SoundScan method of tabulating records sold, country albums zoomed up the Top 200 album chart, a likely indication that country sales long had been underreported. Today, *Billboard's* 200 Top Albums chart, based on the number of records sold regardless of genre, shows that country performers such as Southern rocker Travis Tritt, neotraditionalist Alan Jackson, bluegrass-tinged Vince Gill, and balladeer Reba McEntire sell as many records as do major rock acts.

The Role of Television and Radio. Cable television, which by 1993 boasted two country-music channels reaching a combined 69 million homes, also has been a major boost to country's new success, as has radio. Thanks to listeners who could not understand rap and could not tolerate heavy metal, country radio gained unprecedented numbers of new fans. An Arbitron study in 1991 found that country had overtaken the top-40 format in popularity, and that, in gaining 6 million new listeners between 1990 and 1991, it had emerged as the second-most-popular music format, behind adult contemporary—which lost 8 million listeners in the same period. By 1993 more than 2,500 radio

stations—more than 25% of the total—were programming country music, making it the most predominant format.

Some radio listeners may have turned to country as a way to stave off the economic blues. "Whenever times get bad, people return to their roots," says Steve Berger, the president of Nationwide Communications, Inc., in Columbus, OH, which counts 15 radio stations among its holdings. "Country had a good five-year run starting in about 1978, when, as today, we were coming out of a recession. It ties in with today's new sincerity. It'll have another good five-year run."

Country Becomes a Fad. The question is, can one really call this new, more commercial music "country," since it eschews the grisly topics of early country such as train wrecks, and now relies as much on synthesizers as pedal steel guitar? When Brooks sings Billy Joel's "Shameless," is it country because Brooks delivers it in a cowboy hat? It has become confusing.

It hardly seems to matter, though, since the United States by 1993 seemed obsessed with all things vaguely country-and-western—a nostalgic return to seminal television heroes like Hopalong Cassidy and Roy Rogers and Dale Evans, perhaps. But since the modern-day cowboy is often the hard-calloused construction worker, it is no wonder that the United States is celebrating, as Joe Diffie puts it in his hit single, the "Honky Tonk Attitude." In the past two years, country dance clubs like Denim and Diamonds in Santa Monica, CA, and Coyote's in Louisville, KY, have sprung up across the country faster than jimson weed.

The old honky-tonks were often smoky places with sticky barstools and live music—usually about romantic misery. They were working-class places where the pipe fitter with busted

Long-established stars of country music, like Loretta Lynn (below), retain the respect and admiration of fans of both new- and old-style country; many have become even more successful due to the new spotlight on the genre.

knuckles went for a beer and maybe even a fight at the end of the day. What pass for honky-tonks now are usually squeaky-clean bars with polyester cacti and often canned music, frequented by Garth Brooks clones of every income and lifestyle. "People come out to dance more and drink less," explains Coyote Calhoun, co-owner of Coyote's, and also program director for Louisville's WAMZ radio. In short, these clubs are country discotheques.

Many of today's most prominent country performers are young women. Emmylou Harris, Kathy Mattea, Trisha Yearwood, Pam Tillis, Patty Loveless (left to right above, with backup singer)*, and Mary-Chapin Carpenter* (with guitar) *all have emerged as stars in the past few years.*

"There's no tradition—it's a contrived atmosphere," insists Mary Jane Nalley, owner of Gruene Hall, the oldest honky tonk in Texas, which started in 1878 as a community meeting place, and where, even today, no one ever line dances.

Apart from the Brooks phenomenon, and the success of the newer performers who emulate his style, the so-called country "boom" may be more a discovery and promotion than anything else. Country always has had a reigning superstar of any time period, like Willie Nelson, who sold 4 million copies of his 1978 album *Stardust*. But today the genre is producing several multi-platinum acts at once. "The boom that began with Garth Brooks shows no signs of letting up," *The New York Times* proclaimed in 1992. Yet not all of Nashville is ready to grandstand. "I think we're making progress, but I don't think we can call it a boom unless country's 50 per cent of the market, with ten Garth Brookses," says Rick Blackburn, president of Atlantic Records/Nashville. "We don't want to break our arms patting ourselves on the back yet."

But with country continuing to join forces with other forms of popular music—including Celtic, rock, folk, jazz, and blues—the genre has taken a firm—and apparently quite accurate—stand in representing itself as "America's Music."

© AP/Wide World

CULTS IN AMERICA

By Darrell Turner

More than 25,000 couples representing 120 countries were married in a mass wedding ceremony in Olympic Stadium in Seoul, South Korea, on Aug. 25, 1992. The ceremony was sponsored by the Unification Church and was the largest multiple wedding on record. Although the exact definition of what constitutes a cult continues to be debated, the Unification Church, which was founded by Sun Myung Moon, is generally labeled as such.

The fiery demise in April 1993 of the Branch Davidians and their leader, David Koresh (*see* accompanying article), concluded a standoff that renewed concerns about the nature and role of cults in America.

Reports of the unconventional lifestyle and beliefs of the Davidians in their compound in Waco, TX, and the violence that left four federal agents and more than 80 Davidians dead recalled an earlier notorious example of cult violence—Jim Jones and the People's Temple in Guyana. Jones had moved several hundred of his followers to the South American country from California in 1977. Several relatives of members told Rep. Leo Ryan (D-CA) that they believed Jones was exploiting his followers sexually and financially and urged an investigation. Ryan, a congressman who was known for his penchant for personal involvement, flew to Jonestown, Guyana, to see for himself in November 1978. He was killed by Jones' followers, after which more than 900 people, including Jones, died in a mass murder-suicide.

A Gallup Poll found that the Jonestown tragedy was the best-known news event of 1978. Similarly, by the end of 1993,

millions of people recognized the name of David Koresh, although a year earlier he and the Branch Davidians were virtually unknown. While the Jonestown deaths led to calls for government investigations of religious cults, the government assault on the Davidians' compound led to widespread appeals for restraint in dealing with marginal religious groups, even if they are armed heavily and considered dangerous. The Koresh tragedy also prompted warnings against government agencies trying to determine what is or is not a cult.

What Is a Cult?. "Under the religious liberty provisions of the First Amendment, government has no business declaring what is orthodox or heretical, or what is a true or false religion," according to a statement issued by 16 religious and civil-liberties groups, including the American Civil Liberties Union and the National Council of Churches, after the Waco events. In fact, defining a cult is a problem even for nongovernmental organizations. A tendency of some religious groups to use the term for others that do not share their beliefs has led to the cult label being applied to such groups as the Roman Catholic Church, Jews for Jesus, and the Lubavitcher Hasidim.

An inclination to label extremist religious groups as fundamentalist also has muddied the waters. The fundamentalist tag has been used in books and articles about people—including Koresh, Jones, and the Rev. Sun Myung Moon—simply because they quoted the Bible frequently, even though their interpretations would make such Christian fundamentalists as the Rev. Jerry Falwell or the Rev. Bob Jones III shudder. Anticult movements that arose in the late 1960s and early 1970s have used the term "destructive cults" to emphasize objectionable behavior rather than beliefs. But there is also considerable disagreement on what constitutes dangerous lifestyles and whether members of cult groups are free to leave at will or are held captive through brainwashing.

About the Author. Darrell Turner was an associate editor for the Religious News Service in New York City for a number of years. In 1993 he moved to Fort Wayne, IN, where he maintains his interest in religious news, writing on various topics in the field on a free-lance basis.

© David Fitzgerald/Sipa

The role of cults in society again came to the forefront in 1993 as David Koresh led his group of Branch Davidians to their doom near Waco, TX, in the spring. A 51-day standoff between Koresh and his group and law-enforcement officers received much attention—and not just from the news media. At least one entrepreneur, left, sought to capitalize on the standoff by selling T-shirts.

© Pozanik/Gamma-Liaison

The shaven heads, saffron dress, and chanting of the Hare Krishnas became familiar sights and sounds on U.S. streets during the 1970s. Bhaktivedanta Swami Prabhupa had imported the movement—the International Society of Krishna Consciousness—from India.

"The term 'cult' has become virtually meaningless," according to Michael Barkun, professor of political science at Syracuse University. In an article in the June 2-9, 1993, issue of *The Christian Century*, he wrote that "it tells us far more about those who use it than about those to whom it is applied. It has become little more than a label slapped on religious groups regarded as too exotic, marginal, or dangerous." And Robert C. Fuller, professor of philosophy and religious studies at Bradley University, Peoria, IL, has noted that "we should be careful not to become overly suspicious of all small or dissenting religious groups." He stated that history is full of examples of movements that, "although far outside the mainstream American society, were nonetheless admirable in their pursuit of religious and moral purity."

Barkun and other observers have pointed out that groups that have existed for a long time often are moved from the category of cult to sect, as has happened with such movements as Christian Science, the Jehovah's Witnesses, Mormons, and Seventh-day Adventists—of which the Branch Davidians were a distant splinter. The process also works the other way. Jim Jones started out as an ordained minister in the mainstream Christian Church (Disciples of Christ) and still retained that official status at the time of his death. Carl Raschke, professor of religious studies at the University of Denver, said the Branch Davidians began as a sect in 1959 when they left a group that had seceded from the Seventh-day Adventist Church and later became a cult when Koresh, then known as Vernon Howell, took over in 1989.

Deprogramming. Allegations by former members of brainwashing and mind control in controversial religious movements and documentation of sexual abuse in such groups as the People's Temple and Branch Davidians have fueled attempts to abduct members of so-called cult groups and return them to a "normal" state of mind through a process known as deprogramming. In some cases, deprogrammers have cooperated with police in their activities. In others, they have been arrested and even imprisoned on kidnapping charges. In both situations, deprogrammers have been hired by various parents of group members.

The Rev. Dean Kelley, director of civil and religious liberty for the National Council of Churches, has charged that "forcible deprogramming is the most serious stain on religious liberty facing this country in the later half of the 20th century." In contrast, Marcia Rudin, director of the International Cult Education Program in New York, said, "You have to balance out things. The wrong done to the cult member in the cult is so much larger than the wrong done by the parents."

The Rev. George Robertson, an independent Baptist minister who heads an antideprogramming group in Baltimore called Friends of Freedom, said that although deprogramming is not in the news as much as it once was, the number of such incidents and the people perpetrating them is greater than ever. According to Robertson, deprogramming incidents today often involve members of fundamentalist or Pentecostal churches. He said such churches are often small, local congregations that are not

(Continued on page 68.)

Jim Jones, left, an Indiana-born minister, founded the People's Temple in the mid-1960s. Based in San Francisco and Los Angeles, the Temple initially won acclaim for its volunteer work. After the group came under fire in 1977, Jones moved it to a jungle compound in Guyana. While in that South American nation to investigate the group in late 1978, Rep. Leo J. Ryan (D-CA) was assassinated on an airstrip. Subsequently, more than 900 of Jones' followers committed suicide at his summoning.

David Koresh and the Branch Davidians

David Koresh, above, was born Vernon Howell in Houston, TX, in 1959. He became associated with the Branch Davidians about 1980 and began to claim to be the messiah.

© Acikalin/Sipa

On April 19, 1993, fiery death came for David Koresh, the leader of the fundamentalist Branch Davidians, and some 72 of his disciples, including as many as 17 children. The siege ended in a conflagration at the cult's 77-acre (31-ha) spread, called Mount Carmel, about 10 mi (16 km) east of Waco, TX. The end, which followed a 51-day standoff between Koresh and his group and law-enforcement officers, came much in the way that Koresh—who called himself a prophet, the Lamb of God, and Jesus Christ—had foretold: a fiery battle between Koresh and his followers and the forces of authority.

Some disaffected members of the cult that the 33-year-old Koresh ruled—the fundamentalist Branch Davidians, a disavowed sect of the Seventh Day Adventist Church—said that Koresh had amassed an arsenal of weapons at his compound in preparation for a flaming confrontation with the law. Marc Breault, who described himself as Koresh's right-hand man from 1986 through 1989, said: "Koresh would use fire as a metaphor, saying fire would destroy the world for a new beginning." Such a conclusion was one that Koresh, whose visions of himself were grandiose, probably relished. He was obsessed with the Book of Revelation, the apoc-

alyptical book of the Bible that refers to a flaming lake and other fiery images. It also envisions a new heaven and a new earth, a holy city for the faithful, and the destruction of evil.

"If the Bible is true," Koresh said, "then I'm Christ. But so what? Look at 2,000 years ago. What's so great about being Christ? A man nailed to the cross. A man of sorrow acquainted with grief. You know, being Christ ain't nothing." Koresh also identified with the "Lamb" that is described in the Book of Revelation as having the power to uncover the Seven Seals—including "the Four Horsemen of the Apocalypse"—that also obsessed him.

A senior official of the Federal Bureau of Investigation (FBI) corroborated the cultists' account of Koresh's preaching. "From the middle of the 1980s on, [Koresh] has been preaching that their group will end up in a violent confrontation with law enforcement and that this will be a fulfillment of his prophecy," the official said.

David Koresh. David Koresh had a troubled background. Born in Houston, TX, in 1959 to a single mother, he was named Vernon Howell at birth. (He later called himself David Koresh, and in 1991 legally changed his name. The name Koresh derives from the Persian by way of Hebrew and means Cyrus, the name of the Persian monarch who conquered Babylon and who is mentioned in three books of the Bible. The word came to mean any great king. Koresh also named one of his sons Cyrus.)

Details of Koresh's early life and upbringing are meager, but it is known that as a child he suffered from learning disabilities. At an early age he became devoted to the Seventh Day Adventist religion and to the Bible. Despite his learning problems he developed a marked ability to quote from memory long passages from the Bible. In 1977 he dropped out of high school in Garland, TX, a suburb of Dallas. Around 1984 he came to Mount Carmel, where he became associated closely with Lois Roden, leader of the Branch Davidian sect. After her death in 1986, Koresh and seven of his followers fought a gun battle with Lois' son, George Roden, for control of the group. Koresh's trial in 1988 for attempted murder ended in a deadlocked jury; the charge later was dismissed.

Koresh began aggressively recruiting converts to the Branch Davidian faith and to the compound in Waco. He reportedly impressed his followers with sermons on the Bible that sometimes lasted 17 hours. Men and women lived separately at the compound, but Koresh was reportedly free to take any "wife" he fancied. Many of the children living in the compound were reputed to be his children.

Koresh's Branch Davidians were headquartered at Mount Carmel, above, a 77-acre (31-ha) spread east of Waco, TX. By 1993 authorities believed that the cult had stockpiled enough food at the compound to survive a long siege.

The 1993 Standoff. Although Branch Davidians had lived in the Waco area since 1935, few outside the immediate area knew much about them until the morning of Feb. 28, 1993. On that day, 100 agents of the U.S. Bureau of Alcohol, Tobacco and Firearms (ATF)—with assistance from the local police—converged on the Koresh compound, attempting to serve warrants alleging that illegal weapons were stockpiled in the compound. A White House spokesman later said there also was "overwhelming evidence" that children in the compound were being abused.

Koresh reportedly knew in advance about the raid and was ready for the officers. In a 45-minute gun battle that began shortly after the agents arrived, four federal agents were killed and 16 others were wounded. After the battle,

Four federal agents were killed and more than a dozen were wounded at Mount Carmel on Feb. 28, 1993, as authorities staged an abortive raid on the compound. The officials wanted Koresh for illegal possession of weapons and explosives. There also were allegations that Koresh had abused children.

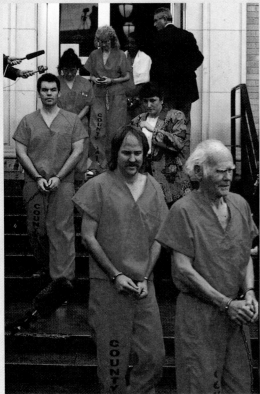

© Bob Strong/Sipa

After the raid, cultists were charged with conspiracy to murder federal agents and possessing firearms during a violent crime. Others were held as material witnesses.

during which DeGuerin conferred again with Koresh. Rumors began to circulate that a break in the impasse was at hand. The FBI then announced that Koresh appeared to be about to give up but said he was awaiting a sign from God before doing so.

Koresh on April 9 sent a letter to the FBI warning that an earthquake would damage the Waco area, including a dam on Lake Waco. (Earthquakes are almost unheard-of in Texas, and no such event occurred.) On April 10, Koresh wrote a second, four-page "letter from God," promising vengeance on Koresh's enemies. Four days later, Koresh said he would end his resistance after he finished a manuscript dealing with the Seven Seals in the Book of Revelation. On Friday, April 16, the FBI began clearing underbrush, debris, wreckage, and motor vehicles from the compound area. One of the cars belonged to Koresh.

At 5:55 A.M. on Monday, April 19, the FBI notified cultists by phone that tear gas would be pumped into the compound. Shortly thereafter, an armored vehicle smashed into a building of the compound near the entrance. When the FBI injected tear gas—in what was described as light concentrations—into the building, cultists inside began firing at the vehicle.

During the morning, armored vehicles repeatedly rammed holes in the building. Each time they did so, cultists fired at the vehicles. Around noon, smoke and flame began to issue from the compound. Fanned by brisk prairie

Koresh claimed that his 2-year-old daughter was among those who had been killed in the compound and that he and others had been wounded. Until the final showdown on April 19, however, there was no further gunplay at the compound during the siege.

On March 1, the day after the gun battle, Koresh spoke on radio, saying that the shooting had been "unnecessary." On the same day, ten children left the compound. On the following day, two women and six more children came out. The trouble seemed destined for resolution when Koresh announced he was ready to surrender if a taped statement were broadcast. His statement was aired on radio and television, but Koresh did not surrender.

After more adults and children left the compound between March 4 and March 12, the FBI on the 18th began using loudspeakers to enable the cultists to hear tapes of negotiations between federal agents and the cult leaders. Also blared at the compound were recordings of Tibetan chants, squealing rabbits, and the singing of Nancy Sinatra.

On March 24, Koresh suspended negotiations. Five days later, he talked again with negotiators and with his lawyer, Dick DeGuerin of Houston. Several days of negotiations ensued,

One of the 21 children who were released by the cult to the custody of the Texas child-welfare agency drew her vision of the Kingdom of Heaven with the Star of David.

© Howell/Gamma-Liaison

© Greg Smith/Saba

Hours after U.S. agents began spraying tear gas and battering holes in the walls of the fortified Mount Carmel on April 19, the compound was engulfed in flames. More than 80 Davidians were killed in the apparent mass suicide.

winds, the fire rapidly spread throughout the compound as those nearby—and millions on live television—looked on in horror. No fire engines were at the scene, but the FBI called the Waco Fire Department at 12:15 P.M. Nine persons who left the compound during the fire were taken to hospitals or to jail. Within 30 minutes, the fire had reduced the compound to a blackened ruin.

In the remains of the compound, investigators found bodies of the cult members, but it was days before Koresh's body was identified. Fire or smoke inhalation claimed most of the victims, but investigators said that Koresh and others, including some of the children, had been shot. The charred bodies of some of the children were found in their mothers' arms. A team of local arson investigators concluded from the presence of accelerants in the compound that the fire had been set deliberately. Except for the nine who left after the fire began, there were no survivors.

The Aftermath. Even before the ashes cooled at Mount Carmel, criticism and questions arose about the handling of the siege by the federal agencies. U.S. Attorney General Janet Reno, who approved the final assault after consulting with President Bill Clinton, took responsibility for the decisions involved. The president in turn

blamed the carnage on Koresh, whom Clinton described as "dangerous, irrational, and probably insane."

Critics, however, asked why agents did not arrest Koresh in Waco, which he was said to visit frequently, before February 28. ATF officials said they never saw Koresh there. Other critics asked how Koresh had learned about the raid before the federal agents moved in. *The New York Times*, however, reported that on February 27, the day before the raid, Waco was "buzzing with talk of the raid," especially after federal agents began pouring into town from Houston, Dallas, and New Orleans. There also were reports that television networks had been alerted on February 27 that a major development in the case was imminent. A late September report by the Treasury Department concluded that the decision to proceed with the raid was wrong "not just in retrospect, but because of what the decision makers knew at the time."

LYNWOOD ABRAM

About the Author. Lynwood Abram is a freelance writer and newspaper correspondent based in El Paso, TX.

The Rev. Sun Myung Moon and his wife, right, wore flower wreaths at a 1981 rally as the businessman turned evangelist pleaded innocent to charges of tax evasion. Moon's supporters and others considered his subsequent conviction and imprisonment to be harassment. Moon's Unification Church has vast holdings, including Bridgeport University in Connecticut and "The Washington Times."

© UPI/Bettmann

part of a national organization, and the deprogramming targets are often adults.

The American Psychological Association has declined to take a stand on whether there is such a thing as mind control or brainwashing as defined by cult opponents. And even if there is, some observers question its effectiveness in the long term. Elizabeth C. Nordbeck, dean of the faculty at Andover Newton Theological School in Massachusetts, has pointed out that about 90% of people who join groups labeled cults voluntarily leave within two or three years. Nordbeck believes that this is "a finding that challenges the familiar depiction of cults as fortress-like enclaves of repression from which victims can exit only through outside intervention."

The Rise of Cults. J. Gordon Melton, director of the Institute for the Study of American Religion in Santa Barbara, CA, believes that "what has been viewed as the rise of cults in America is actually but a single phase of a total global shift in world religion." He cites such trends as the growth of Asian immigration to the West, flourishing of parapsychology, and maturation of metaphysical practices as factors.

Cultism is difficult to quantify because of the differing definitions. Estimates of the number of groups in the United States range from Melton's 700 to the 2,000-5,000 range cited by Margaret Singer, a psychology professor emeritus at the University of California-Berkeley. Membership estimates also vary, particularly because many adherents leave after a few years. Again, Melton is at the low end of the scale with estimates of 150,000 to 200,000, while Singer uses a figure of 10 to 20 million. On the other hand, the Chicago-based Cult Awareness Network believes that there are 2,500 cults in the United States.

The makeup of such groups is diverse. "Cult members are no longer just college-aged young people," said Rabbi A. James Rudin, national interreligious affairs director of the American

Jewish Committee and Marcia Rudin's husband. "Middle-aged men and women are being aggressively recruited into cult groups. And in some cases, entire families join. Thousands of children are born into cults or brought in by their parents or new members."

What attracts people to these movements? Studies have cited such factors as a desire for certainty in a world of rapid change, a search for love and acceptance, and idealism. A study of 41 Jewish families who had consulted a "cult hotline" run by the Jewish Board of Family and Children's Services in New York City was conducted. The results of the study indicated that "cult-involved families, when compared with a control group, were more concerned with political, social, intellectual, and cultural activities." Mel White, an evangelical Christian writer who interviewed several People's Temple defectors, found that they had been attracted to the group because "the Christian people in their experience didn't seem to love each other inside the church. And second, Christian people didn't seem to love the needy outside the church."

Political activities engaged in by people considered cult leaders sometimes have won them respectability outside the religious sphere. This was true of Jones on the left, who won a mayoral appointment to the San Francisco Municipal Housing Authority, and Moon on the right, who was received at the Nixon White House. Anticult groups often have accused such people and their followers of deception in recruiting members. Moon's disciples have organized a number of political groups and seminars that their opponents describe as "fronts" for his Unification Church. In the late 1960s and early 1970s, the Children of God (now known as The Family) used sex as part of a recruiting technique known as "flirty fishing."

However, Melton said that "most groups are and have been quite open and proud of their organization, and many, particularly those whose members adopt distinctive dress, would have a next to impossible task concealing their identity." He noted that the Krishnas' shaven heads and saffron robes make them stand out, and that the Church of Scientology requires prospective members to fill out a form in which they acknowledge their awareness that they are about to participate in a Scientology event.

Both dispassionate scholars and rabid anticultists agree that education—specifically, learning as much as possible about the particular group—is one answer in dealing with cults. To this end, Dean Nordbeck has added that "our presentations must be historically, sociologically, and psychologically sound, representing the research and conclusions of both anticultists and cult defenders."

And as far as the use of the term "cult" is concerned, Karl Meyer noted in a *New York Times* editorial-page notebook column on March 7, 1993, that "an old-time Chicago columnist, Sydney Harris, used to tease his readers with a word game that went like this: My religion is a denomination, yours is a sect, and theirs a cult. Americans who were repelled by the bloody shootout in Waco, TX, would do well to keep that useful declension in mind."

THE U.S. VICE-PRESIDENCY

An Analysis of the Office

By Robert Shogan

Albert Gore, Jr., who had served as a member of the U.S. House of Representatives and as a U.S. senator from Tennessee, was sworn in as the 45th U.S. vice-president by Supreme Court Justice Byron White on Jan. 20, 1993. Gore's close working relationship with Bill Clinton during the presidential campaign and transition period caused political analysts to wonder if the office of vice-president would assume a new role in the Clinton administration.

When Tennessee Sen. Albert Gore was swept into office as U.S. vice-president in November of 1992 along with presidential running mate Bill Clinton, expectations were high that Gore's tenure as Clinton's understudy would mark a break with the pattern of frustration and isolation that for more than two centuries so often has been the hallmark of the vice-presidency. During the presidential campaign, Gore had come closer to filling the role of full partner on the Democratic ticket than any vice-presidential candidate in recent memory. Along with a youthful vigor that made him resemble Clinton, Gore—as a longtime federal legislator—brought with him experience in national affairs that was an important supplement to Clinton's background in state government.

But since Gore was installed as the nation's 45th vice-president on Jan. 20, 1993, his public profile has been clouded by questions all too familiar to occupants of what is nominally the nation's second-most-important office. In place of the partnership relationship established during the campaign, Gore was left to discharge duties that were mainly ceremonial or ancillary. And in addition to being overshadowed by the president, as had been all his predecessors, Gore had the special problem of being overshadowed by the president's wife, Hillary Rodham Clinton, who early in the Clinton presidency assumed responsibilities that shattered all precedent for first ladies.

Evidence of Gore's shrinking public presence came from a *New York Times*/CBS poll published during his first weeks in office, which showed that the proportion of voters who knew too little about Gore to have an opinion about him rose from 14% late in the election campaign to 44%. He became the butt of jokes for comedians, including *The Tonight Show* host Jay Leno, who quipped: "I tell you, if there was an energy tax on people, Gore would be getting a refund." And Gore himself, mindful of his circumstances, read aloud to a reporter the description of his job by an earlier holder of the office, Thomas R. Marshall, Woodrow Wilson's vice-president. Marshall had likened a vice-president to a man suffering a cataleptic seizure. "He cannot speak, he cannot move. He suffers no pain. He is perfectly conscious of all that goes on. But he has no part in it."

But if Gore generally presented a passive appearance to the public, Washington insiders insisted that he was far more active, and influential, behind the scenes. *The Washington Post* reported that Gore was "being taken seriously by the president," not only in such areas as the environment and technology where he could claim expertise, "but as a more experienced hand on

About the Author. As national political correspondent in the Washington Bureau of *The Los Angeles Times,* Robert Shogan has observed firsthand the workings of the executive branch of the U.S. government during three decades. He is the author of *The Riddle of Power: Presidential Leadership from Truman to Bush* (1991) and *None of the Above: Why Presidents Fail & What Can Be Done About It* (1982). Mr. Shogan is a former assistant editor of *The Wall Street Journal* and a correspondent with *Newsweek* magazine.

© Trippett/Sipa

Vice-President Dan Quayle (extreme left) and Speaker of the House Thomas Foley welcomed George Bush to Congress as the president delivered a State of the Union address. According to the U.S. Constitution, the function of the vice-president is to be "president of the Senate." However, he or she "shall have no vote, unless they be equally divided."

A White House luncheon during the 1944 campaign was one of the rare meetings between Franklin Roosevelt and Harry Truman (left). Ending World War II and dropping the atomic bomb on Japan were major issues facing the former Missouri senator after he suddenly assumed the presidency following Roosevelt's death on April 12, 1945. Truman had served as vice-president for 83 days.

the workings of Washington and on the complexities of some foreign-policy issues." And *The Los Angeles Times*—citing Clinton's reported instructions to his cabinet secretaries: "Whenever you get a call from the vice-president, I want you to treat it as a call from me"—claimed that Gore's vice-presidency could become "the most influential in modern history."

It also was pointed out that Gore had been entrusted with helping to fulfill one of Clinton's major campaign promises— "reinventing government"—by being put in charge of the National Performance Review, a six-month study of the workings of every agency in the federal government. "We are determined to move ...from a government preoccupied with sustaining itself to a government clearly focused on serving the people," Gore said of his assignment. On September 7 the vice-president released more than 800 recommendations to streamline "old-fashioned, outdated government," save a total of $108 billion over five years, and cut 252,000 federal jobs by 1998. The job reductions, which would save more than $40 billion over five years, would be accomplished by eliminating various field offices and combining the enforcement and regulatory functions of various agencies. White House aides pointed out that some of the changes required congressional action and the resultant savings would not be realized immediately.

The Modern Vice-Presidency. The mixed signals about Vice-President Gore's role in the Clinton administration are reflective of two axioms that govern the destiny of modern vice-presidents. The first is that because of his propinquity to the president and to the focal point of national media attention in Washington, the modern vice-president is free to make of his job whatever he can—up to a point. And the second rule is that the president establishes where that point is, for no vice-president can be more important than the president wants him to be.

In the past half century, since Franklin Roosevelt vastly expanded the powers and prestige of the presidency, and in the

© AP/Wide World

As the nation's 36th vice-president, Richard M. Nixon represented the Eisenhower administration on numerous diplomatic missions. During the opening of the American National Exhibition in Moscow in July 1959, Vice-President Nixon exchanged views with Soviet Premier Nikita Khrushchev (extreme left) in what became known as the kitchen debate.

process enhanced the importance of the vice-presidency, the impact of vice-presidents on national politics has increased dramatically. Of the ten chief executives who have succeeded Roosevelt, five served first as vice-president. Three of these—Harry Truman in 1945, Lyndon Johnson in 1963, and Gerald Ford in 1974—moved up directly from the vice-presidency: Truman and Johnson after the deaths of Roosevelt and John Kennedy, respectively, and Ford after the resignation of Richard Nixon. Two other former vice-presidents—Nixon in 1968 and George Bush in 1988—won election to the presidency in their own right. In addition, during the same period, four former vice-presidents have been defeated candidates for the presidency: Henry Wallace, who was the standard-bearer for the short-lived Progressive Party in 1948; Richard Nixon, the Republican nominee in 1960; Hubert Humphrey, the Democratic nominee in 1968; and Walter F. Mondale, picked by the Democratic Party in 1984.

Moreover, the new prominence of the modern vice-presidents has allowed them to build constituencies of their own. Among the Republicans, Richard Nixon's aggressive anticommunism won him strong support among conservatives, as did the defense of traditional values by J. Danforth Quayle, Bush's vice-president. On the Democratic side, Wallace, Humphrey, and Mondale were regarded as bulwarks of liberal causes.

Yet even during this era of vice-presidential achievement, rejection and disappointment have been the frequent companions of nearly every vice-president. Mondale, who was credited with helping Jimmy Carter win the presidency in 1976 and was viewed as one of his most trusted advisers, considered resigning the post out of a sense of futility, according to Yale University professor Steven M. Gillon, author of *The Democrats' Dilemma: Walter F. Mondale and the Liberal Legacy.* "I thought there was not much I could do to change things so why break my

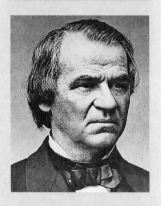

The eight vice-presidents who have assumed the presidency following the death of the chief executive are (top to bottom, page 74): *John Tyler, who succeeded W. H. Harrison in 1841; Millard Fillmore, who took over for Zachary Taylor in 1850; Andrew Johnson, who replaced Abe Lincoln*

health trying," Mondale later said. And on the Republican side, Quayle, though he was Bush's handpicked choice to be his running mate in 1988, was held in so little regard by some within his own party that some influential GOP leaders unsuccessfully sought to persuade Bush to drop him from the ticket when Bush sought reelection in 1992.

The Office's Origin. To understand the inherent problems of the vice-presidency it is necessary to go back to the origins of the office. Like many succeeding generations of politicians, the framers of the constitution had little interest in the vice-presidency itself but instead viewed it as a means to an end. The main end the vice-presidency was intended to serve was to assure an orderly procedure for replacement of a chief executive who had died or become disabled. The office came into being as a by-product of the initial plan for electing a president. Determined that the president of the United States would be a truly national or "continental" leader, the framers of the constitution required under Article II that each presidential elector from each state cast two ballots, at least one of which could not be for a candidate from his state. The Founding Fathers assumed that the electors would cast one ballot for their state's favorite son, and while these votes would be scattered, the other ballot would be cast for a personage of national renown who would gain the majority needed to become president. To make this system more meaningful, it was decided that whichever candidate received the second-highest total of votes would become vice-president.

The vice-president's principal duty, the framers decided, would be to preside over the Senate. John Adams, the first vice-president, made the most of this responsibility, casting the deciding vote to break ties 29 times in eight years—a mark not since equaled. Held in high esteem, Adams ultimately succeeded George Washington as president. But he had few illusions about the vice-presidency, as his oft-repeated comment in a letter to his wife Abigail revealed: "My country has in its wisdom contrived for me the most insignificant office that ever the invention of man contrived or his imagination conceived."

Before long, the development of political parties created unforeseen complications in this system of awarding the vice-presidency to the runner-up in the competition for president. The 1800 balloting resulted in a tie vote between Thomas Jefferson, the candidate for president of the anti-Federalist Party, which ultimately became the Democratic Party; and Aaron Burr, that party's candidate for vice-president. After a prolonged deadlock in the House of Representatives, marked by intrigue and controversy, Jefferson emerged as president and Burr as his vice-president. To avoid a repetition of such a divisive episode, Congress adopted the 12th Amendment to the constitution. Ratified in 1804, the amendment provided for separate election of vice-president and president and made the qualifications for the vice-presidency the same as for the presidency. But reflecting the low regard in which the vice-presidency still was held, drafters of the amendment made no attempt to correct the oversight of the Founding

Fathers by establishing a system for filling a vacancy in the vice-presidency itself.

In fact, by separating the vice-presidential and presidential selection process, the 12th Amendment in effect seemed to institutionalize the insignificance of the vice-presidency. Under the old double-ballot system, the first two vice-presidents, John Adams and Thomas Jefferson, had been elected to the presidency in their own right. But after the amendment's adoption, with the exception of Martin Van Buren—who won the presidency in 1836—and except for those vice-presidents who had succeeded directly to the presidency, no one who held the vice-presidency was able to win election to the presidency for more than a century. Richard Nixon broke that skein in 1968 when he won the White House eight years after his first bid for the presidency as Dwight Eisenhower's vice-president, had fallen short. And in 1988, Bush ended another prolonged jinx when he became the first incumbent vice-president since Van Buren to win the presidency.

Another sign of the low repute in which vice-presidents were held was cited by syndicated columnist Jules Witcover in his book *Crapshoot: Rolling the Dice on the Vice Presidency:* From the time John Calhoun ended his second term in the vice-presidency in 1832, no other vice-president was renominated for the office until James S. Sherman, William Howard Taft's vice-president, was renominated by the Republican Party in 1912.

For most of the first 150 years of U.S. history, vice-presidents became consequential only when they succeeded to the presidency by filling a vacancy in that office. This happened for the first time in 1841 when John Tyler took over from 68-year-old William Henry Harrison, who died only one month into his term from pneumonia he had contracted while delivering, bare-headed, a two-hour inaugural address on a bitter winter's day. Acting decisively to offset the ambiguity in the constitution about whether in the case of a presidential vacancy the vice-president assumed the office itself or just its powers, Tyler immediately took the oath of presidential office. Then in his inaugural address Tyler pointedly declared that his succession meant that for the first time "a vice-president has had devolved upon him the presidential office." Tyler's example meant that on the eight subsequent occasions when vice-presidents filled vacancies in the office of president, the issue of their legitimacy in office never was raised seriously.

But another problem, rooted in the separate balloting for the president and vice-president established by the 12th Amendment, has lingered on through history, often serving to diminish the office. The problem was foreseen during the congressional debate on the amendment. "The question will not be asked is he (a vice-presidential prospect) capable?" Sen. Samuel White of Delaware predicted at the time. "But can he by his name, by his connexions [connections], by his wealth, by his local situation, by his influence or his intrigues best promote the election of president?"

All too often, historians agree, practical political considerations have dominated the vice-presidential selection process and on many occasions have turned out in the long run to have had

Library of Congress

Library of Congress

Library of Congress

The Lyndon Baines Johnson Library

in 1865; Chester Arthur, who followed J. Garfield in 1881; page 75, Theodore Roosevelt, who succeeded William McKinley in 1901; Calvin Coolidge, who took over for Warren Harding in 1923; Harry Truman; and Lyndon B. Johnson, who followed John F. Kennedy in 1963.

© UPI/Bettmann

Gerald Ford (second from right) was the first person to become vice-president under the terms of the 25th Amendment. President Nixon named the House Republican leader from Michigan to the post following the resignation of Vice-President Spiro Agnew in October 1973. Chief Justice Warren Burger (left) administered the oath of office before a joint congressional session on Dec. 6, 1973.

Often political considerations have determined the vice-presidential nominees of both parties. In 1984, Democratic presidential candidate Walter Mondale (below), who had been Jimmy Carter's vice-president (1977-81), chose U.S. Rep. Geraldine Ferraro of New York as his running mate. She was the first woman to run on the national ticket of a major party. The Democratic duo was overwhelmed at the polls by the Republican incumbents—Ronald Reagan and George Bush.

© Mario Ruiz/Picture Group

decidedly impractical consequences. Perhaps the most dramatic example was the case of Andrew Johnson, nominated by the Republicans in 1864 to run with Lincoln in the midst of the Civil War because it was thought his Tennessee origins would broaden the appeal of the ticket. But after Lincoln's assassination made Johnson president and the war ended, his Southern sympathies brought him into bitter conflict with so-called Radical Republicans seeking to overturn the antebellum power structure in the South. The result was that Johnson was the only U.S. president to be impeached, and though he was narrowly acquitted of the charges against him, the controversy severely damaged his presidency.

Still, short-term political considerations continued to play a large role in vice-presidential selection. In 1900, Republican Party bosses schemed to make Theodore Roosevelt William McKinley's vice-president to curb Roosevelt's influence as governor of New York state. In their anxiety to sidetrack the independent-minded TR, the bosses disregarded McKinley's campaign manager, Mark Hanna, who warned: "Don't any of you realize that there is only one life between that madman and the presidency?." Hanna's fears turned out to be prophetic as Roosevelt soon succeeded the assassinated McKinley. But most historians would reject Hanna's low opinion of Roosevelt, whose visage was carved on Mount Rushmore.

Seeking to remedy other long-standing defects in the vice-presidency, Congress once again resorted to changing the constitution, adopting the 25th Amendment, which was ratified in 1967. Spurred by the serious illnesses of President Eisenhower while he was in office and the assassination of John Kennedy,

" Look, it may be a boring, go-nowhere, yes-man job, but it *is* the Vice Presidency. "

the framers of the amendment created for the first time procedures, in the case of presidential disability, for the vice-president to assume the powers of the presidency on a temporary basis. Another section of the amendment provides for filling a vacancy in the office of vice-presidency. This procedure first was used in 1973 by President Nixon, who selected Gerald Ford to replace Spiro T. Agnew. Agnew had resigned the vice-presidency as part of a plea bargain to escape severe punishment in a federal corruption investigation. Then, after Nixon himself resigned in 1974 to head off impeachment in the Watergate scandal, Ford, who replaced him, picked former New York Gov. Nelson Rockefeller as Ford's own replacement.

The Realities of the Office. Yet for all the twists and turns that have marked the course of the vice-presidency during two turbulent centuries, one factor has remained constant: the vice-president's dependence on his president. As history has demonstrated, without the president's goodwill the vice-president can accomplish little, and without the president's good fortune whatever ambitions the vice-president cherishes will come to naught. No one seems to understand these realities better than Vice-President Albert Gore. Though Gore unsuccessfully ran for the presidency once himself and, many believe, would like to do so again, he has shown himself for the present to be primarily the loyal servant of the man who chose him as his running mate, Bill Clinton. "My principal role is that of a general adviser to the president...to help him in every way I can to be the best president our nation has ever had," Gore told reporters not long after taking office.

© Renee Stockdale/Animals Animals

Pets:
A Growing Preoccupation

By Bette LaGow

About the Author. As a freelance writer and editor since the mid-1980s, Bette LaGow has contributed articles on a wide range of topics to regional newspapers and magazines. She is a former editorial correspondent and associate correspondence editor for *Reader's Digest*. An animal enthusiast, Ms. LaGow has written for the American Kennel Club and been the assistant editor of its *American Kennel Gazette*.

Americans' enormous interest in pets was exemplified early in 1993 with the fuss made over Socks, the new "First Pet." Chelsea Clinton's black-and-white cat drew a huge share of media attention and spawned an industry. For example, the Humane Society of the United States (HSUS) and Westin Hotels & Resorts sponsored a Socks look-alike contest, with the $10 entry fee going to the HSUS. But it was not only non-profit organizations that looked to cash in on Socks' newfound fame. Plenty of for-profit entities also hitched their wagons to his star. Entrepreneurs put Socks' likeness on just about anything—jewelry, bumper stickers, key rings, and T-shirts. Several books concerning Socks hit the stands shortly after the Clintons took up residence in the White House.

This outpouring of attention for a presidential pet was not unprecedented. Former President and Mrs. Bush's English springer spaniel, Millie, pulled in nearly $1 million for charity for authoring *Millie's Book* with then First Lady Barbara Bush in 1990. But from the huge amount of attention Socks received, it was obvious that pets are a growing preoccupation in the United States. From an interest in exotic and unique pets, to

pets' use in therapy to help depressed or ill humans, to an increasing concern with *their* inherent rights, domestic animals are a hot topic in the United States today.

Who Are Our Pets? It would seem appropriate that a cat is the current White House pet: Cats have outnumbered dogs as the pet of choice in U.S. households for several years. According to an extensive nationwide study commissioned by the American Veterinary Medical Association (AVMA), there are 57 million cats sharing the lives of Americans, in contrast to 52.5 million dogs. More households (34.6 million) have dogs than cats (29.2 million), but a cat-owning household is more likely to have multiple animals.

Although fish may not be as cuddly as cats or as much fun to play catch with as dogs, they are the next most popular pet, with 24 million in tanks and bowls across the United States. Birds are the pets of choice for 6% of U.S. households—that translates into nearly 12 million feathered friends—and 2% of U.S. pet owners apparently have enough room for the 5 million horses owned nationwide. Rabbits and rodents (hamsters, guinea pigs, and gerbils) round out the most-popular-pet list, with numbers coming in at 4.6 million, 1.3 million, 838,000, and 619,000, respectively.

As for the most popular among the most popular, the Cat Fanciers Association reports the Persian breed has the most registrations in their purebred cat registry, followed by the Maine Coon and the Siamese. Dog lovers opt most often for Labrador retrievers, according to the American Kennel Club's 1992 registration statistics, followed by Rottweilers, cocker spaniels, Chinese shar-pei, and German shepherd dogs.

Exotic Trends in Pet Ownership. Not since John Quincy Adams owned an alligator has a reptile claimed the attentions of a U.S. president. But a growing segment of the pet-owning population is turning its attention to such exotic pets. From snakes to turtles, lizards to iguanas, reptiles are living in U.S. homes in ever-increasing numbers. An estimated 2 million reptiles are owned by U.S. herpetoculturists

© Mike Stewart/Sygma

Following the election of Bill Clinton as 42d president of the United States, Socks, above, his daughter's pet cat, also became a celebrity. The extensive media attention given to Socks was an indication of the preoccupation Americans have with their pets.

(reptile lovers' self-created moniker). This number becomes even more impressive when one considers that many municipalities require special permits and licenses for people to keep reptiles as pets. Some credit the popularity of fictional characters such as the Teenage Mutant Ninja Turtles with bolstering the public's interest in reptiles. The dinosaur mania that has been sweeping the nation for the past several years is another probable factor, especially as concerns lizard ownership. Then, too,

there is the fact that reptiles are relatively low-maintenance pets. For busy people, a pet that needs to eat only a few times a week might have a certain appeal.

> *"Animals are such agreeable friends—they ask no questions, they pass no criticisms."*
>
> *George Eliot*

The Thriving Pet Industry. One thing Americans always have shared with their pets is their money, and this spending is growing by leaps and bounds. According to the Pet Food Institute, Americans spend an estimated $3.9 billion on dog food annually, and $2.4 billion on cat food. In addition to food—of which there is an enormous variety in the marketplace today, including "natural" pet foods, as well as gourmet and life-stage cuisines—Americans also spend a hefty chunk on veterinary care. In 1991 medical expenditures for dogs hovered around $4.6 billion; $2.3 billion was spent on cats, $314 million on horses, and $185 million on birds, according to the AVMA.

Beyond these bare necessities, there are many other opportunities to spend money on pets. The HSUS estimates that one can spend upward of $160 per year on toys and grooming supplies for a dog and another $75 per year on a cat. While this comparison makes a cat seem a veritable bargain, remember the need for about $80 worth of litter annually, which closes the gap. The purchases do not need to stop there, however. There are innumerable gimmicky products snapped up by dedicated dog and cat lovers. Several Texas companies are doing a brisk business selling animal life preservers. And speaking of preserving life, there are health-insurance policies to cover veterinary expenses should one's pet ever be hit by a car or fall victim to cancer or diabetes. Premiums run from $59 to $99 annually. If a pet should suffer from a serious illness, high-tech (and expensive) treatments are increasingly available, from ultrasound and CT scans to chemotherapy treatments, pacemakers, and heart surgery. There are even psychiatrists for emotionally troubled pets.

A booming offshoot industry born of the U.S. love affair with pets is pet sitting. For a fee, pet owners can find someone to come in and care for their pets while they are away on vacation or working long hours. It is a formalized version of the old-fashioned method of asking one's neighbor to feed and water one's dog. Professional pet

According to the American Kennel Club and the Cat Fanciers Association, the Labrador retriever, above right, and the Persian, below, were the most popular breeds of dogs and cats in 1993. The Persian cat has a large broad head, short nose, and very soft fur. The Labrador retriever—which originated in Newfoundland, not Labrador—is known as a strongly built, very active dog.

sitters often carry their own insurance, however, and will spend more time with their charges than would the next-door neighbor. A more recent development in pet care is "aftercare." The term was coined by the International Association of Pet Cemeteries to describe the service provided by their 650 U.S. members. For anywhere from $150 to $400, a grieving pet owner can have a memorial service or a cremation for his or her beloved pet. In the past, if an animal died while at a veterinarian's office, the vet automatically assumed responsibility for disposing of the animal's remains. Today more and more vets are referring people to pet cemeteries, pointing them toward an option that can help smooth the grieving process by providing a dignified sense of closure.

© Robert Pearcy

The Human-Animal Bond. That people would go to the expense and formality of a memorial service for their pets is not surprising. A close relationship between humans and animals has existed since ancient times. Simply put, pets always have made people feel good. Recent research has shown that this feeling has a basis in fact. Aside from easing loneliness, pets indeed may help people get well and stay well, both physically and emotionally. Studies have shown that elderly people require fewer doctor visits when they are bonded with a pet. And it has been well documented that pet owners have consistently lower blood pressure. In fact, the simple act of petting a cat or dog or gazing at fish in an aquarium can produce a drop in blood pressure.

Today, pets are providing their beneficial effects outside the home as well, in hospitals, nursing homes, schools, and prisons—anywhere the residents could use a little accepting, non-

Fish rate behind cats and dogs as the third-most-popular pet. For the fish enthusiast, meticulous care of the tank is a prime responsibility. Meanwhile, piglets, left, have found a following among those who seek a more unusual pet. A Rhode Island breeder has noted that pigs "make wonderful pets—affectionate like a dog, independent like a cat, clean, easy to train." The fact that pigs make noise—a frequent low grunt—can be a drawback, however.

© Lynn M. Stone/The Image Bank

judgmental care and affection. Pet-owning volunteers are providing that help. The Delta Society of Renton, WA, the premier resource and registry for human-animal interaction activities, estimates there are at least 2,000 animal-assisted activity programs nationwide. One such program, administered by the Delta Society, is Pet Partners, in which human/animal teams are trained and certified to visit the types of institutions mentioned above.

A more intense, formalized type of this activity is animal-assisted therapy, in which health professionals either prescribe or personally utilize animals in a therapeutic regimen. "Prescriptions" run from issuing a physically disabled person a dog to groom—thus enhancing strength and motor control—to using an animal to elicit verbal or tactile responses from previously unresponsive patients. One person in this field who has had great success is Dr. Mary Burch of Tallahassee, FL, who uses her own dogs to reach the troubled world of children born addicted to the cocaine derivative crack. As scientific research continues to show that animals can be invaluable in healing the human mind and body, both the study of this phenomenon and the use of pets to help human patients undoubtedly will increase.

What the Future Holds. Will the love affair between Americans and their pets—cats, dogs, iguanas, hamsters, et al—continue? It certainly would seem so, given the growing evidence that having animals in our lives is not only enjoyable, but beneficial to our mental and physical health. Although most pet owners may not go to the extremes of sending their pooch to a therapist or filling kitty's dish with haute cuisine, they still value their pets and appreciate their presence. And the often pampered animals certainly are not complaining!

© Norvia Behling/Earth Scenes

Americans spend billions of dollars annually to feed their pets. With an extensive selection, including "natural" and gourmet varieties, pet food takes up at least an entire aisle at the larger supermarket, above. A veterinarian, right, trims and examines a pet Amazon parrot. With the cost of health care for pets increasing, it now is possible to have pets covered by health insurance.

© Blair Seitz/Photo Researchers

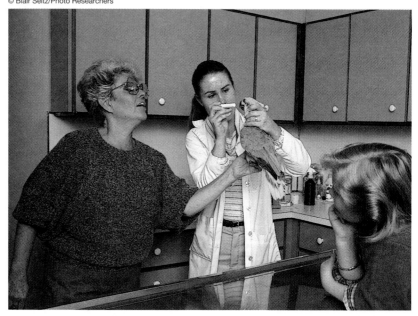

"Great French Paintings from the Barnes Foundation"

On May 2, 1993, at the National Gallery of Art in Washington, DC, an exhibit of 80 of the finest French Impressionist, Postimpressionist, and early modern paintings from the collection of Dr. Albert C. Barnes (1872-1951) went on public view. Cézanne's "The Card Players" (1890-92), Matisse's "le bonheur de vivre" ("The Joy of Life," 1905-06), Picasso's "Acrobat and Young Harlequin" (1905), Renoir's "Leaving the Conservatoire" (1877), and Seurat's "Models" (1886-88) were among the features of the exhibit. In addition, Matisse's tripartite mural, the "Merion Dance Mural" (1932-33), which normally hangs in the main gallery of the Barnes Foundation building in Merion, PA; and the newly discovered and restored "Unfinished Dance Mural" (1931), which was painted to hang in the hall in Merion but was ruled out because it was the wrong size, were shown.

Dr. Barnes, His Art Collection, and the Foundation. Albert Coombs Barnes was born on Jan. 2, 1872, in Philadelphia, PA. His father was a butcher. He worked his way through medical school by playing semiprofessional baseball and boxing. After completing medical school, he turned his attention to the study of pharmacology, codiscovering in the early 1900s and later

Dr. Albert C. Barnes assembled an outstanding collection of paintings during his lifetime (1872-1951). Eighty works from the collection were exhibited in 1993. Georges Seurat's "Models" (top) and Paul Cézanne's "The Card Players" (bottom center)—which normally are part of a "wall-ensemble" at the Barnes Foundation in Merion, PA—were highlights of the show.

Although the Barnes collection features paintings by such giants as Renoir, Van Gogh, Cézanne, Seurat, Picasso, Matisse, and Manet and is considered one of the world's finest private assemblages of art, it had been enjoyed by only a relative few prior to the 1993 exhibition. Works viewed at the historic show included:

VINCENT VAN GOGH
Joseph-Etienne Roulin, 1889
oil on canvas, 26 x 21 ⅝ inches (66.2 x 55 cm)

PABLO PICASSO
Acrobat and Young Harlequin
("Acrobate et jeune Arlequin"), 1905,
oil on canvas, 74 ⅞ x 42 ⅝ inches (190.3 x 107.8 cm)

PAUL CÉZANNE
Still Life with Skull
("Nature morte au crâne"),
1895-1900
oil on canvas 21 ⅜ x 25 ⅝ inches
(54.3 x 65 cm)

HENRI MATISSE
The Music Lesson
("La leçon de musique"), 1917
oil on canvas, 96 ⅜ x 79 inches
(244.7 x 200.7 cm)

PIERRE-AUGUSTE RENOIR
The Artist's Family
("La famille d'artiste"), 1896
oil on canvas, 68 x 54 inches
(173 x 140 cm)

Albert C. Barnes and his dog Fidèle are shown in front of Henri Matisse's "The Red Madras Headdress." Barnes, a medical doctor at the age of 20 who later turned his attention to pharmacology, believed that his art collection should serve as educational tools at the foundation he established in 1922.

manufacturing an antiseptic, Argyrol. His success in the business permitted him to begin to collect art—first with the U.S. painter William Glackens and then on his own. By the early 1920s he had become an obsessive collector, focusing on contemporary American and French Impressionist, Postimpressionist, and early modern works. He also would collect African tribal sculpture, Greek and Egyptian antiquities, and Native American art. In all, Barnes acquired 180 Renoirs, 69 Cézannes, 60 Matisses, and 44 Picassos.

In 1922, Barnes established the Barnes Foundation to "promote the advancement of education and the appreciation of the fine arts." Some 635 of his personal paintings were transferred immediately to the foundation, which was endowed with $6 million. In 1923-24 a 24-room gallery and administrative building for the foundation was constructed in French Renaissance style in Merion, PA. Paul Cret, who designed Philadelphia's Rodin Museum, was its architect. The gallery opened on March 19, 1925.

Barnes' interest in art and education—especially for the working class—caused him to insist that his employees attend class at his factory. As Barnes noted, the course "comprises an objective study of the great traditions of paintings, from the Byzantines to the work of the leading contemporaries, thus showing the continuity of the traditions and how the great artists of each period utilized the contributions of their predecessors as points of departure for their own creative work." In 1931, *The Art in Painting*, Barnes' first book, was published. It remains the basis for the study of art at the foundation. Strict adherence to Barnes' theories regarding art became the focal point of the foundation's classes. John Dewey was the foundation's first director of education. The foundation's galleries were opened only to a limited number of nonstudents, who had to have permission from Barnes or another board member. In essence, the foundation and its collection were more an educational institution than a museum.

In 1950, Barnes decided that Lincoln University, a liberal arts college for black Americans in Oxford, PA, would nominate four of the five trustees of the foundation following his death. (A fifth board position would be reserved for a representative of the Mellon Bank.) A friendship between Barnes and Horace Mann Bond, the president of Lincoln University, had developed in the late 1940s. In deciding the foundation's future, Barnes ignored the establishment of the art world—for which he had little respect.

Following Barnes' sudden death in 1951, the foundation board—which included his widow and a close working associate—adhered to his wishes regarding his art collection. Access

to the galleries remained limited, none of the works left their halls, and no color reproductions of the paintings from the Barnes collection were permitted. Finally in 1961 a judge ruled that if the foundation wished to maintain its tax-exempt status, it would have to open its galleries to the public. Consequently the board agreed to permit 200 persons to view the collection on Fridays, Saturdays, and Sundays. By 1988 the board of directors of the foundation had come under the control of trustees appointed by Lincoln University, and things began to change further. The new board felt that to the extent that was legally possible the Barnes Foundation should be part of the mainstream life of U.S. museums and institutions.

In 1991, Richard H. Glanton, a 43-year-old Philadelphia attorney, was selected as president of the Barnes Foundation. The new president soon asked the court for permission to sell some of the paintings from the Barnes collection to finance needed renovation at the foundation's headquarters. Following an outcry from museum directors, Glanton withdrew his request. He then asked the court for permission to loan 80 paintings from the collection for a world tour. A judge ruled that a one-time exhibit of the works was permissible, and following discussions between Glanton and J. Carter Brown, then director of the National Gallery of Art, the exhibit was organized. Glanton also negotiated a contract to publish two books with full-color illustrations on the collection. One of the publications is the exhibit's 300-plus-page catalog, which was published by Alfred A. Knopf, Inc. and includes more than 300 illustrations. Some of the images were printed in full color for the first time.

© Theo Westenberger/Gamma-Liaison

After becoming director of the Barnes Foundation in 1991, Philadelphia attorney Richard Glanton, above, went to court and successfully challenged Barnes' stipulation that his paintings never be "loaned, sold, or otherwise disposed of." A onetime exhibit, "Great French Paintings from the Barnes Foundation," resulted.

The Exhibit. As Elizabeth P. Streicher, associate research curator in the National Gallery's department of modern painting and the exhibit's coordinating curator, stated, "it was very easy for everyone to choose the 80 paintings in the exhibition. So many of these works are icons in the history of art." These icons, which were displayed on two floors and arranged in chronological order by artist, attracted some 514,000 persons to the National Gallery before the exhibit closed on Aug. 15, 1993. It then was to travel to the Musée d'Orsay in Paris, the National Museum of Western Art in Tokyo, and the Philadelphia Museum of Art.

Editor's Note. The editors are grateful to Laura Linton of the Barnes Foundation and to Deborah Ziska of the National Gallery of Art for reviewing this article. All of the photographs are from "Great French Paintings from the Barnes Foundation: Impressionist, Post-Impressionist, and Early Modern." © The Barnes Foundation, unless otherwise noted.

The Alphabetical Section

Photos, © Sipa

T he year 1993 saw much activity in the area of trade negotiations. After seven years of discussions, the Uruguay Round within the General Agreement on Tariffs and Trade ended in agreement in December. Under the pact the 117 member nations agreed to cut some tariffs and eliminate others in an effort to promote economic stimulation. Sir Leon Brittan *(above left)* and Mickey Kantor *(above right)* represented Britain and the United States, respectively, at the talks. Rice farmers from Japan and South Korea *(top)* protested that the agreement called for the opening of their markets to imports.

Earlier, the U.S. Congress approved legislation implementing the North American Free Trade Agreement (NAFTA) after intense lobbying by the Bill Clinton administration. With the president watching *(bottom page 89)*, Vice-President Al Gore and NAFTA foe Ross Perot held a TV debate on the pact. Mexico also approved NAFTA, and Canada's new Liberal government gave its assent to it. Meanwhile, the 1991 Maastricht Treaty on European unity went into effect on November 1. A second referendum on Maastricht was held in Denmark in May and, unlike in 1992, Danes agreed with the sentiments of the billboard *(page 89)* and supported the treaty.

ABORTION

The abortion debate raged on in 1993, with few signs that this explosive political issue would be resolved anytime soon. The year saw an increase in violent protests by antiabortion activists outside clinics around the United States, as well as the fatal shooting in March of a Florida physician, David Gunn, outside the clinic where he performed abortions.

Legislative Action. With the election of the first pro-choice U.S. president in more than two decades, abortion-rights supporters had looked to 1993 as the year when a woman's right to abortion would be written firmly into law. On January 22, Bill Clinton signed five executive orders on abortion-related issues. "Our goal should be to protect individual freedom, while fostering responsible decision-making, an approach that seeks to protect the right to choose, while reducing the number of abortions," he said. But the judicial system and Congress handed concessions to both sides of the debate, leaving neither with a clear lead as the year drew to a close.

One bill championed by abortion-rights supporters would codify President Clinton's executive order lifting a ban on abortion counseling at about 4,000 family-planning clinics nationwide that receive federal funding. The House of Representatives alone approved the measure lifting the so-called "gag rule" as it reauthorized and increased federal spending for the clinics under Title X of the Public Health Services Act.

In response to the violence of antiabortion protesters and to the U.S. Supreme Court's January ruling that federal civil-rights laws could not be used to protect the clinics, Congress in November handed abortion-rights activists one of their few victories of the year by passing the Freedom of Access to Clinic Entrances Act. The bill would make it a federal crime to obstruct access to abortion clinics by blocking the entrance physically or by threatening, harassing, or injuring a clinic employee or a woman seeking an abortion. It would punish offenders with fines and prison sentences of up to ten years for injury, and with a life sentence in the case of death. Congress rejected claims by antiabortion activists that the bill posed a threat to freedom of speech, as it did not prohibit peaceful demonstrations. The bill was expected to be enacted early in 1994.

Abortion-rights advocates received an unexpected setback when Congress renewed the Hyde amendment banning government-financed abortions as part of the 1994 federal budget. Named for its sponsor, Rep. Henry J. Hyde (R-IL), the amendment has denied access to abortion for poor women since 1976. Beginning October 1, payments for abortion by Medicaid were allowed not only when pregnancy endangers the woman's life, as the amendment previously had specified, but also in cases of rape or incest. States with stricter limits on Medicaid funding of abortion than those outlined, including Colorado and Arkansas, were the object of lawsuits brought by abortion-rights groups late in the year.

A key bill for abortion-rights advocates would codify the Supreme Court's landmark ruling of 1973 in *Roe v. Wade* by establishing a woman's right to have an abortion. Committees in both the House of Representatives and the Senate approved the Freedom of Choice Act, but it remained stalled when neither house took it up for further action. The House version would allow states to restrict the right to abortion under some circumstances after the sixth month of pregnancy, when the fetus can survive outside the womb. The more restrictive Senate bill would allow states to require minors to obtain parental consent before having an abortion.

A challenge to such state parental-consent provisions was defeated November 15, when the Supreme Court let stand a Mississippi rule requiring an unmarried woman under age 18 to obtain both parents' permission before having an abortion or, under extraordinary circumstances, to try to persuade a judge that she is mature enough to make the decision on her own. Physicians and abortion-rights advocates charged in *Barnes v. Mississippi* that such rules pose an "undue burden" on a woman's right to an abortion. In a 1992 ruling, the high court had made it easier for states to restrict abortions as long as they did not pose such a burden.

While the Supreme Court's refusal to interfere with the parental-consent rule was seen as a defeat for abortion-rights advocates, antiabortion groups such as the National Right to Life Committee did not claim absolute victory. They supported legislation in several states to make it even harder for teenagers to have abortions by getting rid of the "judicial bypass" provision enabling young women to obtain permission from a judge to have an abortion.

With the abortion issue still far from resolution, both sides in the debate were gearing up for battle over insurance coverage of the procedure under health-care reform proposals, due to come before Congress in 1994.

Abortion Pill. While Congress and the courts offered few substantive changes in the legal framework surrounding the abortion issue in 1993, technical and commercial developments offered hope for an alternative to surgical abortion. Dr. Etienne-Emile Baulieu, the French researcher who developed the abortion pill, RU-486, announced he would set up a drug firm to produce and market the pill in the United States as soon as the project was approved by the U.S. Food and Drug Administration (FDA). The pill, available in government clinics in France, Great Britain, and Sweden, had been banned in the United States by the Reagan and Bush administrations.

MARY H. COOPER
"CQ [Congressional Quarterly] Researcher"

ACCIDENTS AND DISASTERS

AVIATION

Feb. 8—One hundred thirty-two persons are killed when a passenger jet and a military plane collide shortly after takeoff from Tehran airport, Iran.

March 5—A jet crashes just after takeoff from Skopje, Macedonia, during a snowstorm; 77 are feared dead.

April 16—A military helicopter crashes in central Afghanistan, killing all 15 on board.

April 19—Eight persons are killed, including the governor of South Dakota, when a plane crashes near Dubuque, IA, due to engine trouble.

April 26—More than 70 persons are killed when a passenger jet crashes and burns soon after takeoff near Aurangabad, western India.

April 27—All 71 persons aboard a military plane are killed when it crashes near Tashkurghan, Afghanistan.

April 28—A plane crashes into the Atlantic Ocean near Libreville, Gabon, killing 30 persons, including 18 members of Zambia's national soccer team.

May 19—A Colombian jetliner en route from Panama crashes in the mountains south of Medellín, Colombia; all 132 aboard are killed.

Aug. 28—A Tajik passenger plane taking off in Khorog crashes near the Afghan border, killing 35.

Dec. 1—A commuter plane crashes near Hibbing, MN, in dense fog; all 18 aboard are killed.

Dec. 13—Seventeen are killed when a Laotian airliner crashes into a mountain in north-central Laos.

FIRES AND EXPLOSIONS

Feb. 14—A fire in a department store in Tangshan, China, kills 79 shoppers.

Feb. 17—Seven children alone in a house in Detroit, MI, are killed when fire breaks out and window bars prevent their escape.

Feb. 28—Eight children and one adult are killed when fire strikes an apartment building in Ludington, MI.

Feb. 28—Six persons are left dead by a fire that destroys a three-family residence in Providence, RI.

March 16—Fire breaks out in a hotel in Chicago, IL, killing at least 21.

March 24—A tank truck explodes at a peanut-processing plant in Dakar, Senegal; at least 60 are killed.

May 10—Fire strikes a toy factory west of Bangkok, Thailand, leaving more than 200 workers dead.

July 25—Six children left alone in an apartment building in Philadelphia, PA, die when fire breaks out.

Aug. 5—At least 15 persons are killed in Shenzhen, China, by several huge warehouse explosions.

Aug. 31—Fire spreads through a neighborhood in Laberinto, Peru, killing at least 18.

Sept. 28—A natural-gas pipeline explodes next to a busy highway 40 mi (64 km) west of Caracas, Venezuela, killing 51 motorists trapped in rush-hour traffic.

Nov. 2—At least 39 persons are killed when fire erupts while a crowd is trying to steal fuel from a burst gasoline pipeline in Uong Bi, Vietnam.

LAND AND SEA TRANSPORTATION

Jan. 3—Twenty-five tourists die when their bus crashes into a high-tension power pole near Cancún, Mexico.

Jan. 9—At least 55 persons are killed and 70 are injured when three tour buses collide and burn on a narrow highway in Santo Tomé, Argentina.

Jan. 14—A Polish ferry en route to Sweden capsizes in the Baltic Sea; 50 passengers are left dead.

Jan. 18—Two commuter trains sideswipe each other in Gary, IN, killing seven.

Jan. 30—At least 140 passengers are killed when a Kenyan train plunges into a flooded river.

Jan. 31—A bus is struck by a train at a railroad crossing in Liaoning province, China, killing 66.

Feb. 17—A crowded ferry sinks off the western coast of Haiti, leaving at least 275 passengers dead.

Feb. 28—One hundred forty-seven deportees boarding a ferry from Brazzaville, Congo, to Kinshasa, Zaire, drown when a gangway collapses into the Congo River.

March 28—An express train en route from Seoul to Pusan, South Korea, topples off the tracks and overturns, leaving at least 75 passengers dead.

May 13—Five Amish children are killed and three are injured when a car spins out of control and hits them as they walk along a country road near Wooster, OH.

June 6—A freighter jammed with illegal immigrants from China runs aground off Rockaway Beach in Queens, NY. Passengers flee the ship, and at least six drown.

July 2—More than 230 Philippine pilgrims drown when a floating pagoda collapses during a religious festival on the Bocaue River near Manila.

Aug. 29—A minibus goes off the road and crashes into a wedding party in Porini, Kenya, killing 12 persons.

Sept. 22—Forty-seven persons are killed when an Amtrak train catapults off a 12-ft (3.66-m)-high trestle into a bayou near Mobile, AL, in the deadliest accident in Amtrak's history.

Oct. 10—At least 285 persons are feared dead after a ferry sinks off the western coast of South Korea.

Nov. 10—A bus carrying U.S. and Canadian tourists skids off a highway near Canterbury, England, during a rainstorm, killing ten persons.

Nov. 11—Five rail workers are killed when two freight trains collide head-on and explode near Longview, WA.

Nov. 18—A school minibus crashes near Birmingham, England, killing 12 students and a teacher.

STORMS, FLOODS, AND EARTHQUAKES

Jan. 15—More than a week of heavy rain and flooding leaves at least 25 persons dead in Tijuana, Mexico.

March 12-15—At least 270 persons are left dead after a monster storm, the worst in the 20th century, strikes the U.S. eastern seaboard from Florida to Maine.

March 27—More than 300 persons are feared dead after storms sink cargo boats and an overcrowded ferry in Bangladesh.

May 11—A sandstorm in Gansu province in northwestern China kills at least 47 persons.

June 20—Severe storms and flooding in Bangladesh leaves at least 100 persons dead.

July-Aug.—More than 50 persons are left dead, tens of thousands are homeless, and at least $17 billion damage is done after flooding of the Mississippi and Missouri rivers ravages much of the U.S. Midwest. (*See also* FEATURE ARTICLE, page 44.)

July 12—A major earthquake strikes northern Japan near Hokkaido Island, spawning tsunamis and firestorms; at least 200 are feared dead.

July 24—Four weeks of flooding in southern Asia leave at least 2,100 dead in Bangladesh, Nepal, and India.

July 31—Heavy rains cause flooding in south-central China, leaving at least 41 dead.

Aug. 8—A fierce tropical storm strikes the northern coast of Venezuela, killing 100 persons.

Aug. 27—A dam bursts in Qinghai province, China, causing a flood that leaves at least 200 persons dead.

Sept. 30—Southwestern India is hit with a powerful earthquake, killing 9,748 persons.

Nov. 2—Sixty persons are feared dead after rivers flooded by heavy rains wipe out villages in Atlántida and Colón states north of Tegucigalpa, Honduras.

MISCELLANEOUS

Jan. 14—A volcano near Pasto, Colombia, erupts while a group of scientists is working inside the volcano's crater. At least nine of the scientists are killed.

Feb. 2—The Mayon volcano in Legazpi, the Philippines, erupts suddenly, sending down tons of debris and killing 72 persons.

May 9—A landslide buries a remote gold-mining settlement in southern Ecuador, leaving an estimated 200 persons dead.

Aug. 13—A six-story hotel in Korat, Thailand, collapses, killing more than 100 persons.

Aug. 26—At least 44 persons are killed by a wild elephant rampaging through several villages in northeast India.

Aug. 27—A dam at the Gouhou reservoir in western Qinghai province, China, bursts, leaving as many as 1,200 persons dead.

Oct. 13—At a train station in Borivli, India, at least 45 are killed when they panic and leap off a train they think is on fire, only to be run down by an oncoming train.

Dec. 12—Fifty-four persons are killed when an apartment building in Kuala Lumpur, Malaysia, collapses after being hit by a landslide.

ADVERTISING

In 1993 scandals involving celebrity endorsers, the decline of national brand-name products, and significant developments in the high-tech world of interactive media highlighted a volatile year in the advertising industry.

Controversies. During the National Basketball Association (NBA) play-offs in the spring, Michael Jordan became the target of allegations of heavy gambling. Jordan, who earns an estimated $30 million annually from endorsement deals with companies including McDonald's, Nike Inc., and Quaker Oats Co., acknowledged that he gambled but denied his debts were as large as his critics claimed. The companies supported Jordan and continued to run ad campaigns featuring the star, who announced his retirement from basketball later in 1993. In an unrelated controversy, pop-music superstar Michael Jackson was accused of child molestation by the family of a California boy. Jackson, a longtime celebrity endorser for Pepsi-Cola Co., denied the allegations, and no formal charges had been filed. In November, Pepsi severed its relationship with Jackson when he admitted an addiction to painkillers. And actor Burt Reynolds was dropped as a spokesman by Quaker State Corp. and the Florida Citrus Commission after his acrimonious divorce from Loni Anderson received widespread coverage. These incidents caused advertisers to reconsider the risks of using celebrities to endorse their products.

Meanwhile big-name national brands found themselves under attack by high-quality private-label products. The private-label brands made significant headway among consumers, who began making purchase decisions based on price rather than brand name. National marketers responded by slashing prices to retain market share, with Philip Morris Co. leading the way. In April the tobacco company stunned the marketing community and Wall Street by slashing the price of its flagship Marlboro cigarettes by 40 cents per pack. Other big-name marketers soon followed suit, creating a price-oriented environment at the expense of the big brands.

In yet another controversy, German automaker Mercedes Benz got caught in a public-relations nightmare with a new ad-placement policy that led to accusations of censorship. Mercedes told magazine publishers that its ads must be pulled from any issues carrying negative stories about the company or about Germany itself. Even though most magazines agreed to comply, the request caused such a stir that the automaker soon rescinded it.

Media. For consumer-product marketers, the $33 billion Bell Atlantic-TCI merger marked the advent of a new era of electronic-media opportunities. The merger created a cable giant which would reach millions of U.S. homes, allowing marketers to communicate directly with potential customers. It also would let those customers respond almost instantly, creating unprecedented two-way communication between marketer and consumer. Other media companies, like Time Warner, were involved in similar projects, and more mergers among entertainment and telecommunications companies were expected in the near future. An example of the stakes involved was the heated bidding war between Viacom Inc. and QVC Network Inc. for Paramount Communications Inc.

Account Shifts. Several significant advertising accounts changed hands in 1993, but perhaps one of the most notable developments involved an account that did not go anywhere at all. General Motors Co. put its estimated $140 million Oldsmobile account, handled by Leo Burnett Co. of Chicago, up for review among more than a dozen agencies. In the end, it was Burnett, a long-shot candidate, who held onto the business. In major account shifts, the $80 million BMW of North America auto account moved from Ammirati Puris to Mullen Advertising; Sears Roebuck moved its $40 million apparel account from Ogilvy & Mather to Young & Rubicam; and Reebok International consolidated its $140 million athletic-shoe account at Leo Burnett Co. In a devastating blow for Lintas: New York, the agency lost both the IBM Personal Computer Co. account, worth $40 million, and an estimated $70 million in business on the Diet Coke account. IBM moved to Merkley Newman Harty, while the Diet Coke business was taken over by Lowe & Partners. And Hardee Food Systems Inc. moved its $75 million restaurant account from Ogilvy & Mather to Deutsch/Dworin Inc.

Creative. In February 1993 the long-awaited new commercials for Coca-Cola Co.—produced by the talent agency Creative Artists Agency (CAA) of Beverly Hills—made their debut to generally positive reviews. Coke had stunned the ad industry in 1992 when it hired CAA to create the campaign instead of using its longtime agency, the New York-based McCann-Erickson.

At the International Advertising Film Festival in France, Japanese ad agency Hakuhodo surprised attendees by winning the festival's Grand Prix for two commercials created for Nissin Food Products Co. It was the first time a Japanese agency was awarded the top prize since 1987.

Ad Volume and Acquisitions. The McCann-Erickson ad agency predicted that 1993 ad spending would match or exceed the projected 6% growth in the U.S. gross domestic product. At that rate, ad expenditures would reach almost $140 billion, compared with the $131.3 billion spent in 1992. The agency said an ad-spending recovery was expected in the newspaper industry, which had been in recession since 1989. The three major television networks also were expected to post gains in 1993. Most acquisitions in 1993 were on the media side, although one agency takeover occurred when Omnicom Group acquired TBW in a stock deal.

JOHN WOLFE, *Freelance Advertising Writer*

AFGHANISTAN

In 1993 former resistance groups continued to battle each other in Afghanistan, unable to share power peacefully. Living conditions deteriorated and serious fighting occurred in Kabul and other regions. At year-end the search for peaceful reconstruction continued with some success in outlying areas.

Political Developments. A basic political challenge in Afghanistan was to devise an acceptable system to settle disputes peacefully among former anticommunist resistance groups, whose talents ran more to violence than compromise. Leaders with no experience in such matters had to create from scratch such democratic tools as a working constitution, an electoral system, and a division of political power.

President Burhanuddin Rabbani, 53, whose scheduled four-month term formally expired in October 1992, remained in charge through 1993. In December 1992 he had been reelected formally to a two-year term by the 1,335-member Resolution and Settlement Council. As 1993 began, this group slimmed down to a 205-member parliament charged with selecting a prime minister, writing a constitution, and preparing for elections in 1994.

Rabbani resigned from leadership of his Islamic Society to distance himself from partisan politics. Nevertheless, several political parties formed from other resistance groups boycotted the council that voted Rabbani in. His biggest rival was 44-year-old Gulbuddin Hekmatyar, who termed the president's election illegal and "a declaration of war." Through January and February forces from Hekmatyar's Islamic Party bombarded Kabul with rocket and artillery fire

from bases to the south, while other groups warred within the city.

In the absence of an effective government, various regional and ethnic groups became quasi-independent. In the north, Gen. Abdul Rashid Dostam's Uzbek militia, a multiethnic force originally loyal to the Communists, was headquartered in Mazar-e-Sharif. With 120,000 troops, it was the largest and best-armed military power, with aircraft, armor, and artillery. In the west, the Tajik Ismael Khan ruled Herat and its surrounding provinces, whereas the central highlands were under various splintered Hazara groups, some sponsored by Iran. In the south and east many Pashtuns gravitated to Hekmatyar, and in the northeast Tajiks remained loyal to Defense Minister Ahmad Shah Massoud. The country appeared to be coming apart.

From March to May, however, at meetings in Islamabad and Jalalabad, the eight main parties agreed to a cease-fire and power-sharing until a constitution could be written and elections held. Rabbani remained president, and Hekmatyar took over as prime minister. The two rivals agreed to cooperate in selecting an interim cabinet but did not succeed until August 13. The key ministries of defense and interior were too sensitive to give to one minister and were put under commissioners appointed by field commanders in each province, with Rabbani running the defense commission and Hekmatyar the interior commission. Even after a cabinet was chosen, Hekmatyar so distrusted the security in Kabul that he refused to enter the city. Instead he held cabinet meetings at his headquarters in Charasiab, 10 mi (16 km) to the south.

In August a commission was convened to draft a constitution and prepare for elections in

In March 1993, Afghan military factions announced a peace accord to end months of fighting in Afghanistan. Pakistan's Prime Minister Nawaz Sharif (center) sponsored the peace conference, which was supported by Iran's President Rafsanjani (second from right).

© Eslami Rad/Gamma-Liaison

October. But the 101-article first draft was not ready until September 27, too late for October elections. In addition, its commitment to legal practices followed only by the Sunni branch of Islam so enraged Shiite Muslims that the draft was withdrawn for further study two days later.

Socioeconomic Developments. Despite the cease-fire agreement, there was no letup in the violence, especially in Kabul. Street battles between shifting alliances of contending groups took a huge toll on civilian and combatant lives, and Hekmatyar's forces around the city alternated periodic blockades with rocket and artillery barrages. In February the city was without effective water, electric, telephone, or police service. Rocket attacks killed more than 1,000 civilians and wounded more than 6,000 in the first three months of 1993 alone; they continued intermittently all year. In October fighting between rival factions to the east of Kabul shut the capital's road link to Pakistan, threatening to isolate the city if snows blocked the northern passes. Some 500,000 Kabul residents reportedly fled the city. A food shortage remained critical in many provinces, and epidemics of cholera and typhus threatened.

With the breakdown of the national government, social services suffered badly. The few hospitals able to remain open lacked medicines and equipment. Many orphanages and nursing homes had to close for lack of food and money. Schools and universities in Kabul remained shut, and there was little public transportation.

Some 1.1 million Afghan refugees returned home between September 1992 and March 1993, but Pakistan took in 86,000 new Afghan refugees from the fighting in Kabul and elsewhere. Tehran announced that 400,000 of the 700,000 Afghans in Iran had gone home between April 1992 and February 1993. Bad as conditions were in Afghanistan, some 40,000 Tajiks sought refuge in its northern provinces from a civil war in their country, Tajikistan.

Returning Afghan farmers faced daunting problems on land to which the only attention for more than 13 years had been the planting of some 10 million unexploded mines. The war destroyed and booby-trapped farm holdings to such an extent that few crops could be sown in 1993, and many families again became refugees.

As a stopgap some farmers grew opium—easy to tend and to market in Pakistan, whose illegal laboratories in the past have provided about 20% of the heroin sold in the United States. Afghanistan had the potential to grow 800 tons of opium annually; the rugged 1,400-mi (2 253-km) Afghan-Pakistani border was essentially unguardable.

There were some bright spots. The city and province of Herat made good progress in reconstruction and farming began in other regions. Mine removal continued, although at the cost of many lives. A girls' school opened in Herat, although UN-supplied pencils had to be broken in half to equip all of the 1,800 registrants.

Foreign Affairs. Only a handful of nations, mostly fellow Islamic states, maintained missions in Kabul. More-radical Islamic elements in Afghanistan and neighboring Pakistan and Iran seemed bent on removing from the country all foreign influences, no matter how benign. In February three UN workers were murdered and the UN mission in Kabul was attacked. Ismael Khan had to step in to protect UN activities in Herat. Hekmatyar's rockets were trained periodically on Kabul's International Red Cross hospital, one of the few in the city that remained open. In July, Australian mine-detection training teams were driven from the country because of threats to their security.

During the war some 6,000 unsolicited Arab volunteers served as fighters with the resistance. Later terrorist acts committed by them abroad gave Afghanistan an unenviable and largely undeserved reputation as an exporter of terrorism. Moreover, Afghan resistance veterans reportedly were fighting with Muslims in Tajikistan, Azerbaijan, Myanmar, Kashmir, and Bosnia.

Relations between Afghanistan and most neighboring Islamic states remained good, with plans for improved commerce and communications with Pakistan, Iran, Turkey, and Turkmenistan. Pakistan closed down and forbade Afghan refugee political and military activity on its territory. Only in the north, where the Tajik civil war spilled over onto Afghan territory, was there serious trouble, with Kabul complaining of Russian artillery and air strikes and Moscow accusing the Afghans of aiding Tajik insurgents.

Relations with the United States took an unusual turn in July when the Central Intelligence Agency (CIA) reportedly offered $55 million to buy back 300 antiaircraft Stinger missiles given to the resistance during the war. Hekmatyar said no weapons would be returned.

ANTHONY ARNOLD
Author, "The Fateful Pebble: Afghanistan's Role in the Fall of the Soviet Empire"

AFGHANISTAN • Information Highlights

Official Name: Islamic State of Afghanistan.
Location: Central Asia.
Area: 250,000 sq mi (647 500 km²).
Population: (mid-1993 est.): 17,400,000.
Chief Cities (1988 est.): Kabul, the capital, 1,424,400; Kandahar, 225,500; Herat, 177,000.
Government: *Head of state*—Burhanuddin Rabbani, president (took office June 29, 1992); *Head of government*—Gulbuddin Hekmatyar, prime minister (sworn in June 17, 1993). *Legislature*—bicameral National Assembly.
Gross Domestic Product (1989 est. U.S.$): $3,000,000,000.
Foreign Trade (1991 U.S.$): *Imports*, $884,000,000; *exports*, $235,000,000.

AFRICA

Forces for democratic change clashed with the forces of repression and autocratic rule throughout Africa in 1993. Some nations were steeped in conflict. Military rule returned to Nigeria, and a short-lived coup d'état in Burundi overturned the first democratic election since the country gained independence. The settlement of festering conflicts in Liberia, Angola, Somalia, and Sudan remained elusive, but more hopeful signs were also evident. Democratic elections were held in Senegal, the first open election in 20 years took place in Swaziland, a referendum in Malawi opened the way to elections in 1994, and Mozambique seemed willing to accept a United Nations- (UN-) supervised election as an alternative to internecine warfare. Also, in Rwanda a peace agreement between the government and rebels brought a cease-fire and plans for elections.

While violence continued in South Africa, the country moved closer to majority rule with an election scheduled for April 1994 that would empower a transitional government of national unity. The dramatic changes taking place in South Africa over the past several years were symbolized by the Nobel Prize Committee's decision to award the 1993 Peace Prize to African National Congress (ANC) leader Nelson Mandela and South African President F. W. de Klerk for their political courage in negotiating an end to apartheid and for their efforts to establish the foundation for a nonracial democracy.

Continuing Conflicts. A change in UN and U.S. strategy regarding Somalia, from attempting to capture Gen. Mohammed Farah Aidid to negotiation, resulted in direct peace talks between factions in December 1993. Those talks collapsed, however, when Aidid and rival Ali Mahdi Mohamed were unable to agree on basic issues. Some observers feared that international donors, weary of continued factional fighting, might cut off aid and abandon Somalia. The UN was already in financial difficulties over Somalia because member nations owed an estimated $109 million for the operation. In December the United States and several other nations announced their intention to begin withdrawing their troops. Those departures were expected to create gaps in troop strength, logistics, and intelligence.

Talks in Geneva during July brought an apparent end to three years of bitter civil war in Liberia. The three main factions—the National Patriotic Front, the Armed Forces of Liberia, and the United Liberation Movement in Liberia (ULIMO)—agreed to a cease-fire that took effect on August 1 and a timetable to demobilize and disarm troops, and to create a new transitional government of national reconciliation. In September the UN Security Council voted to send 300 monitors to supervise the disarmament along with the 10,000-member West African force which had been in the country since 1990. Prospects for a lasting political settlement were uncertain, however, because all three of the ethnically based factions feared that they would not be able to win political power in a free election. The National Patriotic Front, led by Charles Taylor, was composed mainly of Gaos and Manos; ULIMO supporters were mostly Mandingos; while the Armed Forces of Liberia received most of its support from the Krahn ethnic group. In November the three groups, with UN encouragement, began a new round of talks in Benin.

Angola seemed bent on self-destruction. After elections in September 1992 and an apparent settlement of the 16-year civil war, Jonas Savimbi, leader of the rebel Union for the Total Independence of Angola (UNITA), refused to accept electoral defeat and renewed hostilities. Angered by UNITA's role in the renewal of hostilities and Savimbi's defiance of all mediation efforts, the Clinton administration announced

© Peterson/Gamma-Liaison

In Burundi, Melchior Ndadaye—who had been elected president in the nation's first multiparty election in June 1993—was ousted in a coup d'état in October. Ethnic fighting between the Hutus, who comprise 85% of the population, and the Tutsis, who have controlled the country, followed the coup, forcing hundreds of persons to move to refugee camps such as the one at left, or to flee the country.

formal recognition of the Marxist Popular Movement for the Liberation of Angola (MPLA) government in May. New rounds of peace talks alternated with outbreaks of intense fighting throughout the year and exploratory peace talks began again only in late October, but there was much doubt that these would be more successful than previous attempts.

None of the continuing conflicts in Africa seemed more intractable than the one in the Sudan. The fight between Arab Muslims from the north and non-Muslims (African Christians and animists) living in the south was complicated further by ethnic differences and personal ambitions in the south and political and religious infighting in the north. The complexity of these interrelationships had compromised all attempts at mediation. The National Islamic Front government (NIF) remained committed to its militant Islamic agenda and allegedly was involved in ethnic cleansing and other human-rights abuses in attempts to subdue the south. The split within the southern rebel Sudan Peoples' Liberation Army (SPLA) that occurred in August 1991 remained unresolved in 1993. Nigeria, Norway, the United States, Zimbabwe, and various states from the Horn of Africa all attempted to mediate during the year with limited success. In August the United States added Sudan to its list of states supporting terrorism. The situation remained unstable as the northern Islamic government threatened renewed military activity and as southern leaders were unable to resolve their differences, particularly over whether the south should declare independence unilaterally.

Coups d'Etat. In October, President Melchior Ndadaye of Burundi and several senior ministers were killed in an attempted coup. Ndadaye, who had been elected in the country's first free multiparty election in June, was the first Hutu and nonmilitary leader to be elected president since the country gained independence in 1962. Ndadaye won 60% of the vote in the presidential election for his Burundi Democracy Front party, which won 65 of the 81 seats for the legislature. The Hutu tribe, which represents 85% of Burundi's 5.6 million people, had been dominated by the minority Tutsi, who controlled the army, the government, and the economy. Ndadaye had replaced most of the country's Tutsi governors, mayors, and government officials with Hutus.

The coup was said to have been led by two Tutsis: former President Jean-Baptiste Bagaza and the army chief of staff, Lt. Col. Jean Bikomagu. Immediately after the coup, ethnic fighting erupted between the Hutus and Tutsis, forcing hundreds of thousands of refugees to flee to adjacent countries. The United States immediately suspended aid but later lifted that suspension when it became clear that the coup had failed. Under the Burundi constitution, in the event of the death of the president, the cabinet acts collectively in place of the president until new elections can be held. Elections were expected to be held sometime in 1994.

Hope that Nigeria could institute civilian-rule government in 1993 was short-lived. President Gen. Ibrahim Babangida voided the June election, which would have replaced military rule with civilian. The abrogation of the election caused considerable internal unrest and international pressure. Babangida was forced to resign and his former minister of finance, Ernest Shonekan, was asked to lead the government. However, in November, Gen. Sani Abacha, who had served in past Nigerian military governments, forced the resignation of Shonekan. Economic stagnation, runaway inflation, and unprecedented levels of corruption fueled the public's lack of confidence in the ability of both military and civilian governments to solve the country's continuing crisis. Soon after taking power, Abacha banned all political parties and meetings and announced that civilian government officials would be replaced by the military. At the same time, he ordered striking labor unions to return to work.

Elections and Politics. In the midst of continuing violence, negotiations proceeded toward South Africa's first nonracial democratic election, scheduled for April 1994. With few options left open, the ruling National Party agreed in September to share power with a multiparty Transitional Executive Committee (TEC) until the election. Negotiators also completed an interim constitution that was ratified by a special session of the parliament in December. Extreme right-wing whites and some black homeland leaders rejected the constitution, threatened to boycott the 1994 election, and sought a political solution that would entrench regional powers.

In a June 14 referendum, 63% of the Malawi electorate voted to introduce a multiparty democracy, a clear rejection of the 30-year rule of Life President H. Kamuzu Banda and the one-party domination of his Malawi Congress Party. While acknowledging defeat in a radio address after the referendum, President Banda said: "The win of the multiparty side of the referendum does not mean that the Malawi Congress Party ceases to exist. Neither does it mean that multiparty advocates have been elected to replace, in any way, the present government...the suggestion that I should resign to be replaced by an interim government is out of the question and unacceptable." However, to avoid a major political confrontation with opposition groups and because of foreign pressure, the government was forced to agree to form a National Executive Council to oversee the transition to the multiparty system and elections scheduled for 1994.

The Rwandan government of President Juvénal Habyarimana and the rebel Tutsi Rwanda Patriotic Front (RPF) signed a peace agreement in Tanzania in April that provided for a transitional government, a united army, and the holding of multiparty elections in June 1995. In October the UN Security Council voted to send a small peacekeeping force to Rwanda to oversee the cease-fire. In September, Swaziland held its

The Black Rhino

Although all five species of rhinoceros—the black and the white in Africa and the Indian, the Sumatran, and the Javan in Asia—have declined in number, the black rhino *(at right)* has been the hardest hit. In the early 1970s as many as 65,000 black rhinos ranged throughout the African savannas; by 1993, only about 2,000 remained in the wild. In all, there are only an estimated 10,000 to 11,000 rhinos still surviving worldwide.

Since the late 1960s, 85% of the world's rhinos have been killed for one thing only: their horns. Rhino horn is used in Asian medicines to cure fevers and is prized for ceremonial dagger handles in Yemen. A horn can fetch as much as $7,000 per pound.

Dehorning. Several years ago, Namibia and Zimbabwe embarked on desperate attempts to discourage poachers and save their rhinos. The programs involved dehorning the survivors. No one knew what effects dehorning would have on the rhinos' behavior: How would mothers protect their young?; Would bulls still fight for dominance? But the grave situation demanded action.

In 1991, Joel Berger and Carol Cunningham went to Namibia to study the dehorned rhinos for the Wildlife Conservation Society. They discovered a number of problems: Rhino horns grow back at a rate of 3.5 inches (9 cm) per year. To be effective, the horns should be removed yearly at a cost of $1,400 per rhino. In areas with predators such as hyenas and lions, all the calves born to mothers without horns died before the age of 1. In addition, mothers with the longest and biggest horns were most successful in rearing calves. It appeared that dehorning would not help save rhinos unless other measures, such as killing the predators, were taken. Additionally, there was debate on what to do

© Anup Manoj Shah/Animals Animals

with the horns of the dehorned rhinos. Zimbabwe, for example, would like to earn money for rhino conservation from the cut-off horns. There was fear, however, that any trade in rhino horns only would increase demand.

Protected Reserves. By 1993, U.S. conservation organizations were trying to put the remaining animals in heavily protected reserves. They also were urging the U.S. Congress to impose trade sanctions on countries that trade in endangered species and their products. An initiative begun in September 1992 by the UN Environment Programme (UNEP) had had some success in increasing the rhino population of certain areas. The black rhino population of Kenya, for example, had grown from about 340 in 1986 to 420 in 1993. UNEP pressure had led to the enforcement of bans on the sale of rhino products in Yemen and the United Arab Emirates. The Chinese government also had made it illegal to buy, sell, trade, or transport rhino horns.

Deborah A. Behler

first free election since 1973. Over the previous 20 years, a state of emergency had been in effect and all political parties had been banned. Voters were allowed to choose candidates for the 55-member lower house of Parliament.

Incumbent President Abdou Diouf was reelected in Senegal after a close race with seven contenders in a February election. The final results were delayed after the opposition alleged that the governing Socialist Party rigged the election. However, Senegal's constitutional court ruled that Diouf received 58% of the vote and his main challenger, Abdoulaya Wade, gained 32%.

Unlike Angola, with its apparent inability to settle its internal civil war, Mozambique took tentative steps in 1993 to maintain and extend the General Peace Accord signed late in 1992 that ended 16 years of devastating civil war between the Front for the Liberation of Mozambique

(FRELIMO) and the rebels of the Mozambique National Resistance (Renamo). The country still had to deal with the demilitarization of former combatants, the distribution of emergency food aid, and eventual democratic elections, for all of which the UN reputedly was spending $1 million to $2 million daily. Hundreds of thousands of Mozambican refugees from neighboring countries had returned and large numbers of internally displaced persons were being resettled.

Other. In December 88-year-old President Félix Houphouët-Boigny, who had ruled the Ivory Coast since independence in 1960, died as the country was edging toward economic and political crisis. Political infighting had split the ruling Democratic Party and the possibility of a military coup could not be discounted.

N. Brian Winchester and Patrick O'Meara
Indiana University

AGRICULTURE

The year 1993 was marked by serious financial stresses on U.S. agriculture from record flooding in the Midwest. Fortunately for consumers worldwide, reserve food supplies were able to fill the gap in supplies from sharply reduced crops. Former centrally planned countries saw a slow but steady progress toward market-directed agriculture. Researchers continued efforts to expand the list of products coming from agriculture, to reduce costs of food and fiber, and to ensure adequate supplies to the growing world population.

World agricultural production fell moderately below past upward trends. Coarse-grain production declined about as much as the record of the last three decades, which occurred with the U.S. drought of 1983. Lower crop production shrank world reserves of grains, oilseeds, vegetable oils, and protein meals. While most countries were spared food shortages, declining reserve stocks would expose supplies in 1994 to production problems if adverse weather struck major grain-producing areas.

United States

Production and Income. Much of the sharp decline in world production was due to extremely high rainfall, record flooding, cool temperatures, and early frost in the U.S. Midwest, the world's largest grain producer. About 13.6 million acres (5.5 million ha) that were intended for corn, soybeans, and grain sorghum did not get planted or had crops destroyed by flooding. Production of peas, snap beans, and sweet corn suffered from bad weather in Minnesota and Wisconsin. In Southeastern states, crops were damaged severely by extreme drought. However, tomato supplies increased with favorable weather in California. Harvests of peaches, pears, apricots, and tart cherries were smaller than in the previous year and brought modestly higher prices.

Livestock- and poultry-feed supplies were more at risk of localized shortages than were major food grains such as wheat and rice. Higher costs for animal feeds hurt production in livestock and poultry sectors, and placed modest upward pressure on U.S. prices for meat, poultry, and dairy products late in 1993.

Rapid growth of integrated pork-production systems propelled North Carolina to the position of Number-3 hog-producing state. Integrated systems coordinate all production and management activities—including the development of breeding stock, production of feeder animals, feed formulation and processing, design and construction of buildings and waste-control systems, feeding, pricing, processing, and marketing—in one business unit or a series of interconnected units. Integrated systems effectively can ensure uniform high-quality, low-fat pork products to meet demands of health-conscious consumers at the lowest possible cost. Similar systems gained prominence in the broiler industry in the southern United States in the early 1960s. The changes had shifted chicken production from an industry of many small farms to one made up of a much smaller number of large production units.

Midwest Floods. Areas of Iowa and neighboring states experienced once-in-500-year floods in 1993. Floods were triggered by record rain that fell from May through August, delaying planting of crops past optimum planting dates, flooding low-lying crops, and bringing cool summer and early fall weather that delayed maturity of corn, soybeans, wheat, sunflowers, and sorghum. In Iowa, one of the hardest-hit states, losses from the unusual weather were estimated to have cut in half net farm income from the previous year. Agricultural losses also were large in Minnesota,

In the U.S. Midwest in 1993, record spring and summer flooding destroyed more than 20 million acres (8 million ha) of choice farmland. The total effect of the disaster on U.S. agriculture still was being calculated as the year drew to a close.

the Dakotas, Missouri, Wisconsin, and neighboring states. Flooding raised discussions of modifying the nation's wetlands policy to encourage conversion of some damaged cropland to permanent wetlands. (*See* FEATURE ARTICLE, page 44.)

Policy and Programs. More than 1 million acres (about 405 000 ha) of U.S. cropland were retired from production in 1993 and placed in the ten-year Conservation Reserve Program. This program has removed nearly 37 million acres (14.9 million ha) of highly erodible and otherwise environmentally sensitive land from crop production. Idling these lands has improved water quality in adjoining streams, reduced soil erosion, and expanded wildlife habitat. It also has helped control surplus grain production that led to a farming financial crisis in the 1980s. Unfortunately, the program also has depressed economic activity in rural areas where large amounts of cropland were retired. Policy makers have examined alternative uses for conservation reserve land for when the contracts with landowners begin expiring in 1995.

Other important agricultural developments included delays in implementing new food-labeling standards, and a continued shift to reduced-tillage and no-tillage methods of crop production to reduce soil erosion and related water-quality problems that affect urban populations.

Economists were examining the potential impact of the unratified North American Free Trade Agreement (NAFTA) on Canadian, Mexican, and U.S. agriculture. In Mexico rapid population growth, a highly urban population, and new marketing facilities brought strong growth in the consumption of fruit and vegetables and growing markets for some U.S. farmers. Some analyses indicated this growth would be accelerated by NAFTA. Several other sectors of U.S. agriculture also anticipated positive benefits from NAFTA, if it is ratified. Sectors fearing negative impact from the agreement included the U.S. wheat, sugar, and citrus industries. Wheat growers expressed concern about strong Canadian wheat competition in both U.S. and Mexican markets. Sugar and citrus growers worried about competition from lower-cost Mexican supplies.

International

Agricultural production rose in parts of Latin America, Canada, China, India, Western Europe, and Southern Africa. Some of these areas had suffered serious weather problems the previous year. Production of some farm products declined in parts of Eastern Europe and the former Soviet Union because of political and economic uncertainty.

Eastern Europe and Former USSR. Dairy, pork, and beef production in most of Eastern Europe and the region that was the USSR declined due to high unemployment and shrinking consumer demand, extreme inflation, and uncertain feed supplies. Animal numbers in the region dropped well below those from the late 1980s and still were sinking. Livestock numbers in many former Soviet republics were nearly one fifth lower than at the end of the 1980s. However, consumer meat supplies did not fall as much as animal numbers, since some breeding stock were slaughtered for meat production. Also, consumer supplies were aided slightly by sales of U.S. pork and dairy products to the former Soviet Union.

The United States, Canada, and Western Europe continued to provide credit for farm-product exports to the region at lower interest rates than commercial credit. Russia was negotiating with international banks to restructure more than $1 billion of outstanding agricultural debt with the United States, which could extend more U.S. credit to Russia in 1994. Political turmoil in Russia, the Ukraine, and Georgia in the fall led to modest additional U.S. food assistance to support the Yeltsin administration and other reform-minded governments and to encourage economic reform.

Crop production in Eastern Europe and the former Soviet Union remained well below previous highs, but several countries harvested larger crops than in 1992. Overall imports of cereals for the area were expected to drop due to reduced consumer demand, better crops, and financing difficulties.

Movement toward a private-enterprise farming and food-marketing system continued at a slow, steady pace. Major impediments were lack of experience with free markets, inadequate information on domestic production and supplies, limited reporting of prices, and lack of risk-shifting mechanisms for forward pricing—such as future markets. Other impediments included lack of a well-developed agricultural credit system and shortages of equipment for small private farms. Despite these limitations, East European and former Soviet farms began basing management decisions on costs and profit incentives reflected by market prices.

China. China is the world's largest producer and consumer of agricultural products because of its huge population. Industrialization continued to challenge agricultural production in 1993. The demand for meat and other products of animal agriculture has grown rapidly in urban population centers, and land has been converted increasingly from agricultural to housing, commercial, and other urban uses. So far, the country has been able to offset loss of cropland through increased uses of yield-increasing production technology. Removing price subsidies for grain and vegetable oils used by urban consumers slowed demand and allowed China to export corn to neighboring countries. However, with China's growing role as a manufacturing and exporting center and a population of more

than 1.1 billion people, economic researchers expect its food-production self-sufficiency to decline in the future. In 1993 rice was grown on more than one fifth of China's cropland, providing about one fourth of the nation's protein intake. Wheat was next in importance, accounting for one fifth of its cropland and a major part of its food imports.

Research and New Product Development

Researchers in North America and Western Europe continued to search for ways to produce more high-quality food products at lower cost with fewer inputs. In meat production, ongoing genetic and nutritional research improved the feed-to-meat conversion ratio in commercial pork-farming operations, so that 1 lb (.45 kg) of meat would be produced for each 3 lb (1.36 kg) of feed fed. Scientists continued plant-breeding activities and other research to enable corn, wheat, and soybeans to produce larger yields from given supplies of soil moisture and plant nutrients. A new U.S. Department of Agriculture computer program helped wheat growers in the Pacific Northwest control outbreaks of yield-reducing diseases. Engineers and designers of harvesting machinery modified designs to adjust for uneven terrain, lodged grain, and other conditions that contribute to harvesting losses.

Agriculture contributes major supplies of fiber to the world's population through wool, cotton, linen (flax), and other materials used for packaging; in 1993 researchers continued work to produce these products at lower cost. Others developed new uses for agricultural products to replace nonrenewable raw materials. Important examples include ethanol derivatives that can extend gasoline supplies and soybean oil that, when added to diesel fuel, can reduce urban air pollution. Ethyl alcohol for motor fuel is manufactured largely from corn and is used widely by U.S. motorists. Similar products are being used in Western Europe and Brazil and are being considered in Japan.

Corn and soybeans have been used as a raw material for numerous industrial products including plastics, protective coatings, paints, ink, packaging materials, disposable diapers, adhesives, and biodegradable garbage bags. Research yielded commercial production of a new building material, called Eviron, which is manufactured from soybeans and waste paper. It can be made to resemble lumber, stone, and other conventional building products. Substantial research also was directed toward maintaining plant and animal health with less reliance on agricultural chemicals. Academics and U.S. Department of Agriculture workers maintained a wide range of plant varieties, many that no longer are used commercially, to provide genetic diversity for major field crops, fruits, vegetables, and horticultural crops. A broad genetic base

© Mark E. Gibson/The Stock Market

As consumers move away from synthetics to natural fibers, cotton production has increased accordingly. U.S. acreage devoted to cotton has jumped by about one third since 1987.

reduces vulnerability to blight, diseases, and other pests that have devastated crops in the past.

Commercial use of bovine somatotropin (BST), a naturally occurring hormone that stimulates milk production in dairy cows, continued to be delayed while BST underwent further testing. Manufacturers were ready to begin commercial production, but were awaiting government approval before selling BST.

Renewable Fuels. Advances in genetic engineering have lowered the costs of processing corn into ethanol for motor fuels. Improved strains of yeast were developed to survive higher concentrations of ethanol and improve corn-processing efficiency. Yeasts are used in fermentation to convert cornstarch to ethyl alcohol (ethanol). Improved fermentation methods reduced the energy needed to process corn, lowering the cost of ethanol production. The motor-fuel market uses about 6% of a normal U.S. corn crop, and plays a key role in clean-air programs in several U.S. cities.

Additional research focused on ways to use other feedstocks to produce ethanol, including crop residues, waste from agricultural processing plants, municipal waste, yard and wood wastes, recycled paper, and new crops grown specifically for energy production. Other research explored ways to use thin sheets of semiporous material to separate ethanol from water and other components of the processed corn. This process would reduce energy needs for distillation.

See also FOOD.

ROBERT WISNER
Iowa State University

ALABAMA

The trial of Guy Hunt, Alabama's first Republican governor in more than a century, on ethics charges and his ouster from the governorship following conviction dominated Alabama news during 1993. Hunt's exit from office set in motion sweeping changes in state government.

The Hunt Trial. On April 12, Governor Hunt went on trial on charges that he illegally diverted $200,000—collected at the time of his first inaugural in 1987 and intended for public purposes—to his own personal use. The prosecution was led by Democratic State Attorney General Jimmy Evans. Hunt contended that he was entitled to the money in repayment for loans he had made to a previous, unsuccessful gubernatorial campaign, and that the trial in effect was a vendetta against him by Evans. The jury deliberated only a little more than two hours before finding the governor guilty. At Hunt's sentencing on May 7, he was ordered to repay the money he had been convicted of taking, pay fines, and perform 1,000 hours of community service during supervised probation. He was not required to go to jail. At year's end, Hunt's conviction still was being reviewed by the Court of Criminal Appeals.

The New Governor. Hunt's conviction caused the gubernatorial office to pass on April 22 to Lieut. Gov. James E. Folsom, Jr., a Democrat who was the son of a former two-term Alabama governor. Most Hunt appointees left their jobs soon after Folsom's accession as the state's 53d governor, and Folsom won considerable praise for appointing blacks and women to important positions in his cabinet. He also was applauded for asking the state Supreme Court on May 10 to dismiss his predecessor's appeal of a January 4 state court ruling that it was illegal for the Confederate battle flag to fly above the newly renovated Alabama Capitol building. The flag had flown there most of the time since 1961.

Education Reform. The major item on the new governor's agenda would be education reform. In response to a suit filed by 22 poorly funded school systems in 1990, State Judge Eugene Reese ruled on April 1 that the state was not living up to its constitutional obligation to provide an adequate education to all students and that reform of school programs with massive infusions of new funds would be required. In order to formulate a remedy that would satisfy the court decision fully, a task force named by Governor Folsom began work on June 21. On October 22, Judge Reese issued another order, this one giving the state until Sept. 30, 1994, to adopt the reform plan recommended by the task force. It was estimated that the plan ultimately would cost approximately $1 billion per year to fund. At year's end the governor and legislators were struggling to develop a consensus on school finances, which could include legalization of revenue-producing gambling casinos.

ALABAMA • Information Highlights

Area: 51,705 sq mi (133 915 km^2).
Population (July 1, 1992 est.): 4,136,000.
Chief Cities (1990 census): Montgomery, the capital, 187,106; Birmingham, 265,968; Mobile, 196,278; Huntsville, 159,789.
Government (1993): *Chief officers*—governor, Jim Folsom, Jr. (D); lt. gov., vacant. *Legislature*—Senate, 35 members; House of Representatives, 105 members.
State Finances (fiscal year 1991): *Revenue*, $9,7671,000,000; *expenditure*, $8,855,000,000.
Personal Income (1992): $68,221,000,000; per capita, $16,496.
Labor Force (August 1993): *Civilian labor force*, 1,958,100; *unemployed*, 142,300 (7.3% of total force).
Education: *Enrollment* (fall 1991)—public elementary schools, 526,473; public secondary, 195,531; colleges and universities, 224,331. *Public school expenditures* (1990-91), $2,475,216,000.

Legislative Sessions. The legislature had met in regular session beginning on February 2, under the cloud of Governor Hunt's looming ethics trial. Little had been accomplished by the time the assembly adjourned on May 17, however, except the passage of a $2.94 billion education budget (which would have to be expanded greatly to satisfy demands for school reform) and an $842 million general-fund budget. The legislature met again in special session in August to consider ethics and campaign-reform legislation. However, the weak measures that cleared the assembly were not to Governor Folsom's liking, and he vetoed both of them on August 31. At the governor's urging, tax-offset legislation was enacted on August 25 which was designed to induce Mercedes-Benz to locate a sports-vehicle assembly plant in the state. On September 30 the German company announced that it would construct the $300 million plant (expected to employ about 1,500 workers) near Tuscaloosa. Thirty states had competed for the plant. This victory offset the loss forecast on June 24 when the federal Base Closure Commission decided to transfer several hundred jobs from the Anniston army depot to Pennsylvania.

Rail Tragedy. On September 22 the worst wreck in Amtrak's history, and one of the most serious rail accidents since World War II, occurred when the Sunset Limited California-to-Florida train—which was carrying 210 passengers and crew—crashed at Bayou Canot near Mobile, causing 47 fatalities. The tragedy occurred when a tow of barges struck a bridge shortly before the train was due to cross it.

Snowstorm. Heavy snows fell on the state during a severe storm that swept the U.S. eastern seaboard, March 12-14. Birmingham received 13" (33 cm), a record for a single storm. Seven fatalities were attributed to the severe weather. President Bill Clinton approved federal storm aid for residents in nine counties.

WILLIAM H. STEWART
The University of Alabama

ALASKA

The collapse of major fisheries throughout Alaska contributed to major social, political, and economic problems in 1993. A disastrous Yukon River chum-salmon run led to an unprecedented decision by the Alaska Department of Fish and Game to close the river system to subsistence fishing, contradicting federal requirements for subsistence preference. Alaska Native villages along the river protested the closure on cultural and economic grounds. Many upriver villages conducted protest fishing in defiance. Meanwhile, extremely low pink-salmon and herring runs in Prince William Sound—which many fishermen blamed on the 1989 *Exxon Valdez* oil spill—caused severe economic problems in a region dominated by commercial fishing. Fishermen blockaded the Valdez oil terminal during the August visit of U.S. Interior Secretary Bruce Babbitt to emphasize their plight.

A Bering Sea Bottomfish Fishery study reported that much of the annual harvest consists of "by-catch" or species that must be dumped because they are either unprofitable or prohibited by federal law. Included in the latter category were some of the salmon bound for Western Alaska rivers.

An August report by the General Accounting Office criticized the *Exxon Valdez* Oil Spill Trustees Council for spending the $900 million settlement from the 1989 Exxon oil spill unwisely. The report cited a lack of financial controls and audits, and claimed that excessive amounts were spent on government studies and unnecessary travel.

Politics. Gov. Walter Hickel filed a $29 billion lawsuit against the federal government for violating the terms of the statehood pact and Alaska's right as a sovereign state to raise revenue. The suit concerned the federal government's withdrawal of more than 100 million acres (40 million ha) of federal lands from development to create national parks and refuges. Hickel claimed that this withdrawal prevented Alaska from receiving 90% of mineral revenues that would be earned if these lands were leased for development.

The Hickel administration, in turn, was sued for moving illegally $800 million in oil-tax settlements to the state's general fund rather than placing it in a special constitutional budget reserve account. The Republican-led coalition of Alaska's Senate and former Democratic Gov. Steve Cowper filed separate suits to stop the funds from being used for capital construction projects across the state.

Finally, during the annual Alaska Federation of Natives conference in October, the U.S. Department of Interior's Assistant Secretary for Indian Affairs Ada Deer announced that 228 Alaska Native villages and organizations had been recognized as having tribal status by the department. This was viewed as a very significant development by Alaska Native leaders, given Alaska's historical position that it will not recognize Native governments within the state.

Environment. A report issued by the Prince William Sound Regional Citizens Advisory Council charged that the Alyeska Pipeline Service Company rigged an air-quality study completed in 1992 to minimize the amount of cancer-causing benzene vapors being released at the company's Valdez tanker terminal. The Alyeska report helped convince the U.S. Environmental Protection Agency (EPA) that a vapor-recovery system was not needed at the terminal. In a related report, an Alaskan oil-industry analyst claimed that oil-company leaders were misleading Alaskans by warning that the cost of proposed environmental requirements could shorten the life of the Trans-Alaska pipeline.

Health. A study in the *Journal of the American Medical Association* reported that Alaska led the nation in the incidence of alcohol-related illness requiring hospitalization among the elderly. Alaska also led the nation in the incidence of hepatitis, primarily in rural, predominantly Alaska Native areas. However, the $1.2 billion cost of implementing improved water systems in rural villages continued to frustrate efforts to resolve the problem.

Other. Animal-rights activists launched a tourism boycott against Alaska in response to the state Board of Game's decision to increase the size of interior Alaska caribou herds by adopting aggressive wolf-hunting tactics. This marked the second year that such a wolf-management plan had been announced, but the 1992 program was rescinded by Governor Hickel in the face of a similar boycott threat.

Patriarch Aleksy II, world leader of the Russian Orthodox Church, made a church outside Anchorage in the village of Eklutna his first stop on a three-week American tour. It was the first visit by a head of the Russian Orthodox Church to Alaska, the church's original gateway to the United States in the late 1700s.

CARL E. SHEPRO, *University of Alaska*

ALASKA • Information Highlights

Area: 591,004 sq mi (1 530 700 km²).

Population (July 1, 1992 est.): 587,000.

Chief Cities (1990 census): Juneau, the capital, 26,751; Anchorage, 226,338; Fairbanks, 30,843; Sitka, 8,588.

Government (1993): *Chief Officers*—governor, Walter J. Hickel (I); lt. gov., John B. Coghill (I). *Legislature*—Senate, 20 members; House of Representatives, 40 members.

State Finances (fiscal year 1991): *Revenue,* $6,355,000,000; *expenditure,* $4,941,000,000.

Personal Income (1992): $13,157,000,000; per capita, $22,419.

Labor Force (August 1993): *Civilian labor force,* 267,400; *unemployed,* 20,600 (7.7% of total force).

Education: *Enrollment* (fall 1991)—public elementary schools, 89,124; public secondary, 29,556; colleges and universities, 30,793. *Public school expenditures* (1990-91), $854,499,000.

ALBANIA

Albania continued to make steady progress on decommunizing the political system and privatizing the economy. However, the Democratic Party government was criticized for its alleged authoritarian leanings. Albanian-Greek relations worsened over the lot of the Greek minority, while the perennial Kosovo problem continued to threaten a wider Balkan war.

Political Disputes. Since the Democrats gained a sweeping victory in the 1992 elections, they had registered some notable successes. Communist controls over the political system were eliminated, pluralism was expanded, and the security forces had been professionalized for the most part. But the government also stood accused by its Socialist opponents of imposing a quasidictatorial system. Democrat leaders in turn accused the Socialists of spreading malicious propaganda in an attempt to reverse the reform process.

The major bone of contention between Democrats and Socialists was the arrest of Socialist parliamentarians charged with misappropriating state funds during their term in office in 1991. In July 1993 the Albanian parliament voted to remove the immunity of Socialist Party leader and former Prime Minister Fatos Nano and placed him under arrest along with several of his colleagues. The arrests led to a two-month boycott of the legislature by Socialist and Social Democrat deputies and a series of rallies organized by their supporters calling for new elections. In September another former prime minister, Vilson Ahemeti, was sentenced to two years in prison for various financial irregularities.

Other opposition parties, including the Democratic Alliance and the Republicans, charged the Democrat majority in the National Assembly with delaying passage of a national constitution. The delineation of executive and legislative powers remained ill-defined and open to abuses. Most opposition forces favored a stronger parliamentary system and complained that President Sali Berisha had acquired various prerogatives during the collapse of communism that enshrined a presidential system without clear constitutional underpinnings.

Although much of the media had been opened to divergent opinions, the state continued to control the main television outlet. The government maintained that television frequencies, like radio airwaves, would be privatized, but in October the authorities passed a restrictive press law according to which newspapers can be confiscated if they publish articles "endangering peace, inciting treason, or undermining state security."

Economic Reforms. The Democrats succeeded in reviving the economy gradually by liberalizing prices, closing unprofitable enterprises, and passing legislation to stimulate private enterprise. Gross domestic product (GDP) was projected to grow by 8% in 1993, the decline in industrial production was halted, and inflation was held to less than 37% as Tiranë strictly adhered to a reform program based on International Monetary Fund (IMF) recommendations. The reform program greatly reduced the budget deficit, stabilized Albania's currency—the lek—and increased exports. By midyear approximately 100,000 people were employed in the private sector, some 65% of them in agriculture.

ALBANIA • Information Highlights

Official Name: Republic of Albania.
Location: Southern Europe, Balkan peninsula.
Area: 11,100 sq mi (28 750 km²).
Population (mid-1993 est.): 3,300,000.
Chief City (mid-1990): Tiranë, the capital, 244,200.
Government: *Head of state*, Sali Berisha, president (took office April 1992). *Head of government*, Aleksander Meksi, prime minister (took office April 1992). *Legislature* (unicameral)—People's Assembly, 140 members.
Gross National Product (1991 est. U.S.$): $2,700,000,000.

© Gianni Giansanti/Sygma

President Sali Berisha (right) welcomed Pope John Paul II to Albania on April 25, 1993. Mother Teresa (extreme left), the 1979 Nobel Peace Prize winner—who is of Albanian extraction—accompanied the pope on his one-day journey. John Paul was the first Roman Catholic pontiff to visit Albania.

Nearly 90% of formerly collectivized land was redistributed, creating a new class of private landowners. However, the program of land distribution accentuated conflicts between the government and the large prewar landowners, who complained that they had not been compensated adequately. They were supported by some opposition parties and ultranationalist organizations.

Despite the introduction of more-liberal laws for foreign capital, new investment lagged, partly because of the unstable Balkan situation and Albania's spartan infrastructure. The country still depended on Western assistance in the form of financial credits for developing communications, housing, and health care, and on humanitarian aid from the European Union (formerly the European Community).

Nationality Conflicts. Albania's relations with two neighbors, Greece and Serbia, gave serious cause for concern. Ties between Tiranë and Athens soured during the summer as a major dispute erupted over the treatment of a Greek Orthodox priest, Archimandrite Maidonis, who had been sent to Albania by the ecumenical patriarch in Istanbul to help rebuild theAlbanian Orthodox Church. Maidonis was expelled in June 1993 for allegedly distributing propaganda advocating that southern Albania be attached to the Greek province of Epirus. The Greek authorities reacted swiftly, expelling tens of thousands of Albanian migrant workers and refugees. Tiranë protested vigorously.

The Maidonis incident also heightened tensions in the Greek-minority areas of southern Albania, where demonstrations and clashes with police erupted. President Berisha sought to appease the Greek minority by holding talks with the Greek Unity Party for Human Rights and pledged to guarantee all internationally sanctioned minority rights. Albanian spokesmen suspected that Athens was intent on destabilizing Albania and distracting attention from the dangerous situation in Kosovo. Foreign Minister Alfred Serreqi claimed that a secret alliance existed between Serbia and Greece designed to keep Albania off-balance.

In Kosovo itself the situation remained highly unstable following the Serbian elections in December 1992, which were boycotted comprehensively by the Albanian majority. Albanian leaders in Kosovo claimed that a silent "ethnic cleansing" campaign was being pursued, designed to persecute and drive out young Albanians. President Berisha called for Kosovo to be placed under a UN mandate in order to avoid major bloodshed. At the same time, he sought to strengthen Albania's political and military ties with the North Atlantic Treaty Organization and with the Islamic world.

JANUSZ BUGAJSKI
Associate Director of East European Studies
Center for Strategic and International Studies

ALBERTA

Elections and provincial cost-cutting made news in Alberta in 1993.

Elections. Premier Ralph Klein's Progressive Conservative (PC) Party won a comfortable victory in the June 1993 provincial election. Klein's party won 51 of the 83 seats, while Laurence Decore's Liberal Party took 32. The PCs had been in power since 1971, but this was their first election under the leadership of Klein, former Calgary mayor. Decore was hampered by his ties to the federal Liberal Party—unpopular in Alberta—and the fact that the Liberals had not governed in the province since 1921. One election surprise was the socialist New Democrat Party (NDP) losing all of its 15 seats. Party leader Ray Martin later resigned the party leadership.

Preston Manning's Reform Party, based in Alberta, ended a 20-year dominance in the province by the PCs in the October 25 federal election. The Reform Party won 22 of Alberta's 26 seats. The Liberals, without representation in Alberta since 1972, won the other four. Before the election, the PCs had held 24 seats, the Reform Party one, and the socialist New Democrats, one.

Senate. Canadian Prime Minister Brian Mulroney, who resigned later in 1993, appointed Calgary lawyer Ron Ghitter to the Senate in Ottawa. Ghitter, 57, a lawyer and PC federal campaign chairman in Alberta, replaced Stan Waters, who died in 1991. Waters had been Canada's only elected senator, and despite pleas to Premier Klein to hold another election, Klein left it to Mulroney to fill the vacancy.

Budget. Provincial Treasurer Jim Dinning unveiled a budget in September that contained neither new taxes nor increases in existing taxes. Dinning announced the accumulated gross debt had risen to C$29 billion from the C$22.6 billion made public in May, but said this was due to

---

ALBERTA • Information Highlights

Area: 255,286 sq mi (661 190 km^2).
Population (June 1993): 2,592,000.
Chief Cities (1991 census): Edmonton, the capital, 616,741; Calgary, 710,677; Lethbridge, 60,974.
Government (1993): *Chief Officers*—lt. gov., Gordon Towers; premier, Ralph Klein (Progressive Conservative). *Legislature*—Legislative Assembly, 83 members.
Provincial Finances (1993-94 fiscal year budget): *Revenues*, $10,110,000,000; *expenditures*, $12,610,000,000.
Personal Income (average weekly earnings, June 1993): $552.53.
Labor Force (August 1993, seasonally adjusted): *Employed* workers, 15 years of age and over, 1,253,000; *Unemployed*, 10.1%.
Education (1993-94): *Enrollment*—elementary and secondary schools, 547,955 pupils; postsecondary—universities, 51,650; community colleges, 27,030.
(All monetary figures are in Canadian dollars.)

© Canapress Photo Service

Premier Ralph Klein, who became leader of Alberta's Progressive Conservatives in 1992, and his wife Colleen were pleased with the outcome of the June 1993 provincial election.

more credible accounting procedures. The Progressive Conservative government had promised to balance the yearly budget by 1996-97, and Dinning said this still could be achieved despite the recession, lower tax revenues, and reduced royalties due to lower oil prices. The 1993-94 deficit was projected at C$2.44 billion, down from C$3.77 billion a year earlier. The reduction was achieved by widespread spending cuts.

Business. Calgary-based Canadian Airlines International, the nation's second-largest scheduled carrier, continued its battle for survival. The airline went ever deeper into debt, but persuaded its employees to invest a portion of their paychecks in the company in return for shares. The airline's future depended on Texas-based American Airlines investing C$246 million in it for a 25% share. The snag was that Canadian Airlines was tied into the lucrative Gemini reservation system with rival Air Canada; American Airlines wanted it instead to join its Sabre reservation system. As the year ended, Canadian Airlines and Air Canada still were fighting battles with various regulatory agencies.

Privatization. The government in September announced plans to privatize all the government-owned retail liquor outlets in the province, with the province maintaining centralized wholesale operations. One hundred thirty-eight stores would be sold to private operators, and the five remaining stores leased out. Union representatives announced plans to fight the proposals, but there was little prospect they could prevent the sell-off. The government expected to make C$400 million per year from the wholesale operations, but said it would save C$67 million annually in retail operating costs. Selling the stores was expected to bring in C$50 million.

PAUL JACKSON, *"The Calgary Sun"*

ALGERIA

In 1993 militant Islamists plunged Algeria into virtual civil war as they extended their attacks against the security forces into a reign of terror aimed at secular intellectuals and foreigners. The efforts of the High State Committee (HCE) to conduct a national dialogue on new political institutions had little impact upon the deteriorating security situation. Redha Malek became prime minister in August in an atmosphere of national crisis.

Political Violence. Despite a curfew imposed in December 1992, armed resistance to the military-backed HCE escalated throughout 1993. In February terrorists very nearly assassinated minister of defense and HCE member Gen. Khaled Nezzar in a car-bomb explosion in Algiers. Although Nezzar narrowly escaped, 15 members of the security forces were killed during that month, while the army killed 26 guerrillas and captured Ikhlef Cherati, a leader of the banned Islamic Salvation Front (FIS) who was considered one of the chiefs of the clandestine Armed Islamic Movement. In March guerrillas infiltrated the Boughezoul barracks, slaughtered 18 soldiers, and escaped with some weaponry. In the ensuing manhunt, 23 guerrillas were tracked down and killed; all in all, the death toll in the violence that began in 1992 climbed to more than 2,000 before year's end.

The sinister campaign against anti-Islamist intellectuals began with a rash of killings in March. Among the victims were the writer and journalist Tahar Djaout as well as known academics and leaders of the medical community. Although some 80,000 people turned out in a march against violence on March 22 and the government expressed its determination to eradicate terrorism, the means were not found to end the mayhem. Other prominent journalists also were assassinated, and the editor of *El Watan*, an anti-Islamist daily, barely eluded an attempt against his life.

In August former Prime Minister Kasdi Merbah was ambushed and murdered. A further

ALGERIA • Information Highlights

Official Name: Democratic and Popular Republic of Algeria.
Location: North Africa.
Area: 919,591 sq mi (2 381 740 km^2).
Population (mid-1993 est.): 27,300,000.
Chief Cities (1987 census): Algiers, the capital, 1,483,000; Oran, 5490,000; Constantine, 438,000.
Government: *Head of state*, Ali Kafi, president (took office July 1992). *Head of government*, Redha Malek, prime minister (took office August 1993).
Monetary Unit: Dinar (24.104 dinars equal U.S.$1, July 1993).
Gross Domestic Product (1990 est. U.S.$): $54,000,000,000.
Foreign Trade (1990 est. U.S.$): *Imports*, $10,122,000,000; *exports*, $13,306,000,000.

© Seghilani/Sipa

During a year of virtual civil war in Algeria, Kasdi Merbah, a former premier and current opposition leader, was assassinated in a coastal resort east of Algiers. The government blamed Islamic fundamentalist extremists for the August 1993 attack which also took the lives of Merbah's son and brother. His supporters (right) expressed their sentiments at his funeral.

escalation occurred in September as two French technical-assistance personnel were slain, the first of several foreigners to be targeted.

Political Maneuvers. Meanwhile the HCE organized a series of meetings with civic associations and political parties—including more moderate Islamic parties than the FIS—over the process of transition back toward elections. In June, President Ali Kafi, head of the HCE, announced agreement upon a formula under which a new three-person council—a president and two vice-presidents—would be named at the end of 1993 to replace the HCE. At the same time, the National Advisory Council would be expanded. Elections, however, were to be delayed for a longer period, perhaps up to three years. General Nezzar appeared to position himself for the new presidential post when he laid down his office of defense minister in favor of retired Gen. Lamine Zeroual and moved another of his allies, Mohamed Lamari, into the post of chief of staff of the armed forces.

The Belaid Abdesselam government, having failed in its primary mission of resuscitating the economy, gave way in August to the Malek government. A former ambassador to the United States and foreign minister, Redha Malek was, like Nezzar, a member of the HCE. He moved to address the sagging economy by naming a market-oriented economist, Mourad Benachenou, as his top economic policy maker. He appointed Selim Saadi, a former military officer, as minister of the interior, a move designed to better coordinate police and army operations.

In October the authorities announced that the dialogue to establish a national consensus would resume. These moves did not reverse the deteriorating security conditions, however, and late in the month the government was reported to have opened talks with some of the imprisoned leadership of the FIS.

Foreign Relations. The domestic crisis placed pressure upon Algerian diplomacy. From February through August, Redha Malek as foreign minister made prompt trips to Tunisia to bolster the Arab Maghreb Union and to Morocco to stem the downturn in relations over the Western Sahara question. In May he traveled to the United States. His most important mission, however, was to enlist French support in the battle against the Islamist guerrillas. Malek and Kafi also visited Egypt.

Economic Affairs. The economy suffered not only from the political strife but also from the weather and a downturn in energy prices. Drought took a heavy toll on agricultural production, which fell by 50%. The global slump in oil prices reduced export revenues with adverse consequences on state-owned industries and overall employment. The government drastically reduced imports from $11 billion in 1992 to $8 billion, causing numerous shortages. Authorities forecast a record budget deficit equivalent to some 40% of the state budget. On top of all of these economic woes came a campaign of industrial sabotage carried out by Islamist sympathizers.

The national oil firm, Sonatrach, signed several contracts for future energy sales, notably with Portugal and with Turkey. The government decided to close down a small number of failing public enterprises while approving measures to assist others in order to save jobs. The government conducted negotiations with the International Monetary Fund (IMF) on policies of structural adjustment throughout the year without reaching agreement.

ROBERT MORTIMER
Haverford College

ANGOLA

Angola's 16-year civil war—which began after the nation gained independence from Portugal in 1975 and ended with a 1991 peace agreement—erupted again in late 1992-93 when the National Union for the Total Independence of Angola (UNITA), a leading opposition party, refused to accept defeat in the September 1992 elections. In the following year, fighting escalated, tens of thousands of people died, and up to 2 million people were displaced.

In January 1993 the troops of the ruling Popular Movement for the Liberation of Angola (MPLA) and UNITA rebels battled to capture or recapture parts of the country they once held. Meanwhile, the United Nations (UN) and other international actors with a stake in the peace process, such as Portugal and the United States, attempted to broker a cease-fire and restart peace talks. Talks that were scheduled for January 1993 ended prematurely and February talks never began. UNITA continued to send confusing signals of war and peace. The UN adopted a resolution in March that placed responsibility for the resumption of war on UNITA.

The situation resembled the crisis at the height of the civil war, with UNITA controlling most of the rural areas and the MPLA government controlling most major cities. Angolan civilians, the major victims of this conflict, alleged that attacks had been made on refugees fleeing the conflict as part of a process of "ethnic cleansing."

By late March the United States and Ivory Coast were helping initiate peace talks. In April talks finally began in Abidjan, the capital of Ivory Coast. The key issues revolved around suspending hostilities, policing such a cease-fire, distributing humanitarian aid, and above all, power-sharing. While the United States did not support any specific proposals on power-sharing, it dispatched Assistant Secretary of State for African Affairs George Moose to urge negotiations between the MPLA and UNITA.

Angered by the role of UNITA and its leader, Jonas Savimbi, in the renewal of hostilities and the defiance of mediation efforts, the Bill Clinton administration formally recognized

© Sam Kiley/Sygma

Loss of life and devastation was heavy in Cuito Cuanavale, above, as civil war resumed in Angola after the UNITA opposition party refused to accept the results of 1992 elections.

the MPLA government in May. The United States felt that a continued refusal to recognize Angola's 1992 democratic election would undermine its commitment to democracy in Africa. Savimbi's refusal to accept the election results and his resumption of the civil war also seemed to cost him political and financial support among conservatives in the international community.

Fighting intensified during the summer, as the MPLA declared a state of emergency and a resumption of all-out war. The UN Security Council met in July and threatened sanctions if UNITA did not participate in peace talks. International support for the MPLA government increased: Great Britain, Russia, and France all considered selling weapons to the MPLA. However, there was little likelihood that the MPLA would receive international troop support. Some observers felt that the war could drag on indefinitely, since neither side seemed willing to stop fighting without improving its bargaining position. UNITA's assault on the government's oil complex cost the MPLA millions of dollars in lost revenue.

Exploratory peace talks began again in late October. Although general terms for a cease-fire were agreed upon two months later, many other issues remained. Angola's ongoing conflict had caused thousands of war-related casualties, a massive internal refugee problem, devastating structural damage, and increasing starvation.

N. BRIAN WINCHESTER
and PATRICK O'MEARA
Indiana University

ANGOLA • Information Highlights

Official Name: People's Republic of Angola.
Location: Western Africa.
Area: 481,351 sq mi (1 246 700 km²).
Population: (mid-1993 est.): 9,500,000.
Chief City (1989 est.): Luanda, the capital, 1,459,900.
Government: *Head of state and government,* José Eduardo dos Santos, president (took office 1979); Marcolino Jose Carlos Moco, prime minister. *Legislature*—People's Assembly.
Gross Domestic Product (1991 est. U.S. $): $8,300,000,000.
Foreign Trade (1990 est.): *Imports,* $1,500,000; *exports,* $3,900,000.

ANTHROPOLOGY

In 1993 investigators reported the discovery of remarkably preserved Neanderthal skulls; a fossil jaw offered insight into the evolution of an ancient ape; and a new African source of fossils and artifacts was announced.

Neanderthal Finds. Spanish paleontologists reported the discovery of three largely complete fossil skulls that apparently represent an early stage of Neanderthal evolution dating to at least 300,000 years ago.

The first unambiguous remains of European Neanderthals—characterized by a large brow ridge, sloping face, jutting jaw, and brain cases slightly larger than those of modern humans—were placed at about 130,000 years old. The new skulls, found in a cave in northern Spain's Atapuerca Mountains, possess some of these Neanderthal features but also have unique attributes, stated Juan-Luis Arsuaga and colleagues of Comprehensive University in Madrid.

The Atapuerca skulls come from two adults and one child, according to the Spanish group. One adult brain case is about the same size as that of the smallest known European and African hominids (members of the evolutionary family that includes humans) from about the same time. The other adult skull includes one of the largest known hominid brain cases of that period. More than 700 fossils from at least 24 hominids had been found thus far at the Spanish cave.

Anthropologists currently disagree as to whether hominids found at various European sites dating to between 500,000 and 130,000 years ago came from one species that consisted of much larger males than females or from two species. Substantial size differences among the ancestral Neanderthals found at Atapuerca lent support to the former theory.

Ancient Ape. An analysis of a fossil jaw found in Africa in 1988 indicated that it belonged to a 14-million to 16-million-year-old ape that was probably a close relative of whatever creature served as a common ancestor for modern apes and humans, said Monte L. McCrossin of the University of California, Berkeley, and Brenda R. Benefit of Southern Illinois University in Carbondale.

The jawbone and its remaining eight teeth, found in western Kenya, belong to the species *Kenyapithecus africanus,* otherwise known only from a few fragmentary fossils, according to McCrossin and Benefit. The specimen came from a relatively young creature, perhaps 6 or 7 years old.

The fossil teeth resemble those of modern apes, such as chimpanzees, more than the teeth of other known groups of ancient apes, the scientists said. A thick jaw held large, jutting teeth at the front of the mouth that *K. africanus* apparently used to crack open hard fruit and nuts before crushing and chewing these foods with cheek teeth.

Excavations in 1993 at the site where the fossil jaw was found yielded several limb bones that probably belonged to a single *K. africanus,* Benefit contended. Unexpectedly, upper portions of an arm bone and leg bone fit onto pieces of a *Kenyapithecus* arm bone and leg bone unearthed at the same location in 1933. Piecing these limbs together would help scientists understand how *K. africanus* moved about.

New African Sites. A team of anthropologists led by Berhane Asfaw of the Ethiopian ministry of culture in Addis Ababa announced the 1991 discovery of a group of sites in southern Ethiopia that eventually may yield large troves of fossils and artifacts from human ancestors.

Excavation of the new sites, known collectively as Konso-Gardula, thus far had unearthed a partial lower jaw and several teeth assigned to *Homo erectus,* generally thought to have been the immediate predecessor of *H. sapiens.* Investigators also found stone tools that resemble those found at other African *H. erectus* sites. The new artifacts consist of pear-shaped stones with sharpened edges and thin pick-shaped tools with triangular points. Bones of large mammals are strewn among the implements and display incisions that may have been made by *H. erectus.*

Sediment layers at Konso-Gardula span the period from about 1.9 million to 1.3 million years ago, Asfaw's group reported. The fossil jaw and stone tools date to approximately 1.4 million years ago. The distinctive sharpened tools favored by *H. erectus,* which have turned up at Asian and European sites extending to 200,000 years ago, may have appeared abruptly around 1.4 million years ago, the anthropologists said. Stone tools found at Konso-Gardula required considerable skill to manufacture and lie scattered in large numbers at several locations, suggesting intensive use of the area by *H. erectus.*

BRUCE BOWER
"Science News"

ARCHAEOLOGY

The excavation of the oldest human burials from the Maya culture, the dating of the oldest known cloth, and the discovery of the only written reference to King David outside of the Bible were among 1993 highlights in archaeology.

Eastern Hemisphere

Ancient Cloth. Microscopic analysis has identified a piece of material found at a Turkish site in 1988 as the oldest known fragment of cloth. The small, calcium-coated specimen dates to about 9,000 years ago. The fabric was found clinging to the handle of a bone tool and may have served as a grip for the implement. Residents of the Turkish settlement, known as Cayonu, apparently produced cloth on a four-sided wooden frame. Weavers interlaced pairs of

© National Museum of Anthropology, Mexico City. Courtesy M.H. de Young Memorial Museum

© Enrique Franco Torrijos. Courtesy M.H. de Young Memorial Museum

During 1993, San Francisco's M.H. de Young Memorial Museum staged the first major exhibit devoted to Teotihuacan, left, Mexico's most-visited archaeological site. The typical Teotihuacan host figure, above, dates from 200-650 A.D.

threads horizontally around single vertical threads held in place on the frame. This method probably was derived from basket-weaving techniques that already were employed in the region.

Horse Figurine. Archaeologists announced the discovery of the oldest known sculpture of a domesticated horse. The 4,300-year-old clay figurine was found during excavations of an ancient Syrian city. The 5-inch (12.7-cm)-long sculpture has exaggerated genitals and may have been used in ceremonies to ensure the fertility of horses. It contains a hole in the muzzle, presumably for a bit to hold reins or a nose ring. And the mane lies flat in a manner unique to domesticated horses. The sculpture suggests that horses played a larger role in the rise of early civilizations than often has been assumed. People in Asia domesticated horses at least 6,000 years ago.

Akkadian Collapse. New evidence indicated that natural causes—a volcanic eruption followed by 300 years of drought and dust storms—initiated the collapse of the Akkadian civilization, the world's first empire, 4,200 years ago. Investigators found the remains of volcanic ash and dust that were carried long distances by wind and deposited atop structures at an Akkadian site in Syria and underneath sand in the surrounding countryside. Soil analysis concluded that low rainfall and reduced water runoff from nearby mountains may have hastened abandonment of the area. Archaeologists already suspected that a drought caused havoc in other areas of the world at the time of the Akkadian collapse.

Biblical Reference. An archaeologist exploring an ancient city in Israel discovered a stone monument containing the only known written reference outside the Bible to King David and the dynasty he founded: the House of David. The style of Aramaic text on the monument and its references to a king of Israel and a king of the House of David suggest that it was built to commemorate a military victory in the 9th century B.C.—a triumph that is cited in the Old Testament. War had broken out between rival kingdoms of Israelites, led by the two rulers mentioned in the text.

Byzantine Town. Excavations at an abandoned town in the remote desert of eastern Egypt yielded the remains of what probably was a major gold-mining outpost for the Byzantine Empire about 1,400 years ago. The site, called Bir Umm Fawakhir, offers a rare look at the lives of ordinary people in Byzantine Egypt.

Archaeologists found evidence of about 200 houses and several outlying settlements. They also discovered pottery fragments that date to the 5th and 6th centuries A.D. and a granite pounding stone that was used to crush gold-bearing quartz. Ancient workers probably used iron picks to chip pieces of quartz that contained gold out of nearby granite cliffs.

Troy's Wall. Excavations indicated that a ditch cut into bedrock, now buried around 3 ft (.9 m) beneath the ground and stretching 13 ft (4 m) thick, protected the Bronze Age city of Troy in the 13th century B.C. At around that time, Troy–located on Turkey's west coast near

Greece–was the site of a fierce battle described in Homer's *Iliad*, a poetic account of the Trojan War. The newly detected ditch lies about 1,300 ft (400 m) beyond the previously known interior sections of the city. Archaeologists found traces of buildings, which suggested that a Bronze Age settlement once stood between Troy's central fortress and the ditch, which apparently served as some kind of an obstacle or fortress against potential invaders.

Greek Shipwreck. Archaeologists found a Greek merchant ship that sank off the island of Alonisos in the Aegean Sea around 400 B.C. It is the largest known vessel from that or any earlier time. The ship may have been up to 85 ft (26 m) long, almost twice as large as most estimates for boats of that era. The wreck was found in 100-ft (30-m)-deep waters among a mound of debris on the seafloor that included nearly 1,000 clay storage jars called amphoras. Also found in the area were numerous black-glazed ceramic wine cups and bowls, a small wine jar, a cooking pot, and a bronze bucket and ladle.

Western Hemisphere

Maya Towns. Mountain jungles in Belize yielded the remains of four Maya settlements where residents exploited local minerals to support a regional trading network more than 1,000 years ago. The discoveries contradict notions that the Maya culture of Central America focused on long-distance trading of jade and other items used by elite social groups.

Each site covers about 4 acres (1.6 ha), excluding surrounding residential areas. People inhabited the towns from about 700 A.D. to 900 A.D., during the "classic" era of Maya civilization. The towns contain remains of plazas, pyramids, raised causeways, and reservoirs. Various minerals occur in and around the sites. These include ocher, which the Maya ground into a red pigment, and granite, which was chiseled into grinding stones. The settlements may have traded goods with major cities that once were located in nearby lowlands.

Hunting Outpost. Archaeologists announced that a prehistoric hunting camp located on a mesa in northern Alaska had been dated to 11,700 years ago, making it the oldest well-documented site of human occupation in North America. Artifacts at the site, including stone spear points and stone tools used to manufacture hunting weapons, may belong to a previously unrecognized culture.

The isolated outpost was discovered during an archaeological survey of the region. Ancient hunters probably climbed up the mesa to scan the area for game and to work on their weapons. A series of radiocarbon dates for bits of charcoal found at the site range from 9,700 to 11,700 years old. Some archaeologists believe that several other North American sites may be slightly older than this camp.

Ancient Text. Investigators deciphered much of the story from the earliest known readable text in the Americas. The story, contained in 21 columns of hieroglyphic writing, was carved into a four-ton stone that was pulled out of a Mexican river in 1986. The story describes warfare and power plays among supporters of a king who reigned in 159 A.D. The hieroglyphics flank a carving of a man wearing an elaborate costume who apparently was the king described in the story.

Researchers believe that the language of the inscriptions may be an ancestral tongue of four related languages now spoken in southern Mexico. The script also contains similarities to Maya hieroglyphics that emerged after 250 A.D. near the Yucatán Peninsula.

Florida Fort. Buried remnants of a 16th-century A.D. Spanish fort discovered in St. Augustine, FL, may be the earliest permanent European settlement in what is now the United States. Excavations uncovered part of a moat and other artifacts linked to a structure archaeologists believe was constructed by Spanish soldiers and settlers in 1565, when the Spanish founded the colony of St. Augustine. Changes in soil color and texture suggested that the moat was 14 ft (4.3 m) wide and 3 ft (0.9 m) deep. A charred post found near the moat indicated that the fort had burned down, consistent with historical accounts of the structure's demise.

Maya Burials. The oldest human burials yet known from the ancient Maya culture were discovered at the Cuello site in Belize. Investigators found five skeletons buried closely together, all of which date to sometime between 1200 B.C. and 900 B.C. One burial revealed a female who was no more than 15 years old clutching a baby in her right arm. Investigators believe that the close spacing of the burials suggests that the individuals had been members of the same family and died within a fairly short period of time. Only a few pottery bowls and jade beads appear in these earliest Maya burials. One skeleton has swollen limb bones that probably were caused by syphilis or a related disease.

Teotihuacan. Interest in Teotihuacan, a large urban center north of Mexico City that flourished in the first eight centuries A.D., remained keen. Archaeological excavations in the area continued to reveal new findings, and a 1993 exhibit at San Francisco's M. H. de Young Memorial Museum showed various items from the culture. Scholars pointed out that the culture probably was older than once believed and that it was divided into more than one period. Experts believe that a major market and pilgrimage center developed in Teotihuacan by the first century and that its residents began to focus on permanent housing in the third century. Most of the Teotihuacanos lived in apartment compounds that were so large archaeologists considered them to be small palaces.

BRUCE BOWER, *"Science News"*

ARCHITECTURE

In 1993 there was growing diversity in the types of buildings architects were asked to create. New projects were often smaller than they had been in the past and there was an increasing shift away from the design of large office buildings to more economical facilities such as community health centers. The larger architectural offices, especially, hurried to reposition themselves to compete in such unaccustomed markets.

Design Diversity. Along with a broadening field of building types, there was an increasing diversity in design, despite stiffer client controls. As a sign of a new internationalism, the 1993 Pritzker Prize for Architecture went to Fumihiko Maki, a Japanese architect noted for modernist design.

The American Institute of Architects' (AIA) annual Honor Awards showed a more inclusive picture of the types of designs accepted by the profession's mainstream. In 1993 the AIA dubbed its annual Honor Awards "Celebrating Pluralism." One recipient, Eisenman Architects' Wexner Center for the Arts at Ohio State University in Columbus, combined several design directions in one building. The basic core was a grouping of International Style white rectilinear forms of the sort that grew popular in the 1930s and became forerunners of current-day modernism. Around these forms were red brick towers that recall those of a late-19th-century fortress-like structure previously standing on the site. They were perhaps an inadvertent bow to postmodernism. The towers were split in two, as if they were coming apart, and a scaffold-like framework was extended across the entry facade. Both elements are hallmarks of deconstructivism, which implies dematerialization and incompleteness. Wexner Center was described as purposely creating tension in audience and performers alike.

Reinforcing Neighborhoods. Most of the other AIA award winners were noted for avoiding individualistic design statements at the expense of established neighborhood character. James Stewart Polshek & Partners created the Seaman's Church Institute in New York City with a simple brick facade that blended with adjacent loft buildings while avoiding overt reference to historic detailing. "A textbook example of contextualism," said the AIA jury report. For the Morton International Building in Chicago, architects Perkins & Will did not introduce a bold departure from the adjacent rectangular mid-century modern buildings. Instead they used subtle relationships of varied glass grids to provide visual refinement.

Among other AIA award winners, the Biodel Education Center on Bainbridge Island in the state of Washington was built with low-scale and indigenous materials. James Cutler Architects blended it into its forest setting so that it resembled a creation of nature. With the Hostos Community College in the Bronx, NY, Voorsanger & Associates Architects helped revive a blighted neighborhood by respecting the scale of the few substantial buildings nearby. A parking structure for Princeton University by Machado and Silvetti Associates ended neighbors' objections by incorporating a wall designed early in the century by McKim Mead & White as a major element of its facade.

Two designs for low-income housing won awards. The large volume of Ron Wellington

Architecture's 1993 Pritzker Prize was won by Japan's Fumihiko Maki, who is noted for his modernist designs. His works include the Iwasaki Art Museum and Annex in Ibusuki, below.

Photos, Courtesy, © Maki & Associates, Tokyo, Japan

Quigley's 202 Island Inn was divided into house-like elements in deference to the scale of the Chinese historic district in San Diego where it is located. In addition, the architect sought design input from local residents, which produced different characters for each element. For Langham Court in Boston, Goody, Clancy & Associates adopted the red-brick vernacular of neighboring buildings and included a central landscaped courtyard that was intended for community use.

Individual Statements. Where an established neighborhood character was lacking, the AIA award winners were notable for creating one. The round high-rise tower of the NationsBank Plaza by Wolf+, Architects was likened by the bank's president to a lighthouse on an otherwise nondescript stretch of Tampa's waterfront. Richard Meier & Partners produced a taut white-enamel and glass International Style headquarters for Canal+ outside Paris that was the clearest statement of individual style among the awards.

There were a number of colorful designs in 1993. Scogin Elam and Bray Architects chose not to ignore a location among gas stations and shopping centers for the Buckhead branch library in Atlanta and took the vernacular to new heights with neon lighting and soaring metal canopies held up by supports set on dizzying angles. Hammond Beeby and Babka used familiar classical and Wild West symbolism and bright materials to enliven youngsters' interest for the Hole-in-the-Wall-Gang Camp for children with cancer and serious blood diseases in Ashford/Eastford, CT. Colton Palms, a retirement home in Colton, CA, also exhibits bright colors and playful forms, with which architects Valerio-Associates enlivened the interests of older adults. The Stretto House in Dallas was designed by Steven Holl, Architect as open pavilions to take full advantage of a spectacular natural site.

As a sign of changing times, only two 1993 AIA-award-winning projects were high-rise towers—NationsBank and Morton International. And, in contrast to recent years' awards, only two awards went to preservation projects: a late-19th-century library designed by Frank Furness at the University of Pennsylvania in Philadelphia restored by Venturi, Scott Brown and Associates; and the Rookery Building of similar vintage in Chicago, which was designed by Burnham and Root and restored by McClier.

Preservation. Despite the lack of awards for preservation projects, they were being completed in record numbers. The construction-industry reporting group F. W. Dodge estimated that nonresidential additions and alterations accounted for 40% of all construction in 1993. The AIA envisioned the year 2000 as the turning point from "The Era of Building to the Era of Rebuilding," when more architects would be working on renovation than new construction.

Conserving older buildings was ingrained in public acceptance. There was a growing trend to conserve all resources, from paper and bottles to buildings. There also was a growing sense of the U.S. past and a sense that other eras (and their physical manifestations) may have been better.

Plans for large city areas called for combining preservation and new construction instead of a strategy of starting afresh. Los Angeles presented a plan by architects Ehrenkrantz & Eckstut for 70 downtown acres (28.4 ha) surrounding its 1939 Union Station, recently renovated by architects Hardy Holzman Pfeiffer. Work was under way on the 1938 Mission Revival style Terminal Annex that called for 11 million sq ft (about 1 million m²) of commercial, residential, hotel, and retail space. In New York, Robert A. M. Stern produced a plan to revive the 42d Street portion of the Times Square redevelopment area—not with wholesale land clearance for major office towers as originally planned, but by reusing existing buildings.

One new type of large-scale renewal project architects faced in 1993 was to adapt former military bases to new uses as the United States scaled down its defense. A competition to remodel one of the bases scheduled for closing, Alameda, CA, was sponsored by *Architectural Record*, and drew entries from both large and small offices.

Buildings of all types were salvaged for new or updated uses. These included schools, shopping centers, office buildings built in the 1950s and 1960s, and one of the world's largest buildings—the Pentagon in Arlington, VA, headquarters of the U.S. Department of Defense. Causes included the need to conform to new building codes, including the Americans with Disabilities Act; technological advance, such as wiring for computers; and—in the commercial sector—the need to attract tenants during a time of great competition. The nation's oldest shopping mall, Market Square, built in the 1920s in Lake Forest, IL, was updated by architect John Vinci. A newer failed shopping mall on a much larger scale, Mizner Park in Boca Raton, FL, was redesigned totally by Cooper Carry & Associates as a mixed-use development containing offices, residential units, and shops.

One code-compliance issue, earthquake resistance, required major structural reinforcement of such landmarks as architect George Herbert Wyman's 1892 Bradbury Building, which was to anchor another Los Angeles renewal area. Restoration architects Levin and Associates used unobtrusive plywood cross-bracing walls between steel columns in locations that would not be seen from the grand multilevel main courtyard-lobby. Architects FFKR skillfully designed exterior poured-concrete shear walls resembling the originals for the early 20th-century Hotel Utah in Salt Lake City.

CHARLES K. HOYT
"Architectural Record"

ARGENTINA

The party of Argentina's President Carlos Saúl Menem captured a strong victory in congressional elections held in October 1993. In November, Menem then cleared a major constitutional hurdle in his quest for reelection in 1995.

Elections. President Menem's Peronist Party, on the strength of its economic program, won the final electoral contest of its six-year term ending in 1995. Peronists gained nine seats in the 257-seat Chamber of Deputies, three short of a majority. The opposition Radical Civic Union (UCR) lost one seat. The biggest win for the Peronists came in the federal district, a UCR stronghold. The October campaign was accompanied by a concurrent scare campaign against journalists in which some were subjected to physical attacks and scores were threatened for criticizing Menem's record.

But the voting also left the Peronists short of the two-thirds congressional majority needed to amend the constitution to permit an incumbent president to succeed himself immediately. On November 14, Menem gained a big step toward that end when the UCR party agreed to constitutional changes that would allow him to seek a second, four-year term in 1995. As a result a scheduled plebiscite on the issue was canceled.

Economic Policies. Almost the entire public sector was expected to be sold by 1995, including railroads, port facilities, and the state insurance system. The sale of 51 companies—including airlines, natural-gas distribution, and telecommunications—had raised $5.6 billion and canceled $12 billion of foreign debt prior to 1993. The privatized companies, previously a drain on the national treasury, contributed $1 billion in taxes during the first half of 1993.

Roughly 45% of the state oil monopoly, YPF, was sold in June. The sale, the year's largest equity offering, earned $3 billion. Analysts believed that, with privatization, 1 million Argentines would purchase YPF stock. Prior to privatizing its largest corporation (and one of the world's 20 largest energy concerns), the Argentine government restructured YPF, reducing the workforce from 51,000 in 1990 to 8,000 by the end of 1993. Proceeds produced by the YPF privatization were earmarked for overdue benefits to old-age pensioners.

One of the more radical economic changes introduced by the government was a private pension scheme. The existing system had absorbed roughly 25% of government expenditures and was collapsing. With a privately funded plan, capital would become available to revitalize state finances, while pension benefits would improve. The labor confederation (CGT) was won over and the Chamber of Deputies approved the scheme in May. A compromise plan cleared the Senate in September. The new plan slightly lowered contributions for employers and employees. Participation in the private plan would be voluntary, with the state program remaining an option.

Privatizing state enterprises had cost 260,000 jobs by August, as the private sector was reducing its workforce by more than 8%. Most jobs lost were in the oil, steel, textile, and sugar industries. Unemployment unofficially approached 14% and underemployment was estimated at 10%. The monthly minimum wage was doubled to $200 in July, but the cost of living had jumped nearly 51% in the 1990s. Church officials complained to the government about the impact of its policies on the middle and lower classes.

Menem reiterated that he would not back off from the neoliberal economic model of his

© Don Rypka/NYT Pictures

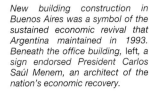

New building construction in Buenos Aires was a symbol of the sustained economic revival that Argentina maintained in 1993. Beneath the office building, left, a sign endorsed President Carlos Saúl Menem, an architect of the nation's economic recovery.

administration. Although the 1993 gross domestic product (GDP) was projected in September to grow more than 5%, it was lower than expected and slowed implementation of a $1.8 billion antipoverty plan introduced early in the year that addressed jobs, housing, and nutrition.

Inflation for 1993 was projected at 8% to 12%, compared with roughly 18% in 1992, reducing pressure on Economy Minister Domingo Cavallo to end an overvalued peso's parity with the dollar. In September, Cavallo suggested that the country might adopt a floating-exchange-rate system within five years. While Cavallo was able to reduce inflation, he failed to narrow the trade gap, expected to widen to $3 billion in 1993. To remedy this shortfall, the government made a $4.5 billion support program available for industry and agriculture to promote international competitiveness and reduce operating costs.

Argentina restructured $19 billion of foreign debt with 750 creditor banks. Payment on the renegotiated portion of the debt would be stretched out over 35 years and the debt servicing burden reduced by one third. The settlement was reached according to the terms of the Brady Debt Reduction Plan, which improved Argentina's place in international financial markets. With this improved status, Argentina appeared to be able to raise between $8 billion and $11 billion in 1993 to cover the year's account deficit. The World Bank extended $750 million in January for debt reduction and privatization, while the International Monetary Fund (IMF) made an additional $460 million available for debt reduction. The Inter-American Development Bank provided $775 million—with $400 million earmarked for debt reduction—late in 1992.

Trade. During a May visit by Brazilian President Itamar Franco, Argentina took steps to make assurances that the Southern Cone Common Market (Mercosur) was still a priority, with Jan. 1, 1995, as the target date to begin regional integration. Among the unresolved problems was an imbalanced exchange rate between Argentina and Brazil. While the Brazilian cruzeiro was devalued frequently, the peso remained at par with the U.S. dollar and its convertibility was reaffirmed in March. Some Argentines believed that the peso was overvalued, but Cavallo opposed devaluating the peso, believing it would end Argentina's "economic miracle."

The Argentine exchange rate lagged far behind domestic price increases, causing the country to be inundated with cheaper industrial and high-technology products from Brazil. The trade imbalance in 1992 was $1.7 billion. Brazil increased its purchases from Argentina in 1993, buying vehicles, crude oil, and wheat, but Argentines bought more products made in Brazil in 1993 than during the previous year, despite a temporary tariff levy of 10% on most imports. Plans moved ahead on other integration projects, including an inland waterway connecting Buenos Aires and São Paulo, utilizing the Paraná, Uruguay, and Teitê rivers. The two countries agreed to share consular facilities and opened pilot projects at some consulates located in Canada and the United States.

Foreign Relations. Contacts with Britain were upgraded when Foreign Secretary Douglas Hurd visited Argentina; he was the highest-ranking British official to do so since the Falklands/Malvinas conflict in 1982. Menem reiterated Argentina's claim to the British-held territory, disputed since 1832. Hurd rejected the Argentine position on ownership of the islands and turned to fishing rights. Even though 60% of the 2,000 islanders' revenues was generated by selling squid-fishing licenses to foreign companies, Argentina had announced the sale of 52 cut-rate licenses that would cost the island's government 35% of its fiscal 1993 revenues. Buenos Aires agreed to limit its licenses to 45. British exports and investment to Argentina rose in 1993.

A visit to the White House in June by President Menem found U.S. President Bill Clinton willing to consider free-trade talks and to expedite the sale of 36 U.S. secondhand Skyhawk bombers to Argentina. Menem indicated that the Argentine Congress soon would act on a bill against the pirating of pharmaceutical patents, a practice believed to cost U.S. firms some $200 million annually. Menem requested that the United States stop marketing subsidized grain in Latin America, a practice which has hurt his country's exports. Menem was the first Latin American head of state to pay an official visit to the new U.S. president. Argentine's armed forces turned the remaining parts of its ground-to-ground Condor missiles over to the United States for destruction in September. With a range of 600 mi (965 km) and the capability to transport nuclear warheads, the weapons were developed with funds and technology from Iraq and Germany.

LARRY L. PIPPIN
University of the Pacific

ARGENTINA • Information Highlights

Official Name: Argentine Republic.
Location: Southern South America.
Area: 1,068,297 sq mi (2 766 890 km²).
Population (mid-1993 est.): 33,500,000.
Chief Cities (mid-1990 est., incl. suburbs): Buenos Aires, the capital, 11,382,002; Cordoba, 1,166,932; Rosario, 1,096,254.
Government: *Head of state and government,* Carlos Saúl Menem, president (took office July 8, 1989). *Legislature*—Senate and Chamber of Deputies.
Monetary Unit: Peso (.9901 austral equal U.S.$1, financial rate, Dec. 20, 1993).
Gross Domestic Product (1991 est. U.S.$): $101,200,000,000.
Economic Indexes: *Consumer Prices* (1992, 1988 = 100), all items, 269,861.0; food, 241,460.0. *Industrial Production* (1991, 1980 = 100), 99.
Foreign Trade (1992 U.S.$): *Imports,* $14,872,000,000; *exports,* $12,235,000,000.

ARIZONA

In political news, U.S. Sen. Dennis DeConcini (D) announced in September 1993 that he would not run for reelection in 1994. The three-term senator had been rebuked by the Senate Ethics Committee for his role in the Charles Keating, Jr., savings and loan scandal and was facing a primary-election challenge from Arizona Secretary of State Dick Mahoney. Republican U.S. Representative John Kyl also had planned to run against him and by late 1993 was considered a shoo-in for the Republican nomination. Several Democrats, including Mahoney, expressed interest in running, and the Democratic primary was considered a toss-up.

Gov. J. Fife Symington signed gaming compacts with more than a dozen of the state's Indian tribes. In 1992 federal marshals had seized gambling machines on the reservations because no agreements with the state had been reached. Several casinos now were in operation and more were planned, including one at the Grand Canyon. The constitution of the Navajos, the state's largest tribe, currently prohibited gaming, but amendments were planned to permit a casino to be built on tribal land on Lake Powell, along Arizona's northern border.

Health Issues. A deadly respiratory disease was detected, first among the Navajos. Marked by a swift onset of cough, fever, and muscle aches, the ailment leads to respiratory collapse within hours. Half the cases were fatal, and no cure was known. As the disease spread, tribal president Peterson Zah denounced those who characterized it as "Navajo plague." Within six months researchers at the Centers for Disease Control and Prevention had identified the cause as a variety of hantavirus passed through the excretions of deer mice. A surge in the rodent population was attributed to a wet winter and an abundance of pine nuts. Residents were urged to avoid disturbing the animals' nests and to seal their homes to keep the mice out.

"Killer bees" made their first appearance in southern Arizona. The African honeybees had been working their way north since they were released accidentally in Brazil nearly 40 years earlier. They first were detected in early summer along the Mexican border, and experts were stunned to find more than 50 swarms in the state by the end of the year, some as far north as Phoenix. While the only casualties thus far had

---

ARIZONA • Information Highlights

Area: 114,000 sq mi (295 260 km^2).

Population (July 1, 1992 est.): 3,832,000.

Chief Cities (1990 census): Phoenix, the capital, 983,403; Tucson, 405,390; Mesa, 288,091; Glendale, 148,134; Tempe, 141,865.

Government (1993): *Chief Officers*—governor, J. Fife Symington (R); secretary of state, Richard Mahoney (D). *Legislature*—Senate, 30 members; House of Representatives, 60 members.

State Finances (fiscal year 1991): *Revenue*, $9,016,000,000; *expenditure*, $7,872,000,000.

Personal Income (1992): $66,386,000,000; per capita, $17,323.

Labor Force (August 1993): *Civilian labor force*, 1,750,200; *unemployed*, 97,700 (5.6% of total force).

Education: *Enrollment* (fall 1991)—public elementary schools, 490,242; public secondary, 166,738; colleges and universities, 272,971. *Public school expenditures* (1990-91), $2,469,415,000.

Eight scientists from the Biosphere 2 project emerged in September 1993 from the giant greenhouse located near Tucson, AZ. The group had been sealed inside the structure for two years in order to study the ecology of closed systems.

© Greg Smith/Saba

been a few family dogs, local firefighters were practicing rescue techniques. Standard fire-fighting foam seemed to disable the swarms effectively.

Biosphere 2. After two years, the Biosphere 2 was opened officially in September. Eight persons had been sealed within the 3-acre (1.2-ha) glass structure north of Tucson to assess a closed system's ecology. The $150 million project had been subject to considerable criticism. A scientific review committee chaired by Thomas Lovejoy, a biologist from the Smithsonian Institution, disbanded early in the year after criticizing the project's research design. John B. Corliss, an oceanographer who had explored the 8,000-ft (2 438.4-m) depths off the Galápagos Islands, then was appointed director of research. The eight "Biosphereans" lost an average of more than 13% of their original body weight and 35% of their average cholesterol counts during their two-year confinement. The project was plagued by a lack of oxygen, and extra supplies had to be piped in twice during the experiment. Eugene Odum, director emeritus of the University of Georgia's Institute of Ecology, maintained that the Biosphere was too small to support eight persons.

PETER GOUDINOFF, *The University of Arizona*

ARKANSAS

Politics dominated news in Arkansas in 1993.

Politics. The year opened with attention focused on the state as former Gov. Bill Clinton prepared to become president. The inauguration of the 42d president drew thousands of Arkansans to Washington, DC, many of whom assumed positions in the Clinton administration.

State Sen. Jerry Jewell (D-Little Rock) was the first black to be elected president pro tempore of the Senate. He thus also became the first black to serve as acting governor when Jim Guy Tucker, who had moved from the lieutenant gov-

ernorship to the governorship following Clinton's resignation from the post in late 1992, was in Washington for the presidential inauguration. As acting governor, Jewell attracted considerable attention when he granted executive clemency to two inmates in the state penitentiary and pardoned two other convicts who had been paroled.

The office of lieutenant governor was vacant for six months until Republican Mike Huckabee defeated Democrat Nate Coulter to become the first Republican in more than ten years to hold a statewide office. State Auditor Julia Hughes Jones changed her political affiliation from Democrat to Republican.

Legislative. The 79th General Assembly of the Arkansas legislature met for 88 days—the longest session in a decade. Highlights of its work included passage of a state civil-rights bill which prohibited discrimination on the basis of race or sex for all employers with nine or more employees; major revision in the state criminal-justice system, including a network of "community punishment centers" for nonviolent offenders; the establishment of a commission to prepare sentencing guidelines for judges and new procedures for sentencing in felony trials; increased licensing fees for nine state agencies; a revision in workers'-compensation rules to require more specific details on the injury; and stronger environmental-safety laws prohibiting new solid-waste landfills, incinerators, and hazardous-waste disposal or storage within 12 mi (19.3 km) of existing landfills. Legislators refused to approve an abortion bill that would have required a 24-hour waiting period.

Constitutional Amendments. Legislators agreed to submit three proposed constitutional amendments to the electorate in November 1994. The amendments would allow the governor to appoint a lieutenant governor when that office becomes vacant; ask voters to approve or reject some form of bingo games, which presently were illegal; and call for a "use tax" that would be earmarked for the Game and Fish Commission. A constitutional amendment to limit terms in office for most elected state officials was declared unconstitutional by a circuit-court judge.

Health and Environment. Health Department officials banned consumption of fish caught in the Ouachita and Saline river basins after random tests found unusually high levels of mercury in fish from those areas. The source of contamination was not determined.

Education. The State Board of Education revised the 1984 standards for public schools by increasing graduation requirements and establishing a two-track academic program—one for college preparatory and another for vocational training. A new math-and-science high school, previously authorized by the General Assembly, began its first year of operation in July.

C. FRED WILLIAMS
University of Arkansas at Little Rock

ARKANSAS • Information Highlights

Area: 53,187 sq mi (137 754 km²).

Population (July 1, 1992 est.): 2,399,000.

Chief Cities (1990 census): Little Rock, the capital, 175,795; Fort Smith, 72,798; North Little Rock, 61,741; Pine Bluff, 57,140.

Government (1993): *Chief Officers*—governor, Jim Guy Tucker (D); lt. gov., Mike Huckabee (R). *General Assembly*—Senate, 35 members; House of Representatives, 100 members.

State Finances (fiscal year 1991): *Revenue,* $4,810,000,000; *expenditure,* $4,649,000,000.

Personal Income (1991): $37,817,000,000; per capita, $15,765.

Labor Force (August 1993): *Civilian labor force,* 1,177,500; *unemployed,* 70,200 (6.0% of total force).

Education: *Enrollment* (fall 1991)—public elementary schools, 315,147; public secondary, 123,371; colleges and universities, 94,340. *Public school expenditures* (1990-91), $1,510,092,000.

ART

The year 1993 was marked by a lack of premieres of blockbuster art exhibitions. A new museum devoted to the works of Norman Rockwell opened in the spring (*see* pages 120-21) and a number of renovations were completed. The art market continued to be a buyer's market.

Exhibitions. A major show of beautiful but rarely seen paintings was entitled "Great French Paintings from the Barnes Foundation." Featuring 81 paintings from Impressionist, Postimpressionist, and early modern styles, it appeared at the National Gallery of Art in Washington, DC, from May 2 to August 15. (*See* FEATURE ARTICLE, pages 83-87.)

One of the best modern-art surveys during 1993 was a show entitled "Picasso and the Age of Iron," with 170 works by such artists as Alexander Calder, Alberto Giacometti, Pablo Picasso, and David Smith. The theme of the show was the development of assemblage and forged iron. It was shown at New York City's Guggenheim Museum from March 19 to May 16 and at the Modern Art Museum of Fort Worth, TX, from early August to early October.

New York City's Museum of Modern Art (MoMA) hosted three major exhibitions of modern artists. "Max Ernst: Dada and the Dawn of Surrealism" included 200 paintings, drawings, and collages done between 1909 and 1929. The show traveled to the Menil Collection in Houston in late May and to the Art Institute of Chicago in September after its sojourn at MoMA from March 12 to May 2. Also appearing at MoMA, from Oct. 13, 1993, to Jan. 11, 1994, was a retrospective of another major surrealist, Spain's Joan Miró. Celebrating the 100th anniversary of the artist's birth, the first full-scale retrospective included approximately 350 works. At MoMA, too, was "Latin American Artists of the Twentieth Century," an in-depth examination of Latin American modernism, which included 300 works by 90 artists. (One third of the selection was contemporary.) After premiering in the Plaza de Armas, Seville, Spain, and appearing at the Centre Georges Pompidou, Paris, in 1992, it was at MoMA during the summer of 1993.

One of the artists in the Latin American exhibition, Frida Kahlo—the Mexican artist and beleaguered wife of Diego Rivera, who has become something of a cult figure—was given a retrospective with 70 paintings, prints, and drawings at the Houston Museum of Fine Arts during the summer.

Most of the shows of contemporary art were retrospectives of well-known artists. Two that opened in October spotlighted abstract expressionist Willem de Kooning and the celebrated pop artist Roy Lichtenstein. De Kooning's works—50 paintings, drawings, and sculptures dating from 1939 to 1989—were a part of Washington's Hirshhorn Museum collection and premiered there in anticipation of the artist's 90th birthday in 1994. Works by Roy Lichtenstein were featured at the Guggenheim Museum in New York with more than 130 paintings and sculptures. Both shows would travel to other museums in 1994.

Appearing at the Los Angeles Museum of Contemporary Art (LA MOCA) was a show of contemporary art that was not a retrospective of an artist but rather a theme show, "Rolywholyover: A Circus." It was billed as "a composition for museum by John Cage," with 200 works by more than 50 artists. The title of the show came from James Joyce's *Finnegans Wake* and was meant to suggest revolution and dynamic movement. It included music and dance performances, film and video screenings, readings, and a selection of Cage graphics. Installed according to chance procedures, the show opened in September and was to travel to other museums after

The Smithsonian Institution's Freer Gallery of Art reopened in May 1993 after extensive renovation. The museum's northeast corner features James McNeil Whistler's famous Harmony in Blue and Gold: The Peacock Room, left, 1876-77.

closing in late November. The 1993 Biennial Exhibition at New York's Whitney Museum of Art highlighted works that were basically political or at least social. Eighty-two artists were exhibited at the Biennial from early March until mid-June.

The Los Angeles County Museum of Art hosted two exhibits of 19th-century painters, beginning in October. "Friedrich to Hodler: A Romantic Tradition" included 100 German and Austrian paintings from the Oskar Reinhart Foundation in Winterthur, Switzerland. The "Friedrich to Hodler" show premiered in Berlin, but "The Golden Age of Danish Painting" premiered in Los Angeles in late October with 100 works created between 1780 and 1850. Both shows would travel in 1994.

Seventeenth-century Dutch and Flemish art was featured in two shows in September. "Judith Leyster: A Dutch Master and Her World" opened at the Worcester Art Museum in Worcester, MA, after premiering at the Frans Hals Museum in Haarlem, the Netherlands, in the summer. The first retrospective of the most famous woman painter of the Netherlands' Golden Age, the show included 42 paintings, of which 18 were by Leyster. Premiering at the Boston Museum of Fine Arts was "The Age of Rubens," which was the first major exhibition of Flemish Baroque painting ever organized in the United States. It included about 125 works with more than 30 by Rubens. It would travel in 1994.

A major show of non-European art, "Korean Arts of the 18th Century: Splendor and Simplicity," featured textiles, paintings, sculptures, ceramics, and lacquers. It opened at the Asia Society in New York in October after premiering at the National Museum of Korea in Seoul.

Drawing shows were highly diverse. One, by the German artist Joseph Beuys, appeared at New York's MoMA, the Los Angeles Museum of Contemporary Art, and the Philadelphia Museum of Art. The show, entitled "Visions of Antiquity: Neoclassical Figure Drawings," featured 125 drawings from the period between 1760 and 1830, including works by William Blake, Henry Fuseli, Antonio Canova, and Jean-Auguste-Dominique Ingres. It premiered at Los Angeles in late July then moved to Philadelphia. Finally, "Giambattista Tiepolo: Master of the Oil Sketch" appeared only at the Kimbell Museum of Art in Fort Worth from September 18 through December 12.

Museums. After a two-year, $12.4 million renovation, the Metropolitan Museum in New York reopened its 19th-century European painting and sculpture galleries in September. Philippe de Montebello, the Metropolitan's director, described the result as "a permanent blockbuster." A part of the installation was the splendid gift of 53 works from the collection of Mr. and Mrs. Walter H. Annenberg, which included Van Gogh's "Wheat Field and Cypresses." (The latter had been purchased by Annen-

berg for $57 million.) Other gifts received by the Metropolitan Museum included $5 million from A. L. Levine, a Palm Beach, FL, shopping-center developer. The gift would be used to convert a former sculpture court in the Lila Acheson Wallace Wing into a gallery of 20th-century art.

The National Gallery of Art in Washington was the recipient of one of William N. Harnett's most famous trompe l'oeil paintings, "The Old Violin" (1886). The painting was valued in excess of $5 million.

A number of museums reopened after renovation and construction. Among these were the Cincinnati Art Museum, which unveiled its renovated galleries in January after a two-year overhaul by local architect Michael Moose at a cost of $10.5 million; and the Denver Art Museum, which reopened its permanent collection galleries after a $9.3 million renovation. In May the Freer Gallery at the Smithsonian Institution in Washington reopened after four and one-half years of renovation and $26 million in costs. An underground exhibition gallery links the Freer with the neighboring Sackler, the Smithsonian's second Asian museum. The Sackler Gallery itself received $2.8 million in 1993 from an anonymous donor. An addition to the Dallas Museum of Art, designed by Edward Larrabee Barnes, offered space for 7,000 American objects.

Also exciting was the reopening of the Jewish Museum in New York City in June. The landmark Warburg Mansion was expanded intelligently and unusually to double its space by Kevin Roche at a cost of $50 million. Opening to the public in November was the Frederick R. Weisman Art Museum of the University of Minnesota, formally called the University Art Museum, which formally moved into its new quarters in July. The $10.5 million, 41,000-sq-ft (3 809-m^2) facility was designed by Santa Monica architect Frank O. Gehry. A long-anticipated unveiling was the New Orleans Museum of Art's $23 million, 55,550-sq-ft (5 161-m^2) expansion and renovation by Eskew Felson Architects.

Personnel Changes. In September, Richard E. Oldenburg, the director of New York's MoMA since 1972, announced his resignation, effective June 30, 1994. Under his leadership, MoMA had undergone a major expansion, staged several blockbuster exhibits, and seen its endowment and attendance increase. John Elderfield, organizer of MoMA's Matisse retrospective in 1992, was promoted to the museum's new position of chief curator at large.

Michael E. Shapiro gave up the directorship of the Los Angeles County Museum of Art. An art historian by training, he had held the post for only ten months. Jay Gates, director of the Seattle Art Museum, took over as director of the Dallas Museum of Art; and Sherri Geldin, formerly an associate director of the Museum of Contemporary Art in Los Angeles, replaced Robert Stearns as director of the Wexner Center

To mark the centennial of the birth of Spain's Joan Miró, a major retrospective of his works was held at the *Miró Foundation, left, in* Barcelona from April 20 through Aug. 30, 1993. Much of the exhibit was shown at New York City's Museum of Modern Art in the fall.

for the Arts in Columbus, OH. Thomas N. Armstrong 3d, former director of New York's Whitney Museum, was appointed director of the Andy Warhol Museum, currently under construction in Pittsburgh. Mark Rosenthal, formerly consultative curator of the Guggenheim Museum in New York, became the new curator of 20th-century art at the National Gallery of Art in Washington, DC.

The Art Market. The top prices for paintings in 1993 went to the Impressionist and modern categories, unlike sales in 1991 and 1992 where Old Master paintings brought the highest prices. The top price for a painting sold during the May auctions at Sotheby's and Christie's went for Paul Cézanne's "Still Life with Apples" at $28.6 million. The painting was sold at Sotheby's on May 11. Henri Matisse's "Fatma, The Mulatto" (1912) went for $14.3 million—also at Sotheby's May 11 sale. At the same sale, Pierre-August Renoir's "Femme dans un jardin" fetched $6.7 million, and at Christie's London sale in June, a Renoir of a young girl with a basket of flowers brought $8.47 million. However, except for such superb paintings, the auction market was very much a buyer's market. For example, at the same auction where the Cézanne sold for $28.6 million, another Cézanne sold for $1 million and yet another simply did not sell.

The contemporary market suffered the greatest losses and could be summed up in one word—volatile. Even great artworks did not bring top prices. Jackson Pollock's "Number 19, 1948" brought $2,422,500 at Christie's May sale. Also at Christie's, Roy Lichtenstein's "White Brushstroke I" sold for $728,500. Meanwhile at Sotheby's, Willem de Kooning's "Untitled"—a black and white abstraction—sold for $965,000, while Mark di Suvero's "Che Raro Senza Eurydice" brought $470,000 at the same sale. There was speculation that auction houses no longer have the clout they once did in determining prices. They no longer set the price for the con-

temporary market, partly because they do not offer top-notch work. For example, 12 Warhol works were put up for sale at Sotheby's May auctions and only two sold.

Nineteenth-century paintings enjoyed a remarkable renaissance during 1992-93. A number of artists broke records. The prices for American paintings continued to rise, with American Impressionism realizing the highest prices. The top price and a record for an American Impressionist work went to Childe Hassam's "The Room of Flowers" from 1894 for $5.5 million at Sotheby's May auction. William Merritt Chase's pastel "Peonies" from 1897 was purchased for $3.9 million. Paintings by Winslow Homer showed strength. Western art held its own; prices of Hudson River paintings waned.

Old Master paintings not only have survived the economic downturn of the early 1990s but have held their own better than any other market. A drawing by Michelangelo entitled "The Holy Family with the Infant Baptist at Rest on the Flight into Egypt" brought $6.3 million at Christie's London July sale. Not in the best condition, the work was purchased by the J. Paul Getty Museum in Malibu, CA. At Sotheby's, Canaletto's "A View of Rivadegli Schiarone, Venice, Looking East" brought $2,642,500. Dutch food, wine, and banquet pictures continued their comeback. Italian Baroque pictures also continued to bring top prices.

November auction sales brought some optimism, although prices were not that impressive. Sales of Impressionist and modern art totaled $64.1 million at Christie's and $93.4 million at Sotheby's. A collection of 88 Picassos, including "Women and Children at the Seashore," was sold for $32 million. Matisse's "The Wine Press" (1951), sold at Sotheby's for $13.7 million, brought the highest single price.

MARGARET BROWN HALSEY
*New York City Technical College
of the City University of New York*

The New Norman Rockwell Museum

On April 3, 1993, the centennial celebrations for Norman Rockwell's birth were launched with the opening of the new Norman Rockwell Museum in Stockbridge, MA. The museum is devoted to exploring the work of Norman Rockwell and his role in the profession of illustration. The much-heralded new gallery building, set on 36 scenic acres (15 ha) overlooking the Housatonic River, is the first museum in the United States to be designed by renowned architect Robert A. M. Stern. This facility houses the largest collection of original Rockwell art in the world.

The museum was founded with the help of Norman and Molly Rockwell in 1969 and is committed deeply to art appreciation and education.

Using the Rockwell collection as a framework, the museum's exhibitions and programs explore the artist's work within the larger cultural, social, and political context of his lifetime (1894-1978).

Concurrent with the inaugural of the museum building, Norman Rockwell's last studio was opened to the public for the first time. The preservation of Rockwell's studio, which was moved to the site in 1986 and was reinstalled just as he left it, offers visitors a unique opportunity to experience intimately the environment where the artist's work took shape.

Since the opening of the new museum—a more modest one existed in Stockbridge for more than 20 years—the number of visitors almost has

The new Norman Rockwell Museum, right, in Stockbridge, MA—the town in which the artist lived from 1953 until his death in 1978—was designed in New England style by Robert A. M. Stern. The museum's portico entrance leads into a reception area featuring wall murals taken from "Stockbridge Main Street at Christmas."

Photos, © Peter Aaron/Esto, from Norman Rockwell Museum

© 1960 The Curtis Publishing Co. from Norman Rockwell Museum

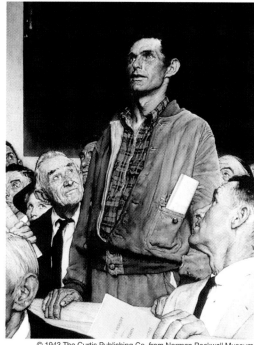

© 1943 The Curtis Publishing Co. from Norman Rockwell Museum

The museum's collection high-lights such Rockwell works as "Triple Self-Portrait," above. Perhaps his most famous works—the "Four Freedoms" paintings, including "Freedom of Speech," above right—are displayed in an octagonal gallery. The series had been used to sell war bonds during World War II. Rockwell painted "The Problem We All Live With," right, for a 1964 issue of "Look" magazine.

© 1967 The Norman Rockwell Estate from Norman Rockwell Museum

tripled, a testament to the perennial popularity of Norman Rockwell's work. In fact, no one in the history of American illustration has had the impact and longevity of Norman Rockwell. A master of the art of illustration, Rockwell was a highly skilled artist and technician who kept pace with the enormous social changes of his century. These skills formed the foundation for his singular gift for observing and communicating the essential, ordinary moments of American life—moments that many neglect to see. From the doughboys of World War I to man's first steps on the moon, Rockwell's images quietly tell the story of a people with traditional values, strongly rooted in a deep optimism.

Now a part of the fabric of popular culture, Rockwell's pictures mirror American society throughout the dynamic period of the 20th century, offering the viewer an opportunity for self-reflection in a rapidly changing world. His work grows increasingly popular today, drawing a broad cross section of the public, ranging from first-time museum visitors to collectors and connoisseurs. The museum plans to meet the on-going needs of its diverse audience through a variety of revolving exhibitions and educational programs.

BEATRICE M. SNYDER
Manager of Public Affairs
The Norman Rockwell Museum

ASIA

During 1993, movements toward regionalism in Asia advanced along both economic and security lines. With respect to the latter, Asia-wide security consultations were inaugurated under the auspices of the Association for Southeast Asian Nations (ASEAN). Along the former, most Asian states attended a regionwide economic summit under the auspices of the Asia-Pacific Economic Cooperation (APEC) forum in Seattle, WA, in November.

APEC. Formed in 1989, APEC includes Australia, Brunei, Canada, China, Hong Kong, Indonesia, Japan, the Republic of (South) Korea, Malaysia, New Zealand, the Philippines, Singapore, Taiwan, Thailand, and the United States. It encompasses the world's fastest-growing economies, whose aggregate gross national product (GNP) increased an impressive 25% between 1988-92, with trade expanding a phenomenal 50% over the same period. Dedicated to trade liberalization, APEC has become an important ingredient in the Bill Clinton administration's Asia policy, demonstrating Washington's commitment to a "new Pacific community." It ties into the U.S. president's plans to revive the economy and create jobs linked to expanding trade and investment flows. Clinton's invitation to APEC heads of state to attend the summit underscored Asia's economic importance to the United States' future.

While most APEC leaders welcomed the summit invitation, there were a few holdouts, the most prominent being Malaysia's Prime Minister Mahathir Mohamad. Malaysia and Indonesia oppose too strong an institutionalization of APEC, fearing that ASEAN—as a subregional organization—would be subordinated to the stronger economies of northeast Asia and the United States. Instead, Malaysia has promoted an East Asian economic grouping that would exclude North America and Australia-New Zealand. The Malaysian idea for an East Asian Economic Caucus (EAEC) would create a Japan-led, exclusively Asian economic consultation group to present a single voice at trade negotiations.

While the Bush administration objected to EAEC as exclusionary, Clinton has adopted a less confrontational posture. Nor has Japan been an enthusiastic backer of the Mahathir proposal. Japan does not want to see exclusionary economic blocs formed anywhere. In 1993, therefore, Malaysia modified its original proposal. It now links the EAEC to APEC and thus to the broader Asia-Pacific forum, while at the same time tying it to the ASEAN economic-ministers' meetings.

The Security Dimension. Although a growing dialogue regarding Asian security matters was initiated at the annual ASEAN postministerial conferences, it quickly expanded to cover the whole Asia-Pacific region. The talks were motivated by the uncertainties of a regional security environment in which China appeared to be increasing its power-projection capability just as the old Cold War superstructure was disintegrating. Thus, the July 1992 ASEAN foreign-ministers' conference for the first time openly called on the United States to retain a military presence in the region.

In light of these changes, President Clinton altered U.S. policy toward regional security discussions in a July 1993 speech in South Korea. Although reassuring U.S. allies in Asia that bilateral arrangements would be honored, the president endorsed security dialogues among Pacific countries, even urging neighboring states to explore joint security arrangements on their own. Clinton noted that the diversity of security interests in Asia precluded the creation of a single institution to cope with them; but he also proposed a number of overlapping security activities from multilateral discussions on specific issues—such as the Spratly Islands—to confidence-building measures, such as the discussion of defense doctrines and transparency in weapons-acquisition plans.

Shortly after Clinton's address, the ASEAN ministerial meeting in Singapore inaugurated a Regional Forum to discuss political and security issues for all of Asia. Consisting of all six ASEAN states and the association's regular dialogue partners—the United States, Japan, Canada, the European Community, South Korea, Australia, and New Zealand—the Regional Forum also includes Russia, China, Vietnam, Laos, and Papua New Guinea. It is scheduled to convene annually, as will another new group created exclusively for ASEAN senior foreign ministry and defense officials. This latter body, which will meet before the Regional Forum, well may serve to hammer out a common ASEAN position for the larger gathering.

At the top of the U.S. agenda for the Regional Forum will be efforts to halt the spread of weapons of mass destruction. For the ASEAN states, concerns will focus on a peaceful resolution of the South China Sea islands disputes and on an effort to develop ASEAN's Treaty of Amity and Cooperation into a regional code of conduct. ASEAN has identified Australia, New Zealand, the United States, Japan, and China as a core group that should be persuaded to accede to the treaty. At bottom, Regional Forum promoters hope that potential antagonists at least can agree to address their differences without hostility.

In Northeast Asia, South Korea also expressed interest in subregional dialogue through which China, Japan, Russia, and the United States would promote stability on the Korean peninsula. This plan was intended to pressure North Korea to abandon nuclear-weapons development in exchange for diplomatic recognition and economic aid.

SHELDON W. SIMON
Arizona State University

ASTRONOMY

Astronomers and space scientists had a bittersweet year in 1993. There were spectacular discoveries, especially concerning small bodies in the solar system and a new type of object in our galaxy. And there was optimism that repairs on the Hubble Space Telescope (HST), which was launched in 1990 with defective optics, had corrected the flawed equipment. In December astronauts from the shuttle *Endeavour* installed an enhanced camera, corrective lenses, and new solar panels and gyroscopes. On the other hand, a high-profile mission to Mars ended abruptly on August 21, when contact with Mars Observer was lost inexplicably. This was the United States' first return to the red planet since 1976, and the catastrophic failure occurred just three days before the space probe was to begin orbiting Mars to survey its landscape. (*See also* SPACE EXPLORATION.)

Remarkable Comet. The most amazing comet in history was discovered on March 24 at Palomar Mountain in California. It was actually a chain of some 20 individual comets stretched out like a string of pearls. Just eight months earlier the parent body had passed 11,000 mi (18 000 km) from Jupiter's surface and was ripped apart by the planet's gravitational field. The fragmented comet gave astronomers an unprecedented opportunity to study how its pieces evolve and interact. However, this chance to study the comet was expected to last only until July 17-22, 1994, when the fragments of Comet Shoemaker-Levy would strike back at the planet that shattered it. Jupiter itself is not in peril, for the fragments are too small to endanger the large planet.

Although the impacts are predicted to occur on the side of Jupiter turned away from Earth, the vaporization of each fragment could produce a fireball 100 mi (161 km) wide that might be seen by light reflected off the planet's satellites. Nevertheless, the planet's rapid rotation will carry "ground zero" into view a few hours after each impact. Observations with HST indicate the fragments are about 2 mi (3 km) across, large enough to cause spectacular wrenchings in the planet's atmosphere that might be visible in amateur telescopes. To take advantage of this unprecedented opportunity to see "planets in collision," astronomers were planning special monitoring programs for observatories both on Earth and in space.

The Perseids. Unprecedented media attention was given to the 1993 Perseid meteors, since there was the possibility that this steadfast annual shower could turn into a once-in-a-lifetime storm on the night of August 11-12. The hoped-for "thousands of meteors an hour" did not materialize, but the Perseids did produce one of their finest displays ever. This was especially true for sky-watchers in Europe, where hundreds of meteors per hour were seen.

Photos, © T.R. Laure (NOAO), NASA

New photographs of the core of the M-31 galaxy in Andromeda taken by the Hubble Space Telescope revealed that there are two nuclei of densely clustered stars in the spiral galaxy (bottom photo). The top photo is a ground view of the galaxy, 40,000 light-years across; the middle shot also is a ground view, 2,000 light-years across; and the Hubble view is 40 light-years across.

Meteors result from dust particles shed from comets that burn up in the Earth's atmosphere. A strong Perseid showing was predicted for 1993 because Earth crossed the dust stream of the meteors' parent body, Comet Swift-Tuttle, only nine months after the comet itself passed by. Experts anticipated enhanced Perseid activity during 1994 and several years beyond—always on August 11. Incidentally, in 1992 astronomers had announced that there was a remote possibility that Comet Swift-Tuttle would strike the Earth in 2126. Fortunately, refined studies of the comet's motion determined that the comet definitely will miss the planet.

Doomsday Asteroid. Other eras were not so lucky at avoiding celestial bodies. In 1980 scientists first suggested that an asteroid impacted Earth 65 million years ago and was responsible for the extinction of the dinosaurs as well as about 80% of all other extant species. Later, a crater centered in what is now the Yucatán Peninsula of Mexico was identified as the probable relic of that cataclysm. There was one problem: The crater, called Chicxulub, was only 110 mi (175 km) across. Scientists believe that a celestial body big enough to cause worldwide destruction would have left a bigger scar.

In 1993 geologist Virgil Sharpton and others showed that Chicxulub is, in fact, at least 185 mi (300 km) across. Such a hole would require an impactor some 20 mi (32 km) in diameter, which is big enough to yield the energy needed for the fatal task—an energy equivalent to a billion Hiroshima-size atomic bombs. Such an impact would have ravaged the planet with dust, firestorms, and acid rain. There is now no doubt that Chicxulub is one of the largest craters on Earth and marks the biggest hit the planet has taken since multicellular life-forms developed roughly 1 billion years ago.

Although events such as Chicxulub occur only every billion years or so, much smaller asteroids continue to threaten contemporary life. As more and more studies sample these "tiny" bodies that brush past Earth, it is becoming increasingly evident that they are vastly more numerous than was thought a few years ago. For example, in May 1993 an asteroid dubbed 1993 KA_2 missed Earth by only 87,000 mi (140 000 km)—one third of Earth's distance from the moon—in the closest such encounter known. The impact of an object of this size, approximately 33 ft (10 m) in diameter, would be powerful enough to devastate an area of the Earth many miles wide.

Dark Matter. For decades astronomers have known that what they see in the universe represents 10% or less of the matter that must exist. The evidence for that unseen, or dark, matter comes from its gravitational effects on objects that can be seen, such as the motions of galaxies in clusters and the rate at which individual galaxies rotate. Theories to explain this phantom matter range from so-called black holes (with huge masses and such fierce gravitational fields that nothing can escape them) to undiscovered kinds of elementary particles (with essentially no mass or gravity).

In 1993 several groups of scientists independently announced the discovery of at least one form of dark matter. Called Massive Compact Halo Objects (MACHOs), these bodies are probably large, Jupiter-size planets or failed stars that contain less than 30% of the mass of the Earth's sun.

Two groups discovered MACHOs by measuring the brightness of millions of stars in the direction of the Large Magellanic Cloud, a companion galaxy to our Milky Way. They found three stars that experienced several-fold *symmetrical* brightening and fading *at all wavelengths* over several months. This behavior is consistent with a phenomenon called gravitational lensing. When a MACHO in our galaxy passes between us and a distant star, such as in the Large Magellanic Cloud, the star's light is bent and focused, causing it to become amplified.

The MACHO detections now must undergo a difficult confirmation process. For example, if all the dark matter in the universe were contained in MACHOs, which is highly unlikely, only one star in a million or so would undergo gravitational lensing in any one year. Indeed, one team monitored 3.3 million stars for a year before recording its first promising signal. Furthermore, it must be proved that the observed light enhancements in fact were caused by dark matter and not by low-mass stars that abundantly populate our galaxy.

The importance of this discovery, and the quest to identify dark matter, is enormous—the very foundation of scientific understanding of the universe depends on it. If MACHOs prove to be commonplace, explaining their existence could require the revision of some theories that describe the earliest stages at which the universe came to be.

Chinese Calendar. The planets move around the sky in complex rhythms, which historians have seen reflected in the 4,000-year-old Chinese calendar. Yet for centuries one question persisted: "What celestial event marked the beginning of that calendar?"

Two researchers, Kevin Pang and John Bangert, answered this question. The calendar began on March 5, 1953 B.C. Melding a sophisticated computer program to an ancient text, Pang and Bangert replicated the appearance of the sky as it was described at the time of the calendar's origin. Their match involved a remarkable clustering of celestial bodies and events—the unique combination of dawn, the beginning of spring, and the appearance of the sun, new moon, and all five naked-eye planets in the constellation of Pegasus. Such a rare occurrence at a propitious time of year indeed would seem to be a fitting point at which to start a calendar.

Leif J. Robinson, *"Sky & Telescope"*

AUSTRALIA

Australian events in 1993 were shaped by old and new issues as the nation assessed its prospects in an expanding world. A dominant theme concerned the search for opportunities for closer involvement in the Pacific region's dynamic growth—an aim brought to the fore in the Asia-Pacific Economic Cooperation (APEC) forum in Seattle in November. On the domestic front, Prime Minister Paul Keating enjoyed a surprising electoral victory, the economy began to show symptoms of a revival, and Sydney was chosen to host the 2000 Summer Olympics.

Politics. The general-election result in March demonstrated the political acumen of Keating's Australian Labor Party (ALP). Preelection opinion sampling had given a clear lead to the Liberal-National Party opposition coalition headed by John Hewson. However, Keating's uninhibited campaign that denigrated Hewson's plan for a goods and services tax (GST) was buttressed by church leaders who expressed fears concerning the effects of the GST on the less privileged. The opposition's support was weakened further when campaigning by the union movement, focused through the Australian Council of Trade Unions (ACTU), stirred fears concerning the opposition's hard-line proposals for workplace reform through enterprise bargaining.

By concentrating its efforts in key middle-ground electorates, the ALP was able to win a sufficient number of these electorates by wafer-thin margins to produce an overall House of Representatives majority of 12—a result described by one leading newspaper as "freakish" under the circumstances. However, the ALP suffered losses in the Senate, controlling only 30 of the 76 Senate seats while the Liberals held 36. Minor parties owned the remaining ten seats, holding a balance

of power which soon proved pivotal in forcing the government to modify some aspects of the budget and other key measures.

The surprise election victory effectively removed dangers of factionalism reemerging within the ALP caucus. By contrast, the Liberals were disconcerted in defeat and faced difficulty in maintaining a united party image. Hewson was able to maintain his leadership in spite of incipient challenges. Opinion sampling generally showed strong public support for the Liberals, with the ALP trailing.

At the state level, the political fallout from Royal Commission inquiries into the earlier collapse of government-owned savings banks in Victoria and South Australia continued to give the ALP a tarnished image. The ALP was out of favor everywhere except Queensland, where the effects of the recession were muted and unemployment was consistently below the national average.

In Victoria, which was hit severely by recession, the Liberal-National Party coalition moved forward with its stringent reforms designed to cut deficits. During its first year in office, the party secured high credit ratings on the state's debt, which had ballooned under a 1983-92 Labor administration. In Western Australia's election, the Liberals won office in time to find the state's economy picking up strongly, thanks to high gold prices and comprehensive mining expansion.

At the national level, newly-emerged issues—including a proposed change from constitutional monarchy to republic, supported by Keating and the ALP—proved contentious. Also raising controversy was the issue of resolving complex aspects of land rights arising from the 1992 Mabo case—a high-court judgment which proclaimed for the first time the underlying existence of native title. Legislation introduced by Keating in November aimed to estab-

© Tassa Taraboulsi/Saba

Australia's Prime Minister Paul Keating and his wife Annita waved to supporters after his successful bid for reelection was sealed in elections on March 13, 1993. Keating and the Australian Labor Party defeated an opposition coalition that had been favored to win as the nation struggled through a persistent economic downturn.

lish federal primacy in determining the scope and application of native title in relation to rangelands leased for pastoral or mining purposes. This plan gained the support of Aboriginal groups but was criticized by influential mining interests and ran counter to the restrictive state legislation drafted by the new pro-mining administration in Western Australia, a state where vast areas remained sensitive to native-title claims. Hewson opposed the federal legislation, declaring it went "too far."

Economy. After a three-year economic slump, signs began to appear in 1993 that consumer and business confidence was growing, in spite of 11% unemployment, growth of only 2.2%, and continuing balance-of-payments deficits. Major elements contributing to the improved outlook were interest rates—at the lowest level in 30 years—and the fiscal stimulus provided by expanded federal expenditures at an increased deficit level.

The removal of debt excesses from the 1980s continued, as corporate balance sheets showed strengthened earnings. For example, the four main banks reported a turnaround from gross 1992 losses of A$400 million (after bad-debt provisioning) to solid profitability.

The rural sector's problems persisted. Wool growers continued to suffer severely, with returns still below cost in most cases. Government measures were designed to alleviate the survival difficulties facing many rural producers as a result of heavy debt problems.

Supported by improved corporate profits, the stock market rose 35% over the year to a seven-year high. A marked rise occurred in the number of share owners as a result of widespread public support for major stock-market floats. On the Australian Stock Exchange nearly 100 newly listed companies raised a total of A$5 billion in capital. Another A$8 billion was raised as additional capital by established corporations, with much through dividend reinvestment. The federal government secured more than A$1 billion by selling its stock in the Commonwealth Bank.

Over the year, recession-induced weakness in house prices gave way to increased demand in home building. The trend was strongest in Perth and in Brisbane and other areas of Queensland.

The Budget. In presenting a stimulatory 1993-94 budget providing a A$16 billion deficit which was 3.8% of gross domestic product (GDP), Treasurer John Dawkins emphasized the government's aim of achieving a federal deficit of 1% of GDP by 1996. Toward this end, promised income-tax cuts were adjusted and immediate increases made to various indirect taxes—including gasoline, alcohol, and tobacco—and to the general wholesale-sales tax. The year's revenue was forecast at A$99 billion or 23.3% of GDP and total outlays at A$115 billion or 27.5%. Employment-program provisions again were boosted (up A$1.6 billion) and social-security and welfare outlays increased.

AUSTRALIA • Information Highlights

Official Name: Commonwealth of Australia.
Location: Southwestern Pacific Ocean.
Area: 2,967,896 sq mi (7 686 850 km²).
Population (mid-1993 est.): 17,800,000.
Chief Cities (mid-1990 est.): Canberra, the capital, 310,100; Sydney, 3,656,500; Melbourne, 3,080,900; Brisbane, 1,301,700.
Government: *Head of state*, Elizabeth II, queen; represented by Bill Hayden, governor-general (took office February 1989). *Head of government*, Paul Keating, prime minister (took office Dec. 19, 1991). *Legislature*—Parliament: Senate and House of Representatives.
Monetary Unit: Australian dollar (1.4728 A$ equal U.S.$1, Dec. 20, 1993).
Gross Domestic Product (1991 U.S.$): $280,800,000,000.
Economic Indexes: *Consumer Prices* (1992, 1980 = 100), all items, 227.3; food, 214.0. *Industrial Production* (1991, 1980 = 100), 129.
Foreign Trade (1992 U.S.$): *Imports*, $40,696,000,000; *exports*, $42,417,000,000

Immigration Program. The planned intake of new settlers again was lowered, to 70,000 per year. A changed national mood was evident: The long-running commitment to a large immigration program that had been a key element of national economic thinking since 1945 should end.

Meanwhile, some 30,000 Chinese students holding refugee status in Australia since the 1989 Tiananmen Square uprising were granted permanent-resident status along with an estimated 10,000 relatives, and another 22,000 asylum-seekers were told they would gain residence if they qualified under established guidelines. Within Australia, population movements were shaped strongly by employment prospects in Queensland and Western Australia. These states recorded steady inflows—reported at up to 1,000 per week—from Victoria and New South Wales.

Foreign Affairs. The principal thrust of Keating's foreign policies was to enhance trade relationships and establish broader ties within the Asia-Pacific region rather than with Great Britain. The earlier initiative of former Prime Minister Robert Hawke to establish APEC as a clearinghouse was advanced to Keating, who tried to build APEC into an active forum for the economic advancement of all constituent nations.

In November, Australia's contingent of 1,500 service personnel returned home after the United Nations (UN) peace team's assignment in Cambodia was completed.

Other Events. On Sept. 23, 1993, Sydney was awarded the bid to host the 2000 Summer Olympics. The city was selected in a close vote over Beijing, China, as well as four other cities that were eliminated earlier in the process. The millennium Olympics were expected to bring billions of dollars and tens of thousands of jobs to the nation.

R. M. YOUNGER
Author, "Australia and the Australians"

AUSTRIA

For Austria, 1993 was characterized by economic stagnation and political debate about the nation's evolving role in Europe.

Government. The Social Democratic and People's Party coalition—headed by Social Democrat Chancellor Franz Vranitzky and Vice-Chancellor Erhard Busek of the People's Party—remained in power throughout 1993 without any changes to the government cabinet. Among the major issues the Austrian government addressed were tax and university reforms, immigration, and a federal budget consolidation. New federal elections were due in 1994.

Immigration was a controversial domestic issue in 1993. Under the leadership of its populist, right-wing chairman, Jörg Haider, the Austrian Freedom Party promoted a ten-point referendum addressing the issues of immigration and the status of foreigners in Austria with the slogan "Austria First." The Freedom Party initiative met considerable resistance from across the political spectrum and contributed to a split within the party.

In February, Heide Schmidt—the Freedom Party's presidential candidate in 1992—formed a new political "club" in the parliament, the Liberal Forum. Schmidt and others from the Freedom Party's liberal wing wished to distance themselves from the increasingly acrimonious and populistic format of the Freedom Party under Haider and hoped to provide a new political base for liberal forces in Austria. The formation of a new political party during a legislative session was unprecedented in the nation's history. The party's viability would be tested in 1994 elections.

In July a new immigration law went into effect. It introduced rigorous new requirements for residence permits and visas for foreigners, as well as quotas for the respective federal provinces. The new law caused considerable criticism and confusion. Proponents emphasized the necessity of revising the nation's liberal asylum policy, restricting immigration, and preventing illegal immigration. Critics argued that the law was too restrictive and did not provide adequately for political asylum or family unification for foreigners legally residing in Austria.

Economy. The Austrian economy experienced a recession in 1993, although its end seemed to be in sight by late in the year. This slump reflected the general trend of Western European economies and was influenced particularly by the poor economy of Germany, Austria's most important trade partner. Austria's exports, imports, and industrial production all dropped approximately 5%, and the Austrian gross domestic product (GDP) shrank 0.7%.

The sagging economy hit Austria's large nationalized steel and petrochemical industries especially hard and fueled debates about their future reorganization and privatization. Some of the problems these industries experienced were attributed to competition with Eastern European countries that have entered Western markets with cheaper products.

European Integration. On Jan. 1, 1993, the European Economic Area (EEA) was established. This pact was made between the seven-member European Free Trade Association (EFTA)—to which Austria already belonged—and the 12-member European Community (EC). It was designed to ease trading conditions among the 19 member states and is viewed as a transitional arrangement to facilitate integration of EFTA members into the EC.

In February, Austria began negotiations with EC authorities in Brussels over the conditions of full membership, with 1996 as a target date for such membership. Austria was concerned particularly about negotiating favorable agreements with the EC regarding transit traffic in the Alps, ecological issues, agrarian subsidies for Alpine farmers, and the status of Austrian neutrality. However, EC authorities expressed reservations about extending exceptional arrangements to Austria and about the compatibility of Austrian neutrality with the defense and security interests of the EC. Public-opinion polls indicated that the Austrian public had mixed feelings about EC membership.

Foreign Affairs. Austria continued to provide asylum for more than 60,000 refugees who had fled from Bosnia-Herzegovina in 1992.

Austria normalized its diplomatic relations with Israel, which had been tense during Kurt Waldheim's presidency (1986-92). The election of career diplomat Thomas Klestil to the Austrian presidency in 1992 and a visit of Federal Chancellor Vranitzky to Israel in 1993 contributed to the normalization process.

LONNIE JOHNSON
Author, "Introducing Austria"

AUSTRIA • Information Highlights

Official Name: Republic of Austria.
Location: Central Europe.
Area: 32,375 sq mi (83 850 km²).
Population (mid-1993 est.): 7,900,000.
Chief Cities (1991 census): Vienna, the capital, 1,533,176; Graz, 232,155; Linz, 202,855; Salzburg, 143,971; Innsbruck, 114,996.
Government: *Head of state,* Thomas Klestil, president (took office July 8, 1992). *Head of government,* Franz Vranitzky, chancellor (took office June 16, 1986). *Legislature*—Federal Assembly: Federal Council and National Council.
Monetary Unit: Schilling (11.531 schillings equal U.S. $1, Oct. 18, 1993).
Gross Domestic Product (1991 U.S.$): $164,100,-000,000.
Economic Indexes (1992): *Consumer Prices* (1980 = 100), all items, 151.9; food, 143.6. *Industrial Production* (1980 = 100), 134.
Foreign Trade (1992 U.S.$): *Imports,* $54,116,000,-000; *exports,* $44,430,000,000.

AUTOMOBILES

With both new-car and truck sales forging ahead, the U.S. auto industry posted a strong recovery in 1993 from the recession of the early 1990s. Ford Motor Company and Chrysler Corporation set the sales pace as total vehicle volume for the first eight months of the year spurted 8.0% from the comparable 1992 period to 9,368,364 units.

Beset by a lack of popular new models and 1992 top-level management shakeup, industry leader General Motors managed to raise its January-August sales by only 4.5%. But Ford rose 12.3% and Chrysler 25.4%, reflecting strong demand for a number of their newly introduced cars and light trucks, minivans, and sport-utility vehicles. The rise of the Big Three—Chrysler, Ford, and GM—cut into the market share collected by the imports for the first eight months of 1993. Late-summer results indicated, however, that the Japanese makes, steadily boosting production at their "transplant" U.S. facilities, were regaining ground. Combined sales of GM, Ford, and Chrysler vehicles in the eight-month period totaled 6,939,648 units, up 10.9% from a year earlier and equal to a 74.1% market share. Japanese brands edged up 1.8% to 2,145,385, but their penetration declined from 24.3% to 22.9%. European makes fell 11.5% to 207,099, reducing their share from 2.7% to 2.2%.

Upbeat performances in the marketplace brought each of the Big Three significant turnarounds in profits, which had vanished during the recession years. GM reported a net profit of $1.4 billion in the first half of 1993, compared with a loss of $869.9 million in the same period of 1992; Ford raised its first-half profit from $610 million to $1.3 billion; while Chrysler more than tripled its actual second-quarter net to $685 million from $178 million after taking a one-time accounting charge for retiree health care that resulted in a paper net loss of $3.4 billion for the first half. Chrysler's first-half sales of $21.9 billion marked an all-time high in the history of the auto company.

Welcome news for the Big Three in 1993 was the upturn in new-car sales, spurred by improved consumer confidence following the 1992 presidential election, growth in retail-sales incentives—particularly short-term lease plans—and, certainly not least, continued strong sales of pickup trucks, minivans, and utility vehicles. The truck sector accounted for a record 38.5% of the industry's January-August sales in 1993, up from 35.6% in 1992, as unit volume surged to 3,602,046 from 3,093,030.

In addition, domestic auto manufacturers and dealers benefited from a wave of "buy American" sentiment. This trend was spurred by substantially improved quality of U.S.-made cars vis-à-vis the Japanese, whose products admittedly had led the world in "fit and finish" in the 1980s, as well as in performance reliability. The Japanese yen's persisting strength against the U.S. dollar also resulted in a widening price gap between Japanese vehicles sold in the United States and competitive domestic units, a marketing condition which carried over into the 1994-model season.

The recession's end for the Big Three gave rise to "cautiously optimistic" forecasts for 1994 sales from the new chief executive officers of Chrysler Corporation and General Motors—Robert J. Eaton and John F. (Jack) Smith, Jr., respectively, and the retiring chairman of Ford Motor Company, Harold A. (Red) Poling. Eaton, successor to the retired Lee A. Iacocca, predicted that industry sales could reach a decade high of 15 million cars and trucks in 1994. Chrysler's recovery was aided by brisk introductory sales of its first restyled truck in 20 years, the Dodge Ram, and its new luxury LH cars and Dodge/Plymouth Neon subcompacts. Peaceful settlement of Ford's collective-bargaining contract with the United Auto Workers (UAW) in September, in a market in which five of the ten top-selling vehicles came from Ford, prompted Poling to raise his projection of the 1994 volume to "more than 14.5 million." (Alexander J. Trotman, English-born president and chief operating officer of Ford's worldwide group, succeeded Poling as Ford's chairman on November 1. He took over as president as well.)

Smith, who became GM's CEO in November 1992 after a management shakeup which promoted him to president earlier that year, faced a tougher recovery road than either of his two domestic competitors. GM's North American activities were only barely in the black during 1993, and it lacked modernized car models in many high-volume segments. GM's unfunded pension liability debt reached $19 billion as its cost burden per vehicle assembled far exceeded that at Ford, Chrysler, Toyota, or Honda at comparable U.S. plants. Nevertheless, Smith—GM's first nonchairman CEO in 30 years—forecast that his cost-cutting moves and organizational restructuring would sustain "slow growth back to GM's position of traditional financial

The 1995 Aurora © General Motors

strength." A spate of newly designed car models was on tap for a mid-1994 debut from Chevrolet and Oldsmobile.

At a late September White House ceremony, the Clinton administration and auto executives said that the government and the auto industry would cooperate to develop a well-priced auto that is three times more energy-efficient than ones currently manufactured.

New Models. Oldsmobile, at 96 the oldest of the GM car divisions, was seeking a reversal of fortunes with the May 1994 launch of its new flagship sedan, the 1995 Aurora. Olds sales plunged from three 1-million-car years in a row in the mid-1980s to 400,000 in 1992 and 1993, in a stark signal of GM's sales descent. The Aurora, highlighting modernistic styling and a version of GM's new 32-valve V-8 "Northstar" engine introduced on the 1993-model Cadillac Seville and Eldorado models, is an effort to recapture customers lost to such Japanese luxury cars as Honda Acura, Toyota Lexus, and Nissan Infiniti. The division name "Oldsmobile" does not appear anywhere on Aurora's badging. It was to be followed in the fall of 1994 by a two-door Buick Riviera variant of the same platform.

Among smaller domestic cars, Ford's recast Mustang sports coupe and Chrysler's Dodge and Plymouth Neon subcompact sedan were featured new models. The updated Mustang followed by one model year redesigned Chevrolet Camaro and Pontiac Firebird coupes in the

The 1995 Neon   © Chrysler Corporation

sporty segment, while Neon returned Chrysler to the crowded subcompact field after a four-year absence. Neon and Mustang offered dual front-seat airbags. The Chrysler subcompact also had the unique "cab-forward" styling of the automaker's year-old LH luxury sedans, increasing roominess for passengers while incorporating rakish styling cues.

On tap also for introduction were three new midsize models from Chevrolet—Lumina, Monte Carlo, and Impala; a restyled subcompact platform for three GM division lines—Chevrolet Cavalier, Pontiac Sunbird, and Buick Skylark; a front-wheel-drive minivan from Ford, called Windstar; and new compact cars from Chrysler.

The Imports. A major redesign of the Honda Accord was followed by the Japanese automaker's decision to build all of its U.S.-sold Accord and Civic cars at its plants in the United States and Canada, stopping exports from Japan because of the cost benefits gained from production in North America. The Accord had been the top-selling car in the United States for three years in a row until Ford's Taurus, benefiting from lower prices and lease terms, outsold it in 1992 and 1993. Honda planned to cut its Japanese workforce by 40,000 workers over the next three years as a result of the Accord transfer. Honda, meanwhile, was seeking a quieter and smoother-riding car. Its 1994 Accord featured a more-programmed automatic transmission and a redesigned interior.

Suggested list prices for 1994-model Japanese cars in the United States were raised between 4% and 6% to reflect the yen's high value against the dollar. The increasingly competitive U.S. market cost another import dropout, as Isuzu abandoned the passenger-car market to concentrate on trucks.

Germany's luxury-car manufacturers, BMW and Mercedes-Benz, announced plans to build assembly plants in the United States. A merger was consummated between France's Renault and Sweden's Volvo, effective Jan. 1, 1994.

MAYNARD M. GORDON
Detroit Bureau Chief
"Dealer Business Magazine"

WORLD MOTOR VEHICLE DATA, 1992

Country	Passenger Car Production	Truck and Bus Production	Motor Vehicle Registrations
Argentina	220,498	41,445	5,841,600
Australia	279,550	4,858	9,649,500
Austria	23,479	4,491	3,812,334
Belgium	222,680	75,392	4,391,497
Brazil	814,423	257,141	13,204,925
Canada	1,024,739	943,758	16,805,096
China	180,000	900,000	6,114,089
Comm. of Ind. St.	930,000	600,000	24,500,000
Czechoslovakia	202,450	26,608	3,613,017
France	3,329,490	438,310	28,830,000
Germany	4,863,721	330,221	40,702,786
Hungary	12,000	6,000	2,240,000
India	153,867	170,518	4,667,749
Italy	1,476,627	209,860	30,721,000
Japan	9,378,694	3,120,590	59,914,623
Korea, South	1,306,752	422,944	4,247,816
Malaysia	117,773	11,414	2,400,000
Mexico	778,413	304,678	10,700,000
The Netherlands	94,019	22,973	6,173,693
Poland	200,000	30,000	7,350,580
Spain	1,790,615	331,272	15,152,132
Sweden	293,499	63,096	3,943,497
United Kingdom	1,291,880	248,453	26,429,283
United States	5,663,284	4,038,218	188,371,935*
Yugoslavia (former)	118,391	9,250	4,540,000
Total	34,766,844	12,611,490	595,306,648**

*U.S. total does not include Puerto Rico, which has 1,562,171 vehicles.
**World total includes 456,032,819 cars and 139,273,829 trucks.
Other countries with more than one million registrations include Algeria, 1,270,000; Bulgaria, 1,450,019; Chile, 1,030,000; Colombia, 1,468,606; Denmark, 1,900,416; Finland, 2,218,067; Greece, 2,592,334; Indonesia, 3,001,508; Iran, 2,200,000; Iraq, 1,000,000; Ireland, 1,069,129; Israel, 1,012,639; Morocco, 1,006,865; New Zealand, 1,867,649; Nigeria, 1,400,000; Norway, 1,948,974; Portugal, 2,448,200; Romania, 1,629,000; Saudi Arabia, 4,500,000; South Africa, 5,324,749; Switzerland, 3,376,829; Taiwan, 2,700,000; Thailand, 2,727,509; Turkey, 2,621,249; and Venezuela, 1,909,000.
Source: American Automobile Manufacturers Association.

BALTIC REPUBLICS

In 1993 the Baltic nations of Lithuania, Latvia, and Estonia celebrated the second full year of their independence—restored after the collapse of the Soviet empire—as well as the 75th anniversary of their independence from the Czarist Russian Empire. Several salient issues from 1992 remained volatile during 1993, but on the whole, the three states made progress toward viable statehood. As the year began the issues of Russian troops in the region and the treatment of Russian minorities continued to rile relations with Russia, and the economies sputtered along in the three countries. At the end of the year, the minority question remained fractious, but Russian troop levels in the region had dropped and the economies had improved.

Political Developments. In February, Lithuania completed a swing to the left which began with the parliamentary elections of 1992. Algirdas Brazauskas, a Social Democrat and former leader of the Lithuanian Communist Party, was elected president. In June 1993 parliamentary elections were held in Latvia under a restrictive election law which excluded resident Russians, who constituted 34% of the population. In the Estonian local elections of November—the first free municipal elections there since World War II—the large Russian minority which had been excluded from the parliamentary elections of 1992 was permitted to participate. In the towns and cities where they were concentrated, the Russians' voter turnout was high, and their candidates gained control of several municipal councils. In the Estonian capital of Tallinn, Russians won 42% of the seats on the city council. As a result, a Russian became the council's deputy chairman.

Pope John Paul II visited the three countries in September, an event of political and spiritual significance. The visit was the pope's first trip within the former Soviet Union since the collapse of the USSR in 1991. His initial stop was in largely Catholic Lithuania, where he was received by President Brazauskas, the former Communist leader. Moving on to the other two Baltic countries, the pope, who expressed a hope of visiting Russia some time in the future, pointedly avoided being drawn into the disputes Latvia and Estonia had with Russia over troops and minority rights.

Troops and Minority Rights. Just before the pope arrived in Vilnius, the last Russian troops were withdrawn from Lithuania. Within a few months all remaining Russian equipment also was removed and former Soviet military bases were turned over to the Lithuanian government. During a visit to Lithuania in November by Prime Minister Viktor Chernomyrdin of the Russian Federation, the Russians agreed to discuss possible compensation to Lithuania for the 50-year Soviet occupation. Russia's adherence to the agreed-upon troop-withdrawal timetable and willingness to talk about compensation was seen as a reward for Lithuania's previous automatic conferral of citizenship on all residents, including Russians, who composed 9% of the population. While Lithuanian-Russian ethnic relations were relatively untroubled, Lithuania's relationship with its Polish minority—7% of the population—remained strained.

In contrast, Russian troops remained in Latvia and Estonia, and ethnic relations between native speakers and the large concentrations of Russians were troubled. Depending on who was counting (the Russian army or the Latvian government), there were either 17,000 or 27,000 Russian troops stationed in Latvia at the start of 1993. Latvia had been the command center for the Northwestern Soviet Army, and many bases and much military equipment remained there. Despite President Boris Yeltsin's October 1992 decree halting troop withdrawals, negotiations between Russia and Latvia resumed in early 1993.

Progress was hindered by Russia's complaints about ethnic discrimination in Latvia. The June parliamentary elections were closed to most Russian settlers, and the passage of an exclusionary citizenship deepened Russia's concerns. In addition, the law on public associations was amended in a way which could be disadvantageous to ethnic-Russian organizations in Latvia. U.S. Secretary of State Warren Christopher, who visited Latvia in October, was careful not to get entangled in the twinned issues, and thus not to offend either side's sensibilities. Toward year's end, however, Russia and Latvia were moving toward a possible deal on the troops—Russia would retain use of an important antimissile radar base for six years in return for withdrawal. Although Latvian nationalist groups rejected the deal, the Latvian leadership was

---

BALTIC STATES • Information Highlights

Nation	Population (in millions)	Area (sq mi)	(km²)	Capital	Head of State
Estonia	1.6	17,413	45 100	Tallinn	Lennart Meri, president
Latvia	2.6	24,749	64 100	Riga	Guntis Ulmanis, president
Lithuania	3.8	25,173	65 200	Vilnius	Algirdas Brazauskas, president

	Estonia		Latvia		Lithuania	
Ethnic	Estonian	61.5	Latvian	52.0	Lithuanian	79.6
Breakdown	Russian	30.3	Russian	34.0	Russian	9.4
	Other	8.2	Other	14.0	Other	11.0

Throughout the Baltic Republics anticrime units—including the one at left undergoing a training exercise in Tallinn, Estonia—were created to combat organized crime. A surge in smuggling, theft, prostitution, and murder has been attributed to organized crime in the region.

considering the possibility of allowing the Russians to use the base for another two years.

In Estonia ethnic relations with the Russians also were quite strained, but fewer Russian troops remained in the country. Late in 1993, Russia offered to withdraw the remaining 3,000 troops in return for concessions by the Estonian side, including their willingness to provide $23 million to build housing in Russia for the officers of the withdrawing forces.

Economy. During the winter of 1992-93 the region, and Lithuania in particular, suffered through an energy crisis. The country had been dependent upon Russia for fuel supplies, and had been unable to pay for the quantity needed. Apartments were cold and factories worked at half-speed. But the economies of all three Baltic countries began to stabilize during 1993, and as the 1993-94 winter approached, citizens were told that the energy situation would be under control with heat and hot water assured.

During 1993, Lithuania and Latvia followed Estonia's example and made their currencies convertible on Western exchange markets to facilitate trade with the West. The move also was to encourage Western private investment once investors became able to repatriate profits in hard currencies. Lithuania also established trade links with countries of the former USSR in central Asia, and was the first of the Baltic states to negotiate a trade accord with Russia late in the year. Although Lithuanian nationalists protested, many recognized that Russia could become an immense market for Baltic goods.

Nonetheless, significant economic problems beset the region, including Western European trade barriers, the impoverishment of parts of the population, and rising unemployment. The Baltic states, like the newly independent states of Eastern Europe, were having difficulty penetrating Western European markets. The European Common Market's protectionist tariffs, designed to protect internal producers against cheaper goods from the East, were hindering the ability of the new states to export their products. In addition, as the Baltic states abandoned a command economy and a Soviet-style welfare state, retired persons and other vulnerable groups had been hurt by rising prices and ram-

pant inflation. Although all three countries began to control inflation during 1993, revenue to fund social policies remained tight.

Unemployment was another inevitable concomitant of marketization, and the Baltic states were not spared. As privatization progressed and inefficient, loss-producing firms were scaled back or closed, people were thrown out of work. New commercial structures absorbed some workers, but unemployment grew. In Lithuania an unemployment rate of 1.5% was acknowledged, but the rate of "hidden" unemployment was much higher, including workforces on half-time and employees without any work kept on the payroll. This situation was worse in Latvia, where 5.5% of the labor force officially was unemployed, plus an estimated 12%-14% incidence of hidden unemployment.

Foreign Affairs. The Baltic republics continued their progress in rejoining the community of independent nations. The region was visited by the U.S. secretary of state, the French minister of defense, and the pope. The three states contributed troops to United Nations (UN) peacekeeping forces. International agreements were signed with Finland, Sweden, Belarus, France, and Russia. Baltic representatives participated in the Council of Europe and the Conference on Security and Cooperation in Europe (CSCE). The CSCE became a medium for Baltic-Russian relations over contentious issues. The Baltic states, led by Lithuania, persuaded the CSCE to issue a resolution calling for the full withdrawal of Russian troops from the region. Russia, in turn, filed complaints with the CSCE and the UN on the treatment of Russians in Estonia and Latvia.

All three states were alarmed by the fall crisis in Moscow. Subsequently, the publication of the new Russian military doctrine in November became a source for concern. At a press conference, Russian Defense Minister Pavel Grachev explicitly remarked, with reference to Latvia and Estonia, that he favored linking "the pullout of troops to the protection of Russian speakers." Thus, in terms of relations with Russia, the year ended for two of the three Baltic republics as it had begun—with unresolved differences.

ROBERT SHARLET
Union College

BANGLADESH

The political and economic outlook for Bangladesh brightened during 1993. Democratic consolidation moved closer to reality, and the economic-liberalization program of the Bangladesh Nationalist Party (BNP) began to show growth. March storms and July floods, however, took their toll. The problem of the Rohingaya—Muslim refugees from Myanmar—continued to tax the nation's resources.

Politics. Actions taken to stem public corruption began to show results. Students and teachers now could receive jail terms for cheating on examinations. A special Securities and Exchange Commission was set up in July to oversee market operations and to ensure fair trading practices. Prime Minister Khaleda Zia also took steps to open communication within the BNP. A September amendment to the party's constitution abolished the electoral college which was used to select the party chief and instituted an election every two years by members of the party council using secret ballots. Rank-and-file party members were encouraged to air their views and complaints. A clear message went to all party officials that the local base must be strengthened through greater party democracy.

The prime minister extended the idea of reconciliation to other parties. Paying homage to Sheikh Mujibur Rahman, founder of the country and the Awami League Party, she called for more parliamentary debate and less political agitation in the streets. Some viewed this as a move to highlight differences between her style and that of Awami League (AL) leader Sheikh Hasina Wajed, and perhaps to attract some of the AL's members who had formed a new party, the People's Forum.

The Communist Party of Bangladesh split in two in June over ideology and strategy. The party's majority formed a reform group dedicated to "democracy, development, nationalism, and social justice," according to party officials. The smaller faction remained wedded to Leninist orthodoxy.

Social Issues. Repatriation of Pakistanis stranded in Bangladesh since 1972 finally began, following an agreement signed in 1992 with Pakistan. The cost was being borne jointly by the Saudis and Pakistan. Although some Rohingaya migrated to the Middle East, most remained in Bangladesh in camps where conflicts between them and the local population continued to demand attention. Without safety guarantees, few Rohingaya refugees were willing to return home. Outbreaks of a virulent form of cholera spread not only in Bangladesh but in India as well.

Prime Minister Zia received credit from observers for efforts in behalf of women's education, economic self-sufficiency through small-business loans, and human rights. Birth rates have fallen from nearly 3% to less than 2.4%.

Economics. With the government emphasizing performance and productivity and the World Bank providing guidance, public-sector enterprises did better. Loan-default rates fell, and managers seemed better able to control their union employees. Wage negotiations between the government and unions staved off a mid-July strike supported by 15 opposition parties.

The economy grew by 5% during the 1993 fiscal year that ended in June. Most of the growth came from a 4.4% growth in agriculture. The government's deficit fell from 8% of the gross domestic product (GDP) to 5%, and inflation slowed from an annual rate of 9% to 3%. Exports also increased by 25%, generating foreign exchange; however, imports also rose by 16%. The main impediment to more growth was investment—which at 13% of GDP was up compared with 1992's 12.1%, but still was far below the 18% needed to ensure a targeted overall annual growth rate of 6%-7%. To encourage investment, the government relaxed foreign-exchange rules, began reviewing tariffs, and started freeing the taka in stages. The government also sought to attract foreign capital through various ventures, including permitting Singapore to train its military in Bangladesh. The World Bank's consortium pledged $2.15 billion in aid—$120 million more than what was requested, but 14% less than 1992.

The Grameen Bank received recognition for its work with the rural poor—especially women. Its default rate was 2%, while the commercial banks faced a 70% default rate for agricultural loans and 90% for business loans.

Foreign Relations. Bangladesh's relations with its neighbors remained problematic. With Bengali immigrants to India facing a forced repatriation, the Bangladesh parliament passed its first resolution critical of India.

The South Asian Association for Regional Cooperation (SAARC) in April discussed abolishing tariffs among the seven members, but Bangladesh was concerned that such a move would be advantageous to India and detrimental to its own interests.

ARUNA NAYYAR MICHIE, *Kansas State University*

BANGLADESH • Information Highlights

Official Name: People's Republic of Bangladesh.
Location: South Asia.
Area: 55,598 sq mi (144 000 km²).
Population (mid-1993 est.): 113,900,000.
Chief Cities (1991 census): Dhaka, the capital, 3,637,892; Chittagong, 1,566,070; Khulna, 601,051.
Government: *Head of state*, Abdur Rahman Biswas, president (took office Oct. 10, 1991). *Head of government*, Khaleda Zia, prime minister (sworn in March 20, 1991). *Legislature*—Parliament.
Monetary Unit: Taka (39.75 taka equal U.S.$1, July 1993).
Economic Index (1992): *Consumer Prices* (Dhaka, 1980 = 100), all items, 309.4; food, 288.1.
Foreign Trade (1992 U.S.$): *Imports*, $3,737,000,000; *exports*, $2,131,000,000.

BANKING AND FINANCE

The U.S. banking industry finally put its financial crises firmly behind it during 1993. But even as the banks and savings and loan associations reaped record profits, they found themselves challenged to adapt to new policies of the Bill Clinton administration. Some of the policies proposed by the administration, which throughout the year emphasized expanding the flow of credit to small businesses and the disadvantaged, were considered by expert observers of the industry to be as dramatic in their potential effects on banking as the administration's much more famous health proposals would be on medicine.

Expanding Profits. For most of the year profits at the nation's banks increased more rapidly than the general economy expanded. Favorable interest rates—especially a relatively wide gap, or "spread," between the cost of short-term deposits and the earnings from longer-term loans—allowed banks to increase their earnings and rebuild their capital. At the same time, the improving economy allowed borrowers to repay their loans more easily without defaulting.

By the end of the third quarter of 1993 banks already had earned more than they had in the full year 1992. Bank failures fell to the lowest level in 11 years, the Federal Deposit Insurance Corporation (FDIC) reported at year's end. Some 42 banks failed in the year, almost two thirds fewer than in 1992, when 120 failed.

S&L Cleanup. As a result of the new breathing room, the Clinton administration was able by year's end to persuade Congress to pass what was expected to be the last legislation needed to pay for the cleanup of the savings and loan crisis of the 1980s. The new legislation enabled the Resolution Trust Corporation (RTC) to resume the process of resolving the failed thrifts, whose assets had been seized by the government. The legislation made up to $26.3 billion available to the RTC and its eventual successor, The Savings Association Insurance Fund. The RTC was to complete its liquidation of the failed thrifts by the end of 1995.

The RTC, criticized for years for sloppy management of the S&L crisis, experienced continuing disarray during the year. Although the administration put into place a series of reforms of the agency's practices, the RTC was without a chief executive officer for the entire year, as the nomination of Stanley Tate, a Republican real-estate developer from Florida, never was considered by the Senate. Tate finally withdrew from consideration.

New Legislative Agenda. At the start of the year the administration had made clear that the RTC legislation was only the first step in what it wanted to be a broad agenda of changes for the banking industry. President Clinton, sensing that the flow of credit through the economy was a crucial element of his overall economic plan, showed even before he was sworn into office that he had a deep personal interest in the banking industry, highlighting his concern at an economic summit meeting in Little Rock, AR, in December 1992. But while there were modest legislative efforts early in the year and a series of regulatory changes affecting banking, the administration by and large followed a strategy of getting the RTC bill enacted before taking up many other items on its agenda.

The administration's agenda for banking had three main elements, which were introduced one at a time as the year went by. First was an effort to reduce regulations that were blamed for restricting the availability of credit. Second was a broader effort to expand credit in poor and minority communities, through a combination of regulatory proposals and legislation. The House and Senate passed slightly differing versions of this legislation but did not complete the work of reaching a final agreement by the end of the year. And third—requiring two further pieces of legislation that Congress did not consider during 1993—was a proposed broad reorganization of the whole industry and its regulatory apparatus, by allowing an expansion of interstate banking and consolidating all the bank regulatory agencies into a single agency.

Regulatory Relief. Throughout the 1992 presidential campaign, Clinton had been told by voters that small businesses were having a hard time getting credit because of the tighter regulations that were imposed during the 1980s as a result of the earlier crisis in the industry, when too many weak loans led to widespread bank failures. So early in 1993 his newly inaugurated administration ordered regulators to come up with a package of regulatory changes that would ease the flow of credit, especially to small business, without undermining bank safety.

The package, announced in March, contained several elements. It revised regulations on how examiners would rate loans to businesses that are not in default but are deemed troubling because of things like incomplete documentation. In effect, as long as a borrower continued to make payments, examiners would be discouraged from requiring a bank to set aside reserves or otherwise restrict so-called character loans. The regulations also set new, more lenient standards for making appraisals of real estate when property is used as collateral for a commercial loan. And the rules allowed banks to pool small business loans together for purposes of examinations. That way, as long as the portfolio as a whole appeared healthy, problems with a single loan would not prevent the bank from continuing to make such loans. Also, bank examiners were instructed to act more flexibly—and their decisions were subjected to appeals by banks.

Credit Expansion. The credit crunch appeared to ease during the year, perhaps as a result of these regulatory changes and perhaps because loan demand picked up as the economy gained steam under the impetus of falling interest rates. In August the Federal Reserve Board (Fed)

reported that banks had become noticeably more willing to lend to businesses. But the Fed said the administration's regulatory changes had not been in place long enough to have a wide effect.

Bank executives surveyed by the Fed said they had relaxed their terms and requirements for commercial loans, although standards for real-estate loans stayed tight. One reason banks seemed more willing to lend as the year progressed may have been a new rule requiring them to recognize the interest-rate risks in their holdings of federal securities. For some time analysts had said that banks would lend to the government rather than to the private sector unless the inherent risks of holding federal securities were accounted for.

Community Development Program. During the campaign, President Clinton had promised repeatedly to establish a network of 100 "community development banks" modeled on the South Shore Bank of Chicago, one of a few banks in the country that had operated profitably by focusing its attention entirely on loans in poorer communities. In the end he produced a program to spur lending in these communities that looked somewhat different from his original plan, and Congress still was considering how to structure the program when the year ended.

President Clinton's program, rather than setting up a number of new depository institutions, created a federal fund that would provide capital to existing organizations that encouraged lending in poor communities. Among the types of institutions that would qualify for grants were not only community-development banks, but also community-development loan funds, credit unions, and the like. The program would cost $384 million over its first five years—not a great sum, but enough to test whether the approach was workable. As passed by the Senate, the bill would limit participation by conventional banks.

In the House of Representatives, however, the program was modified in a way that made it more attractive to conventional banks. They would have to pay lower deposit-insurance premiums to the extent that they increased their loans into poorer communities. That provision would reduce the amount of direct-capital subsidies available to other institutions specializing in lending to the poor. The House and Senate were expected to resolve their differences in 1994.

Interstate Banking. On another legislative front, the administration was ready by autumn to declare its support for legislation that would give the banks the right to operate more freely across state lines. Without interstate-banking legislation, banks must create separate subsidiaries to operate in more than one state, a cumbersome and costly deterrent to expansion.

Treasury Secretary Lloyd Bentsen said that he favored an approach allowing bank-holding companies that now maintain separate operating subsidiaries in more than one state to merge their operations into a single bank with branches in each state, as long as the states permit it. Banks that now operate in only one state would be able to open branches in another, as long as the states agreed. The administration favored interstate banking because it believed this would make the banks healthier and increase the supply of credit.

Proposed Regulatory Reform. In November the administration took another step with broad potential consequences for banking when it proposed to create a single agency to regulate the entire banking industry. Dividing the job among four agencies no longer made sense, the administration said. It proposed creating a Federal Banking Commission to do the work of the Comptroller of the Currency, which is responsible for national banks; the Federal Reserve Board, which regulates bank-holding companies; the Federal Deposit Insurance Corporation, which insures deposits at banks and savings and loan associations; and the Office of Thrift Supervision, which regulates the savings and loans.

The Federal Reserve would continue to control the nation's money supply and perform other important functions, but it would lose regulatory power over the nation's biggest banks. For this reason, the Fed opposed the change, and its prospects were uncertain.

Another administration proposal with potentially broad consequences would change greatly how the regulatory agencies enforce the Community Reinvestment Act (CRA), an important piece of legislation that was enacted in 1977 but had been considered imperfect.

The CRA requires federally insured depository institutions to meet the needs of their communities, including low- and moderate-income segments, by providing loans, branches, and other services in all areas. It was meant to combat "redlining," the practice of discriminating against poor and minority groups by refusing to do business in their neighborhoods. The law had been called overly burdensome, inconsistent, and unpredictable, and full of paperwork by the banks, while community groups had called it ineffective.

President Clinton early in the year ordered regulators to propose regulations that would "replace paperwork and uncertainty with greater performance, clarity and objectivity," and in December the Comptroller of the Currency, joined by other agencies, proposed a major change in the rules that would presume banks to be in compliance so long as they appeared reasonably active in the poorer regions. The proposals won wide support among many banks and community or consumer groups, but they were not praised universally. The final rules were not published by the end of 1993, as comments were being considered. There was considerable resistance among members of the Federal Reserve board of governors, and it was not clear in what form the rules eventually would be imposed.

JOHN H. CUSHMAN, JR.
"The New York Times"

BELGIUM

The unexpected death of King Baudouin I and accession of Albert II to the throne dominated events in Belgium during 1993, a year otherwise notable for economic recession and devolution of federal powers.

Politics. Prime Minister Jean-Luc Dehaene, in keeping with his pledge to further constitutional revisions, won Parliament's approval of a new initial article for the constitution, proclaiming a federal state consisting of three regions: Brussels, Flanders, and Wallonia. The national government retained responsibility for defense, foreign policy, social security, taxation, and justice. Most other matters ranging from education to trade and the environment devolved to the regions and their parliaments.

In March, Parliament deadlocked over the last $1.04 billion in budget cuts required to bring Belgium's national deficit within striking distance of the 3% of gross domestic product (GDP) limit set by the European Community (EC) for participation in the projected EC economic and monetary union. The four-party coalition had agreed on some $2.23 billion in reductions, including a four-year increase of 2% in income and corporate taxes. But Walloon Socialists insisted that wages and salaries be linked to the cost-of-living index, and Flemish Christian Democrats opposed any reduction of family allowances.

When an initial agreement could not be reached, Dehaene offered his resignation to King Baudouin, but the king asked Dehaene to negotiate a solution. Dehaene succeeded, raising revenues by obtaining agreement on the sale of some state assets and on strong accounting measures that were intended to reduce tax evasion and fraud. On April 1, Parliament voted its confidence in the government and approved the austerity measures. In June the legislature supported a law banning corporate funding of political parties and declared individual donations to parties as not tax deductible.

Royal Death. King Baudouin—at the age of 62—died from a heart attack on July 31, while vacationing in Spain. The Belgians' fifth king was introspective and reticent to take a major role in Belgian politics, no doubt bearing scars from the criticism of the rule of his father (King Leopold III) that led to Baudouin's swearing in as king in 1950, accession to power in 1951, and the abdication of Leopold III. Nevertheless, Baudouin had helped stabilize the rivalries between Walloons and Flemings. His loss at a critical point in the devolution process caused political leaders to feel the need for a truly experienced hand at the palace.

Baudouin and Queen Fabiola had no children and many observers expected that the heir apparent, Baudouin's 59-year-old brother Albert, would allow the throne to pass directly to his son, Philippe, 33. But Dehaene and others believed that the "spirit of continuity" was critical,

---

BELGIUM • Information Highlights

Official Name: Kingdom of Belgium.
Location: Northwestern Europe.
Area: 11,780 sq mi (30 510 km²).
Population (mid-1993 est.): 10,100,000.
Chief Cities (Dec. 31, 1991): Brussels, the capital (incl. suburbs), 951,217; Antwerp (including suburbs), 465,783; Ghent, 230,232; Charleroi, 206,903; Liège, 196,303; Bruges, 116,717.
Government: *Head of state,* Albert II, king (acceded Aug. 9, 1993). *Head of government,* Jean-Luc Dehaene, prime minister (sworn in March 7, 1992). *Legislature*—Parliament: Senate and Chamber of Representatives.
Monetary Unit: Franc (36.57 francs equal U.S.$1, commercial rate, Nov. 1, 1993).
Gross Domestic Product (1991 est. U.S.$): $171,800,000,000.
Economic Indexes (1992): *Consumer Prices,* all items (1980 = 100), 164.7; food (1988 = 100), 108.7. *Industrial Production* (1980 = 100), 119.
Foreign Trade (1992 with Luxembourg, U.S.$): *Imports,* $125,058,000,000; *exports,* $123,066,000,000.

---

while Belgium underwent so much change and difficult economic times. Albert agreed to serve, was confirmed by Parliament, and was crowned Albert II on August 9. (*See* page 17.)

Economics. Recession in Germany, France, and the Netherlands hit Belgium hard, as more than two thirds of Belgium's exports are to those countries. The German Bundesbank's efforts to keep German interest rates high to curb inflation there conflicted with the interests of Belgium and other EC nations that wished low rates to stimulate their economies. EC revisions of the European Monetary System, allowing greater fluctuations of currencies against each other, were welcomed in Brussels but also raised concern regarding the possibility of any future European Monetary Union. In anticipation of that union, the National Bank of Belgium was declared officially independent, and the treasury was barred from borrowing from it.

Despite the recession, University of Cambridge experts determined Brussels to have the best economic potential of 178 regions in Europe. Steel tariffs that were imposed temporarily by the United States were removed when the U.S. International Trade Commission rejected many of them because U.S. companies had not been harmed significantly by the pricing practices of European steel exporters.

Foreign Affairs. Troops were sent to Zaire on January 30 to protect Belgian nationals from rioting soldiers in Kinshasa. In subsequent weeks, Belgium, France, and the United States pressured—with only limited success—Zairian ruler Mobuto Sese Seko to transfer some of his power to the parliamentary government. Belgian troops were also active in United Nations operations in Somalia. On July 1, Belgium took over the presidency of the EC and moved to reinvigorate implementation of the Maastricht accords of 1991.

JONATHAN E. HELMREICH, *Allegheny College*

BIOCHEMISTRY

In biochemistry, the period 1992-93 was highlighted by advances involving Huntington's disease, amyotrophic lateral sclerosis, Alzheimer's disease, and colon cancer.

Huntington's Disease (HD). The neurodegenerative illness known as Huntington's disease typically strikes people in their 30s and 40s, destroying their physical and mental abilities and causing death within ten to 20 years. James Gusella and colleagues at Massachusetts General Hospital had determined that the HD gene resided near the tip of chromosome 4. Because of the complexities in working near the tip of a chromosome and the gene's peculiar instability, the HD gene remained elusive.

In 1993, Gusella and colleagues successfully isolated the HD gene. It consists of about 210,000 genetic subunits, or nucleotides. One end of the gene has repeating nucleotide triplets represented by the chemical initials CAG. These trinucleotide repeats are the unstable part of the gene and the site of Huntington's mutation. In normal individuals, the gene has 11 to 34 CAG repeats. But in HD patients, the gene has from 42 to 100 repeats. A mutation apparently causes the expansion of trinucleotide repeats. The greater the number of the repeats in the abnormal HD gene, the earlier the disease seems to develop and the more severe are its symptoms. The normal version of the HD gene encodes a protein, but what the protein does in the body remained unknown during 1993.

Amyotrophic Lateral Sclerosis (ALS). Amyotrophic lateral sclerosis (ALS) is a devastating neurodegenerative illness that deteriorates nerve cells in the lower brain and spinal cord, causing muscular atrophy, paralysis, an inability to swallow, speech loss, and, finally, respiratory failure. It is commonly known as Lou Gehrig's disease. The symptoms usually appear at around age 50, and death ensues within five years.

The biochemical puzzle behind ALS was solved in 1993 when scientists discovered that the gene for ALS resides on chromosome 21 and successfully isolated the gene. They found that the normal version of the gene encodes an enzyme called superoxide dismutase (SOD). SOD scavenges highly toxic molecules called free radicals and converts them into less toxic hydrogen peroxide or oxygen. For this chemical conversion to occur, two identical molecules of SOD link to form a dimer, which is an active form of the enzyme. In ALS patients, SOD molecules do not form proper dimers and thus free radicals accumulate until the disease manifests itself. Knowing that ALS is caused by free radicals, scientists are working to develop drugs that can deactivate the dangerous molecules.

Alzheimer's Disease (AD). Alzheimer's disease (AD) afflicts about 4 million Americans with memory loss, declining motor coordination, and psychosis. Typically, the brain tissue of AD patients is clogged with hard plaques formed from proteins called ß-amyloid and with cord-like structures called neurofibrillary tangles. Researchers suspect that these substances can destroy the brain tissue around them. Most AD patients have the late-onset form of the disease, which begins after the age of 65. In 1993 scientists at Duke University discovered that the gene for late-onset AD is located on chromosome 19 and that the gene codes for a common protein, lipoprotein E-4 (ApoE-4). ApoE-4 normally helps transport cholesterol in the blood. A person may have two, one, or no copies of ApoE-4.

Working with 42 families afflicted with late-onset AD, the Duke group found that patients with two copies of the ApoE-4 gene had eight times the risk of developing AD compared with people without any copies of ApoE-4. Even in those individuals who inherited one copy of ApoE-4, the risk of developing AD was two- to fourfold higher than in those without any ApoE-4 at all. Furthermore, the presence of ApoE-4 lowered the age at which AD began from about 84 years of age when no ApoE-4 was present, to age 68 when two copies were present. Researchers suspect that ApoE-4 helps kill nerve cells by sticking tightly to ß-amyloid circulating through the blood and encouraging the formation of thick fibrous plaques in the brain. The linkage of ApoE-4 to AD provides a powerful diagnostic tool.

Colon Cancer. Biochemists have been exploring the involvement of oncogenes and tumor-suppressor genes in various cancers. Oncogenes normally regulate cell growth and development but, when mutated, they malfunction and cause cells to grow out of control. Tumor-suppressor genes normally keep cell growth in check, but when mutated, they lead to uncontrolled cell division, which eventually can result in tumor formation.

Two collaborating international teams of biochemists at Johns Hopkins University and the University of Helsinki identified a new type of cancer gene that does not make cells divide—like altered oncogenes and tumor-suppressor genes can—but instead causes thousands of mutations throughout the chromosomes. As a result, segments of genes either are repeated or deleted. Apparently, the newly discovered gene induces genetic instability by causing mistakes to occur during DNA replication before a cell divides. If mistakes go uncorrected or are induced, mutations steadily accumulate, which explains why cancer generally develops after the age of 40. The newly discovered gene, carried by one in 200 people, leads to colon cancer and a variety of other cancers. The gene has not yet been isolated.

PREM P. BATRA
Wright State University

BIOGRAPHY

A selection of profiles of persons prominent in the news during 1993 appears on pages 137-51. The affiliation of the contributor is listed on pages 591-94; biographies that do not include a contributor's name were prepared by the staff. Included are profiles of:

ARAFAT, Yasir

Standing on a platform on the White House lawn with U.S. President Bill Clinton and Prime Minister Yitzhak Rabin and Foreign Minister Shimon Peres of Israel, Palestine Liberation Organization (PLO) leader Yasir Arafat in September 1993 achieved the improbable zenith of a unique career. The man denounced for decades by Israel as a terrorist leader, and before 1988 a pariah also to the United States, was there to give formal approval to preliminaries of peace with Israel.

Obnoxious as Arafat was to Israel, and despite his prominence as a Palestinian leader and spokesman, he never has been among the most extreme of Palestinian nationalists. From the mid-1970s on, and especially in the 1980s, Arafat indicated from time to time that he was open to compromise, thus causing fissures within the Palestinian movement. A fundamental weakening of the PLO's economic and political position in the aftermath of the

Yasir Arafat

© H.H.A./Sipa

1991 Persian Gulf war presumably provided in 1993 the motive for this, the greatest imaginable compromise.

Background. Arafat's birth and early years are shrouded in uncertainty. He was born on Aug. 24, 1929; but, while he has claimed to have been born in Jerusalem of distinguished lineage, close associates have said he was born in Cairo, and his family came from Gaza. He attended high school in Cairo and went on to study at Cairo University's prestigious school of engineering. While still a student, he became involved in politics. He joined the League of Palestinian Students in 1944 and served as its president (1952-56). His activities gained the favorable eye of Gen. Abdel Nasser, who recently had come to power in Egypt. In 1956, Arafat was cofounder of the Al-Fatah movement, which may be described as the core of the PLO. He continued to work as an engineer and contractor in Egypt and Kuwait, but by the mid-1960s began to devote himself full-time to politics. He became chairman of the PLO in 1968; and, though his title has varied from time to time, he has continued to be the best-known figure in the movement ever since. He already had been involved in military strikes—or terrorist actions—against Israel for a decade, but his great achievement was to build the PLO into an effective political and economic umbrella organization for all groups espousing Palestinian nationalism.

By the late 1960s he had moved to Jordan. He was able to win financial aid and political support from wealthy Arab states. A landmark was the recognition by the Arab heads of state in 1974 of the PLO as "the sole legitimate representative of the Palestinian people." Meanwhile, Arafat in 1970 had suffered the first of many resounding defeats when his creation in Jordan of a virtual state-within-a-state was found intolerable by King Hussein, whose troops routed Arafat's forces and drove them out of Jordan. Arafat and his organization took refuge in Lebanon until driven out of there after the Israeli invasion of 1982. They subsequently have been headquartered in Tunis, 1,500 mi (2 413 km) west of Palestine.

Arafat has adhered consistently to two principles: that the PLO should be free of control or influence from any Arab state; and that it should be nonsectarian and non-ideological. The growth of Islamic fundamentalism has created splits between Arafat's *Fatah* and the more extreme Palestinians, a difference exacerbated by Arafat's 1988 public acceptance, made at U.S. nudging, of the idea of coexistence with Israel. Arafat is unquestionably a man with a flair for leadership; and he is, above all, a survivor. Personally, he has survived several assassination attempts as well as a 1992 air crash in the Libyan desert. He also has emerged undefeated, if not unscathed, after serious political mistakes, perhaps the gravest being his support for Iraq in the Iraq-Kuwait dispute in the Gulf war.

In November 1991 he married Suha Tawil, a Palestinian Christian. She was 28 at the time.

See also MIDDLE EAST.

ARTHUR CAMPBELL TURNER

© Markel/Gamma-Liaison

Bruce Babbitt

BABBITT, Bruce

When the White House disclosed in the spring of 1993 that President Bill Clinton was considering naming Interior Secretary Bruce Babbitt to a Supreme Court vacancy, foes of Babbitt's efforts to promote conservation protested. They feared that a post on the high court would give Babbitt's views a more enduring influence. But criticism also came from ardent environmentalists who had lobbied to get Babbitt named to the cabinet and who were convinced that no replacement could measure up. To avoid trouble, Clinton soon backed away from the idea of Mr. Justice Babbitt.

This was not the first time that the 55-year-old former Arizona governor's willingness to advocate controversial ideas has brought him mixed blessings. When he sought the 1988 Democratic presidential nomination, Babbitt advocated a national sales tax, which he claimed would reduce the deficit while leaving the economy relatively unscathed. Economists applauded the idea, but rank-and-file Democratic voters turned thumbs down; their reaction hastened Babbitt's early exit from the competition. "The fascinating thing about American Democracy is that we tend, historically, to postpone coming to grips with change," Babbitt said after dropping out of the race. "What I've been trying to do in the last five or six months is drive the other candidates toward the water hole."

Babbitt's pro-conservation record as a Western governor had won him friends among environmentalists around the nation, and he had cemented those ties by serving as president of the League of Conservation Voters. The high hopes raised by his cabinet appointment were diminished early in his tenure when the Clinton White House, under pressure from Western senators, backed off a pledge to raise royalties and grazing fees charged to miners and ranchers. But Babbitt immediately launched a series of hearings throughout the U.S. West to bring together the many interests involved in the use of the 280 million acres (113 million ha) of federal grazing land, and in August 1993 it was announced that grazing fees for ranchers using U.S. land would more than double over the next three years. The move was seen as a clear victory for Babbitt, who stated that new regulations regarding mining and timber and water rights also would be forthcoming over the next months.

Background. The scion of a wealthy Flagstaff, AZ, family that made its initial fortune by running Indian trading posts, Bruce Edward Babbitt was born in Los Angeles, CA, on June 27, 1938, and grew up in Flagstaff. He at first planned a career in mining. Toward that end he majored in geology as an undergraduate at Notre Dame and took a master's degree in geophysics from the University of Newcastle in England. However, shocked by the exploitation of miners he witnessed during a visit to Bolivia, Babbitt decided instead to become a lawyer. "I saw so much human misery...I thought how can I live in an ivory tower?" he said later. Following graduation from Harvard Law School in 1965 (he had taken time out in 1964 to join the memorable civil-rights march in Selma, AL), he entered private practice in Phoenix. He won election as state attorney general in 1974.

It was mainly fate that ushered Babbitt onto the national political scene. In 1978 the incumbent governor of Arizona died and Babbitt, as attorney general, was next in line. He took full advantage of the opportunity, winning two four-year terms from the electorate and gaining national recognition as one of a new breed of Democratic governors with fresh approaches to the role of government in an era of shrinking resources. But in his second term, he angered organized labor—an important Democratic Party interest group—by calling out the National Guard to settle a United Steelworkers strike.

Babbitt—who bears a resemblance to actor Donald Sutherland—and his wife Hattie have two sons, Christopher and T.J.

ROBERT SHOGAN

BARKLEY, Charles Wade

Charles Barkley just *knew* it would turn out this way. Get Charles out of Philadelphia and put him into the uniform of another National Basketball Association (NBA) team and his life and career just would have to explode. And he was right. Boy, was he right.

Barkley, who spent the first eight years of his pro basketball career with the 76ers, became the most valuable player in the NBA for the 1992-93 season, emerging from the long shadow of Michael Jordan of the Chicago Bulls. But unlike Jordan, who—despite appearing in many commercials and making numerous endorsements—stays out of the public spotlight as much as he can, Barkley actually courted more and more attention during his wonderful season. "This is my career," he says, "but that doesn't mean you can't enjoy yourself too. I love the attention. Yes I do." Blessed with a great sense of humor, an outgoing personality, and a zest for life, he is the perfect public figure, a man unaffected by autograph seekers and those demanding yet anoth-

Charles Barkley

© AP/Wide World

er small piece of his time. Flamboyant yet thoughtful, he also is outrageous at times, speaking what is on his mind, often without a lot of careful thought. But, hey, that is just Charles.

The season of glory for Barkley actually began early—during the 1992 Summer Olympics in Barcelona, Spain. While playing on the gold-medal-winning U.S. team, Barkley used the spotlight to establish himself as a truly elite player. He was the best on that all-star squad, better than even the low-key Jordan. That momentum continued into the NBA schedule. Anchored by Barkley's consistent play, the Suns finished with the top record in the league. Barkley averaged 25.6 points, 12.2 rebounds, and 5.1 assists per game—leading the Suns in all three categories. He was fifth in the NBA in scoring and sixth in rebounding. For Phoenix, the reward was obvious: the best record in the 25-year history of the franchise. To the regret of Phoenix fans, however, Barkley indicated that he would retire after the 1993-94 season.

Background. Charles Wade Barkley was born Feb. 20, 1963, in Leeds, AL. He attended Auburn University and was the Southeastern Conference (SEC) player of the year his junior season. He passed up his senior year to enter the NBA draft and was the fifth pick overall—by the 76ers—in the 1984 draft. He left Auburn as its eighth all-time leading scorer and led the SEC in rebounding for three straight seasons. Despite not being very tall (6'6", or 1.98 m), Barkley soon became one of the NBA's most effective inside players. He was chosen to the All-NBA team four times as a 76er and once as a Sun and has played in seven consecutive All-Star games.

One of the best talkers in the league, he is chosen perennially by sportswriters as the NBA's best interviewee. Off the court, he plays golf and loves to watch television, especially sporting events and soap operas. His book—*Outrageous! The Fine Life and Flagrant Good Times of Basketball's Irresistible Force*, written with Roy S. Johnson—was published in 1992.

He is separated from his wife, Maureen. They have one child, Christiana.

PAUL ATTNER

BONDS, Barry Lamar

Although slugger Barry Bonds was expected to be the top prize in baseball's bountiful free-agent market during the winter of 1992-93, he stunned the baseball world when he signed a six-year, $43.75 million deal with the San Francisco Giants. He immediately set out to justify the lavish contract with the finest season of his outstanding eight-year career.

Bonds reached personal peaks in virtually every hitting category and won the National League's most-valuable-player (NL MVP) award. The fleet left fielder also received his fourth Gold Glove for defensive excellence and made the All-Star team for the third time.

Bonds began the 1993 season like a man on a mission. As NL Player of the Month in April, he hit .431 with seven home runs and 25 runs batted in (RBIs). As the summer progressed, his phenomenal production slowed down, but he still made a spirited bid to become the NL's first Triple Crown winner (leadership in batting average, home runs, and RBIs) since 1937. At the season's close, Bonds led the league with 46 home runs, 123 RBIs, a .458 on-base percentage, and a .677 slugging percentage—the NL's best since 1948. Bonds' .336 batting average was the league's fourth best.

Bonds' output helped San Francisco surge to contention in the NL West. The Giants occupied first place for 124 days before the Atlanta Braves—racing to a third straight NL West title—passed them on September 12. The Giants completed the season with 103 wins and 59 losses, the second-best record in the major leagues.

Background. Barry Bonds was born on July 24, 1964, in Riverside, CA. Bonds grew up in San Carlos, CA, as the son of a local sports hero, Bobby Bonds, who hit 332 home runs and stole 461 bases during a 14-year major-league career. With the Giants, Barry was reunited with his father, who served as the batting and first-base coach with the team.

© Focus on Sports

Barry Bonds

Barry played baseball, football, and basketball in high school, and was selected by the San Francisco Giants in the 1982 amateur draft. When they refused his request for a $75,000 signing bonus, however, Bonds decided to go to Arizona State, where he garnered All-America honors. He began his pro career after the Pittsburgh Pirates made him a first-round selection in the 1985 amateur free-agent draft. He spent the first seven years of his career with Pittsburgh.

Bonds is the only man ever to hit .300 with 30 home runs, 100 RBIs, 100 runs scored, and 50 stolen bases in one season. He also has recorded two 30/30 seasons (30 steals and 30 home runs), and he barely missed a third in 1993. In this category, he is chasing the all-time mark of his father, who notched five 30/30 seasons.

The younger Bonds won MVP awards in 1990 and 1992 and finished a close second in 1991. In those three seasons, the Pirates qualified for the National League Championship Series without reaching the World Series. Bonds has performed poorly in postseason situations, hitting .191 with one home run in 20 play-off games.

Although he is bright and articulate, Bonds often has been regarded as petulant and moody. An on-field shouting match with Pittsburgh manager Jim Leyland in 1991 got widespread exposure on national television.

Bonds is married to the former Susann (Sun) Branco. They have two children, Nikolai and Shikari.

DAN SCHLOSSBERG

CAMPBELL, Kim

The political fortunes of Kim Campbell endured a dramatic year of highs and lows in 1993. On June 13, Canada's Progressive Conservative Party chose Campbell as its federal leader, and 12 days later, she became Canada's 19th prime minister. She was the first woman to hold that office. Only four months later, in an October 25 election, Campbell and the Progressive Conservatives suffered an overwhelming defeat to Jean Chrétien and the Liberal Party. Campbell was ousted as prime minister and lost her own seat in the House of Commons as her party surrendered all but two of its 153 seats. In December she resigned as party leader.

Background. Born in Port Alberni, B.C., on March 10, 1947, and christened Avril Phaedra, Campbell grew up in Vancouver's Kerrisdale suburb, the daughter of a lawyer and judge. She renamed herself Kim in 1959 after her mother left the family to work as a caretaker on yachts in the Caribbean and Mediterranean.

Campbell studied political science at the University of British Columbia, where she met Nathan Divinsky, an older, right-wing mathematics professor and chess master. They married in 1972 while she was pursuing a doctorate at the London School of Economics. She returned to Vancouver with Divinsky but without a degree.

In 1980, Campbell was elected to the Vancouver school board—joining her husband—and entered law school. She divorced Divinsky in 1982 and soon succeeded him as chair of the school board. She ran for a provincial legislative seat as a Social Credit Party candidate in 1983, lost, and went to work for British Columbia's Premier William Bennett. When Bennett retired in 1986, Campbell ran for his job and finished last out of 12 candidates. The winner, Bill Vander Zalm, never forgot a Campbell comment: "charisma without substance is a dangerous thing." She won a provincial legislative seat in 1986, but there was no room for her critical positions in Vander Zalm's government.

Although it appeared that Campbell's political life was over, Prime Minister Brian Mulroney wooed her for the Progressive Conservatives. In 1988, Campbell ran for the House of Commons and beat her opponent by only 269 votes. Mulroney appointed her as minister for Indian affairs (1989), minister of justice (1990), and minister of national defense (1993). As justice minister, she sponsored an abortion-regulation law; as defense minister, she backed a controversial helicopter purchase and accepted gays in the armed forces. She was a fiscal conservative and an enemy of affirmative action.

In February 1993, when Mulroney announced that he would step down in June, most Progressive Conservatives saw Campbell as the only successor. But at a party convention in June, Campbell needed two rounds of balloting to defeat the surprisingly strong Jean Charest. As prime minister, Campbell distanced herself from Mulroney. She demonstrated a folksy style at both international summits and local Canadian festivals. She and her ministers developed an agenda of reform, but they had little time to execute these policies in light of their defeat at the polls in October.

DESMOND MORTON

CHRÉTIEN, Joseph-Jacques Jean

Canada's Liberal Party, led by Jean Chrétien, emerged from the general election of Oct. 25, 1993, with the most parliamentary seats and therefore with the right to be asked to form Canada's next government. This the 59-year-old politician from Quebec did as he named a "problem solving" cabinet and was sworn in as the nation's 20th prime minister on November 4.

During the election campaign, Jean Chrétien's popularity and long government experience were assets, but critics insisted that he was "yesterday's man," bereft of ideas and policies. His opposition to sovereignty in Quebec's 1980 referendum and his opposition to the 1990 Meech Lake proposal to recognize Quebec's distinctiveness left him little support in his native province, once a Liberal stronghold. The Conservative Party—having chosen Kim Campbell from British Columbia as its new leader in 1993—believed that they had dried up Chrétien's popularity in the West and planned to defeat him as a high-spending Liberal. Instead they underestimated Chrétien's capacity to charm voters with a folksy, populist style and a straightforward promise to treat widespread unemployment as more important than Canada's large deficit. In fact, immediately after taking office, the Chrétien government moved to institute a program to create 120,000 jobs in the public sector and cancel a major helicopter purchase by his predecessor.

Background. Joseph-Jacques Jean Chrétien was born in Shawinigan, Que., on Jan. 11, 1934, the 18th of 19 chil-

© Canapress Photo Service

Jean Chrétien

dren of a paper-mill worker. The future politician was educated at St. Joseph's Seminary in Trois-Rivières and was graduated in law from Laval University in 1957.

First elected to Parliament from Shawinigan in 1963, Chrétien got his chance in 1965 when Prime Minister Lester Pearson selected him as parliamentary secretary. He entered the government as a minister of state in 1967 and as minister of national revenue in January 1968. Pierre-Elliott Trudeau, Pearson's successor, found Chrétien a loyal and popular subordinate and promoted him to the Indian affairs and northern development ministry in July 1968. In 1976, Chrétien became president of the Treasury Board (responsible for the civil service), and later that year minister of industry, trade and commerce; and in 1977 he was designated minister of finance.

In Trudeau's new government in 1980, Chrétien was appointed minister of justice; and as minister of energy, mines, and resources in 1982, Chrétien took over the government's controversial National Energy Policy. In 1984 he became deputy prime minister and secretary of state for external affairs. That gave him a springboard to challenge the favorite, John Turner, to succeed Trudeau in the leadership spot. Embittered by his 1,862-to-1,368 ballot defeat, he did little to avert Turner's stunning defeat by Brian Mulroney's Conservatives three months later. He left Parliament in 1986 to join a major law firm.

While claiming to have abandoned politics, Chrétien kept his ambitions alive with his best-selling memoirs, *Straight From the Heart*; frequent speeches; and a discreet organization. When Turner lost his second election in 1988, Chrétien's turn as Liberal leader became inevitable. At a party convention in Calgary on June 24, 1990, he was elected as the new leader of the Liberal Party of Canada. Chrétien's first-ballot victory was achieved with little more than ringing insistence on his love for Canada. Attempts by rivals to smoke out specific policies and ideas failed. After winning a New Brunswick by-election, the future prime minister returned to Parliament in December 1990.

Prime Minister Chrétien married Aline Chainé of Shawinigan on Sept. 10, 1957. They have three children. A birth defect left Chrétien deaf in his right ear and his mouth somewhat distorted.

DESMOND MORTON

CHRISTOPHER, Warren

"We are the inheritors of a new world," veteran diplomat Warren Christopher said when U.S. President Bill Clinton selected him as his secretary of state. "We need bold new thinking to guide us." To those who wondered whether the reserved and taciturn 67-year-old Christopher was the best choice to forge a new role for the United States in the changing post-Cold War world, Clinton responded: "I don't think you can make changes in an area this important unless you know what also has to be maintained, unless you have people of real seasoning and judgment."

No one questioned that Christopher had been well seasoned by the challenges he had faced in both domestic and foreign policy for more than three decades. In 1967, President Lyndon B. Johnson assigned Christopher, then deputy attorney general, to make an on-the-spot inspection of the racial rioting in Detroit, MI. There, Christopher helped the president in his decision to send in federal troops to restore order. In 1980, President Jimmy Carter designated then Deputy Secretary of State Christopher, whom he later described as "the best public servant I ever knew," as his representative in Algiers to negotiate the release of U.S. hostages from Iran. And in 1991, Christopher was recruited by Tom Bradley, mayor of his hometown of Los Angeles, to direct a review of the Los Angeles city police force after the videotaped beating of Rodney G. King.

But despite all that, critics contended, Christopher's strengths were as a skilled tactician and negotiator rather than as a creative thinker. Christopher "preferred to litigate issues endlessly...and to have an excessive faith that all issues can be resolved by compromise," wrote former Carter national security adviser Zbigniew Brzezinski.

Christopher's early record under Clinton was mixed. He gained some success by launching an aid plan for Russia and getting Arab-Israeli peace talks under way again. But his efforts to define the U.S. role in ending the war in Bosnia-Herzegovina bogged down in controversy at home and abroad.

At one point, when a senior State Department official suggested to reporters that U.S. willingness to defer to European nations on Bosnia reflected an overall decision to wield less power abroad, Christopher immediately and publicly rejected that idea. "When it is necessary we will act unilaterally to protect our interests," he declared. But some complained that the episode gave the impression of confusion within the State Department.

Background. Warren Christopher's outlook on life reflects his memories of the Depression in the little town of Scranton, ND, where he was born on Oct. 27, 1925. His father, a bank cashier, was forced to sell off the belongings of lifelong friends at foreclosures. "I think that gave me a good deal of my sympathy for people and my liberal leanings," the younger Christopher later said.

After the family moved to Los Angeles, Christopher won a scholarship to Redlands University, then transferred to the University of Southern California. Following service in the navy, he was graduated from Stanford Law School, where he was president of the Law Review. After graduation he clerked for Supreme Court Justice William O. Douglas, forging a relationship that strengthened his liberal beliefs. Christopher and his wife, the former Marie Josephine Wyllis, have four children—Lynn, Scott, Thomas, and Kristen.

See also UNITED STATES—*Foreign Affairs.*

ROBERT SHOGAN

CHUNG, Connie

On June 1, 1993, Connie Chung took her place as coanchor, with Dan Rather, of the *CBS Evening News*. The move by CBS—which hoped to boost its sagging news ratings and give Rather a chance to do more field reporting—was a surprise to most industry watchers, as well as to Chung herself. With a new newsmagazine-type program, *Eye to Eye with Connie Chung*, set to debut on June 17, she already had a full schedule. The new position was a welcome challenge for Chung, however, who is an ambitious—some say workaholic—achiever. With her appointment, she became only the second woman ever to anchor a nightly TV network news program regularly.

Despite three national Emmy awards as well as several years on the Washington, DC, political beat, Chung has the reputation among some insiders of being a journalistic lightweight, if a talented interviewer. Critics questioned her suitability as an anchor, calling her a glorified news reader rather than a true reporter. No one disputed, however, that her personal charisma and warmth would stand her in good stead with the sometimes difficult Rather. With her

Warren Christopher

Connie Chung

high-profile position on the nightly news and the weekly magazine program, Chung would have every chance to prove her mettle.

Background. Born in Washington, DC, on Aug. 20, 1946, Constance Yu-hwa Chung was the tenth and youngest child of William Ling, a diplomat, and Margaret Chung. Her five oldest brothers and sisters died in China before her parents left for the United States in 1944. Chung entered the University of Maryland as a biology major, but switched to journalism after her junior year; she received her bachelor's degree in 1969.

Chung began her career as a copy clerk at WTTG, a Washington, DC, television station. Within a few years, she was a network correspondent in CBS' Washington bureau, reporting on major political stories: George McGovern's 1972 presidential campaign, President Richard Nixon's trip to the USSR in 1972, and the Watergate scandal in 1973-74. She became known for her willingness to work hard and for her determination and assertiveness in obtaining stories and interviews.

In 1976, Chung moved to Los Angeles to become a news anchor at a CBS affiliate, winning local Emmy Awards for her work in 1978 and 1980. She also hosted *Terra, Our World,* an acclaimed PBS documentary that won a Peabody Award. Chung was anxious to move back into national reporting as the 1984 presidential campaign loomed. To this end, she returned to New York City to join NBC as a political correspondent for the *NBC Nightly News.* While at NBC, Chung hosted several prime-time specials that tainted her reputation as a serious journalist— shows such as *Life in the Fat Lane, Stressed to Kill,* and *Scared Sexless.* After rejoining CBS in 1989, she anchored two newsmagazines and was rotating anchor and contributing correspondent for the network's 1991 Gulf war coverage. She had anchored the Sunday edition of the *CBS Evening News* since 1989 and had been a frequent substitute anchor for Rather.

Chung has been married to Maury Povich, who is the host of a syndicated daytime talk show, since 1984. They have homes in New York City and New Jersey.

CLAPTON, Eric

Eric Clapton, a major figure in blues and rock music for almost 30 years, received six Grammy Awards in 1993. His recently tragic personal life had brought him into the spotlight; Clapton's rare ability to translate his raw emotions

Eric Clapton
© Reuters/Bettmann

and pain into music touched audiences and critics alike. Despite his long career and immense popularity in the United States and his native England, Clapton previously had been awarded only two Grammys. But his most recent album, *Unplugged,* with its quiet, beautiful reflection on his son's death, "Tears in Heaven," and a thoughtful remake of one of his best-known songs, "Layla," finally caught the attention of the National Academy of Recording Arts and Sciences.

Background. Eric Patrick Clapton was born March 30, 1945, in Ripley, England. He was the son of Patricia Clapton and Canadian soldier Edward Fryer, whom he never met. Clapton was raised by his maternal grandparents. He was given his first guitar at age 14, and by 18 had become proficient enough to join the Yardbirds, which became one of the most influential bands of the time. Clapton quit the group at the height of its popularity in 1965 to join the more blues-oriented Bluesbreakers. By this time, his spectacular talent had inspired fans to pen "Clapton Is God" graffiti throughout London.

The Bluesbreakers achieved unprecedented popularity for a blues group after Clapton joined up, with its 1966 self-titled album reaching Number 6 on the British pop charts. Once again, however, Clapton left a band at its peak, quitting in 1966 to form Cream with drummer Ginger Baker and bassist Jack Bruce. Although it always remained grounded in the blues, Cream became one of the all-time classic rock bands, setting trends and changing the face of 1960s popular music.

After two years and four albums, Cream broke up, due largely to conflict among its three talented, strong-willed members. Clapton's next band, retaining Ginger Baker and adding Rick Grech and Steve Winwood, was Blind Faith. Although popular—its debut album, *Blind Faith* (1969), reached Number 1—it was short-lived.

The year 1970 was a landmark one for Clapton. He released his first solo album, *Eric Clapton,* which produced a popular hit, "After Midnight." He then founded yet another new band, Derek and the Dominos, which released the album widely believed to contain some of Clapton's greatest work: *Layla and Other Assorted Love Songs.* The cut "Layla," about a troubled love affair, became his best-known song.

After 1970, Clapton went into decline, becoming addicted to heroin and alcohol. Although he conquered his heroin problem in 1974, he remained troubled by alcoholism until the late 1980s. His life began to turn around in 1986 with the birth of his son, Conor, to Italian actress Lori Del Santo. Clapton toured worldwide after releasing his masterful *Journeyman* album in 1989. However, in 1990 he was shocked by the death in a helicopter crash of bluesman and friend Stevie Ray Vaughan and three members of Clapton's road crew. And in 1991, the tragic death in a fall of 4-year-old Conor caused more suffering. He, as always, poured the grief into his music. *Unplugged* (1992) became his biggest-selling record and "Tears in Heaven" his most popular song ever.

Clapton was married to Pattie Boyd Harrison, the former wife of Beatle George Harrison, from 1979 until 1989. She was the inspiration for "Layla." Clapton enjoys art collecting, horse racing, and fly fishing.

EASTWOOD, Clint

For more than 20 years Hollywood's top box-office draw, known primarily as a hero of action and Western films, Clint Eastwood finally gained recognition in 1993 as a serious filmmaker. His dark Western, *Unforgiven* (1992), won an Academy Award for best film, and Eastwood captured an Oscar as best director. He also received the Directors Guild of America award for his directing work on *Unforgiven.*

Although the film was the 16th feature he directed, Eastwood always had been better known for the memorable, often violent, characters he created through his roles. The films he chose to direct had become increasingly serious during the past years. *Bird* (1988), a biography of jazz saxophonist Charlie Parker, was awarded a prize at the Cannes Film Festival for outstanding technical achieve-

© Steve Starr/Saba

Clint Eastwood

ment, and Eastwood captured a best director Golden Globe Award for the film. However, the film proved unpopular with the public.

After his unprecedented critical success with *Unforgiven*, however, Eastwood completed the transition from genre movie star to respected actor and filmmaker. And he continued his success in 1993 with a starring role in the critically praised *In the Line of Fire*, a thriller in which he portrayed a U.S. Secret Service agent. Eastwood certainly had come a long way from his role in the TV series *Rawhide* (1959-66).

Background. Clinton Eastwood, Jr., was born May 31, 1930, in San Francisco, CA, son of Clinton and Ruth Eastwood. His family moved often during his childhood, and Eastwood attended eight different grammar schools. After high school, he worked at various jobs—including as a lumberjack and steelworker—until being drafted into the U.S. Army in 1951. He entered show business in the early 1950s, and got his break with a cowboy role in the TV series *Rawhide*, beginning in 1959. The show ran until 1966.

Seeking career growth, in 1964 Eastwood starred in an Italian "spaghetti western," *A Fistful of Dollars*, which established him as a star in Europe. He followed the film with two sequels, *For a Few Dollars More* (1965), and *The Good, the Bad, and the Ugly* (1966). He gained fame at home when the trilogy was released in the United States in 1967. Eastwood formed a production company in 1968 and made a string of popular, although seldom memorable, movies. Despite the critical drubbings he received for his laconic acting style, by 1969 he was the world's top box-office draw. With a series of movies during the 1970s and 1980s featuring Eastwood's character Dirty Harry, he became something of a legend, but began taking chances in less violent, more humorous roles.

Eastwood had tried directing for the first time in 1971's *Play Misty for Me*. As time went on, he increasingly mixed audience-pleasing movies with quieter, more reflective films that, although not as strong commercially, often were more popular with critics and had personal meaning to him.

Eastwood has a grown son and daughter, as well as another daughter born in August 1993. He served a two-year term as mayor of Carmel, CA, from 1986 to 1988.

ELDERS, Minnie Joycelyn

On Sept. 8, 1993, Joycelyn Elders was sworn in as the U.S. surgeon general, becoming the first African American and only the second woman to serve in that office. As surgeon general, Elders holds the top post in the Public Health Service and commands the rank of a three-star admiral.

Her nomination to the post had been approved by the U.S. Senate, 65-34, after two months of sometimes bitter debate in the legislature. Much of the controversy surrounding Elders' nomination concerned her positions on social, rather than medical, issues. She long has been an outspoken advocate of expanded birth-control and abortion availability, health care for the poor, and sex education—all positions that raised opposition from conservative foes. She is well-known for a sharp tongue and an unwillingness to compromise her ideals.

Most members of the U.S. Senate, however, agreed that Elders' straight-talking populist style and dedication to public health would be well-suited to the high-profile post. The surgeon general's most visible responsibility is to advocate and lobby for sound health policy. Elders attributes much of her commitment to public health to her own hard-earned experiences.

Background. Minnie Joycelyn Jones was born on Aug. 13, 1933, in Schaal, AR, the oldest of eight children. Her parents, Haller and Curtis Jones, were rural sharecroppers. She never saw a physician prior to her first year in college. When Elders was only 15 years old, she received a scholarship to attend Philander Smith College in Little Rock, AR. At the age of 18—already a college graduate—she joined the U.S. Army as a first lieutenant and was trained as a physical therapist.

After leaving the army, Elders began a long period of medical and scientific schooling. She attended the University of Arkansas Medical School (UAMS), using funds from the army's GI bill, and was graduated in 1960. She worked as an intern at the University of Minnesota Hospital in Minneapolis and as a pediatric resident at the University of Arkansas Medical Center in Little Rock. Upon the completion of her residency, Elders obtained a master's degree in biochemistry. In 1976 she joined the faculty at UAMS as a professor of pediatrics. She received board certification as a pediatric endocrinologist in 1978. Elders became an active medical researcher in the field. She wrote more than 150 articles based on her studies of growth in children and the treatment of hormone-related illnesses. She also has received honorary medical degrees from Morehouse College, the University of Minnesota, and Yale University.

In 1987, Elders was appointed as director of the Arkansas Department of Health by Gov. Bill Clinton. In this office, Elders built an impressive record by expanding the state's services in child immunization, HIV testing, prenatal care, breast-cancer screening, and various in-home medical services.

M. Joycelyn Elders is married to Oliver Elder, a retired high-school basketball coach. They are the parents of two grown sons.

Joycelyn Elders

© Reuters/Bettmann

FREEH, Louis J.

New York judge Louis Freeh was sworn in as the fifth director of the Federal Bureau of Investigation (FBI) on Sept. 1, 1993. It marked a new era for the FBI and for Freeh, a return to his beginnings. After graduating from law school, he had gone to work for the Bureau as a special agent (1975-81). Now, after serving in the U.S. attorney's office for New York's Southern District and being named a U.S. district court judge by President George Bush in 1991, he was coming back to where he had started his distinguished career.

Freeh had made a name for himself while at the FBI in heading its investigation of waterfront racketeering—an investigation resulting in some 125 convictions. Then, while at the U.S. attorney's office, he headed the Organized Crime Task Force, which became famous for its work on the "pizza connection" case, the largest criminal investigation ever undertaken by the U.S. government.

Due largely to the influence of his glowing record and reputation as a talented, diligent investigator, the 43-year-old Freeh was confirmed quickly and unanimously by the Senate as FBI director. Some critics, however, questioned whether his career had given him sufficient experience to manage the huge bureaucracy of the FBI, with its 20,000 employees and almost $2 billion budget. Although his new responsibilities might prove a difficult challenge, it appeared that Freeh was confident in his role and indeed came to the job with definite goals in mind. At the time of his nomination by President Bill Clinton, Freeh stressed that a priority of his tenure would be to recruit a more ethnically diverse mix of agents, and during the confirmation hearings, he stated that "The FBI must have only one rule—the rule of law. The FBI must have only one duty—to protect all of the American people against crime and violence."

Background. Louis J. Freeh grew up in Jersey City, NJ. He received both his undergraduate (1971) and law (1974) degrees from Rutgers University. (He earned a graduate degree in criminal law from New York University Law School in 1984.) After getting his law degree, Freeh realized his boyhood dream of becoming an FBI agent, joining the Bureau in 1975. After the successful waterfront investigation, he received a special commendation from then FBI Director William Webster, and later served as an FBI supervisor in Washington.

While at the U.S. attorney's office, Freeh served as assistant, deputy, and associate U.S. attorney. In addition to the "pizza connection" case, he headed the investigation of the 1989 murders of federal judge Robert Vance and National Association for the Advancement of Colored People (NAACP) official Robbie Robinson. Following the conviction of Walter Leroy Moody for the crime, Freeh was given the attorney general's award for distinguished service.

Freeh and his wife, Marilyn, have four young sons and, until his appointment, had resided in New York.

GERGEN, David

When U.S. President Bill Clinton hired David Gergen to help steady his presidency after his first wobbly months in office, politicians in both parties were startled. As communications director for Republican President Ronald Reagan, Gergen had helped to promote the very same economic policies which Democrat Clinton had vowed to reverse.

But a closer look at Gergen's career made clearer the logic of his May 29 appointment as counselor to the president. This hardly would be the first time the 51-year-old Gergen had changed sides. Raised as a Democrat in North Carolina, he voted for Democratic standard-bearer Hubert Humphrey in 1968, three years before he went to work as a speech writer for Richard Nixon, the Republican who defeated Humphrey and was the first of three Republican presidents Gergen would serve.

More fundamentally, Gergen's main impact in public life stemmed from his technical skill at influencing the press and the public, rather than from his commitment to partisan causes or ideological beliefs. "I see myself as moderately right of center, but very interested in seeing if there are not innovative new answers," Gergen—who had

© Cynthia Johnson/Gamma-Liaison

David Gergen

been an editor and columnist at *U.S. News and World Report* before going to the Clinton White House—told *The Washington Post*. "The country really wants people in this city to get together and stop all this savage partisanship." In announcing Gergen's appointment, Clinton himself struck the same note, declaring: "The message here is we are rising above politics."

During his tenure in the Reagan administration, Gergen's pragmatic view of politics had fostered suspicion among some of the president's conservative advisers even as Gergen worked to carry out the "Reagan Revolution." But his grasp of communications skills helped him make his mark. After studying the first 100 days of every chief executive since Franklin Roosevelt, Gergen concluded that presidents who started off with a coherent and concise policy agenda accomplished the most. This insight—incorporated in what became known as the 100-Day Plan, which Gergen coauthored—was credited widely with contributing to Reagan's strong beginning in the White House. More specifically, it was Gergen who suggested that Reagan take maximum advantage of the goodwill toward him that followed the abortive attempt on his life in 1981 by making his first post assassination-attempt appearance a speech to a joint session of Congress. The warm public response helped overcome resistance to Reagan's controversial economic program on Capitol Hill.

Once on the job for Clinton, Gergen—who also had served as a commentator on *The MacNeil-Lehrer Newshour*—moved quickly to improve the new president's uneasy relationship with the press. He immediately reversed the order to close the door linking the press briefing room with the rest of the White House, an edict which had caused widespread resentment among reporters. But it remained to be seen whether he could help solve some of Clinton's deeper-rooted problems, which Gergen himself often had pointed out in his previous role as a journalist. "He's not only gone off track, he's going around in circles," Gergen had said of Clinton's performance during a television interview little more than two weeks before his appointment.

Background. David Richmond Gergen was born May 9, 1942, in Durham, NC. A graduate of Yale University and Harvard Law School, he served in the navy for three years. In addition to his work for Presidents Nixon and Reagan, he served as communications director for President Gerald Ford and later was a resident fellow of the American Enterprise Institute, a Washington-based think tank. He lives in McLean, VA, with his wife Anne and their two children, Christopher and Katherine.

ROBERT SHOGAN

GINSBURG, Ruth Bader

The announcement by U.S. Supreme Court Justice Byron R. White that he was retiring from the court after 31 years began what seemed an agonizing three-month wait until President Bill Clinton picked a successor. But in the end, his selection of federal appeals court judge Ruth Bader Ginsburg met with near-unanimous approval. Ginsburg, 60, is a pioneer in expanding legal rights for women. But she is regarded widely as a moderate—more liberal than most members of the high court but cautious about giving judges expansive power to implement social change. Her intelligence and soft-spoken humor quickly won over the Senate Judiciary Committee, and she was confirmed by the full Senate by a vote of 96-3. Her opponents were three conservative senators who voiced unease primarily with her support of abortion rights.

Ginsburg became the 107th member of the high court and is only the second woman in history to serve as a justice. (Her new colleague Sandra Day O'Connor is the first.) Her appointment marked the first time in 26 years that a Democratic president named someone to the nation's highest court. The most recent previous Democratic appointee was Justice Thurgood Marshall, who died in January 1993, 18 months after his retirement. He was picked by President Lyndon B. Johnson in 1967. White himself had been the last remaining Democratic nominee on the high court when he retired.

At her confirmation hearings, Ginsburg called the right to abortion "something central to a woman's life, her dignity." She earlier had encountered questions from women's-rights groups for criticizing the reasoning in *Roe v. Wade*, the 1973 Supreme Court decision legalizing abortion. Ginsburg was less forthcoming on some other subjects, particularly the death penalty. But her position on capital punishment is not pivotal, since the other eight justices regard it as constitutionally permissible.

Background. Ruth Bader was born in Brooklyn, NY, on March 15, 1933, the daughter of Nathan and Celia Bader. She was graduated with honors from Cornell University, where she majored in government, in 1954. That same year, she married Martin Ginsburg, whom she had met at Cornell. The couple attended Harvard Law School, where she was one of nine women enrolled in a class of 400. When her husband was graduated and went to work as a New York tax lawyer, Ginsburg switched to Columbia Law School and was graduated tied for first in her class.

Ruth Bader Ginsburg

© Robert Trippett/Sipa

No one offered Ginsburg a job as a lawyer, and she began her career clerking for a federal judge. Due to this experience she developed a lasting interest in women's rights. She later gained prominence as a teacher on the faculties of Rutgers University and Columbia Law School. She emerged during the late 1960s and early 1970s as a leading women's-rights advocate, arguing six cases before the U.S. Supreme Court as counsel for the American Civil Liberties Union. She was appointed in 1980 by President Jimmy Carter to the U.S. Circuit Court of Appeals in Washington, DC.

Justice Ginsburg's husband is considered among the nation's foremost U.S. tax lawyers. The couple listed assets of more than $3 million in a financial disclosure report. They have two grown children, Jane Carol and James Steven.

JIM RUBIN

GIULIANI, Rudolph William

Rudolph William Giuliani, the grandson of Italian immigrants and the son of a Brooklyn tavern owner, was elected New York City's 107th mayor in November 1993 at the age of 49. His election immediately merited several historical footnotes. In a city where Democratic voters heavily outnumber Republicans, Giuliani was the first Republican mayor in a generation and only the third in this century. He was the first who had not held elective office before. And he was the first to defeat an incumbent mayor in a general election in 60 years. The 1993 campaign amounted to a rematch between Giuliani and David N. Dinkins, who won by a two-percentage-point margin in 1989 to become New York City's first black mayor.

Background. Growing up in Brooklyn—where he was born on May 28, 1944—and on Long Island, Giuliani first considered becoming a Roman Catholic missionary. But he applied his zeal to the law instead. After being graduated from New York University Law School in 1968, he clerked for a U.S. district judge for two years and then served as an assistant U.S. attorney. From 1975 to 1977 he was a member of the U.S. Justice Department under President Gerald Ford. It was during this period that the Kennedy Democrat switched political parties. After practicing law during the Jimmy Carter years, he joined the Reagan administration in 1981 as associate attorney general. Two years later, he was named the U.S. attorney for the Southern District of New York, a premier federal prosecutor's job that earned him national prominence in law enforcement. He was the first Italian American to hold that post. His office investigated insider trading on Wall Street, won convictions of leading organized-crime figures, and pursued official-corruption cases that rocked New York City politics and prompted tighter curbs on contracting and conflicts of interest.

Giuliani resigned as U.S. attorney to run for mayor in 1989. He emerged bruised from a Republican primary and found himself facing Dinkins, the Manhattan borough president who had defeated the three-term incumbent, Edward I. Koch, for the Democratic nomination. The campaign revolved around issues of competence and corruption, but race undoubtedly played a part in the outcome, too. In a heavily Democratic city, Dinkins won by the smallest margin in any mayoral race since 1905. In the years between his defeat and his second try for the mayoralty, Giuliani practiced law.

If the question of the 1993 campaign was who most embodied change to weary New Yorkers, the answer was Giuliani. The Dinkins campaign sought to make an issue of Giuliani's temperament. Was the Republican candidate too volatile in an already overheated city? Giuliani began his campaign with fuzzy images of his childhood in Brooklyn, where he was a Yankee fan in Dodger territory, and his private life as the husband of television newscaster Donna Hanover and the father of two young children. He ended his campaign by invoking Dinkins' theme from four years earlier: urging New Yorkers to vote their hopes, not their fears. Whatever the voters' motivations, Giuliani won, by a margin of just less than three percentage points. After win-

© Rick Maiman/Sygma

Rudolph Giuliani

ning on a can-do, anticrime platform, Giuliani promised a largely nonpartisan administration that would reflect New York's diversity. *See also* NEW YORK CITY.

SAM ROBERTS

GRISHAM, John

The position of John Grisham as one of today's most popular American fiction writers was enhanced in 1993. Not only was his latest work, *The Client*, high on the best-seller lists, but his three earlier works—*A Time to Kill*, *The Firm*, and *The Pelican Brief*—were among the five leading-selling paperbacks. In all, some 20 million copies of his books were in print by early 1993, and *The Client* hardly had reached the stands. In addition, the film version of *The Firm* was a summer blockbuster and the movie adaptation of *The Pelican Brief* was released late in the year.

The popularity of Grisham's novels is illustrated further by the fact that the membership of The Literary Club and Doubleday Book Club—both of which promote his books—has increased by some 33% since the beginning of the 1990s. Although some critics question the literary merits of Grisham's works, Barnes & Noble even issued a T-shirt with a caricature of the 38-year-old attorney turned author. He thus joined some 15 people of letters, including William Shakespeare and Charles Dickens, in being so honored by the book chain.

In light of Grisham's background as a lawyer, it is not surprising that the plots of all four of his books center on the legal profession. His 1993 effort, *The Client*, concerns a young boy who jeopardizes his own life after trying to stop a suicide and hires a 52-year-old woman lawyer for protection. Grisham's previous novel, *The Pelican Brief* (1992), also featured a woman of strong character—Darby Shaw, a Tulane University law student who seeks to unravel the mysteries behind the murders of two U.S. Supreme Court justices.

A Time to Kill, Grisham's first novel, is the story of a Southern lawyer who, before an all-white jury, defends a black Vietnam veteran who has shot and killed two young white men after they raped his 10-year-old daughter. Although the novel did not sell well initially, it is considered by many to be his best. It also is somewhat biographical, for in 1987, Grisham accidentally witnessed a young girl testifying against a man charged with raping her. Grisham considered the moment the most emotional one of his life and simply "had to write it down." *A Time to Kill* was fol-

lowed in 1991 by *The Firm*, which tells of Mitchell Y. McDeere, a recent Harvard Law School graduate who accepts a high-paying, frills-included position with a Memphis law firm only to discover that it is controlled by the mob. It was *The Firm* that turned John Grisham into a commercially successful writer.

Background. John Grisham was born in Arkansas in 1955. His father was a construction worker and his mother was a homemaker. After being graduated from Mississippi State, he received his law degree from the University of Mississippi. He then practiced law in Southaven, MS, and served two terms in the state legislature. A growing cynicism regarding the legal profession led him to switch careers.

The best-selling writer is married to the former Renée Jones. They are the parents of a son and a daughter and now live in a Victorian home on a 70-acre (28-ha) site outside Oxford, MS.

HOSOKAWA, Morihiro

The selection in 1993 of Morihiro Hosokawa, 55, to be prime minister of Japan was a sign of the transition of political power to a younger generation. The new prime minister—the second-youngest since World War II—was a product of the postwar era. He was different in other ways as well. Hosokawa became the first prime minister in 38 years not drawn from Japan's perennial-majority Liberal Democratic Party (LDP), instead rising out of a coalition of seven non-LDP, noncommunist parties. For the first time since 1955, the cabinet included no members of the LDP.

The turning point in Hosokawa's career had come in May 1992, when he resigned from the LDP and founded the Japan New Party (JNP), which was to be dedicated to breaking up "the overly centralized bureaucratic government." In the (upper) House of Councillors election in July 1992, the JNP won four seats (including Hosokawa's). In local elections, especially for the Tokyo assembly in June 1993, the party did so well that the media began to refer to the "JNP boom." By the eve of the Group of 7 summit in Tokyo in July, Hosokawa was important enough to be met by U.S. President Bill Clinton at the U.S. Embassy.

Prior to the lower house election on July 18, 1993, the JNP cooperated with the small, dissident Harbinger Party. They campaigned successfully on a platform opposing the LDP, and the JNP won 36 seats with a popular vote of more than 5 million (8.1%). Then on July 23, Prime Minister

John Grisham

© Ann States/Saba

Kiichi Miyazawa resigned. The JNP and Harbinger Party joined five opposition parties on July 29 to form a coalition dedicated to the displacement of the scandal-ridden LDP government. Eventually the coalition nominated Hosokawa as a compromise candidate.

In the upper house on August 6, Hosokawa garnered 132 votes of 240 cast; in the lower house, he won the support of 262 members out of 503 voting. On August 10, in his first press conference, the new prime minister stressed the need to reduce Japan's trade surplus, particularly with the United States. However, he would not support opening the Japanese rice market, nor would he set targets for imports as demanded by President Clinton. He also stated that Japan's moral stance should be enhanced by an apology to Asian neighbors for aggression and atrocities during the war.

Although Hosokawa lent his coalition a new air of cleanliness in politics, his cabinet was weakened by the inclusion of politicians previously linked to "money politics." Also, the JNP felt pressure due to major policy differences with its political allies.

Background. Morihiro Hosokawa was born in Tokyo on Jan. 14, 1938. Scion of an aristocratic, wealthy family from Kyushu, he was the grandson of former Prime Minister Fumimaro Konoe (1937-39, 1940-41). At one point in his career, he played the role of an ancestor, Lord Kawatochi Hosokawa, in a samurai movie.

After being graduated from Sophia University in 1963, Hosokawa became a reporter on the daily *Asahi Shimbun*. He and his wife, Kayoko, were married in 1971. During the same year, he ran as an LDP candidate for the upper house and served, as its youngest member ever, for two six-year terms. In 1983 he was elected head of Kumamoto prefecture, becoming the youngest governor at that time. He served two four-year terms and resigned in 1991, firmly believing that such a political position should not be held indefinitely.

ARDATH W. BURKS

LIMBAUGH, Rush

During 1993, talk-show host Rush Limbaugh merged conservative politics and a flair for irreverent comedy to become a ubiquitous media personality. Limbaugh's brash style of improvisational commentary could be found on more than 500 radio stations, in a best-selling book, and on a late-night TV show. His popularity was fueled by his bold exhibitions of reactionary opinion—always fun-loving, if politically incorrect.

Limbaugh was not afraid to criticize political heavyweights or ridicule special-interest groups. Homosexuals, environmentalists, minorities, homeless advocates, feminists, and certainly President Bill Clinton all were targets of his censure. His programs and writings provoked his audience—friend and foe alike—with fiery views of a world lost to liberal ideas, advocating a return to conservative social and political values.

On his radio and television programs, both called the *Rush Limbaugh Show*, Limbaugh blended serious political and social commentary with humor using monologues, listener phone calls, and planned comedy. He is well known for his loud, fast-talking performances and large physical presence.

Background. Rush Hudson Limbaugh 3d was born in Cape Girardeau, MO, in 1951. His parents were both prominent and politically active citizens in their Mississippi River community. His father was a distinguished lawyer and a Republican Party leader, while his mother, Millie Limbaugh, was a longtime Republican committeewoman. Limbaugh's paternal grandfather was an ambassador to India during the Eisenhower administration, and his uncle was appointed as a federal district-court judge by President Ronald Reagan. Like his parents, Limbaugh developed conservative political and social principles and the skill of expressing them with humor.

Limbaugh, who had obtained a radio broadcaster's license at age 16, became a popular radio talk-show personality in Sacramento, CA, in 1984. In 1988 he moved to

© Jacques Chenet/Gamma-Liaison
Rush Limbaugh

New York City and launched a syndicated radio program, the *Rush Limbaugh Show*; thus began his fast climb to fame. More than 15 million followers listen to Limbaugh's three-hour show, which airs on weekdays. His book, *The Way Things Ought To Be*, is a collection of his most popular and memorable bits from the radio program. It has sold more than 2 million copies and enjoyed a long reign as the top nonfiction book in the United States. Limbaugh got his television debut as a guest host on *The Pat Sajak Show* in 1990. His self-named television program attained surprising success in 1993, with more than 200 stations broadcasting the nightly talk show.

Limbaugh also has published a monthly commentary newsletter and is a popular lecturer. A second Limbaugh book, *See, I Told You So*, appeared in late 1993 and was selling well as the year ended. He owns a share in his radio show's distributor, along with John McLaughlin, creator of *The McLaughlin Group*. Limbaugh was expected to earn $5 million in 1993.

Crown Prince NARUHITO and Masako OWADA

On the morning of June 9, 1993, Crown Prince Naruhito of Japan married Masako Owada in a Shinto sanctuary in the Imperial Palace, Tokyo. Some 800 guests—including members of the imperial family (but not Emperor Akihito or Empress Michiko), the bride's family, and leaders of three government branches—attended the quiet, 15-minute ceremony. No foreign guests were invited.

After the ritual, about 200,000 people lined the 2.6-mi (4.18-km) motorcade route from the palace to the couple's provisional residence in Minato Ward. The huge turnout reflected the popularity of the Japanese royal family, which regularly enjoys a 96% approval rating in public-opinion polls. (*See* page 301.)

Background. The crown prince, affectionately known as "Naru-chan," was born on Feb. 23, 1960. As a youth, he lived with his parents and attended primary and secondary schools in Tokyo. After being graduated from Gakushuin University, he became the first future emperor to study abroad, at Merton College in Oxford, England (1983-85). A serious student, he wrote a thesis on Japanese maritime transportation in the medieval period. Due largely to his familiarity with the West, Naruhito—who would become the 126th emperor in a family which has reigned for 1,300

years—represents a modern, more democratic and internationalized imperial institution.

Born Dec. 9, 1963, Masako Owada is the eldest daughter of Hisashi and Yumiko Owada. Her father was the most senior Japanese career diplomat prior to his retirement in August 1993. As a child, she lived for a time in the USSR when her father was stationed in Moscow. Owada attended a Catholic junior high school in Tokyo. After one year in senior high, she moved to the United States (her father was teaching at Harvard University), attending Belmont High School in Boston, MA. She majored in economics at Harvard and was graduated in 1985. Owada studied at the University of Tokyo, then passed the rigorous diplomatic-service examination. By then she could boast of fluency in English, French, and German, and "useful" knowledge of Spanish and Russian.

The crown prince first met Owada in October 1986 at a palace party. She politely put off Naruhito's first marriage proposal as she began a promising career in the foreign ministry. In 1988 she left for Britain on a two-year ministry assignment. Upon her return, she plunged into work on U.S.-Japan trade problems.

Imperial functionaries, frustrated over Naruhito's failure to find a bride, imposed a news blackout on his efforts to win Owada. *The Washington Post* first broke the embargo, reporting that on Dec. 12, 1992, Owada finally had accepted Naruhito's proposal. Japanese media then launched a tsunami of coverage which culminated on January 19 in a news conference mounted by the engaged couple. From the beginning, the crown prince stated, he had developed a "strong and good impression" of Owada: they shared deep interests in music, sports, history, politics, and economics. She in turn described him as "frank, considerate, and patient."

Despite the volume of media activity thereafter, coverage was less frenetic than in 1959, when then Prince Akihito married Michiko. Nor was all the commentary this time of the fairy-tale variety. Some of Japan's venerable peerage complained that Masako was "overly Americanized." Some Japanese media and officials demanded an apology from U.S. magazines for their "disrespectful" coverage. (For example, a *Newsweek* English-language cover heralded "The Reluctant Princess"; the Japanese-language edition, however, referred to "The Birth of a Princess.") In any case, Owada was the first career woman to become crown princess. (Empress Michiko was the first commoner in the role.) Her marriage sent a mixed signal to Japanese women of a new generation known as *shinjinrui*, emphasizing the dilemma between successful career and family duty.

ARDATH W. BURKS

RABIN, Yitzhak

The 1993 peace accord between Israel and the Palestine Liberation Organization (PLO) showed the prime minister of Israel, Yitzhak Rabin, playing a role totally different from that in which he figured during most of his life. The superbly efficient military man became the chief figure on the Israeli side in the peacemaking act. While Israel's Foreign Minister Shimon Peres—not Rabin—engaged in the actual negotiations with the PLO, it was the prime minister who sanctioned the talks and was responsible for the new peace.

Yet it would be easy to make too much of this contrast. Not an ideologue, Rabin always has been a pragmatist, ready to deal as well as is possible with reality.

Background. Yitzhak Rabin was born on March 1, 1922, in Jerusalem. (He is the only native-born Israeli, or *sabra*, who has held the office of prime minister.) His Russian-born Zionist parents emigrated to Palestine when it was governed by Britain as a League of Nations Mandate. He was graduated from the Kadoorie Agricultural School but soon embarked upon a military career. He was a member of Haganah, the Jewish defense force, before and after World War II, but during the war he attended Staff College in England and fought in the British army. He was a brigade commander in the war

© Uzi Keren/Contrasto/Saba

Yitzhak Rabin

that accompanied Israeli independence in 1948 and thereafter continued to achieve rapid promotion. He became deputy chief of staff in 1960 and chief of staff in 1964. Rabin was the architect of victory in the rapid and total Israeli triumph in the Six-Day War of 1967. He deservedly became a popular hero following this achievement, despite a curious collapse from exhaustion shortly before the war.

Rabin was the Israeli ambassador to the United States from 1968 to 1973, and in that post he developed a firm conviction that U.S. goodwill was of supreme importance to Israel. Prime Minister Golda Meir named Rabin labor minister in March 1974, and he suddenly became prime minister when she resigned a month later. His first three-year term as prime minister was not conspicuously successful, although it included steps toward peace with Egypt and the spectacular rescue of Israeli hostages at Entebbe, Uganda. He resigned in 1977 in the wake of an overblown scandal—the technical offense that he and his wife continued to have a bank account in Washington. As defense minister (1984-90), Rabin vigorously combated the Palestinian unrest *(intifada)* that began in 1987.

Rabin's pragmatism, which his opponents call inconsistency, can be seen in a number of his actions since he became prime minister for a second time in July 1992. Rabin's Labor Party was elected with the claim to be a more flexible peacemaker than the previous Likud government. As premier, Rabin moved quickly to curtail further Jewish settlements on the West Bank. This won an end to the U.S. ban on loan guarantees to Israel. He also offered some limited self-government to the Palestinians. On the other hand, the prime minister also engaged in some decidedly confrontational policies in regard to Palestine. He deported some 400 Hamas militants to Lebanon in December 1992, sealed off the Israeli-occupied territories in March 1993, and bombed southern Lebanon in July 1993.

He verbally demonstrated his pragmatism when he was asked about the proposed accord with the PLO, led by Yasir Arafat, an old wartime adversary: "Peace is made with enemies, not friends."

Taciturn in manner and blunt when he speaks, Rabin lacks many of the skills often supposed necessary for success in politics. He and his wife Leah have been married since 1948. They have one son and one daughter.

See also ISRAEL; MIDDLE EAST.

ARTHUR CAMPBELL TURNER

RENO, Janet

By the time President Bill Clinton settled on Janet Reno to be the United States' first female attorney general, he had been forced to discard two other women as candidates for the job because both had hired illegal aliens as babysitters. But the fact that Reno was only the third choice for the job did not prevent her from soon ranking near the top of the Clinton administration in the eyes of the public. In June a *U.S. News & World Report* poll showed that 67% of Americans approved of the way Reno was doing her job at the Justice Department, compared with only 41% who had a positive view of President Clinton's own performance.

Because the 54-year-old Reno's law-enforcement career was founded on her 15 years of service as chief prosecutor for Dade county, FL, some legal authorities complained that she lacked adequate background in federal law enforcement. But at her initial press conference after being named attorney general, the 6'1" (1.85-m) Reno bolstered her imposing physical presence with blunt answers to sensitive questions. On abortion rights, she said flatly: "I'm pro-choice." On capital punishment, while personally opposed to the death penalty, she pledged: "When the evidence and the law justify the death penalty, I will ask for it."

But probably the most dramatic Reno response came April 19, 1993, after the pumping of tear gas into the Branch Davidian compound near Waco, TX, by law-enforcement officials had led to the mass suicide of members of the religious cult who had been besieged by federal lawmen for 51 days. "I made the decisions," Reno said. "I'm accountable. The buck stops with me..." (*See* FEATURE SECTION, page 60.) And Reno was similarly forthright on July 19 when she recommended that the president dismiss FBI Director William S. Sessions because of allegations of unethical behavior.

Background. Janet Reno was born in Miami, FL, on July 21, 1938. The future attorney general grew up in a cypress-log house in Miami built by hand by her parents. She earned a bachelor's degree from Cornell University, where she majored in chemistry, before being graduated from Harvard Law School. Following about ten years of private practice, Reno joined the Dade county state attorney's office as an assistant in 1973. Single and childless, she was known as a workaholic who guarded her privacy intensely. Nevertheless, after being appointed top prosecutor in 1978, she was able to build the political support to win election to the job five times.

Reno's tendency to turn public-corruption cases over to federal authorities for prosecution led critics to charge that she was afraid to challenge the local power structure. But her supporters claimed that federal prosecutors had a better chance of gaining convictions because the rules of evidence under state law favor the defense. By and large, Reno was known for combining toughness in law enforcement with a concern for the underlying social causes of crime, demonstrated by her advocacy of children's rights and juvenile justice reform.

In 1980, Reno's failure to gain conviction of four Miami police officers who beat a black man to death triggered an outburst of inner-city violence and fostered bitter feelings against her in the black community. But when Clinton picked her to be attorney general, Democratic Rep. Carrie Meek—herself a black who represents a large black constituency in Miami—called her a "tough prosecutor, but very, very fair."

ROBERT SHOGAN

RIORDAN, Richard J.

Wealthy businessman Richard J. Riordan, a Republican, became the new mayor of Los Angeles, CA, in 1993, succeeding Tom Bradley, who had held the post for 20 years. Riordan took over the mayoralty at a difficult time. There was a considerable increase in immigration, both legal and illegal, to the area; the city was experiencing a major economic downturn, which mirrored both world conditions and the end of the Cold War; and a damaging 1992 riot energized by the problems of poverty and race relations had left its mark.

In his successful campaign for mayor, after a primary featuring 52 hopefuls, Riordan's runoff opponent was Michael Woo (D), a member of the city council and the son of a prosperous banker. Woo was clearly behind from the start, leading to negative campaigning. Television refused to treat this seriously, while the public remained apathetic. Neither candidate offered specific proposals for the city's many ills, except that both favored a large increase in the number of police.

In his first try for public office, Riordan defeated Woo by a margin of 54% to 46%. His victory was not due so much to his outspending Woo—in part with $6 million of his own money—as to various other factors. These included the voters' perception that Riordan seemed to be the only one who could connect businesses to the rebuilding of the city's economy, and Woo's inability to make the necessary inroads into ethnic-group support, especially of blacks. About 85% of Riordan's support came from non-Hispanic Caucasians, but 14% of black voters, 31% of Asians, and 43% of Latinos voted for him, too. Woo was hurt by apathy and by an abiding skepticism among voters generally concerning the ability of government to help much with ghetto economic problems. During his initial months in office, Riordan concentrated on learning the job and moved with uncharacteristic caution.

Background. Richard J. Riordan was born in Flushing, NY, on May 1, 1930, and grew up in the prosperous New York City suburb of New Rochelle. He was the youngest son of William O. Riordan, president of Stern Brothers department store and a man involved in many public and private activities. The future mayor attended Santa Clara University, then was graduated from Princeton. He was first in his class at the University of Michigan Law School, then moved to Los Angeles in 1956 and engaged in various business ventures.

Among other things, Riordan became the principal partner in a law firm, a partner in an investment-banking firm, a member of many boards of directors, and outright

Janet Reno

© Robert Trippett/Sipa

owner of many businesses. He also was a generous phi-lanthropist and did fund-raising and legal work for the Catholic archdiocese. He contributed to many political campaigns, sometimes to both sides.

Boundless energy, along with drive, competence, and some luck, have been Michael Riordan's hallmarks. His work style is one of long hours and quick decisions. He is known for an ability to spot commercial value in techno-logical developments. The new mayor also is self-confi-dent, wants to have his own way, leaves details to others, and is reluctant to lose or sometimes even to compromise. Such characteristics can lead to success in business, but are not considered ideal for politics.

Mayor Riordan's twin sister was stillborn; three of his other siblings died at young ages; and he lost two of his own children as young adults. His two marriages have failed. All this personal tragedy seems to cause him to lose himself in his work. He lives in the posh Brentwood section of the city in a mansion with several dogs and some 40,000 books.

CHARLES R. ADRIAN

ROSTENKOWSKI, Dan

During 1993, U.S. Rep. Dan Rostenkowski (D-IL) was a central ally in the House of Representatives for the new Bill Clinton administration. As a key House supporter of Clinton's program, the powerful chairman of the House Ways and Means Committee not only was instrumental in the enactment of the administration's budget and deficit-reduction plan but was counted on to play a key role in the forthcoming consideration of major Clinton legislative pro-posals regarding health care and welfare reform. At the same time, Rostenkowski came under fire for his role in the House Post Office scandal which had surfaced in 1991-92. On July 19 it was revealed that Robert V. Rota, the former House postmaster, had told prosecutors that he had helped Congressman Rostenkowski embezzle $21,300. Rota had pleaded guilty to one count of conspir-acy and two counts of embezzlement. The announcement was seen as a step toward Rostenkowski's indictment. The investigation of the case continued throughout the fall.

Dan Rostenkowski

© Richard Bloom/Saba

Background. Daniel Rostenkowski was born in Chica-go, IL, on Jan. 2, 1928, the son of Joseph P. and Priscilla Rose Rostenkowski. His father served in the Illinois House of Representatives, as a Chicago alderman, and as U.S. collector of customs. The Rostenkowskis lived in a house the future congressman's grandfather had built in Chica-go's near northwest side after immigrating from Poland. His mother operated a tavern on the street level of the house, which was a gathering spot for Polish-Americans.

Rostenkowski attended St. John's Military Academy in Delafield, WI. After serving in the U.S. Army in Korea for two years, he gave up his dream of playing professional athletics and attended night classes in business at Loyola University in Chicago. He then followed in his father's footsteps and began his political career, winning election to the Illinois General Assembly in 1952 and to the state Senate in the two subsequent elections. With the support of Chicago's Mayor Richard Daley, Rostenkowski ran for a U.S. congressional seat in 1958. He captured an over-whelming 75% of the vote and has been reelected to every succeeding Congress.

As a Congressman, Rostenkowski has been a sup-porter of civil-rights and social-welfare legislation. He also has been a strong backer of the military and was in favor of U.S. involvement in Vietnam until March 1971, when he realized that he no longer could explain the purpose of U.S. policy in Southeast Asia to high-school students in his district. Rostenkowski was elected chairman of the House Democratic Caucus in 1966 and 1968 and was appointed chief deputy to the House Democratic whip in 1976. Following the 1980 elections, he decided to let go a chance to become House majority whip to take over as chairman of the House Ways and Means Committee, on which he had been serving since 1964. The Illinois Demo-crat also was serving as a chairman of the Joint Commit-tee of Taxation and as a member of the Democratic Steer-ing and Policy Committee in 1993.

Rostenkowski married LaVerne Pirkins on May 12, 1951. They are the parents of four grown daughters.

SHALIKASHVILI, John M.

On Oct. 5, 1993, Gen. John Shalikashvili was con-firmed by the U.S. Senate as chairman of the Joint Chiefs of Staff. Shalikashvili was sworn in a few weeks later, on October 25, becoming the first foreign-born citizen to hold this top military position. He succeeded Gen. Colin Powell, who had been appointed to the position by President Ronald Reagan and was retiring.

In nominating General "Shali" to the post on August 11, President Bill Clinton called him "a soldier's soldier, a proven warrior, a creative and flexible visionary who clear-ly understands the myriad of conflicts—ethnic, religious, and political—gripping the world." Sam Nunn, chairman of the Senate Armed Services Committee, later referred to the general as "a true American success story and out-standing military leader."

Background. John Malchase David Shalikashvili was born June 27, 1936, in Warsaw, Poland. He was the son of a military officer from the Soviet republic of Georgia—who fought in World War II in a Nazi-organized unit—and a Pol-ish mother. His grandfather was a Russian Czarist general. The family fled to Germany in 1944 to avoid the destruc-tive westward march of the Russian Red Army.

At the age of 16, with the aim of finding a better life, Shalikashvili moved to the United States and settled in Peoria, IL. He perfected his command of English from careful observation of John Wayne movies. In 1958 he was graduated from Bradley University with a degree in mechanical engineering and entered the U.S. Army.

Shalikashvili began a long climb through the military ranks. He was commissioned a second lieutenant in the Artillery upon his graduation from officer candidate school in 1959. By 1968 he was leading troops in Vietnam as a major, after serving command and staff positions in the United States and abroad. Two years later, he received a master's degree in international affairs from George Wash-ington University. He then held several significant com-

Gen. John Shalikashvili

mand posts in the United States, Italy, and Germany and attended the Army War College. In 1981 he was promoted to brigadier general and six years later to major general. He developed a reputation as a talented military thinker who handled success without flamboyance.

In 1989, as a lieutenant general, Shalikashvili assumed duties as deputy commander in chief of U.S. Army forces. He commanded Operation Provide Comfort, the mission to save Iraqi Kurds from starvation and Saddam Hussein after the Persian Gulf War in 1991. After the completion of this command, he returned to Washington to serve as assistant to the chairman of the Joint Chiefs of Staff. Observers characterized him as not only a veteran military leader, but as a keen diplomat too. In June 1992 he assumed the position of commander in chief of the U.S. European Command, Stuttgart, Germany, and supreme allied commander, Europe. He was considered to be a leading military authority on the crisis in the Balkans and on the former Soviet republics in the post-Cold War era.

General Shalikashvili is married to the former Joan Zimpleman. They are the parents of one son, Brant.

THOMPSON, Emma

Although British actress Emma Thompson was a relative unknown, it still was not surprising that she won the best actress Oscar at the March 1993 Academy Awards for her role in *Howards End* (1992). Her brilliant and versatile work in *Howards End* and several other films had made her a favorite of knowledgeable filmgoers; she has been compared to such luminaries as Katharine Hepburn and Vanessa Redgrave. While plum roles now are falling her way, Thompson is quick to point out that she still is "surprised to have become an actor... I had tremendous resistance to the notion of women as a kind of romantic ideal, as something to be wondered at, as something beautiful. The thing I wanted to be was that kind of woman who could be strong and independent and jolly, but make people laugh, and break down all that."

Background. Emma Thompson was born April 15, 1959, in London, England, to Phyllida Law and Eric Thompson, both actors. Her younger sister Sophie was a successful child actress. With "no aspirations to perform," Thompson majored in English literature at Cambridge. After joining the celebrated Cambridge comedy troupe, "Footlights," however, she found her niche. "Footlights" had spawned Monty Pythoners John Cleese and Eric Idle, among others. Due to a lack of good comedic material for women, Thompson cowrote, codirected, and coproduced the group's first all-female revue, the successful *Woman's Hour* (1983).

Turning to acting and song and dance after college, Thompson landed a starring role on the Strand during 1985 in *Me and My Girl*. In 1987 she was featured in a BBC miniseries, *Tutti Frutti*, and later that year starred in another BBC miniseries project, *Fortunes of War*. It was during that show that she met her future husband, actor-producer-director Kenneth Branagh of the Royal Shakespeare Company. Since the two married in 1989, her work often has been connected with his, and they have been praised and mocked as the film world's "golden couple." Most notably, Branagh directed his wife in Shakespeare's *Henry V* (1989), *Dead Again* (1991), *Peter's Friends* (1991), and another Shakespeare adaptation, *Much Ado About Nothing* (1993). Thompson's other film credits include *The Tall Guy* (1989), *Impromptu* (1991), and *Remains of the Day* (1993). In 1988 she attempted a one-woman BBC comedic series, *Thompson*, which was based largely on work she had done for *Woman's Hour*; due to various problems, however, the show ultimately failed to find an audience.

Thompson's other honors include a best actress award from the British Academy of Film and Television Arts, and a London Evening Standard Film Award for her work in both *Peter's Friends* and *Howards End*. In 1993 she branched out into screenwriting, beginning work on a screen version of Jane Austen's *Sense and Sensibility*, commissioned by *Dead Again* producer Lindsay Doran. She also was filming a role in *In the Name of the Father*.

Thompson and Branagh make their home in London and enjoy reading Shakespeare together during their limited free time.

Emma Thompson

BIOTECHNOLOGY

The year 1993 brought approval of an HIV gene-therapy trial, a novel means of detecting drug-resistant bacteria, the discovery of a fungus that produces an anticancer drug previously obtained only from a rare tree, a warning on the use of silver dental amalgams, and the use of a deep-freeze process to preserve stocks of experimental animals.

HIV Gene Therapy. The National Institutes of Health gave its approval for a preliminary gene-therapy trial involving ten people who are infected with HIV but who are not sick.

By fall 1993, Drs. J. Galpin and D. Casciato were planning to take a disabled mouse virus—one that is unable to cause disease in humans—and transfer into it an HIV gene for an envelope protein. They were intending to inject this engineered mouse virus into five project participants once a month for three months. Five other subjects would comprise a control group that would receive injections without the virus. The researchers planned then to monitor the number of killer T cells present in the immune systems of all ten people. If the transferred HIV gene increased the incidence of T cells in the experimental group—which would indicate improved immune-system function—without causing severe side effects, five more individuals then would receive a higher dose of the gene.

A Biological Indicator Molecule. The firefly enzyme luciferase catalyzes a reaction that causes the compound *luciferin* to produce light and helps identify drug-resistant bacteria.

Tuberculosis (TB) kills 3 million people worldwide each year. Unfortunately, strains of the bacterium *Mycobacterium tuberculosis* have emerged that are resistant to one or more of the 11 drugs now used to combat the disease. And since the bacteria grow slowly, it can take two to three months before they can be identified in a patient's sputum.

Dr. W. R. Jacobs and colleagues developed a new test that can be completed in several days. They transfer the gene for the enzyme luciferase to a virus that infects *M. tuberculosis*. A patient's sputum sample is split into 11 test tubes, each containing one of the available drugs for TB. The engineered viruses are added to each sputum sample, where they invade the bacteria that are present in the sputum. Each sample then is placed in a culture dish containing luciferin. If the bacteria are resistant to a particular drug, they live and reproduce, and light is produced.

Taxol From a Fungus. A few years ago, it was discovered that the chemical compound *taxol* could shrink tumors greatly in about 30% of women whose ovarian cancers resisted other therapies. However, the source of taxol was the bark of the Pacific yew tree, which was in danger of extinction from logging operations. As a result of its short supply, taxol treatments run as high as $10,000 per patient. In an effort to find an alternative source of this effective anticancer drug, Drs. G. Strobel and A. Stierle of Montana State University collected and tested more than 200 fungi that they found growing under the bark of yew trees. They discovered a new species of fungus, which they named *Taxomyces-andreanae*, that was capable of producing taxol.

As expected, the yield of the drug is extremely small, but the biotechnology firm Cytoclonal Pharmaceuticals purchased the rights to commercialize the taxol-producing fungus. Hopefully, this will result in an ample and more affordable supply of this drug.

Potential Dental Hazard. Silver amalgam is the most common filling for dental cavities. In addition to silver, it contains tin, copper, zinc, and mercury. Dr. A. O. Summers discovered that many people with tooth fillings had intestinal bacteria which were resistant to the poisonous effects of mercury. Many of these bacteria were also resistant to various antibiotics.

The above results spurred Drs. M. J. Vimy and F. L. Lorscheider to experiment with six monkeys. First, they measured the proportion of mercury-resistant bacteria in the animals' intestinal tracts. Silver dental amalgams then were placed in the monkeys' mouths. Within two weeks there was a significant increase in the proportion of mercury-resistant intestinal bacteria. Many of these bacteria were also resistant to various antibiotics.

Subsequently, the silver dental amalgams were removed from four of the six animals. In these four monkeys, researchers identified a gradual but noticeable decrease in mercury-resistant intestinal bacteria. There appears to be a link between the presence of silver dental amalgams and the incidence of antibiotic-resistant bacteria.

Cryopreservation. Much of the research in biology and medicine has been made possible by the availability of massive stocks of experimental animals, notably the roundworm, *Caenorhabditis elegans,* and the mouse, *Drosophila.*

Long-term maintenance of stocks carries the risk that genetic changes will affect an animal strain due to either inadvertent selection or inbreeding. An entire stock also can be lost as a result of an accident. A new technique was developed that permits preservation of stocks without these problems by deep freezing embryos at about -320°F (-196°C), the temperature of liquid nitrogen. Only about 25% of embryos survive the process and develop into adults. Four companies now offer cryopreservation, storage, and rederivation services for mice. These processes will be extended to other species in the future. It also has been proposed that cryopreservation be used to build up stocks of endangered species.

LOUIS LEVINE
Department of Biology
City College of New York

BOLIVIA

Bolivia installed a new president on Aug. 6, 1993, after a campaign rife with paradoxes.

New President. The country's new chief executive is Gonzalo Sanchez de Lozada of the National Revolutionary Movement (MNR), a 62-year-old mining executive who was educated at the University of Chicago and, as a result of long residence in the United States, speaks Spanish with an American accent. His vice-presidential running mate was an Aymara Indian, Victor Hugo Cardenas, who was born in a mud hut along the shores of Lake Titicaca and whose first language is Aymara. In September, Cardenas, formerly a professor at the University of La Paz, became the first indigene in Bolivian history to head the national government when he became interim president while Sanchez de Lozada attended the United Nations General Assembly in New York City.

No candidate won a majority of the vote in the June 6 presidential election, and under Bolivian law the choice fell to the National Congress. Sanchez de Lozada, popularly known as "Goni," won 34% of the popular vote while his principal opponent, Gen. Hugo Banzer Suarez of the National Democratic Action Party, finished with 21%. Banzer, who was the military dictator of Bolivia from 1971 to 1978, ran on the ticket of the Patriotic Accord Alliance with vice-presidential candidate Oscar Zamora, a former Maoist revolutionary.

Sanchez de Lozada had finished first in the popular vote in the 1989 presidential election, but Banzer, who came in second, threw his support to third-place finisher Jaime Paz Zamora, who became president. This time, however, Banzer conceded defeat a few days after the election and instructed his supporters in the Congress to vote for Sanchez de Lozada.

Agenda. Sanchez de Lozada campaigned on an anticorruption platform and also promised Bolivia's Indians, who comprise more than half of the country's nearly 8 million people, that he would increase their political power, permit the use of native languages in public schools, and work for social equity.

As planning minister in the regime of President Victor Paz Estenssoro in the mid-1980s, Sanchez de Lozada had been one of the architects of the New Economic Policy (NEP) that cut Bolivia's runaway inflation rate of 14,000% in 1985, reduced the government's deficit, and pared down bloated publicly owned corporations.

On assuming the presidency, he pledged to continue the reform program and to spur the privatization of government-owned industries—a process he called "capitalization." By the end of 1993, the annual economic growth rate had held steady at 3.5% and inflation was under 10%.

In August, Bolivia signed an agreement with Brazil for a long-planned pipeline project to

---

BOLIVIA • Information Highlights

Official Name: Republic of Bolivia.
Location: West-central South America.
Area: 424,162 sq mi (1 098 580 km²).
Population (mid-1993 est.): 8,000,000.
Chief Cities (mid-1988 est.): Sucre, the legal capital, 95,635; La Paz, the actual capital, 1,049,800; Santa Cruz de la Sierra, 615,122; Cochabamba, 377,259.
Government: *Head of state and government,* Gonzalo Sanchez de Lozada, president (took office Aug. 6, 1993). *Legislature*—Congress: Senate and Chamber of Deputies.
Monetary Unit: Boliviano (4.265 bolivianos equal U.S.$1, June 1993).
Gross Domestic Product (1991 U.S.$): $4,600,000,000.
Economic Index (1992): *Consumer Prices* (La Paz, 1991 = 100), all items, 112.1; food, 115.8.
Foreign Trade (1992 U.S.$): *Imports,* $1,177,000,000; *exports,* $737,000,000.

---

carry natural gas from Santa Cruz to São Paulo. Completion of the 1,370-mi (2 200-km) pipeline is scheduled for 1996. The cost of $2 billion was to be financed by the World Bank, the Inter-American Development Bank, and the Andean Development Corporation.

Emergency and Military Challenge. In September, President Sanchez de Lozada announced an "emergency plan" to alleviate the crisis in the country's crucial tin industry. During 1992-93 some 220 small mining companies had shut down, with a loss of 35,000 jobs. World tin prices had dropped to an all-time low of $1.99 per lb, compared with a production cost of $2.30 per lb.

In October, President Sanchez de Lozada faced the first serious challenge to his government and unexpectedly dismissed the top echelon of Bolivia's military commanders. The armed forces reportedly had been involved in the smuggling of arms and drugs, and rumors of a potential military uprising had swept the country.

Environment. Scientists say the rate of deforestation of Bolivia's rain forest is nearly as great as in Brazil, with more than 3,000 trees taken off land belonging to indigenous groups in two years.

RICHARD C. SCHROEDER
Consultant to the Organization of American States

BRAZIL

Although facing endemic political corruption, four-digit inflation, and high unemployment, Brazil's President Itamar Franco and other leaders showed belated interest in embracing modernization and reform.

Politics. Scandals placed a question mark over the future of civilian rule in Brazil. On Dec. 29, 1992, President Fernando Collor de Mello turned power over to Franco, his vice-president, as the Senate prepared to impeach him for graft, extortion, and tax evasion practiced by his confidants. In September 1993 authorities broke up a

prostitution ring run by a congressional staff worker for the benefit of federal deputies. Meanwhile, 12 deputies reportedly switched parties in return for $50,000 payments.

A major scandal struck Franco's fledgling administration in October. Former congressional and federal budget director José Carlos Alves dos Santos accused 32 politicians of channeling millions of dollars from the federal budget into their own bank accounts. He leveled his charges after being arrested by police, who found $2 million and 212 lbs (79 kg) of gold in his attic and in safe-deposit boxes in a search that was spurred by an investigation into the suspected murder of his wife. Among those accused of kickbacks were Franco's chief of staff Henrique Hargreaves, Regional Integration Minister Alexandre Costa, three state governors, the president of the Senate, and the leader of the largest party in the Chamber of Deputies.

In addition, Paulo César Farias, a central figure in the influence-peddling scandal that forced President Collor de Mello from office in late 1992, reportedly was preparing a dossier that could expose the wrongdoing of even more Brazilian politicians.

These scandals prompted Franco to offer his resignation if Congress determined that advancing the general elections, scheduled for October 1994, would lift the nation from its political and economic crisis. Franco often appeared to be a reluctant leader who did not want the office. Congressional leaders rejected the offer, largely based on fears that a socialist would win an early election. Franco's move also forced the 44-member Parliamentary Commission of Inquiry (CPI)—headed by Sen. Jarbas Passarinho, a highly respected retired colonel—to launch an investigation. Few legislators wanted to face angry voters prematurely, and the president's mere offer to resign sparked declines in both the São Paulo and Rio de Janeiro stock markets.

These revelations fed the public's mounting distaste for politicians. In June respondents to a poll conducted in Rio de Janeiro ranked Congress near the bottom of national institutions in terms of trust (15%) and credibility (5%). In contrast, the armed forces, which held power until 1985, emerged near the top of the survey with a 58% rating. Indeed, officers became increasingly critical of civilian politicians as part of a growing, nationalist-tinged "mobilization" movement in the military. A November poll revealed that most people in Rio and São Paulo believed that the "big fish" would escape the CPI's net.

Brazil's next elections were expected to be especially important. For the first time in more than 43 years, voters would choose a president, governors, and members of congress simultaneously. In accord with an April 21 plebiscite, Brazil would remain a presidential republic. Voters overwhelmingly rejected restoring a monarchy or creating a parliamentary system. But despite compulsory voting for literate citizens aged 18 to 70, abstention was high and almost 20% of the voters cast blank or spoiled ballots.

In light of such discontent, political scientists suggested reforming the electoral system. Nineteen of the nation's 30 political parties held seats in Congress, and many parties owed allegiance to regional bosses who had to be bribed to support some legislation. One proposed change would reduce the number of parties by requiring a party to win a certain percentage of the national vote before gaining representation.

A possible new electoral system aside, the cast of candidates showed few signs of changing. Among the "old faces" who were expected to seek the presidency once again were Luiz Inácio (Lula) da Silva of the Workers' Party; former President José Sarney; São Paulo Mayor Paulo Maluf; and Rio de Janeiro Gov. Leonel Brizola. These veteran politicians devoted more time maneuvering for position in the upcoming campaign than they did seeking solutions to Brazil's critical political, social, and economic ills—including the appalling violence that plagued São Paulo and Rio, where the police were accused of massacring street children.

Economy. President Franco began 1993 by introducing the financial-movements tax. The government estimated the tax would raise $7.2 billion in revenue and help narrow the $13 billion budget deficit. Despite protests from business interests, the measure passed easily. Franco hoped his efforts to rouse the economy would facilitate renegotiations with the International Monetary Fund (IMF). The IMF froze a $2.1 billion loan to Brazil in 1992 and warned that the country would have to present an acceptable economic program before new negotiations occur. Brazil remained the largest debtor of any developing nation in the world.

Thanks to robust domestic consumption and good harvests, Brazil's economy grew by almost

---

BRAZIL • Information Highlights

Official Name: Federative Republic of Brazil.
Location: Eastern South America.
Area: 3,286,473 sq mi (8 511 965 km²).
Population (mid-1993 est.): 152,000,000.
Chief Cities (mid-1991 est.): Brasília, the capital, 1,841,028; São Paulo, 9,700,111; Rio de Janeiro, 5,487,346; Belo Horizonte, 2,103,330.
Government: *Head of state and government*, Itamar Franco, president (sworn in Dec. 29, 1992). *Legislature*—National Congress: Senate and Chamber of Deputies.
Monetary Unit: New cruzeiro (238.25 new cruzeiros equal U.S.$1, Dec. 8, 1993).
Gross Domestic Product (1991 est. U.S.$): $358,000,000,000.
Economic Indexes (1992): *Consumer Prices* (São Paulo, 1988 = 100), all items, 2,104,739; food, 2,027,886. *Industrial Production* (1980 = 100), 92.
Foreign Trade (1992 U.S.$): *Imports*, $20,542,000,000; *exports*, $36,207,000,000.

5%, up from a 1% decline in gross national product (GNP) registered in 1992. However, prices continued to rise—with September's 35.3% inflation rate the highest in three years. In a symbolic attack on hyperinflation, Brazil introduced the cruzeiro real, a new currency worth 1,000 old cruzeiros, in midyear. High unemployment continued to grip the nation.

Neither President Franco nor Finance Minister Fernando Henrique Cardoso—Brazil's fifth since 1990—sought to institute the wage and price freezes favored by the two former presidents. Instead, the chief executive's program included a mix of big spending and big cutting. He earmarked roughly $8 billion in agricultural subsidies and $8.6 billion for health care, announced plans to trim state-enterprise budgets by 10%, and proposed selective tax increases. Also promised were stricter tax collections and more privatization.

While the central government was slashing expenditures, governors in many states were boosting their expenditures, convinced that the central bank would cover their mounting outlays. After a brief confrontation with the state executives, Cardoso called in $40 billion in debts owed by their governments and issued a decree prohibiting state banks from lending beyond their means and threatening to cut off revenue transfers to any state that failed to meet its monthly debt payment.

In October, Cardoso took advantage of congressional debates about revising the constitution to urge greater foreign investment and privatization in such sectors as oil, electricity, and telecommunications. The proposal sparked a battle that pitted Cardoso, others in the Franco administration, and elements of the business community against the political left. The former wanted to control public finances, curb inflation, and modernize inefficient state firms; the latter sought to preserve such social benefits as job security and early retirement for civil servants. The telegenic finance minister could emerge as a presidential candidate in the 1994 election if he could win this battle.

Brazil boasted a $10.3 billion trade surplus in the first nine months of 1993, 9% less than in the same period in 1992. In hopes of increasing earnings from coffee, Brazil signed a pact with the Central American states and Colombia, agreeing to store 20% of their annual coffee exports to restrict supply. The accord—combined with fears of a frost in Brazil—spurred an increase in coffee prices in New York.

A number of countries dispatched representatives to Brasília to expand trade with the world's ninth-largest economy. The recent privatization of Brazilian ports and a reduction in tariffs gave impetus to commercial contacts.

Foreign Relations. German Foreign Minister Klaus Kinkel visited Brasília to discuss investment in Brazil's recently completed—and soon to be privatized—nuclear-power plant. Kinkel

© A. Sassaki/Gamma-Liaison

Itamar Franco, above, succeeded Fernando Collor de Mello as Brazil's president as 1992 ended. Scandals and economic difficulties were dominant during Franco's first year as chief executive.

also suggested that Brazil sign the Nuclear Non-Proliferation Treaty. In October, India's foreign minister came to discuss trade opportunities.

Brazil and China agreed to construct jointly two satellites worth $50 billion. The satellites, scheduled to be launched in 1996, symbolized cooperation and goodwill between two large and increasingly important developing countries.

French Prime Minister Edouard Balladur visited Brazil to gain support for his government's protection of agricultural products in General Agreement on Tariffs and Trade (GATT)-sponsored worldwide trade talks. Balladur hinted that France, which sits on the IMF's Administrative Council, would support Brazil's efforts to regain funding from that organization. In November a top U.S. Treasury official attempted to convince Brazil to open its financial markets to U.S. banks—arguing that countries that fail to afford access would find restrictions placed on their banks operating in the United States.

Brazil hosted the annual Ibero-American conference in Salvador, Brazil. Leaders of 21 Latin American nations, Portugal, and Spain called for end to the U.S. embargo against Cuba.

GEORGE W. GRAYSON
College of William & Mary

BRITISH COLUMBIA

The political agenda in British Columbia (BC) was dominated by environmental concerns during 1993. An April decision to allow logging in 45% of the Clayoquot Sound forestland on the west coast of Vancouver Island and some logging under special management in a further 17% of the sound was very controversial. A violent demonstration against this decision disrupted the opening of the spring session of the legislature, and during the summer and fall there were more than 800 arrests of protesters. The BC government also was criticized for failing to permit adequate participation by native Indian representatives in the Clayoquot decision.

Mounting international environmentalist pressures led Premier Michael Harcourt to propose a forestry-practices code that banned large forest clear-cuts, increased finances for noncompliance from C$2,000 to C$1 million, and based cutting rights on past logging performance. In contrast, a June decision to protect 2.5 million acres (1 million ha) of the Tatshenshini-Alsek wilderness on the Yukon and Alaska border from mining development was acclaimed widely.

Budget and Finance. The 1993-94 provincial budget had expenditures estimated at C$18.99 billion and revenues at C$17.46 billion, thus requiring borrowings of about C$1.6 billion. Health-care funding was estimated to increase by 4% to C$6.2 billion. Revenue measures included a 10% increase in the personal-income surtax, a 0.5% increase in the general corporate-income-tax rate, and increases in various other taxes. A new capital-investment job-creation program was announced, together with the formation of a BC Transportation Financing Authority.

Government and Politics. In a fall cabinet shuffle, only three ministers retained their previous portfolios in the 19-member New Democratic Party (NDP) cabinet. Also, Liberal Party opposition leader Gordon Wilson lost a September party-leadership vote to retiring Vancouver Mayor Gordon Campbell after revelations about a personal attachment to former house leader Judi Tyabji. In November former Social Credit Deputy Premier Grace McCarthy was successful in her third bid since 1986 for party leadership.

In October federal elections, the Reform Party garnered most of BC's seats in the House of Commons, winning 24. The Liberal Party captured six seats and the NDP won two seats.

BC's native peoples also were in the news in 1993. A new provincial treaty commission was given the task of negotiating aboriginal land claims, and a summer BC appeals-court decision modified a 1991 land-claim judgment against the Gitksan-Wet'suwet'en peoples, recognizing that aboriginal rights had not been extinguished.

In March an agreement was reached with health-care labor unions on the implementation of health-care reforms to restructure the delivery of public-health services and shift employment from acute-care hospitals. The long-standing medicare-contract dispute with the province's doctors was resolved later in the year.

Legislature. Major legislative initiatives at the spring sitting of the legislature included extension of human-rights and multiculturalism protections and a revision of the entire framework for local elections. A public-sector employers' council also was established.

Economy. The BC economy outperformed the rest of Canada's economy. A low Canadian dollar, more housing starts, and restrictions on timber supply in the Pacific Northwest helped boost lumber exports to the United States. Weak European demand, however, had an adverse impact on the pulp and paper industry. Consumer spending grew by nearly 10% due to a buoyant economy, low interest rates, and reduced levels of cross-border shopping. While unemployment averaged 10%, full-time employment grew by 2.2%.

NORMAN J. RUFF, *University of Victoria*

BRITISH COLUMBIA • Information Highlights

Area: 365,946 sq mi (947 800 km²).
Population (June 1993): 3,377,000.
Chief Cities (1991 census): Victoria, the capital, 71,228; Vancouver, 471,844; Kelowna, 75,950; Prince George, 69,653; Kamloops, 67,057.
Government (1993): *Chief Officers*—lt. gov., David C. Lam; premier, Michael Harcourt (New Democratic Party). *Legislature*—Legislative Assembly, 75 members.
Provincial Finances (1993-94 fiscal year budget): *Revenues,* $17,460,000,000; *expenditures,* $18,990,000,000.
Personal Income (average weekly earnings, June 1993): $559.88.
Labor Force (August 1993, seasonally adjusted): *Employed* workers, 15 years of age and over, 1,575,000; *Unemployed,* 9.5%.
Education (1993-94): *Enrollment*—elementary and secondary schools, 646,780 pupils; postsecondary—universities, 46,410; community colleges, 30,620.
(All monetary figures are in Canadian dollars.)

BULGARIA

While Bulgaria remained a relative oasis of stability in the Balkans during 1993, the country continued to be racked by political infighting, sputtering economic reform, and growing concern over armed conflicts on its doorstep.

Politics. In October 1992, Prime Minister Filip Dimitrov of the Union of Democratic Forces (UDF) lost a vote of confidence and was forced to resign. In December 1992 a loose alliance of the formerly Communist Bulgarian Socialist Party (BSP) and the predominantly Turkish Movement for Rights and Freedoms (MRF) installed a nonpartisan "cabinet of experts" under the premiership of centrist economist Lyuben Berov.

During the first few months of 1993, the UDF coalition of 15 democratic parties became

increasingly fragmented over the pace of "de-Communization" and economic reform. The UDF leadership refused to cooperate with the Berov government, elected Stefan Savov as the new caucus leader in the Grand National Assembly, and adopted a hard-line position claiming that "de-Communization" was being sabotaged by vested interests in the BSP. Savov advocated tough legislation to bar former high-ranking Communists from top government positions. The UDF's unyielding position on the issue helped garner public support for the Union and led to confrontations with President Zhelyu Zhelev, the UDF cofounder who favored a more measured approach.

UDF supporters staged several large demonstrations in Sofia, demanding Zhelev's resignation for his failure to prosecute former Communists for crimes they allegedly committed while in office. In July, Vice-President Blaga Dimitrova resigned, charging that BSP supporters were seeking to restore communism, an accusation dismissed as exaggeration by observers. After the change of government in December 1992 and another cabinet reshuffling in June 1993, the Socialists gained further influence in the interior and defense ministries. Despite UDF opposition, the Berov administration easily survived a confidence vote in July and received full backing from the BSP and MRF. Even centrist UDF parliamentary members seemed willing to work with Berov. General elections were expected in 1994.

The Economy. Preliminary statistics showed that the steep decline in Bulgaria's gross domestic product (GDP) and industrial production slowed in 1993. GDP was projected to grow by about 2% for the year. However, enormous problems remained: By midyear unemployment stood at 17%, while the rate of privatization failed to meet expectations. Although the government adopted a plan of action for large-scale privatization, by midyear only three large state companies had been sold off. On the other hand, more than one half of the retail trade was in private hands and by June, 170,000 small-scale private firms were registered.

The privatization of collective agriculture continued apace. Under a revised land law, agricultural plots were to be returned to their former owners. By July nearly 35% of the land was possessed by private farmers, and this percentage was expected to double by year's end. Some managers of collective farms and the old Communist *nomenklatura* system opposed the privatization, while uncertainty remained about the productivity of small family plots. Many farmers moved to pool their land in cooperatives.

Bulgaria continued to receive World Bank and International Monetary Fund (IMF) loans for energy and transportation projects, but was criticized for a slow pace of privatization and inadequate financial reform. The London Club of foreign creditors prepared to initiate a substantial debt reduction. In 1993, Bulgaria's net

---

BULGARIA • Information Highlights

Official Name: Republic of Bulgaria.
Location: Southeastern Europe.
Area: 42,823 sq mi (110 910 km²).
Population (mid-1993 est.): 9,000,000.
Chief Cities (Dec. 31, 1990 est.): Sofia, the capital, 1,141,142; Plovdiv, 379,083; Varna, 314,913.
Government: *Head of state,* Zhelyu Zhelev, president (took office August 1990). *Head of government,* Lyuben Berov, prime minister (took office December 1992). *Legislature*—Grand National Assembly.
Monetary Unit: Lev (26.5 leva equal U.S.$1, April 1993).
Gross National Product (1991 U.S.$): $36,400,000,000.
Economic Index (1992): *Industrial Production* (1980 = 100), 79.
Foreign Trade (1992 U.S.$): *Imports,* $4,239,000,000,000; *exports,* $4,071,000,000.

---

external debt was $13 billion. Foreign investment remained comparatively low.

Foreign Affairs. Bulgaria was spared serious social and ethnic tensions common throughout the Balkans. However, the continuing recession, growing economic disparity between rich and poor, and regional unemployment aggravated the position of some minorities. In southern Bulgaria, Turks, Pomaks (Muslim Slavs), and Roma (Gypsies) especially were affected by economic decline amid charges of racial discrimination in employment and housing. In addition, ethnic-based parties remained constitutionally prohibited, although minority rights were strengthened. The activities of extreme nationalist groups waned somewhat as the BSP distanced itself from xenophobic organizations to boost its popularity and entered into an informal coalition with the MRF.

Concerns lingered that the Yugoslav conflict would spill into the neighboring republic of Macedonia, whose Slavic population has historical connections to the Bulgarian nation. Suspicions persisted that a destabilized Macedonia would raise nationalist and expansionist demands within Bulgaria. To counter any potential Balkan conflict, Sofia pursued cooperative relations with two key neighbors—Turkey and Greece—by signing security agreements and pursuing economic opportunities. In June, Bulgaria assumed leadership of the Foreign Ministers Council of the Black Sea Economic Cooperation for six months. The country also obtained an association agreement with the European Community (EC), providing for a gradual opening of markets and financial and technical assistance. The government unsuccessfully sought compensation for losses incurred from maintaining an embargo on rump Yugoslavia, estimated at nearly $1 billion since sanctions were imposed in mid-1992.

JANUSZ BUGAJSKI
Center for Strategic and International Studies

BURMA. *See* MYANMAR.

BUSINESS AND CORPORATE AFFAIRS

More sharply than in any recent year, 1993 events in the world of business defined the emerging performance standards of executives and the companies they led. The demand for a higher level of achievement came from shareholders, directors, customers, and technological growth that could change markets with a single new product. And, as in the 1980s, the growing numbers of foreign companies in the global arena of business also added to the pressures to improve performance.

The misfortunes of the International Business Machines Corporation (IBM) exemplified the changing corporate scene. Although it had eliminated about 100,000 jobs since 1985, the big computer maker began another downsizing early in the year after announcing a 1992 loss of $4.97 billion. In reaction to this, the largest fiscal-year blot of red ink in U.S. corporate history, IBM stock fell to less than $50 per share; this left the company with a total market value of less than $27 billion—less even than that of Microsoft Corporation, a software company it once had nurtured. Founded in 1975 by Bill Gates, then in his early 20s, Microsoft was only a fraction of IBM's size in terms of sales, but investors valued it and its products as entrees to the future. Software, components, and chips to run computers, rather than the production of brand-name computers, were seen as the industry's future. (*See* SPECIAL REPORT, page 160.)

Changes at the Top. After an unpleasant board meeting, John Akers resigned as IBM chairman and was replaced by Louis Gerstner, who left the chairmanship of R.J.R. Nabisco. It was the first of many top executive changes during the year. In short order, Paul Lego, Westinghouse Electric chairman, and James Robinson III, chairman of American Express, were out of work. John Sculley left the chairmanship of Apple Computer for a similar job with Spectrum Information Technologies, a small but growing company where he would receive a multimillion-dollar salary and option package. Kay Whitmore was replaced as chairman of Eastman Kodak by George Fisher, who shocked the business world by leaving the top job at Motorola, where he had accomplished a highly successful modernization. Change at the top was seldom routine, as in the case of Harold Polling, who retired and was replaced as chairman of Ford Motor by the promotion of Alexander Trotman.

Structural Changes. Change was not restricted to top executives. Mass job terminations were announced weekly as companies—unable to raise prices because of fierce competition or because they were caught in defense cutbacks—sought to eliminate expenses and raise productivity. Plants were closed and work was consolidated at other sites. Some large companies divested themselves of entire divisions. For example, Eastman Kodak made plans to remove itself from the chemical business, in which it had been a major operative for many years.

Mergers and Acquisitions. In contrast to downsizings, merger and takeover activity produced some of the biggest news—and rumors as well—of the year, especially among companies seen as links in the so-called information highway. Almost any company successfully involved in information creation, gathering, transmission, or reception was viewed by Wall Street as a potential acquirer or acquiree.

In June, MCI Communications, a long-distance carrier, sold 20% of its stock to British Telecommunications for $4.3 billion, and the New York Times Company purchased the *Boston Globe* for $1.1 billion—the highest price ever paid for a newspaper property. In August, AT&T said it would acquire McCaw Cellular Communications, the nation's largest cellular-telephone company, for $12.6 billion. Almost simultaneously, QVC Shopping Network, headed by Barry Diller, who only recently had left media magnate Rupert Murdoch's 20th Century Fox, a motion-picture producer, offered multibillions for Home Shopping Network. He dropped that effort, and then vied with Viacom Incorporated chairman Sumner Redstone for the right to acquire Paramount Communications. With bidding nearing $10 billion, the victor remained in doubt as the year ended. And, though it was being pursued itself, Paramount, the parent company of Simon & Schuster, bought Macmillan, Ltd., a major book publisher. The $553 million deal was expected to be completed in 1994 and would create the world's second-largest book publisher after Germany's Bertelsmann A.G.

Meanwhile, Bell Atlantic Telephone acquired Tele-Communications, the nation's largest cable company, and Liberty Media, its programming affiliate, in a $21.4 billion deal—the biggest ever. Joining the fray, Turner Broadcasting bought two successful Hollywood companies—New Line Cinema and Castle Rock Entertainment—for $600 million. Two giant toy manufacturers merged when Mattel purchased Fisher Price in a stock swap valued at about $1 billion. And Sears Roebuck & Company continued to return to its core business of retailing when it sold Coldwell Banker Residential Group in a leveraged buyout by senior management and a private investment group.

The Balance Sheet. While such deals produced front-page headlines, companies large and small saw results from their intense efforts to cut costs and improve productivity. Profits were surprisingly high for many companies, and the surprise continued throughout the year. Third-quarter results for the component companies of the Standard & Poor's 500-stock index were estimated to be at least 20% higher than in the similar period a year earlier. Between 60% and 70% of

John C. Malone (at podium) and Raymond W. Smith (near left)— the chief executive officers of Tele-Communications Inc. and Bell Atlantic, respectively—outlined plans for the merger of their companies in mid-October 1993.

© Glifford/Gamma-Liaison

companies reported improvements, and results from 17 of 25 industry groups showed similar results. Financial-company profits of $3.9 billion were 84% higher, as banks benefited from low interest-rate margins and strong trading profits.

Results were especially impressive for U.S. automotive companies. Car and small-truck sales ran at a rate of 14 million units for the first half of the year. The quickening pace showed up immediately in profits. After losing $13 billion in 1992, each of the Big Three—General Motors, Ford, and Chrysler—reported profits of more than $500 million in the first quarter alone. And the good news continued. In the third quarter, industry profits totaled $1.8 billion, compared with a loss of $1.4 billion in the like period a year earlier. (*See also* AUTOMOBILES.)

The fortunes of airlines also seemed to improve, but the industry remained troubled. After losing nearly $1 billion in 1992, American Airlines turned profitable for two quarters but then was closed by a five-day pre-Thanksgiving strike that, said its chairman, cost $10 million per day. Urged by President Bill Clinton, the company agreed to arbitrate its dispute with attendants. Simply to stay in business, Northwest Airlines gave unions a financial interest and a voice in management in return for $1 billion in concessions.

The scene was nearly as glum in the still highly profitable pharmaceutical industry, in part because President Clinton's proposed health-care plan would restrain prices, and partly because of criticism—much of it from the administration—that high prices denied benefits to many people. In contrast, the securities business enjoyed record-high trading activity, and the gambling industry grew more swiftly than any other, largely because of new casinos on Indian lands. (*See* GAMBLING.)

Aircraft manufacturers strained to make the transition to peacetime pursuits. Boeing won close to $3 billion in orders from United Parcel Service, but Lockheed and McDonnell Douglas still were competing for foreign military orders late in the year. Small-business sentiment was mixed: While companies developed niches in technology and health care, surveys by the National Association of Independent Business showed that members were concerned deeply about taxes and regulations—more so even than about competition, worker quality, and wages.

Crime and Fraud News. Much news reflected poorly on business. Prudential agreed to pay $371 million to settle charges that it had defrauded investors in $8 billion of partnership deals in the 1980s. And in Florida and Texas, Metropolitan Life was being investigated for allegedly misrepresenting insurance products. The $20 billion fraud involving Bank of Credit and Commerce International continued in the news; Clark Clifford, chairman of First Washington Bank, was deemed too ill for trial and charges against him later were dropped. Clifford's protégé, Robert Altman, was cleared of eight felony charges, but more criminal and civil suits lay ahead. The underfunding of corporate pension plans worsened; late in the year the Pension Benefit Guaranty Corporation said obligations of the 50 most underfunded private plans exceeded assets by $38.5 billion at the end of 1992, a $9 billion rise in one year.

Some events were embarrassing: NBC was caught doctoring tests that made GM pickup trucks appear to be fire-prone. Some events were odd, as in the spate of unfounded claims that objects were found inside Pepsi Cola cans. Some events were tragic, such as the intrafamily battle between Herbert Haft, 72, and his wife and son over control of assets within the huge Dart Group, a conglomerate he and his wife founded.

JOHN CUNNIFF
The Associated Press

The IBM Story

On Jan. 26, 1993, the board of directors of the International Business Machines Corporation (better known as IBM) announced that it was starting a search to replace Chairman John F. Akers. His demise—he became the first chief executive to be pushed out before retirement in IBM's 80-year history—was a sign of how far things had deteriorated at a company that only a few years earlier had been renowned as a model of management excellence and a standard-bearer of U.S. technological prowess. IBM's decline seemed to be a magnified example of some of the key trends in U.S. business—the failure of large corporations to compete, the relentless workforce shrinkage that is called "downsizing," the willingness of big institutional shareholders to push for change at lagging companies, and the new activism in corporate boardrooms as chief executives no longer can take the support of directors for granted.

Only a month earlier, after announcing that IBM would cut its workforce by a further 25,000 people, reduce its research-and-development spending by $1 billion, and suffer another year of multibillion-dollar losses, Akers had given a spirited defense of his stewardship of the world's largest computer company. Although admitting that the company's transformation was difficult and painful, he insisted that the course was the right one and he planned to stay at the helm. "The IBM board supports this management," Akers said. "The board supports me. And I do not plan to step aside." Yet, by the next month, the board obviously had other plans for the company's future.

IBM's problems, to be sure, had been evident for years. Primarily, the company had failed to see during the 1980s the rapid shift in computing away from big mainframe machines and toward workstations and desktop personal computers based on the low-cost microprocessor—the computer-on-a-chip that serves as the electronic brain of the smaller machines. Even when IBM did recognize the shift to microprocessor technology, it proved incapable of adjusting quickly enough to the new business model of faster-moving markets and leaner operations. It was IBM's inability to get ahead of the game and its being reduced to seemingly endless rounds of cutbacks and losses, year after year, that finally prompted some changes. And 1993 was the year the board, led by James E. Burke—an outside director and retired chairman of Johnson & Johnson—took action with its ouster of Akers.

The January announcement by IBM that it would look for a new chief executive set off the most closely followed, widely handicapped executive search in the history of corporate America. Burke and a few other IBM outside directors did much of the spadework themselves, using the search as a vehicle for reeducating themselves about the computer business. They met with leading industry executives who had no interest in taking over at IBM, like Andrew Grove of the Intel Corporation, the top chip maker; and Bill Gates of the Microsoft Corporation, the dominant software producer. But they spoke more seriously with candidates who at least flirted with the idea of joining the company, including John Sculley of Apple Computer, Lawrence Bossidy of Allied-Signal, John Young of Hewlett-Packard, and George Fisher of Motorola.

A New Era. The board eventually chose an outsider to the computer industry who was, however, a proven manager: Louis V. Gerstner, Jr. (*See* accompanying sidebar.) Burke, the director who led the two-month search, insisted that Gerstner had been the board's first choice all along, though some accounts disputed that. Still, Gerstner was always one of the front-runners and, in the end, was the person who ended up inheriting the challenges and the choices facing the company. After joining IBM in April, Gerstner spent a few months traveling the globe and meeting with IBM customers, rivals, and employees. He also brought in some key outsiders as part of his inner circle, including Jerome York of the Chrysler Corporation, who became IBM's chief financial officer; and Gerald Czarnecki, a former banker and turnaround specialist, who became senior vice-president for personnel.

Some analysts expected Gerstner, a sharp financial manager, to sell off parts of IBM as a quick way to give shareholders more cash. Yet that option was rejected early on. At the company's annual meeting in Tampa, FL, on April 26, the new chairman told a questioner that one does not fix a big, high-tech company like IBM by simply "throwing a fragmentation grenade into it."

The first big move came on July 27, when IBM reported its financial results for the second quarter of 1993. Gerstner announced an $8.9 billion program to cut the company's costs sharply, trimming the payroll by another 35,000 people and getting rid of factories and equipment. The huge charge against profits included the cost of payments to 50,000 workers who had taken advantage of a generous worker-buyout program announced before the change in leadership. Most of the new round of 35,000 cuts were to be in Europe and Asia, and would be done gradually, to be completed by the end of 1994. The U.S. and Canada operations had borne the brunt of earlier job-reduction programs.

With the new round of cutbacks, the IBM worldwide workforce would be 225,000 by the end of 1994, down from a peak of 407,000 in April 1986. To conserve cash, the dividend payment for shareholders was reduced for the second time in 1993; these were the only dividend cuts in the company's history. With the big second-quarter deficit, IBM's losses since 1991 totaled $16 billion.

The cost-cutting drive was applauded on Wall Street as a constructive first step, but analysts and other computer executives noted that the larger challenge was to lay out an overall strategy, or vision, for the company. Gerstner's reply was that the immediate task at hand was to get costs under control. "The last thing IBM needs right now is a vision," he said. "What it needs are tough-minded, market-driven strategies in each of its businesses." Later, he elaborated by saying that a company with $60 billion in yearly revenues does not have a problem selling its products and services. The real problem, he repeated, was controlling costs.

The Future. In the two weeks after IBM reported its huge loss for the second quarter to cover the costs of further streamlining, Gerstner expressed his confidence in the company's future with his own money: He bought more than $700,000 worth of IBM stock at prices ranging from $42 to $45 per share, less than half the price of IBM shares a year earlier.

There were some hopeful signs for the beleaguered company. IBM's personal-computer business, which lost an estimated $1 billion in 1992, turned around with a vengeance in 1993, regaining sales lost to smaller, more nimble rivals and returning to profitability. Accordingly, IBM introduced a new family of personal computers in the fall. The new line is intended for the home market and is equipped with features ranging from ultra-fast chips to CD-ROM players. In an alliance with Motorola and Apple, IBM also had developed its own microprocessor, the Power PC chip, which promised to provide competition for the industry leader, Intel. And the Power PC project, based in Austin, TX, would develop a family of chips that IBM intended to use in everything from handheld computers to the next-generation replacements for mainframes.

For the future, Gerstner spoke in 1993 of making IBM the "premier solution-provider to our customers," offering hardware, software, and services. IBM's technology, he said, was second to none. There are advantages to being a big company, if it is run properly. And IBM would have to run fast if it were to make up for the decline of its traditional business. From 1990 to 1993, IBM's sales of hardware—the machines from mainframes to laptops—had declined from $44 billion to $29 billion, Salomon Brothers Incorporated estimated. The biggest falloff by far was in the sales of mainframe computers. Like Akers before

© Nick Maiman/Sygma

LOUIS V. GERSTNER, JR.

Louis V. Gerstner, Jr., 51 years old, formerly served as a consultant at McKinsey & Company and as president of the American Express Company. He came to IBM from RJR Nabisco Holdings Corporation, where he was chairman and chief executive officer. The Dartmouth- and Harvard-educated Gerstner would be well-paid for his labors at IBM: he was to receive a 1993 salary of $2 million, plus an annual incentive bonus of $1.5 million linked to the company's performance; options on 500,000 IBM shares; and a payment of $5 million to compensate him for the income and benefits he left at RJR Nabisco.

Born on March 1, 1942, in New York City, Gerstner is married and is the father of a daughter and a son. The Gerstners reside in Greenwich, CT. He also has served as a member of the board of the New York Times Company.

him, Gerstner was counting mainly on growth in software and services to make up for lost hardware sales; however, thus far it was not enough for a turnaround.

Whether Gerstner could succeed in reviving IBM would not be known for a few years at least. A couple of profitable financial quarters as cost-cutting measures take effect would not be sufficient proof of recovery. Both in terms of technology and business strategy, IBM needed a new basis for sustained profitability and continued growth, one that was not yet evident.

Like its decline, IBM's efforts to bounce back would be watched closely, because the challenge it was facing—how to retool a big, traditional company to become successful in an era of fast-changing technology—was the same one confronting large corporations worldwide.

See also COMPUTERS.

STEVE LOHR

CALIFORNIA

The slowness of California's economy to rally from the recession dominated state concerns in 1993. School-reform efforts, immigration issues, and disastrous brush fires also made news.

The Economy. Late in 1993, California's unemployment rate remained the highest among the industrial states; experts expected a slow recovery because of cutbacks by government and military contractors, continuing layoffs resulting from a merger of the state's two largest banks, and the continuing influx of would-be workers from other states and abroad.

The legislature responded to calls for improving the business climate and creating jobs by authorizing valuable tax credits for industry even as state revenues were declining. It also provided aid for some home buyers and simplified the environmental-review process.

Population. Despite the laying off of thousands of defense-plant workers—some of whom left the state—and the exodus of others after 1992's Los Angeles riots, by Sept. 30, 1993, the state's population reached 31.5 million. A total of 237,492 persons immigrated legally into the state, a 23% increase from 1992; more than half came from Asia. In addition, at least 100,000 illegal immigrants arrived. All but about 6% of the total went to urban areas. Anxieties about new arrivals relying on welfare or displacing other workers caused some politicians to urge federal laws to limit immigration, especially illegal immigration. But many experts saw the immigration as healthy for the economy.

Government and Budget. California voters continued to doubt the effectiveness of government. Six of seven statewide ballot propositions were defeated. The public's deep concern with urban violence was reflected by the fact that the only proposition to pass would make a temporary .5% sales-tax increase permanent because it was pledged to promote police and fire protection.

The other propositions involved schools, low-cost housing, and a change in budget rules. Although Republican Gov. Pete Wilson's popularity dropped throughout the year, Republicans made small gains in elections to fill legislative vacancies.

In contrast to 1992's record 63-day impasse between governor and legislature, the 1993 budget was signed before the start of the new fiscal year—the first time this had been done since 1986. The governor item-vetoed 2.25% from the conference-committee agreement. Balance was achieved only by taking $2.6 billion from local governments—already strapped for funds—and giving this amount to schools, and by rolling over some of the previous year's state debt. The $52.1 billion budget reflected an absolute reduction for the second straight year. Amounts for every major function were reduced except for prisons and schools. However, schools would not be compensated for enrollment increases. Welfare grants would be cut, community-college and state-university fees would be increased, and renters would lose their tax credit.

Education. In recent years, California school enrollment had been expanding without an equivalent increase in appropriations per child. Perhaps more importantly, reform efforts had not helped raise the state's education rating to the high position it once had held. In 1993, over the objections of the California Teachers Association, the legislature followed Minnesota in allowing up to 100 schools to operate as "charter" schools: they would be free to plan their own programs and would be exempt from the state education code.

In statewide voting, a proposal to require a simple majority instead of a two-thirds vote for school-bond elections was defeated. The much-publicized plan for California to provide vouchers which could be used to pay about one half the cost of attending private schools was defeated soundly, 70% to 30%. Once voters learned there was no benefit for public schools and that taxpayers' costs would increase, the proposal was doomed. It lacked mainstream support and was opposed by public-school personnel.

Workers' Compensation. After years of conflict among the interests involved and with a compromise between governor and legislature, a series of bills was enacted to reform the state code on workers-compensation insurance. The most controversial and heavily lobbied part of the package deregulated rates and divided large and small insurance firms, with the former goal successful.

Fires. With the six-year drought finally ended, California's reservoirs again were full, but the greater growth of flora justified fears of brush fires. At least 26 such blazes challenged southern California firefighters during the year. Perhaps 19 were cases of arson, including the two most destructive—at Laguna Beach and Calabasas-Malibu. The latter fire took the lives of three area residents.

CHARLES R. ADRIAN
University of California, Riverside

CALIFORNIA • Information Highlights

Area: 158,706 sq mi (411 049 km²).

Population (Sept. 1993 est.): 31,500,000.

Chief Cities (1990 census): Sacramento, the capital, 369,365; Los Angeles, 3,485,398; San Diego, 1,110,549; San Jose, 782,248; San Francisco, 723,959; Long Beach, 429,433; Oakland, 372,242.

Government (1993): *Chief Officers*—governor, Pete Wilson (R); lt. gov., Leo T. McCarthy (D). *Legislature*—Senate, 40 members; Assembly, 80 members.

State Finances (fiscal year 1991): *Revenue*, $90,784,000,000; *expenditure*, $85,640,000,000.

Personal Income (1992): $662,786,000,000; per capita, $21,472.

Labor Force (August 1993): *Civilian labor force*, 15,186,200; *unemployed*, 1,371,700 (9.0% of total force).

Education: *Enrollment* (fall 1991)—public elementary schools, 3,720,302; public secondary, 1,386,843; colleges and universities, 2,024,274. *Public school expenditures* (1990-91), $22,748,218,000.

CAMBODIA

In 1993 the United Nations (UN) left Cambodia after completing an ambitious peacekeeping mission. It ended a 24-year civil war, disarmed troops, repatriated hundreds of thousands of refugees, and supervised a free election which led to the formation of a new government.

Politics. Under an international agreement signed in 1991, elections for a constituent assembly were held in May 1993, with hundreds of international observers risking their lives to monitor the polls. In their first free elections since the 1960s, the Cambodian people gave Prince Norodom Ranariddh's royalist Funcinpec Party 45% of the vote. He defeated Hun Sen's Cambodian People's Party, which had ruled Cambodia since it was installed by the Vietnamese army in 1979. Ranariddh and Hun Sen formed a coalition government led by Ranariddh.

The Maoist Khmer Rouge boycotted the election and tried to disrupt it by kidnapping and murdering election workers and threatening violence against anyone who voted. It also tried to build popular support by accusing the Vietnamese minority in Cambodia of being a subversive element and massacring innocent Vietnamese civilians. Yet by year's end the Khmer Rouge was in disarray, with many of its officers and peasant soldiers defecting to the government.

Prince Ranariddh benefited from the popularity of his father, Norodom Sihanouk, who first was crowned king in 1941. He later abdicated the throne but continued to head the government until ousted in a 1970 coup. He became a figurehead leader of the Khmer Rouge, and later its chief opponent. In a September 24 ceremony in the royal palace, Sihanouk was sworn in as constitutional monarch. Immediately after becoming king, Sihanouk named Prince Norodom Ranariddh as first prime minister and Hun Sen as second prime minister. He also ratified a new constitution, which had been approved by the 120-member National Assembly. In a letter to King Sihanouk the United States recognized the new government immediately and said that it wished to establish diplomatic relations promptly.

Although Prince Ranariddh seemed to lack his father's charisma, he was one of the most respected members of the royal family. He taught political science before moving to the Thai border in the early 1980s to build and lead a royalist guerrilla movement against Hun Sen's Vietnamese-backed regime in Phnom Penh.

Ranariddh's half brother, Prince Norodom Chakrapong, led a brigade in Ranariddh's army until 1991, when he defected to Hun Sen's regime. He then gained control of the ministries of aviation, tourism, industry, and communications. In the 1993 election he tried to defeat Ranariddh by attacking his supporters with his private army and refusing to let Ranariddh fly into Phnom Penh airport. After Ranariddh won

---

CAMBODIA • Information Highlights

Official Name: Cambodia.
Location: Southeast Asia.
Area: 69,900 sq mi (181 040 km²).
Population (mid-1993 est.): 9,000,000.
Chief City (1991 est.): Phnom Penh, the capital, 900,000.
Government: *Head of state*, Norodom Sihanouk, king (acceded Sept. 24, 1993); *Heads of government*, Prince Norodom Ranariddh, first premier (named Sept. 24, 1993); Hun Sen, second premier (named Sept. 24, 1993). *Legislature*—National Assembly.

---

the election, Chakrapong briefly declared himself ruler of a seven-province secessionist state, but the revolt collapsed from firm resistance by Ranariddh and most foreign powers. The armies of Hun Sen and Ranariddh then joined forces to attack the Khmer Rouge and reduce the section of the country under its control.

Economics. The Hun Sen regime that ruled Cambodia from 1979 to 1993 repaired some of the havoc caused by three years of Khmer Rouge rule (1975-78). Roads and railroads were rebuilt, but they often were destroyed again by the Khmer Rouge. Rice production and factory output rose gradually during the 1980s. But by 1993, the economy had not yet reached the modest level of prosperity achieved before Sihanouk was overthrown in 1970.

The UN mission in Cambodia cost $2 billion-$3 billion, mostly to support an army of 20,000 soldiers and civilian administrators. They laid a fragile foundation for economic recovery by enforcing a truce, removing land mines, and supervising the election. Once those tasks were complete, the UN mission ended, leaving the task of economic reconstruction to the new government.

Foreign Affairs. Major power rivalries, which bedeviled Cambodia in the past, largely had been replaced by an internal factional struggle among Ranariddh, Hun Sen, and the Khmer Rouge. Their ability to work together—or at least to prevent another civil war—would be needed to attract badly needed foreign investment.

Cambodia's neighbors appeared more likely to make trouble for the new Khmer government. Vietnam backed Hun Sen, while Thailand supported the Khmer Rouge. Early in 1993, Sihanouk accused Vietnam of moving border markers. He also tried to shame Thai leaders by implying they were too weak to prevent Thai generals from supporting the Khmer Rouge. Although he was in failing health, Sihanouk's diplomatic skills seemed necessary to deal with these difficult neighbors.

In February 1993, France's President François Mitterrand became the first French leader since Charles de Gaulle in 1966 to visit Cambodia, a former French colony. President Mitterrand urged all Cambodians to honor the UN-supervised peace process.

PETER A. POOLE
Author, "Eight Presidents and Indochina"

CANADA

For most Canadians, it was another year of recession, vanishing jobs, and shrinking prospects. It was a year of three prime ministers: Brian Mulroney, Kim Campbell, and Jean Chrétien. It was a year when the same people who had defeated the 1992 constitutional referendum demolished two of the three national parties and altered Canadian politics forever. The year 1993 was one to remember.

Political Economics. In an election year, the government desperately needed better times and the experts apparently obliged. On January 21 at 9 A.M., Statistics Canada officially announced that Canada's recession was over. Few believed it. Housing starts fell by 20%, mortgage interest rates fell below 6%, and—in a sign of bad times—Calgary's Palliser Hotel canceled its annual but expensive Range Men's Dinner. Corporate giants also continued to stumble. The once-solid Edper Group had to sell Macmillan-Bloedel Ltd. of Vancouver and the brewing giant, John Labatt. Its Royal Trust stumbled into the protection of the separately owned Royal Bank, and Bramalea needed creditor protection.

Molson's Breweries, one of Canada's oldest companies, fell under the control of Miller Brewing of Milwaukee. Claude Castonguay's Laurentian Group, once a proud symbol of Quebec's mastery of business, collapsed into the Desjardins group of credit unions. Similar debt loads undermined Bertin Nadeau's Unigesco; its best-known companies, Provigo and Loeb, were taken over by Quebec's Caisse des dépôts. Other major failures undermined Quebec's corporate self-confidence and its credit rating.

The year's most spectacular corporate battle was between Canada's two big debt-loaded airlines. Owners of Canadian Airlines International (CAI) sought survival in a deal with the owners of American Airlines; Air Canada, once crown-owned, tried to force a merger. CAI's 6,000 staff members, veterans of the merger of six former airlines, fought for their young company (and their jobs) by cutting their wages to buy shares.

Economics and Environment. A country in deep economic difficulties discovered that it was up against the limits of hitherto dependable sources of natural wealth. Newfoundland, entering the second year of a two-year moratorium on fishing the northern cod, learned that the disastrous depletion of stocks continued. Was it abnormally cold water, an uncontrolled seal population, or continued overfishing by foreign fleets outside Canada's 200-mi (370-km) limit that caused the depletion? Fishing communities had no doubt which answer they wanted. There was violence in outport towns when government officials enforced the ban. At Shelburne, N.S., local fishermen blockaded a Russian ship delivering fish to a local packing plant until the fisheries department agreed to their terms.

Newfoundland not only was robbed of most of its historic staple industry—with one in five out of work—but its dream of an oil-rich future was shaken when Gulf Canada pulled out of the C$5.2 billion Hibernia offshore-oil development. With offshore oil to cost at least $35 per barrel and world prices at $25, only the government would continue the project. Another project driven by the hope of investment and jobs was the "fixed link," an 11-mi (18-km) causeway and bridge between the provinces of Prince Edward Island and New Brunswick.

Canada's Liberal Party leader Jean Chrétien and his wife Aline greeted supporters following the party's overwhelming victory in the Oct. 25, 1993, elections. The 59-year-old Quebecer took office as Canada's 20th prime minister on November 4.

© Bayne Stanley/First Light

Members of "Protectors of Mother Earth" protest the April 1993 decision of the provincial government of British Columbia to permit additional logging in an old-growth forest around Clayoquot Sound on the western side of Vancouver Island.

Yet economics could drive British Columbia—Canada's richest province—to an environmentally unpopular policy, too. Its New Democratic Party (NDP) government inherited a C$9.5 billion forest industry that had ravaged the province's woods but which also was its biggest source of jobs and exports. After an anxious search for a compromise between loggers and environmentalists, NDP ministers announced that, subject to safeguards, Macmillan Bloedel could log part of the old-growth rain forest of Clayoquot Sound. Environmentalists were outraged. After supporting them in earlier fights for the Stein Valley, Carmanah Valley, and South Moresby, the NDP had betrayed them. Greenpeace, the Sierra Club, the Western Canadian Wilderness Committee, and other groups mobilized behind the Friends of Clayoquot Sound. Throughout the summer, the Vancouver Island towns of Tofino and Ucluelet rang with protests, roadblocks, injunctions, and mass arrests, which were interrupted occasionally by rallies of loggers.

Environment, economics, and health affected government revenue. Canada's smokers—made defiant by health warnings, no-smoking areas, and ostracism—felt little compunction in avoiding taxes that raised prices 690%. Federal attempts to tax cigarettes leaving Canada backfired when manufacturers threatened to move production (and jobs) to the United States. However, almost all the exports returned as contraband, often through Indian reserves where

natives were immune from cross-border duties. Akwasasne, a Six Nations reserve straddling New York, Ontario, and Quebec, was a center of the traffic where rival gangs battled, huge fortunes were rumored, and federal and provincial police seemed helpless.

Labor and Jobless Recovery. While statisticians claimed that the economy was improving, unemployment grew to 1.55 million in June—10.5% of the workforce. Many of the unemployed were highly skilled. It was, experts added,

---

CANADA • Information Highlights

Official Name: Canada.
Location: Northern North America.
Area: 3,851,792 sq mi (9 976 140 km²).
Population (mid-1993 est.): 28,100,000.
Chief Cities (1991 census): Ottawa, the capital, 920,857; Toronto, 3,893,046; Montreal, 3,127,242.
Government: *Head of state,* Elizabeth II, queen; represented by Ramon Hnatyshyn, governor-general (took office January 1990). *Head of government,* Jean Chrétien, prime minister (took office Nov. 4, 1993). *Legislature*—Parliament: Senate and House of Commons.
Monetary Unit: Canadian dollar (1.3064 dollars equal U.S.$1, Nov. 10, 1993).
Gross Domestic Product (2d quarter 1993 est., C$): $709,248,000,000.
Economic Index: *Consumer Prices* (1992, 1980 = 100), all items, 189.3; food, 168.7.
Foreign Trade (1992 U.S.$): *Imports,* $122,477,000,000; *exports,* $134,223,000,000.

THE CANADIAN MINISTRY

Jean Chrétien, prime minister
David Anderson, minister of national revenue
Lloyd Axworthy, minister of human resources development and minister of Western economic diversification
Ethel Blondin-Andrew, secretary of state for training and youth
Raymond Chan, secretary of state for Asia-Pacific
David Michael Collenette, minister of national defense and minister of veterans affairs
Sheila Copps, deputy prime minister and minister of the environment
André Cuellet, minister of foreign affairs
David Charles Dingwall, minister of public works and government services and minister for the Atlantic Canada Opportunities Agency
Michel Dupuy, minister of Canadian heritage
Arthur C. Eggleton, president of the Treasury Board and minister responsible for infrastructure
Joyce Fairbairn, leader of the government in the Senate and minister with special responsibility for literacy
Sheila Finestone, secretary of state for multiculturalism and the status of women
Jon Gerrard, secretary of state for science and research and development
Ralph E. Goodale, minister of agriculture and agri-food
Herbert Eser Gray, solicitor general of Canada and leader of the government in the House of Commons
Ron Irwin, minister of Indian affairs and northern development
Lawrence MacAulay, secretary of state for veterans
Roy MacLaren, minister for international trade
John Manley, minister of industry
Sergio Marchi, minister of citizenship and immigration
Diane Marleau, minister of health
Paul Martin, minister of finance and minister responsible for the Federal Office of Regional Development—Quebec
Marcel Massé, president of the Queen's Privy Council for Canada, minister of intergovernmental affairs and minister responsible for public service renewal
Anne McLellan, minister of natural resources
Douglas Peters, secretary of state for international financial institutions
Ferdinand Robichaud, secretary of state for parliamentary affairs
Allan Rock, minister of justice and attorney general of Canada
Christine Stewart, secretary of state for Latin America and Africa
Brian Tobin, minister of fisheries and oceans
Douglas Young, minister of transport

"a jobless recovery." Headlines reported mass layoffs, including in the vaunted high-tech industries. Job growth was in so-called "McJobs," the minimum-wage service sector. Fewer jobs at higher pay meant shrinking tax revenue and higher spending to support the unemployed and welfare cases. The federal government finally pushed through tough changes to Unemployment Insurance (UI). Workers who quit their jobs without just cause would be denied benefits. Under pressure, the government agreed that any woman who claimed that she had quit because of sexual harassment would have her case heard.

Plans to use more of UI for retraining were complicated because provinces had constitutional control of education.

Ottawa also cut its financial transfers to provinces for health, higher education, and, for richer provinces, social welfare. Until 1989, Ottawa had funded half of Ontario's main welfare program; by 1993 its share was only 28%. Faced with a ballooning deficit, Ontario's NDP government slashed spending, raised taxes, and opened negotiations with 950,000 provincially funded employees—from police to professors—to give up C$3 billion in wages. Furious unions denounced the NDP for its proposed "social contract," though alternate threats and concessions persuaded most to accept a compromise by the August 1 deadline. Other provincial governments ignored collective bargaining and simply ordered enough unpaid holidays to meet their savings, but unions vowed vengeance on the NDP since it had been "their" party since 1961.

Foreign Policy. Like most U.S. unions, Canadian labor opposed the North American Free Trade Agreement (NAFTA) negotiated in 1992, but its views carried no weight with the Mulroney government or its business allies. Neither did those of other critics who worried about Mexico's environmental and human-rights record or insisted that fears of an exclusive European Community (EC) had been exaggerated. While some companies hoped to increase Canada's C$3.5 billion annual trade with the huge Mexican market or to benefit from cheaper labor, other supporters feared that staying out of NAFTA would encourage a U.S.-centered "hub and spoke" development of bilateral agreements between Washington and countries in the Western Hemisphere. With his own future in doubt, Mulroney ensured that Canada would be the first of the NAFTA partners to ratify the agreement, even without the side deals negotiated by the Bill Clinton administration. In summer negotiations, the government persuaded Washington not to use sanctions against Canada to enforce treaty provisions. Trade Minister Tom Hockin insisted that they merely would arm U.S. protectionists to harass Canadian exporters, as had happened repeatedly under the 1989 free-trade agreement.

As prime minister, Kim Campbell played a tougher role with Washington than had her predecessor. "It's a great day for Canada," she claimed when Canada won its arguments using sanctions to enforce NAFTA. At the Tokyo summit of major industrial nations, she exacted an apology from President Clinton for ignoring Ottawa when consulting allies about the June 26 bombing of Iraq. Campbell urged officials to prevent U.S. magazines from producing split runs in Canada—Canadian advertising but U.S. editorial material.

Defense. For the Canadian military forces, 1993 was a difficult year. Adm. John Anderson replaced Gen. John De Chastelain as chief of the

(Continued on page 170.)

Leadership and the Elections

By 1993, Canada's Progressive Conservative (PC) government led by Brian Mulroney had been in office for more than eight years. Reelected in 1988 with a mandate for its free-trade agreement with the United States, the government also imposed a 7% goods and services tax (GST); cut transfer payments to provinces; and struggled to find a constitutional formula to reconcile Quebec, natives, regions, and special interests. Having failed to broker a deal on constitutional reform with the ten premiers in 1990, the government spent two years building another package of constitutional compromises called the Charlottetown Accord. Despite backing from all ten premiers, four native organizations, and the three national parties, Canadians defied their leaders and defeated the plan on Oct. 26, 1992. Separatists led by Lucien Bouchard and Jacques Parizeau convinced most Quebecers that the accord was grossly inadequate; elsewhere, most Canadians agreed with Reform Party leader Preston Manning that the changes went too far. Outside Quebec, political leaders agreed that the issue of constitutional change had taken up too much of the national agenda. Quebecers desiring sovereignty insisted that Canada had muffed its last chance to keep the province in the Confederation.

A Change of Leader. Brian Mulroney began 1993 convinced that he could overcome his unpopularity as he had in 1988. On January 4 he shuffled ten of his ministers. Five retired. Among the changes was the appointment of the first woman defense minister, former Justice Minister Kim Campbell (*see* BIOGRAPHY).

Mulroney also heard appeals that he step down. The man who had electrified TV audiences in 1984 by denouncing Liberal patronage made 15 Senate appointments in four months. Those named ranged from party fund-raisers to a hotel manager who once had loaned him a luxury suite. Other Mulroney appointments included his wife's hairdresser. Mulroney delayed his departure from the leadership position to make sure that his despised party rival went first. On February 20, Joe Clark told a Calgary audience he was through with politics. On February 24, after a farewell tour to Washington and Europe and memorial dinners with his political and personal friends, Brian Mulroney made his announcement: He would resign in June.

Mulroney was the only Conservative leader in the 20th century to win two consecutive majorities. In that time, Mulroney had forced through free trade with the United States, slashed spending, and raised consumption taxes. He still faced

---

The need to take Quebec out of the Confederation was the campaign message of Lucien Bouchard, below left, the leader of the Bloc Québécois. In turn, the Liberal Party's Jean Chrétien, right, emphasized the importance of creating jobs.

© Pono Presse Int./Gamma-Liaison   © Mike Pinder/First Light

© Bayne Stanley/First Light

Discontented Canadians of all political persuasions were attracted to the Reform Party. Its leader, Preston Manning, above, promised to end the budget deficit in three years.

the same C$35 billion deficit he had inherited and a doubled national debt.

The Leadership Campaign. Insiders had expected powerful ministers to run for the Conservative leadership. One by one, however, they—Trade Minister Michael Wilson, 55; Finance Minister Donald Mazankowski, 57; External Affairs Minister Barbara McDougall, 55; and Health Minister Benoit Bouchard, 52—announced they were resigning, not running. Others sniffed the prospects, counted the cost of campaigning, and backed off. It seemed to be a cakewalk for Kim Campbell, 45, a brash star of Mulroney's second term, who had been elected to Parliament from Vancouver in 1988. As the new defense minister, she was holding her third portfolio in three years. With few Ottawa friends and liberal views on gay rights and abortion, Campbell should have been an outsider but by March 25, when she announced her candidacy for the party post, her bandwagon was jammed with hopeful Tories, including Perrin Beatty and Bernard Valcourt, who themselves might have been candidates. Conservative Quebec nationalists like Gilles Loiselle and Marcel Masse promised backing in return for continued decentralization. The media reveled in an attractive candidate with a sharp wit and the promise of a new, more inclusive style of politics.

The only alternative was Environment Minister Jean Charest, 34—bright, likable, perfectly bilingual but best remembered as a minister who had resigned after allegations of trying to influence a judge. Polls showed Campbell with 38% of Tory delegates and 68% on a second ballot; Charest had 5% backing. Three backbench members of Parliament (MPs) hardly registered. Then the race began. Ashamed to be uncritical, journalists dug

out details of Campbell's two failed marriages, her insensitive quips, and her participation in the right-wing politics of British Columbia. Critics complained of her drive to take credit. Her manager, Ross Reid, urged her to run a no-risk, low-profile campaign. As an underdog with nothing to lose, Jean Charest brought style and specifics to two televised leadership forums. When Campbell called opposition parties "enemies" of Canadians, her new politics looked nasty.

The Convention. By June 11, when Conservatives launched their convention in an Ottawa arena, Charest had become a popular favorite, with backing from former Prime Minister Joe Clark. Campbell had the money, organization, and precommitted delegates to win. Once on her bandwagon, early supporters dared not jump off; their careers depended on her victory. After soaring so high, Charest's performance in a June 12 leaders' debate lost some of its style. Other critics of the front-runner split among Alberta M.P. Jim Edwards—whose Western, right-wing backers hardly could stomach another Quebec leader—and backbench MPs Garth Turner and Patrick Boyer. On Sunday, June 13, the contest took only two ballots:

	1st Ballot	**2nd Ballot**
Kim Campbell	1,664 votes	1,817 votes
Jean Charest	1,369	1,630
Jim Edwards	307	
Garth Turner	76	
Patrick Boyer	53	

A New Broom. On June 25, Governor-General Ramon Hnatyshyn summoned Campbell to become Canada's 19th prime minister. Conservatives privately rejoiced that Mulroney was gone, but so was his easy fluency in French and his amazing ability to keep a quarrelsome party together.

Normally a preelection budget would have cheered up voters with tax cuts and new spending. Finance Minister Mazankowski had done his best in April. He avoided tax increases despite a C$9 billion shortfall in revenue, promised spending cuts that would come mostly in 1994, and insisted that the deficit from his C$159.6 billion budget would be only C$32.6 billion—C$2.9 billion lower than in 1992. Critics split, some denouncing the preoccupation with the deficit, others warning that International Monetary Fund (IMF) officials might land in Ottawa "like invading aliens" if Canada's C$630 billion debt was not cut.

In her leadership campaign, Campbell had insisted that a five-year deficit-cutting plan—without cutting to social programs or transfer payments to the provinces—was her top priority. As defense minister, she had defended the government's C$6 billion helicopter purchase; in midsummer she cut the order to 47, claiming a saving of C$1 billion. Insiders insisted that the

saving might be more like C$160 million, mostly after 2000. Opposition parties promptly declared there should be no helicopters at all.

The Pre-Election. By midsummer it was hard to believe that Jean Chrétien (*see* BIOGRA-PHY) ever would be prime minister. Starting with a daylong swing across Canada on July 1, Canada's national holiday, Kim Campbell spent the summer of 1993 practicing her promised "politics of inclusion." She danced the twist in Toronto, opened the Highland Games, and went to Quebec City to hand over the management of manpower retraining. In a major speech she promised to tighten up the pensions of MPs, allow more free votes, and force lobbyists to report their political connections. By August, Campbell's popularity dragged Tory support to near parity with the Liberals. Even Liberals privately dismissed their leader Chrétien as "yesterday's man." Other polls convinced them that Canadians were much more concerned about the deficit than with Chrétien's priority: jobs.

Once launched, the 1993 election campaign was unlike any other. The voters' list, compiled for the 1992 referendum, was a year out of date. Millions who had moved during the year had the unusual chore of adding their names. With 23 parties active in the campaign, there was little room for outside lobbyists like the right-wing National Citizens' Coalition. The Progressive Conservatives, Liberals, and New Democrats had virtually full slates of candidates. Lucien Bouchard's Bloc Québécois (BCs) ran candidates only in Quebec; the Reform Party ran only outside Quebec. To the fury of smaller parties, only the five were accorded the status of the national parties by the broadcast media. Debates were held in French and English, with the comments of the unilingual Manning being translated simultaneously in the French-language session. The National Party, led by former Edmonton publisher Mel Hurtig, raged at its exclusion. Magician Doug Henning's Natural Law Party—which ran more than 200 candidates on behalf of transcendental meditation, yogic flying, and "heaven on earth"—took its exclusion more philosophically.

The New Democratic Party (NDP)—thanks to the fury provoked by its provincial counterparts and an uninspired program—plummeted steadily through the year from its usual 18% to a mere 7% when the election was called. The fortitude of party leader Audrey McLaughlin and her occasional eloquence on behalf of social-democratic values could not save her 43-member caucus from virtual annihilation. Equally evident was the dominance of Lucien Bouchard and the Bloc in Quebec. Conservatives, backed for two elections by nationalists, also faced annihilation. Only Jean Chrétien, despised by Quebec opinion leaders and hated by nationalists, could challenge the Bloc.

© Moe Doiron/Sygma

Kim Campbell, above, signs a copy of her biography. Although the leader of the Conservatives was judged a good campaigner, the electorate rejected her and her party at the polls.

In early September, racked with controversy and resentment of Manning's authoritarian style, the Reform Party seemed no stronger than the NDP. With the election call, support surged. Unhappy NDPers, Liberals, and Conservatives wanted a party that rejected the Trudeau-Mulroney legacy. Campbell's Western origins were irrelevant. On the deficit, Manning was even tougher: He would eliminate it in three years. Federal spending on Medicare and higher education would be spared, but the provinces would have the right to run health insurance their way, including user fees and private coverage. Audiences cheered promises of free votes on hanging and a federalism in which all provinces and citizens would be equal. They heard an ill-veiled reminder of past favors to Quebec, minorities, and immigrants. To show he was no bigot, Manning fired an overtly racist candidate in Toronto. Throughout the two-month campaign, the Reform Party aroused the only perceptible grassroots excitement.

Jean Chrétien was the other surprise. "Yesterday's man" had more style, skill, and staying power than his critics. Like Manning, Chrétien appealed to a better time with none of Reform's mean spirit or sacrifices. Media treated him generously, as though it were unfair to press him too hard. When Campbell claimed that a 45-day campaign was too short to discuss complex issues, she seemed arrogant; when Chrétien told reporters to wait for his ideas on how to replace the GST until he was prime minister, it seemed reasonable. The only memorable Liberal promise—C$6 billion for municipal infrastructure and job creation, only a third of it from Ottawa—hardly seemed enough for 1.6 million unemployed, but it was remembered chiefly because

Tories and Reformers thought it wildly extravagant. Bland and insubstantial, the Liberal campaign passed muster because no one seemed to expect more than a seldom-available "Red Book" and folksy reassurance.

Less popular than the Liberals, the PCs had the country's most acclaimed leader and huge funds. Almost immediately, Campbell slipped. Would she solve unemployment? No, said Campbell, it would take until 2000. It sounded candid and heartless. Despite a summer in office, Campbell's ministers had no program for deficit-cutting or reforming unemployment insurance. In the leaders' debate, the defining moment came when Lucien Bouchard demanded that Campbell tell him the size of the deficit. A furious prime minister refused. Next day, Garth Turner gave the number—C$35 billion—far higher than Mazankowski's prediction. The Conservative had bet everything on Campbell and she was irrelevant. From then on, only Chrétien, Manning, and Bouchard mattered.

The Outcome. On October 25, Liberals swept the tradition-bound, impoverished ridings of Atlantic Canada with their message of hope. Defecting NDPers and Conservatives gave them all but one of Ontario's 99 seats and most of Manitoba. Reform resisted the Liberal tide in Saskatchewan and overwhelmed Conservatives and New Democrats all the way to the Pacific. But each Western province contributed a handful of Liberal seats. As for Quebec, Jean Chrétien's St. Maurice was one of the few French-speaking ridings to resist the Bloc Québécois sweep.

Bouchard's 54 seats sufficed to give him the symbolic and practical advantages of becoming the leader of Her Majesty's Official Opposition in Parliament.

Though the NDP's Audrey McLaughlin saved her seat in the Yukon, winning only eight seats was short of the 12 the NDP needed for official party status in Parliament. No one had foreseen the same fate for the PCs. Voters cut the founding party of Confederation to a mere two seats, one of them held by Jean Charest.

CANADIAN GENERAL ELECTIONS
(preliminary)

Party	Seats			Votes (%)		
	1984	1988	1993	1984	1988	1993
PC	211	170	2	50	43	16
Lib	40	82	177	28	32	41
NDP	30	43	9	18	20	7
BQ	–	–	54	–	–	13
Ref	–	–	52	–	2	19
Other	1	–	1	4	3	4
TOTAL	282	295	295	100	100	100

Not for generations had so many seats—close to 70%—changed hands. What remained was for the Conservatives to name a new leader to succeed Campbell, who resigned in December, and retreat as gracefully as they could, for Jean Chrétien to appease as many of his newly elected followers as he could, and for the Bloc and Reform to exploit future opportunities.

DESMOND MORTON

defense staff. The general took over as Canada's new ambassador to Washington. The acerbic but popular Maj. Gen. Lewis MacKenzie, a hero of the UN's 1992 peacekeeping operations in Sarajevo, took early retirement. On July 30, Canadians hauled down their flag at their two North Atlantic Treaty Organization (NATO) bases in Germany and concluded Canadian Forces Europe after 30 years.

Short of forces for its UN commitment in Somalia, the defense department sent an airborne battalion, a unit with more fighting spirit than discipline. While most of the troops did well in the heat and dust of Belet Uen, the alleged torture and killing of a Somali intruder became a national scandal when Campbell's staff tried to cover it up. Four soldiers were accused of the crime, and the command officer ultimately was stripped of his command and charged with negligence. The media demanded to know what Campbell had known about the incident. Criticism was sharpened when a few soldiers in the Airborne were accused of associating with racists. Campbell also was tagged with another defense decision, the C$6 billion purchase of helicopters to equip new patrol frigates

and provide updated search-and-rescue service. Critics insisted that, with the Cold War over, the money could be spent better on day care or deficit reduction.

Justice and Life. If the election suggested that Canadians had moved to the political right, there was much to confirm the trend and a few 1993 events to justify it. Parliament created the new offense of criminal harassment to protect women from men who made their lives miserable. The possession of child pornography also was designated a crime, with the burden of proof on the accused to prove he or she had not committed the offense. Toronto women demanded that *Playboy* and *Penthouse* be removed from newsstands; their mere presence, they said, created a hostile environment. On the other hand, women who bared their breasts were acquitted of indecent exposure. Judge Katie McGowan declared that they met "community standards of tolerance." A federal panel of 13 women issued a C$10 million, 464-page report on violence against women.

See also articles on individual provinces.

DESMOND MORTON
Erindale College, University of Toronto

The Economy

After a strong start early in 1993, the Canadian economy lost momentum during the summer months but began to pick up speed again in September.

Early Indicators. The process of recovery had begun during the first half of the year when investment in business plant and equipment grew significantly and manufacturers began to build their stocks for the first time since the final quarter of 1989. In June output of crude oil and natural gas rose by 3.4%, while oil- and gas-drilling activity had soared 17% to a level 81% higher than in the fourth quarter of 1992.

The sale of big-ticket items showed improvement as consumer spending rose 0.5% during the second quarter and by 1.5% on a year-over-year basis. Manufacturers boosted their output in June by 0.2%, following two monthly declines, with 13 of 21 groups recording higher production. Services output grew 0.2% after increasing 0.3% in April and 0.1% in May. In July the seasonally adjusted value of building permits rebounded with a 9.5% increase to C$2.24 billion. All regions reported increases in the value of building permits, varying from 1.2% in the Prairie provinces to 22.1% in the Atlantic region.

Employment. Such upsurge in sector growth during the first half of 1993 caused part-time employment to grow by 121,000 jobs, while full-time jobs fell by 2,000. Overall the seasonally adjusted unemployment rate during the period averaged 11.3% as compared with 11.05% for the last half of 1992. By November the unemployment rate had fallen to 11.0%. The number of jobs increased by 0.5% in November after dropping in October.

In response to Canada's high unemployment, negotiated wage settlements were at a historic low in September and averaged less than 1% for the first nine months. Two thirds of the new wage agreements called for some type of wage freeze or rollback.

Dwindling Growth. Signs of dwindling economic growth emerged during the summer of 1993. In July, while construction activity was booming, output in transportation and equipment, primary metals, iron and steel, and mining fell by 3.5%, 2.9%, 4.8%, and 3.8%, respectively. Construction activity, due to poor performance by the nonresidential construction sector, slipped as seasonally adjusted value of building permits for August fell 3.1% to C$2.17 billion.

In foreign trade, monthly gains in exports became slow as August exports edged down to C$14.89 billion, following three consecutive months of higher sales of forestry and energy products. Between July and August imports rose by C$473 million to reach C$14.16 billion. Consequently, Canada's merchandise-trade surplus was cut substantially. However, exports, especially forestry products and industrial goods, rebounded in September. Imports also grew in September.

Higher August output of metals and transportation equipment could not counter weakness in residential construction, coal production, and oil- and gas-drilling activity. In addition there was widespread slack in the services sector, including government services, wholesale, transportation, and personal services. This was offset only in part by gains in insurance, finance, and real estate. Transportation and wholesale trade picked up in September.

Outlook. Overall the engine of Canadian economic growth registered a 3.6% increase in seasonally adjusted real gross domestic product (GDP) during the second quarter and 3.7% in the third. This compared favorably with the 1.9% growth rate experienced in all of 1992 and the 0.7% increase for 1991. Prospects for even greater growth in the final quarter of 1993 were considered good.

R. P. SETH
Mount Saint Vincent University

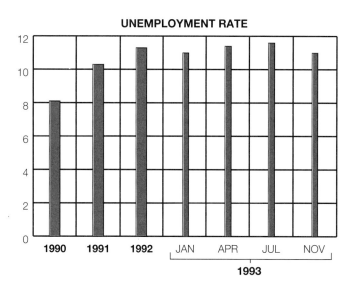

UNEMPLOYMENT RATE

1990 — 1991 — 1992 — JAN — APR — JUL — NOV
1993

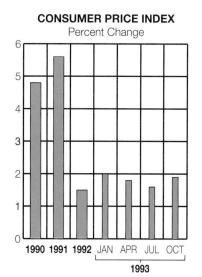

CONSUMER PRICE INDEX
Percent Change

1990 — 1991 — 1992 — JAN — APR — JUL — OCT
1993

In Toronto, The Princess of Wales Theatre—the first privately built hall for live theater to be constructed in Canada in nearly 90 years—opened in May 1993 with David Mirvish's C$12 million production of "Miss Saigon."

The Arts

Canada's art organizations had another tough year as government endowment for cultural programs continued to shrink in 1993. The Canada Council—a major funding source for the arts—was cut 10% (more than C$9 million), the government-owned Canadian Broadcasting Corporation (CBC) was trimmed by C$23 million, and Telefilm Canada lost C$12.6 million. This reduced financing for the various arts forced cultural organizations to find funding elsewhere and to mount more commercial-oriented productions, but despite this constraint, many individuals and organizations still produced excellent work during the year.

Architecture. Douglas Cardinal, designer of the Canadian Museum of Civilization in Hull, Que., was chosen as principal designer of the Smithsonian's National Museum of the American Indian in Washington, DC. The facility will combine traditional native elements and high-tech equipment. Jerusalem's new city hall, designed by Canadian architect Jack Diamond and integrating old and new buildings, was dedicated in June. Toronto's Edwardian-inspired Princess of Wales Theatre, designed by Peter Smith and adorned with Frank Stella murals, opened in May.

Visual Arts. Robert Davidson's retrospective "Eagle of the Dawn," spanning 30 years of work, opened at the Vancouver Art Gallery. This highly acclaimed Haida artist displayed 208 pieces, including totem-pole models, masks, carved wooden panels, bronze sculptures, jewelry, screen prints, and paintings. The National Gallery of Canada exhibited "The Crisis of Abstraction in Canada: The 1950s," a collection of 158 paintings and sculptures by 62 artists that documented the impact of abstraction on Canadian artists of the period. The gallery also unveiled new acquisitions, including an important early landscape by Lawren Harris, "Decorative Landscape," and a controversial abstract, "No. 16," by U.S. artist Mark Rothko.

The focus of the Art Gallery of Ontario's annual Perspectives exhibit, a showcase for new Canadian talent, was Micha Lexier's mixed-media pieces. Drawing rave reviews was "The Earthly Paradise: Arts and Crafts by William Morris and his Circle from Canadian Collections," perhaps the most elaborate and comprehensive exhibit in the gallery's history.

Robin Collyer represented Canada at the Venice Biennial with sculptures made from odd media like vacuum-formed plastic and aluminum ventilation equipment. Montreal artist Zoya Niedermann's "Arch Figures"

won the Fujisankei (Japan) Bienniale sculpture competition.

Performing Arts. *The Stillborn Lover,* by internationally acclaimed Canadian author Timothy Findley, opened at Toronto's Grand Theatre to excellent reviews. Set in the 1970s, Findley's play covers such themes as homosexuality and homophobia, friendship and love, and trust and betrayal. An adapted production of Margaret Laurence's novel *The Stone Angel* also opened to critical acclaim at Theatre Passe Muraille in Toronto. Writer-director Michael Hollingsworth's *The Life and Times of Mackenzie King* opened at The Theatre Centre in Toronto. This historical comedy sweeps through the turbulent years of King's political career in madcap fashion. *The Cape Breton Summertime Review* combined the humor of Cape Bretoners with Gaelic music, under the direction of Sandra Balcovske and Leon Dubinsky.

The highlight of the 1993 Stratford Festival was Canadian playwright Sharon Pollock's new play, *Fair Liberty's Call.* Set in 1785 in New Brunswick, the play combines history, poetry, and mystery. Also well-received were productions of Shakespeare's *Antony and Cleopatra,* directed by Richard Monette; *A Midsummer Night's Dream,* directed by Joe Dowling; and *King John,* directed by Robin Phillips. Brian Macdonald's stylish *The Mikado,* by Gilbert and Sullivan, also was praised highly. The Shaw Festival mounted successful productions of Shaw's *Saint Joan, Candida,* and *The Man of Destiny.* Also well-received was *The Silver King,* an obscure Victorian melodrama written by Henry Arthur Jones, and directed by Christopher Newton.

The Canadian Opera Company's *The Bartered Bride,* marvelously staged and acted, and a sumptuous *Carmen,* starring Jean Stilwell, were much admired, but both were eclipsed by its Robert Lepage production of Bela Bartok's *Bluebeard's Castle* and Arnold Schoenberg's *Erwartung,* a double bill that played to rave reviews at the Edinburgh Festival— where it took the £50,000 Scotsman Festival Prize.

Five philanthropists endowed the National Ballet with C$1.6 million that funded new productions and allowed older ones, such as *The Taming of the Shrew* and *Romeo and Juliet,* to be rejuvenated. The company's first performance of James Kudelka's *The Miraculous Mandarin,* starring Karen Kain and Jeremy Ransom, brought grace and beauty to a dark subject. Les Grandes Ballets Canadiens took New York by storm, especially with James Kudelka's poetic *Désir.*

Canadian composer R. Murray Schafer, who pioneered "acoustic ecology," was honored at a Banff, Alta., conference named after his *The Tuning of the World* and at the annual music festival at Sharon, Ont., which presented a wide selection of his works.

© The Shaw Festival, Photo by David Cooper

The 1993 Shaw Festival featured a production of the 1899 historical drama "The Marrying of Ann Leete," with Ann Baggley and Roger Honeywell, above, in the leading roles.

Film. The annual Montreal World Film Festival, which screened 229 films, opened with the Quebec film *Le sexe des étoiles* ("The Sex of the Stars"), directed by Paule Baillargeon. Toronto's Festival of Festivals presented international and Canadian films, opening with the world premier of David Cronenberg's *M. Butterfly,* based on David Henry Hwang's Broadway play. The festival also launched the Canadian debut of *Kanehsatake: 270 Years of Resistance,* by Alanis Obomsawin. This award-winning National Film Board documentary is seen from an aboriginal perspective and is based on the 1990 conflict between Mohawks and the military at Oka, Que. Also highly praised were François Girard's *Thirty-Two Short Films About Glenn Gould,* Denys Arcand's *Love and Human Remains,* and David Wellington's *I Love a Man in Uniform.*

Featured at the Vancouver International Film Festival were two British Columbian films: *Digger*—directed by Rob Turner and starring Olympia Dukakis, Leslie Nielsen, Adam Hann-Byrd, and Joshua Jackson—is a heartwarming story of two boys who learn about love, life, and death; *The Lotus Eaters,* a comedy about the changing moral climate in a small gulf-island community during the 1960s, was directed by Paul Shapiro. Tara Frederick and R. H. Thompson starred in the latter, with Sheila McCarthy receiving special recognition.

Shadow of the Wolf—one of the few films about the Inuit, and Canada's most expensive film to date—was directed by Jacques Dorfmann. This Canada-France coproduction was based on the novel *Agaguk* by Yves Thériault.

DOUGLAS R. CRONK
Open University of British Columbia

© Robert Trippett/Sipa

President Clinton met with leaders from the Caribbean (l-r)—Hubert Ingraham of the Bahamas, Patrick Manning of Trinidad and Tobago, Guyana's Cheddi Jagan, L. E. Sandiford of Barbados, and Jamaica's P. J. Patterson—at the White House on Aug. 30, 1993.

CARIBBEAN

The Caribbean region experienced sluggish economic growth in 1993, although the prospects for improvement were enhanced—according to a study by the Inter-American Development Bank (IDB)—by recent reforms and measures undertaken by several of the region's governments.

The political panorama of the region was dominated by continuing turmoil in Haiti (*see also* HAITI). Caribbean leaders strongly supported international efforts to end the violent stalemate between Haiti's de facto military rulers and its exiled president, Jean-Bertrand Aristide.

As debate mounted in the United States and Canada over implementation of the proposed North American Free Trade Agreement (NAFTA) among the two countries and Mexico, the Caribbean countries pushed hard for safeguards against the erosion of their commercial advantages in the U.S. and Canadian markets under preferential trade programs.

The Caribbean countries also continued efforts to forge closer economic and political ties with the mainland countries of Central and South America and began exploring cooperation with Cuba, raising concern in the United States.

Economy. The Caribbean continued to be mired in sluggish conditions. The region's GDP declined slightly in 1990 and 1991, and rose by only 0.3% (compared with 3% for Latin America and the Caribbean combined) in 1992. Preliminary estimates for 1993 indicated little change.

According to the *Economic and Social Progress in Latin America* report issued by the IDB, "The subregion, which accounts for less than 3% of the total GDP of Latin America, performed poorly in comparison with the region

as a whole. The slowdown of business activity in the industrialized countries hampered the growth of tourism, a primary source of foreign exchange earnings for many countries, while export revenues declined as a result of terms of trade deterioration and weak demand in the major world markets."

The main exception to the dismal economic performance of the Caribbean was the Dominican Republic, where a stabilization program launched in 1990 began to bear fruit. Government economists projected year-end 1993 growth in that nation at 5% and said that its inflation rate in the first quarter of 1993 was a low 1.5%.

Commodities. Sugar, a dominant export of the Dominican Republic and important for several countries of the region, suffered from a cut in the tariff-rate quota by the United States for the third consecutive year. The quota limits the amount of sugar that may enter the United States at low tariffs or duty-free. To protect domestic growers, the United States cut its quota by 16%.

In another major commodity development, the Caribbean found itself embroiled in controversy with Latin American neighbors when the European Community (EC) announced early in 1993 a preferential program for imports of bananas from the Caribbean islands and restrictions on imports from Latin America. The General Agreement on Tariffs and Trade (GATT) ruled that the EC program violated international trading rules, but the dispute continued through the year.

NAFTA. Caribbean leaders warned that political turmoil could erupt in the region if the United States did not guarantee Caribbean countries trade terms equal to those that Mexico would enjoy under NAFTA. The countries of Central America and the Caribbean had been receiving

preferential treatment for their exports under the U.S. Caribbean Basin Initiative (CBI) and under a similar scheme offered by Canada.

Caribbean leaders from Guyana, Barbados, the Bahamas, Jamaica, and Trinidad and Tobago pressed their NAFTA case in an August meeting with U.S. President Bill Clinton. Clinton ordered a study to gauge the potential impact of NAFTA on the Caribbean. In addition, legislation was introduced in the U.S. Congress to guarantee CBI beneficiary countries parity with Mexico for at least three years if NAFTA is approved.

Section 936. Caribbean CBI beneficiary countries also were distressed in August when the U.S. Congress, in a budget-cutting move, reduced tax benefits available to U.S. firms operating in Puerto Rico under Section 936 of the U.S. Internal Revenue Code. President Clinton originally had planned to eliminate the tax breaks altogether, but congressional opposition forced a compromise for reduced benefits. Tax-exempt funds deposited in Puerto Rican banks by Section 936 companies have been a source of low-cost loans for development projects since 1985. For eight years, some $650 million in Section 936 funds were made available to CBI countries in Central America and the Caribbean. Anticipating the action by Congress, the government of Puerto Rico suspended the program of low-interest loans in May.

Politics. In March the People's National Party (PNP) won a landslide victory in elections held in Jamaica. The incumbent PNP took 52 of 60 parliamentary seats and Percival Patterson became prime minister on April 5. The elections seemed to end a long rivalry between Michael Manley of the PNP and Edward Seaga of the Jamaica Labor Party (JLP). Manley was prime minister from 1972 to 1980 and again from 1989 to 1992, when he retired in poor health. Patterson then took over as party leader and prime minister. The defeat was expected to send Seaga, prime minister from 1980 to 1989, into retirement. Violence marred the election campaign. Twelve persons were killed in interparty rioting and dozens were injured. Homes and businesses were damaged by looting and burning. Patterson condemned the violence and vowed to help forge a more peaceful and prosperous Jamaica.

The government changed hands in Belize, the former British colony on the Central American mainland. Prime Minister George Price unexpectedly called an election for the end of June, 15 months ahead of schedule. Price hoped to catch the opposition United Democratic Party (UDP) off guard, but the tactic backfired due to widespread questions about domestic security. The UDP won 16 seats in the legislature, while Price's People's United Party (PUP) captured 13. UDP leader Manuel Esquivel, prime minister from 1984 to 1989, returned to head the government.

Price had signed an agreement with Guatemalan president Jorge Serrano ending Guatemala's 139-year claim to the territory of Belize, and when Serrano was forced out of the presidency, Belizeans feared that Guatemala might renew its claim, although Guatemala later reaffirmed its acceptance of current borders. The fear was compounded by Great Britain's announcement that it would give up responsibility for Belize's defense and phase down its military presence from 1,500 troops to 200 over a 15-month period.

Cuban Relations. Caribbean leaders, at a July summit meeting in Nassau, the Bahamas, approved a cooperative agreement with Cuba that created a joint commission to explore technical cooperation in tourism, agriculture, biotechnology, and other areas. The Caribbean Community and Common Market (CARICOM) chiefs consented to a request by the Cuban government to delete language in the accord referring to human rights and democracy. Members of the U.S. Congress expressed alarm at the agreement. The United States has maintained a long-standing policy of isolating the Castro government in the Western Hemisphere and has enforced a trade embargo against Cuba.

Retirements. Joaquín Balaguer in the Dominican Republic and Vere Bird in Antigua and Barbuda both said they would not run in general elections scheduled in 1994. Balaguer was in poor health and had undergone surgery in August. He said, nonetheless, that he was under "heavy pressure" from his Social Christian Reformist Party (PRSC) to seek a seventh term. In Antigua, Bird's two sons, Lester and Vere Jr., were named as leaders of the ruling Antigua Labor Party.

In Barbados, Henry Forde resigned as leader of the opposition Barbados Labor Party (BLP) for health reasons in July. The resignation was believed to strengthen the chances of Erskine Sandiford of the ruling Democratic Labor Party (DLP) for a third consecutive term as prime minister in elections to be held in 1995.

RICHARD C. SCHROEDER, *Consultant*
Organization of American States

Percival J. Patterson led Jamaica's social democratic People's National Party to an overwhelming victory in March 1993. He was inaugurated for a full term as prime minister on April 5.

© Najlah Feanny/Saba

CENTRAL AMERICA

After more than a decade of serving as a battleground for competing U.S. and Soviet interests, the Central American nations looked to a future of peace in 1993. Human-rights questions still haunted the people and civil strife had not disappeared in every nation, but there was a sense of hope in the region.

While there were signs of impending progress, the majority of Central Americans still were worse off in 1993 than before the 1980s began. Serious economic problems, which appeared to be endemic to Central America, also have lingered throughout the region as a residue of the dislocations of war. Perhaps 2 million Central Americans left their homes during the Cold War—many for the United States—seeking jobs, food, and safety. Crime, hunger, and underemployment were rising everywhere. National infrastructures sat in disrepair. The economic problems were aggravated by the fact that when reconstruction needs were so great, the richer nations were suffering from their own economic dislocations and could offer much less than in the recent past.

Whenever serious problems that disturbed the U.S. government have been absent, Central America traditionally has been ignored by Washington. This dynamic has been helpful at times, but Central Americans often wondered if they must behave as nuisances to attract Washington's attention. After nearly one year in office, President Bill Clinton had not elaborated much of a Central American policy.

Much of the U.S. role in Central America during the 1980s already had been subjected to extensive speculation and rumor, followed by investigations and denials. But under pressure from the U.S. Congress, two departments—state and defense—and the Central Intelligence Agency (CIA) released 12,000 formerly classified documents in November about the roles of former Presidents Ronald Reagan and George Bush in waging the Cold War in Central America. The documents showed that the two men regularly received intelligence data on right-wing assassinations in El Salvador, yet continued to support the perpetrators because of their opposition to communism. Between 1980 and 1991, El Salvador received $6 billion in military aid even though the two presidents knew that the Salvadoran military was run by officers who ordered or took part in death-squad activities.

For example, the CIA called the late Roberto D'Aubuisson, former head of El Salvador's Nationalist Republican Alliance (ARENA), the "principal henchman for wealthy landowners and a coordinator of the right-wing death squads that have murdered several thousand suspected leftists." The documents referred to D'Aubuisson as "perhaps mentally unstable" and as a trafficker in drugs who directed the assassination of

© Engle/Gamma-Liaison

Many Guatemalan Indians, who had been in exile in Mexico, returned to their homeland in 1993. Less violence in Guatemala and worsening conditions in Mexico led to the repatriation.

Archbishop Oscar Arnulfo Romero in 1980. The documents also indicted as death-squad organizers Vice-President José Francisco Merino López and the mayor of San Salvador, Armando Calderon Sol, who frequently has been mentioned as the next president of the nation. In order to continue giving military aid to El Salvador, President Reagan certified that the nation was making progress in the matter of human rights even as he was receiving embassy reports of the massacre of hundreds at El Mozote in 1981. Congress planned to investigate the testimony of dozens of U.S. officials.

Belize. By the narrowest of margins, Belize voters changed their ruling party in 1993. On June 30, Manuel Esquivel defeated George Price for the post of prime minister in a vote so close that the tallying took all night. Price had defeated Esquivel in a 1989 election. Esquivel's United Democratic Party also captured the House of Representatives, winning 16 of the 29 seats to take control of that body away from Price's Peoples' United Party. Price's defeat came as a surprise to most observers. He undoubtedly lost some votes because of new attention to an old boundary dispute with Guatemala when he failed to persuade the British to keep a small detachment of troops in Belize. In July, Esquivel reopened the boundary question, saying that Price had made too many concessions to Guatemala. The new prime minister declared his

intention to hold a public referendum on the matter. Guatemala consistently had denied any plans to use force to change the border.

In May, Belize hosted the First World Conference on Tourism and the Environment. With the aid of private international groups, the nation has set aside hundreds of thousands of acres of land for parks and sanctuaries. Perhaps no Latin American nation could boast a better environmental record. Ironically, the very policies designed to save the environment and the many Mayan ruins created a new environmental threat—tourism. Providing hotels and other facilities for the growing number of visitors has endangered the nation's rain forests. The 185-mi (300-km) barrier reef already has suffered damage. The people and the government appeared determined to find a balance between development and preservation. The greatest danger was posed by illegal immigration by peasants from other Central American nations, who have burned the rain forests for pasture or cropland.

In 1992, Belize had become the 45th member nation of the Inter-American Development Bank (IDB). This could translate into additional sources of credit to bolster the economy, which was small but growing steadily, averaging 9% growth in the 1980s. Probably the first project for the IDB would be modernizing the Southern Highway out of the capital (Belmopán) to the south. Belize's economic prospects looked strong. Although sugar sales declined due to external quotas, most other agricultural production rose. Citrus exports, rice, and many fisheries enjoyed recent increases. The sale of unfinished lumber was limited due to a new government policy.

In July the U.S. Federal Aviation Administration (FAA) prohibited Air Belize from landing in the United States, alleging inadequate training of the line's personnel.

Costa Rica. After several weak years, Costa Rica's economy took an upward turn in 1993. Early figures reported to the government predicted economic growth for the year to be roughly 5%, with inflation down from 21% in 1992 to 12% in 1993. Unemployment was estimated at 4%. The economic growth was driven largely by increases in exports, up 16% in spite of a decline in sales of coffee. The value of tourism approached $500 million in 1993, double its 1991 value. The nation enjoyed a large increase in investment, accompanied by a 10% increase in manufacturing of nontraditional items.

Some of the new investment resulted from the transferring of companies from the United States, such as Levi Strauss, which moved a factory to Costa Rica (from Texas) in 1990. An estimated 700 foreign corporations were located in Costa Rica. Much of the growth was credited to economic reforms required by international lenders, to a decline in interest rates, and to a reduced state role in foreign exchange, lower tariffs, and the sale of public-sector holdings.

In July 75,000 government workers struck for higher wages, claiming that inflation outpaced the 5% raise that most of them had been granted. The raise also was in the face of a far larger pay increase the members of the National Assembly just had voted for themselves. Many schools and hospitals were forced to close briefly. The strike was settled in fairly quick fashion, and the workers received a small increase.

In 1993 the nation faced two serious hostage situations. The first of these concerned Nicaraguan politics and merely took place in Costa Rica. In March three heavily armed Nicaraguans took over the Nicaraguan embassy in San José, capturing about 25 people, including the Nicaraguan ambassador to Costa Rica, Alfonso Robelo. The men had three demands: the dismissal of Humberto Ortega, chief of the army, and Antonio Lacayo Oyanguren, presidential minister; $5 million for the church in Nicaragua to distribute to handicapped veterans of the recent civil war; and $1 million for the kidnappers' movement. The Nicaraguan government flatly rejected the demands. About ten days later the Robelo family paid $250,000 ransom, all of the hostages were released unharmed, and the kidnappers were given safe conduct out of the country.

The other major incident more directly concerned Costa Rica. In April five gunmen occupied the Supreme Court building in San José, seizing 19 justices who were in the building at the time. The kidnappers demanded $20 million in cash, safe conduct to a South American country without an extradition treaty with Costa Rica, and the release of some unspecified prisoners in local jails. President Rafael Angel Calderón declared he would not negotiate over ransom, but families of some hostages paid $150,000 for their release. The gunmen were offered and accepted passage to Guatemala and released the prisoners. At the airport the kidnappers were tricked into giving up their weapons on the grounds that Guatemala would not permit them to enter the country with guns. The men then were captured and sent to jail. Government critics charged that the incident was caused by the government's failure to maintain the disability pension of the group's leader.

El Salvador. The civil war in El Salvador ended in 1992, but after 12 years of bitter strife every family was affected in some way. Getting the nation back to normal was proving to be as difficult as ending the war. Part of the United Nations- (UN-) sponsored settlement was an agreement to make a thorough investigation of the many murders and other human-rights violations that took place during the war. In March a UN commission charged six men with the 1989 shooting of six Jesuits and two women, under orders from the minister of defense and five top ranking officers. They also charged that the late Roberto D'Aubuisson, then leader of the right-wing ARENA, had ordered the assassination of

Archbishop Oscar Arnulfo Romero in 1980. Finding many rights violations by both sides in the war, the UN asked that guilty rebels be banned permanently from politics and guilty officers be dismissed from the service.

Defense Minister General René Emilio Ponce offered to resign, and the government claimed that 100 officers already had been forced out. But President Alfredo Cristiani went on TV to call for a general amnesty, meaning that large numbers of officers never would be punished for their crimes. The ARENA-controlled National Assembly endorsed the request; some judges even began letting convicted men out of jail.

Six months of stalemate followed as the UN pressed for adherence to the peace treaty. Probably more of a factor was the withholding of financial aid by the United States, which cost El Salvador at least $11 million. President Cristiani finally replaced General Ponce with a less known and probably less "tainted" general as defense minister, and ordered massive changes in the army's command structure. The military "class of 1966," which ran the army during the height of rights abuses, saw its influence destroyed. But the only people charged with human-rights violations during the war who seemed likely to serve their sentences were the five convicted of killing and raping four U.S. church workers. Cristiani did not follow the UN recommendations to replace many Supreme Court justices, and the army resumed its patrolling of the countryside looking for "criminals."

The UN had an unprecedented role in El Salvador. Never before had the agency set up human-rights offices prior to a cease-fire and then kept officials on to supervise reforms and establish peace. Late in 1993 the UN still had 600 military police in El Salvador, helping to build a police academy. Some 800 representatives were expected to observe the 1994 presidential election. UN leadership believed that the cease-fire had been observed properly, but the rebel Farabundo Martí National Liberation Front (FMLN) did not destroy all its weapons, and the government stalled on its military reforms. Unrest still was apparent.

During the civil war five separate rebel organizations worked closely together against the government. But more peaceful conditions and the announcement of a presidential election for March 1994 brought about schisms and disorganization. Rubén Zamora hoped to hold the FMLN together for his presidential nomination.

The government estimated that the civil war had destroyed nearly $2 billion in infrastructure. In particular, roads and bridges needed repair before the economy could return to normal. The land-reform program was far behind schedule, but with funds from the United States and the UN, El Salvador created a land bank to help thousands of peasants (currently squatters), former soldiers, and former guerrillas obtain land.

Guatemala. The nation of Guatemala faced political disturbances caused by the rising cost of living and a frightening increase in crime rates. In May, President Jorge Serrano Elías suspended the constitution and dissolved Congress and the Supreme Court, saying that he was cleansing the nation of corruption. These actions followed weeks of public protest. In the next week, President Serrano suspended basic constitutional rights and attempted to impose public censorship. But he began losing most of his support and was forced to resign under pressure by the army on June 1. He then went into exile.

The congress rejected Vice-President Gustavo Espina Salguero's bid for the presidency, and selected Ramiro de León Carpio—a lawyer who had been a human-rights ombudsman since 1988 and champion of the Indians—to be president until elections would be held in 1995. He would not be eligible to run at that time. He faced grave problems, including what to do about more than 100 congressmen accused of accepting bribes; the absence of any organized party of his own; finding a cooperative cabinet; enforcing the human-rights settlements in the peace treaty; and controlling the power of the military. Just one month into his term, his cousin was assassinated.

Although President de León was limited by the terms of his presidency, he announced an education program for the military, a road-building schedule, elimination of many of the abusive perquisites of government officials, and an effort to heal the divisiveness of the civil war.

Repatriation of Guatemalan Indians from Mexico continued in January 1993. Escorted by UN officials, hundreds of Indians began their homeward trek from various sites. About 1,300 walked from Yucatán alone. Once the Guatemalan Indians in Mexico numbered

CENTRAL AMERICA • Information Highlights					
Nation	Population (in Millions)	Area (sq mi)	(km²)	Capital	Head of State and Government
Belize	0.2	8,865	22 960	Belmopan	Minita Gordon, governor-general Manuel Esquivel, prime minister
Costa Rica	3.2	19,730	51 100	San José	Rafael Angel Calderón Fournier, president
El Salvador	5.2	8,124	21 040	San Salvador	Alfredo Cristiani, president
Guatemala	10.0	42,042	108 890	Guatemala City	Ramiro de León Carpio, president
Honduras	5.6	43,278	112 090	Tegucigalpa	Roberto Reina, president
Nicaragua	4.1	49,998	129 494	Managua	Violeta Barrios de Chamorro, president
Panama	2.5	30,193	78 200	Panama City	Guillermo Endara, president

With El Salvador trying to revamp in 1993 following 12 years of civil war, more than 2,000 women—known as "Mujeres 1994"—paraded through the capital city of San Salvador in August to present a platform for better living conditions for the nation's women.

© AP/Wide World

45,000, but many have drifted back home through the years or have migrated elsewhere. The return of the exiles probably reflected a small decline in violence in Guatemala, but many Indians claimed that their return merely signified worsening conditions in Mexico. Several thousand more migrated home in May. They posed a double problem for the government: getting them relocated and dealing with their desires for self-government.

Honduras. In November citizens elected a new president, Roberto Reina of the Liberal Party. Reina defeated his opponent, Oswaldo Ramos Soto, by a wide margin. Reina vowed to reform two of the nation's biggest challenges: political corruption and the military.

In February, President Rafael Leonardo Callejas ordered 4,000 troops with tanks and artillery into San Pedro Sula, the nation's second-largest city, following the execution-style slaying of three business and professional men. While the purpose of the murders was not clear, their importance was obvious from the government's resolute response. As usual in Central American nations, human-rights groups blamed the military for the assassinations.

The end of the Cold War had a trickle-down effect upon Honduras. During much of the Reagan-Bush era, the United States used Honduras as a base for support of the contras in Nicaragua. As its reward, Honduras received vast amounts of financial aid, including unprecedented military assistance. From 1983 to 1990, Honduras had received $1.2 billion in total economic assistance from the United States. However, Honduras had received little new money or credit from the U.S. government since 1990. Some of the slack was picked up by the IDB: $50 million was granted to modernize agriculture; $60 million awarded to bolster credit programs; and $55 million went to upgrade the San Pedro Sula infrastructure.

In spite of this funding, poverty remained the norm for most Hondurans. Unemployment was calculated at about 25%, and 70% of the rural population lived below the poverty line. A congresswoman charged that Honduras had tolerat-

ed the sale or theft of hundreds of children for adoption, largely by North American citizens. She alleged that about some 800 children disappear from Honduras annually, taken off the city streets or carried away from hospitals, concealed for a time in Tegucigalpa or another large city, then sold abroad. In 1991, U.S. citizens alone adopted 450 such children, paying thousands of dollars for each one. The adoption process usually was handled legally—except for the kidnapping. These procedures put Honduras in violation of the International Rights of Children convention and could lead to sanctions.

In November three days of torrential rain brought heavy flooding to Honduras. The storms were centered in Yoro and Colón provinces, battering the Atlantic coast of the nation. More than 100 persons lost their lives, at least 15,000 were temporarily homeless, and extensive crop damage occurred.

Nicaragua. Although criticism of President Violeta Barrios de Chamorro abounded, she clung to her office. Encouraged by former President Daniel Ortega, transport workers struck in September over higher fuel prices and new vehicle taxes. This was the fourth serious episode in two months, but in this case the strikers were a mixture of Sandinistas and contras, sending a message that the poor of all types were uniting. Traffic halted, stores shut down, and markets closed. After four days the government yielded on the vehicle tax but not on the fuel tax.

Nicaragua remained one of the poorest nations in Latin America. Many Nicaraguans believed that one solution to this poverty was a radical redistribution of agricultural lands. The Chamorro government had promised to implement a significant land-reform program, but little of the plan had been accomplished. Several hundred former contras received small parcels of land, but most of these veterans did not get a proper deed or title, and many sold out. Others so badly lacked irrigation that they could not farm and soon went bankrupt.

Substantial U.S. aid was not forthcoming, in part because of Nicaragua's failure to compen-

After rebels of no clear ideology robbed banks and terrorized the residents of the Nicaraguan town of Estelí in July 1993, federal troops were sent in and fierce fighting resulted. At right, civilians come to the aid of an injured soldier at the height of the disturbance.

© AP/Wide World

sate foreigners for expropriated property. The U.S. State Department released $50 million in April after almost a year of suspension. In August aid was held up again because of the explosion of a hidden weapons cache, revealing a link between Nicaraguan rebels and an international group specializing in terrorism. Although the civil war ended in 1990, at least 20,000 veterans still were in the field, disturbing and frightening the government. One group held the Nicaraguan embassy hostage in Costa Rica.

Perhaps the worst display of dissatisfaction occurred in July when 150 rebels of no clear ideology attacked the town of Estelí, robbing banks, demanding benefits promised by the government, and terrorizing citizens. President Chamorro sent in troops with tanks and artillery; 40 persons were killed during the recapturing of the town. Chamorro blamed Daniel Ortega for stirring up the poor masses. In August leftists and rightists exchanged kidnappings, perhaps as much to show strength as to accomplish anything.

Early in her term, President Chamorro acquired a strong following for her attacks on inflation and reduction of the threat from the two major military forces. But unemployment was rising out of control and the economy was stagnant. To cope with a major complaint, she removed the chief of intelligence, Col. Lenín Cerna, a Sandinista, and replaced him with a civilian. She also promised that Gen. Humberto Ortega, Daniel's brother, would be relieved as head of the army in 1994. One poll alleged that 50% of the people thought they were better off under the Sandinistas than under Chamorro. The Sandinistas were the largest political party, controlling the army, police, and Supreme Court. The U.S. government was unhappy with some of President Chamorro's policies but saw little alternative to giving her grudging support.

Panama. In January the U.S. Department of Justice decided not to proceed on marijuana-smuggling charges against former dictator Manuel Noriega, already serving a 40-year sentence for participating in cocaine trafficking, racketeering, and money laundering. The U.S. government concluded that the cost to pursue the relatively minor marijuana charge would not be justified.

In August, Panama's government confirmed that arms dealers had been trying to ship millions of dollars' worth of illegal weapons and ammunition from Austria and the Czech Republic to Bosnia, falsely declaring Panama the destination. Panama helped block the sales, and the arms never reached Bosnia.

In September 1993 seven soldiers were cleared of responsibility in the 1985 killing of Hugo Spadafora, who had been a leading opponent of Noriega. In some communities reaction to the verdict was so bitter that police had to use tear gas to disperse the rioters.

Although Panama had not been a pawn in the Cold War, it was hurt by a U.S. embargo designed to destroy Noriega. That action ceased, but much of the damage lingered and the Panama economy still suffered. The United States resumed financial aid in 1990, but subsequent amounts appeared to be declining. Small amounts of aid came from the IDB to bolster credit for small businesses and to study the impact of future loans.

In May Panama invited offers by private groups to purchase military installations being abandoned by the United States due to the canal treaties. They covered 250,000 acres (100 000 ha) and were assessed at $40 billion.

Panama was among the Latin American nations developing a nature-conservancy program. It had a unique opportunity: During the years of canal construction many animal species had been trapped on islands in Gatun Lake. These regions are administered by the Smithsonian Tropical Research Institute.

THOMAS L. KARNES, *Arizona State University*

CHEMISTRY

Developments in chemistry in 1993 included new ways to produce and modify fullerenes, studies of giant molecules, and the synthesis of a material that may be harder than diamond.

Fullerenes. Since their discovery in 1985, fullerenes have enjoyed chemistry's spotlight. Their hollow, pure-carbon structures suggest many practical applications, and great effort has gone into modifying these compounds, either by tacking chemical groups on their exteriors or by placing atoms inside them.

In 1993 several groups, for example, reported methods for attaching exterior polar chemical groups to fullerenes to allow the compounds to dissolve in water. This advance may have applications in biomedicine and industrial catalysis. Two teams also reported techniques to attach fullerenes to solid surfaces, which may allow the formation of molecular layers with special mechanical, electrical, and optical properties. Yale University researchers reported that by heating fullerenes to high temperatures in inert gases they could insert neon or helium atoms inside the hollow compounds. These inclusion compounds raise the possibility of introducing radioactive atoms that could identify sources of pollutants. The neon fullerene was described as the first known compound of that inert gas.

Fullerene chemistry has lacked a simple, inexpensive method to produce materials in large amounts. Carbon-arc synthesis remains expensive and difficult. During 1993 two groups reported progress using intense heating from solar-energy furnaces to vaporize carbon rods and form fullerenes. The solar process may have some practical advantages, especially in reducing suspected destruction of the product that occurs in carbon-arc synthesis.

A California chemist also described a method to purify the popular 60-carbon fullerene, C_{60}, from the sootlike material that is formed in the synthesis process. The method depends on the fact that C_{60} has less tendency to form complexes with certain acids—and therefore precipitate out of the mixture—than do other fullerenes. Separately, fullerenes were found in glassy rocks called fulgurites at a site in Colorado, showing that fullerenes can be produced naturally by the action of lightning. Naturally produced fullerenes were discovered once before, in coal-like rocks from Russia.

The most dramatic development in fullerene chemistry, however, was the announcement by two research teams that fullerene derivatives exhibit biological activity against the AIDS virus. The teams independently saw that the round C_{60} fullerene species might have the correct shape and properties to tie up critical enzymes of the AIDS-causing virus, HIV. Both teams had Fred Wudl of the University of California, Santa Barbara, synthesize suitable, water-soluble derivatives, and subsequent test-ing confirmed the anticipated antiviral activity, the first example of biological activity by a fullerene. Although the new compounds are less potent than some existing drugs, the discovery may lead to more effective agents.

Dendrimers. Dendrimers—a name derived from the Greek word for tree—are large, highly branched compounds built by attaching layers of smaller chemicals called monomers about a central core. Typically the monomers have three bond-forming chemical groups that can act as "hooks" for attachment. In the first round of synthesis, three monomers might attach to the core, leaving six hooks dangling on the outside. Monomers then can be attached to each of these six hooks, leaving 12 hooks exposed. After several stages, the product is a large, lacy structure with numerous functional groups on the outside. Possible applications range from the controlled delivery of drugs and agricultural agents, to the manufacture of coatings and adhesives.

Although the dendrimer concept has been known for almost two decades, technical problems have stalled practical exploitation. In 1993 researchers at the University of Michigan announced that they had produced a giant hydrocarbon dendrimer composed of 127 phenylacetylene monomer units. The compound has the chemical formula $C_{1398}H_{1278}$ and a molecular weight of 18,054—the largest dendrimer yet reported. One potential application envisioned by these chemists involves attaching light-absorbing groups to the structure that could capture light energy and funnel it to a central unit where it might be converted to chemical energy. Meanwhile, the Dutch chemical company DSM announced that it had developed methods to synthesize polypropyleneimine dendrimers in large amounts, so chemists can obtain commercial supplies for research and development.

Other Events. In 1989, Marvin Cohen, a physicist at the University of California at Berkeley, predicted on theoretical grounds that a material constructed from units of carbon nitride might be harder than diamond. A number of research groups took up the challenge to prepare the proposed material. In 1993 a team of Harvard University chemists reported that they had made a thin film of it. The team then turned its efforts to purifying the material. Preliminary tests indicated that the film was hard, stable to heating, and stuck well to surfaces, possibly portending use as a diamond substitute.

Element 106 was discovered in the 1970s at the Lawrence Berkeley Laboratory in California, but the creation of an extra-heavy element is not considered secure until it has been confirmed independently. Confirmation is difficult, since Element 106 lasts for a split second, but an independent research team reported in 1993 that it had produced the element and verified its properties.

PAUL SEYBOLD
Wright State University

CHICAGO

Chicago was gripped by a recurring budget crisis in 1993 as schools lacked the money to begin classes in September for the city's 411,000 students. The teachers' union and the Chicago Board of Education could not reach a contract agreement that Chicago taxpayers could afford without additional state aid that was not forthcoming. A federal judge ordered the schools opened as the two sides, with Mayor Richard M. Daley as a mediator, worked to reach some compromises to reduce school spending.

Mayor Daley abandoned plans for a grandiose entertainment center and casino in Chicago when he could not win support from Gov. Jim Edgar and legislators in Springfield. The mayor wanted to bail out the public-school system with tax revenues from the casino. He also tried to win approval for riverboat gambling along the Chicago River. That too met resistance from state leaders, who opposed more competition for the state lottery and other riverboat casinos outside the city that earn much of their revenue from Chicago gamblers.

Business. Chicago-based Sears Roebuck & Company, once the nation's biggest retailer, underwent major restructuring in 1993. Among the changes was the termination of the unprofitable Sears catalog, a U.S. institution since 1896. More than 13 million Sears Big Books—produced by Chicago's R. R. Donnelley & Company—were in print at the time. Sears also closed 113 unprofitable stores and dismissed more than 50,000 employees.

Commonwealth Edison Company, the city's largest public utility, agreed to refund $1.34 billion and to reduce rates by 6% to 3.3 million electric customers in Chicago and Northern Illinois. In what Commonwealth Chairman James O'Connor called "the rate case from hell," the giant utility gave up a decade-old fight with consumer groups over rate hikes to fund four new nuclear-power plants. The Illinois Commerce Commission had approved the rate hikes, but the Illinois Supreme Court ruled in favor of the consumer groups and declared that consumers were burdened unjustly with paying for unnecessary generating capacity. Edison's refund was the second-largest in U.S. utility history, surpassed only by a previous refund by the company of $418 million for invalidated rate increases. Homeowners got an average refund of $221.

Crime. Chicago's violent crime rate of 30.3 per 1,000 residents was the fourth-worst in the nation, exceeded only by Atlanta, Miami, and St. Louis. Police Superintendent Matt Rodriguez blamed the worsening crime picture on crack cocaine and gang warfare. A new antiloitering law aimed at gang members and persons under 17 was enacted to stem gang activity. A judge declared the law unconstitutional, but city officials vowed to enforce the ordinance while they appealed the ruling.

Transportation. Chicago commuters continued to grapple with the rebuilding of the Kennedy Expressway, the main artery between the Loop and O'Hare International Airport, and with new rates for buses and trains on the Chicago Transit Authority (CTA). Fares for rush-hour rides on CTA trains and buses were $1.50, one of the highest rates in the nation.

The good news for travelers was the opening of the $618 million international terminal at O'Hare. The new facility was the last major project in a $1 billion airport improvement. It was built to handle up to 80 international flights a day for 30 airlines.

ROBERT ENSTAD, *"Chicago Tribune"*

CHILE

On Dec. 11, 1993, Chile held its second consecutive free presidential election since nearly 17 years of military rule came to an end in 1989. Meanwhile, the Chilean economy remained strong and new trade agreements were initiated.

Familiar Names. The presidential candidates evoked a strong sense of déjà vu. The winner, Eduardo Frei Ruíz Tagle, is the son of former Chilean President Eduardo Frei (1964-70). The

A new international terminal at O'Hare Airport—one of the world's busiest—was opened in 1993. The $618 million facility, which was financed through airport revenue bonds, features an automated, laser-read baggage sorting system and signs that change to greet passengers in 17 languages.

younger Frei was scheduled to take office in March 1994. His chief opponent was Arturo Alessandri, the nephew of former President Jorge Alessandri, who defeated the elder Frei for the presidency in 1958. Also running in the record field of seven candidates was Gonzalo Townsend Pinochet, the nephew of Augusto Pinochet—Chile's military dictator from 1963 to 1989 and still commander of the armed forces.

Frei, 52, had 58% of the vote, compared with 24% for his closest rival, Alessandri. A far-right candidate, Jose Pinera, finished third with 6.5%, and Manfred Maxneff, the candidate of a small leftist coalition, received 5.5%. Despite Frei's personal landslide, his eight-party coalition, the Concertación por la Democracia, failed in its bid for a two-thirds majority in the 120-seat House of Deputies and for control of the 47-seat Senate.

Domestic Challenges. The most immediate challenge facing the Frei administration in 1994 would be the consolidation of Chilean democracy. Four years after the return of civilian rule to Chile, relations between the military and the government remained tense. The Chilean military was upset by the government's ongoing investigations into human-rights abuses committed during the Pinochet years. Military officers did not face potential trials or prison terms in the probes; they were shielded by an amnesty decreed by Pinochet before he left office for human-rights crimes committed between 1973 and 1978. But the government was attempting to bring to light the names of up to 500 officers responsible for torture, murder, and disappearances during those years.

To protest the investigations, the army engaged in sporadic saber rattling. On May 28 army commandos in full battle gear carrying antitank weapons and assault rifles prowled the streets of Santiago in a daylong show of force. President Patricio Aylwin had been absent from the country during the incident. When he returned, he attempted to mollify the army by proposing legislation to appoint special judges to hear testimony from military officers in secret. Left-wing members of the government protested that the bill was soft on the military, and Aylwin withdrew it in September.

On September 11 the army celebrated the 20th anniversary of the coup d'état that ousted elected President Salvador Allende and brought Pinochet to power with a Mass and a 21-gun salute. Counterdemonstrators took to the streets of Santiago and in an ensuing melee, two civilians were killed and more than 100 persons were arrested by riot police.

Economy. Pinochet left one legacy that the Aylwin government welcomed and built upon: sound economic policies and an open approach to international trade. The Chilean economy grew by an annual average of 6% between 1989 and 1992 and hit a Latin American high of 10.4% growth in 1992. Unemployment dropped from 6% in 1992 to 4.4% in 1993. Public-sector

---

CHILE • Information Highlights

Official Name: Republic of Chile.
Location: Southwestern coast of South America.
Area: 292,259 sq mi (756 950 km²).
Population (mid-1993 est.): 13,500,000.
Chief Cities (June 15, 1992): Santiago, the capital, 4,545,784; Concepción, 314,953.
Government: *Head of state and government*, Patricio Aylwin, president (took office March 1990). *Legislature*—National Congress: Senate and Chamber of Deputies.
Monetary Unit: Peso (411.17 pesos equal U.S.$1, official rate, Dec. 7, 1993).
Gross Domestic Product (1991 est. U.S.$): $30,500,000,000.
Economic Index (Santiago, 1992): *Consumer Prices* (1980 = 100), all items, 893.3; food, 909.1.
Foreign Trade (1992 U.S.$): *Imports*, $10,129,000,000; *exports*, $9,986,000,000.

---

finances were in the black and the nation's debt was reduced from $12.2 billion at the end of 1989 to $9.4 billion in 1993.

The growth rate appeared to slow during the first half of 1993, but still reached a healthy 7.4%. Exports were down by $800 million and government economists forecast a year-end merchandise deficit of $400 million, Chile's first deficit in more than a decade.

To stimulate further growth, the Chilean Congress approved a new investment law in March. It allowed foreign firms to repatriate capital after one year of operations in Chile and lowered the corporate-tax rate from 49.5% to 42%—the first change in Chilean investment rules since 1974.

Trade. International trade remained a major contributor to Chile's strong economic performance. In October, Trade Minister Jorge Marshall Rivera reported that Chile's exports were growing rapidly, rising from 28% of gross national product (GNP) in 1985 to 37% in 1993. Intraregional trade with other Latin American countries accounted for much of Chile's commerce, even though the country did not participate in any of the region's trade-integration movements such as the Andean Pact.

During the year, Chile aggressively pursued bilateral trade agreements with several neighboring countries. In March, Chile and Venezuela signed a free-trade agreement to eliminate import tariffs on 90% of traded goods by 1997. The following month, Chile signed a bilateral pact with Bolivia providing for zero tariff levels on 80 reciprocal products over a ten-year period. In October a bilateral agreement was negotiated with Ecuador for the promotion and protection of investment. And during the year, work was begun on a pipeline to carry oil from Argentine fields to Chile. The two countries also were cooperating on the development of oil deposits in the Strait of Magellan.

RICHARD C. SCHROEDER, *Consultant to the Organization of American States*

CHINA

Perhaps the most important news about the People's Republic of China in 1993 was not news of an event but that of a recalculation. In May the International Monetary Fund (IMF) decided to revise its method of calculating gross national product (GNP) in developing countries. The new method uses buying power in the economy itself to evaluate the product of that economy. Applying the new method to China, the IMF determined that its per-capita income was not $370 per year, but $1,600, and that the Chinese economy ranked not tenth in the world, but third—after those of the United States and Japan. The fund's projections suggested that China will have the world's largest economy by the year 2010.

Accelerate, Brake, Accelerate. China's aging paramount leader, Deng Xiaoping, had endorsed China's rapid shift to a market economy in February 1992. The results of that endorsement were very rapid economic development and, during the first half of 1993, an inflation rate exceeding 20% in China's large cities. In response to those signs of overheating, newly appointed Executive Vice-Premier Zhu Rongji published a 16-point prescription in July designed to cool down the economy—to land the aircraft smoothly, as one analogy had it, before it crashed.

Vice-Premier Zhu's prescriptions were effective: In August and September both the rate of growth and the rate of inflation declined measurably. But in late October, Deng returned to the stage, concerned, perhaps, lest death remove him from the scene during a retrenchment that his conservative rivals might transform into a permanent retreat into the socialist past. "Socialism," he was quoted as having pontificated, "means *rapid* development."

Deng's remark proved fatal to Zhu's plan to cool the Chinese economy. The communiqué of the Third Plenum of the 14th Central Committee, which met in Beijing in mid-November, while light on detail, nonetheless made clear that, torpedoes be damned, the Chinese economy would—for the near term at least—move full steam ahead. At year's end there was little evidence of controls in place that would avoid the overheating of the Chinese economy effectively. The last time this happened was in 1988, and it resulted in the unrest that came close to unseating the Chinese Communist Party in 1989.

Rural Discontents. That outcome was averted in 1989, at least in part because the discontent was confined to China's cities. It was not clear that that would be the case were a similar outbreak of civil disorder to take place in 1994. Rural residents of China had many reasons to be dissatisfied and, during 1993, took to the roads and lanes of their villages in record numbers to express that dissatisfaction.

As the economic reforms began in 1978, the ratio of rural to urban income was about one to three. Economic reform was initiated in the countryside, and as a result rural incomes advanced much more quickly than those in the cities in the early 1980s. By 1985 the ratio was less than one to two. As urban economic reform took off in the late 1980s, however, the urban economy grew much faster than the rural

China's Premier Li Peng and India's Prime Minister P.V. Narasimha Rao (right) agreed to a "series of confidence-building measures," including a mutual troop reduction along their frontier in the Himalayans, in Beijing in September 1993.

© Anderson/Gamma-Liaison

economy. In 1993 the rural economy was growing at between 3% and 4%, while the urban economy was growing at more than six times that rate. As a result, the ratio of rural to urban income in 1993 was about one to four.

There were, in addition, other reasons for rural discontent. There was a regulation on the books that peasant families' taxes should not exceed 5% of their income. A significant number of local governments in China's countryside, however, went bankrupt in 1993 for lack of tax revenue. Those local governments on the brink of doing so attempted to avoid this extremity by imposing what were estimated by one government source as more than 1.1 million new taxes, fines, fees, tolls, and levies nationwide, such that many families were paying far in excess of the 5% ceiling to the local government.

The "Gold Coast" Strategy. Deng's endorsement of rapid development in China's coastal provinces and cities has resulted in another fault line along which one can expect seismic activity in the wake of Deng's demise. Per-capita income in the southwest province of Guizhou, statistically China's poorest region, was approximately one tenth of per-capita income in the city of Shanghai. Differential growth rates were causing this gap to grow, not to shrink. However, there were growing rivalries among enclaves along the gold coast itself: Guangdong with its economic ties to Hong Kong, Fujian with its links with Taiwan, Shandong with South Korea, and Manchuria with Japan. Despite this competition, the coastal cities shared a growing independence from the center. Guangdong, for example, in 1978 drew 80% of its provincial expenditure budget from central funds. In 1993 that number was 2%.

Ethnic Differences. If China were to break up in the wake of some future political upheaval, it is unlikely that, except in certain isolated cases, the breakup would be along ethnic lines. Some 94% of the Chinese population is of the same Han ethnic stock. The remaining 6% is made up of members of more than 50 ethnic minorities. Tibet is an obvious and much-discussed case of potential ethnic separatism, which accounts for its having been subjected periodically to martial law by the People's Liberation Army (PLA).

It is not the only case. In Xinjiang, the autonomous region just north of Tibet, at least three persons were killed in June when a bomb blast destroyed a tourist hotel in the capital city of Kashgar. In Qinghai, Muslims took to the streets in October. At least nine lost their lives in the subsequent effort to restore order.

Political Holding Pattern. Frenetic activity in the economic sphere was accompanied by an eerie calm in the political sphere in anticipation of the storm that, it is assumed, will follow the demise of Deng Xiaoping. The National People's Congress met in March, and appointments to senior positions were announced. These appointments served to identify the principal contenders in a struggle for succession.

© AP/Wide World

China's President Jiang Zemin and U.S. President Bill Clinton met in Seattle, WA, in November. China's trade surplus with the United States and human rights reportedly were discussed.

Jiang Zemin, head of the Chinese Communist Party and designated by Deng Xiaoping as the "core" of the next generation of political leadership, was named president of the People's Republic. Li Peng retained the post of prime minister. Zhu Rongji, as noted above, became executive vice-premier. Qiao Shi, whose career had been primarily in China's security apparatus, became head of the National People's Congress. Li Ruihuan was named head of a hitherto rather inactive advisory council known as the Chinese People's Political Consultative Conference.

Premier Li Peng, a key player in the game of succession, appeared to suffer a significant setback during the summer, when he disappeared from public view. It first was announced that he was suffering from a cold. Subsequent reports confirmed that he had suffered a heart attack. While he returned to public life by mid-fall, his schedule and his portfolio had been reduced, and it appeared that his chances of retaining a major position following Deng's death had declined.

Meanwhile, the political legitimacy of the world's last major ruling Communist Party continued to decline. Despite this, paradoxically, party membership continued to grow at a rate of more than 5%, reaching a total of 57 million. Applicants for membership were abundant: The party reported that it accepted only one in 13 of those who applied. A majority of new members were drawn from the rural sector. The apparent disjunction between the party's popularity and its ability to attract new members is explained by the fact that career advancement in China continued to be facilitated by party membership.

Honoring Mao. The centenary of the birth of the former chairman of the Chinese Communist Party, Mao Zedong, was celebrated on December 26. It was a strange observance: Although he

China's economy was undergoing rapid marketization during 1993. With more than 80% of the populace now watching television, new sets were in strong demand.

was lauded as an unparalleled revolutionary leader and political theoretician, virtually all of the precepts associated with him had been abandoned by his successors. While the current political and economic system was described as "market socialism" or "socialism with Chinese characteristics," there was very little left that was recognizably socialist. Mao, nonetheless, remained a popular figure in China.

Sprouts of Democracy. Deng's plans for reform seemed to be the reverse of those in effect in Russia. There political reform was seen as a necessary precursor to repairing the country's serious economic disarray. In China, by contrast, Deng had succeeded in altering the economy radically while keeping a lid on democratization. Despite this, there were signs during the year that the system was becoming a bit more democratic despite Deng's obvious disdain.

In the southwest province of Guizhou party-approved candidates for governor were defeated by an upstart who ran against them, and the upstart, unprecedentedly, was allowed to take the seat he had won. In a similar vein, more than 10% of the delegates at the National People's Congress, known in the Western press as China's "rubber stamp legislature," abstained or voted against Li Peng for prime minister.

Loosening the Government's Grip. China's economic liberalization has loosened considerably the government's ability to control the lives of its citizens. This is particularly true with regard to the control of the flow of information. More than 80% of the Chinese population watch television, programming for which is controlled closely by the state. Recently, however, more

than 500,000 satellite dishes have given viewers in China's large coastal cities access to international programming over which the government has no control whatsoever.

Mindful of what is, from their point of view, the baneful effects of the free flow of information and tasteless MTV, the government outlawed the private ownership of satellite dishes in the early fall. By year's end, however, satellite dishes (the majority of which are manufactured in plants owned by the army) still were available for illicit purchase, and no plan appeared in place for removing those already in use.

Military Expansion. Not only satellite dishes were being marketed to eager Chinese consumers by the army. Nearly 90% of the output of the extensive network of factories owned and run by the military was devoted to the production of consumer goods. Some 20% of all domestically produced consumer goods on the Chinese market were manufactured and sold by the military, and the profits were returned to the army's coffers. The army profited as well from the extensive sale of arms abroad—sales that the U.S. government was often at pains to curtail. These profits, combined with the substantial budget increases enjoyed by the military each year since it came to the aid of the conservatives in suppressing the prodemocracy demonstrators in 1989, have provided the PLA with the wherewithal to engage in something of a shopping spree in the neighboring states that once were linked in the Soviet Union. Russian President Boris Yeltsin reported in the fall that Russian arms sales to China in 1992 amounted to nearly $2 billion.

This military expansion disturbed many of China's neighbors. Observing China's growing economic power, they were wary of the potential for a concomitant expansion of China's military presence in East Asia, particularly in the wake of the reduction in U.S. force levels in the region. A specific instance of this concern was the Spratly Islands in the South China Sea, sovereignty over which was claimed not only by China, but also by Taiwan, the Philippines, Indonesia, Vietnam, and Malaysia. In the early months of the year, China's naval presence in the island chain was expanded. In an effort to allay mounting suspicions of its intentions, however, in the late fall, China reached an informal agreement with Vietnam that called for "shelving" the dispute over sovereignty in the islands and cooperating in exploration for oil.

One State, Two Headaches. Negotiations with Britain over the composition of Hong Kong's government in the run-up to the transfer of sovereignty in 1997 began in April, but little or no progress had been made by year's end. The Chinese continued to profess outrage over Hong Kong Gov. Chris Patten's modest proposals for democratizing the process of selecting members of Hong Kong's Legislative Council. They threatened to create their own "second kitchen," or shadow government, and to install it in place of the Hong Kong government—which in their view was selected illegitimately—as soon as sovereignty is transferred. Frustrated by China's intransigence, Patten submitted the least controversial of his proposals to the Hong Kong Legislative Council in mid-December.

Beijing appeared equally concerned over changes under way in the political system on Taiwan. The same offer of "one state, two systems" was extended to Taiwan as was used as the basis for negotiating Hong Kong's future in the mid-1980s. Despite the initiation of direct talks with Taiwan in late April, however, the prospects of reunification on China's terms still seemed very remote, and sentiment on Taiwan for political independence grew steadily.

Mitigating China's tendency to act rashly with regard to Hong Kong and Taiwan was the fact that economic ties between China and those two areas had become very close in recent years. Hong Kong was the leading source of foreign investment for China. Taiwan was not far behind, with annual trade and cumulative investment that each reached the figure of $10 billion in 1993.

Least-Favored-Nation. Relations between China and the United States were sour and were likely to become sourer in the near term. President Bill Clinton, following through on a campaign pledge, issued an executive order in May that renewed China's most-favored-nation (MFN) status for 1993, but attached conditions to its further renewal in 1994. The conditions called for "significant improvement" in the observance of human rights by the Chinese government. Also to be negotiated during the year were outstanding issues concerning China's trade surplus with the United States (which the U.S. government calculated to be in excess of $20 billion) and China's arms sales abroad. Not unexpectedly, China's Foreign Minister Qian Qichen said the "politicization" of trade regulations was "unacceptable" to China.

Taking up a case of what it described as an illicit sale of weapons, the Clinton administration imposed sanctions on China in August. Washington described China's transfer of missile parts to Pakistan as in violation of the Missile Technology Control Regime—an agreement to which China was not a party, but which it had agreed to follow. Both the Chinese and Pakistani governments protested the decision, arguing that neither was technically in violation of the regime. Later that month the U.S. government was embarrassed when a joint Saudi-Chinese inspection of a Chinese ship, the *Yinhe*—accused by Washington of carrying ingredients for chemical weapons—revealed no such cargo on board.

Both sides appeared to have hoped that President Jiang Zemin's meeting with President Clinton in Seattle in November would begin the process of mending fences. Newly emboldened, some said, by China's growing economic clout, Jiang began the meeting by reading to Clinton a lecture on the inviolability of China's sovereignty. Although Clinton's spokesperson tried to put a good face on the meeting, little appeared to have been accomplished.

A State Department report prepared at year's end said that little or no progress had been made on the human-rights front in China and predicted that, unless substantial efforts were made in the early months of 1994, MFN would not be renewed. With China's political leaders on tenterhooks awaiting the passing of Deng Xiaoping, the possibility of China's meeting the U.S. conditions appeared dim.

JOHN BRYAN STARR
China Institute, New York

CHINA • Information Highlights

Official Name: People's Republic of China.
Location: Central-eastern Asia.
Area: 3,705,390 sq mi (9 596 960 km²).
Population (mid-1993 est.): 1,178,500,000.
Chief Cities (Dec. 31, 1990 est.): Beijing (Peking), the capital, 7,000,000; Shanghai, 7,830,000; Tianjin, 5,770,000.
Government: *General Secretary of the Chinese Communist Party*, Jiang Zemin (chosen June 1989). *Head of government*, Li Peng, premier (took office Nov. 1987). *Head of state*, Jiang Zemin, president (took office March 1993). *Legislature* (unicameral)— National People's Congress.
Monetary Unit: Yuan (5.8105 yuan equal U.S.$1, official rate, Dec. 31, 1993).
Gross National Product (1989 est. U.S.$): $413,000,000,000.
Foreign Trade (1992 U.S.$): *Imports*, $80,315,000,000; *exports*, $84,635,000,000.

CITIES AND URBAN AFFAIRS

Crime, racial polarization, and decaying infrastructure continued to dominate urban news in 1993.

Fiscal Stress and Crime. The inability of cities to pay for current expenditures or meet capital needs plagued many of the nation's mayors as municipal revenues continued to decline and taxpayers resisted tax increases. In July 1993 the National League of Cities reported virtually no growth in municipal revenues and said that the necessity of balancing the city budget often resulted in service reductions or modifications.

The U.S. Conference of Mayors blamed federal mandates for some of the cities' financial problems. Congress continued to require local governments to do such things as improve environmental quality or provide equal access for the disabled but did not fund such costly endeavors. Mayor Richard M. Daley of Chicago estimated that compliance with the various federal mandates cost his city $160 million annually.

Philadelphia's Mayor Edward Rendell had to make significant cutbacks to prevent the bankruptcy of his city. He froze the salaries of unionized workers and slashed the health-benefits package for city workers. He also made significant alterations to work rules and privatized some functions. Cleveland Mayor Frank White also sought savings in this fashion.

Memphis, TN, Mayor W. W. Herenton proposed annexing his city with Shelby county as a means of forestalling decline. In the 1970s and early 1980s, several other central cities—including Jacksonville (FL), Nashville (TN), and Indianapolis (IN)—formed metropolitan governments by merging with their counties. Although Memphis makes up three quarters of Shelby county's population today, there is movement out of the central city. Herenton's proposal was unusual because it was the first such plan proposed by an African American. In the other cities, African-American officials feared a dilution of minority voting power and therefore opposed such mergers.

There also has been debate in several cities about the benefits of various tax and monetary incentives to lure and retain business in urban locales. In 1993, New York state legislators debated the wisdom of sales-tax waivers and other monetary incentives. New York City officials insisted on the continued need for their utilization.

The crime problem in major U.S. cities remained staggering. The National Center on Institutions and Alternatives found that in Washington, DC, 42% of African-American males between the ages of 18 and 35 were either in jail, on probation or parole, or awaiting arrest. In October, Mayor Sharon Pratt Kelly called on the national government for assistance in patrolling Washington's streets (*see also* WASHINGTON, DC). Central-city areas contain large areas of very high unemployment, and unemployment of males aged 18-25 has been linked to a variety of crimes.

President Clinton and the Cities. With the inauguration of the first Democratic president in 12 years, many of the nation's mayors had hopes of greater presidential responsiveness to the ills of major cities. On January 24 a group of mayors presented President Bill Clinton with a wish list of 7,000 ready-to-go construction projects. These included plans for housing, streets and highways, bridges, schools, parks, and other infrastructure needs. But while the economic-stimulus program that Clinton proposed as his first legislative request contained allocations for urban public works, legislators severely pared the proposal and did not address urban-infrastructure needs because of the huge federal deficit.

Former Michigan Supreme Court Justice Dennis Archer (center), *his wife, and his son were delighted with the returns from the November 1993 mayoralty race in Detroit. The Democratic candidate defeated county prosecutor Sharon McPhail, also a Democrat, by a margin of 57% to 43%. Calling crime "the most pressing issue" facing Detroit, the mayor-elect promised to put more policemen on the city's streets and implement a plan of neighborhood policing.*

President Clinton and Attorney General Janet Reno strongly supported the so-called Brady bill—to mandate a waiting period before handguns can be purchased—which became law in late November. The Clinton administration also was sympathetic to measures to take assault rifles and other weaponry off city streets. Clinton's proposed health-care reform was seen as good for many central cities where public hospitals and clinics treat a disproportionate number of the medically indigent. The Clinton administration also proposed redirecting federal aid for elementary and secondary education from more prosperous districts to inner-city schools and those in rural areas. To remain eligible for funding, districts would have to demonstrate increases in reading and math standards.

Elections. Many of the urban mayoral elections of 1993 clearly showed the principal tensions of race and crime that beset urban areas. In Los Angeles, where crime and the economy were major campaign issues, a white Republican businessman, Richard Riordan (*see* BIOGRAPHY), defeated Democrat Michael Woo, an Asian-American city-council member. Los Angeles still was reeling from the economic devastation that occurred during the riots following the not-guilty verdicts delivered in the Rodney King beating case in 1992. Although minorities outnumber whites in Los Angeles, the majority of voters are white. Riordan replaced five-term incumbent Tom Bradley, Los Angeles' first African-American mayor. (*See also* LOS ANGELES.)

In Detroit another five-term mayor, Coleman Young—the first African American to hold that office—also stepped down. Detroit, too, has economic problems. By 1993, 46% of Detroit's children were living below the poverty line. Dennis Archer, a former Michigan Supreme Court justice who stressed cooperation with the largely white suburbs, outpolled Sharon McPhail, a Wayne county prosecutor who attacked Archer's moderation, to become Detroit's second black mayor.

Race was an issue in New York City where the African-American incumbent David Dinkins, a Democrat, faced a challenge from Rudolph Giuliani (*see* BIOGRAPHY), running as a Republican and Liberal candidate. Dinkins had defeated Giuliani four years before, but Giuliani prevailed by a similar 2% margin in 1993. Dinkins had been hurt badly by the riots in the Crown Heights section of Brooklyn in 1991. The riots had exacerbated already-tense Jewish-black relations. (*See also* NEW YORK CITY.)

St. Louis elected its first black mayor, Democrat Freeman Bosley, Jr., in a city where blacks are 43% of the electorate. Again, crime was a major issue. Candidates discussed increases to the police force and metal detectors in the schools as St. Louis' murder rate soared. Some of those killed and some perpetrators were under 14 years of age. (*See also* MISSOURI.)

LANA STEIN
University of Missouri-St. Louis

COINS AND COIN COLLECTING

The year 1993 was one of discovery and recovery in coin collecting, as the U.S. Mint launched two new commemorative coin programs and the numismatic industry experienced an upturn in bullion prices and market activity.

The Mint's first commemorative coins of 1993—a gold $5, silver $1, and silver 50-cent piece—celebrated the U.S. Bill of Rights and the role that James Madison played in its adoption. A portion of the proceeds was earmarked for the James Madison Memorial Fellowship Foundation to further education about the Bill of Rights in secondary schools.

To mark the 50th anniversary of World War II, the Mint released gold $5, silver $1, and copper-nickel 50-cent coins. Surcharges included in the price of each were paid to the American Battle Monuments Commission to help fund a memorial in Washington, DC, in honor of World War II U.S. armed forces, and to the Battle of Normandy Foundation to erect a U.S. D-Day and Battle of Normandy Memorial in Normandy, France.

The designs for both the Madison and World War II coins were selected by open competition. Sales of the coins exceeded the Mint's hopes, and some of the specially packaged issues were expected to sell out before the end of 1993.

The International Olympic Committee continued its numismatic celebration of the 100th anniversary of the modern Olympic movement with the second in a five-year series of commemorative gold and silver issues. The Centennial Coin Program's 1993 offering—a $200 gold coin and two $20 silver pieces struck by the Royal Australian Mint—highlighted the spirit of "Participation, Friendship and Fair Play."

Nineteenth- and 20th-century U.S. gold coins proved to be the best buys in 1993. Prices for common-date gold issues had dropped drastically between 1985 and 1990, but rising gold values made the series more appealing.

In May 1993 the long-missing Cohen specimen of the legendary 1804 Draped Bust dollar was recovered by Swiss authorities. With its recovery, all 15 known examples of this rarity—each valued at approximately $1 million—were accounted for.

According to an American Numismatic Association survey of nearly 27,000 hobbyists across the country, it was felt that U.S. coins and paper money need a face-lift. A majority of respondents favored changing the designs of circulating U.S. coinage and reintroducing a dollar coin, and nearly half expressed dissatisfaction with the current process of choosing themes for commemorative coinage. As for the nation's paper currency, survey participants indicated that U.S. bills should be more colorful, but should retain their present designs. To combat counterfeiting, respondents suggested watermarks and holograms.

BARBARA J. GREGORY
American Numismatic Association

COLOMBIA

The prospect of presidential elections in 1994 produced a marked increase in political activity in Colombia during 1993. Despite continued guerrilla activity, the Colombian economy continued to outperform its neighbors.

Politics. A September poll showed that the race for the presidency was a virtual tie between the two major-party candidates: Andres Pastrana from the Social Conservative Party and Ernesto Samper from the Liberal Party. Although both men faced challenges from other candidates within their own parties, it appeared likely that these two would fight it out for the presidency in May 1994. Antonio Navarro, the Democratic Alliance (AD) candidate, found himself with only 11% of the preference, less than the 14% that voted for "no one." Long-term political alienation seemed to be diminishing, as the same poll revealed that, for the first time since the 1960s, more than half of voters planned to cast ballots in the upcoming elections.

Meanwhile, the popularity of President César Gaviria Trujillo, which fell precipitously in 1992 due to an electrical shortage and the government's inability to capture Pablo Escobar—former king of the Medellín drug cartel—was rising. In May only 35% of the populace approved of his handling of the presidency, but by September this percentage had risen to 47%. In November, Escobar was killed by security forces in Medellín.

Although the nation's two main guerrilla groups—the Revolutionary Armed Forces of Colombia and the National Liberation Army—formed a unified command, rebel activity decreased in 1993. Colombia, with some 77 murders per day, still was designated as one of the world's most violent countries by the World Health Organization.

Economy. The economy continued to perform creditably during the year, with an estimated 4.1% increase in per-capita gross national product (GNP). Inflation was moderate by Latin American standards, with a monthly increase in the cost of living of 1.5%. Colombia attracted more than $5 billion in foreign investment during 1993. The United States continued to be the largest single source of outside capital, with more than 65% of the total. However, Japan was rumored to be seriously considering large new investments in Colombia.

Colombian exports continued to surpass imports. Coffee, still the nation's main foreign-exchange earner, continued to enjoy strong and stable prices. Oil production, spurred by new production from the Cusiana field, reached 466,700 barrels per day by midyear. There was talk of limiting this production to 300,000 barrels to prevent early exhaustion of the field.

Society. Colombia remained a poor nation with a large gap between rich and poor. With the poverty line in Colombia drawn at U.S.$60 per month, the percentage of poor in the country rose from 42% of the population in 1970 to 46% in 1990. At the same time, the extremely poor—defined as those with incomes of less than U.S.$30 per month—remained constant during the period at 22%.

The Colombian government became increasingly frank about the prevalence of AIDS in the nation, estimating that there were 3,844 people with AIDS and another 3,406 infected with the HIV virus. Public attitudes toward sex also appeared to be changing. An October poll conducted by the newspaper El Tiempo indicated that 86% of the population approved of the use of contraceptives and 71% saw nothing wrong with premarital sex. Only on the subject of abortion did traditional attitudes prevail, as nearly 82% of respondents condemned the practice.

ERNEST A. DUFF
Randolph-Macon Woman's College

COLOMBIA • Information Highlights

Official Name: Republic of Colombia.
Location: Northwest South America.
Area: 439,734 sq mi (1 138 910 km²).
Population (mid-1993 est.): 34,900,000.
Chief City (Oct. 15, 1985): Bogotá, the capital, 4,154,404.
Government: *Head of state and government*, César Gaviria Trujillo, president (took office August 1990). *Legislature*—Parliament: Senate and Chamber of Deputies.
Monetary Unit: Peso (686.46 pesos equal U.S.$1, Nov. 18, 1993).
Gross Domestic Product (1990 est. U.S.$): $45,000,000,000.
Economic Index (1992): *Consumer Prices* (1980 = 100), all items, 1,417.6; food, 1,576.5.
Foreign Trade (1991 U.S.$): *Imports*, $4,967,000,000; *exports*, $7,269,000,000.

COLORADO

Gang violence, arguments over gay rights, a spreading tax revolt, and a visit by Pope John Paul II dominated news in Colorado during 1993.

Crime and Judicial News. The Colorado legislature reduced sentences on some nonviolent crimes to reduce the spiraling costs of new prisons by $12 million. But after a series of highly publicized gang shootings in Denver, Gov. Roy Romer called the legislature back into special session in September to add $40 million to the budget to curb youth crime. At Romer's urging, legislators outlawed possession of handguns by minors except for hunting or target practice and also approved an 80-bed "boot camp" for violent juveniles. But judges in Arapahoe county and Denver challenged the constitutionality of parts of the law.

Aurora voters showed their concern with crime by approving a .25% sales tax to expand

The 500-seat Joan and Irving Harris Concert Hall, constructed by the Aspen Music Festival and School at a cost of $7 million, opened in August 1993. The Aspen Chamber Symphony, *left*, rehearses for the opening performance.

© Jeffrey Aaronson/Network Aspen

the city's police force, and a .5% sales tax was passed in Adams county to build a new criminal-justice center.

Denver District Judge Jeffrey Bayless issued a temporary restraining order stopping enforcement of Amendment 2, which prohibits the state or local governments from including homosexuals as a protected class in civil-rights laws. The amendment had been approved by Colorado voters in 1992. The Colorado Supreme Court issued a 6-1 decision upholding Bayless. While the rulings addressed technical issues, legal experts predicted that the court would rule that Amendment 2 violates the equal-protection clause of the U.S. 14th Amendment. Judge Bayless issued such a ruling in mid-December.

In April the 10th U.S. Circuit Court of Appeals in Denver ruled that Colorado had the power to oversee the cleanup of hazardous waste at the federally owned Rocky Mountain Arsenal. Some 22 other states joined Colorado in the suit to seek oversight over the cleanup of federal facilities in their states.

Elections and School Budgets. On November 2 voters in a statewide referendum rejected a proposal to reinstate a .2% sales tax on some items designed to raise $13 million annually to promote the state's tourism industry. Voters in suburban Douglas county, Lakewood, and Greenwood Village killed proposals to subsidize retail-business outlets. But voters looked more favorably at school-bond issues, passing an $81 million plan in rapidly growing Douglas county and an $89 million bond issue in Boulder.

A school-board election in Littleton attracted wide attention as voters ousted three incumbents in favor of a "back-to-the-basics" slate. Littleton was regarded as a pacesetter in educational reform in Colorado, but critics argued that these reforms sacrificed academic values for vague social goals.

To comply with a tax and spending limit adopted in 1992, the legislature trimmed public-school budgets by about 4%. The legislators also passed a school-reform bill.

Other. Colorado hosted young people from around the globe for World Youth Day. President Clinton greeted Pope John Paul II in Denver and an estimated 375,000 people watched the pontiff celebrate mass at Cherry Creek State Park....The opening of Denver's new airport, originally scheduled for late in 1993, was postponed to March 1994, largely due to design changes requested by airlines....Colorado's cable-TV giant Tele-Communications Inc. announced a merger with Bell Atlantic Corp. The merged company would rank fifth on the Fortune 500 list....The Colorado Rockies set a major-league-baseball attendance record of more than 4.4 million in their inaugural year, though they finished sixth in the seven-team National League West.

BOB EWEGEN, *"The Denver Post"*

COLORADO • Information Highlights

Area: 104,091 sq mi (269 596 km²).
Population (July 1, 1992 est.): 3,470,000.
Chief Cities (1990 census): Denver, the capital, 467,610; Colorado Springs, 281,140; Aurora, 222,103; Lakewood, 126,481.
Government (1993): *Chief Officers*—governor, Roy Romer (D); lt. gov., C. Michael Callihan (D). *General Assembly*—Senate, 35 members; House of Representatives, 65 members.
State Finances (fiscal year 1991): *Revenue*, $7,863,000,000; *expenditure*, $6,992,000,000.
Personal Income (1992): $71,654,000,000; per capita, $20,648.
Labor Force (August 1993): *Civilian labor force*, 1,798,400; *unemployed*, 95,200 (5.3% of total force).
Education: *Enrollment* (fall 1991)—public elementary schools, 435,621; public secondary, 157,409; colleges and universities, 235,108. *Public school expenditures* (1990-91), $2,642,839,000.

COMMONWEALTH OF INDEPENDENT STATES *See* RUSSIA AND THE COMMONWEALTH OF INDEPENDENT STATES.

COMMUNICATION TECHNOLOGY

Communication-technology advances in 1993 opened up new possibilities for the future.

Pager Technology. Pagers—or beepers, as they are commonly known—became increasingly popular. Once used primarily by physicians, pagers now were being used by everyone from teenagers to business owners to stay in touch.

One of the biggest popularity draws for pagers recently has been their cost—much lower than that of cellular phones. In addition, their usefulness has increased greatly. At one time, all a pager could do was beep to alert its carrier to get to a phone to return a call. Most pagers now display a number to which to return a call, and also can play back recorded voice messages in some cases, or display typed messages. Their look has been updated, too, with bright colors and a wristwatch-size model.

The Federal Communications Commission (FCC) in 1993 boosted the advance of pager technology by assigning a block of radio frequencies for satellite paging services. These new services would allow pagers to send and receive brief messages to or from anywhere in the world.

Other Wireless Communications. The wireless communications market expanded rapidly in 1993. Telephone companies got into the act, joining forces with cellular-phone-service providers to create "personal communication networks." In the most prominent example of this trend, AT&T bought McCaw Cellular Communications, the leading cellular-service provider. And in September the FCC set aside blocks of radio frequencies to be auctioned off to providers of wireless communications services. The FCC planned to award more than 2,500 licenses, ultimately bringing as many as seven new wireless services to every U.S. town. It was estimated that some 60 million Americans would subscribe to the new services by the end of the 1990s.

The new wireless networks—much like present cellular-phone services—would consist of "cell sites," or radio relay stations, scattered throughout a city. The sites' antennas would be connected into a wider network that would route calls from one location to another nationwide.

On-line Developments. Telephone companies invested in the cable-television industry, preparing for a merging of television, telephone service, and computing into one technology brought into homes via coaxial cable capable of carrying huge quantities of information. US West and Time Warner, for instance, planned an interactive cable system that would allow viewers to choose among hundreds of TV channels, order pay-per-view events and movies, and send and receive electronic mail (E-mail).

Also during 1993, an "information highway" where people could play games and communicate with one another was developed jointly by Sierra, a computer-game company, and AT&T. The Sierra Network is an on-line game service for personal-computer owners. Subscribers can use household phone lines to play interactive games, send and receive E-mail, or chat with others. Prior to the release of this system, such on-line gaming was impossible due to the limited ability of phone lines to transmit data. With this network, however, the games themselves are installed as software onto the user's system. When the user connects with the network, only the information needed for game playing is transferred over the phone lines.

Political E-Mail. On June 1, 1993, the White House announced that it now could receive letters via E-mail. Any person with access to a personal computer and a modem easily could send a letter to President Bill Clinton. The mail arrives through commercial on-line services and the information highway called the Internet.

ROBERT FIERO
Consultant, Alpha-Byte Computer Services

The Video Phone

In September 1992, AT&T released the long-awaited VideoPhone 2500. This new technology heralded a drastic change in the way people could communicate with one another, as it now became possible to see the person one is speaking with in full-color motion video. The Video-Phone 2500 is the first such device to employ regular phone lines. Although the device itself still was expensive—about $1,000 by late 1993—the cost of using it was the same as for an ordinary phone, and it could be plugged into a standard jack. A prototype of a video pay phone also was produced by AT&T; it would incorporate a teletypewriter (TTY).

The video phone is a modem device, similar in many ways to the modems used with computers.

Signal compression is used to transmit scanned pictures over telephone lines. Video images are displayed on a 3.3-inch (8.38-cm)-diameter LCD screen in full color, at a rate of two to ten frames per second. The user can adjust the focus; this in turn changes the number of frames per second displayed. The higher the quality of focus, the slower the rate of display will be. The moving image on the screen appears jerky—rather like an early motion picture—due to the low number of frames transmitted per second. Standard TV transmissions, for example, are sent at 30 frames per second.

Although this new technology would appear to be the wave of the future, its high cost and limited capabilities destined it to remain a novelty item, at least for the near future.

ROBERT FIERO

COMPUTERS

Fierce competition raged among manufacturers of personal computers, developers of operating systems, and producers of microprocessors in 1993. Battle lines also were drawn between government and private industry over the development of security systems and data superhighways.

Personal Computers. The personal-computer (PC) industry continued to be roiled by a price war—a benefit to buyers but an often deadly struggle for PC makers, who were forced to cut profit margins. As IBM and Compaq entered mass-market channels by virtually matching the prices of "clone" computers, they gained market share at the expense of smaller companies. Weaker manufacturers disappeared or filed for bankruptcy protection. Other companies, such as NeXT, withdrew from the hardware business entirely. Even major companies trimmed their staffs. Apple Computer announced it would lay off 2,500 employees, and Groupe Bull planned to lay off 3,000 workers. (*See also* BUSINESS AND CORPORATE AFFAIRS—*The IBM Story.*)

Numerous new PC models were introduced, most offering lots of computing power at a low price. Especially popular were ultralight "subnotebook computers" such as Hewlett-Packard's Omnibook 300 and IBM's ThinkPad 500, which weighed 2.9 lbs and 3.8 lbs (1.3 kg and 1.7 kg), respectively. Gadget lovers moved toward even lighter pen-based computers known as personal digital assistants (PDAs). Apple began selling the Newton MessagePad, a palm-sized PDA that weighs about 1 lb (0.45 kg) and has a touch-sensitive screen activated by a penlike stylus. Newton recognizes both printed and cursive handwriting by matching words written on its screen with those in its expandable 10,000-word dictionary. It also can send and receive wireless messages, communicate with other computers via modem, and be plugged into PCs.

Operating Systems. The operating system controls the running of other software and enables all a computer system's hardware to work together. The most widely used PC operating system is Microsoft DOS. The latest major revision—DOS 6.0—was introduced in 1993; it featured data compression, built-in virus protection, and an improved memory-management system.

Another introduction from Microsoft was Windows NT, a multitasking operating system that supports the Windows graphical user interface. It is designed specifically for computers linked in networks. IBM also introduced a multitasking operating system for the work-group environment, OS/2 Version 2.1.

Microprocessors. Intel began shipping Pentium microprocessors, the fifth generation of chips in its 8086 family and the successor to its highly popular i486 processor. The Pentium is a 32-bit processor featuring 3.1 million transistors—nearly three times as many as the i486. Models with speeds of 60 MHz and 66 MHz were available. Pentium is compatible with previous 8086 generations, enabling it to run software created for earlier generations. Its power and flexibility make it suitable for a range of sophisticated network applications. Competing against Pentium will be the MPC601 Power PC, a RISC microprocessor jointly developed by Motorola, IBM, and Apple. It also is available in 60 MHz and 66 MHz versions. (RISC, or Reduced Instruction Set Computer chips, have a limited set of instructions, which makes them much faster than conventional chips.)

Data Highways. Anyone with a computer and a modem can go on-line, or access a variety of computer networks via telephone. For millions of computer users, the network of choice is actually an amalgamation of more than 11,000 interconnected networks known as Internet. By 1993, Internet linked 15 million to 30 million people in 137 countries. It was being used to exchange messages, share research findings, retrieve public-domain data, collaborate on projects, engage in teleconferences, and so on.

A more ambitious data highway was proposed in 1993 by the Clinton administration. The plan would invest federal funds in a nationwide fiber-optic network that would link every home, business, classroom, and library in the nation by 2015. The plan was supported by educators and public-interest groups, but opposed by businesses which would have difficulty competing.

Privacy and Security. Among issues to be addressed as organizations go on-line are privacy and security. Hackers often find it surprisingly easy to access everything from individuals' medical and credit records to corporations' marketing plans and investment strategies.

An effective security technique is encryption, or the coding of data prior to storage or transmission to prevent unauthorized access; a special password or decoder is needed to translate the data back into its original form. Businesses and civil libertarians are eager to ensure that all communications remain private, but law-enforcement agencies want to have the ability—with a court's authorization—to tap into communications among criminals and people viewed as national-security threats. The solution, in the government's view, is a national encryption standard to which it or its representatives would hold the special code keys.

The Clinton administration supported Clipper, a data- and voice-encryption standard developed by scientists at the National Security Agency (NSA). But computer-industry personnel severely criticized Clipper, and executives in other industries made it clear that they would not buy Clipper products. Later in the year, a group of companies led by Novell, the leading developer of corporate networking software, announced an encryption scheme that they planned to promote as an industrywide standard.

JENNY TESAR, *Author*
"The New Webster's Computer Handbook"

CONNECTICUT

In Connecticut the major events of 1993 concerned casino gambling, gang wars, a corporate merger, an effort to bring professional football to Hartford, and Gov. Lowell P. Weicker Jr.'s decision not to seek a second term.

Politics and Legislation. In announcing his decision not to seek reelection, Governor Weicker said he wanted to spend more time with his family. He was elected in 1990 as a third-party candidate after an 18-year career as a Republican U.S. senator. He was often at odds with the state GOP's leadership and left the party to run for governor on the A Connecticut Party (ACP) ticket. Lt. Gov. Eunice Groark, his running mate in 1990, said she would run for governor in the 1994 election as the ACP candidate. Groark, as presiding officer of the state Senate, cast the tie-breaking vote in 1993 that led to a law banning the retail sale of semiautomatic weapons. In 1991 she had broken a Senate tie that led to adoption of a personal-income tax.

The legislature, for the first time in 20 years, adopted a biennial budget, of $8.6 billion for 1993-94 and $9.04 billion for 1994-95. The budget satisfies a constitutional cap that voters approved in 1992. Governor Weicker signed legislation authorizing construction of a 70,000-seat stadium in Hartford in a campaign to get the National Football League's New England Patriots to move from Foxboro, MA.

In November 2 elections, Michael P. Peters, a firefighter and former Democrat who turned independent, defeated Hartford's three-term Mayor Carrie Saxon Perry; Waterbury's Mayor Edward D. Bergin (D), Bridgeport's Mayor Joseph Ganim (D), and Danbury's Mayor Gene Eriquez (D) were returned to office; and Joseph DeStefano (D) was chosen as mayor of New Haven. Linda A. Blogoslowski (R) was the first woman to be elected mayor of New Britain.

Casino Gambling and Land Claims. Proponents of legalized casinos in Hartford and Bridgeport spent more than $1 million lobbying the state legislature without even getting a vote. Governor Weicker pledged to veto any casino bill and struck a deal with the Mashantucket Pequots, owners of the state's only casino, that swayed legislators to table the casino issue. The Pequots promised to give the state at least $100 million annually from slot-machine revenues if other slot machines were prohibited in the state. The Pequots' Foxwoods High Stakes Bingo & Casino in Ledyard became the leading revenue producer among U.S. casinos in 1993. (*See also* GAMBLING.)

Efforts of the Mashantucket Pequots to have tribe-owned land near the Ledyard reservation declared part of the reservation and the claim of the Golden Hill Paugussett Indians to land in the Bridgeport area caused turmoil. The legislature authorized a task force to study the land claims. Granting the Indians' claims would remove the land from tax rolls, and the claims in the Bridgeport area clouded the status of real-estate transfers.

Gang Warfare. Latino street gangs battled in state cities, but in Hartford it was open warfare

In September 1993, Connecticut Gov. Lowell Weicker signed a $252.1 million bond issue to build a 70,000-seat stadium in Hartford. The legislation was part of a campaign to lure pro football's New England Patriots to move to Hartford.

CONNECTICUT • Information Highlights

Area: 5,018 sq mi (12 997 km²).

Population (July 1, 1992 est.): 3,281,000.

Chief Cities (1990 census): Hartford, the capital, 139,739; Bridgeport, 141,686; New Haven, 130,474; Waterbury, 108,961.

Government (1993): *Chief Officers*—governor, Lowell P. Weicker, Jr. (I); lt. gov., Eunice Groark (I). *General Assembly*—Senate, 36 members; House of Representatives, 151 members.

State Finances (fiscal year 1991): *Revenue,* $9,816,000,000; *expenditure,* $11,115,000,000.

Personal Income (1992): $89,036,000,000; per capita, $27,137.

Labor Force (August 1993): *Civilian labor force,* 1,807,300; *unemployed,* 117,400 (6.5% of total force).

Education: *Enrollment* (fall 1991)—public elementary schools, 355,463; public secondary, 125,587; colleges and universities, 165,824. *Public school expenditures* (1990-91), $3,427,201,000.

as The Latin Kings and Los Solidos fought an eight-hour gun battle on June 8. Sporadic shootings continued into the fall. Eight gang members and an innocent bystander were shot to death and several people were wounded. The violence was reduced as state police troopers joined city police in patrolling streets and warring gangs made an October truce. The Hartford truce was broken in late October with a shooting death. Two slayings in New Britain and one in Windham in early November were linked to gang feuding.

Other News. Hartford-based insurance giant Travelers Corp. and Primerica Corp., a New York financial firm, agreed to merge. Travelers' shareholders would receive $4.1 billion of Primerica stock. The new company would be named Travelers and headquartered in New York.

Jesse Campbell, who rose through the Hartford Police Department's ranks, became the city's first black police chief. And the Right Rev. Clarence Coleridge, a native of Guyana, became the 13th bishop of the Episcopal Diocese of Connecticut, the Episcopal Church's first diocese in America, dating back to 1784.

ROBERT F. MURPHY, *"The Hartford Courant"*

CONSUMER AFFAIRS

The general attitude of U.S. consumers in 1993 was illustrated by a headline in *USA Today:* "Consumers Still Shaky." People continued to lack confidence in the economy. Nonetheless, there were various signals that the U.S. economy was improving and some evidence that consumer confidence in the economy was also on an upswing. Retail gains, for example, reached double-digit increases over 1992 monthly levels. The multitude of economic actions advocated by the Bill Clinton administration in health care, deficit reduction, and tax reform received high approval ratings from consumers. The budget deficit was down 10% from the fiscal-year 1992 figure. Thus, by year's end 1993 it appeared that consumers were cautious but optimistic.

Government Action. Federal-government involvement in consumer protection had reached low levels during the administrations of Presidents Ronald Reagan and George Bush. President Clinton, however, appeared more supportive of the need to protect consumers. Various Clinton appointees exhibited interest in pursuing aggressively both the environmental and economic problems confronting consumers. This contrasted, however, with state, county, and city consumer-protection-agency efforts. These agencies appeared to continue the downward trend in their effectiveness that began in the 1980s. The general decline was attributed for the most part to budgetary constraints at these levels.

Nutrition Information. The most substantive federal consumer legislation to take effect in 1993 was the Nutrition Labeling and Education Act (NLEA). Provisions of the law related to health claims became effective in mid-1993. The remaining measures, which pertained to nutritional labeling, would go into effect by mid-1994. The law would affect almost all processed food, and was to be administered by two federal agencies, the U.S. Food and Drug Administration (FDA) and the U.S. Department of Agriculture (USDA), for meat and poultry labeling.

The NLEA, which was the first major change in food labeling since 1974, included provisions to eliminate much of the confusion that had permeated supermarket shelves for decades. Among other stipulations, it stated that information regarding nutritional content must be disclosed on labels and expressed in uniform terms. Also, definitions for serving sizes and terms such as "low-fat" and "light" were standardized. If consumers proved willing to read the new labels, the NLEA could have a dramatic effect on improving the nutrition of families throughout the United States.

Other Consumer Laws and Regulations. There were several other federal consumer-protection measures implemented in 1993. All provisions of the Truth in Savings Act became law in 1993. This act requires that savings institutions specify the uniform annual percentage yield (APY), which allows consumers to compare savings rates offered by different banks. Another law, the Telephone Consumer Protection Act (TCPA), restricts the manner and time period in which a solicitor may call consumers. The Federal Communications Commission (FCC) re-regulated cable-television rate charges, and also required cable companies to be more receptive to subscribers' service requests. The Federal Trade Commission (FTC) established standards for advertising and programming directed toward children, as well as for 900-number advertisements and disclosures.

MEL J. ZELENAK
University of Missouri-Columbia

CRIME

The election of a Democrat to the White House seemed to carry the promise that the deadlock over enactment of a sweeping federal crime bill would be broken in 1993. But as President Bill Clinton's first year in office ended, the battle over crime legislation had not been won completely, although the Brady bill, which requires a five-day waiting period for purchase of a handgun, had been signed into law.

While Democrats controlled both houses on Capitol Hill, consensus over key features of the package was slow to develop. Clinton's plan contained many of the same ingredients as the measure that was shelved in 1992 during the presidential campaign. Clinton requested passage of the Brady bill and proposed a ban on the import of assault pistols. The Federal Bureau of Investigation (FBI), departing from its usual neutrality on issues with political overtones, expressed support for a waiting period on gun purchases.

To attract conservative support, the measure included a provision to make 47 felony crimes—ranging from assassination of a member of Congress to drive-by shootings—punishable by death. Also, the plan would require death-row inmates to appeal within six months of conviction when claiming that their rights were violated. The measure also called for $150 million for ten military-style boot camps for young, first-time offenders; and $3.4 billion over five years to put 50,000 additional police officers on the streets.

Another issue that spurred controversy was the handling of mandatory minimum offenses for federal convictions. Attorney General Janet Reno was among the most prominent critics of mandatory sentences, particularly for lesser offenses such as selling small amounts of drugs. Many federal judges complained that they have been stripped of discretion in sentencing; others said mandatory minimums crowd the prisons unnecessarily, making it much more difficult to keep violent offenders behind bars. Clinton also tried to drum up support for his anticrime package by linking it to the administration's top domestic priority: health-care reform. "Violent crime crowds our emergency rooms and drains our medical resources. And it is siphoning away our humanity," he said.

Debate over the crime legislation was waged against a backdrop of mounting gang violence and widespread availability of guns, particularly among the young. Every 14 minutes someone in the United States died from a gunshot wound, nearly half in homicides, according to law-enforcement officials and other experts. They also noted that firearms killed more teenagers than cancer, heart disease, AIDS, and all other diseases combined. The *New England Journal of Medicine* published a study that said keeping a gun at home nearly triples the chance someone will be killed on the premises.

Moreover, authorities said youth gangs were spreading from the big cities to the suburbs. One survey reported that 36% of suburban teenagers knew someone who had been killed or injured from gunfire, surprisingly close to the 40% of city-dwelling teenagers.

In an important development, the drive to enact state and federal laws to make stalking a crime gained momentum. About 40 states have passed such laws in the aftermath of actress

After a summer of testimony in 1993, a jury in Sonora, CA, found Ellie Nesler (near right) guilty of voluntary manslaughter for the killing of Daniel Mark Driver, who was accused of molesting her son. The jury also ruled that the 41-year-old single mother was sane at the time that she entered a courtroom and opened fire on Driver. The case gained attention throughout the United States.

Rebecca Schaeffer's shooting death in 1989 in California at the hands of an obsessed fan. A bill was introduced in Congress that would impose a prison term of up to ten years anytime a stalker crosses state lines or uses the mail or telephone to deliver a threat. Meanwhile, civil libertarians were monitoring these laws to make sure they were not too broad or too vague.

Crime Rates. The FBI's latest study said violent crimes reported to police edged up in 1992 due to increases in aggravated assaults and rapes. But the total number of crimes reported dropped 2.9% from 1991 to 14.4 million, the first annual decline since 1984. FBI Director Louis J. Freeh (*see* BIOGRAPHY) said the news was not cause for celebration. "Any reduction in crime is welcome," he said, "but the amount of violent crime and other grave offenses nationwide remains intolerable. Crime is shockingly high in a country where the rule of law should prevail."

The FBI said police got reports of 1.9 million violent crimes—murder, forcible rape, robbery, and aggravated assault; and 12.5 million property crimes—burglary, larceny-theft, and motor-vehicle theft. Violent crime increased 1.1%, while property crime declined 3.5%. Also, the number of reported crimes per 100,000 U.S. inhabitants dropped 4% to 5,660—the lowest level since 1987. The violent-crime rate in this category fell 0.1% and the property-crime rate dropped 4.6%. The rates take into account the nation's increasing population.

But some crime experts found little solace in the latest statistics. "What I see happening is younger people are committing more violent acts," said Geoffrey P. Alpert, professor of criminology and criminal justice at the University of South Carolina in Columbia. "Where many young people used to start their criminal careers with minor and property crimes, we're seeing them become more violent very, very quickly."

"There's been a growth in the kind of murders that trouble us the most, stranger-to-stranger homicides, which scare people especially when it spreads out to shopping malls, parking lots, and highways," said Alfred Blumstein, dean of the Heinz School of Public Policy and Management at Carnegie Mellon University in Pittsburgh.

The FBI said the number of homicide victims who knew their attackers declined from 55% in 1982 to 47% in 1992. And the FBI said firearms were used in 68% of the homicides in 1992, compared with 61% in 1988. Experts also warned that the FBI figures on crime may not be complete. Many crimes such as burglaries and larcenies never may get reported because people believe the police will not investigate them.

The Death Penalty. By mid-October 1993, U.S. states had executed 34 prisoners, more than in any year since 1962. Texas led the way with 14 executions. There were 31 executions in 1992. The number of men and women on death rows nationwide swelled to nearly 3,000. Death-penalty opponents said the quickening pace of executions reflected growing impatience by many judges with capital-punishment disputes and drawn-out appeals. Federal courts are increasingly willing to let the states act, they said.

In an unusual dispute, New York state demanded the return of Thomas Grasso from Oklahoma—even though the convicted killer said he wanted to be executed in Oklahoma rather than be imprisoned in New York. Grasso was convicted of killing elderly residents in both states. New York officials said he must serve a term of 20 years to life for the New York killing. New York's Gov. Mario Cuomo is an outspoken opponent of the death penalty.

Major Crimes. The randomness of violent crime shocked the nation during the summer when it was learned that the father of basketball superstar Michael Jordan had been killed. Two teenagers were arrested and charged with murdering James Jordan in his car as he napped on a North Carolina roadside. His body was found nearly two weeks later in a South Carolina creek by a fisherman and was identified using dental records. Prosecutors said they intended to seek the death penalty for defendants Larry Martin Demery and Daniel Andre Green, both 18. Michael Jordan later announced his retirement from the Chicago Bulls, fueling speculation his father's death played a role in his decision, although the younger Jordan denied this connection.

Four Muslim fundamentalists—claiming their innocence—went on trial in New York City, accused in February's World Trade Center bombing that killed six persons and injured more than 1,000. Prosecutors said the terrorist attack had shattered Americans' sense of security. The bombing occurred as tens of thousands of people in the world's second-tallest buildings were going about their lunchtime business. The defendants allegedly mixed chemicals to create the bomb and carried it to the Trade Center in a rented van that one of them had reported stolen the day before the attack. The defendants were Mohammad Salameh, 26; Ahmad Ajaj, 27; Mahmud Abouhalima, 33; and Nidal Ayyad, 25. Sheikh Omar Abd al-Rahman, a blind Egyptian cleric, allegedly inspired those accused in the Trade Center bombing and was charged—along with 14 others—with conspiracy in a separate sedition case. (*See also* TERRORISM.)

Florida, one of the nation's leading vacation attractions, was struck by a wave of tourist killings. In one of the most notorious cases, four teenagers were charged in the shooting death of British tourist Gary Colley, 34, and the wounding of his female companion, Margaret Ann Jagger, 35, at an interstate rest stop. The suspects in the case ranged in age from 13 to 17.

In New York, Joey Buttafuoco pleaded guilty to statutory rape, which brought him a six-month jail term. For 18 months, the 37-year-old Long Island body-shop man had denied that he ever had had sex with Amy Fisher, the teenager

© Dan Groshong/Sipa

Deputy District Attorney Janet Moore, right, was the lead prosecutor at a 1993 headline trial stemming from the 1992 Los Angeles riots. Two defendants were tried in connection with the videotaped attack against truck driver Reginald Denny and other victims during the rioting. Damian Monroe Williams was found guilty of mayhem and four counts of misdemeanor assault and acquitted of five other felony counts. Henry Watson was found guilty of a misdemeanor assault and acquitted of three other felony charges. The jury remained deadlocked on an additional assault count against Watson.

who shot Buttafuoco's wife. Fisher is serving five to 15 years in prison. The case seemed to capture the public imagination, becoming the subject of three made-for-television movies. An even more lurid tale developed in Manassas, VA, when Lorena Bobbitt, 24, cut off her husband's penis after, she said, he raped her. She said she had endured years of sexual and physical abuse. She faced charges of malicious wounding. Her husband, John Wayne Bobbitt, 26, was acquitted of marital sexual assault.

Joel Rifkin admitted strangling or suffocating 17 prostitutes over two years, authorities in New York said. He reportedly told police he picked up prostitutes around New York City, had sex with them, and then killed them. He was arrested when police found a decomposed body in his pickup truck after he ran a stop sign.

In Boston radical fugitive Katherine Ann Power was sentenced to eight to 12 years in prison for driving a getaway car in a 1970 bank robbery—that left a Boston policeman dead—intended to raise money for opposition to the war in Vietnam. Power, 44, surrendered to authorities after 23 years in hiding—including 14 years on the FBI's "most wanted" list. She had settled in a small Oregon town, gotten married, and had a son.

In Louisiana, Rodney Peairs was acquitted of manslaughter in the 1992 shooting death of a Japanese exchange student. In effect, the jury decided in favor of the right of citizens to protect their homes from perceived threats. The victim was Yoshihiro Hattori, 16, whom Peairs said he mistook for an assailant when the teen mistakenly went to Peairs' door in Baton Rouge look-

ing for a Halloween party. Peairs had yelled "freeze." But the student, apparently not understanding the term, continued to approach. During a trip to Japan, President Clinton expressed his sympathy to the victim's family.

Late in the year horrific crimes in California and New York compelled Americans to focus even more on the problem of violent crime. Polly Klaas, age 12, was abducted in October from her Petaluma, CA, bedroom. Nine weeks later the alleged killer led police to her body. In New York racial hatred seemed to be the motive behind the December killing of six passengers on a Long Island commuter train. The Jamaican-born gunman, Colin Ferguson, shot 23 persons in all.

White-Collar Crime. In the so-called BCCI bank scandal, lawyer Robert Altman was acquitted by a New York jury of four criminal counts. Altman and law partner Clark Clifford, the former defense secretary and adviser to presidents, were charged with helping BCCI—the Bank of Credit and Commerce International—trick bank regulators so a group of Persian Gulf businessmen could gain control of a major Washington bank. Clifford, recovering from heart surgery, did not stand trial with Altman; federal charges against him were dismissed without prejudice. The case was only a small part of the global scandal in which some $12 billion was lost by tens of thousands of investors.

In October, Stew Leonard, Sr., the owner of a successful Connecticut supermarket, was sentenced to more than four years in prison and fined $947,000 for his role in a tax-fraud scheme.

See also LAW; PRISONS.

JIM RUBIN, *The Associated Press*

CUBA

Government mismanagement, the loss of economic aid from the former Soviet Union, and a natural disaster made 1993 one of the worst years in Cuba since Fidel Castro came to power in 1959. The Cuban government had hoped that the economy, reeling from three difficult years, would stabilize as a result of a series of sweeping reforms that it had put into effect. But the economic improvement did not materialize and the future, Castro conceded, looked grim.

Economy. The Cuban government initiated a series of economic policies that it hoped would boost the nation's troubled economy. The most important of these changes—one which negated a principal tenet of socialism that Castro long had proclaimed as a central doctrine—was the legalization of hard-currency holdings, previously a criminal offense. Following legislation passed in August, Cubans were allowed to maintain bank accounts in foreign currency and buy products in special dollar stores.

Among the other economic moves made to stir the economy were the creation of more-independent farm units able to make financial and market decisions which had been under the domain of Havana central planners; the permission to operate small private businesses in the service sector; and the proposed sale or rent to foreign investors of 132 state enterprises—including a petroleum refinery, a beer brewery, a sugar refinery, and Cuba's fishing fleet. The new economic plan also included a reduction by 40% of Cuba's 180,000-strong armed forces and a drive to increase international tourism, one of the few growing sources of foreign exchange.

According to Western estimates, Cuba's economy declined 10% in 1993, while foreign trade dropped to $3.5 billion from $5.5 billion in 1992. The production of sugar, Cuba's main export crop, reached only 4.2 million metric tons, the lowest in 30 years, to account for a $450 million revenue loss.

The so-called "Storm of the Century" hit Cuba in March, causing more than $1 billion in losses in agriculture and making the existing severe food shortages even worse. Electric-power outages, due to fuel shortages, also reached severe levels, forcing shutdowns of many workplaces, including government ministries.

Despite the economic crisis, the rigidly controlled economy did not respond easily to changes, which were opposed by some hard-line officials. Rather than initiating reforms, the Cuban government had sanctioned existing conditions, such as the long-existing dollar black market or the sale of produce by farmers directly to customers and not to state agencies. There were no indications that Havana was contemplating substantial reforms that would move Cuba toward a free economy and political pluralism.

Social Issues. Economic ills deepened social problems. The government admitted an increase in serious crime, prostitution, alcoholism, and suicide. And political opposition remained weak and disorganized despite the proliferation of minute human-rights and dissident groups. Their leaders were harassed constantly and often were jailed or deported. Most Cubans—preoccupied with the daily difficulties of power outages, transportation problems, and getting their small food rations—did not challenge the government actively.

Domestic Politics. The army and security apparatus appeared to remain loyal to Castro. The 67-year-old "Maximum Leader" appeared to remain in command of strong physical and intellectual faculties. However, younger leaders were coming to the fore, among them Carlos Lage Davila, 41, the presumed Cuban economic

© Lee Celano/Saba

Three Cuban men rolled a rusted refrigerator through the crumbling streets of old Havana. The nation's economy continued its fall into crisis during 1993 as anticipated reforms never appeared and Cubans had to endure meager food rations and power outages.

czar; Ricardo Alarcón de Quesada, 55, a former foreign minister who was named president of the National Assembly of People's Power (Cuba's one-party parliament); and Alarcón's successor, the 37-year-old Roberto Robaina González.

The Roman Catholic Church emerged in 1993 as a potentially important factor in political change. In September 11 Cuban bishops, in a pastoral letter later endorsed by Pope John Paul II, urged all Cubans, including those abroad, to solve in a "fraternal dialogue" the country's problems. Among the problems cited in the document were one-party rule, "excessive control of state security organs," the "high number of prisoners," and "discrimination because of political and philosophical ideas or religious belief." Several officials, but not Castro himself, criticized the pastoral letter, which also called for the end of the 31-year U.S. trade embargo against Cuba. The embargo, which according to Havana had been responsible for many of the nation's economic woes, was tightened late in 1992 by the Cuban Democracy Act, which prohibited foreign subsidiaries of U.S. firms to do business with Cuba.

Foreign Affairs. On several occasions Cuba appeared willing to talk to the United States about solving all outstanding issues, but there were no signs of an early Washington-Havana thaw. Among the issues that Cuba was ready to tackle were reparations for $1.8 billion in U.S. properties seized after 1959, but not, as Castro said, to "negotiate the revolution, socialism, or the national sovereignty." However, small matters were agreed upon by Cuba and the United States successfully, among them the gradual repatriation of 1,500 Cuban-born convicted criminals held in U.S. jails and the return by Cuba of two suspected U.S. cocaine traffickers. The year ended with Castro's estranged daughter defecting to the United States.

Hoping to spur a gradual economic bottoming out in 1994, Cuba looked all over the world for foreign investors. The 13 members of the Caribbean Community and Common Market (CARICOM), despite strong objections from the United States, began discussions with Havana

about tourist-sector cooperation, while Colombia reestablished diplomatic relations with Cuba. Russia, in an effort to protect its Cuban investments, resumed limited aid to Havana.

Meanwhile, a French oil consortium started drilling wells off the coast of Cuba. If this particular venture was successful, it could help solve Cuba's most pressing economic shortfall. Commenting on the country's economic direction in his annual speech on July 26, Castro said, "Who would have thought that we, so doctrinaire, we who have fought foreign investment, would one day view foreign investment as an urgent need?"

GEORGE VOLSKY, *University of Miami*

CYPRUS

For yet another year Cyprus remained a divided island republic in 1993, just as the country had been since 1974 when Turkey invaded and took over large territories in the north. In these northern territories, the Turkish Cypriot Rauf Denktash held the title of president of the Turkish Republic of Northern Cyprus, a political entity unilaterally proclaimed in 1983. In the south the Greek-Cypriot-controlled, internationally recognized government of the Republic of Cyprus held sway and refused to accept officially the de facto partition which the Turkish invasion of 1974 had brought about.

Presidential Elections. President George Vassiliou of the Republic of Cyprus, a Greek Cypriot, failed to win a majority in a presidential election held on Feb. 7, 1993, forcing a runoff on February 14. He then lost his post to Glafcos Clerides, a veteran politician who had served as interim acting president in 1974 during the Turkish invasion. Clerides began a five-year term with the major task of seeking some solution to the island's division.

United Nations Efforts. Attempts were continued under the auspices of United Nations (UN) Secretary-General Boutros Boutros-Ghali during the year to find a way to reconcile the Greek and Turkish Cypriots, represented respectively by Clerides and Denktash. Yet again, as the case has been over the decades with any attempts made at mediation, no settlement was found, nor seemed even near. The UN continued to maintain a peacekeeping force in Cyprus (UNFICYP) which had been deployed since the 1960s to prevent clashes between the Greek and Turkish Cypriots.

Chief concerns for the Greek Cypriots included an arrangement for some 200,000 persons who had fled from the north in the wake of the 1974 invasion, the ascertainment of what had happened to those still missing as a result of the invasion, and the removal of the Turkish armed forces and thousands of Turkish settlers who had been brought into the north. The Greek Cypriots accused Denktash of delaying the quest for a solution. On the Turkish Cypriot side, there

---

CUBA • Information Highlights

Official Name: Republic of Cuba.
Location: Caribbean.
Area: 42,803 sq mi (110 860 km²).
Population (mid-1993 est.): 11,000,000.
Chief Cities (Dec. 31, 1989 est.): Havana, the capital, 2,096,054; Santiago de Cuba, 405,354; Camagüey, 283,008; Holguín, 228,053.
Government: *Head of state and government*, Fidel Castro Ruz, president (took office under a new constitution, December 1976). *Legislature* (unicameral)—National Assembly of People's Power.
Gross National Product (1991 est. U.S.$): $17,000,000,000.
Foreign Trade (1991 U.S.$): *Imports*, $3,690,000,000; *exports*, $3,585,000,000.

CYPRUS • Information Highlights

Official Name: Republic of Cyprus.
Location: Eastern Mediterranean.
Area: 3,571 sq mi (9 250 km^2).
Population (mid-1993 est.): 700,000.
Chief Cities (1982 census): Nicosia, the capital, 48,221; Limassol, 74,782.
Government: *Head of state and government*, Glafcos Clerides, president (took office March 1, 1993). *Legislature*—House of Representatives.
Monetary Unit: Pound (0.502 pound equals U.S.$1, June 1993).
Gross Domestic Product (1990 U.S.$): $5,500,000,000.
Economic Index (1992): *Consumer Prices* (1980 = 100), all items, 180.0; food, 198.2.
Foreign Trade (1992 U.S.$): *Imports*, $3,291,000,000; *exports*, $1,003,000,000.

seemed to be no reason to seek a change in the status quo to a settlement that might be disadvantageous for them.

Royal Visit. Great Britain's Queen Elizabeth II and the Duke of Edinburgh attended a Commonwealth Heads of Government conference of 50 nations in the Republic of Cyprus during October. The queen's visit provoked acrimonious demonstrations by small, vocal Greek Cypriot groups recalling the Cypriot struggle for independence from Britain in the 1950s and protesting the Turkish presence in the north. President Clerides tried to downplay the extent of such protests, but the hostile attitude toward the queen provoked anti-Cypriot comments in the British press.

The Nadir Case. On May 4 a Turkish Cypriot, Asil Nadir, former head of the Polly Peck business conglomerate in Great Britain, jumped bail there and fled to northern Cyprus while he was under indictment on various charges leveled at him by the British Serious Fraud Office. The disclosure that Nadir had been friendly with Michael Mates, a minister in the British government, precipitated an enormous political storm in Britain and caused Mates to resign his office. Nadir steadfastly refused during the year to return from northern Cyprus while various allegations, innuendoes, and rumors continued to circulate concerning the matter.

GEORGE J. MARCOPOULOS, *Tufts University*

CZECH REPUBLIC

On Jan. 1, 1993, the Czech Republic emerged as yet another independent country in Eastern Europe after the Slovaks and the Czechs chose to divide. The western two thirds of Czechoslovakia—the so-called "historic lands" of Bohemia, Moravia, and a portion of Silesia—became the territory of the Czech Republic.

The Czech-Slovak dissensions that led to the separation had begun as early as 1918, when Czechoslovakia was born following World War

I. But these dissensions gained momentum when ethnic rivalries, long suppressed under Communist rule, erupted in the aftermath of the Communist collapse. The proverbial last straw was the adverse effect that the post-Communist economic reforms had on Slovakia's economy. Since the Slovak economy had a larger share of inefficient Soviet-style plants than did the Czech economy, the conversion to a free-enterprise system hit the Slovaks much harder than the Czechs. The Slovak unemployment rate shot up four times higher than that of the Czechs. Slovak nationalists blamed this inequity on "Prague centralism" and alleged Czech disregard of Slovak needs.

In elections held in June 1992, the ferociously nationalistic Movement for Democratic Slovakia prevailed overwhelmingly in Slovakia, while the Czech Civic Democratic Party (ODS), committed to the concept of a strong federal government, won decisively in Czech lands. The partition of the country thus became inevitable.

The Political System. The constitution of the Czech Republic, adopted on Dec. 16, 1992, provided for a parliamentary government. The legislative branch is a bicameral Parliament: a 200-member Chamber of Deputies elected for a four-year term and an 81-member Senate elected for a six-year term. As of November 1993 the Senate remained to be established. Executive authority was vested in the president of the republic and a council of ministers headed by a chairman (prime minister). The president is elected by both houses of the Parliament for a five-year term. He appoints the chairman and the members of the council of ministers, who must have the confidence of the Chamber of Deputies to stay in office.

A Constitutional Court was created to guarantee the constitutionality of all legal rules and procedures, staffed by 15 judges appointed for a ten-year term by the president with the consent of the Senate. The regular court system consists of four levels of courts staffed with judges appointed for life. The basic units of local government are communities headed by communal assemblies elected every four years. Appended to the constitution is an elaborate Bill of Fundamental Rights and Freedoms granting all the inhabitants comprehensive human, political, cultural, economic, social, and ethnic rights.

The former Czechoslovakian president, Václav Havel, was elected as the first president of the Czech Republic, and the former prime minister of Czechoslovakia and the leader of the ODS, Václav Klaus, was appointed as prime minister.

Economy. The gradual conversion of the state-run economy of the Communist era into a market-oriented free-enterprise system continued unabated in 1993. The privatization of state-owned enterprises gathered momentum as its Czech promoters no longer had to cope with Slovak allegations about the adverse impact of privatization on Slovakia's economy. By midyear the private-sector share rose to 60% in services,

In August 1993, Václav Havel (far right), the first president of the Czech Republic, shared a toast in a Prague pub with Russian President Boris Yeltsin (near right), who visited Havel and the capital city on the occasion of the 25th anniversary of the Soviet invasion of Czechoslovakia. The two leaders signed a Czech-Russian friendship treaty during their summit.

© Reuters/Bettmann

58% in construction, 29% in agriculture, and 18% in industrial production. In September an additional 770 state enterprises with a book value of 145 billion crowns (roughly $4.8 billion) were scheduled to be sold to private entrepreneurs.

The performance of the economy improved somewhat in 1993. By the end of 1993 the gross national product (GNP) was expected to increase by 0.9%, which would be the first such increase since the ouster of the Communist regime in 1989. Labor productivity in small (and mostly privately owned) enterprises rose by an impressive 21% above the same period of 1992. As of March 1993 foreign investments in the Czech economy amounted to $1.4 billion, and by September, Czech hard-currency reserves reached $5.6 billion. Foreign trade increased by 15.4% in the first seven months of 1993. At the end of July, the state budget had a healthy surplus of some 6 billion crowns (roughly some $200 million). By August unemployment stood at a low 3.0%.

However, problems connected with the transition to a new system persisted. Industrial production fell by 5.2% and construction by 5.4% in the first half of 1993. Labor productivity in state enterprises with more than 26 employees decreased by 5.5% compared to the first half of 1992. Many industrial enterprises, commercial establishments, and construction firms were insolvent. Grain harvest was expected to be some 2.8% to 10% below the seven million tons

that had been hoped for, so hundreds of thousands of tons would have to be purchased abroad. By June 1993 consumer prices rose 12.1% above their levels for the first half of 1992, and further increases were expected. Even though the Czech Republic and Slovakia remained in a customs union, the partition of Czechoslovakia and the growing Slovak difficulties in paying for imports had an adverse impact on Czech-Slovak trade and caused Czech exports to Slovakia to drop by 33% in the first half of 1993. An estimated 70,000 Czech families were living below the poverty level.

Czech-Slovak Relations. The partition of Czechoslovakia was handled in a civilized and peaceful manner. Some 16 treaties and agreements were concluded to provide for the division of federally owned property and assets, border regulations, use of federal archives, legal assistance, health care and social security, the protection of the environment, and weapons registration. Both parties agreed that intangible property would belong to the republic in which it was located, while most tangible assets and federal property located abroad would be divided by a ratio of two to one, the approximate population ratio of the two republics.

Some controversies arose, such as the division of the Czechoslovak State Bank's assets and Slovak demands that the Czech Republic pay to use the Czechoslovak flag as the flag of the Czech Republic and that Slovakia be compensated for several Slovak villages that the Czechoslovak government had exchanged for Polish territory that became part of the Czech Republic. (*See also* SLOVAKIA.)

Foreign Affairs. In June the Czech Republic joined the Council of Europe and in October an agreement was signed providing for its affiliation with the European Community (later the European Union). The Czech Republic was elected to serve as a nonpermanent member of the United Nations Security Council for a two-year term beginning in January 1994.

EDWARD TABORSKY
University of Texas, Austin

CZECH REPUBLIC • Information Highlights

Official Name: Czech Republic.
Location: East-central Europe.
Area: 30,450 sq mi (78 864 km²).
Population (mid-1993 est.): 10,300,000.
Chief Cities (Dec. 31, 1990 est.): Prague, the capital, 1,215,076; Brno, 392,614; Ostrava, 331,504.
Government: *Head of state*, Václav Havel, president (took office Jan. 1, 1993). *Head of government*, Václav Klaus, prime minister (appointed January 1993). *Legislature* (bicameral)—Senate and Chamber of Deputies.
Monetary Unit: Crown (29.21 crowns equal U.S.$1, commercial rate, Dec. 20, 1993).

DANCE

Leading dance personalities—Agnes de Mille, Alwin Nikolais, and Rudolf Nureyev—died in 1993, and economic hardship caused a growing number of U.S. dance troupes to curtail their seasons or perform without live orchestras. Despite this bleak note, there were spectacular highlights, such as the New York City Ballet's Balanchine Celebration, the France Danse festival at the John F. Kennedy Center for the Performing Arts in Washington, and superb dancing from U.S. and foreign troupes.

Ballet. The two-month celebration that presented 73 ballets (from 1928 to 1981) by George Balanchine was a historic and unprecedented survey of a single choreographer's output. Peter Martins, City Ballet's artistic director, organized this festival to commemorate the tenth anniversary of Balanchine's death. He invited dancers from other U.S. companies and from abroad to appear in the more-than-six-hour closing performance on June 27 at Lincoln Center in New York. "Balanchine does not belong just to City Ballet," he said, explaining that the foreign guests reminded audiences that Balanchine's ballets were danced throughout the world.

Nevertheless, it was for the City Ballet, founded in 1948 by Balanchine and Lincoln Kirstein, that the choreographer produced most of his work; the celebration was a chronological presentation of many ballets that the company had performed over the decades. Balanchine works created elsewhere and never transferred to the City Ballet were excluded, as were ballets dropped from the repertory and now forgotten.

The prolific nature of Balanchine's creativity, however, assured a huge stylistic variety.

Public interest was piqued by the revival of ballets from the 1940s and 1950s that more recent generations of City Ballet viewers never had seen. These works were *Haieff Divertimento, Bourrée Fantasque, Symphonie Concertante, Glinka Pas de Trois, Minkus Pas de Trois,* and *Sylvia Pas de Deux. Valse-Fantaisie* was given in two different versions, from 1953 and 1967.

There was some criticism that the celebration was overextended, but the event attracted sold-out houses and closed in triumph with a *Dinner with Balanchine* program, portions of which later were broadcast nationally over the Public Broadcasting System. During intermissions at this last performance, the audience was served food that was linked thematically to the Russian, European, and American phases of Balanchine's career.

Earlier in the year, the company presented an innovative but uneven premiere that referred to U.S. history: *Jazz (Six Syncopated Movements)* was choreographed by Martins to a commissioned score by Wynton Marsalis.

American Ballet Theatre (ABT), the City Ballet's friendly rival, continued amid severe financial constraints in its first season under a new artistic director, Kevin McKenzie. Performance standards were high, but the major novelties in the spring season were two ballets originally created for other troupes. Both were based on well-known 18th-century tales of vice and perdition. Christian Holder's *Les Liaisons Dangereuses*, set to Mozart, was clever but too dependent upon mime; Kenneth MacMillan's familiar *Manon* was performed with impressive

Students from the School of American Ballet joined with members of the New York City Ballet to perform in the "Balanchine Celebration," marking the tenth anniversary of George Balanchine's death and featuring performances of 73 of his ballets.

© Paul Kolnik

ensemble spirit. Among the company's dancers, the young Paloma Herrera was visibly on the rise. Nina Ananiashvili of the Bolshoi Ballet appeared as a guest in *Swan Lake.*

In December, McKenzie choreographed a new version of *The Nutcracker*, with a modified libretto by the playwright Wendy Wasserstein. The premiere at California's Orange County Performing Arts Center received mixed reviews.

The Joffrey Ballet under Gerald Arpino's direction delivered one of the year's most talked-about premieres—*Billboards.* Set to music by Prince, the four-part rock ballet attracted enthusiastic young audiences on a national tour that began at the University of Iowa. Critics found more style than substance in the separate segments choreographed by Laura Dean, Charles Moulton, Margo Sappington, and Peter Pucci.

Feld Ballets/NY featured premieres by Eliot Feld: *Blooms Wake, Frets and Women, The Relative Disposition of the Parts*, and *Hadji.* The Boston Ballet won acclaim with a new production of *The Sleeping Beauty.*

Modern Dance. The Martha Graham Dance Company invited Twyla Tharp, the first choreographer not associated with the troupe, to create a premiere. Tharp surprised all by using klezmer music in *Demeter and Persephone*, an abstract treatment of mother-daughter relations and a valid homage to Graham, who died in 1991. Another premiere for the Graham company was Pascal Rioult's *Harvest.*

Earlier, while appearing with her own troupe, Tharp presented workshop performances of her choreography and a popular audience-participation event: She invited viewers onstage to learn a dance segment. Tharp also danced in a new solo, *Fever.*

Merce Cunningham's premieres were *Enter, Touchbase,* and *Doubletoss,* and Paul Taylor's premieres were *Spindrift* and *A Field of Grass.* The Alvin Ailey American Dance Theater paid tribute to its late founder with *Jukebox for Alvin*, by Garth Fagan, and *Hymn*, with choreography by company director Judith Jamison and a script written and recited onstage by the actress Anna Deavere Smith. Erick Hawkins explored partnering in his company's *Each Time You Carry Me This Way.* Trisha Brown's new works were *Another Story as in Falling* and *M.G.: The Movie.*

Younger choreographers showed greater emotional expression, even in what looked like pure-movement pieces, as in Mark Morris' *Mosaic and United*, a mysterious work that featured Mikhail Baryshnikov. Morris was more playful in *Home*, but a darker piece was *Grand Duo*, which had the fervor of a revival meeting.

Love and death, especially as related to AIDS, continued to be dominant themes in Bill T. Jones' choreography. His premieres included *Achilles Loved Patroclus* and *War Between the States.* A related subtext was felt in *Landscape*, a solo about inconsolable grief that Christopher Gillis had choreographed for his sister Margie Gillis. Christopher Gillis, a leading male dancer in Paul Taylor's company, died later of AIDS. "A Demand Performance," an AIDS benefit organized by the fashion and dance worlds, was dedicated to Gillis; his sister's own solo, *Torn Roots, Broken Branches*, visibly moved the audience.

A memorable dramatic performance came from Gary Chryst as a man awaiting death in *Dämmerung.* This theatrical study in disintegration, presented at the American Dance Festival in Durham, NC, was choreographed by Martha Clarke, an alumna of Pilobolus. Pilolobus itself attempted a sketchy treatment of the novel *Finnegans Wake* in a premiere called *Rejoyce.*

Foreign Companies. The Kennedy Center's France Danse festival, devoted to French dance, showed off the dazzling dancers of the Paris Opera Ballet in *La Bayadère*, an opulent production staged by Rudolf Nureyev a few months before his death. The company, directed by Patrick Dupond, offered an equally interesting triple bill of 20th-century revivals—*Icare* and *Suite en Blanc*, both by Serge Lifar, and Roland Petit's 1945 masterpiece of poetic realism, *Le Rendezvous.*

France Danse came up with a more surprising success when the Ballet du Rhin staged *La Fille Mal Gardée* with bawdy touches that harked back to its premiere in 1789. Unlike more familiar versions that use modern ballet technique, this reconstruction was choreographed in the style of 18th-century Baroque dance. Four French modern-dance groups also took part in the festival.

Varieties of Canadian dance were represented by four visiting companies. James Kudelka's *Désir*, a passionate and physically daring suite of duets, and his *Private Dances*—both danced by Les Grands Ballets Canadiens—left a strong impact. Originality was the hallmark of Christopher House's work for Toronto Dance Theater, Robert Desrosiers' *Black and White in Color*, and Marie Chouinard's version of *Le Sacre du Printemps.*

Other visitors included the Bavarian National Ballet from Munich, the Royal New Zealand Ballet, and the experimental Indonesian choreographer Sardono, whose *Passage through the Gong* was part of the Next Wave festival at the Brooklyn Academy of Music.

Obituaries. In addition to Nureyev and the choreographers Agnes de Mille, known for her Broadway choreography and dramatic ballets, and Alwin Nikolais, a pioneer in mixed media, other choreographers who died in 1993 included John Butler, Manuel Alum, and Louis Falco. (*See also* OBITUARIES.)

Awards. Choreographer Talley Beatty received the Samuel H. Scripps-American Dance Festival Award for lifetime achievement and Arthur Mitchell, director of Dance Theater of Harlem, received the Kennedy Center Honors.

ANNA KISSELGOFF, *"The New York Times"*

DELAWARE

Delawareans witnessed the first major political transition in 16 years as Thomas Carper was inaugurated governor on a cold, sunny day in January 1993. In taking his oath of office, Carper, a Democrat, succeeded four terms of leadership by Republican Governors Pierre duPont and Michael Castle. Castle also took his oath of office in January as Delaware's only member of the U.S. House of Representatives. Carper had vacated the House seat to run for governor. Castle, who was prohibited by law from seeking a third term as governor, became one of only a few former governors to enter the U.S. House.

The other significant transition in the state involved the inauguration of James Sills as mayor of Wilmington, Delaware's largest city. Sills is the first African American to hold that office. The wheels of government moved slowly as both Carper and Sills replaced most of the key department heads in their administrations. There were few new legislative proposals as the appointments of new cabinet secretaries were announced, confirmation hearings were held, and the new officeholders began to pick up the reins of power.

Legislative Session. A major uproar occurred during the opening days of the 1993 legislative session as information filtered out to the public about the recommendations of a state compensation commission to increase significantly the salaries of most high-ranking state officials, including legislators, cabinet members, and judges. These pay increases were to go into effect automatically, unless the legislature voted to turn them down. Public opposition to the pay raises mounted steadily, but the legislature recessed its January session for six weeks without voting on the pay raises, allowing them to take effect.

A firestorm of public protest erupted as the state Senate was gaveled into recess with members of the minority caucus on their feet calling for a vote on the pay raises. A deluge of telephone complaints, talk-show dialogue, and demonstrations persuaded Governor Carper, who had been inaugurated only a few days earlier, to call the legislature back into session to vote on the pay plan. It was voted down, and the bruised legislators went home to take up the issue later. The remainder of the legislative session was quiet, with no significant legislation being passed.

Economy. Corporate layoffs in the chemical and automotive industries dominated economic news in Delaware in 1993. The biggest shock occurred with the announcement by the General Motors Corporation that it planned to close its Delaware assembly plant in 1996. This would mean the loss of more than 6,000 jobs in direct and related employment. The du Pont company also announced the elimination of some 4,000 jobs in Delaware.

The Delaware unemployment rate remained below the national average during 1993. In September the rate was 5.4%, compared with the national average of 6.7%. Manufacturing jobs showed the biggest decline, while government and service jobs increased slightly. There was no net gain in jobs in the local economy.

Sports. Professional baseball returned to Delaware after an absence of more than four decades. The Wilmington Blue Rocks opened their first season at the new 5,400-seat Legends Stadium in Wilmington. The Carolina League team, a part of the Kansas City Royals organization, was an immediate success. The team attracted the highest home-game average attendance in the league and had the second-highest seasonal attendance in the league. It placed first in its division for the season and won the divisional play-offs, but lost in the final league championship series.

JEROME LEWIS, *University of Delaware*

DELAWARE • Information Highlights

Area: 2,045 sq mi (5 295 km²).
Population (July 1, 1992 est.): 689,000.
Chief Cities (1990 census): Dover, the capital, 27,630; Wilmington, 71,529; Newark, 25,098; Milford, 6,040.
Government (1993): *Chief Officers*—governor, Tom Carper (D); lt. gov., Ruth Ann Minner (D). *General Assembly*—Senate, 21 members; House of Representatives, 41 members.
State Finances (fiscal year 1991): *Revenue,* $2,443,000,000; *expenditure,* $2,318,000,000.
Personal Income (1992): $15,301,000,000; per capita, $22,201.
Labor Force (August 1993): *Civilian labor force,* 380,700; *unemployed,* 19,000 (5.0% of total force).
Education: *Enrollment* (fall 1991)—public elementary schools, 74,555; public secondary, 27,641; colleges and universities, 42,988. *Public school expenditures* (1990-91), $534,003,000.

DENMARK

A second referendum on ratification of the 1991 European Community (EC) Treaty on European Union (the Maastricht Treaty) and domestic politics dominated 1993 news in Denmark.

Maastricht Treaty. The Danes reversed their 1992 rejection of the Maastricht Treaty in a second referendum on May 18, 1993. A total of 56.8% of Danish voters voted yes and 43.2% voted no to ratification of the treaty. That was an increase of 47.5% in the yes vote. Voter turnout increased by 2.4% to 85.5%. All parliamentary parties except the right-wing Progressive Party campaigned for a yes vote, but the left-wing Socialist People's Party, which had campaigned for a no in 1992, was split deeply on the issue. The party switched sides as a consequence of the Edinburgh Agreement, which was negotiated in December 1992 and stipulated that Denmark could "opt out" on several EC actions toward

Denmark's Prime Minister Poul Nyrup Rasmussen savored the positive results of a national referendum on the Maastricht Treaty for European Union on May 18. Social Democrat Rasmussen had taken the helm of a four-party coalition government in January when Prime Minister Poul Schlüter resigned under fire after 11 years in power.

© Regis Bossu/Sygma

unity, including a single currency, a single defense policy, a single judicial and immigration policy, and anything which may threaten the Danish welfare state. The agreement, legally binding for all 12 EC countries and with the same duration as the treaty, substantiated the Danish government's claim that the 1993 referendum was not a simple repeat of the 1992 referendum, which would have been constitutionally questionable.

Politics. Denmark changed government on Jan. 25, 1993, when a four-party government led by Social Democrat Poul Nyrup Rasmussen replaced the Conservative-Liberal government led by Poul Schlüter, in power since 1982. The three other parties in the new government were the Center Democrats, led by Mimi Jakobsen, who took over as minister of industrial coordination; the Radical Liberals, led by Marianne Jelved, the new minister of economics; and the Christian People's Party, led by Jann Sjursen, the new minister of energy. The new government declared the battle against unemployment to be its key priority, and in June parliament passed a tax reform, which will reduce the marginal income-tax rate from the world's largest, 68% in

1993, to 62% in 1998. Fiscal policy was eased moderately to create new jobs in 1994.

Schlüter's resignation had been a direct result of the publication on Jan. 14, 1993, of a Special Judges Report on the rights of Sri Lanka's Tamil refugees in Denmark in 1987. The report, commissioned by the government, stated that families of the refugees had been denied—effectively and illegally—their right to join their next of kin in Denmark, and that then Minister of Justice Erik Ninn-Hansen knowingly had administered this policy. The report further stated that the prime minister did know or should have known about the attempt to cover up these illegal procedures, since changed. Faced with the loss of crucial parliamentary support from the Radical Liberal Party, Schlüter, surprised by the findings, chose to resign. Impeachment proceedings were set in motion against Ninn-Hansen, but not against Schlüter.

Economic Affairs. Unemployment continued to rise through 1993, exceeding 350,000—close to 12% of the labor force. But unemployment apart, the Danish economy was performing better than that of neighboring Germany in terms of growth, inflation, and trade. In the fall, inflation was a mere 1.2%, or less than half of Germany's rate. Despite this fact, the Danish currency was devalued by the markets in 1993—initially by 8% but later in the fall by 3%—after the European Monetary System (EMS) de facto collapsed on Aug. 1, 1993. Since 1982 it had been the policy of the Danish Central Bank and government to keep the Danish exchange rate as close to the German mark as possible, and from 1987 to 1993 the parity did not change at all. With EMS currencies allowed to fluctuate by as much as 15% as the result of an August 1993 agreement, the Danish currency, the krone, for all practical purposes was floating freely for the first time since 1972.

Foreign Affairs. In October the Danish and Polish governments signed an agreement on joint military maneuvers and possibly joint United Nations (UN) peacekeeping forces. Denmark also supported Polish aspirations for closer ties with the North American Treaty Organization (NATO).

LEIF BECK FALLESEN, *Boersen, Copenhagen*

DENMARK • Information Highlights

Official Name: Kingdom of Denmark.
Location: Northwest Europe.
Area: 16,629 sq mi (43 070 km²).
Population (mid-1993 est.): 5,200,000.
Chief Cities (Jan. 1, 1992 est.): Copenhagen, the capital, 1,339,395 (incl. suburbs); Århus, 267,873; Odense, 179,487.
Government: *Head of state*, Margrethe II, queen (acceded Jan. 1972). *Head of government*, Poul Nyrup Rasmussen, prime minister (took office Jan. 1993). *Legislature* (unicameral)—Folketing.
Monetary Unit: Krone (6.7410 kroner equal U.S.$1, Nov. 11, 1993).
Gross Domestic Product (1991 U.S.$): $91,100,000,000.
Economic Indexes (1992): *Consumer Prices* (1980 = 100), all items, 185.5; food, 169.0. *Industrial Production* (1980 = 100), 136.
Foreign Trade (1992 U.S.$): *Imports*, $33,613,000,000; *exports*, $39,577,000,000.

DRUGS AND ALCOHOL

The U.S. government's "war on drugs," first declared in 1971, took on a different cast in 1993. The Clinton administration took steps to rethink the fight against the importation and use of cocaine, heroin, marijuana, and other illicit drugs. The administration began increasing emphasis on drug treatment and education, and scaling down the $1.1 billion annual effort to interdict drug smugglers abroad.

Antidrug Efforts. Congress and the administration agreed to cut $231 million in federal drug education and treatment programs out of the president's $13 billion antidrug budget, which was weighted heavily toward interdiction efforts. Administration officials said, however, that the government was committed to a treatment- and education-oriented program.

"I want drugs to be considered as more of a public-health problem than as a criminal-justice problem," said Lee P. Brown, the former New York City police commissioner who, on June 21, took over the White House Office of National Drug Control Policy—a position newly elevated to Cabinet status. Brown unveiled the outline of a new interim program drug-fighting strategy focusing on lessening domestic demand—as opposed to a program emphasizing foreign interdiction—in an appearance before the Senate Judiciary Committee on October 20. He also told the committee that a final, more detailed plan would be drawn up in early 1994.

The president's National Security Council reportedly concluded that efforts to combat drug smuggling abroad largely had failed and recommended steps to redirect efforts. In September, Congress approved significant funding cuts for foreign antidrug operations, primarily in Peru, Bolivia, and Colombia—where most of the world's coca is grown, processed into cocaine, and distributed. The Drug Enforcement Agency undertook a new plan that focused on stopping a handful of Colombian drug kingpins who are responsible for about 80% of international cocaine traffic and two organized crime leaders in Myanmar and Pakistan who are believed to control the bulk of the world's heroin trade.

Drug Use. Nationwide U.S. surveys released in 1993 reported that drug use among some younger segments of society, which had been declining steadily since the early 1980s, was rising. The annual survey compiled for the federal government by the University of Michigan's Institute for Social Research, released April 13, found that reported use of marijuana, cocaine, and LSD by eighth-graders was higher in 1992 than in 1991. The survey also reported that marijuana and cocaine use among high-school seniors continued to drop, while LSD use among seniors was unchanged from 1991. In July the researchers released more statistics that reported that marijuana and LSD use among college students and young adults increased markedly in 1992 compared with the year before, while cocaine use remained about the same.

In October the federal government's Substance Abuse and Mental Health Services Administration reported an 18% annual increase in cocaine-related visits to hospital emergency rooms in 1992, a 34% increase in heroin-related emergencies, and a 48% increase in marijuana-related emergencies. "These are the highest levels ever," said Daniel Melnick, a Health and Human Services senior official.

Alcohol. Researchers in 1993 reported slight declines in alcohol use among college students and young adults in 1992. Nevertheless, use of alcohol—a substance health officials consider the nation's most abused drug—remained a significant public-health problem. Federal health officials estimated that some 10 million adult Americans were alcoholics or had serious drinking problems that accounted for untold billions

Lee P. Brown, a former municipal police chief, took over as head of the Office of National Drug Control Policy in the Clinton administration. In October 1993 he discussed the administration's Interim National Control Strategy with members of a Los Angeles youth group (right). The administration's overall drug-control program was to be released in early 1994.

of dollars in health-care costs, decreased productivity, and treatment.

Alcohol abuse remained a big problem among students. "Heavy party drinking remains widespread [among college students], and alcohol use on college campuses is extraordinarily high by anybody's standards," said Lloyd Johnston, the head of the University of Michigan drug- and alcohol-use survey.

In April, then U.S. Surgeon General Antonia C. Novello reported that nearly half the nation's 20 million seventh- through 12th-graders said they drank alcohol; that 8 million drank weekly; and that nearly 500,000 drank five or more drinks in a row every week. "At any one time across the country 7 million students are able to walk into a store and buy alcohol without an ID," Novello said. Her successor, Joycelyn Elders, favored including new alcohol taxes in the Clinton administration's proposed health-care plan. Heavy drinkers "have become a public-health problem that we have to address," Elders said, "and the industry that created the problem needs to help pay for it."

MARK LEEPSON, *Freelance Writer*

ECUADOR

During 1993, Ecuadorian President Sixto Durán Ballén—in his first year in office—took steps to create a more open and market-driven economy, but this progress at times was blocked by political and public opposition and even terrorism.

Political Opposition. While President Durán Ballén pursued economic liberalization, his cabinet split into two camps. The "social front" favored gradual reform, was led by Interior Minister Roberto Dunn Barreiro, and included the ministers of social welfare, health, and labor. The "economic front" was led by Vice-President Alberto Dahik and Finance Minister Mario Rivadeneira and included more hard-line ministers. Tensions were resolved in July when the president replaced two ministers from each faction with associates of the vice-president. Durán Ballén promised social programs to soften the impact of his austerity measures, but the hard-line faction clearly had won.

The congress was reluctant to support the president's economic program. The president's Republican Unity Party (PUR) was small and disorganized, lacking a majority even with conservative support. The congress was dominated by a broad opposition coalition—ranging from moderate conservatives to the extreme left—that elected Liberal Samuel Belletini as congressional president. The congress delayed approval of a state-modernization bill—the cornerstone of the president's economic program—for more than seven months. The legislation authorized the privatization of some 160 state-owned companies and the reduction of about

ECUADOR • Information Highlights
Official Name: Republic of Ecuador.
Location: Northwest South America.
Area: 109,483 sq mi (283 560 km²).
Population (mid-1993 est.): 10,300,000.
Chief Cities (1990 census): Quito, the capital, 1,100,847; Guayaquil, 1,508,444; Cuenca, 194,981.
Government: *Head of state and government,* Sixto Durán Ballén, president (took office August 10, 1992). *Legislature* (unicameral)—Chamber of Representatives.
Monetary Unit: Sucre (1,894.01 sucres equal U.S.$1, floating rate, Nov. 4, 1993).
Gross Domestic Product (1991 U.S.$): $11,500,000,000.
Economic Index (1992): *Consumer Prices* (1981 = 100), all items, 4,360.8; food, 6,172.2.
Foreign Trade (1992 U.S.$): *Imports,* $2,491,000,000; *exports,* $3,008,000,000.

120,000 jobs (out of a total of 400,000) in the public sector.

Economy. Despite intense political opposition, the Durán Ballén administration posted modest economic gains, lowering inflation from an annual rate of 60% to 46%, stabilizing exchange and interest rates, building foreign reserves, and reducing the fiscal deficit from 7% to 2% of gross domestic product (GDP). However, the deficit would have been much larger if the government had not boosted oil production nearly 20%. Nevertheless, Ecuador failed to resume payment on its $12.2 billion foreign debt. Negotiations with the International Monetary Fund (IMF) for a two-year standby agreement continued fruitlessly.

Antigovernment Protests. The president's toughest challenge was to maintain public order. When he proposed utility-rate hikes as part of negotiations with the IMF, popular unrest grew. On May 26 a general strike occurred, led by the United Workers' Front (FUT), an umbrella organization representing some 400,000 workers, and the Confederation of Indigenous Nations of the Ecuadorian Andes (CONAIE). Several people were injured in confrontations with police and more than 100 people were arrested. While labor, students, and indigenous groups actively had challenged the president's austerity plan from its inception, this strike marked the first time that they presented a united front. The alliance had lasted only two days when the FUT called off the strike, citing government intransigence. Leaders of CONAIE, representing Ecuador's 2 million to 3 million Indians, opposed the FUT's move and continued the struggle by blockading highways.

Sol Rojo (Red Sun), a Maoist terrorist group, also protested the government's economic policies with a series of bombings of public installations. A large military operation directed against Sol Rojo led to three deaths and spurred charges that the army had used excessive force.

MICHAEL COPPEDGE, *Johns Hopkins University*

EDUCATION

By 1993—ten years after the official launching of public-education reform in the report, "A Nation at Risk"—leaders of U.S. education had realized that there were no simple, silver-bullet solutions to improving schools. While increased student achievement remained uneven, much more complex ideas about what needed to be done had surfaced by 1993 than were found in early solutions such as increased graduation requirements or minimal competency testing.

The Clinton Administration. These goals were evident as national education policy changed hands. The new Bill Clinton administration in Washington, DC, brought, as expected, different ideas about how to shape federal education policy. However, in 1993 state policy making stole the show, and those developing policies for the new administration wrote state-based initiatives into every major piece of legislation.

This shift to a partnership with states might have been expected, considering President Clinton's own experience at state-level education reform in Arkansas and as chair of the Education Commission of the States. With his appointment of two former governors to the top positions in the U.S. Department of Education—his good friend and mentor, Richard Riley of South Carolina, as secretary of education; and former Vermont Gov. Madeleine Kunin as Riley's deputy secretary—a state view of federal policy was assured.

The framework for this partnership was the Goals 2000: Educate America Act. Unlike the Bush administration's America 2000 plan, the Clinton legislation aimed to create fundamental reforms in all schools rather than a model in each congressional district. It also focused on improvements in the public-school system and would not extend funding to nonpublic schools. At the core of Goals 2000 would be state action plans incorporating school and local-community proposals. These plans were to set standards geared to national performance standards that define what all students should know and be able to do in core subject areas.

At the same time, the legislation called for the development of student performance assessments matched to the higher content standards. States would be encouraged to create better assessment systems that meet criteria to be established by the nonpartisan National Education Goals Panel. The most controversial part of the proposal concerned a third category of standards—those guaranteeing "opportunity to learn." The Clinton administration favored voluntary standards, such as information about the availability of resources and preparation of teachers that parents and other taxpayers could use to decide if schools were performing well. Some members of Congress, however, wanted a stricter definition that would insist upon equal opportunities being in place before schools or students could be assessed. The final compromise called for states to submit standards—but the whole process would be voluntary.

With the Clinton administration's plan finalized, the proposal for reauthorization of the Elementary and Secondary Education Act then fell into place. This act, for example, would require states to submit plans under Chapter I, the federal compensatory education program that spells out how eligible children will be helped to meet the standards adopted by the state for all students. Chapter I students also would be assessed by the systems developed in each state that meet national criteria. A focus on state leadership appeared again in the National and Community Service Trust Act, the first major piece of education legislation introduced by the new administration and passed by Congress. (*See* SIDEBAR, page 211.)

Finally, among the early legislative initiatives of the administration was one focused on expanding various types of school-to-work pro-

U.S. SCHOOLS—A STATISTICAL PROFILE*

ENROLLMENT.   U.S. public-school enrollment has been rising, especially in the lower grades, during the 1990s. Private-school enrollment, which declined during the 1980s—in part because many Catholic schools closed—also has been increasing. At the same time, with the economy in a downturn and the job market tight, many unemployed or underemployed people returned to school. This has led to an increase in college enrollment.

	1970	1980	1985	1993 projection
Public				
Elementary	27.49	24.19	24.22	26.55
Secondary	18.40	16.68	15.19	16.42
College	6.42	9.45	9.47	11.18
Private				
Elementary	4.05	3.99	4.19	4.25
Secondary	1.31	1.33	1.36	1.18
College	2.15	2.64	2.78	3.17

TEACHERS.   The number of teachers has increased in accordance with enrollment trends.

	1970	1980	1985	1993
Public				
Elementary	1.13	1.19	1.24	1.46
Secondary	.92	1.00	.97	1.03
Higher	.31	.49	.53	.61
Private				
Elementary	.15	.21	.25	.26
Secondary	.08	.09	.10	.11
Higher	.16	.19	.21	.26

GRADUATES.

	1970	1980	1985	1993
High School				
Public	2.59	2.75	2.41	2.28
Private	.30	.30	.26	.26
College				
Bachelor's	.79	.93	.99	1.10

*All figures in millions.

Students at the University of Bridgeport in Bridgeport, CT, were overjoyed when the Board of Governors of the State Department of Higher Education voted to reaccredit the university through June 30, 1995. The private, 1,400-student institution had run into financial difficulty in 1992 and had been taken over by the Professors World Peace Academy, which is financed almost entirely by the Unification Church.

© Steve Miller/NYT Pictures

grams, including youth apprenticeships. Not only did this proposal call for state plans, but it joined the Department of Education and the Department of Labor in managing the plan. Indeed, collaboration across federal departments was one of the policy principles that emerged in the first year of the Clinton administration. The "reinventing government" thrust of the administration, led by Vice-President Albert Gore, Jr., not only called for eliminating or consolidating small programs in the Department of Education, but also for greater coordination among the Departments of Labor, Education, and Health and Human Services in planning and in granting waivers.

Most of the debate over the reauthorization of Chapter I was expected to center on the targeting of funding to the neediest schools, a move that would eliminate funding in many schools enrolling low numbers of eligible children. At the same time, schools would be given much greater flexibility in deciding how to serve low-income children through an expansion of school-wide plans under Chapter I. All of these measures were aimed at making individual schools more accountable for achieving better results. And, instead of losing funds if student achievement improved, schools would continue to receive funding as long as they enrolled large numbers of poor children.

Several other trends were evident at the federal level in 1993. The administration wanted to put a high priority on staff development in all subject areas, so that teachers would be prepared for more challenging content standards, new assessments, and the goal of helping all students perform at higher levels. Charter schools also were proposed, as long as they were developed within the public-school system. And an Office of Educational Technology was created to coordinate such projects as distance learning and education's role in the proposed national telecommunications network.

This last initiative reflected a breakthrough in thinking and in use of advanced technologies in schools that finally emerged in 1993. Timid and traditional views about computers and other technologies heretofore had dominated their use, but research and experience began to change these views, allowing technology to be integrated into learning across all disciplines rather than used as an add-on or for basic skills instruction. The best evidence of this change was a growing investment in the training of teachers to use new technologies.

State Financing. One by one, state structures for the funding of public education fell before court decisions in 1993, creating the largest group of successful challenges to school finance plans in 20 years. The most sweeping one was in Alabama, where a circuit court ruled the state's entire education system unconstitutional and called for the state to "reinvent" the state education system, much as Kentucky did four years earlier. The plan presented to the court would call for almost $1 billion a year more than at present to cover the cost of equalized funding and improvements to schools. State finance systems in Massachusetts, Tennessee, North Dakota, and New Jersey were among those declared unconstitutional; but in Michigan, it was the state legislature that threw school financing into a turmoil. The problems of a small school district, Kalkaska—forced to close months before the end of the school year because of financial problems—illuminated the flaws in overreliance on property taxes to support schools. As a result,

lawmakers repealed local property-tax funding of schools as of the 1994-95 school year. They then had to come up with a way to raise the $6.3 billion shortfall, with Gov. John Engler calling for plans to provide grants to students for use at any public school and to create charter schools. In August the problem grew even more complex, as Governor Engler abolished state property taxes, which had provided 65% of Michigan's public-school funding.

Reform Update. By the fall of 1993, seven state legislatures had approved the establishment of charter schools. Launched in Minnesota in 1991, the charter-school movement contends that like-minded educators or others should be allowed to receive charters to operate their own autonomous schools. California followed with its own law in 1992, then five additional states passed such laws in 1993. Supporters see charter schools as a way to shake up "mainline" schools, as well as provide a low-cost and less-controversial alternative to vouchers. One early supporter, however, withdrew his endorsement of the concept, largely because charter laws were not protecting teacher rights. American Federation of Teachers (AFT) President Albert Shanker not only came out as opposed to charter schools, but also discontinued an AFT center on school reform, opting for more traditional efforts at improvements through new standards and assessments.

Another major initiative at radical reform, the Edison Project of entrepreneur Chris Whittle, redrew its plans for a national system of private schools, supposedly because the project had not attracted the necessary funding. Instead, Whittle said the project would focus on managing existing schools.

States seeking to adopt or implement another prominent reform strategy—outcomes-based education—ran into unexpected controversy. Supporters of the strategy explain that it is an attempt to focus on what students actually know and how they use their knowledge—the results of schooling—rather than determining school success by the number of hours spent on a subject or credits earned. However, such changes came under severe attack by conservative

National Service Plan

Water still was covering much of the flooded land of the U.S. Midwest when the Iowa Conservation Corps organized hundreds of young people to fan out across the state and help communities begin to recover from the devastating summer of 1993. The corps' work was funded by an emergency grant from the Commission on National and Community Service, a modest federal program begun in 1990.

The Iowa Conservation Corps, like almost 60 similar youth corps around the United States, illustrates the genesis of a burgeoning interest in community service. It was the work of the corps, as well as service-learning programs in schools, higher-education community-service activities, and network building among many interested groups and individuals—all given seed money by the Commission—which laid the foundation for one of the first major legislative initiatives of the Bill Clinton administration to win approval on Capitol Hill.

The National and Community Service Trust Act was signed into law in September 1993 and immediately began its work. On October 1 the Corporation for National and Community Service set up business, replacing the earlier Commission and ACTION, which had housed domestic volunteer programs such as VISTA and the National Senior Volunteer Corps. The new AmeriCorps established under the act initially would allow up to 20,000 young people to earn almost $10,000 each for education costs in return for two years of community service. In addition to funding programs, however, the act would institutionalize community service as a joint federal, state, and local priority. For years, youth service had existed on the fringe of efforts in which schools and communities were interested—a nice thing to do but not very important. The new act required every state wishing to participate in the program to set up a broad-based commission that would plan and administer community-service grant programs. The states would be expected to build upon existing service programs in schools, youth corps, and college campuses, thus giving the movement a stability it had not known in the past.

Both formula grants and competitive grants administered by states must address education, human, public-safety, and environmental needs. The funds could be used for community or full-time youth corps; training for service-learning programs in schools; campus-based service; programs where disadvantaged youth meet housing and community needs in low-income areas; and intergenerational, after-school, and rural programs, as well as those focused on alleviating hunger. The act also established the Civilian Community Corps or CCC—an initiative inspired by the Depression-era corps that put unemployed young men to work on public projects. This was but a small part of the new act; it would establish residential programs in excess military facilities around the country and use military personnel to administer them.

The grant process was to begin in early 1994, and the first projects probably would be selected by the summer of 1994.

ANNE C. LEWIS

groups—often affiliated with religious organizations—which accused outcomes-based education of undermining family values and straying from basic skills instruction. State education-restructuring plans in Virginia, Pennsylvania, and Ohio were among those that had to be modified to overcome such objections.

In California, Proposition 174, which would have provided $2,600 worth of school vouchers for each of the state's 5.8 million students, was defeated overwhelmingly in November, with 70% of those casting ballots voting down the measure. The initiative, which had strong support from conservatives, was opposed by California's political establishment—including Republican Gov. Pete Wilson. Voucher plans thus far had been voted down in all three states where they were presented; the other two states were Colorado and Oregon.

The Tracking Issue. With the rhetoric of education reform insisting that all children can learn at high levels, the traditional practice of tracking by ability came under mounting criticism. Over the past few years, research findings on tracking were consistent—it harms students placed in remedial classes and does not greatly benefit students placed in enrichment classes. However, public and parental perceptions of the worth of gifted education, as well as their belief that mixing abilities will lower standards, make it politically difficult to create heterogeneous grouping. Nevertheless, de-tracking appeared on many school-board and state-reform agendas, as well as in a major project of the College Board, EQUITY 2000, that encourages college-preparatory content for students in low-income schools, beginning in the middle grades. Preliminary evidence from EQUITY 2000's six pilot district-wide sites indicated that low-income students were succeeding, on average, in classes with much higher expectations.

Another aspect of tracking that came under reform efforts is was vocational education. A report from the Southern Regional Education Board found that its consortium formed to integrate vocational and academic content, especially in science and math, improved student outcomes and fostered more collegial planning among teachers. Setting higher standards for students not planning to attend four-year institutions also was part of the Clinton administration's early agenda. The Goals 2000 Act included the establishment of a National Skill Standards Board that would promote the development of a national system of voluntary skill standards in major occupations. Seen as a companion piece to the National Education Goals Panel, this board would certify skill standards that, in turn, would set high standards for vocational students.

Assessment Issues. As national policy moved toward replacing norm-referenced standardized tests with a range of alternatives—performance tests, portfolios, and exhibitions, among them—both the technical quality of new tests and their impact on equity came under question. For several years, the National Assessment of Educational Progress (NAEP) had been using a proficiency scale of 0-500 to determine the level of mastery in the subjects covered by its national sample assessments; and its 1992 assessment in math grouped student scores into three levels: basic, proficient, and advanced. At least four national reports raised questions about these testing methods; the National Academy of Education went so far as to recommend that the reporting on levels be stopped until more reliable tests were developed. However, the governing board for NAEP said it would continue the process, while working to refine it.

A RAND Corporation study of the Vermont portfolio assessment system found the rater reliability to be flawed, but it also said instruction in writing and mathematics had been improved because of the new assessment system. The New Standards Project administered its first full-scale performance assessments in fourth- and eighth-grade reading and math, involving samples from states and districts representing about one half of the K-12 students in the country. Also, Kentucky's new system of performance and portfolio testing met the developers' reliability standards.

All of these ventures into alternative assessments produced an important side benefit, according to evaluations. The use of trained teachers to develop scoring rubrics for the new types of tests became a successful method of helping teachers understand higher content standards. Nevertheless, the transition to new forms of testing created concerns among testing experts familiar with equity issues. While not defending current methods of standardized testing, they cautioned against using untried testing systems as high-stakes tests—those used for crucial decisions such as promotions or graduation—unless equity issues had been considered and especially only if all students had been given equal opportunities to learn the content.

Higher Education and Adult Education. After months of debate, Congress reached a compromise in 1993 on the student-loan program, designing a phase-in of government-administered loans. By 1997, up to 60% of student-loans were to be administered directly by the government.

The first in-depth survey of adult literacy based on knowledge rather than years of school completed revealed that one half of college graduates have literacy levels considered only in the middle range or below on a scale of 1-5 devised by the survey group, the Educational Testing Service. The survey also found that young adults between the ages of 21 and 25 have considerably lower literacy skills than did a similar age group tested in 1985. The decrease was attributed largely to the increase of English-language-deficient young people. Overall, about 47% of the adult population demonstrated low levels of literacy.

ANNE C. LEWIS, *Education Policy Writer*

Physical Education Today

Reform is under way in the United States in the manner in which physical education is taught.

New Thoughts. Under the new way of thinking about physical education, competition and athletics are not the focus; rather, activities that include all youngsters—and teach all children to be physically active—are in. In shifting from such longtime physical-education content as sports and games, proponents of the new approach emphasize how physical education fits into other educational programs and supports a healthy lifestyle. Under the new system, children will develop muscular strength, cardiovascular endurance, and flexibility while learning effective and efficient body management.

Physical competence and health-related fitness for all are the primary goals of the program. The new physical education is emphasized especially at the elementary-school level, but is important at the secondary-school level as well. Proponents focus on teaching skills which will promote lifelong physical activity. With the nation realizing the need to lower health-care costs, the drive to change physical education to an effective preventive medicine has accelerated. Increasingly, programs make use of new high-tech equipment, including heart monitors that help screen amounts of exercise and computerized fitness equipment.

The reform has its roots in the 1980s, when physical education was identified as an important component of the nation's health objectives. Increased public awareness and growing research evidence that regular lifelong physical activity is important in reducing risk of disease also provide support for the goal of quality physical-education programs for all students.

The National Association for Sport and Physical Education (NASPE)—which represents the nation's physical educators—recommends that all students in grade K-12 receive daily physical education and that a certified instructor plan and implement the program. In support of the reform program, NASPE offers a Definition and Outcomes outlining what students should achieve in physical education. NASPE considers a physically educated person to be one who has learned the skills necessary to perform a variety of physical activities, participates regularly in physical activity, is physically fit, knows the implications and benefits of physical activity, and values physical activity and its contributions to a healthful lifestyle.

Support for Sport Programs. The new ideas about physical education clearly distinguish between the excellence required of all individuals and that required of competitive athletes. Schools also should provide sports programs to give physically gifted students opportunities to develop special talents.

The President's Council on Physical Fitness and Sports—of which Florence Griffith-Joyner and Tom McMillen were named cochairs by President Bill Clinton in 1993—represents the federal role in sport and physical fitness. As a part of the Department of Health and Human Services, the Council is the lead agency in promoting achievement of the Healthy People 2000 goals relating to physical activity and fitness. The Council also promotes numerous sport programs for citizens of all ages.

JUDITH C. YOUNG
*National Association for Sport
& Physical Education*

© Keith Myers/NYT Pictures

EGYPT

Hosni Mubarak secured a third term as president of Egypt in October 1993, but he faced increasing peril from militant Islamic groups and popular unrest caused by continuing economic problems. However, Mubarak succeeded in strengthening Egypt's international standing through astute foreign policy and personal diplomacy.

Domestic Unrest. Threats from militant Islamic fundamentalist groups continued to disrupt internal stability as several bloody confrontations arose between security forces and militants, whose targets included government officials, Coptic Christians, foreign tourists, and intellectuals and writers critical of the fundamentalists. Islamic militants set off explosions in and around Cairo, planting bombs near public places such as police posts, metro stations, the Egyptian Museum, and the Pyramids. Several times the Islamic Group, one of the most active antigovernment factions, issued threats to foreigners not to visit Egypt. As a result the tourist industry, one of the chief sources of foreign currency, suffered. The government estimated that attacks on tourists since late 1992 had resulted in the loss of some 4 million visitors and $1 billion in revenues.

Attempts to control the militants included the massive use of force, large-scale public trials, and legislation to cope with the causes of civic unrest. Throughout the year there were armed crackdowns leading to battles between fundamentalists and security forces in Cairo, Aswan, and Asyut. This antiterrorist campaign was the most extensive since the 1981 assassination of President Anwar Sadat.

To strengthen the hand of security authorities, the Peoples Assembly passed a tough new antiterrorism law imposing a death sentence on anyone with ties to "terrorist" groups. Scores of militants arrested by the authorities were put on trial, yielding more than 20 death sentences—the largest number of such sentences in several years. By August 14 militants had been hanged—including five in one day—in the largest number of executions during a single year of Egypt's modern history.

In February the legislature passed a law invalidating election of officers in trade unions and professional organizations unless at least 50% of the membership voted. The law was intended to prevent the Muslim Brotherhood—which previously had won elections with low voter turnout—from controlling these organizations.

Other measures to stem increased support for Islamic fundamentalists included plans to revamp religious education in schools beginning in 1994 and to take control of 120,000 nongovernment mosques established by private groups, because many were centers of antigovernment agitation. Egyptian intellectuals and leaders of the Coptic community called on the government to survey its television programming and cultural activities to instill greater tolerance toward minorities. They charged that official policy dehumanized non-Muslims and marginalized Copts in the school system and the governing establishment.

Amnesty International, Middle East Watch, and Egyptian human-rights groups criticized the government's intensified use of force against militants and new legislation that permitted trials to be transferred from civil to military courts "in cases that require quick measures."

Attempts by "independent" Islamists to mediate disputes between Egypt and its militant fundamentalist opponents were criticized by the nonreligious opposition as lending legitimacy to factions such as the Islamic Group and Islamic Jihad. When Minister of the Interior Abdal-Halim Moussa considered an offer by Muslim intellectuals to mediate between fundamentalists and security authorities, President Mubarak replaced him with Police General Hassan al-Alfi, who categorically rejected any mediation with such "illegal entities."

Economy. Disaffection with the government was exacerbated by more than 20% unemployment among the country's workforce and by another 20% who were underemployed. With insufficient work, the market was unable to absorb many of the 400,000 to 500,000 annual newcomers to the workforce. According to a United Nations estimate, 23% of the population lived in absolute poverty. One in three Egyptian workers lived on an income of less than $25 per month, and the average monthly pay of government employees was about $50. Half the population still was illiterate.

Foreign aid and remittances sent by Egyptians working abroad helped prevent an economic collapse. About 2.5 million Egyptians, one seventh of the working-age population, sent some $5.5 billion home from foreign countries, providing one of the principal sources of foreign-currency earnings. Egypt had received more than $35 billion in U.S. military and eco-

---

EGYPT • Information Highlights

Official Name: Arab Republic of Egypt.
Location: Northeastern Africa.
Area: 386,660 sq mi (1 001 450 km²).
Population (mid-1993 est.): 58,300,000.
Capital: Cairo.
Government: *Head of state*, Mohammed Hosni Mubarak, president (took office Oct. 1981). *Head of government*, Atef Sedki, prime minister (took office November 1986). *Legislature* (unicameral)—People's Assembly.
Monetary Unit: Pound (3.3405 pounds equal U.S.$1, free-market rate, Nov. 18, 1993).
Gross Domestic Product (1991 est. U.S.$): $39,200,000,000.
Economic Index (1992): *Consumer Prices* (1980 = 100), all items, 649.3; food, 692.4.
Foreign Trade (1992 U.S.$): *Imports,* $8,357,000,000; *exports*, $3,104,000,000.

Israel's Prime Minister Yitzhak Rabin (right) stopped in Cairo in mid-September to update Egypt's President Hosni Mubarak (left) on the new Israel-Palestine Liberation Organization peace accord.

© Frederic Neema/Sygma

nomic assistance since 1975, to rank after Israel as the largest recipient of U.S. foreign aid. The United States has its largest overseas aid operation since Vietnam in Egypt.

Because of Egypt's assistance in the Persian Gulf war against Iraq, some $13 billion of its military debt to the United States and other Western nations and $3 billion in military loans owed to the Club of Paris Western creditors were forgiven in 1993. As a result, Egypt's budget deficit decreased from about 20% of gross domestic product (GDP) to less than 3%. The government was able to take steps to lower inflation to less than 10%, stabilize the currency exchange rate, reduce many subsidies on consumer goods, and remove interest-rate controls. These steps helped bolster cash reserves to about $11 billion in 1993.

Egypt began a second phase of economic reform, including greater efforts to privatize business, liberalize trade, and sell off state-owned companies. However, efforts to diminish the large trade deficit were difficult because of the need to pay foreign currency for food imports that provide more than 40% of Egypt's annual requirements.

Foreign aid has helped improve Egypt's road network, telecommunications, water supply, and access to consumer goods. In the last decade improvements to health services led to a declining birth rate and an increasing life expectancy.

Politics. In the legislature there was no effective political opposition to President Mubarak's National Democratic Party, which controlled more than 85% of the seats. In July the Peoples Assembly nominated Mubarak to run for a third term as president in a national referendum in which he was the only candidate. In the referen-

dum held on October 4, participants could vote either "yes" or "no" for the single candidate. Mubarak won with about 96% of the vote. He continued to govern Egypt under a series of emergency decrees, declaring that "until we have stability and economic reform, this is the best way to run the country."

Foreign Affairs. Mubarak's greatest successes were in foreign policy. Egypt played an important role as an intermediary between Yitzhak Rabin and Yasir Arafat prior to the 1993 agreement between the Palestine Liberation Organization (PLO) and Israel. There were several meetings between Israeli and Palestinian officials in Cairo leading up to the agreement.

In Mubarak's visits to Arab states, he attempted to form a coalition that contained Iran. Egypt was also part of the seven-member Arab League committee seeking to find a peaceful solution to the dispute between Libya and the West over the Lockerbie airplane bombing.

Egyptian security authorities also worked closely with U.S. officials, leading to the arrest of several men accused of involvement in the New York City World Trade Center bombing on February 26. Among those arrested in the United States was Sheikh Omar Abd al-Rahman, leader of Egypt's Islamic Group, who had fled from Egypt where he also was indicted for terrorist activity.

In July, Mubarak met with Sudan President Omar Hassan al-Bashir for the first time in two years to negotiate differences over a border dispute and charges by each country of intervention in the internal affairs of the other.

DON PERETZ
State University of New York, Binghamton

ENERGY

Whatever the causes of the U.S. economy's sluggish performance in 1993, energy prices were not among them. Two decades after the Organization of the Petroleum Exporting Countries (OPEC) launched the first energy crisis, oil—still the United States' leading source of energy—was cheap and in abundant supply. Crude petroleum stood at less than $15 per barrel in November, several dollars less than in 1992.

Sluggish demand was partly responsible for the low price of oil, as the anemic economic recovery in the United States and most of the rest of the industrialized world meant that industry and individual consumers used less energy than usual. The International Energy Agency estimated that demand for petroleum products in 1993 fell by 200,000 barrels per day to less than 66 million barrels per day. The drop marked the first decline in world oil consumption since 1983.

Another factor driving up oil supplies and driving down prices was disarray within OPEC during the first half of the year. In the quest for higher revenues, some producing countries—notably Kuwait—overshot their production targets, causing a slight glut of the oil market and driving down prices. Oil prices rose somewhat after the 12 OPEC members agreed in September to abide by a new production ceiling of 24.5 million barrels per day for the next six months.

OPEC's exercise in self-discipline was a pale reflection of the cartel's devastating impact on world energy supplies in 1973. The initial embargo and two later supply cutbacks directed by OPEC produced U.S. gas lines and raised the price of gasoline from 39 cents per gallon before the embargo to $1.38 by 1981. After the early 1980s, however, OPEC lost its grip over the international oil market, as revenue-hungry members exceeded production ceilings and non-OPEC countries such as Britain boosted production outside the cartel's control. Prices gradually fell, and by 1993 the price of a gallon of gasoline in the United States stood at $1.12. While that was much more than the 39-cent gasoline cost before the 1973 embargo in current dollars, it actually amounted to 13 cents less if inflation is taken into account.

Domestic Oil Production. In 1993, U.S. oil reserves continued their steady decline. As a result, domestic oil producers were unable to keep up with the demand for gasoline, heating oil, and other petroleum products. Growing demand and falling domestic production contributed to a long-term trend that in 1993 brought the U.S. dependency on foreign sources of oil to close to 50%, up from just 36% at the time of the 1973 OPEC oil embargo. The Independent Petroleum Association of America predicted that 1994 would mark the first time ever that the United States would rely on foreign suppliers for most of its oil.

Those predictions were based in part on the disappointing results of oil-exploration projects in Alaska's Beaufort Sea. The exploration's major sponsor, Atlantic Richfield Co., announced in October that it would downsize its operations, limiting future oil-exploration projects to the lower 48 states and focusing its efforts increasingly on natural gas. The disappointing results in Alaska dashed hopes of stemming the decline of domestic oil production, which was about 2 million barrels per day less than in 1973.

© AP/Wide World

In November 1993 the Organization of the Petroleum Exporting Countries (OPEC) decided against cutting back its oil-production ceiling of 24.5 million barrels per day. According to Indonesia's Subroto (center), OPEC's secretary-general, the cartel's producers did not see why they should curb their output and let other oil exporters poach their customers.

Changes in energy policy were not a major factor for the domestic oil industry's performance in 1993. Early in the year, the Clinton administration proposed a tax on nearly all forms of energy, based on British thermal units (BTU), a measure of heat consumption. That proposal failed under heavy industry lobbying and was replaced with a less onerous transportation tax: a 4.3-cent increase in the federal tax on gasoline and diesel fuel, effective on October 1. As the year drew to a close, the administration prepared to introduce tax incentives to help the domestic oil and natural-gas industries.

While exploration projects yielded disappointing results in the United States, new discoveries of oil elsewhere added to the global supply of known petroleum reserves. A new oil source that could generate as much as $3 billion in export earnings by 1997 was discovered in 1993 in eastern Colombia. In Asia exploration continued in China's far west and off the shore of Vietnam.

Meanwhile, political and economic problems stymied oil production in other parts of the world. Iraq, a member of OPEC, was prohibited from exporting oil under United Nations sanctions. As a result of Russia's economic crisis, oil output plummeted in the rich Siberian oil fields, and some 22,000 oil wells lay idle for much of the year.

Coal. With reserves sufficient to meet expected demand for the next 300 years, coal remained the most abundant fossil fuel found in the United States. Long an important heating fuel for schools, hospitals, and other large buildings, coal became a leading fuel for electric-power plants after the 1973 oil embargo. Domestic coal consumption grew by more than half from 1973 to 1988.

However, mounting concern over acid rain and air pollution caused by burning coal prompted many utilities to turn increasingly to natural gas during the 1980s. By 1993 coal use had stalled, and consumption stood at about the 1988 level. Phased out of heating systems for many large buildings where it contributed to urban smog, coal use was limited largely to the production of electric power. Even in this market, coal was expected to yield to cleaner-burning natural gas. The use of coal as an energy source was projected to fall by at least 25% by the year 2010.

Coal's greatest promise appeared to lie in further development of coal-liquefaction technology, which permits the production of liquid fuel similar to gasoline from coal. The object of many years of Energy Department research, synthetic oil produced by coal liquefaction has been kept off the market because of its cost. A barrel of synthetic oil from coal cost about $35 in 1993, some $15 more than petroleum. But with fast-dwindling domestic oil reserves and the continued concern over the reliability of foreign sources of oil, coal liquefaction seemed likely to become a viable energy source in the future.

Natural Gas. Of the three fossil fuels, only natural gas appeared certain to continue increasing in demand in coming years. More abundant than crude oil, domestic supplies of natural gas continued to satisfy a large portion of demand. Imports, mostly from Canada, accounted for only about 5% of the gas sold to U.S. consumers in 1993.

Gas became an increasingly attractive alternative to coal for electric utilities because it is cleaner and contributes far less to air pollution. Gas also appeared poised to take an even more prominent place in the energy mix as Clean Air Act regulations forced many heavily polluted states and localities to find alternatives to gasoline for fueling vehicles. Despite pollution-reduction efforts, cars and trucks continued to be the main source of air pollution in heavily populated areas such as Southern California and the Eastern seaboard.

By 1993 about 30,000 natural-gas vehicles were being used in commercial and local government fleets. By 2010 as many as 2 million cars and trucks were expected to run on natural gas, bridging the gap between gasoline-driven and nonpolluting electric cars. Some analysts, who doubted that Americans ever would accept electric cars because of their high cost and low performance, predicted that natural-gas vehicles would become the cars of the future.

Nuclear Energy. In addition to coal, nuclear power initially was thought to offer a reliable source of electricity in the wake of the 1973 embargo. Between 1973 and 1989, the number of licensed nuclear reactors grew from 35 to 112. But nuclear energy's promise faded amid safety concerns prompted by the 1979 reactor accident at Three Mile Island. Since then, no new reactors have been ordered in the United States, and the number of units licensed to operate had fallen to 109. With the prospect that more nuclear-power plants would be decommissioned and shut down, some analysts predicted that nuclear power would be phased out within the next two decades. Despite the fading importance of nuclear energy, reactors still supplied about 20% of the nation's electricity in 1993. In some areas, nuclear power's portion of the energy mix was as high as 45%.

Renewable Energy. Hydroelectric dams, solar energy, wind power, geothermal power, and energy tapped by burning municipal waste continued to provide electricity in limited areas of the country. Because they are the only types of fuel that are not certain to run out some day, these renewable energy sources hold promise for a future when fossil fuels no longer are available for general use.

With the exception of hydroelectric dams, however, the continued affordability of oil

depressed the market for alternative energy sources in 1993, despite the positive prognosis for renewables over the long term. In November, Mobil Corp. announced it was closing down its solar-energy program. Set up in the wake of the 1973 oil crisis when soaring oil prices triggered extensive research into alternative energy sources, the program sold photovoltaic solar cells to utilities but failed to generate adequate profits. That left Amoco Corp. as the sole U.S. oil company with an active solar-energy program. Despite these setbacks, renewable energy accounted for 10% of domestic energy production, more than twice the level before the 1973 embargo.

Conservation and Environmental Protection. Not generally thought of as a type of fuel, conservation efforts actually are one of the most important ingredients in the mix of energy resources, accounting for billions of dollars in annual savings in expenditures. The energy crises of the 1970s and early 1980s launched successful public campaigns that urged consumers to save energy. For the most part, consumers in the United States continued to choose energy-efficient appliances, install energy-saving lighting, and upgrade their home insulation into the 1990s.

But consumers proved far more erratic in their conservation efforts when it came to automobiles. With gasoline prices at historic lows, U.S. consumers in the late 1980s and early 1990s wanted more powerful cars, and Detroit's Big Three automakers satisfied that demand. But environmental concerns stymied the return to inefficient gas-guzzlers. Going beyond federal clean-air regulations, the state of California in 1990 passed legislation requiring that 2% of the vehicles that automakers sell there be "zero-emission" models, beginning with the 1998 model year. The only vehicles that meet that requirement are models that run on electric batteries.

Detroit's Big Three automakers—Ford Motor Company and Chrysler and General Motors corporations—formed the United States Advanced Battery Consortium in January 1991 to develop a battery-driven vehicle that would meet U.S. consumers' demand for high performance comparable to gasoline-fueled cars. The consortium soon bogged down, however, amid disputes over the companies' legal rights, leaving Detroit ill-prepared to meet the 1998 deadline.

Detroit's dilemma grew when 12 Eastern states from Maine to Virginia chose to adopt the California emissions standards as well. Reluctant to assume the high cost of developing mass-market electric vehicles by the 1998 deadline, Detroit fought back in 1993. But in November the automakers lost an important battle when a U.S. District Court in Boston denied their appeal for a preliminary injunction to prevent Massachusetts from enforcing the state's low-emission-vehicle program, due to be phased in beginning in 1995.

While U.S. automakers were fighting requirements to modernize automotive technology, some of their foreign competitors were busy developing new engines. Japan's Mazda Motor Corp., for example, in the fall of 1992 demonstrated a hydrogen-powered car that leapfrogs the cumbersome electric-battery engine, producing a clean but more powerful vehicle. Hydrogen-driven cars still presented technical problems, however, and were not expected to enter full production before the year 2000.

While they continued to fight the California emissions standards, the Big Three endorsed a Clinton-administration project to develop "clean cars" for the future. The project, which was expected to cost $1 billion, would enable the automakers to spend more time developing alternative technology than they would be allowed under the California standards. Detroit reportedly signed on to the plan on condition that the federal government force the Northeastern states to drop their plans to adopt the California standard.

Voluntary Emissions Plan. Another Clinton-administration proposal with potentially far-reaching implications for energy technology was a plan announced in October to reduce emissions of carbon dioxide and other gases thought to cause global warming, which are by-products of fossil-fuel combustion. The administration's plan, which depends heavily on voluntary compliance by the nation's businesses, called for reducing auto emissions and developing solar and other renewable energy sources to roll back emissions to 1990 levels by the year 2000.

In October new regulations aimed at curbing harmful emissions from vehicles took effect. Gas stations in California and other localities were required to start selling "winter gas," a fuel that includes more oxygen to reduce carbon monoxide and other pollutants and that costs several cents more per gallon. At the same time, new regulations took effect requiring trucks, buses, and other diesel-fueled vehicles to start using a new formula of diesel fuel containing 90% less sulfur, the main source of particulates, or soot, from these vehicles. The Environmental Protection Agency (EPA) projected the new fuel would reduce soot emissions by more than one third by 1995. The new regulations applied to road vehicles but not to railroads, ships, or tractors and other agricultural equipment. Although these and other new regulations were expected to add as much as 6 cents per gallon to the cost of diesel fuel, ample oil supplies in late 1993 had lowered that estimate to only a few cents per gallon.

See also AUTOMOBILES; ENVIRONMENT.

MARY H. COOPER
"The CQ [Congressional Quarterly] Researcher"

ENGINEERING, CIVIL

The field of civil engineering had a year marked by significant completions, innovative techniques, and reorganization during 1993. The year saw the successful execution of several important projects, including new highways and an unusual bridge replacement. Engineers continued to give special consideration to environmental issues in many of these efforts.

The U.S. Army Corps of Engineers, the nation's largest construction entity, was reorganized to trim the costs of this organization. And civil engineers also faced some prominent project postponements and cancellations in 1993, including the Superconducting Super Collider in Texas and the Chunnel under the English Channel in Europe.

Award-winning Highway. Many civil engineers consider the new Interstate 70 through Glenwood Canyon in Colorado to be an example of civil engineering at its finest. The 12.5-mi (20-km), $490 million highway opened in October 1993 and was the final link in Interstate 70, which stretches between Baltimore, MD, and Cove Fort, UT. The new highway winds through the White River National Forest in Colorado, one of the premier natural settings in the United States, without detracting from the outstanding scenery. The new highway was presented with the 1993 Outstanding Civil Engineering Achievement Award, an annual honor given by the American Society of Civil Engineers.

Glenwood Canyon, located roughly 150 mi (241 km) west of Denver, is about 2,000 ft (610 m) deep and 300 ft (91 m) across at its widest point. The Colorado River runs through it, carving out a gorge in its path. The four-lane Interstate 70 replaces a two-lane road—the only year-round link between the popular ski resorts of Vail and Aspen, CO—that was built in the 1930s. People who drove this narrow road had to face the fear of being forced into the Colorado River or into a head-on collision with oncoming traffic. Plans to widen the highway were discussed in the 1960s, but opponents warned that any construction would damage the canyon's environment. However, as this project progressed, the highway alignment was shifted by as little as 2-3 inches (5-7.6 cm) to satisfy environmental constraints.

Because of the environmentally fragile nature of the route through Glenwood Canyon, engineers and policy makers took more than a decade to plan this stretch of Interstate 70 and another 12 years to construct the highway. The

A new stretch of Interstate 70 through Glenwood Canyon in Colorado, completed in 1993 after 12 years of construction, utilized innovative design techniques to traverse a perilous and scenic area without disrupting the environment. The French Creek Viaduct (left) doubled the capacity of the highway without disturbing the canyon walls, while the tunnels at Hanging Lake (below) incorporated a low-impact support system never before used in the United States.

Photos, © Colorado Department of Transportation

Colorado Department of Transportation project included two 4,000-ft (1 219-m)-long tunnels, 39 bridges and viaducts, state-of-the-art incident-detection and management facilities, and a traffic-management system that kept as many as 18,000 vehicles per day moving during the peak of construction.

But the greatest environmental effort in the Interstate 70 project was reserved for the 7,000-ft (2 134-m)-long Hanging Lake Viaduct and tunnels, which were designed to hide vehicles traveling around picturesque Hanging Lake. This lake lies at the top of a steep 1,000-ft (305-m) climb. The two 4,000-ft (1 219-m) tunnel portions of the Hanging Lake system featured the first use of rock reinforcement as permanent support in the United States. This technique required no active structural support. Instead, rock bolts, placed around the circumference of the tunnel, were used to reinforce the rock surrounding the opening, creating a self-supporting rock arch.

Natchez Trace Parkway. The final phase of parkway construction along the historic Natchez Trace—a 450-mi (724-km) route between Natchez, MS, and Nashville, TN, that has existed since the 18th century—was completed during 1993. The work to finish the final portion of the project featured the first use of precast segmental bridge arches in the United States. The arches support an $11 million bridge superstructure as it crosses Route 96 near Franklin, TN. The bridge is 1,572 ft (479 m) between abutments, with a main arch span of 582 ft (177 m).

Bridge Replacement. Changes in the Mississippi River's water depth and alignment through the years forced the retirement in 1993 of the 105-year-old Hannibal, MO, swing bridge. Although the bridge's twin navigation openings of 159 ft (48 m) and a vertical clearance of 20 ft (6 m) once had been adequate, the swing span and its pivot pier recently had begun to pose an obstruction and safety hazard to passing barges and boats.

The bridge's owner, Norfolk Southern Railroad, Atlanta, came up with a novel and less expensive strategy to replace the old bridge. In June 1993 another bridge owned by Norfolk Southern—the unused 400-ft (122-m)-span vertical-lift bridge in Florence, AL, that crossed the Tennessee River—was barged in as a replacement. According to Norfolk officials, this switch saved approximately $1 million in construction costs and as many as 12 months of construction time. The U.S. Coast Guard agreed to pay for much of the construction costs for the bridge replacement.

Los Angeles Port. Geotechnical investigations were completed in 1993 for the beginning of Port of Los Angeles' 2020 Plan expansion. Construction was expected to begin in 1994. The $550 million plan calls for the creation, through dredging, of more than 1,000 acres (405 ha) of new land in the Port of Los Angeles to accommodate nearly 20 new container-cargo terminals. Ultimately, contractors will dredge a new main access channel down to an 85-ft (26-m) depth and extend it 3 mi (5 km) seaward from the existing outer harbor breakwaters.

Corps of Engineers. At the beginning of 1993 the U.S. Army Corps of Engineers, the nation's largest construction entity, announced its first major reorganization since 1942. Under the reorganization, more than 2,600 jobs in Corps offices across the United States would be eliminated by 1995, saving an estimated $115 million per year.

A major portion of the Corps' work dominated the news during the summer and early fall of 1993 when the Mississippi and Missouri rivers flooded, causing billions of dollars of damage throughout the Midwest. Since 1927 the Corps had built and dredged $25 billion worth of levees, dams, and channels along the Mississippi River and its tributaries, including the Missouri River. While the two rivers once had spread across the floodplains at times, the complex system of levees that the Corps built funnels water into reservoirs that are filled and emptied at the Corps' discretion.

Although almost all of the levees built by the U.S. Army Corps of Engineers held during the flooding in the Midwest during 1993—most of the levees that failed were built privately—the U.S. government began to rethink the Corps' long-standing mandate for flood prevention along the rivers. In recent years, flood damage from the rivers has cost an average of $2 billion annually, despite the costly work by the Corps. Many federal government officials began to argue that in the future the Corps should be charged with the responsibility of managing the floodplains, reducing flood damage before it becomes too costly, rather than trying futilely to prevent floods.

Canceled and Postponed Projects. The Superconducting Super Collider (SSC) project in Waxahatchie, TX, which was proving to be a showcase for innovative underground design and building techniques, was canceled by the U.S. Congress late in 1993. The cost of building the SSC was estimated initially at $4.5 billion, but more recent estimates by the U.S. Department of Energy had grown to more than $11 billion. Before the SSC lost its funding, work was 65% complete on 70 mi (113 km) of tunnels and 43 vertical shafts. (*See* PHYSICS.)

In addition, the long-awaited opening of the Chunnel—the first dry-land connection between Great Britain, France, and Belgium—again was delayed due to unexpected construction and financial problems. The Chunnel, which runs 23 mi (37 km) under the English Channel, was expected to become fully operational for freight and passenger service by May 1994. Construction of the tunnel began in 1987.

TERESA AUSTIN
Freelance Engineering Writer

ENVIRONMENT

In his Earth Day speech on April 21, 1993, President Bill Clinton vowed to "take the lead" in tackling the global buildup of greenhouse gases—pollutants that could lead to a catastrophic global warming. He pledged to develop a national plan to bring U.S. emissions of these gases back to 1990 levels by the year 2000. The resulting Climate Change Action Plan was unveiled on October 19. Carbon-dioxide (CO_2) releases associated with fossil-fuel use accounted for most of the U.S. greenhouse-gas emissions. Not surprisingly, many of the roughly 50 separate initiatives in the new Clinton plan focused on energy-conservation measures and other activities to reduce CO_2 emission levels. The administration launched several other environmental initiatives within the plan.

On April 2, President Clinton and other leading members of the administration met with representatives of the various factions in the Pacific Northwest logging dispute to "move beyond confrontation." The White House later issued a plan that sought to consider the interests of both the environmentalists and the timber industry. (*See also* SPECIAL REPORT, page 224.) The president also renewed his campaign pledge to elevate the Environmental Protection Agency (EPA) to Cabinet status and proposed replacing the Council on Environmental Quality with a new environmental advisory body.

The fact that the population of the African black rhino had declined from 25,000 in the early 1970s to some 2,500 in the early 1990s—due in part to poaching—was causing concern. (*See also* AFRICA/SIDEBAR.)

Biodiversity. In February, U.S. Secretary of the Interior Bruce Babbitt (*see* BIOGRAPHY) announced another major environmental initiative: a National Biological Survey. Peter Raven, director of the Missouri Botanical Garden, noted that about half of the estimated 650,000 species living in the United States had not yet been described in published reports. In October a National Academy of Sciences (NAS) committee on biological diversity, headed by Raven, issued a report with recommendations about the biological census. Rather than focus on unknown species or those threatened with extinction, the NAS panel argued that the survey should attempt to catalog all species, estimate their numbers, and describe their living conditions. Related studies should evaluate the ability of entire ecosystems, not just single species, to survive and function in ways that would preserve the health of the planet—such as controlling floods and erosion, modulating climate, and cleansing waters.

Surveys like the NAS report were called for in the UN Convention of Biological Diversity, a document drawn up at the 1992 Earth Summit in Rio de Janeiro, Brazil. Though President George

© AP/Wide World

U.S. Secretary of the Interior Bruce Babbitt (left) and local officials inspect a wildlife refuge in the Everglades. Efforts to restore the Florida ecosystem continued in 1993.

Bush refused to sign the proposed treaty in 1992, Bill Clinton embraced its goals to protect Earth's species, their habitats, and the environmental systems that support both. On June 4, 1993, the United States signed the pact. On September 30, Mongolia adopted the document, providing the convention with the minimum number of ratifications (30) needed for it to become law. On December 29 the treaty went into effect.

Ozone Hole. A layer of ozone high in the atmosphere ordinarily shields the Earth from the sun's biologically harmful ultraviolet light. But scientists have been documenting a serious and growing seasonal thinning in the ozone over Antarctica. In October this ozone "hole" registered a new record for size and magnitude. Between August and October, 70% of this ozone was destroyed and ozone thinning covered an area about the size of North America—15% larger than ever before.

Scientists traced most of the ozone thinning to chlorine and bromine pollutants released into the atmosphere by human activities. However, the June 1991 eruption of the Mount Pinatubo volcano seeded the atmosphere with tiny sulfuric-acid droplets. Lingering quantities of these may have increased the ozone-quashing potency of the chlorine, according to scientists with the National Oceanic and Atmospheric Administration.

Not restricted to southern polar skies, ozone thinning has been documented around the

globe. Canadian researchers reported that seasonal thinning over Toronto was greater during 1993 than at any time since 1960. The resulting ultraviolet-radiation levels reaching Earth's surface there have been increasing about 5% per year in winter—and almost 2% annually during the summer. High levels of ultraviolet radiation have been linked to cancer. However, the scientists said the health risks posed by the changes were uncertain because the changes that they documented represent "large fractional increases in small numbers."

Smog Ozone. The presence of ozone in Earth's lower atmosphere can aggravate respiratory problems in the sick and elderly. In March a U.S.-Canadian research group reported in the journal *Science* that ozone, the primary irritant in smog, can withstand breakdown long enough to travel from the United States to Europe. Their data indicated that eastern North America unintentionally exported 16% of its ozone across the Atlantic.

In November a team of California researchers reported that healthy adults can sustain serious tissue damage to their airways during exercise in the presence of moderately high levels of ozone. The concentration used in the study—0.2 parts per million in air—was roughly twice the permissible ozone level for outdoor air in the United States, and a level that typically would trigger a city to issue an "ozone alert."

Dioxin. "Veterans and the American public have a solid reason to believe that their concerns about exposure to Agent Orange, dioxin, and other toxic chemicals are at long last being taken seriously," Sen. Thomas Daschle (D-SD) said at a congressional hearing on July 27. He was responding to a report issued earlier in the day by the NAS. It found strong evidence linking three cancers and two other disorders in U.S. military veterans with their exposures to dioxin-tainted herbicides in Vietnam.

The Department of Veterans Affairs—formerly the Veterans Administration (VA)—already was compensating Vietnam veterans for three of the disorders that the NAS report linked to herbicides: chloracne (a disfiguring skin disease), soft-tissue sarcoma, and non-Hodgkin's lymphoma. At the Senate hearing, Secretary of Veterans Affairs Jesse Brown announced his agency immediately would extend VA coverage to all Vietnam veterans with the two newly linked conditions—Hodgkin's disease (a blood-system cancer) and porphyria cutanea tarda (a liver ailment causing skin blistering).

Researchers in Milan, Italy, also reported finding an excess of certain cancers in persons who had lived downwind of a 1976 chemical accident that had caused the highest known human exposures to dioxin. While some cancers in the Italian study matched those linked to herbicides in the NAS Vietnam veterans analysis, a few were unexpected—such as cancers of the liver, gallbladder, and bile duct.

Drinking Water. In 1992 research linked chlorinated-water consumption to increased incidence of bladder or rectal cancer. The study, however, could not identify whether chlorine or by-products of chlorination might be responsible.

Scientists with the National Institute of Environmental Health Sciences helped resolve that issue with a study published in the *Journal of the National Cancer Institute*. The study showed that neither chlorine or chloramine—the two common agents used for disinfecting municipal drinking water—appeared to pose a toxic risk. However, the trihalomethanes produced when chlorine was used to disinfect water caused high rates of liver and kidney disease and high rates of cancer in mice and rats. The EPA's office of drinking-water standards reviewed the data and said it likely would influence new regulations for lowering allowable levels of trihalomethanes in public water systems.

But the Natural Resources Defense Council (NRDC) charged that changing those rules alone would not protect consumers. A two-year investigation of drinking-water contamination released in September concluded that government agencies failed to enforce many regulations. EPA's records for 1991 and 1992 reflected 250,000 reported violations of the Safe Drinking Water Act. Yet state and federal agencies acted on only 3,200 of these, NRDC noted, largely because enforcement agencies lacked sufficient people and finances to follow up identified problems.

NRDC issued a number of recommendations to cope with the problem, such as strengthening existing regulations and allocating more money to enforcement. In a September statement, EPA Administrator Carol Browner maintained that "Americans can rest assured that their drinking water is among the safest in the world." However, she added that the EPA had begun an overhaul of drinking-water-protection rules, "one that agrees with most of the recommendations made today by the NRDC in its report."

Pesticides in Food. "If you eat, you eat pesticides," says Richard Wiles of the Environmental Working Group (EWG), a food-policy organization in Washington, DC. His group and the NAS published related studies in June arguing that the pervasiveness of pesticide residues on fruits and vegetables posed a low but unnecessary toxic risk to consumers—especially children. "We're not talking about a food panic here," says Philip J. Landrigan of the Mt. Sinai School of Medicine in New York City, who chaired the NAS panel. But, he added, "basic changes are needed in the current regulatory system" if the safety of children is to be maintained.

Wiles' group studied pesticide-residue levels on foods from 1990 through 1992—especially fruits and vegetables making up a large part of a child's diet. The data came from 17,000 food samples tested by the FDA and 3,000 analyzed for supermarkets by other labs. EWG found that

Environmentalists demonstrate against Norway's May 1993 decision to resume commercial whaling in defiance of an International Whaling Commission hunting ban. Norway had announced that it would allow the killing of 296 minke whales in 1993; nearly half would be used for scientific research.

© AP/Wide World

two or more pesticides had been detected on 62% of sampled oranges, 44% of apples, and at least 25% of cherries, peaches, strawberries, celery, pears, grapes, and leaf lettuce. In some cases, a food contained residues of eight different pesticides. In fact, Wiles' data indicate that the average U.S. 1-year-old child has consumed enough of some toxic pesticides to exceed the federal government's usual acceptable-risk level.

NAS pointed out that while food frequently contains residues of more than one pesticide, the U.S. government has set exposure limits as though exposure to each pesticide occurs alone. But because some pesticides may exert their potential toxicity in similar ways or by acting on similar organs, NAS pointed out, their combined exposures may prove more risky than anticipated by current regulations.

Prompted in large measure by these reports, the EPA, FDA, and Agriculture Department pledged to revamp regulations affecting pesticide residues. New proposals unveiled on September 21 included speeding the federal review of all pesticides that was under way and outlawing any pesticide whose lifetime cancer risk exceeds one in 1,000,000—based on reasonable estimates of population exposures from food and other routes.

Oil Spills. On January 11 the oil tanker *Braer* broke up in heavy seas off Scotland's Shetland Islands, spilling millions of gallons of crude oil into the North Sea. Most of the oil, however, dispersed before fouling nearby shores.

If the March 1989 *Exxon Valdez* spill had occurred under more turbulent conditions, perhaps its 10.8 million gallons of crude oil would

not have caused so much damage. But the calm weather that followed the spill led to a catastrophic oiling of Alaska's Prince William Sound. And in February 1993 scientists who had been involved in the cleanup and spill-assessment activities met in Anchorage, AK, to offer the first public reports on the spill's effects.

An estimated 500,000 birds succumbed to oiling. Area seals, otters, and killer whales also suffered large losses that biologists believed probably resulted from an oiling in the early days after the spill. Though populations of bald eagles and several other birds have rebounded to prespill numbers, not all have been so lucky. Several biologists at the Anchorage meeting reported on species of birds that have failed to breed since the spill.

The damage would have been even more serious if Exxon had not spent $2.5 billion and recruited up to 10,000 people to clean oil-stained beaches and wildlife. But even after such aggressive measures, some 324,000 gallons of oil remained on Alaskan beaches in 1993, federal scientists noted. Despite these reports, Exxon issued an April 26 statement saying that Alaska "has almost fully recovered" from the *Valdez* spill. The oil company reported that area wildlife apparently has coexisted with petroleum for hundreds of years. Exxon geologists reported new data showing that a series of natural coastal oil deposits have been seeping crude oil for more than a century, contaminating—without apparent ill effect—the water and sediment in supposedly pristine Prince William Sound.

JANET RALOFF
Environment/Policy Editor, "Science News"

The Timber Industry–
Environmentalist Conflict

On April 2, 1993, in Portland, OR, President Bill Clinton sat down with the battling factions in the Pacific Northwest logging dispute—the timber industry and coalitions of environmental groups—to try to "move beyond confrontation to build a consensus on a balanced policy to preserve jobs and to protect the environment."

It was, by any standards, a tough agenda, given that the decade-long confrontation between loggers and conservationists had engendered bitter feelings and what appeared to be mutually exclusive positions. How does one protect spotted owls, salmon, and more than 600 other species of wildlife that depend on old-growth (at least 200-year-old) forests—much of it in 23 million acres (9.3 million ha) owned by the federal government—while retaining abundant supplies of lumber and other wood products in order to keep people at work? Indeed, the participants in the Northwest dispute were not the only ones who framed the issue in such stark and uncompromising terms. A newspaper headline before the conference declared simply that at stake at the summit were "4,600 owls vs. 32,100 jobs."

Perhaps it was to show just how complex the issues really were that the president brought with him to Portland Vice-President Al Gore, Interior Secretary Bruce Babbitt, Agriculture Secretary Michael Espy, Labor Secretary Robert Reich, Commerce Secretary Ron Brown, Environmental Protection Administrator Carol Browner, Deputy Budget Director Alice Rivlin, and Science and Technology Adviser John Gibbons.

The Background. Although the timber-based economy of the Northwest had been in decline for at least 20 years, the descent really had become pronounced since the restrictions imposed on the industry as a result of the spotted-owl controversy. Nearly a decade earlier, environmentalists began a movement to save the spotted owl—which lives in the old-growth forests of coastal Washington, Oregon, and northern California—from extinction. They said it was being threatened by the timber industry's practice of clear-cutting, in which entire swaths of trees are leveled, cleared, and burned. Worse still, said environmentalists, was the fact that the forest tracts on which timber companies were doing this were owned by the federal government, which had sold the rights to the companies. But since the spotted owl has been declared endangered, the government must act to protect its habitat under the Endangered Species Act.

As the environmentalists pressed their case, various government agencies, including the Department of the Interior, tried to find a solution to the problem. However, since 1991 almost all the logging in federally owned forests has been halted because of various court injunctions in favor of the owl and other endangered species. One judge in the Federal District Court in Seattle has issued a number of rulings that said that past timber-cutting levels were in violation of environmental laws. It is estimated that since 1991, the courts have banned logging on millions of acres in 17 national forests and five Bureau of Land Management parcels in the Northwest.

The Northwest fishing industry, dependent as it is on salmon, also has been near collapse as logging operations have taken their toll. In 1988 sport and commercial fishing generated about 62,000 jobs and injected about $1.25 billion into the local economy. By 1992 the industry take was less than $200 million. The salmon-fishery industry claimed that prior cutting of the forests had caused erosion and other definite damage to the environment.

Obviously, the human dimensions to the problem are as compelling as the environmental ones. According to one report, in 1990 there were 145,000 people working in the timber and related forest-products industries, but by 1992 that number had dropped to 125,000. But the logging industry has said that as many as 30,000 jobs have been lost since 1990 as the timber sales from public lands have dropped to about 10% of 1991 levels. In March 1993 government projections showed that more than 30,000 additional workers would stand to lose their jobs if the logging restrictions continued to be enforced. So at the timber summit the president listened to paper- and logging-company executives, lumberjacks, environmentalists, scientists, area university economists, and mayors from small and fiscally strapped lumber towns. He promised to propose a new, fair policy in 60 days.

The Clinton Plan. The White House plan, which was announced on July 1, would:

• Allow for logging of about 12 billion board feet from old-growth forests on federally owned land in the Northwest over the next decade. (A board foot is one foot square by one inch thick.) This annual harvest of about 1.2 billion board feet is far below the 5 billion board feet taken each year under Forest Service guidelines during the 1980s.

• Set aside about 7 million acres (2.8 million ha) of old-growth reserves—which amount to four fifths of the remaining ancient forests—as limited cutting areas. Logging would be allowed on dead

© J. Lotter/Tom Stack & Associates

and dying trees, and there would be some trimming of live ones. However, this could be done only where it did not threaten the spotted owl.

• Establish no-logging buffer zones around streams that are deemed sensitive and around entire watersheds that are to be protected. It is hoped that the limited logging activity in these areas would help the return of salmon and other fish and avoid endangering other wildlife.

• Set up ten special management zones where experimental timber-harvesting techniques would be used. Those areas would range from 78,000 acres (32 000 ha) to 380,000 acres (154 000 ha) each.

• Ask Congress to provide about $1.2 billion in economic assistance to hard-pressed timber communities over the next five years. The money, most of which would come from funds already budgeted to the Forest Service and Interior Department, would finance business development and planning, small business zones, new jobs in forest and river restoration, worker retraining, schools, roads, and community centers. About $270 million of that amount would be for fiscal 1994. Further, Congress would be asked to encourage more domestic milling of U.S. lumber by eliminating the estimated $100 million in annual federal subsidies and tax breaks for timber companies that export logs mainly to Japan and Pacific Rim countries for milling.

The White House plan was presented to the Federal District Court in Seattle as an environmental-impact statement. The court had to approve the plan before the injunctions against logging on public lands could be lifted. At the same time, a 90-day period of public comment was allowed.

According to most analysts familiar with the situation, the Clinton plan would not end the warfare between those that have contested the way the forest should be managed. Predictably, the maximalists of both stripes leveled criticism at the president's plan. Each side contended that not nearly enough was done. Labor and timber-industry groups wanted higher harvest levels and greater economic-assistance packages than were offered, while environmental and conservation groups said that even the reduced logging levels in the plan were too high to protect the already badly damaged and endangered ecosystem of the Northwest.

Indeed, reports suggested that even President Clinton was not completely satisfied with the plan, but he accepted it as the best possible one. However, it did appear that at least the first step toward some balance between jobs and the environment in the Northwest had been taken, and that more than a decade of stalemate was about to be broken. As the president noted when he presented his plan, it "establishes new adapted management areas to develop new weapons to achieve economic and ecological goals and to help communities shape their own future."

NEIL SPRINGER

ETHIOPIA

The year 1993 was one of turbulence in Ethiopia. Eritrea, Ethiopia's northernmost region, declared its independence; domestic strife was on the increase; and the country was busy preparing for national elections to be held in January 1994.

Eritrea. On May 24, 1993, Eritrea formally declared itself a nation. In an independence referendum held in April, 98.25% of the Eritrean electorate voted in a United Nations-monitored vote and 99.8% voted in favor of independence. A three-decade struggle to secede from Ethiopia finally had resulted in independence. Ethiopia's government, one of the first to recognize the new state, indicated that it would work closely with the transitional government of Eritrea to help it gain economic vitality. (*See* SPECIAL REPORT.)

Domestic Affairs. The transitional government of Ethiopia, led by President Meles Zenawi, initiated a campaign to silence and intimidate its critics. In January security forces clashed with more than 2,000 university students protesting Eritrea's pending independence. Some students were killed and scores were

wounded by soldiers with bayonets. In April, 40 faculty members at the University of Addis Ababa were fired for criticizing the Meles government, while several southern parties were dismissed from the transitional government for disagreeing with state policies. And in July, Professor Asrat Woldeyes, president of the All Amhara People's Organization (AAPO), was jailed on charges of inciting war. The AAPO has

---

ETHIOPIA • Information Highlights
Official Name: Ethiopia.
Location: Eastern Africa.
Area: 471,776 sq mi (1 221 900 km²).
Population (mid-1993 est.): 56,700,000.
Chief Cities (1988 est.): Addis Ababa, the capital, 1,686,300; Asmera, 319,353; Dire Dawa, 117,042.
Government: *Head of state,* Meles Zenawi, transitional president (took office 1991). *Legislature*—Council of Representatives (transitional; established 1991).
Monetary Unit: Birr (5.00 birr equal U.S.$1, May 1993).
Gross Domestic Product (1990 est. U.S. $): $6,600,-000,000.
Economic Index (Addis Ababa, 1992): *Consumer Prices* (1980 = 100), all items, 230.9; food, 236.3.
Foreign Trade (1991 U.S.$): *Imports,* $472,000,000; *exports,* $189,000,000.

Eritrea

Eritrea, a region of more than 3 million people sitting on a sliver of land stretching 750 mi (1 207 km) along the Red Sea in northeast Africa, became a new nation in 1993. Located in an area known as the Horn of Africa, Eritrea is bounded by the Red Sea on the north and east, Sudan on the north and west, Ethiopia on the south, and Djibouti on the southeast. It was formerly the northernmost region of Ethiopia. On May 24, 1993, Eritrea declared itself independent after battling Ethiopia in a 30-year war for independence. It subsequently joined the United Nations.

History. Eritrea first enters recorded history as far back as 3000 B.C., when the pharaohs of Egypt and local leaders on the Red Sea coast of Eritrea engaged in commerce. The country was also part of the original empire of Aksum (the first Ethiopian state), which flourished from 300 to 500 A.D. As such, Eritrea was linked to the earliest history of Ethiopia. After the 16th century, following a period relatively independent of foreign influence, the region was dominated by the Ottoman Empire, then by Egypt, and again by Ethiopia. In 1885, Italy invaded, and in 1889, Ethiopian Emperor Menelik II signed the Treaty of Wuchale, granting Italy control over large parts of Eritrea. In 1890, Eritrea was proclaimed an Italian colony. After World War II, Great Britain occupied the area. In 1952, Eritrea was federated with

Ethiopia; it was incorporated into the Ethiopian empire in 1962.

From 1962 to 1991, Eritrea battled to secede from Ethiopia. Fighting first under the banner of the Eritrean Liberation Front (ELF), a largely Christian-led organization, and after 1970 under the authority of the Eritrean People's Liberation Front (EPLF), a Muslim and Christian group, Eritreans fought for their independence. By the time Ethiopia was defeated in 1991, more than 200,000 Eritreans had died. Almost 100% of Eritrean citizens voting in an April 1993 referendum chose independence.

People, Land, and Economy. The population is divided between Christians and Muslims. The varied population includes Tigrinya-speaking Coptic Christians, Tigrinya-speaking Muslims, and the Saho- and Afar-speaking Danakil. Arabic and Italian also are spoken.

Crisscrossed by volcanic remains, dry river valleys, and plateau slopes, Eritrea long has suffered from desiccation. With erratic rainfall, the country is poor agriculturally; crop yields have declined. Few mineral sources exist, though small deposits of gold and copper are mined and salt is produced. Eritrea began its independence engulfed in drought and devastated by the war against Ethiopia. The main cities have been torn apart by the scorched earth policy that Ethiopia

been in the forefront in condemning the Ethiopian government for engaging in policies leading to ethnic divisions. In addition, dozens of AAPO representatives were abducted and jailed.

According to the U.S. State Department's yearly report on human rights, Ethiopia was guilty of violations of rights in the areas of disappearances, political killings, denying freedom of association, and arbitrary arrest.

National Elections. The term of the transitional government was to run until January 1994. At that time national elections were scheduled. Voters were to select a constituent assembly which would pass a new constitution. During 1993 an 11-member executive committee was formulating a draft of such a constitution. It would be Ethiopia's fourth constitution since 1931.

The Economy. Ethiopia continued to confront formidable economic problems. Unemployment was more than 40%. Hundreds of thousands of soldiers of the former government had not been integrated into society, and many of them had turned to banditry. Although the 1993 rains were the best in years, the droughts of the past decades continued to have a residual effect.

The Ethiopian currency was undergoing devaluation, while the national bureaucracy was being slimmed down radically. The government freed farm prices in accordance with a free-market economy that was introduced in 1992. And many thousands of Ethiopians who had fled the regime of Mengistu Haile-Mariam returned to the country to help in reconstruction.

Foreign Affairs. Because of its border with Somalia, Ethiopia was greatly concerned with the ramifications of warfare in that country. As a result, Ethiopia hosted a series of meetings from January to April 1993 to help bring about reconciliation among the various warring Somali clans. At the end of March in Addis Ababa, 15 Somali factions agreed to form a transitional national council to run Somalia until a national government was formed.

Italy donated $698,000 to the ministry of health to rebuild medical facilities in the Wollo region that were devastated by years of warfare between various Ethiopian factions. The donation was to be used to rebuild the hospital in Dessye and to buy medicine and medical equipment.

PETER SCHWAB
State University of New York at Purchase

---

conducted. Villagers fled and rural land was destroyed. The capital, Asmara (population 375,000), and the ports of Massawa and Assab are in disrepair. Seventy percent of Eritreans are in need of food aid, and thousands of refugees who had fled to the Sudan returned in 1993.

Government. The new government consists of the leadership of the EPLF. Isaias Afewerki,

the secretary-general of the EPLF and the head of state of Eritrea, has said that a constitution will be written and governmental elections held by 1995. A provisional government, led by Afewerki and consisting of the president and a National Assembly, will hold power until the planned elections take place.

PETER SCHWAB

© Robert Papstein/Sipa

ETHNIC GROUPS, U.S.

Although an off year for U.S. elections, the year 1993 saw a redrawing of the political map in U.S. cities as ethnicity resurged as a defining element in politics. In August activists hoped a "march on Washington" would revive national commitment to civil rights 30 years after Martin Luther King, Jr.'s famous "I Have a Dream" speech. But deep divisions between and within racial groups persisted. The failure of the commemorative civil-rights march to capture the public imagination reflected the lack of consensus on civil rights in 1993.

Politics and Racial Tensions. City politics entered a new phase in 1993 as many of the first generation of black mayors either retired or were turned out of office. Those who retired included Atlanta's Maynard Jackson, Detroit's Coleman Young, and Los Angeles' Tom Bradley. In Hartford, Carrie Saxon Perry, the first black woman elected mayor of a major U.S. city, lost her run for a fourth term. In the nation's most-watched mayoral race in New York City, former prosecutor Rudolph Giuliani defeated Mayor David Dinkins in a bitter contest that turned on issues of race and crime. Dinkins' defeat marked the first time an incumbent black mayor of a major U.S. city lost a bid for reelection to a white candidate.

A new breed of so-called "pragmatic idealist" black mayors emerged, emphasizing such issues as crime, jobs, and schools, and seeking managerial reform and private-sector assistance rather than stressing civil rights and pursuing federal support to solve urban problems. Mayor Michael White of Cleveland—who won a second term—and Mayors-elect William Johnson of Rochester, NY, Dennis Archer of Detroit, and William Campbell of Atlanta embodied the trend. Many of the "pragmatists" sought to avoid divisive campaigns, distancing themselves from such controversial figures as Louis Farrakhan.

Racial and ethnic concerns served as political backdrops in other cities. In June white millionaire Richard Riordan (R) defeated Asian-American city councilman Michael Woo (D) to become mayor of racially divided Los Angeles. His promise to heal the city was eased in October when a Los Angeles jury acquitted several blacks of first-degree attempted-murder charges in the beating of a white trucker during the 1992 riots. Two convictions and two acquittals in the federal trial of four policemen accused of violating motorist Rodney King's civil rights also had defused racial tensions in April.

Detroit escaped racial violence when a jury convicted two police officers of murder and assault against a black driver who had been stopped for an alleged drug violation. Memphis

The Congressional Black Caucus, which included 40 members and was led by Maryland Democratic Rep. Kweisi Mfume (center), sought a more influential role in national affairs—especially budgetary matters—in 1993.

© Terry Ashe/Gamma-Liaison

also avoided a racial explosion in May when a jury acquitted black U.S. Rep. Harold Ford of federal fraud and conspiracy charges in a racially charged trial. In Orlando a not-guilty verdict in the trial of a Latino Miami police officer accused in the deaths of two blacks stirred protest in Miami but no violence.

Other events suggested eased racial tensions in south Florida. In May black leaders ended an economic boycott of the region's tourist industry, launched in 1990 to protest local politicians' snub of South African nationalist leader Nelson Mandela's visit to Miami. Also in May a newly elected, ethnically diverse Metro-Dade County Commission unanimously repealed an English-only law that had been passed in 1980 to protest the influx of Hispanic culture. In November former Mayor Steve Clark beat Miriam Alonso, who had appealed to ethnic solidarity. Clark, a white, received an endorsement from Cuban-born outgoing mayor Xavier Suarez and substantial support from Cuban voters.

Race-conscious voting policies attracted considerable attention in 1993. In June the Supreme Court ruled that a North Carolina congressional-redistricting plan designed to benefit blacks was guilty of gerrymandering and was unconstitutional, thus questioning all radical efforts to redraw voting districts to benefit minorities. In November black clergy in New Jersey responded with outrage to Republican campaign strategist Ed Rollins' claim that the Republican gubernatorial campaign had attempted to suppress the black vote by paying off black ministers and Democratic workers to keep black voters home on election day. Republican Governor-elect Christine Todd Whitman and black ministers disputed the charges. When coupled with reports of voting frauds using Latino and other minority voters in such places as Philadelphia in 1993, the New Jersey case heightened national concerns generally about the exploitation of minority voters.

In November, Puerto Rican voters, concerned with maintaining their ethnic cultural identity, rejected a proposal to seek statehood. Race intruded into U.S. foreign-policy debates in Washington. Events in Haiti and Somalia led the Congressional Black Caucus and other black leaders to rethink their long-standing opposition to U.S. military intervention. Meanwhile the Bill Clinton administration's support of the North American Free Trade Agreement (NAFTA) angered black congressmen who feared job loss for blacks. In California, Gov. Pete Wilson (R) inflamed both the state's anti-immigrant fever and racial tensions in August when he urged the federal government to deny citizenship and benefits to U.S.-born children of illegal immigrants.

Public Opinion and Public Policy. The NAFTA debates and the California case pointed to growing American nativism amid new waves of reports of a growing Hispanic population and "white flight." A Newhouse News Service analysis of the 1990 census indicated that U.S. society

© Alan Weiner/Gamma-Liaison

BENJAMIN FRANKLIN CHAVIS, JR.

Benjamin F. Chavis, Jr., executive director of the United Church of Christ Commission for Racial Justice, was named the new executive director of the National Association for the Advancement of Colored People (NAACP) in April 1993. As the first new head of the NAACP in 15 years, Chavis indicated that he would open the organization to Hispanics, Native Americans, and Asian Americans. He was one of the "Wilmington 10" who were jailed for burning down a grocery store in North Carolina until a federal judge overturned the decision in 1980. Born on Jan. 22, 1948, in Oxford, NC, Chavis has a doctorate degree in divinity from Howard University.

was becoming divided as non-Hispanic whites fled the sunbelt in California, south Florida, and lower Texas where large numbers of new immigrants had settled. Illegal immigration became a principal political issue in California.

Concerns about illegal immigration gained wide attention in the summer when thousands of Chinese were found trying to enter the country illegally as a packed steamer ran aground in New York and other vessels were intercepted carrying illegal Chinese immigrants off the California coast. The Immigration and Naturalization Service (INS) began a crackdown on illegal Chinese immigration in New York, New Jersey, and California. Polls indicated that most Americans thought immigration laws were too lax. (*See also* SPECIAL REPORT, page 450.)

Civil-rights groups accused President Clinton and the news media of stirring anti-immigrant bias with their handling of the undocumented-nannies controversy during hearings on Clinton cabinet nominees. Also fueling nativism was an April U.S. Census report showing that the number of U.S. residents who spoke

a foreign language at home, particularly Spanish, jumped by more than one third from the 1980s to roughly 15%.

Renewed nativism grew along with rising white resentment toward affirmative action and other race-based programs. Cases involving speech codes prohibiting racial and ethnic slurs and the destruction of college newspapers by black student groups angry about editorial policies at schools divided blacks and whites on college campuses nationwide. The decision of Secretary of Education Richard Riley in March to support scholarships for minority students as a means to enhance diversity relieved university concerns about financial-aid policies that had been challenged in 1992, but added to discussions about "race-favoring" in higher education. In November a U.S. District Court ruled that a scholarship program limited to blacks at the University of Maryland was constitutional because of the school's history of racial discrimination.

Civil Rights. Black civil-rights organizations, citing the Urban League's "State of Black America" report which painted a picture of high black unemployment and victimization by violence, called on the government to step up economic aid and rights enforcement. In May the Supreme Court barred insurance "redlining" in the sale of homeowners' insurance, and the Congress, in deference to its black members, refused to renew the United Daughters of the Confederacy patent to the Confederate flag. But the Clinton administration was criticized for not filling key posts in the Departments of Justice and Labor and the Equal Employment Opportunity Commission (EEOC) with minorities. The flap over Clinton's nomination and then the withdrawal of civil-rights lawyer Lani Guinier as assistant attorney general in June angered civil-rights activists. In October the Federal Bureau of Investigation (FBI) continued efforts to increase diversity by appointing its first Hispanic assistant director and a black assistant director.

Charges of racism were common. In February, Shoney's restaurants agreed to a $105 million award to blacks the company had passed over in hiring and promotion, and signed a consent decree to adhere to a detailed equal-opportunity policy for ten years. In May a class-action suit was filed against Denny's restaurants for discriminating against black customers in California. After similar complaints in Maryland, the parent company signed an agreement with the National Association for the Advancement of Colored People (NAACP) to improve minority relations and employment. In July race-bias complaints were filed against Denny's in 12 states.

Blacks. Concerns about public health dominated the news. In an annual report on the state of the nation's health released in September, the U.S. Department of Health and Human Services reported that blacks suffered disproportionately high mortality rates from such major causes of death as heart disease, and that infant-mortality rates among blacks were twice those of whites. Inner-city violence remained a major cause of death among young black males. In May black leaders in Congress had forced the Clinton administration to shelve a proposed major study into the causes of violence, which approached violence as a public-health problem, because the study targeted inner cities. More encouraging was a U.S. Census study released in September that reported that, although their earnings continue to lag behind those of whites, far more blacks completed high school and college in 1992 than had done so in 1980. But concerns about the strength of black entrepreneurship lingered. In August the Johnson Products Company, once the nation's biggest black-owned company, announced it was being purchased by a white-run firm.

Hispanics. Despite the appointments of Henry Cisneros as secretary of housing and urban development and Federico Peña as secretary of transportation, Hispanic activists were concerned about the number of Hispanics appointed in the Clinton administration. A perception that Hispanics were being left out of policy making was echoed loudly in California, as Hispanic students staged protests at University of California campuses and other colleges to demand more Hispanic teachers and the introduction of more courses devoted to Hispanic culture. Differences between Hispanic groups surfaced during the year amid reports of a growing preference of farm-labor contractors for hiring Mexicans rather than Puerto Ricans for migrant labor work, even in states not sharing a border with Mexico.

Native Americans. In August, Ada Deer, a Menominee tribal chairwoman, was sworn in as head of the U.S. Bureau of Indian Affairs; she was the first Native American woman to head a major federal-government post. Her office faced widespread pollution on reservations—a key public concern among Native Americans in 1993. In August, Navajos protested the difficulty in collecting compensation due them since 1990 for radiation-related illnesses suffered working in uranium mines on their reservation. Various Indian groups complained about commercial waste-management companies that have approached poor tribes, with some success, to locate garbage or hazardous-waste-disposal facilities on their reservations. A report issued by the Environmental Protection Agency (EPA) in June revealed that Indians and other minorities suffered disproportionate exposure to lead, sulfur, carbon monoxide, and other pollutants.

In response to such health threats, Indians and other minorities initiated numerous lawsuits against local and state governments and businesses for civil-rights violations. The environmental-justice argument first articulated by Native Americans forged a powerful new alliance of racial and ethnic minorities in 1993.

RANDALL M. MILLER
Saint Joseph's University, Philadelphia

© Chesnot/Sipa

Leaders from the 12 European Union (formerly European Community) nations gathered in Brussels, Belgium, in December 1993. The issue of severe unemployment in Europe, including the community's inability to create new jobs, dominated the summit.

EUROPE

Europeans had expected 1993 to be a year of hope. In Western Europe it was to open with the implementation of the Single Market of the European Community (EC) and to progress to the more complete European Union (EU), embracing foreign and monetary affairs, with ratification of the Maastricht Treaty approved by EC leaders in December 1991. In Eastern Europe the post-Communist governments hoped that their market reforms—with Western aid—would begin to show concrete results. Continuing recession throughout the continent, combined with the outbreak of fierce ethnic conflicts from Bosnia to the Caucasus, sullied this hope, and made Europeans skeptical of the capacity, and in many cases of the probity, of their political and economic leaders.

Continuing Recession. The slump in West European production was the worst since that of 1974-75. The growth of gross domestic product of the EU as a whole was expected to be negative, dragged down by the unified German economy, which may have fallen as much as 2%, but also by drops in production in Belgium, France, the Netherlands, and Spain. Of the major economies, only Britain's seemed likely to achieve more than a still paltry 1% growth. The impact on European employment was disastrous. EU's unemployment averaged more than 10%, or 17 million people; and more than half of those had been unemployed for more than a year. Unemployment was most severe in the poorer countries like Spain, where it reached 21%; but not even far stronger economies such as France's, with 3.2 million unemployed, or

Britain's with 2.9 million, seemed able to staunch the loss of jobs.

Analysis of the causes of the recession gave little cheer for the future. The initial shock was identified as the unpredicted cost of German unification, which forced Germany to maintain high interest rates, to which the rest of the EU was tied; reduced Germany's capacity to import; and left a large budget deficit. Little chance was seen of an immediate improvement. Worse, Europe's competitive position in world markets was seen to be worsening. Europe's labor costs, and especially Germany's—swollen from years of higher benefits and increasing vacation time and by massive social-security taxes—were pricing European goods out of world markets. Even investment in research and development had fallen behind that of the United States and Asia.

Nor were proposed solutions likely to be immediately effective. The most widely accepted remedy was to increase the freedom and thus the volume of world trade by concluding the so-called Uruguay Round of negotiations within the General Agreement on Tariffs and Trade (GATT), which by December had limped on for seven years. Although agreement was reached that month, the political clout of the French farmers—dramatized by often-violent demonstrations—had led the French government to threaten to force the EU to veto the agreement on agricultural trade, even though it was supported by all other EU members.

Other proposals posed seemingly imminent threats to the interests of the working class, and roused vehement opposition. Efforts were made to cut down wage increases. German employers

231

reneged on their promise to increase wages in eastern Germany, but were compelled to rescind this decision after widespread strikes. Governments, most notably the Social Democratic one in Spain, eroded their left-wing support by attempting to persuade the unions to accept wage freezes. An austerity plan presented by the Belgian government in November provoked a paralyzing general strike.

Two favored methods for cutting the public deficits were a reduction in the welfare state and privatization of nationalized industry. In France the conservative government of Edouard Balladur attempted to cut the staggering $18 billion debt of the health system, which was absorbing more than 9% of GDP, by raising compulsory contributions and discouraging doctors from excessive prescribing. Even Sweden, a model of welfare-state spending since the 1920s, attempted to cut its budget deficit, which had reached 14% of GDP, by lowering illness and unemployment benefits and raising workers' contributions. To reduce the burden of pension payments, France increased the number of years a person must work before receiving a state pension. The Belgian austerity program included a wage freeze and heavy cuts in medical benefits.

Privatization appealed to countries like Italy and France, where nationalized industries were failing to compete with private companies. Italy speeded up its attempts to sell off parts of the public sector, which controlled 40% of the economy. The Balladur government in France proposed to offer 21 companies for sale, including the Renault automobile company, two major banks, and the state airline, Air France. However, an attempt in October to make Air France more attractive to buyers by reducing its workforce by 4,000 caused violent demonstrations and compelled the government to drop its restructuring plan.

Since many large companies, such as Germany's Mercedes-Benz, were downsizing to make themselves more competitive, governments proposed a variety of plans to make hiring the unemployed financially attractive. Italy ended the indexing of wages to inflation. The French government took over some of the social-security payments normally paid by employers. The most risky experiment, however—proposed in France and Germany—was to cut the workweek to four days, with only a small reduction in wages, to share work with the unemployed.

Political and Social Backlash. In addition to expressing their discontent in demonstrations and strikes—which were especially angry in Madrid, Paris, and Brussels—Europeans turned against the governments then in power. In Italy, where judicial investigators were uncovering evidence of 40 years' corruption—especially in demanding or accepting bribes for awarding government contracts—that extended to the

highest levels of politics and business, the voters in April approved by sweeping majorities eight reform referendums, including ending the proportional representation regarded as responsible for debasing the parliamentary system. In France in the elections of March-April, the governing Socialist Party's representation in the National Assembly was reduced from 282 to 70, while the Center-Right coalition increased its number from 257 to 460. Although Spain's Socialist Prime Minister Felipe González was reelected to a fourth term in June, he did not win a majority of seats in parliament and became dependent on the support of the regional Basque and Catalán parties. Although some observers felt that Western Europe was following Eastern Europe in rejecting the doctrine of state socialism, in countries where conservatives were in power they also were in disfavor. Both Prime Minister John Major in Britain and Chancellor Helmut Kohl in Germany saw their approval ratings plummet. In Greece, 74-year-old Socialist leader Andreas Papandreou was swept back into power in October by an electorate disenchanted with four years of austerity, inflation, and high unemployment.

Europe's growing immigrant population became another scapegoat. A substantial segment of the public, although not a majority, turned against immigrants, both those who had established themselves in the past four decades of economic growth and those seeking, for political or economic reasons, to be admitted. Although much of the resentment arose from fear of competition in the labor market, the more vocal and occasionally violent fringe was influenced by feelings of religious or racist distrust. The legal immigration of workers, especially from North Africa into France and from Turkey into Germany in the boom years after 1950, had left those countries with large, unassimilated groups of immigrants, making up nearly 1.8 million people of Arab or African background in France and a similar number of Turks in Germany. They became the target of criticism of such xenophobic political groups as the National Front in France and of the violence of neo-Nazis in Germany.

After 1985 the number of those entering Western Europe either to seek work or to escape persecution had risen dramatically, especially after the fall of Communist governments in 1989-90 made it possible for Eastern Europeans to emigrate. Moreover, fighting in the former Yugoslavia in 1991-93 caused a massive flight, with more than 300,000 entering Western Europe between January 1992 and June 1993. The majority went to Germany because of its liberal asylum laws. To halt the influx, most European countries started sending back asylum seekers to "safe" countries from which they had embarked. Germany paid its eastern neighbors to patrol their borders more effectively, and its

As 1993 began, ceremonies were held in Bratislava, the Slovak capital, above, to mark the splitting of Czechoslovakia into two separate nations—the Czech Republic and Slovakia. The division had been agreed to by Czech and Slovak leaders in 1992.

political parties united to restrict the right of asylum in Germany. In June the French government made immigration and naturalization more difficult, and increased the police's powers to search for illegal immigrants. Fearful that the abolition of internal boundaries with EU would permit illegal immigrants to enter, the nations of Britain, Denmark, and Ireland decided to keep their passport controls, even though the other nine members had accepted an agreement made in June 1990 to abolish such controls.

The EC: Between Hope and Disillusionment. The EC had expected 1993 to bring renewed economic progress, with the entry into force of the single European market on January 1 and the probable ratification of the Maastricht Treaty later in the year. At the summit in Edinburgh in December 1992, Denmark was permitted to opt out of the monetary and defense commitments in the Maastricht Treaty in the hope that its voters would reverse their narrow rejection of the treaty the previous June. The single market—in which barriers to service activities like insurance and banking as well as industrial and agricultural trade were to be removed, in accordance with the Single European Act of 1986—largely was implemented, with immediate beneficial results in stimulating economic contact across borders. The Danish voters approved the Maastricht Treaty in May, and the British parliament ratified the treaty shortly thereafter. A final challenge to the treaty's constitutionality was overthrown in October by the German Constitutional Court.

Although a special summit in Brussels was held on October 29 to celebrate the conversion of the EC into the European Union (EU) on the treaty's taking effect on November 1, early achievement of the treaty's goals seemed unlikely. The European Monetary System created in 1978 to maintain close linkage of national currencies had been weakened in 1992 when Britain dropped out. Faced with speculative market pressure, the members were compelled in August 1993 to agree that their currencies could be traded as much as 15% above or below their central rate, making it unlikely that a common EU currency could be created as planned in 1997 or even at the fallback date of 1999. The EC'S inability to meliorate the conflict in Bosnia, other than with humanitarian aid, showed that the new union was even more unlikely to formulate a common defense or foreign policy.

The former Communist states of Eastern Europe were disappointed in EC's reluctance to liberalize trade relations or to welcome them to membership. Although Romania and Bulgaria were admitted to associate membership, their trading privileges were less generous than those offered to Hungary, Poland, and Czechoslovakia (which split into the Czech Republic and Slovakia early in 1993) in December 1991. Exports of agricultural goods, steel, and textiles were restricted. EC refused to set a possible date for the membership of Poland, Hungary, and the Czech Republic, and at the Copenhagen summit spelled out high standards of political and economic stability they first must meet before being granted EU admission.

F. ROY WILLIS
University of California, Davis

FAMILY

Recognition of the importance of families grew in 1993 as a federal family-leave bill finally was put in place in the United States. Economic setbacks, however, continued as U.S. poverty levels reached near-record highs.

Family and Medical Leave Act. In 1993, Congress passed and President Bill Clinton signed a bill entitling workers to 12 weeks of unpaid leave for the birth or adoption of a child; serious illness; or the serious illness of a child, spouse, or parent. The law, which went into effect August 5, continues health benefits and guarantees the same or a comparable job when the employee returns. While well-intentioned, the law would not help at least one third of U.S. workers, since it applies only to companies with 50 or more employees. Also, many families cannot afford to take unpaid leave.

Passage of the bill culminated eight years of effort by members of Congress, women's groups, labor, and business. Former President George Bush twice had vetoed earlier versions of the bill. Previous variations which would have applied to companies with 15 or more employees never got through Congress.

Poverty. Poverty continued to be a major problem in the United States. The U.S. Census Bureau reported that the number of poor people grew in 1992 by 1.2 million, to 36.9 million. This was three times faster than the growth rate for the population as a whole, and brought the proportion of U.S. citizens living in poverty to 14.5%—the highest rate since 1983's 15.2%. (A family of four with annual cash income of $14,335 or less is considered poor.)

The increase in poverty was attributed to continuing unemployment following the 1990-91 recession. The highest poverty rates in the United States are found in the South, where 40% of the poor live. The poverty rate for blacks was 33.3%; for Hispanics, 29.3%; for Asian Americans, 12.5%; and for whites, 11.6%.

The Census Bureau also found a slight increase in poverty among young children. The poverty rate for those under 6 years old was 25%, and was 21.9% for those under 18.

Children's Health. Infant mortality continued at a high rate, but there was slight improvement. The Centers for Disease Control and Prevention (CDC) reported in March 1993 that the U.S. infant-mortality rate fell in 1990 to a record low, with 9.2 babies out of every 1,000 newborns dying before reaching the first birthday. This was down from 9.8 deaths per 1,000 births in 1989, but the United States still ranked 20th among 23 developed nations in its infant-mortality rate. Japan has the lowest rate, with five deaths per 1,000 births. The CDC attributed the U.S. decline in infant mortality to new methods for treating underdeveloped lungs, a major cause of death in newborns.

Worldwide efforts were under way to reduce infant deaths in 60 developing countries by immunizing at least 80% of children against six major illnesses. UNICEF reported that 12 developing nations already had immunized more than 90% of their children, while ten other nations had immunized 80%.

In the United States, the CDC estimated that between 37% and 56% of preschool-age children were at risk for major childhood illnesses because they had not received all 15 recommended immunizations.

Changing Family Structure. Nontraditional families continued to grow in number in 1993 and to be recognized as families. Sharp increases were reported in the number of women who had babies without getting married. The Census Bureau found that nearly 24% of the nation's unmarried women aged 18 to 44 have children, up from 15% a decade earlier.

Single-parent families were particularly numerous in the African-American community. Researchers found that a black child born in 1993 had only a 20% chance of growing up with two parents. Two of three first babies born to black women 34 years old or younger were born out of wedlock. White women, too, were having more children without being married. Twenty-two percent of white women between 15 and 34 had their first child out of wedlock. The most rapid rise came among educated, professional women. From 1982 to 1992, the percentage of out-of-wedlock births to college-educated women rose from 3% to 6.4%, and to professionals, from 3.1% to 8.3%.

Even for families where there were once two parents present, changes were occurring as more fathers gained custody of their children after divorce. The proportion of single-parent households headed by fathers rose to 14% in 1992, up from 10% in 1980. More than 4% of all children now were living with a single father. There also were more known instances of gay and lesbian partners raising children. More gay parents have gone public, and more judges have allowed gay men and lesbians to adopt children in recent years, although homosexuality also was used during the year as a reason to remove a child from a parent's care.

Child Care. Child care, and the hiring of domestic help in general, received attention in 1993 when a nominee for U.S. attorney general withdrew from consideration because she had employed illegal aliens to care for her children and had not paid the necessary taxes. The incident pointed out the difficulties many parents have in finding affordable child care. According to 1988 Census Bureau statistics, 57% of all U.S. women with children under the age of 6 are in the labor force. Of these children, 37% are cared for in someone else's home, 28% in their own homes, 26% in an organized child-care facility, and 8% by their mothers at work.

KRISTI VAUGHAN, *Freelance Writer*

Current Issues in Adoption Policy

Adoption made the headlines in 1992-93 as several celebrated cases focused the public's attention on critical issues facing child welfare. Such publicized cases as those of Gregory K., a 12-year-old who sued his biological parents for divorce because he lived in foster care most of his life; Jessica, a toddler who was caught in a custody battle between her biological parents and her custodial parents, who wanted to adopt her; and Kimberly Mays, a teen who was switched at birth and sued to remain with the father who had reared her, raised the age-old questions of nature versus nurture and of whose rights should be paramount in rulings on family-law cases. The three cases also reflected a backlash against current child-welfare policies undermining the permanency of relationships for children in favor of biology.

There was an astoundingly high level of agreement among the public in each of the three cases: The child should remain permanently with the nurturing—rather than the biological—parent. But the law, the courts, and the system did not always reflect this consensus. Although Gregory K. was successful in his suit and Kimberly Mays was allowed to remain with the father who reared her, the U.S. Supreme Court ruled that Jessica must be returned to her biological parents.

Approximately 50,000 U.S. children are adopted by nonrelatives each year. Slightly more than half of those children are infants and the others are older children or children with special needs. In 1992, Americans adopted more than 6,500 children from other countries. It is estimated that 650,000 children come into the foster-care system each year, and that adoption will be the plan for approximately 10% of them. The plan for the vast majority of children is to return them to their biological parents.

As children enter foster care at alarmingly high rates—often after severe abuse and neglect—and stay longer, many critics of the child-welfare system are questioning where children fit into the scheme. The thrust of the system since the mid-1980s has been to provide intensive services for "family preservation." Critics are concerned that social workers, as in Gregory K.'s case, increasingly are unwilling to terminate parental rights even when the evidence shows there is no family to be preserved. The public consensus appears to be: "Families should be preserved, but they should be the families who are nurturing the children."

Since the early 1970s, there have been efforts to challenge the permanency of adoption by anti-adoption forces who advocate "open" adoption (continued involvement by the biological family in the child's life) and the retroactive opening of sealed adoption records to "undo" the adoption by reconnecting adopted persons with their biological family. These efforts have prompted some of the 2 million Americans who want to adopt to seek adoption in other countries. A 1993 Government Accounting Office report showed that 10% of Americans who adopt a child from overseas do so because of the perceived impermanence of U.S. adoptions. This biological bias has fueled discussions about the rights of uninvolved fathers. Few states have addressed the issue adequately and judges are left to decide how far the state, birth mother, and prospective adoptive parents must go to protect the rights of a man who has not claimed any interest or responsibility. The U.S. Supreme Court has ruled essentially that a father's rights are commensurate with the amount of responsibility he has undertaken; however, other courts have ruled on a more lenient standard.

The issues of the best interest of the child and the rights of fathers, in balance with the rights of the other parties, will continue to be debated hotly. They are central to an attempt to draft a uniform adoption act. Other areas of debate include what role advertising should play in the adoption process, what constitutes appropriate expenses in adoption cases, how to measure the qualifications of prospective adoptive parents, and whether and when children available for adoption should be placed with families of other races or ethnic backgrounds. The latter issue involves questions about the proper role of intercountry adoption in a comprehensive child welfare program. These often-emotional and complex issues are most likely to be resolved satisfactorily when the child's needs are considered paramount.

Amid this new adoption-rights movement is increased reporting of adults who were adopted who search for their biological parents. While less than 5% of adopted adults or birth parents search for one another, the possibility has created concern for many who fear their privacy may be violated. The risks of such searching may be greater for all parties who may encounter individuals with problems or unrealistic expectations.

The challenge for adoption is to balance the rights and needs of all parties who may benefit. The evidence is clear that adoption has been a successful social institution. There is consensus that, as with any institution, there is room for improvement. The continuing debate will focus on which changes will be most beneficial.

MARY BETH SEADER
National Council for Adoption

Photos, © Cavalli/Sipa

In a fashion season that featured costumey dressing, the printed, Czarist coat (above) *and the Trotskyite brown fur coat and hat and laced-up boots* (below) *found inspiration in historic Russia.*

FASHION

Fashion's theme for 1993 could be entitled "Runway v. Reality." The designer showings in Europe and the United States were more notable for the celebrity models and audiences and the outrageous staging and gimmicky costuming than they were for either a designer's vision or wearable fashions. Fashion presentations became made-for-television events and theatrical spectacles staged for press coverage. Designers titillated audiences with fashions in sheer fabrics or of abbreviated size for a rarely tasteful skin show that promoted the rivalry between the buxom, brash, and celebrated "supermodels"—dominant in 1992—and the "waifs," a group of undernourished innocents that were touted as fashion's new look. In addition, they reran the tired drama of the wandering hemline and paraded a virtual history of past fashion trends that "inspired" their current collections. Punk looks, complete with tattoos, brightly colored cropped hair, and body-piercing jewelry were revived by Jean Paul Gaultier, while Scarlett O'Hara pranced the runway in hoop skirts at John Galiano. Vivian Westwood showed bustle-skirted Edwardian-style fashions. There were tweedy Trotskyites and Czarist Cossacks at Ralph Lauren; Shaker simplicity and stark monastic chic at Calvin Klein; and the romantic ruffles and flourishes of the *Three Musketeers* and *Beau Brummel* at Richard Tyler, Bill Blass, and Chanel. These mixed messages left audiences dazed and retailers desperate for trends that would invigorate a stagnant retail market.

Hemlines were on the rise again, at least at some designers' shows. Karl Lagerfeld, who in 1992 had lowered hemlines after declaring the short skirt passé, revived his thigh-high looks. Yves St. Laurent also favored the short skirt but added wide lace banding to the hems. Other designers hedged their bets by showing all lengths.

Waistlines rose, too. Trendy skirts and trousers featured high-rising, wide waistbands—many resembling corselets—and there was a revival of the empire waist in dresses, jumpers, and tunics. Other high-waisted looks were achieved by hiking up trousers, jeans, or skirts with suspenders or showing them anchored above the waist with belts or drawstrings.

Another trend was the focus on the midriff as the latest erogenous zone. It was bared via cropped tops, shrunken sweaters, and shirts wrapped and tied under the bust—all shown with low-slung pants or skirts or sarongs tied at the hip. Midriff exposure also was achieved with waistline cutouts on dresses, tunic tops slit high in front, or jackets and vests left unbuttoned to show off the midsection.

Shape and Fabric. Silhouettes were softer and very fluid. Even in tailored clothes, the hard edges were gone as were shoulder pads, linings,

and most mannish affectations, except in those styles reflecting the influence of Beau Brummel romanticism or touched by the Edwardian influence. Softer, lighter, and more drapable fabrics reflected this change. There was an abundance of soft knit and woven fabrics, such as jerseys and crepes, as well as fluid silks and microfibers. Handkerchief-weight linens and cottons were important, as were sheer fabrics such as georgette, chiffon, or voile, which were used for the provocative body-baring looks on the runways. In this category there were also lace and crochet looks in mohair, cotton, or wool that ranged from openwork—net versions as gossamer as a cobweb—to heavier types such as Clunys or guipures and crunchy crochet looks resembling antimacassars or bedspreads.

Important too were crinkled, wrinkled, or Fortuny-pleated fabrics. Lightweight linens, silks, and cottons provided a look that appealed to designers. Issey Miyake corrugated pleats, shaping them into fashion sculptures; Romeo Gigli crimped his Grecian chitons; and Donna Karan had her wrinkled linen resort dresses tea-stained for a vintage look.

But the most ubiquitous fabric of the year by far was velvet. It was plain or panne, crushed or cut, printed, embossed, and tie-dyed and mixed with spandex fibers for a stretch version used for jeans, leggings, and body-hugging dresses. Velvet was so popular that it was seen in virtually every category of apparel (including lingerie and outerwear) and in accessories at every price level.

Color. The color palette was subdued and limited to black (the premier color of 1993); neutrals such as beige, taupe, gray, and ivory; and soft pastel shadings of other colors. Brights, which were so strong in past years, were banished and the only prints shown were vintage florals or ethnic patterns.

Silver replaced gold as the glitz factor. Designers mined silver for everything from sportswear looks like football jerseys and baseball jackets to sexy halter dresses and fancy pants that lit up the night.

Dresses. This was a strong year for dresses, primarily minimalist shapes like the tube; body-skimming chemises or cassock-like shifts; and Donna Karan's empire-waisted dresses, which mixed stretch velvet bodices with wool gauze skirts, spawning a surge of less expensive look-alikes. The apron dress, worn alone or as a jumper over shirts or blouses, was another favorite dress look. But the dress of the year was the slip dress, which was featured by designers and promoted by mass merchandisers in every popular fabric and color. It was shown by itself or layered over T-shirts, tank tops, body suits, or pants; it was worn in pairs, sheer over solid, or in contrasting colors or lengths.

Accessories. Accessories in 1993 were minimal and were used to add authenticity to period looks rather than as embellishment. Antique jewelry in the form of brooches or cameos were

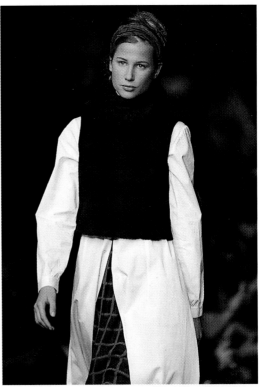

© Daniel Simon/Gamma-Liaison

A trend also developed around austere, ecclesiastically-inspired fashions that included a vest over an open tunic (above) *and a cassock-like, floor-length empire-waist shift* (below).

© Cavalli/Sipa

Creating a waif-like look, popular during the 1993 fashion year, was a close-to-the-body, long, minimalist-style dress and a skirt-and-jacket ensemble—both in neutral tones (left). Popular accessories included a crocheted hat and heavy-duty black boots as well as jewelry of shoestring-like tie chokers and a single long necklace strand. Offering a contrast was a black, short-skirted ensemble (right) that represented a more traditional approach. Black flats—popular 1993 footwear—and black hosiery completed the outfit.

popular costume pieces for the Edwardian looks. Necklaces, earrings, and other jewelry items, when shown at all, were delicate and small in scale. Crosses, however, were the exception and were the most extravagant and popular jewelry symbol in pins or necklaces. They were worn with the austere, ecclesiastically-inspired fashions.

Footwear that laced—like granny boots, oxfords, and leg-wrapping Grecian sandals—was a high-fashion look in 1993, as were pumps with high toplines, ankle wraps, or instep straps. These styles were done with various heel heights and often featured platform soles. Flats, however, were most prevalent, with ballet slippers, espadrilles, thongs, and Birkenstock-type sandals the most important look.

Menswear. In menswear the rule was that there were no rules. A sportswear approach that stressed comfort, practicality, and versatile wardrobe options was the trend. Sweaters instead of shirts were worn with suits, for exam-

ple, and hearty hiking boots cradled feet on the trading floor as well as on the trail. Even the classic three-piece suit combo of vest, trousers, and jacket became basic components of a separates-style expandable wardrobe concept.

There was a strong return to the tried-and-true classics such as traditional single-breasted suits, cashmere sweaters, corduroy or twill trousers, and the plain white shirt—which was updated with a band collar. Outerwear favorites such as the parka, balmacaan, and barn coat were other strong and popular looks, all cut for a relaxed boxy fit that was less continental and more "country casual."

This casual approach extended to accessories, which tended toward sturdy shoes; richly colored ties in classic paisley, plaid, or foulard patterns; tweedy caps or soft fedoras; and chronograph-type watches.

ANN ELKINS
Fashion Director, "Good Housekeeping"

FINLAND

In 1993, Finland continued its reorientation from East to West, both politically and economically breaking the bonds imposed during the Cold War.

The EC and Political Affairs. Finland started negotiations to join the European Community (EC) in February. Though EC negotiators have expressed doubts, Finland plans to adhere to the original timetable, which would make it a member of the EC on Jan. 1, 1995. In stark contrast to the other Nordic countries, polls showed that popular support for Finnish EC membership increased through 1993. Fifty-three percent of Finns supported membership in a September poll, with 35% against. The issue of membership was scheduled to be decided by a referendum in the fall of 1994.

The main stumbling block in the negotiations with the EC was Finnish agricultural policies, which provide higher subsidies than those in the EC Common Agricultural Policy. Finland requested a special deal to reflect the adverse climatic conditions that make Finnish agriculture less competitive. However, the Finnish government's economic policy favored forcing industry to adapt to EC markets. There also was a strong Finnish desire to participate in any future security policy of the EC within the framework of the West European Union (WEU). Finland did not rule out membership in the North Atlantic Treaty Organization (NATO), but it was not a pressing issue.

One of the strongest supporters of the EC membership was Martti Ahtisaari, a former United Nations envoy and front-runner for the Finnish presidency in elections scheduled for January 1994. The incumbent, Mauno Koivisto, was not seeking reelection. Though Ahtisaari is a Social Democrat like Koivisto and also is opposed to the Center Party government led by Esko Aho, he is considered a nonpartisan personality. This election would be the first time the president was chosen by popular vote, and may strengthen the influence of the office. The government, meanwhile, announced that it intended to introduce legislation to curb the powers of the presidency.

Finland's former Trade and Industry Minister Kauka Juhantalo was impeached by parliament in June, after allegations that he linked his own loan interests in a bank to the provision of government support to a large engineering company in which the bank had a large stake. Juhantalo denied the charges at the start of the proceedings in October.

Economic Affairs. In 1993 the share of Finnish exports going to the former Soviet Union was less than 2.5%—only one tenth the level of exports to this area in the 1980s. Finnish trade with its neighbor thus had dropped to a level comparable with that of major West European countries.

The deep recession caused by the collapse of the Soviet market was alleviated in 1993 by dou-

ble-digit growth in exports to the EC. Such trade accounted for more than 55% of Finland's total exports. The nation started a slow move out of recession in 1993. However, growth in output was close to nil for the year, and only 1% growth was expected in 1994. With unemployment at 20%—the highest in the Nordic countries—Finland was far from its success-story profile of the mid-1980s. Dropping interest rates helped banks, which received the first installment—20 billion marks (about $3.3 billion)—on a major government bailout in January. Finland's largest bank, KOP, predicted a breakeven by the end of 1994, but total bailout costs for the sector may reach 70 billion marks (about $11.7 billion) by 1995.

LEIF BECK FALLESEN, *Editor in Chief*
"Boersen," Copenhagen

FINLAND • Information Highlights

Official Name: Republic of Finland.
Location: Northern Europe.
Area: 130,127 sq mi (337 030 km²).
Population (mid-1993 est.): 5,100,000.
Chief Cities (Dec. 31, 1991 est.): Helsinki, the capital, 497,542; Espoo, 175,670; Tampere, 173,797.
Government: *Head of state*, Mauno Koivisto, president (took office Jan. 27, 1982). *Head of government*, Esko Aho, prime minister (took office April 1991). *Legislature* (unicameral)—Eduskunta.
Monetary Unit: Markka (5.8240 markkaa equal U.S.$1, Dec. 1, 1993).
Gross Domestic Product (1991 est. U.S.$): $80,600,000,000.
Economic Indexes (1992): *Consumer Prices* (1980 = 100), all items, 204.8; food, 188.0. *Industrial Production* (1980 = 100), 125.
Foreign Trade (1992 U.S.$): *Imports*, $20,744,000,000; *exports*, $23,520,000,000.

FLORIDA

In 1993, Florida's economy showed marked improvement after a prolonged recession, but the state continued to experience long-term economic problems exacerbated by murderous assaults on tourists and the closing of military bases.

President Bill Clinton chose several Floridians for his new administration, including Attorney General Janet Reno; Environmental Protection Agency head Carol Browner; and Jeffrey Watson, a presidential special assistant.

The Economy. Ravaged by Hurricane Andrew in 1992, south Dade county continued to rebuild, aided by federal funds and the government's commitment to reopen Homestead Air Force Base. Still, many businesses had not reopened, and the rebuilding effort was hindered by bureaucratic delays and unscrupulous contractors and roofers.

The state's unemployment rate remained high, although Florida's new-job creation was above the national average. The state's per-capita income dropped to 22d among the states in 1993.

A Dade county, FL, policeman offers assistance to tourists leaving a rental-car agency. The murder of several foreign tourists in Florida during 1993 adversely affected the state's major industry.

© Tony Savino/Sygma

Tourism, Florida's most important industry with annual revenues of $30 billion, declined slightly, partly as a result of the murders of several foreign visitors. The crimes caused widespread fears, jeopardizing the Sunshine State as a tourist destination. Two white men received life sentences for setting fire to Christopher Wilson, a black man from New York.

The conclusion of a long-term, black-led boycott of Dade county enhanced the prospects for tourism there.

Politics. In May the Metro-Dade Commission repealed Dade county's controversial "English only" language ordinance.

Former Metro-Dade Mayor Steve Clark defeated Miriam Alonso in a fractious Miami mayoralty election in November. The Cuban-born Alonso insisted that the office was a "Hispanic seat," and had urged the city's overwhelmingly Spanish-speaking electorate to vote for her on that basis. In nearby Hialeah, Raul Martinez,

appealing felony convictions, won another term as mayor. Alcee Hastings, a federal judge before his impeachment and conviction in the U.S. Congress, took office as a U.S. representative in January.

Crime. Protester Michael F. Griffin allegedly killed Dr. David Gunn during a demonstration outside a Pensacola abortion clinic....William Lozano, a former Miami policeman, won acquittal on two counts of manslaughter in the 1989 deaths of two blacks after an appeals court overturned an earlier conviction....David Paul, former head of Miami-based Cen Trust Bank, was found guilty in federal court of 68 counts of fraud....Former U.S. Rep. Lawrence J. Smith received a brief prison term for tax evasion and filing false campaign-finance reports.

The Florida legislature approved 32,000 new prison beds but found funding for just one third of them. In a special session of the Florida legislature, lawmakers enacted a juvenile-crime bill prohibiting youths from possessing guns.

Environment. Following five years of legal battles over Everglades pollution, federal and state officials and sugarcane producers reached a tentative agreement on a $465 million plan to restore the world's largest freshwater marsh. The sugar industry was to pay most of the cost.

Legal. In June the U.S. Supreme Court ruled unconstitutional a ban imposed by the city of Hialeah on ritual animal sacrifice, citing violation of religious guarantees. In a nationally publicized case, a Sarasota judge ruled that 14-year-old Kimberly Mays, switched soon after birth with another baby, was not required to maintain contact with her biological parents.

Sports. The Florida Marlins, one of two new major-league-baseball expansion teams, played their first season in Miami and the Florida Panthers, a new professional hockey team, debuted there in the fall. Jacksonville was selected as the site of a new pro-football team.

PAUL S. GEORGE
Miami-Dade Community College, Wolfson Campus

FLORIDA • Information Highlights

Area: 58,664 sq mi (151 939 km²).

Population (July 1, 1992 est.): 13,488,000.

Chief Cities (1990 census): Tallahassee, the capital, 124,773; Jacksonville, 672,971; Miami, 358,548; Tampa, 280,015; St. Petersburg, 238,629.

Government (1993): *Chief Officers*—governor, Lawton Chiles (D); lt. gov., Buddy MacKay (D). *Legislature*—Senate, 40 members; House of Representatives, 120 members.

State Finances (fiscal year 1991): *Revenue*, $25,754,000,000; *expenditure*, $25,168,000,000.

Personal Income (1992): $262,929,000,000; per capita, $19,494.

Labor Force (August 1993): *Civilian labor force*, 6,581,500; *unemployed*, 469,200 (7.1% of total force).

Education: *Enrollment* (fall 1991)—public elementary schools, 1,427,613; public secondary, 504,518; colleges and universities, 611,781. *Public school expenditures* (1990-91), $9,045,710,000.

FOOD

The year 1993 saw reduced U.S. and world food production, efforts to improve U.S. food labeling, a new emphasis on food safety, and moves to integrate nutritional concepts into school lunches.

Food Supplies. Per-capita world food supplies tightened modestly in late 1993 despite improved food production in Africa, due largely to record summer flooding in the U.S. Midwest region. The lowest U.S. corn production in six years and smaller feed-grain and oilseed crops resulted. Feed grains and oilseeds provide livestock and poultry feed, with a small share of production going for industrial uses and direct consumer items such as sweeteners, vegetable oil, cornstarch, textured protein products, and breakfast cereal. Supplies of grain-based consumer items were not affected noticeably. However, more-expensive animal feeds increased U.S. meat and dairy-product prices. Costs of some processed vegetables also rose modestly in response to damage from the Midwest flooding.

In Japan bad weather cut rice production and forced the government to allow imports. Japan long had resisted opening its rice market to imports, despite U.S. pressure to do so.

Food Safety. Planned changes in U.S. food labeling were slowed by complexities in implementing the new system. Product safety won greater attention in the food industry and among government regulators, with emphasis on hygienic conditions and reduced risk of pesticide contamination.

Surveys indicated many people would pay a premium for produce tested and certified free of pesticide residues. More than 60% of U.S. consumers surveyed by the U.S. Department of Agriculture were concerned about health risks from additives, preservatives, and pesticides. Research indicated U.S. fruit- and vegetable-grading systems may encourage pesticide use. Grades emphasize physical appearance, but contain no information about chemical use. Pesticides are used in production partly to meet appearance standards. The Food and Drug Administration (FDA) Pesticide Monitoring Program indicated two thirds of the fresh fruit and vegetables sold contained no pesticide residues and only 2% contained residues slightly above government standards.

Existing regulations required that containers for shipping fresh fruit and vegetables indicate what pesticides were used after harvest. However, labeling did not include pesticides used prior to harvest and was not required when the product was offered for retail sale.

The Congressional Office of Technology Assessment noted that future work in food safety must address testing of genetically engineered products, including genetically altered vaccines for livestock, transgenic plants and animals used for food production, and growth enhancers. In some areas, organic fruits and vegetables provide pesticide-free alternatives for consumers. While no federal standards existed for such products, work was under way to develop standards. More than one half of the U.S. states had regulations or standards for organic products.

The Clinton administration proposed modified standards for nonorganic foods to allow traces of carcinogens in food—provided that they pose no significant health risks. Industry officials wanted to change existing regulations that call for zero tolerance on carcinogens, since testing equipment can detect traces of chemicals that may be far below levels posing health risks.

Meat Inspection. Several persons died and hundreds were affected by a January outbreak of bacteria-tainted meat in the U.S. Northwest. The U.S. Department of Agriculture and the food industry thereafter began to improve meat inspection to reduce the chance of bacterial or pathogen contamination in meat and poultry. The work encompassed manufacturing, handling, processing, and transportation, as well as preparation of meat at restaurants and other retail establishments. Studies indicate risks from such contamination, while small, are much greater than from pesticide contamination.

Food-safety work included educational programs for workers in food industries. A food-safety-risk-assessment concept for meat inspection was being developed at the recommendation of the National Academy of Sciences. The system involves analysis of various factors affecting product quality in each operation.

School Lunches and Fast Foods. Proposed modifications in U.S. school-lunch programs included lower-fat menus. Several fast-food firms provided school-lunch services or partial food service in schools.

Fast-food chains grew rapidly in 1993. Some firms used mobile units—providing food for outdoor concerts, athletic events, and similar activities—and food service to office complexes. Fast food accounted for one third of U.S. consumers' spending on away-from-home meals. To meet growing competition from fast-food firms, supermarkets increased deli offerings and meat processors expanded offerings of snack foods.

Other News. The American Heart Association (AHA) planned to use its heart-and-torch logo on packages of food products that meet government dietary guidelines—which call for ten grams or less of fat per 3-oz serving. The AHA, however, indicated that the logo would be withheld from products that meet the standard if they are made by firms with tobacco businesses.

In June the Pepsi-Cola Co. and the FDA were faced with a potential nationwide tampering scandal—in which consumers in more than 20 states claimed to find syringes or other objects in soda cans. The charges were found to be largely unfounded and led to more than a dozen arrests. *See also* AGRICULTURE.

ROBERT N. WISNER, *Iowa State University*

FOREIGN AID

On Sept. 30, 1993, U.S. President Bill Clinton signed into law the foreign-aid bill for fiscal year 1994. It appropriated $13 billion for foreign operations, including payments to multilateral institutions and development agencies, bilateral economic and military aid to individual countries, and export assistance. Reflecting the diminished security threat after the Soviet Union's collapse and mounting concern over the federal budget deficit, the total appropriation was $1 billion less than in the previous year.

Primary Recipients. The bill provided Russia and the other republics of the former Soviet Union—the United States' Cold War adversary—with $2.5 billion in economic assistance. That placed the former Soviet republics second only to Israel, which received $3 billion, as principal recipients of U.S. foreign aid.

Congressional approval of the president's request for the former Soviet states marked one of Clinton's few clear foreign-policy victories during his first year in office. He introduced his intention to help the economically troubled republics following an April summit meeting with Russian President Boris Yeltsin in Vancouver, B.C. Lawmakers initially protested, citing Russia's arms sales to developing countries and continued military presence in the Baltic states.

Clinton succeeded, however, in convincing Congress of the importance of supporting the region's economic-reform effort and won approval of his full request. The aid was to be used to help dismantle the Soviet nuclear arsenal, provide food and medicine, promote bilateral trade, and privatize government-owned industries. After the violent uprising in Moscow against Yeltsin in October, Clinton reaffirmed his support for the reformist president and pledged to speed delivery of the assistance.

A surprise breakthrough in peace negotiations between the Palestine Liberation Organization (PLO) and Israel in September prompted the Clinton administration also to pledge $500 million over five years to help rebuild the Gaza Strip and the West Bank as Israel withdraws troops from the occupied territories.

Fiscal Pressures. Because more than half of the appropriation was directed to the Middle East and the former Soviet Union, the overall reduction in foreign assistance came at the expense of other programs. For example, the law provided $1.9 billion for multilateral financial institutions, including the World Bank—some $500,000 less than President Clinton had requested. About $5.9 billion was appropriated for development assistance and other programs administered by the Agency for International Development (AID)—a 10% cut from fiscal 1993. Spending was reduced for international narcotics-control programs, development aid for sub-Saharan Africa, and economic aid for Eastern Europe and the Baltic states.

Although Congress easily passed the spending bill, less progress was made in the redrafting of foreign-aid policy in light of the dramatically changed international situation in the post-Cold War era. The 1961 law governing foreign-aid policy long had enabled lawmakers to reward countries friendly to the United States in a world that was polarized between East and West. Events since 1989 had prompted critics to call for fundamental changes in the way aid was distributed.

But efforts to change the law encountered several obstacles. One was flagging popular support for overseas programs, which cost about $28 billion per year when foreign spending by the departments of Agriculture, Treasury, Defense, and State, and agencies such as the Peace Corps were taken into account. Although these programs amounted to less than 2% of the federal budget, the disappearance of a Soviet threat made many Americans less willing to send tax dollars abroad. Objections to foreign aid grew with reports of inefficiency and waste.

Reform. In September a high-level Clinton administration panel completed work on proposals to redraft the foreign-aid law to help the United States respond more quickly to changes in international conditions. The panel recommended broad reforms that would enable the administration to define general policy goals, such as fostering democracy or ending arms proliferation, and decide which countries would receive funds to carry them out. It also would eliminate congressional mandates, or earmarks, that enable legislators to channel funds toward favored countries or projects overseas. The panel also recommended spending less for military aid, which has accounted for more than one third of all U.S. foreign assistance, and more for economic development and humanitarian assistance. This would benefit multilateral institutions, such as the World Bank and relief agencies.

Although the administration's proposals were controversial, both the House Foreign Affairs and Senate Foreign Relations committees were prepared to include reform of the 1961 foreign-aid law in a foreign-aid-authorization bill—the first such legislation since 1985. But that effort appeared doomed as the Clinton administration was not expected to submit its proposals to Congress formally in time for lawmakers to act on them before the end of 1993. Meanwhile, AID administrator J. Brian Atwood announced plans to reorganize the agency to mirror the administration's reform proposals. Atwood wanted AID to reduce its overseas presence from 108 countries to 50, and he promised to reduce the agency's workforce of 55,000 and sharpen its policy objectives. He announced that AID would concentrate on four interrelated goals: curbing population growth, building democracy, protecting the environment, and fostering economic development.

MARY H. COOPER
"CQ [Congressional Quarterly] Researcher"

FRANCE

National elections in France ushered in a new center-right government during 1993 and signaled the beginning of the end for Socialist President François Mitterrand. The country's worst economic downturn of the post-World War II era left 12% of the workforce unemployed by the end of the year—a devastating blow to the French psyche that encouraged isolationist thinking in politics, the economy, and culture.

There were many signs that France was responding to growing global competition—in disparate fields such as agriculture, motion pictures, and high technology—by turning its back on the outside world and shifting inward. Although this tendency belied France's position as the fourth-largest exporter in the world—and second-largest exporter of farm products and services after the United States—it seemed to comfort a country of 58 million rendered leery of the world by recession and the adverse political conditions in Europe.

A clear sign of a change in French thinking came in March, when voters turned out the ruling Socialist majority by electing an overwhelmingly center-right National Assembly. The rout was considered a historic defeat for the Socialists, who garnered only 19% of the vote. The new majority, composed primarily of the Gaullist Rally for the Republic (RPR) and the moderate Union for French Democracy, claimed 460 of the Assembly's 577 seats. The Socialists and their allies only captured 54 seats and were reduced to such devastation by the elections that many analysts doubted they could return as a solid force within the decade. Yet the results for the right were not all bright. The new majority won with just more than 40% of the vote, with abstentions attaining nearly one third.

When President Mitterrand named Gaullist Edouard Balladur as the new prime minister, he seemed to have called on a man of the times: serious and careful to avoid grandiose promises about rapidly improving the French economy. Balladur, a former finance minister, quickly set about reducing France's mounting debt by cutting spending and increasing government withholding. But he also emphasized the need to safeguard the cradle-to-grave social protection that the French have come to expect. Having witnessed firsthand the crippling social protests of 1968, when French workers brought the country to a halt, Balladur remained haunted by the possibility that widespread social unrest could occur once again.

Domestic Affairs. The Socialists' unequivocal national defeat led a number of prominent right-wing leaders, including Paris mayor and former prime minister Jacques Chirac, to call for Mitterrand's resignation. But Mitterrand declared a determination to complete his second seven-year mandate to May 1995. This opened the way to France's second period of "cohabitation" between a president and prime minister of different political parties. Within weeks the Mitterrand-Balladur "odd couple" appeared to be operating smoothly, with Balladur running daily affairs and Mitterrand providing what the public considered a "wise father figure" for the country. Mitterrand adjusted quickly to his new, more modest role, noting in his traditional Bastille Day televised interview that "If I had the impression that the interests of France were being compromised, that's when I would say something."

On May 1, the international day of labor and a holiday of particular symbolism to France's Socialists, former Socialist Prime Minister Pierre Bérégovoy committed suicide, shocking the country into deep introspection. Considered the architect—as longtime economics minister—of the "strong franc" policy that rid France of its traditionally high inflation, Bérégovoy suffered

© Chesnot/Witt/Facelly/Sipa

Following the victory of France's conservative parties in March 1993 elections, Edouard Balladur (left), 63-year-old former finance minister and member of the neo-Gaullist Rally for the Republic Party, succeeded Socialist Pierre Bérégovoy (right) as the nation's premier.

© Reuters/Bettmann

Following the Socialists' defeat at the polls, former Premier Michel Rocard, above, took over as the party's leader. He also was the Socialists' likely 1995 presidential candidate.

from evidence that, under his tenure, France experienced a growing gap between the haves and have nots. Reportedly depressed by the harsh defeat voters handed his government in the March elections, Bérégovoy also was said to have been unable to overcome press and judicial scrutiny of an interest-free loan he obtained from an industrialist to purchase a modest Paris apartment. For many French, the suicide was the cry of a modest man—too poor for a college education—who never felt at home in the class-conscious public administration through which he rose to govern.

In June the National Assembly approved a series of propositions from the new government designed to control legal and illegal immigration. In announcing the reforms, Interior Minister Charles Pasqua declared as their objective "zero immigration"—a politically popular goal in the midst of a recession, but one considered both unrealistic and economically undesirable by most analysts. The new laws limited family-reunification guarantees and grounds for asylum, while facilitating expulsion. The most controversial measures included allowing for random police identity checks and limiting means by which French nationality can be obtained. Under the new measures, French nationality is no longer automatic for children born in France to parents from former French colonies. Sociologists warned that France would develop a generation of "country-less" youths who would be easy targets for discrimination. Reform proponents said such children would place more value on the nationality they chose.

In July a scandal engulfing the Olympique de Marseille (OM) soccer team erupted to dominate the news. The 1992 European-championship team was accused of offering money to three players from a rival team to fix a game. The scandal tarnished the image of the already suffering Mediterranean port city of Marseille, and embroiled OM's owner, Bernard Tapie—a flamboyant businessman, former Socialist-gov-

ernment minister, National Assembly member, and Mitterrand protégé—in deep controversy. By the end of the summer, OM was banned from European Cup competition, and in October a beleaguered Tapie announced he soon would leave the club, but little else about the scandal was clear.

During 1993 the Socialists chose a new party leader, 63-year-old Michel Rocard. He was expected to be the party's candidate in the presidential elections scheduled for 1995.

On November 18, Mitterrand officially opened the Richelieu wing of the Louvre Museum, a project that added 70% to the museum's capacity and marked the completion of the major segments of the billion-dollar "Grand Louvre" expansion. After the controversial pyramid entrance by architect I. M. Pei opened in 1989, and underground parking, shopping, and archaeological exhibits opened early in 1993, the Richelieu wing allowed a doubling of exhibition space to 555,000 sq ft (51 560 m^2), making the Louvre "the world's largest cultural complex," according to Culture Minister Jacques Toubon. The grand Louvre project was expected to be completed by 1997 at a final cost of more than $1 billion.

Economy. France started the year having registered one of the best economic performances for 1992 of all the large developed countries, with 1.1% growth and 2% inflation. But a rapid deterioration left economists predicting the gross domestic product (GDP) would shrink by at least 1% in 1993, while unemployment climbed to 11.8%. The gloomy prospects led to renewed attacks on the French franc, reflecting a growing sentiment among analysts and currency speculators that France would be obliged to abandon its "strong franc" policy in order to lower interest rates and prime a recovery.

Yet even though the Bérégovoy government went down in defeat defending the "strong franc," and even though unemployment continued to grow throughout the year, the Balladur government stuck hard by the franc. Interest rates were kept high, despite industry complaints, to maintain the French currency's parity with the German deutsche mark.

In June the president of the National Assembly, a member of the RPR like Balladur, called for a complete reversal of the government's economic policy in order to favor job creation. At the same time other indications surfaced to suggest discord within the majority on economic policy. In July a new report projecting almost 500,000 more unemployed by the end of the year and sinking economic prospects for Germany, France's principal trade partner, further weakened the franc's underpinnings. On July 23, Balladur insisted the franc would not be devalued, but by August the hemorrhaging in the European Monetary System (EMS) was so critical—with European central banks losing billions of dollars to prop up their currencies—that Euro-

pean Community (EC) economic ministers were forced to act.

The tight fluctuation bands of the EMS were loosened on October 2 such that the system ceased to exist except in name. The franc weakened somewhat against the mark, but the Balladur government refused its new monetary freedom and stuck by a high-interest-rate, low-inflation policy. In November some private analysts continued to predict a devaluation of the franc to ease unemployment, but Balladur insisted there would be no wavering in his policy.

In July the government announced a list of four public companies to be privatized by the end of the year: Elf Aquitaine oil company, Rhône-Poulenc chemical group, Banque National de Paris, and Banque Hervet. The government expected $8 billion in proceeds, with more sales expected in 1994.

Long-standing French hostility toward an international trade-liberalization agreement that would touch the country's agriculture exports grew more strident under the RPR government. Balladur insisted his government wanted an accord, but one that did not include a hard-won farm trade agreement that was reached between the EC and the United States in November 1992 but never accepted formally by individual EC countries. By midyear polls showed most French people considered an agreement in the Uruguay Round of international trade talks would be a "Gattastrophe," a common French play on words on the General Agreement on Tariffs and Trade (GATT), under the auspices of which the 115-nation negotiations were organized. Many citizens believed that GATT had led to a U.S. invasion of France's farm sector, motion-picture industry, and other vital business interests.

In September, Culture Minister Jacques Toubon declared such U.S. film blockbusters as *Jurassic Park* a "menace" to French culture. With U.S. movies already taking 60% of the French market—a smaller percentage than in other European countries—Toubon said France needed to protect its productions from being crowded out. He noted that *Jurassic Park* opened in France in 450 cinemas, compared with *Germinal*, the biggest film production in French cinematic history, which opened on only 350 screens. Toubon and numerous French film stars and intellectuals demanded an "exception" for cultural products in international trade rules.

On September 20 the French government won an agreement from its EC partners to seek "clarifications" of the EC-U.S. agriculture agreement, a move touted by Balladur and numerous French ministers as a major success for France and a sign that France no longer was isolated in Europe in its tough stance on GATT. But the United States immediately said it would not reopen what it considered a closed chapter, leading France to make a growing number of declarations about U.S. intransigence. But by late November the United States had accepted several key modifications and a GATT accord was negotiated in December. (*See* INTERNATIONAL TRADE AND FINANCE.)

In October, Air France was struck by what started as a wildcat strike among the company's ground staff that paralyzed the international carrier for eight days and cost the already unprofitable company $200 million. After heavy losses in 1992 and projections of at least $600 million in losses in 1993, company president Bernard Attali developed a restructuring plan calling for 4,000 job cuts and salary reductions. But ground crews reacted violently to the plan, saying it hit the company's low-income earners disproportionately. Initially the government stood fast by Attali and his plan, calling it "irrevocable." But as Paris' two principal airports remained paralyzed by striking workers and public opinion sided with the workers, the government revoked the restructuring plan and forced Attali's departure.

The government cited what looked increasingly like a workers' "revolt" to explain its about-face, while employees of other loss-making public companies said the "Air France effect" undoubtedly would bolster their resolve to battle any job- or pay-cutting restructuring plans. The government vowed a new loss-cutting plan for Air France, but promised it would "share the hardships" more equitably than the first.

But the Air France strike rang like alarm bells for the government, suggesting deeply troubling prospects for social peace and giving new urgency to efforts to limit ever-rising unemployment. In November, with government support, the Senate voted to experiment with a 33-hour workweek at organizations that increased their staffs by 10%. It was similar to an idea that the government had opposed and defeated in the National Assembly only a month earlier.

International Affairs. In January, Foreign Minister Roland Dumas stunned the country's political leadership by suggesting that France should

---

FRANCE • Information Highlights

Official Name: French Republic.
Location: Western Europe.
Area: 211,208 sq mi (547 030 km²).
Population (mid-1993 est.): 57,700,000.
Chief City (1990 census): Paris, the capital, 2,152,423,000.
Government: *Head of state*, François Mitterrand, president (took office May 1981). *Chief minister*, Edouard Balladur, prime minister (took office March 1993). *Legislature*—Parliament: Senate and National Assembly.
Monetary Unit: Franc (5.9170 francs equal U.S.$1, Nov. 22, 1993).
Gross Domestic Product (1991 est. U.S.$): $1,033,700,000,000.
Economic Indexes (1992): *Consumer Prices* (1980 = 100), all items, 194.4; food, 191.0. *Industrial Production* (1980 = 100), 114.
Foreign Trade (1992 U.S.$): *Imports*, $238,908,000,000; *exports*, $231,940,000,000.

François Mitterrand (left) was welcomed to Cambodia by Prince Norodom Sihanouk (right) on Feb. 11, 1993. Two days earlier, the French president had become the first Western leader to visit Vietnam since it had been reunited under Communist rule in 1976.

© Bernard Bisson/Sygma

liberate "by force, if necessary," detention camps discovered in Bosnia-Herzegovina. Several days later the aircraft carrier *Clemenceau* was sent into the Adriatic Sea, but the saber rattling went nowhere. Throughout 1993, France maintained a cautious policy towards any forced intervention in the Bosnian conflict.

When U.S. Secretary of State Warren Christopher visited Paris in April seeking support for proposed "surgical strikes" against Serbian positions besieging Sarajevo and for rearming of Bosnia's Muslims, the new foreign minister, Alain Juppé, explained French opposition to both plans. The French, with more than 5,000 UN-commanded "blue helmet" troops in the former Yugoslavia, feared such preferential action by the international community would lead both to reprisals against the French soldiers on the ground and to the halt of humanitarian-aid efforts.

In March, French General Phillipe Morillon, commander in chief of UN forces in Bosnia, won kudos for his high-profile efforts to secure humanitarian aid for the Bosnian enclave of Srebrenica. Morillon's actions won public support for the government's emphasis on humanitarian aid and further dampened French interest in a more interventionist role.

Gradually, however, the government's position on Bosnia faced mounting criticism by a growing circle of French intellectuals who saw in the opposition to intervention a reflection of France's historic links to Serbia. At least twice during the year, President Mitterrand suggested an eventual use of force to stop the Bosnian bloodshed or to guarantee the passage of humanitarian aid, but in neither case did the president go on to push the threat with France's European or other Western allies.

In February, Mitterrand traveled to Vietnam and Cambodia. The stop in Vietnam was the first visit by a French president to the former French colony since 1945. During what was viewed as a trip to boost French political, economic, and cultural ties to a quickly developing region of the world, Mitterrand described the French war in Indochina as a "mistake" and declared that the "American embargo no longer serves any purpose."

Palestine Liberation Organization (PLO) leader Yasir Arafat visited Mitterrand on October 21 and was received with most of the honors reserved for a head of state. Addressing the PLO leader as "Mr. President," Arafat's title as the head of the PLO executive committee, Mitterrand promised to intervene with his European colleagues to accelerate EC financial aid to the occupied territories. Having been largely absent from Middle East diplomacy since the Madrid peace talks in 1991, France was seen to be using the Arafat visit to signal its desire to return to a region where it had a traditional interest.

As full ratification and a beginning of implementation of the EC's Maastricht Treaty approached, Mitterrand continued to vaunt the virtues of a tightly integrated Europe based on the Maastricht model of economic and political union. But Balladur said Europe's future was in more cooperation among nations and not in centralized power. Since Balladur was the leading candidate for the presidency in 1995 elections, Europe's shift away from a federal vision of leaders like Mitterrand or German Chancellor Helmut Kohl to a more decentralized form of cooperation seemed to be gaining momentum in France.

HOWARD LAFRANCHI, *Paris Bureau*
"The Christian Science Monitor"

GAMBLING

The growth of commercial gaming in America between 1982 and 1993 was substantial, continuing a trend that began in 1964 when a lottery began operation in New Hampshire. Casino gaming in particular had expanded rapidly in the United States since 1988; available in two states that year, it could be found in approximately 19 by 1993.

In 1992 all legal gaming industries—casinos, lotteries, pari-mutuel wagering, charitable gaming, legal bookmaking, card clubs, and Indian-operated gaming—generated gross revenues after prize payment of almost $30 billion, on a handle (total amount wagered) of $329.9 billion. In contrast, 1982 gross revenues from legal gaming were $10.4 billion, on a handle of $125.8 billion. Gross revenues for the various gaming industries in 1992 were: casinos, $10.1 billion; lotteries, $11.5 billion; pari-mutuels, $3.7 billion; Indian-run gaming, $1.5 billion; others, $3.1 billion.

Casino Growth. Legal casinos, found only in Nevada and Atlantic City, NJ, as recently as 1988, had spread rapidly in a number of forms. Small-stakes casinos opened in the remote mining town of Deadwood, SD, in 1989; this formula was duplicated in three Colorado towns in 1991. Riverboat casinos were authorized in Iowa, Illinois, Mississippi, Louisiana, Missouri, and Indiana between 1989 and 1993. Land-based-monopoly urban casinos were legalized for New Orleans, LA, and for Montreal, Que., and Windsor, Ont., in 1993. The Montreal casino opened in October 1993.

Indian-operated casinos achieved legality as a result of a 1987 U.S. Supreme Court decision, the related passage of the Indian Gaming Regulatory Act of 1988, and subsequent negotiated state compacts. Many significant Native American gaming operations occurred due to favorable court decisions, notably in Connecticut, Wisconsin, and Arizona. By the end of 1993, Indian-run casinos existed in those states as well as in Minnesota, Washington state, New York, Michigan, South Dakota, Iowa, Colorado, and California. Tribes in other states either were negotiating with states for casinos, or were filing suits for the right to operate casinos. Estimated gaming revenue in all Indian casinos in 1992 was about $1.1 billion.

Las Vegas—with the largest concentration of casinos in the world—also joined the expansion between 1989 and 1993, opening several "mega-casinos." The five largest new casinos cost approximately $3 billion to construct, and added about 17,000 hotel rooms to the city.

New Lottery Tactics. The lottery industry reacted to increased competition from casinos and flattening sales for traditional lottery products by introducing more casino-style games, such as Video Lottery Terminals (VLTs) and Club Keno, in a number of jurisdictions. Gross revenues from VLTs in South Dakota—the first state to introduce them—approximated $150 million in 1992 from about 6,000 VLTs. Nationally, lottery sales rose 12.0% in 1992 over 1991, after declining 0.6% in 1991 from 1990. Much of the 1992 growth was attributable to the opening of the Texas lottery and to VLT and Club Keno expansions in specific states.

The Future. It seemed likely that the rest of the 1990s would be marked by continuing proliferation of casino-style gaming, in the form of riverboat casinos, land-based casinos, monopoly urban casinos, or "non-casino casino-style" gaming—like VLTs, Club Keno, or slot machines and gaming devices in age-restricted commercial locations.

The primary government motivations for legalizing casinos have been to capture job-creation and tourism-generation benefits, whereas the spread of lotteries has been motivated more by tax-revenue generation. However, as gaming continued to spread, the proportion of customers from outside the region would decline for most destinations, which dissipating the economic spin-offs. Furthermore, few jurisdictions yet had come to grips with the myriad social costs associated with the excessive and problem gambling that accompanies the spread of commercial gaming.

WILLIAM EADINGTON
University of Nevada, Reno

© Tony Savion/Sipa

The United States' largest Indian-owned casino—Foxwoods in Connecticut, right—grossed more than $400 million in its second year of operation, making it one of the world's most profitable casinos. An expansion was to include two more casinos, a hotel and theme park, golf course, and museum on Native American history.

GARDENING AND HORTICULTURE

Plant lovers throughout the world benefited in 1993 from the introductions of new plants. Potted plants, woody stemmed plants, annuals—both flower and vegetable—and perennial plants were among the year's winners.

New Evaluation for Potted Plants. The year 1993 was the first one during which consumers were made aware of FloraStar, a program sponsored by the floral industry and designed to evaluate and promote superior new cultivars of potted plants for indoor and outside culture. The first FloraStar awards were released in 1990, but only to the wholesale trade.

FloraStar award winners for 1993 included two torenias, "Burgundy Clown" and "Blue & White Clown," hybrids of an old-fashioned garden flower with color only on the sides of the petals. "Burgundy Clown" and "Blue & White Clown" have a solid ring of bright color outside, while the rest of the blossom is a pure, crisp white with yellow throat. Torenias need a bright location with moist soil.

All-America Rose Selections for 1994. Rose connoisseurs and amateur growers will appreciate hybrid teas "Secret" and "Midas Touch," and grandiflora "Caribbean," the 1994 All-America Rose Selection (AARS) winners.

Hybrid tea "Secret" is described as "a rose lover's dream." With fully double blossoms of creamy petals edged with coral-pink emitting a strong, spicy, fruity fragrance, "Secret" is a vigorous, upright growing plant standing 4 to 4.5 ft (1.22 to 1.37 m) tall. Introduced by Conard-Pyle Company, "Secret" was hybridized by Daniel Tracy of E.G. Hill Co., Richmond, IN.

Hybrid tea "Midas Touch" is an upright, well-branched plant with bright yellow blossoms of a mild musk fragrance with a backdrop of dark green, semiglossy foliage. "Midas Touch"—hybridized by Jack Christensen, Ontario, CA—was introduced by Jackson & Perkins, Medford, OR. It was the first yellow hybrid tea rose to win an AARS award in 19 years.

Grandiflora "Caribbean" is a sure winner with warm orange blossoms kissed with sunny yellow on an upright, well-branched plant. It was hybridized by Germany's Wilhelm Kordes and introduced by Jackson & Perkins, Medford, OR.

All-America Selections for 1994. All-America Selections (AAS) announced the 1994 honorees as Cucumis sativus "Fanfare," Lycopersicon esculentum "Big Beef," and Lavandula "Lady." The winners were determined on the basis of tests conducted in 34 flower trial gardens and 26 vegetable trial sites across North America.

Cucumber "Fanfare" is an F1 hybrid slicing cucumber on a short 2-ft to 2.5-ft (.61-m to .76-m) vine; its size makes it ideal for growing in confined spaces. "Fanfare" was introduced by Petoseeds, Saticoy, CA, and is tolerant of diseases and viruses.

Tomato "Big Beef," also developed by Petoseed Co., is an F1 hybrid and an early producer of bright red, superior-quality fruits. It exhibits improved disease resistance.

Lavender "Lady," developed by W. Atlee Burpee & Co., Warminster, PA, received the only 1994 Flower Award presented by the AAS. "Lady" is the first English lavender grown from seed that flowers consistently as a bedding plant.

All-America Daylily Selections Council Winner for 1994. The All-America Daylily Selection Council recognized the first All-America Daylily, Hemerocallis "Black Eyed Stella." Hybridized by Jack Roberson of American Daylily & Perennials, Grain Valley, MO, from more than 3,000 hybrid crosses, "Black Eyed Stella" is a hardy, continuously blooming cultivar combining a glowing yellow with a dark red eye.

RALPH L. SNODSMITH
Ornamental Horticulturist

Winners of the 1993 FloraStar awards included torenias "Burgundy Clown" and "Blue & White Clown," right. These plants are new hybrids of an old-time garden flower. The FloraStar awards are sponsored by the floral industry and aim to promote superior new cultivars of potted plants.

GENETICS

The year 1993 brought increased information on the genetics of drug resistance in bacteria and of homosexuality in human males. Researchers also developed a better understanding of the genetics of the disease amyotrophic lateral sclerosis, left-right organ polarity, and reproductive success in social insects.

Microbial Drug Resistance. Mutations that render pathogens resistant to therapeutic drugs usually produce new enzymes which either destroy the drug or pump it out of the bacterial cells.

In the case of the tuberculosis-causing bacterium *Mycobacterium tuberculosis,* researchers have discovered that resistance to the frequently used drug *isoniazid* involves the loss of the ability to produce an enzyme. An Anglo-French team headed by Drs. D. Young and S. Cole reported that isoniazid-sensitive strains of bacteria contain a gene *katG* that controls the production of the enzyme *catalase-peroxidase.* In isoniazid-resistant strains of the bacteria, the *katG* gene is either missing or nonfunctional, and the enzyme is absent as a result.

Scientists now believe that isoniazid itself has no antituberculosis activity, but requires the catalase-peroxidase enzyme to convert it into an active form. How the active form of isoniazid kills the *M. tuberculosis* bacteria is still unknown.

Male Homosexuality. Twin and adoption studies have shown that there is a considerable genetic component in both female and male homosexuality. In a study of the role of the X chromosome in male homosexuality, Dr. D. Hamer and colleagues at the National Institutes of Health obtained DNA samples from 40 pairs of homosexual brothers. Using 22 known genetic markers spread over the entire X chromosome, they looked for sets of markers that the brothers had in common.

Of the 40 pairs of brothers, 33 pairs shared a set of five genetic markers located in a region designated as Xq28. The probability that these markers occurred together by chance is so small that the researchers are 99.5% certain that there is a gene in this area of the X chromosome that can predispose a male to homosexuality. These findings cannot explain all male sexuality, nor do they identify which genes might indicate female homosexuality.

Amyotrophic Lateral Sclerosis (ALS). Also called motor neuron disease or Lou Gehrig's disease, amyotrophic lateral sclerosis (ALS) involves the degeneration of the large motor neurons of the brain and spinal cord that control muscles. This deterioration leads to progressive paralysis of the individual. The average manifestation of ALS is at 52 years, and death usually occurs within five years. About 10% of all cases of the disease are hereditary. The gene is an autosomal dominant.

Dr. T. Siddique at Northwestern University in Chicago and colleagues elsewhere reported that the gene linked to inherited ALS controls the production of the enzyme *superoxide dismutase* (SOD). Fully functional SOD helps cells get rid of superoxide free radicals that are extremely toxic to the cells, especially those of the nervous system. In all cases of inherited ALS, the SOD produced is defective because of an altered amino-acid sequence which leads to a buildup of superoxide free radicals. The death of motor neurons proceeds very slowly and the subsequent effect on muscles is not apparent until adulthood.

Left-Right Organ Polarity. In all mammals, the spleen and stomach normally are located on the left side of the abdomen, while the liver's major lobe is found on the right side. This arrangement establishes a left-right polarity of these visceral organs. In humans there is a recessive gene, *situs inversus viscerum,* that reverses this polarity in homozygous individuals. In mice there is a similar recessive gene, *inversus viscerum,* that has the same effect.

Dr. P. Overbeek and colleagues at the Baylor College of Medicine in Houston transferred a gene for pigment production to an albino strain of mice, and observed a recessive mutation that reversed the left-right polarity of the internal organs. These two mutations are located on different chromosomes, demonstrating that organ polarity in this species is under the control of more than one gene. The same circumstances also may exist in humans.

Reproductive Success. In the fire ant *Solenopsis invicta,* a social insect, colonies have either a single queen (monogynous) or many queens (polygynous), although only one of the queens in a polygynous colony actively reproduces. Drs. L. Keller of Harvard University and K. Ross of the University of Georgia examined actively reproducing queens from polygynous colonies for the genotype frequencies of 11 enzyme-producing genes. They hoped to determine whether any of the various genotypes were advantageous or disadvantageous for the reproductive success of the queen.

The investigators found that only the genotypes for the gene *Pgm-3* were not in their expected frequencies. The gene *Pgm-3* codes for the enzyme *phosphoglucomutase,* which is important in the energy-transforming biochemical pathway of all organisms. The gene has two alleles: "a" and "b." In polygynous colonies none of the queens were *Pgm-3a/Pgm-3a* homozygotes. In contrast, queens from monogynous colonies carried this genotype in high frequency. These findings demonstrate that selection for reproductive success can be determined by a group's social structure.

See also Medicine and Health.

Louis Levine
Department of Biology
City College of New York

GEOLOGY

Deadly earthquakes and volcanoes shook the globe in 1993, with major quakes in India, the Mariana Islands, and Japan. Scientists also discovered important information about dinosaurs and the inner Earth.

Earthquakes. The year's most damaging earthquake struck southwestern India on September 30, killing nearly 10,000 persons. This tremor, the worst to hit India in 50 years, measured magnitude 6.4 on the Richter scale. Geologists believed the quake was linked to the collision of the tectonic plate carrying India into the Asian plate. Over millions of years, this movement has buckled the crust to form the Himalayan mountains and has compressed the Indian subcontinent.

On August 8 an earthquake measuring magnitude 8.1—the strongest to rock the Earth in four years—struck the Mariana Islands in the Pacific Ocean. However, the quake caused no deaths because of its remote location and because it was centered deep below the Earth's surface. The Mariana shock occurred from the stress as two tectonic plates in the region collided.

A major quake hit the west coast of northern Japan on July 12, causing fires and tsunami waves that were as high as 100 ft (30.6 m). At least 200 persons died in the disaster, and communities as far away as South Korea were damaged. The magnitude 7.8 quake originated under the seafloor near Japan's Hokkaido Island. A magnitude 7.5 jolt also rattled Hokkaido Island's port of Kushiro on January 16. A month earlier, on December 12, a magnitude 7.5 quake rocked Indonesia's Flores Island, triggering an 80-ft (24-m) tsunami and killing some 2,200 persons.

The year's most important seismologic event in the United States was an earthquake that did not happen. In the mid-1980s the U.S. Geological Survey predicted that California's notorious San Andreas fault would generate a strong tremor near the town of Parkfield before the beginning of 1993—an earthquake that never occurred. This was the first and only official prediction made by federal scientists, who based the forecast on Parkfield's history of regular earthquakes in the 19th century. Scientists still believed an earthquake would hit the town within a few years, but the failure of the original prediction reduced their confidence in seismology's ability to foretell the timing of major earthquakes.

In the Pacific Northwest, geologists discovered signs of a mammoth prehistoric quake that ripped through the region of present-day Seattle 1,000 years ago. The quake originated on a newly discovered fault that runs beneath downtown Seattle. Geologic traces found around Puget Sound reveal that the prehistoric tremor created a tsunami that flooded many waterside sites in the region. The quake also triggered avalanches in the mountains and pushed up land on one side of the fault by 20 ft (6 m). Seismologists believed the same fault could trigger large quakes in the future, although it could be centuries before the next big one occurs.

Volcanoes. Two years after the catastrophic eruption of Mount Pinatubo in the Philippines, that nation continued to make volcanic news. In February the Mayon volcano erupted several times, killing at least 72 persons and forcing

In India in late September 1993, nearly 10,000 persons were killed and about 30,000 were injured by an earthquake measuring 6.4 on the Richter scale. The Osmanabad area, including the town of Latur, below, was hit hard.

60,000 others to flee their homes. The mountain had been dormant since 1984. Volcanologists believed Mayon could be preparing for a large eruption in the near future.

A small eruption of the Galeras volcano in the Colombian Andes killed six volcanologists and three tourists who were working inside the crater on January 14. The scientists were studying Galeras because it is the most active of Colombia's volcanoes and threatens some 400,000 people who live on the flanks of the mountain. This event underscored the danger researchers face in the crater of an active volcano.

To lessen the hazards of such studies, engineers and geologists created a robot to collect information in volcanic craters. The scientists tested the spiderlike robot, called Dante, at Antarctica's Mount Erebus. Researchers have tried for decades to climb into Erebus' inner crater, but small blasts continually have thwarted those attempts. Dante was designed to climb down the steep crater walls and collect samples of gases bubbling out of a lava lake on the crater floor. The mission failed, however, when a cable connected to the robot broke as it started its descent.

Paleontology. In the badlands of northwestern Argentina, U.S. and Argentine researchers found the remains of a dog-sized creature, called *Eoraptor,* that ranks as the most primitive known dinosaur. It was a carnivorous hunter that walked upright on its hind legs. It lived during the end of the Triassic period, 230 million years ago, when the first known dinosaurs appeared.

Paleontologists studying the fossilized leg bone of a *Tyrannosaurus rex* believed they had found the remains of red blood cells that may contain dinosaur DNA. Other researchers extracted protein molecules from dinosaur fossils. If researchers could prove the DNA or protein came from dinosaurs, such molecules might solve enduring phylogenetic questions such as whether birds evolved from dinosaurs—a theory held by many paleontologists but widely disputed by ornithologists.

In Mongolia researchers discovered the 75-million-year-old remains of a birdlike creature with a strange forelimb. The animal, called *Mononychus,* resembled a bird except for short stubby arms that ended in a single large claw. The flightless creature may have been a bird that lost the ability to fly, somewhat like modern ostriches and penguins.

An artist who specializes in painting dinosaurs discovered evidence that disputes the accepted picture of the largest dinosaurs: the plant-eating sauropods. Researchers traditionally have envisioned brontosaurus and other sauropods with smooth, scaleless skin. However, skin impressions from one particular sauropod revealed an animal with a pebbled exterior and large bumps. It also had cone-shaped spines as tall as 7 inches (18 cm) running down its back.

Paleobotanists devised a technique to trace atmospheric changes over millions of years by studying fossilized leaves. Scientists know that plants that grow in a carbon-dioxide-rich atmosphere develop fewer pores, so they can count the number of pores on ancient leaves to measure how much carbon dioxide the air once held. Scientists are eager to learn how carbon-dioxide gas—a heat-trapping compound that helps set the Earth's temperature—affected the ancient climate. This research also may help experts predict how carbon-dioxide pollution will change the future climate.

Plate Tectonics and Inner Earth. By timing the speed at which earthquake waves pass through the planet, geoscientists detected the first evidence of a plume of hot rock rising toward Earth's surface. Researchers have hypothesized the existence of such plumes in order to explain volcanic-island chains such as the Hawaiian Islands, but they never found signs of one in the mantle, the layer of the planet directly below the crust. Mantle plumes are thought to start deep in the planet and rise toward the surface. As the moving tectonic plates pass over a plume, the rising current of hot rock burns a series of successive holes in the crust, creating a volcanic chain.

Two research teams used computer models of the Earth's interior to help explain how the ocean floor is recycled. Scientists long have known that ocean crust is created and destroyed by a conveyor-belt-like process. Rock is formed at underwater volcanic mountain ranges, and then is carried to the edges of ocean basins where the crust plunges back into the Earth in deep trenches. But what happens after that has remained a mystery. Some researchers believe the crust sinks all the way down through the mantle to the core of the planet, while others believe the crust remains trapped in the upper mantle close to the Earth's surface. New computer models suggest that both processes occur. In simulations, the ocean crust remains trapped in the upper mantle until enough accumulates to spill into the lower mantle. Eventually, the rock rises back toward the surface, where it is recycled into new ocean crust.

Geoscientists discovered evidence of a fiery volcano hidden beneath Antarctica's mile-thick frozen ice cap. They suspect the volcano is active because the ice surface is depressed above the mountain as if ice were being melted from below. The volcano probably erupted sometime in the last few centuries. This is the first active volcano found under ice in Antarctica—98% of which is covered with ice. Researchers think many other volcanoes exist in this part of the Antarctic continent, which slowly is being torn apart by the movement of Earth's plates.

RICHARD MONASTERSKY
"Science News"

GEORGIA

Georgians cheered for the Atlanta Braves, continued preparation for the 1996 Olympic Games, and enjoyed economic growth in 1993. Gov. Zell Miller (D) announced that he would seek reelection in 1994.

Olympics. Groundbreaking began on the Olympic Stadium, but not until a compromise was reached between the Fulton County Commission and the Atlanta Organizing Committee for the Olympic Games (ACOG). The commissioners, led by Martin Luther King 3d, raised objections over taxpayer liabilities and the number of parking spaces, which would disrupt neighborhoods near the stadium. ACOG officials threatened to locate the stadium outside Fulton county, but backed down, and the groundbreaking began. The symbolism attached to the King family name made Commissioner King's support crucial to the success of the stadium deal and other Olympic projects.

Economy. The state enjoyed its best economic performance since 1985. A 12% increase in state tax collections resulted in a budget surplus. Boosts came from Atlanta, where taxable sales soared, and from increases in metropolitan-area construction activity. Foreign investment in Georgia rose by $1 billion. The Georgia lottery, launched in 1993, was expected to provide funds to improve the public-education system.

Legislation. Lacking support in the state House of Representatives, Governor Miller dropped efforts to eliminate the confederate battle flag from Georgia's state flag. Enacted were·measures allowing public schools to waive state regulations impeding innovative programs and providing for life-without-parole prison sentences for persons convicted of certain crimes. Legislative proposals that provided for background checks on handgun buyers, the suspension of licenses for first-time drunk drivers, restrictions on sex education in schools, and legislative-office term limits were defeated.

GEORGIA • Information Highlights

Area: 58,910 sq mi (152 576 km²).

Population (July 1, 1992 est.): 6,751,000.

Chief Cities (1990 census): Atlanta, the capital, 394,017; Columbus, 179,278; Savannah, 137,560.

Government (1993): *Chief Officers*—governor, Zell Miller (D); lt. gov., Pierre Howard (D). *General Assembly*—Senate, 56 members; House of Representatives, 180 members.

State Finances (fiscal year 1991): *Revenue,* $13,866,000,000; *expenditure,* $13,286,000,000.

Personal Income (1992): $124,803,000,000; per capita, $18,485.

Labor Force (August 1993): *Civilian labor force,* 3,292,200; *unemployed,* 160,700 (4.9% of total force).

Education: *Enrollment* (fall 1991)—public elementary schools, 868,130; public secondary, 309,439; colleges and universities, 277,023. *Public school expenditures* (1990-91), $4,804,225,000.

Politics. Atlanta Mayor Maynard Jackson underwent heart surgery and did not seek reelection. Bill Campbell, a 40-year-old lawyer and city councilman, emerged victorious in a three-way race to succeed Mayor Jackson, but only after he defeated Michael Lomax in a November 23 runoff election. The third candidate was Myrtle Davis, also a city-council member. All three had been criticized for seeking campaign funds from New York brokerage firms vying for Atlanta's bond business. Martin L. King 3d was defeated by state Rep. Mitch Skandalakis in the contest to succeed Lomax as chairman of the Fulton County Commission.

Weather. A late spring blizzard dumped 2 ft (.6 m) of snow on metropolitan Atlanta and northern Georgia, resulting in 12 deaths, widespread loss of electricity and phone service, and the closing of interstate highways. This storm, along with a record-breaking summer heat wave, adversely affected Georgia's $4.4 billion agricultural industry.

People and Baseball. President Bill Clinton chose Georgians Stuart Eizenstat and James Laney as ambassador to the European Community and ambassador to Korea, respectively. U.S. Rep. Newt Gingrich, a former teacher, was criticized when he went to Kennesaw State College to teach a history course on "renewing American civilization." The course was funded partly by a Gingrich-led political action committee, and the state Board of Regents prohibits employees of the university system from holding federal or state office.

The Atlanta Braves, the baseball team that refused to lose in 1993, finally ran out of miracles and was defeated by the Philadelphia Phillies in the National League Championship Series.

KAY BECK, *Georgia State University*

GEORGIA, REPUBLIC OF

Georgia began to resemble a garrison state in 1993, as the republic was engulfed in two major civil wars. Political stability and civil normalcy fell victim to the imperatives of a two-front war. At times, the national political system—and the state itself—appeared ready to collapse under the weight of military defeat.

In a feat that seemed almost miraculous, President Eduard Shevardnadze and the Georgian army survived the year, although not without heavy political and military losses. The already tottering economy was reeling from inflation above 1,000%; a truce between Georgia and its South Ossetian province held, but the enclave became de facto independent; the Abkhazian province was lost to secessionists after bitter combat, with thousands of Georgians and Russians becoming refugees; and a well-armed rebellion led by former President Zviad Gamsakhurdia, who had been ousted in 1992, nearly cut the country in half before being repulsed.

President Eduard Shevardnadze (second from right) *had a difficult year in 1993 as the Republic of Georgia experienced an inflation rate exceeding 1,000% and civil war on two different fronts.*

© Pascal Beaudeon/Sipa

Abkhazi War. The conflict in Abkhazia, nominally a civil war between the Georgian republic and a rebellious minority of a different nationality, was in fact an international war. The Abkhazians, a small ethnic group compared to the several million Georgians, declared their independence in 1992 and touched off a civil war in Georgia. Militarily, the situation appeared to be stalemated in spite of Georgia's numerical superiority, but in 1993 the scale of fighting in the province escalated sharply.

The forces on the Abkhazian side grew in strength, were equipped with better weapons, and became militarily more competent. Fruitlessly, President Shevardnadze attempted to draw the attention of President Boris Yeltsin of Russia and the international community to the conflict, pointing out that the Abkhazians were receiving weapons from Russia and being assisted by Russian military professionals fighting as mercenaries. Although Russia's Defense Minister Pavel Grachev and the Russian government consistently denied any official complicity, or even knowledge of the renegades, the actual position of Russia remained ambiguous.

During the summer and fall, the Abkhazis and their allies began to prevail, launching a final offensive against the Georgian-held Abkhazi capital of Sukhumi. Shevardnadze rushed to the city to be with his troops, futilely appealing to the outside world for help. As the encirclement was completed and the battle became more deadly, the president finally was persuaded

to leave before Sukhumi fell to the triumphant Abkhazis. The Georgian forces were driven out of the secessionist province in disarray, followed by many thousands of non-Abkhazi civilians fleeing the war zone. Most poignant were the multitudes of Georgian refugees, driven into the mountains without adequate clothing or shelter as early winter came on. Many Russian refugees were more fortunate, being evacuated by Russian naval forces in the Black Sea.

The Gamsakhurdia Rebellion. Former President Gamsakhurdia had gathered loyal forces in western Georgia. Despite promises to assist the fight against the Abkhazians, Gamsakhurdia's well-equipped rebel army attacked the retreating Georgian army, driving its demoralized troops eastward as the rebels took town after town along the main east-west railway line, threatening to cut the country in half. Emboldened by his military victories, Gamsakhurdia called for Shevardnadze's resignation.

To save his faltering presidency and preserve the Georgian state, Shevardnadze reluctantly succumbed to Russia's diplomatic request to allow some 20,000 Russian troops to remain in former Soviet bases in the country, and he also agreed to apply for Georgian membership in the Commonwealth of Independent States. Following these accords, Georgia was extended Russian military assistance that had been sought in vain. Russian troops secured the railway line, allowing the Georgian army to regroup and drive Gamsakhurdia's rebels back into the west, where they were defeated in November.

Shevardnadze survived 1993, but his prospects were insecure. The Abkhazian front had reopened as Abkhazi forces attacked Georgian villages on the perimeter of their breakaway province. So long as Shevardnadze was leading a nation at war, he could expect domestic support. Some observers, however, thought the deals he made with the Russians eventually might cost him dearly with his nationalistic compatriots.

ROBERT SHARLET
Union College

GEORGIA • Information Highlights

Official Name: Republic of Georgia.
Location: Western Asia.
Area: 26,911 sq mi (69 700 km^2).
Population (mid-1993 est.): 5,500,000.
Chief City (1991 est.): Tbilisi, the capital, 1,279,000.
Government: *Head of state*, Eduard A. Shevardnadze, speaker of Parliament (elected Oct. 11, 1992). *Head of government*, Otar Patsatsia, prime minister (took office Aug. 1993). *Legislature*—Parliament.

Outside the Parliament in Bonn, a crowd of some 10,000 demonstrators rallied on May 26, 1993, to protest the impending passage of a law which tightened Germany's asylum policy. The new law—backed by strong right-wing support—was approved by a wide margin.

GERMANY

Germany continued to endure the problems and pitfalls of unification in 1993. While the eastern region waited in vain for an economic upturn, western Germany fell into a deep recession, increasing tensions within the long-divided country. Western Germans questioned whether their eastern compatriots appreciated the sacrifices they were making, while Germans in the East felt colonized by Westerners they considered arrogant and selfish.

Politics. German politics was dominated by preparations for the "super election year" of 1994, when new local or state governments were going to be chosen in 11 of the 16 states. In addition, a national election to select a new parliament and chancellor as well as elections to the European Parliament were planned. Finally, the Federal Council, composed of members of the national and state parliaments, was scheduled to select a new federal president early in 1994. None of the major parties escaped 1993 without some scandal involving important political figures, as German voters showed increasing dissatisfaction with all established parties.

Chancellor Helmut Kohl dismissed his transportation minister over alleged misuse of public funds for private purposes. The Christian Democratic (CDU) interior minister had to go when security police used excessive force in arresting fugitive members of the Red Army terrorist gang. The Free Democratic Party (FDP), a junior coalition partner in the Kohl government, lost its

national chairman and economics minister in January when it was revealed that he had used his influence to help a relative start a new business.

Kohl was dealt one of the worst defeats in his 11-year chancellorship in November when he had to withdraw the candidacy of his hand-picked choice for federal president, the East German Steffen Heitmann. While there was widespread support for an "Easterner" to occupy the largely symbolic post of president, Heitmann's nomination drew heavy criticism from his own party. Some of his remarks—that women should spend more time in the home and that Germans should not be singled out for special blame because of the Third Reich—drew praise from the far right and damaged Kohl and the Christian Democrats.

Also in November a close ally of Kohl, Werner Münch, the CDU chief executive of the eastern state of Saxony-Anhalt, together with the entire state government, resigned after admitting that they had received secret salary and expense payments from the state treasury.

The major opposition party, the Social Democratic Party (SPD), had its own problems in 1993, which prevented it from making sizable inroads into CDU support. In April the party's leader and SPD chancellor candidate for the 1994 election, Björn Engholm, resigned over allegations that he had lied to parliamentary investigators. In June, Rudolf Scharping, the chief executive of the Rhineland-Palatinate state, was chosen in a vote by party members as the SPD's new leader. Under Scharping the

party's move to the center, begun during Eng-holm's tenure, continued. Observers expected the SPD to wage a campaign focused on the economy and, specifically, jobs.

Scharping's biggest challenge was to unite the party for the election. The SPD was divided sharply over whether or not German troops should be sent overseas in support of United Nations (UN) peacekeeping operations. In September another major figure in the party, Oskar Lafontaine, provoked more division by proposing that wage increases in the former East Germany be linked to productivity rather than automatically rising to Western levels by the mid-1990s.

The FDP spent most of the year opposing the government's new hard-line law-and-order proposals, which included easier use of wiretapping for government agencies and Kohl's plans to deploy German troops overseas.

Germany's two Green parties benefited from growing discontent within the major parties. Most opinion polls gave the combined parties more than 10% of the vote. While the eastern Greens were more concerned with economic issues than were their affluent Western colleagues, the two parties merged in January and made plans to field a common slate of candidates in 1994.

After two years of delays the Kohl government finally agreed on a timetable to move the capital from Bonn to Berlin by the year 2000. In October the Defense Ministry became the first government department to move its main headquarters to Berlin. Even after the move to Berlin was complete, however, eight of the government's 18 ministries would remain in Bonn.

The Economy. The European recession hit the German economy hard in 1993. For the first time since 1982 the economy failed to grow. The gross domestic product (GDP) dropped by 1.9% and unemployment reached 9.7%. Declining exports and a sharp drop in investment by German companies were major causes of the slump.

Germany's economic woes were strained by supporting the former East Germany at a cost of almost $100 billion per year, and by declining tax revenues due to the recession. In an effort to reduce a record national debt of almost $1 trillion, the Kohl government proposed about $45.2 billion in budget cuts over three years. Some health-care costs were capped, unemployment benefits were reduced, pension levels were frozen until 1995, and family allowances for the children of foreign residents and asylum-seekers were eliminated. The SPD criticized the cuts as an attempt to finance unification by unfairly burdening the poor, the elderly, and the unemployed. The SPD wanted to reduce spending by cutting the defense budget and farm subsidies.

To provide a long-term plan to finance unification, the government in March—after extensive negotiations with both the opposition SPD and all 16 states—passed a Solidarity Pact which called for higher income taxes beginning in 1995, a $9.2 billion cut in federal spending, $30.7 bil-

lion to speed up the renovation and privatization of government-owned housing, a hike in the states' share of the national sales or value-added tax, and increased financial support from the old states to the eastern regions.

The government's attempts to reduce the deficit even included plans to impose tolls on motorists using the Autobahn, Germany's fabled superhighway system, and eventually to privatize the system, the second-largest in the world. Use of the system had been free. The Kohl government also announced plans to begin selling parts of the state-run railway system in 1994.

The poor economy and stiff foreign competition also affected some of Germany's marquee firms. Volkswagen, Europe's largest automaker, reached an agreement with its unionized workforce to reduce the workweek to four days (28.8 hours) and wages by 10%, beginning in January 1994. The plan was part of an extensive restructuring that would cut personnel costs by 20% by 1995. Daimler-Benz, Germany's largest industrial company, responding to record losses, announced plans to eliminate 40,000 jobs—more than 20% of the company's workforce—by the end of 1994.

Throughout 1993 business and government leaders warned that Germany's high wages, short workweek, long vacations, and frequent holidays were endangering its competitive position in the world economy. Hourly labor costs, including fringe benefits, averaged $22.50 in 1993, the highest in Europe. Public-opinion polls found that about 75% of Germans would accept lower wage increases or a wage freeze in exchange for job security. A four-day workweek with a partial pay reduction also had wide-

Rudolf Scharping was chosen in June 1993 as chairman of Germany's opposition Social Democratic Party. The 45-year-old state governor planned to seek the chancellorship in 1994.

© Regis Bossu/Sygma

German Chancellor Helmut Kohl (left) and U.S. President Bill Clinton met for the first time in Washington, DC, on March 26, 1993. The two leaders discussed trade issues and foreign policy, including critical developments in the Balkans and in Russia.

spread support provided that it would reduce unemployment.

Labor Unrest. The frustration of many eastern Germans over the poor economy was evident in May when some 30,000 metal workers went on strike for a promised pay hike that would have brought their wages closer to levels in the West. It was the first legal strike in the East in more than 60 years, since strikes had been outlawed under the Nazis and the Communists. The strike was called when employers balked at a 26% pay raise scheduled for April, citing eastern Germany's low productivity and the recession. Unit labor costs in the East were more than 50% higher than in the West, while Eastern productivity was only 30% of Western levels. After ten days the strike ended in compromise. The workers received the promised wage hike but full wage parity with West Germans, originally set for 1994, would not be reached until 1996.

Right-wing Attacks. Violence against foreigners continued in 1993. In May the nation was shocked by the bombing of a home in Solingen which killed five Turkish immigrants. Several youths associated with radical right-wing skinhead groups were arrested for the crime. In October a band of some 15 skinheads attacked an African-American member of the U.S. luge team training in the eastern German town of Oberhof.

Throughout the year justice officials were criticized for their leniency in dealing with rightists or neo-Nazis. Four of the five skinheads accused of the Solingen deaths were released by the police for lack of evidence. In the eastern city of Dresden two of the three defendants found guilty of killing a Mozambican laborer were given probation and fines and the third was sentenced to only two and one-half years in prison. A man who confessed to stabbing tennis star Monica Seles at a match in Hamburg to prevent her from competing against his idol, German Steffi Graf, was set free because, according to the court, his mental condition made him not responsible for his actions. He was not banned from attending further matches.

The government's efforts to combat right-wing violence included the outlawing of several fringe groups and a campaign against Germany's right-wing music scene. In February police in raids in nine of the country's 16 states seized records, cassette tapes, and compact discs, along with weapons, from the studios and homes of producers and rock musicians suspected of glorifying Nazism and promoting racism and violence.

Following the attack in Solingen, the government proposed new measures to make German citizenship easier to obtain. The existing 80-year-old law had been based more on ethnic heritage than on place of birth or length of residence. People with German ancestors who never had lived in Germany and did not speak the language had a stronger claim to citizenship than did children born and raised in Germany but without German parents. From July on, anyone who had lived legally in Germany for 15 years was entitled to citizenship. The high fees for citizenship application were reduced or eliminated.

To reduce the influx of foreigners, the parliament in May amended Article 16 of the constitution, which had granted unconditional rights to political asylum. Since July 1, 1993, emigrants from European Community (EC)—later European Union—nations or secure third states (states in which the Geneva refugee convention and the European human-rights convention were in force) were not allowed to seek political asylum. Asylum-seekers from states in which there was no political persecution also would be turned away unless they could prove that they were victims of persecution. War refugees would be allowed to remain in the Federal Republic for the duration of the war but would not be granted political asylum.

With the passage of the asylum law, support for right-wing, antiforeigner parties declined. The strongest of these groups, the Republicans, saw their support drop below the 5% minimum needed for parliamentary representation.

Social Issues. In May, Germany's highest court, the Federal Constitutional Court, ruled that a pro-choice abortion law passed in 1992 was unconstitutional. The decision met sharp criticism from feminists, especially those from the former East Germany, where abortions had been available easily before unification. The court ruled that while abortion was illegal, women who had abortions in the first trimester of pregnancy would not be prosecuted pending new legislation. The judges also banned the state health system from paying for abortions.

In October the country was shocked when it was revealed that more than 300 hospital patients had been given transfusions of blood infected with the AIDS-causing virus, HIV. The blood products had been purchased from a private company in Koblenz, which allegedly failed to screen its supply properly; some of its supply came from Eastern European countries. Under the existing system the responsibility to test blood rested with the private companies which supplied it and not with the government. As a result of the scandal it was expected that all blood products would be placed under public control.

The Communist Heritage in the East. Efforts to bring the Communist rulers from the former East Germany to trial continued in 1993, but with mixed results. In January the former head of the East German state, Erich Honecker, was allowed to leave Germany for Chile. But in September two of the remaining defendants in the trial of several top leaders—former Defense Minister Heinz Kessler and his deputy, Fritz Strelitz—were convicted and sentenced to five-to-seven-year prison terms for inciting border guards to shoot East Germans who sought to flee to the West. The convictions of Kessler and Strelitz were followed in October by a guilty verdict for Erich Mielke, the longtime boss of the former East Germany's secret police. Mielke was sentenced to six years in prison for the 1931 murders of two police officers. Charges connected with his secret police leadership were still pending, but it was doubtful whether Mielke, 85, would be brought to trial again.

In December the former East German spymaster, Markus Wolf, was convicted of treason and bribery and sentenced to six years in prison. Wolf, the elusive "spy without a face," who inspired novelists of Cold War espionage, once had directed more than 4,000 agents. In the 1970s one of his moles reached the top level of the West German chancellor's office. His eventual discovery brought down the government of Chancellor Willy Brandt in 1974. Another top agent, operating under the code name "Topaz," worked at the North Atlantic Treaty Organization (NATO) headquarters in Brussels. Wolf charged that his prosecution was motivated by revenge and had no legal basis, since he had been a citizen of a sovereign state and had behaved no differently than an agent from a Western spy organization.

Foreign Policy. Though content to be an "economic giant" and a "political dwarf" during the Cold War, Germany continued to redefine its role in world politics in 1993. While the Kohl government actively sought permanent German membership on the UN Security Council, the question of German military participation in UN peacekeeping operations was a subject of strong debate both within the government itself and between the CDU and the opposition SPD.

In July some 1,700 German soldiers were sent to Somalia, where they provided logistical support for other UN forces. This mission marked the first deployment of German troops since World War II. Later in 1993, German troops were sent on a humanitarian mission to Cambodia.

The refusal of the powerful Bundesbank to lower interest rates in July touched off another crisis in the European Monetary System (EMS). The bank's decision caused a massive sell-off of French francs as the French currency dropped below the level allowed by the EMS. By keeping interest rates higher than in other West European countries, the bank put the deutsche mark and German interests ahead of the general European economy, much to the dismay of the government.

In October at a special EC summit, Frankfurt was chosen as the site for the future European Central Bank. The decision helped the Kohl government contain growing criticism of the Maastricht Treaty on European unity within his party and governing coalition. Many Germans feared that a single European currency would be weaker than the coveted deutsche mark.

DAVID P. CONRADT
East Carolina University

GERMANY • Information Highlights

Official Name: Federal Republic of Germany.
Location: North-central Europe.
Area: 137,931 sq mi (356 910 km²).
Population (mid-1993 est.): 81,100,000.
Chief Cities (1990 est.): Berlin, the capital, 3,433,700; Hamburg, 1,640,100; Munich, 1,219,600.
Government: *Head of state*, Richard von Weizsäcker, president (took office July 1, 1984). *Head of government*, Helmut Kohl, chancellor (took office Oct. 1982). *Legislature*—Parliament: Bundesrat and Bundestag.
Monetary Unit: Deutsche mark (1.7100 D. marks equal U.S.$1, Dec. 16, 1993).
Gross Domestic Product (1991 est. U.S.$): $1,331,400,000,000.
Economic Indexes (1992): *Consumer Prices* (1980 = 100), all items, 139.3; food, 131.1. *Industrial Production* (1980 = 100), 124.
Foreign Trade (1992 U.S.$): *Imports*, $408,358,000,000; *exports*, $430,315,000,000.

GREAT BRITAIN

In Great Britain, 1993 was a year few would want to repeat. It opened with the tragic abduction and murder of a toddler in Liverpool by, allegedly, two other young boys. And it continued with one political fiasco after another and a relentless escalation of violence in Northern Ireland. As unemployment topped 3 million, Britons were found to be downcast about the future. In a Gallup opinion poll published by *The Daily Telegraph* in February, nearly half of the 1,030 Britons interviewed said they would move to another country if they could.

Domestic Politics. For Prime Minister John Major's Conservative government, the year was a difficult one. Most of the Conservative government's political energies were expended in the first half of the year on the battle to ratify the Maastricht Treaty for European political and monetary union. In February the Labour Party, the main parliamentary opposition party, announced that it would fight the government's plans to opt out of the treaty's so-called "social chapter," which would regulate workers' rights across the European Community (EC). Meanwhile, in Major's own party, right-wing "Euroskeptics" fought to keep Britain out of the Maastricht Treaty altogether, believing that the treaty threatened national sovereignty. Led by former Prime Minister Margaret Thatcher, who had become something of a nemesis for her successor, the Tory Euro-rebels agitated unsuccessfully for a national referendum on the treaty.

After a series of humiliating setbacks for the government, the treaty finally was ratified in August. Major was forced to rely on the support of the ten Ulster Unionists in the House of Commons. Speculation was rife that Major had made a deal to gain their backing. The Unionists were reported to want, among other things, a parliamentary select committee devoted to the affairs of the province. "Nothing was asked for, nothing was offered, nothing was given," said Major to a largely disbelieving Parliament and public. The battle over Maastricht left the Conservative Party badly wounded and divided.

But Maastricht was only part of the government's troubles. A judicial inquiry into the sale of arms-related exports to Iraq drew in several high-ranking government officials. More fundamentally, the Conservatives, after 14 years in power, appeared unable to solve the nation's most serious problems, including unemployment above 10%, brought on by the longest British recession since the 1930s. A government proposal to impose a value-added tax on domestic heating fuel also riled voters. In local elections held in May, the Conservatives paid a heavy price, losing control of all but one county council and also losing a vital parliamentary seat to the centrist Liberal Democrats.

A besieged Major reshuffled his cabinet, ousting Chancellor of the Exchequer Norman Lamont in the process, but his troubles were far from over. A poll conducted by Gallup for *The Daily Telegraph* indicated that he had the lowest approval ratings of any prime minister since such polls began. And, less than a week later, Lamont

Britain's Prime Minister John Major, extreme right, was the first European leader to be invited to the Clinton White House. He discussed aid to Bosnia, trade, and other issues with the president, Feb. 24-25, 1993. Troubles at home helped make 1993 a difficult year for the British leader.

inflicted another blow. In a speech before a packed House of Commons, the former chancellor accused Major's government of weakness.

The summer brought little relief. Michael Mates, the Northern Ireland security minister, was forced to resign when it was revealed that he had supported a former Tory Party benefactor, Asil Nadir, who, awaiting trail for fraud, had jumped bail and fled to Cyprus. And the Conservatives faced allegations that the party had received extensive funding from foreign sources.

In September the Labour Party, led by John Smith, voted narrowly to reform voting procedures that had been seen as giving trade unions undue influence within the party. That same month, Britain was shocked by the election of neo-fascist Derek Beackon to an east London local council, the first-ever electoral win by the unabashedly racist British National Party.

In October the country was gripped by the hype surrounding the publication of Lady Thatcher's memoirs, *The Downing Street Years*. Given the much-publicized tension between predecessor and successor, Major got off fairly lightly in the book.

At the Conservative Party conference in Blackpool in October, Major called on delegates to "put unity back at the center of the party." Home Secretary Michael Howard delivered his proposals for tackling crime, including a plan to end a defendant's right to silence.

Economy. Chancellor Lamont's public assurances that he saw the "green shoots" of an economic recovery had become something of a national joke by early 1993. But the hilarity had an anxious note; the tenacious three-year recession had left many Britons bitter and wary. In January, Major sought to kick-start a recovery by reducing the country's base lending rate to 6%.

By April there appeared cause for real rejoicing: Figures released at the end of the month indicated that the gross domestic product (GDP)—which excludes oil—had increased in the first quarter of the year by about 0.6% over the previous quarter; at last, the recession was deemed to be over. The ensuing months saw successive drops in unemployment figures, rises in manufacturing output, and a headline inflation rate that was below 2%. But, as *The Economist* pointed out in August, public confidence remained low. Two months later, *The Economist* itself was outlining reasons for caution: Though the recovery continued, the economy remained "weak"; the nation's trade deficit for the first seven months of the year had risen to £8.7 billion (about $12.9 billion); unemployment remained high and had increased again in both July and August; and the public-sector borrowing requirement, or national debt, quickly was approaching £50 billion ($74 billion).

In November the headline inflation rate fell to 1.4% and the underlying inflation rate, which excludes mortgage payments, dropped to 2.8%, the lowest in 25 years. The government, boosted

---

GREAT BRITAIN • Information Highlights

Official Name: United Kingdom of Great Britain and Northern Ireland.

Location: Island, western Europe.

Area: 94,525 sq mi (244 820 km²).

Population (mid-1993 est.): 58,000,000.

Chief Cities (mid-1991 est.): London, the capital, 6,803,100; Birmingham, 994,500; Leeds, 706,300; Glasgow, 687,600; Sheffield, 520,300.

Government: *Head of state*, Elizabeth II, queen (acceded Feb. 1952). *Head of government*, John Major, prime minister and First Lord of the Treasury (took office November 1990). *Legislature*—Parliament: House of Lords and House of Commons.

Monetary Unit: Pound (0.6757 pound equals U.S.$1, Nov. 17, 1993).

Gross Domestic Product (1991 est. U.S.$): $915,500,000,000.

Economic Indexes: *Consumer Prices* (1992, 1980 = 100), all items, 207.2; food, 177.5. *Industrial Production* (1991, 1980 = 100), 115.

Foreign Trade (1992 U.S.$): *Imports*, $222,655,000,000; *exports*, $190,052,000,000.

---

by the inflation figures, cut the base lending rate. Chancellor of the Exchequer Kenneth Clarke won praise for his budget package, a mix of tax increases and spending cuts intended to tackle the national debt.

Northern Ireland. For Northern Ireland, 1993 proved to be a year of shocking atrocities and surprising turns. As the year opened, roundtable talks among the British and Irish governments and the main Northern Irish parties continued to be blocked by hard-line Unionist politicians opposed to any involvement by the Irish government in the affairs of the North. And the British government was reportedly unhappy about a proposal by U.S. President Bill Clinton to appoint a special envoy to the province.

In March two young boys were killed when two bombs planted by the Irish Republican Army (IRA) exploded in the English town of Warrington. The deaths provoked outrage in Ireland and Britain. Loyalist terrorists, who were responsible for more civilian deaths in Northern Ireland than even the IRA, promptly took revenge by ambushing and killing four Catholic workers.

In April, London was rocked by a massive explosion in the financial district. One person was killed and dozens were injured by the bomb, which had been planted by the IRA. The financial district eventually was sealed off by a police cordon. In May it was reported that John Hume, a British parliamentarian and leader of the nonviolent, nationalist Social Democratic and Labour Party, had embarked on peace talks with Gerry Adams, president of Sinn Fein, the political wing of the IRA. "Our object is to bring about a lasting peace," Hume told *The New York Times*. "We are not talking about a ceasefire, but about a total cessation of all violence."

By the autumn, Hume was confident that he had made real progress in his talks with Adams. Then, on October 23 an IRA bomb exploded in

a fish-and-chips shop in the Protestant section of Belfast; ten persons were killed, including Thomas Begley, one of the terrorists who planted the bomb. Adams enraged Unionist politicians by carrying the coffin during Begley's funeral procession. Loyalist terrorists went on a rampage to avenge the deaths and, in one incident, murdered six Catholics and one Protestant in a County Londonderry pub.

As funeral followed funeral, the province descended into a morass of fear and despair, which gave the search for peace renewed urgency. But neither London nor Dublin seemed prepared to accept proposals partly devised by Adams, and such was the British government's anger over the October 23 bombing that Adams was banned from the British mainland. Still, Hume remained convinced that his proposals were the province's "best hope for peace in 20 years." After a meeting with Major, he told British reporters that Northern Ireland would have peace "within a week" if his proposals were given a chance. Many in Northern Ireland, fed up with the violence that had left some 3,100 people dead, seemed willing to see if Hume could succeed where all others had not.

In early November, according to *The Independent* newspaper, the Irish government had shifted emphasis "in favor of the Hume-Adams initiative." According to that newspaper, Albert Reynolds, the Taoiseach (prime minister) of the Republic of Ireland, had devised peace proposals that he hoped to discuss with Major at a planned summit in December. Reynolds was reported to be willing, if others also compromised, to put to a national referendum his country's constitutional claim to Northern Ireland, a claim that long had been a stumbling block in negotiations with British and Unionist politicians.

On November 28, *The Observer* revealed that the British government had been meeting secretly with the IRA for months, just weeks after Major stridently had denied such action. In early December, Major and Reynolds met to discuss peace, and by midmonth a peace initiative was announced. This vague document stated that Britain would not obstruct a united Ireland if both Northern and Southern Ireland agreed to this marriage, as well as to declarations to curtail violence. The peace process generally was well-received in domestic circles and the international community, but it was unclear as the year ended how long this guarded optimism might last.

Foreign Affairs. As 1993 began, Britain and its allies were forced to confront an old enemy: Iraqi President Saddam Hussein. On January 13, Britain participated in air strikes in southern Iraq, intended to punish Hussein for his continued defiance of the United Nations. Prime Minister Major defended the raid as "limited and in proportion" to the scale of Iraqi transgressions.

February 14 was the fourth anniversary of the Iranian *fatwa*, or death sentence, that forced Salman Rushdie, author of *The Satanic Verses*, into hiding. Although the British government had protected Rushdie from the beginning, it had been reluctant to press Rushdie's case openly, lest British-Iranian relations be damaged further. But in early February, Douglas Hogg, a British foreign minister, met with Rushdie at the foreign office, signaling a change of policy. In a statement, a foreign-office spokesman said that Iran's failure to repudiate the *fatwa* was preventing "the establishment of full and friendly relations between London and Tehran." At a news conference in Tehran on the anniversary of the *fatwa*, Iran's Foreign Minister Ali Akbar Vellayati warned Western governments not to link "the destiny of bilateral relations between Iran and themselves to the destiny of this one person." In May, Rushdie also met with Prime Minister Major.

In April, Major outlined his vision of a "new Europe" that would be "larger, more open, and less intrusive" than the tightly knit, federalized Europe not long ago imagined by European politicians. According to *The Economist*, Major found some support for his views at an EC summit in Copenhagen in June.

Also in April, Lady Thatcher upbraided Major and other Western leaders for failing to take decisive action to help besieged Muslims in Bosnia-Herzegovina. The former prime minister called on Western governments to help arm the Muslims and to launch air strikes against Serbian positions. In the House of Lords, Thatcher said that the arms embargo against the Muslims left them "defenseless in the path of a determined dictator-aggressor." The British government, however, believed that military action against the Serbs would imperil the UN peacekeeping and humanitarian mission in the region. In August the government airlifted a critically ill 5-year-old Bosnian girl named Irma Hadzimuratovic to London for medical care. The story helped focus international attention on the plight of the Bosnian ill and injured. A subsequent airlift of 21 Bosnians in need of emergency medical treatment was more controversial; the government was accused of treating it like a public-relations exercise.

In September, Britain joined the United States in backing Russian President Boris Yeltsin in his clash with the Russian Parliament. Major said Yeltsin's political foes wanted to "paralyze reform." That same month, the Libyan government announced that it would not oppose the planned trial in Scotland of two Libyans accused of the 1988 bombing of Pan Am Flight 103 in which 270 persons were killed, but continued its refusal to extradite the men for trial.

Royalty. As the year began, the government was reported to be mulling over proposals to curb some of the excesses of the British press; the lurid reporting of the marital difficulties of some of the royals had angered government officials. In January an Australian magazine printed the transcript of a telephone conversation, allegedly between Prince Charles and his sup-

posed paramour, Camilla Parker-Bowles. The text, which contained embarrassingly vivid language, was picked up by some British newspapers. In February, Queen Elizabeth II took the highly unusual step of seeking legal damages from *The Sun* newspaper, which had printed leaked text of her annual Christmas message two days before it was broadcast.

That same month, it was announced that the queen had agreed to pay tax on her personal income. On April 29 the queen announced that she would be opening Buckingham Palace to the public, for the first time ever, for eight weeks over the summer to raise money for Windsor Castle, which had been damaged badly by fire in 1992. Although crowds proved lighter than originally expected, the experiment was deemed a success and was expected to be repeated (*see* page 423).

In May, *The Sun* printed a transcript of an alleged face-to-face argument between Prince Charles and Princess Diana; the tabloid claimed that the conversation had been tape recorded by MI5, Britain's domestic security service. Home Secretary Kenneth Clarke said in a news conference that "it does look as if someone is bugging the Royal Family," but he added that reports of government involvement were "nonsense." Later that month, a daylong debate on the future of the monarchy was held at, ironically, the Queen Elizabeth II Conference Center in London. In September a program to modernize Buckingham Palace was announced. In October, Prince Charles visited Glasgow, where he told a conference on urban regeneration that poor housing endangered the very fabric of society. On a visit that same week to the Oxford Center for Islamic Studies, the prince condemned Saddam Hussein for the "unmentionable horrors" to which he was subjecting the Madan, or Marsh Arabs, of southeast Iraq. His remarks provoked the ire of Saddam Hussein's son Uday, who, according to British press reports, published an article in an Iraqi newspaper mocking Prince Charles for "shedding tears for the Iraqis while he himself is sinking deep in adultery and family intrigues."

In November the public gaze returned to Princess Diana after she was reported to have left a public engagement early in tears. The princess said she had a migraine. Others, including her former stepgrandmother, writer Dame Barbara Cartland, suggested that she had experienced a relapse of bulimia, a disease she reportedly had suffered from in the past, while others suggested that she was nearing a breakdown. At a charity function in London, the princess faced the rumors squarely, telling her audience that they were "very lucky" to have her there that day. "I am supposed to be dragged off the minute I leave here by men in white coats," she said wryly, adding, "If it is alright with you, I thought I would postpone my nervous breakdown to a more appropriate moment."

Several days later, *The Sunday Mirror* and its sister paper, *The Daily Mirror*, printed pho-

© AP/Wide World

Norman Lamont, who was blamed widely for Britain's economic doldrums, was dropped as chancellor of the exchequer in May. He later criticized the Major government in a speech before Parliament.

tographs of the princess that were taken secretly as she exercised at a private health club. The government thundered again about press intrusion into the private lives of public figures, and the princess' lawyers issued a flurry of writs.

Other News. Environmentalists were dismayed when a tanker ran aground off the Shetland Islands in January, spilling crude oil into the Bay of Quendale. That same month, historians and critics argued furiously over a new biography of Sir Winston Churchill by historian John Charmley that suggested that the revered prime minister was wrong to have considered nothing less than Germany's complete surrender in World War II. In February, Prime Minister Major filed libel actions against two magazines that had run articles discussing rumors that he had had an extramarital affair; the actions later were settled out of court. In April it was announced that the opening of the Channel Tunnel was to be delayed yet again, until 1994.

In July a royal commission unveiled its recommendations to overhaul the British justice system; one of its most controversial proposals was that the automatic right to a trial by jury be eliminated. In October the House of Commons approved overwhelmingly the Church of England's plans to ordain women priests. And Britain's Privy Council, the final court of appeal for nearly two dozen Commonwealth countries, voted that two Jamaicans should have their death sentences commuted to life imprisonment, as their 14-year detention on death row constituted "inhuman and degrading treatment and torture." The ruling would affect the fates of hundreds of other death-row prisoners.

SUZANNE CASSIDY, *Freelance Journalist, London*

261

The Arts

With Britain just emerging from its longest recession since World War II, arts companies scrambled in 1993 to attract revenue. Hopes were pinned on a national lottery approved by Parliament in October to benefit the arts, sports, heritage, and charities. The lottery also will finance a Millennium Fund to create capital projects to mark the turn of the century.

Theater. Progress was made in 1993 on the reconstruction of Shakespeare's Globe Theater. On April 23 actor Sir John Gielgud led the dedication of the site on which the original Elizabethan theater is being recreated at a cost of about £20 million (c. $30 million). In June, Harold Pinter directed the British premiere of David Mamet's controversial *Oleanna* at the Royal Court Theater and in September Pinter's own play, *Moonlight,* premiered at the Almeida Theater in London. It was Pinter's first full-length play since 1978. That same month, the playwright deposited his literary archive in the British Library. It was also a big year for director Sir Peter Hall, who had five productions on London stages. A 1993 highlight was Dame Maggie Smith's performance as Lady Bracknell in an Aldwych Theater revival of Oscar Wilde's *The Importance of Being Ernest.* The work was directed by Nicholas Hytner, who also directed the Royal National Theater's revival of Rodgers and Hammerstein's *Carousel,* transferred to the West End by Cameron Mackintosh in September.

The year also saw the long-awaited opening of Andrew Lloyd Webber's new musical, *Sunset Boulevard,* based on Billy Wilder's film. Directed by Trevor Nunn, with a book by Christopher Hampton and starring Patti Lupone, it had record advance bookings, but earned mixed reviews. Other notable productions included Sam Mendes' staging of the Brian Friel classic, *Translations,* at the new Donmar Warehouse; a West End production of Shakespeare's *Much Ado About Nothing,* starring Mark Rylance and Janet McTeer; and *City of Angels,* the Broadway musical written by Larry Gelbart. The Royal National staged premieres of Tom Stoppard's *Arcadia,* and *Perestroika,* the second part of Tony Kushner's Pulitzer-winning *Angels in America.* At the Royal Shakespeare Company, Kenneth Branagh took the title role in *Hamlet.* The company also staged Stoppard's *Travesties* and the London premiere of *Wildest Dreams,* new from Alan Ayckbourn.

Music. London's four orchestras were shocked to learn that the Arts Council, the quasi-governmental body that distributes government cash to arts organizations, had decided that it would be able to finance only the London Symphony Orchestra and one other London-based orchestra in the future. The London Philharmonic, the Philharmonia, and the Royal Philharmonic Orchestra were left to compete for the

© Today from Rex USA, Ltd.

Andrew Lloyd Webber's new musical, "Sunset Boulevard," starring Patti Lupone (above), opened in London in 1993. It scored $9 million in advance sales, but received mixed reviews.

remaining Arts Council cash. The Arts Council's decision sparked a public outcry. At Covent Garden the Royal Opera House pressed ahead with its plans for a £150 million (c. $222 million) development project, for which it hoped to attract national-lottery cash. In October pop star George Michael went to the British high court seeking to be released from his 15-year recording contract with the Sony Corporation, which he said was squelching his creativity. Musical highlights included four Barbican Center concerts celebrating the music of Oliver Messiaen; the Royal Opera's production of Tchaikovsky's *Eugene Onegin;* and a Kronos Quartet festival at the Barbican.

Dance. Officially, 1993 was the Year of Dance in Britain; unofficially, it was a year of turmoil. At Covent Garden the Royal Ballet attracted criticism for what some regarded an overly conservative and limited repertoire. At the English National Ballet, Derek Deane was appointed artistic director; he replaced Ivan Nagy, who left five months before his contract expired. Deane, a former senior principal dancer with the Royal Ballet and resident choreographer of the Teatro dell' Opera in Rome, was the company's third artistic director in three years. A change of lead-

ership also was announced at the Rambert Dance Company. Christopher Bruce, a former Rambert dancer and associate choreographer, succeeded Richard Alston, who left suddenly late in 1992. Bruce would not take up his new position until early 1994 because of his commitment as resident choreographer of the Houston Ballet. Among the year's highlights were performances of the Kirov Ballet at the Coliseum, and the Royal Ballet's presentation of Mikhail Baryshnikov's 1978 version of *Don Quixote.* In July the 19th-century Savoy Theater, which had been gutted by fire in 1990, reopened with a gala performance by the English National Ballet.

Visual Arts. In June the Tate Gallery opened a new £3.3 million (c. $4.9 million) gallery in the Cornish seaside town of St. Ives. The Tate Gallery St. Ives, overlooking Porthmeor Beach, showcases the works of the 20th-century artists who belonged to the St. Ives "school." The Tate also proceeded with its plans to reorganize its collection in a radical new form. A new Tate Gallery of Modern Art is to be created at a cost of more than £50 million (c. $74 million) on a London site still to be determined. The new gallery would be devoted to international modern art of the 20th century. On the Tate's present site would be created the Tate Gallery of British Art, devoted to showing the development of British art from about the 16th century through the present.

Notable exhibitions of 1993 included one at the Whitechapel Art Gallery showing 55 recent paintings by the British figurative artist Lucian Freud. At the Royal Academy of Arts and the Saatchi Gallery there was a huge exhibition of "American Art in the 20th Century," and, at the National Portrait Gallery, "Thomas Eakins and the Heart of American Life." A Frank Lloyd Wright gallery opened at the Victoria and Albert Museum in January and the National Portrait Gallery opened a series of new galleries to house its later-20th-century portraits..

Film and Television. The battle over the direction and future of the British Broadcasting Corporation (BBC) continued to rage in 1993 as John Birt, the corporation's director-general, presided over a radical program to cut costs and bureaucracy. His methods drew fire from many, including dramatist Dennis Potter and senior BBC foreign correspondent Mark Tully. Not all the drama was off-screen, however. Among 1993 BBC television highlights was a drama about Northern Ireland titled *Love Lies Bleeding* and *The Snapper,* based on Roddy Doyle's uproarious sequel to *The Commitments,* directed by Stephen Frears. Channel 4 aired a six-part adaptation of Armistead Maupin's cult classic, *Tales of the City.*

For the big screen, Kenneth Branagh directed a sumptuous *Much Ado About Nothing,* his second effort at bringing Shakespeare to the cinema. Branagh and his Oscar-winning wife, Emma Thompson, took the lead roles. The ailing British film industry took another hit when it was announced that Elstree Studios, where both Alfred Hitchcock and Steven Spielberg made films, was likely to be demolished.

SUZANNE CASSIDY

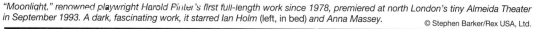

"Moonlight," renowned playwright Harold Pinter's first full-length work since 1978, premiered at north London's tiny Almeida Theater in September 1993. A dark, fascinating work, it starred Ian Holm (left, in bed) and Anna Massey.

© Stephen Barker/Rex USA, Ltd.

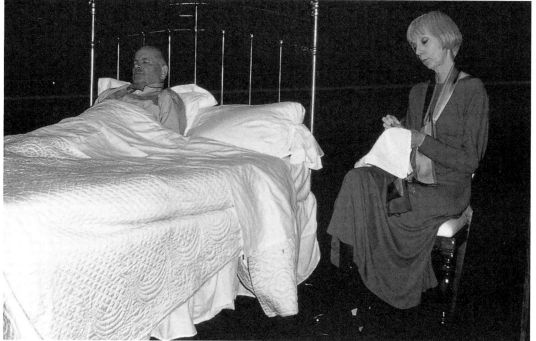

GREECE

The triumphant return of Andreas Papandreou to power as prime minister in October with his Panhellenic Socialist Union (PASOK) dominated political events in Greece during 1993, while upheavals in the Balkans and the continued occupation of part of Cyprus by Turkey drew Greece's greatest attention in foreign affairs.

Politics. For most of the year, Prime Minister Constantine Mitsotakis and his New Democracy Party held power, but his majority of only one in Parliament made him extremely vulnerable to attacks against his government's actions. His longtime implacable political foe, former Prime Minister Andreas Papandreou, and PASOK kept emphasizing their opposition. Mitsotakis even was criticized by members of his party.

On June 30, Antonis Samaras, former New Democracy foreign minister, formed a new party, Political Spring. Samaras had been dismissed from his ministry by Mitsotakis in 1992 when the two clashed over Greece's policies toward the independence of the former Yugoslav republic of Macedonia, located to the north of Greece. When Samaras called for New Democracy members to join him, the party clearly was plunging into disunity. In September 1993, following a defection by New Democracy parliamentary deputies that caused Mitsotakis to lose his majority, he was forced to call for dissolution of Parliament and the scheduling of elections.

Held on October 10, the elections returned Andreas Papandreou and his PASOK party to power for the first time since 1989. PASOK received 170 seats in the 300-seat Parliament, New Democracy 111, Political Spring ten, and the Communist Party nine. For Papandreou and his party, previously embroiled in controversies, allegations, and corruption trials stemming from

events during his tenure from 1981 to 1989, it was a personal triumph. Mitsotakis in defeat resigned as head of New Democracy and was followed by Miltiades Evert, former mayor of Athens.

Foreign Affairs. The question of Greek recognition of the former Yugoslav republic of Macedonia raised enormous nationalist passions in Greece, as the newly independent republic refused to yield on Greek insistence that the name Macedonia not be used in the official designation. Fearing that the utilization of the name Macedonia by the independent republic was an indication of irredentist claims on Greek Macedonia, the Mitsotakis government while in office tried to find some compromise on how its neighbor should be designated officially, perhaps through the use of an epithet in the name.

A further irritant for Greece was the independent republic's refusal to yield on the question of using a 16-ray symbol, variously called

© Argyropolus/Sipa

After the Panhellenic Socialist Union (PASOK) scored a landslide victory in Greek elections on Oct. 10, 1993, Andreas Papandreou, right, the party's 74-year-old leader, returned to the nation's prime ministership, a post he had held from 1981 to 1989.

either the Star of Vergina or the Sun of Vergina, on its flag. This ancient royal symbol was connected to Alexander the Great, and the Greek government regarded its use as an attempt by the newly independent republic, inhabited chiefly by Slavs and Albanians, to usurp the glories of classical Greece.

Although the United Nations did admit the new country as a member in April under the temporary name of "The Former Yugoslav Republic of Macedonia," the controversial flag with the Vergina symbol was not raised outside UN headquarters at that time. All attempts at mediating the name and flag controversy between Greece and the new country failed during Mitsotakis' term. Papandreou in his electoral campaign and after taking office in October indicated that his would be a more hard-line policy.

With Albania, relations remained strained over the treatment of the Greek Orthodox minority there, and during the year the Greek government in a show of strength expelled thousands of illegal Albanian immigrants from Greece. But the borders were hard to patrol, and illegal immigrants still seemed able to enter Greece with minimum difficulties.

Talks aimed at finding a peace for Bosnia's warring factions were held in Greece in May under Mitsotakis' sponsorship amid much publicity. At first hopeful, these led to no substantive agreement among the contesting parties.

Meanwhile the continued Turkish occupation of northern Cyprus after 19 years remained an irritant in Greek-Turkish relations, since no solution appeared in sight.

Economics. While in power, Mitsotakis' government continued to pursue a three-year austerity program that he hoped would improve the Greek economy, seen by most authorities as the weakest in the European Union (formerly the European Community). This organization, of which Greece is a member, gave the country substantial subsidies during the year for economic development. Mitsotakis' program included attempts to proceed with a further decrease in an already curbed inflation rate, and it called for forms of privatization regarding state-owned sectors of the economy, such as the public transportation system and telecommunications.

The austerity program, as the October election results showed all too clearly, proved very unpopular in the country. Once in office, Papandreou announced reversals in the privatization plans and indicated that his government would return to the kind of heavy spending that had characterized his 1980s term of office. The change of government in October and the uncertainty as to the future economic policies of the PASOK regime caused some unease among Greece's fellow members in the European Union.

See also THE YUGOSLAV WARS OF SECESSION, page 26.

GEORGE J. MARCOPOULOS
Tufts University

HAITI

More than two years after the member countries of the Organization of American States (OAS) imposed an embargo on Haiti and launched diplomatic efforts to force the return of ousted President Jean-Bertrand Aristide, the situation remained deadlocked. A review of U.S. policy toward Haitian refugees was under way as 1993 drew to a close.

A United Nations-brokered peace accord was signed at midyear by President Aristide and the Haitian military, that country's de facto rulers, but attempts to implement the accord failed. By year's end the military appeared to be hunkering down for a long stay in power.

International efforts had focused on securing Aristide's return to the presidency, but Lt. Gen. Raoul Cedras, the army commander who drove Aristide into exile, resisted heavy pressure to permit the president's restoration. Robert Malval, Aristide's appointed prime minister, tried vainly to negotiate with Cedras and simultaneously to persuade Aristide to compromise with the military. Late in the year, Malval threatened to resign his essentially powerless post unless the impasse with the army was broken.

An Embattled Junta. During the first half of 1993, an intense diplomatic effort was mounted jointly by the United Nations (UN) and the Organization of American States (OAS) to resolve the Haitian crisis. Dante Caputo, an Argentine diplomat who served as chief negotiator for both international organizations, shuttled back and forth between Port-au-Prince, the Haitian capital, and New York and Washington, offering numerous proposed compromises to the Haitian army and President Aristide, who remained in exile in the United States.

In May a plan was readied for an international observer force of 500 foreign police to be sent to Haiti for peacekeeping. Aristide was persuaded to accept an amnesty for military personnel involved in the 1991 coup. The United States and other countries agreed to resume economic aid, cut off after Aristide's ouster.

HAITI • Information Highlights

Official Name: Republic of Haiti.
Location: Caribbean.
Area: 10,714 sq mi (27 750 km²).
Population: (mid-1993 est.): 6,500,000.
Chief City (1987 est.): Port-au-Prince, the capital, 797,000 (incl. suburbs).
Government: *Interim prime minister*, Robert Malval (took office Aug. 30, 1993). *Legislature*—suspended.
Monetary Unit: Gourde (5.0 gourdes equal U.S.$1, buying rate, July 1991).
Gross Domestic Product (1990 est. U.S.$): $2,700,000,000.
Economic Index (Port-au-Prince, 1992): *Consumer Prices* (1980 = 100), all items, 250.7; food, 223.9.
Foreign Trade (1991 U.S.$): *Imports*, $374,000,000; *exports*, $103,000,000.

Photos, © AP/Wide World

Deposed Haitian President Jean-Bertrand Aristide (above) addressed the United Nations on Oct. 28, 1993, to build international support for a total trade blockade against Haiti to help him regain power. Right-wing demonstrators in Port-au-Prince (right) cheered Aristide's failure to return as president and demanded his immediate replacement.

In June, with the two sides apparently still far apart, the UN Security Council unanimously voted to impose a worldwide oil and arms embargo on Haiti, along with a global freeze on the government's financial assets. The Security Council action reinforced the more limited economic embargo imposed by the OAS after Aristide was overthrown.

As the widened embargo was announced, Marc Bazin, who had served as prime minister under the military regime, abruptly resigned. Bazin, a former official of the World Bank, reportedly had lost the military's support because of his failure to head off the economic sanctions.

Increased Pressure from Abroad. The increasing international pressure succeeded in bringing Aristide and Cedras to New York in early July for negotiations on the terms of restoring Aristide to the presidency. Representatives of both sides, meeting on Governor's Island in New York Harbor, signed an agreement on July 3 setting October 30 as the date for Aristide's return to Haiti. A new prime minister to be named by Aristide would head an interim government until that date. Cedras and other military officers would resign before then. They would not be prosecuted for their part in the 1991 coup, but could face charges brought by individual victims of violence.

In return, the UN and the OAS agreed to lift the trade, oil, and arms embargoes immediately and to authorize the resumption of economic aid. In the United States the Clinton administration pledged $37.5 million as part of a larger package to be offered as soon as the agreement was implemented.

On July 26, Aristide named Robert Malval, a nonpolitical owner of a printing business, as prime minister. Quickly confirmed by the Hai-

tian legislature, Malval was to serve as interim head of government until December 15.

Diplomatic Breakdown. Within a few weeks, the nascent peace process began to break down. On September 8 anti-Aristide rioting broke out at the city hall in Port-au-Prince, led by so-called "attachés," armed gangs under the control of the police. Three days later, gunmen—also described by witnesses as "attachés"—invaded a church service and gunned down Antoine Izmery, a wealthy financial backer of Aristide. Violence continued to mount in the capital and on October 4, Justice Minister Guy Malary, appointed by Aristide, was assassinated along with his bodyguard and driver.

Even before Malary's death, it was apparent that Aristide would not be able to return by the October 30 deadline. Then, on October 11, U.S. and Canadian military engineers—sent to Haiti as an advance party of a 1,200-person UN training and peace-monitoring force—were prevented from landing at Port-au-Prince by a hostile mob. Two days later the UN Security Council voted to reimpose the oil embargo against Haiti and to refreeze the government's financial assets. President Clinton said that the United States would consider stationing U.S. warships off Haiti to enforce the embargo. Aristide, in an address to the UN on October 29, called for a "total embargo . . . by air as well as by sea."

The embargo and other sanctions exacted a heavy toll on Haiti. Factories shut down and power outages were frequent. A study by public-health experts at Harvard University, released in November, found that up to 1,000 children were dying each month from malnutrition and lack of proper medicines.

Refugees. Shortly before his inauguration, President-elect Clinton, reversing a campaign

pledge, said he would enforce the policy of the outgoing Bush administration toward Haitian "boat people"—refugees trying to escape by sea. The new president subsequently ordered the U.S. Coast Guard to intercept the refugees on the high seas and forcibly return them to their homeland. Clinton said the interception policy was necessary to avoid a massive flow of Haitians to the United States. President Aristide supported the U.S. policy and asked his countrymen to stay put.

In June the U.S. Supreme Court, voting 8 to 1, upheld the interception policy, saying a U.S. law requiring deportation hearings did not apply to aliens picked up in international waters.

U.S. Cross-Purposes. In October, Brian Latell, the chief Latin American analyst of the U.S. Central Intelligence Agency (CIA), told a congressional committee that Aristide was mentally unstable and had undergone psychiatric treatment in a Canadian hospital. Aristide supporters denounced the CIA report as "character assassination," and in December the *Miami Herald* said its own investigation showed that the claim that Aristide had been hospitalized was false. *The New York Times* meanwhile reported that key Haitian leaders had been in the pay of the CIA, raising questions about the impartiality of the CIA report.

RICHARD C. SCHROEDER, CONSULTANT
Organization of American States

HAWAII

Lingering effects from a devastating hurricane and a delayed recession left Hawaii in a serious financial bind in 1993.

Tourism. A year after Hurricane Iniki lashed the northern islands causing more than $1.7 billion in damage, much of it on Kauai, less than half of Kauai's 8,200 hotel rooms were back in operation. The reopening of two Sheraton hotels at Poipu was postponed. Insurance disputes also prevented repairs on major hotels.

Legislation. Much of the 1993 state legislative session was devoted to hurricane relief as well as to the creation of a tourism-promotion fund. When efforts to build a state-financed convention center on Oahu provoked furious controversy, legislators had to reconvene in a special August session to approve the plan. Disagreements about the purchase price of $350 million could delay the project further. The Honolulu city government also was interested in building a convention center.

Economy. The Hawaii Visitors Bureau issued continued gloomy forecasts, predicting the current tourism slump would continue well into 1994. In an effort to spur travel from Europe— one of the few areas with continued high tourist traffic—Gov. John Waihee went to Germany and other countries to promote tourism. Waihee's trip came as statistics showed personal income in

---

HAWAII • Information Highlights

Area: 6,471 sq mi (16 759 km²).
Population (July 1, 1992 est.): 1,160,000.
Chief Cities (1990 census): Honolulu, the capital, 365,272; Hilo, 37,808; Kailua, 36,818; Kaneohe, 35,448.
Government (1993): *Chief Officers*—governor, John D. Waihee III (D); lt. gov., Benjamin J. Cayetano (D). *Legislature*—Senate, 25 members; House of Representatives, 51 members.
State Finances (fiscal year 1991): *Revenue*, $4,916,000,000; *expenditure*, $4,510,000,000.
Personal Income (1992): $25,255,000,000; per capita, $21,779.
Labor Force (August 1993): *Civilian labor force*, 579,700; *unemployed*, 26,000 (4.5% of total force).
Education: *Enrollment* (fall 1991)—public elementary schools, 126,855; public secondary, 47,892; colleges and universities, 57,302. *Public school expenditures* (1990-91), $827,579,000.

Hawaii grew only 2.9% in 1992, falling behind inflation. Median home prices rose 8.5% to $385,000, and a 40% gap existed between Hawaii's cost of living and that of the mainland United States.

Honolulu, rated by *Money* magazine as seventh among U.S. "Best Cities" in 1992, dropped to number 124. Hawaiian Airlines, the oldest private carrier in the islands, filed for bankruptcy. The Hyatt Waikoloa hotel on the island of Hawaii was put up for sale at a fraction of its original $360 million cost. Japanese investors, who spent more than $2.1 billion in Hawaii during their 1989 peak year, became scarce.

Politics. Governor Waihee normally would have taken most of the political heat for the mounting woes. But he was a lame duck, nearing the end of his second four-year term and barred from seeking reelection. Waihee's future political plans were unknown, but he was a close friend of President Bill Clinton.

Gubernatorial aspirants such as Honolulu's Mayor Frank F. Fasi and Democratic Lt.-Gov. Ben Cayetano strengthened their political treasuries and alliances in anticipation of a bitter 1994 campaign. Fasi is a Republican who also has run as a Democrat and as an independent in prior bids for the governorship.

Other News. A state forester accidentally cut down the last known *Xylosma crenatum* tree, not knowing it was on the endangered-species list . . . . Hawaii gained a new island when the U.S. Senate voted to return the island of Kaha'olawe, which had been used for military purposes, to state control within ten years . . . . The 100th anniversary of the U.S.-backed overthrow of Hawaii's last monarch, Queen Liliuokalani, stirred efforts to gain sovereignty for native Hawaiians along the lines of that given to the American Indians. Organizers began celebrating the anniversary 17 years earlier and have drawn increasing numbers to the annual rallies.

CHARLES H. TURNER
Freelance Writer, Honolulu

HONG KONG

Sino-British tensions regarding Hong Kong increased in 1993 when British Gov. Christopher Patten awarded a large airport contract to a consortium over Beijing's objection and when he received a Taiwan official and permitted a Chinese dissident to visit Hong Kong. On March 17, Lu Ping, director of the Hong Kong and Macao Affairs Office, said that China would set up a shadow government if the political impasse over Patten's democratic-reform proposals for the scheduled 1995 election was not solved. In April, Beijing appointed a second group of local residents as advisers on Hong Kong. In contrast with the group appointed in 1992, most of the new advisers were younger and more active in Hong Kong's politics.

On September 15, Patten threatened to submit his proposals to the council if there was no progress in the Sino-British talks. In turn, on September 24, China released a statement from its paramount ruler Deng Xiaoping that Hong Kong would be taken over before 1997—the year in which Hong Kong is to come under China's control—if serious disturbances occurred in the territory. China had established a special 6,000-troop force which would garrison Hong Kong in 1997. The 12th round of Sino-British talks began on September 26, but Governor Patten announced on October 6 that negotiations with China were failing and threatened to press on with his reforms without China's support.

Three political camps divided Hong Kong. The pro-Beijing camp was represented by the Democratic Alliance for Betterment of Hong Kong. The democratic camp included the United Democrats of Hong Kong, the Meeting Point, the Association for Democracy and People's Livelihood, and the Hong Kong Democratic Foundation. The conservative camp, willing to cooperate with Beijing, was comprised of the New Hong Kong Alliance, the Liberal Democratic Federation, and the Cooperative Resource Center (CRC). In July 1993 the CRC was organized as the Liberal Party, Hong Kong's first political party.

Economy. With economic confidence damaged, the Hong Kong stock market was devalued significantly early in 1993. However, China continued to invest large sums in Hong Kong firms through investment companies. Critics said that the involvement of a Chinese political body in commercial ventures would give companies an advantage in dealings in Hong Kong and would affect the stock market during political negotiations.

The monetary integration between Hong Kong and China continued. In 1993 about 30% of Hong Kong's banknotes were circulating in China. In March travelers from China were permitted to take roughly $1,000 in Renminbi (the "people's money") with them to Hong Kong, where it increasingly was accepted.

DAVID CHUENYAN LAI
University of Victoria, British Columbia

HOUSING

The U.S. housing market continued to expand in 1993, extending a cyclical recovery that began in early 1991. The recovery continued to be quite uneven across areas of the country. Furthermore, the expansion occurred entirely in the single-family component of the market as the multifamily component declined to the lowest level on record. In the process, the national home-ownership rate moved up to the highest level in a decade, approaching 65% by late in the year.

The 1993 single-family housing expansion was driven by falling mortgage interest rates. The U.S. Federal Reserve held monetary policy steady during the year, and an improving inflation situation along with falling rates abroad fostered continuation of a downslide in interest rates that had begun in early 1989. By late 1993 the cost of mortgage credit was down to the lowest levels since the late 1960s. Long-term fixed-rate mortgage yields fell below 7% and yields on adjustable-rate mortgages approached 4%.

Falling mortgage interest rates stimulated levels of home buying that far exceeded job growth and household formations in the United States during 1993. The historically low interest rates encouraged many renter households to shift to home ownership for the first time. This process unleashed pent-up buyer demand that had built up in the rental-housing stock during the 1980s when the affordability of home ownership was much less favorable.

There were few shifts in federal housing policy during the first year of the new Democratic administration under President Bill Clinton. Clinton's first budget package retained the substantial tax advantages of home ownership and reauthorized two subsidy programs designed to assist moderate-income, first-time home buyers as well as low-income renters. Despite such policies, many young renters still lacked the resources to cover the up-front cash costs of home ownership, and many low-income renters found the availability of decent and affordable apartment units to be lacking seriously. Homelessness remained a high-profile U.S. problem.

During 1993 government statisticians raised estimates of underlying housing demand in the United States because of upward revisions to projections of net immigration. Stronger immigration trends promised to have a profound impact on future housing demand.

Uneven Recovery. Total housing starts rose by 6% in 1993 to 1.27 million units, following an 18% increase in 1992. Single-family starts climbed by nearly 8% to 1.11 million units, the best performance since 1987. One the other hand, multifamily starts fell by 6% to 160,000 units, less than one fourth the peak production levels of the mid-1980s. The seven-year downslide in multifamily starts apparently hit bottom in mid-1993, and production levels were improving

slightly as the year drew to a close. Federal reauthorization of a tax-credit program which subsidizes production of privately owned rental housing for low-income people provided some support to the multifamily sector in late 1993.

The 1993 U.S. housing recovery also was uneven by geographic region. The Northeast region posted very little improvement as both New England and the Middle Atlantic states struggled with weak economic conditions and previously overbuilt housing markets. The Midwest retained a historically large share of national housing-market activity despite a spate of bad weather and the Mississippi River floods. The South posted the strongest growth, paced by Florida and other parts of the South Atlantic area as well as by Texas and other parts of the West South Central area. The Mountain states did well in the West region, but sizable contraction in the California housing market resulted in a decline in housing starts along the Pacific coast.

Rent v. Own. During the 1980s and the early 1990s, home-ownership rates fell substantially for the types of households that historically had been the principal first-time home buyers in the United States. From 1980 to 1992, the rates of home ownership fell by about 10 percentage points for households in the 25- to 34-year-old age group, and this pattern was evident for married couples as well as for other types of households in this age group.

Erosion of affordability conditions was the dominant factor behind this erosion of home-ownership rates. High interest rates and soaring home prices relegated many would-be buyers to rental accommodations, while household surveys consistently showed that the dream of home ownership still was alive and well. Thus, a large backlog of potential home buyers was building up in rental housing during the 1980-1992 period; indeed, regaining the home-ownership losses of the 1980s for the first-time home-buyer group would add as many as 3 million owners to the demand side of the equation in future years.

In 1993 a sizable amount of this pent-up demand shifted from rental housing to home ownership. As a result, rental-vacancy rates held around the historic highs of the late 1980s, despite a plunge in completions of multifamily units to about one fifth of the peak completion rates of the 1980s. The shift of renters to owners also showed up in the home-ownership rates for younger households in 1993. However, the improvement was only a small fraction of the massive erosion in home-ownership rates that occurred during the previous 12 years for these types of households.

Demographic Revisions. In 1993 the U.S. Census Bureau raised the government's population projections for the balance of the 20th century to reflect higher levels of immigration in the wake of changes to immigration law in 1990. Demographers took the new population projections into account and raised estimates of household

growth for the 1990s. In fact, Harvard University's Joint Center for Housing Studies estimated that total household growth for the 1990s would exceed household formations for the 1980s slightly, a major change in perspective.

The upward revisions to household formations have powerful implications for the long-term housing outlook in the United States. As 1993 ended, average annual housing starts for the 1990s were estimated at 1.35 million units. In view of the below-trend years already on record for the first four years of the 1990s (averaging 1.17 million), the prospects for housing starts during the balance of the 1990s averaged about 1.5 million units per year. Furthermore, the new forecasts of household formations continued to favor single-family housing much more than the multifamily sector.

International Comparisons. Home-ownership rates in most developed countries increased in 1993 as governments continued to shift away from sponsorship of public rental housing and, in some cases, introduced subsidies, tax preferences, and other incentives for home ownership. In Belgium, Canada, Finland, Japan, Norway, and Great Britain home-ownership rates now were comparable to those in the United States. In Australia, Italy, New Zealand, Spain, and Singapore the rate was even higher. In Austria, France, Germany, the Netherlands, and Sweden—where rents are controlled and public housing is a well-entrenched, heavily subsidized institution—home-ownership rates still were well below the U.S. level.

A shift away from public housing and toward private markets has occurred in the former Communist countries of East Europe and in the less-developed world as well. A shift in policy by the World Bank encouraged the trend. Private-property rights, mortgage-lending institutions, adequate infrastructure development, and accommodative regulatory regimes were being implemented in many less-developed countries in support of this trend.

In 1993 construction activity in many industrialized countries declined, reflecting the economic recession that continued to plague much of the developed world. Japan, Britain, Australia, and New Zealand, however, experienced recoveries in home building, and Germany apparently showed some further increase after a big jump in 1992. Japan continued to lead the developed world in terms of the number of units built, recording more than 1.4 million housing starts in 1993.

In the United States less than 20% of the units built in 1993 were needed to replace homes lost from demolitions, disasters, or conversions to other uses. In Japan construction was dominated more heavily by replacement demand, and demolitions were common as a result of the limited supply of available land and the presence of many older and substandard units.

KENT W. COLTON
and DAVID F. SEIDERS
National Association of Home Builders

HUMAN RIGHTS

After two weeks of divisive debate, government delegates from 171 nations attending the 1993 World Conference on Human Rights in Vienna adopted a 12,000-word Declaration and Program of Action on human rights on June 25. Boutros Boutros-Ghali, secretary-general of the United Nations, lauded the declaration as "a new vision for global action for human rights into the next century." But Pierre Sané, secretary-general of Amnesty International, described the meeting as "a summit of missed opportunities," and criticized its declaration as dealing "with the past instead of addressing the challenges of the future."

The idea for the conference was approved by the UN General Assembly in 1989, soon after the Berlin Wall fell. It was hoped that the conference would accelerate worldwide momentum toward democratization and improve the UN's ability to promote human rights with a mandate that updated the 1948 UN Universal Declaration of Human Rights. However, the conference may have fallen short of fulfilling some of those high expectations.

The declaration did advance the cause of women's rights. The 1948 Declaration, while briefly referring to "the equal rights of men and women," did not address distinct human-rights problems faced by women. In contrast, a 1,000-word section of the Vienna Declaration covers a broad range of women's issues—including sexual harassment; violence against women in public and private life; and gender bias in courts, health care, education, and employment—and urges the UN to give these issues much higher priority. Charlotte Bunch, director of the Center for Women's Global Leadership at Rutgers University, called the Vienna Declaration "a major half-step forward," which will become "a full step" as its recommendations for UN activities are implemented.

On other major issues, however, governments were split badly. Before and during the Vienna conference, a coalition of China and about 50 countries often accused of autocratic rule took the offensive by promoting their human-rights approach, which favors economic development over democracy and rejects outside pressures on human rights as violations of national sovereignty. "Behind the smokescreen of lofty rhetoric," says Douglas Payne of Freedom House in New York, who attended the parallel conference of nongovernmental organizations in Vienna, "their goal was clear: to be able to reap the benefits of international trade and aid without being held accountable to either their own citizens or to the principles of the Universal Declaration."

The Vienna Declaration restates some of the basic principles of the 1948 Declaration, including "that all human rights derive from the dignity and worth inherent in the human person and that the human person is the central subject of human rights and fundamental freedoms." Regarding practical issues, however, the declaration tends to make the *government* the "central subject" and to subordinate the rights of ordinary people. It places freedom of the press and the work of nongovernmental organizations, for example, under "the framework of national law." The declaration also implies that development assistance and special trade benefits should not be tied to human-rights performance. However, the declaration contains no forthright language, only nuances, to endorse the autocratic view.

A major tactical victory by China and its allies was to exclude representatives of nongovernmental organizations (NGOs) from most drafting committees and conference sessions, even as observers. Human-rights organizations such as Amnesty International exerted some influence on the declaration, however, through separate sessions well covered by the media and through contacts with governmental representatives of individual countries. In a promising sign the UN General Assembly in December agreed to give human-rights monitoring a high priority within the UN bureaucracy by creating the post of high commissioner for human rights. The position's mandate is neither as explicit about investigating human-rights violations as the West wanted nor as restrictive as China and others wished. As a result, the commissioner's role would depend largely on who is appointed and that person's personal leadership.

ASEAN and India. Three months after the Vienna meeting, Southeast Asian nations met to formalize their first joint human-rights position. Meeting in Kuala Lumpur, officials from Brunei, Indonesia, Malaysia, the Philippines, Singapore, and Thailand—the Association of Southeast Asian Nations (ASEAN)—unanimously adopted a charter called the Kuala Lumpur Declaration of Human Rights. Three of the nations—Indonesia, Malaysia, and Thailand—were under U.S. scrutiny for violations of worker rights that may deprive them of special U.S. trade benefits.

Spelling out what only was implied in the Vienna document, the declaration adopted at the ASEAN assembly stated: "Human rights should not be used as a conditionality for economic cooperation and development assistance. Universal promotion and protection of human rights should take place in the context of international cooperation based on respect for national sovereignty."

India also created a National Human Rights Commission, led by a retired Supreme Court justice, to probe alleged human-rights abuses by its armed forces in violence-torn Kashmir. India already had specialized human-rights commissions focusing on women, minorities, and disadvantaged castes and tribes.

ROBERT A. SENSER

HUNGARY

Throughout 1993, Hungary's major political parties made preparations for the 1994 general elections. The governing Hungarian Democratic Forum (HDF) was torn by the emergence of an ultranationalist faction and by the death of Prime Minister Jozsef Antall, the party leader, on December 12. Interior Minister Peter Boross replaced Antall at year's end.

Political Landscape. There were increasing signs of competition during the year among Hungary's major political parties, yet Hungary remained the only East European country where a government elected during the fall of communism had survived its full term in office.

At the beginning of the year, Prime Minister Antall conducted a cabinet reshuffle to consolidate the position of HDF centrist forces. The move was intended to marginalize the populist-nationalist wing of the party led by writer and former Deputy President Istvan Csurka, who in 1992 had published an inflammatory anti-Semitic article.

Csurka's supporters had established a new ultranationalist movement, Hungarian Way, which damaged Hungary's reputation as a model post-Communist state. A number of parliamentary deputies from the HDF and its coalition partner, the Independent Smallholders Party (ISP), displayed sympathy toward Csurka's views. In June, Csurka was expelled from the HDF and established the new Hungarian Justice Party (HJP) with the support of ten parliamentary deputies.

The largest opposition party, the Alliance of Free Democrats (AFD), criticized the government for its hesitant approach toward extremists such as Csurka. The Alliance also was racked by internal conflicts on two main issues: the treatment of former Communist officials and the pace of economic reform. AFD liberals opposed introducing legislation to exclude former Communists from prominent positions. Much of the AFD rank and file favored calling former officials to account for their Communist-era policies. There were also AFD-leadership disputes between social democrats, preferring a slower privatization pace, and free-market liberals.

The second-largest opposition party, the Alliance of Young Democrats (AYD), also underwent some major reorganization in an effort to expand its influence. The party's 35-year age limit was abolished and its formerly loose structure was centralized. Opinion polls indicated that the AYD was the most popular party in the country. The post-Communist Hungarian Socialist Party also gained support, particularly among social groups hit hardest by the reform program.

Economic Record Balance. The Hungarian economy showed both positive and negative trends. The drop in gross domestic product (GDP) slowed from 12% in 1991 to 4.5% in 1992; by the fall of 1993 the GDP had dropped

---

HUNGARY • Information Highlights

Official Name: Republic of Hungary.
Location: East-central Europe.
Area: 35,919 sq mi (93 030 km²).
Population (mid-1993 est.): 10,300,000.
Chief Cities (Jan. 1, 1992 est.): Budapest, the capital, 1,992,343; Debrecen, 214,712; Miskolc, 191,623.
Government: *Head of state*, Arpád Goncz, president (elected August 1990). *Head of government*, Peter Boross, prime minister (took office Dec. 1993). *Legislature* (unicameral)—National Assembly.
Monetary Unit: Forint (98.18 forints equal U.S.$1, Dec. 27, 1993).
Gross Domestic Product (1991 est. U.S.$): $60,100,000,000.
Economic Indexes (1992): *Consumer Prices* (1980 = 100), all items, 460.1; food, 405.4. *Industrial Production* (1980 = 100), 74.
Foreign Trade (1992 U.S.$): *Imports*, $11,222,000,000; *exports*, $10,685,000,000.

2%-3%. Industrial production in the first seven months of 1993 was up by 2.5% over the same 1992 period, although agricultural output was affected by bad weather. Exports declined, and the currency was devalued several times.

Hungary's 200,000 small and medium-sized private firms accounted for about 40% of economic output, with an average of 1,100 new companies starting businesses each month. The country's positive economic news was generated by the private sector and by hard-currency exports. According to midyear statistics, unemployment dropped to 12.6%, down from 13% in the spring. However, it was unclear whether the figure represented real improvement or reflected seasonal employment trends. The government also planned to launch a mass privatization program in early 1994 in order to transform the substantial state sector. A broad-based voucher-type program was to be introduced. Citizens would obtain long-term, low-rate credit vouchers that could be exchanged for shares at privatization sales.

On the negative side, the annual inflation rate was recorded in September at 22.3%, with the price of foodstuffs rising by more than 30% during the previous 12 months. The government's biggest headache was its large budget deficit. The proposed budget for 1994 envisaged a record-high deficit, where debt servicing would account for 19% of total expenditures. The budget deficit became a source of conflict with the International Monetary Fund (IMF). A settlement finally was reached in June whereby Hungary would be provided with new IMF credits and World Bank loans on condition that the budget deficit be reduced in 1994.

Hungary continued to attract the lion's share of direct foreign investment in Eastern Europe, estimated at more than 40%. By the end of 1992, cumulative foreign investments reached $5 billion. Budapest finalized free-trade agreements with the other Visegrad states (Poland, Czech Republic, and Slovakia), whereby customs duties would be

reduced over the next five years. Hungary also signed trade agreements with the seven-member European Free Trade Association (EFTA) to cover industrial and agricultural products.

Nationality Questions. Hungary made significant strides in ensuring legal rights for its ethnic minorities. In July 1993 parliament passed a law granting a wide array of collective rights to a dozen small minorities, thus enabling them to establish "self-governing councils" and obtain seats in the National Assembly, and ensuring free contacts with co-nationals in neighboring states.

One key objective of the government was to encourage the granting of collective rights to the nearly 3 million ethnic Hungarians in Romania, Slovakia, and the Serbian province of Vojvodina. Budapest feared that the position of Magyars in these states could deteriorate seriously, given the rise of nationalist sentiments. The authorities in Bucharest, Bratislava, and Belgrade seemed unwilling to provide full minority guarantees for the Hungarian population, fearful of raising ethnic tensions and irredentist demands. Only neighboring Ukraine agreed to ensure collective rights for its Hungarian minority.

Budapest remained concerned particularly about the situation in Serbia, where the economic embargo contributed to the raising of political and social tensions. Relations with Romania and Slovakia were not all negative, as military agreements with the former and economic accords with the latter contributed to lessening tensions.

JANUSZ BUGAJSKI
Center for International and Strategic Studies

ICELAND

The year 1993 saw Iceland deep in recession, facing the highest unemployment rates seen in decades. Fish stocks had declined drastically in recent years, and fishing quotas were cut to allow for recovery.

Economy. Falling prices for seafood products (accounting for more than 70% of Iceland's export revenues) coincided with the quota cuts and dealt a severe blow to Iceland's primary economic sector. The fishing fleet reacted by fishing greater quantities of other species and seeking new fishing grounds outside Icelandic waters. Icelandic fishing in a "loophole" in the Barent Sea, claimed by Norway and Russia, caused international tension in the latter half of the year.

Unemployment was about 5% of the work-force early in 1993, although it dropped below 4% toward the year's end. While Iceland's unemployment rate was low compared to other European countries, the impact was great because unemployment had been negligible for many decades, and Iceland had not developed a system of unemployment benefits comparable to those of its neighbors.

Stringent government measures to maintain economic stability and minimize inflation yielded the lowest inflation rate (about 4%) in more than 30 years, while wages were frozen and purchasing power fell. Stability was maintained, in spite of two devaluations within six months—by 6% in November 1992 and 7.5% in June 1993. Interest rates remained high until government measures pressured banking institutions into lowering their rates in November. By year's end, the economy looked healthier, with an estimated 1% rise in the gross domestic product (GDP). There was concern over Iceland's foreign debt ($3.6 billion in 1992; 49.6% of GDP), and the 1994 budget boded another year of belt-tightening.

The coalition government of the Independence (conservative) and Social Democratic parties went through a period of unpopularity and discord in 1993, when a breakup seemed more than possible. But with economic prospects looking better, the coalition seemed secure enough to last to the end of its electoral term in 1995.

European Economic Area. The European Economic Area (EEA), the new free-trade area formed by the European Community (EC)—now the European Union (EU)—and European Free Trade Association (EFTA) and taking effect on Jan. 1, 1994, proved controversial. In spite of serious doubts over the significance of the agreement to Iceland, it was ratified by the Althing (parliament) in January, after demands for a referendum had been rejected. There was some debate on the issue of whether Iceland should apply for membership in the EU.

The future of the U.S.-manned, North Atlantic Treaty Organization (NATO) naval air base at Keflavík was a recurring and unresolved issue. Negotiations between Icelandic and U.S. authorities were conducted, with security—guaranteed by the United States under a bilateral defense treaty—only one of the issues at stake. (Iceland has no armed forces, but is a founding member of NATO.) Many Icelanders also were concerned about the economic consequences of the base closing.

ANNE YATES
Freelance Writer and Translator, Reykjavík

ICELAND • Information Highlights

Official Name: Republic of Iceland.
Location: North Atlantic Ocean.
Area: 39,768 sq mi (103 000 km²).
Population (mid-1993 est.): 300,000.
Chief City (Dec. 1, 1991 est.): Reykjavík, the capital, 99,623.
Government: *Head of state*, Vigdís Finnbogadóttir, president (took office Aug. 1980). *Head of government*, David Oddsson, prime minister (took office April 1991). *Legislature*—Althing: Upper House and Lower House.
Monetary Unit: Króna (72.17 krónur equal U.S.$1, selling rate, Dec. 1993).
Gross Domestic Product (1991 U.S.$): $6,500,000,000.
Foreign Trade (1992 U.S.$): *Imports*, $1,692,000,000; *exports*, $1,515,000,000.

IDAHO

In a state known for resisting federal intrusion, Idaho juries repudiated major federal prosecutions in 1993.

Crime. Acquitted of federal murder charges was white separatist Randall Weaver—whose wife and son died along with a federal marshal in a 1992 shoot-out with federal agents—and his codefendant Kevin Harris. Boise jurors in July exonerated Weaver—whose mountain cabin in the northern part of the state had been the scene of a two-day shoot-out following an 11-day siege in 1992—and codefendant Harris of murdering a federal marshal. Harris went free; Weaver later was sentenced to 18 months in prison and fined $10,000 on charges related to a failure to appear in a 1991 federal weapons case. It was when federal marshals went to find him as a fugitive that the shoot-out began. Following a request from U.S. Sen. Larry Craig (R), U.S. Attorney General Janet Reno later ordered an investigation of the incident.

Acquitted in a separate trial was Frank Crnkovich, a former Shoshone county sheriff accused of protecting and shaking down gambling and prostitution operations in the county's historic mining towns.

In other Idaho court cases, former U.S. Rep. George Hansen (R), who had served time in federal prison for campaign-finance-disclosure violations, was sentenced to four years in prison for leading a multimillion-dollar check-kiting operation. Lt. Gov. C. L. "Butch" Otter (R) was convicted of drunken driving.

Public Finances. The Republican-controlled legislature rejected a call by Gov. Cecil Andrus (D) for significantly increased public-school support and a tax shift away from the unpopular property tax. Organizers of an initiative limiting property tax to 1% of market value that failed in the 1992 election began circulating a similar measure for the 1994 ballot. The Idaho Supreme Court instructed a reluctant trial judge to hear a lawsuit brought by 47 of the state's 113 school districts alleging the state had failed to honor its constitutional directive to provide for thorough schools.

Politics. With four-term Governor Andrus announcing his retirement at the end of his current term in January 1995, candidates in both parties began lining up to succeed him. Among the Democrats, Attorney General Larry EchoHawk in September joined a race already featuring state Sen. John Peavey and former Sen. Ron Beitelspacher. In the Republican Party, former Lt. Gov. Phil Batt led a field including Boise businessmen Larry Eastland and Chuck Winder. Party activist Helen Chenoweth of Boise and Port of Lewiston Manager F. Ron McMurray both began campaigns for the Republican nomination to challenge 1st District U.S. Rep. Larry LaRocco (D).

Natural Resources and the Environment. Despite Governor Andrus' continued pressure for drawing down Snake River dams to rescue Idaho's dwindling salmon runs, the U.S. Army Corps of Engineers and the National Marine Fisheries Service said no drawdowns would be conducted until 1996. Andrus, claiming officials were stalling until either he or the salmon disappeared, already had filed suit to force an earlier date.

In March, Representative LaRocco introduced federal legislation designating an additional 1.2 million acres (485 830 ha) of wilderness in his district. This was the same amount Governor Andrus and former U.S. Sen. James McClure (R) had proposed unsuccessfully for the entire state.

The state and the U.S. Navy reached an agreement in August that allows the storage of spent nuclear fuel at a federal atomic reservation near Idaho Falls.

JIM FISHER, *"Lewiston Morning Tribune"*

IDAHO • Information Highlights

Area: 83,564 sq mi (216 432 km²).

Population (July 1, 1992 est.): 1,067,000.

Chief Cities (1990 census): Boise, the capital, 125,738; Pocatello, 46,080; Idaho Falls, 43,929.

Government (1993): *Chief Officers*—governor, Cecil Andrus (D); lt. gov., C. L. Otter (R). *Legislature*—Senate, 42 members; House of Representatives, 84 members.

State Finances (fiscal year 1991): *Revenue*, $2,584,000,000; *expenditure*, $2,305,000,000.

Personal Income (1992): $17,634,000,000; per capita, $16,523.

Labor Force (August 1993): *Civilian labor force*, 531,700; *unemployed*, 31,400 (5.9% of total force).

Education: *Enrollment* (fall 1991)—public elementary schools, 161,458; public secondary, 64,222; colleges and universities, 55,397. *Public school expenditures* (1990-91), $708,045,000.

ILLINOIS

Floods took a heavy toll in Illinois in 1993, while there was good economic news for the state from the federal government. Illinois was the scene of some unusual crimes during 1993, and politicians got an early start on the 1994 campaign.

Floods. The damage to Illinois' crops, land, and property from the 1993 Midwest floods was extensive. Little towns were wiped out. Thousands of persons fled their homes as the Mississippi and Illinois rivers overflowed their banks in floods that were among the worst in Illinois history. Among the flood casualties was Valmeyer, a town of 900 south of St. Louis. After the town was covered by 14 ft (4.3 m) of water, most residents moved to higher ground, leaving behind the skeletal remains of crumbling and rotting buildings.

Government assistance for property damage from the flood was estimated at $883 million, according to the Federal Emergency Management Agency (FEMA). The Insurance Information Institute estimated that insurance claims for

flood damage in Illinois would reach $655 million. Additionally, federal flood payouts of $2.5 billion were expected for crop losses. (*See also* FEATURE ARTICLE, page 44.)

Crime. Restaurant owners Richard and Lynn Ehlenfeldt and five of their employees were slain in Palatine, a suburb northwest of Chicago. Robbery was the apparent motive for the carnage in the fast-food chicken and pasta business on January 8. A task force of local and state police and the Federal Bureau of Investigation (FBI) was formed to investigate the slayings. Although a number of persons were identified as suspects, no one was charged in the mass killings.

Forensic pathologists took a new look at the mysterious deaths of children from sudden infant death syndrome (SIDS) after Gail Savage, 30, of Wauconda, was charged with killing her three babies by suffocating them with a blanket. Authorities at first believed the first baby death in 1990 was caused by SIDS. But subsequent deaths in 1992 and 1993 aroused their suspicion, because multiple SIDS deaths in the same family are extremely rare. An investigation concluded the babies could not have died of natural causes or any hereditary defects. Confronted with such information, Savage confessed she placed a blanket over the faces of her infants because they cried. A forensic pathologist in Lake county who conducted autopsies on the infants said it is impossible to distinguish between suffocation and SIDS.

Children were the subject of another Illinois crime in the "home alone" case. David and Sharon Schoo of Kane county took a nine-day vacation to Mexico in December 1992, leaving their daughters—Nicole, 9, and Diana, 4—home alone. The parents' arrests spawned national headlines and debate over the issue of child abandonment. The case was resolved when the parents were placed on probation after admitting to child neglect. State's Attorney David Akemann of Kane county said he was convinced the Schoos were guilty of more serious charges.

© AP/Wide World

Robert H. Michel, a member of the U.S. House of Representatives since 1957 and its Republican leader since December 1980, announced in 1993 that he would not seek reelection in 1994.

But he said a trial and jail sentence would have consumed tax dollars and time that better would be spent on violent criminals. The children were given up for adoption.

Military Bases. Illinois was a big winner in the battle to keep military bases open as President Bill Clinton and the Defense Base Closure and Realignment Commission selected the Great Lakes Naval Training Center in North Chicago as the U.S. navy's only recruit-training center. Existing boot camps in Orlando, FL, and San Diego, CA, would be moved to Illinois, bringing in thousands of new recruits and an estimated 9,000 jobs. The decision was heartening to Illinois officials because Great Lakes was on the list of bases considered for closure. It was estimated the Great Lakes expansion would infuse $450 billion annually into the economy of northeastern Illinois. (*See also* MILITARY AFFAIRS.)

Politics. U.S. Rep. Robert H. Michel, the Republican leader of the U.S. House of Representatives, announced plans to retire after the 1994 election. The 70-year-old Michel has served in the House for 19 terms, spending 13 years as minority leader. Eager to regain the governor's office after being shut out for 16 years, a threesome of prominent Democrats announced their candidacies for the party's 1994 gubernatorial primary. They were State Comptroller Roland Burris, the first black to run for the Illinois governorship; State Sen. Dawn Clark Netsch of Chicago, the first woman to seek the office; and Richard Phelan, president of the Cook County Board in Chicago. The winner of the primary was expected to face Gov. Jim Edgar (R).

ROBERT ENSTAD, *"Chicago Tribune"*

ILLINOIS • Information Highlights

Area: 56,345 sq mi (145 934 km²).

Population (July 1, 1992 est.): 11,631,000.

Chief Cities (1990 census): Springfield, the capital, 105,227; Chicago, 2,783,726; Rockford, 139,426.

Government (1993): *Chief Officers—governor,* Jim Edgar (R); lt. gov., Bob Kustra (R). *General Assembly—Senate,* 59 members; House of Representatives, 118 members.

State Finances (fiscal year 1991): *Revenue,* $25,092,000,000; *expenditure,* $24,619,000,000.

Personal Income (1992): $255,651,000,000; per capita, $21,980.

Labor Force (August 1993): *Civilian labor force,* 6,131,500; *unemployed,* 468,200 (7.6% of total force).

Education: *Enrollment* (fall 1991)—public elementary schools, 1,327,834; public secondary, 520,332; colleges and universities, 753,297. *Public school expenditures* (1990-91), $8,932,538,000.

INDIA

Early in 1993, India appeared a troubled country, plagued by persistent violence that followed the destruction of an ancient Muslim mosque in Ayodhya, Uttar Pradesh, in December 1992. Prime Minister P. V. Narasimha Rao's position was weakened by divisions within the ruling Congress Party and by electoral reverses in May and November. He managed to survive, however, and to press forward with his program of economic liberalization and reform. The economic picture was generally brighter than it had been for some years. Violence in Punjab ebbed significantly, but remained at high levels in Kashmir. India played an active role in foreign affairs throughout the year.

Politics. The government faced a new crisis in January as ten days of clashes in Bombay between Hindus and Muslims left at least 600 dead. In March bomb blasts killed some 250 persons in Bombay and 70 more in Calcutta. In order to provide stronger leadership in Maharashtra, where Bombay is located, and perhaps to get the leading rival of his party out of New Delhi, Prime Minister Rao sent Defense Minister Sharad Pawar to Maharashtra to resume his former post as chief minister. In a major reshuffling of his cabinet in January, the prime minister replaced 14 ministers and appointed a full-time external-affairs minister.

In March, at a meeting of the All India Congress Committee, Rao beat back a challenge from within the party by supporters of Arjun Singh, minister for human resources and development, and won a strong endorsement of his policies, particularly his economic-reform program. Meanwhile the major opposition party, the Bharatiya Janata Party (BJP), tried to capitalize on dissatisfaction with the Congress government and a rising tide of Hindu fundamentalism in the country and to broaden its agenda to a more moderate course. In a series of by-elections on May 19 for two Lok Sabha seats

and 16 state assembly seats in eight states, the BJP won almost as many seats as the Congress.

Rao's position was weakened further in June by an assertion of Harshad Mehta, the central figure in a financial scandal that was a nationwide sensation in 1992, that he had made an illegal donation of 10 million rupees (about $322,000) to Prime Minister Rao's campaign. Rao denied this allegation, and eventually the investigation of the charges against him were dropped; but many Indians remained convinced that he somehow was involved in the scandal. Soon thereafter, Rao survived a vote of no confidence in the Lok Sabha by a margin of only 14 votes. He could not have survived if he had not received support from former members of the Janata Dal, the second-most-important opposition party in the Lok Sabha.

After the Ayodhya crisis the Rao government had dismissed the governments in four major states where the BJP had been in power: Uttar Pradesh, Madhya Pradesh, Himachal Pradesh, and Rajasthan. In November state assembly elections were held in all four of these states and also in the state of Mizoram and the Union Territory of Delhi. The results reflected disillusionment with politicians generally. The BJP failed to regain control of any of these states, winning a majority only in the Delhi assembly. The Congress Party got a majority in Madhya Pradesh and Himachal Pradesh, and also did well in Rajasthan; but in Uttar Pradesh, India's most populous state, it nearly was decimated.

In one of the most hopeful developments of 1993, years of violence appeared to end in Punjab, after a decade in which some 25,000 people died. In May 1993 not a single civilian or security person was killed, compared with 340 fatalities in May 1992. The ebbing of the conflict between Punjabi (mostly Sikh) militants and security forces was due to a variety of factors, including firm measures by the Congress government of Punjab, headed by Beant Singh, and a decline in popular support of the militants. To a consider-

© AP/Wide World

As 1993 began, clashes between Hindus and Muslims were widespread in Bombay, India. Hundreds were killed in the riots. In a highly Muslim-populated downtown area of the city, left, Indian soldiers sought to impose a dawn-to-dusk curfew.

able degree the people were able to return to a relatively normal life. A peaceful by-election was held in Jalandhar for a seat in the national Lok Sabha, and was won by the Congress candidate.

No such improvement occurred in Kashmir, where hundreds of people were the victims of a continuing struggle between Kashmiri separatists and the sizable Indian Army and security forces stationed in that state. The situation escalated in October, when Indian security forces killed at least 40 Kashmiri protesters and laid siege to Srinagar's Hazratbal mosque, Kashmir's holiest Muslim shrine, where militants had taken refuge. The strong-arm measures of the Indian government and its failure to restore law and order in the Valley of Kashmir were criticized widely in international circles and were a major factor in exacerbating already tense relations between India and Pakistan.

The Economy. In late March 1993, the government released a survey of the economy. The report indicated that reforms begun during 1991 were beginning to bear fruit, despite the enormous financial scandal of 1992 and the political turmoil and sectarian violence that rocked the country after the destruction of the Muslim mosque in Ayodhya in late 1992. The government reported significant increases in agricultural production and a reduction in inflation from a high of more than 16% in 1991 to 7%. Growth in the gross domestic product (GDP) for fiscal year 1993-94 was projected at 4%.

The survey also pointed to weak spots in several sectors of the economy. Industrial production had increased by only 4%, about half of the expected amount. Exports had risen only by 3.4%, as a consequence of the worldwide recession and a drastic decline in exports to rupee-payment countries (mainly Russia), whereas imports had increased by 16.5%. The trade deficit was more than $6 billion by the end of fiscal year 1992-93. India had a dubious distinction as one of

the largest international debtors among the developing countries. Its external debt had risen to $72.7 billion, with further increases projected.

On February 27, Finance Minister Manmohan Singh presented the 1993-94 budget to the Indian Parliament. It reflected the government's determination to press forward with its economic-liberalization program and to integrate India more fully into the global economy. The finance minister announced that the rupee, which had been devalued several times in recent years, would be made fully convertible in the trade account and that sweeping cuts would be made in import and excise duties. The budget included increased expenditures for agricultural development, education, health, infrastructure, defense, and allocations for the eighth five-year plan (1992-97). The overall budget deficit was estimated to be 43 billion rupees (about $1.4 billion), compared with 72 billion rupees (about $2.3 billion) in fiscal year 1992-93.

The budget was greeted with some praise in India and abroad. International lending agencies, notably the World Bank; its soft-loan affiliate, the International Finance Association; and the Asian Development Bank offered some optimism about India's economic prospects, but they also noted that much depended on the implementation of current policy and on further economic reforms. Within India there was considerable criticism from opposition parties, but less than had been expected, and from those who felt that the proposed cuts would affect them adversely. Many Indians also objected to India's alleged subservience to foreign lending agencies, the United States, and other major donors. In midyear the trade deficit was reduced by record growth in exports in the first four months of fiscal year 1993-94. The trade deficit for the first five months of the fiscal year shrunk to about 10% of its level in the corresponding period of the 1992-93 fiscal year.

By summer there were many other signs that the growth rate in 1993-94 was likely to be around 4.5%. In September the International Monetary Fund, in a generally positive report on India's economic achievements and prospects, urged the Indian government to step up its liberalization program in key areas of the economy. The economic reforms continued, but at a slower pace.

Foreign collaboration, joint ventures, and direct foreign investment increased significantly in 1993, particularly in high-technology fields. The United States, India's major trading partner, accounted for much of the foreign investment. While the investment trend was encouraging, India received a total of only $380 million in foreign investment in two and a half years.

In late December a long-awaited parliamentary report on the securities scandal led to the resignation of the finance minister—an action that was rejected by the prime minister.

Foreign Affairs. In its external relations, India was handicapped by internal instability and by

---

INDIA • Information Highlights

Official Name: Republic of India.

Location: South Asia.

Area: 1,269,340 sq mi (3 287 590 km²).

Population (mid-1993 est.): 897,400,000.

Chief Cities (1991 census): New Delhi, the capital, 301,297; Bombay, 9,925,891; Calcutta, 4,399,819.

Government: *Head of state,* Shankar Dayal Sharma, president (elected July 1992). *Head of government,* P. V. Narasimha Rao, prime minister (sworn in June 21, 1991). *Legislature*—Parliament: Rajya Sabha (Council of States) and Lok Sabha (House of the People).

Monetary Unit: Rupee (31.034 rupees equal U.S.$1, official rate, Dec. 1, 1993).

Gross Domestic Product (1992 est. U.S.$): $328,000,000,000.

Economic Indexes: *Consumer Prices* (1992, 1980 = 100), all items, 299.6; food, 307.9. *Industrial Production* (1991, 1980 = 100), 212.

Foreign Trade (1992 U.S.$): *Imports,* $23,255,000,000; *exports,* $17,908,000,000.

its difficult relations with most of its neighbors, especially Pakistan. Tensions with Pakistan increased during the year. India accused its neighbor of assisting militants and separatists in the Indian-held portion of Kashmir and of continuing its efforts to internationalize the Kashmir dispute. Indians were indignant because Pakistan's representatives attempted to raise the Kashmir question in various international and regional associations, including the General Assembly of the United Nations (UN), the Commonwealth summit, and the summit meeting of the South Asian Association for Regional Cooperation (SAARC) in Dhaka, Bangladesh.

The Dhaka summit was postponed twice because Prime Minister Rao was absorbed in crises arising from the aftermath of the Ayodhya affair. At this summit, which ended with the approval of the Dhaka Declaration and the signing of a preferential trade agreement, India's prime minister became the new chairman of SAARC.

Rao also showed his interest in developing closer and more cooperative relations with other Asian nations. During the year he made official visits to Thailand, Iran, four Central Asian republics of the former Soviet Union, China, and South Korea. His visit to China was significant in view of the strained relations between the two Asian giants since 1959. This standoff ended with an important agreement regarding a long-festering border dispute. The two nations committed themselves to a mutual reduction of troops along their disputed border and to a peaceful resolution of their boundary dispute.

India was the object of sharp criticism at the UN World Conference on Human Rights in Vienna in June; but its delegation, led by Finance Minister Singh, ably defended India's human-rights record. Its claims were strengthened by acknowledgments by several international human-rights organizations that the Indian record had improved substantially, although much greater improvement was needed. In September the Indian government—in a decision that was criticized widely in India—announced that it would send some 4,600 troops as part of the UN peacekeeping force in Somalia.

Indian-U.S. relations remained officially good, but were subject to many strains. Indians were irritated in April when U.S. Trade Representative Mickey Kantor put India back on the Special 301 trade hit list for alleged failure to protect intellectual-property rights. Indians blamed U.S. pressures on Russia for the decision of the latter country to back off from a deal to transfer cryogenic rocket equipment and technology to India, and they seemed to resent U.S. pressure on India to adhere to the Nuclear Non-Proliferation Treaty and to improve relations with Pakistan. Indians were pleased with the nomination of former Congressman Stephen Solarz, a staunch friend of India, to succeed Thomas Pickering as the U.S. ambassador to India.

Among the distinguished visitors to India during the year were Britain's Prime Minister John Major, Russia's President Boris Yeltsin, Spain's Prime Minister Felipe González Márquez, German Chancellor Helmut Kohl, Ireland's President Mary Robinson, and King Carl XVI Gustaf and Queen Silvia of Sweden. Of special interest was the official visit of Israel's Foreign Minister Shimon Peres in May—the first such visit by a leading Israeli official.

Natural Disasters. During the summer of 1993, floods caused heavy loss of life and destruction of property in nearly half of India, from Assam in the northeast to Gujarat in the west. More than 1,200 Indians perished by drowning or flood-related diseases. The floods brought devastation to areas inhabited by more than 30 million people. The worst-affected area was Punjab, where more then 300 people lost their lives and hundreds of acres of rich farmland were submerged. Floods are annual occurrences in India, but the 1993 floods were among the worst that the country ever had experienced.

On September 30 the worst earthquake in more than 50 years brought devastation to large areas of southwest and south India. At least 35 villages in the southern part of the state of Maharashtra were destroyed. The southern states of Karnataka, Andhra Pradesh, and Tamil Nadu also were affected seriously. Original estimates of the dead varied from 30,000 to 60,000 persons, but later estimates reported that the casualties neared 10,000. Many thousands were injured, and some 130,000 were left homeless. Assistance to the living victims of the quake was promptly forthcoming from official and unofficial agencies in other countries, international relief agencies, the government of India and many of the Indian states, and Pakistan, Bangladesh, and other South Asian nations. The UN acted as the coordinator for much of the international relief effort.

NORMAN D. PALMER
Professor Emeritus, University of Pennsylvania

INDIANA

Debates over the budget, taxes, and gambling marked 1993 in Indiana.

State Budget. Indiana's state government nearly came to a halt in June when Senate Republicans engaged in an acrimonious budget battle with Democratic Gov. Evan Bayh and the Democratically controlled house. The regular session of the state legislature had ended on April 29 without a two-year state budget being enacted. The central point of contention was taxes. Governor Bayh contended that rising Medicaid costs and his proposed 4% increase in spending on education in each of the next two years required new revenues that he thought could be raised through an 18-cent-per-pack increase in the cigarette tax and revenues from

the legalization of riverboat gambling on the Ohio River and Lake Michigan.

When a special legislative session in June deadlocked over the budget issue, college-student loans were held up, layoff notices for state employees were prepared, and state universities scrambled to find ways of staying open if the impasse was not broken by midnight June 30, when the old budget ended. The legislative drama heightened in the Senate on June 16 when Lt. Gov. Frank O'Bannon (D) called a recess in the middle of a vote on a Democratic compromise that Republicans were about to defeat in order to allow the administration to lobby some Republican senators. After 40 hours, Republican Senate President Pro Tempore Robert Garton wrested control of the Senate gavel from Lieutenant Governor O'Bannon and ended the recess in a move of uncertain legality. Finally, only hours before state government had to shut down, a Republican compromise budget backed by House Democrats was passed and then repassed over Governor Bayh's veto. The new budget rejected the cigarette tax, but it did retain the legalizing of riverboat gambling, subject to local approval.

Gambling. In November several counties along the Ohio River and two counties and two cities on Lake Michigan held referendums on whether to allow gambling. In Evansville, the state's third-largest city, the pro-gambling forces had the open or tacit support of most political and civic leaders and a preelection media blitz funded mainly by casino corporations. The

---

INDIANA • Information Highlights

Area: 36,185 sq mi (93 720 km²).
Population (July 1, 1992 est.): 5,662,000.
Chief Cities (1990 census): Indianapolis, the capital, 741,952; Fort Wayne, 173,072; Evansville, 126,272.
Government (1993): *Chief Officers*—governor, Evan Bayh (D); lt. gov., Frank L. O'Bannon (D). *General Assembly*—Senate, 50 members; House of Representatives, 100 members.
State Finances (fiscal year 1991): *Revenue*, $12,288,000,000; *expenditure*, $11,548,000,000.
Personal Income (1992): $104,204,000,000; per capita, $18,405.
Labor Force (August 1993): *Civilian labor* force, 3,001,100; *unemployed*, 129,800 (4.3% of total force).
Education: *Enrollment* (fall 1991)—public elementary schools, 676,487; public secondary, 280,507; colleges and universities, 290,301. *Public school expenditures* (1990-91), $4,379,142,000.

---

opponents of gambling, led by a number of churches, mounted a grassroots, door-to-door effort. In the end the pro-gambling forces won, but with only 51.8% of the vote. In the rest of the state, four counties and two cities voted for gambling, while four counties voted against it.

Economy. Overall, 1993 was a good year for Indiana farmers. Crop estimates as of October 1 indicated that soybean production would be up 18% from 1992 due to more acres planted and an all-time record average per acre yield of 47 bushels. Wheat production was up 55% over

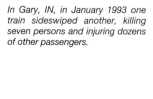

In Gary, IN, in January 1993 one train sideswiped another, killing seven persons and injuring dozens of other passengers.

© AP/Wide World

1992's disease-reduced crop, while corn production was down 17% due to fewer acres planted and the previous year's record yields.

Other good economic news included a federal study that showed that the average income of Hoosiers in 1992 was $18,405, an increase over the 1990 mean of $16,814, and that 57 of 92 counties had real personal-income gains between 1986 and 1991. Indiana's unemployment rate of 6.5% in 1992 was below the national average of 7.4%. The unemployment average for the first seven months of 1993 dropped further and was 5.9%.

Other News. Two commuter trains heading in opposite directions crashed in Gary in January, killing seven persons and injuring dozens of others....In the town of Huntington, citizens established a museum commemorating native son and former Vice-President Dan Quayle.

THOMAS E. RODGERS
University of Southern Indiana

INDONESIA

Indonesia's President Suharto was elected to his sixth uncontested term of office during 1993 in a nation buoyed by a long period of substantial economic growth.

Domestic Politics. On March 10, 1993, President Suharto was elected unanimously to a five-year term as president. Suharto, who led the military in crushing a communist coup in 1965, replaced President Sukarno in 1967 and was elected president in 1968. Voting for the presidency was done by the 1,000-member People's Consultative Assembly (MPR), which is composed of the 500 legislators of the House of Representatives and 500 presidential appointees. It was dominated by the government's political party, Golkar, and the armed forces. However, well before the MPR session, the Muslim-based Development Unity Party and the Christian-secular Indonesian Democratic Party had endorsed the president.

INDONESIA • Information Highlights

Official Name: Republic of Indonesia.
Location: Southeast Asia.
Area: 741,097 sq mi (1 919 440 km²).
Population (mid-1993 est.): 187,600,000.
Chief Cities (1990 census): Jakarta, the capital, 8,227,746; Surabaya, 2,473,272; Bandung, 2,058,122; Medan, 1,730,052.
Government: *Head of state and government*, Suharto, president (took office for sixth five-year term March 1993). *Legislature* (unicameral)—House of Representatives.
Monetary Unit: Rupiah (2,102.03 rupiahs equal U.S.$1, Dec. 1, 1993).
Gross Domestic Product (1991 est. U.S.$): $122,000,000,000.
Economic Index (1992): *Consumer Prices* (1988-89 = 100), all items, 132.2; food, 127.4.
Foreign Trade (1990 U.S.$): *Imports*, $21,837,000,000; *exports*, $25,675,000,000.

Expectations that this would be the 71-year-old Suharto's last term focused attention on the choice of a vice-president. That office went to 57-year-old Gen. Try Sutrisno, newly retired as the head of Indonesia's military and a Muslim. This designation positioned General Try as the leading contender to succeed Suharto in 1998.

With his office secure, President Suharto made efforts later in the year to initiate a reconciliation process with domestic political opponents, particularly the retired military critics of the regime in the "Petition 50" group. This opening was symbolized by the invitation to tea extended by the president to retired military chief Gen. Abdul Haris Nasution.

Economy. The World Bank continued to find Indonesia's economic performance impressive. This opinion was shared by its assistance donors who, meeting in Paris on June 30, pledged a record $5.1 billion in foreign aid for the year. A new deregulation package unveiled during the year was designed to stimulate already burgeoning non-oil exports and enhance the competitiveness of domestic industries. Some initial concern was expressed about the composition of the economic team in the new cabinet, as Muslims linked to the economic nationalism of the politically powerful technology minister B. J. Habibie displaced senior Christian ministers. Suharto's naming of some of the former ministers as special presidential advisers was seen as a reassuring sign that no radical changes in economic policy were envisioned.

Foreign Affairs. Human-rights issues continue to affect Indonesia's relations with Western liberal democracies. The situation led to a cooling of Indonesian relations with the United States. The status of East Timor—a former Portuguese colony that was recovered by Indonesia in 1975—was the center of U.S. concerns. Congressional concern about Indonesia's human-rights record in the province led to a suspension of U.S. military-training aid to Indonesia and the prohibition of the transfer of four used U.S.-built F-5 aircraft from Jordan to Indonesia. A wider array of sanctions was on the congressional agenda. Indonesian Foreign Minister Ali Alatas expressly rejected "conditionalities" on aid of a political character, warning that the impact on U.S.-Indonesian relations would go beyond the military-aid relationship.

U.S.-Indonesian ties were strained further by the U.S. investigation of workers' rights in Indonesia. Complaints by human-rights groups and U.S. labor unions had led to a U.S. government review. U.S. Trade Representative Mickey Kantor set a February 1994 deadline for an improvement in Indonesian practices, after which Indonesia would face the curtailment of trade concessions granted under the Generalized System of Preferences (GSP). GSP covered about 14% of Indonesia's exports to the United States.

DONALD E. WEATHERBEE
University of South Carolina

INDUSTRIAL PRODUCTION

Paced by strength in business equipment throughout much of the year, and a closing surge in motor vehicles and parts, U.S. industrial production grew faster in 1993 than that of other large industrial nations, several of which still were mired in recession.

Productivity Growth. After the economy weathered midspring weakness, the Federal Reserve reported seven straight months of rising output, the strongest of them coming as the year ended, when new-car models and the strongest sales of the year convinced wary automakers to raise output, helping to offset a steady decline in defense industries.

A rebound in manufacturing, which accounted for 85% of industrial output and which had languished through the summer months, was accompanied by what once was considered an anomaly, a steady decline in employment. Between February and October that sector of the economy lost nearly 250,000 jobs, reducing the total to 17.7 million workers, 697,000 fewer than in 1991. Growth in productivity, roughly translatable to output per man-hour, provided the explanation. From 1988 through 1992, productivity had grown at no more than 1.5% annually, and it actually had declined in 1991. With the exceptions of April, May, and July, it grew at 4% or better in every month of 1993, thanks to restraint in pay increases; improved technology; better management; and workers who seemed more dedicated, skilled, and better trained.

The production improvements were in contrast to those of other large industrial nations. While Canada's production also rose at a healthy rate, and that of Great Britain improved to a lesser degree, the economies of Japan, France, Germany, and Italy were less fortunate. All of those nations suffered production declines, the worst of them being in Germany and in Japan, where production fell to its lowest levels since 1989. Some industry analysts said it made the gains in the United States more meaningful, since they came without any significant rise in merchandise exports.

Still, the gains failed to eliminate the fears of doubters. There were many, their numbers supported over the past couple of years by the economy's fits, starts, and blips that had raised hopes and then dashed them. The statistic they eyed now referred to capacity utilization. By November 1993 it had risen to 83% from 80.8% a year earlier, approaching the 85% level at which economists traditionally began to fear inflation. Others maintained, however, that with the economy more global now than it had been when that inflation-fear level was set, and especially with plentiful unused capacity abroad, such fears were exaggerated.

Economic Changes. Reports from the Commerce Department and the Federal Reserve documented indisputably the vast economic changes that newspapers bannered and radio and television aired every evening. The biggest of these was the transition from the military-defense posture of the late and unlamented Cold War to one that relied far less on machinery and more on electronic surveillance and communications.

So-called national-defense purchases, which had fallen more than $8 billion in 1992, fell even more sharply in 1993, by $11 billion to just more than $303 billion as the year ended. The sharpest declines were in military equipment, with expenditures down to an annual rate of $64 billion from more than $73 billion in 1992. The cutbacks included spending on aircraft—to $20.7 billion from $22.7 billion, missiles—to $11.3 billion from $14.3 billion, and ships—to an annual rate late in the year of $10.5 billion from $12.1 billion in 1992.

In contrast, spending for military-electronics equipment rose to $6.6 billion from $6.3 billion.

With the future in mind, GM electric cars are produced at the company's Tech Center in Warren, MI. Overall the U.S. auto industry enjoyed an excellent year in 1993.

The cuts, after years of acute military alertness, caused serious disruptions in many states, especially on the East and West coasts. Reflecting this, California actually had an outflow of workers and its economy remained in the doldrums even as other areas recovered.

Since many airlines were experiencing difficulties at the same time, restraining them from new-equipment purchases, the impact on the aircraft industry and its suppliers was especially harsh. The immediate impact of the change to a more peacetime economy was painful, and the comments of Frank Shrontz, chairman of the Boeing Co., probably applied also to the other big manufacturers, McDonnell Douglas and Lockheed: "We are going to be very prudent about hiring back people and will be trying to make up some of that increased requirement in efficiency," he said. He added that it was too early to tell whether Boeing and four European partners would launch a "superjumbo" jet seating up to 800 passengers.

Automotive Rebound. The U.S. automotive industry was in far healthier condition, having gone through a transition of its own during the previous decade, during which outmoded facilities were closed and newer plants were equipped with the latest technological advances, particularly in the areas of computerization and electronic monitoring. As a result, the industry's design, production, and service facilities were in much better shape than before. Output for the model year, which ended September 30, soared more than $18 billion to a total of $200.6 billion. Commerce Department figures showed a 4% gain to $119.6 billion for cars and a 20% jump to $81 billion in truck production. New motor-vehicle sales rose to 13,981,000 units from 12,871,000 a year earlier. Significantly, domestic automakers improved their market share against Japanese imports; in all, imports fell to 2,011,000 units in the model year from 2,140,000 a year earlier.

Information-Processing Advance. Equally impressive was the production of information-processing and related office and computing machines. All industry, commerce, households, and educational institutions found themselves in a blossoming information age, which until recently had been referred to more often in the future tense. Hardly an institution of any sort existed that could not benefit from (and perhaps not survive without) the new technology and concepts. Computers and various products of electronic surveillance monitored the engine performance of new cars, tracked mail and cargo shipments, changed teaching methods, and brought libraries into homes. The newest computers were designed and wired to receive the products of a growing electronic information highway. Vice-President Albert Gore likened the developing and integrating cable, radio, and telephone systems to the building decades before of the nation's interstate-highway system. While corporations did the building, products and concepts to be utilized by the system often originated in creative small enterprises and even in the home offices of individuals.

Developments were reflected in the official industrial-production indices. While the Commerce Department reported in November that overall production reached an index of 112.2 in October—meaning it was 12.2% higher than the 100% base-measuring year of 1987—information-processing equipment soared to 162.6, compared with 134.6 for 1992. The real highflier, however, was in the "office and computing machines" category, which leaped from an already high 168 in 1992 to 242 as the year neared an end, an astonishing gain that documented the huge change gathering momentum in the industrial United States.

While most of the new-age items were practical products essential for business and personal use, some of the most imaginative were designed for an experimental fringe of the market and for entertainment and amusement. Wrist telephones could be purchased for $1,000, and a handheld computer/organizer with built-in databases and the ability to tap into regular computers could be had for the same price. Sports fans could buy for slightly less a pair of glasses with a built-in TV, making it possible to watch the football game while raking the leaves. Some products were utterly frivolous, and amid the proliferation there were many destined inevitably for the scrap heap. Useful or not, they pointed to a world in the making of which 1993 was probably only the experimental beginning. It was a harshly competitive world; despite demand, profits of computer makers were poor.

INDUSTRIAL PRODUCTION

Major Industrial Countries
1987 = 100 (seasonally adjusted)

	Canada	France	Germany	Great Britain	Italy	Japan	United States
1987	100.0	100.0	100.0	100.0	100.0	100.0	100.0
1988	105.3	104.6	103.9	104.8	105.9	109.3	104.4
1989	105.2	108.8	108.8	107.0	109.2	115.9	106.0
1990	101.8	110.9	114.1	106.7	109.4	121.4	106.0
1991	98.1	111.2	117.4	102.5	107.1	123.7	104.1
1992[p]	98.5	110.0	116.0	102.0	106.5	116.5	106.5
1993[*]	102.6	107.2	106.2	105.3	103.4	111.9	110.8

[p] preliminary
[*] July estimate
Source: National data as reported by Department of Commerce.

Construction and Other Industries. While newer industries proliferated, some traditional ones did well too. Commercial and industrial construction remained weak, a result of vast overbuilding during the 1980s, but home building rebounded. It was largely responsible for bringing total new expenditures above $500 billion for the year, compared with $436 billion in 1992 and only slightly more than $400 billion in 1991. The pace of new private housing ran at close to 1.4 million units as the year ended, the best year since 1988. More than 1.25 million units were one-family homes; multifamily construction, especially of apartment houses, showed little or no sign of emerging from the depths.

The lumber and lumber-products industry and the furniture industry responded to the housing improvement, with both showing production gains for the year. Iron and steel production showed slight gains, but electrical-machinery output grew strongly. Though weak early in the year, construction supplies picked up as the year ended. Metal mining, which had fared better than most industries since the late 1980s, showed small gains. Coal production remained about the same as in the year before, but crude oil and natural gas showed slight increases. Gas and electric utilities grew in harmony with the economy. Chemicals, rubber and plastics, paper, leather, and the products made from them strengthened over 1992, although the leather category still had not regained its levels of the late 1980s.

There was little mystery to why certain industries fared poorly. Under continued warnings of health problems associated with smoking, tobacco products, which had gained in 1992, fell well below their 1987 benchmark. Printing and publishing weakened in spite of an enormous diversity of magazines and specialty publications, a result primarily of declines in the newspaper industry and inroads into communications by the new electronic media. And apparel products lost some of their market share to imports from the lower-wage nations of Asia and Latin America.

Overall, however, U.S. industry stood out in 1993 not only for its gains but for the promise that was indicated for the future. The self-imposed austerity of the previous few years, and the technological creativity and efficiency forced upon it by competition and recession, seemed to be paying off.

JOHN CUNNIFF
The Associated Press

INSURANCE, LIABILITY

For the second year in a row, devastating natural and man-made disasters struck various parts of the United States, causing billions of dollars in damages that translated into claims paid by property casualty insurance companies. Beginning with a blizzard that struck the Eastern seaboard early in the year, the string of disasters included the bombing of New York City's World Trade Center, a series of unusually severe tornadoes and hailstorms in the Midwest, and the flooding in nine Midwestern states that drove thousands of people from their farms and homes (*see* FEATURE ARTICLE, page 44).

These disasters alone cost the insurance industry more than $5 billion in losses. Then, in November a series of fires in southern California swept 152,000 acres (61 538 ha) and destroyed more than 720 buildings, adding an estimated $250 million to the industry's losses. The high claims figure for 1993 came just one year after the industry's biggest losses ever—$22 billion—related to the Los Angeles riots as well as to extensive property damage caused by natural disasters, including Hurricane Andrew's sweep through south Florida.

Despite the soaring losses, the liability-insurance industry remained not only solvent but so well capitalized that insurance rates in most parts of the country did not rise dramatically in 1993. The reason for the industry's financial strength lay in the investment side of the business, which profited from falling interest rates. By selling off $250 billion worth of bonds in 1992, the industry reaped $9 billion in capital gains, a windfall that went far toward offsetting its underwriting losses. Meanwhile the Travelers Corporation agreed in September to merge with Primerica Corporation, forming one of the largest and most diverse financial companies in the United States.

Congressional Action. The insurance industry came under heavy criticism in 1993 in Congress, which offered up, but failed to act upon, several bills aimed at addressing allegedly unethical business practices. Bolstered by support from the Bill Clinton administration, lawmakers introduced a bill to reduce the industry's immunity from antitrust law, which consumer advocates long had charged enabled insurers to fix prices. Two separate bills were aimed at determining whether insurance companies "redline" minority neighborhoods, denying coverage to business and home owners in these areas because of the racial makeup of local residents.

The industry stood to gain, meanwhile, from a product-liability measure that was approved by the Senate Commerce Committee in November. The measure, similar to one the committee had defeated narrowly in 1992, would provide greater protection from lawsuits for manufacturers and the distributors of their products, as well as their insurers. The measure would allow federal courts to penalize a plaintiff who refuses to settle a lawsuit and later loses the case when it goes to trial. The bill also fully would protect defendants from liability in cases where the plaintiff was under the influence of alcohol or drugs at the time of an accident and was mostly responsible for it.

MARY H. COOPER
"The CQ [Congressional Quarterly] Researcher"

INTERIOR DESIGN

Harmony with nature, individuality, and furniture with a simple elegance summed up interior-design trends in 1993.

Styles. Traditional met contemporary in several influential new furniture collections. Classic, stately forms were stripped of embellishment, lightened in color, and softened in texture or finish. By this transformation, once-formal period styles gained a livability and freshness more fitting for today's casual lifestyles. Notable among neoclassic-influenced collections were Lane's Gear Collection by Raymond Waites and Classic Statements by Drexel Heritage, with its pale maple veneers and solids. Traditional 18th- and 19th-century European forms gained fresh interpretation by a trip to the Caribbean in Colonial West Indies-inspired collections like the West Indies-Whim Museum Collection from Milling Road and the Mark Hampton Collection for Hickory Chair.

The year also brought Mission, Shaker, and country looks, nearly all in light-stain woods. The American Tapestry Collection from Lineage was inspired by American country antiques.

Colors. Nature continued to inspire color trends in 1993. Soft earth shades from pale beige to bark brown reflected the yearning for a natural environment. Western styles, still in evidence, took their browns from saddle-leather tones. Green was also strong, with forest colors prevailing. Neutrals were a favorite.

Blues appeared in sea and sky shades, as well as the captivating blue hue of the fabrics of Provence. Yellow tended toward raffia, summer straw, and light sisal tones. Reds arrived in soft seashell hues to vibrant floral pink tones, also turning up in the deep spectrum of winestain and loganberry.

Fabrics and Accessories. Upholstery manufacturers turned to apparel leaders and found a new casual look. Sherrill's Ruff Hewn collection and Bernhardt's Ready-to-Wear boutique typified the trend. Soft washed denim—along with flannel, corduroy, and twill—made the transition from relaxed clothing to relaxed sofa and chair silhouettes. In prints, animal and mosaic patterns, muted awning or tailored stripes, paisleys with plaids, and tea-stained florals predominated. Silver and gold sparked a new Gilded Age in accessory line introductions, making a distinctive contrast to the natural colors and textures prevalent elsewhere.

Furniture. Wood mixed with iron continued to be popular. In a sign of the trend toward harmony with nature, some occasional furniture was made of twig or stone. Contemporary wicker designs were an attractive way to update country or Colonial furniture.

Colors and finishes included distressed painted finishes as well as tortoiseshell, verdigris, and rust. Lighter stains added appeal to the golden-toned mahogany in the West Indies-Whim Museum Collection at Milling Road and Stickely's Mission furniture. Woven raffia added surface interest to Lane's Gear group.

Floor Coverings. Tibetan rugs—including some with African-influenced patterns—offered new excitement. Computer-generated needlepoints continued their development at Michaelian & Kohlberg. Fresh looks for sisal included with tapestry trimming and cotton interweaving. Deeply textured medieval-style matting also offered an attractive alternative.

CARLA BREER HOWARD, *"Traditional Home"*

Interior design in 1993 saw Milling Road, a division of Baker Furniture, introduce the West Indies-Whim Museum Collection, featuring mahogany pieces that were hand-sawed and cured in the sun.

INTERNATIONAL TRADE AND FINANCE

For much of the world, the hard economic times began to fade in 1993. Moreover, ratification of the North American Free Trade Agreement (NAFTA) and successful completion of the Uruguay Round of talks by the General Agreement on Tariffs and Trade (GATT) augured well for future economic growth.

Signs of Economic Recovery. The United States' economic recovery, after a slow first half, picked up speed. With Britain in the vanguard, Europe probably began its march back from recession in the summer. Canada's economy grew at a moderate rate, about 2.7%.

Japan's prolonged slump, however, dragged on, with retail sales falling for the 17th consecutive month in October. Moreover, a pileup of bad loans at commercial banks prompted a sharp downturn in stocks. In late November and December prices on the Tokyo Stock Exchange plunged to their lowest level of the year.

In the rest of Asia rapid growth prevailed. China was in an inflationary boom. For five months the government talked of austerity, but after a meeting of the Communist Party Central Committee in November that talk faded. Growth in total national output in 1993 was estimated at an astonishing 13%. Inflation was running at about 21%. China's trade deficit was expected to amount to $10 billion, compared with a $4 billion surplus in 1992. By the end of September foreign companies already had signed an enormous $83 billion in contracts with Chinese entities.

The newly industrializing nations of Asia—Singapore, Thailand, Hong Kong, Taiwan, and Malaysia—grew at an average real rate of approximately 8.7% in 1993, far above the 2.2% anticipated by the International Monetary Fund (IMF) for the world and the 1.1% it predicted for the industrial countries. The IMF expected unemployment in 1993 in these industrial countries to reach 32 million, 3 million more than in the severe 1982 recession.

With such slow growth, inflation in the industrial countries decreased. This trend was helped by the failure of the Organization of the Petroleum Exporting Countries (OPEC) to reach agreement on lower production quotas. As a result, by late November crude oil prices had declined 20% for the year.

Protectionist Fears Fade. Ratification toward the end of the year of NAFTA by the U.S. Congress and Mexico's National Congress, with Canada's assent, caused a great sigh of relief among free-trade enthusiasts (*see* SPECIAL REPORT, page 286). Approval paved the way for conclusion in December of the 116-nation Uruguay Round of world-trade-liberalization talks under the auspices of the Geneva-based GATT, after some seven years of tough negotiations and crises. At the 11th hour, European Union (EU)—formerly the European Community (EC)—and French officials finally agreed with U.S. officials on farm issues; this probably was the stickiest item in the broad GATT agenda. A dispute over restrictions on the distribution of U.S. films in the EU was left unresolved by agreement. Also, Japan and the United States agreed on a plan to open Japan's market to rice imports.

World Trade. Success in the GATT round would produce important gains for the world. A study by the World Bank and the Organization for Economic Cooperation and Development estimated that it would add $220 billion to the economies of the seven major industrial nations (the Group of Seven)—the United States, Canada, Britain, France, Italy, Germany, and Japan—in the next decade.

According to the IMF, the value of world merchandise trade, measured in U.S. dollars, grew about 7% in 1992, the latest data year available. That was well above the previous year's 4% gain. The economic malaise in 1993 may have muted world trade, at least compared with the vigorous 13.5% annual gains recorded in 1986-90. In real terms, world trade grew 4.5% in 1992 to $3.7 trillion, the GATT estimated. Commercial services amounted to another $960 million.

Asia-Pacific Economic Cooperation (APEC). On November 20, President Bill Clinton met with 14 Asian-Pacific leaders on Blake Island near Seattle, WA. Clinton spoke of an "Asian-Pacific community" that would play "an increasingly vital role for our nation and the world" by working together to expand trade, lower tariffs, and create new high-tech jobs. The group of leaders announced they would be willing to reduce or eliminate tariffs on a number of industrial and agricultural goods as part of the overall Uruguay Round. The decision by APEC, a four-year-old body, was modeled on a similar one made the previous July by the EC, Japan, Canada, and the United States. The two agreements together covered about $250 billion in trade, or about 5% of world trade in goods and services. U.S. exports in 1992 to the Asian members of APEC (Brunei, China, Taiwan, Hong Kong, Indonesia, Japan, South Korea, Malaysia, Philippines, Singapore, and Thailand) amounted to about $128 billion, while imports were $215 billion. These were substantially greater than the $95 billion in U.S. exports and $111 billion in imports with the EC in the same year.

World Stock Prices. Most investors in the major stock markets enjoyed husky gains in 1993. The Dow Jones index for the entire world was up 18.24%, and 25.77% excluding the United States in U.S. dollar terms. Asian and Pacific markets, excluding Japan, had risen a hefty 89.16%. Even the sputtering Japanese stock market had risen 18.82%. The 14 European stock markets were up an average 22.41%, according to the Dow Jones World Stock Index. Germany, Switzerland, Sweden, Denmark, Norway, the Netherlands, and Spain had climbed

21% to 32%. Canadian shares had risen 15.71%. U.S. stocks were up 28.90%. As U.S. stock indexes kept breaking records, concern rose about whether stocks were overpriced.

The Former Soviet Bloc. With considerable fanfare, the Group of Seven (G-7) foreign and finance ministers, meeting in Tokyo April 15, offered Russia $28.4 billion in aid. It was the first such meeting ever called to discuss a single issue, coming two weeks after President Clinton's summit with Russian President Boris Yeltsin, when the United States promised $1.6 billion. Most of the $28.4 billion consisted of loans and credits. It was intended to stem inflation, running about 20% per month, and help with the transition to a market economy. The money was to come from the World Bank, International Monetary Fund (IMF), and the European Bank for Reconstruction and Development—not from the budgets of the G-7 members. Another $15 billion of Russian debts were to be rescheduled.

In June the IMF did make a $1.5 billion loan to Russia. The World Bank provided $600 million for "rehabilitation." But further loans were held up until Russia could get its economic reforms back on track, IMF Managing Director Michel Camdessus said before his multilateral agency's annual meeting in Washington in late September. By then Russia's inflation was running 30% per month. President Clinton signed a bill on September 30 providing $2.5 billion in economic and technical aid to Russia and other former republics of the Soviet Union. He and the Congress had acted with unusual speed on the legislation to give a boost to Russian President Yeltsin, then facing a serious clash with the Russian parliament.

On October 4 troops and tanks loyal to Yeltsin crushed an armed uprising by his opponents with an assault on the Parliament building. That victory not only greatly enhanced Yeltsin's political power, but gave him control of the central bank. Under the direction of parliament, the bank had been making massive and inflationary grants of credit to state enterprises. Behind the scenes, Russia's Committee for the Management of State Property was dismantling communism at a rapid pace. By November one third of Russian industry had been privatized—a pace which would complete the job in a year or two. A slower pace of economic transformation nevertheless appeared inevitable after right-wing gains in parliamentary elections in December.

In Eastern Europe real growth in output for the year ending Dec. 31, 1992, ranged from 5% in Poland (the best in Europe) to minus 7.1% in Slovakia and minus 5.1% in Romania, according to estimates of PlanEcon Europe. Albania grew 3% and Hungary 1.7%. Bulgaria slipped 4.6% and the Czech Republic 1.6%. Germany's economic slump, the divorce between the Czech and Slovak republics, and the civil war in former Yugoslavia were a drag on these postcommunist nations.

Germany. German reunification continued to be expensive. Bonn transferred about $120 bil-lion to the former East Germany, about two thirds of it in welfare and jobless benefits. Unemployment was near 50% in some areas in the eastern states. East German output grew about 7% to 8% in real terms in 1993, a rate insufficient to bring the region's productivity near that of western Germany in any short span of years. Many citizens in the former West Germany resented these costs. For them, they meant more taxes and an effort by the Bundesbank to restrain inflation with high interest rates. As the recession in western Germany became clear, the Bundesbank brought down interest rates gradually throughout 1993. But in real terms the economy shrank 2%. Economists were concerned about high costs in the nation's industry.

Group of Seven Economic Summit. Meeting in Tokyo on July 6-9, the leaders of the seven major industrial democracies agreed to provide $3 billion in additional aid to Russia and pledged to push for economic growth and lower trade barriers. The $3 billion in loans, grants, and export credits, however, was mostly a reallocation of funds previously committed, and was to be made available over 18 months. The money was to be directed more precisely toward putting state-owned companies into private hands. There was no other major economic accomplishment.

Developing-Country Debt. At the annual meeting of the IMF and World Bank in late September in Washington, various proposals to end the developing-country debt crisis were considered. But little in the way of solutions for the debtors was found. These debts stood at a record $1.5 trillion. But a United Nations report in September noted: "The international financial system is no longer in danger."

Latin American debtors had improved their situation significantly, with foreign investors returning to Argentina, Mexico, and Chile. The debt remained primarily a problem for Africa south of the Sahara, with nearly one third of the debt, and for the former USSR. Less than one fifth still was owed by Latin American nations.

Foreign-Exchange Markets. Europe faced another attack on the European Monetary System after the German Bundesbank did not drop an important interest rate as expected on July 29. The next day the Bundesbank spent $35 billion worth of French francs and other currencies in a vain effort to prevent their devaluation against the mark. But at an emergency meeting of EC finance ministers and central bankers that stretched into early August 2, an agreement was reached to let their currencies rise and fall by as much as 15% against each other. In essence, Europe almost had returned to floating rates where the market determines currency values. It was a blow to tighter European economic unity. The other major change was a sharp revaluation of the Japanese yen against the dollar. *See also* EUROPE; FOREIGN AID; STOCKS AND BONDS.

DAVID R. FRANCIS
"The Christian Science Monitor"

The North American Free Trade Agreement

The North American Free Trade Agreement (NAFTA)—which Canada, Mexico, and the United States concluded in 1992 and which was approved by the U.S. Congress late in 1993 after heated debate and much presidential lobbying— will eliminate most tariffs and many other trade barriers among the three nations over ten to 15 years. In essence it creates a free-trade area embracing 365 million people with a total output exceeding $7 trillion. NAFTA's greatest political and economic importance will be for Mexico. In anticipation of its ratification by the U.S. House of Representatives on Nov. 17, 1993, stock prices rose and the Mexican peso strengthened on the foreign-exchange market.

The controversial deal was seen as the crowning achievement of the administration of Mexican President Carlos Salinas de Gortari. He had imposed on his nation a series of tough economic reforms, including privatization of important state enterprises and the voluntary lowering of tariffs to an average 10%. NAFTA further opens Mexico to the influences of the United States. Mexico hoped the pact would encourage enough investment to accelerate economic growth from a modest inflation-adjusted 1% in 1993.

For the United States, the deal might add $5 billion in 1994 to the approximately $50 billion in exports to Mexico in 1993, according to one estimate. The impact of those extra exports on the $6.4 trillion U.S. economy will be barely measurable within the overall growth rate, economists note. During the political debate prior to NAFTA's approval, the opponents—including organized labor and various public-interest groups—and proponents of the deal offered widely differing estimates of its effect on U.S. jobs. However, during 1993 the U.S. economy was adding about 150,000 jobs per month. If that continues, economists said, it would overwhelm any likely job losses from NAFTA. However, NAFTA was expected to result in some job dislocations should U.S. companies step up Mexican investments.

In the case of automobiles, the pact eliminates tariffs after eight years only if 62.5% of a car's cost represents North American materials or labor. After ten years, U.S. producers no longer would have to produce cars in Mexico to sell there. Strict rules would eliminate tariffs on textiles and apparel only for goods made from North American-spun yarn or from fabric made from North American fibers. About half of existing tariffs and quotas would be eliminated immediately on farm goods. Those on politically sensitive crops—such as U.S. corn sold to

Former Presidents Gerald Ford, Jimmy Carter, and George Bush; Vice-President Al Gore; and the congressional leadership were at the White House on Sept. 14, 1993, when President Bill Clinton signed three supplemental amendments to NAFTA.

© AP/Wide World

Mexico or Mexican peanuts, sugar, and orange juice sold in the United States—would be lifted over 15 years. Foreign investors would be treated no less favorably than domestic investors, with exceptions and varying phaseout periods. Mexico would continue to forbid foreign investment in oil and gas exploration, production, and refining, but would open its energy market downstream from these areas. Limits on foreign investment in Mexican banks, insurers, and brokerage firms would be lifted over seven to 15 years.

Mexico approved NAFTA following the U.S. vote, and on December 2, Canada's new Liberal Party Prime Minister Jean Chrétien announced that his government would support the pact after winning concessions from the United States. Canada's Conservative-led Parliament had approved NAFTA in the spring, but it never was proclaimed formally pending the federal elections. The free-trade agreement was scheduled to go into effect on Jan. 1, 1994.

DAVID R. FRANCIS

IOWA

During 1993, Iowa sustained the greatest flood damage in its history—a "500-year" flood hit all of the major rivers in the state. The yearly rainfall recorded was the highest in Weather Bureau history. Flood-damage estimates reached more than $31 million for roads and bridges and almost $35 million for water and sewage systems, with the city of Des Moines being without water for two weeks and without drinkable water for three weeks. Other urban damages climbed into the millions in Des Moines, Iowa City, Cedar Rapids, and Davenport, with smaller cities also seeing staggering damage estimates. The federal government agreed to pay 90% of the damage, while the state agreed to pay the remaining 10%. Iowa State University and the University of Iowa sustained more than $13.4 million in damages to university buildings. Iowa tourism was off by more than 20%. (*See also* FEATURE ARTICLE, page 36.)

The Legislature and Legislation. In 1993 the Republicans held a one-vote majority in the House of Representatives, while the Democrats were in control of the Senate. The House and Senate passed only 189 bills—in contrast with 263 bills passed in 1992—of which Republican Gov. Terry E. Branstad vetoed 11. A budget allocation of $3.525 billion was enacted, an increase of only $120 million over 1992. This was less than the state was expected to collect by some $80 million, an amount designated to reduce the deficit created by a decade of accounting procedures.

Probably the most important bill enacted in 1993 dealt with reform in the welfare system. The new law was considered to be a model piece of legislation. Other new legislation called for higher fees for motorcyclists who ride without a helmet, a requirement that motorcyclists under 19 wear helmets, another rewrite of the ethics law for lawmakers, renewal of driver's licenses by mail, minimum fines established for all criminal offenses, and a protection for children who testify in court. No changes were agreed to concerning the state's restrictive gambling laws.

Economy. Unemployment was at a 15-year low in August—only 3.2%—while employment was at an all-time high with more than 1.5 million Iowans working.

Because of the flooding conditions, the Iowa corn harvest was 40% lower than the record corn crop of 1992. Soybean harvests also were lower, but by only 24%.

The Court and Politics. Governor Branstad appointed the second woman—Marsha Teraus, a lawyer from Vinton—to the nine-member Iowa Supreme Court. She was the 101st justice to serve on the Iowa Supreme Court.

Attorney General Bonnie Campbell announced her candidacy for the Democratic nomination for governor in 1994. However, a primary fight with former Democratic U.S. Rep. Dave Nagel loomed as a distinct possibility. Governor Branstad was expected to run for a fourth four-year term, with no primary opposition. U.S. Rep. Fred Grandy indicated an interest in the governor's seat if Branstad chose not to run. A poll released by the Campbell committee claimed there was a dead heat between Campbell and the incumbent governor.

Education. Enrollment in the three state-supported universities again declined in the 1993-94 academic year. The University of Iowa was again the largest university in the state, with just more than 27,000 students.

RUSSELL M. ROSS
University of Iowa

IOWA • Information Highlights

Area: 56,275 sq mi (145 753 km²).

Population (July 1, 1992 est.): 2,812,000.

Chief Cities (1990 census): Des Moines, the capital, 193,187; Cedar Rapids, 108,751.

Government (1993): *Chief Officers*—governor, Terry E. Branstad (R); lt. gov., Joy C. Corning (R). *General Assembly*—Senate, 50 members;

House of Representatives, 100 members.

State Finances (fiscal year 1991): *Revenue*, $7,137,000,000; *expenditure*, $6,820,000,000.

Personal Income (1992): $52,103,000,000; per capita, $18,526.

Labor Force (August 1993): *Civilian labor force*, 1,594,900; *unemployed*, 51,000 (3.2% of total force).

Education: *Enrollment* (fall 1991)—public elementary schools, 348,231; public secondary, 143,132; colleges and universities, 171,024. *Public school expenditures* (1990-91), $2,136,561,000.

IRAN

The Islamic revolution in Iran appeared to reach a crisis point during 1993. In an election year, President Ali Akbar Hashemi Rafsanjani had his rivals and troubles. No clear line of policy was followed, especially regarding the economy. Observers saw a growing sense of disillusion and frustration among the Iranian people.

Domestic Affairs. In February 1993 there were grave incidents which spoke of increasing political unrest in Iran. These events contrasted sharply with the official celebrations of the 14th anniversary of the Islamic revolution that were held on February 11.

On February 10, Rafsanjani's motorcade was ambushed at a crossroads in northwest Tehran. In the course of the attempt five of the attackers, members of the *Babak Khorramdin* underground organization (BKO), were killed by the president's Revolutionary Guards, and three were captured. *Babak Khorramdin* derived its name from a Persian who fought Arab invaders in the seventh century. Not much was known of its principles except that it opposed the ruling regime. The group was well-armed and had made other deadly attacks that were successful. The ambush against Rafsanjani apparently was set by elite commandos using machine guns and rockets. There was reason to suppose that some members of BKO were in the regular armed forces. In an act of retaliation, the BKO killed five members of the Revolutionary Guards two days after the failed ambush.

Possibly even more serious, suggesting a fissure within the theocracy itself, were reports of the arrest on February 9 of the once-powerful Ayatollah Hossein Ali Montazeri, an outspoken and widely respected cleric with a large personal following. During the Ayatollah Khomeini's later years, Montazeri was his designated successor until he resigned in March 1989, three months before Khomeini's death. Montazeri continued to be regarded as the most senior Shiite clergyman, but he repeatedly attacked the policies of Rafsanjani and of Ayatollah Khamenei, Iran's spiritual leader, as disastrous. As a result, he was confined to the holy city of Qum. His arrest apparently resulted after he attacked the religious hierarchy in lectures to his students. The government claimed that he had been taken to a safer place.

In other political developments, Mohammad Hossein Naqdi, a member of the opposition National Council for Resistance, was killed in Rome on March 16 and Mohammad Hassan Arbab of the opposition Mojahedin-e Khalq ("People's Fighters"), was assassinated on June 6 in Karachi, Pakistan.

The electoral campaign for the presidency concluded on June 11 when Rafsanjani was reelected to a second four-year term. Despite this success, the election was not a ringing endorsement of Rafsanjani or his policies. Though four other candidates were entered, some reports claimed there was a "purge" of other possible opponents. Rafsanjani won easily with 63% of the vote, but his nearest rival, former Labor Minister Ahmed Tavakoli, gained almost 4 million votes (24%). There were more than 250,000 spoiled ballots and the turnout of voters was only 56%. The results were much less clear-cut than in the election of 1989, when Rafsanjani garnered nearly 95% of the vote in a 70% turnout.

Reelected to a second term and with a Majlis (legislature) that was dominated by supporters elected in 1992, Rafsanjani appeared to be in a stronger position than he actually was. This became apparent on August 16 when the Majlis refused to endorse the reappointment of Finance Minister Mohsen Nurbakhsh—a reflection of public criticism of spiraling inflation and a growing debt problem. In policy terms, Nurbakhsh had been in favor of pro-Western and free-enterprise moves. In an end run around the opposition, Rafsanjani appointed Nurbakhsh vice-president in charge of economic affairs.

For the first time public demonstrations were directed against the Rafsanjanis as a family, and especially against the president's younger brother Mohammad, director of official radio and television. The president's rival (and occasional collaborator) Seyyed Ali Khameini seemed to be behind the agitations.

The Economy. Financial measures taken during the summer did not fulfill their objectives, and Iran's economy grew steadily worse, leading to the resignation in November of Mohammad Hussein Adeli, governor of the central bank. Rafsanjani then made a reversal on economic policy, imposing strict import quotas and reintroducing controls.

Inflation accelerated to a rate of more than 100%. Low oil prices were a principal reason for the fiscal difficulties, but a fundamental problem was also the high rate of population growth. The Iranian central bank carried out a substantial devaluation of the rial on March 27. This was followed by wild exchange fluctuations for three weeks and a further devaluation on April 17. In

---

IRAN • Information Highlights

Official Name: Islamic Republic of Iran.

Location: Southwest Asia.

Area: 636,293 sq mi (1 648 000 km²).

Population (mid-1993 est.): 62,800,000.

Chief City (1986 census): Tehran, the capital, 6,042,584.

Government: *Head of state and government,* Ali Akbar Hashemi Rafsanjani, president (took office August 1989). *Legislature* (unicameral)—Islamic Consultative Assembly (Majlis).

Monetary Unit: Rial (66.036 rials equal U.S.$1, March 1993).

Gross National Product (1991 est. U.S.$): $90,000,000,000.

Foreign Trade (1990 U.S.$): *Imports,* $15,900,000,000; *exports,* $17,800,000,000.

June, Iran successfully rescheduled some $3 billion of short-term foreign debt, payments being deferred with the cooperation of French, German, and Japanese lending banks. Late in August measures were announced that were intended to revive industry and loosen monetary controls.

Disasters. On February 25 the Iranian news agency reported that flooding in several provinces had created the worst natural disaster to hit the nation since an earthquake in 1990. The floods killed some 500 persons; damaged or washed away more than 150,000 buildings; ruined 395,000 acres (160 000 ha) of farmland, 9,300 mi (15 000 km) of road, and hundreds of bridges; and killed about 250,000 head of livestock. The total damage was estimated at $1 billion. The government appealed for international assistance and two United Nations (UN) agencies sent teams.

The flood followed an air crash on February 8 at the Tehran airport. An Iranian airliner with 132 on board collided on takeoff with an airforce jet and exploded. There were no survivors.

The Rushdie Affair. An issue which symbolizes the world's difficulty in accepting Iran's behavior as innocuous was the official death sentence, or *fatwa*, given to the British writer Salman Rushdie, author of *The Satanic Verses*, in February 1989. In January, Rafsanjani reaffirmed the *fatwa* first proclaimed by Khomeini. The cash award for Rushdie's death offered by an Iranian foundation had grown since 1989 to $3 million. Others connected with the publication of Rushdie's book have been murdered or hurt.

A courageous reply to the Iranian vendetta against Rushdie was the anthology *For Rushdie*, published in Paris by Editions La Découverte. The book—an anthology of poetry and prose composed by Arab and Islamic authors—honored Rushdie and affirmed the principle of free speech.

Foreign Relations. In February pronouncements, President Rafsanjani made half-hearted gestures to project a conciliatory image to improve Iran's relations with the West, particularly the United States. These moves seemed linked to the new U.S. administration. In January, Rafsanjani said that a condition needed to resume normal relations with the United States would be the freeing of Iranian assets frozen since 1979. He also asked "world thinkers" to reassess attitudes toward the Islamic Republic. He later repudiated charges of Iranian aggression and support for terrorism. However, these olive branches did not seem tied to actual policy changes. Iranian crowds continued to chant the customary slogans denouncing the United States and Israel. Foreign observers viewed with skepticism the establishment in May by the Majlis of a human-rights committee with a mandate to defend "legitimate personal and social liberties" in Iran and the world.

Meanwhile, the U.S. State Department claimed that Iran was "the world's worst sponsor of state terrorism," citing its support of militant

© Eslani Rad/Gamma-Liaison

During 1993, Ali Akbar Hashemi Rafsanjani, above, was elected to a second term as president of Iran, survived an assassination attempt, and faced increasing opposition at home.

Islamic activity in the Sudan and Egypt, and its growing nuclear- and chemical-weapons capability. The charges were repudiated hotly by the Iranian foreign ministry. Egyptian President Hosni Mubarak publicly accused Iran of inciting violence and committing murders in Egypt.

In May, Salman Rushdie met with British Prime Minister John Major. Iran retaliated by imposing much higher visa costs on British businessmen visiting Iran. President Clinton also met Rushdie in November, but later said that he had not meant to offend Muslim opinion. The dispute between Iran and the United Arab Emirates and the Arab League over islands in the Persian Gulf continued. Iran's Foreign Minister Ali Akbar Vellayati visited the Gulf countries in May.

The Iranian arms buildup continued. In May, Iran and the Ukraine signed economic agreements. Subsequently, Iran acquired cruise missiles from the Ukraine. Iran also pursued closer relations with nearby republics of the old Soviet Union. Two of three Russian submarines (Kilo class) purchased by Iran had been delivered by August 1993.

ARTHUR CAMPBELL TURNER
University of California, Riverside

IRAQ

In 1993 the Iraqi government, led by Saddam Hussein, continued quietly to resist the terms accepted at the end of the Persian Gulf war in 1991 and the conditions laid down thereafter. Iraq also continued minor military actions not

quite objectionable enough to provoke major retaliation, although occasional reprisals occurred. Hussein made a determined effort to rebuild Iraq's strength. The theory behind these actions apparently was that coalition opponents, particularly the United States, eventually would tire of constant vigilance against Iraq's actions. Other problems and threats would arise, the alliance against Iraq would unravel, and Iraq would have a freer hand. Aspects of the theory already were proving true.

In domestic politics, Hussein's government continued to strike ruthlessly at all possible opponents.

Military Encounters. A series of military confrontations involving U.S. planes occurred in 1993. For example, U.S. aircraft patrolling the northern exclusion zone dropped bombs at a dam site in the province of Ninawa on April 9, in retaliation against aircraft fire. Nine days later, U.S. aircraft destroyed a radar installation some 35 mi (55 km) south of Mosul.

Major U.S. attacks on Iraq occurred in January and June. The first conflict arose over various Iraqi infractions, but particularly in response to the Iraqi ban on United Nations (UN) flights carrying weapons inspectors into central Iraq. On January 10, U.S., British, and French aircraft attacked missile sites and antiaircraft installations in southern Iraq, accidentally hitting an apartment building in Basra. On January 17, U.S. warships in the Gulf launched cruise missiles against the nuclear-weapons facility at Zaafaraniyah, near Baghdad. One stray missile hit a hotel in Baghdad, reportedly causing 19 deaths. On January 18 more planes struck, and on January 19, Saddam Hussein agreed to allow UN flights. However, in a reaction to the attacks, he had proclaimed another *jihad* on January 14, calling on Arabs everywhere to rise in protest.

In June, U.S. forces conducted a missile attack on Iraqi intelligence headquarters in Baghdad to retaliate for an alleged Iraqi conspiracy to kill former President George Bush during a visit to Kuwait in April. Suspects in the attempt were put on trial in Kuwait, but some investigators doubted Iraqi involvement. International reaction to the June attack—like attitudes to the January one—was not unanimous. Britain, Russia, and Germany approved; France and Italy were less enthusiastic. The Arab League, Jordan, Egypt, and Turkey all had reservations.

Campaign Against Sanctions. The UN Security Council continued to reconsider and renew sanctions against Iraq every 60 days. Iraq devoted considerable diplomatic energy to gaining repeal of the economic embargo, and international opinion began to tilt in that direction, especially on humanitarian grounds. The Turkish foreign minister in February argued to end the sanctions, and Iraqi officials canvassed Russian, Algerian, and Jordanian contacts on the same theme.

Economic interests also played a part. Turkey and other creditor states wanted Iraq to be able

© Bob Strong/Sipa

Iraq's populace felt the effects of continued international sanctions during 1993 as the nation sought to rebuild following the 1991 Persian Gulf war. High inflation was a major problem.

to sell oil to meet payments on its loans. In March, Turkey and Egypt reopened consular offices in Iraq closed since 1990. In September, Turkey announced the resumption of certain exports to Iraq. There was little doubt that other states were conducting a good deal of trade with Iraq in defiance of sanctions, and that some Iraqi oil was being sold illicitly. In November, Iraq announced that its Gulf ports were again operational and ready to deal in goods not prohibited by the UN embargo. The Shatt al-Arab was dredged to Basra. These measures reduced Iraq's dependence on the Jordanian port of al-Aqaba.

Weapons Inspection. UN inspectors continued to visit Iraqi arsenals and arms-manufacturing plants during the year, as perennial disputes with Iraq about its activities lingered. In April stockpiles of irradiated uranium were taken out of Iraq by a UN team. Other such measures were carried out at times, but no one was sure how much Iraq was concealing. Iraq appeared to be behaving in these matters in a more conciliatory fashion. However, in June a major dispute arose over Iraqi refusal to allow installation of monitoring cameras at two missile-test sites. A compromise was achieved in July which permitted the cameras to be installed, though not activated. The cameras were activated on September 24. After some Iraqi opposition, the UN also

instituted low-level helicopter flights for additional surveillance.

UN Security Council Resolution 715, adopted in October 1991, created a permanent regime of inspection. This resolution long had been unacceptable to Iraq and led to a prolonged discussion in the fall of 1993. On November 26, Iraq announced its readiness to comply completely. Rolf Ekeus, head of the UN commission on Iraqi weapons destruction, described this as a major breakthrough. In late 1993, Ekeus and Tariq Aziz, Iraqi deputy prime minister, wrote a draft of what Iraq had to do to be in complete compliance—and thus, presumably, to earn an end to the regime of sanctions. In late December the oil embargo remained.

Kuwait Border. Iraq resented the new demarcation of the border with Kuwait determined by the UN in November 1992 which entered into force on Jan. 15, 1993. The new line ran slightly north of that set in the 1991 cease-fire and gave Kuwait control over the former Iraqi naval base of Umm Qasr. Iraq made incursions into the area in January to remove armaments and equipment from the base. The 300 unarmed UN observers in the border area were impotent to prevent the action.

The Southern Zone. The "no-fly zones" north of the 36th parallel and south of the 32d limited Iraq's control of its territory. In the southern zone, however, there was no U.S. or UN ground presence as in the Kurdish north. Iraq took advantage of this absence to root out all opposition in the region. The marshy flatlands were peopled largely by Shiite Arabs. Iraq drained the marshes, while the population was destroyed or moved in an operation of great cruelty. These and other acts were described in a report by Max van der Stoel, UN special rapporteur on human rights in Iraq. The UN Security Council had not acted on the report by year's end.

Internal Affairs. Impartial reports confirmed that international sanctions on Iraq had caused immense hardship, especially to the poor, the ill, the young, and the old. The sanctions had increased the death rate and imposed economic dislocation. Since 1990 wages had increased by

at least 100%, but prices had risen 6,000%. Industry was hampered and medical supplies were scarce. On the other hand, reports showed that Iraq was militarily stronger than had been supposed. Far more of its elite forces and its military equipment—especially tanks and planes—had survived than believed earlier.

Iraq reduced its economic burdens by an act of bad faith with a May 4 decree to recall the popular 25-dinar Swiss-printed notes. For six days, people were allowed to exchange the old notes for new notes, but Iraqi borders, particularly those with Jordan, were closed to prevent foreign note-holders from exchanging them.

Opposition to Hussein. Credible details about a failed coup d'état in Baghdad emerged in July. Some 300 to 400 persons were arrested and executed, including Jasim Mukhlus and Gen. Bashir al-Talib, both former ambassadors. Many of the conspirators came from Takrit, Saddam Hussein's native area and power base. Large-scale executions apparently continued through August and September.

Perhaps due to the attempted coup, Hussein replaced Prime Minister Muhammad Hamzah al-Zubaydi in September with Finance Minister Ahmed Hussein, and reshuffled a number of other cabinet posts. Meanwhile, two distinguished Iraqi envoys—Hamid el-Jubouri, ambassador to Tunisia, and Husham el-Shawi, an Oxford-educated ambassador to Canada—defected and sought asylum in Britain in August.

ARTHUR CAMPBELL TURNER
University of California, Riverside

IRELAND

Politics, the economy, and negotiations regarding the situation in Northern Ireland dominated events in Ireland during 1993. On May 27, Ireland's President Mary Robinson paid an official visit to London, where she had a private talk with Queen Elizabeth II.

The general election of November 1992 reduced the number of seats held by the reigning Fianna Fail party to 68, thus forcing Ireland's prime minister, Albert Reynolds, to seek a partner in order to form a coalition government. After the second-largest party, Fine Gael (45 seats), had spurned an alliance, the Labour Party—whose numbers had doubled at the election—overcame its aversion to collaborating with the center-right party and agreed on Jan. 8, 1993, to share power with Fianna Fail.

To achieve this unprecedented coalition with Labour, Reynolds conceded six of the 15 cabinet posts to Labour and committed the new government to a five-year program of social and economic reforms. The coalition commanded 101 of the 166 seats in the Dail (lower house of the Irish parliament), thus giving it an overall majority of 36. Labour's popular leader, Dick Spring, occupied the second-highest position in the cabinet

IRAQ • Information Highlights

Official Name: Republic of Iraq.
Location: Southwest Asia.
Area: 168,434 sq mi (436 245 km²).
Population (mid-1993 est.): 19,200,000.
Chief City (1987 census): Baghdad, the capital, 3,844,608.
Government: *Head of state and government*, Saddam Hussein, president (took office July 1979).
Monetary Unit: Dinar (0.311 dinar equals U.S.$1, selling rate, August 1993).
Gross National Product (1989 est. U.S.$): $35,000,000,000.
Foreign Trade (1990 U.S.$): *Imports*, $4,834,000,000; *exports*, $392,000,000.

as deputy prime minister and minister for foreign affairs (including responsibility for relations with Northern Ireland). The Dail endorsed the coalition on January 12 by a margin of 102 to 60 votes.

The Economy. While Labour hoped to steer the coalition in the direction of a more radical social policy aimed at easing the burdens of poverty and unemployment, Reynolds and Spring realized that stimulating the sluggish economy took precedence. They also wanted to defend the parity of the Irish punt (pound) within the European Monetary System. Facing an unemployment rate of close to 20% and worried about the modest increases in gross national product, national income, and industrial as well as agricultural productivity since 1991, the government announced plans for a subsidy of 270 million pounds (about $385 million) from the European Community (EC) that would create 30,000 jobs.

During January several small countries in the EC lowered their interest rates, which resulted in heavy pressure on the Irish pound. To the government's dismay the EC then decided to realign European currencies in order to preserve the exchange rate mechanism (ERM). Even though Reynolds and Spring had pledged to resist devaluation, they had little choice but to approve the pound's devaluation by 10%.

Legislation. The much vexed question of birth control surfaced again in the spring, when the Dail debated a measure that abolished the age limit on the sale of condoms. Although the Roman Catholic Church opposed yielding to the pro-choice lobby, no effective opposition emerged in the Dail and the bill passed on June 3 without a formal vote. After a long campaign by the champions of gay rights, the Dail agreed on June 24 to end the ban on consensual homosexual relations between persons over 16.

Anglo-Irish Relations. While the overall level of political violence in Northern Ireland had fallen in the past few years, the Provisional Irish Republican Army (IRA) continued to set off bombs in public places in England and the north from time to time. And yet Protestant terrorists killed more people in 1993 than did the Provisional IRA. In March two IRA bombs exploded in a shopping mall in northwest England, leaving two boys dead. This outrage gave rise to angry protests in England, while in Dublin several women organized a rally outside the general post office—the central site of the Easter 1916 rebellion. On March 28 well more than 10,000 people gathered there to applaud speakers who denounced the IRA and pleaded for peace.

The carnage caused by an IRA bomb inside a crowded fish shop in the Protestant Shankill area of Belfast on October 23, killing ten and injuring more than 50, seemed to dash any hope for negotiation. Leading Irish and British politicians condemned the atrocity and braced for the inevitable backlash, which came a week later in a pub frequented by Catholics in Greysteel, county Londonderry. Several Protestant terrorists sprayed the room with bullets, leaving seven dead (one a Protestant) and six wounded.

Although he called the Shankill bombers "scum" who had committed "cold-blooded murder," Britain's Prime Minister John Major did not abandon his quest for peace. On October 29 he and Reynolds met privately at an EC summit meeting in Brussels and agreed to invite leaders of the militant Unionists and the IRA to discuss a settlement so long as the men of violence renounced the bomb and the bullet. In a joint statement they declared: "New doors will open and both governments would wish to respond imaginatively to the new situation."

British-Irish Accord over Northern Ireland. After months of secret conversations among representatives of the British and Irish governments, the IRA, Sinn Fein, Protestant paramilitaries, and some leading politicians in the north, Prime Ministers Major and Reynolds signed an agreement on December 15 declaring their resolve to end the sectarian violence by creating a "framework for peace" based on the consent of the people. Seeking to heal the wounds of communal conflict and to promote mutual trust and cooperation, the two premiers affirmed the right of the majority in Northern Ireland to decide "whether they prefer to support the Union or a sovereign united Ireland." Both governments promised to respect the civil rights of the two communities, while Reynolds undertook to amend those clauses in the Irish constitution that claimed dominion over Northern Ireland.

Although the agreement raised hopes for a peaceful solution to the conflict that has killed more than 3,100 persons and injured thousands since 1968, the men of violence refused to lay down their weapons without concessions. The agreement did, however, force both sides in Northern Ireland to choose between the politics of accommodation and "no surrender."

L. PERRY CURTIS, JR., *Brown University*

IRELAND • Information Highlights

Official Name: Ireland.
Location: Island in the eastern North Atlantic Ocean.
Area: 27,135 sq mi (70 280 km²).
Population (mid-1993 est.): 3,600,000.
Chief Cities (1986 census): Dublin, the capital, 920,956 (incl. suburbs); Cork, 173,694; Limerick, 76,557.
Government: *Head of state*, Mary Robinson, president (took office Dec. 3, 1990). *Head of government*, Albert Reynolds, prime minister (took office Feb. 11, 1992). *Legislature*—Parliament: House of Representatives (Dail Eireann) and Senate (Seanad Eireann).
Monetary Unit: Pound (0.6989 pound equals U.S.$1, Dec. 27, 1993).
Gross Domestic Product (1991 est. U.S.$): $39,200,000,000.
Economic Indexes (1992): *Consumer Prices* (1980 = 100), all items, 223.2; food, 476.0. *Industrial Production* (1980 = 100), 208.
Foreign Trade (1992 U.S.$): *Imports*, $22,417,000,000; *exports*, $28,280,000,000.

ISRAEL

The dominant event for Israel in 1993 was the signing of an agreement with the Palestine Liberation Organization (PLO) in September that called for mutual recognition and outlined steps toward a peace settlement. A similar agreement was brokered with Jordan to break an impasse in peace talks that originated in 1991. Division within Israel over the peace process and other issues was reflected in municipal elections, and in rifts within the Labor Party-led government coalition and the opposition Likud bloc.

Peace Process. Indications of changing Israeli attitudes toward the Palestinians began in January 1993 when the Knesset (parliament) repealed a 1986 law barring contacts with the PLO, which had been labeled a "terrorist" organization. This was followed by statements from Labor Party leaders calling for direct negotiations with the PLO and for withdrawal of Israeli forces from the Gaza Strip, occupied since 1967.

By summer reports circulated about "back channel diplomacy" between Israel and the PLO in Oslo, Norway. The secret talks led to the signing of an agreement on September 13 between Israel and the PLO at a public ceremony in Washington, DC, sealed by a historic handshake between Prime Minister Yitzhak Rabin and PLO Chairman Yasir Arafat (*see* BIOGRAPHY). This "Declaration of Principles" provided for mutual recognition and for gradual extension of self-government to the Palestinian inhabitants of Gaza and of the West Bank beginning in the town of Jericho.

Also known as the "Gaza-Jericho First" agreement, the pact created a five-year transition period prior to a final settlement. Transfer of authority from Israel to the Palestinians was to begin late in 1993. Elections were scheduled to be held by July 1994 for a Palestine Interim Self-Government Authority (PISGA), which would have executive and legislative powers and would establish a Palestinian police force to replace the Israeli army. The agreement included protocols calling for establishment of a joint Israeli-Palestinian Committee for Economic Cooperation, and for creation of joint programs related to electricity, water, transport and communications, trade, labor relations, social welfare, and the environment. Talks on the permanent status of the West Bank and Gaza were to begin by December 1995.

After the September agreements, Israel and the PLO began direct negotiations in Egypt on implementation. The critical issues included the withdrawal of Israeli troops and the release of some 10,000 Palestinian prisoners held by Israel. Negotiations were threatened by violence in the occupied territories as Arab dissidents attacked Jewish settlers, who retaliated with mass demonstrations against the Rabin government. The Knesset approved the agreement by a bare majority after a stormy three-day debate.

The agreement with the PLO aided discussions with Jordan, which also signed an agreement on principles with Israel. In November, Foreign Minister Shimon Peres and Jordan's King Hussein met in Amman to discuss economic cooperation and the outlines of a peace treaty. They also agreed to coordinate their relations with the PISGA.

Peace negotiations between Israel and Syria and Lebanon remained in limbo. Relations between Israel and the two countries deteriorated during July as a result of clashes between the Islamic fundamentalist Hezbollah and Israeli forces in Israel's south Lebanon "security zone." The clashes escalated into "Operation Accountability," Israel's heaviest air offensive against southern Lebanon since the mid-1980s. Hundreds of Lebanese homes were destroyed and

Ehud Olmert, 47-year-old member of Israel's parliament from the Likud Party, was elected mayor of Jerusalem in November 1993. He had defeated Teddy Kollek, who held the post for 28 years.

hundreds of thousands of Lebanese fled north during the bombing. A U.S.-brokered truce halted the fighting in August. After "Operation Accountability" ended, Rabin praised Syrian President Hafiz al-Assad for helping to guarantee the cease-fire agreement. Despite repeated rumors of a breakthrough in the negotiations with Syria, the impasse over the future of the Golan Heights that Israel seized from Syria in 1967 remained.

Progress in negotiations with the PLO helped open Israel to establish relations with other Arab and Third World nations. Rabin made the first public visit by an Israeli leader to Morocco, followed by a trip to China with stopovers in Kenya, Singapore, and Indonesia. Israel's Deputy Foreign Minister Yossi Beilin became the highest-ranking Israeli to participate in a public conference in Tunisia. In October, Israeli officials reported negotiations with Qatar on a multibillion-dollar project to bring natural gas to Eilat for shipment to Europe.

Domestic Affairs. Prime Minister Rabin had indicated that he regarded the outcome of October municipal elections as a test of support for the peace initiatives of his Labor-led coalition government, and the results left him disappointed. Turnout for the election was only 36% of registered voters, one of the lowest participation rates in Israel's history.

In the 100 municipal races in the Jewish sector, Likud won 36, while the Labor Party captured 20. Labor won 20 of the 56 Arab municipalities and independents won the others. Likud lost all four of its Arab municipalities, but captured several local councils and mayoralties in former Labor strongholds. Likud's biggest victory came in Jerusalem, Israel's capital and largest city, where 83-year-old incumbent Teddy Kollek, who had been mayor since 1965, lost to Ehud Olmert, one of Likud's young guard. In Tel Aviv, Roni Milo, another of the Likud younger generation,

won. In March the Knesset elected Ezer Weizmann to succeed Chaim Herzog for a five-year term as Israeli president. Weizmann, formerly affiliated with the Labor Party and Likud, was a popular figure known as an outspoken dove.

Two new chief rabbis were chosen by the country's 150 rabbinical electors. Rabbi Yisrael Meir Lau, 56, was selected to represent the Ashkenazi or Central and East European Jews, and Rabbi Eliahu Bakshi-Doron, 52, to represent Sephardic Jews of North African and Middle East origin. The outcome seemed to strengthen the position of the Sephardic Torah Guardians or Shas Party, the only Orthodox religious faction to join Rabin's coalition government. In September, Rabbi Lau held a historic meeting with Pope John Paul II, indicating the Vatican's support for Israel's peace accord with the PLO.

After Likud lost the June 1992 Knesset election, 77-year-old Yitzhak Shamir had retired as the party's leader. In March 1993, Likud elected in his place 44-year-old Benjamin Netanyahu, who adamantly opposed any territorial concessions in the peace negotiations and condemned recognition of and negotiations with the PLO. Netanyahu won 52% of the votes cast by Likud members, alienating the second-strongest candidate, former Foreign Minister David Levy, who received 26% of the votes. Some feared that Levy, an immigrant from Morocco, might abandon Likud along with his large Sephardic constituency.

Rabin's Labor-led coalition was endangered by continuing squabbles between the Shas Party and the left-of-center Meretz Party. Shas leaders threatened to leave the government if Meretz leader Shulamit Aloni was not removed as education minister. A crisis was averted by a cabinet reshuffle in which Aloni and the leader of Shas, Aryeh Deri, were given new ministries. However, the coalition again was shaken when charges of corruption and misuse of funds were raised against Deri. Rabin attempted to postpone a decision about Deri's future, but in October the Knesset voted to lift Deri's parliamentary immunity. The next day the Jerusalem District Court indicted him for taking bribes, falsifying documents of nonprofit organizations, and violating public trust when he was minister of interior. His Shas Party threatened to withdraw from the coalition and to withhold its Knesset votes from government support, thus undermining Rabin's parliamentary majority.

In July, Israel's Supreme Court overturned the conviction of 73-year-old John Demjanjuk, a former U.S. citizen sentenced to death for World War II crimes. The court ruled that there was reasonable doubt about whether Demjanjuk was indeed "Ivan the Terrible," a Nazi death-camp operative. After several delays caused by efforts to prosecute him further, Demjanjuk was released and returned to the United States.

See also MIDDLE EAST.

DON PERETZ
State University of New York, Binghamton

ISRAEL • Information Highlights

Official Name: State of Israel.

Location: Southwest Asia.

Area: 8,019 sq mi (20 770 km²).

Population (mid-1993 est.): 5,300,000.

Chief Cities (Dec. 31, 1990 est.): Jerusalem, the capital, 524,500 (including East Jerusalem); Tel Aviv-Jaffa, 339,400; Haifa, 245,900.

Government: *Head of state,* Ezer Weizman, president (took office March 1993). *Head of government,* Yitzhak Rabin, prime minister (took office July 1992). *Legislature* (unicameral)—Knesset.

Monetary Unit: Shekel (2.8805 shekels equal U.S.$1, Nov. 22, 1993).

Gross National Product (1991 est. U.S.$): $54,600,000,000.

Economic Indexes: *Consumer Prices* (1992, 1980 = 100), all items, 87,143.6; food, 82,681.0. *Industrial Production* (1991, 1980 = 100), 141.

Foreign Trade (1991 U.S.$): *Imports,* $16,906,000,000; *exports,* $11,889,000,000.

ITALY

Public outrage exploded in Italy in 1993 as investigating magistrates uncovered more evidence that many politicians had demanded huge kickbacks before approving governmental contracts. The public also vented its anger at an electoral system that had enabled Christian Democrats to dominate every government since 1945.

Political Corruption and Reform. In February 1992, Antonio Di Pietro, a magistrate in Milan, launched his "Operation Clean Hands" investigation into the system of bribes being paid to politicians for public business. Milan was dubbed "Kickback City" (*Tangentopoli*). By the end of 1993 the probes had spread across Italy. Almost 3,000 prominent politicians and businesspeople were notified they were under investigation. The public cheered on the magistrates.

Typically, companies had to pay bribes equal to 5% to 20% of a contract's value, and the money was distributed to political parties. Experts calculated that such corruption had cost up to $20 billion since 1980. Parties hardest hit by "Operation Clean Hands" were the Christian Democrats and their major coalition partner, the Socialists. While no party emerged unscathed, the least hurt were the former Communists—who had shed their old dogmas and now called themselves the Democratic Party of the Left (PDS). The Communists, even though consistently Italy's Number 2 party, always were excluded from the executive branch of government after the Cold War began in 1947.

Because of the political dynamics of the Cold War, the large Christian Democratic Party was able, under Italy's multiparty system, to dominate every coalition government for more than four decades and thus to enjoy immense opportunities to dispense patronage. With the recent end of the Cold War, many Italians have argued it is time to halt arbitrary exclusion of former Communists from cabinet posts and to move toward an electoral system based on fewer parties that alternate in political power.

Governmental and Socialist Party Shake-ups. Italy began the year with a wobbly coalition government headed since June 1992 by Giuliano Amato, a Socialist (PSI), and also composed of Christian Democrats (DC), Social Democrats (PSDI), and Liberals (PLI). It was Italy's 51st government since World War II. In late February 1993, Amato had to shuffle his cabinet after the resignations of two senior ministers—Finance Minister Giovanni Goria and Health Minister Francesco DeLorenzo—who were linked to the corruption scandals. Goria later was absolved.

Earlier in February the longtime secretary of the Socialist Party, former Premier Bettino Craxi, had to resign the leadership of his party amid allegations of taking bribes in Milan, his power base. One of the charges had to do with Milan's Banco Ambrosiano, which had collapsed in 1982. A potential successor to Craxi, Claudio Martelli, had to quit his governmental post as justice minister. He was accused of using a Swiss bank account to funnel bribes to the Socialist Party. Giorgio Benvenuto was chosen to be the next secretary of the PSI—but three months later resigned after failing to persuade Socialist colleagues in Parliament who were under investigation to resign their seats.

© AP/Wide World

Firefighters and authorities inspect the damage near the famed Uffizi Gallery in Florence, Italy, in late May 1993. A car bomb had exploded near the museum, killing five persons and injuring 30 others. Investigators suspected Mafia involvement in the explosion.

Reflecting the scandals that were engulfing the Socialists and the Christian Democrats, Premier Amato's new cabinet included ten ministers who were either technocrats or who had only loose ties to political parties. This marked a sharp contrast from recent Italian tradition, in which the premier had been dominated by political party bosses.

On March 30, Franco Reviglio (PSI) resigned as minister of finance. He was the fifth cabinet officer in the Amato government to resign in six weeks. He was under investigation for financial irregularities at ENI (Ente Nazionale Idrocarburi), the huge state holding company for energy that he headed from 1983 to 1989. Still another Socialist in the cabinet, Defense Minister Salvo Ando, was notified April 21 he was under investigation for a vote-buying scheme that was connected with organized crime in his native city, Catania, Sicily.

Giulio Andreotti and the Mafia. In a new political twist, Giulio Andreotti—the 74-year-old Christian Democratic wheelhorse who had held the premiership no less than seven times between 1972 and 1992—disclosed on March 27 that he was being investigated for political corruption and collusion with the Mafia in order to obtain votes for the Christian Democratic Party in Sicily. A lengthy document released by Italy's anti-Mafia parliamentary commission found that Andreotti's close Christian Democratic ally in Sicily, the late Salvatore Lima, had helped Cosa Nostra bosses avoid jail terms and had helped transfer anti-Mafia officials away from Sicily.

Two of the Mafia informers making charges against Andreotti were Tommaso Buscetta and Francesco Marino Mannoia. Buscetta, now residing in the United States under the federal witness protection program, was one of the Mafia's most famous turncoats. In the wake of new charges, the full Senate eventually lifted Andreotti's parliamentary immunity. He hired a U.S. defense lawyer.

Arrest of Mafia Bosses. Meanwhile, Salvatore (Toto) Riina, said to be "boss of bosses" of Italy's organized-crime families, was arrested in Sicily in January. His close associate, Giuseppe Montalto, was arrested in Palermo on February 5. He was suspected in the 1992 killing of Salvatore Lima. On May 18 authorities seized Benedetto ("Nitto") Santapaola, boss of the Catania Mafia and presumed mastermind of the Mafia's alliances with Colombian cocaine cartels. He also was believed to have plotted the 1992 assassinations of leading anti-Mafia prosecutors Giovanni Falcone and Paolo Borsellino.

Referendum of April 18-19. Amid the ever-growing revelations of scandals, Italians voted overwhelmingly in a referendum on April 18-19 to support a series of eight measures calling for major governmental reforms. Support for the measures meant only that existing laws would be abolished. Parliament would have to pass new laws to implement the proposals. The referendum was the result of a reform campaign by Mario Segni, a Sardinian and son of former Italian President Antonio Segni. He had resigned on March 29 from the scandal-tainted Christian Democratic Party.

The most important referendum measure called for an end to the strict system of proportional representation (P.R.) for elections to the Senate. The measure proposed that three quarters of the seats be selected on an Anglo-American "first past the post" system in individual election districts, with the remaining one quarter to be decided by P.R. The measure won 82.7% support, leading observers to expect that Parliament would have to enact a similar electoral change for the Chamber of Deputies. The only opposition came from small parties that stood to lose representation under a new system: the neo-Fascist Italian Social Movement (MSI); the Sicily-based clean-government party, La Rete (Network); and a hard-line, rump Communist faction, the Reconstructed Communist Party (PRC).

Another measure that would terminate state financing for political parties got 90.3% of the vote. State funding has been estimated to be worth $53 million per year to the parties. Abolition of the ministry for state share-holdings garnered 90.1% support. Abolition of the ministry of agriculture and transfer of its functions to regional governments won 70.1% approval. A similar proposal for the ministry of tourism got 82.2% of the vote.

The New Ciampi Government. Following the referendum, the government of Premier Amato resigned. He was succeeded on April 29 by Carlo Azeglio Ciampi, who pledged a program of reform. Unlike all other postwar premiers, Ciampi was not a member of Parliament. He had headed Italy's central bank. Antonio Fazio succeeded him in that important post.

Premier Ciampi's new government came under a serious threat just hours after taking power, when the Chamber of Deputies resisted lifting the immunity of a key figure in the political scandals, former Socialist Premier Bettino

---

ITALY • Information Highlights

Official Name: Italian Republic.
Location: Southern Europe.
Area: 116,305 sq mi (301 230 km²).
Population (mid-1993 est.): 57,800,000.
Chief Cities (Dec. 31, 1990): Rome, the capital, 2,791,354; Milan, 1,432,184; Naples, 1,206,013.
Government: *Head of state*, Oscar Luigi Scalfaro, president (sworn in May 28, 1992). *Head of government*, Carlo Azeglio Ciampi, prime minister (sworn in April 26, 1993). *Legislature*—Parliament: Senate and Chamber of Deputies.
Monetary Unit: Lira (1,675.50 lire equal U.S.$1, Nov. 19, 1993).
Gross Domestic Product (1991 est. U.S.$): $965,000,000,000.
Economic Indexes (1992): *Consumer Prices* (1980 = 100), all items, 280.7. *Industrial Production* (1980 = 100), 111.
Foreign Trade (1992 U.S.$): *Imports*, $188,712,000,000; *exports*, $178,471,000,000.

Craxi. In secret balloting, the Chamber voted to lift his immunity in the most serious cases involving corruption—but only those in Rome. Angered at Parliament's failure also to lift Craxi's immunity for cases in Milan (his power base), magistrates in that city appealed to Italy's Constitutional Court for an overruling.

In protest of the Chamber's leniency toward Craxi, three members of Ciampi's cabinet from the Democratic Party of the Left (PDS) resigned April 29. So did the sole Green Party member of the cabinet. But after Ciampi outlined his government's plans on May 6, the PDS and another key opposition party, the rapidly growing Northern League of Umberto Bossi, announced they would abstain in the confidence vote on May 7, thus enabling the new government to survive. Ciampi appointed four technocrats to replace the outgoing ministers.

Scandals and Bombings. In May it was revealed that Cesare Romiti, chief executive of Fiat, Italy's largest private-sector company, was under investigation. He was the latest of scores of businessmen linked to the scandals. Next it was the turn of Carlo De Benedetti, head of the Olivetti computer and publishing empire, to confess that Olivetti had paid kickbacks to secure government contracts. Also arrested was Franco Nobili, chairman of Italy's huge state holding company, the IRI (Institute for Industrial Reconstruction). Romano Prodi was named the new head of IRI, which the government was seeking to privatize. Two accused industrialists committed suicide in Milan in July: Raul Gardini of the Ferruzzi conglomerate and Gabriele Cingari, head of the ENI energy holding company.

Five persons were killed and more than two dozen were injured on May 27 when a car bomb exploded near the Uffizi Gallery in Florence. Three paintings were destroyed and 30 others damaged, including works by Rubens. More than 100,000 people joined a protest march in Florence. Investigators suspected Mafia involvement. The gallery was reopened partially on June 20. On May 14 a car bomb exploded in the Parioli district of Rome, injuring 23 people. On June 2 a bomb was defused near Parliament. Car bombs exploded near Rome's St. John Lateran Church and near Milan's Teatro alla Scala the night of July 27-28, killing five persons.

Local Elections and Electoral Reform. Municipal elections were held in 1,200 cities on June 6 and 20 under a new system of direct voting for mayors. Voters pummeled the centrist parties that had been discredited by the corruption scandals. Substantial gains were made in the north by the populist Northern League (which won control of Milan), and by the Democratic Party of the Left (PDS) in central and southern regions. Nationwide, the Christian Democrats lost half of their 1990 vote.

In a subsequent round of municipal elections held on November 21 in Palermo, Naples, Rome, Genoa, Venice, and Trieste, the center parties virtually collapsed. The Christian Democratic Party got less than 10% of the vote. The Socialist Party also was crushed.

The chief gainers were parties on the far left and far right—the Democratic Party of the Left (PDS) and the neo-Fascists (the Italian Social Movement or MSI). In only one city did a candidate for mayor achieve an outright victory, which required an absolute majority. This was in Palermo, where Leoluca Orlando—a former Christian Democrat who had formed a new anti-Mafia party, La Rete—was the winner.

Elsewhere, runoff elections had to be held on December 5 between the top two candidates. In Naples, Alessandra Mussolini, the neo-Fascist granddaughter of the former dictator, got 29% of the vote in the first round, but lost in the second with 44% to 56% for the PDS candidate, Antonio Bassolini. In Rome, Gianfranco Fini, leader of the MSI, lost with 48% to 52% for Francesco Rutelli, a Green who was backed by the former Communists. The PDS bloc also won in the northern cities of Genoa, Venice, and Trieste. These changes in Italian voting patterns may be an indication of what could be expected in the spring 1994 parliamentary elections that would occur under a new system of voting.

On August 4, Parliament's electoral reform bill was signed. It provided for a "first past the post" system (like that in Britain and the United States) for three quarters of the seats in both the Chamber of Deputies and the Senate. The remaining 25% of the seats were to be distributed on the basis of proportional representation. Parties winning less than 4% of the vote would not be entitled to seats in the lower chamber, but could win representation in the Senate. New parliamentary elections were expected in 1994.

Economy. Italy's economy continued to be poor. Unemployment stood at 10.9% in August 1993, up from 10.3% one year before. Industrial production was 3% less than the preceding year. In July employers and labor unions reached a compromise to tie national pay raises to inflation for four years.

Foreign Policy. Italian military units continued to assist peace efforts in Bosnia. To help the UN relief program in Somalia, Italy sent the largest military contingent after those of the United States and Pakistan. Italy felt especially knowledgeable about Somalia, since it once had been Italy's colony (1905-41), and Italy had administered it as a UN trusteeship (1950-60). But after the deaths of some Italian soldiers and what was viewed as a major shift in UN-U.S. policy in Somalia in 1993, Italy expressed sharp disagreement with efforts to capture Gen. Mohammed Farah Aidid and to disarm his clan supporters in Mogadishu. Italy pulled its troops out of that city in late summer and planned to bring all its forces home by year's end.

CHARLES F. DELZELL, *Vanderbilt University*

JAPAN

Japan experienced a year of great change in 1993. At the United Nations (UN) in New York on September 28, when U.S. President Bill Clinton first met Japan's new prime minister, Morihiro Hosokawa (*see* BIOGRAPHY), Clinton told reporters that both were former governors elected "with a mandate for change." Hosokawa had been nominated by a coalition dedicated to reform. On August 6 he was chosen as prime minister, terminating almost four decades of rule by the Liberal Democratic Party (LDP).

The Imperial Family also felt the effects of continued change. In 1959 the present ruler, Emperor Akihito, had married a commoner, now Empress Michiko. On June 9, 1993, Crown Prince Naruhito was wed to another non-noble, a bright young officer from the Foreign Ministry, Masako Owada (*see* BIOGRAPHY; SIDEBAR, page 301).

Domestic Affairs

In December 1992 the LDP leader, Prime Minister Kiichi Miyazawa, had appointed his second cabinet to offset criticism of "money politics" in the perennial majority party. The latest scandal had involved a trucking company, Tokyo Sagawa Kyubin, which was investigated for offering bribes to some 100 politicians. On March 25 the former vice-president of the LDP, Shin Kanemaru, was freed on bail after having been questioned about evasion of more than $8 million in income taxes. The approval ratings for the Miyazawa cabinet plunged to 21% in public-opinion polls. On April 6 the resignation of 70-year-old Foreign Minister Michio Watanabe, a likely successor, further weakened the cabinet.

Party Politics. In January when the regular Diet session convened, the LDP mustered 274 members, a majority in the 512-seat (lower) House of Representatives. Within one week in late June, on the eve of a general election, 54 of these members quit the party to form dissident groups. With only 99 (of a total of 252) seats in the (upper) House of Councillors, the LDP could be outvoted by opposition parties in the upper chamber of Parliament.

Hosokawa had been the first to leave the LDP. In July 1992 he had formed the Japan New Party (JNP) and promptly won four seats in the House of Councillors on a reform platform. The JNP did so well in the Tokyo Metropolitan Assembly election (June 27) that the party predicted later successes.

Although the LDP held its own in the Tokyo election, the party met stiff resistance in the Diet, where the opposition hammered away at Japan's slumping economy and Miyazawa's failure to fulfill promises for electoral reform. On June 18 the lower house passed a motion of no confidence in the government (with 39 LDP members voting against their own party). Miyazawa immediately scheduled a general election for July 18.

On June 19 ten lower-house members defected from the LDP and founded the Buddhist Harbinger (*Sekigake*) Party, with Masayoshi Takemura as its leader. This loss was followed by the departure of 44 more LDP members, who on June 23 formed the Japan Renewal Party (JRP) with a former finance minister, Tsutomu Hata, as nominal head. The Japanese media speculated that the real JRP architect of the emerging coalition was former LDP Secretary Ichiro Ozawa. Nonetheless, Sadao Yamahana, chairman of the major opposition force, the Social Democratic Party of Japan (SDPJ), told reporters he regarded Hata as "an appropriate candidate" to become the prime minister. Presiding LDP Secretary-General Seiroku Kajiyama, an archrival

© Satoru Ohmori/Gamma-Liaison

Morihiro Hosokawa, second from left, 55-year-old founder of the Japan New Party, and members of his new coalition government which was formed in August 1993, enjoy a toast. Hosokawa's appointment as prime minister ended 38 consecutive years of rule by the Liberal Democratic Party in Japan.

of Ozawa, challenged voters to choose between a stable government under the established party (LDP) or an unstable coalition.

Hata (JRP) met with four opposition-party leaders on June 27 to plan a reform-minded coalition which might be able to succeed the Miyazawa government. Present were Yamahana (SDPJ), Koshiro Ishida (*Komeito*), Keigo Ouchi of the Democratic Socialist Party (DSP), and Satsuki Eda, head of a small socialist group (*Shaminren*).

The general election held on July 18 had been triggered by the no-confidence motion of a month earlier. The results from the polling were confusing. The LDP remained the largest party in the lower house but failed to win a majority. Miyazawa first promised to retain his position but later resigned from the LDP presidency in favor of the chief cabinet secretary, Yohei Kono, 55. The three new conservative parties showed strength in the election. Meanwhile, the Socialists, a perennial opposition party, suffered their worst setback in history. Taking responsibility, SDPJ chairman Yamahana resigned and was succeeded by Tomiichi Murayama.

On July 29 the original coalition was expanded to include seven non-LDP, noncommunist parties, which decided to field Hosokawa (JNP) as candidate for prime minister. At this time, the 512 seats in the House of Representatives were distributed as follows: LDP—225, SDPJ—70, JRP—55, Komeito—52, JNP—36, DSP—15, Japan Communist Party (JCP)—15, Harbinger—13, Shaminren—4, independents and small parties—27. The LDP continued to hold 99 seats in the House of Councillors but the coalition commanded 130.

On August 6 the Diet selected Hosokawa as prime minister over Kono and on August 9 the former governor took the oath of office, thus terminating 38 years of LDP political dominance. The public strength of the coalition, however, masked some inherent weakness.

For example, Hosokawa (JNP) appointed the heads of all the other coalition parties to his cabinet. Takemura (Harbinger) took over the powerful position of chief cabinet secretary; Hata (JRP) became deputy prime minister and foreign minister. Yamahana (SDPJ) resurfaced as minister in charge of electoral reform. Ishida (*Komeito*) became director of the management and coordination agency; Ouchi (DSP), minister for health and welfare; and Eda (*Shaminren*), director of the science and technology agency. Four key portfolios—foreign affairs, finance, international trade and industry, and defense—rested in JRP hands. The coalition covered a spectrum of policy colors.

Three women were appointed to the new cabinet. Equally important, Hosokawa persuaded the lower house to elect Takako Doi, 64—the first woman to have chaired a major party (SDPJ)—to be speaker of the lower house. In the July election, Doi, a constitutional scholar, was elected to her ninth consecutive term from a Hyogo district. She was expected to help curb the influence of the left wing of the SDPJ.

In late August the administration tackled the issue—"money politics"—which had brought down two previous leaders (Toshiki Kaifu and Miyazawa). The new coalition government agreed on political-funding controls and a modified electoral system. The reform program would reduce the lower house to 500 seats: 250 from single-seat constituencies and 250 national seats based on proportional representation. In October the LDP unveiled its reform plan. The government's political-reform agenda was well-received by the public. In September, just one month after establishment of the Hosokawa regime, the cabinet received a record-high 71% approval rating in an *Asahi Shimbun* poll.

Economy. On March 31 the Economic Planning Agency (EPA) announced that the gross national product (GNP) for fiscal 1992 had grown only 0.8% in real terms, the lowest growth rate since 1974. The economy actually shrank (-0.5%) in the April-June quarter, according to the EPA. Financial reports released May 27 showed that 11 major commercial banks posted declines in pretax profits in fiscal 1992 as they struggled with problem loans.

Meanwhile, the Miyazawa cabinet obtained Diet passage of the fiscal 1993 budget by a narrow vote just before the beginning of a new fiscal year on April 1. Expenditures in the budget totaled $603 billion, including almost $72 billion on public works which were intended to stimulate the economy.

Soon thereafter, on April 13, the government announced an additional stimulus package, the largest in the nation's history. The core of the package was expenditures of $92 billion on infrastructure: welfare, education, high-speed rails, new airports, and telecommunications. On

---

JAPAN • Information Highlights

Official Name: Japan.

Location: East Asia.

Area: 145,882 sq mi (377 835 km²).

Population (mid-1993 est.): 124,800,000.

Chief Cities (March 31, 1991 est.): Tokyo, the capital, 8,006,386; Yokohama, 3,210,607; Osaka, 2,512,386; Nagoya, 2,097,765.

Government: *Head of state*, Akihito, emperor (acceded Jan. 9, 1989). *Head of government*, Morihiro Hosokawa, prime minister (took office Aug. 9, 1993). *Legislature*—Diet: House of Councillors and House of Representatives.

Monetary Unit: Yen (107.32 yen equal U.S.$1, Nov. 18, 1993).

Gross Domestic Product (1991 U.S.$): $2,360,700,000,000.

Economic Indexes (1992): *Consumer Prices* (1980 = 100), all items, 128.6; food, 128.2. *Industrial Production* (1980 = 100), 142.

Foreign Trade (1992 U.S.$): *Imports*, $233,548,000,000; *exports*, $340,483,000,000.

September 16 the Hosokawa cabinet added $57 billion in tax incentives, low-interest loans, and increased public-works spending. The government also announced plans to simplify regulations and to pass on the benefits of the yen's rise in value to consumers. On September 21 the Bank of Japan cut the official discount rate to an all-time low of 1.75% to shore up business.

Demographic Developments. Japan's population approached 124 million at the end of fiscal 1992, according to a Home Affairs Ministry survey. A record-low growth rate of 0.3% produced an average household of only 2.88 persons, smaller than ever before. Influx into the three big metropolitan areas—Tokyo, Nagoya, and Osaka-Kyoto—slowed while rural areas grew in population. Saitama Prefecture, just north of Tokyo, showed the nation's largest population gains for the seventh year in a row.

Foreign Affairs

Japan's new leader, Prime Minister Hosokawa, changed the nation's foreign stance as well. In August, upon taking office, he made a formal apology to the world for Japan's past "acts of aggression." In a speech delivered in English to the UN General Assembly in New York on September 27, Hosokawa expressed a "sense of remorse" over wartime deeds. He indicated that Tokyo was prepared to assume additional UN responsibilities.

U.S. Relations. After Miyazawa's first summit meeting with President Clinton in Washington on April 16, the prime minister called Japan's huge trade surplus "embarrassing" and pledged to reduce it. In October, Japan's Finance Ministry reported that the trade surplus with the United States for the month of September was $5.67 billion. The surplus was fueled by the yen's surge against the dollar to a postwar high (111 yen = $1), in part a reaction to Clinton's blunt support of a stronger yen. Indeed, by midyear the bloated surplus reflected an even higher level (100 yen = $1). However, by early November it began a slow fall (107 yen = $1).

As a positive aftermath of the Tokyo summit meeting between the seven major industrial nations (G-7) on July 10, the United States and Japan agreed on a new "framework" for trade relations. Negotiations on access to specific sectors—government procurement, regulatory reform, the automobile industry, and direct investment—began and were reaffirmed in September in a meeting between Hosokawa and Clinton at the UN in New York City. Moreover, the arrival in Tokyo of a new U.S. ambassador, 65-year-old Walter F. Mondale, sounded a new tone in ongoing trade negotiations. Highly respected by the Japanese, the former U.S. vice-president brokered an agreement on October 26 opening up the critical arena of construction projects. He planned to avoid threats of sanctions wherever possible.

Nonetheless, a joint survey (*New York Times*-CBS News-Tokyo BS News) revealed that a majority (55%) of Americans believed that Japan was taking advantage of the United States, while most Japanese (77%) felt that the United States was making unfair trade demands. In December, Prime Minister Hosokawa announced that Japan reluctantly was opening its rice market to imports.

Russian Relations. Moscow pressed Tokyo for assistance to bolster Russian reforms. The Japanese continued to respond cautiously to these efforts because of a petty territorial dispute that dated back to the end of World War II.

Japan had normalized relations with the USSR in the 1950s but a peace settlement awaited agreement on the status of four small islands in the southern Kurils, occupied by Russia since 1945. On April 15 in a preliminary meeting in Tokyo, G-7 and European Community (EC) ministers offered Russia some $40 billion to support President Boris Yeltsin in his April 25 referendum. Yeltsin acknowledged Japan's share ($1.82 billion) but, hard-pressed at home, postponed an official visit to Tokyo for the second time.

The Tokyo meeting of advanced nations in July was called the "G-7+1" summit, because Yeltsin attended as a guest. When President Yeltsin informally talked with Prime Minister Miyazawa, they agreed on an official meeting to be held in the fall. Finally, in talks held October 12-13 in Tokyo, Yeltsin followed Hosokawa's precedent by apologizing for the "inhuman" treatment of Japanese prisoners by Soviet troops after the war. He also pledged to honor a 1956 declaration by which the USSR had promised to return two of the islands off Hokkaido upon conclusion of a bilateral peace treaty.

The Two Koreas In July 1992, Tokyo released a report contending there was no evidence to sustain the charge that during the Pacific War, Japan's Imperial Army had recruited "comfort women" to provide sex for soldiers on the mainland. After countless women—mainly Koreans—had testified to the contrary, on Aug. 4, 1993, the government made public some 100 documents which admitted that military authorities had been in constant control of women forced into prostitution. Chief Cabinet Secretary Kono apologized on behalf of the government. South Korea's Foreign Minister Hang Sung Joo concluded that the apology removed "one of the major stumbling blocks" in the way of smooth relations between Seoul and Tokyo.

The Democratic People's Republic of Korea (North Korea) remained the only Asian nation with which Japan had no formal relations. Tokyo was disturbed by a declaration March 12 by Pyongyang that the regime would withdraw from the Nuclear Nonproliferation Treaty. North Korea had stated that the move was in protest against U.S.-South Korea "Team Spirit" military exercises. The spokesman for the Japanese

A ROYAL WEDDING

A major 1993 news event in Japan was the marriage of Crown Prince Naruhito to Masako Owada on June 9. The wedding, held in a Shinto sanctuary on the grounds of the Imperial Palace, was steeped in centuries-old tradition. The couple wore elaborate ceremonial robes *(below left)* similar to those of their ancestors. Some 800 guests attended, but—as Japanese tradition dictates—not the emperor or empress. Following the ceremony, the couple rode through the streets of Tokyo in a celebratory parade attended by about 200,000 well-wishers, *below right;* that afternoon, the newlyweds formally reported their marriage to Emperor Akihito and Empress Michiko in a solemn ceremony *(above)*. In the days following the marriage, six imperial banquets accommodating 2,700 guests were held to mark the occasion.

Emperor Akihito, extreme right, front row, greeted Boris Yeltsin during his October 1993 visit to Japan. The disputed Kuril Islands were the focus of discussions between the Russian president and Japanese leaders.

© Iwasa/Ochihara/Sipa

Foreign Ministry, Ambassador Masamichi Hanabusa, stated the move would bring "grave repercussions" to the two Koreas and to the world.

Pyongyang also was embroiled with the International Atomic Energy Agency, which had been denied access to two nuclear sites near Yongbyon, North Korea. A watchdog group gave the North Koreans until March 25 to cooperate with inspections. After interminable negotiations, on June 12 at the UN in New York, First Deputy Foreign Minister Kang Sok Ju told U.S. delegates that Pyongyang had announced a delay in treaty withdrawal.

Just two weeks before, however, a different threat had come over the horizon from Korea. An intermediate-range Rodong-1 missile covered 300 mi (483 km), about half its range, to splash down in the Sea of Japan. Capable of carrying chemical or even nuclear warheads, the weapon presumably could have reached Japan's second-largest city, Osaka. Foreign Minister Kabun Muto announced that Japan would mount countermeasures against the North Korean weapons system.

In Tokyo, en route to Seoul in early November, U.S. Secretary of Defense Les Aspin unveiled a suggested U.S.-led missile-defense program. Japan was regarded by the United States as the ally most vulnerable to missile attack. In Seoul, Aspin was urged by both South Korea and Japan to counsel Washington to defer pressure against Pyongyang.

The Rest of Asia. Analysts in Beijing claimed that China absorbed at least 3% of Japan's total overseas investment in 1992. The total came to more than $750 million, a $200 million rise from the previous year. Joint ventures developed in cement production, oil in the Xinjiang region, and automobile manufacturing.

A Foreign Ministry report released June 11 revealed that Japan had provided more than $11 billion in official development assistance (ODA) in 1992. The total was about a 3% increase over 1991 expenditures and held Japan's position as the world's top donor. Indonesia was the top recipient, followed by China, the Philippines, India, and Thailand.

United Nations. In his first visit to Japan, in a February interview with Kyodo News Service, UN Secretary-General Boutros Boutros-Ghali expressed the hope that the nation would alter its constitution so as to participate in more heavily armed peacekeeping operations. Better received was his suggestion that problems in the new world order called for a "democratized" United Nations. The secretary-general hinted that Japan, along with Germany and Brazil, needed to play larger roles in world affairs. In Tokyo, although the wish was expressed subtly, this meant that Japan should have a permanent seat on the UN Security Council.

In fact, Japan was a leading contributor—financially at least—to international organizations. As a Ministry of Finance report revealed, in 1992, Japan's contribution rate to the UN budget was more than 12% (surpassed only by the United States, which gave 25%). Japan also ranked second in contributions to the International Monetary Fund and to the World Bank.

Moreover, after a successful year in Cambodia, Japan's first peacekeeping force from its Self-Defense Forces (SDF) closed base and returned home in September. Already, another contingent of Japanese soldiers had been dispatched, in mid-May, on a second peacekeeping mission to Maputo, Mozambique, to oversee general elections.

Disasters. In July a major earthquake, measuring magnitude 7.8, struck the western coast of northern Japan with tsunami waves and significant structural damage. At least 200 persons were killed by the quake, which originated in the vicinity of Hokkaido Island.

In July an explosion at a factory in Niihima on the southern island of Shikoku sharply limited global production capacity for computer memory chips. More than 50% of epoxy resin used to seal the chips had been produced at the factory.

ARDATH W. BURKS, *Rutgers University*

JORDAN

Jordan's foreign and economic policies continued to attempt a delicate balancing act during 1993. As a small nation torn between Western influence and Islamic tradition and wedged between two historically bitter enemies—Iraq and Israel—Jordan has had to tread warily to avoid major conflict. Political problems remained exacerbated by economic difficulties caused by refugees and interruptions to normal trade. Jordan continued to need Western aid, especially since aid from wealthier Arab states had been lacking since 1990.

However, despite these hazards, Jordanian internal policy showed one clear line of purpose: the development of its form of government from a constitutional monarchy into a genuine multiparty democracy. And in foreign policy, Jordan pushed ahead with breakthrough peace talks with Israel. Though clearly a gamble, the political reforms and involvement in Middle East peace efforts earned a strong vote of approval in general elections that were held in November.

Much of the year was spent watching and waiting for developments, particularly concerning the dragging negotiations between Israel and Jordan and the Palestine Liberation Organization (PLO). Questions lingered about what role Jordan would have in a new regional configuration if an agreement was reached, and about whether or not—and under what electoral rules—the general election due in the fall actually would take place. Answers to these questions finally came late in the year.

Foreign Relations. King Hussein continued his policy of distancing Jordan cautiously from Saddam Hussein of Iraq, and of trying actively to further the Middle East peace process. On June 18 in Washington, he met U.S. President Bill Clinton for the first time—the ninth U.S. president he had dealt with. At the time, King Hussein had been aware only in general terms that secret PLO-Israel negotiations had been in progress.

On September 14, Jordan signed its own "agenda for peace" with Israel, and two weeks later the king's brother, Crown Prince Hassan, met with Israel's Foreign Minister Shimon Peres in Washington, with President Clinton in attendance. Hassan and Peres then announced plans to set up committees to normalize economic relations between the two countries.

The King's Health. The health of King Hussein, 57, remained a major concern. He underwent major surgery for cancer at the Mayo Clinic in Rochester, MN, in August 1992. A checkup in December 1992 showed no signs of the disease's recurrence and tests at the end of June 1993 showed "no traces of the cancer." Physicians indicated that the monarch's overall health was excellent. The king's illness and recovery evoked an upsurge of sympathy for him which continued through 1993 and, paradoxically,

strengthened his position. On May 2 he celebrated 40 years on the throne—an extraordinary record of survival. Most Jordanians never have known any other ruler. In this emotional climate, Jordanian politics during 1993 had a restrained quality. Even the normally fundamentalist Islamists adopted this air and strove to present themselves as loyal moderates.

Domestic Politics. The fractious parliament elected in 1989, in which the Islamists constituted the largest bloc, adjourned for what proved to be the last time on March 31. In March an Islamist attempt to enforce segregation by sex in schools and swimming pools was defeated. The Jordanian Bar Association also elected an executive committee with a centrist majority. The legal registration of political parties, permitted since July 1992, proceeded, and 22 had been registered formally by the fall.

On May 29 the king replaced his old friend, Zaid Ibn Shaker, as prime minister with Abdul Salam Majali, head of the Jordanian delegation to the peace talks. A number of cabinet changes also were made.

On August 4 the king dissolved the existing parliament—Jordan's eleventh—and called new elections for November 8, to be held under new electoral laws. The former bloc-voting system was replaced by a one-man, one-vote system that was expected to reduce the Islamist representation. Despite the changing situation created by the PLO-Israeli accord in September, the election was held as scheduled.

The result was the first major democratic setback for Islamic fundamentalists in the Middle East. The Islamic Action Front (IAF), though the best-organized party, lost six of its former 22 seats in the elected lower house, leaving conservative and moderate deputies in control. The election was a tough defeat for the IAF, which had based its platform on opposition to peace talks with Israel. One of the three women elected was Toujan al-Faisal, a strongly secular pro-

---

JORDAN • Information Highlights

Official Name: Hashemite Kingdom of Jordan.
Location: Southwest Asia.
Area: 35,475 sq mi (91 880 km²).
Population (mid-1993 est.): 3,800,000.
Chief Cities (Dec. 31, 1991 est.): Amman, the capital, 965,000; Zarqa, 359,000; Irbid, 216,000.
Government: *Head of state,* Hussein I, king (enthroned May 2, 1953). *Head of government,* Abdul Salam Majali, prime minister (took office May 29, 1993). *Legislature*—Parliament: House of Representatives and Senate.
Monetary Unit: Dinar (.687 dinar equals U.S.$1, Dec. 1, 1993).
Gross Domestic Product (1991 est. U.S.$): $3,600,000,000.
Economic Index (1992): *Consumer Prices* (1980 = 100), all items, 233.4; food, 211.8.
Foreign Trade (1992 U.S.$): *Imports,* $3,257,000,000; *exports,* $1,194,000,000.

Western journalist and feminist bitterly opposed by fundamentalists.

The Economy. Although Jordan still faced massive financial problems, particularly with its foreign indebtedness, the financial situation generally became less desperate. The International Monetary Fund (IMF) and other monetary institutions were sympathetic to Jordan's plight, especially in light of its progress toward democracy. In February the "Paris Club" of donors gave $380 million in loans and grants to ease the balance of payments for the year.

A report issued early in 1993 showed that the Jordanian economy had lost more than $570 million during 30 months of U.S. sanctions against Iraq, as transit traffic through the port of al-Aqaba was reduced to a trickle. On the other hand, money brought into Jordan by several hundred thousand Jordanians expelled from Kuwait and other Gulf countries helped generate a massive economic boom and much new construction. An unfortunate side effect of this infusion was a widening gap between the well-off and the poor. Despite boom conditions, almost one third of the population lived in poverty. A severe and unjust blow to individuals was the Iraqi repudiation in May of its 25-dinar "Swiss" notes. Many of these were held by Jordanians, and personal savings estimated at $250 million were wiped out. *See also* MIDDLE EAST.

ARTHUR CAMPBELL TURNER
University of California, Riverside

KANSAS

In the spring and summer of 1993, Kansas was hit hard by excessive rainfall and flooding which caused significant crop losses. In September, Gov. Joan Finney surprised Kansans by announcing that she would not run for a second term.

Agriculture and Floods. In some areas of Kansas, rainfall totals were 20 inches (50 cm) above normal by July, causing flooding along the Kansas River and the Missouri River in northeast Kansas. Among the hardest-hit areas were Manhattan, near the Tuttle Creek Reservoir constructed after a 1951 flood; farmland and communities downriver; and Elwood. As of November 1, Kansans had received $22.4 million in crop-disaster payments and at least 9,000 farmers had more than 33% of their crops destroyed.

Excessive rain and flooding damaged more than 2.85 million acres (1.15 million ha) of wheat and 1.47 million acres (595 350 ha) of sorghum, soybeans, and corn. In spite of the damage, Kansas wheat production was 388.5 million bushels—7% greater than in 1992—allowing the state to regain its ranking as the nation's largest wheat producer. Other crops which matured in late summer did not enjoy this success. Corn production was down 7% from 1992, the sorghum crop was 30% smaller, and soybean

production dipped 16%. (*See also* THE GREAT FLOOD OF '93, page 44.)

Politics. On September 4, Governor Finney (D) announced that she would not seek a second term. She had been involved in several controversies since taking office, including conflicts with the state attorney general and the legislature. Several short-lived appointments and resignations had dampened her administration. U.S. Rep. Jim Slattery (D) announced his intention to run for governor.

Government. The Kansas legislature conducted its business during a short 92-day session. Workers-compensation reform was a major topic, following revelations of several large settlements to the retired commissioner of insurance and several others associated with administering workers-compensation claims. The maximum awards for permanent partial disabilities were limited, caps on legal fees were enacted, the position of assistant attorney general was created to investigate and prosecute abusive practices, and awards given in cases when related preexisting conditions are documented were reduced.

The legislature also approved refinements and additional funding for a school-finance formula that was enacted in 1992 and established a uniform $3,600 base for state aid per pupil. Several school districts challenged the law in court. Concern that an additional $100 million would be needed to fund the program in fiscal year 1995 led to frugal spending for other state agencies.

Other newly enacted legislation included stronger laws against driving and boating under the influence, revisions to sentencing guidelines enacted in 1992, and a new procedure to negotiate and approve tribal-state gambling compacts.

Kansas may face a settlement exceeding $100 million to retired military personnel living in the state following a ruling by the U.S. Supreme Court that questioned exposing federal pensions to income taxes while exempting state and local

---

KANSAS • Information Highlights

Area: 82,277 sq mi (213 098 km²).
Population (July 1, 1992 est.): 2,523,000.
Chief Cities (1990 census): Topeka, the capital, 119,883; Wichita, 304,011; Kansas City, 149,767.
Government (1993): *Chief Officers*—governor, Joan Finney (D); lt. gov., James L. Francisco (D). *Legislature*—Senate, 40 members; House of Representatives, 125 members.
State Finances (fiscal year 1991): *Revenue*, $5,249,000,000; *expenditure*, $5,134,000,000.
Personal Income (1992): $48,807,000,000; per capita, $19,348.
Labor Force (August 1993): *Civilian labor force*, 1,328,000; *unemployed*, 64,000 (4.8% of total force).
Education: *Enrollment* (fall 1991)—public elementary schools, 325,126; public secondary, 120,264; colleges and universities, 167,699. *Public school expenditures* (1990-91), $1,938,012.

pensions. Little progress was made in legal negotiations between the military retirees and the state.

Other. A Wichita doctor whose clinic already had been a target of antiabortionists was shot in both arms in August. A woman from Grants Pass, OR, was arrested on assault charges.

PATRICIA A. MICHAELIS
Kansas State Historical Society

KENTUCKY

Political corruption, legislative ethics, campaign-finance reform, and the health-care system captured headlines in Kentucky during 1993.

Other important developments included state-revenue shortfalls of $264 million, public debate over casino gambling, reform of the Kentucky Lottery Commission, establishment of off-track betting parlors, a comprehensive review of cutting government waste, and the appointment of the first female Supreme Court justice. Economic changes included the state takeover of Kentucky Central Life, a rise in homebuilding starts, fiscal distress and stagnant tax bases, plant closings, a decline in the national basic tobacco quota, and the completion of Toyota's plant expansion in Georgetown.

Corruption. A three-year federal probe of corruption involving banking, health-care, and horse-industry legislation in the state produced more than 15 indictments and reached a climax with the extortion and racketeering convictions of the speaker of the House and a top aide to former Gov. Wallace Wilkinson. And in three unrelated federal investigations, the husband of former Gov. Martha Layne Collins, Lexington's county attorney, and Jefferson county's sheriff were convicted of crimes involving political corruption.

The Legislature. In the wake of these scandals, the General Assembly selected some new leaders and produced tough laws on legislative ethics and campaign finance. Reforms included limitations on taking anything of value from lobbyists, creation of a Legislative Ethics Commission, a 35% limit on the share of campaign money (up to $5,000) that legislators can get from PACs, a "revolving door" rule banning former lawmakers from becoming lobbyists for two years, a ban on speaking fees for legislators, and strict lobbying-reporting requirements.

Because of a crisis in Medicaid funding and 450,000 uninsured Kentuckians, Gov. Brereton Jones, with widespread public support, tried to attain universal health-care coverage and mandated cost controls. Lobbied extensively by health-care special interests and small business employers, lawmakers refused to overhaul the financially strapped health-care system. Instead legislators passed a new tax levied on all health providers to fund Medicaid, set up the Kentucky Health Care Data Commission, and created a task force directed by legislative leaders to develop further comprehensive health-care reform.

KENTUCKY • Information Highlights

Area: 40,410 sq mi (104 660 km²).
Population (July 1, 1992 est.): 3,755,000.
Chief Cities (1990 census): Frankfort, the capital, 25,968; Louisville, 269,063; Lexington-Fayette, 225,366.
Government (1993): *Chief Officers*—governor, Brereton Jones (D); lt. gov., Paul Patton (D). *General Assembly*—Senate, 38 members; House of Representatives, 100 members.
State Finances (fiscal year 1991): *Revenue*, $9,951,000,000; *expenditure*, $9,048,000,000.
Personal Income (1992): $63,261,000,000; per capita, $16,848.
Labor Force (August 1993): *Civilian labor force*, 1,774,000; *unemployed*, 118,000 (6.7% of total force).
Education: *Enrollment* (fall 1991)—public elementary schools, 466,170; public secondary, 179,854; colleges and universities, 187,958. *Public school expenditures* (1990-91), $2,480,363,000.

Politics. More than 7,600 people filed for city and county offices, apparently attracted by the first-ever five-year term due to the 1992 amendment's provision of one less election year. Although Lexington elected its first female mayor and county attorney, women and blacks captured few local offices. Kentucky remained last in the nation in percentage of female state legislators.

Romano L. Mazzoli, a Democrat who has served 12 terms in the U.S. House of Representatives, said he would not seek reelection.

Education. An unprecedented number of school officials, charged with official misconduct and/or incompetence, were dismissed by the State Board for Elementary and Secondary Education in several eastern Kentucky counties. Since 1990 more than 375 Family Resource and Youth Services Centers and 625 local school councils—models for the nation—have been created. The first results from statewide testing of fourth-, eighth-, and 12th-graders, however, were disappointing.

Mines. Costain Coal Inc. pleaded guilty and agreed to pay $3.75 million in fines in connection with charges stemming from an 1989 mine explosion that killed ten miners. Miners in June joined a United Mine Workers strike against selected mines.

PENNY M. MILLER, *University of Kentucky*

KENYA

The ruling Kenya African National Union (KANU) retained power following elections, but only because opposition parties could not form a united front. KANU used increased patronage to maintain domestic support, stifling economic reforms demanded by international donors, whose financial help seemed vital to Kenya's economic future.

Politics. In December 1992, President Daniel arap Moi was elected to a third five-year term in

Tribal clashes that began during Kenya's 1992 presidential-election campaign continued into 1993. One group of Kikuyu families, who were driven from their farms in the Rift Valley by supporters of President Daniel arap Moi, were forced to form a refugee camp near the town of Elburgon, Kenya, right.

© Betty Press

an election marred by corruption and violence. Clashes that began during the election left more than 1,000 dead and 200,000 homeless in the Rift Valley, where KANU supporters attacked Kikuyu and other backers of the opposition. With only 36% of the popular vote, and most of his previous cabinet and all KANU representatives from the Kikuyu or Luo—the two largest ethnic groups in Kenya—defeated, Moi's government had little credibility. His stature was damaged further when he reappointed his old cabinet members and appointed an in-law, Musalia Mudavadi, as minister of finance.

After antigovernment outbursts in January, Moi suspended parliament until March. Opposition parties opted against a boycott and rejoined the National Assembly. Kenneth Matiba, head of the Forum for the Restoration of Democracy (FORD) Asili, became the leader of the opposition, joined by FORD Kenya and the Democratic Party.

Economy. Prior to a meeting with the International Monetary Fund (IMF) in March, Kenya implemented a series of economic reforms—aimed to win the aid of the IMF—that tightened public expenditures, floated the shilling for commercial transactions, and devalued the exchange rate for official transactions. The reforms caused a drop in the value of the shilling and a 60%-80% rise in the cost of basic commodities. Following a decision to permit exporters to retain foreign exchange in their own accounts, Kenya's own reserves became dangerously low and shortages emerged. Fearing opposition, the government suspended the reforms and rejected the IMF reform package completely.

Rapidly rising prices arose from corruption as the money supply was expanded late in 1992. To help finance its election campaign, the government had sold public land, printed excess currency, transferred public-sector pension funds, and paid export incentives to KANU loyalists.

Following Kenya's rejection of IMF proposals, Western donors met in Paris to reiterate their refusal to reestablish aid. Kenya argued that a serious economic deterioration would have broad regional ramifications and threatened to remove forcefully more than 500,000 refugees estimated to be residing along its northern borders.

In order to control inflation, the government vowed to curtail central-bank lending to private banks, to invest all public-sector pension funds in government securities, and to sell more treasury bills. While government spending grew by 27%, the government vowed to limit the budget deficit to 3% of gross domestic product (GDP).

The success of these measures depended upon the finance minister's ability to wrest control of public spending away from KANU stalwarts and upon the speed with which the government trimmed public services and privatized the economy. Success in these areas would reestablish public discipline in finance and curtail the government's use of public funds to maintain power. Economic problems made such measures even more critical. The economy grew by 0.4% in 1992, the lowest rate since 1984, and agriculture declined by 0.4%. Employment dropped for the third straight year, inflation increased 8% from 27.5% in 1992, and debt grew to 76% of the GDP. Servicing this debt required more than one third of the country's export revenue, so Kenya stopped making payments on most of its $7 billion international debt.

WILLIAM CYRUS REED
The American University in Cairo

KENYA • Information Highlights

Official Name: Republic of Kenya.
Location: East Coast of Africa.
Area: 224,961 sq mi (582 650 km²).
Population (mid-1993 est.): 27,700,000.
Chief Cities (1989 est.): Nairobi, the capital, 1,286,200; Mombasa (1985 est.), 442,369.
Government: *Head of state and government*, Daniel T. arap Moi, president (took office Oct. 1978). *Legislature* (unicameral)—National Assembly, 188 elected members, 12 appointed by the president.
Monetary Unit: Kenya shilling (64.20 shillings equal U.S.$1, June 1993).
Gross Domestic Product (1990 est. U.S.$): $8,500,000,000.
Economic Index (1992): *Consumer Prices* (Nairobi, 1990 = 100), all items, 154.5; food, 166.9.
Foreign Trade (1991 U.S.$): *Imports*, $1,839,000,000; *exports*, $1,130,000,000.

KOREA

For the first time in 32 years, South Korea installed a civilian president in 1993, Kim Young Sam, who introduced a series of anticorruption and democratic reforms that appeared to be enjoying success. Meanwhile, North Korea threatened to withdraw from the nuclear non-proliferation regime, setting off a charged diplomatic tug-of-war. This issue and overall relations between North and South Korea remained tense at year's end.

Republic of Korea (South Korea)

Politics and Government. A longtime opposition political leader, Kim Young Sam, took office as the 14th president of the Republic of Korea on February 25, 1993, promising reform and the creation of a "New Korea." Three broad areas of reform were stressed in the ensuing months: civilian control over and depoliticization of the military, creation of a "kinder and gentler" government, and anticorruption campaigns.

Within two weeks of Kim's inauguration, the army chief of staff and the commander of the powerful military-security unit were dismissed. Eventually, all service chiefs and key military commanders who were suspected of supporting the preceding regimes were replaced. Specially targeted for removal were members of the secret *Hanahoe* (One Mind) fraternity within the army, of which former Presidents Chun Doo Hwan and Roh Tae Woo had been charter members. Charges of bribery, kickbacks, and other irregularities were leveled against a dozen high-ranking military officers. By midyear all top military officers had taken an oath of noninterference and political neutrality. President Kim successfully established firm control over the military, allaying fears that a defiant military would challenge the first civilian commander in chief in more than 30 years.

Attempts to eradicate the vestiges of an authoritarian past and to create a more humane bureaucratic culture took many forms. A university professor, Kim Deok, was appointed the director of the much-feared Agency for National Security Planning. He promptly trimmed the organization and publicly disavowed secret police activities. As a symbolic gesture of openness, the streets leading to the presidential mansion, Blue House, were opened to civilian traffic for the first time in two decades.

More substantive was the decision to permit the rehiring of teachers who had been dismissed for unauthorized union activities and to release and restore the civil rights of more than 41,000 political dissidents and criminals. Efforts also were made to improve the efficiency and public accountability of bureaucracy. Simplified red tape and shorter response times for bureaucratic action were advertised. Immediately noticeable

to those familiar with the Korean street scene in past decades was the virtual cessation of violent student demonstrations and the removal of the helmeted riot police from busy street corners. Korea appeared to be a more civil and free society administered by a leadership that had become more sensitive to the needs of the people than in the past.

The campaign to stop corruption in public life started with the unusual announcement by President Kim that he would accept no political funds from businesses. He then proceeded to disclose his and his family's financial assets. Upon his urging, more than 1,100 high officials, including the members of the National Assembly, made similar disclosures. In May the Public Officials Ethics Law was enacted, which required everyone in public service to register their assets or to resign. Any irregularity or hint thereof was to be investigated. Public outcry against those with excessive wealth that could not be explained forced the resignation and retirement of scores of bureaucrats and more than a dozen lawmakers, including the speaker of the National Assembly, Park Jyun Kyu.

Coupled with widely publicized prosecution of former cabinet ministers on charges of bribery and other abuses, the disclosure campaign created anxiety among officeholders and an exciting spectacle for the public. A public-opinion survey conducted 100 days into President Kim's term showed an impressive approval rating of 81% in support of his reform program. President Kim displayed unexpected vigor, conviction, and political skill in executing his reform measures.

To appease his critics, Kim replaced Prime Minister Hwang In Sung with Lee Hoi Chang, a former Supreme Court justice who in his most recent capacity as director of the audit board had been the president's chief agent in the anticorruption campaign. This change also signaled Kim's continuing drive to purge the government of holdovers from the previous military-led administrations in the name of reform.

After becoming president of South Korea in February 1993, Kim Young Sam (r) named Hwang In Sung (l) as premier. In December, Kim changed premiers, appointing Lee Hoi Chang.

© Reuters/Bettmann

Foreign Affairs. Foreign policy never had been Kim Young Sam's strong suit. Nevertheless efforts were made to highlight a foreign-policy orientation which differed from that of previous administrations. Kim offered a New Diplomacy which, according to his foreign minister, entailed five fundamentals: globalism, diversification, multidimensionalism, regional cooperation, and future orientation. This policy emphasized the pursuit of a more independent and mature foreign policy befitting a country coming into its own. Nine foreign heads of state visited Korea in 1993—a measure of Seoul's growing international standing. In a July visit, U.S. President Bill Clinton reassured Seoul of the United States' firm security commitment in Korea. In November, Japanese Prime Minister Morihiro Hosokawa formally apologized for Japan's past occupation of Korea in a tone that was more sincere than any previous statement from a Japanese leader.

South Korean-U.S. relations remained a key concern of Seoul in 1993. In the face of loud internal protests and after prolonged negotiations, Korea granted some trade concessions to the United States in financial services, intellectual-property rights, and agricultural exports to pave the road to the General Agreement on Tariffs and Trade (GATT) in December.

Seoul anxiously watched U.S. negotiations to open North Korea's nuclear sites to international inspection. Seoul hoped that the U.S. response to Pyongyang would be as firm as possible without provoking the North to lash out in desperation. Close consultation between the two allies was critical but each nation had different priorities. During a visit to Washington in November, President Kim reportedly persuaded President Clinton to abort an offer to North Korea that would have granted significant concessions such as economic aid or diplomatic recognition before North Korea would allow nuclear inspection. President Kim also insisted that his government should have the final say on whether to suspend the joint U.S.-South Korean military exercise, known as Team Spirit, during 1994.

Economy and Trade. South Korea's economy in 1993 began to accelerate slowly from the sluggish pace of 1992, when the annual growth rate had declined to 4.7% from 8.4% in 1991. The gross national product (GNP) in 1992 was $295 billion. Under the slogan of creating a "New Economy," the Kim government aimed at a 6% growth rate but had to settle for an estimated 4.9% rate—a respectable rate by most standards. This "setback" was attributed partly to a poor harvest caused by a cool summer, but it also could be explained by an uncertain business environment under new political leadership.

Perhaps the most noteworthy economic event of 1993 was the inauguration of a so-called real-name system in banking. The need for this system long had been recognized. For decades Korean bank depositors were able to open accounts using fictitious names rather than their own, allowing people to conduct secret financial transactions. Past political leaders did not eliminate the system. In August, President Kim used his emergency power and ordered the closure of all nonreal-name accounts after a two-month grace period. Despite initial misgivings, 95% of targeted bank accounts, worth an estimated $7 billion, were transferred to real-name accounts. The long-term effect of this shock treatment on the economy was expected to be positive.

South Korea's exports continued to grow at a steady rate of 4.8% in the first ten months of the year. However, imports continued to outpace exports, creating a negative trade balance of more than $2 billion in late October. This deficit nevertheless signified a substantial improvement in the balance of trade; it was less than half of the 1992 shortfall of more than $5 billion. South Korea's trade with the United States showed a small surplus at the end of October 1993 of $360 million.

Although South Korean-U.S. trade was roughly in balance, much U.S. pressure was exerted to reduce Korea's protective barriers. Much publicity and emotion were focused on the question of opening the Korean rice market as part of the Uruguay round of the GATT talks. Only days before the December 15 deadline, the Seoul government agreed in principle to admit foreign rice into South Korea. Angry street demonstrations ensued and President Kim publicly apologized for the decision.

Democratic People's Republic of Korea (North Korea)

Domestic Affairs. The 81-year-old self-proclaimed Great Leader Kim Il Sung remained the head of the government and the ruling Korean Workers' Party in 1993, but his son, Kim Jong Il, clearly was assuming an ever-growing role as the de facto decision maker. In April the Supreme

---

SOUTH KOREA • Information Highlights

Official Name: Republic of Korea.
Location: Northeastern Asia.
Area: 38,023 sq mi (98 480 km²).
Population (mid-1993 est.): 44,600,000.
Chief City (1990 census): Seoul, the capital, 10,612,577.
Government: *Head of state and government*, Kim Young Sam, president (formally inaugurated Feb. 25, 1993). *Legislature*—National Assembly.
Monetary Unit: Won (808.4 won equal U.S.$1, August 1993).
Gross National Product (1992 est. U.S.$): $294,500,000,000.
Economic Indexes (1992): *Consumer Prices* (1980 = 100), all items, 213.0; food, 227.7. *Industrial Production* (1980 = 100), 344.
Foreign Trade (1992 U.S.$): *Imports,* $81,775,000,000; *exports,* $76,632,000,000.

During a visit to South Korea on July 10-11, 1993, U.S. President Bill Clinton inspected the demilitarized zone between North and South Korea, left, and spoke to U.S. military personnel guarding the zone. The U.S. president also told South Korea's parliament that more-restrictive economic sanctions could be imposed against North Korea if that nation did not permit international inspectors to visit its nuclear-energy sites.

© Reuters/Bettmann

People's Assembly (SPA) elected the younger Kim, 51, chairman of the National Defense Commission, reconfirming his control over military affairs. This new title for the "Dear Leader" was particularly significant because the 1992 revision of North Korea's constitution highlighted the preeminence of the commission in the governing machinery of the country. Kim Jong Il also was identified publicly as the source of major decisions such as the proclamation of a high military alert in March (at the time of Team Spirit exercises) and North Korea's declaration of withdrawal from the Nuclear Non-Proliferation Treaty (NPT) shortly thereafter.

Yon Hyong Muk, the chief North Korean negotiator who signed the pact of reconciliation and nonaggression with South Korea in December 1991, was replaced as premier of the Administration Council (the cabinet) by Kang Song San, a former premier. Although Kang had been identified as a technocrat, not a fanatical ideologue, this reshuffle and subsequent personnel changes announced in December 1993 seemed to signal a turn toward hard-line politics.

Further economic deterioration in 1993 may have been linked to the political shift. The third seven-year plan (1987-93) experienced serious setbacks. Negative economic-growth rates were reported for 1990, 1991, and 1992. The plan's failure was announced formally at the December meeting of SPA—an act of rare candor on the part of the North.

In January, China followed Russia in demanding cash payments for its exports to North Korea—a severe blow to a nation strapped for hard currency and dependent on Chinese oil. Reports of food shortages became more frequent. Efforts to turn the economy around included North Korea's continuing participation in the United Nations (UN)-sponsored five-nation Tumen River Basin project; a delegation from Pyongyang attended a workshop in Seoul in November when inter-Korean relations were very frosty. Three new laws on foreign invest-

ment, similar to those adopted by China with much success, were passed by the Supreme People's Assembly in April. It was clear, however, that North Korea would continue to place politics ahead of the economy.

Nuclear-Weapons Issues. North Korea became the object of growing international attention to its nuclear development. For several years reports had discussed North Korea's suspected nuclear-weapons production, but many observers were reassured by the signing of the inter-Korean agreement to keep the peninsula nonnuclear in December 1991 and Pyongyang's accession in January 1992 to allow inspections by the International Atomic Energy Agency (IAEA).

However, Pyongyang dashed such hope by a sudden announcement on March 12, 1993, of its withdrawal from the NPT, charging IAEA's alleged lack of impartiality. On June 11, following days of intensive negotiations in New York with U.S. Assistant Secretary of State Robert Gallucci, North Korea's First Deputy Foreign Minister Kang Sok Ju announced "unilateral suspension" of its withdrawal. A second round of U.S.-North Korean meetings took place in July without any agreement. The third round, expected to meet within two months, did not materialize by year's end. Nor had there been

---

NORTH KOREA • Information Highlights

Official Name: Democratic People's Republic of Korea.
Location: Northeastern Asia.
Area: 46,540 sq mi (120 540 km²).
Population (mid-1993 est.): 22,600,000.
Chief Cities (1986 est.): Pyongyang, the capital, 2,000,000; Hamhung, 670,000.
Government: *Head of state and government*, Kim Il Sung, president (nominally since Dec. 1972; actually in power since May 1948). *Legislature* (unicameral)—Supreme People's Assembly. The Korea Workers' (Communist) Party: General Secretary, Kim Il Sung.
Gross National Product (1991 est. U.S.$): $23,300,000,000.

A North Korean cruise ship lies at anchor north of Tokyo, Japan, and represents one of the North's few contacts with the outside world. With international concerns growing that the North was developing nuclear weapons and with its economy experiencing negative growth, North Korea became even more isolated in 1993.

any IAEA inspections since February 1993. In the meantime, North Korea developed and tested a 620-mi (1 000-km) range ballistic missile, called Rodong 1, capable of reaching western Japan. Other reports indicated that Iran and Syria wanted to buy the missiles from North Korea.

U.S. concerns focused on nuclear proliferation and destabilization of military equilibrium in the region of East Asia. The United States employed a carrot-and-stick ploy: economic and technical aid, diplomatic recognition, and cancellation of the annual Team Spirit exercise on the one hand, and the threat of a range of unspecified sanctions through the United Nations on the other. Washington wanted to act in consultation with other interested countries, especially South Korea, Japan, and China—a process that had been difficult.

The most likely military use of a North Korean nuclear weapon would be deterrence. Even after the withdrawal of U.S. tactical nuclear weapons from Korea in 1992, South Korea and Japan remained covered by the U.S. nuclear umbrella. While the deterrence factor should not be ignored, North Korea also benefited from increased diplomatic leverage. This new strength brought the United States to the conference table after Washington had been reluctant for several years to go beyond low-level contacts in Beijing despite overtures from Pyongyang.

As the year drew to a close, the nuclear issue remained unsolved, giving rise to talks of a military showdown. The seven known North Korean nuclear plants on the IAEA list, including two reactors in Yongbyon, continued to operate.

China, the only remaining ally of North Korea, openly had favored a nonnuclear Korea but insisted on a diplomatic solution without resorting to sanctions. Japan, preoccupied with its own internal political turmoil, had stood on the sideline without reactivating the on-and-off negotiations with North Korea that had languished since May 1992. UN Secretary-General Boutros Boutros-Ghali visited Seoul and Pyongyang during the 1993 Christmas season.

The Two Koreas

Contrary to expectations that a civilian government in Seoul would improve relations between the two Koreas, 1993 failed to show any progress in the inter-Korean dialogue. The momentum built in 1991-92 from the pact of reconciliation and nonaggression, a nonnuclear declaration, and eight rounds of premier-level conferences seemed almost lost.

South Korea's President Kim in his inaugural address made an emotional reference to the fact that blood was more important than ideology. His aides repackaged Seoul's unification formula to highlight the three stages of exchange, federation, and an ultimate political union. Seoul ignored Pyongyang's protest and resumed in March Team Spirit exercises that had been suspended in 1992, in response to the North's unwillingness to open nuclear sites to international inspection. The North responded by announcing withdrawal from the NPT. The chilly atmosphere did not improve even after Seoul allowed repatriation of Yi In Mo, a 76-year-old former Communist guerrilla who had been imprisoned for more than three decades in the South.

When South Korean Premier Hwang In Sung proposed in May to meet his northern counterpart, the latter responded by proposing yet another format for the dialogue: an exchange of special envoys at the vice-premier level to prepare a summit conference. The reason for the proposed change was not clear, but Seoul, after some hesitation, decided to go along as long as the nuclear issue would be the first item for discussion.

In October three meetings of lower-level officials to prepare for the exchange of special envoys were held but little substantive progress was reported. The North called off a meeting scheduled in November, blaming U.S. and South Korean unwillingness to suspend Team Spirit in 1994.

HAN-KYO KIM
University of Cincinnati

KUWAIT

Continued tension with Iraq and economic reconstruction dominated Kuwait during 1993.

Security and Foreign Relations. Kuwaitis felt threatened as Iraq maintained its claim to Kuwait and kept more than 600 Kuwaitis prisoner to apply pressure.

On Oct. 11, 1992, Kuwait had agreed to buy 236 tanks from the United States at a cost of about $4 billion. When Iraqis moved into border zones that the United Nations had awarded to Kuwait, U.S. President George Bush sent 1,250 U.S. troops, who arrived on Jan. 15, 1993, just days before Bush left office.

On April 14-16 now former President Bush visited Kuwait, where he spoke to parliament. Iraqi intelligence agents planned to assassinate him, but they were detected and 17 were arrested in Kuwait on April 26. An investigation by the U.S. Federal Bureau of Investigation (FBI) confirmed Iraqi complicity, and on June 26 the United States bombed Iraqi intelligence headquarters in Baghdad.

Kuwait began June 10 to dig a security trench along its border with Iraq; when completed the trench was to be 120 mi (193 km) long, 9 ft (2.7 m) deep, and 16 ft (4.9 m) wide. Since Kuwaitis realized their safety depended chiefly on United Nations and U.S. protection, Kuwait aided the UN peacekeeping mission in Somalia by sending about 100 soldiers, and the government supported U.S.-backed Palestinian-Israeli peace talks by ending in June an indirect boycott of firms doing business in Israel.

Economic Reconstruction. As the recovery from the Iraqi occupation continued, Kuwait needed large sums of money from oil production to pay for rebuilding its infrastructure.

The Organization of the Petroleum Exporting Countries (OPEC) had kept in force at its Nov. 27, 1992, meeting a special rule allowing Kuwait to pump as much oil as it could; however, this policy was changed at the next OPEC meeting on Feb. 16, 1993, when Kuwait was limited to a quota of 1.6 million barrels per day. Kuwaiti Oil Minister Ali Ahmed al-Baghli, rejecting an OPEC offer on June 10 to increase its quota by only 10%, said on June 20 that Kuwait gradually would increase oil production to 2 million barrels per day. By September, Kuwait had reached or exceeded that level of production, and OPEC set a new and more realistic quota of 2 million barrels per day on September 28. Because of more money from oil, the government was able to reduce its budget deficit, although it had to draw down its foreign-cash reserves.

Political Changes. After the Oct. 5, 1992, parliamentary elections in which opposition groups won a majority of the 50 seats, Emir Jabir al-Ahmad al-Sabah on October 17 appointed a new cabinet, chaired by Prime Minister Crown Prince Saad al-Abdallah al-Sabah. Although key posts still were controlled by the royal family, the emir added to the cabinet opposition deputies, including the oil, justice, and commerce ministers. Parliament elected Ahmed Saadun as its speaker October 20; Saadun, who also was in the opposition, had been speaker in 1986.

KUWAIT • Information Highlights

Official Name: State of Kuwait.
Location: Southwest Asia.
Area: 6,800 sq mi (17 820 km²).
Population (mid-1993 est.) 1,700,000.
Chief Cities (1985 census): Kuwait, the capital, 44,335; Salmiya, 153,369; Hawalli, 145,126.
Government: *Head of state*, Jabir al-Ahmad al-Sabah, emir (acceded Dec. 1977). *Head of government*, Saad al-Abdallah al-Sabah, prime minister (appointed Feb. 1978). *Legislature*—National Council.
Monetary Unit: Dinar (0.300 dinar equal U.S. $1, August 1993).
Gross Domestic Product (1991 est. U.S.$): $8,750,000,000.

© Gustavo Ferari/Gamma-Liaison

Schoolgirls joined in welcoming George Bush to Kuwait on April 14, 1993. The Kuwaiti government presented the visiting former U.S. president with the nation's highest civilian medal in gratitude for his "efforts in liberating Kuwait" during the 1991 Persian Gulf war and for his "services toward world peace and understanding."

The parliament gradually gained additional powers during 1993, particularly as a financial scandal involving Kuwaiti investments in Spain showed that the administration of government needed oversight to stop abuses. In August the royal family gave parliament the right to obtain more information on financial matters, but the government also closed six human-rights organizations. On August 31 parliament passed a law on the repayment and cancellation of debts—a prerequisite for the personal financial recovery of many Kuwaitis.

WILLIAM OCHSENWALD
Virginia Polytechnic Institute
and State University

LABOR

After years of stormy weather, the climate for U.S. labor improved somewhat in 1993 while labor relations in other industrialized countries deteriorated as a result of economic recession.

United States

Signs of Economic Recovery. During the year the U.S. economy showed increasing signs of recovery, growing at a 2.8% annual rate in the third quarter, up from 1.9% in the second quarter. The Commerce Department noted that growth would have been even greater without the effects of a Mississippi River valley flood in the Midwest, a drought in the Southeast, and a decline in auto production.

Third-quarter employment increased by 1.5% over the same period in 1992, and the unemployment rate declined from 7.6% to 6.7%. In December the unemployment rate dropped sharply to 6.4%. All age groups—adult men, adult women, and teenagers—shared in the decrease in unemployment as did white, African-American, and Hispanic workers. Despite the improvement, the Bill Clinton administration considered the unemployment rate unacceptably high.

This was underscored by a Labor Department report that the government had been underestimating unemployment substantially, particularly among women, for at least a decade. The department discovered a bias in its survey methodology wherein women who were seeking jobs were described erroneously as homemakers, and therefore were not counted as being in the workforce. Under the redesigned survey to correct for this bias, the nation's unemployment rate in the 12 months through August 1993 was 7.6%, rather than the 7.1% previously reported by the Labor Department. The corrected rate for women was 6.8% rather than 6.0%, and for men 6.9% rather than 6.7%. The Labor Department also discovered that, in addition to undercounting jobless women, it was miscounting laid-off employees and discouraged workers.

Productivity, as measured by output per hour in the nonfarm business sector, rose by 3.9% during the third quarter, the largest increase since the first quarter of 1992. Unit labor costs in the nonfarm sector declined by 0.4%, the first quarterly decrease since 1987. Gross average weekly earnings rose by 2.9% during the first three quarters of 1993, while the Consumer Price Index for urban wage earners edged up by 2.5%, resulting in a 0.4% gain in real wages. However, after adjustment for inflation, real weekly earnings in September still were 6.9% below the level of 1983.

Worker-Management Relations. The Departments of Labor and Commerce appointed a panel of former cabinet officers and representatives of labor, business, and academia to explore the state of worker-management relations and labor law. The commission was chaired by John T. Dunlop, a former labor secretary (1975-76) and professor emeritus at Harvard University. In a background paper the commission listed four key facts relevant to its mission of reporting ways to encourage employees and managers to work together to improve the nation's competitiveness and standards of living.

• First, the U.S. economy had not performed well in recent years in meeting the needs of many workers and firms.

© AP/Wide World

Richard Trumka, right, president of the United Mine Workers of America, addressed a September 1993 rally in support of a strike against the nation's largest coal companies. The walkout began in the spring and ended in December with the ratification of a new five-year contract.

• Second, the U.S. system of labor relations, historically developed in labor-management conflict and partisan politics, was ill-suited to deal with current and future economic problems.

• Third, U.S. labor laws were not well-suited to take account of increased diversity of the workforce.

• Fourth, the complex and growing number of federal and state laws, administrative rules, and court rulings governing employee-management relations had produced costly litigation without efficient resolution of workplace problems.

On the positive side, the commission noted that some employers and unions had introduced a range of employment-involvement practices. The commission supported such programs and deemed them a long-term gain for workers and employers.

AFL-CIO Membership. Membership in AFL-CIO unions in 1993, as reported to the biennial AFL-CIO convention, dropped by 633,000 to about 13.3 million, a 5% decline from 1991. The 1993 figure was just 122,000 higher than the membership in 1971 but above the low point of 12.7 million in 1987. Mergers reduced the number of unions from 90 to 85.

Most unions showed drops in membership with only two—the Service Employees International Union (SEIU) and the American Postal Workers Union (APWU)—showing substantial gains. SEIU membership increased by 38,000 to 919,000 and APWU membership was up by 21,000 to 249,000 over 1991, the year of the last convention. The largest membership losses were suffered by the United Brotherhood of Carpenters and Joiners (86,000), the United Auto Workers (79,000), the International Brotherhood of Teamsters (63,000), and the International Association of Machinists (60,000). The Teamsters, with 1.3 million members, continued to be the largest union in the AFL-CIO, followed by the American Federation of State, County, and Municipal Employees with 1.2 million members, the United Food and Commercial Workers with 997,000, and the SEIU with 919,000. These membership figures did not include unions not affiliated with the AFL-CIO; the largest of these was the National Education Association, with more than 2 million members.

Family and Medical Leave. One of the first results of the change in administrations in Washington was the enactment of the Family and Medical Leave Act. This was a top priority of Bill Clinton during his campaign and the first major legislation passed by Congress and signed by the president. The law became effective on Aug. 5, 1993.

The act applies to employers of 50 or more employees. Covered employers must allow eligible employees to take up to 12 weeks of unpaid leave during any 12-month period for any of the following reasons: one, the birth of a child to the employee or the employee's spouse; two, adoption or acceptance of a child for foster care;

U.S. EMPLOYMENT AND UNEMPLOYMENT
(Armed Forces Excluded)

	1992	1993
Labor Force	127,414,000	128,138,000
Participation Rate	66.4%	66.1%
Employed	117,737,000	119,489,000
Unemployed	9,667,000	8,649,000
Unemployment Rate	7.6%	6.7%
Adult Men	7.2%	6.4%
Adult Women	6.5%	5.7%
Teenagers	20.4%	17.9%
White	6.7%	5.9%
African American	14.2%	12.7%
Hispanic	11.7%	10.1%

N.B. Third-quarter average, seasonally adjusted.
Source: U.S. Bureau of Labor Statistics

three, the need to care for a spouse, son, daughter, or parent with a serious health condition; and four, a serious health condition that makes the employee unable to perform job functions.

When both parents of a newborn or adopted child work for the same firm, the employer is required to grant only a total of 12 weeks of leave. But 12 weeks of leave must be provided to each spouse in order to care for a child with a serious health condition. Employers must continue to provide group health insurance to an employee on leave on the same terms as were provided while the employee was at work.

North American Free Trade Agreement. In a major victory, President Clinton succeeded in having Congress ratify the North American Free Trade Agreement (NAFTA) in November. NAFTA provides for decreasing and eventually eliminating, over 15 years, tariffs on almost all products and services passing among the United States, Canada, and Mexico.

Starting from what appeared to be almost certain defeat in the House of Representatives, President Clinton prevailed by a vote of 232 to 200 in that chamber. The Senate, where there was strong support from the outset, approved NAFTA shortly thereafter.

The major issues in the debate over NAFTA were its potential effect on jobs and the environment. The AFL-CIO, fearing the loss of jobs to Mexico, was opposed strongly to NAFTA and lobbied vigorously for its defeat. Many environmental organizations opposed NAFTA because of concern that U.S. firms would move to Mexico to avoid more stringent environmental-protection laws in the United States. The Clinton administration argued that, while some jobs would be lost through movement of firms to Mexico to take advantage of much lower wages and benefits, more jobs would be gained through exports to Mexico, especially among higher-skilled, professional and technical employees. With respect to the environment, the administration noted that it had negotiated side agreements that would lead to raising environmental standards in Mexico.

The AFL-CIO, which strongly had supported the president's election, felt that he had let the unions down by sacrificing jobs of U.S. workers

In March 1993 steelworkers at Krupp Stahl A.G. staged a protest in Duisburg-Rheinhausen, Germany, after the company announced the closing of a local plant and the elimination of some 2,000 jobs. Germany experienced unusually high unemployment during 1993, with some 3.72 million Germans looking for work.

© Reuters/Bettmann

for benefits to agriculture, business, and financial institutions. Many labor leaders were bitter toward the administration and Democratic members of Congress who had voted for NAFTA. The House of Representatives majority was achieved through more Republican than Democratic votes, indicating that on this issue the president was out of step with his party. As 1993 ended, it remained to be seen whether the president and the labor movement would mend their rift over the NAFTA issue and work together to pass other legislation important to the unions, including health-care reform, prohibiting the hiring of permanent replacements for striking workers, and increasing the minimum wage. These were measures on which Republicans, who voted for NAFTA, could not be counted to vote for administration proposals.

International

Italy. In July 1993 the Italian government, the major trade-union confederations, and the employers' organizations agreed to a new constitution for industrial relations. It provides the framework for a national incomes policy related to inflation and reforms the previous confused structure of collective bargaining. The central agreement regulates workplace union representation and introduces a degree of flexibility into the labor market.

The agreement abolished the previous pay-indexation system. In future there were to be three bargaining rounds every four years: company bargaining, national bargaining over pay, and national bargaining over other terms and conditions of employment. In effect the new approach followed the German system of four-year collective agreements with biennial pay negotiations.

The pact introduced a more participatory approach to company bargaining on issues other than those negotiated at the sector level. The agreement recognized the need of employers to have a responsible counterpart in the workplace to that of union representation. It was important because it revealed a high degree of maturity by employers and unions in the current unstable political situation in Italy.

The general secretaries of the three main confederations—CGIL, CISL, and UIL—withdrew their representatives from the governing bodies of several social-security institutions. The corruption scandal in the trade unions mirrored the bribery revelations among political leaders. For example, four national officials in CGIL and UIL were jailed during the year for receiving 174 million lire (c. $117,000) in exchange for allegedly agreeing to 170 job cuts in a major company.

Great Britain. A new survey based on interviews with nearly 5,000 managers and employee representatives in more than 2,000 workplaces covering 1,143,019 employees found a major decline in representation of workers by unions and in the coverage of collective bargaining, particularly in the public sector. The study concluded "that the traditional, distinctive 'system' of British industrial relations no longer characterized the economy as a whole."

Factors influencing this development were changes in the structure of the economy in the 1980s and the disappearance of many larger establishments in older manufacturing industries where trade unions were important. There also were changes in internal business structures, the privatization of much of the public sector, changes in labor laws, and the need to meet growing competition overseas. However, in workplaces where trade unions and collective bargaining persisted, there was little change.

The Trade Union Congress meeting in September elected John Monks general secretary, succeeding the retiring Norman Willis. The congress was marked by a strong pro-union speech by Labour Party leader John Smith. Monks' keynote address promised a new-style pragmatic unionism relevant to the modern world of work. The days of "overmighty unions are yesterday's history," and that period had been succeeded by "dictatorship by the bad employer," he said. He urged a change in industry "through security and partnership, not through fear and coercion."

Germany. As of the beginning of 1993, membership of German Trade Union (DGB)-affiliated unions was slightly more than 11 million, a decrease of about 800,000 as compared with the previous year. The decline was concentrated in the former East Germany, where the total of 3.4

million represented a fall of 18.4%. The decrease in the former West Germany, where membership stood at 7.6 million workers, was only 0.2%.

The sharp decline in eastern Germany was attributed by the DGB to large losses in employment resulting from deindustrialization. Particularly affected was the textile and clothing industry, in which output was only 10%-20% of output in 1989. Union membership in this industry was down by 45%.

The stagnant total membership in western Germany hid an increase of 2.0% in female membership at the same time that male membership was declining by 1.0% from the previous year. Women constituted 35% of all union members in Germany in 1993. Union wages in western Germany declined in real terms during the first six months of the year. While wage raises in eastern Germany actually kept pace with inflation, wages there still were far below those in western Germany.

Volkswagen (VW) A.G., Europe's largest automaker, and the I.G. Metal Union reached an agreement in November to reduce costs by putting production workers at its six plants in Germany on a four-day workweek and cutting production workers' pay by nearly 10%. Production workers were to begin working a four-day week of 28.8 hours on Jan. 1, 1994.

VW, which had been suffering from severe sales decreases and high production costs, offered workers a choice: accept the shorter workweek and a cut in pay or lose 30,000 of the company's 100,000 jobs by the end of 1995. The union accepted the reduced workweek. It expressed satisfaction with the agreement, stating that monthly base pay would be preserved by spreading traditional holiday bonuses and vacation pay over the year.

Reaction to the agreement from within Germany was mixed. A board member of the German Trade Union Association said that the VW agreement would serve as a pilot for other labor contracts. But the chairman of the Democratic-Christian Social Association of Medium-Sized Companies called the agreement "a decision against the market economy." Economists said the shorter workweek was not a longer-term solution for VW or for German industry.

Europeans already work fewer hours per week than workers in the United States, Japan, or Pacific Rim countries. In Germany the workweek averages 37 hours and nearly all workers get six weeks of paid vacation plus an additional month's pay as a holiday bonus in December. Public-opinion polls found a majority of Germans supporting the idea of a shorter workweek with lower pay if it meant maintaining employment.

France. In 1992, the latest year for which figures were available, 95,000 employees in France took parental leave without pay. Although the law extends to both men and women, 99% of those using this right were women. The Ministry of Labour considered the number of employees taking advantage of the law relatively low, as about 1 million households were eligible. Most employees using the parental-leave law worked in the private sector and in public employment outside civil service. Of every 100 employees taking parental leave, 83 were blue- or white-collar, 13 were middle-level professionals and managers, and four were senior cadres.

Japan. Faced with a loss of $300 million—and unwilling to dismiss white-collar workers—Mazda Corporation decided to shift 500 such workers to the assembly line for a three-month period, replacing contract workers. This contrasts with the practice of U.S. companies, which have laid off thousands of workers to become more efficient.

Japanese companies employ an estimated 2 million more workers than are needed. If they were laid off, the unemployment rate would climb to 5.6% from the late 1993 level of 2.6%. The unemployment rate also was kept artificially low by not counting women, who are the first to be let go and who do not seek other jobs. The government does not wish to see unemployment rise and is pressuring companies to maintain payrolls.

European Community (EC). European Economic Commission (EEC) institutions advertising themselves as equal-opportunity employers still set a maximum age in their advertisements. The EEC justified its policy on the ground that it wished to recruit staff able to serve for many years. These practices on hiring would be illegal in the United States, Canada, and New Zealand. An Equal Opportunities Review (EOR) survey, looking at 4,000 job advertisements during the "European Year of Older People," found almost one third specified an age qualification.

British employers appeared to signal that "you're over the hill at 45" in advertisements for employment. Some 30% stated an age preference as compared with 27% in a similar survey four years earlier. Some 80% of advertisements giving an age preference set an age limit of 45 years for applicants. For clerical, secretarial, and administrative jobs, 35 years or younger was specified. Despite claiming they were equal-opportunity employers, the survey found, many employers excluded applicants on the basis of age.

In a study of how Europeans spend their time, the following data were reported:

Work: Forty-eight percent of Europeans spend an average of seven hours and 20 minutes at work each weekday. British workers claimed to work six hours and 25 minutes per day, while workers in Portugal reported working nearly two hours longer. The proportion of the population working varied widely among countries. In Central European countries, 57% of the population was working as compared with 36% in Greece, 38% in Spain, and 39% in Ireland.

Life Satisfaction: 95% of Danes, Dutch, and Finns were satisfied with their lives, while in Central Europe only 72% of Czechs, 65% of Poles, and 58% of Hungarians expressed satisfaction.

JACK STIEBER, *Michigan State University*

LAOS

In 1993, Laos continued slowly to open itself to outside influences and worked on developing its economy.

Politics. While continuing to allow no political opposition, Laos' Communist rulers cautiously were opening the economy to market forces. In 1993 they began publishing the annual budget and laws governing economic activity, which previously had been secret.

The modest reforms were consistent with the course set by former President Kaysone Phomvihan, who died in November 1992. Prime Minister Khamtay Siphandon, 68, succeeded him in the key job of party chairman. Nouhak Phoumsavan, 78-year-old former chairman of the National Assembly, became president. Two younger political leaders who seemed likely to play increasingly important roles in Laos were Deputy Prime Minister Khamphoui Keoboualapha and Phao Bounnaphonh, who was in charge of government coordination.

Economics. The Mitraphap bridge, the first to span the Mekong River, would link Vientiane, the capital of Laos, to Nongkhai, Thailand. The bridge was being built by Australia and was to be opened by the king of Thailand in April 1994. It already had led to a building boom on both sides of the river, and would increase greatly the volume of goods and people crossing the river boundary. But many Lao worried that it also would bring pollution, crime, AIDS, and other modern problems.

The isolated mountain villages where most of Laos' 4 million people live in stark poverty have been changed very little by the opening of the country to foreign trade and investment. But in towns strung along the Mekong valley, cars, motorcycles, and TV sets now were commonplace for a small, newly rich business class. A new garment industry, mostly run by foreigners, had become the top export earner, surpassing the traditional sale of electric power and logs to Thailand. But inflation was down to 6% and the value of the kip, the national currency, remained stable.

Among government plans to promote economic growth were the encouragement of large-scale farming for export to Thailand; the development of hydroelectric power and mineral resources; and participation in a regional upgrading of roads, railroads, and tourist facilities linking Laos to China, Thailand, Vietnam, and Cambodia.

Foreign Relations. With the end of Russian aid and Vietnam's focus on its own internal problems, Laos was more on its own in 1993 than at any time in the 20th century. Thai businessmen were gaining a dominant role in the Lao economy, and the nation was dependent on the World Bank, International Monetary Fund (IMF), and Asian Development Bank for large capital-investment projects. Relations with the United States never were broken, and now were focused on resolving the status of Americans missing in action during the Vietnam war and on finding ways to curb opium production in Laos.

PETER A. POOLE
Author, "The Vietnamese in Thailand"

LATIN AMERICA

Corruption, long a factor in Latin American politics and business, but widely ignored by governments and the media, emerged as a volatile political issue throughout the region in 1993. Meanwhile, the military, frequently a potent political force in most countries, receded into the background as civilian governments strengthened their grip on the reins of power.

Politics. The first victim of Latin America's new demand for honesty in government was Brazil's President Fernando Collor de Mello, who was forced out of office in December 1992 on charges of pocketing millions of dollars in a kickback scheme. This political upheaval was followed in May by controversy surrounding Venezuelan President Carlos Andrés Pérez, who was suspended for misusing a discretionary fund of $17 million. He denied the fund was diverted for his own use, but in September the national Congress voted to make the removal permanent.

Also in May, Guatemalan President Jorge Serrano Elías dissolved the Congress and the Supreme Court, saying he did so to "purge the state of all its forms of corruption." Serrano's "auto coup" was similar to the action of Peruvian President Alberto Fujimori, who suspended Peru's Congress and constitution in 1992 in the face of rising civil unrest, military pressure, and a strong leftist guerrilla insurgency. Serrano's attempt, however, backfired. The Guatemalan military refused to support him and within a few days he was forced to resign and leave the country. In his place, the national Congress installed an unlikely choice: Ramiro de León Carpio, a crusading human-rights advocate and a frequent critic of the military. De León Carpio quickly fired Guatemala's defense minister and shuffled the military command.

The focus of Paraguay's 1993 presidential election was not corruption but the end of military domination of the government. A businessman, Juan Carlos Wasmosy, was elected in May, and in August he became the country's first

---

LAOS • Information Highlights

Official Name: Lao People's Democratic Republic.
Location: Southeast Asia.
Area: 91,430 sq mi (236 800 km²).
Population (mid-1993 est.): 4,600,000.
Chief City (1990 est.): Vientiane, the capital, 442,000.
Government: *Head of state:* Nouhak Phoumsavan. *Head of government,* Khamtay Siphandon. *Legislature* (unicameral)—Supreme National Assembly.

freely elected president since Paraguay achieved independence in 1811. He replaced Gen. Andrés Rodríguez, who in 1989 ousted Gen. Alfredo Stroessner to end 35 years of dictatorial rule and put Paraguay on the road to democracy.

Economy. During 1993 most of the nations of Latin America experienced, for the third consecutive year, moderate economic expansion, gradual price stabilization, alleviated debt burden, and significant inflows of external capital, according to the United Nations Economic Commission for Latin America and the Caribbean (ECLAC). "There is no possibility of a regression to the upheaval that characterized the 1980s," the commission said.

ECLAC projected year-end growth for the region at slightly more than 3%. However, the commission declared, the regional performance would be affected strongly by the behavior of the global economy and by an anticipated recovery of output in Brazil. Twelve Latin American countries were growing by between 3% and 5%, and only four by less than 3%. Meanwhile, Argentina and Chile were growing by more than 5%.

ECLAC reported that most countries of the region maintained or lowered their inflation rates during the year. Excluding Brazil, where the inflation rate accelerated, the region's annual weighted increase in consumer prices was about 19%, down from 22% in 1992.

Fiscal stability, achieved through the large-scale adjustments of recent years, also was preserved in 1993. However, the commission noted, as the hemisphere's economies return to normal after the "lost decade" of the 1980s, fiscal stability will become more difficult to maintain as the growth of tax receipts declines and government spending increases.

The region's cumulative external debt was expected to rise by 5% to 6% above the 1992 year-end level of $438 billion, due to the increasing acceptance of Latin American bonds in international markets and the expansion of commercial credit. However, a drop in interest rates was expected to bring debt service—as a proportion of exports of goods and services—down to about 16%, compared with 19% in 1992.

Latin America also continued the dramatic reversal of the capital flight of the 1980s and the resumption of investment-capital inflows to the region. Net capital inflows during 1993 appeared to exceed $50 billion, only slightly less than the record level achieved in 1992. According to the Inter-American Development Bank, Mexico was the leader in attracting both new capital and repatriating the flight capital of previous years. Lesser, but still significant, beneficiaries included Argentina, Brazil, Chile, Colombia, Peru, and Venezuela.

Trade. Economic expansion in the region sustained a strong demand for imports, and Latin America's merchandise trade balance, which turned negative in 1992, rose slightly to $14 billion in 1993. Of the total deficit, $6.4 billion was registered in trade with the United States. Overall, imports rose by about 9%, while exports grew by less than 6%. Economic-integration agreements completed in the last few years bolstered intraregional trade, which has become the "most dynamic element of the region's export sector," the ECLAC said.

In August the Western Hemisphere's three biggest trading partners—Canada, Mexico, and the United States—completed negotiations of supplementary accords to the proposed North American Free Trade Agreement (NAFTA), setting the stage for an intense debate in the U.S. Congress over approval of the tripartite pact. The side agreements covered labor and environmental standards and protection against sudden import surges. Opponents of NAFTA, including organized labor and some environmental groups, said the supplemental accords were not strong enough to win their backing and support for NAFTA. Nevertheless, Congress approved the pact.

During the year a feud erupted between banana-exporting countries in Latin America and those in the Caribbean over a European Community (EC) plan to tariff and limit banana imports from Central and South America and to give preference to imports from former European colonies in the Caribbean. Acting on a Latin American complaint, the General Agreement on Tariffs and Trade (GATT) ruled that the European plan would violate international trade rules.

In another commodity development, world coffee exporters—most of them in Latin America—formed a new Association of Coffee Producing Countries (ACPC) and agreed to withhold from the market as much as 20% of their output to strengthen sagging coffee prices. The ACPC denied it would be a producers' cartel, but the United States withdrew in protest from the International Coffee Organization, which included both producing and consuming nations.

Drugs. After years of U.S. funding efforts to halt the production and trafficking of illegal drugs—mainly cocaine—in Latin America, the new Clinton administration said that it would reduce its international drug-fighting budget sharply. Bolivia, Colombia, and Peru principally were affected by the U.S. decision. Key Latin leaders and U.S. officials agreed that the antidrug crusade had failed and argued that a new strategy was necessary. U.S. officials said that some of the money cut from international antidrug programs might be shifted to domestic efforts.

Other. Enrique Iglesias of Uruguay was sworn in for a second five-year term as president of the Inter-American Development Bank, the principal finance institution for Latin development. Iglesias is a former foreign minister of Uruguay and was executive secretary of ECLAC (1972-85). In its annual report, the Bank reported it had approved a record $6 billion in 1992 for 90 loans to finance economic and social development in Latin America and the Caribbean.

RICHARD C. SCHROEDER, *Consultant*
Organization of American States

LAW

For the first time in more than a quarter century, a Democratic president appointed a new U.S. Supreme Court justice in 1993. President Bill Clinton's nominee, Ruth Bader Ginsburg, succeeded retiring Justice Byron White and joined Sandra Day O'Connor to become the second woman ever on the nation's highest court. Most legal experts predicted Ginsburg would slow the steady conservative march engineered by previous Republican administrations. Justice Ginsburg—elevated from the U.S. Circuit Court of Appeals in Washington, DC—had a far smoother confirmation process than most recent Supreme Court nominees. She was confirmed by a vote of 96-3, as three senators voted against her, expressing displeasure over her support of abortion rights. (*See also* BIOGRAPHY.)

The high court's 1992-93 term was a relatively calm one. A slow move to the political right continued, as the justices handed civil-rights proponents some notable setbacks and chipped away at the separation between church and state. Some observers said the high court demonstrated an aversion to activism that matched the values of the court's moderate conservatives. The centrists included Justices O'Connor, David Souter, and Anthony Kennedy. Justice Souter surprised some observers with sharply worded dissents against some key conservative victories. Justice Kennedy was in the majority more than any other member of the high court, dissenting only six times in 107 cases. Chief Justice William Rehnquist and Justices Antonin Scalia and Clarence Thomas usually were allied on the right; and Justices Harry Blackmun and John Paul Stevens were the most liberal members on the court.

Retired Justice Thurgood Marshall, who stepped down in 1991, died in January at the age of 84. (*See also* OBITUARIES.) The Library of Congress opened Marshall's files to the public, angering the justices. Rehnquist asked the library to close the files, but the library argued it was following Marshall's wishes to let the public see his papers. Later in the year, the court considered taking action to prevent distribution of a tape-and-book set of famous oral arguments. Professor Peter Irons planned the distribution despite signing a statement agreeing to use the arguments only for private work.

In the lower courts, there were convictions in the Los Angeles police beating case of Rodney King. In Miami another racially charged case ended with the acquittal of a Hispanic police officer who killed two blacks. Some vexing social issues also arose in court, including the case of a girl who won a "divorce" from her biological parents and the case of a couple forced to return their adopted baby to her biological parents. The trial of a libel case in which a famous psychoanalyst said he was defamed by a writer ended

© Trippett/Sipa

Byron White, 76, gave up his seat as the current longest-serving justice on the U.S. Supreme Court at the end of the 1992-93 term. He had joined the high court in 1962.

inconclusively. A white separatist was acquitted in the killing of a federal marshal in Idaho.

United States

Supreme Court. In two important cases involving the rights of minorities, conservatives maintained a narrow sway. The justices, voting 5-4, made it harder for workers trying to prove job discrimination based on race, sex, or religion. The majority said fired workers do not win such bias claims automatically solely by proving that an employer is lying to defend an apparently discriminatory action. Workers may have to show further evidence that the employer intended to discriminate (*St. Mary's Honor Center v. Hicks*).

By the same 5-4 split, the justices opened the way to challenges against oddly shaped legislative districts that appear designed to help elect members of racial minorities. At issue was a congressional district in North Carolina that stretched along a narrow 160-mi (257-km) path and included parts of ten counties. The high court said it appeared to be a case of gerrymandering to elect black legislators. The court majority concluded that the state must demonstrate a compelling interest to abandon geographical compactness and contiguity in such cases (*Shaw v. Reno*). In this case, the members of the minority were Justices White, Stevens, Blackmun, and Souter. Justice Souter chastised the majority for, in his words, mistakenly applying affirmative-action principles to the voting-rights case.

The high court lowered some barriers between church and state and also moved to protect members of a religion who claimed unconstitutional interference by the government. The justices unanimously ruled that an ordinance unconstitutionally banned ritual animal sacrifice by adherents of the Santería religion *(Church of the Lukumi Babalu Aye v. City of Hialeah)*. The justices also voted 9-0 to rule that public-school systems that permit after-hours use by community groups must permit religious organizations to use the buildings and grounds on the same terms *(Lamb's Chapel v. Center Moriches School District)*. The court split, 5-4, in permitting public schools to provide a sign-language interpreter to students who attend religious school—the first time the court let a public employee participate directly in religious education *(Zobrest v. Catalina Foothills School District)*.

There was no ruling during the term that directly affected the right of a woman to have an abortion. But the justices barred federal judges from using a post-Civil War law—designed to protect freed slaves—to halt blockades of abortion clinics *(Bray v. Alexandria Women's Health Clinic)*.

In an important free-speech case, the court upheld so-called "hate crime" laws that provide stiffer penalties when violent attacks are motivated by bias. The court unanimously upheld a Wisconsin law *(Wisconsin v. Mitchell)* similar to those in about 25 states. The court said a city could not ban advertising brochures automatically from newspaper vending machines on public property *(Cincinnati v. Discovery Network)*. The court also ruled that not all FBI sources said to be confidential are protected automatically from having their identities disclosed under the Freedom of Information Act *(U.S. v. Landano)*.

In the area of criminal law, the court said police do not always need court warrants to seize drugs discovered when people are frisked for weapons *(Minnesota v. Dickerson)*. In an unexpected win for prisoners' rights, the court ruled that an inmate's right to be free from cruel and unusual punishment may be violated by exposure to secondhand cigarette smoke *(Helling v. McKinney)*. The court said death-row inmates almost always are barred from getting federal-court hearings to make belated claims of innocence *(Herrera v. Collins)*. The court also said federal courts lack authority to overturn state convictions flawed by procedural error unless a violation actually harmed the defendant's case *(Brecht v. Abrahamson)*. But the court said a state criminal conviction, regardless of the evidence, must be overturned if the judge did not instruct the jury properly to find guilt beyond a reasonable doubt *(Sullivan v. Louisiana)*.

The court ruled that the constitutional ban on excessive fines limits how much money and property government agents may seize from drug dealers in a case of a man who lost his business and home after selling two grams of cocaine to an undercover agent *(Austin v. U.S.)*. The court also extended protection to people who innocently accept property paid for by drug proceeds. That case involved a woman ordered to forfeit her house bought by a boyfriend who was a drug dealer *(U.S. v. A Parcel of Land)*. The court let the government seize all assets from pornographers convicted of selling some obscene materials, although there also must be limits to protect against excessive fines *(Alexander v. United States)*. Maintaining the status quo, the court refused to bar federal-court access for prisoners who claim their convictions were tainted because they were questioned by police without first being warned of their right to remain silent. The case involved a man who had lost an argument in state court that his Miranda rights were violated and then turned to the federal courts for help *(Withrow v. Williams)*.

The court upheld the Bush and Clinton administrations' policy of intercepting fleeing Haitians at sea and returning them to Haiti without asylum hearings *(Sale v. Haitian Centers Council)*. The justices also upheld the Senate's shortcut procedure for conducting impeachment trials of federal judges, letting a group of senators conduct the proceedings and then report to the full Senate *(Nixon v. U.S.)*. And the court gave federal judges considerable leeway to decide when novel scientific theories can be used as evidence. The judges are not bound by an old rule that required the evidence to be accepted generally by scientific peers before it is admissible, the court said *(Daubert v. Merrill Dow)*.

A ruling long anticipated by the nation's business community failed to materialize as the justices ruled the Constitution does not bar massive punitive-damage awards intended to punish or deter wrongdoing. The court upheld an award 526 times the actual monetary damages suffered *(TXO Production v. Alliance Resources)*. The court upheld Internal Revenue Service rules that strictly limit the ability of taxpayers to claim deductions for spare rooms in their homes that are used for business purposes, ruling that a home office is deductible only if it is the location of a person's most important professional activities. The ruling denied a deduction to an anesthesiologist who did paperwork at home but practiced his profession in hospitals *(Commissioner v. Soliman)*. The court retroactively applied a 1989 ruling that could require many states to give big refunds to retired federal workers who were denied a tax break given to retired state workers *(Harper v. Virginia)*.

Local Law. In Los Angeles two police officers, Stacey Koon and Laurence Powell, were convicted in federal court of violating the civil rights of black motorist Rodney King in a beating that was captured on videotape. Koon, Powell, and two other white officers were

Several cases involving adoption issues came to the forefront during 1993. In Iowa, Roberta DeBoer (extreme right) and her husband Jan DeBoer were ordered to return 2$^1/_2$-year-old Jessica (on swing) to her natural parents. The DeBoers had raised Jessica since shortly after her birth.

acquitted on state charges in 1992, a decision that touched off days of deadly rioting in the city. Koon and Powell each were sentenced to two years in prison on the federal charges by a sympathetic judge. The sentences angered civil-rights leaders and others in the community who said they were too lenient, and the federal prosecutors planned to appeal. But there was no repeat of the street violence. Meanwhile, two black men accused of beating white trucker Reginald Denny in the 1992 rioting that followed the first verdict in the King case were acquitted, for the most part, in a Los Angeles trial (*see also* CRIME).

A steady drizzle and persistent police patrols were credited with keeping Miami relatively calm in the aftermath of the acquittal of Hispanic police officer William Lozano in the 1989 deaths of two blacks: a speeding motorcyclist who was shot fatally and a passenger who died in a subsequent crash. The deaths touched off three days of widespread rioting in 1989, but after the verdict there were only sporadic incidents of looting, rock- and bottle-throwing, and random gunfire.

A jury in Austin, TX, handed out a 40-year sentence to Joel Valdez, convicted of raping a woman at knifepoint after she asked her attacker to wear a condom to protect herself against disease. The first grand jury to hear the case had refused to indict Valdez, which provoked an outcry from women's groups.

Kimberly Mays went to court in Sarasota, FL, to sever ties from her biological parents, Ernest and Regina Twigg. The 14-year-old was raised by Robert Mays since she was switched mistakenly at birth with another child. The court ended visitation privileges for her biological parents. The 2-year-old child known as baby Jessica was taken from Jan and Roberta DeBoer, who had raised her since birth, and returned to her biological parents, Dan and Cara Schmidt. The Schmidts had fought since 1991 to get their daughter back after Cara, then unmarried, gave up custody of her newborn. The legal battle ended when the Supreme Court refused to delay the return of Jessica to the Schmidts. (*See also* SPECIAL REPORT, page 235.)

In San Francisco a federal jury deadlocked on monetary damages after deciding that writer Janet Malcolm defamed psychoanalyst Jeffrey Masson by fabricating quotes in an article in *The New Yorker*. The case earlier had been the subject of a Supreme Court ruling that an author can be sued if contrived quotes change the spirit of the speaker's comments. A federal judge ordered a new trial on all issues.

White separatist Randy Weaver and a supporter were acquitted in federal court in Boise, ID, of the 1992 killing of a federal marshal in a shoot-out at a remote mountain cabin. Weaver was convicted on two minor counts. The death of William Degan had led to an 11-day standoff before Weaver surrendered.

In New Jersey, Sol Wachtler—formerly New York state's chief judge—was sentenced to 15 months in prison for harassing a former lover—Manhattan socialite Joy Silverman.

JIM RUBIN
The Associated Press

Gay Rights in the United States

Gay and lesbian Americans long may remember 1993 as the year their concerns moved into the national political spotlight. The issue of gays in the military captured particular prominence, along with notable child-custody cases, a controversial law in Colorado, and scientific research into the origin of sexual orientation.

Gays in the Military. Democratic presidential nominee Bill Clinton had raised the hopes of gays during the 1992 election campaign by vowing to strike down the long-standing ban against homosexuals in the armed services. The muted reaction to Clinton's proposal apparently persuaded his advisers that eliminating the ban would pose no problems.

But when Clinton moved to fulfill the pledge shortly after his January 20 inauguration, he ran into fierce opposition from members of Congress, military leaders, and ordinary citizens. In an effort to buy time, White House officials announced on January 27 that the president had decided to delay for six months an executive order permanently lifting the ban. In the meantime, they said, enforcement of the existing policy would be suspended.

Clinton's move failed to mollify either homosexual-rights activists or their opponents. This issue was a key theme at the March on Washington for Lesbian, Gay, and Bi[sexual] Equal Rights held on April 25. "End the ban now!" marchers chanted as they paraded down Pennsylvania Avenue to a rally attended by some 300,000 persons. Homosexual military personnel who stood on the podium in uniform received rousing applause.

Clinton did not address the rally, but asked Rep. Nancy Pelosi (D-CA) to read a letter of support on his behalf. In a speech that day in Boston, the president defended his decision to allow homosexuals to serve openly in the military. "This is not about embracing anybody's lifestyle," he said. "This is a question of whether if somebody is willing to live by the strict code of military conduct, if somebody is willing to die for their country, should they have the right to do it? I think the answer is yes."

Over the next few weeks, however, Clinton's resolve to end the gay ban seemed to waver. The president's thinking seemed swayed by Senate Armed Forces Committee Chairman Sam Nunn (D-GA), who opposed lifting the ban, and Rep. Barney Frank (D-MA), one of two avowed homosexuals in Congress. Senator Nunn suggested that the armed services adopt a permanent "don't ask, don't tell" policy under which military personnel would not be asked about their sexual orientation but would be prohibited from being open about it.

Meanwhile, Frank proposed that off-base conduct be exempt from military supervision, which would enable gay and lesbian service personnel to be open about their orientation off-base without fear of disciplinary action. Frank described his approach: "Don't ask, don't tell, . . . don't listen, and don't investigate."

Clinton's final decision, contained in a July 19 directive issued by Defense Secretary Les Aspin, closely followed the Nunn formula. Homosexuals could serve in the armed forces, he said, provided they did not disclose their sexual orientation or engage in homosexual behavior. Meanwhile, military commanders were barred from investigating the sexual proclivities of service personnel solely on the basis of suspicion or hearsay. The policy was to take effect October 1, the scheduled retirement date of Gen. Colin Powell, chairman of the Joint Chiefs of Staff.

Clinton acknowledged that his policy was not a "perfect solution." However, he said any move to terminate the ban would have met with "certain and decisive reversal by the Congress, and the cause for which many have fought for years would be delayed, probably for years."

Though the Clinton compromise fell short of both sides' expectations, it seemed to have a soothing effect on public opinion. However, controversy flared up again in August with the disclosure that a study commissioned by the Pentagon had concluded that the military ban on homosexuals could be removed without impairing national defense. The report was prepared by the RAND Corp., a California think tank with long-standing ties to the Defense Department.

The report said that while concerns about allowing known homosexuals to serve were not groundless, "the problems do not appear insurmountable, and there is ample reason to believe that heterosexual and homosexual military personnel can work together effectively." It also asserted that "open homosexual military personnel are likely to be rare, at least in the foreseeable future. Homosexuals in the military will be under enormous informal pressure to 'stay in the closet,' even without any explicit requirement to do so." The RAND study was made public at the insistence of congressional Democrats who wanted the contents revealed before the House and Senate debated the fiscal 1994 defense-authorization bill, which included language legalizing a restrictive policy on gays in the military.

This strategy failed. The House and Senate versions of the defense bill contained identical provisions codifying a slightly revised version of the existing prohibition on gays in the armed forces. The measures reaffirmed the Pentagon's

ban on homosexual conduct by military personnel, barring even private disclosures to a friend that one is gay or bisexual.

Some commentators felt the language approved by Congress was substantially more restrictive than the policy announced by Clinton in July. Others disagreed, noting that the legislation left it to the defense secretary to decide whether to resume asking recruits about their sexual orientation, which left intact the administration's decision to end that practice. As the executive and the legislative branches sparred, the federal judiciary emerged as a third party in the gay-ban debate. In September, Judge Milton Schwartz of U.S. District Court in Sacramento, CA, said the military's long-standing policy on homosexuals was unconstitutional and ordered the reinstatement of a sailor discharged for homosexuality in 1982. This ruling applied only to Pentagon policy in effect prior to Clinton's proposed changes.

In a similar decision on September 30, Judge Terry Hatter, Jr., of U.S. District Court in Los Angeles declared that the military cannot discharge or otherwise change the status of service members because of their homosexuality. He also threatened to impose fines of $10,000 per day if the military failed to comply. The central figure in the case was Navy Petty Officer Keith Meinhold, who was discharged in 1992 after acknowledging on national television that he was gay. In an earlier ruling, Hatter ordered the navy to reinstate Meinhold.

Pending further legal developments, Hatter's latest decision left military policy on homosexuals in limbo. The day after he issued his ruling, the Pentagon suspended its ban on homosexuals. Then on October 12 it announced that it would ask the Supreme Court to delay enforcement of Hatter's order. A three-judge panel of the U.S. Court of Appeals in San Francisco already had rejected a similar Pentagon request.

A Long Island, NY, mother, right, *went to Washington in April 1993 to join some 300,000 other Americans in a rally supporting the rights of gays and lesbians in the United States.*

© Michelle V. Agins/NYT Pictures

© Nina Berman/Sipa

Local Issues. In Colorado a battle over homosexual legal rights entered a climactic phase. The key issue was a ballot measure approved in 1992 that barred legal protection for gays and lesbians. Supporters of the measure, known as Amendment 2, opposed the granting of "special rights" solely on the basis of sexual preference.

Amendment 2 was scheduled to take effect January 15, but on that day, Judge Jeffrey Bayless of Denver District Court suspended implementation of the measure until his court determined whether or not it violated the constitutional rights of Colorado homosexuals. The Colorado Supreme Court upheld the injunction, saying a citizen's fundamental rights could not be submitted to popular vote. A trial on Amendment 2's constitutionality began in Denver District Court October 12, with Bayless presiding.

Measures to enhance gay rights were on voting ballots in various locales in November 1993. Voters in Cincinnati overwhelmingly repealed a 1992 ordinance protecting gays from discrimination; a similar law was defeated in Lewiston, ME; and a nonbinding vote on gay rights went down to defeat by a margin of three to two in Portsmouth, NH. Meanwhile several states were considering ballot measures for 1994 that would prohibit legal protection for gays.

In stark contrast to the furor in Colorado, a Minnesota law protecting homosexuals against discrimination in housing, employment, and education went into effect August 1 without incident. Minnesota thus became the eighth state to extend civil-rights protection to homosexuals, joining California, Connecticut, Hawaii, Massachusetts, New Jersey, Vermont, and Wisconsin.

For some homosexuals, parental rights raise the most painful legal issues of all. In recent years, gay and lesbian couples with children have won acceptance in numerous cities with sizable homosexual communities. Moreover, a nationally televised CBS program *(Other Mothers)* presented a sympathetic portrait of such a family. Nonetheless, many Americans still recoil from the idea of homosexuals raising children.

This attitude found expression in a widely publicized child-custody case that pitted Sharon Bottoms, a lesbian living in Richmond, VA, against her mother, Kay. In September, Henrico county Circuit Court Judge Buford Parsons, Jr., awarded custody of Tyler Bottoms, 2, to his grandmother. Parsons said Sharon Bottoms' lesbian relationship was immoral, making her an unfit parent.

Another legal case involving a lesbian mother turned out differently. On September 10 the Massachusetts Supreme Court allowed surgeon Dr. Susan Love and her lesbian companion to adopt Love's 5-year-old daughter. The child was conceived through artificial insemination with sperm supplied by the companion's cousin. Both women received full parental rights under the court's ruling. The biological father also waived any adoption rights to the child. This case was the first of its kind in Massachusetts, but similar adoptions have been approved by courts in Alaska, California, New York, Oregon, Vermont, and Washington, DC.

Homosexuals continued to make headway in 1993 in another important area—health-care coverage. Over the past decade or so, dozens of local governments and businesses across the country have adopted policies extending health insurance and other benefits to the "domestic partners" of their employees. In many cases, the partner is of the same sex as the employee. Among the companies offering such coverage to homosexuals for the first time in 1993 were Apple Computer Inc., Home Box Office Inc., and Warner Bros.

Defining Homosexuality. Debate on the legal status of gays and lesbians often has centered on the nature of homosexuality. Opponents of gay rights argue that homosexuality is a freely chosen "lifestyle" that can be changed or discarded at will, while most gays and lesbians contend that homosexuality is either an inborn trait or an immutable and healthy psychological condition that is developed early in life.

The distinctions between these two interpretations are crucial. If opponents of gay rights were proved correct, their claim that homosexuals are seeking undeserved "special rights" would gain credence. But if homosexuals could show that their sexual orientation was fixed at birth, their case for broader civil-rights protections would seem stronger. Consequently, medical studies attempting to trace the origins of homosexuality often stir heated controversy.

In one such study, published in the journal *Science*, scientists at the National Institutes of Health (NIH) reported that they had uncovered evidence suggesting some gay men inherited genes that predisposed them to be homosexual. The researchers found that 33 of 40 pairs of homosexual brothers had identical regions on a tip of the X chromosome—indicating that genes in that vicinity may have influenced the men's homosexuality. Although the findings did not establish the existence of a specific "gay gene," they raised the possibility that there are genes which increase the chances a male will be gay. A number of previous studies also have cited evidence that points to a biological basis for sexual orientation.

The reaction of gay-rights leaders to the NIH study generally was restrained. While some of them felt that this research represented progress in the right direction, others concluded that establishing a biological cause of homosexuality would do little to overcome opposition to their cause.

RICHARD L. WORSNOP

International Law

Innovation in international law again was driven in 1993 by armed conflict, specifically in the former Yugoslavia. Most significantly, the international community established, for the first time since the Nuremberg and Tokyo trials after World War II, an international war-crimes tribunal. The Tribunal, so-called, which held its inaugural meeting at The Hague in November, was composed of 11 judges. It was mandated to try individuals accused of having committed grave breaches of humanitarian law, crimes against humanity, and acts of genocide in the territory of the former Yugoslavia.

The Tribunal was to sit in two trial chambers and one appeals chamber. Allegations concerning possible violations were to be investigated by a prosecutor. If endorsed by a trial judge, indictments could be issued by the Tribunal. As the Tribunal was established by a mandatory United Nations (UN) Security Council resolution, states were obliged to cooperate with it and surrender suspects who may be found in their territory. However, the tribunal was dependent on such cooperation; it did not have the authority to try suspects in absentia.

In addition to cases against individuals that might be brought in future before the Tribunal, the Federal Republic of Yugoslavia (Serbia and Montenegro) was charged with state responsibility for having supported, conducted, and controlled acts of genocide in the territory of the Republic of Bosnia-Herzegovina. On April 8, after having found that the Belgrade government might have to answer a prima facie case arising from such activities, the International Court of Justice issued an interim order instructing the government to refrain from them. The court was constrained to reiterate its order in September in light of the Belgrade government's failure to comply.

In November the Republic of Bosnia-Herzegovina announced its intention to bring an action in the World Court against Great Britain for failure to fulfill its obligation actively to prevent genocide, which is established in the 1948 Genocide Convention. An alternative legal action also was under consideration.

Former Yugoslavia provided the occasion for further developments in international jurisprudence. The Badinter Arbitration Commission, a legal advisory body attached to the UN/European Community (Union) peace conference on former Yugoslavia, considered at some length issues of succession of states. This area of international law had been the subject of prolonged codification efforts by the International Law Commission. However, as the resulting draft convention failed to attract a significant number of ratifications, the law in this area remained unclear. Although the work of the Badinter Commission could have amounted to an important precedent, the commission failed to grapple with the issue in a comprehensive and convincing way. (*See also* FEATURE ARTICLE, page 26.)

Nuclear Nonproliferation Issues. Succession issues created difficulties with respect to other newly independent states, in particular the former Soviet republics. Considerable problems were encountered in the area of arms-control treaties, which had been intended to cover the entirety of the USSR's territory. The failure by some republics to embrace the Nuclear Nonproliferation Treaty (NPT) unconditionally led to international tensions. The question of whether or not there exists an international obligation to comply with the mandates of nonproliferation irrespective of membership in the NPT was raised even more dramatically by the proposed withdrawal of North Korea from the treaty, and its refusal to permit international inspections of its nuclear facilities. The United States threatened to seek the imposition of sanctions by the UN Security Council if North Korea were to persist in its policy.

Sanctions and Other Issues. Sanctions were maintained, and even tightened, against Libya, in connection with the failure of that state to surrender the suspects in the terrorist bombing of Pan Am Flight 103 over Lockerbie, Scotland, in 1988. Tripoli initially had hinted at the possibility of encouraging the two suspects to make themselves available for trial in the United States or Great Britain.

Sanctions also were kept in place against Iraq, despite the effort of the Baghdad regime to break through its economic and political isolation. Iraq's legal campaign at the UN was hampered by Baghdad's renewed challenge to the Iraq-Kuwait boundary, which had been confirmed by a UN demarcation commission and the UN Security Council, and by allegations concerning the mistreatment of the marsh Arabs in southern Iraq.

The UN compensation commission for victims of Iraqi atrocities received some funds during the year, derived from Iraqi assets seized abroad, and it began to engage in its substantive work. The U.S.-Iran Claims Tribunal, which had been operating for more than a decade, proceeded in its work of settling claims arising out of the revolutionary turmoil in Iran in 1979 and 1980.

Codification work on state responsibility, crimes against the peace and security of mankind, and other issues progressed in the UN International Law Commission. The International Committee of the Red Cross convened a diplomatic conference that adopted a helpful declaration on strengthening humanitarian law. On the other hand, the UN human-rights conference, convened in Vienna over the summer, almost ended in disaster. A number of less-developed nations proceeded to challenge even the fundamental concepts of human rights—which, it had been thought, were no longer controversial. (*See also* HUMAN RIGHTS.)

MARC WELLER, *University of Cambridge*

LEBANON

In spite of isolated political kidnappings and new incidents of political intimidation by government authorities, most of Lebanon experienced another year of relative peace in 1993. The nation continued its recovery from more than 15 years of conflict that ended in 1990.

Numerous encouraging signs were visible. A number of governments—including those of all the Persian Gulf countries—announced that their embassies soon would reopen in Beirut. Many major foreign air carriers began to offer service to and from Beirut International Airport. And Lebanon hosted many prominent foreign dignitaries, including the foreign ministers of Italy, the United States, and Egypt; a former French prime minister; and the emir of Kuwait—the first Arab head of state to visit Lebanon since 1975. Syrian officials, including the vice-president, foreign minister, and prime minister, traveled to Lebanon frequently.

Domestic Politics. The government of Prime Minister Rafiq al-Hariri completed its first full year in office and remained actively involved in the reconstruction and rebuilding of Lebanon's tarnished international image.

However, numerous political problems arose from the corrupt nature and inefficiencies of the Lebanese government. Cabinet ministers fought continually and openly amongst themselves, while the "three presidents"—President Elias Hrawi, Prime Minister al-Hariri, and Assembly Speaker Nabi Birri—were in constant conflict, frequently shuttling back and forth between Beirut and Damascus to seek Syrian support for their postures.

Lebanese public sentiment held the government guilty of neglect, as the services that had collapsed during the war years failed to improve and as the cabinet appeared much more interested in personal politics and enrichment than in administering the country. When the widely respected minister of electricity and water resources, George Frem, refused to go forward with a project in which the bid price appeared inflated and the circumstances suspect, he unceremoniously and illegally was demoted, reinforcing the image of a corrupt government.

In spite of its fractiousness, the Lebanese government embarked on an active campaign of censorship, closing a television station, suspending several newspapers, and banning books and plays. Security forces harassed opposition groups and leaders. Critics attributed the closed political climate to the Syrian control that had dominated contemporary Lebanon for several years, but the initiatives often appeared purely Lebanese in origin.

Security. Parts of Israel's self-declared "security belt" in southern Lebanon suffered through continuing violence, caught between the pro-Israeli South Lebanon Army and the Lebanese resistance led by Hezbollah, a fundamentalist

© AP/Wide World

In late July 1993, Israeli forces conducted air raids and artillery strikes against bases and villages in southern Lebanon in retaliation for Hezbollah attacks on northern Israel.

Muslim movement. Intermittent Hezbollah attacks produced heavy Israeli retaliation.

In late July, after Hezbollah ambushes in the "security belt" and rocket attacks on Israeli proper, Israeli aircraft, artillery, and naval forces laid siege to the south and attacked other parts of Lebanon. One product of this conflict was a controversial secret agreement. Under the terms of this accord, Hezbollah eschewed attacks on Israeli territory and Israel restrained retaliation for attacks in the "security belt." In essence the pact contained the struggle inside southern Lebanon itself.

The Economy. The Lebanese economy, often considered a barometer of political confidence, had been largely stagnant since the end of the war, but foreign-aid pledges picked up during 1993. The World Bank, predicting annual gross-domestic-product (GDP) growth of 8% for five years, extended a loan of $175 million to Lebanon, and several Persian Gulf states made pledges of additional funding. However, there was a real question as to whether or not the pledges from the Gulf nations would be honored in view of competing demands on Gulf states' aid. European and some Gulf countries also extended limited loans or grants for specific projects or needs.

Most economic assistance was tied to the government's controversial and ambitious Horizon 2000 reconstruction program that envisages $10 billion in reconstruction funds over the ten-year period between 1993 and 2002. The program was buffeted about in the parliament,

Members and supporters of Hezbollah, a fundamentalist Muslim movement, demonstrated their solidarity by parading in downtown Beirut in support of a victim killed in the July bombing—Israel's most intense offensive against Lebanon since 1982.

where some critics argued it was unrealistic, while others feared that the magnitude of foreign investment would weaken Lebanon's sovereignty.

Syrian Relations. The public held the perception that Lebanon's political, economic, and social future continued to depend upon the nature of its relationship with Syria. In 1993, Syria further institutionalized its grip on Lebanon. The two countries promulgated a nexus of treaties complementing those already signed, and formally launched the Syrian-Lebanese Higher Council established by an earlier treaty.

In August the Lebanese government—without securing Syrian acquiescence—agreed to send additional army forces to the south to try to arrest the spiraling violence there. Almost immediately thereafter, following a quasi-public chastisement of Lebanese leaders, Syria announced that the Higher Council would begin to function and named a member of the Syrian National Socialist Party as its secretary-general. The vague and sweeping powers of the Higher Council appeared to supersede some aspects of Lebanese sovereignty in deference to Syrian-Lebanese cooperation.

Foreign Affairs. The United States continued to demand Syrian withdrawal from Lebanon in accordance with the Taif agreement of 1989. However, when the U.S. Congress passed a resolution calling for such withdrawal, the pro-Syrian Lebanese parliament and senior officials of the Lebanese government protested that this action constituted interference in Lebanon's domestic affairs and that a series of treaties between Lebanon and Syria effectively superseded the Taif accords. Nevertheless, similar appeals were made by the United States to Syrian Foreign Minister Farouk al-Sharaa during his October visit to Washington.

Lebanon continued to participate in the Arab-Israeli peace process, but following Lebanese statements unwelcome in Damascus, the Syrian leadership moved to ensure tighter control over all initiatives of the Lebanese delegation. Indeed, all other participants acknowledged openly that the Lebanese could not move in negotiations ahead of Syria and that any peacemaking progress between Israel and Lebanon would in fact be determined by Syria, rather than Lebanon. *See also* ISRAEL; SYRIA.

ROBERT D. McLAURIN
Abbott Associates, Inc.

LEBANON • Information Highlights

Official Name: Republic of Lebanon.
Location: Southwest Asia.
Area: 4,015 sq mi (10 400 km²).
Population (mid-1993 est.): 3,600,000.
Chief Cities (1982 est.): Beirut, the capital, 509,000; Tripoli, 198,000.
Government: *President*, Elias Hrawi (took office November 1989); *premier*, Rafiq al-Hariri (named Oct. 22, 1992). *Legislature* (unicameral)—National Assembly.
Monetary Unit: Lebanese pound (1,716 pounds equal U.S.$1, Dec. 7, 1993).
Foreign Trade (1990 est. U.S.$): *Imports*, $1,800,000,000; *exports*, $700,000,000.

LIBRARIES

While most libraries continued to sustain massive funding cuts during 1993, others succeeded in getting bond issues approved, and still others began exploring alternative revenue sources. Librarians and library advocates entered the third year of a massive public-relations program emphasizing the centrality of libraries in the information age, and changes were made in the leadership of several of the United States' major libraries.

Funding. As in the past several years, many libraries sustained massive cuts necessitating staff reductions and closures. Chicago closed its 91-year old Municipal Reference Library, which housed every document issued by the city since 1871 (including some which predated Chicago's Great Flood). The city planned to move some, but not all, of the 50,000 documents to its public library.

New Orleans closed all of its 15 sites on Fridays, and nine Baltimore County Public Library branches were closed permanently, including one site that had circulated more than 700,000 items in 1992.

Oregon's Multnomah County Public Library debated becoming the first public library in the nation to charge for telephone reference service by using a 900- or 976-exchange telephone number that would bill users by the minute. Charging for such basic services would, however, violate one of the profession's basic tenets: to support free access to information. The Ventura County Library Services Agency in California considered using telemarketing to raise $400,000 in donations over a three-year period. Both studies resulted from the constant decrease in tax revenues which traditionally have supported public-library services.

Other libraries were successful in increasing their funding bases. The Birmingham, AL, public library passed its fourth bond issue in a decade, and students at the University of North Carolina at Chapel Hill voted to pay $2.50 each semester to build a student-endowed library fund. U.S. Bank donated $57,600 to the Sacramento (CA) Public Library to allow the central library there to open on Sundays for the first time, while the New York Public Library's branches were slated to be open six days a week, beginning in mid-1994, for the first time since 1947.

Illinois passed its most significant library legislation in 25 years. The state's "Live & Learn" program, financed through automobile fees, was expected to generate $18.9 million annually for the state's libraries. This would increase state funding of Illinois' libraries by nearly 60%.

Major Library Events. The Library of Congress, the nation's largest library, marked the reopening of its renovated Great Hall in 1993 with a $2 million exhibition entitled "Rome Reborn: The Vatican Library and Renaissance

Culture," which included 200 of the Vatican Library's most valuable prints, manuscripts, books, and maps.

Severe flooding throughout the U.S. Midwest did little damage to libraries, primarily due to state regulations and volunteer efforts. Some libraries sustained damage, but almost all had been reopened by late fall 1993. To save books at the height of the flooding, volunteers helped move them to the upper stories of libraries in several cities. In Des Moines, IA, for example, about 50 volunteers formed a human chain to move more than 10,000 books between 3:00 A.M. and 6:00 A.M.

Timothy Healy, president of the New York Public Library, died suddenly on Dec. 30, 1992. Paul LeClerc, a Voltaire scholar and president of Hunter College since 1988, was to take over as NYPL's new director in January 1994. The NYPL will mark its centennial in 1995. And on May 5, 1993, Carla Hayden—formerly chief librarian of the Chicago Public Library—was named director of Baltimore's Enoch Pratt Free Library; she succeeded Anna Currie.

Associations. More than 17,000 people attended the American Library Association's (ALA's) 112th annual conference June 24-30 in New Orleans. Presided over by ALA President Marilyn Miller, the conference had as its theme "Empowering People Through Libraries." Hardy Franklin, director of the District of Columbia Public Library, was inaugurated as the association's new president at the end of the conference, and Boston Public Library Director Arthur Curley was welcomed as the president-elect. Roger Parent, the association's deputy executive director, resigned to become executive director of the American Association of Law Libraries, succeeding Judith Genesen.

"In the Human Cause" was the theme of the Canadian Library Association's 47th annual conference held June 16-20 in Hamilton, Ont. The conference was presided over by President Margaret Andrewes, and Patricia Cavill was welcomed as first vice-president/president-elect.

CHARLES HARMON
Headquarters Librarian
American Library Association

LIBRARY AWARDS FOR 1993

Beta Phi Mu Award for distinguished service to education for librarianship: Kathryn Luther Henderson, University of Illinois Graduate School of Library and Information Studies

Randolph J. Caldecott Medal for the most distinguished picture book for children: Emily Arnold McCully, *Mirette on the High Wire*

Grolier Award for unique contributions to the stimulation and guidance of reading by children and young people: Michael L. Printz, Topeka West High School

Joseph W. Lippincott Award for distinguished service to the profession of librarianship: John G. Lorenz, National Commission on Libraries and Information Science

John Newbery Medal for the most distinguished contribution to literature for children: Cynthia Rylant, *Missing May*

© Anmar Abd Rabbo/Sipa

A poster pays homage to Libya's Col. Muammar el-Qaddafi. UN-imposed sanctions not only posed political problems for Qaddafi but also isolated the nation internationally in 1993.

LIBYA

United Nations sanctions on international air traffic to and from Libya—imposed in 1992 to pressure the government to comply with a UN resolution demanding that it surrender two suspects in the bombing of a Pan American airliner over Scotland in 1988—isolated Libya, created economic hardships for its people, and exacerbated tensions within the country's ruling circle during 1993. The sanctions failed, however, to accomplish their objective of bringing the accused Libyans to trial. This prompted the United States, Great Britain, and France to initiate a campaign to institute even more rigorous restrictions.

Continued Sanctions. As the United Nations prepared to review the impact of the existing sanctions in April, the Clinton administration lobbied unsuccessfully to toughen them with the imposition of a worldwide boycott of Libyan oil. Few members of the world body supported such a tactic, and several Western European countries that import large amounts of oil from Libya strongly opposed it. Faced with this resistance, the United States joined other members of the Security Council in voting to extend the sanctions without altering them.

Col. Muammar el-Qaddafi, the Libyan leader, argued that the absence of an extradition treaty between his country and either the United States or Great Britain prevented him from compelling the suspects to give themselves up to British or U.S. authorities. Although he maintained that Libya's offer to try the two suspects complied with both international law and the UN resolution, he also put forward several alternatives in an attempt to reach a compromise. These included suggestions to hold the trial in a neutral country or to create an international tribunal under the auspices of the UN or the Arab League. Qaddafi also raised the possibility of his personal intervention to persuade the two men to surrender voluntarily if, in return, Western diplomatic relations with Libya were restored.

Rejecting all of these proposals, the British and U.S. governments announced in August that they would ask the Security Council to enact a series of harsher sanctions on Libya if the suspects had not been handed over by October 1. France, which sought to question Libyan intelligence agents concerning the destruction of a French airliner over Chad in 1989, lent its support to the Anglo-American demands. The new sanctions closed loopholes in the existing ones and further proposed to reinforce them by freezing Libyan assets abroad and banning the sale to Libya of equipment used in the refining and transportation of oil. They did not, however, embargo the 1.4 million barrels per day of crude oil exported from the country.

Negotiations between UN Secretary-General Boutros Boutros-Ghali and Libyan Foreign Minister Omar Mustapha al-Muntasir, as well as other less formal contacts, took place during the late summer and early fall, leading to a gradual softening of the Libyan position. Libya announced its willingness to provide compensation to the bombing victims' families and, after a series of meetings between Libyan officials and Scottish lawyers, dropped its previously categorical objections to a trial in Scotland. The Libyan government continued to insist, however, that it could not force its citizens to turn themselves over to foreign authorities. The suspects remained in Libya as the October deadline passed, while deliberation of the call for the stronger sanctions was delayed by the Security Council's preoccupation with affairs in Somalia and Haiti.

The ban on air traffic in and out of Libya during 1993 not only inconvenienced travelers by forcing them to go by land to airports in either Tunisia or Egypt for international flights, but also resulted in shortages of consumer and industrial goods. Efforts to isolate Libya even extended to the exclusion of its athletes from international competition.

Domestic Repercussions. Perhaps the most serious consequence of the sanctions was the dissatisfaction they engendered within the Libyan political elite and the military. Existing differences between Qaddafi and his chief deputy, Maj. Abdessalam Jalloud, over the pace of the country's shift toward a more liberal economy

A Libyan Muslim used U.S. dollars to purchase worry beads during a pilgrimage to Israeli-occupied Jerusalem at midyear. The trip by some 200 Libyans had to be cut short when the visitors called for the overthrow of Israel's government.

© Reuters/Bettmann

were aggravated by Qaddafi's willingness to compromise with Great Britain and the United States concerning the Pan Am bombing suspects.

A far more dangerous, and possibly related, threat to Qaddafi materialized with an attempted military coup. Although denied by the official Libyan media, reliable reports from foreign embassies in Tripoli noted the outbreak of rebellions in the city of Misurata and at several other locations in the western portion of the country in October that appeared to have involved several thousand troops. The National Front for the Salvation of Libya, an opposition group that operates from exile but maintains close links with elements in Libya opposed to the regime, confirmed the accuracy of these reports.

Observers speculated that the officers behind the coup may have been reacting to the diminution of Qaddafi's prestige (attributable not only to the travails caused by the increasing isolation of Libya, but also by the country's marginalization in the rapidly changing political environment of the Middle East) and to the military's own deterioration as a result of the unavailability of spare parts due to the UN sanctions. Moreover, close U.S. monitoring of Libyan military activity had enabled Washington to thwart the army's acquisition of missiles from Russia and to terminate the unwitting participation of European countries in the alleged development of a chemical-weapons facility.

In mid-December, Mansur R. Kikhia, a dissident and former high-ranking official, was reported missing in Cairo, Egypt. Opposition members expressed the belief that he had been kidnapped by Qaddafi's agents. Kikhia had served as Qaddafi's foreign minister in the early 1970s and Libya's UN representative in the late 1980s.

Toward the middle of the year, with the UN sanctions causing considerable disruption in Libya, Qaddafi made two eccentric moves that were interpreted widely as efforts to improve his standing in Western capitals. At the end of May he approved a pilgrimage by some 200 Libyans to Muslim shrines in Israeli-occupied Jerusalem. A debacle ensued, however, when the visit was cut short following the Libyans' call for the overthrow of the Israeli government, the liberation of the city, and the creation of a Palestinian state. In July the Libyan government hired Abraham Sofaer, a former legal adviser in the U.S. State Department, to defend it against claims lodged by relatives of the victims of the Pan Am bombing. In the face of vehement protests, however, Sofaer's firm quickly reversed itself and dropped Libya as a client.

KENNETH J. PERKINS
University of South Carolina

LIBYA • Information Highlights

Official Name: Socialist People's Libyan Arab Jamahiriya ("state of the masses").

Location: North Africa.

Area: 679,359 sq mi (1 759 540 km²).

Population (mid-1993 est.): 4,900,000.

Chief Cities (1984 census): Tripoli, the capital, 990,697; Benghazi, 435,886.

Government: *Head of state*, Muammar el-Qaddafi (took office 1969). *Legislature*—General People's Congress (met initially Nov. 1976).

Monetary Unit: Dinar (0.298 dinar equals U.S. $1, July 1993).

Gross Domestic Product (1990 est. U.S.$): $28,900,000,000.

Foreign Trade (1990 est. U.S.$): *Imports*, $5,599,000,000; *exports*, $13,877,000,000.

LITERATURE

Overview

In a year filled with questions about progress in racial equality in the United States, two strong voices that articulated the evolving experiences of the African-American woman captured the attention of the literary community, as novelist Toni Morrison won the 1993 Nobel Prize in literature and Rita Dove was appointed U.S. poet laureate. Both writers have garnered large public followings and have earned critical acclaim with their bold determination to give black women a powerful expression of their problems and triumphs.

Born Chloe Anthony Wofford in Lorain, OH, on Feb. 18, 1931, Toni Morrison was the daughter of two former sharecroppers and was raised in Depression-torn Ohio. Her novels portray troubled black women and men who struggle to find or understand their racial identities as they wrangle with the continuing problems of oppression and prejudice. She is the author of six novels—*The Bluest Eye* (1970), *Sula* (1973), *Song of Solomon* (1977), *Tar Baby* (1981), the Pulitzer Prize-winner *Beloved* (1987), and *Jazz* (1992)—as well as one play and numerous essays. She has taught creative writing at Princeton University since 1989.

The Swedish Academy described her novels as "characterized by visionary force and poetic import." She is the first black woman and the 90th overall winner of the annual literature

Toni Morrison

© Thomas Engstrom/Gamma-Liaison

prize, which carries a monetary award of $825,000.

U.S. Poet Laureate. Rita Dove, winner of the 1987 Pulitzer Prize in poetry, was appointed in May as the seventh poet laureate of the United States, effective October 1. She became the first black woman and the youngest writer—at age 40—to be so honored. In announcing the appointment, which extends for one year, James H. Billington, the librarian of Congress, said it was a pleasure "to have an outstanding representative of a new and richly variegated generation of American poets" in the post. Dove, who has taught poetry at the University of Virginia since 1989, has written four volumes of poetry, one novel, and a collection of short stories.

Anniversaries. The year 1993 marked the 200th anniversary of the death of Italian playwright Carlo Goldoni, an event that was marked by celebration and controversy on the European continent. In addition, 1993 was the 400th anniversary of the birth of English author Izaak Walton, the author of *The Compleat Angler,* a book credited with originating the genre of the fishing novel. Finally, 1993 was the 100th birthday of Beatrix Potter's world-famous and beloved fictional character, Peter Rabbit.

Other Awards. The winner of the Lannan Foundation's annual lifetime achievement award was novelist William Gaddis. V. S. Naipal received the newly established British literature prize for lifetime achievement and Stefan Heym, author of *The Crusaders* (1948), was named winner of the 1993 Jerusalem Prize.

See also PRIZES AND AWARDS.

Rita Dove

© Robert Severi/Gamma-Liaison

American Literature

Perhaps in reaction to the charge that American literature had become too self-absorbed, novels in 1993 were large in scope, inquiring into complex social and political issues. Even those that focused on individuals and family life showed a heightened awareness of cultural context.

Novels. Since some historians have argued that there is no absolute way to know the past, novelists perhaps felt freer to intermingle fantasy, invention, and traditional history. In Philip Roth's *Operation Shylock*, there is a character named Philip Roth who is beset by another character who claims to be Philip Roth. The book is set in Jerusalem, where the false Roth tries to convince Jews to give up Israel and return to Europe, where they would live in the exile that gives them their identity. Roth blurs fiction and reality as he mixes political figures with his own characters. Steve Erickson's *Arc d'X* puts Thomas Jefferson and his putative slave mistress Sally Hemmings into a dystopian novel set in a future Los Angeles. T. Coraghessan Boyle's *The Road to Wellville* is set in a health sanitarium in Battle Creek, MI, run by a man named Kellogg who invented the cornflake. John Calvin Batchelor's *Peter Nevsky and the True Story of the Russian Moon Landing* blends fact and fiction in recounting the U.S.-Soviet space race. Susan Fromberg Schaeffer's *First Nights* features a major character based on actress Greta Garbo. Lewis Nordan's *Wolf Whistle* turns the lynching of Emmett Till in Mississippi into magic realism. Using the setting of a children's hospital for an epic inquiry into present and past civilizations, Richard Powers' *Operation Wandering Soul* intermixes such stories as the Anabaptist Revolt with the Pied Piper of Hamelin.

Novelists also seemed fascinated by the problematic nature of documentation that supposedly reports the past. Carol De Chellis Hill's *Henry*

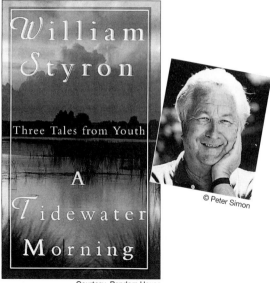

Courtesy, Random House

James' Midnight Song is based on a found manuscript that involves Henry James as a suspect in a homicide that occurred in the office of Sigmund Freud. William McCranor Henderson's *I Killed Hemingway* has a character whose claim to being a murderer inspires his literary memoir. In Cathleen Schine's *Rameau's Niece*, the study of an 18th-century manuscript leads the protagonist to imitate its experiments in love relationships. Schine plays with real literary texts to create a contemporary satire of postmodern academic criticism. Bharati Mukherjee's *The Holder of the World* has contemporary scholars researching the life of a 17th-century woman who leaves the puritanism of the Massachusetts Bay Colony to find her destiny in India with a Hindu prince.

The appeal of politics and history proved irresistible for some first novelists. Bob Shacochis' *Swimming in the Volcano* is a rich, evocative portrait of politicians, expatriate Americans, and struggling natives on an invented Caribbean island. In Jesse Lee Kercheval's *The Museum of Happiness*, the American heroine travels to pre-World War II Paris to fall in love with a fascinatingly divided man from the disputed territory of Alsace-Lorraine.

These ambitious novels perhaps were emblematized by Vikram Seth's *A Suitable Boy*. Placed in an India struggling for independence and populated with historic figures like Prime Minister Nehru, it is a multigenerational family saga running 1,376 pages.

At the same time, much of the strength of the contemporary novel still worked to capture the specific texture of U.S. regional and ethnic cultures. Not necessarily celebratory or nostalgic, these novels often dealt with the harshness of people's lives, hatred, and cruelty. Yet they recognized the richness and beauty of these cultures. Southern fiction remained strong, but writers from throughout the country had discovered the power and burden of a sense of place.

Photo by Vyto Starinskas, "Rutland Daily Herald" ©

Courtesy, Charles Scribner's Sons

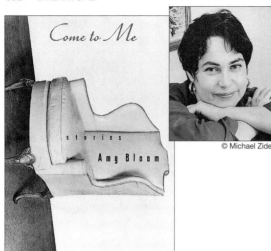

Courtesy, Harper Collins Publishers

© Michael Zide

Courtesy, Villard Books

© Bruce Plotkin

Bobbie Ann Mason's *Feather Crowns* chronicles the life of a Kentucky farm couple at the turn of the century who must survive the fame and sorrow brought to them by having, and then losing, quintuplets. Jeffrey Eugenides' *The Virgin Suicides* also deals with the reaction to five deaths. Ernest J. Gaines' *A Lesson Before Dying* explores race and class tension in 1940s Louisiana. Beverly Coyle's *In Troubled Waters* involves a family at odds with a central Florida community, while Carl Hiaasen's bizarre *Strip Tease* captures the surrealism of south Florida. South Carolina is the setting for T. R. Pearson's comic murder story, *Cry Me a River*; Dori Sanders' *Her Own Place*, an account of a black woman's triumph over adversity; and Pam Durban's first novel, *The Laughing Place*, whose heroine returns from the North to confront her Southern heritage.

Displacement is a constant American-literature theme. New England author E. Annie Proulx's *The Shipping News*, which won the National Book Award, tells of a hapless hero named Quoyle who, with his aunt and daughters, tries to make a new life in the cold, wet world of a Newfoundland fishing town. Fae Myenne Ng's *Bone* tells of the Chinese-American community in San Francisco. Oscar Hijuelos' *The Fourteen Sisters of Emilio Montez O'Brien* follows the adventures of an Irish-Cuban family growing up in Pennsylvania.

Short Stories. In 1993 works by many notable new and established short-story writers appeared. Thom Jones' *The Pugilist at Rest* suggested his coming importance, while Reynolds Price's *The Collected Stories* testified to a lifetime of achievement. But most interesting was that a neglected literary form in the United States, the novella, seemed to be making a comeback, as seen in such collections as Stanley Elkins' *Van Gogh's Room at Arles*, William Styron's *A Tidewater Morning*, and Mary Gordon's *The Rest of Life*.

History and Biography. Significant biographies like Joseph Brent's *Charles Sanders Peirce*, Kenneth S. Davis' *FDR: Into the Storm, 1937-1940*, and Willard Sterne Randall's *Thomas Jefferson: A Life* appeared in 1993. Controversial biographies, however, took the headlines. Joe McGinniss' *The Last Brother*, on Sen. Edward M. Kennedy, was charged with wild speculation and poor research. In another biography of the Kennedys, journalist Richard Reeves provided an appraisal of John Kennedy in *President Kennedy: Profile of Power*. Anthony Summers' *Official and Confidential: The Secret Life of J. Edgar Hoover* accused the long-time head of the Federal Bureau of Investigation (FBI) of flagrant misbehavior.

The most notable trend, however, was the rise of the memoir. This form, long regarded as merely casual reminiscence, has become a complex medium for moral meditation, cultural criticism, and fictionalized autobiography. Lars

© Alen MacWeeny

Courtesy, Little, Brown and Company

AMERICAN LITERATURE: MAJOR WORKS | 1993

NOVELS

Abish, Walter, *Eclipse Fever*
Adams, Alice, *Almost Perfect*
Barthelme, Frederick, *The Brothers*
Batchelor, John Calvin, *Peter Nevsky and the True Story of the Russian Moon Landing*
Baxter, Charles, *Shadow Play*
Bell, Madison Smartt, *Save Me, Joe Louis*
Boswell, Robert, *Mystery Ride*
Boyle, T. Coraghessan, *The Road to Wellville*
Conroy, Frank, *Body and Soul*
Coyle, Beverly, *In Troubled Waters*
Dickey, James, *To the White Sea*
Dobyns, Stephen, *The Wrestler's Cruel Study*
Durban, Pam, *The Laughing Place*
Erickson, Steve, *Arc d'X*
Eugenides, Jeffrey, *The Virgin Suicides*
Gaines, Ernest J., *A Lesson Before Dying*
Gibbons, Kaye, *Charms for the Easy Life*
Hawkes, John, *Sweet William: A Memoir of an Old Horse*
Henderson, William McCranor, *I Killed Hemingway*
Hiaasen, Carl, *Strip Tease*
Hijuelos, Oscar, *The Fourteen Sisters of Emilio Montez O'Brien*
Hill, Carol De Chellis, *Henry James' Midnight Song*
Kauffman, Janet, *The Body in Four Parts*
Kercheval, Jesse Lee, *The Museum of Happiness*
King, Thomas, *Green Grass, Running Water*
Levin, Jenifer, *The Sea of Light*
Mason, Bobbie Ann, *Feather Crowns*
McCourt, James, *Time Remaining*
Miller, Sue, *For Love*
Mukherjee, Bharati, *The Holder of the World*
Ng, Fae Myenne, *Bone*
Nordan, Lewis, *Wolf Whistle*
Oates, Joyce Carol, *Foxfire*
Parker, Michael, *Hello Down There*
Pearson, T.R., *Cry Me a River*
Pesetsky, Bette, *Cast a Spell*
Powers, Richard, *Operation Wandering Soul*
Proulx, E. Annie, *The Shipping News*
Reed, Ishmael, *Japanese By Spring*
Richard, Mark, *Fishboy*
Rodriguez, Abraham, Jr., *Spidertown*
Roth, Philip, *Operation Shylock: A Confession*
Sanders, Dori, *Her Own Place*
Schaeffer, Susan Fromberg, *First Nights*
Schine, Cathleen, *Rameau's Niece*
Seth, Vikram, *A Suitable Boy*
Shacochis, Bob, *Swimming in the Volcano*
Smith, Scott, *A Simple Plan*
Turow, Scott, *Pleading Guilty*
Waller, James Robert, *Slow Waltz in Cedar Bend*
Wilcox, James, *Guest of a Sinner*

SHORT STORIES

Baker, Alison, *How I Came West, and Why I Stayed*
Bloom, Amy, *Come to Me*
Dorris, Michael, *Working Men*
Elkin, Stanley, *Van Gogh's Room at Arles*
Glancy, Diane, *Firesticks*
Gordon, Mary, *The Rest of Life*
Hannah, Barry, *Bats Out of Hell*
Jones, Thom, *The Pugilist at Rest*
Lyons, Daniel, *The Last Good Man*
Price, Reynolds, *The Collected Stories*
Shomer, Enid, *Imaginary Men*
Styron, William, *A Tidewater Morning*
Tallent, Elizabeth, *Honey*
Taylor, Peter, *The Oracle at Stoneleigh Court*
Troy, Judy, *Mourning Doves*
Woiwode, Larry, *Silent Passengers*

HISTORY AND BIOGRAPHY

Anderson, Terry, *Den of Lions: Memoirs of Seven Years*
Ashe, Arthur, and Rampersad, Arnold, *Days of Grace*
Brent, Joseph, *Charles Sanders Peirce*
Brown, Cecil, *Coming Up Down Home: A Memoir of a Southern Childhood*
Davis, Kenneth S., *FDR: Into the Storm 1937-1940, A History*
Dunn, Stephen, *Walking Light: Essays and Memoirs*
Eighner, Lars, *Travels With Lizbeth*
Epstein, Daniel Mark, *Sister Aimee: The Life of Aimee Semple McPherson*
Frohnmayer, John, *Leaving Town Alive: Confessions of an Arts Warrior*
Gooch, Brad, *City Poet: The Life and Times of Frank O'Hara*
Grumbach, Doris, *Extra Innings*
Halberstam, David, *The Fifties*
Heidenry, John, *Theirs Was the Kingdom: Lila and DeWitt Wallace and the Story of the Reader's Digest*
Hemphill, Paul, *Leaving Birmingham*
Kaysen, Susanna, *Girl, Interrupted*
Kolchin, Peter, *American Slavery, 1619-1877*
McGinniss, Joe, *The Last Brother*
Millier, Brett C., *Elizabeth Bishop: Life and the Memory of It*
Morris, Willie, *New York Days*
Raines, Howell, *Fly Fishing Through the Midlife Crisis*
Randall, Willard Sterne, *Thomas Jefferson: A Life*
Reeves, Richard, *President Kennedy: Profile of Power*
Shultz, George P., *Turmoil and Triumph: My Years as Secretary of State*
Silverthorne, Elizabeth, *Sarah Orne Jewett: A Writer's Life*
Summers, Anthony, *Official and Confidential: The Secret Life of J. Edgar Hoover*
Trillin, Calvin, *Remembering Denny*
Trilling, Diana, *The Beginning of the Journey: The Marriage of Diana and Lionel Trilling*
Tuttle, William M., Jr., *"Daddy's Gone to War" The Second World War in the Lives of America's Children*
Utley, Robert M., *The Lance and the Shield: The Life and Times of Sitting Bull*

CULTURE AND CRITICISM

Fishkin, Shelley Fisher, *Was Huck Black? Mark Twain and African-American Voices*
Friedan, Betty, *The Fountain of Age*
Hughes, Robert, *Culture of Complaint: The Fraying of America*
Kidder, Tracy, *Old Friends*
Lewis, R.W.B., *Literary Reflections: A Shoring of Images, 1960-1993*
Moyers, Bill, *Healing and the Mind*
Nozick, Robert, *The Nature of Rationality*
Rich, Adrienne, *What Is Found There: Notebooks on Poetry and Politics*
Said, Edward, *Culture and Imperialism*
Sowell, Thomas, *Inside American Education: The Decline, the Deception, the Dogmas*
Vidal, Gore, *United States: Essays 1952-1992*
West, Cornel, *Race Matters*
Wilson, Edmund, *The Sixties: The Last Journal, 1960-1972*
Wilson, James Q., *The Moral Sense*

POETRY

Alexie, Sherman, *Old Shirts & New Skins*
Ammons, A. R., *Garbage*
Cherry, Kelly, *God's Loud Hand*
Clifton, Lucille, *The Book of Light*
Doty, Mark, *My Alexandria*
Duncan, Robert, *Selected Poems, edited by Robert J. Bertholf*
Goldbarth, Albert, *The Gods*
Hall, Donald, *The Museum of Clear Ideas*
Olson, Charles, *Selected Poems, edited by Robert Creeley*
Rich, Adrienne, *Collected Early Poems: 1950-1970*
Rosenberg, David, *The Lost Book of Paradise*
Seidel, Frederick, *My Tokyo*
Smith, Charlie, *The Palms*
Van Duyn, Mona, *Firefall and If It Be Not I: Collected Poems 1959-82*
Waldman, Anne, *Iovis*

Eighner's *Travels With Lizbeth* garnered the most attention. His firsthand account of being homeless, traveling around the country with his dog, and living out of dumpsters was not so much social protest as a delineation of a way of life. Susanna Kaysen's *Girl, Interrupted* depicts the ironies and tragedies of Kaysen's two-year commitment to a fashionable mental asylum at age 17. Calvin Trillin's *Remembering Denny* was not so much about himself as it was an attempt to understand the life of a talented Yale classmate who committed suicide.

© 1993 Joyce Ravid

The Fountain of Age

BETTY FRIEDAN

Courtesy, Simon & Schuster

A battle over contemporary literary history was precipitated by Willie Morris' *New York Days*; a recollection of his embattled editorship of *Harper's Magazine* in the 1960s, it provoked present editor Lewis Lapham to an extensive rebuttal. Former head of the National Endowment for the Arts John Frohnmayer's *Leaving Town Alive: Confessions of an Arts Warrior* gives his account of decisions and mistakes he made in trying to reconcile political pressure groups and artists during the Bush administration.

Two novelists recalled their Southern childhoods in Paul Hemphill's *Leaving Birmingham* and Cecil Brown's *Coming Up Down Home*. Diana Trilling's *The Beginning of the Journey: The Marriage of Diana and Lionel Trilling* candidly tells of the early years and personal lives of these two influential literary critics.

Culture and Criticism. Australian-born critic Robert Hughes' *The Culture of Complaint* trenchantly dissects current trends in social and esthetic polemics. He argues that conservative complaints against the expansion of the literary canon and the study of non-Western cultures are as intellectually bankrupt as are the complaints of those who dismiss their heritage as merely the product of "dead white European males." Stanley Fish's *There's No Such Thing as Free Speech and It's a Good Thing, Too* argued that reason, tolerance, and fairness are simply masks for widespread right-wing oppression. Thomas Sowell's *Inside American Education: The Decline, the Deception, the Dogmas* states that schools have failed because they have succumbed to left-wing power.

In *United States: Essays 1952-1992*—Gore Vidal's enormous collection of provocative and perceptive literary, cultural, and historical essays—the author demonstrates that intelligence and learning still can differentiate between foolishness and achievement. The eminent literary critic R. W. B. Lewis' *Literary Reflections: A Shoring of Images, 1960-1993* shows a similarly impressive range of reference. With *The Sixties: The Last Journal, 1960-1972*, Edmund Wilson brings to a close a fascinating account of the life of a brilliant writer who seems to have known everyone of importance to our cultural history. Adrienne Rich's *What Is Found There: Notebooks on Poetry and Politics* is a collection of thoughts, memories, and favorite passages by one of the most significant U.S. poets.

Edward Said's *Culture and Imperialism* argues that the British sense of empire had a pervasive but generally unacknowledged effect on English literature, not only in writers like Rudyard Kipling but in such figures as Jane Austen and Charles Dickens. Shelley Fisher Fishkin's *Was Huck Black? Mark Twain and African-American Voices* invites a reexamination of the American literary classic by pointing out that the speech patterns of Huckleberry Finn were influenced by Twain's friendship with the black community. Tracy Kidder's *Old Friends* and Betty Friedan's *The Fountain of Age* both celebrate the possibilities of the elderly living dignified and meaningful lives despite debilitating illnesses and the approach of death.

Not only the U.S. national situation, but the entire human condition, was being rethought. Robert Nozick's *The Nature of Rationality* speculates on evolution's role in the development of reason. James Q. Wilson's *The Moral Sense* argued that, despite the evidence of war and crime, humans have an innate disposition to social interdependence and a sense of justice.

Poetry. Perhaps the most audacious book of poetry in 1993 was the biblical scholar David Rosenberg's *The Lost Book of Paradise*, in which he uses fragments of ancient texts to imagine an unorthodox Garden of Eden inhabited by a male and female snake, and creates a commentary on the poem as if written by a woman scholar from the time of Solomon. Also ambitious was A. R. Ammons' *Garbage*, a book-length poem meditating on the power of poetry and language to deal with the world and humanity's place in it.

Native American poet Sherman Alexie's *Old Shirts & New Skins* skillfully intermingles rage and insight in poems on such figures as Marlon Brando and General Custer. Lucille Clifton's *The Book of Light* celebrates women of the present and past. Adrienne Rich's *Collected Early Poems: 1950-1970* demonstrates the development of her voice as a major American poet.

JEROME STERN, *Florida State University*

Photos, Courtesy, Doubleday

BILL MOYERS

HEALING · AND · THE MIND

Children's Literature

Children's books remained a potent force in the literary marketplace of the United States during 1993, accounting for approximately 40% of bookstore sales, but the industry's growth had leveled out. Publishers continued to hang their hats on the multicultural hook, offering books featuring African-American, Hispanic, and Asian-American characters. More books were published simultaneously in English and Spanish, and old favorites were reissued in Spanish-language editions.

Another trend was books focusing on U.S. history, both in story and song. Most notable was *From Sea to Shining Sea: A Treasury of American Folklore and Folk Songs,* collected by Amy L. Cohn. Featuring illustrations from 11 Caldecott Medal and four Caldecott Honor book artists, the book traces U.S. history, reflecting its multicultural roots, through 140 folk songs, tales, poems and stories—from Longfellow's "Paul Revere's Ride" to Woody Guthrie's "This Land is Your Land."

Other books that showed young readers history in new and innovative ways were Virginia Hamilton's *Many Thousands Gone,* which traces the history of slavery in the United States through individual profiles; Paul Fleischman's *Bull Run,* which looks at the Battle of Gettysburg from the perspective of 16 Northerners and Southerners; Russell Freedman's insightful biography of Eleanor Roosevelt; and for younger audiences, a

The 1993 Newbery Medal winner

© Courtesy, Orchard Books, New York

The 1993 Caldecott Medal winner

Courtesy, G.P. Putnam's Sons

biography of Abe Lincoln by Edith Kunhardt incorporating folk-art paintings.

In award news, the winner of the 1993 Newbery Medal was Cynthia Rylant for her look at love and death in *Missing May.* Emily Arnold McCully was awarded the 1993 Caldecott Medal for her story of turn-of-the-century Paris, *Mirette on the High Wire.*

Picture Books. As in recent years, picture books continued to be the largest slice of the children's-literature pie in 1993. Famous names dominated, often combining their talents. For instance, the hilarious *Parents in the Pigpen, Pigs in the Tub* was a collaboration between Amy Erlich and artist Steven Kellog, in which a family and their farm animals switch abodes. *The Sorcerer's Apprentice* by prizewinning poet Nancy Willard featured pictures by distinguished illustrators Leo and Diane Dillon.

The most discussed book of the year probably was *Down in the Dumps with Jack and Guy* by Maurice Sendak. Using two lesser-known Mother Goose rhymes as his text, Sendak confronts the problems of homelessness, poverty, urban blight, and terror through his art. Though some found the book a controversial piece for children, Sendak's artistry is undeniable.

Middle-Grade Books. As the number of middle-grade readers increased due to the baby boomlet, beginning chapter books established a niche in the marketplace. Aimed at 7- to 9-year-olds, these books are a step beyond easy readers and look more like the novels children's older friends and siblings read, a feature new readers enjoy. Two notable characters to come out of

SELECTED BOOKS FOR CHILDREN

Picture Books

Aliki. *Communication*
Carle, Eric. *Today is Monday*
Carrick, Carol. *Whaling Days*
Johnson, Paul Brett. *The Cow Who Wouldn't Come Down*
McMullan, Kate. *Nutcracker Noel*
McPhail, David. *Pigs Aplenty, Pigs Galore*
Rayner, Mary. *Garth Pig Steals the Show*
Rosenberg, Liz. *Monster Mama*
Rylant, Cynthia. *The Dreamer*
Say, Allen. *Grandfather's Journey*
Trivizas, Eugene. *The Three Little Wolves and Big Bad Pig*
Van Allsburg, Chris. *The Sweetest Fig*
Woods, Audrey. *Rude Giants*
Yep, Laurence. *The Man Who Tricked a Ghost*

The Middle Grades

Appelbaum, Diana. *Giants in the Land*
Atkin, Beth S. *Voices From the Fields*
Blume, Judy. *Here's to You, Rachel Robinson*
Cooper, Susan. *The Boggart*
Fieffer, Jules. *The Boy on the Ceiling*
Griffin, Pen. *Switching Well*
Hamilton, Virginia. *Plain City*
Krull, Kathleen. *Lives of the Musicians*
MacBride, Roger Lea. *Little House on Rocky Ridge*
McCully, Emily Arnold. *The Amazing Felix*
Mills, Claudia. *Dinah in Love*
Orlev, Uri. *Lydia, Queen of Palestine*
Sills, Leslie. *Visions*
Vos, Ida. *Anna is Still Here*
Waddle, Martin. *Stories from the Bible*
Wilcox, Charlotte. *Mummies & Their Mysteries*

Junior High and Young Adult

Dickinson, Peter. *A Bone from a Dry Sea*
Gee, Maurice. *The Champion*
Johnson, Angela. *Toning the Sweep*
Klause, Annette. *Alien's Secrets*
Lawrence, Jacob. *Harriet and the Promised Land*
Lewin, Ted. *I Was a Teenage Professional Wrestler*
Mazer, Harry. *Who is Eddie Leonard*
Tamar, Erika. *Fair Game*
Verhoeven, Rian, and van der Rol, Rudd. *Anne Frank: Beyond the Diary*

this genre were Marvin Redpost, a boy whose imagination gets him into no end of trouble, from the series by Louis Sacher, and the feisty young heroine Junie B. Jones, from the series by Barbara Park.

Series books continued to dominate the market, but did not proliferate as they once had. Books like Lois Lowery's *The Giver* and Tor Seidler's *The Wainscott Weasel* were strong entries in the fantasy genre.

Junior High and Young Adult. Although fewer young-adult books were being published, their quality remained high, especially when written by authors who did not condescend to their audience. Two notable entries were Suzanne Fisher Staples' *Haveli*, about a young woman's life in Pakistan; and *Celebrating the Hero* by Lyll Becerra deJenkins, in which a teenager must face the truth about her grandfather—a man she always thought was a hero.

See also LIBRARIES.

ILENE COOPER
Editor, Children's Books, "Booklist" magazine

Canadian Literature: English

Despite economic and political uncertainty, Canadian literature continued to flourish in 1993. Nonfiction works concentrated on politics, finance, and biographies. Some established poets and fiction writers resurfaced after long absences, while promising newcomers stretched the boundaries of their art.

Nonfiction. Prime Minister Brian Mulroney's resignation inspired two reviews of his political record: Lawrence Martin's *Pledge of Allegiance: The Americanization of Canada in the Mulroney Years*, and Mel Watkins' *Madness and Ruin: The Legacy of the Conservatives*. Kim Campbell, Mulroney's successor as head of the Progressive Conservatives and Canada's first female prime minister, spurred such biographies as *The Politics of Kim Campbell* by Murray Dobbin and *Kim Campbell: The Making of a Politician* by Robert Fife. Campbell and the Conservatives later suffered a major electoral defeat. Former Prime Minister Pierre Trudeau's autobiography, *Memoirs,* was hailed as the publishing event of the year.

Two books explored Canada's political dilemmas. David Orchard's *The Fight for Canada* details U.S. military, cultural, and political invasions, while Jeffrey Simpson's *Faultlines: Struggling for a Canadian Vision* analyzes eight Canadians who embody the new politics and power struggles that face Canada.

The fall of the Reichmanns, the world's largest real-estate developers, is chronicled in Peter Foster's *Towers of Debt: The Rise and Fall of the Reichmanns*. Also compelling is Maj.-Gen. Lewis MacKenzie's autobiography, *Peacekeeper: The Road to Sarajevo*, which charts a military career that culminated in the command of the UN mission to Sarajevo in June 1992.

Correspondence between the late Margaret Laurence, one of Canada's most honored literary figures, and poet Al Purdy comes alive in John Lennox's *Margaret Laurence–Al Purdy: A Friendship in Letters*. Poet Irving Layton is celebrated in Henry Beissel and Joy Bennett's *Raging Like a Fire*. And Farley Mowat, always irreverent and controversial, celebrates his own childhood in *Born Naked*.

Poetry. Leonard Cohen published *Stranger Music: Selected Poems and Songs*, a collection that covers 40 years of writing and performing. Two other notable collections are Roy Miki's *George Bowering Selected Poems 1961-1992*, and Dennis Lee's jazz-inspired *Riffs*. Joanne Arnott faces her First Nations and European roots in *My Grass Cradle*, a collection exploring personal abuse, poverty, and family relationships.

Fiction. Timothy Findley resurfaced with *Headhunter*, which explores humankind's relentless march toward self-destruction, as Joseph Conrad's Kurtz runs loose in the heart of modern Toronto. Margaret Atwood returned in 1993 with *The Robber Bride*, her eighth novel.

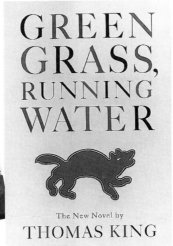

© Timothy Francisco

Courtesy, Houghton Mifflin Company

Thomas King's "Green Grass, Running Water," the story of a Blackfoot family in Alberta, was considered one of Canada's leading novels of 1993.

First Nations lives and voices gained prominence in works like Thomas King's *Green Grass, Running Water*, a portrayal of a Blackfoot family in Alberta. Lee Maracle's *Ravensong* evokes the suffering of a Native American community devastated by a flu epidemic, a symbol of the impact of European culture.

Carol Shields' ingenious *The Stone Diaries* explores parallels between life and fiction within a tale of exiled Orkney stonemasons in middle-class North America. In *Gentleman Death*, Graeme Gibson comes to terms with mortality through a humorous 56-year-old novelist. Set on the Niagara frontier during the American Revolution, Douglas Glover's *The Life and Times of Captain N* depicts the horrors of war and the collision of cultures.

David Adams Richards completes his trilogy with *For Those Who Hunt the Wounded Down*, which delves into the dark reaches of rural New Brunswick, and Nino Ricci adds a sequel, *In a Glass House*, to his award-winning *The Lives of the Saints*. In *Away*, Jane Urquhart traces generations of Irish immigrants who settle in Ontario.

Among notable collections of short stories are Mavis Gallant's *Across the Bridge*, her first collection in seven years. Isabel Huggan's *You Never Know* seemed headed for high praise. The postmodernist stories in M. A. C. Farrant's *Raw Material* are anything but ordinary. J. Jill Robinson and Regina's Diane Warren explore women's relationships in *Lovely In Her Bones* and *Bad Luck Dog*, respectively. Finally, *The Journey Prize Anthology* contains fiction from the best of Canada's new writers.

DOUGLAS R. CRONK
Open University of British Columbia

English Literature

Setting, whether viewed in terms of the spirit of place or its authenticity, took center stage in English fiction in 1993. Meanwhile political history was the dominant force of the year's English nonfiction.

Fiction. The compelling backdrops of 1993 English fiction were divided between the close-to-home and the exotic. Recent events in Bosnia heightened interest in the appearance of translations of the Nobel Prize-winning novelist Ivo Andric. A new translation of *The Damned Yard and Other Stories* exhibits Andric's wit, beauty, and power. Translations of two works by the politically beset Algerian novelist, Rachid Mimouni—*The Honour of the Tribe*, a novel, and *The Ogre's Embrace*, a collection of stories—expanded his audience.

Celebrating the new voices of women writing fiction in some of the many languages of India, *Separate Journeys*—edited by Geeta Dharmarajan—was sure to appeal to readers of all of them. Gita Mehta's new novel, *A River Sutra*, is an artful medley of stories centered in the rich cultural flux of India. On the theme of the shifting empire, Amit Chaudhuri's poetic novel, *Afternoon Raag*, ranges from impressions made in England to vast India and finally to an artistic home in Calcutta. Sam Watson's novel, *The Kadaitcha Sung*, provides readers with glimpses into a world of the Aborigine people, into the vitality of its land-oriented imaginative and visceral reality. A capacity for lengthy fiction was confirmed by the favorable reception of Vikram Seth's 1,349-page *A Suitable Boy*, intertwined tales told with avuncular fondness and set in the historical north of India in the turbulent 1950s.

The realms of fantasy have had many guides, but few have been more cunning than Gabriel García Márquez, whose new collection of stories appeared under the title *Strange Pilgrims*. Ben Okri followed his Booker Prize winner, *The Famished Road*, with *Songs of Enchantment*, West African tales of fantasy and vision. Meanwhile, the character and action of Iris Murdoch's *The Green Knight* are removed to the mythic rather than being set in the familiar social reality of her other fiction. Sebastian Falkes' *Birdsong*,

his fourth novel, uses the historical period prior to World War I to detail the horror of life and death in the trenches. The action of Tim Parks' sixth novel, *Shear*, centers around a Mediterranean quarry and the distance between it and the protagonist's London home. Sharon Olds' *The Father* advances unflinchingly into the emotions centered around the death of her father. The tumultuous world of Northern Ireland during the 1960s is witnessed through the eyes of a 10-year-old boy in Roddy Doyle's *Paddy Clarke Ha Ha Ha*. It captured the 1993 Booker Prize.

The family saga continued to provide narrative structure and motive for the characters of the new novel of Roy Hatlersley, *Skylarks's Song*. Village life has its own intense traditions, as shown in the new novel of 80-year-old Sybil Marshall, *A Nest of Magpies*. *Smoke Signals: Stories of London* was a collection of sponsored stories. Also new on the scene is Jonathan Mallabeir's *The Prince of Wales and Stories*, a triumph of a deliberately manipulative art—manner over substance—that successfully reclaims fiction from what otherwise passes as reality. With *The Night Manager*, John Le Carré turned to the post-Cold War era for his brand of action.

In the recognition category, the newly established David Cohen British Literature Prize was awarded to V. S. Naipaul for lifetime achievement, and the Sunday Times Award for Excellence in Writing was given to Martin Amis. Salman Rushdie's *Midnight Children* received a special Booker Prize as the best British novel of the past 25 years.

Nonfiction. Robert Bartlett's *The Making of Europe: Conquest, Colonization and Cultural Change, 950-1350* asserts that by the beginning of the 14th century, Europe—by virtue of religious and social belief, economic and technological development, and the institution of universities—had come to possess a cultural identity at once both united and diverse. With an eye warily cast toward implications for the present, the editors R. Ahmann, A. M. Birke, and M. Howard presented *The Quest For Stability: Problems of West European Security, 1918-1957*, a series of 20 essays offering much to interest both students and historians of international relations. Happily for the many who cannot read Welsh, *A History of Wales*, a monumental and detailed work, was translated into English by its author, John Davies. And Jonathan Bardon provided the lengthy *A History of Ulster*, which concentrates most heavily on the recent, troubled times in this province.

Robin Horron's *Patterns of Thought in Africa and the West: Essays on Magic, Religion and Science* collects many of the author's important, if debatable, essays on those subjects in one volume. The relation of humans to nature and the nature of humans are of increasing concern, and one work beyond the sometimes shrill voice of the activist is *Landscape, Natural Beauty*

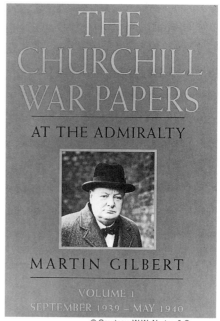

© Courtesy, W.W. Norton & Company

and the Arts, edited by Salim Kewal and Ivan Gaskell. Jason Goodwin's *On Foot to the Golden Horn: A Walk to Istanbul* reports on an elegantly recorded journey made in 1934 by Patrick Leigh Fermor. Goodwin gives a firsthand look at the present conditions of central Europe.

Beginning what would be a long publishing venture, *The Churchill War Papers, Volume One: September 1939-May 1940*, editor Martin Gilbert supplies the professional and armchair historian with much—more than 1,300 pages—to reconsider. Books abounded on English royalty, and among those that put monarchy in general into favorable perspective is Veronica Maclean's *Crowned Heads: Kings, Sultans and Emperors: A Royal Quest*. The NCR Book Award for Non-Fiction went to Peter Hennessy for his *Never Again: Britain 1945-1951*.

Poetry. The poetry published during the year displayed a chorus of bardic voices that continued to win interest. In *Walking to Santiago*, Neil Curry uses the pilgrimage route to create poetry that may lack supporting myth or personal conviction, but does expose a familiar modern soul and attend quietly to detail along the way. Among the poets whose works appeared from small presses, those of special promise included Lavinia Greenlaw's *Love From a Foreign City* and John F. Deane's *Far Country*. The appearance of the *Collected Poems, 1935-1992* of F. T. Prince acknowledges a skillful master of the long poem and the lyric. The formidable volume of R. S. Thomas' *Collected Poems 1945-1990* reassures his lasting reputation, as does Ray Fuller's *Last Poems*.

DONALD L. JENNERMANN
Indiana State University

World Literature*

The year 1993 was an excellent one in world literature, in quantity and in quality. Particularly impressive were the efforts of writers from India, China, Egypt, and Central Europe.

Asia. In *Red Sorghum*, Mo Yan wove five novellas into a seamless family portrait covering three generations in a township of Shandong province, China, concentrating on the lawless 1930s and the Japanese occupation but also touching on the Cultural Revolution and the post-Mao reform movements of the 1980s. Mo's countryman Su Tong reissued his novella "Wives and Concubines" with two other narratives under the title *Raise the Red Lantern,* capitalizing on the fame of the Academy Award-nominated 1992 film of that name by Zhang Yimou. The rechristened title story follows the fortunes of a young female student forced to give up her studies and marry into the household of an aging merchant, where her presumption and sensuality spark a series of intrigues that lead inexorably to tragedy.

Japan's wildly popular novelist Haruki Murakami brought out a collection of short stories titled *The Elephant Vanishes.* A pervasive sense of emptiness marks these tales and their characters, but the author's whimsy, imaginative flair, and infatuation with things Western enliven them all, including "The Dwarf," a parody of mass production in which the narrator works in the ear department of an elephant factory. (Elephants take too long to gestate and grow to maturity on their own, the reasoning goes; hence the need to manufacture them.) Harumi Setouchi, one of Japan's leading women authors, was introduced to Western readers via the translation of her best-selling novel *Beauty in Disarray,* which centers on the life of a young woman during the Meiji era, when Japan transformed itself from a feudal society into a modern state.

India's Vikram Seth created what was literally the year's biggest literary sensation with the publication of *A Suitable Boy,* the 1,350-page tale of a quiet 19-year-old northern Indian girl named Lata and her efforts to find a husband in 1950, as the world's largest and youngest democracy prepares for its first general election. Stately, conservative in style and temperament, kindly and charming in disposition, and all-encompassing in its social and geographic reach, the work is a major accomplishment by any measure and possesses the fullness of life of the great 19th-century European realist novels it emulates so well. In her carefully constructed novel *A River Sutra,* Gita Mehta follows the experiences of an Indian bureaucrat who retires to run a government rest house in the jungle by the sacred Narmada River, only to discover that the river's teeming traffic of people, stories, and passions make it the last place on earth where he should have expected to be able to withdraw into contemplative solitude. The grand old man of Indi-

an letters, R. K. Narayan, issued three novellas under the title *The Grandmother's Tale.* The lead story concerns a young bride's search for the child-groom who deserted her shortly after their arranged marriage, thus depriving her of all status and value; the other two works involve a small-town official and petty racketeer and a would-be romance novelist who joins forces with her gifted chef of a husband to write a best-selling cookbook.

Near East. The Jordanian-born writer Abdelrahman Munif completed his epic Cities of Salt trilogy in 1993 with *Variations on Night and Day.* Where *Cities of Salt* and *The Trench* traced the development of the sultanate of Mooran (a thinly disguised Saudi Arabia) from the 1930s discovery of oil by British and U.S. groups through the 1950s, *Variations* returns to the opening decades of the 20th century to reveal how Sultan Khureybit consolidated his power and created Mooran as a modern nation-state. In the novellas *The Well of Life* and *The Thread,* published together in a single volume, Nawal El Saadawi—Egypt's most celebrated woman writer—presented two quasi-surreal narratives about oppressed women wherein everything that occurs is cast as strange and inexplicable, all actions occur with the compulsive necessity of nightmare, and the reader constantly is made aware of a didactic message. Naguib Mahfouz, Egypt's 1986 Nobel Prize winner, saw his 1960s novella *Adrift on the Nile* make its belated appearance in translation; a rather static tale centered on the evening gatherings of a group of complacent and superfluous older men and their *kif*-clouded, self-indulgent discussions, the work unfortunately now seems quite dated in both style and social import. Latife Tekin, one of Turkey's finest young writers, made her debut in translation with *Berji Kristin: Tales from the Garbage Hills,* a largely plotless but wholly provocative and enjoyable novel that uses humor, fantasy, and playful exaggeration to depict the plight of migrants from the countryside struggling to survive in Istanbul.

Africa, West Indies. South Africa's André Brink brought out the English version of his captivating 1988 novella *Cape of Storms,* a mythic tale—told from the nominally native perspective of the fabled giant T'kama—of the first encounter between Europeans and Africans five centuries ago when Vasco de Gama sailed around the Cape of Good Hope. In *The Powers That Be,* Brink's countryman Mike Nicol recounts the story of Enoch Mistas, a black youth with a Bible chained to his wrist and strange voices in his head who leads a messianic rebellion against an imperious, bewildered government.

Caryl Phillips of St. Kitts followed up his successes of *Higher Ground* (1989) and *Cambridge* (1991) with *Crossing the River,* presenting four interrelated narratives involving a U.S. tobacco planter who sets out for West Africa in 1841 in

*titles translated

search of a former slave of his who is now a missionary. In *From the Heat of the Day* the Guyanese novelist Roy Heath charted his typical "downward path to wisdom," as one critic stated, here focusing on the vicissitudes in the marriage of a middle-class woman and a once-ambitious provincial who settles for the dull but steady life of a postal clerk.

French. Of the many fine works of fiction and poetry published in French in 1993, perhaps none had a more powerful impact than the late Hervé Guibert's *Paradise,* a novel in which fiction is replaced progressively by autobiography as the protagonist and his female companion take ill during a foreign jaunt with what seems at first only some inconvenient infection but slowly, inexorably, tragically comes to be known for what it is—AIDS. It robs the narrator of vitality, strength, memory, lucidity, and ultimately life. Another, very different sort of posthumous work to appear was *Conte bleu,* a surrealistic prose poem by the late grande dame of French letters, Marguerite Yourcenar, about mysterious jeweled treasures, an exotic slave girl, avaricious European traders, ruthless pirates, and fantastical sea creatures. The *conte* was issued together with two other short tales: "The First Evening," written by Yourcenar with her father and first published in 1929; and "Maleficence," a curious piece first issued in 1933. *The Secret* by Philippe Sollers bends the conventions of the spy thriller into what one critic termed "a static but highly combative analytic novel" that takes off from a lengthy foray into the papal-assassination plot and expands its attention to encompass narcotics trafficking, sperm banks, genetic engineering, the international media, and ethnic cleansing.

Central and Eastern Europe. From the outstanding Czech novelist Ivan Klíma in 1993 came *Judge on Trial,* an emotionally wrenching epic tale of justice, conscience, and memory set amid the aftermath of the 1968 invasion; originally issued in *samizdat* form in 1978 but only now published for the first time, the work generally is regarded as Klíma's masterpiece, a vivid and compelling portrait of a generation forced to witness the dissolution of its ideals and the destruction of its accomplishments. In *The Little Town Where Time Stood Still,* Klíma's countryman Bohumil Hrabal offered a more easygoing, low-key, and seemingly effortless account of two family histories, one in "a far-off country of which we know nothing" but which closely resembles the interwar Czech republic, the other in postwar Czechoslovakia dominated in all aspects by communism. A personal biography of Czech President Václav Havel by Eda Kriseova, his friend and press adviser, was presented in the West. It was published in Czechoslovakia in 1990. With *The Inner Side of the Wind,* Serbian novelist Milorad Pavic produced another of his imaginatively inventive fictional experiments, recasting the ancient story of Hero and Leander in a double narrative. The tales begin literally at opposite ends of the book and are set simultaneously in the 17th and 20th centuries.

The Hungarian Péter Lengyel's 1988 novel *Cobblestone* became available to a worldwide audience in English translation, presenting "a philosophical mystery for the millennium" (1896's 1,000-year celebration of the founding of the Magyar nation) that is at once a suspense tale about a gang of safecrackers in fin-de-siècle Austria-Hungary and an informative lesson in Central European history. The Romanian émigré author Norman Manea followed up his dual success of 1992 (the essay volume *On Clowns* and the short-story collection *October, Eight O'Clock*) with another volume of short fiction, *Compulsory Happiness;* its four novellas present an appalling panorama of human cruelty and suffering. Albania's Ismail Kadare saw his controversial 1990 fable on totalitarianism, *Palace of Dreams*, rendered into English and also brought out a new work, *Claire de Lune,* a brief novel of manners and morals revolving around the efforts of a modern-day virgin named Mary to clear her name and honor amid the calumnious lies of neighbors and acquaintances and the mysterious birth of a child. And in *Fear*, Russia's Anatoly Rybakov presented a stunning account of the Stalinist purges through the story of a young school-newspaper editor whose one casually impolitic remark sends him to prison and subsequently into Siberian exile during an era of mass arrests, torture, sham trials, terror, and death on an unimaginable scale.

Other. Dacia Maraini produced perhaps the year's best-received and best-selling novel in Italy, *Isolina*. The book fleshes out the true story of a poor but fun-loving and attractive young girl whose body was found floating in the river at Verona in January 1900, the victim of a botched abortion. The Basque novelist Bernardo Atxaga (nom de plume of Joséba Irazu Garmendia) enjoyed worldwide success with *Obabakoak,* a wildly imaginative set of tales revolving primarily around the Basque town of Obaba but ranging widely in space and time and in styles of writing. Brazil's grand old man Jorge Amado saw his 1944 novel *The Golden Harvest* rendered into English for the first time and distributed worldwide in celebration of his 80th birthday; an astonishingly fertile and detailed recreation of Brazilian plantation life in the first third of this century, the work is a sheer delight in its realism and the vibrancy of its storytelling and characterization. And from Mexico came Elena Poniatowska's *Tinísima*, a massive but vividly readable account of the life and trajectory of Tina Modotti, an Italian-born photographer, social militant, and Communist who lived in Mexico in the 1920s and participated actively in the country's cultural, intellectual, and political life.

WILLIAM RIGGAN
"World Literature Today"

LOS ANGELES

In 1993, Los Angeles elected someone other than Tom Bradley mayor for the first time in 20 years. The area continued to suffer sharply economically, and witnessed headline trials in connection with the 1991 beating of Rodney King and the 1992 riots (*see also* CRIME; LAW).

Election. Businessman Richard Riordan (*see* BIOGRAPHY) defeated Michael Woo in the city's mayoralty race. The electoral contests for city council operated for the first time under rules of partial public financing and spending limits. Partly as a result, four new members were selected for the council, including two who defeated incumbents.

Recovery. By late in the year some 60% of the structures devastated during the 1992 riot had been repaired or rebuilt. Mayor Riordan, in his inaugural address, called for more personal responsibility and less dependence upon state and federal programs in the recovery. The city in fact was given little federal aid and most rebuilding was done on an ad hoc basis. RLA (Rebuild L.A.), the private agency intended to lead and organize riot recovery, was not effective in recruiting large corporations to provide jobs in the ghetto and was reorganized to serve as broker in the development of small businesses.

Budgets. Both the city and county endured another year of very tight budgets. Faced with a decline in assessed evaluation following the recession and 1992 riot, it still was necessary by law to balance the budgets. But raising tax rates was politically impossible. For the city, this required a $190 million budget reduction and the laying off of 128 more employees. Since 1990, 2,434 city positions had been eliminated. Mayor Riordan cut still another $150 million from the Bradley budget. But the new mayor's hope to sell the main library to a private corporation and lease it back to the city was rejected by the council. And Riordan's idea of leasing the main airport to private firms was dropped. Other than police and fire services, practically all functions were trimmed to the extent allowed by law.

Schools. Plans for year-round schools and a major educational reform plan, the Los Angeles Educational Alliance for Restructuring Now (LEARN), foundered. The former encountered parental objections and budget problems. Only one regular school made the change, though more than 200 multitrack schools and 100 centers for specialized schooling will be on a year-round calendar. LEARN was developed by business, educational, teachers'-union, and other interests and was two years in the making, but the compromises did not jell and were opposed strongly in the end by leaders of the teachers' union and others. LEARN's future remained in doubt late in the year.

Efforts to break up the giant school district continued. Meanwhile it sought to modify its bilingual teaching program, which had been criticized severely by state officials, whose report said middle- and high-school students were not learning English adequately. In some suburbs thousands of parents volunteered to do janitorial, library, and even instructional tasks to help overcome budget shortages. The Compton district, in fiscal and educational trouble, was forced to ask the state for an emergency loan of $10.5 million. In acting, state authorities gave broad authority to a substitute administrator. The University of Southern California received a $120 million cash gift from the Walter H. Annenberg Foundation for developing programs in the communication arts.

© Steve Starr/Saba

On June 8, 1993, Republican businessman Richard Riordan, shown with his sister-in-law Terry (left), walked through the streets of Los Angeles after casting a vote for his own successful mayoral candidacy. Riordan, 63, defeated city-council member Michael Woo to succeed Democrat Tom Bradley, who had been the city's mayor for two decades.

Functions and Leaders. The powerful county administrative officer, Richard B. Dixon, was forced to leave in February because of policy differences with the county Board of Supervisors. Sally R. Reed, 50, who had held a similar position in Santa Clara county in northern California, was selected to fill the office. The landmark Central Library, first built in 1926 and badly damaged in a 1986 arson fire, was reopened in October after extensive reconstruction.

The newly created Metropolitan Transportation Authority named Franklin White, 51-year-old transportation commissioner for the state of New York, as its first chief executive officer. The arrangement combines into one agency a special district and a county department, former rivals. The growing multibillion-dollar Metro Rail subway system was subjected to investigations into contract and management practices.

The canals in the Venice section of the city were reopened after being rebuilt. Public areas were repaired following half a century of controversy concerning financing and method. The project restored the 88-year-old waterways to something like their original condition.

CHARLES R. ADRIAN
University of California, Riverside

LOUISIANA

Gambling fever began sweeping Louisiana in late 1993, as riverboat gambling went on-line and a compromise was reached on who would operate the New Orleans land-based casino, projected to be the biggest in the world. The state also struggled with economic problems, crime, and a political scandal.

Gambling. Louisiana's first gambling boat went into operation on Lake Pontchartrain in New Orleans in the fall, and 14 others were gearing up, from Shreveport on the Red River in northwestern Louisiana to the bayou country in the southeast. Some authorities, including state

© AP/Wide World

In a trial of international interest in Baton Rouge, LA, Rodney Peairs was acquitted of manslaughter charges that arose when he fatally shot a teenage Japanese exchange student.

Riverboat Gaming Commission Chairman Ken Pickering, called for more boats, but Gov. Edwin Edwards said he wanted to maintain a cap of 15 boats statewide.

Edwards' chief interest was the rapid development of the New Orleans casino, which would be built just blocks from the Mississippi River near the famed French Quarter. A heated dispute arose over who would operate the casino when the city gave the site lease to developers of the Grand Palais Casino, and the state gaming board gave preliminary approval for the license to Harrah's Casino Management. After Edwards applied public pressure for a compromise, the competitors agreed to share interest in the enterprise. The casino in New Orleans and the gambling boats joined the lottery and video poker machines as legal forms of gambling new to Louisiana in the 1990s. To help deal with social problems caused by gambling, the state mandated that toll-free help lines be set up and that the number be posted in all gambling outlets.

Budget. In spite of new gambling revenues, the state still struggled in 1993 to balance the budget. A special legislative session called by Edwards in March failed to solve budget problems when lawmakers could not agree on new taxes or heavy cuts. In the regular session ending in June, the legislature did come up with a balanced $10.9 billion budget, raising almost $120 million in sales taxes on previously exempt food and drug items, and in corporate income taxes. About $60 million for higher education was cut, with $40 million of that being made up by higher college tuitions. Other state departments also were cut and almost 3,000 state jobs were lost.

Violence. The state received international notoriety when a Baton Rouge man shot and killed a 16-year-old Japanese exchange student who approached the man's house in costume while looking for a Halloween party. Yoshihiro

---

LOUISIANA • Information Highlights

Area: 47,752 sq mi (123 677 km²).
Population (July 1, 1992 est.): 4,287,000.
Chief Cities (1990 census): Baton Rouge, the capital, 219,531; New Orleans, 496,938; Shreveport, 198,525.
Government (1993): *Chief Officers*—governor, Edwin W. Edwards (D); lt. gov., Melina Schwegmann (D). *Legislature*—Senate, 39 members; House of Representatives, 105 members.
State Finances (fiscal year 1991): *Revenue*, $10,764,000,000; *expenditure*, $10,537,000,000.
Personal Income (1992): $68,055,000,000; per capita, $15,874.
Labor Force (August 1993): *Civilian labor force*, 1,871,100; *unemployed*, 138,200 (7.4% of total force).
Education: *Enrollment* (fall 1991)—public elementary schools, 572,772; public secondary, 192,817; colleges and universities, 197,438. *Public school expenditures* (1990-91), $2,987,448,000.

Hattori knocked on the door of Rodney Peairs' suburban home and scared his wife, who slammed the door and told her husband to get his gun. Peairs, armed with a handgun, confronted Hattori in his carport, and shot the youth when he failed to heed Peairs' order to "freeze." A Baton Rouge jury acquitted Peairs of manslaughter.

Violence plagued the entire state. Statistics released in 1993 showed that in 1992, Louisiana ranked first among all states in homicides per capita and the New Orleans metropolitan area was ranked first in murders per capita. In 1993, New Orleans was on its way to its highest murder rate ever, averaging more than one homicide per day.

Tuition Scandal. In June it was revealed that New Orleans Mayor Sidney Barthelemy—who earned more than $90,000—had awarded a Tulane University scholarship to his own son under legislation that dates back to the 1880s. Subsequent revelations showed that many legislators also had given scholarships to relatives or close political friends. After much negative publicity, the scholarship process was reformed.

JOSEPH W. DARBY III
"The Times Picayune," New Orleans

MAINE

Facing the continued diminution of the state's defense-based industries throughout 1993, Maine's economy remained sluggish as business and government sought to maximize returns from its other leading income producers. Meanwhile the state prepared for elections in 1994.

Economy. There were indications that the state's economic health was improving. A midyear Maine business index compiled by the Center for Business and Economic Research at the University of Southern Maine showed a modest upturn from the recession's nadir in 1991.

New markets were being developed for Maine forest products and the continuing

increase in tourism revenues held firm. By the end of November, more than 20 million board feet of Maine timber had been shipped to new markets in China and Turkey. And the total number of vehicles that crowded the Maine Turnpike during the 1993 tourist season was up by nearly 2 million over comparable figures for 1992.

But not all economic news was good. Bath Iron Works, Maine's largest industrial employer, continued to downsize its skilled workforce from a high of 12,000 in 1991 to 8,500. The same situation prevailed at pulp and paper manufacturers, which collectively generate the state's largest payrolls.

As the emphasis on the health of Maine's economic recovery focused on resource-based industries, industry leaders worked to safeguard their critical resources. Lobstermen discussed and compiled a new lobster-management plan designed to limit pressure on the resource and ensure the fishery's future. Meanwhile, the Northern Forest Lands Council concluded three years of research and began formulating recommendations to help ensure the continued productivity and preservation of the timber tracts that occupy more than 90% of Maine's land area.

As the year ended, there was good news for Maine's boat builders when the U.S. Congress repealed the two-year-old 10% luxury tax on all pleasure craft costing more than $100,000.

Politics. With gubernatorial and legislative elections scheduled for November 1994, political incumbents and new candidates spent much of 1993 in public debate over the best ways to revive the Maine economy. As the year ended, no less than 16 men and women had initiated gubernatorial campaigns to succeed Gov. John R. McKernan, the Republican who would have served the constitutional consecutive two-term limit.

Maine had seen independent Ross Perot challenge both major-party candidates in the 1992 presidential election, so much attention was paid to three unaffiliated candidates running for governor. Among Democrats, discussion focused on former two-term governor Joseph Brennan, who announced that he would run for the office once again.

The aspirations of candidates for the Maine House and Senate would be affected by the results of a referendum in November 1993 that placed an eight-year limit on previously unlimited terms.

Sports. In Portland a $1.5 million upgrade of the city's Hadlock Field neared completion; the project was in preparation for the spring arrival of the Maine Sea Dogs, the state's first AA minor-league professional baseball team.

And Mainers were watching to see if the University of Maine's hockey team could retain the national intercollegiate championship it won early in 1993. The entire team attended a presidential reception at the White House. The team's success had helped much of Maine get through a severe winter that brought the "Storm of the Century."

JOHN N. COLE, *"Maine Times"*

MAINE • Information Highlights

Area: 33,265 sq mi (86 156 km²).

Population (July 1, 1992 est.): 1,235,000.

Chief Cities (1990 census): Augusta, the capital, 21,325; Portland, 64,358; Lewiston, 39,757; Bangor, 33,181.

Government (1993): *Chief Officer*—governor, John R. McKernan, Jr. (R). *Legislature*—Senate, 33 members; House of Representatives, 151 members.

State Finances (fiscal year 1991): *Revenue*, $3,222,000,000; *expenditure*, $3,515,000,000.

Personal Income (1992): $22,360,000,000; per capita, $18,100.

Labor Force (August 1993): *Civilian labor force*, 654,300; *unemployed*, 49,600 (7.6% of total force).

Education: *Enrollment* (fall 1991)—public elementary schools, 156,764; public secondary, 59,636; colleges and universities, 57,178. *Public school expenditures* (1990-91), $1,070,965,000.

MALAYSIA

The era of leadership by Malaysia's Prime Minister Mahathir Mohamad began to wind down in 1993 as a new generation of political leadership emerged. The nation continued to enjoy one of the strongest economies among the world's newly industrializing countries.

Domestic Politics. The year's pivotal political event was the November 4 election for United Malay National Organization (UMNO) deputy president. This post within Malaysia's dominant political party is tantamount to a guarantee for gaining the position of deputy prime minister, which eventually leads to the prime ministership. The contest was initially between Minister of Finance Anwar Ibrahim and Deputy Prime Minister Ghafar Baba. Mahathir gave some evidence early on of preferring not to see a change of the old guard, but Anwar won in a landslide. Ghafar Baba withdrew from the race and resigned from the cabinet, leaving a space open for the new UMNO deputy president. On December 1 the prime minister appointed Anwar as deputy prime minister, with a full cabinet reshuffle expected in January 1994.

Anwar's supporters from his *pasukan wawasan* (vision team) also won control of lower UMNO party posts. However, the new team was split between Islamic and economic factions. A second splintering factor was that many votes for Anwar came from Sabah, the independent-minded East Malaysian state separated from West Malaysia by some 400 mi (650 km) of South China Sea.

Other political events also challenged UMNO leadership. UMNO continued to pressure political figures in Sabah to join the government. On the mainland, a top official of Semangat '46, an opposition party, was forced to give up his party post in order to maintain participation in the Malaysian labor movement. Although Malaysia has kept a good reputation in this area, the government did not favor a strong labor movement.

Economy. The economy continued to flourish in 1993, with more than 8% real growth in gross domestic product (GDP) and growth in investment predicted at 15%. Exports and imports were expected to advance by roughly 10%. Future economic growth could be stalled by bottlenecks created by the poor infrastructure.

Malaysia was the first ASEAN (Association of Southeast Asian Nations) member to undertake substantial tariff cuts to meet the goals established by the ASEAN Free Trade Area (AFTA). Tariffs on some 1,100 items were to be reduced or eliminated by 1994.

Defense. Malaysia continued to modernize and increase investment in its defense. Malaysia concluded deals to buy U.S. and Russian fighter planes. The Russian deal suggested that the prime minister was willing to demonstrate some independence from the West. The Malaysian

navy also was given approval to purchase 27 offshore patrol boats. Meanwhile, the United States announced that it was restoring military-training assistance to Malaysia.

Foreign Policy. Prime Minister Mahathir raised some eyebrows by his absence in November from the Asia Pacific Economic Cooperation (APEC) forum in Seattle. He had been miffed at the United States' failure to support his East Asian Economic Caucus (EAEC). Mahathir then threatened Australia with diplomatic and trade sanctions following comments by Prime Minister Paul Keating that Mahathir was recalcitrant. In December, Malaysia banned Australian television programs and news. However, the matter was defused by year's end.

Malaysian police and military forces participated in UN operations in Mozambique, Cambodia, Bosnia, and Somalia during 1993. Malaysia also signed an agreement with Indonesia to enforce stronger antipiracy and pro-environmental policies in the Strait of Malacca.

PATRICK M. MAYERCHAK
Virginia Military Institute

MANITOBA

In Manitoba in 1993 the provincial government struggled to control a budget deficit and put forth legislation regarding French-speaking schools and no-fault insurance.

The Budget and Legislation. When the provincial budget was released in early 1993, for the fifth year in a row there were no significant new taxes. However, inflationary costs were to be funded by a series of compulsory unpaid "holidays" for all provincial-government employees. The government extended these holidays to teachers, university professors, and health-care workers. The reductions in wages were roughly 2.5%. Employee pension contributions were to remain as before, since the nominal salaries were not decreased.

Record amounts of summer rain fell in Manitoba in 1993. Winnipeg, the province's capital and largest city, was hit by nearly twice the usual level. Basement flooding in the city, which is built on flat ground, was common.

© "Winnipeg Free Press"

The legislation allowed employers to override existing wage settlements and was unpopular with many employees, particularly health-care workers, who voted against the Progressive Conservative (PC) government in a by-election in a hitherto-safe seat in northeastern Winnipeg. Also unpopular was the cutting of about 500 government jobs over a period of a few months.

Other revenue-raising measures included the extension of the province's 7% sales tax to cover a broader range of items, and an increase in the gasoline tax of one cent per liter. Tax credits were cut for pensioners, homeowners, renters, and those on welfare and worker's compensation. Finance Minister Clayton Manness forecast 1993-94 spending of C$5.4 billion and a deficit of C$367 million.

In other legislation the government moved to establish a separate francophone school board, institute no-fault insurance, and rewrite the provincial parks and liquor acts.

Elections. Besides the by-election in northeastern Winnipeg, there were four other by-elections in which the New Democratic Party (NDP) and the Liberals each gained two seats. The Conservative majority dropped from three seats to one. The one-seat majority for Premier Gary Filmon duplicated the position of his predecessor, Howard Pawley of the NDP. Pawley also had had a one-seat majority, and was overthrown in 1988 when a rebellious backbencher voted against his government.

In the October federal elections, the Liberals swept Manitoba, taking 13 seats, compared with the five they had held. The NDP dropped from two seats to none, and the Reform Party gained one. The biggest change came for the PC Party, which dropped from seven seats to none. The PCs had 37% of the vote in 1988, but only 12% in 1993. Most of their voters shifted to the Reform Party, which took 22% overall. The Liberals rose from 37% to 45%, mostly at the expense of the NDP.

Flooding. For the second summer in succession, Manitoba was hit by record amounts of rainfall. The resultant flooding in southern Manitoba was the worst in two decades. Winnipeg had almost double its normal rainfall, 16.8 inches (42.78 cm) between June 1 and August 15, compared with the usual 9.1 inches (23.1 cm). There was widespread basement flooding in the city, which is built on very flat ground. The suburb of Transcona was particularly hard hit.

Other News. Métis leader Yvon Dumont, a self-employed general contractor, was appointed Manitoba's lieutenant-governor....Paul Edwards, a Winnipeg lawyer, was elected as the new provincial Liberal leader.

MICHAEL KINNEAR, *University of Manitoba*

MANITOBA • Information Highlights

Area: 250,946 sq mi (649 950 km²).
Population (June 1993): 1,101,000.
Chief Cities (1991 census): Winnipeg, the capital, 616,790; Brandon, 38,567; Thompson, 14,977.
Government (1993): *Chief Officers*—lt. gov., Yvon Dumont; premier, Gary Filmon (Progressive Conservative). *Legislature*—Legislative Assembly, 57 members.
Provincial Finances (1993-94 fiscal year budget): *Revenues*, $5,033,000,000; *expenditures*, $5,400,000,000.
Personal Income (average weekly earnings, June 1993): $490.24.
Labor Force (August 1993, seasonally adjusted): *Employed* workers, 15 years of age and over, 490,000; *Unemployed*, 9.4%.
Education (1993-94): *Enrollment*—elementary and secondary schools, 221,820 pupils; postsecondary—universities, 20,860; community colleges, 4,570.
(All monetary figures are in Canadian dollars.)

MARYLAND

News in Maryland in 1993 centered on the addition of the game keno to the state lottery and passage of health-insurance legislation.

State Government. During the year, Gov. William Donald Schaefer added the controversial game keno to Maryland's lottery, prompting outcries from gambling opponents, unsuccessful efforts in the legislature to kill the game, and a federal investigation into how the contract was awarded. Keno got off to a slow start, but close to the year's end, state officials announced that they expected to raise about $60 million per year with the game.

The General Assembly passed legislation making health insurance more available to employees of small businesses. The law also included reforms to ease physician malpractice-insurance costs, but did not require employers to assume a portion of health-insurance premiums for their workers. A "clean cars" law was passed, as Maryland set stringent auto-emissions standards beginning with the 1996 model year.

Politics. The nomination of Democratic delegate John S. Arnick for a state judgeship was derailed when a woman lobbyist complained that he had used vulgar and offensive language toward her. The former House majority leader and judiciary-committee chairman eventually withdrew his name from consideration after having resigned his House seat. In October he was reappointed to his seat when the man picked to replace him died.

After Baltimore's Mayor Kurt Schmoke (D) and state Attorney General J. Joseph Curran, Jr. (D) announced that they would not run for governor in 1994, Democrats were left with Prince George County Executive Parris Glendening, Lt. Gov. Melvin A. Steinberg, Sen. Mary Boergers, and Sen. American Joe Miedusiewski as possible gubernatorial candidates. On the Republican side, Congresswoman Helen D. Bentley, state delegate Ellen R. Sauerbrey, and Bill Shepard—who ran unsuccessfully against Schaefer in 1990, were the front-runners.

Scandals. Ronald Walter Price, a former Anne Arundel county teacher, was convicted of having sex with one current and two former high-school students and was sentenced to 26 years in prison. The case led to the resignation of the county school superintendent, who was accused of burying allegations about teacher-student sex. Price agreed to testify in student sex cases against other teachers. Three other teachers were indicted for having sex with students, and one was acquitted.

The U.S. Naval Academy was rocked by the largest cheating scandal in its history as well as charges of a cover-up. The cheating, which began in December 1992, involved a junior-level electrical-engineering exam. In March the academy announced that an initial investigation found that 28 students had seen the pilfered exam before the test. Eleven were convicted by midshipmen-run hearing boards. Six midshipmen were recommended for expulsion to Secretary of Navy John Dalton, who declined to decide before another investigation was complete. The probe was expected to implicate up to 100 more midshipmen.

Sale of the Orioles. Baltimore Orioles owner Eli Jacobs, a New York-based investor who was facing bankruptcy, was forced to auction off his baseball team for $173 million, a record for a professional sports franchise. The buyers assumed ownership in October and announced that the Orioles would remain in Baltimore.

DAN CASEY, *"The (Annapolis) Capital"*

MASSACHUSETTS

Responding to difficult economic times, Republican Gov. William F. Weld and Massachusetts legislators focused on budget and growth issues during 1993. The unemployment rate, as high as 9% in 1992, hovered around the 7% mark in 1993.

Economy. Economic growth in Massachusetts sputtered during the year. While there was some improvement in the unemployment rate, the number of jobs continued to shrink. This trend was seen continuing as key business sectors in the Bay State—defense, computers, banking, and insurance—reorganized, making more job cuts.

Such giants of the Massachusetts defense industry as Raytheon, manufacturer of the Patriot missile, and General Electric, builder of jet engines, scrambled to reorient their operations in the face of projected U.S. defense cuts. And the computer industry, an economic mainstay in the state, continued a long recession. Wang Laboratories, once a model of success, struggled to emerge from bankruptcy as a much smaller company. Other major computing-equipment manufacturers, such as Digital Equipment Corporation, were downsizing.

MARYLAND • Information Highlights

Area: 10,460 sq mi (27 092 km²).

Population (July 1, 1992 est.): 4,908,000.

Chief Cities (1990 census): Annapolis, the capital, 33,187; Baltimore, 736,014; Rockville, 44,835.

Government (1993): *Chief Officers*—governor, William Donald Schaefer (D); lt. gov., Melvin A. Steinberg (D). *General Assembly*—Senate, 47 members; House of Delegates, 141 members.

State Finances (fiscal year 1991): *Revenue*, $12,479,000,000; *expenditure*, $12,576,000,000.

Personal Income (1992): $114,115,000,000; per capita, $23,249.

Labor Force (August 1993): *Civilian labor force*, 2,586,300; *unemployed*, 177,000 (6.8% of total force).

Education: *Enrollment* (fall 1991)—public elementary schools, 543,492; public secondary, 192,746; colleges and universities, 267,931. *Public school expenditures* (1990-91), $4,184,858,000.

Thomas Menino was joined by members of his family as he acknowledged his election as mayor of Boston, MA, on Nov. 2, 1993. Menino, who became the city's acting mayor in July after Raymond L. Flynn resigned to become U.S. ambassador to the Vatican, was to serve the remaining two years of Flynn's term.

© Eileen M. Counihan

Government and Politics. Governor Weld and the legislature tangled repeatedly over the issues of "privatization," or contracting out work currently performed by state agencies and departments to private firms. The issue, central to the governor's plan to streamline state government, was opposed strongly by the legislature, sensitive to the political clout of state workers. Some legislators mounted a direct challenge, filing a bill that would limit executive-branch options in contracting out work.

The $15 billion budget for fiscal year 1994—passed in June after months of wrangling—was seen in some circles as a milestone. It included a major component of public-school reform, adding $175 million in state aid to city and town school budgets.

On the plus side, Weld pointed to the fourth increase in Massachusetts' bond rating, to "A-plus." Wall Street rating agencies in 1991 had classed the state's bonds among the poorest risks in the nation. The new rating was expected to save millions of dollars in interest costs.

Another issue that captured much attention was a proposal to build a sports "megaplex" to house the New England Patriots National Football League (NFL) franchise along with a major convention facility. The Patriots were being wooed by Connecticut and St. Louis, MO. The question of providing state funding for the proposed sports complex was debated hotly. Weld advocated a controversial $700 million funding scheme with revenues from new offshore gambling boats and other gambling licenses. Other advocates of the complex proposed more conventional bond financing, while yet others questioned whether state funds should be used at all. An attempt to resolve the issue by year's end failed.

Boston's mayoral office became vacant in July when Raymond L. Flynn, first elected in 1983, resigned to become U.S. ambassador to the Vatican. City Council President Thomas Menino became acting mayor, and in November won over former state representative James Brett.

Lewis Death. In a sports-related occurrence that dominated the news for weeks, Boston Celtics captain Reggie Lewis, 27, collapsed and died at a workout on July 27. Lewis had fainted during an April game. In May he was pronounced unfit to play by one team of doctors but switched hospitals and medical consultants, who diagnosed a non-life-threatening condition. Lewis' death raised the issues of medical advice and care of sports figures with health problems.

HARVEY BOULAY, *Rogerson House*

MASSACHUSETTS • Information Highlights

Area: 8,284 sq mi (21 456 km²).

Population (July 1, 1992 est.): 5,998,000.

Chief Cities (1990 census): Boston, the capital, 574,283; Worcester, 169,759; Springfield, 156,983.

Government (1993): *Chief Officers*—governor, William Weld (R); lt. gov., Argeo Paul Cellucci (R). *Legislature*—Senate, 40 members; House of Representatives, 160 members.

State Finances (fiscal year 1991): *Revenue*, $18,727,000,000; *expenditure*, $20,349,000,000.

Personal Income (1992): $142,828,000,000; per capita, $23,811.

Labor Force (August 1993): *Civilian labor force*, 3,145,100; *unemployed*, 220,300 (7.0% of total force).

Education: *Enrollment* (fall 1991)—public elementary schools, 615,990; public secondary, 230,165; colleges and universities, 419,381. *Public school expenditures* (1990-91), $4,906,828,000

MEDICINE AND HEALTH

Health-care reform, pushed by skyrocketing medical costs and millions of uninsured people, dominated medical headlines during 1993, stirring a growing sentiment that the United States needed universal health-care coverage. (*See* FEATURE ARTICLE, page 36.) Within the health-care community, additional areas of consensus also developed: the need to aggressively combat infectious diseases, to encourage exercise and better nutrition, to take steps to limit exposure to secondhand tobacco smoke and other pollutants. Mental-health experts helped focus attention on the public-health aspects of violence among young people. Much concern also was expressed about bioethical dilemmas such as cloning and physician-assisted suicide.

Overview

Infectious Diseases. The Centers for Disease Control and Prevention (CDC) announced that a measles epidemic in the United States was over, thanks to a massive inoculation campaign. During the first six months of 1993, only 175 cases were reported to the CDC, a 99% drop from the nearly 14,000 cases reported for the first half of 1990, when the epidemic was at its height.

In contrast, the incidence of tuberculosis continued a dramatic rise. The rate of increase in the United States slowed during 1993, due largely to more aggressive surveillance and treatment. But in many parts of the world, said Arata Kochi of the World Health Organization, tuberculosis "is out of control." The disease claims the lives of 3 million people each year, more than all other infectious diseases combined. The epidemic's expansion was tied to insufficient funding for control programs and treatment, particularly in poor countries. Efforts also were complicated by the emergence of drug-resistant strains of the tuberculosis bacterium.

Another ancient scourge, diphtheria, spread rapidly through Russia and into other former republics of the Soviet Union. The epidemic was attributed to lack of immunization, coupled with social and economic upheavals.

A new or previously unrecognized strain of hantavirus was found to cause a deadly disease that surfaced in 1993, primarily in the U.S. Southwest. The virus appeared to spread through airborne particles from the urine, droppings, and saliva of deer mice, causing a severe respiratory illness that led to at least 21 deaths in 11 states.

As a pandemic caused by one strain of cholera bacteria continued unabated, a new strain swept across India and Bangladesh and into Thailand. Health officials could not predict how rapidly the new strain would spread, noting that people who survived infections from older strains were not immune to attacks by the new strain.

Initial safety tests of a vaccine for Lyme disease were successful, leading to hopes that the vaccine might be available commercially by the mid- to late 1990s. However, there are many different strains of the Lyme bacterium, making a definitive vaccine more difficult to develop. Researchers at Rocky Mountain Laboratories reported that genetic factors are involved in determining the molecular makeup of the outer surface of the Lyme bacterium, which enable the microorganism to alter its outer coat and perhaps help it avoid the body's immune-defense mechanisms.

AIDS. The number of cases of acquired immune deficiency syndrome (AIDS), a disease caused by the HIV virus, continued to rise. In the United States, where a new, expanded definition of AIDS went into effect in 1993, there were 339,250 reported cases by October 1993, including 204,390 deaths. AIDS became the leading cause of death in men aged 25 to 44, and the fourth-leading killer of women in the same age group.

About 1 million people in the United States were believed to be infected with the HIV virus, which meant that they could infect other people even though they may not yet have shown symptoms of AIDS. Worldwide, an estimated 14 million people were infected with HIV, and experts feared that unless stronger preventive measures were taken, this number would soar to 30 million to 40 million people by the year 2000.

The United Nations Development Program noted that sexually active teenage girls were emerging as the "leading edge" of the AIDS epidemic, with higher rates of infection than older women or young men. In the United States a study of 270,000 youths found 4.2 girls per 1,000 infected, compared with 2.0 per 1,000 boys. Noted the UN report, "It is plausible that women become infected more easily than men, possibly at all ages and most definitely when they are in their teens and early 20s and after menopause."

Another group at high risk of infection is intravenous-drug users. Despite legal, political, and religious opposition, needle-exchange programs—which allow addicts to exchange used needles for clean ones—have been organized in dozens of communities. Federal studies of such programs concluded that they were effective as an AIDS-prevention strategy and did not result in any measurable increase in drug use.

Though scientists' understanding of the physiology of HIV viruses continued to grow, translating such knowledge into effective vaccines and treatments was fraught with frustration. Hopes for one drug after another have been dashed. For instance, experimental vaccines that were effective against HIV viruses grown in laboratories turned out to be useless against HIV viruses taken from humans.

Participants at the ninth international AIDS meeting in Berlin stressed that prevention was the only way to stop the spread of HIV. They urged increased education, the promotion of

condom use, maintenance of safe blood supplies, and expanded needle-exchange programs. Yet they and other AIDS experts were dismayed by the world's prejudices and inertia. "The AIDS epidemic is an emergency, but society is responding as if it were not," said Lars O. Kallings, an AIDS researcher from Sweden.

Cardiovascular Disorders. Preventive medicine and alternative therapies received a boost when Mutual of Omaha Insurance Co., one of the nation's major health-insurance providers, said it would reimburse heart-disease patients participating in a therapy called the "reversal program." It was the first time that a non-surgical, nonpharmaceutical therapy for heart disease qualified for insurance reimbursement. The program, developed by Dean Ornish at the Preventive Medicine Research Institute, uses exercise, a low-fat vegetarian diet, stress-management techniques, and participation in support groups to retard and even reverse heart disease.

More than 550,000 Americans undergo either angioplasty or bypass operations annually to treat coronary-artery blockages, the main cause of heart attacks. A study directed by Spencer B. King 3d of Emory University found that the two techniques were equally effective in treating people who have blockages in two or more coronary arteries. Angioplasty was less enervating and less costly than bypass. But within three years of the operations, 22% of the angioplasty patients needed a bypass and 40% needed a second angioplasty procedure. In contrast, only 12% of the bypass patients needed further surgery.

Contradicting earlier studies, researchers at Oxford University in England reported that three drugs commonly used to treat heart attacks offer little or no help in reducing the death rate from heart attacks. The drugs were magnesium; nitrates, such as nitroglycerin; and captopril. Studies conducted in Italy and China confirmed the captopril and nitrate findings.

Cancer. In December two independent teams of researchers reported an important genetic discovery that was expected to improve substantially the identification and treatment of a common type of colon cancer. Scientists isolated a gene that, when observed in a defective form, predisposes people to hereditary nonpolyposis colorectal cancer, a familial disorder that strikes more than 20,000 people every year. Researchers anticipated that a genetic screening test could be developed before the end of 1994 that would be offered to those with a family history of the disease. This test would allow patients with the mutation to be identified before cancerous growth began, significantly improving the odds of successful treatment.

Record numbers of U.S. men were diagnosed with prostate cancer and were undergoing surgery or radiation therapy. Scientists with the Prostate Patient Outcomes Research Team concluded, however, that older men with early prostate cancer may benefit more from "watchful waiting" than from surgery or radiation. The researchers reported that since prostate cancer is slow-growing, many patients would die of other causes before their tumors became dangerous.

Health-care reform was a major issue in the United States in 1993. On October 27, Hillary Rodham Clinton, the chair of the president's task force on such reform, joined President Bill Clinton in unveiling the administration's plan at the Capitol.

© Jose R. Lopez/NYT Pictures

© AP/Wide World

In June 1993, Kristine Gebbie—a former nurse, state health official, and member of the presidential commission on AIDS—was named to the new federal position of AIDS policy coordinator.

Two large studies provided new evidence that having a vasectomy may increase a man's risk of developing prostate cancer. The studies, led by Edward Giovannucci of Harvard University, found that the risk of prostate cancer was up to 89% higher among men who had had vasectomies more than 20 years earlier than among men who had not had vasectomies. Also, the risk of developing prostate cancer increased as more time passed since a vasectomy was performed. Scientists have found no biological explanation for a link between vasectomy and prostate cancer and note that the great majority of U.S. men who develop prostate cancer never had vasectomies.

The first direct proof that sunscreens lower the risk of skin cancer was reported by Australian researchers. Studying 588 adults during one summer, the researchers found that those who used a sunscreen with an SPF-17 rating before going outside developed fewer precancerous growths, known as solar keratoses, than adults who used a lotion without sunblock.

Diabetes. The Diabetes Control and Complications Trial, scheduled to be a ten-year study comparing two types of treatment for Type I (insulin-dependent) diabetes, was stopped earlier than planned so that its dramatic findings could be shared with all diabetics. The study compared conventional treatment, in which diabetics received one or two shots of insulin daily, with a more rigorous therapy in which diabetics were put on a special diet and either received three or more injections daily or relied on an insulin pump to deliver insulin continuously to their bloodstream. The latter procedure reduced fluctuations in blood-sugar levels and significantly

delayed or prevented blindness, kidney failure, and other complications of diabetes.

Roughly 50% of people with Type I diabetes ultimately develop kidney disease, which eventually destroys the kidneys and necessitates either dialysis or a kidney transplant. A study involving 30 medical centers in the United States and Canada reported that captopril, widely prescribed for treating high blood pressure, can postpone kidney failure sharply.

Diet and Exercise. Several major studies provided new evidence of the benefits of vitamins. A study by Chinese and U.S. scientists of rural residents in north-central China showed that vitamin supplements reduced the risk of dying from cancer and other diseases. One study found that vitamin A can slow vision loss in people suffering from retinitis pigmentosa and another suggested that vitamin A reduces women's risk of breast cancer. Two studies involving more than 120,000 adults linked daily supplements of vitamin E with significant declines in heart attacks and other coronary problems.

A study that tracked 51,000 male health professionals suggested that a high-fat diet, particularly one rich in butter and fats from red meats, affects the development of prostate cancer. Such a diet does not appear to increase the risk of developing prostate cancer but, rather, increases the chances that the disease will progress to an advanced, lethal stage.

In a major shift from previous administrations, the U.S. Department of Agriculture began placing greater emphasis on nutrition, announcing that it would double the amount of fresh produce available in school lunches and reduce the amount of fat and salt. "We can't continue to deep-fry our children's health," stated Secretary of Agriculture Mike Espy.

The low-fat diet of rural Chinese long has been extolled by nutritionists. But the food typically ordered by Americans in Chinese restaurants came under fire in a report from the Center for Science in the Public Interest. The consumer advocacy group found that U.S. diners avoided the steamed vegetables and fish that are traditional Chinese staples, and ordered dishes high in fat and salt instead.

New guidelines from the National Cholesterol Education Program (NCEP) urged physicians to measure levels of beneficial high-density lipoprotein (HDL) in initial cholesterol testing, even if the total cholesterol level was within the desirable range of less than 200 milligrams per deciliter (mg/dL). The recommendation reaffirmed that a low level of HDL (less than 35 mg/dL) was a risk factor for coronary heart disease. In contrast, an HDL level of more than 60 mg/dL appeared to protect against heart disease. The NCEP also emphasized the cholesterol-lowering benefits of weight loss in overweight people and physical activity.

The CDC reported that almost 60% of Americans over age 18 are physically inactive,

and only 22% are active at levels recommended for good health benefits. Meanwhile, evidence of the benefits of regular exercise continued to mount. A study at the University of Connecticut School of Medicine found that daily 30-minute bicycle rides reduced blood pressure in men with mild hypertension. A University of Washington project found that men aged 60 to 82 who exercised four or five times a week experienced a significant improvement in their body's ability to break up blood clots that otherwise might block arteries. Two studies evaluating long-term survival rates showed that men who exercised lived longer and decreased their risk for heart attacks.

Exercise programs were found to save money too. For example, the Canadian Life Assurance Co. of Toronto provided a gym and exercise classes for its employees. The company annually saved $679 per worker on insurance claims as compared with a similar company that had no exercise program; this equaled a $6.85 return for each $1 invested in the fitness program.

Environmental Medicine. According to the American Lung Association, 66% of the 1991 U.S. population lived in areas that violated federal clean-air standards for ozone, lead, carbon monoxide, and three other pollutants. This was an increase from 60% of the population in 1988. Air pollution causes or exacerbates a variety of respiratory problems and reduces the body's ability to absorb oxygen. At greatest risk are children and elderly people with respiratory problems, and people of all ages with asthma.

The dangers of soot and other particulate matter in the air were stressed by epidemiological studies from the U.S. Environmental Protection Agency (EPA) and the Harvard University School of Public Health. The studies suggested that particle pollution causes 50,000 to 60,000 deaths annually in the United States—far more than any other form of pollution.

The EPA designated environmental tobacco smoke (ETS), known as secondhand smoke, as a human carcinogen, responsible for some 3,000 lung-cancer deaths annually among U.S. nonsmokers. The EPA also said that secondhand smoke caused serious respiratory problems for infants and young children. The CDC announced preliminary results in a study of 23,000 people to determine the presence of smoke remnants in blood serum. Cotinine, a by-product of nicotine, was found in the blood serum of all of the first 800 people tested. Levels were generally highest in smokers, but even children as young as 4 tested positive. Analyses by Michael Siegel, working with the CDC, found that waiters and bartenders, who are exposed to higher-than-average levels of secondhand smoke, have a 50% higher risk of getting lung cancer than does the general public.

The massive evidence of the dangers of secondhand smoke triggered a surge of smoking restrictions, especially after First Lady Hillary Rodham Clinton banned smoking in the White House. The Postal Service banned smoking in its 40,000 facilities. State governments banned smoking in state and municipal buildings. Many restaurants also instituted bans on smoking.

In September the Clinton administration presented a series of reforms of the nation's pesticide laws to reduce the risks posed by these chemicals. The action followed release of a National Research Council report which argued that current federal regulations were based on adult exposure to pesticides. These regulations did not consider variations in pesticide exposure between children and adults; take into account that infants and children have different growth rates, diets, and eating patterns than adults; or recognize that children's bodies may react differently than adults to foreign substances. The report recommended that the government learn more about the dangers of pesticides in children and adults; find out what residues remain on food; and study children's eating patterns to determine their exposure to pesticides.

Yet another study linked the pesticide DDT to breast cancer. The study, headed by Mary Wolff at the Mount Sinai School of Medicine in New York, found that women with the highest exposure to DDT were four times more likely to develop breast cancer than were women with the least exposure. DDT was phased out in 1972 in the United States, but it is known to accumulate in fatty tissues.

A study from the Institute of Medicine linked Agent Orange and other herbicides used during the Vietnam war with Hodgkin's disease and the rare metabolic disorder porphyria cutanea tarda. Three other diseases—non-Hodgkin's lymphoma, soft-tissue sarcoma, and chloracne—had been linked previously to the herbicides.

Polluted drinking water resulted in an outbreak of intestinal illness among Milwaukee residents, affecting thousands and contributing to six deaths. The illness was caused by a parasitic protozoan, cryptosporidium, which is present in the intestinal tracts of humans, cattle, and other animals. The parasite apparently entered Lake Michigan in farm runoff, then passed through a water-treatment plant while employees were testing a new sanitation chemical.

Benito Marinas, a civil engineer at Purdue University, developed a chemical process to remove lead permanently from faucets and other lead-containing components, resulting in lead-free drinking water. Lead poisoning can cause kidney and liver damage in children and adults, but it takes its greatest toll on the young, impairing memory, reaction time, and the ability to concentrate. Contaminated drinking water, deteriorating lead-based paint, urban soil and dust, and ceramic glazes are the major sources of elevated blood-lead levels in U.S. children.

JENNY TESAR
Freelance Science Writer

Electricity and Cancer—A Connection?

One of 1993's most highly publicized health scares developed after a Florida man charged that his wife's death from brain cancer was caused by her heavy use of a portable phone. Although no evidence was submitted to prove that such phones can cause cancer, the incident intensified public concerns that electrical devices pose health hazards.

During operation, portable phones—like power lines, appliances, office equipment, and other electrical sources—produce electromagnetic fields (EMFs). A growing number of studies have shown statistical correlations between prolonged exposure to EMFs and disease.

The strongest evidence links EMFs to various forms of cancer, especially childhood leukemia. For instance, a 1992 long-term study in Sweden reported that children who live near high-voltage power lines suffered three times the normal rate of leukemia. Study findings, however, often are contradictory. One Swedish study found increased incidences of leukemia and brain cancer in workers exposed to EMFs. In contrast, a 1993 U.S. study followed more than 36,000 electric-utility workers and found that those with the highest exposure to EMFs did not have especially high cancer rates.

In addition, many who link EMFs and cancer admit that the risks are slight compared with other risks of modern living. One of the Swedish researchers who reported a connection between EMFs and leukemia noted that only one of the some 70 cases of childhood leukemia that are reported in Sweden each year might be due to high-voltage power lines. Meanwhile, a much greater number of children are killed by other causes, such as traffic accidents.

Some researchers have linked EMFs with miscarriages, birth defects, nervous-system problems, and immune-system disorders. In 1988 researchers in one study found that women who used computer video display terminals (VDTs) for 20 hours weekly during the early months of pregnancy had almost twice as many miscarriages as women doing other office work. But in a 1991 study, the National Institute for Occupational Safety and Health found no correlation between computer work and miscarriages.

Despite the statistical correlations, no cause-and-effect relationship between EMF exposure and disease has been demonstrated. Thus other factors may be causing illnesses. For example, people living near power lines may receive high exposure to carcinogenic herbicides that control plant growth beneath the wires. Laboratory studies have shown that EMFs, including those produced in U.S. homes, can cause biochemical changes in living cells. But researchers have been unable to produce cancer in laboratory animals using such EMFs.

Scientists are divided over the link between EMFs and disease, an uncertainty that is echoed by government policy makers. While Sweden established low-emission standards for VDTs, the U.S. Environmental Protection Agency did not follow suit, arguing that it did not "believe there is sufficient information about the health effects of EMFs to write responsible guidelines for VDTs or other sources."

As the debate continues, electric utilities are moving to reduce exposure from power lines and facilities, and appliance manufacturers are redesigning products to cut EMFs. People also can minimize EMF exposure by maximizing their distance from field sources, since the strength of electric and magnetic fields diminishes rapidly with distance.

JENNY TESAR

Medical Ethics

During 1993 such topics as physician-assisted suicide, fetal-tissue transplants, the abortion pill, and human-embryo cloning received prime attention in the field of medical ethics.

Physician-Assisted Suicide. The care of dying patients is a vexing ethical problem for the medical profession. Despite considerable advances in pain control and comfort care, some patients still suffer intolerably before death. Some such patients rather would die than continue living and a few request assistance from their physicians.

Dr. Jack Kevorkian, a retired Michigan pathologist, continued to focus attention on the debate over physician-assisted suicide. Between 1990 and the end of November 1993, Kevorkian had been involved in the deaths of 20 persons. After each of the first three deaths, murder charges were brought against the doctor, but subsequently were dismissed. In 1991, Michigan suspended his license to practice medicine, as did California in 1993. Despite efforts to curtail Kevorkian, he continued to help ailing people kill themselves.

On Dec. 15, 1992, Michigan Gov. John Engler signed the state's anti-assisted-suicide bill. Unlike in most other states, assisted suicide had not been a crime in Michigan. The bill was to become effective March 30, 1993, but the state legislature moved the date up to Febru-

Dr. Jack Kevorkian talks to reporters and supporters during a break in a court hearing in Detroit. The retired pathologist continued during 1993 to help ailing patients commit suicide. He was jailed twice for his attempts to challenge the constitutionality of Michigan's 1992 law banning physician-assisted suicides.

ary 25 after Kevorkian increased his activities in anticipation of the bill's enactment.

Michigan's law temporarily criminalizes assisted suicide and creates a commission to develop recommendations for permanent "legislation concerning the voluntary self-termination of life." The temporary ban expires six months after the commission issues its recommendations. The American Civil Liberties Union (ACLU) challenged the constitutionality of the law. A Michigan court struck down the law on technical grounds, but an appellate court reinstated it.

The Michigan law was declared unconstitutional in December 1993 by a judge presiding over a case involving Kevorkian. The doctor meanwhile had been jailed in yet another case in Oakland county, where authorities said the ruling of unconstitutionality was not binding in their jurisdiction and refused to release Kevorkian. He was freed later in the month after promising to assist in no more suicides for the time being.

The Michigan Medical Society subtly changed its position regarding assisted suicide in 1993. After contentious debate, the society officially adopted a stance of "no position" on both assisted suicide in general and the Michigan law in particular. Some commentators expected other state medical societies to follow this lead and moderate their opposition to assisted suicide. On the other hand, the American Medical Association remained adamantly opposed to physicians helping terminally ill patients kill themselves.

Fetal-Tissue Transplants. Two days after taking office as president, Bill Clinton reversed a number of abortion-related restrictions to mark a radical shift in federal policy. One of his actions was to lift a five-year-old ban on federal funding for transplantation research that uses fetal tissue. The use of fetal tissue for treating a host of intractable diseases and illnesses such as Parkinson's disease and diabetes has raised hopes for patients and their families. In the meantime, however, this practice has created considerable controversy, primarily because the tissue usually

is obtained from electively aborted fetuses. Lifting the ban, imposed by the Department of Health and Human Services (HHS) in 1988, was expected to increase dramatically research using tissue from electively aborted fetuses.

RU-486. President Clinton also asked HHS and the Food and Drug Administration (FDA) to "determine whether there is sufficient evidence to warrant exclusion of RU-486 from the list of drugs that qualify for the personal use importation exemption." RU-486 is the world's first abortion pill and first was approved for general distribution in France in 1988. The FDA had banned its importation to the United States since 1989. The president also directed HHS to "assess initiatives" by which the department could promote the "testing, licensing, and manufacturing" of RU-486 and other antiprogestins in the United States. The pill, which works only during early pregnancy, chemically interrupts the pregnancy. The result is a medically controlled early miscarriage. By the end of 1993, more than 150,000 women had abortions with RU-486 in France, Sweden, and England—the only countries besides China where the drug has been available. (*See also* ABORTION.)

Cloning Embryos. The October announcement by researchers at George Washington University that they successfully had cloned human embryos touched off a heated debate in ethics circles. The technique was developed to help infertile couples to conceive artificially, by producing extra embryos. It also could allow for the storing of embryos indefinitely, which possibly could lead to a market where embryos are bought and sold. The new medical procedure also would allow parents to have an entire family of twins or identical twins of different ages. Such possibilities raised numerous ethical questions, involving the uniqueness of human beings and the rights of individuals to control their own embryos. The debate over the entire issue of human-embryo cloning was continuing as the year came to a close.

REINHARD PRIESTER
Center for Biomedical Ethics
University of Minnesota

Mental Health

Stirring new evidence that mental illnesses involve interactions between biological vulnerabilities and environmental factors was reported in 1993 as researchers gained new understanding about the role of genetics and biological and psychosocial environmental factors. Mental illnesses affect roughly 22% of the adult U.S. population. The most severe mental illnesses—including manic-depressive illness, schizophrenia, and severe depression—affect some 5 million U.S. adults. However, less than 30% of mentally ill individuals seek any help for their problems during a given year and far fewer see psychiatrists and other professionals skilled at diagnosing and treating these illnesses. Efficacy rates for treatments of major mental disorders (60%-80%) parallel or exceed those for other illnesses.

Cost Offsets. Severe mental disorders exact a $148 billion annual toll in treatment, lost productivity, and other indirect costs in the United States. The National Institute of Mental Health (NIMH) calculated in 1993 that providing full insurance coverage for treatment of the severely mentally ill would save more than $2.2 billion annually. While full coverage for mental-health care would lead to added costs, the NIMH contended that this would be offset by a dip in the use of general medical services by these chronic patients and by reduced federal disability payments. Adequate coverage also would provide an incentive for general health practitioners to improve their ability to diagnose, treat, and refer patients with mental illness.

Treatment. The well-regarded theory that mental illness involves brain dysfunction which can be corrected by treatment was supported by an NIMH-supported study that pinpointed a change in brain activity associated with clinical improvement following psychological and medication treatment. The same brain changes seen in positron emission tomography (PET) scans of obsessive-compulsive-disorder patients following successful drug treatment also were observed after cognitive/behavioral therapy.

Human Brain Project. NIMH announced that it would lead interested federal agencies in developing a Human Brain Project, using recent advances in mathematics and computer technology—including fiber-optic networks and massive databases—to help scientists manage the knowledge explosion in the neurosciences.

Neural Communications. Evidence was mounting that nitric-oxide and carbon-monoxide gases serve as "neuromessengers" in the brain, causing scientists to rethink long-held assumptions about how neurons communicate. Researchers discovered a naturally occurring brain cannabinoid chemical called anandamide that works through the same receptors on cell surfaces which mediate the effects of marijuana. Further characterization of such novel brain systems could help develop medicines with unique properties for treating anxiety, depression, and other illnesses. The first links between specific genes, their functions within brain cells, and specific behaviors also emerged in 1993.

Brain Imaging. The use of functional (fast) magnetic resonance imaging (MRI), which provides real-time "movies" of the brain at work, was explored in 1993. This noninvasive technique uses powerful magnets and radio waves to track changes in oxygen use and reveal brain sites active during transient experiences, such as the act of remembering. Previously, the only ways to visualize activity within the living human brain precisely used infusions of radioactive tracers, which yielded only static images and which could be used only in limited quantity on a given individual. Already revolutionizing basic neuropsychology, functional MRI promised to yield important insights into mental illness.

Schizophrenia. NIMH scientists reported replicating in rats a process thought to occur in schizophrenia: early damage to the brain's limbic system that mysteriously does not affect the individual's functioning until young adulthood. Rats that experienced early chemical damage to a limbic brain structure appeared normal until after puberty, when they became hyperactive in response to stress. Remarkably, a dopamine-blocking drug commonly used to treat schizophrenia prevented the abnormal behavior.

A similar pattern of response to stress was observed in rats that sustained damage to the prefrontal cortex—which helps regulate limbic dopamine activity during stress—in adulthood. Since this brain area does not develop fully until after puberty, researchers proposed that early limbic damage might interfere with communications between the two brain areas, stunting prefrontal functioning and hence the organism's ability to cope with stressors. Functional brain-imaging studies have shown that schizophrenic patients perform poorly on tasks requiring activation of the prefrontal cortex and show impaired ability to activate that brain structure. MRI studies also reveal subtle structural abnormalities in patients' limbic systems.

Alzheimer's Disease. Some nose cells stem from the same evolutionary roots as brain cells, and thus may hold clues to detecting Alzheimer's disease and to better understanding and treating the illness. NIMH scientists detected abnormal processing of the beta-amyloid protein—known to be abnormally high in Alzheimer's patients' brain cells—in cultured olfactory neurons. They found levels of a parent chemical, beta amyloid's precursor protein, to be 700% greater in patients' nose cells than those from controls. They also were able to reverse these increases with two commonly available drugs: theophylline and isoproterenol, suggesting potential clinical applications in treating Alzheimer's patients.

FREDERICK K. GOODWIN, M.D.
Director, National Institute of Mental Health

© Alan Weiner/Gamma-Liaison

The "storm of the century" spread snow, ice, and wind across one third of the United States—from the Gulf Coast to New England—in mid-March 1993. In Atlanta, above, which was shut down by the storm, children enjoyed a rare treat, sledding.

METEOROLOGY

Several U.S. regions took turns hosting record storms or other unusual weather events in 1993, while researchers continued to study the long-term directions of the atmosphere.

"Storm of the Century." The first outstanding weather event of 1993 in the United States was the intense low-pressure system that wreaked havoc from the Gulf Coast to New England in mid-March. The "storm of the century" earned its name by spreading snow, ice, and wind over one third of the country. Damage and cost estimates topped $6 billion, with insured losses exceeding $1.6 billion—the fourth-costliest storm in U.S. history and by far the most costly extratropical storm. More than 200 deaths were reported in 13 states, and some 50 persons were lost at sea in the surrounding waters. Transportation was paralyzed; interstate highways and major airports from Atlanta to Maine were closed. Power outages were widespread, as repair work was delayed in many areas due to the extent of damage and difficulty in travel after the storm.

More than 1 ft (.3 m) of snow fell from Alabama to Maine, with more than 3 ft (.9 m) at the North Carolina-Tennessee border. Record low pressures were recorded all along the East Coast, and low-temperature records were set after the storm passed. Coastal areas saw winds and storm surges that equaled the effects of a moderate hurricane.

Midwestern Flood. The year's second outstanding U.S. weather event was an unprecedented series of storms that repetitively produced excessive rainfall in the Midwest during the spring, summer, and fall. Dozens of precipitation records were shattered and the resulting runoff drove many rivers, including the Mississippi and Missouri, to record crests. Scores of flood-control levees failed despite the efforts of residents and volunteers to provide sandbag reinforcement. At one point, 1,000 mi (1 609 km) of the Mississippi and Missouri were closed to barges, while a 200-mi (322-km) stretch of the Mississippi River was without a safe bridge crossing. The area around St. Louis was particularly hard hit since both the Missouri and Mississippi rivers were flooding. Regular barge traffic was allowed only intermittently until the fall due to continuing flooding.

Agricultural production in the region suffered significant losses, not only due to direct flood damage, but also because excessively wet fields prevented timely planting and cultivation. The summer was also very cool, and early killing frosts hit parts of the upper Midwest. (*See* FEATURE ARTICLE, page 44; AGRICULTURE.)

Ozone Depletion. Several major producers of chlorofluorocarbons (CFCs) announced that they would terminate production by the end of 1994, rather than the previous deadline of 1995 or the original date of 2000 specified in the Montreal Protocol. The ozone hole over Antarctica again set records in October. Ultraviolet radiation in central Chile, well away from Antarctica, was about 30% above normal levels. In one encouraging development, researchers reported studies in which several types of bacteria degraded hydrochlorofluorocarbons (HCFCs) biologically. HCFCs were chosen as an interim replacement for CFCs, to which they are chemically similar, because they degrade more quickly. This study opened the possibility of removing HCFCs from the atmosphere faster.

The Bill Clinton administration announced a plan for U.S. compliance with the 1992 Earth

Summit accord, which called for developed nations to limit greenhouse gases to 1990 levels. The plan featured some 50 measures, most of which depended on government-industry cooperation. The emphasis on voluntary cooperation brought criticism from environmental groups, while the need for any action continued to be debated.

Another study reported that Arctic air pollution had decreased over the previous ten years. This change was credited largely to decreased emissions in Western Europe and Russia.

NWS Modernization. The National Weather Service (NWS) continued to modernize the tools that provide weather information in the United States. Early field experience with the Automated Surface Observing System (ASOS) led to revised instrumentation for temperature, wind, humidity, and present weather. ASOS was intended to replace human weather observers in many cases, so reliability under extreme conditions was critical. The NWS also moved forward with a new computer system that was expected to link all observational and forecasting resources for the meteorologist. A third aspect of modernization was the realignment of staffing at weather-forecast offices. Congressional concern with maintaining levels of service led to a mandate that all office closings be planned carefully, with oversight from an interagency committee.

Satellites. The uncertainty of space travel was reinforced in August when a newly launched polar-orbit weather satellite, NOAA-13, suddenly went silent. Data from the spacecraft indicated that a wire connecting the solar panels to the electrical system broke, depriving the instruments of electrical power. The mothballed NOAA-9 was reactivated to fill the gap. The next NOAA satellite was due for launch in May 1994.

Meanwhile, preparations continued for the first launch of the new model of Geostationary Operation Environmental Satellite (GOES) in April 1994. Repeated delays in developing the new GOES forced the United States to borrow Meteosat-3 from the European Space Agency (ESA) in 1993 to cover the eastern United States. In response to these developments, the United States and ESA announced an agreement on geostationary-satellite cooperation. This plan called for the United States to have two operational satellites routinely, while ESA would maintain one operational and one back-up satellite.

Field Experiments. The Greenland Ice Sheet Project continued drilling and achieved the deepest core ever attained in Greenland—10,013 ft (3 052 m). This core provided a 250,000-year snowfall record. Preliminary analysis indicated a number of very rapid shifts in the climate, sometimes in as little as a decade.

Weather Highlights. The lingering effects of Mount Pinatubo's eruption continued to be felt in 1993. By July the aerosols that the eruption had injected into the stratosphere had settled out substantially, but global average surface temperatures continued to be slightly below average. This occurred because it took some time for the atmosphere-ocean system (particularly the ocean) to warm up to "normal" conditions.

At the same time, the El Niño begun in 1992 moved to a mature stage, but then persisted and even strengthened as 1993 ended. Such behavior was rare and raised interesting questions about how variable the El Niño might be.

The weather news for 1993 was dominated by increased precipitation throughout the United States and the globe. A seven-year drought in California ended decisively early in 1993 as the heaviest winter precipitation since 1983 fell. By late March the snowpack in the Sierra Nevada stood at 150% of normal, and reservoirs stood at 92% of capacity, compared with 69% in 1992. The winter was also wet in the central and eastern United States, the Andes Mountains, central Europe, central Asia, and southern Africa—where a long drought was broken. Hawaii and the Pacific Northwest were the only U.S. regions with drought conditions at winter's end. Immediately after the "storm of the century," the mid-Atlantic and New England states experienced flooding due to rapid warming and heavy rains.

In addition to the flooding in the Midwest, the Ukraine experienced a similarly wet, cool summer, while Nepal, eastern India, and Bangladesh experienced the heaviest summer monsoon in 58 years, with attendant losses of 7,000 lives and housing for 6 million.

Despite nearby flooding, the states from Alabama to Maryland endured a summer that was several degrees above normal and that produced less than 50% of average rainfall. Other severe droughts occurred in Greece and in southeastern India, with Madras essentially out of water for most of the summer despite nearby flooding.

During the fall southern California experienced a devastating series of brush fires. These fires were driven by Santa Ana winds—hot, dry winds blowing out of the east—and fed by vegetation that had grown luxuriantly from the record rains the previous winter. The fire danger receded after rain arrived in November.

Tornado activity continued the trend of previous years, with above-average numbers of sightings, but below-average numbers of deaths. The greatest loss of life was associated with the "storm of the century," when some 20 tornadoes killed at least 40 persons in Florida.

Hurricane activity was relatively low in the United States, although Central and South America saw significant damage. There were eight named storms, of which three reached hurricane status. Hurricane Emily posed the only significant threat to the U.S. mainland, but turned back to sea as forecast after crossing the Outer Banks of North Carolina.

GEORGE J. HUFFMAN
Science Systems and Applications, Inc.

MEXICO

Mexico continued to witness many changes in 1993 as President Carlos Salinas de Gortari's administration moved into its fifth year. The government completed a surprising cabinet shuffle and a reversal of presidential involvement in gubernatorial elections. Relations with the United States were bolstered by the approval of the North American Free Trade Agreement (NAFTA) in the U.S. Congress. Continuing human-rights concerns were highlighted by the murder of Cardinal Juan Jesús Posadas Ocampo.

Politics. During the year, President Salinas shifted his political approach to a hard-line strategy. In the past, Salinas had intervened in some state elections and reversed official voting by forcing the government's candidate to resign, replacing him with an interim candidate. But the administration changed its strategy in November 1992 elections by threatening the personal and business interests of opposition-party candidates—especially those from the Democratic Revolutionary Party (PRD)—to prevent public protest over election results. Opposition parties had used postelectoral demonstrations to attract attention to alleged fraud, demanding presidential intervention. Salinas reversed his strategy to answer increasing frustration within his own Institutional Revolutionary Party (PRI).

Salinas reinforced his new hard-line approach in March by shuffling his cabinet members. He removed his secretary of government, Fernando Gutiérrez Barrios. Salinas replaced him with Patrocinio González Blanco Garrido, governor of the southern state of Chiapas, who was known for repressing peasants, opposing the Catholic Church on abortion, and ignoring human-rights complaints. Salinas also replaced his attorney general, Ignacio Morales Lechuga, with the head of the government Human Rights Commission, Jorge Carpizo McGregor, a respected jurist and human-rights activist. Carpizo's appointment received favorable reactions in Mexico and abroad and was seen as a counterbalance to González Blanco.

The cabinet reshuffling fueled speculation about the presidential-succession process, which generally heats up in the fall of the president's penultimate year in office. Elections were scheduled for August 1994. Normally, the incumbent president designates his own successor and nominates him as the PRI candidate. This process usually occurred in September or October, but Salinas, who remained popular in public-opinion polls, delayed his announcement. The leading candidates for his party's nomination were Social Development Secretary Luis Donaldo Colosio, Treasury Secretary Pedro Aspe Armella, and Mexico City Mayor Manuel Camacho Solís. On November 28, Colosio received the nod.

Policy Changes. Several new, unexpected political reforms occurred in 1993. The government announced in the summer that it would seek, for the third time in four years, to alter Mexico's electoral laws. The proposed changes included regulations on the financing of political parties and on campaign spending, and modest moves to strengthen opposition parties.

The Senate voted to alter Article 82 of the constitution, which required that presidential candidates be children of Mexican-born parents. Several prominent cabinet members as well as Vicente Fox—one of the National Action Party's (PAN's) most eligible figures—were ineligible to run for president for this reason. The new law overcame PRI opposition to changing the constitution and permitted a naturalized citizen with one foreign-born parent who has resided in Mexico for 20 years to run. The reform would not go into effect until the 1999 presidential succession. Observers saw this constitutional change as a government attempt to obtain PAN support for other proposed electoral reforms.

Mexican President Carlos Salinas de Gortari (extreme left) and U.S. President-elect Bill Clinton met at the governor's mansion in Austin, TX, on Jan. 8, 1993, to discuss immigration and the North American Free Trade Agreement—a historic economic pact which later was approved by both nations.

Economics. The Salinas administration survived months of worries over the NAFTA negotiations after the pact won passage in the U.S. Congress in November. Both governments' trade representatives finally accepted side agreements in arduous negotiations before NAFTA went to Congress. Many U.S. Democrats opposed the treaty, but the pact passed after vigorous efforts by President Bill Clinton and Republicans in Congress. The U.S. approval of NAFTA gave a large boost to President Salinas and his agenda of economic reform and internationalization.

Confidence in government policies grew in many foreign financial circles. Foreign holdings of Mexican government securities rose from $2.5 billion in 1990 to more than $20 billion in June 1993. The Mexican government claimed that the gross national product grew at an annual rate of 3.8% between 1989-91. The administration also signed a new pact with business and labor in an attempt to maintain single-digit inflation.

A controversy arose when it was revealed that 38 of Mexico's wealthiest families had been approached by government-party officials to donate millions of dollars to party coffers. This meeting ironically took place on the same day that Salinas proclaimed the PRI no longer would be "the party of the government." The news drew loud denunciations in the media, and the party shortly thereafter withdrew its requests for donations.

The Salinas government also continued its economic privatization program, selling the remaining government-owned banks back to the nation's private sector. The Finance Ministry also approved several new banking chains proposed by prominent investors. Public-sector participation in the gross domestic product declined to 8% in 1993 from 25% in 1983.

Social Welfare. The Salinas administration continued to increase spending in the social sector. In his 1992 State of the Nation address, the president announced that social expenditures as part of the public-sector budget had increased steadily since he took office, accounting for 40% in 1988, 50% in 1990, and an estimated 60% in 1992. Much of this funding was generated by revenues from privatization sales.

The administration's human-rights record continued to receive widespread attention. The government's failure to eliminate human-rights abuses, particularly to ferret out government and military officials associated with drug trading and corruption, was accentuated by Cardinal Juan Posadas' assassination in May. One of only two Mexican cardinals, Cardinal Posadas was in charge of the archdiocese of Guadalajara and had become increasingly outspoken against the immorality of drugs. The government investigation, in the hands of new Attorney General Jorge Carpizo, alleged that Posadas was killed in cross-fire between drug traffickers in a case of mistaken identity. Although the Vatican and the Mexican episcopate publicly accepted the government's version, privately most clergy and bishops disagreed with this conclusion.

The government's reputation for controlling the press was illustrated when Zachary Margoulis, a U.S. journalist with the English-language daily *The News,* was dismissed after he reported a Los Angeles court's charges against Manuel Bartlett, governor of Puebla and former government secretary. Margoulis wrote that Bartlett and other officials allegedly were linked to drug trafficking and the death of a U.S. Drug Enforcement Agency (DEA) agent.

Foreign Affairs. U.S. President Clinton inherited excellent relations between the two countries, a consequence of the personal relationship between George Bush and Salinas, and U.S. ambassador John Negroponte's skillful diplomatic efforts. The Clinton administration, however, initially did not give the same attention to Mexico as had its predecessor. This created some difficulties for President Salinas, especially concerning NAFTA, to which President Bush had made a strong commitment. But in the end, the Clinton administration waged an aggressive battle to encourage Congress to pass NAFTA. This passage was greeted with satisfaction and relief by Salinas. Mexico had sacrificed a great deal in reducing its tariffs radically as a show of good faith anticipating the agreement, and was unlikely to be as trusting in the future if NAFTA had died in Congress.

The change in U.S. administrations was a critical variable in the relations between the two countries in 1993. Although Mexico reportedly asked the Clinton administration to retain Ambassador Negroponte until a vote on NAFTA, President Clinton appointed James Jones, a former Democratic congressman and head of the American Stock Exchange, as the new U.S. representative. Jones, who strongly favored NAFTA and had many contacts in Congress, helped persuade Democrats to support Clinton's position on the treaty.

MEXICO • Information Highlights

Official Name: United Mexican States.
Location: Southern North America.
Area: 761,602 sq mi (1 972 550 km²).
Population (mid-1993 est.): 90,000,000.
Chief Cities (March 1990 census): Mexico City (Federal District), the capital, 8,236,960; Guadalajara, 1,628,617; Nezahualcóyotl, 1,259,543.
Government: *Head of state and government*, Carlos Salinas de Gortari, president (took office Dec. 1988). *Legislature*—National Congress: Senate and Chamber of Deputies.
Monetary Unit: Peso (3.110 pesos equal U.S.$1, floating rate, Nov. 19, 1993).
Gross Domestic Product (1991 est. U.S.$): $289,000,000,000.
Economic Indexes (1992): *Consumer Prices* (1980 = 100), all items, 21,334.8; food, 18,745,7. *Industrial Production* (1980 = 100), 128.
Foreign Trade (1992 U.S.$): *Imports*, $48,138,000,000; *exports*, $27,531,000,000.

One of the few incidents which threw a pall over U.S.-Mexican relations in 1992 was the kidnapping—funded by the Drug Enforcement Agency (DEA)—of physician Humberto Alvarez Machain, an alleged participant in the murder of DEA agent Enrique "Kiki" Camareno Salazar. After being acquitted by a U.S. judge in 1993, Alvarez Machain announced that he would sue both Mexican and U.S. officials for violating his civil rights.

Since Mexico reestablished relations with the Vatican and eliminated restrictions against the Catholic Church, Salinas continued to improve his ties with the clergy. Cardinal Posadas' murder severely jeopardized this relationship, since the public speculated that Posadas knew of criminal drug ties to the government. The Mexican episcopate also increased tensions between the Church and the government in June when it alleged that a connection existed between some military officials and the drug trade. Nevertheless, the administration benefited from a visit by Pope John Paul II in August, which legitimized their relations at the highest levels.

RODERIC AI CAMP, *Tulane University*

MICHIGAN

Detroit voters elected a new mayor in 1993 to succeed the retiring Coleman Young. The trials of white Detroit police officers accused of fatally beating a black man claimed national news coverage, as did the legal proceedings against Dr. Jack Kevorkian. Michigan Gov. John Engler focused his efforts on public-school reform.

Detroit Election. Mayor Young, one of Detroit's most celebrated politicians, did not seek reelection, citing failing health at age 75. Dennis Archer, an African-American lawyer who resigned from the Michigan Supreme Court to seek the office, was elected November 2 after a sometimes bitter campaign against Young's chosen successor, Sharon McPhail, an African American who had hoped to become the city's first female mayor. Archer, 51, who advocated change from Young's ironfisted leadership, was elected by a margin of 57%-43%. After the election, Archer visited the governor and state legislators in an effort to heal rifts which had developed between the city and the rest of the state.

As Young, Detroit's first black mayor, prepared to leave office, he would be remembered as a charismatic and confrontational leader who served 20 years by addressing the concerns of the city's increasingly black population, reorganizing a police department once viewed as racist by many residents, and enticing investment to the city. But he also was criticized for deteriorating public services.

School Reform. Governor Engler initiated a reform of Michigan's public schools and the way they were financed. State lawmakers in July granted the biggest property-tax break in Michigan history, scrapping $6 billion in local property taxes historically used to pay for public schools. The action set the stage for a new school-funding plan, but differing financing proposals threatened to deadlock the legislature. The law outlawing property taxes took effect Dec. 31, 1993. Without a new way to pay for schools, many districts faced chaos and perhaps closings in the 1994-95 school year.

In the meantime, the governor's proposals to create educational competition by allowing parents to choose schools in their district—including tax-supported "charter schools" established by nonprofit, nonreligious organizations—came under fire. The Michigan Educational Association asked its members for a $90-per-member contribution to help defeat the proposals.

Police Trial. The trials of three white police officers accused of fatally beating a black man aroused strong emotion in Detroit. After a 13-week trial, two of the officers—Larry Nevers and Walter Budzny—were found guilty of second-degree murder by a Detroit jury. Nevers was sentenced to a term of 12 to 25 years in prison, and Budzyn to an eight- to 18-year sentence. The third officer, Robert Lessnau, accused of assault with intent to do great bodily harm, was acquitted by a judge. The verdicts and sentences were seen by many as polarizing race relations between mostly black Detroit and its mostly white suburbs.

Dr. Kevorkian. Physician Dr. Jack Kevorkian, who was known as "Dr. Death," continued to make headlines by assisting terminally ill people to commit suicide. Reacting to his actions, Michigan in February made assisting in a suicide a crime. Kevorkian—who had been present at the deaths of 20 people—challenged the law as unconstitutional. He later was charged twice with violating the law and he was jailed on November 30. In mid-December a state judge struck down the law. *See also* MEDICINE AND HEALTH—*Medical Ethics.*

CHARLES THEISEN, *"The Detroit News"*

MICHIGAN • Information Highlights

Area: 58,527 sq mi (151 586 km^2).

Population (July 1, 1992 est.): 9,437,000.

Chief Cities (1990 census): Lansing, the capital, 127,321; Detroit, 1,027,974; Grand Rapids, 189,126; Warren, 144,864; Flint, 140,761.

Government (1993): *Chief Officers*—governor, John Engler (R); lt. gov., Connie Binsfeld (R). *Legislature*—Senate, 38 members; House of Representatives, 110 members.

State Finances (fiscal year 1991): *Revenue*, $24,505,000,000; *expenditure*, $24,037,000,000.

Personal Income (1992): $185,713,000,000; per capita, $19,680.

Labor Force (August 1993): *Civilian labor force*, 4,686,700; *unemployed*, 306,200 (6.5% of total force).

Education: *Enrollment* (fall 1991)—public elementary schools, 1,156,876; public secondary, 434,244; colleges and universities, 568,491. *Public school expenditures* (1990-91), $8,545,805,000.

MICROBIOLOGY

The year 1993 brought the discoveries of an antimicrobial steroid and a species of giant bacteria, and new findings regarding the infectious nature of peptic ulcers. The reemergence of cholera and the widespread occurrence of contaminated shellfish threatened the health of many people.

A New Antimicrobial Steroid. In the fight against infectious microorganisms—bacteria, protozoa, and fungi—there are numerous antibiotics available that are produced by molds. These antibiotics—such as *penicillin, ampicillin,* or *streptomycin*—are peptide compounds, composed of strings of amino acids. In addition, there are a few antimicrobial steroid compounds that have been isolated from plants. Steroids are lipids—consisting of four carbon rings—to which other molecules may be attached.

In 1993, Drs. M. Zasloff and K. Moore of the University of Pennsylvania discovered a new antimicrobial steroid called *squalamine.* It is produced by sharks and is the first antimicrobial steroid found in animals. In laboratory tests, squalamine proved effective against highly virulent strains of *Staphylococcus, Streptococcus*, and *Candida.* If squalamine proves to be effective in subsequent tests using mammals, it will be an important new antimicrobial compound available for fighting various infectious diseases.

A Reemergent Killer. Cholera is caused by the bacterium *Vibrio cholerae.* Infection usually results from drinking water contaminated by the feces of an infected person. The bacterium is an intestinal parasite that produces a toxin that causes profuse diarrhea and vomiting. If lost fluids are not replaced, coma and death follow within 24 hours.

Although cholera is endemic to India and spreads periodically to other countries, it has been absent from the Western Hemisphere for most of the 20th century. Unfortunately it appeared in South America in early 1991, and by the end of 1992, more than 700,000 cases had been reported, including 6,000 fatalities. About 100 cases of cholera also have been reported in the United States.

Although it is impossible to predict the course of this latest cholera outbreak, attempts to eradicate the disease will require that people throughout the world have access to safe drinking water.

Giant Bacteria. Different single-celled organisms usually are characterized by their sizes. Among the smallest organisms are bacteria, which average one micrometer ($\frac{1}{1,000,000}$ of a meter or $\frac{1}{25,000}$ of an inch) in length. The unaided human eye can see a dot as small as 100 micrometers—the length of a paramecium, a single-celled animal.

In 1985, Israeli scientists studying the surgeonfish in the Red Sea discovered a very large one-celled organism that was 0.5 millimeter ($\frac{1}{2,000}$ of a meter or $\frac{1}{50}$ of an inch) long in the fish's intestinal tract. They gave the newly discovered organism the scientific name *Epulopiscium fishelsoni* and concluded that it was an extremely large one-celled animal, since it was about five times longer than the average paramecium.

In the early 1990s, Drs. N. R. Pace and E. R. Angert at Indiana University extracted the genetic material from *E. fishelsoni* and compared it with the DNA of different one-celled organisms. They found that *E. fishelsoni* was a true bacterium, even though it was 500 times larger than the average bacterium. This discovery means that scientists no longer will be able to use size as a definitive means of characterizing one-celled organisms.

Contaminated Shellfish. Mussels, clams, scallops, and oysters feed on microscopic organisms that inhabit their surrounding waters. Among such microorganisms are *diatoms*—one-celled marine plants—belonging to the species *Nitzschia pungens.* Diatoms produce a chemical compound called *domoic acid* that does not appear to harm shellfish. However, when this compound is ingested by humans who have eaten contaminated shellfish, it causes vomiting, diarrhea, difficulty in breathing, seizures, and—in severe cases—death.

The first outbreak of domoic-acid poisoning occurred among people who ate blue mussels cultured in marine beds off the eastern coast of Canada. More recently, razor clams from the coastal waters of the Pacific Northwest and California have been found to be contaminated. Experts do not yet know how these diatoms spread, nor have they discovered an antidote for this potentially fatal poison.

A New Infectious Disease. It previously was assumed that peptic ulcers—those found in the esophagus, stomach, and intestines—were caused by stress, diet, smoking, drinking, or other factors that result in an excess secretion of acid by the stomach. Peptic ulcers generally are treated with the prescription of antacids. Unfortunately, the recurrence rate after completion of this treatment is 95% over a two-year period.

Dr. E. Hentschel and colleagues at the University of Vienna treated one group of ulcer patients with antibiotics, while a control group was given a placebo. Researchers found a recurrence rate of only 8% in patients who were treated with antibiotics, compared with 86% in patients receiving the placebo. The bacterium associated with peptic ulcers was isolated and named *Helicobacter pylori.* Since bacteria often mutate to antibiotic resistance, researchers are trying to develop an effective vaccine against *H. pylori* infection.

See also MEDICINE AND HEALTH.

LOUIS LEVINE
Department of Biology
City College of New York

MIDDLE EAST

Genuinely new and unexpected developments are the exception in the Middle East. However, the accord between Israel and the Palestine Liberation Organization (PLO) signed in September 1993 was a refreshingly unforeseen event. Under the agreement, Israel and the PLO committed themselves to share a land that they both had claimed. (*See also* SPECIAL REPORT.)

A New "Great Game" in Central Asia. The disintegration of the USSR continued to have an effect on the area. The old gambit played by various Middle East nations of exploiting U.S. and Soviet rivalry had ended. During 1993 the only outside power with major influence in the region was the United States. The newly independent countries that emerged in former Soviet Central Asia and west of it opened a new arena of geopolitical maneuvering. Turkey and Iran had become the great rivals for influence and economic advantage in the former Soviet republics, but Israel and other states also exhibited interest in the region. Radio broadcasts, trade missions, and personal visits to the republics were deployed.

Continuations. The Kurds—whether in Iraq, Iran, or Turkey—were allowed to lapse into their usual status of a forgotten people. During 1993 they were harassed in Iraq, and less so in Iran. The more numerous and militant Kurds of Turkey continued their eight-year armed uprising and committed various terrorist acts.

A disquieting trend that continued was the arms buildup in the Middle East, where money was available to take up some of the slack resulting from defense cutbacks in Russia and the United States. A prime example of the trend was the International Defense Exhibition in Abu Dhabi in February—billed as "the largest and most sophisticated arms bazaar in history." Yet in reality, Persian Gulf security remained an unsolved problem. Iran and Iraq continued to be military threats, hardly to be exorcised by purchases of sophisticated weapons and occasional meetings of the Gulf Cooperation Council.

Islamic Fundamentalism. Iran was involved deeply in fanning the flames of Islamic fundamentalism. It supported the Shiite fundamentalist party Hezbollah in Lebanon, backed the fanatical regime and trained terrorists in Sudan, incited opposition and murder in Egypt, and encouraged the fundamentalist movement to penetrate Africa.

Prospects for Democracy. Although democracy has been a fragile plant in the Middle East, several actions in its favor occurred in the region during 1993. For example, Jordan conducted a successful election; Egypt's President Hosni Mubarak pondered democratic moves to broaden the base of his rule; Yemen held out promises of a more democratic future; and Turkey gained the nation's first woman prime minister, Tansu Ciller.

ARTHUR CAMPBELL TURNER
University of California, Riverside

SPECIAL REPORT/MIDDLE EAST

The Israel-PLO Accord

The totally unlikely agreement reached between Israel and the Palestine Liberation Organization (PLO) at the end of August 1993, and formalized at the White House on September 13, provided basically for the beginnings of Palestinian self-government in areas limited at first to the Gaza Strip and Jericho. The accord thus brought together in a compact the sworn enemies of many decades.

This was so extraordinary an event that it is difficult to think of any parallels. One has to go back to the visit of Egypt's President Anwar el-Sadat to Jerusalem in 1977 to find anything at all comparable in terms of surprise, improbability, and potential for good. The Sadat visit to Jerusalem was an icebreaking gesture that led to the Camp David negotiations of 1978 and the Egyptian-Israeli peace treaty of 1979. By that treaty, Israel traded land for peace on a massive scale, yielding back to Egypt the Sinai Peninsula, seized in the 1967 war—an area vastly larger than that of Israel proper.

© Reuters/Bettmann

A group of joyous Israelis rallied on Sept. 4, 1993, in support of Labor Prime Minister Yitzhak Rabin and the recently negotiated peace accord with the Palestine Liberation Organization.

© Stephane Compoint/Sygma

Throughout the Gaza Strip, East Jerusalem, Jericho (above), and other West Bank towns, thousands of Palestinians gathered to salute the new peace agreement with Israel. Flags and portraits of PLO Chairman Yasir Arafat were everywhere.

The 1979 treaty established diplomatic relations between Egypt and Israel and made war between the two countries unlikely. It, however, did not do all that was hoped for at the time. It did not lead to peace between Israel and its other neighbors—though the events of 1993 are in a sense long-term results. Another quite clear result was the 1981 assassination of Sadat—a fact undoubtedly present in the thoughts of the 1993 peacemakers.

The Washington Talks. The sequence of events leading to the 1993 accord provided an instructive case study in the comparative advantages of open diplomacy and secret, or confidential, negotiation. The public, bilateral sessions in Washington between Israeli and Jordanian-Palestinian delegations continued off and on in 1993. Such talks had been going on since the historic opening in Madrid in October 1991; but now there obviously was a dwindling expectation of actually achieving much, as well as a diminished attendance of participants. The ninth round of these Middle East peace talks opened in Washington on April 27, after having been postponed twice, and continued into May. The gap since the eighth session had ended in December 1992 was the longest since the series began in Madrid. The tenth session opened on June 15 and continued until early July. The 11th session began toward the end of August, but by that time other developments had ousted the Washington talks from center stage, as it became known that other, parallel, talks had been going on—and productively. The Washington conferees on both sides had been kept in the dark until very nearly the last moment.

Still, even if the Washington talks achieved little, the fact that they took place gave some ground for encouragement; and in fact, some parallel ancillary discussions in the U.S. capital did more than that. During the seventh round of bilateral talks in October 1992, Jordan and Israel quietly reached an agreement—confirmed in September 1993—on the major questions between them. Similar side discussions between Israel and Syria at least clarified what were their main points of issue.

The Secret Negotiations. The series of confidential meetings between Israel and PLO negotiators that led to the accord were no simple matter. Although Israeli citizens had been forbidden legally from 1986 until January 1993 to have any dealings with the PLO, some contacts in fact continued, especially in academic and journalistic circles. What may be regarded as the germ of the negotiations—a first incident that came about as a result of a suggestion by Terje Larsen, director of a research institute in Oslo, Norway—was a breakfast meeting at a London hotel on Dec. 4, 1992, between Yair Hirshfeld, a political scientist at Haifa University, and Ahmed Suleiman Khoury (known in PLO circles as Abu Alaa), administrator of the PLO's finances. The meeting had the sanction of

Yossi Beilin, Israeli deputy foreign minister in the government of Yitzhak Rabin (*see* BIOGRAPHY).

There was a further meeting in January, and the fateful Oslo meetings began on January 20 and continued for eight months. That these talks were kept secret from the public was an astonishing feat. The circle of those who knew about them was kept rigorously tight. For many months in Israel the only ones who knew were Rabin, Israel's Foreign Minister Shimon Peres, Beilin, and a couple of others. PLO Chairman Yasir Arafat (*see* BIOGRAPHY) was equally careful about security.

The negotiators held 18 meetings over the eight months—14 of them in Oslo, the rest in various places, including Tunis. Most but not all of the Oslo meetings took place at a government-owned country estate, where the cover story was that the negotiators were a group of professors holding a conference. Major credit for what was achieved must go to Norway's Foreign Minister Johan Jorgen Holst and his immediate aides for facilitating the meetings.

Success in maintaining secrecy about the so-called "Oslo Channel" no doubt was due largely to the fact that it was only one of several "back channels" where Israel and the PLO were conducting informal conversations, and so was not thought to be of unique significance. In fact, Peres at first had greater hopes from some meetings that were taking place in Cairo. But in April 1993, Rabin instructed Peres to strengthen the Israeli team in Oslo, and in May and June distinct progress was made.

"Gaza first"—the idea of Israel's giving up a not particularly desirable piece of territory—had been around in Israel for some time; but when Arafat indicated that this was an inadequate concession, the addition of Jericho made the difference. The PLO also made great concessions in resting content—for the moment—with creating an administration in these two areas; and, above all, in agreeing to postpone discussion of much more intractable matters, including the status of Jerusalem, for two years. The great symmetrical concession was mutual recognition by each of the two parties of the legitimacy of the other. Such was the outline of the agreement that began to emerge late in August.

A Propitious Moment. There were special circumstances in 1993, rendering mutual concessions possible, that had not existed earlier. Arafat and the PLO were in unprecedented difficulties. Their financial support from Saudi Arabia and other Persian Gulf states had disappeared because of Arafat's backing Iraq in the Gulf war of 1991. Political and financial support from the Soviet Union also was gone with the disintegration of that entity. The *intifada*—a Palestinian uprising against Israel—had been going on in Israeli-administered territories since December 1987, but only had made Israeli rule difficult, not

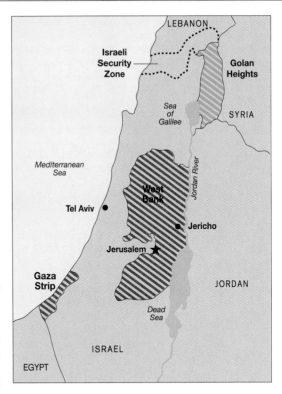

impossible. Arafat's own control of the PLO, and even of his own Fatah group, was being questioned. There was pressure for a settlement from Mubarak and other Arab leaders.

On the Israeli side, Rabin's Labor Party had won Israel's 1992 election with a policy of striving for peace even by making territorial concessions. He was obliged to explore possibilities in that direction, even though as a wary and skeptical former general he held views that did not differ all that much from those of his Likud opponents. For both sides, a more fundamental underlying factor was the increasing prominence of the fundamentalist Islamic group Hamas, which bade fair both to undermine Arafat's position and to make Israeli rule in the territories more costly and difficult. For both sides, it had become a case of "if not now, maybe never."

Final Approaches. Events accelerated remarkably in late August and early September. On August 19 the Israeli and Palestinian representatives initialed the final draft of the accord and referred it back to their principals for approval. The Israeli cabinet approved in principle on August 31 the arrangements for Palestinian self-government. Later, on September 9, they approved the mutual-recognition formula, a point important to Arafat. He had a difficult time securing PLO backing. On September 2 he convened a meeting in Tunis of the Executive Committee of his own Fatah—the largest and most moderate group within the PLO. Three days of acrimonious debate procured an endorsement

by September 4. Then on September 8 followed the meeting of the Executive Committee of the PLO; only 13 of the 18 members assembled. Next day the Committee voted, nine to three, to approve. Two extremist groups boycotted the meeting. Arafat did not convene the PLO National Council to endorse the accord.

On September 10, Arafat and Rabin exchanged letters of crucial significance, with Holst of Norway acting as courier. The key portions of Arafat's letter said: "The signing of the Declaration of Principles marks a new era in the history of the Middle East....The PLO recognizes the right of the State of Israel to exist in peace and security....The PLO commits itself to the Middle East peace process and to a peaceful resolution of the conflict between the two sides....The PLO renounces the use of terrorism and other acts of violence....The PLO affirms that those articles of the Palestinian Covenant which deny Israel's right to exist...are now inoperative and no longer valid." Rabin's letter to Arafat said, "I wish to confirm to you that...the government of Israel has decided to recognize the PLO as the representative of the Palestinian people and commence negotiations with the PLO within the Middle East peace process."

The Ceremony. On Rabin's instructions, Peres flew to California on August 26 to let a surprised U.S. Secretary of State Warren Christopher know of developments. Then on September 10 the Clinton administration offered to host the ceremony of the final signing, at the same time resuming relations with the PLO, intermitted in June 1990. The consequence was the historic ceremony on the White House lawn on the brilliant morning of September 13, where before the assembled diplomatic corps and several hundred specially invited guests, the accord was formalized. Peres signed for Israel, Mahmoud Abbas for the PLO. Since the United States and Russia were cosponsors of the Middle East peace conference, Christopher witnessed for the United States and Russia's Foreign Minister Andrei Kozyrev for Russia. Then, in an intensely symbolic gesture, Rabin and Arafat shook hands.

President Clinton opened and closed the ceremony. Among the guests, Peres spoke first, then Abbas, Rabin, and Arafat. Rabin and Peres spoke in English, the PLO leaders in Arabic. Rabin's speech did not gloss over the bitter enmities and the lives lost of the past but pointed out: "We say to you today in a loud and clear voice: Enough of blood and tears! Enough!"

The Accord. What was signed on September 13—the "Declaration of Principles on Interim Self-Government Arrangements" and associated annexes—runs to several thousand words. The principal aim is declared to be "to establish a Palestinian Interim Self-Government Authority, the elected Council, for the Palestinian people in the West Bank and the Gaza Strip, for a transi-

tional period not exceeding five years, leading to a permanent settlement based on Security Council Resolutions 242 and 338." There are provisions for election of the council under international supervision. The council would have limited legislative authority, with control over taxation, health, education, social welfare, culture, tourism, and the establishment of a police force. Israel would retain authority for external defense and overall security, though not in Palestinian population centers, and for controlling border crossings. An agreement would be concluded "within two months from the date of entry into force of this Declaration of Principles" (i.e., by December 13) on the arrangements for the withdrawal of Israeli forces from the Gaza Strip and Jericho area. Complete Israeli withdrawal from these areas was to be completed within another four months. These areas were, in other words, to be the test case for Palestinian self-government.

Further points in the projected timetable were these: By July 1994 the council would be elected and would have competence over the West Bank and Gaza, though the major questions of Jerusalem and of Palestinian refugees outside Israel would be held over for later discussion. Talks on permanent status must be begun by April 1996, and a permanent settlement should be in place by April 1999. In the meantime, Israel would continue to be responsible for external security and—significantly—for the security of all Israelis in the territories.

Aftermath. The months immediately following the signing of the accord gave no clear indication of whether the daring initiative would succeed. It was a compromise in which both sides conceded much, and as such it was detested by many in both the Palestinian and Israeli camps. It was acclaimed internationally, and even the Arab countries—except for Libya and Syria—were persuaded by Arafat to give approval. But in the areas involved, there were continued outbreaks of violence, initiated by Palestinian extremists and Israeli settlers, leading to some 40 deaths by the end of the year.

Meanwhile, the discussions in Cairo to implement the accord did not go smoothly, partly because of ambiguities in the accord itself. What, for example, was "the Jericho area"? The Israelis defined it as constituting 20 sq mi (52 km^2), the Palestinians as 140 sq mi (363 km^2). Also, the December 13 deadline to begin self-rule in the Gaza Strip and Jericho had to be extended for at least ten days after Rabin and Arafat could not agree on "security arrangements." These areas, in fact, are not economically viable and possibly never will be. In recognition of this, the wealthiest countries, in a conference in Washington on October 1, pledged almost $2 billion over the first five years to support Palestinian self-government

See also ISRAEL.

ARTHUR CAMPBELL TURNER

MILITARY AFFAIRS

Both in the United States and in Russia, the major successor state to the former Soviet Union, military authorities and strategists continued during 1993 to reconfigure military doctrine and forces to meet the uncertainties of a changed world. In contrast to the period from 1947 to 1991 when Washington and Moscow focused on each other and their allies, the modern panorama contained more varied possibilities for international violence than in the past. Also making headlines in 1993 was the establishment of a new policy that loosened the ban on homosexuals serving in the U.S. military (*see also* SPECIAL REPORT/LAW, page 321).

U.S. Restructuring. On September 20 the U.S. Senate voted to seal the nation's third round of military-base closures since 1988. Congress approved the recommendations of the Defense Base Closure and Realignment Commission, which was created by President Bill Clinton to help depoliticize the effort to downsize the military. The commission recommended the full closure of 130 bases and major cuts at 45 other sites.

In its first year in office, the Clinton administration sought to address a radically changing national security scene by downsizing the military while increasing its capabilities to respond rapidly to potential threats. Policy guidance for the military restructuring was provided by a study of future requirements termed the "Bottom-Up Review: Forces for a New Era." Commissioned by Secretary of Defense Les Aspin, the study concluded that the United States should be prepared to fight two major regional wars at the same time.

For planning purposes the study assumed that the two major regional conflicts for which the United States should prepare would be an attack by a remilitarized Iraq against Persian Gulf states and an assault by North Korea upon the Republic of Korea. While such conflicts would not threaten the United States directly, they would jeopardize important U.S. interests and allies. The size of the conflicts anticipated by the Bottom-Up Review could involve up to 750,000 enemy personnel under arms, 4,000 tanks, 1,000 combat aircraft, and 1,000 Scud-type missiles possibly carrying nuclear, biological, or chemical warheads.

While the United States once relied upon nuclear weapons to deter a war with the former Soviet Union, more-recent planning depends on the presence of conventional forces overseas, joint exercises with allies, and other maneuvers to deter regional conflicts. However, the United States developed a four-stage response strategy for regional conflicts if deterrence should fail. The first phase called for U.S. forces to back up an ally under attack to halt an invasion as quickly as possible. In the second stage, the United States and other coalition forces would build up while enemy forces were reduced. In the third phase, allied forces would seek to defeat the enemy by using large-scale, air-land envelopment reminiscent of the last days of the Gulf war. Lastly there would be the establishment of regional stability based on the presence of U.S. and allied military units which could enforce compliance with war-termination agreements.

To provide the ability to fight two simultaneous regional conflicts, U.S. planning called for six types of supporting capabilities: airlift capacity; equipment prepositioning; battlefield surveillance, command, control, and communications; advanced munitions; aerial refueling; and sealift capacity. To support U.S. participation in regional conflicts and in peace-enforcement and intervention operations such as the one in Somalia, the Bottom-Up Review called for a new force structure including the following capability: ten active Army divisions with five in reserve; 11 aircraft carriers with one in reserve, roughly 50 attack submarines and 350 other ships; 13 fighter wings with seven in reserve; and up to 184 bombers for the delivery of conventional munitions. The Marines would be authorized with a total force strength of 174,000.

According to the Bottom-Up Review, the United States should maintain 100,000 troops in Western Europe and a similar number in northeast Asia, mostly in South Korea. The Seventh Fleet would continue to patrol the western Pacific, backed by combat aircraft based in Japan and on the island of Okinawa. Navy ships would continue to patrol the Persian Gulf, while heavy equipment for a brigade would be kept in Kuwait for use by rotating contingents of troops. Access to ports and bases and transit rights for aircraft would be maintained with African nations. In Latin America, U.S. military units would promote democratic armed forces and help combat drug traffickers. U.S. troops would continue to protect the Panama Canal in concert with Panamanian troops until the canal reverts to full Panamanian control in 1999.

During the Cold War rivalry with the Soviet Union and its allies, the United States invested heavily in strategic nuclear forces to deter a nuclear attack. Now, with the dissolution of the Warsaw Pact and the USSR, the threat of nuclear war was at its lowest point in decades. However, the Pentagon argued that the United States should maintain a nuclear capability to hedge against an unpredictable future which includes unanswered questions regarding the disposition of the nuclear forces from the former Soviet Union.

The U.S. effort envisioned to provide an impenetrable shield to protect the nation from ballistic missile attack—dubbed Star Wars or the Strategic Defense Initiative (SDI)—was modified by the Clinton administration. The SDI Organization was renamed the Ballistic Missile Defense Organization, and the effort was scaled back to focus on defending against missile attacks upon U.S. forces in the field, and

defending the continental United States against a limited attack by "terrorist" states.

Disarmament. Tens of thousands of nuclear warheads remained in Russia and in the former Soviet republics of Ukraine, Belarus, and Kazakhstan. In theory the number of such weapons would be reduced greatly under the terms of the Strategic Arms Reduction Treaty (START) I and II agreements negotiated with the United States. However, substantial obstacles remained to implementing the agreements fully, such as the ratification of START I by Ukraine and the accession to the Nuclear Non-Proliferation Treaty by Ukraine and Kazakhstan. Even after START I and II were implemented, it would take nearly ten years for the reductions to be made.

Given these uncertainties, the Pentagon posited two guidelines for sizing U.S. strategic nuclear forces during the final years of the century: provide an effective deterrent within START I and START II limits, and maintain a base that can be bolstered if new threats arise. The force which was planned to meet these requirements included 18 Trident submarines carrying SLBMs, 94 B-52H intercontinental jet bombers, 500 ICBMs, and 20 B-2 Stealth bombers.

The end of the Cold War and the return home of many U.S. troops from overseas prompted the creation of an integrated command structure for the continental United States called the U.S. Atlantic Command (USACOM). The organization placed most Army, Navy, Air Force, and Marine personnel under the command of a four-star officer based in Norfolk, VA. The task of USACOM's first commander, Navy Adm. Paul Miller, was to train forces to conduct cooperative operations, including missions of humanitarian aid and disaster relief.

Russian Military Restructuring. Several months after the publication of the Bottom-Up Review, the Russians made public their new post-Soviet-era military doctrine. According to Russian Defense Minister Pavel Grachev, Moscow considered no nation to be its enemy. In place of the United States and North American Treaty Organization (NATO) countries, the new threats identified by the Russian defense doctrine were potential hostilities from nationalist and separatist groups within or upon the borders of Russia, including efforts to undermine the Russian constitutional order.

The new Russian doctrine also contained the threat to use nuclear weapons first to defend Russia against a nonnuclear attack. This statement broke from a long-standing Soviet position that it would not be the first to introduce nuclear weapons into a conflict, but U.S. officials viewed the new policy as only propaganda. The Russians indicated their downsized army would emphasize airborne and other kinds of rapid-reaction capability, and the potential to participate in UN peacekeeping operations.

NATO. In a fall meeting of NATO members, Defense Secretary Aspin recommended that all former Soviet republics and East European members of the former Warsaw Pact be invited to become NATO partners. The rationale behind the proposal was that the old enemies should band together to work against a future which Aspin said could contain "a handful of nuclear weapons in the hands of terrorists." Additional cooperative efforts would include joint participation in peacekeeping missions, disaster-relief operations, search-and-rescue missions, and crisis-management activities. The NATO defense ministers endorsed the U.S. plan.

Proliferation of Nuclear Weapons. The announcement in the spring by North Korea that it intended to withdraw from the Nuclear Non-Proliferation Treaty (NPT) underscored a major military concern of the Clinton administration, Russian President Boris Yeltsin, and many others. The worry was that while 157 nations were signatories of the NPT, North Korea might join Israel, India, Pakistan, Iraq, and Iran as actual or potential possessors of nuclear weapons in the near future. The United States engaged in a series of negotiations to convince North Korea to remain in the NPT and open up its nuclear facilities for international inspection.

By 1993 much of the national-security community believed that Pakistan had developed atomic weapons or had the capability to do so. Gen. Aslam Beg, former Pakistani army chief of staff and former supervisor of the nation's nuclear program, reportedly had claimed that Pakistan possessed nuclear weapons that were developed to be used in a war with India should conventional forces prove ineffective, but he subsequently denied the statement.

President Clinton called for the strengthening of the NPT when it comes up for renewal in 1995 and for an expansion in the authority of the International Atomic Energy Agency (IAEA) to conduct on-site inspection and monitor potential nuclear-weapon-fabrication capabilities. The United States continued to support the Missile Technology Control Regime as a means to impede the sale of components which could be used to build ballistic missiles by "rogue" and "terrorist" states.

Despite a specific warning from Clinton, China tested a nuclear weapon in the fall. This action spurred pressure on the U.S. government to resume testing. Counterpressures upon the president argued that the United States should refrain from testing nuclear weapons to reaffirm the precedent against such testing shared with Moscow. These same critics noted China had possessed nuclear weapons since 1964, and that one test did not endanger U.S. security.

South Africa's President F. W. de Klerk admitted in 1993 that his nation clandestinely had manufactured six primitive atomic bombs in the 1970s and 1980s. In 1989 the government decided to dismantle the weapons and decommission the plant which produced highly enriched uranium fuel for the weapons. In 1991,

South Africa signed the NPT and opened up its nuclear facilities to IAEA inspection—the first nation to disarm its nuclear arsenal. This encouraged disarmament advocates that other nations might make the same decision.

Questioned U.S. Intervention. While the outlines of the future U.S. military-force structure grew clearer, it was uncertain how the forces would be used in situations such as Somalia and Haiti that were not major regional conflicts. The subject of whether the United States was the world's "911" number was addressed by President Clinton before the UN in the fall. He cautioned the world that "the United Nations simply cannot become engaged in every one of the world's conflicts," and noted that, "if the American people are to say yes to UN peacekeeping, the United Nations must know when to say no."

The intervention of U.S. forces in Somalia and Haiti caused some members in Congress, mostly Republicans, to seek restraints on the president's power to commit troops overseas. The effort was reminiscent of the War Powers Resolution passed by Congress during the Vietnam war. But a proposal by Sen. Don Nickles (R-OK) to require congressional permission before the president could place forces overseas under UN command failed.

Retirements and Appointments. As the year drew to a close, Defense Secretary Aspin suddenly resigned, and President Clinton named Bobby Ray Inman, a former intelligence official, as his successor. Inman withdrew his nomination in mid-January 1994, however. Gen. Colin Powell, the first black chairman of the Joint Chiefs of Staff, who oversaw the Persian Gulf war victory, retired on September 30.

To succeed General Powell, President Clinton named Gen. John Shalikashvili (*see also* BIOGRAPHY), who was serving as the Supreme Allied Commander in Europe, as the new chairman of the Joint Chiefs of Staff. Gen. George Joulwan, commander of U.S. forces in Latin America, then was named to succeed General Shalikashvili as NATO commander.

Acting on a campaign promise to make his administration "look more like America," President Clinton appointed Sheila Widnall of the Massachusetts Institute of Technology as secretary of the Air Force—the first woman to head a branch of the U.S. armed forces.

In June, Air Force Chief of Staff Gen. Merrill McPeak announced that Maj. Gen. Harold Campbell would be fined $7,000 and be forced to retire because of derogatory remarks made about President Clinton at a banquet. The Uniform Code of Military Justice bars commissioned officers from using "contemptuous words" in reference to their commander in chief.

The Tailhook Affair. Two years after women military personnel were sexually harassed at the Tailhook Association convention in Las Vegas, the Navy still was feeling repercussions from the scandal. Navy Secretary John Dalton said that the Navy's top admiral, Frank Kelso, had shown a "lack of leadership" during the course of the Tailhook investigation and should resign. However, Defense Secretary Aspin overruled Dal-

With a parade in his honor at Fort Myer, VA, Gen. Colin Powell (third from left), the chairman of the Joint Chiefs of Staff since 1989, retired from the U.S. army on Sept. 30, 1993. Both Presidents George Bush and Bill Clinton attended the ceremonies.

© Johnson/Gamma-Liaison

ton, and Admiral Kelso remained as the Chief of Naval Operations. The first of several trials for naval officers accused of sexual misconduct was dismissed by the Navy for lack of evidence.

Illness Among Gulf War Troops. Since the end of the Persian Gulf war in 1991, several thousand U.S. soldiers who served in the region have complained of several mysterious sicknesses. Both veterans' groups and members of Congress have attributed the problems to the possible use of chemical agents by Iraq. In November, Secretary of Defense Aspin said a claim by Czech chemical-warfare experts that traces of chemical weapons were detected in Saudi Arabia during the conflict might be true, but that the amounts of the gases were too small to cause the reported illnesses. The commander of Walter Reed Army Medical Center near Washington, DC, Maj. Gen. Ronald R. Blanck, suggested that the symptoms could have arisen from exposure to air pollution from oil-well fires in Kuwait and spills of ammonia and chlorine near Saudi seaports.

ROBERT M. LAWRENCE
Colorado State University

MINNESOTA • Information Highlights
Area: 84,402 sq mi (218 601 km²).
Population (July 1, 1992 est.): 4,480,000.
Chief Cities (1990 census): St. Paul, the capital, 272,235; Minneapolis, 368,383; Duluth, 85,493.
Government (1993): *Chief Officers*—governor, Arne Carlson (I-R); lt. gov., Joanell Dyrstad (I-R). *Legislature*—Senate, 67 members; House of Representatives, 134 members.
State Finances (fiscal year 1991): *Revenue,* $13,701,000,000; *expenditure,* $12,730,000,000.
Personal Income (1992): $91,512,000,000; per capita, $20,427.
Labor Force (August 1993): *Civilian labor force,* 2,478,200; *unemployed,* 113,700 (4.6% of total force).
Education: *Enrollment* (fall 1991)—public elementary schools, 556,735; public secondary, 216,836; colleges and universities, 255,054. *Public school expenditures* (1990-91), $3,740,820,000.

MINNESOTA

Severe flood damage, legislative upheaval, the state's worst air crash in history, administrative turmoil at the University of Minnesota Medical School, municipal elections, and the conviction of three assailants for the murder of a Minneapolis police officer were major 1993 events in Minnesota. In August the world's largest shopping center—the Mall of America in Bloomington, a Twin Cities suburb—reported drawing 40 million visitors during its first year.

Disaster and Turmoil. As a result of the Great Flood of '93, damage to Minnesota's corn and soybean crops was estimated at $2.5 billion. Of the state's 87 counties, 41 were declared eligible for disaster relief. *(See also* FEATURE ARTICLE, page 44.)

The University of Minnesota moved to fire Dr. John Najarian, a world-recognized pioneer in transplant surgery, as part of a continuing investigation into an allegation that for 22 years he ran an unlicensed program producing drugs designed to prevent rejection of transplant organs. The action followed the resignation of several top administrators after reports of questionable spending of fees received from private patients.

Eighteen persons died in the crash of a Northwest Airlink commuter plane in Hibbing. At the time, Northwest Airlines was continuing its struggle to avoid bankruptcy. After negotiations the airline's employees accepted $800 million in pay cuts in exchange for partial control of the company.

Charges were dismissed against U.S. Sen. Dave Durenberger (R) for defrauding the federal government by obtaining reimbursement for living expenses while staying in an apartment he owned. A suit alleging he had raped a client 29 years ago, fathering a son, was dismissed after blood tests proved negative. Durenberger announced in September that he would not seek reelection.

Legislature. Dee Long resigned the House speakership after a protracted controversy that followed the revelation that the telephone credit card of House Majority Leader Alan Welle had been used by his son and others to charge $80,000 in unauthorized calls. Welle resigned as majority leader, but Long was the target of a continuing attack for having mishandled the affair. She resigned after being embarrassed further when a hidden news camera showed her playing golf when she presumably was attending a legislative conference in San Diego.

Crime, Schools, and Elections. Three young assailants were convicted for the murder of a Minneapolis police officer. But a witness who had identified the triggerman told the court in December that her memory was faulty and that she wanted to recant her testimony. Her action left the final outcome of the proceedings in doubt.

In an unusual departure from established practice, the Minneapolis school board, by a vote of four to three, named Peter Hutchinson and his management consulting firm as superintendent; Minneapolis thus became the nation's first major city to employ a private company instead of a professional educator to manage its system.

In Minneapolis, Sharon Sayles Belton, a 42-year-old Democrat who had served ten years on the city council, was the first woman and the first African American to be elected mayor of Minneapolis. She would succeed Don Fraser, who did not seek reelection after serving 11 years, the longest tenure in the city's history. In St. Paul state Assistant Attorney General Norm Coleman (D) was chosen to succeed Mayor Jim Scheibel, who did not seek reelection.

ARTHUR NAFTALIN
Professor Emeritus, University of Minnesota

MISSISSIPPI

The growth of dockside casinos and a special election to fill an open U.S. congressional seat were of particular interest to Mississippians in 1993. Other highlights included quadrennial city elections and a legislative session that left the governor and legislators embroiled in a post-session legal dispute.

Casino Gambling. In the 12 months immediately following the August 1992 opening of the state's initial floating casino on the Gulf Coast, nine additional dockside casinos became operational—six on the coast and three in counties bordering the Mississippi River. During that year, gross gaming revenues exceeded $500 million and generated higher-than-expected state and county tax payments.

In October, Mississippi Choctaws approved gaming on their reservation, clearing the way for Mississippi's first inland casino in 1994.

Elections. Bennie Thompson, a Hinds county supervisor, received 55% of the ballots cast in a hotly contested April election to fill a U.S. congressional seat vacated by Mike Espy, who resigned to become secretary of agriculture. Thompson's runoff victory over Hayes Dent, a former adviser to Gov. Kirk Fordice, saved the district for the Democrats and assured continued representation by a black congressman.

Municipal elections held in June resulted in gains for Republicans, blacks, and women; but each of those groups continued to comprise only a small percentage of city officeholders.

Democrat Bennie Thompson took the oath of office after winning a special April 1993 election for the U.S. House seat vacated by Mike Espy, the new U.S. secretary of agriculture.

© AP/Wide World

MISSISSIPPI • Information Highlights

Area: 47,689 sq mi (123 515 km²).
Population (July 1, 1992 est.): 2,614,000.
Chief Cities (1990 census): Jackson, the capital, 196,637; Biloxi, 46,319; Greenville, 45,226.
Government (1993): *Chief Officers*—governor, Kirk Fordice (R); lt. gov., Eddie Briggs (R). *Legislature*—Senate, 52 members; House of Representatives, 122 members.
State Finances (fiscal year 1991): *Revenue,* $5,794,000,000; *expenditure,* $5,171,000,000.
Personal Income (1992): $36,936,000,000; per capita, $14,128.
Labor Force (August 1993): *Civilian labor force,* 1,198,700; *unemployed,* 64,900 (5.4% of total force).
Education: *Enrollment* (fall 1991)—public elementary schools, 369,936; public secondary, 134,191; colleges and universities, 125,350. *Public school expenditures* (1990-91), $1,510,552,000.

The Legislature. The regular 90-day session of the state legislature ended May 2 with a record that was both praiseworthy and disappointing. Major successes included pay raises for state employees and teachers, tort reform, and creation of an intermediate court of appeals. A number of high-profile issues—including car-tag reform, reporting requirements for lobbyists, and term limitations for public officials—were left unresolved. A one-day special session held August 9 enacted legislation to replenish a depleted loan-assistance program for the state's expanding poultry industry.

Veto Dispute. Governor Fordice's April 20 line-item veto of more than $60 million from two bond bills angered many legislators, who claimed that such veto power applies exclusively to appropriations bills. The attorney general and the State Bond Commission supported that claim. Three lawmakers filed a suit in Hinds County Chancery Court seeking a judgment as to the constitutionality of the unprecedented vetoes. The court's judge ruled in favor of the legislators.

The Ayers Case. In September, Mississippi's landmark higher-education-desegregation lawsuit was set for retrial in February 1994. This action in the 18-year-old case came more than a year after the U.S. Supreme Court held that vestiges of segregation existed within the system and after litigants were unable to agree upon a plan to remedy the situation.

Other News. U.S. Attorney General Janet Reno directed the Department of Justice to probe a series of hanging deaths in Mississippi jails....Mississippi ended its fiscal year June 30 with a $156 million surplus, and tax revenues continued to run well ahead of projections....On October 1 the state's sovereign immunity expired, allowing citizens to sue in some cases of government negligence....Northeast Mississippi suffered a major economic setback in October when Congress killed funding for NASA's new shuttle booster scheduled for manufacture near Iuka.

DANA B. BRAMMER, *University of Mississippi*

MISSOURI

Floods that stretched from summer into fall inundated Missouri and monopolized the state's news in 1993. The Mississippi and Missouri rivers were quick to take hold and slow to relinquish their grasp, making Missouri the state to be hit the hardest by the flooding. Also making the headlines in 1993 was the conviction of former Missouri Attorney General William Webster on public-corruption charges.

The Flood. During the summer, it seemed as if the rain never would end and the rivers never would stop rising. By late fall, 101 of Missouri's 114 counties had been declared flood disaster areas. At least 31 persons died and tens of thousands were left homeless because of the flooding. Officials estimated that the flooding caused more than $4 billion in property and crop damage, prompting Gov. Mel Carnahan to call the Missouri General Assembly into special session.

Few places were spared. Near the town of Taylor, the Mississippi River grew from its usual width of about 3,000 ft (915 m) to 5.5 mi (8.8 km). In Jefferson City, the state capital, the Missouri River submerged roads into the city, effectively cutting it off from half the state. The flood stormed St. Joseph's water plant and left residents without water for days. (*See also* FEATURE ARTICLE, page 44.)

Politics. Former Attorney General William Webster pleaded guilty to federal charges of conspiracy and misapplication of state funds while in office. A judge imposed a two-year sentence on Webster, once a fast-rising Republican star who ran for governor in 1992. As attorney general, Webster gained national fame arguing before the U.S. Supreme Court against abortion and a patient's right to die.

St. Louis voters elected Democrat Freeman Bosley, Jr., as their mayor; he became the first African American to hold that post....The Mis-

© AP/Wide World

Democrat Freeman Bosley, Jr., St. Louis' Circuit Court clerk, and his wife celebrated in April 1993 as he became the first African American to be elected mayor of the city.

souri General Assembly approved a $310 million tax increase to reform and finance the state's education system.

Crime. Vietnam veteran James Johnson, who contended he suffered from war flashbacks, was convicted of first-degree murder and sentenced to die for a 1991 shooting spree. Johnson killed four law officers and a sheriff's wife. Four Palestinian men, one already in prison for killing his teenage daughter, were indicted in St. Louis for allegedly plotting terrorist acts. Federal prosecutors contended that the four were agents of terrorist Abu Nidal.

After the longest criminal trial in St. Louis history, Jerry Lewis-Bey, national sheikh of the Moorish Science Temple, and six others were sentenced to life in prison for organizing a drug and murder crime ring....Convicted serial killer Ray Copeland—at age 78 the oldest person on death row—died in prison after suffering a stroke.

Other News. The sparkling image of Branson, a booming tourist mecca, was tarnished after two independent investigations uncovered questionable construction and inspection practices....Terminally ill Christine Busalacchi, who had been in a persistent vegetative state since a 1987 car accident, died in March. Her father appealed to the Missouri Supreme Court for permission to remove her feeding tube....Trans World Airlines announced it was moving its headquarters to St. Louis from New York.

Sports. St. Louis, once considered the leading choice, lost in its bid for one of two National Football League expansion franchises. Football fans across the state, meanwhile, exulted in the arrival of legendary quarterback Joe Montana with the Kansas City Chiefs. And two eras came to an end for Kansas City Royals baseball fans, as 21-year veteran George Brett retired and beloved team owner Ewing Kauffman died of cancer.

LANE BEAUCHAMP, *"The Kansas City Star"*

MISSOURI • Information Highlights

Area: 69,697 sq mi (180 516 km²).

Population (July 1, 1992 est.): 5,193,000.

Chief Cities (1990 census): Jefferson City, the capital, 35,481; Kansas City, 435,146; St. Louis, 396,685; Springfield, 140,494; Independence, 112,301.

Government (1993): *Chief Officers*—governor, Mel Carnahan (D); lt. gov., Roger B. Wilson (D). *General Assembly*—Senate, 34 members; House of Representatives, 163 members.

State Finances (fiscal year 1991): *Revenue,* $10,002,000,000; *expenditure,* $9,254,000,000.

Personal Income (1992): $98,963,000,000; per capita, $19,058.

Labor Force (August 1993): *Civilian labor force,* 2,689,500; *unemployed,* 156,400 (5.8% of total force).

Education: *Enrollment* (fall 1991)—public elementary schools, 596,001; public secondary, 231,403; colleges and universities, 297,154. *Public school expenditures* (1990-91), $3,487,786,000.

MONTANA

The Montana legislature's attempts to change the state tax structure dominated events in 1993. But voter reluctance to accept the government changes left Montana with no significant tax reform and a sizable deficit at year's end.

Taxes. The biennial Montana legislature approved two laws to reform the state's tax structure. The bills were designed to raise part of the money needed to eliminate a state-budget deficit that officials believed would reach $336 million in 1993 and 1994. The remaining deficit was to be eliminated through spending cuts.

The first law set an election to ask Montana voters if they wanted a 4% general sales tax. At present, Montana had no general sales tax. Most of the state government was funded with revenue from income taxes, while local and county governments and schools generally got their money from taxes on property. While some of the revenue from the proposed general sales tax was intended to reduce the budget deficit, much of it would have replaced revenue from an associated decrease in property taxes and income taxes.

The second law would increase income taxes by about 10%, with all of the annual $72.2 million in new revenue going to the state government. The income-tax increase, retroactive to the beginning of 1993, was to take effect only if voters rejected the 4% general sales tax in June, however, which they did by a margin of 74% to 26%.

By the end of summer, Missoula law professor Rob Natelson, leading a group called Montanans for Better Government, gathered enough petition signatures to require a vote on the income-tax increase. By mid-September the group had gathered enough signatures to block the state from collecting the additional tax until after the vote, which was scheduled for November 1994. The validity of the petition drive was challenged in lawsuits, however, because state law allows as few as 26,000 signers to force a

vote on any law passed by the legislature. Only 61,000 voter signatures were necessary to suspend the tax collection until after the vote. Gov. Marc Racicot called a special session of the legislature for November 1993 to deal with the deficit through cuts in government spending.

Legislation. State lawmakers also passed a new workers-compensation payroll tax to raise $54 million toward a shortage in the state insurance fund for injured workers. Two bills to mention gays specifically in antidiscrimination laws were killed by the legislature. Governor Racicot vetoed legislation that would have allowed hazardous-waste burning in the state.

Economy. Weather that set records for low temperatures and rainfall during the summer months accounted for a decrease in tourist traffic. Most noticeable was a decrease in traffic from the Midwest, where flooding in the Mississippi Valley kept residents occupied in their home states. While the damp summer accounted for excellent growth in dry-land grains, yields were expected to drop below projections because mud postponed the harvest for as long as six weeks in eastern regions of the state. Western Montana's logging industry continued to struggle under the constraints of environmental restrictions and a sagging demand.

Other. Conservative Supreme Court Justice R. C. McDonough retired after six years and was replaced by James Nelson of Great Falls....Ismay, the state's smallest incorporated town, changed its name to Joe, Montana, in honor of the National Football League quarterback.

ROBERT C. GIBSON
"The Billings Gazette"

MOROCCO

Morocco in 1993 held legislative elections, saw improvement in relations with Europe, and hosted Israel's prime minister.

Elections. The legislative elections resulted in strong gains by the left-wing opposition and the entry of women into the parliament for the first time in Morocco's history. The polling, which generally was seen as free and fair, originally was due in 1990 but was delayed because of the proposed United Nations (UN) referendum on the disputed territory of Western Sahara.

The two main opposition parties—the nationalist Istiqlal and the Union of Popular Socialist Parties (USFP)—settled old disputes and presented a common list of candidates. In the first round of voting for two thirds of the parliament seats in June, the two parties emerged with the largest number of seats, 91, while two other opposition parties won eight seats. But the opposition saw this early victory fade in the second indirect round of voting—cast by representatives from chambers of commerce, professional associations, and trade unions—in September. The remaining 111 seats went mostly

---

MONTANA • Information Highlights

Area: 147,046 sq mi (380 848 km²).

Population (July 1, 1992 est.): 824,000.

Chief Cities (1990 census): Helena, the capital, 24,569; Billings, 81,151; Great Falls, 55,097.

Government (1993): *Chief Officers*—governor, Marc Racicot (R); lt. gov., Dennis Rehberg (R). *Legislature*—Senate, 50 members; House of Representatives, 100 members.

State Finances (fiscal year 1991): *Revenue,* $2,359,000,000; *expenditure,* $2,384,000,000.

Personal Income (1992): $13,397,000,000; per capita, $16,264.

Labor Force (August 1993): *Civilian labor force,* 414,900; *unemployed,* 27,900 (6.7% of total force).

Education: *Enrollment* (fall 1991)—public elementary schools, 112,780; public secondary, 42,999; colleges and universities, 37,821. *Public school expenditures* (1990-91), $719,963,000.

On June 25, 1993, Moroccan voters cast their ballots to select legislators in the first round of a long-awaited election. A fusion of two leading opposition parties dominated the June balloting, but the incumbent center-right parties excelled in the September polling of local councillors.

© Jean Blondin/Sipa

to the center-right parties, which had formed the majority in the outgoing parliament.

The inconclusive results of the elections led to disarray among opposition parties that were divided over whether or not to participate in a future government. The situation was complicated when Abderrahman el-Yousoufi, secretary-general of the USFP, decided to step down after only 18 months as its head. King Hassan II met party leaders in early October to urge them to take part in a future government. The USFP and Istiqlal feared their credibility among voters could suffer if they entered into a coalition with the center-right. The king inaugurated the parliament on October 8 and a member from the center-right Constitutional Union was elected speaker.

After several meetings with the monarch, the USFP, Istiqlal, and a smaller opposition party announced on November 5 they would not be taking part in a future government because of electoral irregularities. The parties also complained they would not have a free hand to govern, as the king retained the right to nominate key ministers. King Hassan responded by accusing the parties of lacking the necessary experience to

occupy the major portfolios. Under the terms of a new constitution, adopted in September 1992, the new government would have greater powers than its predecessors, although the king retained control of defense and foreign policy.

Faced with the opposition's refusal to form a minority government, the king again turned to the outgoing prime minister, Karim Lamrani. Lamrani's new government was composed of nonpartisan technocrats. In response to criticism of the country's human-rights record, the king established a ministry for human rights.

Western Sahara. The year saw little progress toward the long-overdue United Nations-sponsored referendum on the disputed territory of the Western Sahara. The vote was scheduled for early in the year but was blocked by disagreements over voting lists between Morocco and the Polisario front. Both sides claim the former Spanish colony. The Polisario wanted the UN to use a 1974 Spanish census as the basis for the voting lists, while Morocco wanted the UN to accept 120,000 additional people which it says fled the territory during Spanish occupation.

In an attempt to break the deadlock, the UN organized a face-to-face meeting in July between representatives of the Polisario and Morocco in el Aaiún. But the talks broke up. Negotiations resumed in October under the auspices of the UN.

Foreign Relations. Morocco continued attempts to build favorable political and economic relations with Europe. Relations with the French, which had been strained by the presence of leading Moroccan dissidents in the country, improved after the election victory of the right in France. Relations were cemented by the visit of French Prime Minister Edouard Balladur on July 22.

In September, King Hassan received Israel's Prime Minister Yitzhak Rabin on his return to Israel from Washington after the signing of the PLO-Israeli peace accord. Other Israeli officials secretly had visited Morocco, which had been working behind the scenes to promote peace between Israel and Arab states.

Mosque. In 1993 in Casablanca, King Hassan inaugurated the world's second-largest mosque.

ALFRED HERMIDA
BBC's North Africa Correspondent

MOROCCO • Information Highlights

Official Name: Kingdom of Morocco.
Location: Northwest Africa.
Area: 172,413 sq mi (446 550 km²).
Population (mid-1993 est.): 28,000,000.
Chief Cities (mid-1990 est., incl. suburbs): Rabat, the capital, 1,427,000; Casablanca, 3,210,000; Fez, 1,012,000; Marrakech, 1,517,000.
Government: *Head of state,* Hassan II, king (acceded 1961). *Head of government,* Mohamed Karim Lamrani, prime minister (appointed Aug. 11, 1992). *Legislature* (unicameral)—Chamber of Representatives.
Monetary Unit: Dirham (8.879 dirhams equal U.S.$1, April 1993).
Gross Domestic Product (1991 U.S.$): $27,300,000,000.
Economic Indexes (1991): *Consumer Prices* (1980 = 100), all items, 217.7; food, 217.3. *Industrial Production* (1980 = 100), 143.
Foreign Trade (1992 U.S.$): *Imports,* $7,356,000,000; *exports,* $3,977,000,000.

© Gamma-Liaison

Steven Spielberg's 1993 blockbuster "Jurassic Park" told of a theme park featuring living dinosaurs. The movie, with its gripping special effects, captured the imagination of filmgoers and set box-office records.

MOTION PICTURES

In motion pictures, 1993 was the year of the dinosaur. Steven Spielberg's spectacular *Jurassic Park*, about a contemporary theme park with dinosaurs recreated from genetic remains, became an instant box-office rage, leading to stratospheric grosses. After 16 weeks in release, domestic theater receipts reached $326 million, and the foreign total soared to around $400 million. Thus the film already had topped *E.T.*'s record worldwide gross of $701 million and could reach a total of $750 million or more. Spielberg scored an incredible coup by also directing one of the most acclaimed dramas of the year, the powerful, deeply moving *Schindler's List*, a towering artistic work dramatizing the heroism of a Catholic factory owner who saved more than 1,000 Jews destined for Auschwitz.

The other side of the success-story coin was the fizzling of *Last Action Hero*, another intended summer blockbuster from Hollywood. The film, starring Arnold Schwarzenegger, failed with critics and the public alike. With a cost reputed to be some $80 million, by summer's end the film's domestic gross was less than $50 million.

Among 1993 films doing exceptionally well financially were the Disney Company's *Aladdin*, which by mid-October had taken in some $217 million in the United States; *The Fugitive*, a taut action thriller starring Harrison Ford, which grossed more than $167 million; *The Firm*, starring Tom Cruise, which topped $154 million; and

Sleepless in Seattle, a romantic story costarring Tom Hanks and Meg Ryan, which reached some $119 million. Others joining the $100 million club were *In the Line of Fire*, starring Clint Eastwood; and *Indecent Proposal*, which raised the question of whether a woman, played by Demi Moore, would sleep with a rich tycoon, portrayed by Robert Redford, for $1 million.

Artistic Triumphs. With the three-hour film *Short Cuts*, iconoclastic director Robert Altman examined groups of Americans leading lives in emotional turmoil, brilliantly juxtaposing their stories in a film that was at once entertaining and disturbing. *Short Cuts* was honored with the opening-night berth at the New York Film Festival. The Film Society of Lincoln Center announced it would honor Altman in 1994 as the latest cinema great in its pantheon of directors and stars who are celebrated at a gala tribute each spring. Coming after his much-praised *The Player*, Altman's latest gave fresh impetus to his career.

Another high-quality work was *The Age of Innocence*, based on the Edith Wharton novel. It was a triumph for director Martin Scorsese, who convincingly broadened his range. Perhaps the classiest film of the year was Kenneth Branagh's *Much Ado About Nothing*, an exuberant Shakespeare adaptation enlivened by the performances of director Branagh and Emma Thompson. Another excellent film was *The Joy Luck Club*, taken from Amy Tan's best-selling novel.

Robert De Niro, one of the United States' top actors, showed that he could have a whole

new career as a director. His *A Bronx Tale*, in which he also took a leading role, was applauded for its surefooted realization of the memoir by Chazz Palminteri, who also starred and wrote the screenplay. Actor Morgan Freeman also turned director with *Bopha!*, dramatizing the life of a family under South Africa's apartheid. Danny Glover and Alfre Woodard starred.

Peter Weir directed *Fearless*, which examined what happens to survivors of an air crash. Ted Turner Pictures originally envisioned *Gettysburg* as a television series, but the depiction of the Civil War battle was so impressive that New Line Cinema released it as a theatrical film. *Rising Sun*, a vigorous and enjoyable action film from Michael Crichton's novel, starred Sean Connery and Wesley Snipes. Woody Allen reprised his flair for comedy with *Manhattan Murder Mystery*. Allen and costar Diane Keaton were spirited and funny as a couple prying into a possible murder next door.

Kevin Kline excelled in two roles—as U.S. president and his double—in the satire *Dave*. Director Agnieszka Holland offered *The Secret Garden*, a well-received adaptation of Frances Hodgson Burnett's classic novel. Disney dared an unusual animation feature—Tim Burton's ghoulish and original *The Nightmare Before Christmas*.

Year-end Crush. As usual, many films aiming high were released near year's end in hope of capturing holiday business and being remembered at Oscar time. Among these in 1993 were Ismail Merchant and James Ivory's *The Remains of the Day*, with Anthony Hopkins and Emma Thompson, and Alan J. Pakula's *The Pelican Brief*, from the John Grisham novel, starring Julia Roberts and Denzel Washington.

Other late dramatic entries included Oliver Stone's *Heaven and Earth*, rooted in the Vietnam experience; Brian De Palma's *Carlito's Way*, with Al Pacino playing a drug lord; *A Perfect World*, with Clint Eastwood and Kevin Costner in an action thriller directed by Eastwood; *Shadowlands*, teaming Debra Winger and Anthony Hopkins and directed by Richard Attenborough; Jonathan Demme's *Philadelphia*, starring Tom Hanks in a drama about AIDS; and *Six Degrees of Separation*, based on John Guare's play.

Lighter fare included Robin Williams disguised as an English nanny in *Mrs. Doubtfire;* the sequel *Addams Family Values;* a remake of *The Three Musketeers* with Charlie Sheen, Kiefer Sutherland, and Oliver Platt; and *Beethoven's 2nd*, reuniting Charles Grodin with his troublesome St. Bernard.

Impressive Imports. Two of the year's very best films came from abroad. China's *Farewell My Concubine*—showcased by the New York Film Festival and Toronto's Festival of Festivals—was a sprawling, exquisitely photographed epic focusing on the personal lives of Chinese opera stars. China at first banned the film, then relented after some cuts were made.

Also acclaimed was *The Piano*, New Zealand director Jane Campion's film in which U.S. actress Holly Hunter starred. Hunter won the best-actress award at the Cannes Film Festival, and the movie shared the Palme d'Or grand prize with *Farewell My Concubine*.

The Scent of The Green Papaya, a subtle film by Vietnamese director Tran Anh Hung, portrayed the life of a servant and the families for whom she worked in Saigon from 1951 to 1961. The French film *The Accompanist*, directed by Claude Miller, depicted a love story involving an opera singer during World War II and the experiences of her young accompanist. A first feature by director Carlo Carlei of Italy established him as a talented newcomer. His *Flight of the Innocent* grippingly followed the plight of a boy caught in warfare over drugs. Veteran Italian filmmaker brothers Paolo and Vittorio Taviani made the visually stunning *Fiorile*, about successive generations of a controversial family. *Like Water for Chocolate*, a Mexican saga about love, family intrigue, and food, achieved popularity. Actress Liv Ullmann turned director with *Sofie*, a moving drama about a Jewish family in Denmark. Another of the year's best was *Guelwaar*, a masterly and revealing contemporary drama from Senegal by director Ousmane Sembene.

In France complaints accelerated against domination of the market by U.S. films, while French films had limited reciprocal opportunities. But there was little prospect for improvement, as distributors were wary of presenting subtitled films to mainstream U.S. audiences.

English-language imports fared better in the United States, but still struggled. *The Snapper*, a charming comedy from England, was challenging because of its sometimes hard-to-decipher accents. *Bad Behaviour*, a hilarious English comedy about family life, benefited from cleverly daft performances by Stephen Rea and Sinead Cusack. *Orlando*, adapted by director-writer Sally Potter from Virginia Woolf, wittily examined the role of women through the centuries. And Mike Leigh's *Naked* grimly depicted the life of a disturbed, angry London drifter.

Independent Voices. Audiences who find pleasure in films not in the Hollywood mainstream were rewarded by many special efforts in 1993. Steven Soderbergh (*sex, lies, and videotape*) switched gears to write and direct *King of the Hill*, a drama about a boy struggling to survive in the 1930s Depression. Victor Nunez wrote and directed *Ruby in Paradise*, about a young woman (played by Ashley Judd) trying to establish herself in Florida. Franz Kafka's *The Trial* was given a new adaptation that stood in sharp contrast to Orson Welles' baroque version. Harold Pinter's powerful script stressed realistic Kafka for the film directed by David Jones.

One of 1993's most enjoyable films was The Berlin International Film Festival cowinner *The Wedding Banquet*, a U.S.-Taiwan coproduction set in New York, and exploding in complications

MOTION PICTURES | 1993

THE ACCOMPANIST. Director, Claude Miller; screenplay by Miller and Luc Beraud, based on the novel by Nina Berberova. With Richard Bohringer, Ellena Safonova, Romane Bohringer.

ADDAMS FAMILY VALUES. Director, Barry Sonnenfeld; screenplay by Paul Rudnick, based on characters created by Charles Addams. With Anjelica Huston, Raul Julia, Christopher Lloyd, Christina Ricci.

THE AGE OF INNOCENCE. Director, Martin Scorsese; screenplay by Jay Cocks and Scorsese, based on the novel by Edith Wharton. With Daniel Day-Lewis, Michelle Pfeiffer, Winona Ryder.

THE BEVERLY HILLBILLIES. Director, Penelope Spheeris; screenplay by Lawrence Konner, Mark Rosenthal, Jim Fisher, Jim Staahl, based on the television series created by Paul Henning. With Jim Varney, Erika Eleniak, Cloris Leachman, Lily Tomlin, Dabney Coleman.

BLUE. Director, Krzysztof Kieslowski; screenplay by Kieslowski and Krysztof Piesiewicz. With Juliette Binoche, Benoit Regent, Florence Pernel.

BOPHA! Director, Morgan Freeman; screenplay by Brian Bird and John Wierick, based on the play by Percy Mtwa. With Danny Glover.

BOXING HELENA. Written and directed by Jennifer Chambers Lynch, based on a story by Phillipe Caland. With Julian Sands, Sherilyn Fenn, Art Garfunkel.

A BRONX TALE. Director, Robert De Niro; screenplay by Chazz Palminteri. With Robert De Niro, Chazz Palminteri, Lillo Brancato, Francis Capra.

CARLITO'S WAY. Director, Brian De Palma; screenplay by David Koepp, based on the novels *Carlito's Way* and *After Hours* by Edwin Torres. With Al Pacino, Sean Penn, Penelope Ann Miller.

COMBINATION PLATTER. Director, Tony Chan; screenplay by Edwin Baker and Chan. With Jeff Lau, Colleen O'Brien.

DANGEROUS GAME. Director, Abel Ferrara; screenplay by Nicholas St. John. With Harvey Keitel, Madonna.

A DANGEROUS WOMAN. Director, Stephen Gyllenhaal; screenplay by Naomi Foner, based on a novel by Mary McGarry Morris. With Debra Winger, Barbara Hershey.

DAVE. Director, Ivan Reitman; screenplay by Gary Ross. With Kevin Kline, Sigourney Weaver, Frank Langella, Ben Kingsley, Charles Grodin, Faith Prince.

DENNIS THE MENACE. Director, Nick Castle; screenplay by John Hughes, based on characters created by Hank Ketcham. With Walter Matthau, Mason Gamble.

ETHAN FROME. Director, John Madden; screenplay by Richard Nelson, based on the novella by Edith Wharton. With Liam Neeson, Patricia Arquette, Joan Allen.

FALLING DOWN. Director, Joel Schumacher; screenplay by Ebbe Roe Smith. With Michael Douglas, Robert Duvall, Barbara Hershey, Lois Smith, Tuesday Weld.

FAREWELL, MY CONCUBINE. Director, Chen Kaige; screenplay by Lillian Lee and Lu Wei, from the novel by Lee. With Leslie Cheung, Zhang Fengyi, Gong Li.

FATAL INSTINCT. Director, Carl Reiner; screenplay by David O'Malley. With Armand Assante, Sherilyn Fenn, Kate Nelligan, Sean Young, Tony Randall.

FEARLESS. Director, Peter Weir; screenplay by Rafael Yglesias, based on his novel. With Jeff Bridges.

THE FIRM. Director, Sydney Pollack; screenplay by David Rabe, Robert Towne, and David Rayfiel, based on the novel by John Grisham. With Tom Cruise, Jeanne Tripplehorn, Gene Hackman, Holly Hunter, Hal Holbrook.

FLESH AND BONE. Written and directed by Steve Kloves. With Dennis Quaid, Meg Ryan, James Caan.

FLIGHT OF THE INNOCENT. Director, Carlo Carlei; screenplay by Carlei and Gualtiero Rosella. With Federico Pacifici, Manuel Colao, Jacques Perrin, Francesca Neri.

THE FUGITIVE. Director, Andrew Davis; screenplay by Jeb Stuart and David Twohy, based on characters created by Roy Huggins. With Harrison Ford, Tommy Lee Jones.

GEORGE BALANCHINE'S 'THE NUTCRACKER.' Director, Emile Ardolino; adapted from the stage production by Peter Martins. With Macaulay Culkin, Darci Kistler.

GERONIMO. Director, Walter Hill; screenplay by John Milius and Larry Gross, from a story by Milius. With Wes Studi, Jason Patric, Gene Hackman, Robert Duvall.

GETTYSBURG. Written and directed by Ronald F. Maxwell, based on a novel by Michael Shaara. With Tom Berenger, Martin Sheen, Jeff Daniels, Richard Jordan.

THE GOOD SON Director, Joseph Ruben; screenplay by Ian McEwan. With Macaulay Culkin, Elijah Wood.

GRUMPY OLD MEN. Director, Donald Petrie; screenplay by Mark Steven Johnson. With Jack Lemmon, Walter Matthau.

GUILTY AS SIN. Director, Sidney Lumet; screenplay by Larry Cohen. With Rebecca De Mornay, Don Johnson.

HEAVEN AND EARTH. Written and directed by Oliver Stone, based on the books *When Heaven and Earth Changed Places* by Le Ly Hayslip with Jay Wurts, and *Child of War, Woman of Peace* by Hayslip and James Hayslip. With Tommy Lee Jones, Joan Chen, Haing S. Ngor, Hiep Thi Le.

HOUSEHOLD SAINTS. Director, Nancy Savoca; screenplay by Savoca and Richard Guay, based on the novel by Francine Prose. With Tracey Ullman.

IN THE LINE OF FIRE. Director, Wolfgang Petersen; screenplay by Jeff Maguire. With Clint Eastwood, John Malkovich, Rene Russo, Dylan McDermott.

IN THE NAME OF THE FATHER. Director, Jim Sheridan; screenplay by Terry George and Sheridan. With Daniel Day-Lewis, Emma Thompson, Pete Postlethwaite.

THE JOY LUCK CLUB. Director, Wayne Wang; screenplay by Amy Tan and Ronald Bass, based on the novel by Tan. With Kieu Chinh, Tsai Chin, France Nuyen.

JURASSIC PARK. Director, Steven Spielberg; screenplay by Michael Crichton and David Koepp, based on the novel by Crichton. With Sam Neill, Laura Dern, Jeff Goldblum, Richard Attenborough.

KING OF THE HILL. Director, Steven Soderbergh; based on the memoir by A. E. Hotchner. With Jesse Bradford, Karen Allen, Jeroen Krabbe, Lisa Eichhorn.

LAST ACTION HERO. Director, John McTiernan; screenplay by Shane Black and David Arnott, based on a story by Zak Penn and Adam Leff. With Arnold Schwarzenegger.

LIKE WATER FOR CHOCOLATE. Director, Alfonso Arau; screenplay by Laura Esquivel. With Lumi Cavazos.

LOST IN YONKERS. Director, Martha Coolidge; screenplay by Neil Simon, based on his play. With Richard Dreyfuss, Mercedes Ruehl, Irene Worth.

M. BUTTERFLY. Director, David Cronenberg; screenplay by David Henry Hwang, based on his play. With Jeremy Irons, John Lone, Barbara Sukowa, Ian Richardson.

MANHATTAN MURDER MYSTERY. Director, Woody Allen; screenplay by Allen and Marshall Brickman. With Woody Allen, Diane Keaton, Anjelica Huston, Alan Alda.

MENACE II SOCIETY. Directors, the Hughes Brothers; screenplay by Tyger Williams, based on a story by Allen Hughes, Albert Hughes, and Williams. With Tyrin Turner.

In "The Age of Innocence," Daniel Day-Lewis and Winona Ryder are husband and wife. The period film was considered a departure for its noted director Martin Scorsese.

© Sygma

© S. Vaughan/Sygma

Harrison Ford (above) plays the title role in "The Fugitive," a summer hit based on the long-running TV series. It was one of two major 1993 films derived from television.

MRS. DOUBTFIRE. Director, Chris Columbus; screenplay by Randi Mayem Singer and Leslie Dixon, based on *Alias Madame Doubtfire* by Anne Fine. With Robin Williams.

MUCH ADO ABOUT NOTHING. Director, Kenneth Branagh; adapted by Branagh from Shakespeare's play. With Kenneth Branagh, Emma Thompson, Denzel Washington.

MY LIFE. Written and directed by Bruce Joel Rubin. With Michael Keaton, Nicole Kidman.

ORLANDO. Written and directed by Sally Potter, based on the Virginia Woolf novel. With Tilda Swinton.

THE PELICAN BRIEF. Written and directed by Alan Pakula, from the novel by John Grisham. With Julia Roberts, Denzel Washington, Sam Shepard.

A PERFECT WORLD. Director, Clint Eastwood; screenplay by John Lee Hancock. With Clint Eastwood, Kevin Costner, Laura Dern, T. J. Lowther.

PHILADELPHIA. Director, Jonathan Demme; screenplay by Ron Nyswaner. With Tom Hanks, Denzel Washington, Jason Robards, Mary Steenburgen, Antonio Banderas.

THE PIANO. Written and directed by Jane Campion. With Holly Hunter, Harvey Keitel, Sam Neill, Anna Paquin.

POSSE. Director, Mario Van Peebles; screenplay by Sy Richardson and Dario Scardapane. With Mario Van Peebles, Stephen Baldwin, Melvin Van Peebles.

THE REMAINS OF THE DAY. Director, James Ivory; screenplay by Ruth Prawer Jhabvala, based on the novel by Kazuo Ishiguro. With Anthony Hopkins, Emma Thompson, Christopher Reeve, James Fox, Tim Pigott-Smith.

RICH IN LOVE. Director, Bruce Beresford; screenplay by Alfred Uhry, based on the novel by Josephine Humphreys. With Albert Finney, Jill Clayburgh.

RISING SUN. Director, Philip Kaufman; screenplay by Kaufman, Michael Crichton, Michael Backes, based on the novel by Crichton. With Sean Connery, Wesley Snipes, Harvey Keitel, Ray Wise, Cary-Hiroyuki Tagawa.

THE SAINT OF FORT WASHINGTON. Director, Tim Hunter; screenplay by Lyle Kessler. With Matt Dillon, Danny Glover.

SCHINDLER'S LIST. Director, Steven Spielberg; screenplay by Steven Zaillian, based on the novel by Thomas Keneally. With Liam Neeson, Ben Kingsley, Ralph Fiennes.

SEARCHING FOR BOBBY FISCHER. Written and directed by Steven Zaillian. With Max Pomeranc, Joe Mantegna, Joan Allen, Ben Kingsley.

THE SECRET GARDEN. Director, Agnieszka Holland; screenplay by Caroline Thompson, based on the book by Frances Hodgson Burnett. With Kate Maberly, Maggie Smith, Heydon Prowse, John Lynch, Laura Crossley.

SHADOWLANDS. Director, Richard Attenborough; screenplay by William Nicholson, based on his play. With Anthony Hopkins, Debra Winger.

SHORT CUTS. Director, Robert Altman; screenplay by Altman and Frank Barhydt, based on the writings of Raymond Carver. With Andie MacDowell, Bruce Davison, Jack Lemmon, Julianne Moore, Anne Archer, Fred Ward, Tim Robbins, Annie Ross, Lori Singer, Lily Tomlin, Tom Waites, Frances McDormand, Peter Gallagher, Jennifer Jason Leigh, Chris Penn, Lyle Lovett, Buck Henry.

SIX DEGREES OF SEPARATION. Director, Fred Schepisi; screenplay by John Guare from his play. With Donald Sutherland, Stockard Channing, Will Smith.

SLEEPLESS IN SEATTLE. Director, Nora Ephron; screenplay by Ephron, David S. Ward, and Jeff Arch. With Tom Hanks, Meg Ryan.

SLIVER. Director, Phillip Noyce; screenplay by Joe Eszterhas, based on the novel by Ira Levin. With Sharon Stone, William Baldwin, Tom Berenger.

THE SNAPPER. Director, Stephen Frears; screenplay by Roddy Doyle from his novel. With Colm Meaney, Tina Kellegher.

SOFIE. Director, Liv Ullmann; screenplay by Ullmann and Peter Poulsen. With Karen-Lise Mynster.

SOMMERSBY. Director, Jon Amiel; screenplay by Nicholas Meyer and Sarah Kernochan; story by Meyer and Anthony Shaffer, based on the film *The Return of Martin Guerre.* With Jodie Foster, Richard Gere.

SON OF THE PINK PANTHER. Director, Blake Edwards; screenplay by Edwards, Madeline Sunshine, and Steve Sunshine. With Roberto Benigni.

STRICTLY BALLROOM. Director, Baz Luhrmann; screenplay by Luhrmann and Andrew Bovell. With Paul Mercurio, Tara Morice.

THE SUMMER HOUSE. Director, Waris Hussein; screenplay by Martin Sherman. With Joan Plowright, Julie Walters, Jeanne Moreau.

THIS BOY'S LIFE. Director, Michael Caton-Jones; screenplay by Robert Getchell, based on the book by Tobias Wolff. With Robert De Niro, Ellen Barkin, Leonardo DiCaprio.

THE THREE MUSKETEERS. Director, Stephen Herek; screenplay by David Loughery, based on the novel by Alexandre Duma. With Charlie Sheen, Kiefer Sutherland, Chris O'Donnell, Oliver Platt.

TIM BURTON'S THE NIGHTMARE BEFORE CHRISTMAS. Director, Henry Selick; screenplay by Caroline Thompson; devised and coproduced by Tim Burton. (animated)

THE TRIAL. Director, David Jones; screenplay by Harold Pinter, based on the novel by Franz Kafka. With Kyle MacLachlan, Anthony Hopkins, Jason Robards.

UNDERCOVER BLUES. Director, Herbert Ross; screenplay by Ian Abrams. With Kathleen Turner, Dennis Quaid.

VISIONS OF LIGHT: THE ART OF CINEMATOGRAPHY. Directors, Arnold Glassman, Todd McCarthy, and Stuart Samuels. (documentary)

THE WEDDING BANQUET. Director, Ang Lee; screenplay by Lee, Neil Peng, and James Schamus. With May Chin, Winston Chao.

WHAT'S EATING GILBERT GRAPE. Director, Lasse Hallström; screenplay by Peter Hedges from his novel. With Johnny Depp, Leonardo DiCaprio, Mary Steenburgen, Juliette Lewis.

WHAT'S LOVE GOT TO DO WITH IT. Director, Brian Gibson; screenplay by Kate Lanier, based on *I, Tina* by Tina Turner. With Angela Bassett, Laurence Fishburne.

WRESTLING ERNEST HEMINGWAY. Director, Randa Haines; screenplay by Steve Conrad. With Robert Duvall, Richard Harris, Shirley MacLaine.

as a gay Chinese-American man marries a young woman from China to help her get a green card. Another film dealing with immigrants was young director Tony Chan's original, funny, and compassionate *Combination Platter*.

Director Nancy Savoca focused on family life in New York's Little Italy in the 1950s in *Household Saints*. Richard Wilson, Myron Meisel, and Bill Krohn took footage that Orson Welles had shot in Brazil and emerged with *It's All True: Based on an Unfinished Film by Orson Welles*, unveiled at the New York Film Festival.

Robert Rodriguez must be credited with the most daring achievement: With only $7,000, he made *El Mariachi*, a satirical action film shot in Mexico. The piece was picked up by Columbia Pictures. Another independent work that commanded attention was *Menace II Society*, a searing look at gang warfare in Los Angeles by twin brothers Allen and Albert Hughes. *Searching for Bobby Fischer*, directed by Steven Zaillian, was a creative drama about pressures on a child chess genius.

Two exceptional documentaries highlighted the year. *The War Room* was an inside look at Bill Clinton's presidential campaign, captured by D. A. Pennebaker and Chris Hegedus. *Aileen Wuornos: Selling of a Serial Killer*, directed by Nick Broomfield, chillingly revealed the commercial exploitation of Wuornos, a prostitute and lesbian condemned to death for murder in Florida after admitting to seven killings that she claimed were in self-defense.

Business. Film companies continued to reposition themselves through important acquisitions or mergers. The Turner Broadcasting System made a major move by arranging to buy Castle Rock Entertainment and New Line Cinema Corporation for a total of some $600 million in cash and stock. Time Warner owns 20.6% of Turner, and Sony, which owns Columbia, owns 45% of Castle Rock.

A fierce battle broke out for control of Paramount Communications Inc. A deal seemed set when Viacom Inc. was to acquire Paramount for $8.2 billion in what *The Wall Street Journal* said would be the creation of "a multimedia behemoth." However, the revelation that Paramount was for sale triggered further competition—notably by QVC Network Inc. At a later stage, Paramount agreed in December to merge with QVC, but the issue remained unresolved at year's end.

WILLIAM WOLF, *New York University*

MOZAMBIQUE

After nearly 16 years of devastating civil war, Mozambique, one of the world's poorest countries, took tentative steps in 1993 to maintain and extend the general peace accord signed in late 1992 between the Front for the Liberation of Mozambique (Frelimo) government and rebels of the Mozambique National Resistance (MNR or Renamo). While war-weary Mozambicans desperately wanted the uneasy peace to succeed, the country faced numerous challenges.

By late 1993, not one soldier had shown up at any of the United Nations (UN) established checkpoints, in part because of the late arrival of UN troops but also because of continuing political maneuvering between Renamo and Frelimo. When UN-supervised demobilization finally begins, an estimated 20,000 Renamo fighters and 62,000 government troops will be processed.

UN Operation. The UN's Operation in Mozambique (UNOMOZ) included committing more than 6,000 troops and additional support units from various countries. The UN was reputed to be spending $1 million-$2 million per day for peacekeeping operations to prepare the country for democratic elections and for the distribution of emergency food aid. Other international donors warned of a possible suspension of aid unless more progress is made. Hopeful signs included the return of hundreds of thousands of Mozambican refugees from neighboring countries and the resettlement of large numbers of internally displaced persons. Relief agencies predicted that, as a result of the resettlement and improved rainfall, only 1.2 million Mozambicans would require emergency food aid in 1993—a considerable improvement over recent years. On the other hand, the absorption of so many refugees in so short a time period could pose problems.

The UN operation in Mozambique, which was supposed to have ended on Oct. 31, 1993, was extended as a result of a breakthrough in the negotiations between Mozambican President Alberto Chissano and Renamo leader Afonso Dhlakama in late August over problems raised concerning the impartiality of the police and the state-owned media and the nature of regional administration. Renamo, in addition, was demanding millions of dollars to complete its transformation from a guerrilla movement into a political party. Elections scheduled for 1993 were postponed until 1994 at the request of all the major parties to the dispute, who agreed that former combatants must be integrated into a united army and all other forces demobilized first.

N. BRIAN WINCHESTER and PATRICK O'MEARA
Indiana University

MOZAMBIQUE • Information Highlights

Official Name: Republic of Mozambique.
Location: Southeastern coast of Africa.
Area: 309,494 sq mi (801 590 km²).
Population (mid-1993 est.): 15,300,000.
Chief City (1987 est.): Maputo, the capital, 1,006,765.
Government: *Head of state*, Joaquím A. Chissano, president (took office November 1986). *Head of government*, Mário da Graça Machungo, prime minister (took office July 1986). *Legislature* (unicameral)—People's Assembly.
Gross Domestic Product (1991 est. U.S.$): $1,700,000,000.

MUSIC

During 1993 orchestras everywhere were being squeezed anew financially; the Italian mezzo-soprano Cecilia Bartoli reached new heights of stardom as she made her U.S. stage debut; ground finally was broken for the Rock and Roll Hall of Fame and Museum in Cleveland, OH, and Dennis Barre was named director of the Hall of Fame; the renowned tenors Plácido Domingo and Luciano Pavarotti marked their silver jubilees with the New York Metropolitan Opera; and country music gained new levels of respectability and popularity across the United States (*see* FEATURE ARTICLE, page 52). Meanwhile a September 1993 statistical profile in *U.S. News & World Report* pointed out that 16% of the U.S. population had attended an opera or classical-music performance in the previous 12 months; that opera attendance had grown by 35% in the ten-year period 1983-92; and that *The Barber of Seville* was the most widely produced opera.

Classical

The classical-music world tends to change only gradually from year to year, with each season bringing its share of premieres and revivals, tours by renowned orchestras and star soloists, and even the occasional fad. Of course, financial concerns are virtually always in the air, given the expense of running orchestras that employ more than 100 musicians year-round, or of presenting fully staged operas. In 1993 financial worries seemed more pressing than usual, and not only in the United States. In Germany, where government largess had kept the arts afloat, the strains of reunification and the pressures of a recession have led to deep cuts. Italy, too, cut back funding to its opera houses, heretofore considered national treasures. And in England the trend of recent years toward diminishing government support continued apace, leaving London's major orchestras, as well as the country's opera companies, feeling imperiled (*see also* GREAT BRITAIN —*The Arts*).

Suddenly, European arts organizations that never had known life without government subsidy were being forced to emulate their U.S. counterparts in seeking corporate grants and private donations. They were hindered, to a degree, by the fact that European businesses were not structured yet for arts support. And their predicament robbed U.S. institutions of a favorite refrain about how much more enlightened foreign governments were in matters of arts support.

Renowned tenors Luciano Pavarotti (extreme right) and Plácido Domingo marked the 25th anniversary of their debuts with the New York Metropolitan Opera with a rare joint concert that opened the company's 1993-94 season. Both tenors sang roles new to their Met repertories.

U.S. Orchestras. Meanwhile, U.S. orchestras were scrambling to keep afloat amid growing wage and benefits demands by musicians, and an audience which—either because of financial restraints or demographic changes—had started to taper off. Several of the major orchestras had large deficits. The champion was the Cleveland Orchestra, with an accumulated deficit that topped $6 million.

In 1992 the American Symphony Orchestra League published a report that argued that orchestras had expanded their activities beyond their natural bounds. In 1993 the league presented a follow-up study that proclaimed that orchestras could save themselves by rethinking their repertories to reflect the ethnic diversities of the communities and to include more pops concerts and crossover endeavors. Many critics and orchestra managers argued that adopting the league's suggestions would mean jettisoning the classical-music tradition that orchestras were meant to keep alive.

In the meantime, orchestra managements faced greater labor unrest than usual as the 1993-94 season opened. The Kennedy Center Opera House Orchestra, which plays for the Washington Opera and for ballet and theater productions at the Kennedy Center, was on strike for more than a month. The Honolulu Symphony's and Buffalo Philharmonic's seasons were canceled. Disputes raged at the St. Paul (MN) Chamber Orchestra and the Milwaukee Symphony, and the Philadelphia Orchestra came close to calling its first strike since 1966.

Yet for all the financial hand-wringing, orchestral life went on. The New York Philharmonic celebrated its 150th anniversary with gala concerts, museum exhibitions, and commissioned works, including the world premiere of Olivier Messiaen's last work, "Eclairs sur l'Au-Delà." Kurt Masur, in his second season with the orchestra, continued to redefine the Philharmonic's sound, and was rewarded with both critical praise and popular support. The Philadelphia Orchestra, meanwhile, welcomed a new music director, Wolfgang Sawallisch, while the Boston Symphony celebrated the 20th anniversary of its relationship with Seiji Ozawa. And the San Francisco Symphony did something major that U.S. orchestras rarely do: It appointed an American, Michael Tilson Thomas, to be its music director.

Besides the Messiaen work in New York, notable additions to the repertory included Witold Lutoslawski's "Symphony No. 4," which was given its world premiere by the Los Angeles Symphony Orchestra; new "Flute Concertos" by Lowell Liebermann and William Bolcom, both given their world premieres by James Galway with the St. Louis Symphony; an "Oboe Concerto" by John Harbison, unveiled in San Francisco; and the first U.S. performances of Luciano Berio's "Continuo," offered by the Chicago Symphony. Berio also was named to the Charles Eliot Norton chair at Harvard University, and began his series of Norton lectures in October. His predecessors among composers include Leonard Bernstein, Igor Stravinsky, and Roger Sessions.

Composers. There seemed to be a welcome thaw in the decades-long cold war between composers and audiences. Composers who grew up listening to everything—the classics, rock 'n' roll, jazz, 12-tone music, and Minimalism—have come to their work undogmatically and have drawn uninhibitedly on all those influences. Thus, a composer like Christopher Rouse could speak to younger listeners in works like his "First Symphony" and "Bonham," which quote rock riffs from Led Zeppelin and Canned Heat, while at the same time winning unstinting respect from older composers. Rouse was awarded the 1993 Pulitzer Prize in music for his "Trombone Concerto."

The most peculiar fad of 1993, in fact, centered around an unlikely crowd pleaser, the Polish composer Henryk Górecki's "Symphony No. 3." This "Symphony of Sorrowful Songs," as it is subtitled, is a bleak, slow-moving, post-Minimal piece with texts (all sung in Polish) drawn from a 15th-century lament, a prayer scrawled on the wall of a Gestapo prison by an 18-year-old girl, and a Polish folk song. Górecki composed it in 1976. It was recorded several times, and part of it was used as the soundtrack to a French film, *Police*, in 1987. Yet, when a new recording conducted by David Zinman and featuring the young U.S. soprano Dawn Upshaw was released at the end of 1992, the piece took on a life of its own. The recording topped the classical charts in *Billboard* for much of the year. And in England it not only held fast to the top of the classical charts, but sold well enough to climb the pop charts.

Opera. The U.S. opera world was buffeted less severely by financial winds than the orchestra world, but shortages of cash took a toll there, too. Most notably, the country's second-largest company, the New York City Opera, was so strapped financially that what should have been a grand celebration of its 50th anniversary was celebrated modestly as the company worried about its future.

Still, the company's general director, Christopher Keene, held true to the City Opera's image in his programming. Besides giving the first New York performances of Sir Michael Tippett's *A Midsummer Marriage*, he marked the company's anniversary with three world premieres by U.S. composers. The results were mixed. Ezra Laderman's *Marilyn*, about Marilyn Monroe, was derided widely for a muddled and often rather silly libretto and ineffectual music. Lukas Foss' fairy-tale opera, *Griffelkin*—the story of a young devil who is sent to Earth to make mischief, but who ends up excommunicated from hell for doing a good deed—was somewhat better received. Foss wrote the work as a one-hour television opera for NBC in 1956, but later

Cecilia Bartoli, right, delighted audiences with her U.S. stage debut in the Houston Grand Opera's production of the "Barber of Seville." The 27-year-old Italian mezzo-soprano continued to record and also performed in the "Mostly Mozart Festival" at New York's Lincoln Center.

© Paul S. Howell/Gamma-Liaison

expanded it to full length. The consensus was that the expansions undercut the work's charms. That left *Esther*, an opera by Hugo Weisgall on the biblical Book of Esther. Composed in an entirely atonal style, it was a surprise success and showed that atonalism could yield emotionally direct and lyrical vocal music.

Elsewhere in the opera world, William Bolcom's *McTeague* drew lukewarm reviews at the Lyric Opera of Chicago, as did Philip Glass' *Orphée*—based on the Jean Cocteau film script—when it had its premiere at the American Repertory Theater in Boston. Daron Hagen's *Shining Brow*, a work about Frank Lloyd Wright, was considered a promising first effort when it had its premiere at the Madison (WI) Opera.

Laderman's *Marilyn* and Hagen's *Shining Brow* were among the latest examples of a recent operatic trend—building operas around contemporary (or nearly contemporary) figures. Past efforts of this kind included Anthony Davis' *X* (about Malcolm X), Philip Glass' *Satyagraha* (about Gandhi), and John Adams' *Nixon in China* and *The Death of Klinghoffer*. The latter dealt with the hijacking of the *Achille Lauro* and the murder of one of its passengers by Palestinian terrorists. In another of 1993's crop, the Arab-Israeli issue was explored from a different perspective. The composer Steve Reich and the video artist Beryl Korot presented their first theater work, *The Cave*. The title refers to the Cave of Machpelah in Hebron, where the biblical patriarch Abraham is believed to be buried. In the work, video interviews in which Israelis, Arabs, and Americans offer their own points of view about Abraham are woven into Reich's rhythmically spiky instrumental score.

Along similar lines, the electronic-music composer Morton Subotnick presented *Jacob's Room* at the American Music Theater Festival in Philadelphia. A multimedia work using projected images, a computer-generated musical score, and live vocals by Joan La Barbara, the piece draws on everything from Virginia Woolf to Plato to biblical texts in order to evoke the pain of the Holocaust and other recent historical tragedies.

Plentiful as new operas were, the larger companies stuck mainly to the tried and true. At the Metropolitan Opera, a disastrous new "psychological" production of Gaetano Donizetti's *Lucia di Lammermoor* was offset by an appealing new staging of Richard Wagner's *Die Meistersinger*, and a revival of the company's *Ring* cycle. The Lyric Opera of Chicago offered the first installments of a *Ring* as well.

The drawing card for the Houston Grand Opera's production of Gioacchino Rossini's *Barber of Seville* was the U.S. stage debut of Cecilia Bartoli, an Italian mezzo-soprano in her mid-20s whose recordings and recitals have won her a large and enthusiastic following in recent seasons. And the Santa Fe Opera drew sizable crowds for the first U.S. stagings of two early Kurt Weill works, *The Tsar Has His Photograph Taken* and *The Protagonist*, the latest offerings in the Kurt Weill revival that has been apace since the late 1970s.

In the world of starry soloists, Luciano Pavarotti was often in the news. Early in the year he canceled several U.S. and European engagements in order to undertake a weight-reduction program. When he emerged, he did not look notably trimmer, but he was in better shape vocally. In June he gave a free concert in New York City's Central Park, attended by an estimated 500,000 people and televised live around the world. And he and Plácido Domingo celebrated the 25th anniversary of their 1968 Metropolitan Opera debuts with a gala concert that opened the house's 1993-94 season.

Deaths. The contralto Marian Anderson, the first black singer to perform at the Met; pianist Mieczyslaw Horszowski; violinist Alexander Schneider; the flamenco guitarist Carlos Montoya; and conductors Erich Leinsdorf and Maurice Abravanel were among the important musicians who died during 1993. *See also* OBITUARIES.

ALLAN KOZINN, *"The New York Times"*

Popular and Jazz

Among the most significant events of 1993 in popular music were the festivities celebrating the January inauguration of U.S. President Bill Clinton. Performing at inaugural functions in Washington, DC, were Barbra Streisand, Fleetwood Mac, Michael Jackson, Judy Collins, Wynton Marsalis, and Soul Asylum. But this melting pot of musicians was not just an exercise in evoking a great mosaic; it also underscored the fact that Clinton is the first chief executive to grow up in a world with rock 'n' roll. The president is also a jazz buff, and later in 1993 he hosted a jazz concert at the White House, bringing out his saxophone to participate in an impromptu jam session.

The very fact that a baby boomer now was in the White House went a long way to explaining the increased diversity and segmentation of popular music. The term "rock 'n' roll," originally coined to characterize the music of teenage America, now could apply to music appealing to anyone from age 6 to 60. Little wonder, then, that one of 1993's biggest Broadway hits was a lavish version of The Who's late-1960s rock opera, *Tommy*.

This divergence of the marketplace, plus the recent linkage of chart positions to actual sales data in the trade magazine *Billboard*, made it relatively common for a major album to debut at the top of the charts. Among the year's Number 1 debuts were albums by country singer Garth Brooks, pop singer Billy Joel, the rap group Cypress Hill, and the rock band Aerosmith. Sales of country music nearly had doubled over the past two years, and now accounted for about 16.5% of the total (*see* FEATURE ARTICLE, page 52), but rap and so-called "alternative rock" were the choices of younger consumers.

Alternative Rock. Veteran observers of the pop scene were quick to recognize that the new "alternative bands" had clear stylistic predecessors. For while 1993's young bands were reaping the commercial success denied late-1970s punk groups, they also showed the influence of earlier rock acts. New releases by Pearl Jam (*Vs.*) and Nirvana (*In Utero*) proved that the multimillion-selling success of each group's previous album was not a fluke. Their music also showed that Pearl Jam was indebted stylistically to Led Zeppelin, while Nirvana owed more to The Who.

Other bands that flourished in the alternative boom were Belly, Smashing Pumpkins, Stone Temple Pilots, Urge Overkill, and Soul Asylum—which landed on the cover of *Rolling Stone* after years of relative obscurity. Another school of successful newer rock bands followed the hippie-like, improvisational model of the Grateful Dead. Bands working in this style included Blues Traveler, Spin Doctors, and Blind Melon.

Pop and Rock. The sweep of six Grammy awards by Eric Clapton's *Unplugged* (*see* BIOGRAPHY) underscored how an appearance on MTV's acoustic-concert program could reignite a career. Rod Stewart followed suit, scoring his biggest album in years with *Unplugged...And Seated.* Other acts releasing records drawn from *MTV Unplugged* included Neil Young, 10,000 Maniacs, and Arrested Development.

Concert promoters learned that older listeners could be attracted to high-priced concerts at relatively intimate venues. New York City's fall 1993 concert season was dominated by two monthlong runs—a show by Bette Midler and a career retrospective by Paul Simon that attracted attention by including a reunion with Simon's former partner, Art Garfunkel. Singer Tony Bennett won a Grammy for his album of songs associated with Frank Sinatra, *Perfectly Frank.*

© Sipa

Praised for its fresh and innovative take on rap music, the group Arrested Development (left) was presented with the 1993 Grammy Award for best new artist.

Sinatra, meanwhile, released his first album in more than a decade—*Duets*—featuring performances with singers ranging from Bennett to Bono of U2.

Film Soundtracks. Movie soundtracks continued to ring cash registers and bring additional marketing support to films. Whitney Houston's soundtrack to her hugely successful big-screen debut with Kevin Costner, *The Bodyguard*, sold more than 9 million copies in the United States alone, spurred by her hit rendition of an old Dolly Parton song, "I Will Always Love You." An even bigger surprise, however, was the Number 1 success of the soundtrack to *Sleepless in Seattle*, which featured romantic pop songs by such late singers as Jimmy Durante and Nat King Cole. Some genre-related soundtracks, including *Menace II Society* (rap) and *Pure Country* (country), proved to be more popular than the movies they accompanied.

Rap and Rhythm and Blues. Urban popular music continued to be dominated by rawboned rap and high-tech dance music, with various hybrids occupying a middle ground. The Los Angeles rapper Dr. Dre sold more than 3 million copies of *The Chronic*, making it the most popular hard-core rap album in history. Overall, so-called "gangsta" rap continued to be as controversial as it was popular, with some African-American activists complaining that the music promoted violence and disrespect for women. Highly regarded albums with more progressive views were released by rap groups like P.M. Dawn and De La Soul.

Other groups drew on more traditional music styles, like Boyz II Men and Tony Toni Toné, whose hit album declared that the trio were *Sons of Soul*. Janet Jackson continued as the queen of dance music with the tremendous success of her *janet.* album. Meanwhile, Jackson's usually reclusive brother Michael performed during halftime at pro football's 1993 Super Bowl, submitted to a live TV interview with Oprah Winfrey, then spent months on a world tour while dogged by U.S. headlines concerning allegations of child molestation. In November he abruptly canceled the tour and went into seclusion, citing an addiction to prescription painkillers.

Jazz. With a saxophone-playing president welcoming jazz musicians to the White House, and the Lincoln Center Jazz Orchestra touring the United States, jazz continued to cultivate its position in the cultural mainstream.

Two young artists emerged to wide acclaim in 1993. Joshua Redman, the Harvard-educated son of saxophonist Dewey Redman, established his own identity on the instrument with *Wish*, an album featuring an all-star group composed of Pat Metheny, Charlie Haden, and Billy Higgins. Cuban pianist Gonzalo Rubalcaba made his U.S. performing debut at Lincoln Center, playing in the solo, duet, and trio format. Critics were particularly impressed with the stylistic range of the classically trained pianist, who moved easily from playing ruminative solos in the style of

© Christian Ducasse/Gamma-Liaison

Veteran tenor saxophonist Joe Henderson had an impressive year. In addition to performing at two inaugural balls in January, he won a Grammy Award for best jazz instrumental solo.

Keith Jarrett to interpreting pieces by musicians from John Lennon to Ornette Coleman.

Deaths. The jazz world mourned the loss of trumpeter Dizzy Gillespie, the last major link to the birth of bebop. Gillespie was celebrated for creating music that consummated jazz's flirtations with Latin music.

Other losses to the music world included jazz keyboardist Sun Ra; country singer Conway Twitty; zydeco pioneer Alton Rubin, better known as Rockin' Dopsie; and rock guitarist Mick Ronson.

Industry Trends. The U.S. record industry stopped selling compact discs in the cardboard longbox that had come to be regarded as environmentally wasteful. After much discussion of various options, the industry began marketing CDs in the plastic "jewel box" used for packaging throughout the rest of the world.

Consumers showed little interest in two new audio formats designed to play and record digitally: the MiniDisc and the Digital Compact Cassette. An emerging question was how the so-called electronic highway ultimately would affect the distribution of recorded music. Blockbuster Entertainment and IBM investigated a cooperative venture that would let consumers order a recording that would be transferred electronically to the point of purchase, where a digital copy would be generated. The next step presumably would be home delivery, with digital music delivered over a phone or cable line and recorded for playback.

JOHN MILWARD
Freelance Music Writer and Critic

MYANMAR

In 1993, Myanmar tried to maintain a low profile on the international scene. Since strongman Gen. Ne Win resigned in 1988, Myanmar had been a pariah in the world community because of its human-rights record, its military crackdowns, and its refusal to honor the 1990 election results.

Political Oppression. The State Law and Order Restoration Committee (SLORC) continued its authoritarian rule. Nobel Prize winner and opposition-party leader Aung San Suu Kyi began a fourth year under house arrest. The last major dissident, former chairman of the National League for Democracy Aung Gyi, was jailed in April on the pretext of not paying an egg bill. Some observers linked his imprisonment to interviews he gave during one of the government's periodic efforts to court the Western press.

The SLORC also did little to soften its image at home and abroad as it sought to control the drafting of a new constitution. In January several hundred handpicked delegates from ethnic, political, and professional groups were assembled and removed from media and public attention, ostensibly to draft a constitution. Attendees disliked the junta's proposed version, which called for continued military leadership in a centralized authoritarian government. The convention ended in failure, and within days, followers of Aung Gyi were arrested, as were 33 students who were accused of distributing antigovernment propaganda.

Military leaders tried to mollify public opinion, particularly in other nations, but the junta did not reform its policies or loosen its control. Some reports speculated that more conciliatory leadership might be at hand, noting that the regular military promoted Lt. Gen. Maung Aye to be commander-in-chief of the army. He filled a vacancy left by Gen. Than Swe, who became supreme military commander and head of SLORC. Other appointments favored professional soldiers over the rival intelligence service headed by Lt. Gen. Kwin Nyunt—a protégé of the retired but still formidable Gen.

Ne Win. In September the SLORC lifted some martial-law provisions, including the curfew, and released 1,200 political prisoners. Some 1,000 others, including 300 Buddhist monks and 30 opposition members, still were in prison.

Economic Conditions. Poverty and inflation continued to plague the nation in 1993. The UN Development Program reported that prices of staples had tripled in less than five years; the enormous trade deficit was widening; and domestic production was down.

Ethnic Relations. Ethnic warfare in Myanmar has been serious for more than 40 years. The political forces shift frequently, most recently with the disintegration of the Maoist-led Communist Party of Burma (CPB). Ethnic groups control many border areas that are the leading producers of illicit opium and heroin. The Wa hill tribe, producers of more than 60% of the poppies used in the drug trade, offered to halt production if the government would grant political concessions and economic assistance. Secret talks were held with Kachin leaders, and other groups indicated a willingness to end fighting in exchange for a federal constitution allowing some ethnic autonomy. On October 2 the Kachins, the largest of the rebel ethnic factions, signed a cease-fire agreement with the government, which was expected to allow some limited control of their territory and the right to trade with China. The government was working on a similar agreement with the next largest group, the Karens.

International Relations. Myanmar took a defensive stand at a spring human-rights conference in Bangkok, arguing that other countries with different customs and values should not judge Asian nations on their human rights. However, it has been primarily Asian nations, such as Thailand and Japan—perhaps driven by a desire for influence and trade—that have urged Myanmar to improve its image by ending ethnic warfare and political repression.

India softened its sharp criticism of Myanmar's human-rights abuses, opting for "constructive engagement." India was hoping that if it neutralized the 14,000 Burmese exiles in India, Myanmar would do the same with the anti-Indian insurgents within its borders. India also feared that further isolation of Myanmar might increase the nation's dependency on China. Domestic and international interests were worried that China was trying to reassert its historical hegemony over Myanmar.

A February visit to Myanmar by China's Foreign Minister Qian Qichen was the first by a high-ranking Chinese since the political upheaval in 1988. The Chinese just had completed a strategically important, all-weather road linking the two countries. The SLORC had ordered large quantities of military hardware. More than $1 billion in trade was cementing the relationship between the two nations.

LINDA K. RICHTER, *Kansas State University*

MYANMAR • Information Highlights

Official Name: Union of Myanmar.
Location: Southeast Asia.
Area: 261,969 sq mi (678 500 km²).
Population (mid-1993 est.): 43,500,000.
Chief Cities (1983 census): Yangon (Rangoon), the capital, 2,513,023; Mandalay, 532,949.
Government: *Head of government,* Gen. Than Swe (took power April 23, 1992). *Legislature* (unicameral)—National Assembly.
Monetary Unit: Kyat (6.051 kyats equal U.S.$1, April 1993).
Gross Domestic Product (1991 est. U.S.$): $22,200,000,000.
Economic Index (1991): *Consumer Prices* (1980 = 100), all items, 386.7; food, 412.3.
Foreign Trade (1991 U.S.$): *Imports,* $616,000,000; *exports,* $412,000,000.

NEBRASKA

Flooding, agricultural woes, the sesquicentennial of the Oregon Trail, and, of course, college football dominated the news in Nebraska in 1993. Nebraska had the second-highest rise in personal income in the nation during the 1991-93 period, when personal income in the state rose 8.4% annually.

Flooding. Though Nebraska suffered less dramatic consequences from the Great Flood of '93 (*see* FEATURE ARTICLE, page 44) than its neighboring states to the East, flooding of the Missouri River and several smaller streams caused damage in many Nebraska counties from early spring to autumn. By mid-July, estimated damage to crops had reached more than $117 million, with millions of dollars more anticipated in destruction to utilities.

Late planting because of the wet spring weather, coupled with an early frost in some parts of the state, led to fears of a seriously reduced harvest.

Crime. A surprise development focused attention on the small town of Lyons in northeast Nebraska early in 1993 when the prime suspect in a six-year-old murder case was arrested in Florida. Gregory Webb, former Lyons police chief, had disappeared on Dec. 30, 1986, three days after the body of Anna Anton was found in a field 20 mi (32 km) north of Lyons. No clues to Webb's location had surfaced until a Florida man, who had seen the television show *Unsolved Mysteries*, called Nebraska state-patrol authorities and reported the fugitive's whereabouts. Webb pleaded innocent to charges in July.

Oregon Trail Sesquicentennial. Along with states from Missouri to Oregon, Nebraska took part in numerous observances of the 150th anniversary of the Oregon Trail. Chief among these was the Oregon Trail wagon train, which followed closely the main route of the original trail from spring to autumn. Three Nebraska

wagons joined in a train of approximately 15 vehicles, which entered the state along the Kansas border on May 19 and continued the 475-mi (764-km) segment of the journey until it crossed the Wyoming border on June 29.

Miscellaneous. Small Nebraska towns made news. A national Best Small Towns in America contest named the Sand Hills village of Cody, population 177, one of the seven best. Cody's slogan is "A Town Too Tough to Die." The town of Tarnov, population 61, celebrated a dubious distinction on August 16. Fifty years earlier, during World War II, Tarnov was bombed. Six practice bombs, all duds, were dropped mistakenly by the Army Air Corps, causing some damage but no casualties. The town of Gross, with nine residents, attracted some 3,000 people to its centennial celebrations.

In October, *Forbes* magazine reported that Omaha investor Warren Buffett, who became Nebraska's first billionaire only a few years earlier, almost had doubled his wealth in 1992-93—to $8.3 billion—and now was the richest person in the United States.

Big Red Football. A small section of the University of Nebraska's football stadium collapsed

Nebraskans joined in the celebrations marking the 150th anniversary of the Oregon Trail. For a cost of $20 per day, the adventurous could ride a wagon train, which closely followed the main route American pioneers took on their journey west.

© AP/Wide World

on May 17. The collapse was attributed to a flaw in the concrete. There were no injuries, but careful inspections of the entire stadium were made during the summer. The stadium was pronounced safe by the fall, and Husker fans showed no reluctance to being on hand as their team enjoyed an undefeated regular season.

WILLIAM E. CHRISTENSEN
Midland Lutheran College

NETHERLANDS

Economic difficulties dominated 1993 events in the Netherlands as they did in much of Europe.

Domestic and Economic Affairs. In the face of declining revenues, government leaders sharply reduced social-service expenditures and proposed major cuts in defense spending, including a reduction in compulsory military service from 12 to nine months and a reduction in personnel demands from 125,000 to 70,000 troops. These cuts would save an estimated $610 million per year and were made possible by the ending of the Cold War.

Disability-benefit rules were tightened as of August 1 in order to save more than $2 million. New definitions of incapacity to work were framed and medical examinations were made more rigorous to eliminate fraud. In some instances benefits were limited to 70% of the minimum wage rather than 70% of the last wage earned. Citizens were told that they may have to supplement national insurance with private policies. The government also stiffened enforcement of laws against the hiring of illegal immigrants.

The changes were not accepted without protest. The Ministry of Social Services was bombed. The junior party in the government coalition, the Labor Party, experienced considerable stress. At midyear two of its state secretaries were forced to resign in a controversy over their handling of educational policy and the unpopular social-security reforms.

NETHERLANDS • Information Highlights

Official Name: Kingdom of the Netherlands.
Location: Northwestern Europe.
Area: 14,413 sq mi (37 330 km²).
Population (mid-1993 est.): 15,200,000.
Chief Cities (Jan. 1, 1992): Amsterdam, the capital, 713,407; Rotterdam, 589,707; The Hague, the seat of government, 445,287.
Government: *Head of state*, Beatrix, queen (acceded April 30, 1980). *Head of government*, Ruud Lubbers, prime minister (took office Nov. 1982). *Legislature*—States General: First Chamber and Second Chamber.
Monetary Unit: Guilder (1.9271 guilders equal U.S.$1, Dec. 1, 1993).
Economic Indexes (1992): *Consumer Prices* (1980 = 100), all items, 137.1; food, 126.7. *Industrial Production* (1980 = 100), 120.
Foreign Trade (1992 U.S.$): *Imports*, $134,475,000,000; *exports*, $139,944,000,000.

Despite the hard times, Dutch union laborers still fared well. Their average combined hourly wages and benefits ranked below only those of West Germany and Sweden in 1992—$21.64 per hour, well above the figure of $15.89 for the United States or $17.79 for France. Their workweek averaged 39 hours, and they topped all groups with 41 paid holidays each year. Absenteeism averaged 8% of regular workdays.

European Community (EC) statistics for 1991 rated the Dutch economy as the seventh-largest in the EC, with a gross domestic product (GDP) of $287 billion, or 4.6% of the EC's total GDP.

Work began on a plan approved in 1990 to return about 600,000 acres (243 000 ha) of farmland into forests, wetlands, and lakes. This was being done because of fears that the centuries-old manipulation was wreaking havoc with the environment by causing a further sinking of the lowlands and pollution of fields and aquifers.

Euthanasia. After heated debate, the second chamber in February passed the most liberal euthanasia measure in Europe. While euthanasia officially remains illegal and carries a 12-year sentence, the amendment to the 1955 Disposal of the Dead act permits a doctor to administer euthanasia if a 28-point procedure is followed and documented. The guidelines say the patient must be in a "perpetual, unbearable, and hopeless" condition, although not necessarily terminally ill. The patient must have requested death repeatedly while in a lucid state of mind, and a second medical opinion is required.

Right-to-life groups compared the law to Nazi extermination of the disabled, and the Vatican delivered an official protest. The majority of the population, however, rejected such criticism. Surveys indicated that 78% of the people supported the right to ask for euthanasia, and only 11% of the nation's doctors would not participate in administering it.

Foreign Affairs. In February, in reaction to the crime wave disrupting St. Maarten, the Dutch government took direct control of that Caribbean dependency....The Netherlands, along with many other nations, signed a major new treaty banning the use, manufacture, or stockpiling of chemical weapons. The Organization for the Prohibition of Chemical Weapons, which was being established to monitor compliance procedures, would have its seat in the Hague.

A Dutch antinarcotics official kidnapped by Afghans was released in May after being held for more than three weeks....Four U.S. military bases in the Netherlands were listed for closure....A Dutch frigate participated in the multinational embargo of Haiti established in October.

JONATHAN E. HELMREICH, *Allegheny College*

NEVADA

A long legislative session, the opening of massive theme gaming resorts in Las Vegas,

the end of a seven-year drought, and a revitalized economy marked 1993 in Nevada.

Legislative Session. Following Gov. Robert Miller's emergency budget cuts of $144 million in July 1992, the state legislature passed an austere $6.2 billion budget during the last moments of the 1993 biennial session. Because the legislature and the governor had ruled out any major tax increases, new initiatives and programs were not considered.

The final budget included a $15.8 million increase for kindergarten through grade 12 public education and a $10 million decrease for the Nevada community-college and university system. State workers and Nevada's 25,000 public-school teachers received no raises for the 1993-95 biennium.

Reorganization. With a projected $2 billion shortfall, the State Industrial Insurance System (SIIS) was on the verge of bankruptcy. In an effort to reorganize it, the state Senate emphasized cutting workers' benefits. The Democratically controlled Assembly fought for higher taxes on employers. After an acrimonious standoff, the Senate's version prevailed.

Democratic Gov. Bob Miller proposed reorganizing the multitude of state agencies and boards into an umbrella of six super agencies with increased gubernatorial control. The approved plan differed significantly from the governor's, but still created six super agencies and permanently cut 1,482 vacant state jobs. The legislative session adjourned after 166 days, the second-longest session on record.

The Economy and Drought. Nevada's economic rebound was seen in 16 straight monthly increases in sales-tax revenues, with an 11.4% increase in August alone. Unemployment dropped to 6.9% in September and gaming taxes increased throughout the year at a double-digit pace. The economy grew at a 3.8% rate during the second quarter of 1993. Personal income increased by 11% in the June 1991-June 1993 period, the highest growth in the nation.

Above-normal snowpacks during the winter of 1993 brought a respite from seven years of drought. While the snow brought temporary relief, the reservoirs remained below their historic normal levels.

Mega-resorts. Las Vegas responded to the spread of gaming into other states by opening the first of many planned theme resorts (*see also* GAMBLING). The new Luxor with a huge replica of the Sphinx as an entryway, the Treasure Island with a pirate motif and battling galleons, and the MGM Resort and Theme Park with a huge amusement park added a total of 10,475 rooms to Las Vegas' 76,500 existing rooms. The MGM is the world's largest hotel, with 5,200 rooms. The intersection between the Las Vegas Strip and the Tropicana resort now is the site of hotels with a total of 13,567 rooms. The historic Dunes resort in Las Vegas closed after 38 years of operation.

Las Vegas' 23 million tourists in 1993 were expected to increase to 27 million by 1997. Reno's tourist industry was boosted by the start of construction of a national bowling stadium and the announcement of plans for a new theme resort.

TIMOTHY G. HALLER
Western Nevada Community College

NEVADA • Information Highlights

Area: 110,561 sq mi (286 352 km²).
Population (July 1, 1992 est.): 1,327,000.
Chief Cities (1990 census): Carson City, the capital, 40,443; Las Vegas, 258,295; Reno, 133,850.
Government (1993): *Chief Officers*—governor, Robert J. Miller (D); lt. gov., Sue Wagner (R). *Legislature*—Senate, 21 members; Assembly, 42 members.
State Finances (fiscal year 1991): *Revenue*, $3,553,000,000; *expenditure*, $3,436,000,000.
Personal Income (1992): $28,254,000,000; per capita, $21,285.
Labor Force (August 1993): *Civilian labor force*, 713,700; *unemployed*, 46,300 (6.5% of total force).
Education: *Enrollment* (fall 1991)—public elementary schools, 157,713; public secondary, 54,097; colleges and universities, 62,664. *Public school expenditures* (1990-91), $864,379,000.

Nevada—the original U.S. mecca for those who enjoy making a bet—responded to the growth of legalized gambling throughout the nation by introducing theme gaming resorts in Las Vegas. The new Luxor, right, included a replica of the Sphinx at its entrance.

NEW BRUNSWICK

New Brunswick's Liberal government of Premier Frank McKenna raised the banner of fiscal conservatism to new heights in 1993. The province's unique bilingual character was enshrined in the Canadian Constitution, and voters went massively Liberal in the October 25 federal election.

Budget and the Legislature. The provincial budget unveiled March 31 by Finance Minister Allan Maher projected a C$41.5 million operating deficit for fiscal year 1993-94—on spending of C$4 billion—compared with C$137.3 million the year before. And in 1994-95, according to Maher's calculations, the accounts would show a sizable surplus of C$68.4 million.

To demonstrate that it meant business, the government pushed through the legislature on May 6 an act requiring that governments in the future balance their books over the normal four-year term of elected office. The move to fiscal integrity came at a stiff price to tax-weary New Brunswickers. The budget called for a two-percentage-point increase in the provincial income tax and widened the scope of the province's 11% sales tax.

The drug program for senior citizens was slashed by C$11 million, and 500 civil-service jobs were eliminated. Also abolished was the sales-tax exemption for off-reserve purchases by native Indians.

The plan to kill the sales-tax exemption for Indians did not live long. Native groups quickly mounted a widespread series of protest actions, some of which turned ugly. Twenty-four persons were charged with public mischief after the Royal Canadian Mounted Police (RCMP) clashed with a crowd of natives who had erected a roadblock near Fredericton. On Easter Sunday, April 11, the government caved in on the pretext that the new rule needed "clarification": The sales tax still would not apply to items used or consumed on Indian reservations.

Health Protests. Repercussions from the government's restraint program continued on June 29, when several thousand noisy demonstrators marched through downtown Saint John to protest cuts in provincial health services. Reforms introduced in 1992 had forced nearly every hospital in the province to restrict its operations.

Linguistic Equality. The equality of New Brunswick's English and French linguistic communities was written into Canadian fundamental law on March 12. In Ottawa, Gov.-Gen. Ramon Hnatyshyn signed a constitutional amendment enshrining the two groups' equal standing in respect to rights, status, and privileges. The amendment had been ratified earlier by the House of Commons and the provincial legislature. New Brunswick is the only province where such equality is guaranteed constitutionally.

Elections. The Liberals easily held onto the Moncton North seat in a provincial by-election

---

NEW BRUNSWICK • Information Highlights

Area: 28,355 sq mi (73 440 km²).
Population (June 1993): 731,000.
Chief Cities (1991 census): Fredericton, the capital, 46,466; Saint John, 74,969; Moncton, 57,010.
Government (1993): *Chief Officers*—lt. gov., Gilbert Finn; premier, Frank McKenna (Liberal). *Legislature*—Legislative Assembly, 58 members.
Provincial Finances (1993-94 fiscal year budget): *Revenues*, $3,958,500,000; *expenditures*, $4,000,000,000.
Personal Income (average weekly earnings, June 1993): $498.52.
Labor Force (August 1993, seasonally adjusted): *Employed* workers, 15 years of age and over, 288,000; *Unemployed*, 13.0%.
Education (1993-94): *Enrollment*—elementary and secondary schools, 139,830 pupils; postsecondary—universities, 20,310; community colleges, 3,800.
(All monetary figures are in Canadian dollars.)

February 1. However, the Conservatives recaptured Carleton North, a traditional Tory stronghold taken by the Liberals in 1987, in a by-election on June 28. The Liberals captured nine of New Brunswick's ten parliamentary seats in the federal election on October 25.

Unitel. The economy of severely depressed northeastern New Brunswick got a boost on February 1 when Unitel, the telecommunications company, announced its intention to locate a new long-distance phone center in Edmundston.

JOHN BEST, *"Canada World News"*

NEWFOUNDLAND

On Dec. 21, 1992, the city of St. John's, Newfoundland, suffered a major downtown fire. No lives were lost but millions of dollars' worth of property, including a famous landmark, was destroyed by the fire. It was not a good omen for the province for 1993.

Hibernia Oil Field. On January 4, Texaco ended its participation in the Hibernia oil-development project off Newfoundland; 11 days later the other partners—Mobil and Chevron, the government of Canada, and Murphy Oil of Arkansas—increased their participation and the project was back on track. When the first big contract was granted and construction began, Hibernia became the only activity bringing new money into the provincial economy. However, the provincial shipyard at Marystown lost a tender bid for a C$100 million share of the contract, in spite of an upgrading of facilities and manpower.

Aboriginal Issues. A January 26 incident involving the Indians of Labrador drew attention to the devastating conditions in aboriginal communities. Six children, aged between 10 and 16, were found in Davis Inlet sniffing gasoline, apparently attempting suicide. The immediate response was to send the children and members of their families to a rehabilitation program in Alberta. Proposals to move the whole communi-

NEWFOUNDLAND • Information Highlights

Area: 156,649 sq mi (405 720 km²).
Population (June 1993): 577,000.
Chief Cities (1991 census): St. John's, the capital, 95,770; Corner Brook, 22,410.
Government (1993): *Chief Officers*—lt. gov., Frederick William Russell; premier, Clyde Wells (Liberal). *Legislature*—Legislative Assembly, 52 members.
Provincial Finances (1993-94 fiscal year budget): *Revenues*, $3,072,000,000; *expenditures*, $3,475,000,000.
Personal Income (average weekly earnings, June 1993): $526.53.
Labor Force (August 1993, seasonally adjusted): *Employed* workers, 15 years of age and over, 184,000. *Unemployed*, 20.7%.
Education (1993-94): *Enrollment*—elementary and secondary schools, 120,690 pupils; postsecondary—universities, 13,720; community colleges, 4,460.
(All monetary figures are in Canadian dollars.)

ty to a new site foundered because of cost, and the issue remained unresolved at year's end.

On other aboriginal issues, the provincial government made a formal land-claims offer to the Inuit in October, and relations with the Innu (Indians) remained sour so long as the latter refused to restore Newfoundland Hydro meters to their community of Sheshatshit. In October the Innu Nation announced that the meters could be restored.

Elections and the Fishing Issue. The Liberal government of Premier Clyde Wells called an election for May 5. The premier campaigned on the basis of the budget brought down in March, which called for continued wage and program cuts. The government was returned with a new seat distribution of: Liberals 35; Conservatives 16; and New Democratic Party (NDP) 1. In the Nain, Labrador, riding a historical first was achieved when an aboriginal was elected. The serious state of the province's finances was illustrated two weeks after the election, when one of Canada's bond-rating agencies downgraded the provincial credit rating despite the promise of austerity.

The cod-fishing moratorium entered its second, and supposedly last, year with what seemed to observers to be a false air of prosperity. The regular income from federal transfers was being used by 20,000 persons on the northeast coast to upgrade homes and buy new household supplies. But an Inter-Church Coalition for Fishing Communities, formed in January, continued to warn about the long-term social and psychological effects of the ban. In September and October variations of the income-support program had to be extended to the south and west coasts.

The provincial government used the opportunity of the Oct. 25, 1993, federal election to seek support from national political leaders for more overt action to halt fishing in international waters. The election outcome was a sweep of all seven of the province's federal legislative seats by the Liberals.

SUSAN MCCORQUODALE, *Memorial University*

NEW HAMPSHIRE

The year 1993 proved to be one of economic improvement for New Hampshire.

Economy. As 1993 began the state's economic news was at best mediocre, but as the year progressed signs of improvement became evident. The state's unemployment rate declined from an all-time high of 8.6% in February to 5.9% by August. In the summer and early fall, real-estate sales were increasing but still modest by the standards of the 1980s. Bankruptcies and foreclosures also declined from 1992.

Reflecting the somewhat better state economy, state revenues also improved. The 1993 fiscal year ended with a surplus and an 8% increase in tax revenues over 1992. The 1994-95 state budget, however, still relied heavily on federal Medicare funds to stay in balance. Contrasting with these positive signs was a stagnation in manufacturing jobs.

Legislature. Gov. Stephen Merrill (R) and the legislature became involved in several heated controversies during the year, none more acrimonious than one regarding the capital budget. The budget first was vetoed by the governor and approved only in mid-September, after two months of discussion and behind-the-scenes debate. The compromise reduced the capital budget from $65.1 million to $58.4 million. The $4.9 billion state operating budget was approved just hours before the end of the fiscal year on June 30.

Another gubernatorial action angered the Democrats. Merrill appointed Miriam Luce, a Libertarian, to the powerful state liquor commission. By law he had to appoint someone other than a Republican. Previous Republican governors had appointed Democrats.

Several important bills were passed during 1993. After a ten-year battle, the legislature passed a law lowering the legal intoxication level for drivers from .10% to .08%. The first major change in the state's tax system occurred with the passing of the governor's business enterprise

NEW HAMPSHIRE • Information Highlights

Area: 9,279 sq mi (24 032 km²).
Population (July 1, 1992 est.): 1,111,000.
Chief Cities (1990 census): Concord, the capital, 36,006; Manchester, 99,567; Nashua, 79,662.
Government (1993): *Chief Officer*—governor, Steve Merrill (R). *General Court*—Senate, 24 members; House of Representatives, 400 members.
State Finances (fiscal year 1991): *Revenue*, $2,088,000,000; *expenditure*, $2,135,000,000.
Personal Income (1992): $25,100,000,000; per capita, $22,596.
Labor Force (August 1993): *Civilian labor force*, 642,200; *unemployed*, 40,600 (6.3% of total force).
Education: *Enrollment* (fall 1991)—public elementary schools, 129,698; public secondary, 47,440; colleges and universities, 63,718. *Public school expenditures* (1990-91), $888,156,000.

tax, which was designed to broaden the limited base of the business-profits tax. The new tax imposes a .25% tax on wages, making it more difficult for businesses to avoid paying any state tax. The effort to create a state holiday honoring Martin Luther King, Jr., however, failed once again in the legislature.

Jobs. The possible closure of the Portsmouth naval shipyard threatened thousands of jobs in Maine and New Hampshire. The shipyard's fate hung in the balance until late June, when the federal Defense Base Closure and Realignment Commission voted, 6-0, to keep it open.

Other Issues. On July 11 the Lakes Region witnessed the largest sporting event in New Hampshire history when the New Hampshire International Speedway in Loudon hosted a Winston Cup race, attended by an estimated 66,000 racing fans.

Less noticed was the conclusion of six years of work by the state Land Conservation Investment Program and its private counterpart, the Trust for New Hampshire Lands. They spent $50 million to preserve and conserve key parcels of land throughout the state.

WILLIAM L. TAYLOR, *Plymouth State College*

NEW JERSEY

The gubernatorial election dominated events in New Jersey in 1993.

The Election Campaign. The key figure was Gov. Jim Florio, running for reelection in what at the outset seemed like an impossible task, given the unpopularity of his $2.8 billion tax increase in 1990, sweeping Republican gains in the 1991 legislative elections, and allegations of corruption against one of his top advisers. Florio attempted to tone down his stridently liberal image by offering no new taxes in the $15.6 billion budget he sent to the legislature in January 1993. He also dismissed his chief of staff, Joseph C. Salema, whose investment firm of Armacon Securities allegedly benefited from irregularities in underwriting $2.9 billion of New Jersey Turnpike Authority bonds.

For their part the Republicans witnessed a spirited nominating primary contest between Christine Todd Whitman, whose exploitation of the tax issue almost had unseated Sen. Bill Bradley in the 1990 election, and former state Attorney General W. Carey Edwards. Whitman easily defeated Edwards and conservative Jim Wallwork in the June 8 primary. The first woman in New Jersey history to be nominated for governor by a major party, she came from a wealthy patrician background. She and her husband disclosed an annual income for 1992 in the neighborhood of $3 million; she also was forced to pay back Social Security taxes of about $25,000 for two illegal aliens she had employed as nannies.

The campaign between Florio and Whitman featured disagreements over crime and taxes.

© Horodynsky/Sipa

In November 1993, Christine Todd Whitman, a 46-year-old Republican, narrowly defeated incumbent Jim Florio (D) to become the first woman to be elected governor of New Jersey.

On one hand, the Republicans called into question the ban on assault weapons that Florio had backed; on the other hand, Whitman adopted a Reaganesque approach to taxes by calling for a 30% reduction in the income tax, to be phased in over three years. Many doubted the practicality of the tax proposal. As the campaign went on, Florio appeared to be gaining voter confidence, as it was felt that the tax increase, while unpleasant, was necessary. Furthermore, many commentators criticized Whitman for not defining herself clearly to the public and waffling on many of the issues. Shortly before the election many polls gave Florio a commanding lead.

Whitman's narrow victory was thus a major upset. Postmortem analysis generally agreed that the tax issue was decisive, and Whitman announced that she would develop plans to put her rollback plan into effect as soon as possible. Florio was the first incumbent New Jersey governor ever to be defeated for reelection. In the legislative elections, the Republicans retained control of both houses, but the Democrats picked up seats. Another by-product of the

---

NEW JERSEY • Information Highlights

Area: 7,787 sq mi (20 169 km²).
Population (July 1, 1992 est.): 7,789,000.
Chief Cities (1990 census): Trenton, the capital, 88,675; Newark, 275,221; Jersey City, 228,537; Paterson, 140,891; Elizabeth, 110,002.
Government (1993): *Chief Officer*—governor, James J. Florio (D). *Legislature*—Senate, 40 members; General Assembly, 80 members.
State Finances (fiscal year 1991): *Revenue*, $24,743,000,000; *expenditure*, $23,250,000,000.
Personal Income (1992): $210,059,000,000; per capita, $26,969.
Labor Force (August 1993): *Civilian labor force*, 3,942,000; *unemployed*, 280,000 (7.1% of total force).
Education: *Enrollment* (fall 1991)—public elementary schools, 800,696; public secondary, 309,100; colleges and universities, 334,641. *Public school expenditures* (1990-91), $8,784,969,000.

unpopularity of the Florio tax increase was the wide margin of approval given to a referendum that allows voters to recall elected officials after one year in office.

Whitman's election victory came under question, however, when Ed Rollins, her campaign manager, claimed on November 9 that the Republicans had paid $500,000 to suppress the black vote—which normally goes Democratic—in the race. After various testimony and investigations, the New Jersey Democratic Party chairman announced in late November that the party would abandon its effort to have Whitman's victory overturned.

Nonpolitical Matters. The bombing of the World Trade Center in February, as well as the Islamic fundamentalist terrorist plans discovered in June, focused attention on Sheikh Abd al-Rahman, who preached in Jersey City (*see also* TERRORISM)....In a case that gained the spotlight, three Glen Ridge teenagers were convicted of sexually assaulting a retarded schoolmate.

HERMANN K. PLATT, *Saint Peter's College*

NEW MEXICO

New Mexico was dogged in 1993 by issues ranging from health to religion and taxes.

Hantavirus. A mystery illness killed ten persons in northwest New Mexico, and became a concern throughout the U.S. West. Termed *hantavirus*, the sickness led to lung congestion and suffocation, and was found to be spread by fecal remnants from deer mice. Gov. Bruce King's office reported that 15 persons in the state had contracted the virus.

Border Blockade. In September 1993 the southern part of New Mexico along the U.S.-Mexico border saw the U.S. Border Patrol stage a blockade—made up of 450 agents along a 20-mi (32.2-km) stretch beginning in El Paso, TX—in an effort to stop the illegal migration of Mexicans. The first day of the blockade alone, six times fewer immigrants were apprehended by agents

than the day before—an indication that Mexicans feared the blockade and were staying in Mexico.

Sunland Park, NM, on the border, reported reduced crime. However, its neighboring city, Anapra, Mexico, reported high unemployment and increased crime because the blockade was keeping Mexicans from their U.S. jobs. While welcomed by U.S. bureaucrats, the blockade angered Mexicans. The Juarez, Mexico, Chamber of Commerce launched a boycott of U.S. goods.

Ranching and Agriculture. Although President Bill Clinton had won New Mexico in the November 1992 election, his preservationist view of public land lost him many supporters in the state, since tougher regulations meant higher costs for ranchers. The state has 9,000 cattle ranches and 1.3 million head of cattle. In 1993, Interior Secretary Bruce Babbitt called for raising grazing fees over a three-year period. Sen. Pete Domenici (R-NM) launched a Senate filibuster in an effort to delay Babbitt's plan for one year. Despite heated rhetoric over fees and rules, which were not scheduled to take effect until 1994, it was too early to tell by year's end 1993 what impact the new rules would have.

Farmers of the state's prize crop—chile—suffered when the New Mexico Department of Agriculture in the spring pulled 6,400 lbs (2 903 kg) of the crop from stores because of a pest called the chile weevil. Though the out-of-season produce had come from Mexico, it aroused suspicions that New Mexico's crop would be infested as well, which it was. Agriculture officials quarantined much of Dona Ana county after the weevil was found in chile fields there in June. Chile accounts for $59 million in cash receipts for New Mexico farmers. Officials unsuccessfully tried to gain permission from U.S. Agriculture Secretary Mike Espy to prevent Mexican chile from entering the state.

Religion. Roman Catholic Archbishop Robert Sanchez of the Santa Fe archdiocese resigned his post in April 1993 amid allegations of sexual improprieties. Bishop Michael J. Sheehan of Lubbock, TX, was named interim successor and later as Sanchez' permanent replacement.

Other. New Mexican taxpayers were enraged in 1993 by one action of the state legislature. The legislature passed a 6¢-per-gallon gasoline tax to fund education, but it soon was found that the added revenues were not needed. Governor King resisted calls for a special session to repeal the tax, stating that it could be rolled back in 1994....The Vietnam Women's Memorial, designed and sculpted by Santa Fe sculptor Glenna Goodacre, was completed in 1993. Placed beside the Vietnam Veterans Memorial in Washington, DC, it honors the 11,500 military women who served in the war, and the 265,000 in uniform during that time....Albuquerque's annual balloon fiesta attracted a record 1.6 million spectators. Tragically, balloon accidents at the event took two lives.

KEITH WHELPLEY, *"Las Cruces Sun-News"*

NEW MEXICO • Information Highlights

Area: 121,593 sq mi (314 925 km²).
Population (July 1, 1992 est.): 1,581,000.
Chief Cities (1990 census): Santa Fe, the capital, 55,859; Albuquerque, 384,736; Las Cruces, 62,126.
Government (1993): *Chief Officers*—governor, Bruce King (D); lt. gov., Casey Luna (D). *Legislature*—Senate, 42 members; House of Representatives, 70 members.
State Finances (fiscal year 1991): *Revenue*, $4,931,000,000; *expenditure*, $4,527,000,000.
Personal Income (1992): $24,609,000,000; per capita, $15,563.
Labor Force (August 1993): *Civilian labor force*, 735,800; *unemployed*, 54,200 (7.4% of total force).
Education: *Enrollment* (fall 1991)—public elementary schools, 212,836; public secondary, 95,831; colleges and universities, 93,507. *Public school expenditures* (1990-91), $1,134,142,000.

NEW YORK

New York's seldom-shifting political scene displayed some new faces and surprising directions in 1993, but the social currents buffeting the state since the late 1980s—a sluggish economy, high taxes, and rising crime—remained implacable.

Politics. During 1993 two of the four elected state officeholders gave up the jobs they long had held. Under the state constitution, their successors were installed by a joint vote of the Democrat-dominated state legislature.

State Comptroller Edward (Ned) Regan, the sole Republican among state leaders since his 1978 election, announced his resignation in February to become president of an economic institute at Bard College in Annandale-on-Hudson, NY. His Democratic successor was H. Carl McCall, who became the first African American to hold a statewide office in New York. McCall, a Citibank executive with a resume that included service as head of the New York City Board of Education, deputy ambassador to the United Nations, and state senator, immediately launched his campaign for election in November 1994 to fill the final two years of Regan's term.

In September, Attorney General Robert Abrams announced that he would resign after 15 years in office to become a partner in a large Manhattan law firm. Abrams said that he had decided to return to private life after narrowly losing in a 1992 campaign for U.S. senator against Republican Sen. Alfonse D'Amato. Legislators chose G. Oliver Koppell, an Assembly Democrat who had represented a Bronx district since 1970, as Abrams' successor.

Another prominent face left the state scene: Former Chief Judge Sol Wachtler pleaded guilty in March to sending harassing letters to his former lover, a prominent Republican socialite. Wachtler, who was diagnosed as suffering from severe psychological problems, began a ten-month federal prison sentence in September. Gov. Mario Cuomo appointed Judith S. Kaye of the state Court of Appeals to replace Wachtler as chief judge in March. She is the first woman to hold that post.

Other political shifts occurred at the voting booth. Republicans not only took over New York's City Hall for the first time since 1965, but also scored impressive victories elsewhere, wresting the mayor's office from Democrats in Syracuse and Binghamton and holding off determined Democratic candidates in key county executive races in suburban Westchester and Nassau counties. In Buffalo, Rochester, and Albany, insurgent Democrats won control of city halls when incumbents retired.

Polls indicated that many voters had grown increasingly fearful of crime and angry over taxes. A year-end study by *Money* magazine identified New York as having the nation's heaviest tax burden in relation to citizens' ability to pay. Meanwhile, the pace of economic recovery remained slow, although business activity was improved slightly from 1992. In part because of such problems, Cuomo, once viewed as a prime contender for the White House or the U.S. Supreme Court, dropped to his lowest-ever approval rating among voters. At year's end, he was mulling his political future, amid indications that he would seek a fourth term in 1994.

Government. A $59.4 billion state budget for the 1993-94 fiscal year was passed in April. The budget (including federal money) represented an increase of 8.4% over the 1992-93 fiscal year.

The state legislature's annual session was highlighted by the creation of a $100 million Environmental Assistance Fund to enable the state to buy threatened land, close landfills, and improve parks. Legislators also approved a five-year, $21 billion transportation-funding plan to improve roads, bridges, airports, and mass-transit systems. A new 17-cent-per-pack cigarette tax was enacted, raising the tax on cigarettes bought in New York to 56 cents per pack, one of the highest levels in the country.

Crime. In October, Joseph Buttafuoco of Long Island's south shore pleaded guilty to statutory rape involving teenager Amy Fisher, who was serving a five-to-15-year sentence for shooting Buttafuoco's wife. In November he was sentenced to a fine and six months in prison. In December six persons were killed when a man with no prior criminal record went on a shooting spree on a Long Island Rail Road train during rush hour.

Other News. In April, Governor Cuomo signed an agreement that allowed the Oneida Indian Nation near Syracuse to open a high-stakes gambling casino. . . . Rochester's Eastman Kodak Company continued to shrink its labor force, announcing its intention to cut 10,000 jobs worldwide by the end of 1995.

REX SMITH
Editor, "The Record," Troy, NY

NEW YORK • Information Highlights

Area: 49,108 sq mi (127 190 km²).
Population (July 1, 1992 est.): 18,119,000.
Chief Cities (1990 census): Albany, the capital, 101,082; New York, 7,322,564; Buffalo, 328,123; Rochester, 231,636; Yonkers, 188,082; Syracuse, 163,860.
Government (1993): *Chief Officers*—governor, Mario M. Cuomo (D); lt. gov., Stan Lundine (D). *Legislature*—Senate, 61 members; Assembly, 150 members.
State Finances (fiscal year 1991): *Revenue*, $65,715,000,000; *expenditure*, $64,321,000,000.
Personal Income (1992): $432,001,000,000; per capita, $23,842.
Labor Force (August 1993): *Civilian labor force*, 8,482,300; *unemployed*, 667,900 (7.9% of total force).
Education: *Enrollment* (fall 1991)—public elementary schools, 1,862,215; public secondary, 781,778; colleges and universities, 1,056,487. *Public school expenditures* (1990-91), $19,514,583,000.

NEW YORK CITY

For New York City, 1993 was a year of para-doxes. Five persons were killed when foreign terrorism was brought home by the bombing of the World Trade Center in lower Manhattan. Eight illegal immigrants seeking a better life in New York died when the freighter on which they were being smuggled from China ran aground off a Queens beach. Rudolph W. Giuliani (*see* BIOGRAPHY), former federal prosecutor, unseat-ed David N. Dinkins to become the first Repub-lican mayor in a generation. Staten Island, which provided Giuliani with his winning margin, voted to secede from the city that it had joined 95 years earlier.

Reported crime dropped in the city, but not by enough either to redound to the mayor politi-cally or to stifle the circulation battles that peri-odically erupt among the city's tabloid newspa-pers. In 1993 the tabloids became stories themselves; after tumultuous management changes, Rupert Murdoch became owner of the *New York Post* again, and Mortimer Zuckerman, a developer and publisher, bought the *Daily News.* (*See also* SPECIAL REPORT/PUBLISHING.) Also, a late-winter blizzard was followed a few months later by a brutal heat wave.

Terrorism. Muslim fundamentalists were blamed for the explosion that blasted a crater in the basement of one of the World Trade Center's 110-story twin towers on February 26. Four men went on trial for conspiring to make and trans-port the bomb, which caused millions of dollars' worth of damage, stranded office workers and a touring group of elementary-school students in an elevator, closed one of the towers for weeks, and prompted tighter security in government buildings and other public places. Fifteen Mus-lims also were charged in a thwarted plot to blow up several city targets, including the United Nations headquarters and a vehicular tunnel

under the Hudson River between New York and New Jersey. The government alleged that an Egyptian cleric living in New Jersey was the head of a group plotting a "war of urban terrorism."

City Elections. If the Trade Center bombing and the smuggling of illegal immigrants by Chi-nese gangs were tragic reminders of New York's ethnic and racial diversity, the polarization reflected in the mayoral campaign also unsettled many New Yorkers. Dinkins, the city's first black mayor, easily won renomination in the Demo-cratic primary. The more challenging general election was a rerun of the 1989 campaign, which Dinkins barely had won. He presided dur-ing a recession and compiled an uneven record marred by several racial incidents and distin-guished by his success in balancing the budget and enlarging the police force. But in 1993 his coalition of liberal whites, blacks, Hispanics, and loyal Democrats had eroded. Coupled with a higher Staten Island turnout, where voters removed another roadblock to possible seces-sion, the erosion produced a mirror image of the 1989 outcome. Giuliani, running with the Liberal Party's endorsement, just barely won, toppling an incumbent mayor in a general election for the first time in 40 years.

If Dinkins' race was a factor, the outcome also suggested that incumbency was a liability. Elizabeth Holtzman, the city's comptroller, was defeated in the Democratic primary by Assem-blyman Alan G. Hevesi, who won in November. City Council President Andrew Stein abandoned his mayoral campaign, then also decided not to seek reelection to the newly named position of public advocate, which was won by Mark Green, former consumer-affairs commissioner. Voters also overwhelmingly approved a referendum that would limit city officials elected in 1993 and thereafter to two four-year terms.

Education. Another incumbent was ousted, this time by the Board of Education. Joseph Fer-

New York City's Mayor David Dink-ins (left) and Mayor-elect Rudolph W. Giuliani held a postelection meeting at City Hall. In a Nov. 2, 1993, rematch of the 1989 cam-paign, the Republican Giuliani had defeated the Democratic incum-bent by a small margin.

nandez' contract as schools chancellor was not renewed after contentious debate over making condoms available to students without parental consent and over how vividly gay and lesbian lifestyles should be described in guidelines on teaching tolerance. To succeed him, the board's majority chose Ramon C. Cortines, the San Francisco schools superintendent. He inherited another crisis: the belated discovery of potentially hazardous asbestos in school buildings, which delayed the start of classes for weeks and cost more than $100 million to abate.

Obituary. Robert F. Wagner, Jr., the son of a former mayor and grandson of a U.S. senator and himself a former Board of Education president and City Planning Commission chairman, died in November.

SAM ROBERTS
"The New York Times"

NEW ZEALAND • Information Highlights

Official Name: New Zealand.
Location: Southwest Pacific Ocean.
Area: 103,737 sq mi (268 680 km²).
Population (mid-1993 est.): 3,400,000.
Chief Cities (March 1991 census): Wellington, the capital, 325,682; Auckland, 885,571; Christchurch, 307,179; Hamilton, 148,625.
Government: *Head of state*, Elizabeth II, queen, represented by Dame Catherine Tizard, governor-general (took office November 1990). *Head of government*, James Bolger, prime minister (took office November 1990). *Legislature* (unicameral)—House of Representatives.
Monetary Unit: New Zealand dollar (1.7976 N.Z. dollars equal U.S.$1, Dec. 14, 1993).
Gross Domestic Product (1991 est. U.S.$): $46,200,000,000.
Economic Index (1992): *Consumer Prices* (1980 = 100), all items, 285.5; food, 261.6.
Foreign Trade (1992 U.S.$): *Imports*, $9,205,000,000; *exports*, $9,829,000,000.

NEW ZEALAND

New Zealand's 1993 general election on November 6 produced the closest result in the nation's modern political history, with the outgoing National government's massive majority dramatically cut.

Election. Until midyear, polls typically gave the opposition Labour Party a 10% or more margin over a dispirited ruling National Party. A major cabinet reshuffle in March had very little impact and in April a renegade former minister, Winston Peters, theatrically resigned his seat. He won the ensuing by-election with a huge majority and soon after formed a new party, New Zealand First.

The polls had highlighted unemployment, education, the public-health system, and the level of crime as areas in which the National Party was extremely vulnerable among the 2.3 million voters. In April nearly 75% of those polled said they were dissatisfied with Prime Minister Jim Bolger's leadership. As the election neared, however, National's support steadily climbed as confidence in the economy grew. An election-eve poll gave National a 10% lead over Labour. The actual election results gave National 50 seats and 35% of the vote to Labour's 45 seats and 34.5% support. The minor parties, Alliance and New Zealand First, won 18.5% and 8% of the vote, respectively. They each took two Parliament seats. Prime Minister Bolger said he intended to govern for a full three-year term, but with an absence of further controversial economic or social initiatives.

Electoral Referendum. Following the 1992 indicative referendum that showed that a huge majority was in favor of changing the system of electing members of Parliament, a binding referendum was held in September. The change to mixed-member proportional representation was approved, but the final vote of 54% to 46% was far closer than had been anticipated in June. The new system would be in place for the 1996 general election.

Economy and Budget. The New Zealand economy had improved gradually since 1987 under the direction of both the Labour and National parties. The gross domestic product (GDP) rose by 2.8% in the 1993 fiscal year, ending June 30, while inflation—at 1.5%—nearly was extinguished. The value of building permits issued rose 30% in a year and mortgage rates dropped to a 20-year low of 7.5%.

Finance Minister Ruth Richardson delivered a "trust us," "do nothing" budget in July. It made minor adjustments to family-support benefits but did not focus on lowering taxes or the level of unemployment. It focused instead on an economic forecast of a sustained 3% growth rate and a dwindling government deficit (N.Z.$2.3 billion in 1993-94), and hinted at further rounds of government cost-cutting. The government also promised to introduce legislation forcing the ruling party to disclose the state of the public finances before general elections.

Health Reform. The prolonged reform of the public-health system culminated in government-appointed health authorities taking over the public-hospital system in July. A series of polls indicated an overwhelming disbelief in the reform being able to effect any substantial improvement in the quality of health care.

Foreign Affairs. Prime Minister Bolger visited Europe in March, hammering at the importance of the European Community (later the European Union) for the New Zealand export market. Trade issues also were behind Bolger's May visit to the Far East, with several deals being negotiated. The prime minister attended the Asia-Pacific Economic Cooperation (APEC) forum in Seattle in November.

G. W. A. BUSH
University of Auckland

NIGERIA

During 1993, Nigeria's military government, led by Gen. Ibrahim Babangida and the National Defense and Security Council (NDSC), abrogated presidential elections that were held in June. This political turmoil—which began in 1992 when primary results were canceled—helped perpetuate Nigeria's economic difficulties.

Politics. After the disturbances of 1992, the military junta reconstituted itself as the NDSC. Babangida promised to turn over authority to civilians on Aug. 27, 1993, following new elections. The two recognized political parties, the Social Democratic Party (SPD) and the National Republican Convention (NRC), chose their candidates. The NRC selected Bashir Othma Tofa, a Muslim economist from the North, while the SPD fielded Moshood Abiola, a Yoruba media magnate. The NDSC issued a decree specifying the death penalty for anyone speaking or publishing things that undermined the government after former head of state Olusegun Obasanjo criticized Babangida.

The new presidential elections were scheduled for June 12. The pro-military Association for a Better Nigeria (ABN) filed suit for retention of the military and the high court in Abuja ordered a delay two days before the elections. The National Electoral Committee (NEC) allowed the elections to proceed. By June 14, with half of the results reported, it was obvious that Abiola would win. Ultimately he was victorious in 19 of the 30 states. Nevertheless, the high court directed the NEC not to release the results. The NEC complied but appealed the ruling.

On June 23 the NDSC annulled the election. Babangida promised a civilian government by the target date in August but with new rules that prevented Abiola and Tofa from running again. A plan for a bipartisan government was rejected by Abiola, and Babangida withdrew the plan. A new organization, Committee for Democracy, issued a call for civil disobedience as Abiola maintained that he was the rightful president. Demonstrations against the NDSC flared throughout the country, including a violent riot in Lagos in which 25 persons reportedly were killed by the police.

Under pressure from foreign states and Nigerian notables, and abandoned by his fellow officers, Babangida resigned on August 26. Before leaving office he appointed an interim government headed by his former minister of finance, Ernest Shonekan. Shonekan promised new presidential elections in February 1994. However, a new military strongman, Gen. Sani Abacha, ousted Shonekan in November and then selected a cabinet that included numerous allies of Abiola.

Economy. Political uncertainty further eroded Nigeria's poor economy. Falling demand for oil, a chief export, dictated reduced public expenditure. The inflation rate was more than 40% and

---

---

the naira plunged to a low official rate: 32 naira to $1. A nationwide strike by state workers in February threatened briefly to paralyze government operations. Finance Minister Shonekan, introducing a new economic plan in January, appealed for support from creditor nations, particularly Great Britain. Britain promised to write off 50% of Nigeria's debt and reschedule the rest only if Nigeria complied with International Monetary Fund (IMF) guidelines. An attempt to enact an IMF suggestion to remove a government subsidy on gasoline caused threats of strikes and endemic violence. The NDSC quickly gave up the plan. The Paris Club of private investors warned in March that loans could dry up quickly if the arrears in interest payments amounting to $4 billion per year were not paid.

Foreign Policy. The abrogated presidential elections brought protests from Britain and the United States, with both nations urging acceptance of the election results. Britain froze all new economic aid and the U.S. suspended all nonrelief aid, but all foreign states declined any stronger action. In spite of domestic turmoil, Nigeria supported various peacekeeping efforts in Africa, providing most of the military forces of the Economic Community of West Africa (ECOWAS) in Liberia. Troops also were sent to Somalia as part of a United Nations mission.

HARRY A. GAILEY
San Jose State University

NORTH CAROLINA

A 110-day legislative session provided 1993's leading story in North Carolina.

Budget and Financial Matters. A combination of spending cuts, tuition increases, and delayed construction projects enabled the General Assembly to adopt a $9 billion annual budget. Major new spending went to pay raises, education, court personnel and crime control, and economic and technical development. Voters approved a $750 million bond issue for capital improvements for universities, community colleges, state parks, and water and sewer projects.

Unemployment in North Carolina remained well below the national average, but the state lost to Alabama in the competition for a Mercedes-Benz plant, for which the General Assembly conditionally had appropriated $35 million for the training of thousands of workers. Funds also were provided for development of a Global Trans-Park air-cargo facility in Lenoir county.

Legislation and Redistricting. A law that previously prevented a husband from being prosecuted for raping his wife was repealed. A law making breast-feeding in public grounds for a charge of indecent exposure also was repealed.

The U.S. Supreme Court ordered further hearings on a case charging that the gerrymandered 12th congressional district violated the rights of white voters. The system of statewide primary voting for local judicial officials also was challenged.

Education. New funds were provided for teachers' salaries, textbooks, school buses, low-wealth and small school systems, expansion of the Basic Education Program, and experiments in a private-public venture—dubbed "Smart Start"—providing for early childhood education, day care, and health care. An accountability commission was appointed to develop a new test, passage of which would be required for high-school graduation by the year 2000.

President Bill Clinton on October 12 helped celebrate the bicentennial of the University of North Carolina (UNC), the first publicly supported university to open its doors in the United States. Earlier in the year conflict over where to locate a black cultural center at UNC resulted in the arrest of 16 protesters.

Crime and Punishment. The top concern of the citizenry—crime and violence—led to increased appropriations for law enforcement and prisons; and judges were given authority to impose minimum sentences without privilege of parole. The legislature made it a felony for a stu-

© Mark B. Sluder/"The Charlotte Observer"

On Oct. 26, 1993, Charlotte, NC, celebrated the news that the National Football League owners had awarded the city a franchise. The Carolina Panthers would begin play in the 1995 season.

dent to carry firearms or explosives onto school grounds, but possession of knives or brass knuckles on school property remained a misdemeanor. The legal blood-alcohol threshold for driving while intoxicated (DWI) was lowered to .08.

A U.S. Army sergeant from Fort Bragg went on a shooting spree at a Fayetteville restaurant, killing four persons and wounding ten. James Jordan was murdered along a highway, and his bereaved son, famed basketball star Michael Jordan, later retired from the Chicago Bulls.

Miscellaneous News. Benjamin F. Chavis, Jr., was elected executive director of the National Association for the Advancement of Colored People (NAACP)....Joseph A. Herzenberg, first avowed gay person to be elected to a city council in the South (in Chapel Hill), resigned after being found guilty of income-tax evasion....Nannerl O. Keohane became Duke University's eighth president and the only woman to serve as the permanent head of one of the nation's top research universities. She formerly was president of Wellesley College....Jill McCrae of Durham gave birth to quintuplets....For the third consecutive year the NCAA's men's basketball crown remained in the Research Triangle as the University of North Carolina replaced Duke as national champions.

H. G. Jones
University of North Carolina at Chapel Hill

NORTH CAROLINA • Information Highlights

Area: 52,669 sq mi (136 413 km²).

Population (July 1, 1992 est.): 6,843,000.

Chief Cities (1990 census): Raleigh, the capital, 207,951; Charlotte, 395,934; Greensboro, 183,521; Winston-Salem, 143,485; Durham, 136,611.

Government (1993): *Chief Officers*—governor, James B. Hunt, Jr. (D); lt. gov., Dennis A. Wicker (D). *General Assembly*—Senate, 50 members; House of Representatives, 120 members.

State Finances (fiscal year 1991): *Revenue*, $15,266,000,000; *expenditure*, $15,036,000,000.

Personal Income (1992): $123,074,000,000; per capital, $17,986.

Labor Force (August 1993): *Civilian labor force*, 3,448,300; *unemployed*, 157,900 (4.6% of total force).

Education: *Enrollment* (fall 1991)—public elementary schools, 794,773; public secondary, 302,825; colleges and universities, 371,968. *Public school expenditures* (1990-91), $4,544,112,000.

NORTH DAKOTA

Agriculture and the weather overcame politics at the top of the conversation list in North Dakota in 1993.

A 77-day legislative session that ended in April gave way to a spring and summer of wet weather that had farmers and ranchers smiling in the western part of the state and scowling in eastern North Dakota. Thirty-nine of the state's 53 counties were declared federal disaster areas as a result of the Great Flood of '93. (*See* FEATURE ARTICLE, page 44.)

And while 1993 was in many ways a disastrous year for North Dakota crops, the emergence of several agricultural cooperatives was a ray of sunshine for the state.

Agriculture. Much of the grain crop not flooded out by rain fell victim to a disease called vomitoxin, rendering the grain useless as a cash crop or feed for livestock. In addition, the record rains delayed or prevented planting in June and flooded fields in July. The state's Agricultural Statistics Service said crop yields in sunflowers, sugar beets, dry edible beans, hard red spring wheat, durum wheat, winter wheat, barley, rye, and corn were down statewide. Roughly 4 million acres (1.6 million ha) of wheat, mostly in the Red River Valley of the east, were affected by scab disease and vomitoxin.

Prices fell, as did farm income and spending power. Some farmers in western North Dakota who missed the heavy rains and disease found their high-protein wheat selling for as high as an unheard-of $6.50 per bushel.

Cooperatives. The first of the state's cooperatives to open—the $43 million Dakota Growers Pasta Plant in Carrington—accepted its first truckload of durum wheat for processing in late October. Three sugar cooperatives in North Dakota and Minnesota formed the United Sugars Corporation to market their sugar worldwide. Ground was broken in New Rockford for the North American Bison Cooperative plant to produce buffalo meat for restaurants.

Air Bases and Budget. The state's two Air Force bases—the Minot Air Force Base and Grand Forks Air Force Base—were given new life when they were spared from the list of military installations being closed across the United States. State and local officials had campaigned hard in behalf of the bases in Washington.

Human services and elementary, secondary, and higher education all took budget cuts when North Dakota's budget-conscious legislature met from February through mid-April.

Crime. The kidnapping and subsequent murder of tour guide Donna Martz captured the attention of the whole state. Martz, 59, was abducted from the parking lot of a Bismarck motel in late September. A man and woman from Pennsylvania were arrested after Martz was found dead in Nevada in November.

DAVE JURGENS
"The Forum," Fargo, North Dakota

NORTH DAKOTA • Information Highlights

Area: 70,702 sq mi (183 119 km²).

Population (July 1, 1992 est.): 636,000.

Chief Cities (1990 census): Bismarck, the capital, 49,256; Fargo, 74,111; Grand Forks, 49,425; Minot, 34,544.

Government (1993): *Chief Officers*—governor, Edward Schafer (R), lt. gov., Rosemarie Myrdal (R). *Legislative Assembly*—Senate, 53 members; House of Representatives, 106 members.

State Finances (fiscal year 1991): *Revenue*, $1,998,000,000; *expenditure*, $1,793,000,000.

Personal Income (1992): $10,934,000,000; per capita, $17,193.

Labor Force (August 1993): *Civilian labor force*, 311,600; *unemployed*, 12,900 (4.2% of total force).

Education: *Enrollment* (fall 1991)—public elementary schools, 84,941; public secondary, 33,435; colleges and universities, 38,739. *Public school expenditures* (1990-91), $460,581,000.

NORTHWEST TERRITORIES

There was renewed interest in the mining sector in the Northwest Territories (NWT) in 1993. Some C$80 million was spent in exploration, mainly for diamonds.

Mining Potential. Significant diamond finds near Lac de Gras, about 224 mi (360 km) northeast of the capital of Yellowknife, were in the process of being evaluated. If mining was found to be viable, analysts were projecting a relatively large development for the Northwest Territories—about C$700 million and employing up to 500 people.

The steadying of the gold market, in the range of U.S.$375 per ounce, also gave companies the confidence to renew prospecting and to consider reopening mines. The Colomac Gold Mine, north of Yellowknife, was to begin production in the spring of 1994, after having been closed since 1990. Other base-metal mines south of Coppermine, in the Western Arctic, and near Fort Simpson, in the Mackenzie region, were poised for start-up by 1994 or 1995.

Mine Strike. The bitter strike at Royal Oak Mine's Giant Yellowknife Gold Mine ended in December, with the strikers returning to work and court-ordered arbitration under way for remaining areas of dispute. In October the Royal Canadian Mounted Police (RCMP) arrested a striking miner and charged him with murder related to the underground explosion that killed nine workers at the mine in September 1992.

Legislature Building. In November, Jean Chrétien—in one of his first official functions as Canada's new prime minister—took part in the opening ceremonies of the new C$25 million legislative building. The building was funded in part by a public bond issue.

NORTHWEST TERRITORIES
• Information Highlights

Area: 1,304,903 sq mi (3 379 700 km²).
Population (June 1993): 57,000.
Chief Cities (1991 census): Yellowknife, the capital, 15,179; Iqaluit, 3,552; Inuvik, 3,206; Hay River, 3,206.
Government (1993): *Chief Officers*—commissioner, Daniel L. Norris; government leader, Nellie Cournoyea. *Legislature*—Legislative Assembly, 24 elected members.
Public Finances (1992-93 fiscal year): *Revenues*, $1,118,071,000; *expenditures*, $1,150,624,000.
Personal Income (average weekly earnings, June 1993): $702.08.
Education (1993-94): *Enrollment*—elementary and secondary schools, 17,210 pupils; postsecondary—community colleges, 565.

(All monetary figures are in Canadian dollars.)

Iqaluit Financial Crisis. In November the government of the Northwest Territories took direct control of the town of Iqaluit on Baffin Island. The elected mayor and town council were dismissed and a territorial government administrator was appointed until the end of 1994. The territorial government stated that it had taken the drastic measure because the town was in financial crisis. The town owed more than C$5 million to the territorial government.

Native Land-Claims Agreements. In January the Sahtu Tribal Council announced that it had reached a land-claims agreement with the federal government. Under the agreement the 2,200 Sahtu Dene and Metis of NWT's Great Bear Lake region were to gain ownership of 15,999 sq mi (41 437 km²) of land, including more than 695 sq mi (1 800 km²) with subsurface rights. They also were to receive a tax-free payment of C$75 million over a 15-year period. The tribe voted to ratify the agreement in July, and signed it in September. In January the Dogrib Dene, living to the south of the Sahtu, agreed to begin negotiations for a similar agreement.

In July federal legislation was enacted that would create from the NWT a third northern territory, Nunavut, by 1999.

Ross M. Harvey
Government of the Northwest Territories

NORWAY

Politics and the issue of membership in the European Community (later the European Union) dominated the news in Norway during 1993. Meanwhile preparations were on schedule for the 1994 Winter Olympics in Lillehammer.

Politics. The Labor Party, led by Prime Minister Gro Harlem Brundtland, gained four additional seats in the elections to the Norwegian parliament, the Storting, on Sept. 13, 1993. The increase raised Labor's total number of parliamentary seats to 67, and the party formed a new minority government. However, the real election victor was the Center Party, which trebled its representation to 31 seats. Under the leadership of the charismatic Anne Enger Lahnstein, the Center Party had campaigned vigorously against Norway's proposed membership in the European Community (EC). Parties losing seats were the right-wing Progressive Party, the Conservative Party—led by Kaci Kulmann Five, Norway's third principal political leader—and the left-wing Socialist Alliance.

European Community. The Norwegian government upheld its Feb. 1, 1993, application for EC (EU) membership, but the Labor Party was split deeply on whether Norway should join the organization. A referendum after the results of the membership negotiations with the EU are known may be required to resolve the issue. On October 26 the Center Party tabled a motion calling for Norway to withdraw its EU membership application. By late 1993 opinion polls showed that a majority of Norwegians—55% to 60%—were against EU membership, a sharp increase compared with early 1993.

Foreign Affairs. Fears of losing fishing and whaling rights played an important part in turning public opinion against EU membership in 1993. Despite an agreement in January among the Nordic states, Russia, and the EC Commission to set up a Barents Euro-Arctic Council, conflict erupted with Iceland and Russia over fishing in the Barents Sea. An area of 24 sq mi (62 km²) was disputed by Norway and Russia. Despite the alleged threat to fish stocks, trawlers from Iceland, the Faroe Islands, and Russia fished for cod in the region.

In February the U.S. House of Representatives passed a resolution asking the Bill Clinton administration to oppose the resumption of commercial whaling. Despite the House's action and protests from EC countries, Norway resumed whaling on a small scale. The Norwegians claimed that the species hunted was not scarce. (*See* ENVIRONMENT.)

NORWAY • Information Highlights

Official Name: Kingdom of Norway.
Location: Northern Europe.
Area: 125,182 sq mi (324 220 km²).
Population (mid-1993 est.): 4,300,000.
Chief Cities (Jan. 1, 1992): Oslo, the capital, 467,090; Bergen, 215,967; Trondheim, 139,660.
Government: *Head of state*, Harald V, king (acceded January 1991). *Head of government*, Gro Harlem Brundtland, prime minister (took office November 1990). *Legislature*—Storting: Lagting and Odelsting.
Monetary Unit: Krone (7.5305 kroner equal U.S.$1, Dec. 31, 1993).
Gross Domestic Product (1991 est. U.S.$): $72,900,000,000.
Economic Indexes (1992): *Consumer Prices* (1980 = 100), all items, 220.6; food, 224.5. *Industrial Production* (1980 = 100), 171.
Foreign Trade (1992 U.S.$): *Imports*, $26,076,000,000; *exports*, $35,150,000,000.

Foreign Minister Johan Joergen Holst and Norway scored an international diplomatic triumph by providing a secret meeting place in Oslo for representatives of the Palestine Liberation Organization (PLO) and Israel to hold peace talks. The negotiations led to the agreement that was signed in September. (*See* MIDDLE EAST/SPECIAL REPORT.) Holst's predecessor as foreign minister, Thorvald Stoltenberg, had succeeded Cyrus Vance as UN negotiator in the former Yugoslavia.

The Economy. Falling interest rates and rising values of securities alleviated the crisis in Norway's financial sector. After having been rescued from bankruptcy by the government in 1992, several of the nation's biggest banks reported modest profits for the first half of 1993. Major institutional investors joined the government in safeguarding Norwegian control of the key banks, buying shares from the government, which wanted to relinquish control.

Norway's oil and gas activity expanded in 1993, and estimates of total reserves were increased by 30% to 5.6 billion tons of oil equivalent.

Growth in the nonenergy mainland part of the Norwegian economy remained sluggish. Unemployment was up from 1992 and reached 127,000, or 5.8% of the workforce, in September. A government committee led by former Finance Minister Per Kleppe proposed cuts in state expenditure on the welfare state but also new subsidies to agriculture.

LEIF BECK FALLESEN
"Boersen," Copenhagen

NOVA SCOTIA

During 1993, Nova Scotians continued to suffer from a deep recession and were angry when their newly elected Liberal government betrayed its supporters by creating new taxes.

Provincial Election. In late May the Liberals, in a provincial election called by Don Cameron's Conservative government, rode to power on a wave of public discontent with 15 years of scandal-ridden Tory rule. The Conservatives, before declaring the election, tried to improve their political image by adopting budget-deficit-reducing measures, including privatizing Nova Scotia Power and putting Sydney Steel Corporation (Sysco) up for sale. This strategy became ineffective when John Savage, a physician and former mayor of Dartmouth, led a Liberal election campaign geared to job creation and lower deficits with no new taxes, which brought a landslide victory in the 52-seat legislature. Although Cameron retained his seat, he later resigned, and after an August by-election, the Liberals held 41 seats, the Conservatives had eight, and the New Democratic Party had three.

Legislation and Government. The Liberals introduced nearly 40 pieces of legislation, including tough conflict-of-interest legislation and legislation for preventing the sale of tobacco products to minors, as well as changes in the delivery of health, education, and social services.

Initially the Liberal government was preoccupied with firing Tory-appointed senior bureaucrats and nine directors of the Crown-owned Nova Scotia Resources Ltd. It rekindled an old controversy by permitting the opening of stores on Sunday and suffered public wrath for awarding two large untendered contracts to International Business Machines Corporation (IBM) and Proactive Group to act as government consultants. In its first budget it hiked the provincial sales tax by 1%, added 2 cents per liter to the fuel tax, raised the surtax on annual incomes exceeding C$65,000, and forced all public employees to take unpaid holidays for a week. For its part, the government expressed helplessness in tackling a C$396 million Tory budget deficit without raising taxes.

Economy. During 1993 the recession-bound Nova Scotia economy showed signs of slow recovery. Although its seasonally adjusted August unemployment rate rose from 13% to 14.7% in September, most of its sectors recorded lackluster growth. The fishery sector, however—with the depletion of cod and groundfish stocks—had collapsed, throwing 8,000 fishermen out of work. Several fish-processing plants were closed, stifling exports. The Westray coal-mine closure left a stagnant mining sector.

Construction housing starts were also down, and investment in apartment dwellings had dwindled. Similar declines in investment in the primary and manufacturing sectors had liquidated higher investment growth in the financial, commercial, communication, and government sectors. Signs of some growth, however, were recorded when during the first seven months of the year, the value of factory shipments, export trade, and retail trade grew.

R. P. SETH
Mount Saint Vincent University, Halifax

NOVA SCOTIA • Information Highlights

Area: 21,425 sq mi (55 491 km²).

Population (June 1993): 910,000.

Chief Cities (1991 census): Halifax, the capital, 114,455; Dartmouth, 67,798; Sydney, 26,063.

Government (1993): *Chief Officers*—lt. gov., Lloyd R. Crouse; premier, John Savage (Liberal). *Legislature*—Legislative Assembly, 52 members.

Provincial Finances (1992-93 fiscal year budget): *Revenues,* $4,588,000,000; *expenditures,* $4,741,-000,000.

Personal Income (average weekly earnings, June 1993): $495.07.

Labor Force (August 1993, seasonally adjusted): *Employed* workers, 15 years of age and over, 359,000; *Unemployed,* 14.9%.

Education (1993-94): *Enrollment*—elementary and secondary schools, 170,480 pupils; postsecondary—universities, 30,260; community colleges, 2,830.

(All monetary figures are in Canadian dollars.)

OBITUARIES

NUREYEV, Rudolf

Soviet-born dancer: b. near Lake Baikal, USSR, March 17, 1938; d. Levallois, France, Jan. 6, 1993.

One of the great classical dancers of the 20th century, Rudolf Nureyev attracted millions of viewers to ballet through his charismatic presence, flamboyant temperament, and technical bravura. Nureyev owed much of his astonishing impact to the electrifying tension that colored his performances: His celebrated "animal" quality strained against his superb academic form.

As a dancer, Nureyev was at his peak from his defection from the USSR on June 17, 1961, through the 1970s. He gave his last performance onstage in Budapest in February 1992.

Controversy was seldom absent from Nureyev's career, which encompassed his idiosyncratic stagings of 19th-century classics as well as his stormy directorship of the Paris Opera Ballet from 1983 to 1989. But along the way, Nureyev thrilled audiences throughout the West. He projected a sexuality then new to ballet and his modernized interpretation of the classics appealed beyond the dance world. His 15-year partnership with Margot Fonteyn in Britain's Royal Ballet, beginning in 1962, was legendary.

Background. Rudolf Hametovich Nureyev was born on a train traveling along Lake Baikal in Siberia as his mother, Farida, was en route to join her husband, Hamet, an army officer. Nureyev's mother was a Tatar and his father was of Muslim descent from Bashkiria, part of the Russian republic. After living in Moscow for a time, Nureyev and his three sisters moved with their parents to Ufa, Bashkiria's capital.

Nureyev studied ballet and folk dance in Ufa. At 17, he was accepted to the school of the Kirov Ballet in Leningrad (now St. Petersburg). He joined the Kirov in 1958 and was featured prominently in the company's 1961 Paris performances. However, instead of continuing to London with the Kirov, he was ordered back to Russia at Le Bourget Airport.

The dancer's request for political asylum made international headlines and ushered in his multifaceted career. He danced with every major ballet troupe, toured internationally from 1975 to 1991 with his chamber group "Nureyev and Friends," choreographed a few original ballets, and danced as a guest with U.S. modern-dance companies. He acted in two films, *Valentino* (1977) and *Exposed* (1983), and in a touring production of *The King and I* (1989). In 1991, Nureyev embarked on a new career as an orchestra conductor, but fell ill in 1992. He died in a hospital in a Paris suburb.

ANNA KISSELGOFF

HEPBURN, Audrey

Actress and UNICEF goodwill ambassador: b. Brussels, Belgium, May 4, 1929; d. Tolochenaz, Switzerland, Jan. 20, 1993.

Audrey Hepburn, with her aristocratic accent, unique innocence, and delicate, waiflike beauty, epitomized classic Hollywood elegance for two decades. Often cast in films opposite men much her senior—Gregory Peck, Humphrey Bogart, Cary Grant, Rex Harrison, Gary Cooper, Fred Astaire—Hepburn maintained an aura of chaste romanticism. Her ability to make Cinderella transformations in her movies made her one of the most memorable stars of the 1950s and 1960s.

Hepburn left acting for the most part in the late 1960s, and in 1988 became a goodwill ambassador for the United Nations Children's Fund (UNICEF). She traveled extensively in Africa and Latin America to aid starving children. Her last trip, in 1992, drew worldwide attention to the suffering children of Somalia.

Background. Edda van Heemstra Hepburn-Ruston, born in Belgium, was the only child of a Dutch baroness and an English banker. Trapped in the Nazi-occupied Netherlands during World War II, she, her mother, and two older half brothers ate tulip bulbs to survive.

Growing up in Brussels, England, and the Netherlands, Hepburn dreamed of becoming a ballerina. She studied ballet on scholarship and worked as a model in London after the war. Success struck overnight when the French author Colette starred Hepburn in the Broadway musical *Gigi* (1951). Her gamine looks and aura of chic modernity earned her instant popularity.

Hepburn won her first major movie role, as a princess in *Roman Holiday,* in 1953; she garnered the best actress Oscar for the film. In 1954 she was given a Tony Award for her work in *Ondine.* Hepburn earned four more Academy Award nominations, for *Sabrina* (1954), *The Nun's Story* (1959), *Breakfast at Tiffany's* (1961), and *Wait Until Dark* (1967). Her other awards included a special Tony award in 1968, the Cecile B. DeMille and Golden Globe Awards in 1990, and a Film Society of Lincoln Center tribute in 1991, for which her colleagues traveled from around the globe to speak of her professionalism and warm, good humor. In March 1993, she posthumously received the Jean Hersholt Humanitarian Award.

After her role in *Wait Until Dark,* Hepburn went into semiretirement, taking only a few film roles. Her final role was a cameo in 1989's *Always,* as an angel. Hepburn, who had lived in Switzerland since the mid-1950s, was married and divorced twice, first to actor Mel Ferrer and then to Italian psychiatrist Andrea Dotti. She had a son from each marriage.

MARY C. KERNER

MARSHALL, Thurgood

U.S. civil-rights attorney and Supreme Court justice: b. Baltimore, MD, July 2, 1908; d. Bethesda, MD, Jan. 24, 1993.

Even before he became the first black to sit on the U.S. Supreme Court, Thurgood Marshall's place in history was secure. Many regarded him as the most important U.S. lawyer of the 20th century, a leader in the battle for civil rights and racial equality. His most famous legal victory was the landmark high-court ruling in 1954—*Brown v. Board of Education*—that outlawed segregation in the public schools of the United States. Many years after he had argued that case before the Supreme Court, he said: "Segregation is the worst thing that ever happened."

For decades as a young man, he had crisscrossed the nation—particularly the South—fighting the legal battles of the poor and powerless. The phrase "Mr. Marshall is coming" heartened those he represented and inspired countless others who came to rely on his leadership in the early days of the civil-rights movement. Marshall argued dozens of cases before the Supreme Court and won nearly all of them, both as legal director of the National Association for the Advancement of Colored People (NAACP) and as solicitor general, representing the federal government.

In eulogizing Marshall after he died of heart failure at age 84, U.S. President Bill Clinton called him "a fundamental force of change in this nation."

Background. The great-grandson of a slave, Marshall grew up in comfortable but not affluent circumstances in Baltimore. His father, William Marshall, was a headwaiter in a private club; his mother, Norma, was a schoolteacher. He was introduced to the Constitution in grade school when he was required to memorize parts of it as punishment for misbehaving. "Before I left school, I knew the whole thing by heart," Marshall said.

He was graduated from Lincoln University in Pennsylvania, originally planning to study dentistry. Later he enrolled at Howard University Law School in Washington, DC, graduating at the top of his class in 1933. His mother had sold her engagement ring to help pay his way through. Marshall credited his father for instilling in him the will to take on tough battles on behalf of the underdog: " 'Son,' he used to say to me, 'if anyone ever calls you a nigger, you not only got my permission to fight him. You've got my orders to fight him.' "

As the NAACP's top lawyer, Marshall could assemble an elite group that included future judges, Cabinet members, and law professors to discuss tough cases. In 1961, President John F. Kennedy named him to the 2d U.S. Circuit Court of Appeals based in New York City. President Lyndon Johnson picked him to become

© Harris & Ewing

solicitor general—the administration's top courtroom lawyer—in 1965, and two years later appointed him to the high court.

Marshall's tenure there was 24 years, spanning a period of enormous change for the nation and its legal system. At the outset, Marshall was part of a liberal majority among the justices. That began to change in the 1970s with a more moderate to conservative court that often charted a zigzag course ideologically. By the end of his career, Marshall often was a frustrated and even bitter dissenter in cases that pitted individual or minority rights against government authority. Throughout, he stood fast with Justice William J. Brennan, his close friend and fellow liberal, in opposition to the death penalty. Marshall retired from the Supreme Court in 1991, declaring he was "getting old and coming apart." President George Bush picked Clarence Thomas as his successor. After tumultuous Senate confirmation hearings that included charges of sexual harassment against the nominee, Thomas became the second black to sit on the high court.

Marshall was married in 1929 to Vivian Burey, whom he met in Philadelphia while in college. She died of cancer in 1955, and Marshall married Cecilia S. Suyat. They had two sons, Thurgood Jr. and John William. Marshall, at 6'2" (1.9 m), towered over his wife, a Hawaiian of Filipino descent who worked as a secretary for the NAACP in New York.

Marshall, at his death, became only the second Supreme Court justice to be honored by having his casket lie in state at the court. The line of mourners wrapped around the Supreme Court building and included many who said they personally felt a debt of gratitude to him.

See also LAW.

JIM RUBIN

ASHE, Arthur

U.S. tennis star and humanitarian: b. Richmond, VA, July 10, 1943; d. New York City, Feb. 6, 1993.

Few athletes in their lifetimes made so profound a worldwide impact as did Arthur Ashe, the only black man to win the U.S., Wimbledon, and Australian tennis titles. Ashe—who died in New York City on Feb. 6, 1993, at age 49—was revered not only for his prowess on the tennis court but also for his quiet endeavors to bring about social justice and for an unflinching fight against AIDS.

Ironically, Ashe's quiet demeanor and his respect for privacy clouded the final year of a life that was always in the camera's eye and which endured not only poor health but the slings and arrows of unrelenting critics. While Ashe would be the last to say he was on a mission, he pursued his causes with a missionary's zeal. He was an eloquent spokesman and fighter for those who did not have a voice—dedicating himself to bringing down the barriers of privilege, poverty, and racism.

Ashe, who was the first black athlete to be granted a visa to compete in South Africa in 1973, stood tall in the fight against that country's racial policy of separatism; in 1985 he was arrested as an antiapartheid protester. He counted Nelson Mandela of South Africa's African National Congress among his longtime friends. In 1992 he spearheaded a drive to raise $5 million for the establishment of a foundation named after him to combat AIDS, and months later, he went to Washington to stand in the forefront of a protest against the Bush administration's Haitian refugee policy. Many of Ashe's critics, even in the black community, wished he were more aggressive, but his manner was quiet and his message was simple—steeped in the basic value of justice for all.

The cause of Ashe's death was pneumonia brought about by complications from the human immunodeficiency virus (HIV) that causes AIDS, which the tennis star said he believed he contracted from a transfusion of contaminated blood while undergoing heart-bypass surgery for a second time in 1983. He first learned of the infection in September 1988 after he went into New York Hospital for brain surgery. A biopsy disclosed the presence of a parasitic infection linked to AIDS.

Ashe chose not to make his condition public, wishing to protect the privacy of his wife Jeanne Moutoussamy-Ashe and his daughter Camera, who was born in 1986. But on April 8, 1992, after he was told that *USA Today* intended to publish an article about his illness, he made a public disclosure.

Ashe refused to be limited by his sickness. His time was filled with his many pursuits as golfer, public speaker, columnist, television com-

© UPI/Bettmann

mentator, and author of a three-volume history of the black athlete in America. His memoir, *Days of Grace*, written with Arnold Rampersad, was published posthumously.

Background. Born in Richmond, VA, on July 10, 1943, Arthur Ashe, Jr., was the son of a parks policeman, who believed in stern discipline, and a schoolteacher. Ashe made his first tennis strokes at age 7 on the Brookfield Park courts, a segregated playground near his home. He reached the national junior semifinals in 1958 and won U.S. indoor titles in 1960 and 1961. As the fifth-ranked junior in the country, he won a full scholarship to UCLA in 1962, attracting the attention of two of tennis' great stars, Pancho Gonzalez and Pancho Segura, who helped to tutor him.

He joined the Davis Cup team in 1963 and three years later was hailed by Harry Hopman, a renowned tennis teacher, "as the most promising player in the world." Ashe did not disappoint his boosters. He was a 25-year-old amateur fulfilling a three-year commitment in the U.S. Army when he won the first U.S. Open in 1968. By defeating Tom Okker of the Netherlands in the final, he became the first black man to win a tennis Grand Slam event. In 1970 he took the Australian Open and in 1975 he scored a stunning upset over the heavily favored Jimmy Connors in the final at Wimbledon. His career earnings in prize money totaled $1,584,909.

Ashe was on the U.S. Davis Cup team (1981-84) and joined the International Tennis Hall of Fame in 1985. Tennis was such a part of his life that he devoted much of his time and finances to help inner-city youth learn the sport. He also helped organize the Association of Tennis Professionals, a players union.

GEORGE DE GREGORIO

HAYES, Helen

U.S. actress: b. Washington, DC, Oct. 10, 1900; d. Nyack, NY, March 17, 1993.

Dubbed "The First Lady of the American theater," Helen Hayes played more than 70 major roles on the stage during her 60-year acting career. One of the United States' most popular stars for most of the century, Hayes had a vast appeal, attributable largely to her versatile acting style and the vulnerability and warmth she was able to project into her roles. She herself found it difficult to account for her enduring fame; in *On Reflection,* her memoirs—published in 1968—she wrote, "Without the compensation of glamour I am hard put to explain the durability of my career and the loyalty of the audience . . . Perhaps I am just the triumph of Plain Jane."

Background. Helen Hayes Brown was the only child of Francis Van Arnum Brown, a pork and poultry salesman, and Catherine Estelle Hayes Brown, an occasional actress who determined early on that her daughter would have a future on the stage. As a result, Hayes' acting career began when she was only 5 years old. She was graduated from Sacred Heart Academy in Washington in 1917, by which time she already had appeared in several stage productions, including the Broadway play, *The Prodigal Husband* (1914). She garnered her first star billing with a part in the play *Bab* in 1920.

Although taken lightly by critics at first, and noted mostly for her deft touch as a light comedian, Hayes astounded audiences and critics with her performance as a tragic heroine in the drama *Coquette* (1927). Over the years, she starred in many Broadway plays and in films, winning a Tony Award in 1946 for *Happy Birthday* and one in 1958 for *Time Remembered*; two Oscars, for *The Sin of Madelon Claudet* (1931) and *Airport* (1971); and a third Tony Award, for lifetime achievement, in 1980. She also appeared on television, winning an Emmy Award in 1952 and starring in the series *The Snoop Sisters* in the early 1970s and as sleuth Miss Marple in several TV movies during the 1980s. She retired from the stage in 1972 following a performance in *A Long Day's Journey into Night.*

Her many stage performances had included *What Every Woman Knows* (1926, 1938, 1954), *Mary of Scotland* (1933), *Victoria Regina* (1935), *Candle in the Wind* (1941), *Harriet* (1943), *Farewell to Arms* (1950), *Vanessa* (1950), *The Wisteria Trees* (1950), *Mrs. McThing* (1952), *Mainstreet to Broadway* (1953), and *The Skin of Our Teeth* (1955, 1961).

Commenting on the actress' performance in *Mary of Scotland*, Brooks Atkinson, the drama critic of *The New York Times,* noted that "slight as she is in stature [Mary herself was 6' (1.8 m) tall], Miss Hayes raises herself to queendom by the transcendence of her spirit." Of her visibly

© AP/Wide World

aging in *Victoria Regina,* Atkinson remarked upon Hayes' ability "to encompass in one evening the youth, maturity, and venerability of one human being" as a "humbling personal triumph."

Hayes received many honorary degrees—including ones from Columbia University, Smith College, Princeton, and the University of Denver—and distinguished awards, notably the Kennedy Center Honors in 1981 and the Presidential Medal of Freedom in 1986. She was active in the theater world offstage as well as on—she was president of the American National Theater and Academy and honorary president of the American Theater Wing—and volunteered for many causes, serving as national chairwoman of women's activities for the March of Dimes.

She was one of only two actresses to have a Broadway theater named in her honor. The annual Helen Hayes awards, given for artistic achievement in the Washington professional theater, also were named for her. For her epitaph, Hayes said that she wanted a line alleged to have been shouted out to Britain's Queen Victoria on the celebration of her 90th birthday, "Go it, old girl. You've done well."

In addition to her memoirs, the actress authored the novels *Our Best Years* (1986) and *Where the Truth Lies* (1988) and an autobiography, *My Life in Three Acts* (1990).

Hayes married the playwright Charles MacArthur in 1928; he died in 1956. The couple had a daughter, Mary, a novice actress who died from polio in 1949 at age 19. They also adopted a son, James, in 1938, who became an actor—appearing in the TV series *Hawaii Five-O*—and has three children.

MARY C. KERNER

ANDERSON, Marian

U.S. singer: b. Philadelphia, PA, Feb. 27, 1897; d. Portland, OR, April 8, 1993.

A contralto with an affecting, velvety sound and an expressive, remarkably versatile interpretive manner, Marian Anderson was the first black singer to perform at the Metropolitan Opera, and served as an inspiring role model for several generations of black musicians. Her 1939 performance on the steps of the Lincoln Memorial, where she sang for 75,000 people (plus a national radio audience of millions) after being denied the use of Constitution Hall, became a symbol of her quietly dignified, determined way of fighting racial prejudice.

Background. Born in a poor section of south Philadelphia, Marian Anderson began singing in the Union Baptist Church choir when she was 6 years old, impressing the director by singing all four parts of the choir's hymn arrangements. When she was in her mid-teens, her church raised money to help her pay for formal voice lessons, and the Philadelphia Choral Society, a black ensemble, gave a benefit performance on her behalf.

The young singer's first taste of national prominence came in 1925, when she won a vocal competition sponsored by the New York Philharmonic, with which she made her debut later that year. She was intent on continuing her studies, however, and in 1930 went to Europe to search for performance opportunities and to study languages and the art of lieder singing.

Anderson enjoyed greater success overseas than she had in the United States, where her career had stalled because promoters and opera directors were uneasy about hiring a black singer. In Europe she earned praise from all quarters. The Finnish composer Jean Sibelius dedicated a song ("Solitude") to Anderson, and in 1935, Arturo Toscanini told her: "Yours is a voice such as one hears once in 100 years."

The colorful impresario Sol Hurok heard Anderson sing in Paris in 1935, and brought her back to New York for a Town Hall recital on December 30 of that year. A *New York Times* critic, writing about that performance, described Anderson as "one of the great singers of our time."

Although Anderson was singing about 70 recitals a year by the late 1930s, she still made no headway in the opera world. It was not until Jan. 7, 1955—when she was 57 years old, and well past her vocal prime—that her opportunity came at the Metropolitan Opera: She sang the role of Ulrica in Verdi's *Ballo in Maschera.* Newspaper accounts of the performance say that she received a tumultuous ovation.

Because opera was closed to her for most of her career, Anderson's reputation rests on the considerable communicative power that she brought to the recital stage. Her manner–closed

eyes, very few gestures—conveyed stateliness and inner serenity. And her repertory covered considerable ground, from Bach and Handel oratorio selections to Schubert, Brahms, Schumann and Rachmaninoff songs; Verdi arias; and spirituals. Indeed, one of her real achievements was in emphasizing that spirituals deserved a place in the active repertory. She highlighted the form with her sublime readings of "My Lord, What a Morning" and "Crucifixion."

Anderson sang at the inaugurations of U.S. Presidents Dwight Eisenhower and John F. Kennedy. She toured India and the Far East in 1957, and sang for U.S. troops in Berlin in 1961. She was appointed an alternative representative in the U.S. delegation to the Human Rights Committee of the United Nations. She gave benefit concerts for several groups, and sang again at the Lincoln Memorial in August 1963 during the March on Washington for Jobs and Freedom.

In 1964, Anderson began her farewell recital tour at Constitution Hall—the hall she had been barred from in 1939—and gave her final concert at Carnegie Hall on April 18, 1965.

Much honored late in her life, Anderson was awarded a Presidential Medal of Freedom in 1963, was among the first group of artists to receive Kennedy Center Honors in 1978, and in 1984 was the first recipient of the Eleanor Roosevelt Human Rights Award of the City of New York. She was given a National Arts Medal in 1986. In 1980 the U.S. Treasury Department coined a half-ounce gold commemorative medal with her likeness.

Anderson married Orpheus H. Fisher, an architect, in 1943; the couple had no children, and Fisher died in 1986.

ALLAN KOZINN

The following is a selected list of prominent persons who died during 1993.
Articles on major figures appear in the preceding pages.

Abe, Kobo (69), Japanese author; one of Japan's most highly praised postwar writers. He was named a foreign member of the American Academy of Arts and Letters in 1992: d. Tokyo, Japan, Jan. 22.

Abravanel, Maurice (90), Greek-born musical conductor; also conducted orchestras, operas, and ballets, winning a Tony Award for his work in *Regina*: d. Salt Lake City, UT, Sept. 22.

Adzhubei, Aleksei (68), Russian journalist; former editor of the newspaper *Izvestia*. His father-in-law was Nikita Khrushchev: d. Moscow, Russia, March.

Agostini, Peter (80), figurative sculptor; helped establish the Pop Art movement in the 1960s: d. New York City, March 27.

Ahmann, James H. (62), lieutenant general in the U.S. Air Force; served as a combat pilot during the Vietnam War: d. Vienna, VA, Aug. 8.

Albertson, Joseph A. (86), corporate executive; founded one of the nation's largest supermarket chains and helped pioneer the one-stop supermarket concept: d. Boise, ID, Jan. 20.

Alexander, Arthur (53), U.S. Southern soul singer; his music influenced many rock singers: d. Nashville, TN, June 9.

Alexander, Myrl E. (83), former head of the U.S. federal prison system. An innovator in prison reform, he was instrumental in the passage of the 1965 Federal Prisoner Rehabilitation Act. He won the President's Award for Distinguished Service in 1967: d. Corpus Christi, TX, Jan. 14.

Alexandra (71), exiled queen of Yugoslavia; widow of Peter II, the last king of Yugoslavia: d. London, England, Jan. 30.

Allison, Davey (32), stock-car driver; a member of one of stock-car racing's most prominent families. He won the Daytona 500 in 1992: d. Birmingham, AL, July 13.

Ambro, Jerome A. (64), former U.S. congressman (D-NY, 1974-80); as chairman of the New Members Caucus in the House of Representatives in 1974, helped win changes in seniority rules and campaign financing: d. Falls Church, VA, March 4.

Ameche, Don (85), actor; a star in radio and movies during the 1930s and 1940s, he became newly popular with his work in the 1985 film comedy *Cocoon*, for which he won a best supporting actor Oscar: d. Scottsdale, AZ, Dec. 6.

Ames, Leon (born Leon Waycoff) (91), character actor and a founder of the Screen Actors Guild: d. Laguna Beach, CA, Oct. 12.

Andrews, Bert (63), performing-arts photographer; best known for chronicling the history of contemporary black theater. His works are collected in *In the Shadow of the Great White Way: Images from the Black Theater* (1990): d. New York City, Jan. 25.

Anrig, Gregory R. (61), educational tester; headed the Educational Testing Service since 1981: d. Princeton, NJ, Nov. 14.

Antall, Jozsef (61), prime minister of Hungary; the longest-ruling leader in post-Communist Eastern Europe, he was elected in March 1990: d. Budapest, Hungary, Dec. 12.

Anthony, Joseph (80), actor and director; in 1960-61, staged four successful Broadway shows in 11 months: *Best Man, Under the Yum-Yum Tree, Rhinoceros*, and *Mary, Mary*: d. Hyannis, MA, Jan. 20.

Ardolino, Emile (50), director of films and dance documentaries; in 1983 won a best-documentary Oscar for the film *He Makes Me Feel Like Dancin'*: d. Los Angeles, CA, Nov. 20.

Athulathmudali, Lalith (58), Sri Lankan politician; leader of the Democratic United National Front of Sri Lanka. He was assassinated: d. Colombo, Sri Lanka, April 23.

Auger, Arleen (53), opera singer; performed at the wedding of the Duke and Duchess of York in 1986: d. Leusden, Netherlands, June 10.

Baghdadi, Maroun (43), Lebanese filmmaker; famed for his portrayal of Lebanon's civil war. Won a Cannes Jury Prize (1991) for *Out of Life*: d. Beirut, Lebanon, Dec. 10.

Bailey, Charles P. (82), surgeon; pioneered new techniques and instruments for heart surgery: d. Marietta, GA, Aug. 18.

Baldwin, Benjamin (80), architect and interior designer; a leading force in modern American design, he was chosen as a charter member of the Interior Design Hall of Fame in 1985: d. Sarasota, FL, April 4.

Baldwin, Charles (91), former U.S. ambassador to Malaya (1961-64): d. Cockeysville, MD, Aug. 18.

Ballard, Lucinda (87), Broadway costume designer; won the first Tony Award for costume design in 1947. She won a second Tony for *The Gay Life* (1962): d. New York City, Aug. 19.

Barksdale, Don (69), professional basketball player; one of the first blacks in the National Basketball Association. He was a member of the gold-medal-winning 1948 U.S. Olympic basketball team: d. Oakland, CA, March 8.

Bartlett, Hall (70), experimental filmmaker; best-known for directing *Jonathan Livingston Seagull* (1973): d. Los Angeles, CA, Sept. 8.

Baudouin I, King of Belgium (62), reigned for 42 years, since the abdication of his father, Leopold III, in 1950. He helped stabilize the ongoing controversy between the Walloons and Flemish in Belgium: d. Motril, Spain, July 31.

Bauman, Art (53), dancer and choreographer; helped found the Dance Theater Workshop in New York City. His best-known work was *Dialog* (1965): d. New York City, Jan. 27.

Bauza, Mario (82), instrumentalist and bandleader; helped introduce Latin-style music and a series of several dance crazes to the United States in the 1940s and 1950s: d. New York City, July 11.

Bazelon, David L. (83), a U.S. appeals-court judge; his opinions extended the rights of individuals and criminal defendants. He worked to make prisons less brutal and sentencing guidelines more flexible: d. Washington, DC, Feb. 19.

Beam, Jacob D. (85), U.S. diplomat; served as ambassador to the USSR (1969-73): d. Rockville, MD, Aug. 16.

Beech, Olive A. (89), cofounder and former president and chairwoman of Beech Aircraft Company. She was inducted into the Aviation Hall of Fame: d. Wichita, KS, July 6.

Bellaver, Harry (88), character actor; best-known for his role on the television series *Naked City* (1960-64), and for roles on Broadway: d. Nyack, NY, Aug. 8.

Bennett, Wallace (95), former U.S. Republican senator; represented Utah from 1950-74: d. Salt Lake City, UT, Dec. 19.

Berberova, Nina (92), Russian-born writer; her best-known work is her 1969 autobiography, *The Italics Are Mine*. Her fiction also received high praise: d. Philadelphia, PA, Sept. 26.

Bérégovoy, Pierre (67), former prime minister of France. He took office in April 1992, but, facing allegations of corruption and criticism over his economic policies, stepped down after his Socialist Party was defeated in March 1993 elections. Deeply distressed over the accusations he faced, he committed suicide: d. Nevers, France, May 1.

Bernstein, Lord (born Sidney Lewis Bernstein) (94), British businessman; founded Britain's Granada cinema chain and Granada television station, which went on the air in 1956. Was made a life peer in 1969: d. London, England, Feb. 5.

Betts, Jackson E. (89), former member of the U.S. House of Representatives (R-OH); served as a congressman for 22 years (1951-73): d. Findlay, OH, Aug. 13.

Bevans, Margaret Von Doren (75), author, editor, and illustrator of children's books; best-known for her illustrations for *Pat the Bunny* (1940): d. Torrington, CT, July 14.

Bixby, Bill (59), television actor; starred in *My Favorite Martian* (1963-66), *The Courtship of Eddie's Father* (1969-72), and *The Incredible Hulk* (1978-82). At the time of his death, he was director of the series *Blossom*: d. Century City, CA, Nov. 21.

Boone, Sylvia A. (59), scholar of African and women's art; the first black woman to be granted tenure at Yale University: d. New Haven, CT, April 27.

Raymond Burr

Sammy Cahn

Roy Campanella

Cantinflas

Bordley, John Earle (90), researcher and educator; worked to improve treatment of the deaf and hearing impaired. Cofounded the Hearing and Speech Clinic at Johns Hopkins University: d. Baltimore, MD, July 12.

Bortoluzzi, Paolo (55), Italian ballet dancer and choreographer; at the time of his death, was director of the Grand Theatre in Bordeaux, France. Was a guest artist with American Ballet Theatre (1972-81): d. Brussels, Belgium, Oct. 16.

Boulding, Kenneth (83), British-born economist, philosopher, and poet; despite his unorthodox approach and ideas, he received many honors, and became president of the American Economic Association in 1968: d. Boulder, CO, March 19.

Brakefield, Charles (73), radio and television industry executive; served as president of The New York Times Company Broadcasting Group and as vice-president of The New York Times Company (1972-85): d. Memphis, TN, Aug. 13.

Brandon, Henry (77), Czechoslovakian-born British journalist; Washington correspondent for the British *Sunday Times* (1949-83). Made a commander of the British Empire in 1985: d. London, England, April 20.

Brian, David (82), film and television actor; among his films were *Intruder in the Dust* (1949) and *A Pocketful of Miracles* (1961). Starred in the TV series *Mr. District Attorney* (1954-55): d. Los Angeles, CA, July 15.

Bridges, James (57), film director and writer. Two of his films, *The Paper Chase* (1973) and *The China Syndrome* (1979), were nominated for Academy Awards. His other movies include *Urban Cowboy* (1980) and *Bright Lights, Big City* (1988): d. Los Angeles, CA, June 5.

Brooks, John (72), writer; authored three best-selling novels as well as ten nonfiction books on business and finance. He also was a staff writer for *The New Yorker*: d. Southampton, NY, July 27.

Brooks, Patricia (59), opera singer; a lyric soprano known for her unique style. Gave a command performance at the White House for U.S. President John F. Kennedy: d. Mount Kisco, NY, Jan. 22.

Brouwer, Arie R. (58), church leader; general secretary of the National Council of Churches (1984-89): d. Teaneck, NJ, Oct. 7.

Brown, John R. (83), U.S. circuit-court judge; played a major role in many 1950s desegregation cases in the U.S. South. With two other judges, he was the subject of a 1981 book, *Unlikely Heroes:* d. Houston, TX, Jan. 22.

Brusati, Franco (66), Italian film director; among his films were the award-winning *Bread and Chocolate* (1978) and *To Forget Venice* (1980): d. Rome, Italy, Feb. 28.

Buddhadassa Bhikkhu (87), Thai Buddhist monk; founded a monastery in 1932. His nontraditional teachings transformed Thai Buddhism: d. southeast Thailand, July 8.

Buell, Marjorie (88), cartoonist; created the popular Little Lulu character in 1935: d. Elyria, OH, May 30.

Burdett, Winston (79), radio and television correspondent; covered world events for CBS News from the 1940s until 1978: d. Rome, Italy, May 19.

Burgess, Anthony (76), British writer and composer; his bleak futuristic novel *A Clockwork Orange* (1962), was made into a movie by Stanley Kubrick: d. London, England, Nov. 25.

Burke, Kenneth (96), philosopher and writer; won the National Medal for Literature in 1981, and was honored by the American Book Awards the same year. Was a member of the National Institute of Arts and Letters and the American Academy of Arts and Letters: d. Andover, NJ, Nov. 19.

Burkitt, Denis P. (82), Irish-born missionary surgeon and medical researcher; his findings on cancer and nutrition spurred millions to change their diets. Studied a cancer common in Africa, now known as Burkitt's lymphoma. Received the Lasker Award: d. England, March 23.

Burn, Ian (53), Australian artist; a Conceptualist, he exhibited works in the United States and Europe. Helped found the Artworkers Union in Australia in 1979: d. Milton, Australia, Sept. 29.

Burr, Raymond (76), actor; best-known for his television portrayals of defense lawyer Perry Mason and police detective Robert Ironside. *Perry Mason* ran from 1957 until 1966, and the character was re-created for more than 25 TV movies. *Ironside* appeared from 1967-75: d. Dry Creek Valley, CA, Sept. 12.

Butler, John (74), ballet choreographer and dancer; received a *Dance Magazine* award in 1965: d. New York City, Sept. 11.

Butts, Alfred M. (93), inventor of the popular board game Scrabble: d. Rhinebeck, NY, April 4.

Cahn, Sammy (79), music lyricist; wrote the words to many Broadway hits, as well as cowriting several hit songs for Frank Sinatra. Won several Academy Awards. He was president of the National Academy of Popular Music since 1973: d. Los Angeles, CA, Jan. 15.

Callison, Charles (79), Canadian-born U.S. conservationist; served as conservation director and secretary of the National Wildlife Federation (1953-60) and executive vice-president of the National Audubon Society (1960-77). Founded the Public Lands Institute: d. Columbia, MO, Feb. 23.

Campanella, Roy (71), professional baseball player; a catcher with the Brooklyn Dodgers (1948-58), he was one of the first black major-leaguers. His career was cut short by an automobile accident. He was elected to baseball's Hall of Fame in 1969: d. Woodland Hills, CA, June 26.

Cesar Chavez

John Connally

Cantinflas (born Mario Moreno) (81), Mexican comic actor. Made 49 films; best-known for his role as Passepartout in *Around the World in 80 Days* (1956): d. Mexico City, Mexico, April 20.

Carli, Guido (79), Italian economist; guided Italy's recovery after World War II, and led the central bank (1960-75). Was treasury minister from 1989 to 1992: d. Spoleto, Italy, April 23.

Chambers, Albert A., Episcopal bishop; opposed the ordination of women to the priesthood, approved by the Episcopal Church in 1976. After the decision, he performed unauthorized confirmations for dissidents: d. Sun City Center, FL, June 18.

Chapman, Ben (84), professional baseball player during the 1930s and 1940s. Was banned temporarily from baseball in 1943 after striking an umpire: d. Hoover, AL, July 7.

Charteris, Leslie (85), Singapore-born mystery writer; his books featuring the Saint were made into several movies in the late 1930s and were the basis for a television series in the 1960s: d. Windsor, England, April 15.

Chavez, Cesar (66), social activist and union founder; worked to improve the life of U.S. migrant farm workers. Organized the first successful U.S. union of farm workers and was instrumental in getting collective-bargaining legislation passed for farm workers: d. San Luis, AZ, April 23.

Chiles, Harold Edmonds (Eddie) (83), oil executive and former owner of the Texas Rangers major-league baseball team (1980-89): d. Fort Worth, TX, Aug. 22.

Christison, Sir Philip (100), British military general; was the commander to whom the Japanese surrendered in Singapore at the end of World War II: d. Melrose, Scotland, Dec. 21.

Christoff, Boris (79), Bulgarian opera singer; a bass, he was renowned for his performances in the role of Boris Godunov: d. Rome, Italy, June 28.

Cogan, David G. (85), ophthalmologic researcher; considered the founder of the subspecialty of neuro-ophthalmology. Discovered radiation-induced cataracts in atomic-bomb survivors at Hiroshima and Nagasaki: d. Wayne, MI, Sept. 9.

Cohen, Jerry (70), journalist; was lead writer for *The Los Angeles Times'* coverage of the 1965 Watts riots, which won a Pulitzer Prize: d. South Pasadena, CA, May 8 (reported).

Collins, Albert (61), blues guitarist; known as the "Master of the Telecaster," he won a Grammy Award for a collaborative effort, *Showdown* (1985): d. Las Vegas, NV, Nov. 24.

Congakou, Tahirou, former president of Benin; was toppled by a 1965 military coup: d. Cotonou, Benin, June 16.

Conn, Billy (75), professional boxer; former light heavyweight champion. Famed for his 1941 title fight against heavyweight Joe Louis, which he almost won: d. Pittsburgh, PA, May 29.

Connally, John B. (76), former governor of Texas (1963-69); served in the John F. Kennedy and Richard Nixon administrations. Injured when Kennedy was assassinated in 1963: d. Houston, TX, June 15.

Constantine, Eddie (75), actor and singer; U.S.-born, he became a film star in Europe, specializing in the role of the American "tough guy": d. Weisbaden, Germany, Feb. 26.

Copeland, Vincent (77), political and social activist; cofounded the Workers World Party (1959): d. Hoboken, NJ, June 7.

Coyle, Joseph William (Joey) (40), man who gained fame in 1981 for picking up $1.2 million as it fell from an armored car: d. Philadelphia, PA, Aug. 15.

Crichton, Robert (68), author; several of his best-selling works became hit films: d. New Rochelle, NY, March 22.

Crosby, Bob (80), swing-era big-band leader; brother of singer Bing Crosby: d. La Jolla, CA, March 9.

Curtis, Thomas B. (81), U.S. congressman (R-MO, 1951-69); headed three federal commissions. Resigned in 1973 as chairman of the Corporation for Public Broadcasting in a dispute with the Richard Nixon administration: d. Allegan, MI, Jan. 10.

Cusack, Cyril (82), Irish actor; generally regarded as that nation's greatest actor. Among his films were *Odd Man Out* (1947), *The Spy Who Came in From the Cold* (1966), and *My Left Foot* (1989): d. London, England, Oct. 7.

Agnes de Mille

Doris Duke

Federico Fellini

Dizzy Gillespie

Danielewski, Tad (71), theater, movie, and television director; he produced and directed the Emmy Award-winning ABC documentary *Africa* (1967-68): d. Los Angeles, CA, Jan. 6.

Daniels, Wilbur (70), union official and civic leader; formerly a top officer of the International Ladies Garment Workers Union: d. New York City, March 20.

Davydov, Aleksandr Sergeivich (80), Ukrainian chemical physicist; best-known for creating the "exciton theory" during the 1960s: d. Ukraine (reported June 18).

Decker, Bernard Martin (89), U.S. federal judge; ruled in the 1970s that neo-Nazis had the right to march in a parade in Skokie, IL: d. Lake Forest, IL, Nov. 2.

DeFore, Don (80), actor; played Mr. Baxter on the television comedy *Hazel* (1961-65). Also appeared in other TV programs, onstage, and in films: d. Santa Monica, CA, Dec. 22.

deGavre, Chester B. (85), retired U.S. army brigadier general; participated in World War II and the Korean War: d. Onancock, VA, May 16.

de la Torre, Lillian (Lillian de la Torre Bueno McCue) (91), writer of historical mysteries. She was a former president of the Mystery Writers of America: d. Colorado Springs, CO, Sept. 13.

del Mestri, Cardinal Guido (82), Bosnia-Herzegovina-born Roman Catholic cardinal; a Vatican diplomat: d. Nuremberg, Germany, Aug. 2.

DeLoatch, Gary (40), dancer. Was a leading dancer with the Alvin Ailey American Dance Theater: d. New York City, April 2.

de Mille, Agnes George (88), choreographer; won Tony awards for her work in *Brigadoon* (1947) and *Kwamina* (1961). Elected to the Theater Hall of Fame in 1973, she received the Kennedy Center Career Achievement Award in 1980 and the National Medal of Arts in 1986: d. New York City, Oct. 7.

Deming, W. Edwards (93), expert on business management; advised Japan in its industrial reconstruction after World War II: d. Washington, DC, Dec. 20.

DeRita, Curly Joe (83), comedian; the last surviving member of the Three Stooges comedy team: d. Los Angeles, CA, July 3.

Dessauer, John H. (88), German-born chemical engineer and researcher; helped build a small photographic-product manufacturer into the multimillion-dollar Xerox Corporation: d. Rochester, NY, Aug. 12.

De Vries, Peter (83), writer; best-known for his humorous novels, he was a regular contributor to *The New Yorker*: d. Norwalk, CT, Sept. 28.

Diebenkorn, Richard (71), painter; his abstract and figurative works were influenced by the light and open spaces of California: d. Berkeley, CA, March 30.

Dingman, James E. (92), telecommunications engineer; helped develop the Telstar satellite while chief engineer at AT&T. Was director of Comsat (1964-73): d. Vergennes, VT, Aug. 7.

Donahue, Wilma Thompson (92), clinical psychologist; an expert in the psychology of aging, she took part in three White House conferences on aging (1961, 1971, 1981): d. Ann Arbor, MI, Aug. 17.

Donald, James (76), British stage, screen, and television actor. Among his films were *The Bridge on the River Kwai* (1957) and *The Great Escape* (1963): d. Wiltshire, England, Aug. 3.

Donner, Frank J. (82), civil-liberties lawyer; served as director of the American Civil Liberties Union's Project on Political Surveillance from 1980: d. Branford, CT, June 10.

Doolittle, James H. (96), aviation pioneer; as a lieutenant colonel in the U.S. air force, led the first air raid on Japan during World War II. Was awarded the Medal of Honor by President Franklin Roosevelt, eventually attaining the rank of lieutenant general. In 1989 he received the Presidential Medal of Freedom from President George Bush: d. Pebble Beach, CA, Sept. 27.

Dorsey, Thomas A. (93), pianist and composer; known as "the father of gospel music": d. Chicago, IL, Jan. 23.

Douglas, Gordon (85), film director; made many "Our Gang" short films in the 1930s, one of which—*Bored of Education*—won a 1936 Academy Award: d. Los Angeles, CA, Sept. 29.

Dowager Lady Fermoy (84), maternal grandmother of Diana, Princess of Wales: d. London, England, July 6.

Dreyfus, René (88), French-born race-car driver; won the Monaco Grand Prix in 1930. Was awarded the Legion of Honor by France's President Charles de Gaulle: d. New York City, Aug. 16.

Drysdale, Don (56), professional baseball player; a pitcher for the Brooklyn and Los Angeles Dodgers (1956-69), he was inducted into the Baseball Hall of Fame in 1984: d. Montreal, Que., July 3.

du Bois, William Pene (76), author and illustrator of children's books; won the Newbery Award in 1948. Also was founding editor of *The Paris Review*: d. Nice, France, March 5.

Duke, Doris (80), tobacco heiress and philanthropist; president of the Doris Duke foundation, which supported social and health services and cultural programs. She also donated to AIDS foundations: d. Beverly Hills, CA, Oct. 28.

Eagan, Andrea Boroff (49), journalist, educator, and women's advocate. Served (1983-87) as founding president of the National Writers Union: d. New York City, March 9.

Eckstine, Billy (78), bandleader and singer; popular during the late 1940s and the 1950s. His hits included "Everything I Have Is Yours," "My Foolish Heart," and "Blue Moon": d. Pittsburgh, PA, March 8.

Elson, Rev. Edward L. R. (86), Presbyterian church leader; chaplain of the U.S. Senate (1969-81). He baptized and confirmed U.S. President Dwight Eisenhower in 1953: d. Washington, DC, Aug. 25.

Espy, R.H. Edwin (84), religious leader; former general secretary of the National Council of Churches of Christ in the United States (1963-73), and a leader of the U.S. ecumenical movement: d. Philadelphia, PA, Jan. 17.

Falco, Louis, dancer and choreographer; formerly a principal dancer with the José Limón Dance Company, he was an internationally known choreographer of modern dance: d. New York City, March 26.

Fawcett, Gordon Wesley (81), publishing executive; with his three brothers, founded Fawcett Publications, which pioneered the paperback book: d. North Palm Beach, FL, Jan. 17.

Fellini, Federico (73), Italian film director and screenwriter; known for his deeply personal, sometimes bizarre films. Won four Academy Awards for best foreign-language film (1956, 1957, 1963, 1974): d. Rome, Italy, Oct. 31.

Ferris, Leo (76), a founder of the National Basketball Association (NBA): d. Syracuse, NY, June 1.

Fine, Reuben (79), chess champion and psychologist; wrote books on chess and psychoanalysis: d. New York City, March 26.

Fisher, Carl A. (48), Roman Catholic bishop; in 1987 he became the first black bishop in the western United States: d. Lakewood, CA, Sept. 2.

Fisher, Marvin (76), pop-music composer during the 1940s. His songs were recorded by such stars as Nat (King) Cole and Mel Tormé: d. Southampton, NY, Aug. 21.

Fleischmann, Peter F. (71), former president and chairman of *The New Yorker* magazine: d. New York City, April 17.

Ford, Constance (69), actress; appeared in various Broadway plays and several films, and played on the television serial *Another World* for 25 years: d. New York City, Feb. 26.

Fortenberry, Joe (82), captain of the first U.S. Olympic basketball team in 1936, which won the gold medal: d. Amarillo, TX, June 3.

Fosberg, F. Raymond (85), tropical-plant expert; helped found the Nature Conservancy, an environmental group: d. Falls Church, VA, Sept. 25.

Foster, Vincent W., Jr. (48), deputy White House counsel; a friend since childhood of U.S. President Bill Clinton, he apparently committed suicide due to the pressure of his office: d. Fort Marcy Park, VA, July 20.

Freedman, Daniel X. (71), psychiatrist and pharmacologist; former president of the American Psychiatric Association. First showed the link between hallucinogenic drugs and the brain hormone serotonin: d. Los Angeles, CA, June 2.

Gallo, Julio (83), wine industrialist; helped found the giant E&J Gallo winery: d. Tracy, CA, May 2.

Ganilau, Ratu Sir Penaia (75), president of Fiji; before becoming Fiji's first president in 1987, he had served in numerous government posts, including as governor-general: d. Washington, DC, Dec. 22.

Gary, Raymond D. (85), former Democratic governor of Oklahoma in the 1950s; helped ease school integration in the state: d. Madill, OK, Dec. 11.

Gaynor, Florence Small (72), registered nurse; the first black woman to head a major U.S. teaching hospital. Was appointed executive director of Sydenham Hospital in Harlem, New York City, in 1971: d. Newark, DE, Sept. 16.

Gehringer, Charlie (89), pro-baseball player for the Detroit Tigers (1924-42); later served as the Tigers' general manager and vice-president. He was elected to the baseball Hall of Fame in 1949: d. Bloomfield Hills, MI, Jan. 21.

Gentry, Alwyn (48), botanist and senior curator at the Missouri Botanical Garden; an expert in tropical plants, he had collected about 70,000 specimens: d. Ecuador, Aug. 3.

Georgescu, Valeriu (89), Romanian-born oil executive with Standard Oil; became a symbol of Communist oppression in the early 1950s, when the Romanian government refused to allow his sons to leave the country and join their parents in the United States. President Dwight Eisenhower intervened to secure their freedom: d. Geneva, Switzerland, Oct. 30.

Gesell, Gerhard A. (82) U.S. district-court judge; ruled in 1971 that *The Washington Post* could continue to publish information from the Pentagon Papers; sentenced John Ehrlichman, President Richard Nixon's adviser, to prison in the Watergate case in 1974; and presided in Oliver North's 1989 trial on Iran-contra charges: d. Washington, DC, Feb. 19.

Giddens, Kenneth R. (84), former head of Voice of America (1969-77); also was assistant director of the U.S. Information Agency: d. Mobile, AL, May 7.

Gilbert, Ruth (71), stage and television actress; best known for her role as the secretary on *The Milton Berle Show* in the 1950s: d. New York City, Oct. 12.

Gillespie, Dizzy (born John Birks Gillespie) (75), jazz trumpeter; internationally renowned for his musicianship, he revolutionized jazz music by helping to popularize the bebop style: d. Englewood, NJ, Jan. 6.

Gilliatt, Penelope (61), English-born writer and film critic; best known for her film criticisms in *The New Yorker* magazine from 1968 to 1979: d. London, England, May 9.

Giniger, Henry (71), journalist; a foreign correspondent for *The New York Times* after World War II, he chronicled the redevelopment of postwar Europe. Won an Overseas Press Club Award in 1969 for his coverage of Latin America: d. Paris, France, March 7.

Gish, Lillian (99), actress; began her career in 1898 in silent films and appeared in dozens of D.W. Griffith films in the early 1900s. She moved from silent films to "talkies," and later acted onstage and on television as well. Her last film appearance was in *The Whales of August* (1987): d. New York City, Feb. 27.

Golding, William (81), British author; won the Nobel Prize for literature in 1983. His best-known book was *Lord of the Flies* (1954); others included *Rites of Passage*, which won Britain's Booker Prize in 1980: d. Perranarworthal, England, June 19.

Golpaygani, Grand Ayatollah Mohammad Riza (90s), Iranian senior religious figure for Shiite Muslims: d. Tehran, Iran, Dec. 9.

Gould, John Ludlow (Jack) (79), reporter and critic; radio and television critic for *The New York Times* (1944-72). Won the George Polk Award, a Peabody Award, and a Page One Award: d. Concord, CA, May 24.

Granger, Stewart (born James Lablanche Stewart) (80), British-born U.S. actor known for his swashbuckling roles; starred in more than 60 films: d. Santa Monica, CA, Aug. 16.

Greenberg, Simon (92), rabbi and educator; vice-chancellor emeritus of the Jewish Theological Seminary of America. Wrote several books on Jewish affairs: d. Jerusalem, Israel, July 26.

Grinker, Roy Richard (92), educator in psychiatry and psychoanalysis; founder and former chairman of the Institute of Psychosomatic Training and Psychiatric Research and Training at Michael Reese Hospital in Chicago, IL. Studied under Sigmund Freud (1933-35): d. Chicago, IL, May 9.

Grizodubova, Valentina S. (83), Russian pioneer aviator and air commander during World War II. She set aviation records for women in distance, altitude, and speed: d. Russia, April 28.

Grucci, Felix James (87), fireworks expert; achieved an international reputation with his elaborate displays. He created fireworks shows for the 1986 Statue of Liberty celebration and the Lake Placid and Los Angeles Olympics: d. Long Island, NY, Jan. 9.

Gulick, Luther H. (100), administrator and scholar; advised President Franklin D. Roosevelt and other leaders on public management. Served as president of the Institute of Public Administration (1921-62), and as its chair until 1982: d. Greensboro, VT, Jan. 10.

Gwynne, Fred (66), actor; best-known for his role as Herman Munster in the TV series *The Munsters* (1964-66). Also starred in the comedy series *Car 54, Where Are You?* (1961-63): d. Taneytown, MD, July 2.

Habermann, A. Nico (62), computer scientist; founding dean of the School of Computer Science at Carnegie Mellon University, he headed that department from 1980 to 1988: d. Pittsburgh, PA, Aug. 8.

Hajek, Jiri (80), Czech intellectual and human-rights advocate; served as Czechoslovakia's foreign minister during the "Prague Spring" of 1968. A founder of the Civic Forum that led the nonviolent overthrow of Communist rule in 1989, he served as chairman of the Citizens Assembly (1988-92): d. Prague, Czech Republic, Oct. 22.

Haldeman, Harry Robbins (H. R.) (67), chief of staff under President Richard Nixon. He resigned his White House post in 1973 and was convicted in 1975 of trying to cover up the involvement of the Nixon administration in the Watergate scandal. After being released from prison in 1978, he wrote a book about the scandal, *The Ends of Power:* d. Santa Barbara, CA, Nov. 12.

Hamlin, Vincent (93), cartoonist; created the Alley Oop cartoon strip during the 1930s: d. Spring Hill, FL, June 14.

Hani, Martin Thembisile (Chris) (50), South African Communist and antiapartheid leader; he was secretary-general of the South African Communist Party and a prominent member of the African National Congress (ANC). He was assassinated by a white right-wing extremist: d. Boksburg, South Africa, April 10.

Hardy, Harriet L. (87), medical doctor; became the first female full professor at Harvard Medical School (1971). She created an occupational-medicine clinic at Massachusetts General Hospital in 1947: d. Boston, MA, Oct. 13.

Harken, Dwight E. (83), heart surgeon; known as the father of heart surgery, he was the first surgeon to experience repeated successes in operating on the human heart, during World War II. He created the first intensive-care unit: d. Cambridge, MA, Aug. 27.

Harley, John H. (77), expert on environmental radioactivity; former director of the Environmental Measurements Laboratory of the U.S. Department of Energy (1960-80): d. New York City, July 25.

Hawkins, Erskine (79), bandleader, composer, and trumpeter of the swing era: d. Willingboro, NJ, Nov. 11.

Haworth, Edward S. (Ted) (75), motion-picture art director; won an Academy Award for his work on *Sayonara* (1957): d. Provo, UT, Feb. 18.

Hayakawa, Kiyoshi (80), Japanese publisher; founded Hayakawa Publishing in 1945. Introduced Japanese readers to writers from the West: d. Tokyo, Japan, July 9.

Hearst, William Randolph, Jr. (85), journalist and publisher; shared a 1956 Pulitzer Prize for international reporting on the USSR, and won an Overseas Press Club award in 1958. Was chairman of the Hearst Corporation: d. New York City, May 14.

Heinsheimer, Hans W. (93), German-born classical-music publisher; one of the most influential persons in the field in the 20th century: d. New York City, Oct. 12.

Hempelmann, Louis Henry (79), authority on radiation biology; part of the Manhattan Project to create an atomic bomb during World War II, he later directed the health division of the U.S. government's nuclear laboratory: d. Rochester, NY, June 30.

Henize, Karl G. (66), scientist and former astronaut; died while attempting to climb Mt. Everest: d. China, Oct. 5.

Lillian Gish

William Golding

H.R. Haldeman

Henle, Fritz (83), German-born travel photographer; known for his classical black-and-white compositions. He published more than 20 books of travel photographs from around the world, and several guides to amateur photography: d. St. Croix, Virgin Islands, Jan. 31.

Henry, Paul B. (51), U.S. politician and state representative (R-MI); first elected to Congress in 1984: d. Grand Rapids, MI, July 31.

Hepler, Charles D. (74), publisher; was the first at *Reader's Digest* to hold the title of publisher (1968-80): d. Santa Fe, NM, May 24.

Herlihy, James Leo (66), playwright, novelist, and actor; best known for the novels *All Fall Down* (1960) and *Midnight Cowboy* (1965): d. Los Angeles, CA, Oct. 21.

Hersey, John (78), novelist and journalist; won a Pulitzer Prize for fiction for his 1945 novel, *A Bell for Adano:* d. Key West, FL, March 24.

Hester, William (Slew) (80), tennis official; served as president of the U.S. Tennis Association: d. Jackson, MS, Feb. 8.

Hibbert, Eleanor (80s), English novelist. Under several pseudonyms, most notably Victoria Holt and Jean Plaidy, wrote about 200 romantic, historical, and Gothic novels that sold more than 100 million copies and were translated into 20 languages: d. Mediterranean Sea, Jan. 18.

Hoebel, E. Adamson (86), anthropologist; a past president of the American Anthropological Association and the American Ethnological Society: d. St. Paul, MN, July 23.

Hoffman, Philip E. (84), lawyer; former national president of the American Jewish Committee (1969-73) and U.S. representative to the UN Human Rights Commission (1972-75): d. Livingston, NJ, June 6.

Holley, Robert H. (71), biologist; unraveled the genetic code of RNA (ribonucleic acid), a feat for which he shared the 1968 Nobel Prize for physiology or medicine. He also won the Lasker Award (1965) and a National Academy of Sciences award (1967): d. Los Gatos, CA, Feb. 11.

Horman, Edmund C. (87), human-rights crusader. Famed for his investigation of his son's disappearance and death during a 1973 military coup in Chile. His story was the subject of a book and a movie: d. New York City, April 16.

Horszowski, Mieczyslaw (100), Polish-born pianist; a child prodigy, his career spanned almost 90 years: d. Philadelphia, PA, May 22.

Houphuët-Boigny, Felix (88?), president of Ivory Coast since 1960; he was Africa's oldest and longest-serving head of state: d. Ivory Coast, Dec. 7.

Howard, Cy (born Seymour Horowitz) (77), comedy writer, director, and producer; wrote the 1940s radio shows *My Friend Irma* and *Life with Luigi:* d. Los Angeles, CA, April 29.

Howe, Irving (72), editor and critic; founded *Dissent* magazine. Wrote several books, including the 1976 National Book Award winner, *World of Our Fathers:* d. New York City, May 5.

Hungerford, David A. (66), geneticist; codiscovered the first visible genetic abnormality in cancerous cells, which became known as the Philadelphia chromosome: d. Jenkintown, PA, Nov. 3.

Hunt, James (45), British race-car driver; won the 1976 Formula One world championship and other major races: d. London, England, June 15.

Iba, Henry (88), basketball coach; led Oklahoma State to two national championships and coached three U.S. Olympic teams (1964, 1968, 1972). He was elected to the Basketball Hall of Fame in 1968: d. Stillwater, OK, Jan. 15.

Jack, Rev. Homer A. (77), Unitarian minister; founded the UN Non-Governmental Committee on Disarmament in the early 1970s and headed the agency until 1983: d. Swarthmore, PA, Aug. 5.

Jacobsen, Robert (80), Danish abstract sculptor. One of Denmark's most prominent artists, he was known for huge works in welded iron: d. Copenhagen, Denmark, Jan. 25.

Jadid, Salah (63), former military ruler of Syria (1966-70). Was ousted and imprisoned by Hafiz al-Assad in a bloodless 1970 coup: d. Damascus, Syria, Aug. 19.

Janeway, Eliot (80), political economist and author; wrote economic advisory newsletters and syndicated columns for The Chicago Tribune-New York News syndicate. He criticized the economic policies of U.S. presidents from Franklin Roosevelt to Ronald Reagan: d. New York City, Feb. 8.

Johnson, D. Mead (78), business executive; as chief executive officer of Mead Johnson & Co. (1955-68), helped the company grow into a worldwide pharmaceutical giant: d. Palm Beach, FL, Jan. 21.

Jonas, Hans (89), German-born philosopher who fled his native country when Hitler came to power. He became prominent in the new field of biomedical ethics with a book called *The Phenomenon of Life* (1966): d. New Rochelle, NY, March 5.

Jordan, James (56), father of pro-basketball great Michael Jordan; he was robbed and killed while sleeping in his car near a highway: d. near Fayetteville, NC, July 23.

Jordan, Richard (56), actor; won a Golden Globe Award for his role in the NBC miniseries *Captains and the Kings* (1976): d. Los Angeles, CA, Aug. 30.

Juan de Borbón (79), father of the king of Spain, Juan Carlos. He renounced his claim to the throne in 1977 to aid in the legitimization of Spain's parliamentary monarchy during the transition to democracy in Spain after the death of dictator Francisco Franco: d. Pamplona, Spain, April 1.

Kadoorie, Lord Lawrence (94), Hong Kong industrialist; was a force in the transformation of Hong Kong into an industrial powerhouse. Was the first man born in Hong Kong to be named to the British House of Lords: d. Hong Kong, Aug. 25.

Kanin, Michael (83), director, producer, playwright, and screenwriter. He shared an Academy Award in 1942 for writing *Woman of the Year:* d. Los Angeles, CA, March 12.

Kantor, Seth (67), journalist; his adamant refusals to reveal his sources led to court tests of the privilege of journalists under the 1st Amendment: d. Washington, DC, Aug. 17.

Kauffman, Ewing M. (76), owner of the Kansas City Royals major-league baseball team and a philanthropist: d. Mission Hills, KS, Aug. 1.

Keeler, Ruby (82), actress, dancer, and singer; starred in many popular musical films of the 1930s. In 1971, 30 years after retiring, she made a comeback: d. Palm Springs, CA, Feb. 28.

Kelly, Bruce (44), landscape architect; created the Strawberry Fields John Lennon memorial area in Central Park, New York City: d. New York City, Jan. 21.

Kempner, Robert M. W. (93), German-born lawyer; was deputy chief counsel for the United States at the Nuremberg war-crimes trials after World War II: d. Frankfurt, Germany, Aug. 15.

Kerst, Donald William (81), physicist; invented an early acceleration device, the betatron, during World War II. A member of the National Academy of Sciences, he was awarded its Comstock Prize in 1943: d. Madison, WI, Aug. 19.

Khouini, Hamadi (50), Tunisian government official and diplomat; was Tunisia's senior envoy and chief delegate to the United Nations: d. New York City, June 22.

Klein, Robert J. (66), editor and consumer advocate; founding editor of *Money* magazine: d. New York City, June 3.

Klos, Elmar (83), Czech film director; shared an Academy Award with codirector Jan Kadar for *The Shop on Main Street* (1965). Was at the forefront of the New Wave of Czechoslovak filmmaking during the 1960s: d. Prague, Czech Republic, July 19.

Knebel, Fletcher (81), author and newsman; known for his national daily newspaper column, "Potomac Fever," which ran for 13 years (1951-63). Coauthored *Seven Days in May* (1962), a best-selling military thriller: d. Honolulu, HI, Feb. 26.

Knowles, Warren (77), former Republican governor of Wisconsin (1965-71). Called out National Guard troops to the University of Wisconsin's Madison campus to quell student protests in 1969: d. Black River Falls, WI, May 1.

Koenig, Mark (88), professional baseball player; shortstop for the 1927 New York Yankees, considered perhaps the greatest baseball team of all time: d. Willows, CA, April 22.

Krauss, Ruth (91), children's book writer; won the Caldecott Medal for *The Happy Day* (1950) and *A Very Special House* (1954): d. Westport, CT, July 10.

Kulwicki, Alan (38), race-car driver; won the 1992 NASCAR championship: d. Bristol, TN, April 1.

Kunayev, Dinmukhamed A. (81), former Communist Party leader of Kazakhstan (1966-87): d. near Alma-Aty, Kazakhstan, Aug. 22.

John Hersey

Eliot Janeway

Erich Leinsdorf

© Elliott Erwitt/Magnum

© AP/Wide World

© AP/Wide World

Myrna Loy

Jean Mayer

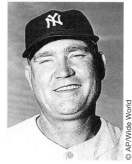

Johnny Mize

Garry Moore

Kusch, Polykarp (82), German-born U.S. physicist. Shared the 1955 Nobel Prize for physics: d. Dallas, TX, March 20.

Lamborghini, Ferruccio (76), Italian automobile executive; founded the industrial company that produced Lamborghini sports cars: d. Perugia, Italy, Feb. 20.

Landau, Ely A. (73), television and film producer; won a Peabody Award for a series of plays mounted for television, *Play of the Week* (1959-61). His best-known film was *Long Day's Journey into Night* (1962): d. Los Angeles, CA, Nov. 4.

Landon, Margaret (90), novelist; her book, *Anna and the King of Siam* (1944), inspired the Broadway musical *The King and I* (1956): d. Alexandria, VA, Dec. 3.

Langmuir, Alexander (83), physician; saved thousands of lives with his work in controlling infectious-disease epidemics. Received the Dana Foundation Award and awards from the American Public Health Association and the Royal Society of Medicine in England: d. Baltimore, MD, Nov. 22.

Larson, L. Arthur (82), top aide to U.S. President Dwight Eisenhower; advocated moderate Republicanism and wrote several books on the Republican Party's philosophy: d. Durham, NC, March 27.

Latch, Edward Gardiner (92), Methodist minister; chaplain of the U.S. House of Representatives (1967-78): d. Gaithersburg, MD, April 9.

Lazar, Irving Paul (Swifty) (86), literary and entertainment agent; represented such luminaries as Humphrey Bogart, Ernest Hemingway, and Richard Nixon: d. Beverly Hills, CA, Dec. 30.

Ledoux, Fernand (96), French actor; he appeared in more than 800 plays and films during one of the longest careers in French theater and cinema: d. Villerville, France, Sept. 21.

Lee, Brandon (27), film actor; the son of late martial-arts film star Bruce Lee, he was shot accidentally while filming a scene for an action film, *The Crow*: d. Wilmington, NC, March 31.

Lee, Pinky (born Pincus Leff) (85), vaudeville comic and star of children's television shows during the 1950s: d. Mission Viejo, CA, April 3.

Leinsdorf, Erich (81), Austrian-born musical conductor; known for his discipline and musical knowledge, he wrote a book on his profession, *The Composer's Advocate:* d. Zurich, Switzerland, Sept. 11.

Leontovich, Eugenie (93), Russian-born actress, playwright, director, and teacher; created memorable roles on Broadway in *Grand Hotel* (1930), *Twentieth Century* (1932), and *Anastasia* (1954). Cowrote *Dark Eyes* (1943), which ran on Broadway for 230 performances: d. New York City, April 2.

Lewis, Reginald "Reggie" (27), professional basketball player; a first-round draft pick in 1987 from Northeastern University, he was the Boston Celtics' captain, and had been an NBA All-Star in 1992: d. Waltham, MA, July 25.

Lewis, Reginald F. (50), lawyer and financier; led the $1 billion acquisition of Beatrice Companies in 1987: d. New York City, Jan. 19.

Lipsky, Eleazar (81), lawyer and novelist; served as legal counsel to the Mystery Writers of America. Published many novels, most with a legal background: d. New York City, Feb. 14.

Lounsbery, Daniel (84), television producer; won two Emmy awards and a Peabody Award: d. Philadelphia, PA, Aug. 22.

Loy, Myrna (born Myrna Williams) (88), film actress; starred in film comedies in the 1930s and 1940s. Her best-known films were *The Thin Man* (1934) and its sequels. She was awarded an honorary Oscar (1991): d. New York City, Dec. 14.

Lussi, Gustave (95), Swiss-born figure-skating coach; coached 16 world skating champions, among them seven Olympic gold medalists: d. Lake Placid, NY, June 24.

MacDonald, Anne Thompson (96), founder of Recording for the Blind, which puts books on tape for blind and learning-disabled students: d. Huntington, NY, Oct. 9.

Manby, C. Robert (73), retired entertainment executive; formerly president and chairman of RKO Pictures (1978-86): d. New York City, Aug. 6.

Mankiewicz, Joseph L. (83), writer, director, and producer of films. Won four Academy Awards for writing and directing the comedies *A Letter to Three Wives* (1949) and *All About Eve* (1950): d. Mount Kisco, NY, March 6.

Mayer, Jean (72), French-born nutritionist; researched the causes of obesity and regulation of hunger. He organized a 1969 White House conference that led to the introduction of food stamps for the poor. Named president (1976) and chancellor (1992) of Tufts University: d. Sarasota, FL, Jan. 1.

Maynard, Robert C. (56), publisher; the first black editor and owner of a major U.S. daily newspaper, *The Oakland* (CA) *Tribune* (1983-92): d. Oakland, CA, Aug. 17.

McCluskey, Roger (63), race-car driver and auto-racing official; was executive vice-president and chief operating officer of the U.S. Auto Club: d. Indianapolis, IN, Aug. 29.

McCollum, Leonard (91), philanthropist and oilman; as president of Continental Oil Company, built the company into the international giant, Conoco: d. Houston, TX, June 13.

McFarland, George "Spanky" (64), former child star; starred in the "Our Gang" and "Little Rascals" comedies during the 1930s and early 1940s. He also was featured in 14 full-length movies, but ended his acting career while still a teenager: d. Grapevine, TX, June 30.

McGrath, Earl James (90), educator; served as commissioner of education under Presidents Harry Truman and Dwight Eisenhower: d. Tucson, AZ, Jan. 14.

Merbah, Kasdi (born Abdallh Khalaf) (55), Algerian politician; served as prime minister (1988-89) and was opposition leader at the time of his assassination: d. Bordj el-Bahri, Algeria, Aug. 21.

Mickelson, George (52), Republican governor of South Dakota since 1986. Was cochairman of the National Governors Association's task force on health care: d. near Dubuque, IA, April 19.

Mikardo, Ian (84), British politician; former chairman of the Labour Party and a member of Parliament for 37 years: d. Stockport, England, May 6.

Mize, Johnny (80), professional baseball player from the 1930s to the 1950s; inducted into the Baseball Hall of Fame in 1981: d. Demorest, GA, June 2.

Montoya, Carlos (89), Spanish-born guitarist and composer; instrumental in developing flamenco into an internationally known musical style: d. Wainscott, NY, March 3.

Moore, Garry (78), star in early television; hosted a variety show, *The Garry Moore Show* (1950-67), and the game shows *I've Got a Secret* (1952-66) and *To Tell the Truth:* d. Hilton Head Island, SC, Nov. 28.

Morgan, Edward (82), radio and television reporter; covered such historic events as the 1956 sinking of the *Andrea Doria* and the assassination of U.S. President John F. Kennedy in 1963. He won the Peabody, DuPont, Polk, and Hillman awards: d. McLean, VA, Jan. 27.

Mori, Taikichiro (88), Japanese real-estate magnate; considered the richest man in the world: d. Tokyo, Japan, Jan. 30.

Morris, Alice S. (90), editor and writer; literary editor of *Harper's Bazaar* (1951-68). Won a lifetime achievement award from PEN International in 1977: d. New York City, Sept. 24.

Morris, John M. (78), gynecological researcher and surgeon; discovered the "morning-after" birth-control pill and helped develop new approaches to cancer treatment: d. Woodbridge, CT, April 8.

Morse, Carleton E. (91), writer for radio; created the longest-running soap opera in U.S. radio history, *One Man's Family* (1932-59): d. Sacramento, CA, May 24.

Mosconi, Willie (80), famed pocket-billiards player; won the world pocket-billiards championship 13 times in 15 years (1941-56): d. Haddon Heights, NJ, Sept. 16.

Most, Johnny (69), radio sports announcer; covered the Boston Celtics professional basketball team's games for almost 40 years. He was famous for his enthusiasm: d. Hyannis, MA, Jan. 3.

Nabiyev, Rakhman N. (62), former president of Tajikistan; governed the nation when it was a Soviet republic (1982-85), and returned to power in 1991. He resigned in 1992 after violent protests: d. Dushanbe, Tajikistan, April 10.

Ndadaye, Melchior (40), president of Burundi; elected in June 1993 in the nation's first democratic election, he was killed in a military coup only three months later: d. Bujumbura, Burundi, Oct. 24 (reported).

Nesbett, Buell A. (83), judge; headed the Alaska Supreme Court after Alaska attained statehood in 1959: d. Anchorage, AK, Aug. 17.

Pat Nixon

Norman Vincent Peale

Nesbitt, Lowell (59), realist painter. His works were depicted on four U.S. Postal Service stamps in 1980. Was the official artist for the Apollo 9 and Apollo 11 spaceflights: d. New York City, July 8.

Newhall, Beaumont (84), photography historian and author; pioneered the chronicling of the art of photography. His books include *The History of Photography, 1839 to the Present (1948):* d. Santa Fe, NM, Feb. 26.

Nikolais, Alwin (82), composer, designer, and choreographer; a pioneer of multimedia dance, he founded his own modern-dance company in the late 1940s. He won the Capezio Award (1982), the Scripps American Dance Festival Award (1985), a National Medal of Arts (1985), and Kennedy Center Honors (1987): d. New York City, May 8.

Nixon, Pat (born Thelma Catherine Ryan), former U.S. first lady, the wife of U.S. President Richard M. Nixon. She was active in many educational and volunteer-aid programs: d. Park Ridge, NJ, June 22.

North, Henry Ringling (83), former owner and manager of the Ringling Bros. and Barnum & Bailey Circus (1936-67): d. Switzerland, Oct. 2.

Nosaka, Sanzo (101), Japanese politician; founder (in 1922) and former chairman of the Japan Communist Party, from which he was expelled in 1992: d. Tokyo, Japan, Nov. 14.

Nouira, Hedi (82), Tunisian politician. He served as finance minister and Tunisia's first central-bank head after independence was gained in 1956. Named as chosen successor to President Habib Bourguiba in 1974, he took over day-to-day governing of the country in the 1970s: d. Tunis, Tunisia, Jan. 25.

Nye, Russel B. (80), historian of U.S. culture and literature; won a 1945 Pulitzer Prize for *George Bancroft: Brahmin Rebel* (1944): d. Lansing, MI, Sept. 2.

Ochoa, Severo (88), Spanish biochemist; won the Nobel Prize in physiology or medicine in 1959 for his discovery of an enzyme that can synthesize RNA: d. Madrid, Spain, Nov. 1.

O'Connell, Helen (73), big-band singer; one of the United States' most popular female singers in the early 1940s: d. San Diego, CA, Sept. 9.

O'Keefe, Richard J. (87), retired U.S. air force major general; commanding officer of the 17th Air Force in Tripoli, Libya, in 1956. Was a former director of air force flight-safety research. He retired in 1960: d. Washington, DC, July 21.

Owles, James W. (46), a founder of the Gay Activists Alliance; became the first openly gay candidate for political office in New York City in 1973: d. New York City, Aug. 6.

Özal, Turgut (66), president of Turkey; led his country toward free enterprise and revitalized the economy during the 1980s. Became prime minister in 1983, and in 1989, after losing popularity due to inflation and autocratic behavior, he had himself elected president—a post traditionally above politics in Turkey: d. Ankara, Turkey, April 17.

Parker, Barrington D. (77), U.S. district judge; presided over the trial of John Hinckley, Jr., who tried to assassinate U.S. President Ronald Reagan in 1981: d. Silver Spring, MD, June 2.

Parker, Theodore A. 3d (40), senior scientist for Conservation International; one of the world's leading ornithologists, he was able to recognize nearly 4,000 species of birds by their sound alone: d. Ecuador, Aug. 3.

Parker, William (49), singer; a lyric baritone, he won several major prizes, including the Kennedy Center-Rockefeller Foundation International Competition for Excellence in the Performance of American Music: d. New York City, March 29.

Parkinson, C. Northcote (83), British historian and author; established a notion known as "Parkinson's law": "work expands...to fill the time available for its completion." The book of the same title became a best-seller in 1958. His writings mixed satire and economic analysis: d. Canterbury, England, March 9.

Peale, Norman Vincent (95), one of the most influential religious figures in the 20th century; advocated optimism and positive thinking, as explained in his book, *The Power of Positive Thinking* (1952). Was one of the first to bring psychiatric tenets into religion. He received two Freedom Foundation awards: d. Pawling, NY, Dec. 24.

Peckham, Robert F. (72), U.S. district judge; issued orders on the desegregation of the San Francisco Police Department and the San Jose Unified School District, and prohibited statewide use of I.Q. tests in California schools, saying they were biased against black students: d. San Francisco, CA, Feb. 16.

Pennel, John (53), pole-vaulter; set eight world records during the 1960s and became the first to break the 17' (5.18-m) barrier: d. Santa Monica, CA, Sept. 26.

Petrovic, Drazen (28), professional basketball player; leading scorer for the New Jersey Nets in the 1992-93 season. A Croatian, he began his basketball career in Europe: d. near Ingolstadt, Germany, June 7.

Pharoun, Henry (92), Lebanese politician; active in Lebanon's fight for independence, he served as foreign minister and in other posts after freedom was achieved in 1943, and designed the Lebanese flag: d. Beirut, Lebanon, Aug. 7.

Philbrick, Herbert A. (78), spy for the U.S. Federal Bureau of Investigation (FBI) during the 1940s. Infiltrated the U.S. Communist Party, later testifying before the House Un-American Activities Committee and helping convict 11 party leaders: d. North Hampton, NH, Aug. 16.

Phoenix, River (23), actor; won praise for his roles in such films as *Stand By Me* (1986), *Running on Empty* (1988), and *My Own Private Idaho* (1991): d. Los Angeles, CA, Oct. 31.

Pizey, Sir Mark (93), British navy admiral; a hero in World War II, he later was commander-in-chief of the Indian navy: d. Burnham-on-Sea, England, May 17.

Pleven, René (91), French politician; twice served as France's prime minister (1950-51; 1951-52), and led the Democratic and Socialist Union of the Resistance Party he had helped found (1946-53): d. Paris, France, Jan. 13.

Polk, Lee (69), television producer, director, and writer; served as director of children's programming at National Educational Television (1970-72) and at ABC (1972-76). He won an Emmy Award in 1986: d. New York City, Feb. 19.

Pollard, Jim (70), professional basketball player for the Minneapolis Lakers in the 1940s and 1950s. Was inducted into the Basketball Hall of Fame in 1977: d. Stockton, CA, Jan. 22.

Pontecorvo, Bruno (80), Italian-born physicist; pioneered the study of neutrinos. After becoming a British citizen, he defected to the USSR in 1950: d. Dubna, Russia, Sept. 24.

Posadas Ocampo, Cardinal Juan Jesus (66), archbishop of Guadalajara, Mexico; was shot by members of a drug cartel, who apparently mistook him for a drug lord: d. Guadalajara, Mexico, May 24.

Premadasa, Ranasinghe (69), president of Sri Lanka; his administration, while tarnished by human-rights abuses, had crusaded for the poor. He was assassinated by a suicide bomber during a parade: d. Colombo, Sri Lanka, May 1.

Price, Vincent (82), actor; best known for his villainous roles in many horror films. He appeared in scores of films and more than 2,000 television programs, as well as onstage: d. Los Angeles, CA, Oct. 25.

Pulitzer, Joseph, Jr. (80), publisher and art collector; chairman of the Pulitzer Publishing Company, he received a special citation from the Pulitzer Prize board for his service to U.S. journalism: d. St. Louis, MO, May 26.

Quesada, Elwood R. (88), aviator; was the first head of the Federal Aviation Administration (1958-61). A member of the U.S. Army Air Corps since 1927, he retired as a three-star general in 1951: d. Jupiter, FL, Feb. 9.

Ra, Sun (born Herman [Sonny] Blount) (79), jazz musician; an innovative bandleader, he combined elements of theater into his surrealist style: d. Birmingham, AL, May 30.

Raczynski, Count Edward Bernard André Maria (101), Polish diplomat; served as foreign minister of the London-based Polish government-in-exile during part of World War II. Also was Polish ambassador to Britain (1933-45): d. London, July 30.

Ramanujan, Attipat K. (64), Indian poet and translator; taught English literature in India, and Indian literature in the United States. Won a fellowship in 1983 from the MacArthur Foundation and received many literary awards in India: d. Chicago, IL, July 13.

Renoir, Claude (79), French cinematographer and grandson of Impressionist Pierre Auguste Renoir; he was praised for his artistic skill in filmmaking: d. Troyes, France, Sept. 5.

Resnekov, Leon (65), cardiologist; known for his pioneering work in the use of electrical shock to restore normal heart rhythms, and in the use of nuclear medicine in heart imaging: d. Chicago, IL, Aug. 17.

Rhoodie, Eschel (60), exiled South African politician; former secretary of information who served as chief propagandist for apartheid. Was forced to resign in 1978 when the information ministry was abolished: d. Atlanta, GA, July 17.

Rich, Stanley R. (76), entrepreneur and inventor; developed a scanning sonar for submarines during World War II: d. Cambridge, MA, Nov. 21.

Ridder, Elizabeth Sullivan (93), philanthropist; served on the national board of the Girl Scouts of America (1946-58; 1961-70), and as national secretary from 1950 to 1968. Received an award from Pope Pius XII in 1942 for her service to the Roman Catholic Church: d. West Palm Beach, FL, Aug. 12.

Ridgway, Matthew B. (98), U.S. army general and former army chief of staff; led U.S. forces in Normandy during World War II and UN forces in Korea. He planned and executed the army's first major

airborne attack during World War II, into Sicily. Appointed chief of staff in 1953 by President Dwight Eisenhower, he retired in 1955. He was awarded the Presidential Medal of Freedom in 1986 and the Congressional Gold Medal in 1991: d. Fox Chapel, PA, July 26.

Ridley, Lord (Nicholas) (64), British politician; served as a minister in all three of Margaret Thatcher's Conservative governments. Was named a life peer in 1992: d. Liddesdale, England, March 5.

Riegels, Roy (84), college-football player for the University of California in the 1920s; became famous when he ran 69 yards in the wrong direction in the 1929 Rose Bowl, costing his team the game: d. Woodland, CA, March 26.

Robinson, Roscoe, Jr. (64), U.S. army general; the first black to become a four-star army general. Served in Korea and Vietnam, and was the U.S. representative to the North Atlantic Treaty Organization's military committee: d. Washington, DC, July 22.

Rodham, Hugh E. (82), father of first lady Hillary Rodham Clinton: d. Little Rock, AR, April 7.

Rogers, Will, Jr. (81), former actor and politician; son of the humorist Will Rogers: d. Tubac, AZ, July 9.

Rome, Harold J. (85), Broadway songwriter. He was elected to the Songwriters' Hall of Fame in 1981 and the Theater Hall of Fame in 1981, and was presented the Drama Desk Award in 1990: d. New York City, Oct. 26.

Rossi, Bruno (88), physicist; a pioneer in cosmic-ray research. Helped to develop space physics and shape government policy for early space exploration. A member of the National Academy of Sciences and the American Academy of Arts and Sciences, he received the U.S. Medal of Science and the Wolf Prize in Physics: d. Cambridge, MA, Nov. 21.

Rubin, Alton, Sr. (Rockin' Dopsie) (61), zydeco musician. A master of this fusion of Cajun, blues, and country styles, he received a 1991 Grammy nomination for his last album, *Louisiana Music:* d. Opelousas, LA, Aug. 26.

Sabin, Albert B. (86), developer of a polio vaccine; researched the nature and method of transmission of the viruses that cause polio, and developed the live-virus polio vaccine. He was elected to the National Academy of Sciences (1951), and won the Lasker Award (1965) and the U.S. National Medal of Science (1971): d. Washington, DC, March 3.

Salant, Richard S. (78), former head of CBS News. During his tenure as president (1961-64; 1966-79), CBS became an industry leader: d. Southport, CT, Feb. 16.

Salisbury, Harrison E. (84), author and journalist; an authority on the Soviet Union, he won a Pulitzer Prize in 1955 for his work as a foreign correspondent for *The New York Times:* d. Providence, RI, July 5.

Sanger, Eleanor (63), television producer; won several Emmy awards for her Olympics broadcasts for ABC: d. West Tisbury, MA, March 7.

Sauvé, Jeanne (70), former Canadian speaker of parliament (1980-84) and Canada's first woman governor-general (1984-90): d. Montreal, Que., Jan. 26.

Schaefer, Vincent J. (87), chemist; invented cloud seeding and created the first artificial snowfall and rainfall during the 1940s: d. Schenectady, NY, July 25.

Schlaefer, Salvador (73), Roman Catholic bishop; was a missionary in Nicaragua for 45 years: d. Bluefields, Nicaragua, Oct. 22.

Schmiechen, Richard (45), film producer; won an Academy Award for the documentary *The Times of Harvey Milk* (1984): d. Los Angeles, CA, April 7.

Schneider, Alexander (84), Lithuanian-born U.S. violinist and conductor; he founded the New York String Orchestra (1968). Won Kennedy Center Honors in 1988: d. New York City, Feb. 2.

Schumacher, Hal (82), professional baseball player in the 1930s. Played for three World Series-winning New York Giants teams: d. Cooperstown, NY, April 21.

Sen, Binay Ranjan (94), Indian diplomat; as director-general of the UN Food and Agriculture Organization (1956-67), he campaigned against world hunger, most notably with the 1963 World Food Congress: d. Calcutta, India, June 10.

Sepulveda, Jesse D., Jr. (7), boy who received a heart transplant at the age of 16 days. The operation began a national debate on medical ethics and led to the creation of an organ-donor system: d. Loma Linda, CA, July 16.

Sharaff, Irene (83), costume designer for films and plays; won five Academy awards and one Tony Award for her work: d. New York City, Aug. 16.

Sharkey, Ray (40), television and film actor; portrayed tough yet vulnerable characters. Best known for his role in the television series *Wiseguy* (1987): d. Brooklyn, NY, June 11.

Sheaffer, Louis (80), Pulitzer Prize-winning biographer; won in 1974 for *O'Neill, Son and Artist,* the second volume of a biography of playwright Eugene O'Neill: d. Brooklyn, NY, Aug. 7.

Sheikh Amin Tarif (95), spiritual leader of the Arab Druse religious sect in Israel. Was named his community's spiritual leader in 1928: d. Julis, Israel, Oct. 2.

Shirer, William L. (89), author and historian; as a foreign correspondent just before World War II, pioneered the use of live transatlantic radio broadcasts. His best-known book is *The Rise and Fall of the Third Reich* (1960): d. Boston, MA, Dec. 28.

Slayton, Donald (Deke) (69), astronaut; one of the first seven U.S. astronauts, he also served as chief of flight operations at the Johnson Space Center: d. League City, TX, June 13.

Smith, Alexis (72), actress; won a Tony for her role in the Broadway musical *Follies* (1971). Also had a successful film career in the 1940s and 1950s: d. Los Angeles, CA, June 9.

Smith, Joseph (91), U.S. army general; headed the post-World War II Berlin airlift operation. From 1951 to 1958 he headed the Military Air Transport Service. Was awarded the Legion of Merit and the Distinguished Service Medal: d. Andrews Air Force Base, MD, May 19.

Smith, Kay Nolte (61), writer of mystery novels. Her first book, *The Watcher* (1980), won the Edgar Allan Poe Award from the Mystery Writers of America: d. Long Branch, NJ, Sept. 25.

Soloveitchik, Joseph D. (90), Russian-born Orthodox rabbi and philosopher; helped break Orthodox Judaism in the United States. Was the unchallenged leader of mainstream Orthodoxy: d. Brookline, MA, April 8.

Stafford, William Edgar (79), poet and educator; won the National Book Award for poetry in 1962 for *Traveling Through the Dark,* and received an American Academy and Institute of Arts and Letters Award (1981): d. Lake Oswego, OR, Aug. 28.

Stark, Dame Freya (100), travel writer; visited many Middle Eastern regions as yet unknown to Westerners. Was named a Dame of the British Empire in 1972: d. Asolo, Italy, May 9.

Stayman, Samuel M. (84), master bridge player and administrator; invented the Stayman Convention, a form of inquiry in bridge bidding: d. Palm Beach, FL, Dec. 11.

Steinbrunner, Chris (59), writer and expert on mystery films and television shows. Was cowinner of the Mystery Writers of America Edgar Award for *Encyclopedia of Mystery and Detection* (1976): d. Queens, NY, July 7.

Stroder, Josef (81), German pediatrician; during World War II, worked to save the lives of Jewish and Polish children. He was awarded Poland's highest honor, the Gold Cross, in 1976: d. Wurzburg, Germany, Nov. 22.

Sulzberger, C.L. (80), journalist; foreign correspondent and columnist for *The New York Times* for almost 40 years. He won a special Pulitzer Prize in 1951 and three Overseas Press Club awards (1951, 1957, 1970): d. Paris, France, Sept. 20.

Suttman, Paul (59), sculptor; best known for Impressionistic works in bronze. Won the Prix de Rome three times during the mid-1960s: d. South Kent, CT, April 21.

Taft, Robert (76), former U.S. representative and senator (R-OH); was the grandson of U.S. President William Howard Taft and son of a U.S. senator: d. Cincinnati, OH, Dec. 6.

Tambo, Oliver R. (75), national chairman and former president of the African National Congress (ANC) in South Africa. He cofounded the Youth League of the ANC with Nelson Mandela in 1944: d. Johannesburg, South Africa, April 24.

Matthew Ridgway

© Harris & Ewing/Globe

Albert Sabin

© Susan Steinkamp/Saba

Oliver Tambo

© Stuart Franklin/Sygma

Conway Twitty

Thomas Watson, Jr.

Frank Zappa

Tanaka, Kakuei (75), Japanese politician; served as prime minister (1972-74), and was influential in Japanese politics until his retirement in the late 1980s, despite being convicted in 1983 of accepting a multimillion-dollar bribe from Lockheed while in office: d. Tokyo, Japan, Dec. 16.

Tata, J.R.D. (Jehangir Ratanji Dadabhoy) (89), Indian industrialist and philanthropist; one of India's most influential figures, he was awarded the country's highest civilian public-service award, the Jewel of India (1991): d. Switzerland, Nov. 29.

Tatum, Donn B. (80), former president and chairman of the Walt Disney Company. Was instrumental in the creation of Walt Disney World in Florida and Tokyo Disneyland: d. Pacific Palisades, CA, May 31.

Taylor, Harold (78), educator; president of Sarah Lawrence College (1949-59). Taught at the New School for Social Research and City University of New York, and hosted a television series, *Meet the Professor* (1962-63): d. New York City, Feb. 9.

Tenzer, Herbert (87), U.S. congressman (D-NY, 1965-69), lawyer, and philanthropist. He was chairman emeritus and a trustee of Yeshiva University: d. Lawrence, NY, March 24.

Theremin, Leon (97), Russian musical inventor; in 1920, invented one of the first electronic musical instruments, known as the theremin: d. Moscow, Russia, Nov. 3.

Todd, Ann (82), British film and stage actress; famous for her role in the classic suspense film, *The Seventh Veil* (1945): d. London, England, May 6.

Trent, William J., Jr. (83), executive director of the United Negro College Fund (1944-64): d. Greensboro, NC, Nov. 27.

Treurnicht, Andries P. (72), South African politician and advocate of apartheid; founded the Conservative Party in 1982 to fight concessions to the nonwhite majority: d. Cape Town, South Africa, April 22.

Triffin, Robert (81), Belgian-born economist; helped establish European currency convertibility after World War II and was involved in the formation of the Common Market. Was made a baron by the king of Belgium in 1989, although he had become a U.S. citizen in 1942: d. Ostend, Belgium, Feb. 23.

Troyanos, Tatiana (54), opera singer; a mezzo-soprano, her repertory spanned all of opera from Monteverdi to Philip Glass: d. New York City, Aug. 21.

Tsiang, S. C. (75), Chinese-born U.S. economist; one of the principal architects of Taiwan's economic "miracle" during the 1960s and 1970s: d. Chicago, IL, Oct. 21.

Tully, Alice (91), philanthropist; an important figure in New York City's music world. Lincon Center's chamber-music hall was named for her: d. New York City, Dec. 10.

Twitty, Conway (born Harold Jenkins) (59), country singer; had more than 50 Number 1 hits: d. Springfield, MO, May 31.

Valvano, James Thomas (47), basketball coach and commentator; led North Carolina State to its 1983 national championship. After being forced to give up coaching in 1990 due to reports of financial irregularities and corruption, he became a television commentator: d. Durham, NC, April 28.

van Well, Günther (72), West German ambassador to the United States from 1984 to 1987: d. Bonn, Germany, Aug. 14.

Venable, James R. (92), lawyer and white supremacist; founded a major Ku Klux Klan faction, the National Knights of the Klan, in 1963. Served as lawyer for Klan leaders questioned by the House Committee on Un-American Activities (1966): d. Lawrenceville, GA, Jan. 18.

Vera (born Vera Neumann) (84), artist and designer; known for her brightly printed scarves emblazoned with her name: d. North Tarrytown, NY, June 15.

Villechaize, Hervé (50), French-born U.S. actor; best-known for his role on the television series *Fantasy Island* (1978-83): d. Los Angeles, CA, Sept. 4.

Vuitch, Milan (78), Serbian-born physician and abortion-rights advocate; brought an early legal challenge to U.S. abortion laws by disputing the constitutionality of the District of Columbia's abortion law in 1969: d. Washington, DC, April 6.

Wallhauser, George M. (93), former Republican congressman and New Jersey government official. Served three terms (1959-64) in the U.S. House of Representatives, representing New Jersey's 12th District: d. Livingston, NJ, Aug. 4.

Wang Zhen (85), vice-president of China; one of China's most powerful and hard-line leaders. A disciple of Mao, he opposed all liberalization of China's Communist ideology and was said to endorse enthusiastically the 1989 crackdown against pro-democracy demonstrators: d. Beijing, China, March 12.

Watson, Thomas, Jr. (79), business executive; led IBM to become one of the world's biggest corporations. After retiring from IBM in 1971, he embarked on a career in public service and served as U.S. ambassador to the USSR (1979-81): d. Greenwich, CT, Dec. 31.

Waymer, David (34), professional football player; a defensive back, he played in the Pro Bowl in 1987: d. Mooresville, NC, April 30.

Weick, Fred E. (93), aviation engineer; revolutionized aviation with ingenious designs making planes more aerodynamic, safer, and easier to fly: d. Vero Beach, FL, July 8.

Wenner, Seymour J. (80), lawyer; an expert on U.S. federal administrative law, he had served as an administrative judge for the Federal Power Commission and the Postal Rate Commission: d. Silver Spring, MD, Sept. 27.

Westmorland, Fifteenth Earl (born David Anthony Thomas Fane) (69), former chairman of Sotheby Parket Bernet. Helped spur the international growth of the auction company, and served as an aide to Queen Elizabeth II for more than 25 years: d. Tetbury, England, Sept. 8.

Weston, Brett (81), photographer; son of Edward Weston, a pioneering modernist photographer. The two often worked together and greatly influenced the development of photography as an art form: d. Hawaii, Jan. 22.

White, F. Clifton (74), political consultant; a prominent conservative, he masterminded the nomination of Barry Goldwater for U.S. president at the 1964 Republican convention: d. Greenwich, CT, Jan. 9.

Wilkerson, Doxey A. (88), education expert and civil-rights leader. Served as a Communist Party leader before resigning publicly from the party in 1957: d. Norwalk, CT, June 17.

Williams, Archie (78), U.S. athlete; won the 400-m race in the 1936 Berlin Olympics. With their victories, he and Jesse Owens foiled Adolf Hitler's plan to showcase Aryan athletes (Williams and Owens were black): d. Fairfax, CA, June 24.

Wilson, John Tuzo (84), geophysicist; an early proponent of the theory of continental drift, now known as plate tectonics: d. Toronto, Ont., April 15.

Wirth, Conrad L. (93), former U.S. National Park Service director; known for his efforts to preserve the United States' open land and waters: d. Williamstown, MA, July 25.

Wise, Gloria E. (56), social-work administrator and activist; best-known for leading a sit-in in Greensboro, NC, in 1960 to protest racial segregation: d. Bronx, NY, June 7.

Wrightson, Earl (77), singer and actor; hosted a television show, *The American Musical Theater,* during the 1950s, for which he won an Emmy Award: d. East Norwich, NY, March 7.

Zappa, Frank (52), composer, guitarist; an iconoclastic leader in progressive rock music, he was best-known for his humorous pop compositions, but also composed classical works: d. Los Angeles, CA, Dec. 4.

Zeppa, Robert (68), surgeon; in the late 1960s, helped develop a lifesaving operation for patients suffering from cirrhosis of the liver. Received a distinguished service award from the American College of Surgeons in 1990: d. Miami, FL, Sept. 2.

Zuckerman, Lord (born Solly Zuckerman) (88), British scientist and author; advised several prime ministers, including Winston Churchill. Advised the Royal Air Force and the Allied forces in the Mediterranean during World War II. He was knighted in 1956 and elevated to life peerage in 1971: d. London, England, April 1.

Zwerling, Israel (76), psychiatrist; was a founding member of the American Family Therapy Association: d. Philadelphia, PA, Nov. 12.

OCEANOGRAPHY

Although an El Niño warming in the Pacific Ocean that began in 1991 continued through 1993, signals indicated that it might be approaching an end. Such a system produces a pool of warm water that spreads across the equatorial Pacific and weakens the normal air circulation; these changes upset weather patterns around much of the globe. There was an unexpected resurgence of warm El Niño conditions in the spring of 1993 that altered weather patterns in Indonesia, the United States, and the Pacific coast of South America. By late summer, sea-surface temperatures were dropping in much of the tropical Pacific—a sign that El Niño conditions might be winding down—but winds and upper-air patterns had not returned yet to normal.

CEPEX and JGOFS. Scientists from more than 15 institutions participated in a Central Equatorial Pacific Experiment (CEPEX) to study the factors that regulate tropical ocean and climate temperatures. Four aircraft, guided by weather-satellite information, explored the atmosphere between 100 and 70,000 ft (30 and 21 336 m) over an area bounded by the Hawaiian islands, Christmas Island, the Marshall Islands, and Fiji. Observations from these planes, ships, and aerial balloons sought to determine the role of clouds and surface evaporation in limiting maximum sea-surface temperatures in the equatorial Pacific—which always exceed 81° F (27° C) but never rise above 90° F (32° C).

CEPEX was established to investigate the mechanism of this apparent thermostat and to develop a global model to predict climate variations based on the interplay of ocean, atmosphere, and clouds in the tropics. A Coupled Ocean-Atmosphere Response Experiment (CARE) was completed in late 1992 in a region along the equator just north of Papua New Guinea as a part of the Tropical Ocean and Global Atmosphere (TOGA) program of the World Climate Research Program. Ships, aircraft, satellites, and other equipment measured the ocean-atmosphere energy exchange over the western Pacific to study the significance of the warm pool in the tropical ocean-atmosphere system.

The Joint Global Ocean Flux Study (JGOFS) report on the study of a North Atlantic plankton bloom in 1989 stressed the interaction of net plankton forms and smaller nanoplankton that are equally critical to oceanic productivity. The importance of nanoplankton was reaffirmed at a station near Bermuda where regular observations in the water column have been collected for years. Time-series observations were made during the spring and summer of 1993. They revealed variations in plankton concentration that were correlated with seasonal changes in incident radiation and water-mass characteristics.

Field Surveys. An international research team studied the physical and chemical characteristics of one of the world's largest and deepest hydrothermal fields, located on the mid-Atlantic Ridge. Scientists investigated both active and inactive zones of the field—known as the Trans-Atlantic Geotraverse (TAG) hydrothermal field—with the submersible ALVIN. Drilling on an active sulfide mound in this field by the Ocean Drilling Program was scheduled to begin in late 1994. Scientists first wanted to advance their understanding of the system in order to determine the mound's structure and to develop a baseline prior to drilling. The area includes hot springs that discharge black smoke at temperatures up to 689° F (365° C), while cooler white smokers and diffuse flows are found toward the margins of the mound. Water and sediment samples also were obtained in the study of the area.

In a complex vent field of the northern Juan de Fuca ridge (Pacific Ocean), U.S. and Canadian scientists tested the capabilities of a remotely operated vehicle (ROV). Samples of fluids were taken from vents—as small as 2 inches (5 cm) across—at depths of more than 1.5 mi (2.4 km). Photographs, video footage, and a variety of geological and biological samples were obtained. The ROV plugged into recorders left by ALVIN in 1991, and collected data recorded since that time.

ODP. The Ocean Drilling Program (ODP) recorded the longest single section of undisturbed core so far obtained, about 1,300 ft (400 m). The program also extended a previous hole in the eastern Pacific to a total depth of 6,562 ft (2 km), which is the deepest penetration of the ocean crust to date, nearly to the level of rocks that are the remains of magma chambers that fed the seafloor pillow-lava eruptions. The hole goes through a level of sediments, a section of pillow and massive lava, a transition zone, and a deep layer of sheeted dikes.

At another Pacific Ocean site, scientists sampled deep crustal structures of rocks crystallized from the roof of a magma chamber. In a second, nearby hole, they also collected peridotites typical of the mantle and of melt zones of magma pushing upward into the crust. These samples substantiated much of the accepted theory of seafloor spreading and provided significant new mineralogical detail about mantle-rock materials.

Sewage Sludge. The proposal for deep seabed waste disposal received further consideration, but was blocked by legislative bans on offshore dumping. As land-based disposal options have become increasingly restricted, many scientists feel that deep ocean isolation of waste is a solution to a pressing problem. Unfortunately, its costs may prove prohibitive.

DAVID A. McGILL
U.S. Coast Guard Academy

OHIO

Ohio benefited from a slowly improving economy, which allowed increased expenditures for some services in 1993, but questions about reforming campaign finance and school funding remained. The largest prison riot in state history also confronted officials in Ohio.

Prison Riot. Nine inmates and one guard at the Southern Ohio Correctional Facility in Lucasville were killed during an 11-day standoff that began on April 11. Four hundred fifty prisoners seized control of a cell block, took 12 guards hostage, and killed inmates who opposed them. The riot allegedly was caused by prisoner dissatisfaction with overcrowding, mandatory health testing, gang-related violence, and racial tensions. Leaders of black Muslim and white-supremacist groups took joint control and negotiated with officials to end the crisis. Ohio Highway Patrol troopers and National Guard soldiers quickly surrounded the buildings, but Gov. George Voinovich, who kept a low profile throughout the ordeal, did not order them to quell the disturbance.

Two guards were released in the following two days, and the prisoners finally surrendered on April 21. American Civil Liberties Union negotiator Niki Schwartz worked out an agreement that assured inmates a review of their grievances and immunity to unlawful retaliation. Lawmakers and officials immediately launched investigations, and a new state budget funded the hiring of 900 additional prison guards. Control over inmates at Lucasville was tightened greatly after the riot.

State Government. The $30.9 billion state budget—up 13% over the previous budget—for the 1993-95 biennium boosted higher-education spending by 5% and mandated a 5% annual ceiling on tuition increases at state universities.

OHIO • Information Highlights

Area: 41,330 sq mi (107 044 km^2).

Population (July 1, 1992 est.): 11,016,000.

Chief Cities (1990 census): Columbus, the capital, 632,910; Cleveland, 505,616; Cincinnati, 364,040; Toledo, 332,943; Akron, 223,019; Dayton, 182,044.

Government (1993): *Chief Officers*—governor, George V. Voinovich (R); lt. gov., Michael DeWine (R). *General Assembly*—Senate, 33 members; House of Representatives, 99 members.

State Finances (fiscal year 1991): *Revenue,* $31,721,000,000; *expenditure,* $27,791,000,000.

Personal Income (1992): $207,769,000,000; per capita, $18,860.

Labor Force (August 1993): *Civilian labor force,* 5,501,800; *unemployed,* 308,900 (5.6% of total force).

Education: *Enrollment* (fall 1991)—public elementary schools, 1,277,403; public secondary, 506,364; colleges and universities, 569,326. *Public school expenditures* (1990-91), $8,407,428,000.

Other programs receiving significant budget increases included elementary and secondary education, environmental protection, and child services. The state planned to raise additional revenue by increasing user fees for state services and extending the sales tax. Final approval of the budget was held up until the legislature, at the governor's insistence, overhauled the medical benefits administered by the state's workers' compensation system.

However, lawmakers failed to reform campaign finance and school funding. Charges surfaced that lobbyists had too much influence on key proposals. Rep. Paul Jones (D-Ravenna) resigned as chairman of the House Health and Retirement Committee in September after it was revealed that he had received speaking fees from medical groups. Jones had supported the effort of Cleveland-based Blue Cross-Blue Shield of Ohio to acquire Cincinnati-based Community Mutual

© Ralf-Finn Hestoft/Saba

An 11-day siege at the Southern Ohio Correctional Facility near Lucasville, OH, ended on April 21, 1993, after inmates and prison officials reached an agreement on improving prison conditions. Five remaining hostages also were freed. During the unrest, family and friends, right, *demonstrated their support for the captured guards.*

Insurance Co. A former legislative aide to a state senator also was reported to have worked on behalf of title insurance companies to kill a proposal to use interest from the companies' escrow funds in the state treasurer's office to fund increased legal-aid services. In another prominent reform issue, no action was taken to equalize education funding across rich and poor school districts. A lawsuit on the issue was pending.

Other. Three-term U.S. Sen. Howard Metzenbaum announced he would not seek reelection in 1994....The Cleveland Indians baseball team played their last season in Municipal Stadium and would move to the new Gateway Stadium in downtown Cleveland in 1994....Tragedy struck Ohio's large Amish community when a speeding motorist hit a group of children walking on a rural road near Wooster, killing five.

JOHN B. WEAVER
Sinclair Community College

OKLAHOMA

Major 1993 news events in Oklahoma included the state legislature's struggle with the economy and finances and a finance scandal that implicated the governor.

Legislation. In 1992 voters had adopted bill SQ640, which required that tax increases be approved by three fourths of the legislature or by a vote of the people. In effect, SQ640 ruled out tax increases as a way to resolve state financial problems. Legislators also had to deal with a sluggish economy that reduced revenue.

To help alleviate mounting money pressures, the legislature dipped into the Rainy Day Fund for $43 million to add to the revenue available for 1993. In appropriations, common education received 38.5% of all funds. Legislators felt this satisfied high-priority education needs set forth by a major education act passed in 1990. Welfare needs were well-publicized, but spending for social services did not rise, receiving 19.7% of

appropriated funds. Higher education was cut, receiving 14.9% of the budget. The cut was alleviated somewhat by provisions for tuition increases. Some lesser agencies were cut up to 9% and the legislature tacked on an estimated $13 million in user fees.

Legislators resorted to some novel measures to enhance administrative efficiency. Oklahoma teaching hospitals were removed from the aegis of the Department of Human Services. And in a sharp reversal of usual practices, state agencies were allowed to retain unexpended funds from the budget year rather than return them to the General Fund, to encourage accountability and long-term planning by the agencies.

Scandals and Controversies. A state scandal arose from a multicounty grand jury that investigated campaign contributions to Democratic Gov. David Walters. Some 20 indictments had been handed down by mid-October. And although some indictments were sealed, most were not. Some prominent citizens pleaded guilty to the misdemeanor offense of contributing more than the legal amount to the campaign. Governor Walters pleaded guilty to a misdemeanor violation in a plea-bargain arrangement that allowed him to remain in office and avoid a jail sentence. Governor Walters resisted calls for his resignation but did announce that he would not run for reelection.

The Corporation Commission was also in the news. The major utilities providing electricity, telephone service, and natural gas challenged decisions by the commissioners, each of whom was elected statewide. And in a bizarre admission, Republican Bob Anthony said that he had served as an informant for the Federal Bureau of Investigation (FBI) in an investigation of allegations that a utility representative tried to bribe a previous commissioner.

State Treasurer Claudette Henry—who had been regarded as a rising star in the GOP—came under fire in a state auditor's report that charged that Henry's chief trader and close friend engaged in trades that involved millions of dollars in excessive payments.

School districts in Oklahoma City and Tulsa were charged by the Internal Revenue Service (IRS) with making money from the issuance of tax-free school bonds. The IRS claimed that school districts issuing the bonds inflated their projections of school financial needs and, in the process, made money for which they owed the IRS substantial sums.

The presidents of the University of Oklahoma and Oklahoma State University resigned under fire within months of each other.

Governors Conference. An August meeting of the National Governors' Association attracted President Bill Clinton and Vice-President Al Gore to Tulsa. The president outlined his health-care plan to the gathering.

HARRY HOLLOWAY
University of Oklahoma (emeritus)

OKLAHOMA • Information Highlights

Area: 69,956 sq mi (181 186 km²).

Population (July 1, 1992 est.): 3,212,000.

Chief Cities (1990 census): Oklahoma City, the capital, 444,719; Tulsa, 376,302; Lawton, 80,561.

Government (1993): *Chief Officers*—governor, David Walters (D); lt. gov., Jack Mildren (D). *Legislature*—Senate, 48 members; House of Representatives, 101 members.

State Finances (fiscal year 1991): *Revenue,* $7,819,000,000; *expenditure,* $7,267,000,000.

Personal Income (1992): $52,847,000,000; per capita, $16,452.

Labor Force (August 1993): *Civilian labor force,* 1,539,900; *unemployed,* 91,600 (5.9% of total force).

Education: *Enrollment* (fall 1991)—public elementary schools, 432,334; public secondary, 155,929; colleges and universities, 183,536. *Public school expenditures* (1990-91), $2,078,673,000.

ONTARIO

In 1993, Ontario's burgeoning budget deficit and Premier Bob Rae's New Democratic Party (NDP) government's attempts to reduce it left few of the province's residents untouched.

Government and Economic Affairs. In April, Treasurer Floyd Laughren unveiled a drastic austerity program to cut C$4 billion from government spending in 1993 and eliminate up to 11,000 jobs. Government efficiency would be improved; provincial institutions, services, and programs were to be closed or scaled down; and welfare payments would be reduced or eliminated. Public-housing rents were raised and grants in many areas cut. Many now would have to pay for drugs that were previously free, and doctors would get lower fees.

These cuts were matched in the May 20 budget with substantial tax increases, the aim being to keep the current deficit to less than C$10 billion. Charges for fees and licenses were raised and the sales tax was extended. The personal-income tax was raised by 3%, to 58% of the federal tax, and the surtax on incomes of more than C$51,000 and C$67,000 was raised to 20% and 30% of provincial tax, respectively. A minimum corporate tax also was introduced. With the plan in place, revenue was expected to rise to C$43.985 billion while expenditure would drop to C$53.144 billion—the first time in 50 years that there has been a year-after-year drop in expenditure.

The most contentious part of the austerity drive was Bill 48. Introduced in June, the bill was intended to gain reductions in the salaries of nearly 1 million public-sector employees. Premier Rae spoke of a "social contract" whereby employees would negotiate wage freezes, rollbacks, and unpaid days off over the next three years. The bill permitted the opening up of collective agreements and allowed settlements to be imposed if no agreements were reached before August 1. This measure alienated the provincial labor movement and many longtime NDP supporters who already were critical of previous government policies they felt betrayed the NDP's social democratic ideology. The Canadian Automobile Workers Union drastically reduced its financial support for the provincial party; many members urged leaving the party altogether.

In another government matter, Rae promised to take the federal government to court over the proposed North American Free Trade Agreement (NAFTA), alleging it violated provincial jurisdiction. Many saw this as a bid by Rae to recoup his standing with NDP supporters—longtime opponents of the Canada-U.S. free-trade agreement.

Relations with Quebec. A long-simmering dispute with the province of Quebec came to a head in September. After negotiations failed, Ontario introduced contracting rules matching those long in place in Quebec. Quebec contractors and subcontractors and Quebec-produced building materials were excluded from Ontario government projects. Private firms were to be encouraged to hire Ontario rather than Quebec contractors, and legislation would be introduced to match Quebec's restrictions on Ontario construction workers. Ontario municipalities would be discouraged from buying Quebec-made buses. The move was welcomed by union and municipal officials.

Energy. Ontario Hydro, one of the world's largest borrowers, with a debt of C$34 billion, outlined plans in March to restructure itself along private business lines. It planned to cut its staff by 4,500, freeze rates for 1994 and hold further increases to the rate of inflation for the rest of the decade, cut capital spending by C$10 billion (33%), and reduce its debt by at least C$13 billion over the next decade.

Election. With the NDP blighted by the provincial government's problems, and the unpopularity of the Conservative federal government, the Liberals swept the province in the October 25 federal election, taking 98 seats. The Reform Party captured one seat, and all other parties were shut out.

PETER J. KING, *Carleton University*

ONTARIO • Information Highlights

Area: 412,580 sq mi (1 068 580 km²).

Population (June 1993): 10,259,000.

Chief Cities (1991 census): Toronto, the provincial capital, 635,395; Ottawa, the federal capital, 313,987; Scarborough, 524,598; Mississauga, 463,388; Hamilton, 318,499; London, 303,165.

Government (1993): *Chief Officers*—lt. gov., Hal Jackman; premier, Robert Keith Rae (New Democrat). *Legislature*—Legislative Assembly, 130 members.

Provincial Finances (1993-94 fiscal year budget): *Revenues*, $43,985,000,000; *expenditures*, $53,144,-000,000.

Personal Income (average weekly earnings, June 1993): $590.50.

Labor Force (August 1993, seasonally adjusted): *Employed workers*, 15 years of age and over, 4,790,000; *Unemployed*, 10.8%.

Education (1992-93): *Enrollment*—elementary and secondary schools, 2,084,600 pupils; postsecondary—universities, 223,700; community colleges, 105,700.

(All monetary figures are in Canadian dollars.)

OREGON

In the 1993 session, the Oregon legislature debated a sales tax and a health-care plan. Meanwhile, a U.S. Senate ethics inquiry into the conduct of Oregon's Sen. Bob Packwood (R) was embroiled in conflict.

Government. The legislature killed a 5% sales tax, but then referred it to the November ballot. The state general fund—derived from income taxes—had been under pressure after passage of the Proposition 5 property-tax cap. General-fund spending on education forced severe budget reductions for all state agencies, and pro-

ceeds from the new tax would be devoted to education. After the legislature adjourned, a Marion county judge declared the referral to be illegal because it sought multiple constitutional amendments. Secretary of State Phil Keisling filed an appeal to the state Supreme Court, which overruled the lower court decision. The proposition failed overwhelmingly in November.

After securing required waivers from the Bill Clinton administration, the legislature passed the Oregon Health Plan, which would extend guaranteed health-care access to 120,000 previously uncovered poor Oregonians. The state's 280,000 uninsured workers, however, would have to wait up to four years before employers would be required to furnish health insurance. The plan limits coverage for treatments based upon medical effectiveness and social value.

The third effort in two years to recall Gov. Barbara Roberts did not amass enough signatures to put a petition on the November ballot. However, Democrat John Kitzhaber, former president of the Oregon Senate, announced that he would run for governor in 1994. His candidacy could mean that Roberts would be Oregon's first sitting governor to face a serious primary challenge in more than 50 years.

Six cities and one county passed measures prohibiting special rights for homosexuals. The initiatives were enacted despite a new untested law prohibiting the enforcement of such measures, and forbid local government from extending minority status to homosexuals and from promoting homosexuality.

Packwood Inquiry. The U.S. Senate Ethics Committee was looking into allegations of sexual misconduct by Sen. Bob Packwood, which arose shortly after he won a fifth term in November 1992. He was accused of making unwanted advances to some two dozen female aides over a 20-year period. In October 1993 the inquiry took a confrontational turn when the committee demanded unrestrained access to Packwood's

© Terry Ashe/Gamma-Liaison

Bob Packwood, a U.S. senator since January 1969, came under fire in 1993 amid allegations that he had made unsolicited advances to some two dozen women over a 20-year period.

extensive private diaries and subpoenaed these documents. Senator Packwood disputed this access and refused cooperation. As the investigation and controversy continued into late November, rumors developed that Packwood was contemplating resigning his Senate seat.

Earthquakes and the Environment. Two serious earthquakes—both registering 5.7 on the Richter scale—hit Oregon. In March a quake centered near Salem damaged the State Capitol rotunda and bridges and buildings in several towns. In September a quake shook the Klamath Falls area, causing two deaths and significant structural damage.

The Trojan nuclear-power plant at Ranier survived a ballot measure calling for its permanent closure, but it nevertheless remained closed by the Portland General Electric Company (PGE). Microscopic cracks in steam-generator tubes had led PGE to slate closure for 1996, but in the end, PGE opted to close the plant early to capture economic savings.

President Clinton's forest plan for the Pacific Northwest was denounced by both environmental and timber interests. The plan would permit the harvesting of 1.2 billion board feet per year from federal lands west of the Cascades in Oregon, Washington, and northern California (*see* ENVIRONMENT/SPECIAL REPORT, page 224).

Prisons and Crime. Inmates at the federal correctional institution in Sheridan burned a building and ransacked the chapel. The institution, built to house some 700 inmates, had a population of 1,296 at the time of the riot.

Alberto Gonzalez of Portland was convicted of attempted murder because he tried to infect a 17-year-old girl with the AIDS virus through unprotected sex. It was believed to be the first conviction on such a charge in the United States.

L. CARL and JOANN C. BRANDHORST
Western Oregon State College

OREGON • Information Highlights

Area: 97,073 sq mi (251 419 km²).
Population (July 1, 1992 est.): 2,977,000.
Chief Cities (1990 census): Salem, the capital,107,786; Portland, 437,319; Eugene, 112,669.
Government (1993): *Chief Officers*—governor, Barbara Roberts (D); secretary of state, Phil Keisling (D); *Legislative Assembly*—Senate, 30 members; House of Representatives, 60 members.
State Finances (fiscal year 1991): *Revenue*, $8,201,000,000; *expenditure*, $7,249,000,000.
Personal Income (1992): $54,840,000,000; per capita, $18,419.
Labor Force (August 1993): *Civilian labor force*, 1,564,500; *unemployed*, 113,900 (7.3% of total force).
Education: *Enrollment* (fall 1991)—public elementary schools, 359,348; public secondary, 139,266; colleges and universities, 167,107. *Public school expenditures* (1990-91), $2,453,934,000.

OTTAWA

Although Ottawa is Canada's federal capital, the city was preoccupied particularly with its status as a provincial municipality in 1993.

Government. In June municipal grants were trimmed from the provincial budget, forcing Ottawa, suburban Nepean, and the regional government to cut their budgets. The cuts were made by postponing some projects, reducing the scope of others, and disposing of surplus equipment. No layoffs were involved.

A bill was introduced in the Ontario legislature to restructure the regional government. A smaller Regional Council with 18 directly elected councilors—rather than area mayors—would be set up. New wards cutting municipal boundaries would be created, limiting the power of existing municipalities. The region would take over tax collection, economic development, sewers and water management, and set standards for land use (including business parks) and the taxi business. Area police would be combined into a single force.

Vigorous opposition subsequently blocked the bill. Suburban politicians feared that lost local control over new business parks would threaten municipal finances, that new ward boundaries would subordinate suburban needs to those of central Ottawa, and that the extra costs of new regional concerns would not be met by local reductions. Police-force amalgamation drew the strongest public opposition. The suburbs feared reduced service if the new force concentrated on downtown crime, while the cities whose forces would be merged also feared higher police costs as the Ontario Provincial Police were replaced in the other regional municipalities.

A provincial fact finder was appointed to look into the region's five school boards that oversee 128,000 students. The action was seen as a prelude to amalgamating the school boards into three. In an attempt to prevent this, the boards were discussing consolidating their support services.

Other News. The city also helped embroil Ontario in a dispute with Quebec. With a 24% unemployment rate in the Ottawa construction industry, truck drivers blockaded two major bridges between Ottawa and Hull in August to protest Quebec's restrictions on Ontario residents working in that province, while some 4,000 construction workers were employed in Ontario. Mayor Jacqueline Holzman of Ottawa called for retaliation by the province and the region considered excluding Quebec firms from its contracts.

Sports. Two new Ottawa professional sports teams played their first seasons. In baseball the Ottawa Lynx set an International League attendance record and made the play-offs. The National Hockey League's Senators had less success—a last-place finish, which led to unsustained allegations that the team threw a game to ensure this finish.

PETER J. KING, *Carleton University*

PAKISTAN

In a year of political turmoil, Pakistan held elections in 1993 and returned Benazir Bhutto to power as head of a weak coalition government.

Politics. Conflict arose early in 1993 between Prime Minister Nawaz Sharif and President Ghulam Ishaq Khan. Nawaz clashed with Ishaq Khan over the 8th Amendment to the Constitution—a provision introduced in 1985 as a condition for lifting martial law—which strengthened the powers of the president as a check upon the prime minister. When Nawaz attempted to organize repeal of the amendment, Bhutto sided with Ishaq Khan.

On April 18, Ishaq Khan dismissed Nawaz amid charges of corruption, appointed a caretaker government under veteran Punjabi politician Balakh Sher Mazari, and scheduled elections for July. The Supreme Court overruled the dismissal on May 26, restoring Nawaz to power.

Further deadlock, combined with Bhutto's demands for elections, led to the unprecedented resignation by both the president and the prime minister, brokered by the army, on July 18. Senate President Wasim Sajjad became acting president and World Bank official Moeen Qureshi became caretaker prime minister. Qureshi's government actively pushed reform. The names of major loan defaulters were published, and the defaulters were not allowed to contest elections. Drug traffickers also were dealt with harshly, including electoral disqualification.

The configuration of forces in the October elections resembled 1990 and 1988 with Bhutto's Pakistan People's Party (PPP) facing Nawaz Sharif's Pakistan Muslim League (PML), plus a variety of religious and regional parties and independents. In March the PML had split, and the dissident faction allied itself with the PPP in the October elections. A third national force in the elections was the Pakistan Islamic Front (PIF), led by Qazi Hussein Ahmed.

The militant regional group, the Mohajir Qaumi Movement (MQM), which dominated

---

Karachi, Hyderabad, and other cities in the Sindh province, also was split into two major factions. The larger faction, under exiled leader Altaf Hussein, boycotted the national polls.

Meanwhile, Bhutto's younger brother, Mir Murtaza Bhutto, filed for several national and provincial contests and threatened to vie with his sister for leadership of the PPP and the legacy of their late father, former Prime Minister Zulfikar Ali Bhutto. Their mother, Begum Nusrat Bhutto, cochairperson of the PPP, sided with Murtaza. He won a seat in the assembly of the Sindh province despite his alleged ties with the terrorist organization al-Zulfikar.

The election results demonstrated the viability of the two major political parties, but neither won a clear mandate. Bhutto's PPP won 86 seats in the National Assembly—compared with 72 for Sharif's PML—but needed support of smaller parties and independents to establish a majority in the 217-seat body. The PML actually outpolled the PPP in popular votes. The PPP also received a majority in Sindh, but the PML won in the Northwest Frontier province. In Punjab, the largest province, the PML won a plurality, but the PPP and its allies combined to form a majority. Baluchistan was so fragmented that no party could win a quarter of the assembly seats.

International observers generally praised the elections as free and fair. Election observers also were mobilized throughout the country by the Human Rights Commission of Pakistan, a nongovernmental organization. The military helped maintain law and order at polling stations, a contribution generally welcomed by the parties and the public. But the elections were not without incident. Former Punjab Chief Minister Ghulam Haider Wyne was killed just before the voting.

Following the parliamentary elections, Farooq Leghari defeated acting President Wasim Sajjad in presidential elections. Leghari, Bhutto's nominee, indicated his willingness to consider repeal of the controversial 8th Amendment.

Economy. Pakistan suffered several economic setbacks in 1992-93, according to the finance ministry's annual economic survey, released in June. Gross-domestic-product (GDP) growth dropped from 7.7% to roughly 3%. Agricultural growth was a negative 3.9%. The balance-of-payments deficit nearly doubled to almost $3 billion. More positively, per-capita income increased 9.6%, total investment 14.1%, and national savings 18.4%.

The restored Nawaz Sharif government introduced a "growth" budget in June, with a total outlay of 332 billion rupees (approximately U.S. $11 billion). But when Moeen Qureshi assumed power a month later, he declared that Pakistan was on the verge of bankruptcy. His caretaker government devalued the rupee, solicited support from the World Bank and International Monetary Fund (IMF), and imposed immediate economic measures. A tax on agricultural income was established.

© d'Archives/Sipa

In Pakistan, Benazir Bhutto, 40, led the Pakistan People's Party back to power in a close 1993 election. She was sworn in as prime minister for a second time on October 19.

Foreign Policy. Relations with India continued to be tense, especially over the continuing turmoil in Indian-held Kashmir. When a series of bombings occurred in Bombay in March, Indians were quick to accuse Pakistan.

Three issues troubled U.S.-Pakistani relations: nuclear proliferation, drugs, and Pakistan's alleged support of rebels in Kashmir. The U.S. Congress considered including Pakistan on a list of terrorist states. Skillful diplomacy and effective Pakistani action against drug lords improved relations. Resumption of U.S. aid for Pakistan remained stymied by the nuclear-weapons issue.

Pakistan hosted a conference of foreign ministers of the Economic Cooperation Organization (ECO) in February, worked with Saudi Arabia and Afghan factions to forge agreements in Afghanistan in March, and received several hundred Bosnian refugees in June. Pakistani peacekeeping troops in Somalia suffered casualties in June when 24 soldiers were killed.

WILLIAM L. RICHTER
Kansas State University

PARAGUAY

As the presidency of Paraguay passed from military to civilian control in 1993, a new civil-military relationship emerged.

Politics. President Andrés Rodríguez held general elections on May 9, as scheduled. His Colorado Party candidate, Juan Carlos Wasmosy, defeated Domingo Laíno of the Radical Liberal Party (PLRA) and Guillermo Caballero Vargas of the newly formed coalition Encuentro Nacional, as verified by some 300 international observers.

Wasmosy took office for a five-year term on August 15, reminding the military in his inaugural address that it no longer was in power. He provoked violent reactions among political parties three days later, however, by naming strongman Gen. César Oviedo as army chief. A key cabinet nomination was Hugo Estigarribia as defense minister—he would be the first civilian to hold the post.

Wasmosy failed to reach an agreement with the opposition-dominated Congress over passage of key administration bills. The first act of the incoming legislators was to repeal a military-organization law which limited the president's role as commander in chief of the armed forces. Those in uniform doubted the weakened Colorados would be able to protect their interests.

Economics. Finance Minister Crispiniano Sandoval endorsed plans for economic liberalization and privatization. He also proposed extending the autonomy of the central bank to promote longer-term development and called for a new banking law to create agriculture and small-business development banks. Funding would come from sales of public enterprises and state-owned Itaipú Power. Since Wasmosy opposed the levying of new taxes, additional funds would be raised through more-stringent tax collection.

Exports were down by nearly 26%—to less than $61 million—in the first two months of 1993, and revenues fell well below expenditures by midyear. One fifth of budgeted revenues were to come from the sale of Itaipú to Brazil, but payments were in arrears. Inflation had topped 24% during Rodriguez' final year in office, and the public debt had grown from less than $200 million to nearly $800 million over the past two years.

Some foreign aid was forthcoming. A $28 million loan from Japan would be used for a communications satellite. In August the International Development Bank (IDB) promised $700 million for health, education, and housing projects. Paraguay would share $130 million from the IDB for the relocation of 50,000 persons displaced by dam construction on the Paraná River.

Foreign Relations. Paraguayan dissatisfaction increased with Mercosur, the fledgling Southern Cone common market encompassing Uruguay, Paraguay, Argentina, and Brazil. Although committed to regional integration, Paraguay

---

PARAGUAY • Information Highlights

Official Name: Republic of Paraguay.
Location: Central South America.
Area: 157,046 sq mi (406 750 km²).
Population (mid-1993 est.): 4,200,000.
Chief City (1992 census): Asunción, the capital, 502,426.
Government: *Head of state and government,* Juan Carlos Wasmosy, president (sworn in Aug. 15, 1993). *Legislature*—Congress: Senate and Chamber of Deputies.
Monetary Unit: Guaraní (1,631.8 guaraníes equal U.S.$1, selling rate, January 1993).
Gross Domestic Product (1991 est. U.S.$): $7,000,000,000.
Foreign Trade (1991 U.S.$): *Imports,* $1,850,000,000; *exports,* $642,000,000.

---

opposed the implementation on Jan. 1, 1995, of a 20% common external tariff. Neither Brazil nor Argentina supported the Paraguayan position. Equally frustrating for Asunción was its inability to be exempted from an Argentine trade barrier increased to 10% late in 1992. The tariff reduced Paraguay's export income by some $10 million per month. Asunción threatened to withdraw from Mercosur over the issue. In July, Mercosur members threatened to expel Paraguay over concessions it had negotiated with members of the General Agreement of Tariffs and Trade (GATT) prior to its admission to GATT. The concessions were well below Mercosur's projected common external tariff.

Human Rights. A former political prisoner appealed to the Organization of American States in August to prevent the Wasmosy government from destroying the so-called "horror files" uncovered in December 1992. These contained information on 15,000 Paraguayans who fell into the hands of former dictator Alfredo Stroessner's secret police and in some cases met with torture, disappearance, and death. Documents researched by the UN Commission on Human Rights and the legislative and judicial branches of the government precipitated action against some of the dictator's henchmen and renewed efforts to bring Stroessner back from exile to face charges. The records confirmed the existence of a "dirty war" in Paraguay in the 1960s and 1970s, as well as its coordination with clandestine police and military activity in neighboring countries.

LARRY L. PIPPIN, *University of the Pacific*

PENNSYLVANIA

Pennsylvania had a quiet year of moderation with neither a dominant issue nor significant government initiatives in 1993.

Politics. One reason for the calm may have been Democratic Gov. Robert P. Casey's rare heart-liver transplant June 14 at the University of Pittsburgh Medical Center. He suffered from

Pennsylvania Gov. Robert P. Casey, surrounded by his wife Ellen and son Matthew, left the University of Pittsburgh Medical Center on July 27, 1993, after undergoing a rare heart-liver transplant. The 61-year-old Democrat subsequently suffered various infections and spent much of the balance of the year recuperating at the governor's mansion in Harrisburg.

© Reuters/Bettmann

amyloidosis, a hereditary liver disease. Lt. Gov. Mark S. Singel served as acting governor during Casey's hospitalization and recuperation.

The Democrats—with a small yet united majority in the legislature—passed the state's $17.4 billion budget on May 28, well before the July 1 start of the fiscal year.

Thomas J. Murphy, 48-year-old Democratic state representative, was elected mayor of Pittsburgh.

Economy. A modest economic upswing continued in the state, led by monthly retail sales increases of more than 5% for all but two months. Although by the fall there were 24,500 more nonfarm jobs than a year earlier, unemployment was at 7.5%, slightly higher than the national average. Unemployment was highest in western industrial cities and lowest in the central east communities. Manufacturing did poorly, with more than 55,000 jobs lost since the economic recovery began in March 1991. Anthony O'Reilly, head of H. J. Heinz of Pittsburgh, announced in April that the company would lay off 10% of its workforce, or 3,600 workers, by the end of 1994.

The United Mine Workers staged a month-long strike in February against Peabody Holding and other large coal producers. The Pittsburgh *Post-Gazette* resumed publication in January, ending a strike by delivery workers that began in May 1992.

Medical News. The same day as Governor Casey's operation, doctors removed a benign brain tumor from U.S. Sen. Arlen Specter (R), who returned to the Senate within a month. A man who received a baboon's liver in Pittsburgh on January 10 died February 5. The state's most highly publicized operation was the separation of the Lakeberg twins, who had shared a damaged heart. Angela survived the August 20 operation, which sacrificed Amy to give Angela a chance at survival. The glow of celebration dimmed when Kenneth Lakeberg admitted on August 25 that he had spent $1,300 of donated funds on a three-day cocaine binge.

Legal Issues. An issue involving the University of Pennsylvania's speech code ended May 24 when five African-American sorority sisters dropped charges of racial harassment against a white student who had called them "water buffaloes" when asking them to quiet their celebration the night of January 13. The women interpreted the term as racial, while the student said it was a mild Hebrew epithet. The women did not believe they would get a fair hearing and dropped the charges. The issue received additional publicity when President Bill Clinton nominated the university's president, Sheldon Hackney, to head the National Endowment for the Humanities. Although Hackney was criticized for not throwing out the women's charges, the Senate confirmed his nomination.

A U.S. District Court judge upheld the 1992 indictment of Congressman Joseph M. McDade (R) for allegedly accepting bribes from defense contractors. Another U.S. District judge ruled in June that former Gov. Richard L. Thornburgh was partly liable for $300,000 in campaign debts to consultant Karl Rove from a 1991 Senate race in which he was defeated.

ROBERT E. O'CONNOR
Pennsylvania State University

PENNSYLVANIA • Information Highlights

Area: 45,308 sq mi (117 348 km²).

Population (July 1, 1992 est.): 12,009,000.

Chief Cities (1990 census): Harrisburg, the capital, 52,376; Philadelphia, 1,585,577; Pittsburgh, 369,379; Erie, 108,718; Allentown, 105,090.

Government (1993): *Chief Officers*—governor, Robert P. Casey (D); lt. gov., Mark A. Singel (D). *Legislature*—Senate, 50 members; House of Representatives, 203 members.

State Finances (fiscal year 1991): *Revenue,* $27,086,000,000; *expenditure,* $26,710,000,000.

Personal Income (1992): $244,814,000,000; per capita, $20,385.

Labor Force (August 1993): *Civilian labor force,* 6,086,700; *unemployed,* 454,400 (7.5% of total force).

Education: *Enrollment* (fall 1991)—public elementary schools, 1,195,012; public secondary, 497,785; colleges and universities, 620,036. *Public school expenditures* (1990-91), $10,087,322,000.

People, Places, and Things

The following four pages recount the stories behind a selection of people, places, and things that may not have made the headlines in 1993 but that drew attention and created interest.

On Sept. 26, 1993, conductor Mstislav Rostropovich, above, who spent two decades in exile from the USSR, returned to Moscow's Red Square to lead the National Symphony Orchestra of Washington in a concert before some 100,000 people. In another sign of the post-Cold War environment, Sergei Nikitich Khrushchev, below, a political scientist and son of the late Soviet Communist stalwart, took up residency with his wife in Rhode Island. Meanwhile, Katherine Ann Power, left, a former anti-Vietnam-war radical, surrendered to Boston officials after living 23 years as a fugitive. She was sentenced to an eight- to 12-year jail term for her role in a 1970 bank robbery that left a police officer murdered.

Now visitors to London not only can view Buckingham Palace's famous gates but can pay an admission fee and tour some of its art-filled rooms, and vacationers in Japan can enjoy some unusual new attractions—large indoor beaches and the world's largest indoor ski center. In 1993, Queen Elizabeth II opened Buckingham Palace, left, to the public to help repair Windsor Castle, which suffered an estimated $50 million in fire damage in 1992. The domed Seagaia complex, below, on the Japanese island of Kyushu began operations in August. It features a chlorinated, salt-free surf, with computer-created waves and an artificial volcano.

Also during 1993 the Ferris wheel, above, celebrated its 100th birthday; dinosaurmania was the new trend; an English-born aristocrat and Democratic Party fund-raiser took charge of the U.S. Embassy in Paris; a lucky throw earned a basketball fan $1 million; a new Hockey Hall of Fame opened; and international chess competition was in disarray. Created by George Washington Gale Ferris, Jr., the original Ferris wheel—which debuted at the Chicago World Columbian Exposition—was 264 ft (80.5 m) tall and could seat some 2,000 riders. The year's top-grossing movie,"Jurassic Park," sparked a wave of dinosaur-inspired consumer products (below left) that soared to popularity, but some critics argued that the film was too scary for young children—the target audience for most of the merchandise. Meanwhile, Pamela Harriman, below right, widow of Averell Harriman, was named U.S. ambassador to France by President Bill Clinton. Don Calhoun (page 425, top left), a salesman from Indiana, sank what might have been the longest and most-profitable basketball shot of the year during a Chicago Bulls home game on April 14. Calhoun, a randomly selected spectator, hit a 75-ft (23-m) toss. In June the new Ice Hockey Hall of Fame, page 425, bottom, opened in Toronto—complete with hockey memorabilia, high-tech video exhibits, and a miniature rink.

© Phillip Hollis/FSP/Gamma-Liaison

In a disputed world championship chess match held during 1993 in London, Russian grand master Gary Kasparov defeated Nigel Short of England, above, by the decisive score of 12.5 to 7.5. For his victory, Kasparov won $1.43 million and the title from the Professional Chess Association, a group that the two chess players created in opposition to the established ruling body of international chess: the International Chess Foundation (FIDE). FIDE did not recognize the Kasparov-Short championship, and held a title match of its own in Jakarta, Indonesia, which saw Anatoly Karpov of Russia defeat Jan Timman of the Netherlands.

© Carl Sissac/"Sports Illustrated"

© Courtesy, Hockey Hall of Fame

PERU

On Oct. 31, 1993, Peruvians ratified a new constitution that consolidated the political and economic reforms of President Alberto Fujimori. The ratification highlighted 1993 news in Peru.

Politics. The "Government of Emergency and Reconstruction" established by the April 1992 presidential coup ended on Jan. 2, 1993, as the Democratic Constituent Congress (CCD), elected in November 1992, assumed legislative power and began to rewrite Peru's 1979 constitution. Its final draft, produced in September, provided for the replacement of the 240-member bicameral legislature with a smaller unicameral legislature, sanctioned the death penalty for terrorists, and cleared the way for Fujimori to run for reelection in 1995.

While the draft constitution was approved in the CCD by a majority that went beyond the progovernment Cambio 90-Nueva Mayoría coalition, it was contested by opposition parties—the Popular Christian Party (PPC) and the Democratic Movement of the Left (MDI). These parties appealed for a greater separation of powers and objected to such broad executive powers as the presidential veto, extensive emergency decrees, and the right to dissolve congress without cause once per term. Other opposition parties—including APRA, Acción Popular, the Liberty Movement of Mario Vargas Llosa, and extreme leftist parties—boycotted the 1992 elections and were not represented in the CCD. Prior to the referendum, Fujimori campaigned openly for a "yes" vote, portraying the vote as a plebiscite on his performance as president. The new constitution was ratified by a wide margin.

Military Investigation. In April a CCD investigative commission turned up allegations that a military death squad was responsible for the disappearances of nine students and a professor from a Lima university in 1992. When the military took to the streets to protest the congressional investigation, President Fujimori, who depended heavily on military backing, voiced unwavering support for the army and accepted a CCD minority report that absolved the military of guilt. The majority report written by the opposition called for the dismissal of army commander Gen. Nicolás de Bari Hermoza for allegedly attempting to cover up the military death squad, and accused Vladimiro Montesinos, head of intelligence and Fujimori's chief security adviser, of directing a military execution squad. De Bari Hermoza and Montesinos were key supporters of Fujimori's pact with the armed forces, but their authority within the military seemed somewhat tenuous because de Bari Hermoza was serving as chief of the army despite a scheduled mandatory retirement and Montesinos was formerly a lawyer for drug traffickers.

Terrorism. President Fujimori announced that his antiterrorism campaign was a success and that the Maoist Shining Path guerrillas would be defeated totally by 1995. The government had weakened the movement by imprisoning leader Abimael Guzmán in 1992 and capturing an estimated 95% of the central committee. The Shining Path thus was operating at a reduced level. Terrorist-related deaths in the first eight months of 1993 were down about 30% from the 1989-92 average. Even high-visibility attacks—such as a car bombing at the U.S. Embassy in July—did not match the skill of past actions. In October, Fujimori told the United Nations that the imprisoned Guzmán had made an offer—which he had rejected—for peace talks. Meanwhile, the pro-Cuban Túpac Amaru Revolutionary Movement (MRTA) nearly was dissolved as many leaders took advantage of a repentance law and renounced armed struggle in exchange for leniency.

The Economy. Peru began emerging from a severe economic recession in 1993. Real gross domestic product (GDP) was expected to grow by 4%, up from a 2.6% decline in 1992; inflation continued to decline, with estimates of 40% for the year, down from 50% in 1992; and foreign reserves rose to $2.54 billion. Relations with the international financial community got off to a shaky start in late 1992 and January 1993, when Economy Minister Carlos Boloña resigned and the International Monetary Fund (IMF) froze its accord with Peru. New Economy Minister Jorge Camet set out to form a "support group" with loans from Japan, Italy, Germany, and the United States, and in March, Peru received a bridge loan from the United States and Japan to cover some $850 million in arrears to the IMF and the World Bank. The United States initially conditioned its assistance on progress in human rights, but later dropped these objections.

Fujimori also announced that the government's ambitious privatization plan would be completed by mid-1995. Companies to be privatized include Petroperu, mining companies, the communications firm ENTEL, and the utilities Electrolima and Electroperu.

MICHAEL COPPEDGE, *Johns Hopkins University*

PERU • Information Highlights

Official Name: Republic of Peru.

Location: West coast of South America.

Area: 496,224 sq mi (1 285 220 km²).

Population (mid-1993 est.): 22,900,000.

Chief Cities (mid-1989 est.): Lima, the capital, 6,233,800; Arequipa, 612,100; Callao (mid-1985 est.), 515,200.

Government: *Head of state,* Alberto Fujimori, president (took office July 28, 1990). *Head of government,* Alfonso Bustamente y Bustamente, prime minister (appointed Aug. 28, 1993). Legislature—Democratic Constituent Congress.

Monetary Unit: new sol (2.10 new sols equal U.S.$1, official rate, Nov. 1, 1993).

Gross Domestic Product (1991 est. U.S.$): $20,600,000,000.

Economic Index (Lima, 1992): *Consumer Prices* (1990 = 100), all items, 884.2; food, 769.9.

Foreign Trade (1991 U.S.$): *Imports,* $2,955,000,000; *exports,* $3,379,000,000.

PHILIPPINES

Philippine President Fidel Ramos completed his first full year in office during 1993, a year of continued struggle against domestic violence and political scandal, modest economic growth, and new foreign-policy initiatives.

President Ramos was not much more popular in 1993 than he was in 1992, when he won the presidency in a seven-way race with a mere 24% of the vote. However, he greatly enlarged his formal party base in the Congress. While he began his presidency with little congressional support and although some have judged his presidency lackluster, many members of Congress scrambled to join his political camp. The nonideological nature of Philippine parties often has led to "turncoatism" or climbing on the bandwagon of the winner. This election was no exception. It was premature, however, to conclude that the president's strength had been enlarged dramatically. He merely may have increased the number of claimants making demands on his patronage.

Domestic Affairs. President Ramos moved to revamp the scandal-ridden Philippine National Police (PNP). Waves of kidnappings of wealthy Chinese residents for ransom, brutal murders, and mounting evidence of corruption had tainted the PNP. In February and April, Ramos forced several hundred high-ranking officials to retire and planned to remove 3,000-5,000 of the officers in the 100,000-member force.

Ramos also moved to appoint a second panel of inquiry in October to investigate the 1983 assassination of Benigno Aquino, the martyred husband of former President Corazon Aquino and then chief political rival of President Ferdinand Marcos. Investigations that occurred while Marcos was in power were considered inconclusive.

Former President Marcos, who died in Honolulu in 1989, was buried in 1993 in his hometown of Batac in the province of Ilocos Norte, but was denied the trappings of a state funeral. The government still was trying to recover some $10 billion he reputedly stole from the nation during his long tenure (1965-86). His widow, Imelda Marcos, apparently thought the funeral might provoke an upsurge in sentiment that would translate to political power for her and her family. Instead she was indicted and then convicted on charges of corruption and was sentenced to 18 to 24 years in prison. She remained free late in 1993, pending an appeal. The government was said to be negotiating with representatives of Marcos for restitution payments in exchange for dropping the criminal charges.

As the only Protestant President in the history of the largely Catholic country, Ramos had several clashes with the Catholic Church, led by the politically powerful Cardinal Jaime Sin, over population planning and the burgeoning AIDS crisis. The nation has one of the highest population-growth rates in Asia. The president and Health Secretary Juan Flavier had insisted on the resignation of health workers unwilling to implement population policies or instruct people in AIDS-safety education. Cardinal Sin insisted that health workers should resist the government orders and be allowed to follow their religion on such issues.

Ramos successfully instituted an amnesty plan designed to bring dissidents from their respective "undergrounds" and forge a new era of reconciliation. Some 30,000 dissidents from several different organizations were offered

Imelda Marcos (center) led the mourners as her husband, Ferdinand Marcos, the former president of the Philippines, was buried in his home province of Ilocos Norte in September 1993. His body had been in Hawaii since his death in 1989.

© Emerito Antonio/Sipa

amnesty. By October 5,100 rebels had surrendered. The Communist New People's Army was estimated to have 12,000 members, Muslim separatist groups numbered about 15,000, and an additional 3,000 were former military men implicated in coup attempts during the previous Aquino presidency. It is unclear how many of those who surrendered were from each group.

Economic Developments. The economic news in 1993 was mixed. In January, Ramos announced his "Philippines 2000" agenda, which included the breakup of monopolies that thwarted technological improvements and constrained trade. The Philippine Long Distance Company and San Miguel Brewery were the first targets.

The banking system also was being overhauled, with a centralized monetary authority developed to replace the discredited central bank. Banking reforms were expected to encourage more foreign investment, as was the government plan to allow foreigners to buy Philippine citizenship for $50,000. The government estimated such a move could bring in massive infusions of capital now limited by restrictions on foreign ownership.

A major target of investment was the Subic Bay investment zone, which had been the home of the United States' largest overseas base until 1992. The Philippine Senate refused to allow the United States to renew its lease on the base. The abandoned area was being promoted for alternative development, including a large industrial park. Planned hotel development was on hold, pending the resolution of environmental issues.

International tourism was expected to set a record in 1993 both because of improvements in stability and the weakened peso, down more than 16% against many international currencies in the first nine months of the year.

The nation continued to labor through an electrical-power crisis, as daily electricity cuts of eight to ten hours exacted a costly toll. Productivity losses as a result were estimated to be $1 billion to $3 billion annually. The situation was exacerbated when the government lost its case against Westinghouse Electric Corporation, which built the controversial and never-used Bataan Nuclear Plant after allegedly giving millions in kickbacks to the Marcos family. At year's end the government appeared to be moving toward a negotiated settlement with Westinghouse that would give the Philippines $49 million in electrical-power capacity in exchange for the government not launching an expensive appeal of the court's decision.

Good news for the economy included record highs on the stock market following the merger of the two leading exchanges, a growth rate of nearly 3% for the gross domestic product (GDP), and new oil discoveries off the Palawan coast that may meet two thirds of the Philippines' oil needs by 1997.

Foreign Policy. President Ramos had three chief thrusts to his foreign policy in 1993: repairing the Philippine relationship with the United States that was bruised badly when the lease on the bases was not renewed; expanding ties with fellow members of the Association of Southeast Asian Nations (ASEAN); and developing alternative aid and investment partners to offset the decline in U.S. participation in these areas.

The most critical issue was redefining the Philippines' once special relationship with the United States. Even after the United States granted Philippine independence in 1946, the relationship often was suffocatingly close. The absence of a foreign military base in the nation for the first time in 400 years left Philippine nationalist groups without a rallying cause. U.S. supporters of Philippine aid were also without a compelling security issue on which to base aid once pledged at more than $200 million annually. In 1993, U.S. aid was expected to be no more than $15 million. President Ramos was expected to visit the United States in November to press for more aid and a resolution of the issue of the thousands of Amerasian children left behind in the wake of the base closure.

In May nine Southeast Asian nations met to discuss the Spratly Islands, which six countries, including the Philippines, claim. No decisions were reached. Ramos also visited Libya to encourage that nation to continue mediation with the Muslim separatists in the southern Philippines. Libya was an important source of foreign remittances from the 35,000 Filipinos working there.

In September, President Ramos visited Indonesia hoping to discuss boundary issues between the two nations and ways to develop a trading alliance known as the East Asian Triangle linking Mindanao in the southern Philippines, Sulawesi in Indonesia, and eastern Malaysia. He also was concerned about the sharp drop of Indonesian investment in the Philippines.

LINDA K. RICHTER
Kansas State University

PHILIPPINES • Information Highlights

Official Name: Republic of the Philippines.
Location: Southeast Asia.
Area: 115,830 sq mi (300 000 km²).
Population: (mid-1993 est.): 64,600,000.
Chief Cities (1990 census): Manila, the capital, 1,601,234; Quezon, 1,669,776; Davao, 849,947; Caloocan, 763,415, Cebu, 610,417.
Government: *Head of state and government,* Fidel V. Ramos, president (sworn in June 30, 1992). *Legislature* (bicameral)—Senate and House of Representatives.
Monetary Unit: Peso (28.26 pesos equal U.S. $1, floating rate, Nov. 10, 1993).
Gross National Product (1991 est. U.S.$): $47,000,000,000.
Economic Index (1992): *Consumer Prices* (1988 = 100), all items, 165.6; food, 157.3.
Foreign Trade (1991 U.S.$): *Imports,* $12,051,000,000; *exports,* $8,840,000,000.

PHOTOGRAPHY

In 1993, despite a continuing economic downturn, photographic markets saw strong growth in products tailored to the casual photographer, including point-and-shoot and disposable cameras. At the same time, photographic equipment traditionally associated with advanced amateurs and professionals—including 35mm single-lens reflex (SLR) cameras, view and medium-format cameras, and enlargers—continued to decline in popularity.

There were promising developments in imaging—a term that describes the intersection of electronic technology, still and motion video equipment, and computers—particularly the growing application of hybrid technology that uses digital imaging processes to manipulate images from conventional photographs.

In the world of auctions, however, traditional photographs were still the big drawing cards. Prices at the spring auctions at Sotheby's and Christie's indicated a strong, but selective, image-driven market. Rock singer Elton John paid a record $193,895 for Man Ray's "Glass Tears."

Hardware and Software. Point-and-shoot 35mm fully automatic cameras accounted for most of the cameras sold. They continued to replace the SLR as the photographer's primary camera. Trends included downsized full-featured cameras, pocket-sized models with zooms, and high-style appearance in color and finish. Nikon's Lite-Touch, which is the size of a deck of cards, was the smallest and lightest autofocus point-and-shoot camera ever made.

Cutting into the low end of the point-and-shoot market were single-use disposable cameras—one of the greatest marketing success stories in photographic history. The disposable camera continued double-digit growth, and 1993 sales were expected to reach 26 million units.

At London's Sotheby's in the spring, rock star Elton John paid a record $193,895 for Man Ray's "Glass Tears," below. Traditional photos sold well at the various auctions during 1993.

© Sotheby's London

© Courtesy of the National Portrait Gallery, Smithsonian Institution, Washington, DC

"Woman with a Goldfish Bowl," a 1923 hand-tinted photograph, was part of the National Portrait Gallery's late 1993 exhibit of the photos of James VanDerZee (1886-1983).

Recent variations included a 3-D camera, a model with 800-speed film and flash, and a camera that had a bounce flash and an 85mm lens for portrait photography.

The SLR cameras continued to lose their customer appeal. Users perceived 35mm SLRs as too complicated and too expensive. In addition, the improved quality of print films allowed less expensive cameras to take better pictures. One significant new SLR camera was Sigma's autofocus SA-300, the first SLR ever made by a lens manufacturer.

In the video market, new cameras featured image-stabilization systems that compensate for vibration, allowing users to shoot jiggleless movies from any distance without a tripod. This technology was developed jointly by Sony and Canon. Some manufacturers also offered video cameras that capture sharper colors by using a new sensor system that can measure each primary color independently.

The big story in the instant-photography sector was Polaroid's Captiva—a compact, 26-oz (.9-g) autofocus SLR. Polaroid hoped that the Captiva would develop a new market for instant cameras under $100. The Captiva does not deliver pictures like traditional instant cameras. Instead the prints are transported to a viewing area and container in the back of the camera.

New York's Metropolitan Museum exhibited a selection of photographs from the Gilman Paper Company Collection, including "Trees with Reflections," right, an 1840s salted paper print from a paper negative, by William Henry Fox Talbot.

The prints are a new, smaller size: about 2 x 3 inches (5 x 7.6 cm).

In the software arena, 400-speed films were improved. They have become an industry standard, even for critical work, producing results comparable to slower films. At the annual Photo Marketing Association trade show, Kodak introduced two revised 35mm color-print films, Gold Ultra 400 and Ektapress Plus 400, as well as a new medium-format film, Kodak Pro 400. Kodak also introduced new Ektachrome Lumiere and Elite slide films, the first slide films to incorporate Kodak's patented T-grain emulsion in blue-, green-, and red-sensitive imaging layers. Fuji also revised Fujichrome 100 in 1993.

From 3M came a new color print film called Advanced Technology Generation (ATG) to help solve a common photography problem—underexposure. 3M claimed that the ATG film could produce high-quality pictures when exposed over a seven-stop range, a feature that could reduce underexposure in many pictures.

Exhibitions and Publications. In late 1992 the Robert Mapplethorpe Foundation made a generous gift to the Guggenheim Museum that included $2 million and more than 200 photographs. The Whitney Museum also initiated a permanent photographic collection. All of New York City's major art museums now were in a position to have strong representation in photography for the first time.

Two significant exhibitions opened at New York City museums. "The Waking Dream, Photography's First Century: Photographs from the Gilman Paper Collection," a well-regarded private collection, opened at the Metropolitan Museum, while "John Heartfield: Photomontages" opened at the Museum of Modern Art as the first extensive showing of the German artist credited with the invention of the photomontage. The show, which earlier had toured Europe, reflected the current popularity of multiple imagery.

"James VanDerZee Photographs" was shown at the National Portrait Gallery in Washington, DC. It is a retrospective of the life of the 20th century's first great African-American photographer, best known for his photographs of the Harlem community between the two world wars.

The autobiography of Richard Avedon, considered one of the most influential photographers of the 20th century, appeared late in the year. To mark its publication, *Newsweek* magazine devoted 30 pages of a September issue to Avedon and his works. Two other noteworthy new books were *Icons,* a collection of Douglas Kirkland's famous images that were altered on a computer, and *Imogen Cunningham: Ideas Without End,* which showed the deceased master photographer's surprising and largely unknown experimentation with double exposures and negative prints.

The Bridges of Madison County, a popular novel by Robert James Waller, presented a compelling story of a *National Geographic* photographer named Robert Kincaid who has an intense four-day relationship with a farmer's wife. The book was complemented with artful photographs of covered bridges. These images and the characters appealed to so many readers that the site in Iowa became a tourist attraction, and the words "a novel" had to be printed on the book jacket to emphasize its fictional nature.

BARBARA LOBRON, *Writer, Editor, Photographer*

PHYSICS

In 1993 important advances were made in the study of neutrinos and anyons, while the future of the Superconducting Super Collider (SSC) was a matter of debate.

Solar Neutrinos. Physicists still were working to solve the puzzling solar neutrino problem: a discrepancy between the number of neutrinos expected to be emitted by the Sun and the number actually measured. This problem has persisted largely because detecting neutral, nearly massless particles which interact very weakly with matter is exceptionally difficult. Until the early 1990s data came only from the neutrino detector at the Homestake Gold Mine in South Dakota and from the Japanese detector Kamiokande II. Giant underground liquid detectors are used, with chemical separation of the very few nuclei which are the end products of the neutrino interaction. Both detectors measured less than predicted, leaving the original solar neutrino puzzle unsolved.

Two new systems, the Russian- (formerly Soviet-) American Gallium Experiment (SAGE) in the Russian Caucasus and the Gallex experiment in Italy, have yielded more promising results. The initial SAGE results did not observe neutrinos, but further measurements observed about 44% of the predicted value. Initial results from Gallex yielded about 63% of the predicted value. One possible explanation for this shortfall—the Mikheyev-Smirnov-Wolfenstein (MSW) effect—states that the predicted number of neutrinos are created in the Sun and then transformed into another type of neutrino during passage to Earth. The MSW theory appears consistent with available experimental data, but neutrino mixing implies that neutrinos have a finite mass.

Neutrino Mass. Questions regarding the controversial massive (17 keV) neutrino have been put to rest. In beta decay the electron and the electron neutrino share the energy released, a relationship that allows physicists to make predictions about the properties of the neutrino. In 1985, John Simpson of the University of Guelph in Ontario observed a "kink" in the energy spectrum about 17 keV less than expected, which was interpreted as evidence for a neutrino with 17 keV mass. Groups at Oxford University in Britain and at the University of California, Berkeley, observed similar evidence for the heavy neutrino. In the early 1990s an Argonne-Berkeley collaboration used a magnetic field to guide the electrons to the detector (instead of collimators and baffles), and observed no kink in the spectrum. Scientists at Berkeley repeated their first experiment with an improved system and found no evidence for a heavy neutrino.

Whether the neutrino has a mass is a fundamental question. In beta decay an electron and a neutrino are emitted; in the rare process of double beta decay, two electrons and two neutrinos are emitted. The observation of double beta decay without neutrino emission would establish that neutrinos have mass. Experiments in progress in underground laboratories in Italy and Spain should place upper limits on the neutrino mass of less than 1 eV, much smaller than the present limits.

Anyons. In quantum mechanics, particles generally are classified into two categories: fermions (such as electrons) and bosons (such as photons). However, physicists now believe that there are quantum particles, called anyons, that are neither fermions nor bosons. Anyons can occur in two-dimensional systems. Anyons violate time-reversal symmetry, a fundamental principle that states that the laws of quantum mechanics do not distinguish between time going forward or backward. Systems which violate time-reversal symmetry show optical effects, absorbing left-handed polarized light differently from right-handed polarized light (optical dichroism). Experiments use these symmetry-breaking effects as signatures of anyons.

Anyons might have applications when electrons are confined to two dimensions. Researchers are attempting to connect anyons with high-temperature superconductors (the copper-oxide planes are essentially two-dimensional). Experiments have been performed on thin films of superconducting material. A group at AT&T Bell Labs observed positive results, while a Stanford University group did not. With these inconclusive results, the existence of anyons remained unproven in 1993.

Superconducting Super Collider. As proposed, the Superconducting Super Collider (SSC)—with a tunnel some 50 mi (80 km) long with two 20 TeV (1 TeV = 1,012 electron volts) colliding proton beams—would have been the world's largest scientific instrument. The cost of the SSC, to be built at Waxahatchie, TX, was estimated originally at $4.5 billion, but 1993 estimates by the U.S. Department of Energy (DOE) exceeded $11 billion. Efforts to obtain international partners for the project were unsuccessful. Meanwhile, SSC contracts were awarded in more than 40 states, and DOE grants and contracts were presented to some 90 universities and institutes.

In 1992 the U.S. House of Representatives narrowly voted to stop funding the project, but a Senate vote restored funding. Joint House-Senate action then continued funding for the SSC for fiscal year 1993. Although the new Clinton administration supported the SSC, the House again voted in 1993 to cancel it. Then, after receiving initial support in the Senate, the SSC was killed in a complicated congressional maneuver in October. A sum of $640 million was approved by Congress to shut down the super collider.

GARY MITCHELL
North Carolina State University

© Chesnot/Sipa

On April 19, 1993, a ceremony was held in Warsaw, Poland, to mark the 50th anniversary of the Jewish ghetto uprising against German Nazis. Israel's Prime Minister Yitzhak Rabin and U.S. Vice-President Al Gore were among the dignitaries in attendance.

POLAND

Poland continued to pursue an agenda of economic reform in 1993, in an economy full of good and bad news. The traumas induced by these reforms had reverberations felt in politics, as elections held in September led to a sharp swing to the political left.

Economy. The economic picture was full of contrasting indicators. Industrial output was reported at 5.4% above corresponding levels for the first quarter of 1992; worker productivity was up 10%; the annual rate of inflation was reported at 39%, roughly equal to the 1992 rate. By midyear, about half of the labor force was employed by private companies and accounted for about 40% of total industrial output. However, unemployment climbed above 15% in June. Polish exports declined and imports increased, creating a $1 billion deficit in the country's foreign trade at midyear. The government's budget was about $1.5 billion in the red.

The World Bank and the International Monetary Fund (IMF) demanded that Poland "hold the line" on inflation and deficit government spending as a condition of any further loans, credit, and other financial assistance. Simultaneously, workers, teachers, state employees, retirees, and farmers all demanded increased pensions, wages, price supports, and benefits to offset increased living costs. This led to political and social tensions. By May 5, 300,000 public-school teachers were on strike for higher salaries and more funds for the school system. Strike action also hit transportation and manufacturing facilities throughout

Poland. On May 30, Solidarity renewed its call for a general strike on behalf of substantial wage increases for all workers. On June 1 government sources announced that 800 coal miners were being laid off, and, more ominously, that it planned to halve the 340,000-strong coal-mine workforce because of reduced demand for coal.

Government Policy. Among the measures taken by the center-right cabinet of Prime Minister Hanna Suchocka was a new value-added tax (VAT) of 22% on most goods. Medicine and some basic foods were among the exempted articles. Excise taxes also were applied to alcohol, tobacco, cosmetics, automobiles, and electronic equipment. The government hoped to lower tax evasion and to raise more revenue for public purposes. On August 28 the zloty was devalued by about 8% of its value against several Western currencies, including the U.S. dollar. The measure was intended to stimulate Polish exports.

The government continued to push forward its policy of privatizing firms to create a more competitive and profit-oriented economy and fulfill its international commitments. In late February a privatization agreement was concluded by leaders of eight trade unions, the Polish government (represented by Labor Minister Jacek Kuron), and the head of an employers' group. State employees were offered incentives—in the form of profit-sharing, stocks, and participation in management—in exchange for agreements to privatize.

Given the attendant problems, privatization faced considerable opposition in the parliament. On April 2 the minister of privatization, Janusz Lewandowski, survived a personal no-confidence

vote in the Sejm by the narrow margin of 175-147 with 51 abstentions. On April 30 the cabinet as a whole survived a 215-178 vote in the Sejm. However, Prime Minister Suchocka and her entire cabinet, opposed by a six-party coalition, suffered defeat in the Sejm on May 28 by the scant margin of one vote when she refused to raise the salaries of nurses, teachers, and other public employees. She had been in office since July 1992, longer than any post-1989 Polish premier.

President Lech Walesa expressed his support for the defeated cabinet when he vetoed, on May 31, a parliamentary measure that would have added $1.3 billion in pension and wage supplements to the budget deficit. However, on June 2, Walesa called for new parliamentary elections to be held on September 19. Walesa asked Prime Minister Suchocka and her cabinet to maintain a caretaker role until the general election.

In a curious return to an initiative undertaken by Poland's authoritarian leader of the 1920s—Józef Pilsudski—President Walesa created his own so-called nonpartisan organization for the support of reforms, with the same acronym as Pilsudski's 1928 entity (BBWR). Walesa distanced himself still further from the remnants of the old Solidarity movement, which he had led until 1989, by refusing to attend its national convention in late June.

Elections. The results of parliamentary elections held on September 19 reflected the frustrations and privations experienced by the Polish electorate since the previous election in 1991. Only half of the eligible voters participated in the elections. The results produced a substantial swing to the left and the emergence of Poland's former Communist Party—renamed the Alliance of the Democratic Left (SLD)—as the largest party. The SLD increased its vote from approximately 12% in 1991 to 20% in 1993. The SLD's ally, the leftist Polish Peasant Party (PSL), received 15% of the vote.

Earlier in the year, President Walesa had signed into law a new electoral provision which required a minimum of 5% of the national vote for any party to have representation in parliament and 8.5% for party conglomerates. This measure was intended to decrease the number of parties occupying legislative seats and thus to make the process of coalition building simpler and more stable. Aided by the new law, the SLD and PSL together controlled 303 seats in the 460-member lower house (Sejm). Under the leadership of Waldemar Pawlak of the PSL, a two-party government was constituted.

The total number of parties represented in the Sejm and the less powerful upper house, the 100-member Senate, was reduced to six (not counting the contingent of four German deputies in the Sejm). The balance of power shifted from right-center to the left. Hanna Suchocka's Democratic Union received roughly 10% of the popular vote and only 72 seats in the Sejm. The former Solidarity controlled 41 seats, Walesa's BBWR won 16 seats, and the rightist Confederation of Independent Poland (KPN) garnered a mere 22 seats. The Catholic Electoral Club coalition failed to get 8.5% of the vote, and received no representation.

The new cabinet pledged to continue reform policies to strengthen private enterprise, but with more concern for the living standards and the economic security of workers, pensioners, and other less privileged strata of Polish society. Some observers expected the pace of Polish market reforms to slow down, while others felt that social policies could jeopardize the government's commitment to fiscal restraint.

Church-State Relations. Among the most significant evidences of the Roman Catholic Church's influence in Polish politics was the passage into law of a highly restrictive abortion measure in February. Signed by President Walesa, who personally supported severe limits on abortion, the law allowed such procedures only in certain situations: if a mother's life and health were endangered according to competent medical opinion; in cases of rape certified by public authorities; and in instances of medically certified damage to the fetus.

The leaders of the Polish Catholic Church and the Christian National Union worked to abolish abortion totally. (It had been accessible to women freely under the Communist regime.) The legislation enacted in February nevertheless was a significant victory for the religious forces and, according to public-opinion polls, was not the preference of most Poles. The Church and its political allies suffered a disappointment, however, in the results of the September elections, when the Catholic Electoral Club coalition failed to win representation in parliament under the new threshold law.

On Oct. 14, 1993, Waldemar Pawlak of the Poland Peasant Party (PSL) was named premier of Poland. The PSL and the Democratic Left Alliance had dominated in September elections.

© Ewa Grochowiak/Sygma

In early April, Pope John Paul II moved to resolve a long-standing conflict between the Polish Church and the Jewish community in Poland and throughout the world. The pope called upon the Carmelite nuns to abandon their convent at Oswiecim (Auschwitz), which was located on the site of the extermination of millions of Jews.

Foreign Affairs. Poland busily forged new post-Cold War relationships during 1993. On April 19, Israeli Prime Minister Yitzhak Rabin and U.S. Vice-President Albert Gore joined with President Walesa for a commemoration of the 50th anniversary of the Warsaw Ghetto uprising.

On May 7, Poland and Germany signed an agreement that provided for a subsidy of $75 million to help Poland pay the expenses of housing and shipping refugees denied entry into Germany along the German-Polish border.

Also in May, Poland agreed to resume interest payments on a $12.1 billion debt to Western nations at a financial conference with members of the London Club. The payments had been suspended in 1989. On June 3 the 24-member Organization for Economic Cooperation and Development (OECD) identified Poland—along with South Korea, Hungary, and the Czech Republic—as potential future members. At a June European Community (EC) summit meeting in Copenhagen, the 12 EC leaders invited Poland—along with Hungary, the Czech Republic, Slovakia, Romania, and Bulgaria—to apply for membership "when political and economic conditions allow." Full EC (later the European Union, or EU) membership for Poland was not expected before 2000.

In mid-July, Poland participated in the Budapest meeting of the ten-nation Central European Initiative with Italy, Austria, Hungary, the Czech Republic, Slovakia, Slovenia, Croatia, Bosnia-Herzegovina, and Macedonia. Discussions involved relations with the EC and the question of refugee movements within Eastern Europe.

On August 25, Russia's President Boris Yeltsin visited President Walesa and others in Warsaw. Agreements were concluded on bilateral trade and on the withdrawal of the last Russian troops from Polish territory by October. A new pact also was formed to build a natural-gas pipeline across Russia and Poland to transport gas to Western Europe. Yeltsin placed a wreath on the Katyn memorial to the victims of Stalin's 1940 executions. He also expressed his "understanding" of Poland's desire to become a part of the North Atlantic Treaty Organization (NATO), but by December, Russian approval seemed doubtful.

ALEXANDER J. GROTH
University of California, Davis

POLAR RESEARCH

Antarctica. The amount of ozone depleted from the antarctic atmosphere reached a new high during September and October 1993. That amount set a record for the lowest values of ozone ever recorded on Earth. This ozone measurement was matched by record increases in the amount of solar ultraviolet radiation reaching Earth's surface. At the South Pole in November the average level of UV-B radiation—the part of the ultraviolet spectrum most harmful to life—was 19% higher than in the two previous years, while levels were 44% higher than in 1992 at McMurdo Station on the coast.

At the edge of the Ross Ice Shelf near McMurdo Station, geologists found remnants of well-preserved wood and a mixture of microscopic marine organisms, all about 35 million to 55 million years old. These fossils ultimately may shed light on Antarctica's link to the world climate and help predict future climate change. On Vega Island near the Antarctic Peninsula, U.S. and Argentine geologists found a fossil bird with the body of a shorebird and the head of a duck. These fossils, the first of a land bird ever found in Antarctica, may illuminate how birds were evolving about 65 million to 70 million years ago.

In June 1993 astronomers who were working at the U.S. Center for Astrophysical Research in Antarctica at the South Pole announced that their antarctic data revealed evidence of cosmic structures that formed roughly 1 million years after the "Big Bang." These new measurements, which confirmed those made by the Cosmic Background Explorer satellite, provided greater detail to describe how structure formed in the universe.

Results of a 1992 investigation by U.S. and Russian scientists of winter processes in the Weddell Sea indicated that there are multiple sources of antarctic bottom water, each with subtle differences in salinity and temperature. In the northern region of the Weddell Sea, scientists discovered that these waters mixed to form the characteristic bottom water that spreads out globally. Other results from the

---

POLAND • Information Highlights

Official Name: Republic of Poland.
Location: Eastern Europe.
Area: 120,726 sq mi (312 680 km²).
Population (mid-1993 est.): 38,500,000.
Chief Cities (Dec. 31, 1991 est.): Warsaw, the capital, 1,653,300; Lodz, 844,900; Krakow, 751,300.
Government: *Head of state,* Lech Walesa, president (inaugurated Dec. 22, 1990). *Head of government,* Waldemar Pawlak, premier (sworn in Oct. 26, 1993). *Legislature* (bicameral)—Sejm and Senate.
Monetary Unit: Zloty (20,380 zlotys equal U.S.$1, Dec. 31, 1993).
Gross Domestic Product (1991 est. U.S.$): $162,700,000,000.
Economic Indexes (1992): *Consumer Prices* (1990 = 100), all items, 243.5; food, 206.6. *Industrial Production* (1980 = 100), 72.
Foreign Trade (1992 U.S.$): *Imports,* $15,913,000,000; *exports,* $13,187,000,000.

117-day expedition included the discovery that the continental slope along the Antarctic Peninsula extends some 62 mi (100 km) further west than previously thought.

Arctic. In May 1993, 200 scientists from the United States, Russia, Norway, Ireland, Finland, Canada, and the International Atomic Energy Agency met in Anchorage, AK, to assess the amount of contaminants in the arctic environment. The Russians revealed that there was no available information on the fate of radioactive materials dumped by the Soviet government at marine sites and that near some Siberian oil fields, radiation exceeded acceptable levels caused by naturally radioactive brines pumped out of the Earth with petroleum. These radioactive materials then remained concentrated in ponds because water would evaporate while the other radioactive particles could not disperse due to the frozen ground.

U.S. earth scientists continued to study the unusual surging behavior of Alaska's Bering Glacier, the longest glacier in North America. The glacier races along at 100 ft (30 m) per day—among the fastest sustained speeds ever measured for a glacier—and spawns thousands of icebergs per hour. By learning more about the causes of this surging, scientists hoped to gain insight into how climate may affect continental-sized ice sheets.

WINIFRED REUNING
National Science Foundation

PORTUGAL

Economic policy loomed large on Portugal's agenda in 1993 as the government sought to deepen its integration with the European Community (EC)—later the European Union (EU)—amid poor economic growth and worker unrest. Municipal elections also were held.

Politics. The ruling Social Democratic Party (PSD) continued to dominate the political scene as Prime Minister Aníbal Cavaco Silva maintained a high profile, despite a 20-point drop in popularity from the early 1990s. The main opposition party, the Portuguese Socialist Party (PSP), remained deeply divided and posed no credible threat to the PSD. Despite a new secretary-general, Carlos Carvalhas, the Portuguese Communist Party continued to lose strength as its hard-line Stalinist legacy appeared increasingly irrelevant to young people.

The PSD sought to downplay the importance of municipal elections held on December 12 because they concerned local issues. However, these issues gave voters an opportunity to express discontent with national leadership. The Social Democrats ran second (33.9%), behind the Socialists (35%), but well ahead of the Communists (12.5%) and the Social Democratic Center (8.5%). Defense Minister Fernando Nogueira, who recruited PSD candidates, feared that his

party's setback would jeopardize his prospects to succeed Cavaco Silva.

Many observers believed that the most effective critic of the Cavaco regime was President Alberto Mário Soares, a former Socialist prime minister, who criticized the social impact of Cavaco's belt-tightening policies. This scolding was expected to end in 1996 when Soares steps down, possibly to be replaced by Cavaco.

Economics. The prime minister's economic objectives included combating inflation, curbing government expenditures, and restructuring industry to spur his nation's integration into the EU. Predictably, these policies sparked dissatisfaction and continued economic hardship, as real unemployment climbed to 7% from 6.7% in 1992. The government tried to control wages as it promoted industrial restructuring. Cavaco imposed a 5.5% salary ceiling on public employees, which sparked strikes by teachers, doctors, and other public employees.

The gross domestic product (GDP) continued a four-year slide, dropping slightly (less than 1%) in 1993. Public and private investment also fell, but austerity measures did cut inflation to approximately 6%, down from 8.9% and 11.4% in 1992 and 1991, respectively.

The Bank of Portugal reported that a strong escudo sparked a fall in exports. Meanwhile, a small surge in imports ensured that the 1993 deficit would approach the $200 million deficit in 1992. Business leaders lamented that an overvalued currency combined with high interest rates would destroy the nation's industrial base. As a result, Cavaco moved to depreciate the escudo slightly within the European Monetary System (EMS), even as he sought to integrate his currency with those of sister European nations. The trade deficit eroded some of the $24.6 billion in foreign-exchange reserves that Portugal boasted at the end of 1992.

The government sought to attract external investment by launching the second phase of its

---

PORTUGAL • Information Highlights

Official Name: Portuguese Republic.
Location: Southwestern Europe.
Area: 35,552 sq mi (92 080 km²).
Population (mid-1993 est.): 9,800,000.
Chief Cities (1981 census): Lisbon, the capital, 807,167; Oporto, 327,368; Amadora, 95,518.
Government: *Head of state*, Alberto Mário Soares, president (took office March 1986). *Head of government*, Aníbal Cavaco Silva, prime minister (took office November 1985). *Legislature* (unicameral)—Assembly of the Republic.
Monetary Unit: Escudo (176.90 escudos equal U.S.$1, Dec. 31, 1993).
Gross Domestic Product (1991 est. U.S.$): $87,300,000,000.
Economic Indexes (1992): *Consumer Prices* (1991 = 100), all items, 108.9; food, 107.5. *Industrial Production* (1980 = 100), 156.
Foreign Trade (1992 U.S.$): *Imports*, $29,726,000,000; *exports*, $17,905,000,000.

ambitious privatization program. Foreigners, formerly restricted to 25% ownership of privatized firms, were permitted to purchase a controlling interest, provided the state approved the transaction. In so doing, Lisbon attempted to placate EU critics, who claimed that the old 25% policy violated the spirit of a single European market. Portugal also wanted to burnish its image in international financial markets.

The difficult economic conditions impeded the sale of Petrogal, the state oil firm and the country's largest firm. Prospective buyers proved reluctant to acquire a relatively inefficient corporation with older technology and a bloated labor force. For his part, Cavaco was reluctant to downsize the company and fire workers during a period of economic hardship.

Foreign Relations. In October, Nelson Mandela, leader of the African National Congress (ANC), visited Lisbon to soothe fears of black rule among the 600,000 Portuguese immigrants in South Africa. Mandela said that the immigrant community could play an important role in South Africa's political transition and that its property would be safe should the ANC come to power.

Lisbon and Washington continued to negotiate the future of U.S. personnel at the Lajes air base in the Azores Islands. After eight bargaining sessions, it appeared late in 1993 that the two countries would sign a Charter on Cooperation and Defense, covering bilateral initiatives in science, technology, culture, and the Azores.

GEORGE W. GRAYSON
College of William & Mary

POSTAL SERVICE

The extent to which the U.S. Congress has been taxing the U.S. Postal Service (USPS) indirectly in recent years to help reduce the federal deficit has been one of the nation's best-kept political secrets. Including fiscal year (FY) 1988, the amount of taxation has averaged more than $1 billion annually.

Finances. The tax story goes back to FY 1979 when the USPS recorded its first surplus since its creation as a government corporation in 1971. Between FY 1979 and FY 1987 the service was in the black five out of eight years. Congress noted this and in 1987 brought the USPS under the terms of the antideficit Gramm-Rudman Act so that the postal surplus could be tapped. Several billion dollars were assessed during the next two years. When the USPS faced a $1.5 billion deficit in FY 1989, Congress agreed to take the service off budget again so it could recoup its losses.

But Congress reneged and continued its assessments. During most of the same period, Congress failed to reimburse the USPS fully for the congressionally mandated below-cost ("revenue foregone") rates given to nonprofit mailers.

In what has become common recently, the USPS ended FY 1993 with a total deficit of $1.766 billion, including an estimated operating deficit of $372 million (including $318 million nonprofit losses unreimbursed), an $857 million assessment by Congress, and $537 million from a onetime debt refinancing. The normal operations of the system, however, were very close to being in the black—within $62 million out of a total budget of nearly $50 billion.

Labor peace was kept by the extension of contracts with the Mail Handlers Union and Rural Letter Carriers Association to November 1994 and November 1995, respectively. Even so, a rate-increase request, the first since 1990, was expected to be filed in early 1994 and take effect in 1995. The Elvis Presley stamp, issued on January 7, had the greatest sale of any U.S. commemorative ever.

Reorganization and an Appointment. Postmaster General Marvin T. Runyon expanded the efforts of his three predecessors to loosen up an organization long criticized as top-heavy and overly bureaucratic. He abolished nearly 25,000 overhead jobs. More than 40,000 employees retired. Runyon also pledged to have better communications with workers and customers. Since taking office in 1992, he had started regular employee and customer surveys, cut the domestic-mail-manual text in half, reduced the top executive level from 42 to 25, and pushed the delegation of authority lower and lower. At the same time he continued to search for 7,000 more managerial jobs to abolish.

Runyon's efforts have been aided by a renewed increase in postal volume after a decline in FY 1991. The FY 1993 volume promised to reach a new high of more than 171 billion pieces. Continued expansion of automation enabled the system to remain the most productive per employee of any postal service in the world. Customers were pleased. The customer-satisfaction index prepared by Opinion Research of New Jersey rose from 87% to 89%.

In an attempt to bypass the need for congressional approval by making an appointment when Congress was in recess, outgoing President George Bush on January 8 appointed Thomas Ludlow Ashley to the Postal Board of Governors. Ashley was a longtime Bush friend, and the president hoped that by appointing Ashley he would have the necessary votes to drop a postal-rate suit that the board had been pursuing in defiance of the Justice Department. A federal-court judge ruled against the appointment,

New Logo and Museum. The USPS in October announced that it would adopt an updated version of its eagle symbol at a cost of more than $6 million....A National Postal Museum opened on July 30 as part of the Smithsonian Institution in Washington, DC. It displays 55,000 domestic and foreign stamps.

Canada. The Canadian Post Corporation reported a surplus of C$26 million for its FY 1993, ending March 31. It was the fourth surplus in five years.

PAUL P. VAN RIPER, *Texas A&M University*

PRINCE EDWARD ISLAND

In 1993, Prince Edward Island (PEI) became the first Canadian province to elect a woman premier, the province's federal electoral map stayed Liberal red, and a contract to bridge Northumberland Strait was signed.

Politics. The year was not a month old when, on January 23, Catherine Callbeck was chosen to lead PEI's governing Liberal Party in succession to Joe Ghiz, who resigned in 1992. She won on the first ballot at a party convention in Charlottetown, easily defeating two male opponents. Two days later she was sworn in as premier.

Callbeck then proceeded to go after her own mandate from island voters; she got it and then some. In a provincial general election March 29, the Liberals took all but one of the legislature's 32 seats. Conservative leader Patricia Mella salvaged the lone Tory seat. Callbeck thus became Canada's first elected female premier—though she repeatedly made clear that she assigned no particular priority to women's issues.

The new premier first had entered the legislature in 1974, later serving as health minister. After taking a break from politics to run her family's hardware business, she was elected federal member of Parliament (MP) for Malpeque in 1988. She resigned her House of Commons seat after winning the provincial Liberal leadership.

Not three weeks after the Liberals' landslide election victory, Callbeck took a broom to her cabinet, sweeping out five ministers and bringing in four new ones for a net reduction of one. The bureaucracy also got a face-lift, with new departments created and existing ones amalgamated.

The contemporary Liberal leaning of PEI voters was confirmed again when Liberal candidates swept all four island ridings in the October 25 federal election—just as in 1988. The lineup of PEI MPs remained the same except in Malpeque, where Liberal Wayne Easter replaced Callbeck.

© Canapress Photo Service

Catherine Callbeck, 53, led Prince Edward Island's Liberal Party to an election victory in March 1993, thus becoming the first woman elected as a provincial premier in Canada.

Budget and Taxation. Fiscal restraint was the theme of Treasurer Wayne Cheverie's budget presentation on June 17. The budget called for a 10% cut in spending on health and social services over a three-year period, and aimed to eliminate the budget deficit over the same period, beginning with a huge drop from C$83.4 million to C$25.4 million in 1993-94. Total spending for the fiscal year was set at C$793 million. Cigarette and gasoline taxes were raised and exemptions from the 10% provincial sales tax eliminated.

Property owners living outside the province would continue to face double taxation as the result of a PEI Supreme Court ruling made public on February 9. The judgment disallowed an appeal against the controversial measure; the appeal was launched by a group representing 8,000 nonresidents with holdings on the island.

Bridge Contract. After more than a century of debate, the way appeared to be open for a fixed link between PEI and the Canadian mainland. Under a contract signed in Charlottetown on October 8, an 8.4-mi (13.5-km) bridge was to be built across the Northumberland Strait to New Brunswick. The contract is between the federal government and Strait Crossing Inc., a Calgary consortium. The signing took place to the accompaniment of demonstrations by protesters, who insisted that the mammoth C$840 million project should be delayed pending a full environmental review. The bridge was scheduled to open in 1997, replacing a long-established ferry service.

JOHN BEST
"Canada World News"

PRINCE EDWARD ISLAND
• Information Highlights

Area: 2,185 sq mi (5 660 km²).

Population (June 1993): 132,000.

Chief Cities (1991 census): Charlottetown, the capital, 15,396; Summerside, 7,474.

Government (1993): *Chief Officers*—lt. gov., Marion Reid; premier, Catherine Callbeck (Liberal). *Legislature*—Legislative Assembly, 32 members.

Provincial Finances (1993-94 fiscal year budget): *Revenues*, $767,600,000; *expenditures*, $793,000,000.

Personal Income (average weekly earnings, June 1993): $455.55.

Labor Force (August 1993, seasonally adjusted): *Employed* workers, 15 years of age and over, 52,000; *Unemployed*, 19.4%.

Education (1992-93): *Enrollment*—elementary and secondary schools, 24,950 pupils; postsecondary—universities, 2,740; community colleges, 1,250.

(All monetary figures are in Canadian dollars.)

PRISONS

Continuing a decades-long trend, the number of U.S. citizens in prison steadily increased in 1993, reaching new heights during the year. Mandatory sentencing for drug offenses now was the principal cause of persons being sent to prison, but was having no apparent impact on reducing the national drug problem. Some challenges and alternative strategies emerged in 1993. The U.S. Supreme Court severely limited the possibilities for the appeal of death sentences, and the number of executions increased. Racial issues continued to vex overcrowded prison systems throughout the country.

In May the Justice Department reported that 1993 began with an official prison census of 883,593. But when account was taken of persons in jail held for less than a year, and those held under a variety of probation and parole programs, the total number of U.S. citizens in government detention rose beyond 5 million.

Mandatory-Sentencing Controversy. As the national policy of a war on drugs became stronger in the early 1980s, critics had called attention to wide discrepancies in the length of sentences handed down for drug convictions in different jurisdictions. Stringent national guidelines were issued in 1986 which excluded mitigating circumstances, including prior arrest records, and imposed mandatory sentences based largely on the amount of drugs in possession at the time of arrest. The number of people going to prison for drug-related nonviolent crimes immediately began to rise. By 1993, drug charges accounted for more than 60% of those sent to prison. And while studies showed that drug use was as widespread among whites as among blacks, the number of minorities arrested and sentenced on drug charges continued disproportionately high.

With almost all U.S. prisons at or above capacity, pressure to release inmates to make space for new prisoners intensified. Forbidden by the guidelines to release nonviolent drug offenders before the full sentence has been served, parole boards turned to those sentenced for violent crimes as candidates for early release. The effectiveness of the antidrug policy came into question on several fronts. One study of federal prisons indicated that of the 17,000 people serving drug sentences of ten years or more, less than 10% were considered management-level dealers. In the view of many, the national policy was crippling the prison system and imposing a burden on taxpayers. The mandatory sentencing policy for drugs also was largely responsible for the sharply rising number of women in prison, which had more than tripled over the last decade and in 1993 totaled more than 51,000. Many judges were particularly frustrated by the policy, and by year's end more than 50 federal judges were refusing publicly to hear any drug cases. U.S. Attorney General Janet Reno characterized the mandatory sentences as costly, unfair, and ineffective, and ordered a review. In July the U.S. House Judiciary Subcommittee on Crime and Criminal Justice began hearings to reexamine rigid sentencing laws. And in October, President Bill Clinton announced a new approach at the federal level to dealing with drug use, in which education and treatment, rather than only incarceration, would be given strong consideration.

Death Penalty. The Supreme Court continued to narrow the possibilities for appeal of execution sentences. In January the court ruled, 6-3, that prisoners producing new evidence of their innocence after lower courts had condemned them to death were not, under most circumstances, entitled to new hearings. Although the decision did not ban new evidence of actual innocence completely, it did rule that such claims would have to meet "extraordinarily high standards to justify an appeal hearing."

In another ruling, the court overturned an appeals-court decision staying the execution of Bobby Ray Fretwell, a convicted Arkansas murderer. The lower courts had stated that an error by Fretwell's court-appointed attorney in failing to make a legal argument which would have avoided the death sentence deprived Fretwell of his due-process right. The Supreme Court held that an attorney's mistake was not a violation of the client's rights. Fretwell was executed.

More than 200 prisoners had been executed since the death penalty was reinstated by the Supreme Court in 1976. The pace of executions accelerated and exceeded 1992's record figure of 31. Some 20 states had enforced the death penalty in recent years, with Louisiana, Texas, and Nevada leading the way. Considerable media attention was given to the hanging in Washington state of Westley Allan Dodd in January; it was the first U.S. execution by that method in 28 years. In Richmond, VA, Charles S. Stamper had been convicted of shooting three coworkers to death. While he was in prison, his spinal cord was injured severely, and he was confined to a wheelchair. After several stays to reexamine his medical condition, he was executed. Death-penalty opponents argued that Stamper was no longer a threat to society and criticized "making the death house wheelchair-accessible."

Racial Issues. Minorities are overrepresented in the prison populations of most states, and racial tensions are often an underlying condition in many facilities, especially where officers are mostly white and inmates are mostly minorities. In April rioting inmates of the Southern Ohio Correctional Facility—70 mi (112.7 km) south of Columbus, the state capital—took over the prison. In the riot's first days, six white inmates were killed, apparently by rioting prisoners. Authorities in the prison, whose population is 55% black, attributed the deaths to racial conflicts.

DONALD GOODMAN
John Jay College of Criminal Justice

PRIZES AND AWARDS

NOBEL PRIZES[1]

Chemistry: Kary B. Mullis, La Jolla, CA, for his discovery of the polymerase chain reaction, which makes such methods as DNA fingerprinting possible; Michael Smith, University of British Columbia, for inventing a method—called oligonu-cleotide-based site-directed mutagenesis—used to splice foreign components into genetic molecules

Economics: Robert W. Fogel, University of Chicago, and Douglass C. North, Washington University; for "applying economic theory and quantitative methods" to the study of world history

Literature: Toni Morrison, United States; her novels, "characterized by visionary force and poetic import, give life to an essential aspect of American reality" (*See* page 330.)

Peace: F. W. de Klerk and Nelson Mandela, South Africa, for displaying "personal integrity and great political courage" in their work to end apartheid; their "constructive policy of peace and reconciliation also points the way to the peaceful resolution of similar...conflicts elsewhere in the world"

Physics: Russell A. Hulse and Joseph H. Taylor, Jr., Princeton University, for discovering the first known binary pulsar and investigating the gigantic gravitational forces exerted by these ultradense stars

Physiology or Medicine (shared): Richard J. Roberts, New England Biolabs, Beverly, MA, and Phillip A. Sharp, Massachusetts Institute of Technology, for the discovery (independently) of split genes, which "has been of fundamental importance for today's basic research in biology as well as for more medically oriented research concerning the development of cancer and other diseases"

[1] $825,000 in each category.

ART

American Academy and Institute of Arts and Letters Awards
Academy-Institute Awards ($5,000 ea.): architecture—Franklin D. Israel; art—Tom Friedman, Mark Greenwold, Gregory Kondos, Donald Lipski, Mary Robertson; music—Stephen P. Hartke, Stephen Jaffe, Christopher C. Rouse, David Sheinfeld

Michael Smith, 61, a British-born professor of biochemistry at the University of British Columbia in Canada, was a cowinner of the 1993 Nobel Prize in chemistry.

© Jeff Vinnick/Saba

Award for Distinguished Service to the Arts: Jacques d'Amboise
Arnold W. Brunner Memorial Prize in Architecture: José Rafael Moneo
Jimmy Ernst Award: John Opper
Gold Medal for Painting: Richard Diebenkorn (posthumous)
Walter Hinrichson Award: Richard Festinger
Charles Ives Fellowship ($10,000): Sebastian Currier
Goddard Lieberson Fellowships ($10,000): James Primosch, Edward M. Smaldone
Louise Nevelson Award in Art: Byron Kim
Richard and Hinda Rosenthal Foundation Award ($5,000): Sharon Horvath

Capezio Dance Award ($5,000): Dance/USA
Avery Fisher Career Grant ($10,000): Anne Akiko Meyers
John F. Kennedy Center Honors for career achievement in the performing arts: Johnny Carson, Arthur Mitchell, Sir Georg Solti, Stephen Sondheim, Marion Williams
Edward MacDowell Medal: Harry Callahan
National Academy of Recording Arts and Sciences Grammy Awards for excellence in phonograph records
Album of the year: *Unplugged*, Eric Clapton
Classical album: *Mahler's Symphony No. 9*, Leonard Bernstein conducting Berlin Philharmonic Orchestra
Country music song: "I Still Believe in You," Vince Gill and John Barlow Jarvis (songwriters)
Country vocal performance: (female) "I Feel Lucky," Mary-Chapin Carpenter; (male) *I Still Believe in You*, Vince Gill
Jazz vocal performance: "'Round Midnight," *Play*, Bobby McFerrin
New artist: Arrested Development
Pop vocal performance: (female) "Constant Craving," k.d. lang; (male) "Tears in Heaven," Eric Clapton
Record of the year: "Tears in Heaven," Eric Clapton
Rock vocal performance: (female) "Ain't It Heavy," *Never Enough*, Melissa Etheridge; (male) *Unplugged*, Eric Clapton
Song of the year: "Tears in Heaven," Eric Clapton and Will Jennings (songwriters)
National Medal of Arts: Walter and Leonore Annenberg, Cab Calloway, Ray Charles, Bess Lomax Hawes, Stanley Kunitz, Robert Merrill, Arthur Miller, Robert Rauschenberg, Lloyd Richards, William Styron, Paul Taylor, Billy Wilder
Praemium Imperiale for lifetime achievement in the arts ($138,000 ea.): Kenzo Tange, Japan (architecture); Maurice Béjart, France (theater and film); Jasper Johns, United States (painting); Max Bill, Switzerland (sculpture); Mstislav Rostropovich, Russia/United States (music)
Pritzker Architecture Prize ($100,000): Fumihiko Maki
Pulitzer Prize for Music: Christopher Rouse
Samuel H. Scripps/American Dance Festival Award ($25,000): Talley Beatty
Wolf Prize ($100,000): Bruce Nauman

JOURNALISM

Maria Moors Cabot Prizes ($1,000 ea.): CANA (Caribbean News Agency, Ltd.), Barbados; Pamela G. Constable, Washington deputy bureau chief, *The Boston Globe*; Edward Seaton, editor in chief, *The Manhattan* (KS) *Mercury*; Patricia Verdugo A., author and journalist, Santiago, Chile; (posthumous) Manuel de Dios Unanue, former editor, *El Diario/La Prensa* and *Cambio XXI*, New York City
National Magazine Awards
Design: *Harper's Bazaar*
Essays and criticism: *The American Lawyer*
Feature writing: *The New Yorker*
Fiction: *The New Yorker*
General excellence: *Newsweek, The Atlantic Monthly, American Photo, Lingua Franca*
Personal service: *Good Housekeeping*
Photography: *Harper's Bazaar*
Public-interest: *The Family Therapy Networker*
Reporting: *IEEE Spectrum*
Single-topic issue: *Newsweek*
Special-interest: *Philadelphia*
Overseas Press Club Awards
Book on foreign affairs: Misha Glenny, *The Fall of Yugoslavia*
Business or economic reporting from abroad: (magazines)— Stephen Baker, David Woodruff, and Elizabeth Weiner,

© Markel/Gamma-Liaison

On Jan. 13, 1993, former U.S. President Ronald Reagan was awarded the U.S. Presidential Medal of Freedom by his successor, George Bush, just before Bush left office.

Business Week, "Detroit South"; (newspapers and wire services)—Peter Carey and Lewis Simons, *The San Jose Mercury News,* "Profits and Power: Japan's Foreign-Aid Machine"; (radio and television)—Tom Gjelten, National Public Radio, "From Marx to Market"

Cartoon on foreign affairs: Don Wright, *The Palm Beach* (FL) *Post*

Daily newspaper or wire-service interpretation of foreign affairs: Marc Fisher, *The Washington Post,* "Transition of a Unified Germany"

Daily newspaper or wire-service reporting from abroad: Roy Gutman, *Newsday,* "Human Rights Abuses in Bosnia"

Magazine reporting from abroad: Orville Schell and Todd Lappin, *The Nation,* "Capitalist Leap: China Plays the Market"

Photographic reporting from abroad (magazines and books)—James Nachtwey, Magnum for *The New York Times Magazine,* "Somalia 1992: The Casualties"; (newspapers and wire services)—Anatoly Morkovkin, The Associated Press, "Ethnic War"

Radio interpretation or documentary on foreign affairs: Deborah Wang and Melissa Block, National Public Radio, "The Journey Home: Cambodian Refugees on the Cusp of Return"

Radio spot news from abroad: Lou Miliano, WCBS Radio News, "Lou Miliano in Somalia"

Television interpretation or documentary on foreign affairs: *Frontline*/BBC/Gwynne Roberts of WGBH, Boston, "Saddam's Killing Fields"

Television spot news reporting from abroad: Don Kladstrup, Steve Schnee, Tim Manning, and Nick Prince, *ABC World News Tonight with Peter Jennings,* "Somalia"

Whitman Bassow Award (for best reporting in any medium on environmental issues): Emily Smith, *Business Week,* "Growth versus the Environment"

Eric and Amy Burger Award (for best entry in any medium dealing with human rights): Karen Lee Ziner, *The Providence* (RI) *Journal-Bulletin,* "What Now Cambodia?"

Robert Capa Gold Medal (photographic reporting from abroad requiring exceptional courage and enterprise): Luc Delahaye, Sipa Press for *Newsweek,* "Sarajevo: Life in the War Zone"

Madeline Dane Ross Award (for foreign correspondent in any medium showing a concern for the human condition): Deborah Scroggins and Jean Shifrin, *The Atlanta Journal-Constitution,* "Women of the Veil"

George Polk Memorial Awards

Career award: Herbert Mitgang, *The New York Times*

Environmental reporting: John-Thor Dahlburg, *The Los Ange-*

les Times, for in-depth reporting of unregulated disposal of radioactive material in the former USSR and its effects on people and nature

Foreign reporting: Roy Gutman, *Newsday,* for a series documenting human-rights abuses in Bosnia

Foreign television reporting: Chris Wallace, Neal Shapiro, Anthony Radziwill, *Prime Time Live* (ABC), for an investigative report on the rise of neo-Nazism in Germany, its U.S. connection, and its effect on German immigrants and Jews

Health reporting: Seth Rosenfeld, *The San Francisco Examiner,* for a series on the Dow Corning Company

Legal reporting: Marianne Lavelle, Marcia Coyle, Claudia MacLachlan, *The National Law Journal,* for reporting on a racial division in U.S. government cleanup of toxic-waste sites and punishment of polluters

Local reporting: *The Los Angeles Times,* for coverage of the Los Angeles riots

Magazine reporting: Lawrence Weschler, *The New Yorker,* for descriptions of injustices against a leader of the Czechoslovak resistance

National reporting: Gregory Vistica, *The San Diego Union-Tribune,* for coverage of the U.S. Navy Tailhook convention

National television reporting: Brian Ross and Rhonda Schwartz, *Dateline* (NBC), for reporting that Wal-Mart purchased many of its clothes from Indian sweatshops employing young children

Op-ed article: Henry Louis Gates, Jr., Harvard University, "Black Demagogues and Pseudo-Scholars," published in *The New York Times*

Photography: Carlos Guerrero, *El Nuevo Herald,* for a photograph of a dazed man holding his last possessions after Hurricane Andrew hit Florida

Radio reporting: Tom Gjelten, National Public Radio, for a broadcast revealing that Serbian militia forces had executed 200 unarmed Bosnian Muslims

Pulitzer Prizes

Beat reporting: Paul Ingrassia and Joseph B. White, *The Wall Street Journal*

Commentary: Liz Balmaseda, *The Miami Herald*

Criticism: Michael Dirda, *The Washington Post*

Editorial cartooning: Stephen R. Benson, *The Arizona Republic*

Explanatory journalism: Mike Toner, *The Atlanta Journal-Constitution,* for "When Bugs Bite Back"

Feature photography: The Associated Press staff

Feature writing: George Lardner, Jr., *The Washington Post*

International reporting: John F. Burns, *The New York Times;* Roy Gutman, *Newsday*

Investigative reporting: Jeff Brazil and Steve Berry, *The Orlando Sentinel*

National reporting: David Maraniss, *The Washington Post*

Public service: *The Miami Herald*

Spot news photography: Ken Geiger and William Snyder, *The Dallas Morning News*

Spot news reporting: *The Los Angeles Times*

LITERATURE

American Academy and Institute of Arts and Letters Awards

Academy-Institute Awards ($5,000 ea.): Ellen Akins, Richard Bausch, Vance Bourjaily, Deborah Eisenberg, Rolf Fjelde, Tina Howe, Denis Johnson, A.G. Mojtabai

Michael Braude Award for Light Verse: Turner Cassity

Witter Bynner Prize for Poetry ($1,500): Patricia Storace

E.M. Forster Award: Sean O'Brien

Gold Medal for Belles Lettres and Criticism: Elizabeth Hardwick

Sue Kaufman Prize for First Fiction ($2,500): Francisco Goldman, *The Long Night of White Chickens*

Rome Fellowship in Literature: Thomas Bolt

Richard and Hinda Rosenthal Foundation Award ($5,000): Robert Olen Butler, *A Good Scent from a Strange Mountain*

Jean Stein Award ($5,000): Stanley Crouch

Harold D. Vursell Memorial Award ($5,000): T. Coraghessan Boyle

Morton Dauwen Zabel Award ($2,500): James Purdy

Bancroft Prizes in American history ($4,000 ea.): Charles Capper, *Margaret Fuller: An American Romantic Life: The Private Years*; Melvyn P. Leffler, *A Preponderance of Power: National Security, the Truman Administration and the Cold War*

Bollingen Prize in Poetry ($10,000): Mark Strand
Canada's Governor-General Literary Awards ($10,000 ea.)
  English-language awards
    Drama—Guillermo Verdecchia, *Fronteras Americanas*
    Fiction—Carol Shields, *The Stone Diaries*
    Nonfiction—Karen Connelly, *Touch the Dragon*
    Poetry—Don Coles, *Forests of the Medieval World*
  French-language awards
    Drama—Daniel Danis, *Celle-là*
    Fiction—Nancy Huston, *Cantique des plaines*
    Nonfiction—François Paré, *Les Littératures de l'exiguïté*
    Poetry—Denise Desautels, *Le Saut de l'ange*
Lannan Foundation literary prizes ($50,000 ea.):
  Lifetime achievement: William Gaddis
  Fiction: Paul West
  Fiction fellowships: Rikki Ducornet, Denis Johnson, Carole Maso
  Nonfiction: Edward Hoagland
  Nonfiction fellowship: Terry Tempest Williams
  Poetry: Denise Levertov
  Poetry fellowships: Cyrus Cassells, Benjamin Alire Saenz
Ruth Lilly Poetry Prize ($75,000): Charles Wright
Mystery Writers of America/Edgar Allan Poe Awards
  First novel: Michael Connelly, *The Black Echo*
  Novel: Margaret Maron, *Bootlegger's Daughter*
  Grandmaster award: Donald E. Westlake
  Motion picture screenplay: Michael Tolkin, *The Player*
National Book Awards ($10,000 ea.):
  Fiction: E. Annie Proulx, *The Shipping News*
  Nonfiction: Gore Vidal, *United States: Essays 1952-1992*
  Poetry: A. R. Ammons, *Garbage*
National Book Critics Circle Awards
  Biography/autobiography: Carol Brightman, *Writing Dangerously: Mary McCarthy and Her World*
  Criticism: Garry Wills, *Lincoln at Gettysburg: The Words That Remade America*
  Fiction: Cormac McCarthy, *All the Pretty Horses*
  Nonfiction: Norman Maclean, *Young Men and Fire*
  Poetry: Hayden Carruth, *Shorter Collected Poems 1946-1991*
National Book Foundation Medal for distinguished contribution to American letters ($10,000): Clifton Fadiman
PEN/Faulkner Award ($15,000): E. Annie Proulx, *Postcards*
Pulitzer Prizes
  Biography: David McCullough, *Truman*
  Fiction: Robert Olen Butler, *A Good Scent from a Strange Mountain*
  General nonfiction: Garry Wills, *Lincoln at Gettysburg: The Words That Remade America*
  History: Gordon S. Wood, *The Radicalism of the American Revolution*
  Poetry: Louise Glück, *The Wild Iris*
Rea Award for the Short Story ($25,000): Grace Paley
U.S. Poet Laureate: Rita Dove

MOTION PICTURES

Academy of Motion Pictures Arts and Sciences ("Oscar") Awards
  Actor—leading: Al Pacino, *Scent of a Woman*
  Actor—supporting: Gene Hackman, *Unforgiven*
  Actress—leading: Emma Thompson, *Howards End*
  Actress—supporting: Marisa Tomei, *My Cousin Vinny*
  Cinematography: Philippe Rousselot, *A River Runs Through It*
  Costume design: Eiko Ishioka, *Bram Stoker's 'Dracula'*
  Director: Clint Eastwood, *Unforgiven*
  Film: *Unforgiven*
  Foreign-language film: *Indochine* (France)
  Music—original score: Alan Menken, *Aladdin*
  Music—original song: Alan Menken and Tim Rice, "A Whole New World" (from *Aladdin*)
  Screenplay—original: Neil Jordan, *The Crying Game*
  Screenplay—adaptation: Ruth Prawer Jhabvala, *Howards End*
American Film Institute's Life Achievement Award: Jack Nicholson
Cannes Film Festival Awards
  Palme d'Or (best film) (shared): Jane Campion, *The Piano* (New Zealand); Chen Kaige, *Farewell My Concubine* (China)
  Grand Jury Prize: Wim Wenders, *Far Away, So Close* (Germany)
  Jury Prize (shared): Ken Loach, *Raining Stones* (England);

Hou Hsiao-hsien, *Puppet Master* (Taiwan)
  Best actor: David Thewlis, *Naked* (England)
  Best actress: Holly Hunter, *The Piano*
  Best director: Mike Leigh, *Naked*
  Camera d'Or (best first-time director): Tran Anh Hung, *Scent of Green Papaya* (France)
  Special award: Elaine Proctor, *Friends* (South Africa)
National Society of Film Critics Awards
  Actor: Stephen Rea, *The Crying Game*
  Actress: Emma Thompson, *Howards End*
  Director: Clint Eastwood, *Unforgiven*
  Film: *Unforgiven*
  Screenplay: David Webb Peoples, *Unforgiven*
  Supporting actor: Gene Hackman, *Unforgiven*
  Supporting actress: Judy Davis, *Husbands and Wives*

PUBLIC SERVICE

Charles A. Dana Foundation Awards for pioneering achievements in health and higher education ($50,000 ea.): Anders Björklun, Marie M. Clay, Fred H. Gage, Priscilla W. Laws, Gay Su Pinnell, Larry R. Squire, Ronald K. Thornton
Frontrunner Awards for women who exemplify leadership, achievement, and pioneering spirit ($25,000 ea.): arts—Maya Angelou; business—Linda Alvarado; government—Janet Reno; humanities—Lorraine Hale
American Institute for Public Service Jefferson Awards
  National Awards ($5,000 ea.):
  Benefiting Disadvantaged: Arthur Ashe (posthumous)
  Public Official: Carla Hills
  Private Citizen: James Burke
  Citizen under 35: Mary Taylor
Kennedy Profile in Courage Award ($25,000): James Florio
Thurgood Marshall Lifetime Achievement Awards for commitment to civil- and human-rights issues: Harry Belafonte, Sidney Poitier
Spark M. Matsunaga Medals of Peace ($25,000 ea.): Jimmy Carter, Ronald Reagan
National Endowment for the Humanities' Frankel Prize: Richard E. Alegria, John Hope Franklin, Hanna Holborn Gray, Andrew Heiskell, Laurel T. Ulrich

Harry Belafonte (below left) and Sidney Poitier (below right) were presented with the first Thurgood Marshall Lifetime Achievement Award by the NAACP Legal Defense and Educational Fund.

© Reuters/Bettmann

National Security Medal (awarded by President George Bush on Jan. 13, 1993): Admiral Jonathan T. Howe

Philadelphia Liberty Medal ($100,000 shared) (awarded by President Bill Clinton on July 4, 1993): F.W. de Klerk, Nelson Mandela

Templeton Prize for Progress in Religion (c. $1,000,000): Charles Wendell Colson, founder, Prison Fellowship

U.S. Presidential Medal of Freedom (awarded by President Bush on Jan. 13, 1993): Ronald Reagan; (awarded by President Clinton on June 22, 1993): Arthur Ashe (posthumous); (awarded by President Clinton on Nov. 2, 1993): Martha Raye; (awarded by President Clinton on Nov. 30, 1993): William J. Brennan, Marjory Stoneman Douglas, Thurgood Marshall (posthumous), Joseph Rauh, Jr. (posthumous), John Minor Wisdom

SCIENCE

Louisa Gross Horwitz Memorial Prize for research in biology or biochemistry ($22,000 shared): Nicole Le Douarin, Collège de France; Donald Metcalf, University of Melbourne, Australia

Bristol-Myers Squibb Award for distinguished achievement in cancer research ($50,000 shared): Gianni Bonadonna, National Tumor Institute, Italy; Bernard Fisher, University of Pittsburgh

General Motors Cancer Research Foundation Awards ($100,000 ea.)
Kettering Award (shared): Bernard Fisher, University of Pittsburgh; Gianni Bonadonna, National Tumor Institute, Italy
Mott Award: Carlo M. Croce, Jefferson Cancer Institute, Philadelphia, PA
Sloan Award: Hidesaburo Hanafusa, Rockefeller University, New York

Albert Lasker Medical Research Awards ($25,000 ea.): Gunter Blobel, Rockefeller University and Howard Hughes Medical Institute, New York (basic medical research); Donald Metcalf, Walter and Eliza Hall Institute of Medical Research, Melbourne, Australia (clinical medical research); (shared) Paul Rogers, former member, U.S. House of Representatives (D-FL) and Nancy Wexler, Columbia University College of Physicians and Surgeons, NY (public service)

TELEVISION AND RADIO

Academy of Television Arts and Sciences ("Emmy") Awards
Actor—comedy series: Ted Danson, *Cheers* (NBC)
Actor—drama series: Tom Skerritt, *Picket Fences* (CBS)
Actor—miniseries or a special: Robert Morse, *Tru* (PBS)
Actress—comedy series: Roseanne Arnold, *Roseanne* (ABC)
Actress—drama series: Kathy Baker, *Picket Fences* (CBS)
Actress—miniseries or a special: Holly Hunter, *The Positively True Adventures of the Alleged Texas Cheerleader-Murdering Mom* (HBO)
Comedy series: *Seinfeld* (NBC)
Directing—comedy series: Betty Thomas, *Dream On* (HBO)
Directing—drama series: Barry Levinson, *Homicide: Life on the Street* (NBC)
Directing—miniseries or a special: James Sadwith, *Sinatra* (CBS)
Directing—variety or music program: Walter C. Miller, *The 1992 Tony Awards* (CBS)
Drama series: *Picket Fences* (CBS)
Miniseries or a special: *Mystery: Prime Suspect 2* (PBS)
Supporting actor—comedy series: Michael Richards, *Seinfeld* (NBC)
Supporting actor—drama series: Chad Lowe, *Life Goes On* (ABC)
Supporting actor—miniseries or a special: Beau Bridges, *The Positively True Adventures of the Alleged Texas Cheerleader-Murdering Mom* (HBO)
Supporting actress—comedy series: Laurie Metcalf, *Roseanne* (ABC)
Supporting actress—drama series: Mary Alice, *I'll Fly Away* (NBC)
Supporting actress—miniseries or a special: Mary Tyler Moore, *Stolen Babies* (Lifetime)
Variety, music, or comedy series: *Saturday Night Live* (NBC)
Variety, music, or comedy special: *Bob Hope: The First 90 Years* (NBC)

George Foster Peabody Awards
Radio: National Public Radio, *Prisoners in Bosnia* (correspondent Sylvia Poggioli); National Public Radio and WBUR, Boston, *Car Talk*; KFFA, Helena, AR, *King Biscuit Time*; American Folklife Radio Project (independent producer David Isay); BBC Radio (institutional award)
Television: Propaganda Films and the Fox Broadcasting Company, *Rock the Vote*; KIRO-TV, Seattle, WA, *When the Salmon Runs Dry*; KNME-TV and the Institute for American Indian Arts, Albuquerque, NM, *Surviving Columbus*; Signifyin' Works, Berkeley, CA, and the Public Broadcasting System, *Color Adjustment*; Canamedia Productions Ltd. and TV Ontario, Toronto, Ont., *Threads of Hope*; HKO Media Inc. and WKBD-TV, Detroit, MI, *Close to Home: The Tommy Boccomino Story*; GPN-Nebraska ETV Network, Lincoln, NE, *Reading Rainbow: The Wall*; WCVB-TV, Needham, MA, *The Incredible Voyage of Bill Pinkney*; NBC, *The More You Know*; MTV, *Choose or Lose Campaign*; CBS and Finnegan-Pinchuk Company, in association with Brand-Falsey Productions, *Northern Exposure: "Cicely"*; CNN, Atlanta, GA, *Larry King Live Election Coverage 1992*; CBS and Granada Television, London, England, *Age Seven in America*; C-SPAN (institutional award)
Personal Awards: Fred Rogers, Daniel Schorr

THEATER

American Academy and Institute of Arts and Letters Awards
Academy-Institute Award ($5,000): David Mamet
Marc Blitzstein Memorial Award for Musical Theater: Sheldon Harnick

New York Drama Critics Circle Awards
Best drama: *Angels in America: Millennium Approaches*, by Tony Kushner
Best musical: *Kiss of the Spider Woman*, by Terrence McNally (book), Fred Ebb (lyrics), John Kander (music)
Best foreign play: *Someone Who'll Watch Over Me*, by Frank McGuinness (Ireland)

Outer Critics Circle Awards
Actor—play: Robert Klein, *The Sisters Rosensweig*
Actor—musical: Martin Short, *The Goodbye Girl*
Actress—play: Madeline Kahn, *The Sisters Rosensweig*
Actress—musical: Tonya Pinkins, *Jelly's Last Jam*
Director—play: Daniel Sullivan, *The Sisters Rosensweig*
Director—musical: Des McAnuff, *Tommy*
Musical: *Tommy*
Play: *The Sisters Rosensweig*
Revival—play: *Anna Christie*
Revival—musical: *Carnival*

Antoinette Perry ("Tony") Awards
Actor—play: Ron Leibman, *Angels in America: Millennium Approaches*
Actor—musical: Brent Carver, *Kiss of the Spider Woman*
Actress—play: Madeline Kahn, *The Sisters Rosensweig*
Actress—musical: Chita Rivera, *Kiss of the Spider Woman*
Choreography: Wayne Cilento, *Tommy*
Director—play: George C. Wolfe, *Angels in America: Millennium Approaches*
Director—musical: Des McAnuff, *Tommy*
Featured actor—play: Stephen Spinella, *Angels in America: Millennium Approaches*
Featured actor—musical: Anthony Crivello, *Kiss of the Spider Woman*
Featured actress—play: Debra Monk, *Redwood Curtain*
Featured actress—musical: Andrea Martin, *My Favorite Year*
Musical: *Kiss of the Spider Woman*
Musical—book: Terrence McNally, *Kiss of the Spider Woman*
Musical—score (tie): John Kander and Fred Ebb, *Kiss of the Spider Woman*; Pete Townshend, *The Who's Tommy*
Play: *Angels in America: Millennium Approaches*
Reproduction of a play or musical: *Anna Christie*
Special award: *Oklahoma!* (50th anniversary)
Pulitzer Prize for Drama: Tony Kushner, *Angels in America: Millennium Approaches*

PUBLISHING

The publishing industries, like many other sectors of the U.S. economy, gave mixed signals of health as 1993 unfolded. People in the newspaper industry seemed particularly unsure about its future direction in the face of continuing economic and technological developments (*see also* SPECIAL REPORT, page 445). The book and magazine industries also awaited a stronger recovery in the U.S. economy. Book publishers continued issuing controversial titles, while the magazine industry foresaw an end to its recent doldrums.

Books. The U.S. Commerce Department forecast that book shipments would increase by 3.4% to $18.2 billion in 1993, with greater growth expected in subsequent years. In 1992 publishers' income from book sales grew a modest 4.4% from 1991, according to the Association of American Publishers. Most publicly traded publishing companies improved operating margins in 1992. The number of hardcover books with sales of more than 100,000 reached an all-time high, further testimony to the recession-proof nature of segments of the industry. Americans purchased 7% more books in 1992 than in 1991, although purchases by those under age 25 dropped by an ominous 25%. U.S. publishers issued about 48,000 titles in 1992, well below the more than 55,000 titles that were published in 1987 and 1988.

Some hopeful economic signs appeared in 1993. Book publishers began the year worried about falling profit margins, a weak economy, and enhanced competition from other sources for U.S. leisure dollars. However, the Book Industry Study Group forecast that book sales would increase by 6.4% in 1993—the largest increase since 1989—and indicated that the industry could see annual compound growth of more than 7% for the next five years.

Some individual titles achieved notable success in 1992-93. Rush Limbaugh's *The Way Things Ought To Be* reached sales of $2.1 million in the final quarter of 1992, making it the fastest-selling hardcover book in history. Intense publicity lifted Madonna's *Sex,* which contains graphic sexual photos, onto the best-selling lists in late 1992. *The Bridges of Madison County,* written by Robert Waller, a novice romance novelist and Iowa college dean, became an unlikely success of 1993. The book, which appealed strongly to middle-aged women, won the American Booksellers Book of the Year prize. In late September, after 58 weeks on the *Publishers Weekly* fiction hardcover best-seller list, it remained in first place. The year also was a successful one for author John Grisham (*see* BIOGRAPHY).

One of the year's most controversial releases was Joe McGinniss' *The Last Brother,* a "biography" of Ted Kennedy that combined fact with fictional thoughts and dialogue attributed to actual people. McGinniss originally approved an unprecedented disclaimer for the title page, but changed his mind and opted for a lengthy author's note that was inserted at the end of the book. The widely censured publication experienced slow sales shortly after its release in July.

In an unprecedented collaboration, rivals Random House and Simon & Schuster agreed to publish jointly the combined memoirs of James Carville and Mary Matalin. Carville and Matalin were top officials in the 1992 presidential campaigns of Bill Clinton and George Bush, respectively. Their ironic offstage romance set the stage for an equally ironic marketing gimmick by the two publishers. Publishers continued to pay big sums to famous people in 1993. Random House landed the future memoirs of retiring Joint Chiefs of Staff Chairman Colin Powell for $6.5 million.

© Richard Howard

In 1993, "The New York Times" acquired "The Boston Globe," one of the last major daily newspapers in the United States not owned by a media chain.

Some significant acquisitions occurred or appeared imminent during late 1993. In October, McGraw-Hill purchased the remaining 50% of Macmillan-McGraw-Hill School Publishing from Maxwell Communications Corporation for about $340 million. McGraw-Hill, which also publishes *Business Week* magazine, already was a partner in the nation's largest elhi publisher. The deal could simplify the ultimate sale of Maxwell. In September cable-television company Viacom and home-shopping company QVC Network made rival bids to acquire Paramount Communications, which includes book publishers Simon & Schuster and Prentice Hall, plus numerous other holdings. If completed, a merger between Viacom and Paramount would be the second-largest in the history of the communications industry, creating one of the world's largest media companies.

The ongoing war between independent bookstores and national chains intensified during 1993. *Publishers Weekly* reported that sales at five of the largest chains increased by a whopping 9.3% during the first three months of 1993. In response to the growth of chain superstores, from 100 at the start of 1992 to about 240 18 months later, a group of 21 large booksellers formed a buying organization, the Independent Booksellers' Consortium. This group will attempt to obtain the same terms from publishers that national chains—which use classic retailing strategies like discounting—enjoy. Independents traditionally have relied upon an intimate understanding of their customers' tastes rather than focusing on these retailing techniques. Some observers fear that large chains will force more independent sellers out of business, putting publishers at the mercy of a few large buyers. In turn, this dynamic ultimately might reduce the selection of titles available to customers.

Magazines. The magazine industry was expected to begin a recovery in 1993. The U.S. Bureau of Labor reported that non-newspaper periodical employment fell by 5.8% to 123,000 in the two years preceding October 1992. After falling 9% in 1991, advertising pages at magazines grew by 2.4% in 1992. In an optimistic forecast, investment bankers Veronis, Suhler and Associates—a firm specializing in publishing industries—predicted that total expenditures for magazines would grow at a 6% annual compound rate through 1997, as compared with 4.2% in the previous five years. However, this rapid growth was not observed in 1993, as ad-page counts increased only slightly during the first half of the year.

About 10,850 titles were published in 1993. The *NRTA-AARP Bulletin* led in magazine circulation with about 22.4 million, followed by *Modern Maturity*. Members of the American Association of Retired Persons receive both titles. *Reader's Digest* and *TV Guide* were in third and fourth place, respectively.

Some notable acquisitions and other deals occurred in 1992-93. At the end of 1992, American Express agreed to let Time Incorporated manage many of its publications, including *Travel & Leisure*. Early in 1993, Lang Communications, with an investment-banker partner, bought out Time's 50% share of *Working Woman* and *Working Mother* to gain full control of both publications. Later in the year, Time, Inc., publisher of 30 magazines and six book operations, announced a decentralization, evidently to quiet rumors that its parent, Time Warner, might sell it. In March, S. I. Newhouse and Condé Nast agreed to purchase *Architectural Digest* and *Bon Appétit* for $170 million from Knapp Communications. Shortly after the purchase, Condé Nast announced that it was folding *HG* (*House & Garden*) and merging its circulation into that of *Architectural Digest*. In September, Reed Elsevier P.L.C., a British-Dutch publishing conglomerate, bought *Official Airlines Guide* for $417 million in cash from the Maxwell Communications Corporation. The deal represented the first major U.S. asset of the now-defunct corporation to be sold by the accounting firm charged with liquidating its assets.

A number of noteworthy redesigns and other changes occurred during 1993. Early in the year, both *Seventeen* and *Mademoiselle* introduced new appearances. One cover of *The New Yorker* depicted a Hasidic man in a passionate embrace with an African-American woman and also contained an unprecedented statement of intent by the artist. The controversial cover illustrated the influence of former *Vanity Fair* editor Tina Brown, who took over at the traditionally staid publication in late 1992. Early in 1993, the humor magazine *National Lampoon* reappeared as a quarterly after a nine-month absence. In June, *MagazineWeek*, one of two important magazines about the magazine industry, abruptly suspended publication. Caspar Weinberger, the former U.S. secretary of defense, took over as chairman of the parent company of *Forbes* magazine. *Time* magazine planned to make entire issues available to readers via computer screens ahead of their newsstand appearances and to introduce computerized communication between readers and its journalists.

The industry continued to face significant legal issues in 1993. The U.S. Supreme Court let stand a $4.375 million judgment against *Soldier of Fortune* magazine for running a "gun-for-hire" ad that wound up recruiting a hit man to kill an Atlanta businessman. The decision threatened the future of the magazine. The U.S. Supreme Court also ruled that publishers can depreciate their subscriber lists for taxation purposes in certain cases. Many publishers lauded the appointment of Ruth Bader Ginsburg (*see also* BIOGRAPHY) —a former American Civil Liberties Union attorney and an advocate of freedom of the press—to the Supreme Court.

DAVID K. PERRY, *The University of Alabama*

The Newspaper Today

In May 1993 the conservative commentary magazine *National Review* published a symposium entitled "The Decline of American Journalism." Focusing primarily on the newspaper industry, contributors painted a picture of a profession choked by monopolistic owners, out of touch with readers' concerns, and stifled by a culture of "political correctness."

Although the symposium may have interpreted a complex industry with the bias of a conservative agenda, newspapers still faced serious, indisputable problems in 1993. By late 1992 about 1,570 dailies—16 fewer than during the previous year and about 190 fewer than in 1980—were being published in the United States. Media chains owned about 75% of these newspapers. The dailies had a combined circulation of about 60 million, down about 600,000 from a year earlier and 2.5 million from 1987. Only about 63% of U.S. adults reported that they read a newspaper daily, down from about 78% in 1970. Total U.S. newspaper employment fell to about 450,000 during 1992 from a high of about 475,000 in 1990.

On the other hand, Sunday and weekly newspapers could report much brighter news. An all-time record of 893 Sunday papers were being published, with a total circulation of about 62.5 million—500,000 more than in the previous year and 8 million more than in 1980. In addition, about 7,400 weeklies existed, with a total circulation of about 55 million. In 1987 about 7,600 weeklies were published, with a total circulation of about 47 million.

Among all media, a category which includes newspapers, magazines, radio, and television, dailies commanded the largest share of advertising expenditures—23.3%—slightly ahead of television's 22.4%. This gap has narrowed substantially over the years, however. In 1960, television received only about 13%.

At times, the newspaper industry seemed uncertain about the future of new forms of electronic delivery. After decades of expectations, electronic newspapers finally became available via personal-computer screens in cities such as Chicago and St. Louis. Many of these services supplemented, rather than duplicated, traditional newspapers by offering features such as background readings and opportunities for computer users to communicate with journalists and their sources. In addition, newspapers began forming partnerships with regional telephone companies. For instance, Cox Enterprises, one of the nation's largest newspaper chains, announced an agreement with Bell South Corporation to deliver Yellow Pages and newspaper classified advertising information via telephone lines in the Southeast. For years, publishers had argued that the telephone companies should be barred from the information-delivery business because their control of telephone conduits gave them an unfair advantage. In May a federal appeals court upheld a ruling allowing regional phone companies to own information services. During the summer, legislation was introduced in Congress to try to sort out the issue.

The New York Situation. The problems that faced newspapers were quite evident in New York City, where four dailies competed in a market that probably can support only two or three. The *Daily News* and the *New York Post* struggled to survive, battling numerous personnel, circulation, and revenue crises. Their competitor,

Photos, © Courtesy, "Chicago Tribune," Chicago Online

The number of U.S. major newspapers offering electronic editions increased in 1993. An on-line version of "The Chicago Tribune," photos, had been introduced in 1992.

The New York Times, acquired *The Boston Globe,* one of the last major dailies not owned by a media chain, in the biggest single newspaper acquisition in U.S. history. Some observers also expected that the fourth daily, Long Island-based *Newsday,* might cut its financial losses in New York City and retreat back to its suburban markets.

The media spotlight shone most brightly on the troubled *Post.* Early in the year, employees accepted a 20% pay cut after owner Peter Kalikow, himself in personal bankruptcy, threatened to close the paper. To make matters worse, the *Daily News* then hired away some of the *Post*'s top editors.

Soon thereafter, a bankruptcy judge granted Abe Hirschfeld, a New York real-estate mogul, ownership of the *Post,* pending transfer of stock. Hirschfeld, who once had admitted he was most interested in the paper's real estate, attempted to fire editor Pete Hamill and dozens of other employees. A few days later, Hirschfeld reversed his earlier action—allowing Hamill to return—after employees loyal to Hamill left his name on the paper's masthead. One edition of the paper had a front-page illustration of founder Alexander Hamilton with a tear falling from his eye and devoted most of the news and editorial space to attacking Hirschfeld. Shortly after Hamill's reinstatement, Hirschfeld again made waves when he refused to rehire some key editorial employees, who kept working for free. In response, Hamill refused, for one day, to run the paper from the newsroom and instead operated out of a nearby diner.

The situation temporarily settled down when former owner Rupert Murdoch assumed management control. Murdoch offered to let Hamill remain as a columnist but he refused. Further problems appeared in July when Murdoch canceled his management agreement with Kalikow and shut down the paper after unions rejected his demands. For two days, until tentative agreements were reached, the *Post* did not publish.

In September a U.S. bankruptcy judge approved an attempt by Murdoch's News Corporation to purchase the *Post* for about $25 million, but the deal still hinged on ratification of ten union contracts. The Newspaper Guild, which represents advertising, clerical, and news employees, soon went on strike after failing to negotiate adequate seniority protection for its members. Once again, the paper did not publish for two days, as Murdoch tried to withdraw from the deal to purchase the *Post* and end his management control of the paper. The crisis ended—and Murdoch completed his acquisition of the paper—when other unions crossed the Guild's picket lines.

At the *Daily News, U.S. News & World Report* owner Mortimer Zuckerman formally took control in January and dismissed 170 employees. In response, The Newspaper Guild staged protests, but these demonstrations died down after other labor organizations opposed them. The 700,000-circulation *Daily News* might be the real winner, in terms of readers and advertisers, if the *Post,* with a 1992 circulation of about 430,000, folded.

The New York Times' planned acquisition of Affiliated Publications, Inc., parent of the *Globe,* was announced in June. The *Times* agreed to pay about $1.1 billion, mostly in new stock, and guaranteed editorial independence for the *Globe* for five years. The *Times* is the nation's fourth-largest daily, with a weekday circulation of about 1.2 million and a Sunday circulation of 1.8 million. The *Globe,* with a circulation of about 500,000 daily and 800,000 on Sunday, is the 13th-largest daily. In August the U.S. Justice Department approved the deal, concluding that it would not reduce competition for readers or for advertisers. The *Times* completed the acquisition in October.

Other Highlights. Among individual newspapers, *The Wall Street Journal* remained the average-daily-circulation leader, with about 1.8 million. *USA Today* and the *Los Angeles Times* followed in circulation. At the Washington Post Company, publisher of the nation's fifth-largest daily, Katharine Graham stepped down as chairman, handing the title to her son Donald. During her 30 years at the helm, the *Post* had gained international recognition for its journalism, especially its exposés of the Watergate scandals. Graham also helped lead the company to spectacular financial success.

As was the case in much of the U. S. economy, publicly held newspaper companies grew only modestly in 1993. Also during the year, some notable newspapers ceased publication. In January the *San Antonio Light* closed suddenly after the U.S. Justice Department allowed its parent, the Hearst Corporation, to buy its local rival, *The Express-News.* The *Pittsburgh Press* died following a lengthy strike started in May 1992. On the other hand, the *Pittsburgh Post-Gazette* resumed publication in January, giving the city a local daily for the first time since the strike began.

In May, William Randolph Hearst, Jr., died. He was editor in chief of Hearst Newspapers and chairman of the executive committee of the Hearst Corporation, among the largest diversified communication companies in the United States. Hearst was the son of William Randolph Hearst, Sr., one of the most important U.S. publishers during the early 20th century and the subject of the 1941 film classic *Citizen Kane.* Robert C. Maynard, former owner of the *Oakland Tribune*—and the first black publisher of a mainstream U.S. newspaper—died in August.

DAVID K. PERRY

PUERTO RICO

During 1993, Puerto Ricans celebrated the 500th anniversary of Christopher Columbus' arrival and voted to retain Puerto Rico's commonwealth status with the United States. Other news centered on the efforts of new Gov. Pedro Rosselló to "reinvent" government and the island's struggle to contain its homicides with use of National Guard troops.

The Plebiscite. On November 14, five days before the island's quincentenary, voters opted to maintain commonwealth status—in place since 1952—with 48.4% of the ballots cast. The statehood option, with 46.2% of the vote, came in second despite a strong campaign effort from Rosselló and his New Progressive Party, which dominated the Senate, House, and 54 of the island's 78 mayoral seats. Those opting for independence tallied just 4.4% of the vote.

The outcome uncovered two distinct truths about the relationship of Puerto Ricans with the United States: It showed that the majority of voters did not want statehood, while another slightly smaller group was not happy with the present commonwealth status and was in fact gaining strength. (In a 1967 plebiscite, commonwealth status took 67% of the vote, compared with statehood's 38%.) Supporters of commonwealth status showed a desire to retain a U.S. association, while keeping their culture and language.

Commonwealth status, however, had experienced a setback earlier in 1993 when the U.S. Congress passed President Bill Clinton's budget act, which included cuts in federal-tax breaks for more than 300 U.S.-based companies with manufacturing operations in Puerto Rico. The cuts meant that the firms would pay $9.89 billion over five years, with pharmaceutical producers paying the most. After their plebiscite victory, pro-commonwealth Popular Democratic Party leaders sought enhancement of Puerto Rico's status in Washington, including a restoration of tax benefits.

Government. On January 2, Pedro Rosselló was inaugurated as Puerto Rico's sixth elected governor. Within weeks, he signed a law making both English and Spanish official languages of the government. The new law repealed a 1991 law that had made Spanish the only official language.

The governor also began an all-out effort to revamp the government, signing into law an eight-year measure to convert the Health Department from a provider of health services for an estimated 1.7 million medically indigent people to an insurer of services. The governor also signed a school-reform measure giving communities more authority and control over their public schools, including a school-voucher system. Another enacted measure involved the merger of the Anti-Addiction Services Department with the Health Department's mental-health division.

As Rosselló worked to restructure the government bureaucracy, he initiated tougher penalties for violent crime offenders and activated the National Guard in the occupation of 27 public-housing projects known as "hot" drug distribution spots or *puntos*. The move marked the first time in island history that police and National Guard troops had taken over public-housing units. Despite these efforts the island's homicide rate continued to surge, with most homicides related to drug-gang feuds.

Celebrations. Dayanara Torres of Toa Alta was voted Miss Universe 1993. The island also celebrated as baseball's Juan González became the American League's home-run leader for the second consecutive year, with 46.

PETER J. ORTIZ, *"The San Juan Star"*

QUEBEC

Two events provided the primary focus of attention in Quebec in 1993—and both had potential impact on the enduring issue of the province's place in the Canadian federal union. One was the stunning breakthrough of an avowedly separatist party, the Bloc Québécois, in the October 25 federal election. The other was the resignation of Robert Bourassa, Quebec's staunchly federalist premier.

Federal Election. The Bloc Québécois (BQ), a political movement dedicated to the goal of an independent Quebec, scored a major victory in the federal election, winning 54 of the province's 75 House of Commons seats. The Liberals won 19 seats and the Conservatives, who in 1988 had taken 63, nearly were wiped out, taking just one. One independent candidate also was elected.

The BQ, though it contested only Quebec ridings, still finished second nationally to Jean Chrétien's Liberals. Both Bloc leader Lucien Bouchard and Chrétien won personal election, Bouchard in Lac-St.-Jean and Chrétien—the new prime minister of Canada—in St.-Maurice.

The election left Bouchard in an anomalous position. While determined to advance the cause of Quebec separatism—he jubilantly hailed the result as a big step along that road—he also was supposed to act as chief of Parliament's "loyal" opposition. Bouchard was quick to point out, however, that the independence issue would be fought primarily on the political battlefields of Quebec itself, where a crucial provincial election was expected in 1994.

Bourassa Resignation. After 27 years in politics, Robert Bourassa decided to call it a day. At

---

PUERTO RICO • Information Highlights

Area: 3,515 sq mi (9 104 km²).

Population (mid-1993 est.): 3,600,000.

Chief Cities (1990 census): San Juan, the capital, 437,745; Bayamon, 220,262; Ponce, 187,749.

Government (1993): *Chief Officer*—governor, Pedro Rosselló (New Progressive Party). *Legislature*—Senate, 27 members; House of Representatives, 51 members.

a September 14 press conference in Quebec City, a tired-looking Bourassa announced that he was resigning as premier—a job he had held for 14 years altogether—to devote more time to his family. Another factor was undoubtedly the skin cancer he had been battling in recent years, though he received a clean bill of health from a Bethesda, MD, institute only two months before bowing out.

Bourassa's departure left a gaping void not only in Quebec politics but in national politics also. In recent years he had become an increasingly ardent champion of the federalist cause in Quebec and a redoubtable opponent of forces bent on separating Quebec from Canada, namely the BQ at the federal level and the Parti Québécois (PQ) at the provincial level. Even as he announced his departure, he took a parting shot at the separatists, branding the notion of an independent Quebec "geopolitical nonsense."

There was no heir apparent to Bourassa's twin posts of Liberal Party leader and premier. However, Treasury Board president Daniel Johnson, Jr., the only declared candidate, was acclaimed party leader on December 14. He planned to take over the premiership in January 1994. Just hours before Johnson's acclamation, Deputy Premier Lise Bacon announced that she was quitting politics.

Other Politics. The PQ recorded its third consecutive provincial by-election victory on July 5, winning handily in the Quebec City-area constituency of Portneuf, which had been a Liberal stronghold since 1973. Roger Bertrand, the PQ candidate, took 51% of the vote against 34% for Liberal standard-bearer Gilles Portelance and 15% for fringe candidates. PQ leader Jacques Parizeau hailed the result as a triumph for the cause of Quebec sovereignty, although Bertrand campaigned mainly on economic issues.

Taxes Go Up. In May, Finance Minister Gerard D. Levesque hit Quebecers with more than C$1 billion in higher income taxes. He raised revenue largely by eliminating a number of obscure tax breaks and introducing a 5% surtax on levies above C$5,000.

Under the new tax rules, a couple with two children and a household income of C$100,000 per year would pay C$1,132 more in taxes. A couple with two children earning barely enough to live would see their tax credits cut by $90. Family allowances and welfare benefits were frozen. Even workers-compensation benefits for on-the-job injuries would be taxed.

The government's intention to hold the line on spending had been signaled earlier, on March 24, when Treasury Board president Johnson tabled 1993-94 estimates that projected an increase of just 0.9% over 1992-93 expenditures.

In the fall, Levesque was replaced by Monique Gagnon-Tremblay, the first woman to hold the post of finance minister.

Signs of the Times. The use of English on outdoor advertising signs, banned since 1977, was restored by the Quebec National Assembly. A bill sponsored by the Bourassa government and passed on June 17 permits English on signs outside commercial establishments so long as French also is used and remains "markedly predominant."

The legislation was opposed fiercely by the PQ and other ultranationalist groups, which warned that it would undermine the position of the French language and lead to the "anglicization" of Montreal. However, Bourassa said that it attested to a new maturity among Quebecers on language matters. Though most Quebecers speak French, language militants see it as constantly under siege from English.

Neighborly Quarrels. A series of tough measures by the neighboring province of New Brunswick, slamming the door against Quebec products and construction workers, provoked an angry response in Quebec City. Industry Minister Gerald Tremblay called the New Brunswick move, announced on April 21, an unacceptable escalation of a long-standing dispute over the mobility of workers, and hinted at retaliation. The New Brunswick action, itself a retaliation, was aimed at shutting out Quebec companies from provincially funded projects.

Several months later, in September, Quebec found itself embroiled in a dispute with its neighbor to the west, Ontario, which imposed restrictions against Quebec similar to those of New Brunswick. In November, Quebec and New Brunswick agreed to accept transborder bids on procurement contracts. A similar truce began to take shape between Quebec and Ontario in December.

Education News. Students attending Quebec's tuition-free junior colleges have an added incentive to study hard. Under a sweeping reform of the system announced in April, those who fail more than five courses in the two-year pre-university program would have to pay $50 per course to continue. Students in the three-year vocational program would be charged the same fees after failing seven courses.

JOHN BEST, *"Canada World News"*

QUEBEC • Information Highlights

Area: 594,857 sq mi (1 540 680 km²).
Population (June 1993): 6,985,000.
Chief Cities (1991 census): Quebec, the capital, 167,517; Montreal, 1,017,666; Laval, 314,398.
Government (1993): *Chief Officers*—lt. gov., Gilles Lamontagne; premier, Robert Bourassa (Liberal). *Legislature*—National Assembly, 125 members.
Provincial Finances (1993-94 fiscal year budget): *Revenues,* $36,580,000,000; *expenditures,* $41,080,000,000.
Personal Income (average weekly earnings, June 1993): $543.48.
Labor Force (August 1993, seasonally adjusted): *Employed* workers, 15 years of age and over, 2,934,000; *Unemployed,* 12.9%.
Education (1993-94): *Enrollment*—elementary and secondary schools, 1,149,460 pupils; postsecondary—universities, 141,350; community colleges, 174,510.

REFUGEES AND IMMIGRATION

The continuation of disparities between rich and poor countries, rising nationalism, violent fragmentation of existing states, and the formation of new national entities generated new masses of refugees and migrants during 1993. Population movement has constituted one of the most important and difficult problems facing Western policy makers in the post-Cold Warera. Although the numbers of people who migrated from the Third World to the developed world and from Eastern Europe to the West grew, the largest portion of refugee movements occurred within the developing world and the post-Communist states of the former Soviet Union and the Balkans.

Escalating Numbers. The number of people seeking asylum around the world had escalated sharply since the beginning of the 1990s. According to a report issued in November 1993 by the United Nations High Commissioner for Refugees, the number of refugees in the world swelled to 44 million. More than half of these refugees (24 million) were exiled within their own countries, but the number of people driven across international lines (20 million) was alarming too.

Within a two-year span, more than 1.2 million people were displaced in the former Yugoslavia and at least 600,000 more took refuge outside the region. The total number of people dependent on international assistance in the former Yugoslavia rose from 500,000 to more than 4 million.

Meanwhile, millions of refugees were found elsewhere around the globe. Hundreds of thousands of Somalis became refugees by fleeing to neighboring Kenya and Yemen and millions more became vulnerable to famine within Somalia as a result of vicious interclan conflict; more than 500,000 people were displaced by the conflict between Azerbaijan and Armenia over Nagorno-Karabakh; 60,000 refugees fled to Afghanistan and 500,000 people were displaced by civil war between clans in Tajikistan; 250,000 Muslim refugees fled widespread harassment and repression in Myanmar's Arakan state to poverty-stricken Bangladesh; mass exoduses in Togo led to nearly 300,000 taking refuge in Benin and Ghana; several hundred thousand fled political upheaval and persecution in Burundi; and up to 100,000 refugees fled from ethnic strife in Bhutan to Nepal.

Refugees Returning Home. Despite the growing number of conflicts, about 2.4 million people returned home to their native countries in 1992. By mid-1993, more than 1.6 million Afghan refugees had repatriated from Pakistan and Iran, despite instability in their native land. Some 350,000 Cambodians also returned home in time to take part in national elections in May. And in Central America, returnees greatly outnumbered remaining refugees. The largest organized repatriation ever attempted in Africa, involving 1.3 million Mozambicans, began in July.

If large numbers of refugees continue to repatriate in the coming years, the focus of concern may shift from repatriation to more long-standing reintegration and development. It has been increasingly evident that—in countries such as Cambodia, Mozambique, Afghanistan, and Ethiopia—one of the preconditions for successful returns is development aid and reintegration assistance aimed at alleviating poverty in countries of origin. Without careful reintegration and reconciliation, returning refugees compete for scarce developmental resources, which can lead to fierce political and economic competition with local populations that did not flee.

Asylum Crisis in the West. There was a rapid increase in the number of asylum applicants in industrialized countries. In 1983 less than 100,000 people requested asylum in Europe, North America, Australia, and Japan. By 1992 the number rose to more than 825,000. In total, approximately 3.7 million asylum applicants

© Hardy A. Saffold/Sipa

During 1993 an increasing number of immigrants from mainland China, Hong Kong, and Taiwan— including the group of Chinese huddled together in a hold on a freighter in San Francisco's harbor (left)—were seeking to enter the United States illegally, causing authorities to take a new look at U.S. immigration policies.

The Illegal Immigrant

The end of the Cold War has cast a spotlight on the dilemmas of open borders in the industrialized countries of the world. There is a perception in the United States that the nation has lost control of its destiny because of an upsurge in illegal immigration. To many Americans, images of Mexicans wading across the Rio Grande, masses of Chinese huddled below deck in an overcrowded freighter in San Francisco harbor, and Haitians clinging to rickety rafts off the Florida coast exemplify a failure to manage the country's borders. This led to fierce political debate over illegal immigration and calls for dramatic policy changes in 1993.

The New Immigration. Immigration to the United States has grown to its highest level since the beginning of the 20th century. Almost 9 million newcomers entered the United States during the 1980s, surpassed only by the years from 1901 to 1910. In addition, by most estimates, at least 2 million illegal immigrants arrived during the 1980s. Added to the approximately 125,000 refugees and 700,000 immigrants that the United States officially admits every year, an estimated 300,000 illegal immigrants enter annually.

Immigration to the United States not only has accelerated rapidly in recent years but it also has assumed a new prominence in U.S. life. The effects of this immigration are felt most immediately at local levels, where some people believe immigrants have overwhelmed educational, health-care, and social-welfare institutions. In the late 1980s, more than 70% of immigrants and refugees settled in just six states—with almost half in California and New York alone. California has about 1.3 million illegal immigrants, and 100,000 more arrive each year. If trends continue, whites in the United States will be outnumbered by other ethnic groups by the middle of the 21st century, while whites in California and Texas will become a minority early in the century.

This new wave of immigration has spurred widespread concern that the identity and social cohesion of the nation are being threatened, particularly as interethnic conflict and economic competition among different minority groups increase. Bitter tensions have flared between blacks and recently arrived immigrants, such as Koreans, while in some communities, immigrants have been used as scapegoats for economic and social problems. Some well-publicized studies have reported that new immigrants use up more public expenditures for education, medical care, and welfare than they pay in taxes. As a result, national public-opinion polls indicate that most Americans now favor tighter immigration controls.

Restrictive Immigration Measures. Several restrictive immigration bills were introduced during 1993 in the California state legislature and the U.S. Congress. The California bills aimed to restrict the access of undocumented aliens to many social services, identify undocumented aliens already in California and report them to the Immigration and Naturalization Service, or keep undocumented aliens out of California altogether.

California Gov. Pete Wilson also proposed a series of federal measures to curb illegal immigration, including a ban on government-paid social services for illegal residents, a constitu-

were recorded during the decade 1983-92. Germany was affected most seriously by the sharp increase, with the number of asylum seekers rising from 121,000 in 1989 to 438,000 in 1992. The majority of recent asylum applicants to Western Europe were from Eastern Europe.

In response to these growing numbers, the advanced industrialized states were increasingly reluctant to let people enter their countries to apply for political asylum and instituted a number of restrictive practices such as visa requirements and carrier sanctions on airlines transporting undocumented entrants. For example, by the middle of 1993, most European countries had imposed visa restrictions on refugees fleeing conflict in the former Yugoslavia. At midyear, Germany introduced legislation to restrict the constitutional right to asylum and entered into agreements with its neighbors in Central Europe and the Balkans to take back their nationals and others who pass through their territories on their way to Germany.

Concern over immigration also shifted political discourse and action sharply to the right in France. After national elections, the French government introduced legislation which reduced access to French citizenship, and strengthened police authority to enforce immigration laws strictly and to arrest and deport individuals who did not possess proper legal documentation.

By year's end, despite movement toward a united Europe following the ratification of the Maastricht Treaty, differences of interests and approaches remained among states regarding refugees and immigration. For example, Britain, Ireland, and Denmark refused to lift internal border controls on foreigners entering their countries.

Across the Atlantic, the United States also took steps to restrict immigration and access to asylum (*see* SPECIAL REPORT). In reaction to several highly publicized abuses of the asylum system in 1993, the Bill Clinton administration took

tional amendment to deny U.S. citizenship to children born in the United States to illegal-immigrant parents, and a tamper-proof legal-resident eligibility card that would be required for all legal residents seeking benefits. The Wilson proposals also would deny ratification of the North American Free Trade Agreement (NAFTA) unless the Mexican government agreed to cooperate in stopping massive illegal immigration from Mexico.

The California bills coincided with federal efforts to restrict immigration and access to asylum. In reaction to highly publicized events such as the terrorist bombing of the World Trade Center in New York in late February 1993, the increased smuggling of Chinese nationals by international criminal rings, and the abuse of the asylum system in 1993, the Bill Clinton administration announced a plan to boost penalties for alien smuggling and to require aliens arriving with false documents to demonstrate a substantial likelihood that they ultimately would win asylum before they could apply. President Clinton also proposed adding 600 agents to the U.S. Border Patrol.

Long-term Approaches. Although controls are a necessary part of an overall response to illegal immigration, enforcement measures alone have been unable to halt this influx. Congress last tried to control illegal immigration with the Immigration Reform and Control Act of 1986. Despite redoubled border-control efforts, sanctions against employers who knowingly hired undocumented aliens, and a program to legalize more than 3 million persons, the number of illegal immigrants has risen to an estimated 3 million.

This immigration crisis has polarized politicians and public opinion over how to develop a long-term policy. The conservative camp calls for

© Sianz de Branda/Gamma-Liaison

The Mexico-California border, above, remains a major point of entry for persons looking for refuge in the United States. Some 100,000 illegal immigrants arrive in California annually.

intense restrictive measures that will tighten control over immigration. On the other hand, liberal policies would require greater U.S. involvement with developing countries to liberalize trade, to increase employment-generating development, and to promote the observance of human-rights conditions. Some economists and demographers argue that a more liberal policy that tries to integrate immigrants into U.S. society could have long-term economic benefits.

GIL LOESCHER

actions to penalize alien smuggling, stiffen asylum-application standards, and increase the number of U.S. border guards. Several restrictive immigration and asylum bills also were introduced in the U.S. Congress.

Preventative Strategies. As the number of refugees continued to grow during 1993, the international community sought new ways to deal with this global problem. There was an increasing emphasis by states and international organizations on preventive strategies which addressed the causes of flight through policy responses, including early warning of impending crises, preventive diplomacy, and improved human-rights efforts. The new emphasis on prevention aimed to reinforce the international community's legal obligation to protect and assist people after they became refugees.

Unfortunately, a shift to a preventive strategy cannot be accomplished easily or quickly. Current humanitarian, political, diplomatic, and economic mechanisms are not developed

sufficiently to cope with the increasingly complex and volatile refugee movements of the post-Cold War period. The most difficult political issues confronting governments and international organizations are how to intervene to prevent refugee flights within countries or across international borders, and how to provide assistance to internally displaced people either when their governments object to intervention or when it is impossible to determine the legitimate authority of the country. Many of the destabilizing effects of refugee movements cannot be dealt with successfully at the national level. Some observers believe that Western governments eventually will have to adopt policy responses to refugees that go beyond conventional border-control and humanitarian measures and actually become part of the countries' national political, economic, and security objectives.

GIL LOESCHER
University of Notre Dame

RELIGION

Overview

During 1993, the world of Judaism paid close attention to historic developments in the Middle East; Pope John Paul II issued the encyclical *Veritatis Splendor* ("The Splendor of Truth") and attended World Youth Day in Denver, CO; an increasing number of women assumed leadership roles in the Protestant denominations; and the status of Islam in the United States came under new scrutiny.

Charles Colson, the founder of the Prison Fellowship—an organization that seeks to bring Christian ministries into prisons—was awarded the 1993 Templeton Prize for Progress in Religion. Colson, 61, had been an adviser to President Richard Nixon and served seven months in jail for his role in the Watergate scandal.

The Church of Latter-Day Saints—the Mormons—remained one of the world's fastest-growing religions and faced controversies regarding its official church history and the ordination of women to the priesthood. Meanwhile the 1993 *Yearbook of American and Canadian Churches* reported that the Church of God in Christ, a black Pentecostal denomination, was the fastest-growing church in the United States—nearly 200,000 members and 600 congregations since 1982. Assemblies of God and the Southern Baptist Convention also were said to have fast-growing membership rates.

Christian Science. The 1993 annual meeting of the First Church of Christ, Scientist was attended by more than 4,000 church members. After controversies in recent years regarding the church's television enterprise, which was discontinued in 1992, and the 1991 publication of a book that opponents claimed violated the church's bylaws, the June 1993 session focused on business as usual or, as church treasurer John Selover noted, "the completion of a turnaround year." In August a Minneapolis jury awarded $9 million to a father whose son had died while under Christian Science treatment through prayer. The First Church of Christ, Scientist; the boy's mother and stepfather; and several persons connected with the church were held liable for the compensatory damages. It was the first time that the Christian Science Church had been held responsible for damages in such a lawsuit.

Far Eastern

Violence between militant Hindu groups and Muslims continued to plague the nation of India during 1993. Local organizations of several Far Eastern religious groups, including Buddhists, Hindus, and Zoroastrians, took the lead in planning the second Parliament of the World's Religions in Chicago in late August. Buddhists were particularly visible during the conference.

Unrest in India. In India the year opened with violence between Hindus and Muslims spreading to the commercial city of Bombay. Estimates of the number of casualties from the rioting ran as high as 1,700. Several prominent Muslims blamed an extremist Hindu movement called the Shiv Sena for the unrest. Bal Thackeray, the 66-year-old leader of the group, told a *Washington Post* interviewer that he was fighting "pro-Pakistani Muslims." He added that any Hindu sheltering such Muslims "must be shot dead." Thackeray's influence is considered so great that the nation's large motion-picture studios have censored films to suit his tastes, and cricket matches with Pakistani teams have been canceled at his demand.

Additional clashes between Hindus and Muslims broke out in the state of Manipur in May. That state had been relatively free of such conflict in the past. In August a bomb destroyed the Madras office of another militant Hindu group, killing at least ten people and injuring four. The targeted organization, the Rashtriya Swayamsevak Sangh, had been banned following the destruction by Hindu mobs of a prominent mosque in the northern town of Ayodhya in December 1992, touching off violence in which about 2,000 people were killed.

Although India's 750 million Hindus far outnumber the nation's 105 million Muslims, many Hindus say the Muslims have gained undue political clout. On the other hand, Prime Minister P. V. Narasimha Rao was criticized widely for failing to take strong action against the Hindus following the violence in Ayodhya and Bombay.

A World Parliament. India's religious tensions surfaced at an early session of the weeklong Parliament of the World's Religions in late August when a Sikh from Punjab denounced Hindus for persecuting his faith. That assertion led to a shouting match that ended when police escorted protesters from the ballroom where the conference was being held. A group of Zen Buddhist delegates objected to prayers being offered to God at the conference, suggesting that such terms as "Great Being" or "Power of the Transcendent" be used instead. "Buddhism is not a religion of God," the Zen group said, "We can practice religion with or without God." In response to such objections, the Global Ethic statement issued at the conclusion of the religion conference conspicuously omitted any mention of God.

The Dalai Lama, the exiled Tibetan Buddhist leader and Nobel Peace Prize winner, delivered the keynote address at the closing session of the parliament. In it, he declared that "all religions carry the same message: compassion, forgiveness, love...and each philosophy, each tradition has a powerful mechanism to do good."

DARRELL J. TURNER
Freelance Religion Writer

Islam

During 1993, militant Muslim organizations in Algeria and Egypt staged antigovernment attacks. Muslim activists in Yemen entered the mainstream of the political system to influence it through the democratic process. The plight of Bosnia's besieged Muslims aroused the compassion of the Islamic world.

Algeria and Egypt. Algeria's Islamic Salvation Front (FIS) continued a guerrilla campaign begun in 1992 when the government canceled elections which appeared likely to bring the FIS to power. Its militants targeted not only police, soldiers, and politicians, but also Algerian intellectuals, journalists, and other public figures who spoke out in support of the country's secular institutions. Hundreds died in these assaults or in police reprisals, while hundreds of FIS sympathizers were imprisoned.

In Egypt *al-Gamaa al-Islamiya* (the Islamic Group) won extensive support, especially among the urban poor, with its condemnations of President Hosni Mubarak's ties with the West and its accusations of widespread official corruption. Its leaders argued that only a return to Islamic law (*sharia*) could solve Egypt's social and economic disorders. In an attempt to undermine the government, *al-Gamaa al-Islamiya* launched raids on police and military posts, government officials, secular intellectuals, and Coptic Christians. Most damaging, however, were its attacks on foreign tourists, which called into question the power of the government and weakened its economic underpinnings, which depend heavily on tourist revenues. In response, the government placed scores of *al-Gamaa al-Islamiya* activists on trial before military tribunals, which imposed harsh punishments, including more than a dozen death sentences. Insisting they did not oppose Islam as such, the authorities simultaneously sought to soothe moderate Muslim opinion by censoring books, films, and plays to eliminate potentially offensive material and by providing more Islamic programming on radio and television.

In both Algeria and Egypt, opponents of the militants accused Iran and Sudan of providing them with monetary support and training. They also pointed out that many of those involved in the Islamist organizations previously had been Afghan *mujahidin*—young men recruited throughout the Muslim world in the 1980s, often by Western intelligence agencies, to serve with the Muslim forces opposing the Soviet occupation of Afghanistan. Their acceptance of the Islamist ideology around which resistance to Soviet control crystallized, in conjunction with the military training they received, made them potent recruits for organizations like the FIS and *al-Gamaa al-Islamiya.* This link to the Afghan resistance was also present among some of the Muslim immigrants to the United States charged with the February bombing of New York's World Trade Center. Sheikh Omar Abd al-Rahman, the Egyptian imam whom many of them regarded as their mentor, was alleged to have recruited volunteers for service in Afghanistan on behalf of the U.S. Central Intelligence Agency (CIA).

Other World Events. In Yemen's first free parliamentary elections in April 1993, an Islamist party, the *Islah,* won approximately one quarter of the seats. *Islah* promoted policies consistent with its commitment to Islam, but as a loyal opposition party. In Jordan, where Islamic political parties had been represented in parliament for several years, King Hussein's August dissolution of that body and the introduction of a new electoral law cast doubt on the government's willingness to allow Islamist groups the latitude it had in the recent past.

Muslims everywhere were frustrated by the reluctance of the world powers to come effectively to the aid of Bosnian Muslims. The Orga-

In Casablanca, Morocco, the Hassan II Mosque was inaugurated by King Hassan II in late August 1993. The $500 million structure, the world's second-largest mosque, features the world's tallest minaret, a laser indicating the way to Mecca, and a retractable roof.

Muslims in the United States

Following the bombing of New York City's World Trade Center in February 1993 and the uncovering in June of an alleged conspiracy to destroy other New York landmarks, U.S. authorities arrested a number of recent immigrants from Middle Eastern and South Asian countries. The disclosure that all were adherents of a New Jersey-based Egyptian imam known for his criticisms of Egyptian President Hosni Mubarak, and of U.S. support for Mubarak, drew attention to Muslims throughout the country. To the dismay of the approximately 5 million U.S. Muslims, many Americans—including media representatives—incorrectly assumed that the actions of these extremists represented the values of Islam.

The Roots of Stereotyping. The tendency of Americans to view Muslims as violent extremists has its roots in the social, economic, and political ills of the Middle East. U.S. support for Israel against the Palestinians, its patronage of the Iranian monarchy prior to the 1979 revolution, and its endorsement of governments in Egypt and Algeria that have repressed domestic Islamist movements all have contributed to making the United States and its citizens targets of Arab or Iranian militants. Over the years, many people in the United States have come to believe that political extremism of this kind epitomizes Islam—a conviction reinforced by the World Trade Center bombing. As a result, U.S. Muslims, whose religion shares many key beliefs with Christianity and Judaism, found themselves forced to refute the simplistic notion that all members of their faith are "terrorists." The absence of significant contact with Muslims has contributed to the willingness of many Americans to accept this stereotypical view.

Islam in the United States. In recent years, Islam has been the most rapidly growing religion in the United States. Persons of Arab ethnicity currently make up about 12% of the U.S. Muslim population, while those of South Asian origin constitute another 25%. However, the largest single ethnic component, comprising some 42% of the total, consists of African-Americans.

Many slaves transported to North America from West Africa during the 18th and 19th centuries were Muslims. Although they were compelled to convert to Christianity, vestiges of Islamic beliefs and practices survived in some areas until emancipation. The first wave of voluntary Muslim immigration began in the late 19th century and consisted principally of relatively impoverished, poorly educated immigrants from the Ottoman Empire.

A few African-Americans turned to variants of Islam as an ancestral faith in the early 20th century, but a more widespread adoption of Islam by black Americans began with the 1933 founding of the Nation of Islam by Elijah Muhammad. Later, during the civil-rights movement of the 1960s, African-Americans found in the Nation of Islam an effective vehicle for the expression of black consciousness. However, Malcolm X and other young leaders of the Nation of Islam, after making a pilgrimage to Mecca and observing the practice of Islam in its heartland, concluded that some of Elijah Muhammad's teachings conflicted with true Muslim beliefs and in fact ran counter to Islamic values of equality and nondiscrimination. Malcolm X and his associates left the Nation of Islam and merged into the Muslim mainstream. They were joined by most other followers of Elijah Muhammad after his death in 1975, although the Nation of Islam under the leadership of Louis Farrakhan continued to promote its founder's radical racial theories.

Because Islam emphasizes correct practice as well as correct belief, and because it regulates every facet of a Muslim's life, the proper observance of rituals is very important. In predominantly Muslim societies, the rhythm of daily life accommodates such rituals as the five daily prayers or obligatory fasting during the holy month of Ramadan, but keeping such practices in a society which makes no adjustment for them requires surmounting considerable challenges. Similarly, adherence to traditional Muslim social norms in terms of dress and relations between the sexes sometimes can lead to discrimination and abusive treatment.

U.S. Muslims hope that, as their community grows and increasing numbers of Americans become more familiar with their beliefs and practices, the U.S. tradition of religious tolerance will forge an atmosphere of acceptance that will dispel negative stereotyping.

KENNETH J. PERKINS

nization of the Islamic Conference went so far as to call for military intervention to alleviate the situation. Although no such operation was undertaken, several Muslim countries, along with the Palestine Liberation Organization (PLO), offered to provide troops to secure "safe areas" for Bosnian Muslims. Other Muslim countries opened their doors to Bosnian refugees. (*See* FEATURE ARTICLE, page 26.)

Indicative of Muslims' commitment to their faith was the August opening in Casablanca, Morocco, of the world's second-largest mosque (smaller only than the Haram al-Sharif in Mecca). Built at a cost of more than $500 million, the Hassan II Mosque combines high-technology features with traditional mosque design.

KENNETH J. PERKINS
University of South Carolina

Judaism

Jews worldwide had to adjust to the dizzying pace of events in the Middle East during 1993. In the United States, various issues caused controversy, and the U.S. Holocaust Memorial Museum was opened in Washington, DC (*see* SPECIAL REPORT, page 456).

Middle East. The assumption of power in Israel by a Labor-led coalition advocating a land-for-peace settlement of the Israel-Arab dispute required adjustments on the part of U.S. Jews. After considerable wrangling, Americans for Peace Now, which advocates Israeli territorial concessions, was granted membership in the Conference of Presidents of Major American Jewish Organizations, legitimizing its position. The American Israel Public Affairs Committee, perceived as too hard-line by the new Israeli government, underwent a leadership shakeup. When the Israel-Palestine Liberation Organization (PLO) rapprochement was announced in September (*see* SPECIAL REPORT/MIDDLE EAST), most leading Jewish organizations expressed cautious optimism.

U.S. Developments. Tensions between Jews and blacks in the United States continued. The report of a New York state task force on the 1991 Crown Heights riots blamed the New York City administration and police brass for their handling of the violence, in which one Jew was murdered. Jews cited the finding as proof that the city—and its black mayor, David Dinkins—were insensitive to Jewish concerns. A Public Broadcasting Service (PBS) documentary entitled *Liberators*, intended to draw blacks and Jews together, movingly described how black soldiers in World War II—themselves victims of racism—liberated Nazi death camps. But it was withdrawn from distribution when doubts were raised about its accuracy.

The Anti-Defamation League (ADL) of B'nai B'rith, one of the best known and most influential U.S. Jewish organizations, came under heavy criticism during 1993 for its undercover work in monitoring anti-Semitism. The organization allegedly engaged in illegal invasion of privacy. The ADL and its supporters rejected the charges and suggested that only political extremists would gain from any weakening of the organization's fact-finding operations.

Gay rights became an increasingly divisive issue among U.S. Jews. In March 1993 the Reconstructionist Rabbinical Association, which years earlier had voted to accept homosexuals into its ranks, approved the performance of commitment ceremonies for gay and lesbian couples. The more traditionalist Conservative movement, however, was wracked by dispute over the issue. At the annual convention of its rabbinical association, a prominent rabbi urged an end to the stigmatization of homosexuality. But the chancellor of the Jewish Theological Seminary responded that "individual autonomy"

must take a backseat to the "wisdom of a tradition born in revelation and tempered by time."

The annual Salute to Israel parade on May 9 in New York City provided a broader focus for the debate over gays and gay rights. Congregation Beth Simchat Torah, a gay synagogue, requested permission to march in the parade. Orthodox groups then refused to participate on the grounds that that implicitly would condone homosexuality. After a tentative agreement was reached to allow the gay synagogue to march without an identifying banner, the Orthodox contingent reneged when the gay congregation's rabbi publicized the matter in a *New York Times* feature article.

Progress was made during the year on an issue of Jewish law that long had vexed observant Jews. Biblical law requires divorce to be initiated by the husband. With the proliferation of divorce in modern times, there were many cases of husbands refusing to give their wives Jewish divorces, or using the opportunity to extort money. The Rabbinical Council of America called upon its members to ostracize husbands engaging in such behavior and to have engaged couples sign a prenuptial agreement stipulating stiff monetary payments to the wife if the couple is estranged and the husband does not deliver a Jewish divorce.

Lubavitch Sect. The messianic interests of the Lubavitch sect of Hasidim reached fever pitch in 1993. Some followers declared that the Rabbi Menachem Schneerson would reveal himself as the messiah at a "coronation" gathering on January 31. The internationally televised event featured a brief appearance by the elderly rabbi, who remained silent in an anticlimax that did not dampen the enthusiasm of the believers.

LAWRENCE GROSSMAN
The American Jewish Committee

Orthodox Eastern

Celebrations in honor of the bicentennial of Eastern Orthodox Christianity in North America began in Alaska in 1993 and were led by Metropolitan Theodosius, primate of the Orthodox Church in America. Patriarch Aleksy II of Moscow joined in the festivities, traveling the route of the original Russian Orthodox missionaries, who went across Siberia to Alaska in 1793. His visit was cut short after he participated in events in Anchorage, Kodiak, San Francisco, and Chicago by his need to return to Russia in light of the political dispute between the parliament and President Boris Yeltsin.

Eastern Europe. Orthodox Church life in Russia and other former Marxist nations continued to blossom with the construction of thousands of new churches, monasteries, parochial schools, and philanthropic associations. Churches in those countries have experienced inner divisions, however, due to ethnic and political disagreements.

The U.S. Holocaust Memorial Museum

© Reuters/Bettmann

The overcast sky in Washington, DC, on April 22, 1993, reinforced the somberness of the occasion: the dedication of the U.S. Holocaust Memorial Museum. The museum is located on federally donated land near the Mall, close to the Washington Monument, and was built with private funds expected to amount to $168 million.

Among the dedication's speakers were President Bill Clinton and Vice-President Al Gore, Israeli President Chaim Herzog, and writer Elie Wiesel. President Clinton and Nobel laureate Wiesel *(at right in photo)* joined Harvey M. Meyerhoff *(left),* chairman of the U.S. Holocaust Memorial Council that planned the museum, in lighting an eternal flame. Addressing the audience from a dais inscribed with the words "For the dead and the living, we must bear witness," President Clinton pointed to the Nazi destruction of millions of innocent men, women, and children as a grim lesson "that knowledge divorced from values can only serve to deepen the human nightmare." Wiesel, the council's founding chairman, added a political note by insisting on the immediate practical application of the lessons of the Holocaust. Referring to the "ethnic cleansing" occurring in Bosnia, he turned to Clinton and said: "Mr. President, this bloodshed must be stopped. It will not stop unless we stop it."

Controversy had accompanied the museum project since its beginnings in 1980: Was this to be a memorial to Jewish victims, or did it have a universal message? What was the rationale for such a museum in the U.S. capital, thousands of miles from the site of Adolf Hitler's evil works? Why a memorial to Holocaust victims and not to American Indians or U.S. black slaves? Would the creation of such a museum spark anti-German feeling? From the standpoint of Jewish group survival, might the money raised for the museum not have been spent more wisely on Jewish education to keep alive the religious and cultural traditions that Hitler had sought to erase? Controversy over such issues, combined with other problems, long had delayed the museum's construction.

Even the successful culmination of the project did not end the disputes. Two weeks before the dedication, the Clinton administration dismissed the chairman and vice-chairman of the museum—Reagan appointees—reportedly because they were so insistent on making the museum "American" that they opposed inviting the Israeli president to speak at the dedication. At the dedication ceremony, Croatian President Franjo Tudjman was jeered for having written disparagingly of Jews. And Serbians, whose people had suffered greatly under the Nazis, were outraged that their president—under fire for his role in fomenting violence in Bosnia—was not invited. Throughout the proceedings, anti-Semitic demonstrators shouted epithets.

Yet the impact of the museum on those who went inside when it opened to the public on April 26 rendered the complaints insignificant. The building itself, designed by architect James I. Freed, "at every twisted turn...evokes the closed, monitored world of the Nazi death camps," wrote Kenneth Woodward in *Newsweek.* This is especially true of the ground-floor Hall of Witness, with its numerous architectural symbols of Nazi terror. In building this area, Freed largely succeeded in his goal: "I wanted to make a scream."

Each visitor is given a computerized card bearing the identity of a Holocaust victim of the visitor's own age and gender. By inserting the card into monitors throughout the museum, the visitor can follow the victim's story. Displays of pictures, artifacts, and tape recordings lead visitors from the Nazi takeover, through the Holocaust years, until the liberation. Bleak exhibits of bunks where prisoners were jammed in, replicas of crematory ovens, arrays of belongings of prisoners, as well as films of the atrocities so explicit they are shielded from children's view, assail visitors. The final stop in the museum tour is the Hall of Remembrance, where visitors can reflect.

LAWRENCE GROSSMAN

Russia, Ukraine, Moldova, Bulgaria, and Estonia all have several Orthodox ecclesiastical bodies claiming legitimacy and vying for popular support. Patriarch Bartholomew of Constantinople, Eastern Orthodoxy's world leader, visited each of these countries, as well as Romania and Serbia, in attempts to solve disputes and reconcile hostile church bodies.

Orthodox Churches in formerly Communist countries also continued to face serious challenges from foreign missionaries, particularly from North America and Western Europe. Legal action intended to limit foreign religious movements in Russia failed to secure Yeltsin's support.

Serbian Orthodox leaders who blamed former Communists for the perpetuation of civil war in the former Yugoslavia visited the Vatican for the first time since the 13th century in a peacemaking effort. They reported wholesale destruction of Orthodox Church life in Croatia, with pastors expelled and hundreds of churches destroyed.

The Orthodox Church in Albania under the leadership of Archbishop Anastas of Tiranë succeeded in increasing its membership, recovering properties, developing activities, and maintaining unity—all while claiming discrimination by the Albanian government and facing disruptive actions from Greek nationalists on the country's southern borders.

Patriarch Bartholomew. In addition to visiting Eastern and Western Europe, Ecumenical Patriarch Bartholomew of Constantinople also traveled to Middle Eastern Orthodox Churches in the patriarchate of Antioch. In July he presided at an extraordinary synod of bishops of the Ecumenical Patriarchate—attended also by Patriarch Parthenios of Alexandria—which censured Patriarch Diodoros of Jerusalem for interference in church affairs outside his jurisdiction. The possibility of a major schism passed when Diodoros complied with measures correcting his uncanonical activities.

Milestones. The Russian Orthodox Archdiocese of Western Europe elected Archimandrite Sergei Konovalov of Brussels as primatial archbishop. He succeeded Archbishop Georges Wagner, who died in April. The Russian Orthodox Theological Institute of St. Serge in Paris elected theologian and ecumenist Father Boris Bobrinskoy as dean.

Archimandrite Sophrony Sakharov, founder of St. John the Baptism Monastery in Essex, England, died in July at age 97. Among Orthodoxy's leading spiritual elders and authors, Sophrony had commented extensively on the life and teaching of the recently canonized St. Silouan of Mount Athos. The greatest modern Romanian Orthodox theologian, Father Dumitru Staniloae, died in October at age 89. He wrote and translated countless books and articles, many while in detention under the Marxist regime.

THOMAS HOPKO
St. Vladimir's Seminary

Protestantism

Women continued to advance in leadership positions in the world of Protestantism during 1993, although most denominations remained wary of granting ordination to avowed practicing homosexuals. Ecumenical relations also took some steps forward during the year.

Women. The Rev. Mary Adelia McLeod was elected bishop of the Episcopal Diocese of Vermont in June, becoming the first woman to head a diocese in the United States and only the second in such a position in the worldwide Anglican Communion. The 116,000-member Mennonite

In Orlando, FL, in June 1993, the 205th General Assembly of the Presbyterian Church (U.S.A.) chose David Lee Dobler as moderator. The assembly also voted to keep its ban on allowing practicing homosexuals to serve as clergy, elders, and deacons.

Church chose Donella M. Clements as its moderator in July, making her the first woman to hold its top position.

The 33,000-member Christian Reformed Church (CRC), which has debated ordination of women for several years, voted at its annual synod in Grand Rapids, MI, in June to allow local congregations to decide individually. Although the resolution must be ratified by a subsequent synod before it can be implemented, it touched off immediate protests by conservatives. Korean-American leaders who opposed the decision met in Los Angeles in October and organized the Christian Presbyterian Church, a breakaway body with 5,659 members in 16 congregations.

A week before the CRC synod took its action, the General Assembly of the 243,000-member Presbyterian Church (U.S.A.) urged the CRC to repent over what it called its "departure from the scriptures in its doctrine and practice." The resolution criticized the CRC for allowing women to preach and teach, failing to remove a celibate homosexual from its clergy ranks, allowing evolutionary theories to be taught at church-related Calvin College in Grand Rapids, and "harassing" conservative clergy.

The Church of England's 1992 decision to open the priesthood to women prompted some opponents, including retired Bishop Graham Leonard of London, to join the Roman Catholic Church. Meanwhile, male priests and bishops who wanted to remain in the Anglican fold asked the General Synod for legal guarantees that they could remain while refusing conscientiously to recognize the ministry of women priests.

Homosexuals. David Lee Dobler, an Alaskan pastor who opposes the ordination of practicing homosexuals, was elected moderator of the Presbyterian Church (U.S.A.). The General Assembly, meeting in Orlando, FL, in June, voted to keep its ban on allowing practicing homosexuals to serve as clergy, elders, and deacons. At the same time, it called for a three-year, churchwide study on the subject. The 396-155 vote for the study touched off a demonstration by more than 60 gay-rights activists, including the Rev. Jane Spahr, a lesbian whose clergy appointment by a congregation in Rochester, NY, was overturned by the denomination's highest court in 1992.

A gay-rights caucus in the American Baptist Churches was denied permission to set up an exhibit booth at the 1.1-million-member denomination's biennial convention in San Jose, CA, in June because of the church's official position that homosexual practice is "incompatible with Christian teaching." However, just before the convention opened, the church's General Board passed a resolution acknowledging "a variety of understandings" on homosexuality.

National Council of Churches. Executives of the National Council of Churches (NCC) voted in May to make plans for a discussion involving representatives of its 32 member churches and of homosexual groups. The largely homosexual Universal Fellowship of Metropolitan Community Churches had been trying unsuccessfully for more than a decade to persuade the NCC to grant it membership or observer status.

Lani J. Havens resigned as director of Church World Service, the NCC's relief and development agency, over what she described as "a lack of organizational clarity." She was succeeded in September by the Rev. Lonnie Turnipseed, a veteran NCC staffer. Meanwhile, the ecumenical organization moved toward a new restructuring in response to a study that found that its "current mode and level of operations are not sustainable in the long term."

Ecumenical News. The Consultation on Church Union (COCU) got a boost in June when the Presbyterian Church (U.S.A.) assembly voted to endorse its plan for mutual recognition of ministers and joint celebration of Communion by nine denominations. The Presbyterians became the third denomination to endorse the plan and the first of COCU's five large mainline members to do so.

Two other COCU member denominations, the 1-million-member Christian Church (Disciples of Christ) and the 1.6-million-member United Church of Christ, held joint national meetings for the first time in St. Louis, MO, in July.

Presidential Involvement. Three former U.S. presidents—Gerald Ford, Jimmy Carter, and Ronald Reagan—agreed to serve as honorary cochairmen of a fund drive to raise $10 million for the "faith and order" work of the National and World councils of churches. Carter, a Southern Baptist, also lent his support to the Cooperative Baptist Fellowship, a group that opposes the fundamentalist policies of the 15.2-million-member Southern Baptist Convention. In May he was the keynote speaker for the group's national meeting in Birmingham.

Although President Bill Clinton is a Southern Baptist, the denomination's annual convention in Houston in June opposed his policies on abortion and homosexual rights. President Clinton invited leaders from 19 denominations in the NCC to meet with him and Vice-President Al Gore at the White House in March.

DARRELL J. TURNER

Roman Catholicism

The activities of Pope John Paul II dominated 1993 developments in Roman Catholicism.

The Vatican. In a powerful show of unity, an estimated 375,000 young Catholics from around the world joined with Pope John Paul II in Denver, August 12-15. In an event called World Youth Day, young people participated in an electrifying display of prayer, education, and fellowship, demonstrating the theme "we are part of something bigger." The pope used the event to call forcefully on the faithful to oppose abortion, euthanasia, and other evils that threaten

human life. During the visit, which began with stops in Jamaica and Mexico, the holy father met with U.S. President Bill Clinton for the first time.

In February, Pope John Paul had taken his tenth trip to Africa, visiting Benin, Uganda, and Sudan. The pope also visited the Baltics and Balkans, two areas radically altered by the fall of communism. In a 12-hour visit to Albania on April 25, the pope ordained four bishops to reestablish the hierarchy in an area where religious activity had been outlawed for 47 years of communist rule. During his visit to Lithuania, Latvia, and Estonia, September 4-10, the pope urged the Baltic countries to avoid ethnic tensions and collaborate ecumenically. The pope appealed for an end to the conflict in the former Yugoslavia and urged the United Nations (UN) to use its "right of intervention" to stop the fighting. Pope John Paul also made his fourth trip to Spain, June 12-17, as part of the International Eucharistic Congress.

The Vatican welcomed the accord between Israel and the Palestine Liberation Organization (PLO). The agreement raised speculation that the Vatican would formalize diplomatic relations with Israel, and an agreement establishing such relations was signed at year's end. Significantly, Yisrael Meir Lau, the chief rabbi of Israel's Ashkenazi Jews, met with the pope outside Rome on September 21. It was the first time a chief rabbi of the Jewish state had met with a pope. The Vatican established diplomatic relations with 16 other countries and exchanged ambassadors with Slovakia. Boston Mayor Raymond Flynn was appointed U.S. ambassador to the Vatican.

The pope also released *Veritatis Splendor* ("The Splendor of Truth"), the tenth encyclical of his pontificate and the first papal encyclical on the foundations of moral theology. Six years in the making, the 183-page encyclical was a renewed call for obedience to church teachings on moral issues and reaffirmed "the genuine concept of human freedom and its relationship with truth." Despite rumors, hospital tests showed the 73-year-old pope healthy and fit nearly a year after undergoing surgery to remove an intestinal tumor. The pontiff fractured his shoulder in November.

The U.S. Church. The Catholic Church in the United States took major steps to confront revelations and allegations of sex abuse by the clergy. The U.S. bishops formed a committee with a sweeping mandate to deal with all aspects of the problem, including formulating plans to help victims, dealing with abusive priests, and screening seminarians. The Vatican and U.S. dioceses developed new policies for dealing with sexually abusive priests, including dismissal from the priesthood. Pedophilia was an expensive financial burden for the church. Chicago's Cardinal Joseph Bernardin announced that the Chicago archdiocese paid out $1.85 million for clergy sex-abuse matters in 1992. In November, Cardinal Bernardin himself was the subject of allegations

© Grafton Smith/Gamma-Liaison

Pope John Paul II addressed some 90,000 people at Denver's Mile High Stadium as ceremonies marking World Youth Day began Aug. 12, 1993. It was the pope's third major U. S. visit.

that he had molested a teenage seminarian almost two decades earlier.

Pedophilia was not the only sexually related issue affecting Catholic leadership. Archbishop Robert F. Sanchez of Santa Fe, NM, the first U.S.-born Hispanic archbishop, resigned in April 1993 after he was accused of having intimate relations with at least three young women in the 1970s and 1980s.

The Catholic Church strongly backed U.S. health-care reform. The bishops unanimously adopted a ten-page resolution placing them squarely on the side of massive reforms but at the same time solidly against coverage of abortion or euthanasia as "health care."

Growth. The 1993 *Annuario Pontificio*, the Vatican yearbook, indicated that there were 404,031 priests worldwide, a very small increase over the previous year. Worldwide, the number of Catholics increased by some 16 million, up to 994 million of the world's 5.4 billion people, or about 18% of the population. In the United States, the number of seminarians increased for the first time since 1982, with the number of post-college seminarians rising 5.3%. Russia's first Roman Catholic seminary opened in Moscow.

DANIEL MEDINGER
Editor, "The Catholic Review," Baltimore

RETAILING

Retailers became more dependent on consumers in 1993. In the recent past, retailers had relied heavily on government, other businesses, and international markets. In 1993, however, these groups did not respond. Continued fiscal problems led to cutbacks in state and federal spending, the worldwide recession helped cause a decline in importance of exports, and the business sector continued to have cutbacks. A bright spot was the growth of the home-shopping industry (*see* SPECIAL REPORT, page 461).

Consumer Confidence. Consumer confidence, a major factor in determining retail success or failure, was on a roller-coaster ride in 1993. During the first part of the year, low consumer-confidence levels were attributed to worries over unemployment, new spending, and tax hikes proposed by the new Clinton administration, as well as the fact that real wages for the average worker had declined 20% over the past 20 years. Toward year's end, confidence rose as consumers better understood and were less anxious about the spending, health, and tax reforms planned by President Bill Clinton and debated in Congress.

Retail Sales. Consumer spending was erratic in 1993. This was reflected in the sales revenues of the largest U.S. retailers. Retail sales were stagnant during the first half of the year, then moved up sharply in the second half. Wal-Mart and K Mart continued as the largest U.S. retailers. Wal-Mart posted sales for the first nine months in excess of $40 billion, up 22% from 1992, while K Mart sales were more than $25 billion for the same period. Sears remained in the third position with sales of nearly $20 billion for the first nine months. Wal-Mart did experience some problems during 1993, however. Its stock, which had exhibited Herculean growth over the past decade, declined more than 25% over a six-month period in 1993. Sears, meanwhile, returned to its original retail focus, ending its catalog operations and cutting back its management force.

Among the year's retailing standouts was Best Buy, an electronics and appliance retailer. It posted same-store sales at double-digit levels throughout 1993. Its sales revenues for the year's first nine months skyrocketed from approximately $700 million in 1992 to nearly $1.3 billion in 1993.

Suffering problems during 1993, however, was the Woolworth Corporation, which announced in October that it would eliminate 13,000 jobs and close 970 stores over several months. About 400 of the stores to be closed were dime stores, which were declining in profitability. Instead, it would devote attention to its more profitable specialty chains, like Foot Locker.

Warehouse Clubs. The growth in warehouse clubs appeared to wither in 1993. Pace, K Mart's

© Ann States/Saba

Sales at Home Depot, an Atlanta-based retailer specializing in do-it-yourself items for the home, have grown at an average annual rate of 50.8% since the early 1980s.

warehouse entry, showed heavy losses. K Mart responded by closing some stores and selling all of the remaining stores to Wal-Mart. Sam's, Wal-Mart's warehouse operation, also lagged in sales revenues throughout most of the year.

Competitive Pressures. Competitive pressures on retailers perhaps reached an apex in 1993. Not only were consumers becoming more price-conscious than in the past, but they also were demanding better services. Concomitantly, retailers were faced with higher costs for employee benefits, higher federal and state taxes, and increasing government regulations. Small-scale retailers appeared to be hardest-hit by business bankruptcies, which approached the highest level ever of filings for the second year in a row. Jamesway Stores was the largest retailer to file for Chapter 11 protection in 1993.

MEL J. ZELENAK
University of Missouri-Columbia

Television Home Shopping

Television home shopping made further gains in 1993. Home shopping began broadcasting nationwide in 1985, and by 1986 sales had reached $160 million. Growth over the next few years was spectacular, with sales of more than $2 billion by 1992. Over the first nine months of 1993, revenues increased 33% over the same period in 1992. This steady gain contrasts with the mostly flat growth of general retail revenues during 1992-93.

The Networks. The meteoric gains of the QVC (Quality, Value, Convenience) Shopping Network reflect the industry's growth as a whole. During the first nine months of 1993, QVC stock nearly tripled. The network exhibited its financial strength with its hostile $9.5 billion attempt to take over Paramount Communications. It also made overtures to merge with its major competitor, HSN (Home Shopping Network)—a move that would create a $2.2 billion mega-network available to two thirds of TV-watching households in the United States. HSN did not fare as well as its main rival in 1993, experiencing losses of $20 million during the second quarter, which caused its stock to plummet. HSN's dilemma was caused in part by various serious legal problems. Nonetheless, most analysts remained optimistic about its future, especially with the QVC merger in the offing.

The two networks together account for 99% of the U.S. home-shopping market. In 1993, QVC could be seen in about 50 million homes, while HSN reached more than 60 million households. The networks' hold on the market appeared to solidify in July when the Federal Communications Commission ruled that cable companies must carry home-shopping channels.

Consumer Acceptance. Home shopping became more widely accepted by U.S. consumers in 1993. The networks were effective in shedding much of the "hurry-or-these-will-be-gone" image that had permeated the industry since its inception. The merchandise offered was of better quality, and the sales presentations became more sophisticated. Liberal return policies and better product information also helped overcome the industry's image problem. Surveys conducted in 1993 indicated that home-shopping buyers were typical of the general U.S. population.

Retailers' Acceptance. Retailers exhibited substantive interest in home shopping in 1993. Spiegel's, Saks Fifth Avenue, and Sharper Image all entered the market, and Macy's planned to launch its own home-shopping channel in mid-1994. The approach offers retailers many advantages. Large inventories may be kept at only a few sites, reducing operating costs; the huge market reached also is impressive.

International Markets. The international market for television home shopping was expanding exponentially, with networks either in existence or planned in Britain, Ireland, Canada, Japan, Mexico, Spain, Portugal, and Germany.

The Future. Home shopping was the fastest-growing segment of the retail market in 1993. The potential for further growth is apparent. New technology like digital compression and interactive systems is already available in some cities. Digital compression of channels will allow cable companies to offer hundreds of viewing options; it is anticipated that several dozen shopping networks will be offered. Interactive systems, already in thousands of homes, make the home buying experience more real: The customer is able to "walk the aisles," selecting items and receiving detailed information about them. Tele-Communications plans to equip more than 1 million homes with interactive systems by the end of 1994.

MEL J. ZELENAK

© Yvonne Hemsey/Gamma-Liaison

Television watching and shopping remain two favorite American pastimes. The combination of the two into a new trend—shopping at home through the television—has created a billion-dollar industry.

RHODE ISLAND

Atop the news in Rhode Island during 1993 was the resignation of the chief justice of the state Supreme Court, Thomas F. Fay. He was battered by accounts of mishandled court funds, favoritism in appointments, and attempted ticket fixing for friends. Impeachment proceedings were launched by the state House of Representatives, but were halted by his October 8 resignation. Calls for reform of the legislative system for electing justices became insistent.

The Legislature. Reform became the watchword for the General Assembly. A bitter struggle for the House leadership was won by a Democratic faction—with Republican support—that promised to "open up" the legislative process. Early in the session several rules reforms were adopted. The Senate also came under new leadership with the defeat of the incumbent majority leader by a reform coalition. Ironically, on October 14 serious ethics complaints were filed against new Speaker of the House John B. Harwood.

When the Assembly settled down to work, it was faced once again with serious budget problems. Gov. Bruce Sundlun proposed severe cuts in human-service spending, $14 million in tax cuts to help improve the business climate, a higher gasoline and cigarette tax, and many fee increases, but no change in the sales or income taxes. These moves were designed to deal with a weak revenue prospect and threatened deficit. Most proposals survived unprecedented long and emotional debates and amendment efforts.

The Economy. The budget problems reflected the poor shape of the state's economy. Like the national economy, Rhode Island showed only scattered signs of improvement. The jobless rate was 7.7% in February, edged up to 8.1% in June, and dropped to 6.6% in July—largely due to a decline in those seeking work. That figure brought Rhode Island down to the national average after long remaining considerably higher.

At midyear, a periodic University of Rhode Island/*Providence Journal-Bulletin* survey showed the economy continuing flat and stagnant. Activity was predicted to pick up, although slowly, during the rest of the year. October Census Bureau reports showed that Rhode Island's median income declined from $33,313 to $30,836—slightly below the national average—from 1990 through 1992, but the state had fewer people under the poverty line than the national average.

The threat of U.S. Navy programs being eliminated cast a shadow over the economy. The state's largest employer, submarine builder Electric Boat, announced immediate and projected employee layoffs in July, but the key Seawolf program was not scuttled. Rhode Island escaped heavy damage from the list of military-base closures released by the federal government.

One spot of good news was the real-estate market. Home sales picked up briskly during the year as mortgage rates and prices dropped.

Credit Unions. Joseph Mollicone, Jr., a former bank president whose alleged huge thefts precipitated a credit-union crisis, returned to Rhode Island and was tried in April. He was convicted and given a 30-year prison sentence. In October the governor announced that final repayments were being mailed to depositors.

Politics. Early candidacies began stirrings for 1994 elections. Democratic State Rep. Patrick Kennedy, son of U.S. Sen. Edward Kennedy, announced his candidacy for the U.S. House of Representatives from the 1st District, and two aspirants for the Republican gubernatorial nomination emerged—U.S. Rep. Ronald Machtley and former U.S. attorney Lincoln Almond.

ELMER E. CORNWELL, JR., *Brown University*

RHODE ISLAND • Information Highlights

Area: 1,212 sq mi (3 140 km²).

Population (July 1, 1992 est.): 1,005,000.

Chief Cities (1990 census): Providence, the capital, 160,728; Warwick, 85,427.

Government (1993): *Chief Officers*—governor, Bruce G. Sundlun (D); lt. gov., Robert A. Weygand (D). *General Assembly*—Senate, 50 members; House of Representatives, 100 members.

State Finances (fiscal year 1991): *Revenue*, $3,305,000,000; *expenditure*, $3,465,000,000.

Personal Income (1992): $19,996,000,000; per capita, $19,895.

Labor Force (August 1993): *Civilian labor force*, 519,100; *unemployed*, 35,600 (6.8% of total force).

Education: *Enrollment* (fall 1991)—public elementary schools, 104,146; public secondary, 37,998; colleges and universities, 79,112. *Public school expenditures* (1990-91), $823,655,000.

ROMANIA

During 1993, Romania continued to stumble toward democracy and international integration. The new government and parliament preserved a measure of political stability, despite a disquieting growth in extreme nationalism. Economic reforms were marred by a slow process of privatization and unrest among disaffected workers. Bucharest avoided any dangerous international disputes, but relations with Hungary simmered.

Politics. The government of Prime Minister Nicolae Vacaroiu, installed in November 1992, faced a series of political challenges. The cabinet, based around the Democratic National Salvation Front (DNSF) and a handful of independents, increasingly was split over economic reform. Vacaroiu and the DNSF remained reliant on parliamentary support. In August numerous cabinet members were replaced, including the reformist Chairman of the Council for Economic Coordination Misu Negritoiu, four ministers, and 16 deputy ministers. The reshuffle indicated that gradualists and even antireformers appeared to be in the ascendancy.

Nationalists from the Romanian National Unity Party and the Greater Romania Party appeared to gain increasing influence in the government. The nationalists obtained representation in the Ministry of Culture through several controversial appointments. The threat of populist nationalism could not be ignored, especially given the weakness and factionalism within the liberal and centrist parties. The opposition coalition, the Democratic Convention of Romania, was riven by internal conflicts. Seeking to gain a clearer, center-left political profile, the ruling DNSF changed its name to the Party of Social Democracy and elected former Foreign Minister Adrian Nastase as party leader.

Economy. Romania's economic performance was mixed. By midyear, industrial production rose slightly over 1992 levels, although industrial stoppages during the year lowered output. Unemployment reached 9.6% in midyear—up from 8.5% in January—and continued to climb into the fall. Inflation remained high, registering an average rate of 13.6% per month in the first five months of 1993. In May the remaining subsidies on basic goods and services were eliminated, dramatically increasing consumer prices.

Romania's foreign debt climbed to $2.5 billion early in 1993, more than double the 1991 figure. Most of the loans were acquired from international institutions to support market reform and industrial development. Further loans from the World Bank and International Monetary Fund were delayed due to Romania's poor economic performance and its inability to meet credit conditions. World Bank officials pointed out that Romanian officials were less determined in their push toward privatization than were other former Communist states. Bucharest calculated financial losses of up to $7 billion from UN sanctions against the former Yugoslavia. Western diplomats considered the figure to be exaggerated.

The Vacaroiu government was elected on the promise that it would intensify economic reforms and protect the disadvantaged sectors of society. This policy proved difficult to implement with a limited state budget. Pro-market reformers were unable to pass major legislation on privatization due to substantial political and bureaucratic resistance. A wave of strikes during the summer of 1993 resulted in substantial economic losses and paralyzed key sectors such as mining and transportation. The strikes were provoked by massive price hikes that followed the removal of subsidies on most goods and services. Labor leaders opposed an economic-reform program that threatened to lay off thousands of workers. Although the government managed to subdue the unrest and avert a major strike through wage concessions, the threat of future unrest remained.

Ethnic Conflicts. Ethnic relations were jeopardized by the growth of nationalist Romanian parties after the 1992 general elections. Following President Ion Iliescu's reelection in September

---

ROMANIA • Information Highlights

Official Name: Romania.
Location: Southeastern Europe.
Area: 91,699 sq mi (237 500 km²).
Population (mid-1993 est.): 23,200,000.
Chief Cities (Jan. 7, 1992 est.): Bucharest, the capital, 2,064,474; Constanta, 350,476; Iasi, 342,994.
Government: *Head of state,* Ion Iliescu, president (took office December 1989). *Head of government,* Nicolae Vacaroiu, prime minister (named Nov. 4, 1992). *Legislature* (unicameral)—Grand National Assembly.
Monetary Unit: Leu (615.000 lei equal U.S.$1, April 1993).
Gross Domestic Product (1991 est. U.S.$): $71,900,000,000.
Foreign Trade (1992 U.S.$): *Imports,* $5,394,000,000; *exports,* $4,031,000,000.

1992, leaders of the sizable Hungarian minority charged that the government was placing DNSF loyalists in local government, education, and the legal system and removing ethnic Hungarians from influence.

The nationalist mayor of the Transylvanian city of Cluj, Gheorghe Funar, continued to provoke Hungarians, placing restrictions on their rallies, cultural activities, and the placement of bilingual signs. At the Third Congress of the Democratic Alliance of Hungarians in January, moderate factions prevailed, but observers believed that an escalation of Romanian nationalism could provoke Magyar militancy. Bucharest tried to defuse tensions by establishing an advisory Council for National Minorities representing some 30 ethnicities. The council proposed various measures to improve minority education and sponsored an accord between government officials and Magyar leaders.

The worst ethnic conflicts were evident in the treatment of the large Roma (Gypsy) population. Human-rights groups reported that Roma communities were subjected to repeated acts of discrimination in housing, employment, and education, and negative stereotypes were spread by the state-run media. Gypsy houses were torched and individuals attacked by mobs in several villages. Roma families claimed they were receiving insufficient police protection.

Foreign Affairs. Romania's relations with Hungary improved as their foreign ministers decided to open new border crossings and develop economic relations. Preparations also were made to sign a new bilateral treaty, but the question of minority rights continued to pose a major stumbling block. Bucharest remained concerned over the situation in Moldova, where a separatist movement threatened Moldovan independence and accentuated calls for swift unification with Romania. In October, Romania was admitted formally as a full member to the Council of Europe and the U.S. Congress restored Romania's most-favored-nation trading status.

JANUSZ BUGAJSKI
Center for Strategic and International Studies

RUSSIA AND THE COMMONWEALTH OF INDEPENDENT STATES

Nineteen ninety-three was year two of transitional politics and economics in Russia and the Commonwealth of Independent States (CIS). It was a difficult year for most of these former republics of the USSR as they struggled to transform their erstwhile Soviet-style polities and economies. Nominally, all aspired to political democracy and market economies, but by year's end aspiration and reality were diverging in Russia and a number of other states, in the region now called the "near abroad." Post-Soviet authoritarian political forms had begun to emerge, along with strange hybrid economic arrangements, combining elements of market spontaneity and vestiges of state control.

The centerpiece of a dramatic year in the region was Russia with its crises, its drive for constitutional reform, and, finally, at the end of 1993, the first post-Soviet Russian elections. The other states in the Commonwealth were not without their own major problems, internal conflicts, and even in a few cases large-scale armed violence. It was Russia, however—deeply divided throughout much of the year over power sharing; the pace of economic change; and, not least, the contradictory visions and ambitions of its president, Boris Yeltsin, and the speaker of the Parliament, Ruslan Khasbulatov—that gripped the attention of its neighbors.

The Commonwealth of Independent States. The CIS began the year as a loose association of ten states, all former union republics of the USSR, including two, Ukraine and Moldova, that opted to remain aloof from the common structure. By the end of 1993, Azerbaijan and Georgia—both of which had declined to join when the CIS was formed in December 1991—were seeking membership, and Moldova and Ukraine were drawing closer. It appeared that the young, multistate, international organization was beginning to knit on the basis of shared mutual interest.

Appearance belied reality, however. If the CIS enjoyed any sense of fragile unity and common purpose in the second year of its existence, it was due to its most powerful member, Russia. The Russian Federation was the driving force, using its economic and military muscle not only to counter centrifugal forces within the CIS, but to forge, and even benevolently "impose," some measure of economic cooperation on its fellow states. In the case of Moldova and Ukraine, Russia used its oil weapon to induce greater economic involvement in the CIS. In Georgia and Azerbaijan, both of which were in deadly battle to preserve their territorial integrity in the face of serious armed challenges, Russia's under-the-table military assistance to their respective enemies, Abkhazia and fellow CIS member Armenia, proved in the end a persuasive reason to seek membership in the new club, the CIS.

From Russia's standpoint it was understood implicitly that it would be a long time before Russian goods found customers in the West, so the objective became to reassemble the former Soviet economy as an internal market—absent, of course, central planners and a ruling Communist Party. Making the CIS work, at least on Russian terms, also filled other needs for

On Oct. 4, 1993, Russian troops loyal to Boris Yeltsin attacked and seized the Russian parliament building from parliamentarians who had barricaded themselves in the structure after voting to impeach the Russian president on September 21 (photos page 465). A debate over proposed constitutional changes was at the center of the crisis, which saw large demonstrations, including the pro-Yeltsin one (right), and increasing violence.

© Jon Jones/Sygma

Moscow. The Russian public was still in shock from the abrupt loss of superpower status, so holding sway over the CIS as well as the Baltics served as a surrogate of sorts for the lost empire. Also, to be credible as a "great power," President Yeltsin and Foreign Minister Andrei Kozyrev understood that the nation would need to have a viable economy and the ability to project power over its sphere of interest.

Thus the CIS—with its charter, clearing agreements, interparliamentary meetings, and legal conferences—had begun to look like an extension of Russian foreign economic policy, resembling to some extent U.S. hegemony over the North Atlantic Treaty Organization (NATO) in its formative years when West Europe still was recovering from World War II. In this sense, then, the second-anniversary conference of the CIS in Askhabad, Turkmenistan, was less a meeting of coequals than a thinly disguised occasion for the projection of Russian influence in its border regions.

Russia's Political Crisis. At the end of 1992 the Seventh Russian Congress of People's Deputies, chaired by Khasbulatov, dealt President Yeltsin several setbacks. Among other things, the president was forced to give up his acting prime minister, Yegor Gaidar, who, as the principal architect of radical economic reform, had aroused the ire of the conservative opposition. The best Yeltsin could achieve was a compromise brokered by Chief Justice Valery Zorkin of the Russian Constitutional Court. This called for both president and parliament to suspend their conflict in favor of a public referendum on the new draft constitution to be held in early April. However, by mid-January, Khasbulatov was hedging his commitment and the referendum deal was coming undone.

In early March, Speaker Khasbulatov convened the Eighth Congress. At this stormy conclave the speaker and his conservative allies canceled the referendum, deprived Yeltsin of certain powers, and attempted to block aspects of his economic policy. U.S. President Bill Clinton, who previously had scheduled a summit with Yeltsin, rushed to mobilize the Western leaders in rhetorical support of their beleaguered Russian counterpart. Buoyed by this lift from the democracies and his impending summit with Clinton, and determined to best his opponents, Yeltsin counterattacked on March 20. In a televised special speech to the nation he announced a state of "Special Rule," a type of emergency power that included suspending parliament until the referendum, reinstated, could be held in April.

Predictably, Yeltsin's extraconstitutional move was opposed quickly by Khasbulatov, along with his own vice-president, Aleksandr Rutskoi, and Chief Justice Zorkin. The speaker called into emergency session the Ninth Congress and the

© Willy/Sygma

© Haviv/Saba

© Reuters/Bettmann

With the Ukraine in a state of deep division and even paralysis in 1993, a group of Ukrainian miners traveled to Moscow in June to bring their case before President Yeltsin.

impeachment process was set in motion. Nonetheless, calm temporarily prevailed and a fresh political deal was cut: The president revised his emergency decree, deleting the parts offensive to the constitution, while parliament agreed to a new referendum date of April 25.

Opening his campaign for a favorable vote on the referendum, Yeltsin flew to Vancouver, Canada, for a largely ceremonial Russian-U.S. summit on April 3-4. Although the United States, given its own sluggish economy, had little to offer the Russian leader other than photo opportunities and a package of symbolic gestures—including some aid—the bottom line was that the leader of the Western democracies had endorsed Yeltsin and his path to the market visibly and dramatically. On his return to Moscow, Yeltsin, a good campaigner, plunged into the ongoing referendum campaign as he and his government ministers fanned out across Russia. Khasbulatov and his allies also mounted a campaign, but it was not as extensive. Both sides, however, promised many public boons to curry favor with the voters.

The conservatives had gambled on the referendum and lost. The turnout was very good; both Yeltsin and his policies received public endorsement, and, confirming parliament's unpopularity, substantial numbers expressed their preference for early parliamentary elections, although not enough to require them. Still, there was a significant negative vote on Yeltsin's policies, signaling substantial and widespread public discontent with the social pain caused by economic shock therapy. Nonetheless, tremendously encouraged by the outcome of what was in effect a plebiscite on his presidency, Yeltsin moved quickly during the spring and summer to consolidate his advantage over parliament.

The Path of Constitutional Reform. Although Russia in 1993 was awash in economic misery,

the persistent crisis was fundamentally political in nature. The failure of the elite successfully to resolve questions of power and, specifically, the shape of the political system in turn manifested itself in a constitutional crisis. Throughout the year until mid-December, Russia was governed by the much-amended, heavily revised 1978 Soviet-period Russian Constitution. In the course of many rounds of amendments, the constitution had become a mass of contradictions, including elements of both parliamentary and presidential forms of government. In effect, both Yeltsin and Khasbulatov could "shop" the constitutional chapters for appropriate clauses to support their competing claims.

In the course of the political crisis of spring 1993, Yeltsin, who never had been quite satisfied with the distribution of powers in the official draft constitution written by a constitutional commission of the Sixth Congress in 1992, set up his own constitutional commission. Yeltsin's group soon produced a competing draft, this one more pro-executive, in which the president exercised more authority over the formation and dissolution of the cabinet or "government," and held a decided advantage over the parliament within the separation-of-powers arrangement. After his success in the April referendum, Yeltsin, moving quickly to maintain his new political momentum, convened a new constitutional convention to bring to a conclusion the long, drawn-out drafting process. The selection of delegates and the internal organization of the convention clearly favored the presidential as opposed to the parliamentary point of view. Yeltsin instructed the body to use *his* draft version of the constitution as a basis for discussion, but he did permit the parliamentary version to be considered also.

In spite of Yeltsin's best efforts, the drafting process continued to be plagued by contention, this time not over the legislative-executive relationship, but concerning the division of powers between the central government of the Russian Federation and its constituent parts, called the subjects of the federation. Of the 89 subjects, 21 were known as republics and enjoyed certain political and economic privileges in relationship to Moscow. Many of the majority of the other subjects, known as regions, objected to this special status and insisted on constitutional equality. The republics resisted. Unable to resolve the dispute, the constitutional convention in July reported out a composite of the two spring drafts, forwarding it to the legislative bodies of the federation subjects for further discussion. Not surprisingly, by August a number of republic and regional legislatures had rejected the draft altogether as being unresponsive to their respective corporate interests.

Crisis and Violence and the Near Abroad. In comparison with Russia's, some of the political conflicts in neighboring states were very intense and intractable. The communal conflict over the

Nagorno-Karabakh region of Azerbaijan had grown into an interstate war between Armenia and Azerbaijan. Georgia was wracked by a two-front civil war (*see* GEORGIA, REPUBLIC OF), and while the civil war had subsided in Tajikistan, cross-border forays by the Tajik opposition continued from Afghan territory. In Moldova the truce between the government and its breakaway province—the so-called Trans-Dniester Republic—held, but another ethnic group with separatist inclinations, the Gagauzi, began to stir again. Elsewhere, in former Soviet Central Asia, superficially changed Communist systems in Uzbekistan and Turkmenistan continued to develop along authoritarian lines. Finally, Ukraine's internal crisis deepened in 1993, complicated by regional and ethnic frictions and extremely vexed relations with Russia.

In Azerbaijan the issue centered on a largely Armenian-populated enclave near the Armenian border. Gradually the ethnic antagonisms grew into a guerrilla war between fighters from neighboring villages. By 1993 the Armenian forces, aided by Russia, had taken control of the contested area, opened a corridor to Armenia, and begun new operations on the perimeter of Nagorno-Karabakh to create a buffer zone against Azeri counteroffensives.

The failure of the Azeri armed forces to protect their own cities and towns produced a major political crisis in Azerbaijan. A charismatic military commander leading a rebel force marched on Baku, the capital, forcing the democratically elected president to flee for his life. In an increasingly familiar pattern, a former Communist Party leader of Soviet Azerbaijan, Geidar A. Aliyev, assumed the presidency of the postcoup state with the rebel leader as prime minister.

In Tajikistan the civil war had ended in victory for the former Communist elite. The peculiar alliance of democratic reformers and Islamic fundamentalists had been defeated and dispersed. Some continuing democratic activism proved controllable through police repression, but the Islamic faction was more intractable. Large numbers of the defeated had fled before the victorious forces and become refugees in neighboring Afghanistan. From there during 1993 contingents of armed Islamic fighters attempted to cross the border into Tajikistan in force, only to be repulsed by Russian border troops. At the December CIS summit, Russia and Tajikistan in fact renewed an agreement by which Russian troops guard the Tajik frontier. So far the incursions had been relatively small in scale, but by late 1993 there were signs that the rebels were planning a major offensive from Afghanistan during spring 1994.

Moldova continued to suffer open secession in its midst by the largely Russian and Ukrainian area calling itself Trans-Dniester. Although recognized by no other country, this secessionist province operated like a sovereign state within Moldova supported by the 14th Russian Army. By year's end there was good news and more bad news for Moldova. While the scheduled withdrawal of the Russian forces was announced, the Gagauzi, a separatist Turkic ethnic group that the Moldovans had contained previously, again were showing signs of activity.

While nothing dramatic occurred elsewhere in Central Asia, Uzbekistan and Turkmenistan, where the former Communist Party leaders were now the elected presidents, continued steadily to develop into post-Soviet authoritarian states. In Uzbekistan human-rights violations abounded, with continuing pressure on any signs of too independent and critical a press, discriminatory workplace dismissals, and arrests of political activists not toeing the official line. Turkmenistan was another throwback to the Soviet era, in which little independent political activity was tolerated, and the president was celebrated publicly in a cult of personality. When Yeltsin visited Ashkhabad for the December CIS summit, Russia and Turkmenistan signed a mutual defense treaty by which Russia extended its military protection over the Turkmen borders with Afghanistan and Iran. Generally, Russia has shown little inclination to encourage democratic development among its Central Asian neighbors; on the contrary, Moscow has operated like a classic postcolonial power intent on preserving its influence and prizing stability above all in its client states.

Finally, Ukraine, the second-most-populous and powerful state on the former Soviet territory,

		Area			
Nation	**Population (in Millions)**	**(sq mi)**	**(km²)**	**Capital**	**Head of State and Government**
Armenia	3.6	11,506	29 800	Yerevan	Levon Akopovich Ter-Petrosyan, president
Azerbaijan	7.2	33,436	86 600	Baku	Geidar A. Aliyev, president
Belarus	10.3	80,154	207 600	Minsk	Stanislav Shushkevich, president
Kazakhstan	17.2	1,049,151	2 717 300	Alma-Aty	Nursultan A. Nazarbayev, president
Kyrgyzstan	4.6	76,641	198 500	Bishkek (Frunze)	Askar Akaev, president
Moldova	4.4	13,012	33 700	Chisinau (Kishinev)	Mircea Snegur, president
Russia	149.0	6,592,741	17 075 200	Moscow	Boris Yeltsin, president
Tajikistan	5.7	55,251	143 100	Dushanbe	Emomili Rakhmonov, acting president
Turkmenistan	4.0	188,456	488 100	Ashkhabad	Saparmurad Niyazov, president
Ukraine	51.9	233,089	603 700	Kiev	Leonid M. Kravchuk, president
Uzbekistan	21.7	172,741	447 400	Tashkent	Islam Karimov, president

COMMONWEALTH OF INDEPENDENT STATES • Information Highlights

© Denis Paquin/AP/Wide World

Boris Yeltsin conferred with Britain's Prime Minister John Major in Brussels, Belgium, in December. The leaders of the West generally supported the Russian president during 1993.

was also one of the most troubled in 1993. Unable to agree among themselves on a forward policy for the transition period, the Ukrainian elite was divided politically, regionally, and ethnically, with the result being policy paralysis. President Leonid Kravchuk and Prime Minister Leonid Kuchma were unable to work together; Kuchma resigned, while parliament increasingly marginalized the president. In foreign policy there was the continuing fractious dispute with Russia over ownership of the Black Sea fleet, control of the Crimean peninsula, and Ukraine's reluctance to part with its nuclear warheads without substantial Western aid as well as security assurances. By early winter 1993 preparations were under way for Ukraine's first post-Soviet parliamentary elections, in March 1994, but no one was forecasting that a new cast of politicians would inspire any greater confidence among a weary and disheartened public.

The CIS Economies and Russian Foreign Policy. The Moscow leadership seemed discreetly intent on rebuilding the former Soviet internal market under the aegis of emerging Russian capitalism. A trade agreement was signed with Lithuania, a currency union established with Belarus, and economic aid to the poorer states of Central Asia ensured. The rationing of Russian energy exports was used as a bargaining chip to draw Moldova and Ukraine into the planned CIS economic union.

Meanwhile, Russian economic reform continued to move forward in fits and starts as Yeltsin in his struggle with parliament tried to keep the social pain within some bounds. Positive indicators included avoiding hyperinflation, stabilizing the ruble, and pushing forward with the privatization of businesses. On the downside, inter-enterprise debt grew exponentially as state companies failed to pay each other for goods and services; wages went unpaid for long periods,

generating labor unrest; social deviance increased, especially business-related crime; and unemployment climbed, reaching perhaps 5 million to 6 million.

The End of the First Russian Republic. During two days in early October the First Post-Soviet Russian Republic came to a fiery end. All the signs that this might happen had been evident earlier in the year: the inability of president and parliament to agree on a new constitution and balanced power-sharing arrangements, the increasing stridency and extremism of the mutual rhetoric, and the tendency of each side to demonize the other. At its midsummer session, the parliament had drawn up amendments to the constitution that would have reduced the president to a political figurehead. On September 21, Yeltsin responded with Decree No. 1400, which dissolved parliament and suspended key parts of the constitution, pending early elections. Parliament reacted by nullifying the decree, impeaching Yeltsin in a rump session, and declaring Rutskoi the new president. The "war of decrees" soon became a siege with police troops surrounding the White House, where conservative parliamentarians with armed supporters were holed up.

On Sunday, October 3, hostilities began with Rutskoi ordering his irregular "troops" to attack the central television studio and Moscow city hall. The next day military units loyal to Yeltsin counterattacked. There was much loss of life and as tank shells set the parliament building on fire, the holdouts led by Khasbulatov and Rutskoi surrendered to Yeltsin's forces. The speaker and vice-president, along with other leading militants, were imprisoned, pending indictment and probably trial. Thus ended the First Russian Republic.

What followed was a brief interregnum during which Boris Yeltsin held all the reins of power. Ordering the production of a new, even stronger presidential draft constitution, Yeltsin decreed elections for a new, restructured parliament along with a referendum on his draft constitution for December 11. This left little time for an election campaign as parties scrambled to organize and field candidates. Thirteen parties and blocs qualified for the election, ranging from communists and nationalists at the extremes with a variety of centrists and reform groups in between.

Russia's Election and the Rise of the Second Republic. The initial election results surprised and dismayed Russian liberals and official Washington, but not close observers of Russia's rocky transition. For the seats in the lower house for which parties vied, candidates on the whole who espoused slower reform and greater social protection for the worker did best, with pro-reform candidates trailing. Thus Communists, the Agrarians, the Women's Party, and the LDP—led by the notorious Vladimir Zhirinovsky—did well. Gaidar's group led the reform parties with a modest showing. Initially the LDP's success in winning nearly a quarter of the party vote caused political hysteria in Russian reform circles, fear

in the near abroad, and great concern in Western capitals. The word "fascism" was on everyone's lips. Then, as returns from single-seat races trickled in, Russia's Choice forged ahead in the State Duma, the lower house of the new Federal Assembly, bringing forth a collective sigh of relief. Voting for the upper house, the Federation Council, elected mostly regional and republic political executives, as expected.

Finally, Yeltsin's customized constitution passed, officially ushering in the Second Russian Republic. U.S. Vice-President Albert Gore arrived in Moscow a few days later, renewing U.S. support for Russian reform and laying the groundwork for President Clinton's scheduled visit in January 1994. In the final days of 1993, President Yeltsin, who had lived through a political lifetime during the preceding tumultuous year, had the last word. Lauding the passage of the first post-Soviet Russian constitution in a statement on December 22, he repeatedly referred to its main import as "stability" rather than democracy.

See also BALTIC REPUBLICS.

ROBERT SHARLET, *Union College*

SASKATCHEWAN

Budget cuts and the trimming of the health-care program made news in Saskatchewan in 1993.

Budget. Finance Minister Janice MacKinnon brought in a cost-cutting budget in March which increased taxes and levies by C$193 million and cut programs and services by C$108 million. The sales tax, fuel tax, and corporation capital-resource surcharge were raised. The school-based dental-care program was ended and a prescription-drug subsidy plan was terminated except for those with low incomes or high drug costs. Mac-Kinnon said she was forced to raise taxes and cut programs because of Saskatchewan's accumulated deficit of almost C$8 billion, including the 1993 deficit of C$296 million.

Senate Appointments. Prior to retiring in June 1993, Prime Minister Brian Mulroney appointed three Saskatchewan residents to the Canadian Senate. Raynell Andreychuk, 48, was named in March. Andreychuk had been a Liberal, but would sit in the Senate as a Progressive Conservative. At the time of her appointment, she had been Canada's ambassador to Portugal. In May, Mulroney named Progressive Conservative member of Parliament (MP) Len Gustafson, 59. Gustafson had nominated Mulroney for the party leadership in 1983. Saskatoon businessman David Tkachuk, 47, was named in June.

Health Care. Saskatchewan residents were shocked to learn that soaring budget deficits were forcing the socialist New Democratic Party government of Premier Roy Romanow to cut acute-care funding to 52 rural hospitals. The hospitals either were to close or to become community

---

SASKATCHEWAN • Information Highlights

Area: 251,865 sq mi (652 330 km^2).

Population (June 1993): 992,000.

Chief Cities (1991 census): Regina, the capital, 179,178; Saskatoon, 186,058; Moose Jaw, 33,593.

Government (1993): *Chief Officers*—lt. gov., Sylvia O. Fedoruk; premier, Roy Romanow (New Democrat). *Legislature*—Legislative Assembly, 64 members.

Provincial Finances (1993-94 fiscal year budget): *Revenues*, $4,631,800,000; *expenditures*, $4,928,-100,000.

Personal Income (average weekly earnings, June 1993): $472.37.

Labor Force (August 1993): *Employed* workers, 15 years of age and over, 440,000; *Unemployed*, 7.9%.

Education (1993-94): *Enrollment*—elementary and secondary schools, 208,040 pupils; postsecondary—universities, 23,340; community colleges, 3,820.

---

health clinics. The New Democratic Party had introduced government-funded medicare and hospitalization to Canada, and it had been a tenet of its philosophy that medicare should be strengthened. However, Health Minister Louise Simard said money was no longer available and studies had shown Saskatchewan had too many hospitals and that a rationalization of services would not endanger patients. Simard also announced funding for all health-care facilities in the province would be cut by 5.5% in 1993.

Federal Election. The October 25 federal election saw Saskatchewan's 14 federal seats split almost evenly between the New Democratic, Liberal, and Reform parties, but at the expense of the Progressive Conservatives (PCs), who lost all four seats they had held. The Liberals, without any representation prior to the election, won five seats. The New Democrats lost five of the ten seats they had held before election day. The Reform Party won the other four.

Crime. Legal proceedings relating to charges of widespread sexual abuse in an unlicensed day-care babysitting center continued into a second year. The scandal, in the small town of Martensville, near Saskatoon, saw nine individuals charged with more than 100 offenses against 15 children over four years. Five of those charged were, or had been, local police officers. Publicity bans were imposed on the news media to protect the children involved and to ensure that all defendants received fair trials. The disclosures had shocked Canada, but many Canadians were equally shocked in 1993 to find that one of the defendants, a Saskatoon police corporal, had been charged wrongly and had run up legal bills of C$50,000 to prove his innocence. Justice Minister Robert Mitchell refused to launch an official inquiry into the mishap until all trials were concluded, probably in 1994.

Death. Former Lt.-Gov. Frederick William Johnson died in 1993 at age 76. Johnson had served as lieutenant-governor from 1983 to 1988.

PAUL JACKSON
"Saskatoon Star-Phoenix"

SAUDI ARABIA

Internal political reforms and the increasing expression of dissident opinions in 1993 marked a new Saudi Arabian governmental phase.

Political Affairs. In August 1993, King Fahd appointed 60 members to a consultative council that had been established by royal decree in 1992, while issuing detailed regulations concerning the council's operations and powers. The all-male council, headed by Justice Minister Mohamed Ibrahim Jubair, consisted of professors, other government employees, physicians, businessmen, retired military officers, journalists, and religious scholars. No princes served as members. The council was to meet at least once every two weeks.

Other reforms included the September royal decrees that outlined new arrangements for provincial governments and local consultative councils, and new rules for the Saudi cabinet. The king retained the prime ministry for himself, but other cabinet ministers would be limited in the future to four-year terms of office; previously there had not been such term limits. The cabinet was expanded to include ministers of state and advisers appointed by royal decree. Despite these steps taken toward greater political representation, King Fahd reacted sharply against Muslim religious groups and civil-rights organizers who objected to government policies. He dismissed several prominent clerics from government employment when they refused to condemn petitioners who asked for stricter religious regulations. The fundamentalist Muslim critics made their criticism known through clandestine audiotapes and speeches in mosques. The king publicly condemned these methods.

Another sign of opposition to the regime took place in May, when a small group of academics and lawyers formed the Committee for the Defense of Legitimate Rights. Senior clerics denounced this group, and the Saudi government soon outlawed it, fired from government posts persons who had belonged to it, and arrested its spokesman.

SAUDI ARABIA • Information Highlights

Official Name: Kingdom of Saudi Arabia.
Location: Arabian peninsula in southwest Asia.
Area: 750,965 sq mi (1 945 000 km²).
Population (mid-1993 est.): 17,500,000.
Capital (1981 est.): Riyadh, 1,000,000.
Government: *Head of state and government*, Fahd bin 'Abd al-'Aziz Al Sa'ud, king and prime minister (acceded June 1982).
Monetary Unit: Riyal (3.7510 riyals equal U.S.$1, Dec. 27, 1993).
Gross Domestic Product (1991 est. U.S.$): $104,000,000,000.
Economic Index (1992): *Consumer Prices* (1981 = 100), all items, 99.7; food, 111.1.
Foreign Trade (1990 U.S.$): *Imports,* $24,069,000,000; *exports,* $44,417,000,000.

Perhaps in reaction to these developments, the number of public executions grew rapidly. From May 1992 to May 1993, more than 100 persons were beheaded. Most of the victims had been convicted of murder or offenses related to drugs or alcohol; usually the trials took place without defense lawyers present. Amnesty International twice cited Saudi Arabia for violations of human rights. Interior Minister Prince Nayif rejected Amnesty International's comments as he maintained that justice in Saudi Arabia was based entirely on the holy law of Islam.

The Saudi government showed an unusually open attitude on one sensitive matter—the size of the population. It released the results of the national census in December 1992, which showed that more than one fourth of the kingdom's residents were foreigners and that the population-growth rate was about 3.5% per year.

International Relations and the Military. The ramifications of the 1991 war against Iraq continued to be felt by Saudi Arabia. As a means to help pay Iraq's international debts, the United Nations Security Council in October 1992 authorized Saudi Arabia to sell Iraqi oil held by the Saudis. And in January 1993, Saudi-based U.S., British, and French airplanes attacked Iraqi missile batteries. Saudi Arabia continued to support the UN sanctions against Iraq and the "no-fly" zones in northern and southern Iraq. Several countries, including the United States, admitted Iraqi refugees who had been sheltered in Saudi camps, but many remained on Saudi soil as the year began.

Saudi Arabia also was involved in other world crisis areas, including Bosnia, Somalia, Israel, and Iran. The kingdom in late 1992 provided money and diplomatic support to the Muslims of Bosnia and decided to send troops to Somalia as part of the UN-directed humanitarian-relief operation. By July 1993 more than 670 Saudi soldiers were in Somalia.

Tense relations with the Palestine Liberation Organization (PLO) were eased somewhat when Mahmud Abbas of the PLO's Executive Committee visited Riyadh in January. In April, Foreign Minister Prince Saud suggested that Saudi Arabia eventually would resume its financial support of the PLO. The Saudi Council of Ministers in September issued a statement backing the agreement between the PLO and Israel, while the United States looked to Saudi Arabia for economic aid to the Palestinians in the Gaza Strip and Jericho.

Again in 1993, as during several earlier pilgrimage seasons, Saudi authorities took severe measures designed to stop Iranian pilgrims from engaging in public political demonstrations in Mecca . . . . In August a Chinese vessel on its way to Iran was intercepted by the United States and escorted to Dammam, where Saudi inspectors searched the ship but did not find any lethal chemicals . . . . Close ties between the United States and Saudi Arabia were reinforced in August when

President Bill Clinton succeeded in persuading King Fahd to buy U.S. civilian airplanes worth more than $6 billion.

Economy and Oil. The extraordinary expenses resulting from the 1991 war with Iraq remained a burden to Saudi Arabia's treasury. In January the new budget was announced; it projected spending at about $52 billion and income of only about $45 billion, although the deficit was less than in 1991 and 1992. Foreign-currency reserves and the balance of trade had improved but still were weak.

Saudi revenue was tied to an oil-production quota authorized by the Organization of Petroleum Exporting Countries (OPEC), and as oil prices gradually declined through most of 1993, OPEC tried to reduce its worldwide production so as to increase prices, even though Saudi Arabia favored pumping more of its oil. By August, Saudi Arabia was producing about 8.3 million barrels of oil per day. At the September OPEC meeting, the kingdom agreed to limit production to 8 million barrels per day.

A major reorganization of the Saudi oil industry began on June 14 when the government-owned Arabian American Oil Company (ARAMCO) gained control of another government-affiliated business, Saudi Arabian Marketing and Refining Company (SAMAREC). The merger of these two units linked the world's largest oil-producing company with the third-largest oil refiner. Saudi Arabia became for the first time the largest producer of oil in the world, surpassing Russia in October 1992.

WILLIAM OCHSENWALD
Virginia Polytechnic Institute and State University

SINGAPORE

Singapore enjoyed a year of continued success in 1993, both in political and economic terms. Strong emphasis was placed on expanding the country's business and corporate enterprises into neighboring economies, particularly Vietnam and China. Singapore hosted the first-ever ASEAN (Association of Southeast Asian Nations) security conference—something that would not even have been contemplated two years earlier. The country elected a new president with greatly enhanced powers. And the World Economic Forum rated Singapore as one of the top newly industrialized countries (NICs) in the world.

Domestic Politics. On September 2, Ong Teng Cheong assumed the revamped and enhanced position of president after receiving 58.7% of the valid votes in an August 29 election. The election was important because it made it clear that the "old guard" of the People's Action Party (PAP) still had a firm hand on the state's tiller. Both the president-elect and his opponent, Accountant General Chua Kim Yeow, were establishment candidates. Ong Teng Cheong was a former deputy prime minister and PAP member. Two other individuals, J. B.

SINGAPORE • Information Highlights

Official Name: Republic of Singapore.
Location: Southeast Asia.
Area: 244 sq mi (632.6 km^2).
Population (mid-1993 est.): 2,800,000.
Capital: Singapore City.
Government: *Head of state*, Ong Teng Cheong, president (took office September 1993). *Head of government*, Goh Chok Tong, prime minister (took office November 1990). *Legislature* (unicameral)—Parliament.
Monetary Unit: Singapore dollar (1.5910 S. dollars equal U.S. $1, Dec. 27, 1993).
Gross Domestic Product (1991 est. U.S.$): $38,300,000,000.
Economic Index (1992): *Consumer Prices* (1980 = 100), all items, 132.2; food, 121.4.
Foreign Trade (1992 U.S.$): *Imports*, $72,216,000,000; *exports*, $63,516,000,000.

Jeyaretnum and Tan Soo Phuan—both Workers' Party members—had their candidacies rejected by the Presidential Election Committee. Jeyaretnum had been an outspoken opposition politician for many years.

The government also continued to limit the sale of offending foreign publications. The latest offender was *The Economist*, which did not print the full text of a government response to one of its articles. *The Economist* followed in the footsteps of *The Far Eastern Economic Review, Asiaweek, Asian Wall Street Journal*, and *Time*. In December two editors from a domestic financial newspaper, the *Business Times*, were put on trial for publishing a government economic forecast without permission.

Such episodes were in contrast to the government's November statement that it intended to develop a 100-channel cable TV system. Singapore wanted to challenge Hong Kong as the media center for the Southeast Asian region. Most satellite dishes already were controlled in Singapore. The seeming contradiction between the social and economic policies of the island ministate appeared unlikely to change soon.

Defense. Singapore, like most of its ASEAN neighbors, participated in the United Nations mission to Cambodia. Some 65 Singapore Armed Forces (SAF) personnel, along with a 75-man police contingent, helped monitor Cambodia's national elections. Singapore continued to work to modernize its defense forces both materially and in concept. The nation purchased nine countermeasure vessels from Sweden to protect its sea lines of communication. And the government announced a plan to integrate its air, land, and sea forces totally by the year 2000.

Singapore continued to raise its defense profile throughout the ASEAN region. In June 300 SAF personnel participated in a joint exercise with the Philippine Army. In July the SAF took part in a military exercise, Malapura VIII/93, with the Malaysian Navy. And in August the SAF joined the United States and Australian air

forces for Pitch Black/93, conducted in the latter's Northern Territory. Additional joint exercises were conducted with Thailand and Brunei.

Economy. Singapore's economy logged another outstanding performance in 1993. Gross domestic product (GDP) rose by 9.8% for the year, the largest increase since 1988. Unemployment and inflation were a low 2.5%. Growth in foreign trade approached 15%. The United States accounted for nearly 40% of the country's exports. The economic growth was spurred largely by the manufacturing and finance sectors.

The government continued its proactive policies to help the country's workers remain competitive. Steps to improve worker education and to encourage immigration of talent into the country were undertaken. The government also hoped to increase workers' stake in the economy (and to raise revenue) with a public offering of Singapore Telecom shares. A plan also was begun to sell Housing Development Board "shophouses" and hawker stalls to small entrepreneurs.

P. M. MAYERCHAK
Virginia Military Institute

SLOVAKIA

On Jan. 1, 1993, the Slovak Republic (Slovakia) was created, along with the Czech Republic, out of the partition of Czechoslovakia into two nations. Slovakia was carved out of the eastern portion of the former state.

Czechoslovakia had been caught in the torrent of ethnic rivalry that swept across Eastern Europe after the collapse of Communist rule. The split was cemented in the wake of national elections in June 1992. A deep rift about the pace of economic reform and the distribution of power between the federal and Slovak state government arose between the Civic Democratic Party, which was victorious in the Czech-inhabited portion of Czechoslovakia, and the Movement for Democratic Slovakia (HZDS), which won the election in Slovakia. Since neither side was willing to compromise, dissolution became inevitable.

Government. Slovakia's constitution, adopted on Sept. 1, 1992, created a parliamentary government. Its legislative body is the National

Council, with 150 members elected to four-year terms. Executive power is vested in the president of the republic, elected for five years by a three-fifths majority of the National Council, and in the prime minister and the council of ministers, who are appointed by the president. On Feb. 15, 1993, Michal Kovač was elected to be the first president of Slovakia, while Vladimír Mečiar, the leader of the HZDS, became the nation's first prime minister.

A constitutional court of ten judges, appointed by the president, was set up to ensure constitutionality. The regular judiciary consisted of courts staffed with judges elected by the National Council for four-year terms. They could be confirmed for life after serving three years. The constitution also included a bill of rights to guarantee the range of freedoms usually contained in Western democratic constitutions, and provided for exclusive state ownership of national resources, such as raw materials, underground water, and rivers.

Economy. A major Slovak argument for loosening ties with the Czechs was that Slovakia's economy was hurt badly by the "shock therapy" decided upon and carried out by Czechoslovakia's federal government. Thus many Slovaks expected that when the conduct of their affairs was fully in the hands of their own leaders, the situation would improve quickly. But this expected upturn did not occur.

In the first half of 1993, gross national product (GNP) fell by more than 6% from the first half of 1992. Unemployment and inflation continued to hover near 12%, the Slovak crown had to be devalued, and the state deficit topped $400 million. Foreign-currency reserves declined and a 20% tariff surcharge was imposed on imports. The privatization of state enterprises slowed, as only 50 industrial enterprises were scheduled to be privatized in the first half of 1993, compared with 633 in the first half of 1992. Although private-sector ownership in many sectors continued to grow in 1993, 73% of industrial enterprises and more than 50% of construction firms remained insolvent.

Growing Dissent. Widespread discontent with the economy began to grow and was bound to affect the country's politics. A poll conducted by the Slovak Statistical Office revealed that 51% of the respondents felt the splitting of Czechoslovakia had been a loss and only 32% "welcomed the separation." In another poll conducted by the Slovak Center of Social Analysis, 78% of respondents found the Slovak government to be incompetent. Prime Minister Mečiar came under increasing criticism, especially for his authoritarian tendencies. His candidate for the presidency, Roman Kovač, was rejected by the National Council, and bitter feuds developed within the HZDS. In June several opposition parties got together in an endeavor to bring about Mečiar's demise.

See also CZECH REPUBLIC.

EDWARD TABORSKY, *University of Texas, Austin*

SLOVAKIA • Information Highlights

Official Name: Slovak Republic.
Location: East-central Europe.
Area: 18,932 sq mi (49 035 km²).
Population (1991 census): 5,274,335.
Chief Cities (1991 census): Bratislava, the capital, 442,197; Kosice, 235,160.
Government: *Head of state*, Michal Kovač, president (took office February 1993). *Head of government*, Vladimír Mečiar, prime minister (took office February 1993). *Legislature* (unicameral)—National Council.
Monetary Unit: Koruna (crown) (32.84 koruna equal U.S.$1, Dec. 27, 1993).

SOCIAL WELFARE

The positive U.S. economic news in 1993—a soaring stock market and falling interest rates, inflation, and unemployment rates—did little to ameliorate the social conditions of the millions of Americans mired in poverty. Outside the United States, 1993 saw a wave of social upheaval brought on by ethnic wars in Europe, Africa, Asia, and the Middle East.

The United States

In the United States the annual Census Bureau survey of family income and poverty reported the highest number of Americans living below the poverty line in three decades. The report, released October 4, found that in 1992 some 36.9 million Americans—about 14.5% of the population—lived below the poverty line, defined as a total cash income of $14,335 for a family of four and $7,143 for a single person. The survey also reported that the nation's median household income was $30,786, nearly $2,000 less than in 1989.

The poverty rate for African Americans, the bureau reported, was 33.3%; for Hispanics, 29.3%; for Asian Americans, 12.5%; for whites, 11.6%; for children under 18, 21.9%; and for children under the age of 6, 25%. Nearly half of all black children under 18 were poor.

Presidential Proposals. President Bill Clinton had promised during the 1992 presidential campaign to change the nation's welfare system. As governor of Arkansas, Clinton had designed a state program to help welfare parents (90% of whom were single mothers) find work and get off welfare. During the campaign the president called for a $6 billion federal-tax credit and job-training program for welfare mothers.

The president reiterated a call to "end to welfare as we know it" in a February address to the National Governors Association. "No one likes the welfare system as it currently exists, least of all the people who are on it," Clinton said. "The taxpayers, the social service employees themselves don't think much of it either. Most people on welfare are yearning for another alternative, aching for the chance to move from dependence to dignity. And we owe it to them to give them that chance."

The president proposed expanding education and training programs for the some 4.5 million families who receive Aid to Families with Dependent Children, the largest federal welfare program. He also promised to expand health insurance and child-care programs, to give tax credits to the working poor, and to crack down on fathers who do not pay child support. The president also called for the institution of a two-year cap on benefits after welfare recipients have completed job-training programs.

President Clinton formed the 22-member Working Group on Welfare Reform, Family Support, and Independence in June to draw up the specifics for a new law that would include his welfare proposals. The group was charged with making its recommendations to the president by the end of 1993. Analysts predicted that the recommendations would be controversial. A new welfare law with Clinton's proposals "will inevitably provoke an acrimonious national debate," said Richard P. Nathan, director of the Rockefeller Institute of Government and the author of a recent book on welfare reform.

Indications of Poverty. A series of reports issued throughout the year painted a dark picture of the state of the nation's social welfare. In New York City officials reported, for example, that the number of city residents receiving welfare had risen to nearly 1.1 million, an increase of some 273,000 in four years. The U.S. Department of Agriculture reported in September that some 27 million Americans in nearly 11 million households—more than 10% of the population—received food stamps, an increase of more than 1.7 million food-stamp recipients from March 1992.

Throughout 1993 the national unemployment rate continued to fall after reaching a high of 7.8% in June 1992. The national unemployment rate was 6.7% in September 1993, according to the U.S. Labor Department. Unemployment rates for August had been significantly higher in populous states such as California (9.0%), Illinois (7.6%), and New Jersey (7.1%). The department also reported that in 1993 1.7 million Americans had been unemployed and looking for work for six months or more and that 1.1 million people had dropped out of the labor force. (*See also* LABOR.)

Poverty and its attendant social ills among blacks and Hispanics remained a large problem. The 18th annual "State of Black America"

As it became apparent that many U.S. children have not been immunized properly, Southern Baptist medical missionaries took to the streets of Philadelphia to administer such vaccinations.

© Stephen Fiorella/Gamma-Liaison

report by the National Urban League, released in January, characterized life among the nation's inner-city blacks as "desperate." The report cited an unemployment rate of 25% and a poverty rate of 50% among urban African-Americans, and a large disparity in the national median family incomes of blacks ($21,548) and whites ($37,783). The nation must address "the jobs deficit, the health-care deficit, the education deficit," Urban League President John Jacob said.

A report issued July 7 by the government's National Center for Health Statistics reported that in 1986, death rates for low-income Americans were significantly higher than the death rates of the nation's more affluent people. Among lower-income black men, the report said, the death rate was 30% higher than the rate for lower-income white men. "The gap between the mortality rate for blacks and the rate for whites has widened over the last ten years," said Dr. Gregory Pappas, an epidemiologist who conducted the study.

The U.S. Health and Human Services Department, in a September report, found that the mortality rate in 1991 among black infants was double that of whites—a rate of 17.6 deaths per 1,000 live births for blacks versus a 7.3 rate per 1,000 births for whites. The report also found that in 1992 32% of Hispanics and 21% of blacks had no health insurance, compared with 11% of whites. Overall, about 37 million Americans did not have health insurance.

The Census Bureau reported in September that although the number of blacks earning college degrees rose in the last decade, blacks with college degrees received significantly lower pay than white college graduates in many jobs. The annual median salary for black college graduates in 1992, the bureau said, was $30,910, compared to $37,490 for whites. Black high-school graduates had a median salary of $18,620, compared with $22,370 for white high-school graduates.

The nation's 22 million Hispanics compose about 9% of the population, but account for 18% of all Americans living in poverty, the Census Bureau reported August 23. That data, based on 1992 statistics, also showed that Hispanic men had median incomes that were about one third less than those of non-Hispanic whites; that nearly half of all Hispanics living in poverty were under age 18; and that Hispanic children accounted for 21.5% of all American children living in poverty, yet made up only 12% of the nation's child population.

The Disabled. In 1990 the landmark Americans With Disabilities Act (ADA) for the first time prohibited private employers from denying jobs to the nation's 43 million physically and mentally disabled persons. That groundbreaking law also gave protection to the disabled from discrimination in public accommodations, transportation, and telecommunications. Regulations implementing the law's major provisions went into effect July 26, 1992, and by the spring of 1993 advocates for the disabled were reporting some of the implications of the law's sweeping changes.

The United Cerebral Palsy Association reported that 76% of the businesses it surveyed had taken steps to comply with the law. Most of the businesses, however, would not reveal the actual measures they said they took. "A lot of companies are sitting back and waiting to see whether [the Department of Justice is] willing to enforce the law," said Pat Wright, chief lobbyist for the Disability Rights Education and Defense Fund. "The make-or-break success of ADA rests on this administration, and I think they realize that."

The National Council on Disability, an independent federal agency, reported in July that some 13,000 discrimination complaints had been filed with the federal agencies—including the U.S. Equal Employment Opportunity Commission and the Justice Department—that monitor the law's compliance. Most complaints, about 48%, were from employees who claimed they were discharged wrongly from work because of their disabilities. About 22% of the complaints were claims that businesses did not make reasonable accommodations for disabled workers, and 13% were from prospective employees who believed they were prevented from getting a job because of their disability.

The U.S. Department of Health and Human Service's National Center of Child Abuse and Neglect issued a study in October that found disabled children were neglected and abused about 1.7 times more often than other children. In about half the cases a child's disability caused the problem. "Children are vulnerable, but children with disabilities are the most vulnerable," said Sen. Christopher J. Dodd (D-CT), who sponsored the law requiring the study. The report showed the "tremendous economic and social pressures that are crushing" many families with disabled children, Senator Dodd said.

International Social Crises

The serious social problems of the United States were dwarfed in 1993 by those faced by hundreds of millions of people in other countries. International media coverage focused on ongoing social turmoil in Somalia, Bosnia, and Croatia.

In Somalia an unprecedented humanitarian-relief effort, aided by U.S. and United Nations military forces, ended a famine that had killed some 100,000 Somalis. But outside intervention did not end anarchy in the capital city of Mogadishu, as a continuing civil war was waged by Somali clan chiefs.

Fierce fighting with many civilian casualties continued in 1993 among Bosnians, Croatians, Serbs, and Muslims in the former nation of Yugoslavia. Other nationalist wars caused extreme hardship for untold millions in dozens of other countries around the world. "The defining mode of conflict in the year ahead is ethnic con-

A steady growth in the urban population of Third World nations has led to a corresponding increase in social problems. This slum in São Paulo, Brazil, left, is but one example of such urban blight.

© Anthony Suau/Gamma-Liaison

flict," Sen. Daniel Patrick Moynihan (D-NY) said early in the year. "It promises to be savage. Get ready for 50 new countries in the world in the next 50 years. Most of them will be born in bloodshed."

A survey published February 7 in *The New York Times* listed 48 countries in which ethnic clashes were causing widespread social upheaval, including large numbers of deaths, serious injuries, severe economic problems, and widespread social dislocation. The survey cited nine nations in Europe, seven in the Middle East and North Africa, 15 in southern Africa, 13 in Asia, and four in Latin America.

Conditions were especially difficult on the Horn of Africa in southern Sudan. The cause was the ongoing ten-year-old war between the nation's Arab Muslim government in Khartoum and the rebelling Sudan People's Liberation Army, made up of black Christians and animists. Millions of Sudanese have been displaced by the fighting, and hundreds of thousands suffered from famine and disease as warring factions continued to block relief supplies and food. Southern Sudan is "the most silent of the major humanitarian crises in the world today," said Jim Kunder, head of the U.S. Agency for International Development's office of foreign-disaster assistance.

A severe drought in Brazil, South America's largest country, complicated the nation's most intractable social problem—the recent migration of millions of poor people to the burgeoning cities of Rio de Janeiro and São Paulo. Tens of thousands of residents of the nine drought-affect-ed states fled to cities in 1993 where they lived with millions of others in rudimentary shantytowns or on the streets, facing extreme poverty, rampant crime, and virtually uncontrolled pollution.

Globally, the movement of tens of millions of people from rural areas to cities, to flee civil unrest and social disintegration, "could become the human crisis of our age," the United Nations Population Fund said in its annual "State of the World Population" report released July 6. The report estimated that 100 million people were living outside their native countries in 1991. The report counted some 35 million refugees in sub-Saharan Africa, as well as some 15 million each in Western Europe, North America, Asia, and the Middle East.

The world's worst refugee problem, the report said, was the movement every year of 20 million to 30 million of "the world's poorest people" from rural to urban areas in Third World nations. About half these immigrants, the report said, were women, many of whom were single parents. Female refugees, the report noted, were more likely to suffer "downward mobility" in their new urban environs than males. (*See also* REFUGEES AND IMMIGRATION.)

On a positive note, one of the century's most severe droughts ended in southern Africa. The rains began in late 1992 and continued through the 1993 rainy reason, ending a drought that threatened the welfare of 120 million people.

MARK LEEPSON
Freelance Writer

SOMALIA

Although the U.S. military forces that were deployed in Somalia in 1992 were replaced by United Nations (UN) troops in 1993, the country remained adrift in a state of virtual anarchy. Unable to agree on military or political goals, individual nations whose troops were under the authority of the UN openly quarreled with the position of UN Secretary-General Boutros Boutros-Ghali. Gen. Mohammed Farah Aidid, a major Somali warlord, confronted and battled with the United States and the UN, forcing both to capitulate.

United Nations Intervention. By the end of 1992, approximately 22,000 U.S. troops and 10,000 troops from other nations were sent to Somalia on a mission to feed the millions of people who were in danger of starvation. On May 4, 1993, the United States withdrew the bulk of its troops and handed over control of food relief to the UN. Deeming the relief operation a success, the United States indicated that this second phase of the military operation would deal with political and economic reconstruction. In the year preceding May 1993, almost 500,000 people died of starvation and civil war. But with the relief operation being successful and famine having ebbed to a trickle, the UN moved to take control of the country's reconstruction.

The UN action in Somalia was the first time the international organization had taken upon itself the role of constituting a new government in a country which had none. By the end of 1993 more than 32,000 UN troops were stationed in the country and offshore. Italy, Pakistan, France, India, and the United States (with 17,500 troops) provided the largest contingents of troops. Other countries that volunteered armed forces included Saudi Arabia, Germany, Kuwait, Canada, Belgium, and Australia.

United Nations Disunity. Disarray within the UN military operation began to arise almost immediately. In June, General Aidid organized an attack which killed 24 Pakistani troops. Aidid had initiated a strategy of opposing UN intervention militarily and fighting against UN troops, maintaining that the UN and the United States were attempting to recolonize Somalia. In response to these heightened aggressions, UN troops went on the offensive to seek out Aidid and his followers.

© Caratim/Sygma

U.S. pilot Michael Durant, who had been captured after his helicopter was shot down by supporters of Somalia warlord General Aidid in late September 1993, was freed in mid-October.

© S. Peterson/Gamma-Liaison

The STARS and STRIPES

U.S. copter pilot freed

Durant reportedly in pain but in good spirits

Phone changes brew confusion

2 airmen discharged, 5 rebuked for salute to Klan

SOMALIA • Information Highlights

Official Name: Somali Democratic Republic.
Location: Eastern Africa.
Area: 471,776 sq mi (637 660 km²).
Population (mid-1993 est.): 9,500,000.
Chief City (1984 est.): Mogadishu, the capital, 600,000.
Government: No functioning government as of December 1993.
Monetary Unit: Shilling (3,800 shillings equal U.S. $1, December 1990).

Italy maintained that the UN command did not comprehend the culture of Somalia and was complicating the nation's political problems. Italy also accused the United States of dictating the military operation in Somalia. In July, Italy threatened to recall its 2,600-member contingent, claiming that the relief mission had turned into a combat operation against Aidid. In response, the United Nations demoted the Italian UN commander in Somalia. Many observers, however, felt that some of Italy's criticism of the operation was correct.

The United States refused to place its 1,600 Rapid Response forces under the control of the United Nations. Its contingent, in opposition to Italian demands for negotiating with Aidid, engaged in a policy of disarming Somalis, destroying arms depots, and seeking to capture Aidid and his followers (many of whom were arrested). Hundreds of Somali civilians and military personnel were killed by U.S. troops.

In early October, Aidid struck back. In fierce fighting in Mogadishu, 18 U.S. troops were killed, scores wounded, and one captured (who soon was released). The confrontation also left at least 300 Somalis dead and hundreds more injured. Public opinion in the United States, repulsed by television images of dead U.S. soldiers being dragged through Mogadishu streets, demanded that Washington rethink its policy in Somalia. By the end of the year at least 35 U.S. troops and one U.S. civilian were among the UN casualties.

UN and U.S. Policies Revised. In September the UN Security Council had voted to set March 1995 as the date for ending peacekeeping operations in Somalia and handing over responsibility for the country to an elected government. It also voted to hold General Aidid responsible for criminal acts, and continued to seek his arrest. The UN also agreed to organize a national police force and to reorganize the judicial system. In moving to promote reconciliation among the warring clans, the UN indicated that it would not continue in Somalia without establishing an exit date.

As U.S. forces continued to face sustained attack by Aidid's supporters, pressure in the United States against continuing the military operations in Somalia grew markedly, particularly after the October killings. In response, U.S. President Bill Clinton announced on October 7 that the United States would withdraw virtually all of its military forces by March 31, 1994, and immediately would halt its search-and-destroy operation against Aidid. Clinton also reported that additional U.S. forces would be sent to Somalia to protect U.S. troops.

Instead of continuing to confront Aidid's forces, the United States enlarged its political goals with these announcements. The new policy attempted to bring the warring factions inside Somalia together in an effort to resolve the various disputes that had flared since 1991. In December 1993 the various Somali factions met in Addis Ababa, Ethiopia—with Aidid being flown there on a U.S. military transport—but they were unable to resolve their differences. Some observers believed that Aidid would try to hold out until March 1994, after which there would be far fewer constraints on his continuing struggle to gain power over Somalia. Indeed, after Clinton's announcement in October, the nations of Norway, France, Italy, Belgium, and Sweden announced that they would withdraw their troops from Somalia by March 1994. And in November the UN announced that its forces would be reduced to roughly 11,000 by March 31, 1994.

The Role of the U.S. Congress. Demonstrating the restiveness of the U.S. public over the growing involvement in Somalia, the U.S. Senate and House of Representatives passed resolutions in September demanding that the Clinton administration limit its Somalia mission or face the cutoff of funds. Congress indicated its outrage over Somalis killing U.S. soldiers and parading their bodies while the troops were there trying to feed Somalis. The nonbinding resolutions called on the president to seek congressional authorization by Nov. 15, 1993 to continue the deployment of troops in Somalia.

Clinton's October 7 announcement was, in part, a recognition of Congress' role in articulating the U.S. public's fury at events that had gotten out of control in Somalia. The U.S. and UN roles were still in conflict, however, as the United States moved to curtail its involvement sharply, while the UN moved to continue in Somalia, though in reduced circumstances, until 1995.

The Future. Until March 1994—the planned pullout date for most U.S. forces in Somalia—the U.S. mission was primarily to defend its troops and to attempt to broker a political settlement. The UN was largely impotent since Aidid had rejected its role, and because Somalis saw the organization as a failure. Multiple Somali factions, particularly those led by Mohamed Ali Mahdi, appeared unlikely to allow Aidid to reach his goal unimpeded. Thus, after March 1994, unless political reconciliation could be achieved, civil strife and its consequences were likely to reemerge in Somalia.

See also UNITED NATIONS.

PETER SCHWAB
State University of New York at Purchase

SOUTH AFRICA

South Africa remained a country of extreme contradictions in 1993. Although all apartheid legislation was repealed, little or nothing had changed for the majority of the population living in townships or rural slums. A postapartheid democracy seemed possible for the first time and yet a significant minority of right-wing white extremists were stockpiling arms for the race war that they assumed would occur eventually. Negotiations were proceeding toward the country's first truly nonracial democratic election in early 1994, but the level of violence continued unabated. Black political leader Chris Hani was assassinated, there were continuing hostilities between the forces of the Zulu Inkatha Freedom Party (IFP) and those of the African National Congress (ANC), and violent urban crime rose.

The Nobel Prize Committee awarded the 1993 Peace Prize to ANC leader Nelson Mandela and President F. W. de Klerk. The committee recognized their great political courage and said, "their constructive policy of peace and reconciliation also points the way to the peaceful resolution of similar deep-rooted conflicts elsewhere in the world."

The year also saw the lifting of sanctions imposed by the United Nations (UN) and others, but whether or not many foreign investors would return to South Africa remained unclear because of violence, economic uncertainty, and the fact that sanctions were not repealed yet from statutes in more than 100 municipalities and 27 states in the United States.

Constitutional Settlement. At the end of June a compromise was reported between the National Party (NP) government and the ANC at multiparty negotiations taking place in Johannesburg. The participants set April 27, 1994, as the date for South Africa's first democratic nonracial election. On July 25, 1993, hundreds of armed white extremists reacted to this settlement by storming Johannesburg's World Trade Center, the site of the constitutional negotiations, smashing through the front of the building in an armored truck. The dramatic two-hour intervention resembled a military operation, as the extremists disrupted the negotiations and held the peace process hostage.

In September, by a vote of 107 to 36 in the white House of Assembly and subsequently by unanimous votes in the Indian and so-called Colored parliaments, the government agreed to share power with a multiparty Transitional Executive Committee (TEC) in the months leading up to the election.

The TEC consisted of 32 members, including one representative from every major political party, and was given the power to override the government on all major issues affecting the election. The TEC reflected the composition of the multiparty forum where negotiations had been taking place and where each of the many

Several black townships erupted in violence following the assassination of Chris Hani, general secretary of South Africa's Communist Party, on April 10, 1993. Some 80,000 mourners later assembled in a Soweto soccer stadium for Hani's funeral.

© Patrick Robert/Sygma

parties had equal weight. The character of decision making in South Africa was expected to be altered fundamentally because most of the TEC members would be black. There would be one seat each for the ANC, the National Party, the Communist Party, and each of the homelands.

At the same time, negotiators completed work on an interim constitution which was ratified by a special session of Parliament in November. During this transition period, the army, the police, the budget, and the bureaucracy would be monitored by specialized subcouncils and the TEC would be empowered to organize a new peacekeeping force which combined the police force and army with former guerrilla fighters. Those monitoring the police, the army, and intelligence would require 75% majorities for decision-making, while those dealing with finance or local government would operate on a two-thirds majority. The TEC also planned to monitor government expenditures and to supervise state television and radio.

Not all political forces in the country accepted the formation of the TEC or the constitutional process it was supposed to implement. An unexpected alliance emerged to challenge the TEC and press for a federal system of government. Fearing a loss of influence, Zulu Chief Mangosuthu Buthelezi of the Inkatha Freedom Party and the homeland leaders of Ciskei and Bophuthatswana joined with extreme right-wing whites of the separatist Conservative Party and the Afrikaner VolksFront (AVF) to form the Freedom Alliance—which rejected the constitution, threatened to boycott the 1994 election, and sought a political solution which would entrench strong regional powers.

On November 18, President de Klerk, Nelson Mandela, and 18 other leaders agreed to an interim constitution which would become the foundation to govern South Africa until a final constitution could be written. The IFP and a number of the white separatist groups did not participate in the final meeting, but de Klerk and Mandela still hoped that they would agree to take part in the April 1994 election in which all South Africans would cast a single ballot for the party of their choice. However, both de Klerk and Mandela were quick to affirm that force would be used if necessary to prevent opponents from disrupting the elections. In warning them, Mandela added that "you are welcome in this country but democracy has no place for talk of civil war."

The new parliament was designed to consist of a 400-member Assembly elected by proportional party representation and a 90-member Senate elected by nine provincial legislatures. The participants also agreed that after the election the homelands would be abolished and those forcibly displaced by apartheid would have the right to claim restitution for their lost land or property. Many whites were concerned that some 3.5 million people would be eligible to claim such restitution.

SOUTH AFRICA • Information highlights

Official Name: Republic of South Africa.
Location: Southern tip of Africa.
Area: 471,444 sq mi (1 221 040 km²).
Population (mid-1993 est.): 39,000,000.
Chief Cities (1985 census, city proper): Pretoria, the administrative capital, 443,059; Cape Town, the legislative capital, 776,617; Durban, 634,301; Johannesburg, 632,369.
Government: *Head of state and government,* Frederik W. de Klerk, state president (took office Sept. 1989). *Legislature*—Parliament (tricameral): House of Assembly, House of Representatives (Colored), and House of Delegates (Indians).
Monetary Unit: Rand (3.3750 rands equal U.S. $1, Dec. 14, 1993).
Gross Domestic Product (1991 est. U.S.$): $104,000,000,000.
Economic Index (1992): *Consumer Prices* (1980 = 100), all items, 514.9; food, 621.6.
Foreign Trade (1992 U.S.$): *Imports,* $18,236,000,000; *exports,* excluding exports of gold, $22,073,000,000.

The elected parliament was given the authority to write the new permanent constitution and to make laws. All parties with at least 5% of voter support would be entitled to have a seat in the 27-member cabinet. A final concession made by de Klerk was to remove a mandated two-thirds majority for key decisions by the cabinet. The final document only required the president to consult the cabinet in "a consensus-seeking spirit." The winning party in the so-called government of national unity thus would have more power than de Klerk had hoped. The leader of the winning party, most likely the ANC, would become president of the country.

The proposed government of national unity faced a debate over the terms of a final constitution and a justiciable Bill of Rights. An impartial commission would present the president with a list from which he would name an 11-member constitutional court which would have the power to interpret the interim constitution. South Africa would be divided into nine new provinces, each of which would have its own police force and wide additional powers. The provinces would select the members of the Senate.

Lifting of Sanctions. Two weeks after the South African Parliament prepared the groundwork for the April 1994 election, the UN General Assembly lifted economic sanctions against South Africa. In advocating this move, Nelson Mandela stated, "the countdown to democracy in South Africa has begun." Mandela asked, however, that the arms and oil embargo remain until after the new government was elected. He also called on the UN Security Council to assist with measures to ensure "free and fair" elections.

Continuing Violence. While nearly 11,000 persons were killed in the three years since the constitutional process began, individual acts of violence throughout 1993 continued to shock even South Africans hardened to random violence.

On April 10, Chris Hani, general secretary of the South African Communist Party (SACP) and a member of the National Executive Committee of the ANC, was shot and killed outside of his house in Boksberg, Transvaal. He allegedly was shot by Januzu Jakub Walus, a naturalized white South African citizen who had emigrated from Poland. Hani was a former chief of staff of the ANC's armed wing, The Spear of the Nation, and once was regarded by the South African security forces as "Public Enemy Number 1." In recent years, while Hani was committed deeply to constitutional negotiations and worked closely with Nelson Mandela to bring about peaceful change, he nevertheless remained also a very popular figure among young black militants.

In an effort to defuse the tension that was building throughout the country among the many thousands of people who supported the charismatic Hani, the ANC organized a week-long campaign of mass protest and memorial services. Despite the intensity of feelings involved and the vast crowds that attended Hani's funeral, South Africa remained relatively peaceful. On April 21 it became clear that Walus was not alone in the assassination plot. Clive Derby-Lewis, a leading member of the Conservative Party, and his Australian-born wife Gaye subsequently were arrested. Derby-Lewis, a member of a number of anticommunist organizations, had connections to Walus through the Stallard Foundation, an extreme right-wing group with a large number of East European émigré members.

In October, Derby-Lewis and Walus were sentenced to death for the assassination of Hani. It appeared unlikely, however, that the death sentences would be carried out because there had been a moratorium on executions since 1990. Limpho Hani, the widow of Chris Hani, said that justice had been incomplete since all the "plotters" were not in court. Gaye Derby-Lewis was acquitted of charges of murder and subsequently appeared as a heroine at an emotional right-wing rally in Pretoria.

On July 25, 11 persons were killed and 52 were injured when five blacks hurled grenades during a church service in St. James Anglican Church in the Cape Town suburb of Kenilworth.

In August, Amy Biehl, a Fulbright scholar from California, was stabbed and beaten to death by black youths while driving three black friends home to the township of Guguletu near Cape Town. Police arrested two teenagers who were members of the Pan-Africanist Students' Organization (PASO). While members of the organization had used the confrontational slogan "one settler, one bullet," some observers saw the unfortunate killing in a larger context of the alienation and frustration of young blacks in the townships.

Early in October the South African army sent a unit to Umtata, capital of the Transkei, and raided the house of Pan Africanist Congress militant Siggibo Mpendulo. He was murdered along with his three sons, ranging in age from 12 to 19,

as well as friends who were there at the time. There was speculation initially over whether or not the raid was authorized by the military without the knowledge of high-ranking members of the government. However, in a subsequent statement, President de Klerk acknowledged that the government had authorized the raid.

Nelson Mandela, the ANC, and other black leaders condemned the murders, especially since de Klerk was a recipient of the 1993 Nobel Peace Prize along with Mandela for negotiating the end of apartheid and the beginning of nonracial democracy. The human-rights organization Amnesty International, while recognizing the significance of the award, said that "it is important not to overlook the simple fact that political violence and human-rights violations persist on a massive scale in South Africa."

Economy. The lifting of sanctions—by the UN, the European Community, and the Commonwealth—and the promise of a new constitutional arrangement greatly increased the chances for an improvement in South Africa's economic conditions, especially since the nation also would become eligible for support from the International Monetary Fund (IMF) and the World Bank. If a new government could contain the violence and the ANC were to reject nationalization, foreign investors were expected to be more likely to return. There was significant interest from many international companies in reinvesting in South Africa. Great interest was shown in a number of investment conferences organized during the year and several companies made plans to return. On his trips abroad, Nelson Mandela made efforts to assure investors that their investments would be safe from government expropriation and that they would be able to repatriate dividends and profits. He also promised that in the future, tax incentives would be provided to facilitate investments. The rate of inflation dropped throughout the year and was forecast to fall to about 6% in 1994, a significant decline from 20% in 1986.

Winnie Mandela. In June, South Africa's highest appeals court upheld the conviction of Winnie Mandela for the 1988 kidnapping of four young blacks but rejected the five-year jail term imposed by a lower court in favor of a fine, compensation to the victims, and a suspended sentence.

Oliver Tambo Dies. On April 24, Oliver Tambo, national chairman of the ANC, died of a stroke in a Johannesburg hospital. The 75-year-old Tambo had been president of the ANC for more than 30 years. When the ANC was banned in 1960, Tambo became its leader in exile. He returned to South Africa in 1990 after Nelson Mandela was released from prison and the ANC was unbanned. Mandela succeeded Tambo as president of the organization in July 1991 when he became national chairman.

N. BRIAN WINCHESTER
and PATRICK O'MEARA
Indiana University

SOUTH CAROLINA

The year 1993 saw South Carolina adopt a major reorganization of state government, the state legislature struggle to pass a balanced budget, and a federal court order that called for legislative and congressional reapportionment.

Government Restructuring. The 1992 deadlock between the Democratic legislature and Republican Gov. Carroll Campbell over Campbell's proposal to reorganize state government under a cabinet system was broken in 1993, largely because key leaders of the House of Representatives joined the forces for reform with their own restructuring proposal. Reorganization was opposed bitterly by state agencies and allied interests, with legislative opposition concentrated in the Senate. Ultimately, a House-Senate conference committee agreed on a compromise that was acceptable to Governor Campbell, who signed the bill into law in June.

The law consolidates a total of 75 separate state agencies into 17, reducing the total number of autonomous state agencies from 145 to 87. The governor was given direct control over 11 cabinet departments, including social services, corrections, revenue and taxation, and a new commerce department consisting of several formerly independent economic-development agencies. The new cabinet significantly increased the administrative powers of the governor and reduced the state's reliance on independent boards and commissions.

Several major agencies of state government were left outside the governor's cabinet, including the Department of Highways and Public Transportation, which long had been criticized as a repository of scandal, legislative pork-barreling, and bureaucratic arrogance. The agency was reorganized into a new Department of Transportation, with a seven-member governing board. The Department of Health and Environ-

© AP/Wide World

Kimberly Clarice Aiken (right), Miss South Carolina, was crowned Miss America at Atlantic City, NJ, on Sept. 19, 1993. She received the scepter from Leanza Cornett, Miss America 1992.

mental Control also would continue to be governed by a citizen board chosen by the governor.

A component of the reorganization was its provision for six administrative-law judges, elected by the legislature, who would hear appeals from decisions of state licensing boards, the Department of Revenue and Taxation, and the Department of Health and Environmental Control.

Thirty-four governing boards remained in place, as did the separate boards of trustees of South Carolina's ten institutions of higher education. With minor exceptions the departments headed by South Carolina's eight statewide elected officials were unaffected.

Economy and Budget. As the end of 1993 approached, unemployment stood at 6.9%. Yet the economic outlook took on a rather gloomy cast as the federal government announced the closing of the Charleston naval base and shipyard. Those shutdowns may take up to 30,000 jobs out of the economy. Tourism, however, continued to grow in the coastal counties, and continued upstate economic vitality was signaled by the construction of a new BMW automobile plant near Spartanburg.

The General Assembly passed a $3.7 billion budget that contained only $130 million in estimated revenue growth. Legislators rejected all proposals for tax or fee increases.

Redistricting and Politics. The U.S. Supreme Court threw out the congressional and legislative districting plan implemented for the 1992 elections. A federal judicial panel gave the General

---

SOUTH CAROLINA • Information Highlights

Area: 31,113 sq mi (80 582 km²).
Population (July 1, 1992 est.): 3,603,000.
Chief Cities (1990 census): Columbia, the capital, 98,052; Charleston, 80,414; North Charleston, 70,218.
Government (1993): *Chief Officers*—governor, Carroll A. Campbell, Jr. (R); lt. gov., Nick A. Theodore (D). *General Assembly*—Senate, 46 members; House of Representatives, 124 members.
State Finances (fiscal year 1991): *Revenue,* $9,413,000,000; *expenditure,* $8,970,000,000.
Personal Income (1992): $58,362,000,000; per capita, $16,197.
Labor Force (August 1993): *Civilian labor force,* 1,817,200; *unemployed,* 130,400 (7.2% of total force).
Education: *Enrollment* (fall 1991)—public elementary schools, 456,039; public secondary, 171,431; colleges and universities, 164,907. *Public school expenditures* (1990-91), $2,493,524,000.

Assembly until April 1994 to draw new districts that provide more representation for South Carolina's African-American minority in Congress and the state House of Representatives.

Political maneuvering began for the 1994 gubernatorial race. Early favorites for the post among the Democrats were Charleston Mayor Joseph Riley, Jr., and Lt.-Gov. Nick A. Theodore, and among the Republicans, U.S. Rep. Arthur Ravenel and former state House Speaker Pro Tem David Beasley.

GLEN T. BROACH
Winthrop University

SOUTH DAKOTA

Weather, prison troubles and the death of the governor highlighted 1993 in South Dakota.

Flood Damage. The Great Flood of '93 was one of the worst natural disasters in South Dakota's history. Seven persons lost their lives in the state due to the floods; damage to such crops as corn, soybeans, wheat, oats, and alfalfa was estimated at $725.7 million; and more than 900 homes were damaged. South Dakotans and residents of eight other states would share in a $6.2 billion federal flood-relief package, including $2.35 billion in payments to farmers to make up for crop losses. The U.S. Army Corps of Engineers suggested a $30 million project to protect Sioux Falls and other Big Sioux River valley communities from future disasters. (*See also* FEATURE ARTICLE, page 44.)

A September frost also diminished the state's agricultural production. In sum, more than $1 billion was lost because of climatic conditions in the state in 1993.

Politics. Following the death of Gov. George Mickelson (R) in an April 19 plane crash in Dubuque, IA, Lt.-Gov. Walter D. Miller, a legislator and rancher from western South Dakota, became governor. He chose Sioux Falls businessman Steve Kirby to finish the term as lieutenant governor. The Miller-Kirby ticket led in polls against other possible candidates for the 1994 gubernatorial election. Former Republican Gov. William Janklow announced his interest in running again for the governorship. Democrats Les Herseth, who lost to Mickelson by a small margin in 1986; Ted Muenster, architect of state governmental reorganization during Richard Kneip's administration; former U.S. Sen. James Abourezk; and Dakota Wesleyan University president Jim Beddow all expressed interest in becoming gubernatorial candidates.

Legislation and the Economy. State legislators appropriated $1.6 billion for fiscal 1994. Nearly 21% of the appropriations was allocated for social services. Higher education, pre-college education and cultural affairs, transportation, and human services received 17.2%, 16.5%, 15.5%, and 7.2%, respectively. Legislators established a ten-member committee to study governmental relations with Indian tribes and passed legislation regulating abortions, perpetuating a moratorium on nursing-home construction, and authorizing local governments to create solid-waste-disposal districts. The legislature also authorized nickel video-lottery machines and increased the state's share of machine-lottery income by 1%. Voters in September, however, defeated a referendum increasing betting limits from $5 to $100 at the state's casinos.

In 1992 sales taxes produced $279 million and video-lottery proceeds totaled $48.8 million. Excise taxes on motor fuel, cigarettes, contract construction, and vehicular purchases accounted for most of the state's additional revenue. South Dakota imposed the lowest state and local tax burdens in the region, at 0.92% of income. Moderate economic growth was evident in a 6.5% increase in average annual income among the state's residents and in a state unemployment rate of 3.1%.

Indian Affairs. The addition of a casino at Crow Creek to four already in operation at other reservations brought steady improvement in tribal economies. Attorneys continued their defense of tribal jurisdiction against state encroachment through litigation in federal courts.

Prison Conditions. Inmates rioted against crowded conditions at a maximum-security prison in Sioux Falls on May 5-6. Designed for 440 prisoners, the facility was housing some 540. The rioters injured guards while presenting 17 demands for change in prison management, health-care delivery, parole procedure, and personal treatment. The cost of repairs at the prison was expected to reach $6.8 million. Corrections Secretary Lynne DeLano, a former superintendent at state correctional facilities in Yankton and Springfield, changed administration and procedure at both the penitentiary in Sioux Falls and the medium-security prison in Springfield. More than 500 inmates at the Yankton minimum-security prison observed the disturbance without incident.

HERBERT T. HOOVER
University of South Dakota

SOUTH DAKOTA • Information Highlights

Area: 77,116 sq mi (199 730 km²).

Population (July 1, 1992 est.): 711,000.

Chief Cities (1990 census): Pierre, the capital, 12,906; Sioux Falls, 100,814; Rapid City, 54,523.

Government (1993): *Chief Officers*—governor, Walter D. Miller (R); lt. gov., Steve Kirby (R). *Legislature*—Senate, 35 members; House of Representatives, 70 members.

State Finances (fiscal year 1991): *Revenue*, $1,597,000,000; *expenditure*, $1,417,000,000.

Personal Income (1992): $12,147,000,000; per capita, $17,081.

Labor Force (August 1993): *Civilian labor force*, 370,900; *unemployed*, 10,000 (2.7% of total force).

Education: *Enrollment* (fall 1991)—public elementary schools, 96,423; public secondary, 35,153; colleges and universities, 36,332. *Public school expenditures* (1990-91), $481,304,000.

SPACE EXPLORATION

During 1993 the world's spacefaring nations orbited numerous satellites for communications, navigation, and Earth-scanning purposes. Remote-sensing spacecraft were used increasingly to monitor such disasters as floods. Previously launched space-borne astronomical instruments continued to reap exciting observations, and the space shuttle *Endeavour* completed a spectacular repair of the Hubble Space Telescope. Several failures also plagued the U.S. space program, including the loss of the Mars Observer spacecraft. And U.S. plans for a permanent space station were altered significantly in 1993 (*see* SIDEBAR).

Shuttle Program. Seven U.S. shuttle flights took place during 1993, although technical snags led to four launch aborts seconds before liftoff.

The five-person crew of space shuttle *Endeavour* STS-54 (January 13-19) deployed the Tracking and Data Relay Satellite-6. During the mission the crew maneuvered the shuttle orbiter to study so-called soft X-ray diffuse background radiation within the Milky Way Galaxy. Life-science and materials-science experiments also were carried out. Astronauts also conducted space walks to evaluate techniques for future space-station construction.

The five-person crew, which included the first Hispanic woman to fly in space, on the shuttle *Discovery* STS-56 mission (April 8-17) operated the Atmospheric Laboratory for Application and Science 2 (ATLAS 2), a set of instruments to measure Earth's ozone layer and solar infrared radiation passing through the stratosphere. The Spartan 201 satellite was released from the orbiter's cargo bay and later retrieved by the crew. It focused its instruments on holes and streamers in the Sun's corona, allowing scientists to deduce their effect on the speed and strength of the solar wind.

Columbia's STS-55 mission (April 26-May 6) carried the long-delayed Spacelab D-2 as a primary payload. The seven-person crew included two German payload specialists who performed experiments in materials science, biology, space technology, Earth observations, and astronomy. Germany paid the National Aeronautics and Space Administration (NASA) $150 million to be involved in the mission and to use the special Spacelab module carried in *Columbia*'s cargo hold. A Biolabor facility measured the effects of microgravity on perch, tadpoles, and plants. Other experiments studied how the heart and body fluids cope with space microgravity. A German-built robot arm was tested in the cargo bay.

A six-person team flew ten days (June 21-July 1) aboard shuttle *Endeavour* on its STS-57 flight. The mission marked the debut of Spacehab, a privately built and owned pressurized module designed to stimulate commercial experimentation in space. Additional studies included a fuel-transfer experiment, a crystal-growth experiment to develop more powerful lasers, and several smaller payloads called Getaway Special experiments. The crew also used the shuttle's robotic arm to pluck from space the European Retrievable Satellite (EURECA), which had been released from the shuttle *Atlantis* in August 1992. Balky antennas on EURECA forced an earlier-than-planned space walk by two astronauts, who secured the antennas and then simulated servicing tasks required for the Hubble Space Telescope repair mission.

The *Discovery*'s STS-51 mission (September 12-22) deployed the Advanced Communications Technology Satellite (ACTS) and the Orbiting

© Johnson Space Center

Spacewalking astronauts F. Story Musgrave (top) and Jeffrey Hoffman performed delicate repairs to the Hubble Space Telescope on Dec. 9, 1993. The space shuttle "Endeavour"'s STS-61 mission corrected the defective optics of the telescope and upgraded the onboard computer processors.

and Retrievable Far and Extreme Ultraviolet Spectrometer-Shuttle Pallet Satellite (ORFEUS-SPAS). The mission had been delayed for some two months by two aborted launch attempts and by a meteor shower. Once in orbit, the five-person crew sent the ACTS on its way, pushed into geosynchronous orbit by an attached Transfer Orbit Stage (TOS). The experimental ACTS was sponsored by NASA to explore communications technologies and uses of the "Ka-band" (30/20 gigahertz) of the electromagnetic spectrum. *Discovery*'s robotic arm dropped off Germany's ORFEUS-SPAS, which carried two ultraviolet telescopes to observe hot, young stars and the 1-billion-degree hot gas bubble that surrounds the solar system to some 600 light-years distance. The German spacecraft later was snared from space and returned to the shuttle cargo bay. Two spacewalking astronauts spent seven hours evaluating tools and foot restraints to prepare for the Hubble Space Telescope repair mission.

Columbia's 14-day STS-58 mission (October 18-November 1) set a record for the longest shuttle flight to date. The cargo hold carried a pressurized module packed with medical experiments designated as the Spacelab Life Sciences flight (SLS-2). The seven-person crew ran extensive medical tests on themselves to study the changes in the cardiovascular system of the human body during microgravity. Use of echocardiographs allowed the astronauts to image their own hearts to study changes caused by exposure to weightlessness. Musculoskeletal and neuro-vestibular experiments also were carried out to augment the medical database regarding long-term spaceflight and its impact on human body functions.

The last shuttle mission of 1993 was the heralded repair of the out-of-focus Hubble Space Telescope. Its primary mirror flawed by improper manufacturing, the orbiting telescope required special corrective optics to realize its powerful observing potential. *Endeavour*'s STS-61 mission (December 2-13) was central to fixing Hubble's blurry condition. Five space walks by two teams of astronauts, a new record for the shuttle program, rejuvenated the telescope after it was grappled in orbit and then positioned in the shuttle cargo bay for servicing. Hundreds of

The Search for a U.S. Space Station

The planned U.S. space station was much in the news in 1993. The U.S. quest to house astronauts in a permanently orbiting research facility above Earth had begun in earnest in January 1984, when President Ronald Reagan committed the nation to build a space station "within a decade." The complex later was christened the space station *Freedom*, to be built in partnership with European nations, Canada, and Japan.

However, the plan has been embroiled in controversy over its funding and scientific utility since it was announced. Proponents have argued that the space station would be the next logical evolution of the U.S. human exploration program and could serve as a long-term research post where important research could be initiated. Opponents have contended that funds allocated for the station would cripple other, more beneficial, areas of space-science exploration.

Driven by the escalating cost of building the initially proposed station—a total cost of more than $30 billion—Congress mandated restructuring the effort. This directive meant reducing the station's crew, the available electrical power, and the size of the station. The changes also pushed back the expected completion date.

Shortly after taking office in 1993, President Bill Clinton determined that the proposed space station still was unaffordable in light of budget constraints. He directed NASA and an independent advisory committee to redesign the station—the fifth restructuring of the space station since 1984. A sweeping assessment of the program was pursued by NASA Administrator Daniel Goldin, resulting in a design called space station *Alpha,* which could be operational in 2003 with a cost tagged at $19 billion. In June an attempt to kill the project was blocked by one vote in the House of Representatives.

Further deliberations among the White House, NASA, and Russia in 1993 opened the door to involving Russia in the international project. In mid-December, U.S. Vice-President Al Gore and Russia's Prime Minister Viktor Chernomyrdin signed an agreement to augment U.S.-Russian space cooperation. The deal included the United States paying Russia $400 million over four years in exchange for up to ten NASA space-shuttle flights to the currently orbiting *Mir* space station. The agreement would give U.S. astronauts a total of 24 months time onboard *Mir*. A review also was initiated to explore the use of Russian space hardware to begin developing the world's first spaceport in 1997, a 200-ton laboratory for a six-person crew. Use of Russian space hardware and expertise was expected to save $2 billion in building expenses.

The multinational space station was slated to be completed in 2001. It would fly the flags of the United States, Russia, France, Japan, Canada, Belgium, Denmark, Germany, Italy, Norway, Great Britain, the Netherlands, and Spain.

LEONARD DAVID

hours of ground simulations and previous shuttle flights permitted the nearly trouble-free maintenance of the huge space-borne telescope. The telescope's gyroscope packages and their electronic control units were replaced and Hubble was outfitted with two new solar wings, a wide-field planetary camera, two magnetometers, and a corrective optics space telescope axial replacement (COSTAR) unit that would focus the light from celestial targets to compensate for Hubble's incorrectly shaped mirror. The space-walking "astro-mechanics" upgraded Hubble's computers to process data more rapidly. The astronauts spent more than 35 hours in space working on the $3 billion orbiting observatory.

First assessments of the overall health of the Hubble following the mission were positive, although first images from the overhauled telescope would not be available until early 1994. NASA's image was strengthened by the apparently successful repair and adjustment of the Hubble Space Telescope in order to allow the facility to fulfill its intended research objectives.

Space Station. Russia's *Mir* space station hosted many cosmonauts during 1993. In January cosmonauts Gennady Manakov and Alexander Poleshchuk replaced Anatoliy Solovyev and Sergey Avdeyev, who had lived in space for five months. A replacement crew of Vasily Tsibliev, Alexander Serebrov, and French researcher Jean-Pierre Haignere arrived at *Mir* in July. Haignere soon returned to Earth with Manakov and Poleshchuk, while the two other crew members remained onboard through year's end. Among the experiments carried out during 1993 by *Mir* cosmonauts was the deployment of a large solar reflector. On February 3-4 a resupply ship undocked from *Mir,* later unfurling a large reflecting disc designed to study the potential of reflecting light on dark areas of Earth.

Space Science. The loss of the U.S. Mars Observer placed a damper on what was otherwise a banner year for scientific revelations. As the first U.S. Mars mission in 17 years, the failure of the Mars Observer to reach the planet stunned space scientists. On August 21, just three days before the probe was to enter orbit around Mars, contact with the craft was lost. One possible failure scenario was that the spacecraft was lost when a fuel line ruptured during a tank-pressurizing procedure. Attempts to reacquire signals from the space probe proved unsuccessful. The lost Observer was viewed as a major setback for the planetary sciences.

Despite its blurred vision, the Hubble Space Telescope peered deep into space to image the collision of two galaxies and the apparent star clusters that were born of the cosmological crash. Hubble observations also supported the theory that a class of active galaxies are fueled by a massive black hole at their center. Astronomers said in July that the Hubble discovered a complex "double nucleus" in the center of M31, a spiral galaxy located in the constellation Andromeda.

© NASA/Johnson Space Center

German payload specialists Ulrich Walter (foreground) and Hans Schlegel ran a battery of tests inside the cargo hold of space shuttle "Columbia" during the spring 1993 STS-55 mission.

Hubble also provided a detailed view of comet fragments hurtling toward a July 1994 impact with the planet Jupiter.

On February 20, Japan's Institute of Space and Astronautical Science (ISAS) boosted into orbit Astro-D, a cooperative X-ray astronomy mission which NASA designed to help scientists understand the physics of a variety of cosmic sources, such as neutron stars, black holes, supernova remnants, and clusters of galaxies.

In March and April a joint endeavor between NASA and the European Space Agency (ESA) attempted to detect, without success, the existence of gravity waves. Three interplanetary spacecraft—the U.S. Mars Observer, the Jupiter-bound Galileo spacecraft, and ESA's Ulysses probe en route to the Sun—were used simultaneously in the radio-science experiment.

In March, NASA's International Ultraviolet Explorer (IUE), lofted in January 1978, recorded the first direct evidence that red supergiants—the largest stars known—end their existence in massive explosions known as supernovae. The IUE focused its instruments on a supernova 12 million light-years away, which had been discovered earlier in 1993 within a galaxy known as M81 in the Ursa Major constellation.

NASA's Compton Gamma-Ray Observatory, shuttle-deployed in 1991, chalked up impressive discoveries in 1993, including the first map of the whole sky in gamma-ray energies. In April the Earth-circling probe observed that mysterious gamma-ray bursts may be more energetic than previously thought and appear to originate far beyond the Milky Way galaxy. In August it was announced that the probe had discovered a powerful X-ray pulsar in the southern constellation Carina. In October, Compton Gamma-Ray detectors spotted titanium 44 and aluminum 26 emissions called gamma-ray lines, linked to

Photographed from the space shuttle "Discovery," the Spartan 201 satellite was released and then retrieved by astronauts during the STS-56 mission in April 1993. It collected data on the Sun's corona for astronomy experiments.

supernova remnants. The detections will enable scientists to unmask hidden supernovae that may be buried deep within the Milky Way. Late in 1993 the satellite reboosted itself to a higher orbit, prolonging its scientific usefulness.

In May, NASA scientists proclaimed that a new radiation belt of cosmic rays around Earth had been pinpointed by the Solar, Anomalous and Magnetospheric Particle Explorer (SAMPEX). The belt was most intense above a 5,000-mi (8 050-km) strip of Atlantic Ocean between the southern tips of South America and Africa.

The U.S. Magellan radar-mapping Venus probe became the first spacecraft to complete a set of fuel-saving "aerobraking" maneuvers around a planet. The Magellan craft skimmed through the top of the thick Venusian atmosphere to change its orbit. From its new orbit, Magellan began high-resolution gravity mapping of the mid- and high-latitude regions of Venus and its poles.

Also in May the Voyager 1 and 2 spacecraft discovered the first direct evidence of the long-sought-after heliopause, the boundary that separates Earth's solar system from interstellar space. The two interplanetary probes have been in space since their separate launchings in 1977.

Making its way to Jupiter for a 1995 rendezvous, the Galileo spacecraft snapped highly detailed images of asteroid Ida in August.

Applications Satellites. Several nations used satellites to monitor the Earth's environment, including charting weather, plotting possible changes in climate, and other applications.

SCD-1, the first Brazilian-built satellite, was rocketed into orbit on February 9 with a Pegasus booster supplied by a private U.S. firm. The small satellite would collect environmental data from numerous ground stations over an expanse of Brazil, such as the valued rain forest.

An Ariane booster launched from Kourou, French Guiana, placed the SPOT-3 Earth-observation satellite into orbit on September 25. France's SPOT series of commercial remote-sensing spacecraft proved useful, along with several U.S. and European satellites, in monitoring flood conditions in the Midwestern United States during 1993. On September 20, India's IRS-1E Earth-observing satellite was boosted spaceward by the Indian Space Research Organization's Polar Satellite Launch Vehicle to monitor flooding in India, but the satellite fell into the sea off Sri Lanka after a stage on the rocket failed.

The U.S. Landsat-6 remote-sensing satellite, lofted on October 5 from Vandenberg Air Force Base in California, also fell to the sea after its kick motor failed to fire. Yet another failure involved a U.S. weather satellite. Blasted into orbit with an Atlas-E rocket on August 9, the National Oceanic and Atmospheric Administration's NOAA-13 fell silent on August 21 due to a power failure aboard the meteorological craft.

China failed to deorbit a recoverable satellite on October 16 after eight days of flight. A one-ton section of the out-of-control satellite crashed to Earth, while another one-ton segment was destined to fall from space in 1994.

Communications Satellites. The building and launching of telecommunication satellites continued to be the most marketable of space businesses. France's Arianespace achieved seven Ariane liftoffs in 1993, placing ten separate satellites into orbit. Ariane boosters launched communications satellites into space for Luxembourg, the United States, Spain, India, and for Thailand's first telecommunications satellite.

U.S. commercial-launcher operators faced mixed reviews in 1993. An Atlas 1 booster stranded a Navy communications satellite in the wrong orbit March 25, but successfully orbited a similar satellite into space on September 3. An Atlas 2 booster rocketed a Defense Satellite Communications System satellite into geosynchronous orbit on November 28. On December 15 the premier flight of an Atlas 2AS rocket powered a telecommunications satellite into orbit. Delta 2 boosters were used to maintain a Global Positioning System—a network of navigation-aiding satellites. The Delta 2 rocket also hurled a military-communications satellite into space for the North Atlantic Treaty Organization (NATO).

While strapped for cash, Russia orbited Gorizont and Molniya satellites for communications purposes and Global Space Navigation System (GLONASS) spacecraft for navigation needs.

LEONARD DAVID
Space Data Resources & Information

SPAIN

Facing political and economic problems in 1993, Spain's Prime Minister Felipe Márquez González and his Socialist Party (PSOE) made a strong showing in parliamentary elections.

Politics. Corruption continued to plague the PSOE. In March government auditors confirmed that two senior party officials sold nonexistent consultancy services to important national companies and banks, and received an estimated $8.5 million in payments that subsequently were funneled to the PSOE. In an attempt to unite a factional party, González moved the legislative elections from November to June. The election announcement followed a PSOE executive-committee meeting called to hammer out differences between two factions: González and the party's secretary-general, supported by conservative cabinet members; and Deputy Secretary General Alfonso Guerra, backed by unions and other leftists.

The Socialists' campaign survived intraparty discord, corruption charges, and a currency devaluation just before the campaign started. The main opposition, the conservative People's Party (PP), claimed that the PSOE's "leftist agenda" was outmoded. The Socialists countered by stressing their experience and the PP's association with late dictator Francisco Franco.

The Socialists diffused some criticism by inviting Judge Baltasar Garzón, a well-known corruption fighter, to run as a PSOE legislative candidate. PP leader José Maria Aznar's failure to offer clear policy alternatives also helped the PSOE. Aznar hoped to benefit from the disintegration of the Democratic and Social Center Party and to win over urban and young voters.

Aznar's inability to exploit PSOE weaknesses enabled the Socialists to triumph. González' party emerged from the June 6 balloting with 39% of the vote and 159 seats in the 350-member Cortés, down from 175 seats. The People's Party captured 35% of the vote and raised its total to 141 seats. The Communist-led United Left coalition held onto its 18 seats. The Catalán nationalist Convergence and Union (CiU) collected 17 seats and the Basque Nationalist Party won its usual five seats.

The outcome left the Socialists without a majority and the option either to form a minority government or forge a coalition with one of the leading regional parties. The fiscal policies of the CiU made the party the leading contender for the PSOE's coalition partner.

After attaining an electoral plurality, the PSOE remained divided. The nomination of Carlos Solchaga, a free-market economist, as party spokesman alienated Guerra's liberal supporters. For the first time since winning power in 1982, the PSOE faced the challenge to court opposition support on some key issues.

Economy. The economy failed to grow in 1993. In February the government unveiled

---

SPAIN • Information Highlights

Official Name: Kingdom of Spain.
Location: Iberian Peninsula in southwestern Europe.
Area: 194,884 sq mi (504 750 km²).
Population (mid-1993 est.): 39,100,000.
Chief Cities (March 1991 est.): Madrid, the capital, 3,010,492; Barcelona, 1,643,542; Valencia, 752,909.
Government: *Head of state,* Juan Carlos I, king (took office Nov. 1975). *Head of government,* Felipe González Márquez, prime minister (took office Dec. 1982). *Legislature*—Cortés Generales: Senate and Congress of Deputies.
Monetary Unit: Peseta (135.75 pesetas equal U.S.$1, Nov. 10, 1993).
Gross Domestic Product (1991 est. U.S.$): $487,500,000,000.
Economic Indexes: *Consumer Prices* (1992, 1980 = 100), all items, 273.4; food, 264.4. *Industrial Production* (1991, 1980 = 100), 119.
Foreign Trade (1992 U.S.$): *Imports,* $99,766,000,000; *exports,* $64,329,000,000.

---

measures designed to create jobs and spur investment. González stated that Spain would continue its economic alignment with the European Community (EC), leave the peseta in the Exchange Rate Mechanism (ERM), create a "social pact" between employers and unions to hold down wage increases, and eventually cut tax rates. The PSOE managed to sell off $1.6 billion worth of public assets, cut unemployment entitlements, and stop indexing civil-service pay. Joblessness stood at 23%, the highest in three years. In addition, the peseta was devalued three times in the twelve months after September 1992. The European Commission estimated that investment fell 5.4%. Still, the government was able to reduce inflation to 4.5%, down from 5.3% in 1992.

In October the government presented the 1994 budget, which Economics Minister Pedro Solbes described as "compassionate, austere, and reactivating." It followed negotiations on the social contract with Basque and Catalán nationalists whose votes were needed to pass the initiative. The government predicted a gross-domestic-product (GDP) growth rate of 1.3% in 1994 and hoped to lower inflation to 3.5%. The "compassionate" part of the budget embraced pensions, unemployment benefits, and health care. The "austerity" portion involved cutting government outlays and freezing public-employee salaries. The state also would increase public-debt interest payments by 14%.

Foreign Affairs. Both González and Foreign Minister Javier Solana expressed support for Russian President Boris Yeltsin. Meanwhile, Solana stated that aid to Equatorial Guinea would continue with assistance conditioned on the country's making progress toward democracy.

In September, French Prime Minister Edouard Balladur met with González to discuss trade and other issues.

GEORGE W. GRAYSON
College of William and Mary

SPORTS

© Tasso Taraboulsi/Saba

© Jason Reed/Reuters/Bettmann

© Yann Guichaqua/Vandystadt/Allsport

Overview

Politics, violence, and other controversy cast an unmistakable shadow onto the world of sports during 1993.

In September the International Olympic Committee awarded Sydney, Australia, the Summer Olympic Games for the year 2000, surprising many observers who anticipated that Beijing, China, would get the nod. Much of the dialogue that accompanied the decision—which delighted residents of the "Land Down Under" (photos above)—focused on China's fast-growing economy and questionable human-rights record.

Violence jumped onto center court as tennis star Monica Seles was the victim of a knife-wielding attacker in April at a minor tournament in Hamburg, Germany. Seles was stabbed in the back by an overzealous fan of another top player (photo, page 489, top right). Although Seles was not injured critically, the physical and psychological damage from the attack kept her from competitive play for the rest of 1993. This unfortunate incident raised questions regarding security for the participants at sporting events everywhere.

And violence seemed to turn its ugly head around the sports globe in 1993. Riots ensued out of victory celebrations in Chicago, Dallas,

© Ralf-Finn Hestoft/Saba

© Claus Bergman/Conti Press/Sipa

and Montreal. Meanwhile, disorder continued to plague the stands of international soccer competition in the elimination rounds for the World Cup. And in addition to the now-familiar hockey fight, sports spectators were witness to innumerable—and more intense—melees on baseball and football fields and on the pro-basketball courts as well.

Fighting for the spotlight among these distractions was the sporting action itself. Repeat championship performances were logged as the Chicago Bulls won a third straight National Basketball Association (NBA) title and as baseball's Toronto Blue Jays took the World Series. Spanish cyclist Miguel Indurain also returned to the winners' circle, snaring his third consecutive Tour de France *(photo, page 488),* while Jeff King won the 1,161-mi (1 868-km) Iditarod Trail Sled Dog Race in record time. Britain's Colin Jackson was just one of the track stars who set a major new mark—12.91 seconds in the 110-m hurdles *(below).*

Steffi Graf won three Grand Slam singles titles in tennis, while the Number 1 men's player, Pete Sampras, took two of the big singles crowns. In the National Hockey League (NHL), the Montreal Canadiens won the Stanley Cup over the Wayne Gretzky-led Los Angeles Kings. The North Carolina Tar Heels won the NCAA basketball championship. And in the most heralded fight of the year, welterweight Julio César Cháves battled Pernell Whitaker to a draw in a bout that most observers felt Whitaker won handily.

Player retirements, particularly a surprise announcement by Michael Jordan of the Chicago Bulls *(above left),* sparked big headlines.

PETER A. FLAX

© Wolfgang Rattay/Reuters/Bettmann

Auto Racing

France's Alain Prost captured his fourth Formula One championship in 1993 by winning seven races. He then retired at age 38, ending a 13-year career marked by 51 Grand Prix wins. Prost's 1993 performance topped Ayrton Senna of Brazil, who posted five Formula One victories.

Nigel Mansell of Great Britain, the 1992 Formula One champion, made a dramatic switch to IndyCar racing, winning five races to capture the IndyCar PPG Cup championship. He became the first racer to win Formula One and IndyCar titles in consecutive years. In his first year on oval tracks, Mansell won four straight races and became the first driver in IndyCar racing's 82-year history to win both the pole and the race in his debut in Australia.

However, inexperience may have cost Mansell the Indianapolis 500 when his unfamiliarity with restarts aided Emerson Fittipaldi's second Indianapolis victory. Fittipaldi, a two-time world champion, slipped past Mansell on a restart with 16 laps to go, and Fittipaldi won by 2.9 seconds over Arie Luyendyk as Mansell finished third.

Winston Cup racing lost two leading drivers in 1993. Defending series champion Alan Kulwicki, 38, was killed in an airplane crash April 1 near Bristol, TN. Davey Allison, 32, died in a helicopter crash on July 13 at Talladega, AL.

The Winston Cup championship was not settled until the final race of the season, the Hooters 500 at Hampton, GA, where Dale Earnhardt clinched his sixth title—one short of Richard

Petty's record. Rusty Wallace took ten races but could not overcome an early-season lead mounted by Earnhardt. Dale Jarrett edged Earnhardt to win the Daytona 500, stock-car racing's premier event.

The Indianapolis Motor Speedway, where no race other than the Indianapolis 500 had been run since 1911, announced plans to hold a Winston Cup 400-mi (644-km) race in 1994.

STAN SUTTON
"Louisville Courier-Journal"

AUTO RACING

Major Race Winners, 1993

Indianapolis 500: Emerson Fittipaldi, United States
Marlboro 500: Nigel Mansell, Great Britain
Daytona 500: Dale Jarrett, United States

1993 Champions

World Championship: Alain Prost, France
IndyCar: Nigel Mansell, Great Britain
NASCAR: Dale Earnhardt, United States

Grand Prix for Formula One Cars, 1993

South African: Alain Prost, France
Brazilian: Ayrton Senna, Brazil
European: Senna
San Marino: Prost
Spanish: Prost
Monaco: Senna
Canadian: Prost
French: Prost
British: Prost
German: Prost
Hungarian: Damon Hill, Great Britain
Belgian: Hill
Italian: Hill
Portuguese: Michael Schumacher, Germany
Japanese: Senna
Australian: Senna

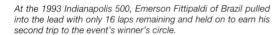

At the 1993 Indianapolis 500, Emerson Fittipaldi of Brazil pulled into the lead with only 16 laps remaining and held on to earn his second trip to the event's winner's circle.

© Reuters/Bettmann

© AP/Wide World

Baseball

The 1993 baseball season was marked by tight division races, an explosive increase in hitting and scoring, and record attendance. The year was also the last time that the leagues would play under the two-division format that had prevailed since 1969. Baseball owners and players approved a plan—intended to raise revenue—that split each league into three divisions, with the three winners and a "wild card" (the second-place team with the best record) to meet in a new play-off system.

Play-offs and World Series. Three of the four leaders at the 1993 All-Star break—the Toronto Blue Jays, Chicago White Sox, and the Philadelphia Phillies—eventually brought home divisional titles, while the Atlanta Braves needed a tremendous second-half surge to win the National League (NL) West. At midseason only two games separated the top five teams in the American League (AL) West, while the fifth-place team in the AL East was only three games behind. A 13-2 September spurt enabled Toronto to clinch first a week before the White Sox wrapped up the AL West. Chicago's eight-game margin of victory helped second-year manager Gene Lamont win AL manager of the year honors from the Baseball Writers Association of America.

Philadelphia opened the season with a 45-17 mark but cooled to permit an unsuccessful late drive by the Montreal Expos. Though the Phillies squandered a June lead of 11 games, the team finished three games ahead of Montreal to become the third team to go from last place to first in one year. In the West the San Francisco Giants could not outlast the Braves. Atlanta overcame San Francisco's ten-game lead of July 22 and took a four-game lead with 16 games to play. The Giants went 13-2 before losing on the last day of the season as the Braves won—the first time a title was decided on the season's final day since 1982. The Giants finished with the most wins (103) of any NL team not in postseason play since 1942, but could not match Atlanta's 54-19 finish—the third-best second-half record in baseball history. The trigger for Atlanta's turnaround was the July 20 arrival of first baseman Fred McGriff. The pitching-rich Braves had ranked last in batting without McGriff but first after he arrived from San Diego.

Although Atlanta was favored heavily to win the play-offs, McGriff and the Braves could not take the National League Championship Series (NLCS). The Phillies took a 4-3, ten-inning victory in the October 6 opener at Philadelphia, then lost consecutive 14-3 and 9-4 verdicts. In Game 4 on October 10, an error by the Braves Mark Lemke allowed two unearned runs—enough for Phillies pitcher Danny Jackson to secure a 2-1 victory over formerly unbeaten postseason hero John Smoltz. Atlanta bats remained silent until the ninth inning of Game 5, but a game-tying, three-run rally fell short when

© AP/Wide World

The outstanding play of center fielder Lenny Dykstra in 1993 helped carry the Philadelphia Phillies from last place to first in one year—and into the World Series.

Lenny Dykstra homered in the tenth for another 4-3 Phils victory. Back in Philadelphia for Game 6 on October 13, Tommy Greene rebounded from a poor Game 2 performance to outpitch Atlanta's Greg Maddux, 6-3, and put the Phils into the World Series. Though he had no decision in the series, Philadelphia starter Curt Schilling won play-off most-valuable-player (MVP) honors.

Toronto's third straight American League Championship Series (ALCS) appearance had a good start when the Jays took the first two games on the enemy turf of Chicago's Comiskey Park. Paul Molitor, whose 4-for-5 performance led a 17-hit Toronto barrage in the opener, had six straight hits, an ALCS record, over the two games. Under Toronto's SkyDome, however, the White Sox tied the series by beating the Jays, 6-1 and 7-4, led by a complete game by Wilson Alvarez in Game 3. In the pivotal fifth game on October 10, Toronto made quick work of ace Chicago starter Jack McDowell for the second time. Roberto Alomar's three-hit, three-steal performance helped Juan Guzman win his second game of the series, 5-3. The Jays' Dave Stewart was even better the next day, however, with a 6-3 win that boosted his career ALCS record to 8-0 and gave Toronto the right to play in the World Series. Stewart, who compiled a 2.03 earned run average (ERA) against the White Sox, won play-off MVP honors for the second time in five years.

© Focus on Sports

World Series MVP Paul Molitor turned in a strong hitting performance—a .500 batting average, six extra-base hits, and eight RBIs—to lead Toronto to a repeat championship.

Professional—Major Leagues
Final Standings, 1993
AMERICAN LEAGUE

Eastern Division	W	L	Pct.	Western Division	W	L	Pct
Toronto	95	67	.586	Chicago	94	68	.580
New York	88	74	.543	Texas	86	76	.531
Baltimore	85	77	.525	Kansas City	84	78	.519
Detroit	85	77	.525	Seattle	82	80	.506
Boston	80	82	.494	California	71	91	.438
Cleveland	76	86	.469	Minnesota	71	91	.438
Milwaukee	69	93	.426	Oakland	68	94	.420

NATIONAL LEAGUE

Eastern Division	W	L	Pct.	Western Division	W	L	Pct.
Philadelphia	97	65	.599	Atlanta	104	58	.642
Montreal	94	68	.580	San Francisco	103	59	.636
St. Louis	87	75	.537	Houston	85	77	.525
Chicago	84	78	.519	Los Angeles	81	81	.500
Pittsburgh	75	87	.463	Cincinnati	73	89	.451
Florida	64	98	.395	Colorado	67	95	.414
New York	59	103	.364	San Diego	61	101	.377

Play-offs—American League: Toronto defeated Chicago, 4 games to 2; National League: Philadelphia defeated Atlanta, 4 games to 2.

World Series—Toronto defeated Philadelphia, 4 games to 2. First Game (Skydome, Toronto, Atlanta, Oct. 16, attendance 52,011): Toronto 8, Philadelphia 5; Second Game (Skydome, Oct. 17, attendance 52,062): Philadelphia 6, Toronto 4; Third Game (Veteran's Stadium, Philadelphia, Oct. 19, attendance 62,689): Toronto 10, Philadelphia 3; Fourth Game (Veteran's Stadium, Oct. 20, attendance 62,731): Toronto 15, Philadelphia 14; Fifth Game (Veteran's Stadium, Oct. 21, attendance 62,706): Philadelphia 2, Toronto 0; Sixth Game (Skydome, Oct. 23, attendance 52,195): Toronto 8, Philadelphia 6.

All-Star Game (Camden Yards, Baltimore, July 13, attendance 48,147): American League 9, National League 3.

Most Valuable Players—American League: Frank Thomas, Chicago; National League: Barry Bonds, San Francisco.

Cy Young Memorial Awards (outstanding pitchers)—American League: Jack McDowell, Chicago; National League: Greg Maddux, Atlanta.

Managers of the Year—American League: Gene Lamont, Chicago; National League: Dusty Baker, San Francisco.

Rookies of the Year—American League: Tim Salmon, California; National League: Mike Piazza, Los Angeles.

Leading Hitters—(Percentage) American League: John Olerud, Toronto, .363; National League: Andres Galarraga, Colorado, .370. (Runs Batted In) American League: Albert Belle, Cleveland, 129; National League: Barry Bonds, San Francisco, 123. (Home Runs) American League: Juan Gonzalez, Texas, 46; National League: Bonds, 46. (Hits) American League: Paul Molitor, Toronto, 211; National League: Lenny Dykstra, Philadelphia, 194. (Runs) American League: Rafael Palmeiro, Texas, 124; National League: Dykstra, 143. (Slugging Percentage) American League: Gonzalez, .632; National League: Bonds, .677.

Leading Pitchers—(Earned Run Average) American League: Kevin Appier, Kansas City, 2.56; National League: Greg Maddux, Atlanta, 2.36. (Victories) American League: Jack McDowell, Chicago, 22; National League: Tom Glavine, Atlanta, and John Burkett, San Francisco, 22. (Strikeouts) American League: Randy Johnson, Seattle, 308; National League: Jose Rijo, Cincinnati, 227. (Shutouts) American League: McDowell, 4; National League: Pete Harnisch, Houston, 4. (Saves) American League: Jeff Montgomery, Kansas City, and Duane Ward, Toronto, 45; National League: Randy Myers, Chicago, 53. (Innings) American League: Cal Eldred, Milwaukee, 258.0; National League, Maddux, 267.0.

Professional—Minor Leagues, Class AAA

American Association: Iowa
International League: Charlotte
Pacific Coast League: Tuscon

Amateur

NCAA: Louisiana State University
Little League World Series: Long Beach, California

Toronto won the 90th World Series in six games—the first team with consecutive titles since the 1977-78 New York Yankees. Toronto took Game 1 at home on October 16, 8-5, using power to overcome three deficits. The Phils rebounded with a 6-4 win in Game 2, but the Jays then won successive 10-3 and 15-14 contests in Philadelphia. The 29-run total of Game 4 made it the highest-scoring postseason game in baseball history. One night later, however, Schilling silenced Toronto's attack with a complete-game, 2-0 shutout to make up for his Game 1 loss and send the series back to Toronto for Game 6 on October 23. Philadelphia closer Mitch Williams, who lost Game 4, again failed to hold a late-inning lead. Given a 6-5 lead in the ninth inning, he gave up a crushing Joe Carter three-run homer—only the second to end a World Series. Paul Molitor, a 37-year-old designated hitter (DH) in his first year with the Blue Jays after 15 years with the Milwaukee Brewers, was named MVP. His 12 hits and six extra-base hits tied records for a six-game World Series.

Regular Season. Shortly after spring training began, baseball had been tinged by a tragic boating accident in which Cleveland pitchers Steve Olin and Tim Crews were killed and Bob Ojeda was sidelined until August. Within weeks, however, this sorrow was superseded by the euphoria of expansion as the Colorado Rockies and Florida Marlins joined the major leagues. With pitching diluted by expansion, 1993 was a hitters' year.

Early in the season, two unlikely players—John Olerud (Blue Jays) and Andres Galarraga (Rockies)—flirted with .400 averages, a mark untouched since Ted Williams hit .406 in 1941. Both cooled but managed to win batting titles. Galarraga hit .370, while Olerud finished at .363

and led both leagues with a .473 on-base percentage and a 26-game hitting streak. The Blue Jays became the first team in the 20th century to take the top three individual batting spots when Paul Molitor and Roberto Alomar finished second and third.

The year's top one-game performance came from Mark Whiten of the St. Louis Cardinals on September 7. He became the 12th player to hit four home runs in a game and tied the single-game mark of 12 runs batted in (RBIs). Meanwhile, Ken Griffey, Jr., of the Seattle Mariners slammed home runs in eight straight games, tying a major-league mark en route to a 40-homer season.

No one matched the season-long performance of San Francisco's Barry Bonds (*see* BIOGRAPHY), who led the National League with 46 home runs, 88 extra-base hits, 123 RBIs, a .458 on-base percentage, and a .677 slugging average. Bonds won his third MVP award in four seasons. His chief competition came from Lenny Dykstra, who led the league with 143 runs scored (the most by an NL player since 1932), 194 hits, and 129 walks. Sammy Sosa became the newest member of the 30/30 club, and the first in Chicago Cubs history, hitting 33 homers and stealing 36 bases. Bonds fell one steal short of his third 30/30 season. Florida outfielder Chuck Carr led the league with 58 stolen bases but trailed Mike Piazza (35 homers and 112 RBIs for the Dodgers) in the NL rookie-of-the-year voting. California's Tim Salmon won AL rookie honors after hitting .283 with 31 homers and 95 RBIs.

New York Yankees pitcher Jim Abbott, born without a right hand, threw himself into the record books with a heroic, 4-0 no-hitter on Sept. 4, 1993, against the Cleveland Indians.

© Focus on Sports

American League MVP honors went to Frank Thomas (White Sox), who hit .317 with a club-record 41 homers, 106 runs, 128 RBIs, 112 walks, 77 extra-base hits, a .607 slugging percentage, and a .426 on-base percentage—ranked near the top of the league in all categories. Juan Gonzalez (Rangers) tied Bonds for the major-league lead in homers, while Albert Belle (Indians) topped the AL with 129 RBIs. Paul Molitor led the majors with 211 hits and became the oldest player (37) to reach 100 RBIs for the first time. Dave Winfield, who previously held Molitor's job as Toronto DH, was wearing a Minnesota Twins uniform when he became the 19th member of the 3,000-hit club, against Oakland on September 16. A two-time former MVP, Baltimore shortstop Cal Ripken, Jr., extended his consecutive-game playing streak to 1,897, only 233 behind Lou Gehrig's record.

George Brett, who collected his 3,000th hit in 1992, announced that he was retiring, ending a 21-year career spent with the Kansas City Royals. Nolan Ryan, who pitched seven no-hitters during a record 27-year career in the majors, and Carlton Fisk, who caught more games than anyone else, also retired. National League hitters probably wished Atlanta's Tom Glavine would retire. He became the first NL pitcher in two decades to produce three straight 20-win seasons. Glavine won 22 games during the season and one in the NL Championship Series. Jack McDowell (White Sox) and John Burkett (Giants) tied Glavine for the major-league lead in wins. Maddux, in his first year with the Braves, finished with 20 wins for the second straight season and won a second straight Cy Young Award, leading the NL with a 2.36 ERA and 267 innings pitched.

In the American League, McDowell, with a record of 22-10 and a 3.37 ERA, won the Cy Young Award. Second in the voting was Seattle southpaw Randy Johnson, who became the 12th man to strike out 300 batters in a season. Kansas City's Kevin Appier had the AL's lowest ERA (2.56), ending a three-year streak by Boston's Roger Clemens. Teammate Chris Bosio pitched the season's first no-hitter, a 7-0 win over Boston in the Kingdome on April 22. Jim Abbott (Yankees) no-hit Cleveland at New York, 4-0, on September 4, four days before Darryl Kile (Astros) pitched another no-hitter in New York, beating the Mets, 7-1. Randy Myers of the Chicago Cubs saved 53 games to top Lee Smith's previous NL record by six. Jeff Montgomery (Royals) and Duane Ward (Blue Jays) had 45 saves each to share the AL lead.

Former All-Star hero Reggie Jackson, who hit 563 home runs, was enshrined in the Baseball Hall of Fame on August 1. No commissioner presided over induction ceremonies because the game's ruling executive council failed to appoint a successor to Francis T. (Fay) Vincent, Jr., deposed by the owners in September 1992.

DAN SCHLOSSBERG, *Baseball Writer*

Basketball

The Chicago Bulls made National Basketball Association (NBA) history by becoming only the third team to win three straight titles when they defeated the Phoenix Suns, four games to two, to take the 1993 championship. The Bulls had beaten the Los Angeles Lakers in 1991 and the Portland Trail Blazers in 1992 to become only the fourth franchise to win back-to-back crowns.

The National Collegiate Athletic Association (NCAA) men's basketball championship went to the University of North Carolina, which beat the University of Michigan, 77-71, in the tournament's final game. It was the second straight year that Michigan had lost in the championship game. The Wolverines fell to Duke in 1992. The National Invitation Tournament (NIT) title went to Minnesota, while Texas Tech won its first NCAA women's championship. In a major off-the-court development, University of California coach Lou Campanelli was fired during the season after his players complained about his verbal abuse.

The Professional Season

The 1992-93 NBA season became a story of one sensational rookie, center Shaquille O'Neal of Orlando; two veterans, Michael Jordan and Charles Barkley (*see* BIOGRAPHY); and two teams, the Chicago Bulls and the Phoenix Suns. O'Neal, the most highly touted rookie to enter the league in years, lived up to expectations with a magnificent season. Barkley, who had been traded in the off-season from Philadelphia to Phoenix, challenged Jordan for most-valuable-player honors, which Jordan had won the previous two seasons. Barkley's Suns also challenged Jordan's Bulls for the NBA championship, trying to break Chicago's two-year domination over the league. It wound up that Barkley's individual achievements were more successful than his team's quest.

The season had not even begun when the first major news story occurred. Magic Johnson, who was attempting a comeback after a year's retirement from the Los Angeles Lakers, decided to return to retirement. He had retired originally after announcing that he had tested positive for the HIV virus.

Regular Season. Chicago did not play particularly well during the regular season, in part because stars Jordan and Scottie Pippen were tired after a summer of playing on the U.S. Olympic basketball team. But the Bulls still won the Central Division title, holding off the Cleveland Cavaliers by three games. However, Chicago did not even have the best record in the Eastern Conference. That honor went to the improved New York Knicks, who made great progress under second-year coach Pat Riley. The Knicks compiled a 60-22 record and finished 12

Chicago's Michael Jordan (23) dominated the NBA play-off finals as his Bulls won their third consecutive championship, defeating the Phoenix Suns in six games. The star guard averaged 41 points per game in the finals and was the series' MVP.

© Nathaniel S. Butler/NBA Photos

games ahead of the Boston Celtics in the Atlantic Division. Phoenix, led by the energetic Barkley, ran away with the Pacific Division, winning by seven games over young Seattle. Defending Western Conference champion Portland, plagued by injuries, tumbled to third place in the Pacific. Houston and San Antonio staged a spirited race for the Midwest Division title, which the Rockets finally won by six games. The Spurs benefited from the hiring of coach John Lucas, who replaced the fired Jerry Tarkanian early in the season. Lucas became the first admitted reformed drug addict to coach an NBA team. Former expansion team Charlotte, led by rookie center Alonzo Mourning, made it to the play-offs for the first time. Not so fortunate was former powerhouse Detroit, which failed to qualify. The Lakers, without Magic, barely made it into postseason play. Pistons coach Ron Rothstein was fired, as was Atlanta coach Bob Weiss and Indiana coach Bob Hill. Cleveland's Lenny Wilkens and the Los Angeles Clippers' Larry Brown resigned and wound up taking jobs with Atlanta and Indiana, respectively.

Jordan won his seventh straight scoring title, averaging 32.6 points, to tie Wilt Chamberlain's NBA record. He also became the second-fastest player in NBA history, behind Chamberlain, to reach 20,000 points for his career. Second to Jordan in scoring was Dominique Wilkins of Atlanta (29.9) and Karl Malone of Utah (27.0). But Barkley won most-valuable-player honors after Phoenix finished with the best record in the league. Jordan finished second in the voting. Utah's John Stockton averaged 12 assists to win his sixth straight assist title. Detroit's Dennis Rodman defended his rebounding crown, averaging 18.3 per game, while O'Neal was second (13.9). O'Neal also was eighth in scoring, fourth in field-goal percentage, and second in blocked shots. He was named rookie of the year, ahead of Mourning. Jordan led in steals and Hakeem Olajuwon of Houston was first in blocked shots.

Jordan, Barkley, Malone, Olajuwon, and Cleveland's Mark Price were named first team all-NBA. Jordan, Detroit's Joe Dumars, Olajuwon, Rodman, and Pippen were named to the all-defensive squad. Riley was coach of the year. Portland's Cliff Robinson won the sixth man award and Olajuwon was named best defensive player. Guard Drazen Petrovic of the New Jersey Nets, who made third-team all-NBA, was killed in a postseason automobile accident. Celtic star Reggie Lewis died from chronic heart problems after collapsing during a workout.

The Play-offs. Based on regular-season standings, the Knicks and Suns should have played for the league championship. But, thanks to Chicago, that was not how it worked out. The Suns struggled throughout the play-offs. They had to rally after losing the first two games of their opening-round series against the Lakers, and they needed a seventh game to down Seattle for the conference championship. New York and

PROFESSIONAL BASKETBALL

National Basketball Association

(Final Standings, 1992-93)

Eastern Conference

Atlantic Division	W	L	Pct.	Games Behind
*New York	60	22	.732	—
*Boston	48	34	.585	12
*New Jersey	43	39	.524	17
Orlando	41	41	.500	19
Miami	36	46	.439	24
Philadelphia	26	56	.317	34
Washington	22	60	.268	38

Central Division	W	L	Pct.	Games Behind
*Chicago	57	25	.695	—
*Cleveland	54	28	.659	3
*Charlotte	44	38	.537	13
*Atlanta	43	39	.524	14
*Indiana	41	41	.500	16
Detroit	40	42	.488	17
Milwaukee	28	54	.341	29

Western Conference

Midwest Division	W	L	Pct.	Games Behind
*Houston	55	27	.671	—
*San Antonio	49	33	.598	6
*Utah	47	35	.573	8
Denver	36	46	.439	19
Minnesota	19	63	.232	36
Dallas	11	71	.134	44

Pacific Division	W	L	Pct.	Games Behind
*Phoenix	62	20	.756	—
*Seattle	55	27	.671	7
*Portland	51	31	.622	11
*Los Angeles Clippers	41	41	.500	21
*Los Angeles Lakers	39	43	.476	23
Golden State	34	48	.415	28
Sacramento	25	57	.305	37

*In play-offs

Play-offs

Eastern Conference

First Round	Charlotte	3 games	Boston	1
	Chicago	3 games	Atlanta	0
	Cleveland	3 games	New Jersey	2
	New York	3 games	Indiana	1
Second Round	Chicago	4 games	Cleveland	0
	New York	4 games	Charlotte	1
Finals	Chicago	4 games	New York	2

Western Conference

First Round	Houston	3 games	L.A. Clippers	2
	Phoenix	3 games	L.A. Lakers	2
	San Antonio	3 games	Portland	1
	Seattle	3 games	Utah	2
Second Round	Phoenix	4 games	San Antonio	2
	Seattle	4 games	Houston	3
Finals	Phoenix	4 games	Seattle	3
Championship	Chicago	4 games	Phoenix	2
All-Star Game	West 135, East 132			

Individual Honors

Most Valuable Player: Charles Barkley, Houston
Most Valuable Player (championship): Michael Jordan, Chicago
Most Valuable Player (All-Star Game): John Stockton, Utah, and Karl Malone, Utah
Rookie of the Year: Shaquille O'Neal, Orlando
Coach of the Year: Pat Riley, New York
Defensive Player of the Year: Hakeem Olajuwon, Houston
Leader in Scoring: Michael Jordan, 32.6 points per game
Leader in Assists: John Stockton, 12.0 per game
Leader in Rebounds: Dennis Rodman, Detroit, 18.3 per game
Leader in Field-Goal Percentage: Cedric Ceballos, Phoenix, .576
Leader in Free-Throw Percentage: Mark Price, Cleveland, .948
Leader in Steals: Michael Jordan, 2.83 per game
Leader in Blocked Shots: Hakeem Olajuwon, 4.17 per game

MICHAEL JORDAN

Basketball superstar Michael Jordan–renowned for his acrobatic, high-flying style of play–stunned the sports world by announcing his retirement from the game on Oct. 6, 1993. His retirement capped a brilliant nine-season career with the Chicago Bulls in which he captured every conceivable honor. Jordan summed up his own legacy: "I have nothing more to prove in basketball."

The 1992-93 NBA season had been no exception, as Jordan led the Bulls to their third straight championship. Unfortunately, Jordan also dominated headlines with off-court controversy and personal misfortune. He was plagued by stories of a high-stakes gambling habit in golf and cards. The Chicago star later suffered a tragic loss when his father, James Jordan, was found shot to death–the apparent victim of a random robbery. However, Jordan maintained that a real lack of further challenges–rather than these distractions–spurred his decision to retire.

Jordan is arguably the most illustrious player in basketball history. He holds the all-time record for career regular-season scoring average (32.3). He captured most-valuable-player honors in three regular seasons, three NBA finals, and one All-Star Game. His streak of seven straight scoring titles had been accomplished only once before–by Wilt Chamberlain.

Jordan also was a member of the University of North Carolina team that won the 1982 national collegiate championship and of the gold-medal-winning teams at the 1984 and 1992 Olympics.

Chicago had an easier time setting up their showdown for the Eastern Conference title. The Knicks won the first two games in New York and seemed on the verge of knocking off the Bulls. But led by Jordan and Pippen, Chicago won the next four games to set up the confrontation with Phoenix in the final round.

After the first two games of that series, both won by Chicago on the Suns' home court, it appeared the Bulls would win the series easily. The Bulls never trailed in the first game, cruising to a 100-92 victory. It was a bit more difficult in the second contest, but Chicago held off a fourth-quarter rally for a 111-108 triumph. The series moved to Chicago, where Phoenix immediately registered a major upset, beating the Bulls, 129-121, in three overtimes to win the third game.

Only one other championship-round game ever had gone to three overtimes. Phoenix used a 9-0 run to pull out the victory, in which Barkley had 24 points and Dan Majerle had 28, offsetting Jordan's 44. Chicago got 55 points from Jordan to take Game 4, 111-105, but Phoenix remained alive with a 108-98 triumph in Game 5. Chicago trailed for most of the contest and could not offset the scoring of Barkley, Kevin Johnson, and Richard Dumas. The series returned to Phoenix, but Chicago ended things quickly with a 99-98

victory in the sixth game. The winning points were provided by guard John Paxon, who made a three-point shot with 3.9 seconds left. Forward Horace Grant then blocked a Johnson shot to end the game. Jordan won his third straight playoff MVP award. The only other franchises to win three straight titles are Boston and the former Minneapolis Lakers.

The College Season

At the start of the 1992-93 college basketball season, the major story revolved around Duke University, which was trying to win its third straight NCAA-tournament title despite the graduation of star center Christian Laettner. But the Blue Devils still had stars Bobby Hurley and Grant Hill. A group of talented teams that included North Carolina, Seton Hall, Florida State, Arizona, Indiana, Kansas, and Michigan—which had lost the 1992 championship game to Duke—was expected to provide Duke with its greatest challenge. The Michigan Wolverines had started five freshmen in the 1992 NCAA final and all were back for the 1992-93 season.

The controversy surrounding California's Campanelli dominated late-season headlines.

COLLEGE BASKETBALL

Conference Champions

Atlantic Coast: North Carolina[r]; Georgia Tech[t]
Atlantic 10: Massachusetts[r, t]
Big East: Seton Hall[r, t]
Big Eight: Kansas[r]; Missouri[t]
Big Sky: Idaho[r]; Boise State[t]
Big South: Towson State[r]; Coastal Carolina[t]
Big Ten: Indiana
Big West: New Mexico State[r]; Long Beach State[t]
Colonial Athletic: James Madison, Old Dominion (tied)[r]; East Carolina[t]
Great Midwest: Cincinnati[r, t]
Ivy League: Penn
Metro: Louisville[r, t]
Metro Atlantic Athletic: Manhattan[r, t]
Mid-American: Ball State, Miami, Ohio (tied)[r]; Ball State[t]
Mid-Continent: Cleveland State[r]; Wright State[t]
Mid-Eastern Athletic: Coppin State[r, t]
Midwestern Collegiate: Xavier, Ohio, Evansville (tied)[r]; Evansville[t]
Missouri Valley: Illinois State[r]; Southern Illinois[t]
North Atlantic: Drexel, Northeastern (tied)[r]; Delaware[t]
Northeast: Rider[r, t]
Ohio Valley: Tennessee State[r, t]
Pacific-10: Arizona
Patriot League: Bucknell[r]; Holy Cross[t]
Southeastern: Vanderbilt (eastern division), Arkansas (western division)[r]; Kentucky[t]
Southern: Tennessee-Chattanooga[r, t]
Southland: Northeast Louisiana[r, t]
Southwest: SMU[r]; Texas Tech[t]
Southwestern Athletic: Jackson State[r]; Southern[t]
Sun Belt: New Orleans[r]; Western Kentucky[t]
West Coast: Pepperdine[r]; Santa Clara[t]
Western Athletic: Utah[r]; New Mexico[t]
[r]regular-season winner; [t]conference-tournament winner

Tournaments

NCAA Division I: North Carolina
NCAA Division II: Bakersfield State
NCAA Division III: Ohio Northern
NIT: Minnesota
NAIA: Hawaii Pacific
NCAA Division I (women): Texas Tech

The decision to let him go was promoted by complaints from his players, who had talked about boycotting games. The Bears later made the NCAA tournament under former assistant coach Todd Bozeman.

Duke wound up struggling somewhat during the regular season, in part due to an injury to Hill. But there was no lack of outstanding teams. Indiana, behind talented scorer Calbert Cheaney, finished ranked Number 1 in the polls; it was followed by Kentucky, under outstanding coach Rick Pitino, and young Michigan. North Carolina won the Atlantic Coast Conference (ACC) regular-season title but lost to Georgia Tech in the ACC tournament final. Arizona dominated the Pacific-10 and Kansas ran away with the Big Eight's regular-season title. Seton Hall was the dominant team in the Big East, while other elite squads included Vanderbilt—which proved Kentucky's equal in the Southeastern Conference—and Cincinnati.

Indiana's Cheaney was awarded the John Wooden Award and the Adolph F. Rupp Trophy as the nation's top player. Other contestants for best player in the country were Kentucky forward Jamal Mashburn, Anfernee Hardaway of Memphis State, Hurley of Duke, J. R. Rider of Nevada Las Vegas, Chris Webber of Michigan, Eric Montross of North Carolina, Rodney Rogers of Wake Forest, and Jason Kidd of California. Other standouts included Glenn Robinson of Purdue, Terry Dehere of Seton Hall, Chris Mills of Arizona, and Nick Van Exel of Cincinnati. Hardaway, Mashburn, Rogers, and Webber all left school early to join the professional ranks. Greg Guy of Texas-Pan American led the nation in scoring with a 29.3 average and Warren Kidd of Middle Tennessee State was the top rebounder with a 14.8 average.

The Tournaments. Along with Indiana, the top seeds in the NCAA tournament were Kentucky, North Carolina, and Michigan. Only Indiana failed to advance to the Final Four. The Hoosiers were upset by Kansas in the final of the Midwest Regional. Kentucky won the Southeast by beating Florida State, North Carolina took the East over Cincinnati, and Michigan survived the West by downing Temple. Duke was upset by California in the Midwest. Highly regarded Arizona lost early in the West.

In the Final Four in the Superdome in New Orleans, Kansas played North Carolina in one semifinal, while Michigan opposed favored Kentucky, which hardly had been challenged in the tournament's early rounds. North Carolina had too much size and strength for Kansas and won easily, 78-68. Michigan also used a height advantage to wear down Kentucky in overtime, 81-78. In the final, North Carolina sophomore Donald Williams made four free throws in the last 11 seconds to secure a 77-71 triumph. It was the second NCAA championship for veteran coach Dean Smith. Michigan's Webber committed the key mistake. With his team trailing, 73-71, and

© Focus on Sports

North Carolina's Donald Williams (21) was high scorer with 25 points as his Tar Heels beat Michigan, 77-71, for the NCAA crown. The sophomore guard was voted MVP of the Final Four.

11 seconds left, he called a time-out. But his team had no time-outs left and the Wolverines were hit with a technical. Williams finished with a game-high 25 points.

In the NIT, junior Ariel McDonald scored 14 of his game-high 20 points in the second half as Minnesota held off Georgetown, 62-61, to win the title. Teammate Voshon Leonard was named MVP. In the women's NCAA tournament, senior Sheryl Swoopes scored 47 points to lead Texas Tech to an 84-82 victory over Ohio State in the final game. Ohio State had beaten Iowa, 73-72, and Texas Tech had downed Vanderbilt, 60-46, in the semifinals. Swoopes was named MVP of the women's Final Four.

PAUL ATTNER
Senior Writer, "The Sporting News"

Boxing

Two unusual championship bouts were contested in 1993. In one of boxing history's more bizarre title fights, Evander Holyfield became the third former heavyweight champion to regain the title when he dethroned Riddick Bowe in a bout on November 6 in Las Vegas, NV. The fight was disrupted by an unexpected visitor from the sky. In another controversial title fight, welterweights Julio César Chávez and Pernell Whitaker fought to a controversial draw in San Antonio, TX.

The Heavyweights. The championship bout was a brutal, no-holds-barred slugfest. The 31-year-old Holyfield, who weighed 217 lbs (98 kg) to Bowe's 246 lbs (112 kg), regained the title on a 12-round majority decision. Two judges voted for Holyfield while one called it a draw.

Holyfield, a 6-1 underdog who often had been maligned as a champion who had not proven himself against topflight opponents, was fighting to regain his pride and to avenge his earlier loss to Bowe, when he had surrendered all three major heavyweight crowns: the World Boxing Association (WBA), International Boxing Federation (IBF), and World Boxing Council (WBC) titles. Late in 1992 the 26-year-old Bowe ceded his WBC title to Lennox Lewis of England.

Holyfield joined Floyd Patterson and Muhammad Ali as the only dethroned heavyweight champions to regain their titles by defeating the man who had taken it away. Holyfield handed Bowe his first defeat. Bowe's record fell to 34-1 with 29 knockouts. Holyfield avenged his only defeat, gaining his 30th victory in a career that includes 22 knockouts. When the pay-per-view television returns were tabulated, the fighters earned $12 million each. Bowe had stayed busy earlier in the year with knockouts of Michael Dokes and Jesse Ferguson.

The fight was interrupted startlingly in the seventh round by a paraglider who descended from the night sky seemingly out of nowhere and crashed into the ring ropes. The paraglider's intrusion gave the bout a surreal quality worthy of a Dali painting. The man, James Miller of Las Vegas, 30 years old, was pummeled at ringside and arrested. He did not have a weapon. The intrusion delayed the fight for 21 minutes as the fighters stood in their corners struggling to keep warm in the 50° F (10° C) evening chill.

In October, Lewis defended his WBC heavyweight crown against Frank Bruno, a journeyman fighter, in a bout that pitted two British heavyweights in a title match for the first time in boxing history. The much-ballyhooed fight was a virtual flop in the ring as Lewis scored a knockout in the seventh round, but gained little critical acclaim. In May, Lewis also scored a one-sided unanimous decision over Tony Tucker in Las Vegas.

The Lighter Divisions. Another bout that generated great controversy was the Julio César Chávez-Pernell Whitaker match in San Antonio.

WORLD BOXING CHAMPIONS*

Heavyweight: World Boxing Council (WBC)—Lennox Lewis, Great Britain, 1992; World Boxing Association (WBA)—Evander Holyfield, United States, 1993; International Boxing Federation (IBF)—Holyfield, 1993.
Cruiserweight: WBC—Anaclet Wamba, France, 1991; WBA—Orlin Norris, United States, 1993; IBF—Alfred Cole, United States, 1992.
Light Heavyweight: WBC—Jeff Harding, Australia, 1991; WBA—Virgil Hill, United States, 1992; IBF—Henry Maske, United States, 1993.
Super Middleweight: WBC—Nigel Benn, England, 1992; WBA—Michael Nunn, United States, 1992; IBF—James Toney, United States, 1993.
Middleweight: WBC—Gerald McClellan, United States, 1993; WBA—John David Jackson, United States, 1993; IBF—Roy Jones Jr., United States, 1993.
Junior Middleweight: WBC—Simon Brown, Jamaica, 1993; WBA—Julio Cesar Vasquez, Argentina, 1992; IBF—Gianfranco Rosi, Italy, 1989.
Welterweight: WBC—Pernell Whitaker, United States, 1993; WBA—Crisanto España, Venezuela, 1992; IBF—Felix Trinidad, Puerto Rico, 1993.
Junior Welterweight: WBC—Julio César Chávez, Mexico, 1989; WBA—Juan Martin Coggi, Argentina, 1993; IBF—Charles Murray, United States, 1993.
Lightweight: WBC—Miguel Angel Gonzalez, Mexico, 1992; WBA—Gusshie Nazarov, Russia, 1993; IBF—Fred Pendleton, United States, 1993.
Junior Lightweight: WBC—Azumah Nelson, Ghana, 1988; WBA—Ganaro Hernandez, United States, 1991; IBF—John John Molina, Puerto Rico, 1992.
Featherweight: WBC—Kevin Kelly, United States, 1993; WBA—Yung-kyun Park, South Korea, 1991; IBF—Tom Johnson, United States, 1993.
Junior Featherweight: WBC—Tracy Patterson, United States, 1992; WBA—Wilfredo Vazquez, Mexico, 1992; IBF—Kennedy McKinney, United States, 1992.
Bantamweight: WBC—Jungil Byon, South Korea, 1993; WBA—Junior Jones, United States, 1993; IBF—Orlando Canizales, United States, 1988.
Junior Bantamweight: WBC—Sungkil Moon, South Korea, 1990; WBA—Katzuya Onizuka, Japan, 1992; IBF—Julio Borboa, Mexico, 1993.
Flyweight: WBC—Yuri Arvachakov, Russia, 1992; WBA—David Griman, Venezuela, 1993; IBF—Pichit Sibranchpagan, Thailand, 1992.
Junior Flyweight: WBC—Michael Carbajal, United States, 1993; WBA—Leo Gamez, Venezuela, 1993; IBF—Carbajal, 1990.
Strawweight: WBC—Ricardo Lopez, Mexico, 1990; WBA—Chana Propaoin, Thailand, 1993; IBF—Ratnaapol Vorapin, Thailand, 1993.

*As of Dec. 26, 1993; date indicates year title was won.

This championship also produced a bizarre outcome and left fight fans bewildered.

The 31-year-old Chávez had not lost in 87 fights (with 75 knockouts), and he was considered by many experts to be the "best fighter pound for pound" in all of boxing. The 29-year-old Whitaker, with a record of 32-1 (15 knockouts), was a southpaw stylist with a diverse arsenal of ring weapons. Many believed he would be the one to stop Chávez' unbeaten streak. Each had held five titles in three weight divisions; the two were fighting for Whitaker's WBC welterweight crown.

Whitaker put on a dazzling show, bewildering Chávez with his bobbing and weaving. Whitaker also appeared to outmuscle Chávez and beat him to the punch—to the surprise of the partisan fans in the Alamodome. Most boxing observers concluded that Whitaker won the fight handily. However, when it was over, two of the three judges scored the 12-round bout a draw, while one judge awarded the fight to Whitaker. The official verdict was called a "majority draw." According to many experts, few bouts in ring annals have ended in such a widely disputed decision.

GEORGE DE GREGORIO
"The New York Times"

Football

The 1993-94 pro-football season will be remembered as the beginning of a new era of liberalized free agency. Many star players, such as defensive end Reggie White, took advantage of new free-agency rules to change teams. Although this movement affected the competitive balance of the National Football League (NFL), the Super Bowl still featured the same teams that had played in the previous title game: the Dallas Cowboys and the Buffalo Bills.

Buffalo entered Super Bowl XXVIII—played before a crowd of 72,817 on Jan. 30, 1994, in the Georgia Dome in Atlanta—looking to avoid a fourth straight title-game loss. But the Bills were outplayed by the Cowboys, 30-13. Dallas running back Emmitt Smith was voted the game's most valuable player after leading the Cowboys' high-powered offense with 132 yards and two touchdowns. The Bills had earned a 13-6 halftime lead, but the Cowboys scored 24 unanswered points in the second half to put the game out of reach. Once again, the Bills hurt themselves in the Super Bowl with costly turnovers. Buffalo's top running back Thurman Thomas fumbled twice, including one ball that was picked up by the Cowboys' James Washington and returned 46 yards for a momentum-turning score in the opening seconds of the third quarter.

In college competition, Florida State won its first national championship by defeating the previously unbeaten Nebraska Cornhuskers, 18-16, in the Orange Bowl. The Heisman Trophy went to the Seminoles' star quarterback, Charlie Ward.

In the Canadian Football League (CFL), Edmonton defeated the Winnipeg Blue Bombers, 33-23, to win the Grey Cup. It was the Blue Bombers' second straight Grey Cup defeat. The CFL also expanded in 1993 to include its first U.S. franchise, the Sacramento Gold Miners.

The Professional Season

NFL Developments. With the introduction of liberalized free agency, NFL player salaries skyrocketed prior to the 1993 season. High-profile players, such as quarterbacks and pass-rushing defensive linemen, began signing contracts that earned them between $2 million and $4 million per year, far above what had been the league standard. Such established stars as White, quarterbacks Bobby Hebert and Wade Wilson, and running back Marcus Allen moved to new teams and lucrative contracts. Payroll costs increased so much in 1993 that observers expected that a salary cap, one which would limit the amount of money teams could spend on player costs, would be in place for the 1994 season. A salary cap would allow NFL teams to make a profit.

In another major financial move, the NFL ended a long association with the Columbia Broadcasting System (CBS), which had been covering the NFL since the 1955 season. CBS was outbid by the Fox Broadcasting Company to televise games from the National Football Conference (NFC). Fox would start telecasting games in the 1994 season and was expected to hire many of CBS' top personnel, including star commentators John Madden and Pat Summerall. Meanwhile, the National Broadcasting Company (NBC) retained the rights to televise games in the American Football Conference after team owners rejected a higher bid from CBS.

In the fall of 1993, NFL owners also selected two cities—Jacksonville, FL, and Charlotte, NC—to gain franchises for the 1995 season. Both ownership groups agreed to pay $140 million to join the other 28 teams in the NFL. Three other cities—Baltimore, St. Louis, and Memphis—had tried and failed to secure a franchise.

Miami coach Don Shula made history on November 14 when he became the winningest

© Mike Powell/Allsport

Dallas running back Emmitt Smith captured his third straight rushing title—despite missing the first two games of the season due to a contract dispute. Smith rambled for 132 yards in the Cowboys' 30-13 Super Bowl triumph over Buffalo and was chosen as the game's most valuable player.

National Football League
Final Standings, 1993

AMERICAN CONFERENCE

Eastern Division	W	L	T	Pct.	Points For	Against
Buffalo	12	4	0	.750	329	242
Miami	9	7	0	.563	349	351
N.Y. Jets	8	8	0	.500	270	247
New England	5	11	0	.313	238	286
Indianapolis	4	12	0	.250	189	378

Central Division	W	L	T	Pct.	For	Against
Houston	12	4	0	.750	368	238
Pittsburgh	9	7	0	.563	308	281
Cleveland	7	9	0	.438	304	307
Cincinnati	3	13	0	.188	187	319

Western Division	W	L	T	Pct.	For	Against
Kansas City	11	5	0	.688	328	291
L.A. Raiders	10	6	0	.625	306	326
Denver	9	7	0	.563	373	284
San Diego	8	8	0	.500	322	290
Seattle	6	10	0	.375	280	314

PLAY-OFFS

Kansas City 27, Pittsburgh 24
Los Angeles Raiders 42, Denver 24
Buffalo 29, Los Angeles 23
Kansas City 28, Houston 20
Buffalo 30, Kansas City 13

NATIONAL CONFERENCE

Eastern Division	W	L	T	Pct.	Points For	Against
Dallas	12	4	0	.750	376	229
N.Y. Giants	11	5	0	.688	288	205
Philadelphia	8	8	0	.500	293	315
Phoenix	7	9	0	.438	326	269
Washington	4	12	0	.250	230	345

Central Division	W	L	T	Pct.	For	Against
Detroit	10	6	0	.625	298	292
Minnesota	9	7	0	.563	277	290
Green Bay	9	7	0	.563	340	282
Chicago	7	9	0	.438	234	230
Tampa Bay	5	11	0	.313	237	376

Western Division	W	L	T	Pct.	For	Against
San Francisco	10	6	0	.625	473	295
New Orleans	8	8	0	.500	317	343
Atlanta	6	10	0	.375	316	385
L.A. Rams	5	11	0	.313	221	367

PLAY-OFFS

Green Bay 28, Detroit 24
New York 17, Minnesota 10
Dallas 27, Green Bay 17
San Francisco 44, New York 3
Dallas 38, San Francisco 21

SUPER BOWL XXVIII: Dallas 30, Buffalo 13

pro coach of all time. With a 19-14 victory over Philadelphia, the Dolphins gave the 31-year coaching veteran his 325th victory. With this win, Shula eclipsed the mark set by the late George Halas, who had coached the Chicago Bears during five decades.

Play-offs. The Dallas Cowboys were favored heavily to repeat as champions of the NFC East. They lived up to that prediction, but the title was not an easy feat. After starting the season with two straight defeats—thanks in part to a contract holdout by star running back Emmitt Smith—the Cowboys had to chase after the revitalized New York Giants all season. But they finally won the title by defeating the Giants in

overtime on the last day of the regular season and began the play-offs viewed as the strongest team in the NFL. The Giants emerged as one of the year's surprise teams, becoming a wild-card play-off entry under first-year coach Dan Reeves, who formerly coached at Denver.

The NFC Central title went to the Detroit Lions, a team that overcame problems at quarterback, starting three different players at that position during the season. The Lions barely outdistanced the Minnesota Vikings and the Green Bay Packers. However, both the Packers and the Vikings still made the play-offs, as wild-card teams.

San Francisco continued a pattern of strong regular-season performances begun in the early 1980s by sweeping to yet another NFC West title. The 49ers were led by quarterback Steve Young, who won a record third straight passing title. The division also produced one of the most disappointing teams, the New Orleans Saints, who failed to make the play-offs after being a dominant team for the first six weeks of the season.

In the AFC, the Houston Oilers—who had hired controversial defensive coordinator Buddy Ryan to help them get into the NFL title game—finished the season with an 11-game winning streak to capture the AFC Central crown and enter the play-offs as one of the favorites to advance to the Super Bowl. The Buffalo Bills also finished strongly and were able to capture home-field advantage throughout the play-offs. Miami had led the AFC East at midseason, but lost its final five games and was beaten out by Buffalo. The Dolphins faltered so badly they failed to make the play-offs. In the same division, the formerly woeful New England Patriots improved considerably under new coach Bill Parcells, the former coach of the New York Giants.

In the AFC West, Kansas City provided the most excitement with the addition of legendary Joe Montana at quarterback. Montana, considered to be one of the greatest quarterbacks in history, left San Francisco in a trade after sitting out almost two years with a bad throwing arm and other injuries. His Chiefs won the division, with the Los Angeles Raiders and Denver Broncos also advancing to the play-offs.

In the play-offs, Montana and the Chiefs were sentimental favorites, particularly if they could play San Francisco in the Super Bowl. That dream matchup almost became a reality. Montana twice rallied the Chiefs to play-off victories, beating Pittsburgh at home and then traveling to Houston, where the Chiefs upset the Oilers. Those victories put Kansas City in the AFC finale against Buffalo, which had overcome windy, freezing conditions to beat the Raiders.

In the AFC championship game, the Bills' running back, Thurman Thomas, put on a sensational show, gaining 186 yards as Buffalo overpowered Kansas City. Montana was forced to leave the game in the third quarter with a concussion, but the Bills already were dominating the game.

© Ron Vesley/Focus on Sports

In his first year as head coach of the New York Giants, Dan Reeves was named the NFL coach of the year for guiding the team to an 11-5 record and into the play-offs.

In the NFC, both Dallas and San Francisco had a relatively easy time advancing to the championship game. In the first round of the play-offs, Green Bay defeated Detroit, while the Giants topped Minnesota. However, neither of these victorious teams could survive the following week, as the Cowboys knocked off Green Bay and the 49ers dominated the Giants. San Francisco thought it was capable of upsetting Dallas in the conference title game, but the Cowboys played a nearly perfect first half to take a 28-7 lead and breezed to a second straight Super Bowl appearance.

Individual Performances. Running back Emmitt Smith of Dallas won his third straight rushing title (1,486 yards) and was chosen the league's most valuable player. He also won the combined yardage title (1,900 yards) to end Thurman Thomas' record four-year streak. Green Bay's Sterling Sharpe caught 112 passes—becoming the first player to have consecutive 100-reception seasons, while San Francisco's Jerry Rice led the NFL in receiving yardage. Other standouts included quarterbacks Troy Aikman of Dallas and John Elway of Denver; linebackers Junior Seau of San Diego, Hardy Nickerson of Tampa Bay, and Greg Lloyd of Pittsburgh; cornerback Rod Woodson of Pittsburgh; and running backs Barry Sanders of Detroit and Jerome Bettis of the Los Angeles Rams.

Off the Field. Several coaches were fired during the season. Richie Petitbon of Washington lasted only one season as the replacement for Joe Gibbs, who had retired unexpectedly in the off-season. Also dismissed were Bruce Coslet of the Jets, Jerry Glanville of Atlanta, and Joe Bugel of Phoenix. Admitted to the Pro Football Hall of Fame were running back Walter Payton, quarterback Dan Fouts, offensive guard Larry Little, and coaches Bill Walsh and Chuck Noll. One probable future Hall of Fame inductee, Lawrence Taylor of the New York Giants, announced his retirement following a distinguished career that established him as perhaps the best outside linebacker in history.

The College Season

After years of disappointment, Florida State head coach Bobby Bowden finally won his first national college-football championship when his Seminoles beat Nebraska, 18-16, on New Year's night in the Orange Bowl. Bowden's teams had been among the strongest in the nation for many years, but the Seminoles always lost at least one game each season, which had cost them a chance to finish Number 1.

In an important November game against Notre Dame, Florida State appeared to continue this unfortunate tradition with an exciting 31-24 loss, which later proved controversial. Notre Dame became Number 1 after the victory but lost the next week at home to Boston College, allowing Florida State to regain the top spot in

---

COLLEGE FOOTBALL

Conference Champions	Atlantic Coast—Florida State Big Eight—Nebraska Big Ten—(tie) Wisconsin, Ohio State Big West—(tie) Utah State, Southwestern Louisiana Pacific-10—(tie) UCLA, Arizona, Southern Cal Southeastern—Florida Southwest—Texas A&M Western Athletic—(tie) Brigham Young, Fresno State, Wyoming
NCAA Champions	Division I-AA—Youngstown State Division II—Northern Alabama Division III—Mount Union
NAIA Champions	Division I—East Central (Oklahoma) Division II—Pacific Lutheran (Washington)
Individual Honors	Heisman Trophy—Charlie Ward, Florida State Lombardi Award—Aaron Taylor, Notre Dame Outland Trophy—Rob Waldrop, Arizona

Major Bowl Games

Alamo Bowl (San Antonio, TX, Dec. 31)—California 37, Iowa 3
Aloha Bowl (Honolulu, HI, Dec. 25)—Colorado 41, Fresno State 30
Blue-Gray Classic (Montgomery, AL, Dec. 25)—Gray 17, Blue 10
Carquest Bowl (Miami, FL, Jan. 1)—Boston College 31, Virginia 13
Citrus Bowl (Orlando, FL, Jan. 1)—Penn State 31, Tennessee 13
Copper Bowl (Tucson, AZ, Dec. 29)—Kansas State 52, Wyoming 17
Cotton Bowl (Dallas, TX, Jan. 1)—Notre Dame 24, Texas A&M 21
Fiesta Bowl (Tempe, AZ, Jan. 1)—Arizona 29, Miami 0
Freedom Bowl (Anaheim, CA, Dec. 30)—Southern Cal 28, Utah 21
Gator Bowl (Jacksonville, FL, Dec. 31)—Alabama 24, North Carolina 10
Hall of Fame Bowl (Tampa, FL, Jan. 1)—Michigan 42, North Carolina State 7
John Hancock Bowl (El Paso, TX, Dec. 24)—Oklahoma 41, Texas Tech 10
Heritage Bowl (Atlanta, GA, Jan 1)—Southern 11, South Carolina State 0
Holiday Bowl (San Diego, CA, Dec. 30)—Ohio State 28, Brigham Young 21
Independence Bowl (Shreveport, LA, Dec. 31)—Virginia Tech 45, Indiana 20
Las Vegas Bowl (Las Vegas, NV, Dec. 17)—Utah State 42, Ball State 33
Liberty Bowl (Memphis, TN, Dec. 28)—Louisville 18, Michigan State 7
Orange Bowl (Miami, FL, Jan. 1)—Florida State 18, Nebraska 16
Peach Bowl (Atlanta, GA, Dec. 31)—Clemson 14, Kentucky 13
Rose Bowl (Pasadena, CA, Jan. 1)—Wisconsin 21, UCLA 16
Sugar Bowl (New Orleans, LA, Jan. 1)—Florida 41, West Virginia 7

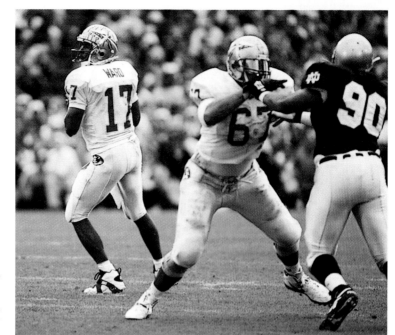

A two-sport standout at Florida State, quarterback Charlie Ward (17) was named the 1993 Heisman Trophy winner by a wide margin. Ward led the Seminoles to victory over Nebraska in the Orange Bowl to gain the national title.

© Brian Masck/Allsport

the Associated Press (AP) writers' poll. Meanwhile, Nebraska, which ended the regular season as the undefeated champion of the Big Eight Conference, was ranked first in the CNN/*USA Today* coaches' poll going into the Orange Bowl.

Bowl Games. When Notre Dame beat Texas A&M in the Cotton Bowl in Dallas to end the season with just one defeat, Fighting Irish coach Lou Holtz felt his team deserved to be ranked ahead of Florida State since his team had won the head-to-head matchup. Both polls put Florida State first and Notre Dame second, renewing calls for a national play-off system in college football.

Florida State's win over Nebraska, which had entered the game as a 17-point underdog, did not come easily. Nebraska took the lead, 16-15, on a 27-yard field goal by Byron Bennett with only 76 seconds left. The Seminoles then drove 71 yards to set up a 22-yard field goal by freshman Scott Brantley with 24 seconds remaining in the game. Nebraska made the most of the final moments, moving quickly to the Florida State 28-yard line, where a 45-yard attempt by Bennett was wide to the left, giving the victory and the national title to Bowden and Florida State.

Notre Dame likewise was pressed in the Cotton Bowl by underdog Texas A&M. The Aggies led for most of the game before Notre Dame rallied behind its running game to pull out a victory. The Aggies led, 21-14, in the third quarter and appeared on their way to ending a two-game losing streak in the Cotton Bowl. But Notre Dame tied the score in the third quarter and then won the game on a 31-yard field goal by Kevin Pendergast with less than three minutes left.

In the Rose Bowl, Big Ten cochampion Wisconsin overwhelmed UCLA of the Pacific-10 Conference, 21-16. Running back Brent Moss rushed 36 times for 158 yards and two touchdowns. UCLA gained 500 total yards and receiver J. J. Stokes caught 14 passes for 176, both Rose Bowl records. The Bruins were thwarted by six turnovers.

West Virginia finished the regular season with an 11-0 record and national-title hopes. But the Mountaineers could not handle Florida in the Sugar Bowl, losing 41-7. The game was tied, 7-7, when Florida's Lawrence Wright returned a second-quarter interception 52 yards for a touchdown. Running back Errict Rhett scored three times for the Gators.

The Best Players. The race for the Heisman Trophy was one of the most lopsided in history. Florida State quarterback Charlie Ward finished with the second-most votes in trophy history and was named college football's best player. Ward was a rare college athlete. He also was a star basketball player on his school's team and was projected to be drafted by professional teams in both the National Football League (NFL) and the National Basketball Association (NBA). In football, he set most of Florida State's career and season passing records but was also particularly dangerous running from the pocket.

Nebraska linebacker Trev Alberts and Ohio State defensive lineman Dan Wilkinson emerged as two of the nation's best defensive players.

Other Divisions. In Division I-AA, Youngstown State defeated defending champion Marshall, 17-5. The victory gave Youngstown its second title in three years. Undefeated Northern Alabama downed Indiana (PA) University, 41-34, scoring on the last play of the game to win the Division II crown, while Mount Union rolled over Rowan College, 34-24, in the Division III title game.

PAUL ATTNER
"The Sporting News"

Golf

The biennial Ryder Cup Match was the golf highlight of 1993. In the September event, the United States defeated Europe, 15-13, at The Belfrey in Sutton Coldfield, England.

Trailing by three points at the end of the Saturday morning foursomes, the United States won three out of four four-ball matches in the afternoon to pull within a point of the Europeans. The surprising doubles team of Chip Beck and John Cook, both seeing their first action in the Ryder Cup, defeated Europe's top team, Nick Faldo and Colin Montgomerie, to provide much of the impetus. In Sunday's singles competition, U.S. players won six matches

GOLF

PGA Tour

Infiniti Tournament of Champions: Davis Love III (272)
United Airlines Hawaiian Open: Howard Twitty (269)
Northern Telecom Open: Larry Mize (271)
Phoenix Open: Lee Janzen (273)
AT&T Pebble Beach National Pro-Am: Brett Ogle (276)
Bob Hope Chrysler Classic: Tom Kite (325)
Buick Invitational of California: Phil Mickelson (278)
Nissan Los Angeles Open: Tom Kite (206)
Doral Ryder Open: Greg Norman (265)
Honda Classic: Fred Couples (207)
Nestle Invitational: Ben Crenshaw (280)
The Players Championship: Nick Price (270)
Freeport-McMoran Classic: Mike Standly (281)
Masters: Bernhard Langer (277)
Deposit Guaranty Classic: Greg Kraft (267)
MCI Heritage Classic: David Edwards (273)
K Mart Greater Greensboro Open: Rocco Mediate (281)
Shell Houston Open: Jim McGovern (199)
BellSouth Classic: Nolan Henke (271)
GTE Byron Nelson Classic: Scott Simpson (270)
Kemper Open: Grant Waite (275)
Southwestern Bell Colonial: Fulton Allem (264)
Memorial Tournament: Paul Azinger (274)
Buick Classic: Vijay Singh (280)
U.S. Open: Lee Janzen (272)
Canon Greater Hartford Open: Nick Price (271)
Sprint Western Open: Nick Price (269)
Anheuser-Busch Golf Classic: Jim Gallagher, Jr. (269)
New England Classic: Paul Azinger (268)
Federal Express St. Jude Classic: Nick Price (266)
Buick Open: Larry Mize (272)
PGA Championship: Paul Azinger (272)
International: Phil Mickelson (+45)
NEC World Series of Golf: Fulton Allem (270)
Greater Milwaukee Open: Billy Mayfair (270)
Canadian Open: David Frost (279)
Hardee's Golf Classic: David Frost (259)
B.C. Open/Ryder Cup: Blaine McCallister (271)
Buick Southern Open: John Inman (278)
Walt Disney World/Oldsmobile Classic: Jeff Maggert (265)
H.E.B. Texas Open: Jay Haas (263)
Las Vegas Invitational: Davis Love III (331)
Tour Championship: Jim Gallagher, Jr. (277)
Lincoln Mercury Kapalua International: Fred Couples (274)
Franklin Funds Shark Shootout: Steve Elkington/Ray Floyd (188)
The Skins Game: Payne Stewart ($280,000)
JC Penney Classic: Mike Springer/Melissa McNamara (265)

LPGA Tour

HealthSouth Palm Beach Classic: Tammie Green (208)
Itoki Hawaiian Ladies Open: Lisa Walters (210)
Ping-Welch's Championship (March): Meg Mallon (272)
Standard Register Ping: Patty Sheehan (275)
Nabisco Dinah Shore: Helen Alfredsson (284)
Las Vegas LPGA at Canyon Gate: Trish Johnson (209)
Atlanta Women's Championship: Trish Johnson (282)
Sprint Classic: Kristi Albers (279)
Sara Lee Classic: Meg Mallon (205)
McDonald's Championship: Laura Davies (277)
Lady Keystone Open: Val Skinner (210)
LPGA Corning Classic: Kelly Robbins (277)
JC Penney/LPGA Skins Game: Betsy King (7 Skins)
Oldsmobile Classic: Jane Geddes (277)
Mazda LPGA Championship: Patty Sheehan (275)
Rochester International: Tammie Green (276)
ShopRite LPGA Classic: Shelley Hamlin (204)
Jamie Farr Toledo Classic: Brandie Burton (201)
Youngstown-Warren LPGA Classic: Nancy Lopez (203)
JAL Big Apple Classic: Hiromi Kobayashi (278)
U.S. Women's Open: Lauri Merten (280)
Ping-Welch's Championship (September): Missie Berteotti (276)
McCall's LPGA Classic at Stratton Mountain: Dana Lofland-Dormann (275)
Sun-Times Challenge: Cindy Schreyer (272)
Minnesota LPGA Classic: Hiromi Kobayashi (205)
du Maurier Ltd. Classic: Brandie Burton (277)
State Farm Rail Classic: Helen Dobson (203)
Ping-Cellular One LPGA Golf Championship: Donna Andrews (208)
Safeco Classic: Brandie Burton (274)
Kyocera Inamori Classic: Kris Monaghan (275)
World Championship of Women's Golf: Dottie Mochrie (283)
Nichirei International: United States 23, Japan 6
Toray Japan Queens Cup: Betsy King (205)
JC Penney Classic: Melissa McNamara/Mike Springer (265)

Senior PGA Tour

Infiniti Senior Tournament of Champions: Al Geiberger (280)
Senior Skins Game: Arnold Palmer ($190,000)
Royal Caribbean Classic: Jim Colbert (199)
Better Homes & Gardens Real Estate Challenge: Mike Hill (202)
GTE Suncoast Classic: Jim Albus (206)
Chrysler Cup: United States
GTE West Classic: Al Geiberger (198)
Vantage at the Dominion: J.C. Snead (214)
Gulfstream Aerospace Invitational: Raymond Floyd (194)
Doug Sanders Celebrity Classic: Bob Charles (208)
Fuji Grand Slam: Lee Trevino (207)
Tradition: Tom Shaw (269)
PGA Seniors Championship: Tom Wargo (275)
Muratec Reunion Pro-Am: Dave Stockton (211)
Las Vegas Senior Classic: Gibby Gilbert (204)
Liberty Mutual Legends of Golf: Harold Henning (204)
PaineWebber Invitational: Mike Hill (204)
Bell Atlantic Classic: Bob Charles (204)
Cadillac NFL Golf Classic: Lee Trevino (209)
Nynex Commemorative: Bob Wynn (203)
Southwestern Bell Classic: Dave Stockton (204)
Burnet Senior Classic: Chi Chi Rodriguez (201)
Ford Senior Players Championship: Jim Colbert (278)
Kroger Senior Classic: Simon Hobday (202)
U.S. Senior Open: Jack Nicklaus (278)
Ameritech Senior Open: George Archer (133)
First of America Classic: George Archer (199)
Northville Long Island Classic: Raymond Floyd (208)
Bank of Boston Senior Golf Classic: Bob Betley (204)
Franklin Quest Championship: Dave Stockton (197)
GTE Northwest Classic: Dave Stockton (200)
Bruno's Memorial Classic: Bob Murphy (203)
Quicksilver Classic: Bob Charles (207)
GTE North Classic: Bob Murphy (134)
Banc One Classic: Gary Player (202)
Nationwide Championship: Lee Trevino (205)
Vantage Championship: Lee Trevino (198)
Transamerica: Dave Stockton (203)
Raley's Senior Gold Rush: George Archer (202)
Ralphs Senior Classic: Dale Douglass (196)
Ping Kaanapali Classic: George Archer (199)
Du Pont Cup: United States 26, Japan 6
Hyatt Senior Tour Championship: Simon Hobday (199)

Other Tournaments

British Open: Greg Norman (267)
Ryder Cup: United States 15, Europe 13
Toyota World Match Play: Corey Pavin
World Cup: Bernhard Langer (272)
Team: United States (556)
U.S. Men's Amateur: John Harris
U.S. Women's Amateur: Jill McGill
U.S. Men's Public Links: David Berganio
U.S. Women's Public Links: Connie Masterson
U.S. Men's Mid-Amateur: Jeff Thomas
U.S. Women's Mid-Amateur: Sarah Ingram
U.S. Senior Men's Amateur: Joe Ungvary
U.S. Senior Women's Amateur: Anne Sander
U.S. Junior Boys: Eldrick (Tiger) Woods
U.S. Junior Girls: Kellee Booth
NCAA Men: Individual: Todd Demsey (278); Team: Florida (1,145)
NCAA Women: Individual: Charlotta Sorenstam (287);
Team: Arizona State (1,187)
British Amateur: Iain Pyman
British Senior Open: Bob Charles (291)
Senior British Amateur: Charlie Green
Dunhill Cup: United States
Grand Slam of Golf: Greg Norman (145)
Sun City Million Dollar Challenge: Nick Price (264)

© Focus on Sports

With three birdies on the last six holes, Lee Janzen, 28, captured the 1993 U.S. Open at Baltusrol Golf Club in Springfield, NJ. He defeated Payne Stewart by two strokes.

ner—both topped the $1 million mark in winnings for the year.

In major men's competition, Germany's Bernhard Langer won his second Masters title in April, and Lee Janzen held off Payne Stewart to win the U.S. Open at Baltusrol in June. Norman won the British Open in July, capped by a final-round 64 that was one of the best major-championship finishes ever. He also won once in the United States and finished third on the money list with $1,359,653.

Senior Tour. The player-of-the-year honors on the Senior PGA tour went to Dave Stockton, who won five times and captured the money title with $1,175,944. Bob Charles, a three-time winner and second in money with $1,046,823, nipped Stockton for the scoring title, 69.59 to 69.71. George Archer and Lee Trevino also won three tournaments each to finish third and fourth, respectively, on the money list.

Jack Nicklaus held off Tom Weiskopf to win the U.S. Senior Open at Cherry Hills in Englewood, CO. Meanwhile, unknown Tom Wargo won the PGA Seniors Championship, and Tom Shaw won the Tradition, the fourth designated major tournament on the Senior tour, at Desert Mountain in Scottsdale, AZ.

LPGA Tour. Honors were contested hotly on the 1993 LPGA tour between Betsy King and Brandie Burton. King won the last event of the season to sweep the money title with $595,992, the Vare Trophy for low scoring average, and Rolex Player of the Year Honors from Burton. Burton won three tournaments, including a major championship in the du Maurier Limited Classic, and was third in money winnings.

Patty Sheehan won the Mazda LPGA Championship and one other tournament and finished second on the money list. Sheehan's fine play earned her player-of-the-year honors from the Golf Writers Association of America, and she also won her way into the LPGA Hall of Fame during the year.

Laurie Merten won the U.S. Women's Open at Crooked Stick in Indianapolis, her first tour victory in nine years. The other major triumph went to Helen Alfredsson, who captured the Nabisco Dinah Shore.

LARRY DENNIS, *"Senior Golfer"*

against three for the Europeans, with three matches halved. Beck, Jim Gallagher, Tom Kite, Davis Love III, and 51-year-old Ray Floyd all had big victories on the final day to help the U.S. team celebrate its second straight Cup victory and to raise its overall Ryder Cup record to 23-5-2. The Cup would be held again in 1995 in Rochester, NY.

South Africa native Nick Price captured player-of-the-year honors on the U.S. PGA Tour. Price won the Players Championship in late March, then won three tournaments in a row during a midsummer hot streak. At the end of the season, Price had won the money title with a record total of $1,478,557 and the Vardon Trophy for low scoring average.

However, Price only won the money title by a scant $20,000 over Paul Azinger, who won the PGA Championship at Inverness in a play-off with Greg Norman and had two other tournament victories en route to the best season of his career. The year ended on a somber note for Azinger after he was diagnosed in early December with non-Hodgkins lymphoma cancer in his right shoulder blade. Azinger's doctors expected him to recover from this illness.

Two other players—Jim Gallagher, Jr., who won the Tour Championship, one other PGA tournament, and starred in the Ryder Cup; and David Frost, another two-time tournament win-

Horse Racing

The $3 million Breeders' Cup Classic was won in 1993 by the 5-year-old French horse Arcangues. Running his first race on dirt, Arcangues went off as a 133-1 shot, marking the biggest upset in the ten-year history of the Breeders' Cup. Ridden by Jerry Bailey, Arcangues covered the 1.25-mi (2-km) Santa Anita course at Arcadia, CA, in 2:00⅘ and finished two lengths ahead of Bertrando, with Kissin Kris third.

Brocco won the $1 million Breeders' Cup Juvenile by five lengths over Blumin Affair and 13

lengths ahead of favorite Dehere, which finished eighth. Gary Stevens rode Brocco over the $1\frac{1}{16}$-mi (1.7-km) course in 1:42$\frac{4}{5}$. Lure successfully defended his 1992 win in the Breeders' Cup Mile. With Mike Smith in the saddle, the 4-year-old won in 1:09$\frac{2}{5}$. Lure's time for the 1993 race was only one second slower than the course record he set in 1992.

Sea Hero, owned by 85-year-old Paul Mellon and trained by 71-year-old Mack Miller, won the 119th Kentucky Derby in Louisville, KY. Ridden by Bailey, Sea Hero went off at almost 13-1 and became the 14th straight nonfavorite to win the 1.25-mi (2-km) race, in 2:02$\frac{2}{5}$. Sea Hero was 13th in the early going and seventh at the head of the stretch before racing past runner-up Prairie Bayou, the favorite, and third-place finisher Wild Gale. Sea Hero paid $27.80, $12.80, and $8.

The Kentucky Derby was the only Triple Crown event avoiding tragedy. Union City broke down in the 1.19-mi (1.9-km) Preakness Stakes at Baltimore, MD, and Prairie Bayou fractured a front leg in the 1.5-mi (2.4-km) Belmont Stakes at Elmont, NY. Both horses were destroyed humanely.

Three weeks before his misstep in the Belmont, Prairie Bayou, a gelding, won the Preakness in a stretch duel with Cherokee Run. Prairie Bayou followed Pine Bluff's triumph and gave co-owners John Ed Anthony and Mary Lynn Dudley their second consecutive Preakness victory. In the Belmont Stakes, Julie Krone rode Colonial Affair to victory to become the first woman to win a Triple Crown race. Unfortunately, Prairie Bayou's death detracted somewhat from Krone's achievement.

Harness Racing. Riyadh won the Cane Pace and Meadowlands Pace but fell short of pacing's Triple Crown by finishing second to Life Sign in the Little Brown Jug at Delaware, OH. Life

© Bill Frakes/"Sports Illustrated"

Colonial Affair, ridden by Julie Krone, won the 125th running of the Belmont Stakes in 1993. Highlighting a 12-year career, Krone became the first woman to take a Triple Crown event.

Sign, driven by John Campbell, prevailed in a half-mile head-to-head duel with Riyadh at the Delaware County Fair Grounds.

American Winner won the Hambletonian, the sport's showcase event for 3-year-old trotters, at East Rutherford, NJ, and also won the Yonkers Trot at Yonkers, NY. But American Winner, trained by former horse-van driver Milton Smith, broke stride while trying to capture trotting's Triple Crown in the 101st Kentucky Futurity in Lexington, KY. Pine Chip, driven by Campbell, defeated Oaklea Bluejay by 6$\frac{1}{2}$ lengths.

STAN SUTTON

HORSE RACING

Major U.S. Thoroughbred Races

Arkansas Derby: Rockamundo, $500,000 (total purse)
Arlington Million: Star of Cozzene, $1 million
Belmont Stakes: Colonial Affair, $1,740,900
Blue Grass Stakes: Prairie Bayou, $500,000
Breeders' Cup Classic: Arcangues, $3 million
Breeders' Cup Turf: Kotashaan, $2 million
Breeders' Cup Juvenile: Brocco, $1 million
Breeders' Cup Juvenile Fillies: Phone Chatter, $1 million
Breeders' Cup Mile: Lure, $1 million
Breeders' Cup Distaff: Hollywood Wildcat, $1 million
Breeders' Cup Sprint: Cardmania, $1 million
Champagne Stakes: Dehere, $500,000
Florida Derby: Bull Inthe Heather, $500,000
Donn Handicap: Pistols and Roses, $500,000
Haskell Invitational Handicap: Kissin Kris, $500,000
Hollywood Gold Cup: Best Pal, $750,000
Iselin Handicap: Valley Crossing, $500,000
Jim Beam Stakes: Prairie Bayou, $600,000
Jockey Club Gold Cup: Miner's Mark, $850,000
Kentucky Derby: Sea Hero, $985,900
Kentucky Oaks: Dispute, $294,200
Mother Goose Stakes: Sky Beauty, $200,000
Pimlico Special: Devil His Due, $600,000
Preakness Stakes: Prairie Bayou, $725,900
Santa Anita Derby: Personal Hope, $500,000
Santa Anita Handicap: Sir Beaufort, $1 million
Strub Stakes: Siberian Summer, $500,000
Suburban Handicap: Devil His Due, $300,000

Super Derby: Wallenda, $750,000
Rothmans International: Husband, $1,038,500
Travers Stakes: Sea Hero, $1 million
Whitney Handicap: Brunswick, $250,000
Wood Memorial: Storm Tower, $500,000

Major North American Harness Races

Breeders Crown Horse and Gelding Pace: Staying Together, $350,000
Breeders Crown Horse and Gelding Trot: Earl, $350,000
Breeders Crown Mare Pace: Shady Daisy, $300,000
Breeders Crown Mare Trot: Lifetime Dream, $300,000
Breeders Crown 2-year-old Filly Pace: Electric Slide, $300,000
Breeders Crown 2-year-old Colt Pace: Expensive Scooter, $300,000
Breeders Crown 2-year-old Filly Trot: Gleam, $300,000
Breeders Crown 2-year-old Colt Trot: Westgate Crown, $300,000
Breeders Crown 3-year-old Filly Trot: Expressway Hanover, $300,000
Breeders Crown 3-year-old Colt Trot: Pine Chip, $300,000
Breeders Crown 3-year-old Filly Pace: Immortality, $300,000
Breeders Crown 3-year-old Colt Pace: Life Sign, $300,000
Cane Pace: Riyadh, $432,800
Hambletonian: American Winner, $1,104,000
Kentucky Futurity: Pine Chip, $157,000
Little Brown Jug: Life Sign, $465,500
Meadowlands Pace: Presidential Ball, $1 million
Messenger Stakes: Riyadh, $328,305
Peter Haughton Memorial: Westgate Crown, $625,250
Sweetheart Pace: Freedom's Friend, $550,250
Woodrow Wilson Pace: Magical Mike, $747,700
World Trotting Derby: Pine Chip, $532,000

Ice Hockey

The Montreal Canadiens brought in a new coach, Jacques Demers, but relied on an old goalie, Patrick Roy, to capture their 24th Stanley Cup championship in 1993. They won 16 of their last 18 play-off games, including a National Hockey League (NHL) record ten straight in sudden-death overtime, and dispatched Wayne Gretzky and the Los Angeles Kings, four games to one, in the final.

After being swept in four straight games by Boston in their division final in 1992, the Canadiens made several changes. They hired Demers as coach to replace Pat Burns, who quit and eventually moved to the Toronto Maple Leafs. They traded for Edmonton's Vince Damphousse, who led them in points during the regular season (97) and the play-offs (23). And they got masterful play-off goaltending from Roy, who won his second Conn Smythe trophy as the most valuable player (MVP) of the play-offs. Roy, who had a very ordinary regular season, outdueled the Kings' Kelly Hrudey in the Cup final as the Canadiens won their first NHL title since 1986.

The Canadiens and Kings did not figure to be in the final, but Pittsburgh's reign as two-time champion ended in its division championship when the New York Islanders shocked the Penguins. Pittsburgh had ended the season undefeated in the last 18 games (17 wins and a tie), but it fell to the Islanders in overtime in the seventh game of the Patrick Division final. The Kings, who never had won more than one play-off round since entering the NHL in 1967, rode the revived Gretzky, who won the play-off scoring title with 40 points. Gretzky only had 65 points in the regular season after missing the first three months with a serious back injury.

Regular Season. The Penguins, even without the cancer-stricken Mario Lemieux for two months, finished with a franchise-high 119 points to win the overall points title. They were 26 points ahead of second-place Washington in the Patrick Division. In all, seven teams had 100 points or more in the expanded 84-game—four more than the year before—season. The Boston Bruins, who captured the Adams Division, had the second-best points total with 109. Two other teams in the Adams—Quebec (104) and Montreal (102)—also exceeded 100 points. The Chicago Blackhawks (106) took the Norris Division, three points ahead of Detroit. The Vancouver Canucks (101) won their second straight Smythe Division title.

Lemieux won his fourth Art Ross trophy as the scoring champion, even with his bout with Hodgkin's disease. He had 160 points in 60 games, 12 more than the runner-up, Buffalo captain Pat LaFontaine, who played 84 games. Boston's Adam Oates was third with 142, with Detroit's Steve Yzerman next at 137. In all, 21 players had 100 or more points, compared with only nine in the 1991-92 season. The admittance of two more expansion teams—Tampa Bay and Ottawa—had a good deal to do with that. Winnipeg rookie Teemu Selanne and Buffalo's Alexander Mogilny tied for the league high in

The Montreal Canadiens were jubilant after they defeated the Los Angeles Kings four games to one to capture the 1993 Stanley Cup. Goaltender Patrick Roy took the Conn Smythe Trophy as the most valuable player of the play-offs.

© David E. Klutho/"Sports Illustrated"

goals with 76. Selanne shattered the NHL rookie record for goals (53), set by New York Islander winger Mike Bossy in 1977-78.

Play-offs. None of the regular-season division champions or teams finishing second got past

ICE HOCKEY

National Hockey League
(Final Standings, 1992-93)

Wales Conference

Adams Division	W	L	T	Pts.	For	Goals Against
*Boston	51	26	7	109	332	268
*Quebec	47	27	10	104	351	300
*Montreal	48	30	6	102	326	280
*Buffalo	38	36	10	86	335	297
Hartford	26	52	6	58	284	369
Ottawa	10	70	4	24	202	395
Patrick Division						
*Pittsburgh	56	21	7	119	367	268
*Washington	43	34	7	93	325	286
*N.Y. Islanders	40	37	7	87	335	297
*New Jersey	40	37	7	87	308	299
Philadelphia	36	37	11	83	319	319
N.Y. Rangers	34	39	11	79	304	308

Campbell Conference

Norris Division	W	L	T	Pts.	For	Goals Against
*Chicago	47	25	12	106	279	230
*Detroit	47	28	9	103	369	280
*Toronto	44	29	11	99	288	241
*St. Louis	37	36	11	85	282	278
Minnesota	36	38	10	82	272	293
Tampa Bay	23	54	7	53	245	332
Smythe Division						
*Vancouver	46	29	9	101	346	278
*Calgary	43	30	11	97	322	282
*Los Angeles	39	35	10	88	338	340
*Winnipeg	40	37	7	87	322	320
Edmonton	26	50	8	60	242	337
San Jose	11	71	2	24	218	414

*In play-offs

Stanley Cup Play-offs
Wales Conference

First Round	Buffalo	4 games	Boston	0
	Montreal	4 games	Quebec	2
	N.Y. Islanders	4 games	Washington	2
	Pittsburgh	4 games	New Jersey	1
Second Round	Montreal	4 games	Buffalo	0
	N.Y. Islanders	4 games	Pittsburgh	3
Finals	Montreal	4 games	N.Y. Islanders	1

Campbell Conference

First Round	Los Angeles	4 games	Calgary	2
	St. Louis	4 games	Chicago	0
	Toronto	4 games	Detroit	3
	Vancouver	4 games	Winnipeg	2
Second Round	Los Angeles	4 games	Vancouver	2
	Toronto	4 games	St. Louis	3
Finals	Los Angeles	4 games	Toronto	3

Stanley Cup Finals

Montreal	4 games	Los Angeles	1

Individual Honors

Hart Trophy (most valuable player): Mario Lemieux, Pittsburgh
Ross Trophy (leading scorer): Mario Lemieux
Vezina Trophy (top goaltender): Ed Belfour, Chicago
Norris Trophy (best defenseman): Chris Chelios, Chicago
Selke Trophy (best defensive forward): Doug Gilmour, Toronto
Calder Trophy (rookie of the year): Teemu Selanne, Winnipeg
Lady Byng Trophy (most gentlemanly player): Pierre Turgeon, N.Y. Islanders
Conn Smythe Trophy (most valuable in play-offs): Patrick Roy, Montreal
Adams Trophy (coach of the year): Pat Burns, Toronto
King Clancy Trophy (humanitarian service): Dave Poulin, Boston
Bill Masterton Trophy (dedication and sportsmanship): Mario Lemieux

NCAA: Maine

the second round in the play-offs. The Blackhawks, who lost to Pittsburgh in four straight games in the 1992 Stanley Cup final, crashed in their opening-round series with the fourth-place St. Louis Blues, losing four in a row. Detroit also went out, losing in overtime in the seventh game to third-place Toronto. The Blues got superb goaltending from Curtis Joseph, but the Maple Leafs managed to win the division final in seven games.

The Kings finally celebrated a division title when they surprised two teams that finished considerably ahead of them—Calgary and Vancouver. The third-place team beat Calgary in six games and the Canucks in the same number. The Canucks had beaten the Kings seven out of nine times during the season, but Gretzky had ten points in the final three games of the series. Vancouver had taken out Winnipeg in their play-off round, also in six games.

In the Adams Division, Boston fell to place Buffalo in four straight games, and Montreal dropped the first two games of the best-of-seven series to Quebec but won four in a row in a heated rivalry between two cities only 120 mi (193 km) apart. The Canadiens humbled the Sabres, who lost Mogilny in the third game with a broken ankle, in a four-game sweep.

The Penguins barely broke a sweat beating fourth-place New Jersey in five games in their first round, but could not handle the inspired Islanders, who played all but the last game without their best player, Pierre Turgeon. Lemieux' back acted up and he was not his usual dominant self, but the Islanders got great goaltending from Glenn Healy to win the final overtime game. The Islanders had won three overtime games against Washington in a six-game, round-one victory.

In the Wales Conference final, Montreal cruised behind the excellent goaltending of Roy to a four-games-to-one victory over the Islanders. New York could not sustain its fire after the Pittsburgh win. In the Campbell Conference, Gretzky scored three goals in the seventh game to carry Los Angeles past Toronto, four games to three.

Gretzky had four points—three assists and an empty-net goal—as the Kings beat the Canadiens in Montreal, 4-1, in the first game of the final. It was the fourth time in the play-offs the Kings had won the first game of a series on the road. The Kings were 77 seconds away from winning Game 2, but Montreal scored on a power play to tie it when Marty McSorley was penalized for using an illegal stick. Then defenseman Eric Desjardins got his third goal of the game, 51 seconds into overtime, for a 3-2 victory. Desjardins became the first defenseman in NHL finals history to score three times in a game.

The Canadiens took Game 3, 4-3, winning their ninth straight overtime game when John LeClair scored on a wild scramble, 34 seconds into the extra period. In Game 4, the Kings fought back from a 2-0 deficit but LeClair scored

again in the 14th minute for a 3-2 win. In the clinching game, center Paul DiPietro, who spent a good portion of the season playing for Montreal's minor-league affiliate, scored two goals as the Canadiens registered a masterful 4-1 victory.

JIM MATHESON
"Edmonton Journal"

Ice Skating

U.S. figure skaters turned in disappointing performances at most international competitions in 1993. It was the first time the United States had won no medals at the world championships since 1964; the nation would be permitted only eight figure-skating entries in the 1994 Winter Olympics, its smallest contingent since 1976. The year's new star at the world championships was Ukraine's Oksana Baiul, a 15-year-old who dazzled the judges and demolished her better-known competitors.

In the European championships, France's Surya Bonaly took her third consecutive gold medal. Dmitri Dmitrenko of Ukraine won the men's championship, and Marina Eltsova and Andrei Bushkov of Russia took the gold for pairs. Russia's Maya Usova and Aleksandr Zhulin won both the European and world ice-dancing crowns.

Speed Skating. Falko Vandstra of the Netherlands won the men's all-around world speed-skating championship, and Gunda Kleeman-Niemann repeated as the women's all-around champion.

Appearing in international competition for the first time, Oksana Baiul, a 15-year-old Ukrainian, won the women's title at the World Figure-Skating Championship.

© Anton Want/Allsport

ICE SKATING

World Figure-Skating Championships

Men: Kurt Browning, Canada
Women: Oksana Baiul, Ukraine
Pairs: Isabelle Brasseur and Lloyd Eisler, Canada
Dance: Maya Usova and Aleksandr Zhulin, Russia

U.S. Figure-Skating Championships

Men: Scott Davis
Women: Nancy Kerrigan
Pairs: Calla Urbanski and Rocky Marval
Dance: Renée Roca and Gorsha Sur

World All-Around Speed-Skating Championships

Men's Overall: Falko Vandstra, Netherlands
Men's 500 meters: Chen Song, China
Men's 1,500 meters: Johann Olav Koss, Norway
Men's 5,000 meters: Falko Vandstra
Men's 10,000 meters: Bart Veldkamp, Netherlands
Women's Overall: Gunda Kleeman-Niemann, Germany
Women's 500 meters: Qiabo Ye, China
Women's 1,500 meters: Gunda Kleeman-Niemann
Women's 3,000 meters: Gunda Kleeman-Niemann
Women's 5,000 meters: Gunda Kleeman-Niemann

Skiing

During the 1993 ski season, Anita Wachter of Austria ended countrywoman Petra Kronberger's three-year reign as World Cup overall champion with an impressive performance in Are, Sweden, and Austrian Marc Girardelli made World Cup history when he won a record fifth overall title. Norway's Kjetil Andre Aamodt, the runner-up to Girardelli, took the giant slalom and the super-giant slalom.

In the U.S. Alpine championships, U.S. and Canadian skiiers fought difficult weather to take home most of the medals, with the U.S. women's team winning 13 out of the 15 available medals. The Canadian men were impressive, sweeping the giant slalom event and winning three of the total five golds. Matt Grosjean of the United States defended his slalom title, and the United States' Diann Roffe-Steinrotter kept her claim to the giant-slalom title for the women.

Norway's Lasse Kjus and Mirian Vogt captured the men's and women's combined, respectively, at the World Alpine Championships.

SKIING

World Cup

Men's Downhill: Franz Heinzer, Switzerland
Men's Slalom: Tomas Fogdoe, Sweden
Men's Giant Slalom: Kjetil Andre Aamodt, Norway
Men's Super-Giant Slalom: Kjetil Andre Aamodt
Men's Overall: Marc Girardelli, Austria
Women's Downhill: Katja Seizinger, Germany
Women's Slalom: Vreni Schneider, Switzerland
Women's Giant Slalom: Carole Merle, France
Women's Super-Giant Slalom: Katja Seizinger
Women's Overall: Anita Wachter, Austria

U.S. Alpine Championships

Men's Combined: Chris Puckett, United States
Men's Downhill: Cary Mullen, Canada
Men's Slalom: Matt Grosjean, United States
Men's Giant Slalom: Thomas Grandi, Canada
Men's Super-Giant Slalom: Cary Mullen
Women's Combined: Julie Parisien, United States
Women's Downhill: Lindsay Roberts, Canada
Women's Slalom: Kristi Terzian, United States
Women's Giant Slalom: Diann Roffe-Steinrotter, United States
Women's Super-Giant Slalom: Picabo Street, United States

NCAA: University of Utah

Soccer

The qualifying round for the 1994 World Cup, soccer's quadrennial spectacle, ended on Nov. 17, 1993, when Argentina became the final country to join the 24-team field. The World Cup—the most popular sports championship on the planet—would be hosted for the first time by the United States in 1994. As the host country, the United States was entered automatically into the field, but the U.S. team showed enough promise against international competition to be considered as a dark horse in the tournament. Germany, the defending champion, also received an automatic bid. The 52-game event was scheduled to be held in nine U.S. cities in July 1994.

The most startling victory by the U.S. team came against England, which lost for only the second time to the United States in an international level match. The United States won, 2-0, with goals coming from midfielders Tom Dooley and Alexi Lallas. The English eventually were eliminated from the World Cup competition.

U.S. players were benefiting from the use of a $3 million training facility in Mission Viejo, CA. Players competing for places on the team were earning up to $70,000 per year, highlighting the seriousness with which U.S. officials were approaching the event. The nucleus of the squad was composed of a dozen players with extensive overseas experience. Despite predictions by officials in other parts of the world that the World Cup would not be popular in the United States, ticket sales were so brisk that every game in the tournament was expected to sell out.

World. A major scandal rocked European soccer circles when Jean-Pierre Bernes, the general manager of the Olympique de Marseille (OM) team, was accused in July of offering money to players on a rival team to fix a match. OM had beaten A.C. Milan in the European Championship Cup in May. Late in the summer OM was banned from European Cup competition.

United States. The University of Virginia won its third straight men's NCAA Division I championship, beating South Carolina, 2-0. On the women's side a perennial soccer power, the University of North Carolina, won another title—the school's eighth consecutive championship—downing George Mason, 6-0.

In professional play, the Dallas Sidekicks won both the regular-season and play-off titles of the Continental Soccer League, beating the San Diego Sockers in the play-off final. The Colorado Foxes defeated the Los Angeles Salsa in overtime, 3-1, in the championship game of the American Professional Soccer League.

PAUL ATTNER

Swimming

A flurry of world records was made late in 1993, as Chinese women set three new short-course marks and a U.S. relay established one new record at a meet in Majorca. At both of the year's big events—the Pan Pacific Championships in Kobe, Japan, and the Phillips 66 Spring National Championships in Nashville—U.S. swimmers dominated but did not set any world records.

World Records. In individual events, Chinese women rewrote the record books at Majorca: Guohoug Dai won the 400-m individual medley (4:29) and Jinyi Le captured the 100-m freestyle (53.01). In relay events, Chinese women won the 800-m freestyle relay (7:52.45), while U.S. men set a mark in the 400-m medley relay (3:32.57).

The year's only other world record came in the men's 100-m breaststroke when Karoly Guttler of Hungary clocked 1:00.95 at the European championships in Sheffield, England. The meet's outstanding performance, however, was reserved for Franziska van Almsick of Germany, who won six gold medals, tying a mark set by another German, Michael Gross, who won six races at the 1985 European championships.

Pan Pacific Championships. The U.S. team dominated the meet, winning 23 races—more than all other nations combined. On the first day of competition, the U.S. winners were Jeff Rouse in the 100-m men's backstroke, Josh Davis in the 200-m freestyle, and Lea Loveless in the women's 100-m backstroke. Hayley Lewis of Australia swam the third-fastest women's 1,500-m freestyle ever—16 minutes, 4.84 seconds. The next day, Jenny Thompson (55.25) and Jon Olsen (49.73) won the 100-m freestyle events for the U.S. team.

The squad made a virtual shambles of the meet on the third day, winning seven of eight events as Thompson, an Olympic champion and world-record holder, won gold medals for the 100-m butterfly and as a member of the 400-m freestyle relay team. Thompson's performance at Kobe, where her 100-m freestyle time was a shade slower than her world record of 54.48, capped a brilliant season. Kieren Perkins of Australia, the world-record holder in the 800-m and 1,500-m, won the men's 400-m freestyle.

Phillips Championship. Pablo Morales was the big attraction at the Phillips 66 Spring National Championships in Nashville. Morales, at the age of 27, had astonished the swimming world by winning the 100-m butterfly gold medal at the 1992 Olympics. That comeback earned him the U.S. Olympic Committee's "sportsman of the year" award. At the age of 28, when most swimmers have retired, he was competing again. Morales turned in the fastest time in the heats, 54.32 seconds, but he faltered in the final, losing to Brian Alderman.

The meet saw other notable efforts. Janet Evans, Olympic champion and world-record holder, won the 800-m freestyle in 8:34.99, her 31st national title. Only Tracy Caulkins (48) and Johnny Weissmuller (36) had more. Also, the fifth-fastest 50-m freestyle ever (22.26) was turned in by Lithuania's Raimundas Marzuolis in a heat. He went on to win the gold in 22.57.

GEORGE DE GREGORIO

Tennis

Sadly for the game of tennis, the most stunning and influential stroke of the year was made with a 9-inch (23-cm) boning knife, held by a deranged German spectator, Guenther Parche. On April 30 he plunged the blade into the back of then Number 1-ranking player Monica Seles during a tournament match at Hamburg and changed the history of the game.

The intent of Parche's disturbing act of violence was to restore countrywoman Steffi Graf as the world's top-ranked women's player. As Seles—a U.S. resident from the former Yugoslavia—missed the remainder of the year recovering from her physical and emotional wounds, Graf, 24 (loser of the Australian final to Seles, 4-6, 6-3, 6-2), indeed did retake the Number 1 ranking.

Graf won a third French Open title over Mary Joe Fernandez of the United States, 4-6, 6-2, 6-4; a fifth Wimbledon over Czech Jana Novotna, 7-6, 1-6, 6-4; and a third U.S. Open over surprising 12th-seeded Czech Helena Suko-

Pete Sampras, a 22-year-old who resides in Tampa, FL, emerged as the Number 1 men's tennis player in 1993. His tournament victories included Wimbledon and the U.S. Open.

© Focus on Sports

va, 6-3, 6-3. Graf also won the season-ending Virginia Slims Championship in New York for a third time, beating Spaniard Arantxa Sanchez Vicario 6-1, 6-4, 3-6, 6-1, to finish with a 76-6 match mark and a female season prize-money record of $2,571,337. Seven other singles titles raised Graf's career total to 79, including 14 majors—pushing her to fifth on the all-time roll.

Seles' Australian triumph was her third, an eighth major well before her 20th birthday. Even though she won one other tournament—for a career total of 32—and posted a 17-2 match record prior to the stabbing, Seles, inactive for most of 1993, declined to a Number 8 ranking. Her removal was the most shocking alteration in the game's flow since 1954 when the great career of Maureen Connolly—with nine major titles by age 19—ended in a horseback-riding accident.

Veteran Martina Navratilova, 37, of the United States completed her 21st professional season and her 19th straight year in the top ten (at Number 3), and was a Wimbledon semifinalist for a 16th time. She won five titles in singles and three in doubles, stretching her all-time career records to 166 and 160, respectively. She also extended her career prize-money record to $19,432,645 after collecting $1,036,119 in 1993.

Conchita Martinez, winner of five titles, and Sanchez Vicario, with four, paired to capture a second Federation Cup for Spain, winning 3-0 in the final over Australia. The Puerto Rico-Belarus coalition of Gigi Fernandez and Natalya Zvereva won 11 tournaments—including the Australian, French, and Wimbledon—but missed out on a doubles Grand Slam with a U.S. semifinal loss to eventual champs Sanchez Vicario and Sukova, 1-6, 6-3, 6-4.

The Men. U.S. players were dominant on the men's side where Pete Sampras, 22, and Jim Courier, 23, battled all year for the top ranking. Although Courier began sharply with his second straight Australian title over Sweden's Stefan Edberg, 6-2, 6-1, 2-6, 7-5, he lost to Spain's Sergi Bruguera, 6-4, 2-6, 6-2, 3-6, 6-3, falling one step short of a third successive French. Then Sampras, high with eight titles and an 83-15 match mark for the year, seized Number 1 by knocking off Courier in the Wimbledon final, 7-6, 7-6, 3-6, 6-3, and defeating the startling 12th seed, Cedric Pioline—the first Frenchman in the U.S. Open final since 1932—6-4, 6-4, 6-3, to take an upset-riddled U.S., his second.

Courier and Sampras gave the United States three major crowns for the second consecutive year. A fading, 33-year-old Ivan Lendl of the United States finished at Number 19, but won two singles titles, lifting his career total to 94, second only to Jimmy Connors' 106. Lendl's winnings, $1,075,876, hiked his record career total earnings to $20,248,503. Sampras set a season financial record, winning $4,574,331.

Although U.S. players won 27 of 88 titles on the male circuit, Germany's Michael Stich beat

TENNIS

Davis Cup: Germany
Federation Cup: Spain

Significant Tournaments

Australian Open—men's singles: Jim Courier; men's doubles: Danie Visser (South Africa) and Laurie Warder (Australia); women's singles: Monica Seles (Yugoslavia); women's doubles: Gigi Fernandez and Natalia Zvereva (Belarus); mixed doubles: Arantxa Sanchez Vicario (Spain) and Todd Woodbridge (Australia).

International Players Championships—men's singles: Pete Sampras; women's singles: Arantxa Sanchez Vicario (Spain); women's doubles: Larisa Neiland (Latvia) and Jana Novotna (Czech Republic).

Italian Open—men's singles: Jim Courier; men's doubles: Jacco Eltingh and Paul Haarhuis (Netherlands); women's singles: Conchita Martinez (Spain); women's doubles: Arantxa Sanchez Vicario (Spain) and Jana Novotna (Czech Republic).

French Open—men's singles: Sergi Bruguera (Spain); men's doubles: Luke Jensen and Murphy Jensen; women's singles: Steffi Graf (Germany); women's doubles: Gigi Fernandez and Natalia Zvereva (Belarus); mixed doubles: Eugenia Maniokova (Russia) and Andrei Olhovskiv (Russia).

Wimbledon—men's singles: Pete Sampras; men's doubles: Todd Woodbridge (Australia) and Mark Woodforde (Australia); women's singles: Steffi Graf (Germany); women's doubles: Gigi Fernandez and Natalia Zvereva (Belarus); mixed doubles: Mark Woodforde (Australia) and Martina Navratilova.

U.S. Open—men's singles: Pete Sampras; men's doubles: Ken Flach and Rick Leach; women's singles: Steffi Graf (Germany); women's doubles: Arantxa Sanchez Vicario (Spain) and Helena Sukova (Czech Republic); mixed doubles: Helena Sukova (Czech Republic) and Todd Woodbridge (Australia); senior men's singles: Gene Mayer; senior men's doubles: Marty Riessen and Sherwood Stewart; senior women's doubles: Betsy Nagelson and Joanne Russell.

A.T.P. Finals—singles: Michael Stich (Germany); doubles: Jacco Eltingh (Netherlands) and Paul Haarhuis (Netherlands).

Virginia Slims Championship—singles: Steffi Graf (Germany); doubles: Gigi Fernandez and Natalia Zvereva (Belarus).

NCAA (Division I)—men's singles: Chris Woodruff, Tennessee; men's doubles: David Blair and Mark Merklein, Florida; women's singles: Susan Gilchrist, Texas.

N.B. All players are from the United States unless otherwise noted.

Sampras for the tour-ending ATP Championship, 7-6, 2-6, 7-6, 6-2, at Frankfurt to slide ahead of Courier to the Number 2 spot.

A Netherlands pairing of Jacco Eltingh and Paul Haarhuis beat the Wimbledon champs, Australia's Mark Woodforde and Todd Woodbridge, 7-6, 7-6, 6-4 to win the ATP Doubles Championship at Johannesburg; this was the pair's sixth title for the season.

Stich led Germany to a third Davis Cup, 4-1 over Australia in the final before a partisan crowd at Dusseldorf. The reign of the 1992 Cup-winning U.S. team lasted only 110 days, ended by a first-round loss to Australia. Top U.S. players Courier and Sampras declined to play in the tournament.

BUD COLLINS
"The Boston Globe"/NBC

Track and Field

Track and field was replete with world-class performances in 1993. The world championships in August produced some Olympian efforts, and the men's mile and the women's 10,000-m run created an unusual stir among aficionados everywhere.

Running Events. Algeria's Noureddine Morceli, 23, shaved almost two seconds off the world record for the mile, long considered track's glamour event. Morceli accomplished the astonishing feat on September 5 at Rieti, Italy, clocking 3 minutes 44.39 seconds to erase the mark of 3:46.32 set by Steve Cram of Britain in July 1985—the largest drop in the mile record in 28 years. Morceli was unbeaten in the 1,500-m and mile during the season.

Three days after Morceli's feat, the National Games in Beijing, China, produced more remarkable performances. The world record in the women's 10,000-m was shattered when Wang Junxia of China lowered the mark by an astronomical 42 seconds. Wang's time of 29 minutes 31.78 seconds topped the 30:13.74 set by Ingrid Kristiansen of Norway in 1986. The record assault continued as Wang broke the 3,000-m record twice—in two days—by a total of 16 seconds with 8:06.11, and Qu Yunxia raced the 1,500-m in 3:50.46, two seconds faster than the old mark. The Chinese were accused of using performance-enhancing drugs, but Chinese officials credited the results to hard endurance training.

At the world championships in Stuttgart, Germany, the U.S. men's 1,600-m relay team of Andrew Valmon, Quincy Watts, Butch Reynolds, and Michael Johnson trounced the previous world record by 1.45 seconds with a time of 2.54.29, while the U.S. 400-m relay team of Jon Drummond, Andre Cason, Dennis Mitchell, and Leroy Burrell tied a world mark of 37.40 seconds. The U.S. team dominated the event, winning 26 medals—13 gold, seven silver, and six bronze.

Meanwhile, the 100-m event at Stuttgart was billed as a showcase for superstars. Linford Christie, the English Olympic champion, was pitted against Carl Lewis, the 32-year-old American who had won three world titles and held the 100-m world record. Also in the field were rapidly ascending U.S. sprinters Cason and Mitchell. The crowd of 45,000 was not disappointed. Christie churned to the tape in 9.87 seconds, only .01 second slower than Lewis' world mark. Cason finished second in 9.92, Mitchell was third in 9.99, and Lewis was fourth with 10.02. Earlier, on July 30, Christie and Lewis had been guaranteed $150,000 each to compete in a special 100-m dash at Gateshead, England. Christie prevailed (10.08), with Lewis finishing third (10.12).

Also at the world championships, Colin Jackson of Wales beat the 110-m hurdles world record by .01 second, with a time of 12.91 seconds. U.S. hurdlers had held the 110-m hurdles mark since 1989.

The men's world 10,000-m record was broken twice in five days by two Kenyan runners. On July 5 at Stockholm, Sweden, Richard Chelimo clocked 27:07.91 to lower the 27:08.23 set by Arturo Barrios of Mexico in 1989. Then on July 10 at Bislett Stadium in Oslo, Norway, Yobes Ondieki became the first to break the 27-minute barrier, with a time of 26:58.38. Ondieki's record was the 50th world standard at Bislett Stadium since 1924.

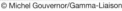

On Sept. 5, 1993, Algeria's Noureddine Morceli, who won the 1,500-m run at the world championships (left), *lowered the world record for the mile to 3:44.39. Also in September, China's Wang Junxia* (right) *set a new world mark for the women's 3,000 meters—8:06.11.*

Field Events. High jumper Javier Sotomayor of Cuba, the Olympic gold medalist and already the world-record holder at 8 ft (2.44 m), raised the mark to 8' 1/2" (2.45 m) at Salamanca, Spain, on July 27. The record book also made room for Jan Zelezny of the Czech Republic, who threw the javelin 313' 10" (95.66 m) at an international meet at Sheffield, England, in August.

GEORGE DE GREGORIO

Yachting

Yachting in 1993 did not escape the worldwide economic recession, as many events either were curtailed or eliminated. Many hearty souls, however, kept the sport afloat and exciting.

A group of Ukrainian sailors who had dreamed of competing in the six-month, 32,000-mi (51 488-km) Whitbread Round the World Race finally got their wish. After trying to find financial backing for nearly three years, skipper Anatoly Verba brought the 63-ft (19-m) *Odessa* to Tampa, FL, where she was completed and outfitted. The crew, which built the boat, lived in ramshackle housing and labored long hours to finish the yacht. It embarked from Tampa in September for Southampton, England, where the Whitbread started.

Another long-distance event, the 28,000-mi (45 052-km) around-the-world British Steel Challenge, also provided seafarers with excitement in an unusual season. Although the race of 67-ft (20-m) steel yachts was marred by an accident in which one sailor dived off the stern of his

yacht and was lost at sea, the finish at Southampton, England, on May 23 gave *Nuclear Electric,* skippered by John Chittenden, a two-hour ten-minute victory over *Group 4 Securitas,* skippered by Mike Golding, for the closest finish ever recorded in a world marathon.

The recession forced cancellations on the Grand Prix match-racing circuit in France, Germany, and Hong Kong. One notable casualty was the Liberty Cup regatta in New York. But somehow, an event most would have expected to go by the wayside—the $50,000 ACY Cup in Rovinj, Croatia, close to the war front in the Balkans—was listed on the Omega Grand Prix schedule.

The Spanish 60-ft (18-m) yacht, *Galicia 93 Pescanova,* was the first to finish on elapsed time in the British Fastnet Race, the prestigious finale to the Admiral's Cup series. Skippered by Javier de la Gandara, *Galicia* beat *Winston,* owned by Dennis Conner, who was competing elsewhere, by 30 minutes in the 605-mi (973-km) race that hosted a fleet of 243.

Rich Wilson of Marblehead, MA, skipper of *Great American II,* and his partner Bill Biewenga of Newport, RI, sailed their trimaran nonstop for 69 days 19 hours to break the 140-year-old San Francisco-to-Boston speed mark by almost a week. In 1853 the famous clipper ship, *Northern Light,* set the previous record of 76 days 6 hours.

Windquest, a 70-ft (21-m) sloop owned by Rich DeVos of Ada, MI, distinguished herself by winning the Chicago-to-Mackinac Island, MI, race.

GEORGE DE GREGORIO

SPORTS SUMMARIES[1]

ARCHERY—World Champions: men: target: Kyung Mo Park, South Korea; indoor freestyle: Gennadi Matrofanov, Russia; indoor compound bow: Kirk Ethridge, Rogersville, TN; women: target: Hyo Jung Kim, South Korea; indoor freestyle: Jennifer O'Donnell, Farmington Hill, MI; indoor compound bow: Inga Low, Roseville, CA.

BADMINTON—World Champions: men's singles: Joko Suprianto, Indonesia; women's singles: Susi Susanti, Indonesia.

BIATHLON—U.S. Champions: men's 10k: Duncan Douglas, Lake Placid, NY; men's 20k: Ian Harvey, Jericho Center, VT; women's 7.5k: Angie Stevenson, Bend, OR; women's 15k: Beth Coats, Breckenridge, CO.

BILLIARDS—World Champions: men's 9-ball: Johnny Archer, Twin Cities, GA; women's 9-ball: Loree Jon Jones, Hillsborough, NJ.

BOBSLEDDING—World Champions: 2-man: Christoph Langen, Germany; 4-man: Gustav Weder, Switzerland.

BOWLING—Professional Bowlers Association Tour: BPAA U.S. Open: Del Ballard, Jr., Richardson, TX; Tournament of Champions: George Branham III, Indianapolis, IN; Bud Light PBA National Championship: Ron Palombi, Jr., Erie, PA; Bud Light Hall of Fame Championship: Bob Learn, Jr., Erie, PA. **Ladies Professional Bowlers Tour:** BPAA U.S. Open: Dede Davidson, San Jose, CA; Sam's Town Invitational: Robin Romeo, Van Nuys, CA.

CANOEING—U.S. Sprint National Champions: men: canoe: 500m: Jim Terrell, Newport Beach, CA; 1,000m: Zsolt Molnar, Newport Beach, CA; kayak: 500m: Peter Newton, Bellevue, WA; 1,000m: Mike Herbert, Rogers, AR; women: kayak: 500m: Traci Phillips, Honolulu, HI; 1,000m: Shirley Dery-Batlik, Costa Mesa, CA.

CASTING—U.S. Champions: men's all-around: Chris Korich, Oakland, CA; men's all-distance: tie, Steve Rajeff, Poulsbo, WA, and Steve Korich, Oakland, CA.

CROSS-COUNTRY—World Champions: men: William Sigei, Kenya; women: Albertina Dias, Portugal. **U.S. Champions:** men: Todd Williams, Knoxville, TN; women: Lynn Jennings, Newmarket, NH.

CURLING—U.S. Champions: men: Scott Baird, Bemidji, MN; women: Bev Behnke, Denver, CO.

CYCLING—World Champions: men's pro road: Lance Armstrong, Austin, TX; men's pro sprint: Gary Newland, Australia; men's pro pursuit: Graeme Obree, Britain; men's points race: Etienne de Wilde, Belgium; women's road: Leontien van Moorsel, the Netherlands; women's points race: Ingrid Haringa, the Netherlands. **Tour de France:** men: Miguel Indurain, Spain.

DOG SHOWS—Westminster: best in show: Ch. Salilyn's Condor, English springer spaniel, owned by Donna and Dr. Roger Herzig, Louisville, KY, and Julia Gasow.

EQUESTRIAN—World Champions: World Cup Jumping: Ludger Beerbaum, Germany; World Cup Dressage: Monica Theodorescu, Germany.

FENCING—World Champions: men's foil: Alexander Koch, Germany; men's saber: Grigory Kirienko, Russia; men's épée: Pavel Korobkov, Russia; women's foil: Francesca Bortolozzi, Italy; women's épée: Oksana Yermakova, Estonia.

FIELD HOCKEY—NCAA Division I: Maryland.

GYMNASTICS—World Champions: men's all-around: Vitaly Scherbo, Belarus; men's floor exercise: Grigori Misutin, Ukraine; men's parallel bars: Vitaly Scherbo; men's still rings: Yrul Chechi, Italy; men's vault: Vitaly Scherbo; women's all-around: Shannon Miller, Edmund, OK; women's floor exercise: Shannon Miller; women's uneven bars: Shannon Miller; women's balance beam: Lavinia Milosovici, Romania; women's vault: Elena Piskun, Belarus.

HANDBALL—U.S. Handball Association: men's one-wall: Albert Apuzzi, New York City; men's three-wall: Eric Klarman, New York City; men's four-wall: David Chapman, Long Beach, CA; women's one-wall: Barbara Canton, New York City; women's three-wall: Anna Engele, St. Paul, MN; women's four-wall: Anna Engele.

HORSESHOE PITCHING—World Champions: men: Alan Francis, Blythedale, MO; women: Cathy Carter, Council Bluffs, IA.

JUDO—U.S. Champions: men's open: Andy Ruggiero, Toms River, NJ; women's open: Colleen Rosensteel, Gainesville, FL.

KARATE—U.S. Champions: men: advanced mandatory kata: Ferdie Alias, San Diego, CA; advanced kata: Gary Sisson, CT; advanced kumite: Carlos Quintero, FL; women: advanced kata: Jill Sokugo, WA; advanced weapons kata: Gwen Hoffmann, NJ.

LACROSSE—NCAA Division I: men: Syracuse; women: Virginia.

LUGE—U.S. Champions: men: Robert Pipkins, Staten Island, NY; women: Cammy Myler, Lake Placid, NY; **World Champions:** men: Wendel Suckow, Marquette, MI; women: Gerda Weissensteiner.

MODERN PENTATHLON—United States: men: Mike Gostigian, Newtown Square, PA; women: Vanessa Richey, San Antonio, TX.

PADDLE TENNIS—U.S. Champions: men: Scott Freedman, Venice, CA; women: Nicole Marios, Los Angeles, CA.

PLATFORM TENNIS—U.S. Champions: men's singles: Scott Staniar, Greenwich, CT; men's doubles: Bill Fielder and Barry Judge, Chicago, IL; women's doubles: Robin Fultin, Stamford, CT, and Diane Tucker, Bedford, NY.

POLO—U.S. World Cup on Snow: Champagne, Pommery; **Rolex Gold Cup:** Cellular One, New York; **International Gold Cup:** Revlon.

RACQUETBALL—U.S. Champions: men's pro: Andy Roberts, Memphis, TN; men's amateur: John Ellis, Stockton, CA; women's amateur: Michelle Gilman-Gould, Ontario, OR.

RODEO—World Champion: men's all-around: Ty Murray, Stephenville, TX.

ROWING—World Champions: men's eights: Germany; women's eights: Romania; men's lightweight eights: Canada. **U.S. Collegiate Champions:** men: Brown; women: Princeton.

SHOOTING—U.S. International: men's trap: Lance Bade, Ridgefield, OH; men's skeet: Todd Graves, Laurel, MS; women's trap: Terry Wentzel, Cincinnati, OH; women's skeet: Connie Schiller, College Station, TX.

SLED DOG RACING: Iditarod (Anchorage to Nome): Jeff King, Denali, AK.

SOFTBALL—U.S. Champions: men's fast pitch: National Health Care Discount, Sioux City, IA; women's fast pitch: Redding Rebels, Redding, CA.

TRIATHLON—U.S. Champions: men's ironman: Mark Allen, Cardiff, CA; women's ironman: Paula Newby-Fraser, Encinitas, CA.

VOLLEYBALL—National Championship: men: Asics, Huntington Beach, CA; women: Nick's Fishmarket, Chicago, IL; **NCAA Division I Champions:** men: UCLA; women: Stanford.

WATER POLO—U.S. Champions: men's outdoor: San Francisco Olympic Club; women's indoor: Sunset, San Diego; men's NCAA Division I: Stanford.

WEIGHT LIFTING—World Champions: men: 54kg: Ivan Ivanov, Bulgaria; 59kg: Nikolai Peshalov, Bulgaria; 64kg: Naim Suleymanoglu, Turkey; 70kg: Yoto Yotov, Bulgaria; 76kg: Altym Orazurdiev, Turkmenistan; 83kg: Pyrros Bimas, Greece; 91kg: Ivan Tchakarov, Bulgaria; 99kg: Victor Tregubov, Russia; 108kg: Timur Taimazov, Ukraine; plus 108: Ronnie Weller, Germany; women: 46kg: Nan-mei Chu, Taiwan; 50kg: Liu Xiuhua, China; 54kg: Chen Xiaomin, China; 59kg: Caiyan Sun, China: 64kg: Li Hongyun, China; 70kg: Milena Trendafilova, Bulgaria; 76kg: Ju Hua, China; 83kg: Shu-Chic Chen, Taiwan; plus 83: Yajuan Li, China.

WRESTLING—National Champions: men's freestyle: 105.5 lbs: Rob Eiter, Clarion, PA; 114.5 lbs: Zeke Jones, Mesa, AZ; 125.5 lbs: Brad Penrith, Lincoln, NE; 136.5 lbs: Tom Brands, Iowa City, IA; 149.5 lbs: Matt Demaray, Madison, WI; 163 lbs: Dave Schultz, Newtown Square, PA; 180.5 lbs: Kevin Jackson, Ames, IA; 198 lbs: Melvin Douglas, Phoenix, AZ; 220 lbs: Kirk Trost, Ann Arbor, MI; 286 lbs: Bruce Baumgartner, Cambridge Springs, PA; women's freestyle: 97 lbs: Debby Weiss, Scottsdale, AZ; 103.5 lbs: Tricia Saunders, Phoenix, AZ; 110 lbs: Shannon Williams, Ontario, CA; 116.5 lbs: Miyuu Yamamoto, Phoenix, AZ; 125.5 lbs: Atina Bibbs, Davenport, IA; 134 lbs: Diana Wesendunk, Hillsbrough, CA; 143 lbs: Sheri Belew-Kennedy, Chowchilla, CA; 165 lbs: Sandra Schmidt, Snowflake, AZ.

[1]Sports for which articles do not appear in pages 490-512.

SRI LANKA

Prospects for political stability, ethnic peace, and economic progress in Sri Lanka seemed brighter as 1993 began than they had been for at least a decade. This encouraging picture was marred by the assassination of the chief opposition leader on April 23 and the nation's president within one week. Civil strife between government forces and Tamil militants, led by the Liberation Tigers of Tamil Eelam (LTTE), continued intermittently. The economy improved.

Politics. On April 23 the most prominent opposition leader, Lalith Athulathmudali, was gunned down in Colombo. He had held important positions in the ruling United National Party (UNP) and in the government, but he had fallen out with President Ranasinghe Premadasa and had formed a new party. Members of this party privately charged that his murder had been instigated by Premadasa. On May 1, while the country was still in shock, Premadasa was blown up by a suicide bomber during a rally in Colombo. The LTTE was blamed widely for the tragedy, but it denied all such allegations.

Premadasa had been a strong and sometimes ruthless leader. He was identified especially with the suppression of a radical Sinhalese group in the south and an unrelenting drive against the LTTE in the north and east. But he also was known for measures of economic liberalization and reform and special programs for the poor. Few Sri Lankans mourned his passing. He was succeeded by Prime Minister Dingiri Banda Wijetunge, who subsequently named Ranil Wickremasinghe as premier. The UNP continued in power, even though its leadership had been weakened and dissatisfaction with many of its policies had been growing. Its position was strengthened by rifts in the main opposition party, the Sri Lanka Freedom Party, led by former Prime Minister Sirimavo Bandaranaike.

A shifting balance of forces was reflected by the results of long-scheduled provincial-council elections in May. The UNP won a majority of the council seats in four of the seven provinces in which elections were conducted, and a five-party alliance called the People's United Front, led by Bandaranaike, gained a majority in two provinces, including the influential Western province where Colombo is located. No voting was scheduled in the merged Northern-Eastern province due to uncertain security. Late in 1993 the government proclaimed that in the Eastern province the situation largely had returned to "normal" and that the LTTE was no longer a major threat there. In the Northern province the LTTE remained in virtual control. On November 11 it won a major military victory over extensive government forces on the Jaffna peninsula.

The large-scale ebbing of the civil conflict was one of the most hopeful developments of the year. In August, LTTE leaders proposed a cease-fire for the first time, to be followed by "unconditional" talks with government representatives. The government responded cautiously but favorably to this overture, but in a short time launched a new offensive against the LTTE.

Both the government and the LTTE had been criticized often, especially by international agencies, for alleged violations of human rights. Most of the foreign agencies reported that the situation in Sri Lanka improved considerably in 1993, but almost all of them insisted that further improvement was necessary.

Economy. Signs of improvements included a reduction of the deficit, an annual growth rate of about 5%, a significant recovery in the production of tea (the nation's largest export crop), a bumper rice harvest that enabled the government to stop rice imports, and a substantial increase in export earnings. Foreign investment, especially in the hotel and banking sectors, increased significantly.

These generally encouraging conditions improved Sri Lanka's international credit standing. International lending agencies praised progress in political stability, the ebbing of civil strife, and human rights; but these agencies pointed out that the progress was only relative. Increased foreign aid came from several countries, mainly Japan and the United States, and from international organizations, notably the Asian Development Bank. In the first half of 1993 aid commitments approached $480 million, mostly in loans with concessional terms.

Foreign Policy. Before his death, President Premadasa was active as chairman of the South Asian Association for Regional Cooperation (SAARC). In January he made an official visit to India, and then met with the leaders of Bangladesh and Pakistan in Dhaka. In April he presided over the SAARC summit, where the Dhaka Declaration was approved and the South Asia Preferential Treaty was signed. His successor, President Wijetunge, was less active in foreign affairs.

NORMAN D. PALMER, *Professor Emeritus*
University of Pennsylvania

SRI LANKA • Information Highlights

Official Name: Democratic Socialist Republic of Sri Lanka.
Location: South Asia.
Area: 25,332 sq mi (65 610 km²).
Population (mid-1993 est.): 17,800,000.
Chief Cities (mid-1990 est.): Colombo, the capital, 615,000; Dehiwala-Mount Lavinia, 196,000.
Government: *Head of state*, D. B. Wijetunge, president (took office May 1993). *Head of government*, R. Wickremasinghe, prime minister (took office May 1993). *Legislature* (unicameral)—Parliament.
Monetary Unit: Rupee (47.97 rupees equal U.S.$1, April 1993).
Gross Domestic Product (1991 est. U.S.$): $7,200,000,000.
Economic Index (Colombo, 1992): *Consumer Prices* (1980 = 100), all items, 396.1; food, 402.1.
Foreign Trade (1992 U.S.$): *Imports*, $3,513,000,000; *exports*, $2,354,000,000.

STAMPS AND STAMP COLLECTING

© U.S. Postal Service

Music had charms for the United States Postal Service (USPS) stamp program in 1993. With much advance hoopla and publicity, the "King of Rock and Roll"—the late Elvis Presley—set the stage for the year with his philatelic debut on January 8. The Presley stamp was the first in the series "Legends of American Music." Elvis joined other rock 'n' roll and rhythm-and-blues artists in a booklet of seven designs. Later in the year, a quartet of country-music stars also was honored in a stamp booklet. One of these performers was Hank Williams, who appeared solo on a separate stamp. Broadway musicals were honored, too, in a booklet of four designs featuring *Showboat, Oklahoma!, Porgy & Bess,* and *My Fair Lady.* The show *Oklahoma!* also was featured on a separate stamp during the year.

The research chemist Percy Lavon Julian was hailed on the 16th Black Heritage Series stamp. Other historic figures receiving philatelic tribute during 1993 were statesman Dean Acheson, boxing legend Joe Louis, and Monaco's late Princess Grace (formerly U.S. actress Grace Kelly)—who was honored in a joint tribute with Monaco.

A February issue commemorated the World University Games held in Buffalo, NY. The centennial of the Cherokee Strip land run was celebrated, and the third issue in the USPS' five-year series observing the 50th anniversary of World War II was released in May. Deaf communication was the theme for a pair of stamps depicting a mother showing the sign-language sign for "I love you." A futuristic look at outer space was illustrated in a "Space Fantasy" booklet of five designs. And a five-design booklet with a Garden Flowers theme bloomed in May.

A block of four designs spotlighted the circus, and another block of four pictured sporting horses. Youth classic books—*Huckleberry Finn, Little House on the Prairie, Rebecca of Sunnybrook Farm,* and *Little Women*—appeared on a block of four. There also were four stamps dedicated to the National Postage Museum in Washington, DC. To mark the quincentennial celebration of Columbus' landing in Puerto Rico, a commemorative stamp was issued in November. Also that month, a stamp was issued to honor the Commonwealth of the Northern Mariana Islands.

The annual Christmas stamps were released in October; the traditional design featured a Madonna, and the contemporary designs came in a block of four. The final stamp of 1993 was dedicated to AIDS Awareness, and displayed the red-bow symbol of recognition.

Several self-adhesive stamps were issued during the year as the forerunner of many more similar issues. Each stamp in the 1993 program mentioned above was categorized as a 29-cent commemorative, except the contemporary and traditional Christmas stamps, which were labeled as 29-cent "special issues."

SYD KRONISH
The Associated Press

SELECTED U.S. STAMPS FOR 1993

Subject	Denomination	Date	Subject	Denomination	Date	Subject	Denomination	Date
Elvis Presley	29¢	Jan. 8	Dean Acheson	29¢	April 21	Rose (self-adhesive)	29¢	Aug. 19
Space Fantasy	29¢	Jan. 25	Horse Racing	29¢	May 1	Deaf Communication	29¢	Sept. 20
Percy Lavon Julian	29¢	Jan. 29	World War II (10 stamps)	29¢	May 31	Country Music	29¢	Sept. 25
World University Games	29¢	Feb. 25	Hank Williams	29¢	June 9	Christmas (contemporary)	29¢	Oct. 21
Grace Kelly	29¢	March 24	Rock 'n' Roll, R&B	29¢	June 16	Christmas (traditional)	29¢	Oct. 21
Oklahoma!	29¢	March 30	Joe Louis	29¢	June 22	Youth Classics	29¢	Oct. 23
Circus	29¢	April 6	American Musicals	29¢	July 14	Puerto Rico	29¢	Nov. 19
Cherokee Strip	29¢	April 7	National Postal Museum	29¢	July 30	AIDS Awareness	29¢	Dec. 1

STOCKS AND BONDS

With a powerful assist from the booming mutual-fund industry, U.S. stocks and bonds turned in strong showings in 1993, extending a bull market dating back to the start of the decade. Stock prices, which had been advancing without so much as a 10% setback ever since the fall of 1990, worked their way ahead erratically, staging no dramatic surprises. But bonds confounded many of the experts as interest rates kept falling, pushing the yield on long-term Treasury bonds below 6% for the first time in a generation.

Trends. The Dow Jones average of 30 industrials, the most widely recognized measure of stock-price trends, crossed the 3,700 level for the first time in the late stages of the year. It closed December 31 at 3,754.09, up 452.98 points, or 13.7%, from the end of 1992. Most broader market indexes also reached new peaks, with those dominated by small stocks slightly outpacing the indicators heavily weighted in favor of big blue chips.

In the credit markets, the short-term money markets stabilized around the lowest yield levels seen since the 1960s. Yields on three-month to one-year Treasury bills hovered around 3% before turning slightly higher in November and December. For the first time since 1983, the Federal Reserve made no change all year in its discount rate, the charge it sets on loans from private financial institutions. The rate had been lowered to 3% from 3.5% on July 2, 1992.

Long-term bonds had a much more eventful year. Prices of 30-year Treasury bonds rose sharply as their yields fell from a little less than 7.5% in late 1992 to around 5.75% in the fall of 1993, before rebounding to 6.25% in December. Enthusiasm for bonds was fed by continued low rates of inflation and a relative absence of credit demand in an economy that still made only modest progress toward recovery from the 1990-91 recession.

Mutual Funds. The strength in both stock and bond prices provided a hothouse environment for the continued growth of mutual funds. By the end of October, according to the Investment Company Institute, assets of the nation's mutual funds stood at just less than $2 trillion, up from $1.558 trillion in October 1992. Assets had reached $1 trillion for the first time in 1990. A similar story on a smaller scale was occurring in Canada, where fund assets topped $100 billion at the end of October, up more than 50% from 12 months earlier, according to Dalbar Publishing's Mutual Fund Market News. The funds continued to attract heavy inflows of money from investors disillusioned with the low returns available on traditional savings vehicles such as bank certificates of deposit. Yields on bank money-market accounts, for example, sagged to a late-1993 average of

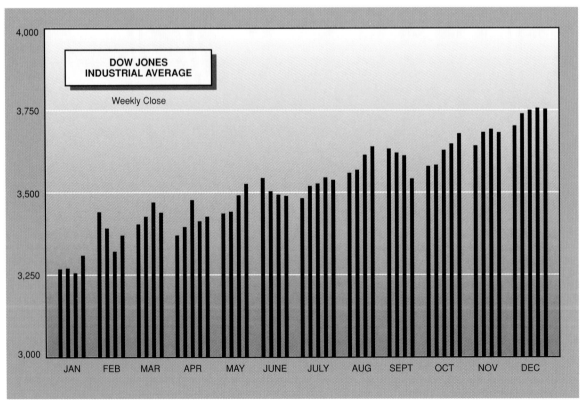

2.35%, as reported by Bank Rate Monitor, from 2.75% 12 months prior.

In some ways, analysts viewed the shift by investors as a positive development in that it directed more of their money toward investments with greater potential long-term returns. But at the same time, worries intensified that some newcomers were assuming risks they did not understand. The Securities and Exchange Commission published survey results which indicated that significant numbers of respondents erroneously believed funds sold in banks or in brokerage firms were backed by government insurance.

There also was much talk that "hot money" in mutual funds could cause problems for the funds and the markets in any future period of turbulence. In a classic vicious cycle, some said, declining markets would prompt fund shareholders to cash in, forcing sales of securities by fund managers that would depress the markets further.

But the many advocates of the funds said that such fears were exaggerated, if not groundless, and that 20 or more years of strong industry growth had established the funds as a prime, solid force in national and world finance. "The so-called 'boom' in mutual funds did not begin in 1993, or even in the 1990s," said the Investment Company Institute. "Contrary to frequent, but incorrect, reports, most of the new money moving into mutual funds from bank CDs is not coming from unsophisticated savers who have never invested. Much of what is invested in mutual funds is long-term money in retirement plans.

"Although mutual funds are not guaranteed or insured, mutual funds are heavily regulated under federal and state securities laws, especially the Investment Company Act of 1940. No mutual funds have 'collapsed' or 'gone bankrupt' since the 1940 act was passed."

The funds' partisans also pointed out that the money entrusted to the industry was dispersed over a wide range of investment types in the United States and, increasingly, abroad as well. For instance, slightly more than $250 billion of assets was accounted for by municipal-bond funds, which enjoyed a surge of interest prompted by passage of 1993 legislation raising marginal tax brackets for upper-income Americans to 36% and 39.6%.

About $50 billion more was invested in funds specializing in high-yield or "junk" bonds, which enjoyed their third straight year of gains after a shakeout in 1989 and 1990. According to the investment firm of First Boston, the default rate on these lower-rated bonds for the first ten months of 1993 shrank to 1% of par value, from a 1991 high of 9%.

Overall, long-term bond and income mutual funds held about $750 billion. Despite some of the lowest rates of return in modern memory, more than $550 billion of fund assets still sat in short-term taxable and tax-exempt money funds. That left a little more than $660 billion in equity, or stock, funds of all types.

New Offerings. Strong demand for stocks and bonds encouraged many new offerings. According to a preliminary Securities Industry Association estimate, the value of U.S. corporate stock and debt offerings made during 1993 surpassed $1 trillion for the first time, with bonds and other debt accounting for all but about $128 billion of the total.

Numerous debt offerings were made simply to refinance old, higher-cost debt, paralleling the continued drive among individual Americans to refinance mortgages and other consumer debts at lower interest rates. But the stock-underwriting business was bubbling as well, producing a long succession of hot new issues that eagerly were gobbled up by investors. In one of the most spectacular of these, the stock of the restaurant operator Boston Chicken debuted at $20 per share in early November and soared immediately to $51 before settling back into the high $30s a few weeks later.

International Markets. When they were not scrambling after new issues, U.S. investors were channeling much money into global and international mutual funds. After three consecutive years in which most foreign stock markets lagged behind Wall Street's gains, many overseas financial centers easily outdistanced U.S. performance in 1993. Through December 1, Dow Jones & Company's world stock index, including some 19 markets outside the United States, showed a gain for the year of 26.16%, against a rise of just 5.83% for the U.S. equity-market index. Markets with the sharpest gains—measured in U.S. dollars—ranged from Hong Kong, up about 69%, and Malaysia, up about 75%, to Finland, up about 68%.

In Tokyo, home of the world's second-biggest market, Dow Jones' index was up about 28%, but much of that rise represented appreciation by the yen against the dollar. In late November, Japanese stocks were hit by a sell-off that wiped out most of the gains they had recorded earlier in the year, as investors in Tokyo grappled with worries about persistent weakness in Japan's economy.

Among the major markets of Europe, all of which were bolstered by hopes for recovery from a lingering economic slump, Switzerland showed a gain of about 31%; Germany 26%; the United Kingdom 14%; France 14%; and Italy 11%.

One impetus behind the rush into international investments was a desire to diversify in markets not quite so picked over as Wall Street's. Another was the belief that new surges of capitalistic energy were creating great growth opportunities in places ranging from Latin America to China. By late in 1993, however, some big advocates of global investing had pulled back a bit.

CHET CURRIER, *The Associated Press*

SUDAN

A civil war, political instability, and economic weakness posed lingering problems in 1993 for Sudan and its leader, Omar Hassan al-Bashir.

Domestic Affairs. In 1993, Sudan's government further developed the system of popular congresses that began in 1991. After establishing local and provincial structures, the Revolutionary Command Council for National Salvation (RCCNS) formally disbanded itself in October. By constitutional decree, the RCCNS transferred power to a council of ministers and a Transitional National Assembly, and appointed Bashir as president in the new system. Officials said these actions would lead to parliamentary and presidential elections in 1994. Opponents of the regime described the changes as new vehicles for the Bashir regime to maintain control of Sudan.

The government continued the program of extending Islamic law that was initiated when it came to power in 1989. The leading figure in defining the Islamist program remained Hassan al-Turabi. Although Turabi held no governmental position, members of his organization—the National Islamic Front (NIF)—occupied most of the prominent cabinet and government positions. Old differences within the NIF leadership over tactics continued in 1993. Turabi appeared to hope for national reconciliation with the older northern Muslim groups. A more exclusive role for the NIF was advocated by others, including Ali Osman, who assumed the cabinet position responsible for religious affairs and social reform in the new governmental structure.

Opposition to the government also became increasingly divided. The National Democratic Alliance (NDA) remained the major organization of opposition groups in exile, but tensions within the NDA continued. Non-Muslim Sudanese in the NDA expressed concern over the formation by two major northern Muslim opposition parties—the Ummah and the Democratic Unionist Party—of an "Islamic Front" as an Islamic alternative to the Bashir regime. Opponents within the NDA felt this contradicted a basic coalition position affirming a need for a fully secular political system.

The civil war in southern Sudan, where the Sudan People's Liberation Army (SPLA) opposed the government, showed few signs of ending. War-related famine remained a major issue as international relief agencies were hindered by the conflict. Some of the year's bloodiest fighting in southern Sudan was between SPLA factions.

Efforts to create a negotiated settlement continued during 1993. Early in the year talks were held in Nigeria under the patronage of the Nigerian president, but divisions within the SPLA and intransigence on the issues of secularism and religion caused the suspension of those talks. Other mediation efforts were undertaken by former U.S. President Jimmy Carter and by an ad hoc group of East African leaders.

The government continued programs to extend Islamic law to the economy and to restructure its economic situation to satisfy international expectations. These efforts were not successful and in August, Sudan's voting rights in the International Monetary Fund (IMF) were suspended.

International Affairs. During 1993, Sudanese-U.S. relations deteriorated significantly. Sudanese nationals were arrested in connection with the bombing of the World Trade Center in New York City in February and a terrorist conspiracy in June. Although no charges of direct Sudanese governmental involvement were made, a Sudanese diplomat at the United Nations was named as having indirect ties with the conspiracy.

Concluding a weeklong African trip in February 1993, Pope John Paul II conferred with Sudan's President Omar Hassan al-Bashir (near right) in Khartoum. The pontiff asked Bashir to find a "constitutional formula" to end Sudan's civil war.

In August the United States placed Sudan on its list of governments supporting terrorism, although it made no specific accusations. The Sudanese government maintained close ties with both the Iraqi and the Iranian governments.

Tensions with Egypt grew early in 1993 due to a border dispute over the Halaib region and Egyptian charges that Sudan supported Islamic militants in Egypt. Relations seemed to improve later in the year, reflected in the meeting of Bashir and Egyptian President Hosni Mubarak in June.

Roman Catholic leaders in southern Sudan continued to criticize the Bashir regime. In February, Pope John Paul II visited Sudan and met with Bashir; at a public event, he condemned the human-rights record of the Sudan government. In October, Turabi met with the pope and other church officials in Rome. Relations between the Roman Catholic Church and the Sudanese government gained increasing significance in 1993.

JOHN O. VOLL, *University of New Hampshire*

SWEDEN

Budget deficits and recession forced an overhaul of Sweden's welfare state in 1993.

Political Changes. On March 9 a commission of independent experts—chaired by economist Assar Lindbeck, a former member for 35 years of the Social Democratic Party and the architect of the welfare state—delivered a blow to the Swedish welfare-state model when it proposed 113 changes in the state system. The proposed changes included allowing the Swedish krona (SKR) to be a free-floating currency, which it de facto had been since late 1992; saving 100 billion SKR (about U.S.$12 billion) on the budget by reducing unemployment benefits and social expenditures; and reducing by one half the size of the membership of Sweden's parliament, the Riksdag, to increase the efficiency of the political decision-making process. The proposal to reduce the parliamentary membership was ignored, but many of the other proposals were welcomed by the minority Conservative-Centre government led by Carl Bildt.

The Budget and Economy. Conservative Finance Minister Anne Wibble presented the budget on April 22 and, with difficulty, secured the necessary support of the right-wing antitax party, New Democracy, led by Ian Wachtmeister. The budget called for reducing the Swedish public-budget deficit from 13% of gross national product (GNP) in 1993 to about 4% in 1998 through savings of 81 billion SKR (about $10 billion). Thirty-five billion SKR (about $4.3 billion) of savings would accrue from freezing public expenditure at 1993 real levels. Another 26 billion SKR (about $3.2 billion) would come from cuts in all kinds of welfare-related income transfers to households, including a reduction in unemployment and child-care benefits. The opposition Social Democratic Party had proposed lower consumption taxes for a limited period to increase consumption and economic growth. Although Wibble's budget passed, public opinion favored the Social Democrats.

Unemployment in Sweden in 1993 peaked at 9.6% in July, dropping to 8.7% in September as exports picked up in response to the devaluation of the Swedish krona by about 20% over 12 months. But employment was almost double that of 1992, and almost four times the figure of 1991. Sweden remained in recession, with negative growth of 1.7%, but positive growth was forecast for 1994.

Foreign Affairs. On February 1, Sweden applied for membership in the European Community (EC). Some of the government parties and the opposition Social Democrat voters remained deeply divided on the EC issue. Pending the expected successful conclusion of membership negotiations, a referendum was planned for the fall of 1994 to decide on EC membership by 1995. Pollsters predicted an uphill fight for EC supporters. In September 1993 only 30% of Swedes said they would vote yes on EC membership, while 44% say they would vote no.

Among the areas of contention was the Swedish government retail-alcohol monopoly.

Relations with Denmark were strained by delays in confirmation of the decision to build a bridge from the southern city of Malmö to Copenhagen, Denmark, which was agreed to in a 1991 treaty. Environmental groups challenged the design of the bridge, and the Centre Party threatened to leave the Swedish government if all environmental demands were not met. Construction was due to start in 1994. Denmark also protested the indefinite postponement of the closure of Sweden's Barseback nuclear plant, only 10 mi (16 km) from the center of Copenhagen.

Defense. To reduce the budget deficit, the Swedish government cut defense spending. Despite a crash of the new JAS Gripen fighter aircraft at an air show, the aircraft's production continued. The hunt for unidentified submarines in inshore waters also continued.

Business. Scandinavian Airlines System (SAS)—which is three-sevenths owned by Sweden and two-sevenths owned by Norway and Denmark, respectively—started merger negotiations with Dutch KLM, Swissair, and Austrian Airlines to create an airline strong enough to survive in Europe's deregulated skies. Negotiations lapsed in November.

Lower interest rates helped banks draw back from the brink of bankruptcy and government takeover. Skandinaviska Enskilda Banken became profitable in 1993's second quarter.

The crown jewel of Swedish industry, the carmaker and industrial conglomerate Volvo, decided to merge its automobile subsidiary with French Renault. Shareholder opposition, however, forced the automaker to abandon the merge plans in December and prompted the resignation of Volvo's longtime chairman.

LEIF BECK FALLESEN, *Boersen, Copenhagen*

SWITZERLAND

An electoral controversy—along with economic and military issues in the international arena—dominated Swiss affairs in 1993.

Politics. On March 3 the combined houses of the Swiss parliament refused to elect the chosen candidate of the Social Democratic Party, Christiane Brunner, to a seat reserved for the party on the seven-member governing Federal Council. Brunner was undermined by anonymous charges that she had posed for nude photographs and had an abortion, which is illegal in Switzerland. She denied the former and refused comment on the latter. The failure of Brunner's candidacy prompted a violent public demonstration by some 10,000 women, plus threats by the Social Democrats to withdraw from the four-party coalition that has governed Switzerland since 1959. On March 10 the two houses responded by electing another woman and Social Democrat, Ruth Dreifuss, to the office.

SWITZERLAND • Information Highlights

Official Name: Swiss Confederation.
Location: Central Europe.
Area: 15,942 sq mi (41 290 km²).
Population (mid-1993 est.): 7,000,000.
Chief Cities (Dec. 31, 1991 est.): Bern, the capital, 134,393; Zurich, 343,106; Basel, 172,768.
Government: *Head of state*, Adolf Ogi, president (took office Jan. 1993). *Legislature*—Council of States and National Council.
Monetary Unit: Franc (1.4650 francs equal U.S.$1, Dec. 8, 1993).
Gross Domestic Product (1991 est. U.S.$): $147,400,000,000.
Economic Indexes (1992): *Consumer Prices* (1980 = 100), all items, 153.8; food, 153.1. *Industrial Production* (1980 = 100), 122.
Foreign Trade (1992 U.S.$): *Imports*, $65,924,000,000; *exports*, $65,783,000,000.

Referendums. To generate much-needed revenues, Swiss voters rescinded an 1874 ban on gambling casinos in March and approved a 20% increase in the cost of gasoline. In June voters rejected an attempt to prohibit the proposed purchase of 34 McDonnell Douglas FA-18 jet fighters until the year 2000 and turned back a companion proposal to limit the number of Swiss military-training sites to forty. In November, Swiss voters approved a value-added tax (VAT).

International Affairs. On June 24, Bern, Geneva, and Zurich were among two dozen European cities subjected to attacks on Turkish targets by Kurdish nationalists. In Bern one person was killed and nine wounded at the Turkish embassy.

Switzerland's highest court on April 8 denied a U.S. effort to obtain nearly $10 million in frozen funds related to the Iran-contra scandal during the Ronald Reagan administration. U.S. officials charged rival claimants to the money, Richard Secord and Albert Hakim, with embezzlement. The court's decision effectively terminated criminal proceedings, but gave the U.S. government the opportunity to file civil claims in the case.

The Swiss government approved the controversial sale of 60 Pilatus PC-9 single-engine aircraft to South Africa, despite protests by the United Nations (UN) and the African National Congress (ANC). To emphasize its commitment to UN peacekeeping efforts, the Swiss government later announced its military would participate in future UN peacekeeping missions.

Economy. Although Swiss voters had rejected participation in the new European Economic Area (EEA) in 1992, Switzerland was granted observer status in the EEA on March 17.

Other News. In July the government announced a three-and-one-half-year experimental program to distribute hard drugs to addicts for free to determine if drugs should be legalized permanently, and to assess the program's impact on crime, prostitution, and the spread of AIDS.

PAUL C. HELMREICH, *Wheaton College*

SYRIA

Syria did not have a year of dramatic change in 1993. The country remained firmly in the grip of President Hafiz al-Assad, an astute and ruthless operator at all levels of politics who remained the loudest drumbeater for Arab unity. The Syrian economy continued to be shaky, though improving. Meanwhile, peace with Israel seemed possible, if not immediate, at year's end.

Domestic Affairs. The cult of exaggerated veneration of Assad, 65, seemed to increase. The celebrations—replete with well-orchestrated "spontaneity"—in December 1993 to mark his completion of 23 years in power were louder than ever. Assad and the ruling clique belong to the Alawi sect of Sunni Islam, regarded by many as heretics. Thus to have remained in command of Syria for 23 years was a formidable achievement.

Assad's age and health fueled speculation about his succession. He had diabetes and had suffered a major heart attack in 1984 and a lesser one in 1992. The likeliest successors to Assad were his son Basil, 32, the president's younger brother and old rival Rifaat, and Vice-President Abdel Halim Khaddam. But Basil was not yet 40, the legally required age to be president, and his interest in politics was uncertain; Rifaat had only just been allowed home after ten years in exile; and Khaddam is an orthodox Sunni.

A former rival of Assad's disappeared on August 19 with the death of Salah Jadid. Jadid, 63, a Baath Party member like Assad, became ruler of Syria in 1966, though without official title, but was ousted and jailed by Assad in 1970. He was said to have died of a heart attack.

An event of some significance was the removal in January of Gen. Ali Douba as head of military intelligence. Douba was promoted to general and named deputy chief of staff. No successor was appointed. Many observers assumed that the head of internal security, Mohamed Nassif, newly promoted to brigadier, would inherit the security service. Douba's removal was welcomed in the West, where some of his intelligence activities had been criticized.

The U.S. National Academy of Sciences announced in March that Syria had the world's worst record of abuses against scientists. The report said 287 scientists had been imprisoned, usually without trial, and 20 others were thought to have disappeared.

The Economy. Assessments of the economy were often contradictory. The picture, in fact, was mixed. Gross domestic product (GDP) increased by 7% in 1992, with further growth anticipated. Inflation—high in the 1980s—dropped to about 12%. Oil production almost had tripled since the mid-1980s, as crude production averaged 570,000 barrels per day, and export earnings from petroleum products were roughly $2 billion per year. The government began encouraging private investment and loosening its tight grip on the economy.

SYRIA • Information Highlights

Official Name: Syrian Arab Republic.
Location: Southwest Asia.
Area: 71,498 sq mi (185 180 km²).
Population (mid-1993 est.): 13,500,000.
Chief Cities (June 30, 1990 est.): Damascus, the capital, 1,378,000; Aleppo, 1,355,000; Homs, 481,000.
Government: *Head of state,* Gen. Hafiz al-Assad, president (took office officially March 1971). *Head of government,* Mahmoud Zubi, prime minister (took office Nov. 1987). *Legislature* (unicameral)—People's Council.
Monetary Unit: Pound (11.225 pounds equal U.S.$1, April 1993).
Gross Domestic Product (1991 est. U.S.$): $30,000,000,000.
Economic Index (Damascus, 1992): *Consumer Prices* (1980 = 100), all items, 843.5; food, 851.6.
Foreign Trade (1992 U.S.$): *Imports,* $3,490,000,000; *exports,* $3,093,000,000.

However, there was a growing gap between the new rich and those on fixed incomes. Also, Western investors were wary of committing funds to a country with a reputation for corruption. Most investment came from Syria, Lebanon, Jordan, and Gulf sources. And the economy's strains were demonstrated in shortages and daily electricity blackouts. Syria continued to be rewarded for its allegiance to the U.S. position in the Gulf war. In May the European Investment Bank loaned Syria $25 million to help finance a new dam.

Foreign Affairs. U.S. Secretary of State Warren Christopher visited Syria during his first Middle East trip in February. Syria endeavored to be seen as favoring the peace process, and was instrumental during the spring in overcoming difficulties to ensure that the sessions of the general Middle East peace conference occurred.

Syria distanced itself from a close relationship with Iran and actively established other links. Turkish Premier Suleyman Demirel visited Syria in January—the first Turkish leader since 1987 to do so. In Damascus in February the foreign ministers of Syria, Iran, and Turkey met to discuss their common problems with Kurdish minorities. In the West, Syria's relations with Germany were especially friendly.

Syria played an important role in helping to end the seven-day Israeli attacks on south Lebanon at the end of May, reportedly by undertaking to take steps with Lebanon to curb Hezbollah attacks from Lebanon on Israel.

The Palestine Liberation Organization (PLO)-Israeli accord in September was an unpleasant surprise to Assad. It broke the ranks of Arab unity and did not help Syria's efforts to regain the Golan Heights—the focal point for Syria in the peace process. In a press conference in Cairo on September 22, Assad ambiguously declared that he neither would oppose the accord nor oppose those who opposed it.

ARTHUR CAMPBELL TURNER
University of California, Riverside

TAIWAN

A major change in the once hostile relationship between Taiwan and the Chinese mainland was effected in Singapore in April 1993 when representatives from the two sides sat down to talks for the first time since 1947. Representing Taiwan was the Straits Exchange Foundation (SEF) and representing China was the Association for Relations Across the Taiwan Straits (ARATS); both organizations were linked closely with their respective governments at the highest level. The SEF delegation was headed by Koo Chen-fu, a close associate of President Lee Teng-hui. Wang Daohan, leader of the ARATS delegation, is a former Shanghai mayor who has worked closely with China's President Jiang Zemin, himself a former Shanghai mayor.

Issues in a New Dialogue. The first meeting was not without problems. The ARATS representatives proposed modifying the agenda to include discussion of direct transportation, postal, and trade links. Taiwan—insisting that these were "political" issues—accused ARATS of attempting to sabotage the talks. Nonetheless, the two sides met three more times before year's end—in Beijing in August, in Xiamen in Fujian province in November, and in Taipei in December.

These subsequent meetings were devoted to discussion of three nettlesome issues. The first was the determination of fishing rights in territorial waters shared by the two sides. The second was the repatriation of illegal immigrants. Taiwan, in need of foreign labor, had authorized visas for some 135,000 immigrant workers; however, fearing an uncontrollable migration from the mainland to Taiwan, the government had restricted the visas to citizens of Thailand, the Philippines, and Malaysia. Nonetheless, an estimated 50,000 citizens of the People's Republic of China had entered Taiwan illegally since 1988. Of these, half had been located and returned to the mainland.

The third issue under discussion was a spate of airplane hijackings by mainland residents who demanded that they be taken to Taiwan, including

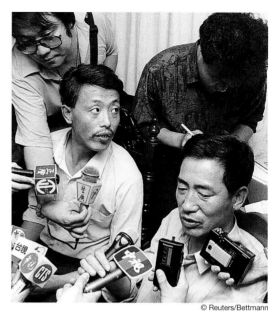
© Reuters/Bettmann

Two Chinese men who commandeered a jet to Taipei in November meet the press. Taiwan blamed the hijacking, the eighth such incident in 1993, on lax airport security on the mainland.

eight such incidents during 1993. The Taiwan side accused China of a lax system of airport security, while China protested Taiwan's insistence that the hijackers be tried, sentenced, and imprisoned on Taiwan.

Conflicting Goals. There were substantial differences between Taiwan's and the mainland's perceptions of the nature of the talks and their ultimate purpose. China issued a white paper on cross-straits relations on August 31. It reiterated Beijing's position that reunification must occur so as to place Taiwan under the control of the government of the People's Republic as a "special administrative region"—a status analogous to that of Hong Kong after 1997, and one that Taiwan authorities rejected.

A conservative minority on Taiwan also favored reunification, but on terms that would allow for a coalition government under which power would be shared by a reformed and democratized Chinese Communist Party and the Kuomintang (KMT), or Nationalist Party. A growing minority favored an independent Republic of Taiwan, with economic links to the mainland. The increasing acceptability of this point of view on Taiwan disturbed the older and more conservative wing in Beijing, who threatened armed intervention to prevent its realization. The majority on Taiwan (and, most probably, on the mainland as well) favored the gradual evolution of the status quo.

Economic Links. Behind this evolutionary process were expanding economic ties between the two political entities. Two-way trade, which reached $7.4 billion in 1992, grew at a rate of more than 30% in 1993 and was projected to reach $10 billion by year's end. Cumulative Taiwanese

---

TAIWAN • Information Highlights

Official Name: Taiwan.

Location: Island off the southeastern coast of mainland China.

Area: 13,892 sq mi (35 980 km²).

Population (mid-1993 est.): 20,900,000.

Chief Cities (Dec. 31, 1991 est.): Taipei, the capital, 2,717,992; Kaohsiung, 1,396,425; Taichung, 774,197; Tainan, 689,541.

Government: *Head of state*, Lee Teng-hui, president (installed Jan. 1988). *Head of government*, Lien Chan, prime minister (appointed Feb. 1993). *Legislature* (unicameral)—Legislative Yuan.

Monetary Unit: New Taiwan dollar (26.40 NT dollars equal U.S.$1, Dec. 31, 1993).

Gross National Product (1990 U.S.$): $150,800,-000,000.

investment in the mainland totaled $10 billion, with more than 10,000 mainland enterprises wholly or partially owned by Taiwanese investors.

While the growth in trade was predicted to slow somewhat as Chinese factories (many of them Taiwanese-owned) increased their output of products for the mainland consumer market that heretofore had been imported from Taiwan, the only potential curb on the growth of Taiwanese investment in the mainland was government regulation seeking to limit Taiwan's economic dependence on its mainland neighbor. The Taiwan economy itself was projected to grow at a rate of 6.3% for 1993. Per-capita income at midyear stood at $10,800, and inflation was just more than 4%. Despite these statistics, plans for the six-year, multibillion-dollar infrastructure-building program were scaled back in an effort spearheaded by opposition-party legislators.

Continuing Democratization. Municipal elections held in November for mayors in 23 cities were the most democratic ever held on Taiwan. A third political party, the Chinese New Party (CNP), joined the KMT, the Democratic Progressive Party (DPP), and a host of minor parties in fielding candidates. In the run-up preceding the election, it was assumed that the KMT would suffer an embarrassing defeat from the DPP, paving the way for a national DPP victory in 1995. To avoid this outcome, President Lee Teng-hui took to the hustings on behalf of KMT candidates, thereby risking his own political future.

Election results vindicated the president's gutsy strategy and greatly strengthened his position in the party. Fifteen of the 23 contested positions went to KMT candidates—one more than they previously had held. The DPP won six (down one), and the remaining two seats went to independent candidates. The CNP polled 3% of the vote, winning no positions. Conceding these encouraging results for the KMT, opponents nonetheless noted that the party took only 47.5% of the total vote—the first time that the ruling party's share of the vote had fallen below 50%.

JOHN BRYAN STARR
China Institute, New York

TANZANIA

Sectarian violence spread in 1993 as Tanzania continued to pursue political and economic reforms.

Political Affairs. Tension between mainland Tanzania and the island of Zanzibar reached a peak when the latter joined the Islamic Conference Organization (IOC) without approval from the mainland government. In January a supermarket in Zanzibar that sold alcoholic beverages was bombed and three months later, Muslims—under the banner of the Council for the Propagation of the Koran (Balukta)—attacked butcher shops in Dar es Salaam that sold pork, which Islamic law forbids.

TANZANIA • Information Highlights

Official Name: United Republic of Tanzania.
Location: East coast of Africa.
Area: 364,900 sq mi (945 090 km²).
Population (mid-1993 est.): 27,800,000.
Chief City (1985 est.): Dar es Salaam, the capital, 1,096,000.
Government: *Head of state*, Ali Hassan Mwinyi, president (took office November 1985). *Head of government*, Joseph S. Warioba, prime minister (took office November 1985). *Legislature* (unicameral)—National Assembly, 233 members.
Monetary Unit: Tanzanian shilling (365 shillings equal U.S.$1, May 1993).
Gross Domestic Product (1989 est. U.S.$): $6,900,000,000.
Foreign Trade (1991 U.S.$): *Imports*, $1,170,000,000; *exports*, $360,000,000.

In response, the government banned Balukta and detained its leader, Sheikh Yahya Hussein, on charges of incitement to overthrow the government. Balukta was alleged to have received support from Iran by way of Kenya's Islamic Party. Three Sudanese also were deported on charges of "sowing the seeds of fundamentalism." The leader of the Democratic Party, Tanzania's largest opposition party, also was detained and convicted of sedition.

President Mwinyi, a Muslim, has vowed to crush the fundamentalists; in January he fired Foreign Minister Ahmed Diria Hassan because of his involvement in Zanzibar's membership in the IOC, which Zanzibar subsequently ended. Tanzania, however, did join the Islam in Africa Organization. The majority of the population in Tanzania is Muslim.

Economy. Tanzania faced a revenue shortfall 25% greater than expected, largely because of lower levels of production stemming from drought in 1992 and the resulting shortages of hydroelectric power. To address future power shortages, Tanzania signed agreements with Burundi for access to power from that country and with the World Bank to construct a 180-megawatt hydroelectric station in Iringa.

In an attempt to reduce its dependence on aid and external loans, which were 42% less than expected during the year, the government presented a budget calling for increased revenue and decreased expenditure. Fees for owning and operating an automobile more than doubled, and excise duties on other items increased by 50%. In order to reduce expenses, the government announced its intention to cut 10,000 jobs from the civil service in 1993 and an additional 20,000 over the following two years.

In a further attempt to open the economy, Meridean BIAO became the second foreign-owned bank, after Standard Chartered, to open a full-service bank. The government also agreed to legalize private radio and television networks.

WILLIAM CYRUS REED
The American University in Cairo

TAXATION

In his first State of the Union address on Feb. 17, 1993, U.S. President Bill Clinton outlined a two-part economic plan to control the rising federal budget deficit and to give a boost to the nation's economy. The first part of the package consisted of a multibillion-dollar economic-stimulus package. The second part of his plan contained major changes to the U.S. tax and expenditure policy to take place starting at the beginning of fiscal year (FY) 1994, which spanned Oct. 1, 1993, to Sept. 30, 1994.

The tax changes, combined with planned spending cuts, were designed to reduce the budget deficit by $500 billion over the following five years. Specifically, Clinton's tax proposals included a new broad-based tax on energy content—measured in British thermal units (BTUs)—as well as increases in the federal personal and corporate income-tax rates. The president also proposed increasing the taxable portion of Social Security benefits for high-income recipients. Finally, Clinton introduced a temporary investment-tax credit for larger firms and a permanent credit for small firms.

President Clinton's economic plan ran into immediate stiff opposition in the U.S. Congress. Republican and some Democratic legislators urged additional expenditure cuts and far fewer tax increases. The first part of Clinton's economic plan, the economic-stimulus package, became the first casualty of this debate over the federal government's need for fiscal restraint.

As required by the U.S. Constitution, the House of Representatives first considered Clinton's proposed tax-policy changes. The resulting House tax bill was similar to the Clinton administration's proposal and consisted of the broad-based energy tax, higher personal and corporate tax rates, and larger portions of Social Security income subject to tax for higher-income retirees. On May 27 the House of Representatives narrowly passed this budget plan by a vote of 219 to 213.

After the budget plan gained passage in the House of Representatives, the Senate took up the deficit-reduction package. In order to pass this legislation through the Senate, the Clinton administration was forced to negotiate away the broad-based energy tax and replace it with an increase in the federal tax on motor fuels. Vice-President Gore, as presiding officer of the Senate, voted to break the 49-49 tie in the upper house, and the bill passed on June 25.

Following these narrow victories, a House-Senate Conference Committee crafted the final version of the deficit-reduction package. In the conference bill, the personal-income-tax rate for upper-income individuals was increased, while the motor-fuels tax was boosted by 4.3 cents per gallon. In addition to these increases, a greater portion of Social Security benefits was subjected to taxation, Medicare employee taxes were increased, and the corporate tax rate was increased. In dra-

matic fashion, the final House-Senate Conference committee bill narrowly passed in the House 218-216 and, once again, the Vice-President's vote of "yea" broke a 50-50 tie in the Senate on August 6. Four days later, President Clinton signed the Omnibus Budget Reconciliation Act.

In addition to these major tax-policy changes initiated in 1993, President Clinton also considered substantial increases in federal taxes—so-called "sin taxes"—on cigarettes and other tobacco products in order to fund part of his universal-health-care proposal.

In state and local tax developments in the United States, only some $3 billion of additional state taxes and fees were passed for FY 1994. In a controversial legislative decision, Michigan eliminated the local property tax as a method of funding the school system.

Meanwhile, on the international scene, China and Germany instituted tax changes and, for the first time, the Pacific island of Tahiti introduced an income tax.

United States

Federal. Federal-tax collections in FY 1993 were estimated at $1,130,029,000,000. Three taxes composed roughly 92% of this revenue. Roughly 45% ($510.39 billion) of the total federal tax collected was drawn from individual income taxes, 38% ($435.83 billion) was collected from social-insurance taxes and contributions for Social Security, and 9% ($105.50 billion) was acquired from corporation-income taxes. Excise taxes, estate and gift taxes, and customs duties and fees constituted the remaining 8% of federal-tax collections.

During FY 1993, U.S. tax law was governed by the Tax Reform Act of 1986 (TRA-86) and the Omnibus Budget Reconciliation Act of 1990 (OBRA-90). The TRA-86 lowered and reduced the total number of personal-income-tax bracket rates—the tax rate applied to the portion of personal income falling into each bracket. The TRA-86 also increased the fixed deduction from gross income available to all taxpayers and it eliminated several personal deductions, or so-called "tax loopholes." The OBRA-90 modified the TRA-86 by reducing the number of marginal tax rates to three: 15%, 28%, and 31%. Taxable family income between $0 and $34,000 faced a 15% marginal tax rate, income between $34,000 and $82,150 was taxed at 28%, and family income greater than $82,150 was taxed at 31%. The deficit-reduction package passed in 1993 raised the top tax rate for those with very high income. The marginal-tax rate for couples earning more than $140,000 was raised to 36%, while those making more than $250,000 had to face a new tax rate of 39.6%.

The deficit-reduction package passed in August 1993 also reversed the policies established by the earlier tax treatment of corpora-

tions. The corporate-tax rate was increased to 35% from the 34% rate established by the TRA-86. A limited investment-tax credit was reinstated that allows small businesses to deduct $17,500 per year in new equipment purchases. In addition to these various changes, business deductions allowed for meals and entertainment were reduced to 50% from 80%.

The fastest-growing portion of total federal taxes remained the social-insurance tax (payroll taxes). In 1993 it remained a flat statutory tax rate of 6.2% that applied to all labor income—so interest and capital gains would not be covered. No tax would be paid on income beyond $57,900. In addition to the employee's share, the employer also was responsible for 6.2% of the employee's labor income. An additional flat tax on the employer and employee of 1.45% of labor income was designated to fund the medical-insurance program (Medicare) for the elderly. Although there was a cap on employee wages subject to the Medicare portion of this payroll tax equal to $135,000—roughly 8% higher than the 1992 cap—the 1993 deficit-reduction package applied the 1.45% rate to all wage income.

Since the combined 7.65% payroll-tax rate did not vary by income level and the 6.2% rate went to zero beyond $57,900, the social-insurance tax was considered regressive. Under a regressive tax, individuals with higher income pay a smaller tax as a proportion of their total income. The regressivity of this tax was reduced, however, when the payments from these taxes—in the form of Social Security, Medicare, and unemployment insurance—were taken into consideration. The newly passed deficit-reduction package further reduced this regressivity, as the Social Security benefits subject to tax for couples with an annual income of at least $34,000 was increased to 85% from the current 50%.

State and Local. State and local government tax revenue equaled roughly $600 billion in FY 1992. States obtained approximately 75% of their tax revenue from income taxes on individuals and corporations, and from sales taxes. On the other hand, local governments received the bulk of their revenue from property taxes, and, in a few localities, income and sales taxes.

Many differences in tax structures and burdens were observed across the nation's 50 states and numerous localities. For example, 14 states did not impose a broad-based personal income tax on their citizenry, and, in the states that did, the numbers and levels of income-tax brackets varied widely, as did the levels of personal exemptions and deductions. In addition, a few states did not impose a general sales tax, and, of the states that did, many exempted food, prescription drugs, and other items.

For FY 1994, 14 states increased or decreased their personal-income taxes, 17 states changed their sales tax, 19 states increased or decreased their corporate-income tax, and 19 states increased fuel taxes and one or all of their "sin taxes"—affecting cigarettes, other tobacco products, and alcohol.

New state taxes and fees of about $3 billion were passed for the fiscal year. About $966 million came from increases in sales taxes in ten states; $553 million from personal-income-tax increases in nine states; $680 million from increases in "sin" taxes on cigarettes, tobacco products, and alcohol in 16 states; $205 million from increases in corporate-income taxes in 12 states; and $255 million from increases in taxes on motor fuels in seven states.

Among the nation's states, California had the largest changes, with an increase in its personal-income tax of $440 million, a growth in its sales tax of $744 million, and a $70 million increase in corporate-income taxes. Several states also decreased their taxes. Of these states, Texas saw the largest decreases in its sales tax ($292 million) and corporate-income tax ($318 million).

Local property, income, and sales taxes also varied across jurisdictions with respect to tax rates, tax base, and the definition of property. One major change in property taxes occurred in Michigan. During the summer the Michigan state government eliminated the local property tax as a source of revenue to fund the state's school systems. This controversial legislation then forced Michigan quickly to design and implement a new school-financing system to take effect for the 1994-95 school year.

International

Several countries or regions changed their tax systems in response to changing political and economic events.

Germany. Germany passed significant corporate-tax cuts. The top rates on corporations were reduced by about 5% on retained and distributed profits. Some allowances that were previously available to corporations were eliminated in order to balance these reductions. Earlier in 1993 the German parliament rejected a plan to increase fuel taxes, sought to pay the increasing costs of unification.

China. China's central cabinet, the State Council, cut fees and taxes on peasant farmers in June and also said that local governments could not impose fees on peasants without central-government approval. In addition, the Chinese government began to tax state-owned and private businesses at the same tax rate of 33%.

Tahiti. In response to insufficient health care and housing, deteriorating roads, and a weak social-welfare system, the French government enacted the first personal-income tax on the Pacific island of Tahiti in June. The top tax rate was 3%, and wages less than $12,000 would be exempt from the tax. The new tax was designed to generate $30 million in 1993.

THOMAS A. HUSTED
The American University

TELEVISION AND RADIO

After years of rumbling discontent and scattered crusades against violence and sleaze on television, the issue finally burst into the sustained glare of media criticism and congressional hearings in 1993.

Beavis and Butt-head became the buzz phrase for how television had gotten out of hand. The cartoon series on MTV (the rock-music cable network) about two insolent, cackling teenage boys, whose mischief included playing with matches, was blamed for a copycat tragedy—the death of a 2-year-old Ohio girl in a trailer blaze set by her 5-year-old *Beavis*-watching brother. MTV immediately moved the show to a later hour and eliminated fire-setting, paint-thinner-sniffing, and other offensive antics. Other programs—such as Nickelodeon's cartoon series, *Rocko's Modern World* (featuring jokes about a tapeworm farm for kids), and Fox's perennial lowbrow favorite, *Married. . .With Children*—also continued to draw complaints.

A cover story in *Newsweek* linked TV's plummet in morals and literacy to the explosion in channel capacity. *Time* magazine noted that public-access cable channels were becoming havens for various extremists, from the Ku Klux Klan to black racists. President Bill Clinton told *TV Guide* that he was "mortified" by some of what he saw on television, and a *Los Angeles Times* poll found that 80% of Americans believed that TV violence was harmful.

Still, the issue was delicate and complex, and one viewer's idea of sleaze could be another's idea of good, graphic realism. A case in point was the American Broadcasting Companies' (ABC's)

In "N.Y.P.D. Blue," a controversial fall television series that won critical acclaim, David Caruso (below) stars as an honest police detective with a partner suffering from burnout.

© 1993 ABC, photo by Craig Sjodin

N.Y.P.D. Blue. Sexually suggestive and explicit in its exposure of a violent world, the police drama caused controversy in its first episodes until a critical consensus emerged that it was one of the best new entries of 1993. Similarly, a much-talked-about episode of the National Broadcasting Company's (NBC's) *Seinfeld*, one of the top-rated shows of 1993, dealt extensively with masturbation—but with witty, teasing euphemisms, avoiding much viewer ire.

Warning Labels on TV Shows. Sen. Paul Simon (D-IL) organized congressional hearings that resulted in the television industry agreeing to a voluntary two-year experimental plan, beginning in the fall of 1993, in which advisories or "warning labels" would run before and during programs in which "violent content is unexpected, graphic, or pervasive." But the action did not appease many critics, who argued that the programmers were tossing the problem back to parents, rather than addressing it through a reduction in violent programming. U.S. Attorney General Janet Reno warned the TV industry that if more significant actions were not taken soon, "government action will be imperative."

Renewals. Once again, the plight of quality drama on television could be summarized in the 1993 Emmy Award-winning programs that either were canceled or threatened with cancellation for poor ratings. NBC's *Homicide: Life on the Street* won a best-director award for the dizzying, on-the-run camera techniques of film-maker Barry Levinson (*Rain Man*), but it was not renewed. *I'll Fly Away,* the fine drama of values and race relations in a Southern town of the 1960s (an Emmy for supporting actress Mary Alice), was dropped by NBC but picked up in reruns by the Public Broadcasting Service (PBS) for the fall of 1993. The Columbia Broadcasting System's (CBS') *Picket Fences*, the thoughtful drama of relationships and life issues in a Wisconsin hamlet, won Emmys for best drama series, best actor (Tom Skerritt), and best actress (Kathy Baker), but barely won renewal in the fall.

Other renewed programs whose reputation for quality was reinforced by Emmy nominations included NBC's drama *Sisters* (starring Swoosie Kurtz); CBS' *Northern Exposure* (Rob Morrow and Janine Turner); Home Box Office's (HBO's) *The Larry Sanders Show* (comedian Gary Shandling); and NBC's *Seinfeld* (Jerry Seinfeld).

These shows, however, were the exception; the tabloid mentality was closer to the rule. The three major networks raced into production with hit sagas of Amy Fisher, the real-life teenager who shot and wounded the wife of her much older lover. Another titillating docudrama, HBO's *The Positively True Adventures of the Alleged Texas Cheerleader-Murdering Mom,* was redeemed by an Emmy-winning turn by Holly Hunter.

Mainly because of Ted Danson's decision not to return, NBC's *Cheers* ended after 11 years. (*See* SIDEBAR, page 529.)

Public Broadcasting Service. A dramatic highlight of 1992-93 was the PBS broadcast of *Tru*, with Robert Morse repeating his solo Broadway tour de force, transformed into a dissolute but still puckish Truman Capote. Morse won an Emmy for his performance.

Two noted British thespians earned Emmy nominations—Helen Mirren for the British series *Mystery!: Prime Suspect 2*, and Maggie Smith (starring opposite Rob Lowe) for her role in Tennessee Williams' psychological thriller, *Suddenly Last Summer*.

Depicting Black America. Producers, black and white, of black-oriented programming were caught between black leaders denouncing demeaning stereotypes and large enthusiastic audiences who did not seem offended at all.

A *New York Times* story, "Black Life on TV: Realism or Stereotypes?", noted the mixed blessings of such HBO productions as *Strapped* and *Laurel Avenue*, which showed courage among inner-city black characters—along with a predilection for drugs, crime, and out-of-wedlock babies. Continuing the debate started in 1991 by Fox's *In Living Color*—the witty sketch comedy that both exploded and exploited stereotypes—the *Times* analysis went on to scorn such characters as the man-chasing Shaneneh, played in drag by comedian Martin Lawrence on Fox's *Martin*, and the shiftless sidekick Malcolm on ABC's *Where I Live*.

One of the "events" of 1992-93, however, was a celebration of black history: CBS' *Queen*, by Alex Haley (*Roots*), starred newcomer Halle Berry as the author's half-Irish grandmother, struggling to find acceptance in the post-Civil War South.

With four new black-oriented comedies in the fall of 1993 (including the bawdy Fox hit *Living Single*, starring rap star Queen Latifah) joining seven continuing black series, there were an unprecedented 11 black-dominated shows running at year's end.

News. In an almost unheard-of public confession, *Dateline NBC* anchors Jane Pauley and Stone Phillips apologized on the air for errors the newsmagazine made in a November 1992 report on the safety of General Motors trucks. The *Dateline* demonstration truck had been rigged secretly with rocketlike sparking devices so that it would burst into flame upon collision. While the report did establish that the trucks' leaky gas tanks posed a hazard, the deception was denounced widely.

It was observed that the debacle grew out of ratings competition from such syndicated "tabloid" news programs as *Hard Copy* and *A Current Affair*, which use dramatic reenactments and other attention-grabbing devices shunned in traditional news practice. A *60 Minutes* interview with the scandal-plagued Woody Allen was offered as a more subtle example of this spicier news sensibility. Nonetheless, it was the great

© CBS/Everett Collection, Inc.

DAVID LETTERMAN

David Letterman, for 11 seasons a staple on late-night television as the star of NBC's "Late Night," in April 1993 switched to CBS as the star of the "Late Show with David Letterman." As such, he posed a strong challenge to Jay Leno of "The Tonight Show" and to the supremacy of NBC in the 11:30 P.M. time slot. At CBS, Letterman landed a three-year contract worth a reported $42 million. Born in Indianapolis, IN, on April 12, 1947, the comedian—noted for his sense of irony—was educated at Ball State University. He worked in local broadcasting in Indianapolis and later was a performer/writer in Los Angeles. His big break came on "The Tonight Show" in 1978, where he later was a guest host. He also hosted a morning show.

contribution of *60 Minutes* to TV journalism that was foremost in viewers' minds during the CBS show's 25th-anniversary season—marked by a special retrospective broadcast.

In the first departure in years from the single-male-anchor format on the three network evening-news programs, *The CBS Evening News* elevated Connie Chung (*see* BIOGRAPHY) to coanchor status with long-running newsman Dan Rather. NBC news anchor Tom Brokaw teamed with *Today's* Katie Couric in *Now*, a new newsmagazine.

The 1993-94 Season. The dominant fall themes on the four broadcast networks were nontraditional families (with a slew of single parents) and stand-up comedians making their debuts as sitcom leads. Two shows that clicked with both themes were ABC's *Grace Under Fire* (comedienne Brett Butler as a divorced moth-

© Twentieth Century Fox

Tom Skerritt and Kathy Baker (above), the stars of "Picket Fences," won Emmys as best performers in a drama series. The show also picked up an Emmy as television's best drama series.

er), and Fox's *The Sinbad Show* (named for its jumbo comedian lead as a single man who adopts two kids). However, the quick cancellation of two other comedian-led series—ABC's *The Paula Poundstone Show* and Fox's *Townsend Television*, with Robert Townsend—led *Variety* to dub the fall a "low-concept season" that had gone overboard on "performer-driven" series.

Despite its voguishly eccentric spelling (and mud-bottom critical reviews), Steven Spielberg's *SeaQuest DSV* on NBC scored high initial ratings with the kind of techno-spectacle the director brought to his movies. While there were no artistic breakthroughs evident at year's end (except perhaps for the aforementioned *N.Y.P.D. Blue* and NBC's *Frasier*, heir to *Cheers* as an intelligent ensemble comedy), the show formulas were at least commercially sound. Also, a number of new series (18 out of 35) received full-season 22-episode orders, twice the renewal rate of the previous season, in a new trend toward letting shows find their audience.

The surprise hit *Dr. Quinn, Medicine Woman* (starring Jane Seymour), returning for its second season on CBS, was credited with sparking a resurgence of Westerns, including the network's *Harts of the West*, with old hand Lloyd Bridges as an ex-con rancher.

David Letterman, after an enormously successful 11-year run on NBC's *Late Night*, switched to CBS in August of 1993 for an hour-earlier time slot (11:30 P.M. on most affiliates) and a spectacular $14-million-per-year salary. The shift caused seismic vibrations up and down the late-night programming landscape. Neither Letterman's timing nor ratings missed a beat, and the move gave CBS its first major late-night talk show, creating fierce competition for the syndicated *Arsenio Hall Show* and NBC's *Tonight Show* with Jay Leno. (Leno had been picked over Letterman to replace Johnny Carson.) Acclaimed as a comedy writer—but unknown as a performer—Conan O'Brien took over Letterman's *Late Night* duties to a mixed reception. Comedian Chevy Chase's new talk show on Fox was canceled after six weeks.

Announced at year's end was the possibility of at least one new national network, with Warner Brothers and Paramount Communications both seeking new inroads for their products. Amid news of an approaching "500-channel television universe," the National Cable Television Association (NCTA) listed 58 new channels that came on line or were scheduled to begin in 1993. They included the Home & Garden Television Network; the Game Channel, featuring game shows and interactive video games; the Golf Network; the Romance Classics Network; Booknet, which focuses on books and films from novels; and the ECO Channel on environmental themes. An NCTA spokesperson projected that the average home would more than double its channel capacity to about 140 channels by the year 2000.

Radio. The decreasing airtime given over to the presentation of artistic performances and cultural news—especially on National Public Radio (NPR), their traditional home—was decried in the media as another sign of the hard economic times. Staffers for financially beleaguered NPR told *Billboard* magazine that coverage of the arts had been slashed roughly in half, with more "hard" news in its place in order to keep member stations from cutting away from the network feed during the "soft," or cultural, segments.

Recession-pinched corporations were forced to withdraw sponsorship of weekly radio broadcasts by major orchestras, so that these mainstays of U.S. cultural life virtually had vanished by the end of 1993.

Howard Stern rode his success as a radio "shock jock" to add a best-selling book on his exploits, *Private Parts*. His picture appeared on the cover of *Time* magazine, and he made a guest appearance on TV's *Donahue*. In typical fashion he proclaimed himself "king of all media." At year's end, however, Arbitron ratings showed that his national radio audience had declined during 1993.

See also PRIZES AND AWARDS.

DAN HULBERT
"The Atlanta Journal and Constitution"

Good-bye to *Cheers*

After 11 years and 275 episodes, NBC's situation comedy *Cheers* made its final bow on May 20, 1993. The event was billed by the network as a "television landmark." Indeed, *Cheers*, the longest-running comedy ever on NBC, was a record-setter. It had finished among the ten most-watched television shows for eight straight years, winning the Number 1 slot in the 1990-91 season. It garnered a record 111 Emmy nominations and won 26 Emmy awards. The show's cast members, unknowns when the show began in 1982-83, by the end were familiar to virtually all TV-watching Americans. And *Cheers*' central star, Ted Danson, earned a reported $450,000 per episode.

Viewers and critics alike were dismayed, however, by the fuss over the series' curtain call. The much-hyped finale was a marathon 98 minutes long. In an indication of the expectations NBC had for the episode (it anticipated 100 million viewers), it charged $650,000 per 30 seconds of ad time. This was a new record for a television series—ads usually run that high only for pro football's Super Bowl.

Despite the grand send-off for the customers and workers at TV's most famous Boston bar, which was watched by some 93 million people, there was more to come. In addition to syndicated reruns, fans could enjoy *Frasier*, a spinoff featuring *Cheers* alumnus Kelsey Grammer as Dr. Frasier Crane, which premiered in fall 1993 to high ratings and favorable reviews.

MEGHAN O'REILLY

TELEVISION | 1993

Some Sample Programs

Americas—A ten-part series on Latin America and the Caribbean. Narrated by Raul Julia. PBS, Jan. 4.

Apollo Theatre Hall of Fame—A concert honoring New York's Apollo Theatre. Hosted by Bill Cosby. NBC, August 4.

Arthur Miller's "The American Clock"—An episodic period drama springing from Miller's recollections of the 1930s Depression. With Mary McDonnell, John Rubinstein, Joanna Miles. TNT, August 23.

Barbarians at the Gate—A made-for-cable movie, adapted from the Bryan Burrough-John Helyar book about the RJR-Nabisco buyout. With James Garner, Jonathan Pryce, Peter Riegert, Joanna Cassidy. HBO, March 20.

Bill Monroe: Father of Bluegrass Music—Tribute to Bill Monroe. with Ricky Skaggs, Jerry Garcia, Emmylou Harris, Marty Start. TNN, May 31.

Billy Ray Cyrus—A special featuring the singer in concert in Reno, NV. ABC, Feb. 17.

Blind Spot—A Hall of Fame TV movie about drug abuse. With Joanne Woodward, Fritz Weaver. CBS, May 2.

Bonanza: The Return—Descendants of the Cartwright clan face a showdown with an unscrupulous tycoon. With Michael Landon, Jr., Ben Johnson, Dean Stockwell, Linda Gray. NBC, Nov. 28.

Call of the Wild—A TV-movie adaptation of Jack London's novel. With Rick Schroeder. CBS, April 25.

The Carol Burnett Show: A Reunion—A retrospective of Burnett's television show. With Carol Burnett, Harvey Korman, Vicki Lawrence, Tim Conway, Lyle Waggoner. CBS, Jan. 10.

Class of '61—TV movie about three friends who are members of West Point's 1861 class. With Clive Owen, Dan Futterman, Joshua Lucas, Len Cariou. ABC, April 12.

Clive James' Fame in the 20th Century—An eight-hour series exploring the nature of fame in this century. Host, Clive James. PBS, June 7.

Columbo: It's All in the Game—TV movie that has Columbo in a battle of wits with a charming sophisticate. With Peter Falk, Faye Dunaway. ABC, Oct. 31.

Cooperstown—Made-for-cable movie fantasy about a former baseball pitcher and his traveling companion, the ghost of his catcher. With Alan Arkin, Graham Greene. TNT, Jan. 26.

The Countess Alice—A *Masterpiece Theatre* telecast about an octogenarian British countess married in the 1930s to a

Prussian count, and a reporter who does a then-and-now article on her. With Wendy Hiller, Zoe Wanamaker, Duncan Bell. PBS, Jan. 24.

The Deadly Deception—A *Nova* telecast detailing an experiment conducted from 1932 to 1972 with 400 black men from Alabama who were misled into thinking that they would receive free treatment for syphilis when in fact treatment was withheld. PBS, Jan. 26.

Fallen Champ: The Untold Story of Mike Tyson—A documentary chronicling the rise and fall of the former heavyweight boxing champion. NBC, Feb. 12.

Family Pictures—A two-part TV movie about a suburban family's attempts to deal with a mentally impaired child. With Anjelica Huston, Sam Neill, Kyra Sedgwick. ABC, March 21.

The Fire Next Time—Two-part TV movie set in the future when global warming causes climatic catastrophes. With Craig T. Nelson, Bonnie Bedelia. CBS, April 18.

Foreign Affairs—A TV movie about two very different Americans who fall in love while in England. With Joanne Woodward, Brian Dennehy. TNT, March 17.

Great Moments from Nova—A 20th-anniversary retrospective of the science series. PBS, Dec. 7.

Gypsy—Television adaptation of the Broadway musical on the life of stripper Gypsy Rose Lee as she grows up with the ultimate "stage mother." With Bette Midler, Peter Riegert, Cynthia Gibb. CBS, Dec. 12.

Healing and the Mind with Bill Moyers—A five-part series dealing with how health can be affected by thoughts and feelings. PBS, Feb. 22.

Hedda Gabler—A *Masterpiece Theatre* dramatization of Henrik Ibsen's stage classic. With Fiona Shaw, Stephen Rea, Nicholas Woodeson. PBS, March 28.

House of Secrets—TV movie about a battered wife who plots to kill her husband with the aid of his former mistress. With Melissa Gilbert. NBC, Nov. 1.

The Incredible Discovery of Noah's Ark—A documentary dealing with the Biblical text and various historical writings pertaining to Noah's ark. CBS, Feb. 2.

Jack—A profile of John F. Kennedy. CBS, Nov. 17.

Judgment Day—The John List Story—A fact-based TV movie about a man who murders his New Jersey family and then establishes a new life for himself in Colorado. With Robert Blake. CBS, Feb. 23.

Katharine Hepburn: All About Me—Katharine Hepburn talks about her life and career. TNT, Jan. 18.

Knots Landing—The longest-running prime-time serial drama ends with a two-hour finale. With Michelle Lee, Joan Van Ark, Donna Mills, William Devane, Nicolette Sheridan, Ted Shackelford. CBS, May 13.

Larry King Extra—Elizabeth Taylor is interviewed. TNT, March 3.

The Last P.O.W.? The Bobby Garwood Story—TV docudrama about a Marine prisoner of war charged with aiding the enemy. With Martin Sheen. ABC, June 28.

A Life in the Theatre—A made-for-cable movie about two stage actors spending a season in repertory. With Jack Lemmon, Matthew Broderick. TNT, Oct. 9.

Lucy and Desi: A Home Movie—A remembrance of the stars of *I Love Lucy* through interviews, stills, clips, and home movies. Hosted by Lucie Arnaz. NBC, Feb. 14.

The Man from Left Field—TV movie about an amnesiac who becomes a coach for a team of Florida youths. With Burt Reynolds, Reba McEntire. CBS, Oct. 15.

A Matter of Justice—A two-part TV movie revolving around a sensational murder case and a child-custody battle. With Patty Duke, Martin Sheen. NBC, Nov. 7.

Men Don't Tell—A TV movie about an abused husband. With Peter Strauss, Judith Light. CBS, March 14.

Mostly Mozart and Mendelssohn Too—A *Live from Lincoln Center* presentation of a concert from the Mostly Mozart Festival. With June Anderson, Andre Watts, Joshua Bell. PBS, July 7.

Murder in the Heartland—Two-part TV docudrama about Charles Starkweather, a killer who terrorized Nebraska in 1958. With Tim Roth, Fairuza Balk, Randy Quaid, Kate Reid. ABC, May 3.

The Odd Couple—A TV movie based on the 1970-75 series. With Jack Klugman, Tony Randall, Penny Marshall. CBS, Sept. 24.

On the Town in Concert—A *Great Performances* concert-style presentation of the Broadway musical. With Frederica von Stade, Tyne Daly, Thomas Hampson, Kurt Ollmann, David Garrison. PBS, Dec. 8.

One on One with Michael Jackson—On a special *Oprah Winfrey*, Jackson is interviewed by the talk-show hostess. ABC, Feb. 10.

The Parallax Garden—A *Playwrights Theater* presentation about a woman who develops a relationship with a backyard scarecrow after her husband leaves her. With Jean Stapleton. Arts and Entertainment, April 13.

Parsifal—A *Metropolitan Opera Presents* telecast of the Wagner opera. With Siegfried Jerusalem. PBS, April 7.

The Parsley Garden—A *Weekend Special* drama adapted from a 1949 William Saroyan short story. With Christopher Miranda. ABC, March 27.

The Portrait—A made-for-cable movie about a retired professor whose artist daughter has returned home to paint a portrait of her parents. With Gregory Peck, Lauren Bacall, Cecilia Peck. TNT, Feb. 13.

Prime Suspect 2—A four-part *Mystery* whodunit, featuring London police detective Jane Tennison. With Helen Mirren. PBS, Feb. 11.

Queen—A three-part miniseries based on Alex Haley's saga of his paternal grandmother. With Halle Berry, Martin Sheen, Ann-Margret, Tim Daly, Jasmine Guy, Paul Winfield, Ossie Davis. CBS, Feb. 14.

The Real McTeague—A documentary by Robert Altman looks at two adaptations of the Frank Norris novel: a 1924 film, *Greed*, and a 1992 opera. PBS, May 26.

Return to Lonesome Dove—Three-part sequel to the 1989 Western miniseries. With John Voight, Barbara Hershey. CBS, Nov. 14.

The Sea Wolf—A TV movie adaptation of the Jack London classic. With Charles Bronson, Christopher Reeve. TNT, April 18.

Sixty Minutes . . . 25 Years—A two-hour tribute offering a behind-the-scenes look at the popular TV newsmagazine. With Mike Wallace, Morley Safer. CBS, Nov. 14.

Skylark—A TV *Hall of Fame* drama, the sequel to *Sarah, Plain and Tall* (1991), in which the family—including Sarah, a mail-order bride—struggles with a drought. With Christopher Walken, Glenn Close. CBS, Feb. 7.

The Sound of Silence—Two-part, made-for-cable movie biography of Alexander Graham Bell. With John Bach. TNT, July 18.

Stolen Babies—A fact-based TV movie about a sinister orphanage manager in Tennessee who ran a baby-stealing ring in the 1940s. With Mary Tyler Moore, Lea Thompson, Kathleen Quinlan. Lifetime, March 25.

Suddenly, Last Summer—A *Great Performances* telecast of Tennessee Williams' one-act drama. With Maggie Smith, Natasha Richardson, Rob Lowe. PBS, Jan. 6.

Telling Secrets—A two-part TV movie involving a complex murder case. With Cybill Shepherd, Mary Kay Place, Ken Olin. ABC, Jan. 17.

There Are No Children Here—A TV movie about a mother struggling to raise her children in a Chicago public-housing unit. With Oprah Winfrey. ABC, Nov. 28.

They—A made-for-cable movie about a blind woman with supernatural gifts who helps a grieving couple. With Vanessa Redgrave, Patrick Bergin. Showtime, Nov. 14.

To Dance with the White Dog—A *Hall of Fame* presentation about an elderly man who finds a strange white dog that becomes a companion after his wife's death. With Hume Cronyn, Jessica Tandy. CBS, Dec. 5.

Tosca—A *Great Performances* telecast of the Puccini opera performed in the actual Roman settings. With Plácido Domingo, Catherine Malfitano. PBS, Jan. 3.

Where Angels Fear to Tread—A *Masterpiece Theatre* presentation of a 1991 British adaptation of E. M. Forster's first novel. With Helena Bonham Carter, Judy Davis, Helen Mirren, Giovanni Guidelli. PBS, Nov. 7.

Wild Palms—A four-part series set in the year 2007 that deals with a technology known as virtual reality. With James Belushi, Robert Loggia, Dana Delany, Angie Dickinson. ABC, May 16.

With a Little Help from Her Friends—Singer Aretha Franklin performs duets with Elton John, Rod Stewart, and others. Fox, May 9.

Zelda—A TV-movie biography of F. Scott Fitzgerald and his wife. With Timothy Hutton, Natasha Richardson. TNT, Nov. 7.

TENNESSEE

Economic progress marked the year 1993 in Tennessee.

The Legislature and Politics. Legislators, encouraged by a financial surplus, adopted a record $11.7 billion budget. State employees received their first salary increase in several years. In lieu of adopting an income tax, legislators made permanent a half-cent increase in the sales tax—thus raising the levy to 8.25%, the nation's highest. Much of the additional funds would be devoted to education. Specifically, the tax would provide an additional $100 million for grades kindergarten through 12, allow some additional funding for reforms included in the Basic Education Program begun in 1992, and provide salary increases for teachers from kindergarten through the university level.

Lawmakers authorized Gov. Ned McWherter to seek federal approval to substitute "Tenn-Care" for Medicaid. The Tenn-Care plan provides health insurance for uninsured workers and present Medicaid recipients alike. Under the plan, Tennessee would use matching federal money to purchase health care in bulk. If properly managed, this should result in substantial savings for the state.

After heated debate, legislators approved student-initiated prayer at nonmandatory school functions, adopted a formal policy against sexual harassment, and reapportioned electoral districts. Equitable reapportionment has been a problem for each Democratic-controlled legislature since the 1962 U.S. Supreme Court decision *Baker v. Carr.* By midsummer the latest reapportionment plan had been declared unconstitutional. Lawmakers were under court order to have a plan in place by the 1994 elections.

With the governor not eligible to succeed himself and with the state's two U.S. Senate and nine U.S. House of Representatives seats before the voters in 1994, dozens of potential candidates surfaced in 1993. Harlan Matthews, who was appointed to the Senate seat vacated when Al Gore became vice-president, was not expected to run for the remaining two years of Gore's Senate term.

Economy. Dry weather during July and August hurt most crops, especially soybeans and corn, both of which are million-dollar industries for the state. Tobacco continued to be the principal money crop. Cotton, aided by consistent hot weather, flourished in the southern counties. In early fall the unemployment rate for the state dropped to 5.5%—a three-year low. Per-capita income increased at a faster rate than in 1992, due to the continued industrialization of the state. Economists projected 2.8% growth for 1994.

Prisons. After more than a decade of federal control, Tennessee prisons were returned to the state after a federal judge—who ruled in 1982 that the state's prison conditions violated the 8th Amendment—noted that problems of over-

crowding, filth, violence, and idleness had been addressed properly. Six new prisons holding 1,000 prisoners each had been opened since the 1982 ruling. Tennessee expected to spend more than $322 million to operate its prisons in 1994.

People. State Supreme Court Justice Martha Craig Daughtrey, the first woman to serve on the state's high court, was appointed to the U.S. 6th District Court....Education Commissioner Charles Smith was named chancellor of the Board of Regents after Otis Floyd, the state's first black chancellor, died of a heart attack....Upholding a Tennessee Supreme Court decision, the U.S. Supreme Court in February refused to hear the appeal of a woman who sued for control of seven embryos she and her husband had conceived in vitro. The husband subsequently had them destroyed.

ROBERT E. CORLEW
Middle Tennessee State University

TERRORISM

A single car bombing in 1993 signaled a historic initiation for the United States into the realm of violent terrorism. The explosion at the World Trade Center in New York City on February 26, 1993, killed six persons, injured more than 1,000 others, and also shattered the myth of the United States' invulnerability to terrorism. Although U.S. citizens and facilities long had been targets of terrorists, these attacks usually occurred overseas. Americans, therefore, felt safe from terrorists at home. This perception of security dissolved with the World Trade Center blast—the largest terrorist bombing ever to take place within the United States.

World Trade Center Blast. The terrorists packed 1,000 lbs (373 kg) of nitrate explosives in a rental van and parked it in the underground garage of the huge office complex. Some 50,000 people were believed to be in the 110-story

"Twin Towers" at the time of the explosion—which caused hundreds of millions of dollars in damages. Dramatic television pictures captured the images of frantic office workers trapped in the skyscrapers as smoke rushed upward through the elevator shafts. Many of them had to walk down scores of flights of stairs in darkness, as the blast blew out power for the elevators and some of the lights.

The real significance of the event, however, was embedded in the symbolism of the target. The terrorist message was clear: If a successful attack could be launched in one of the most populous cities in the United States and against one of the world's most famous business and financial structures, then no city, building, or person in the nation was truly safe from terrorists.

The shock of the World Trade Center bombing still was being felt when another major terrorist plot was uncovered. The Federal Bureau of Investigation (FBI) announced the arrest in June 1993 of several Islamic extremists who were plotting to blow up four targets in New York on or near Independence Day. They planned to set off car bombs at the United Nations headquarters; the Lincoln and Holland Tunnels, which carry tens of thousands of motorists every day between New Jersey and Manhattan; and the Javits Federal Building in Manhattan that houses the FBI and other government agencies.

In August a federal grand jury indicted Sheikh Omar Abd al-Rahman, a blind Islamic cleric, as the leader of a group that conspired to engage in terrorism. Rahman had been tried and acquitted in Egypt for involvement in the 1981 assassination of President Anwar Sadat. While in the United States, he remained the spiritual leader of the extremist Islamic Group in Egypt.

He also had a loyal following of militant and alienated youths from the Middle East who were living in the New York area.

Economic Terrorism. The spread of Islamic extremism to the United States was just one of the newer developments in terrorism in 1993. Another story was the heightened priority that some terrorist groups gave to attacking economic targets. One of the terrorists arrested in connection with the World Trade Center bombing told an FBI informant that "the operation is to make them lose millions and that is what happened."

The United States was not unique in having economic and financial centers attacked by terrorists. In April the Irish Republican Army (IRA) set off a powerful car bomb in London's financial district (City of London), causing hundreds of millions of dollars in damage. The bomb was hidden in a parked truck and killed one person, injuring 44 others. The IRA had set off a similar bomb in the City of London in 1992, killing three persons and causing $1.25 billion in damages.

In addition to the bombing of London's financial district, the IRA was also responsible for several other spectacular terrorist attacks in 1993. On October 23 an IRA member placed a bomb inside a crowded fish shop in a Protestant area of West Belfast, Northern Ireland. The bomb exploded prematurely, killing the IRA member and nine other persons. Protestant terrorists retaliated with several attacks, including the shooting of seven persons in a pub in Londonderry.

In India terrorists set off a series of bombings in March in the financial capital of Bombay—including one blast at the Bombay Stock Exchange—killing more than 250 persons and wounding more than 1,000. In an unrelated inci-

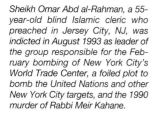

Sheikh Omar Abd al-Rahman, a 55-year-old blind Islamic cleric who preached in Jersey City, NJ, was indicted in August 1993 as leader of the group responsible for the February bombing of New York City's World Trade Center, a foiled plot to bomb the United Nations and other New York City targets, and the 1990 murder of Rabbi Meir Kahane.

© Markel/Gamma-Liaison

As the new director of the Federal Bureau of Investigation, Louis J. Freeh, a 43-year-old former federal judge, will be responsible for the investigation of terrorist incidents in the United States.

dent, 60 persons were killed when a bomb exploded in an underworld bomb factory in Calcutta.

Islamic extremists in Egypt targeted that country's tourism industry with several bombings of tourist buses and shootings in 1993. The result was a dramatic decline in foreign travel to Egypt. The terrorist attacks were aimed to damage the economy—tourism long has been a major source of revenue for the country—and to hasten the downfall of President Hosni Mubarak.

A famous Italian tourist and cultural attraction was also the target of a terrorist attack. In May a car bomb exploded on a street behind the well-known Uffizi Gallery in Florence, killing five persons and wounding 30 others. Several works of art were destroyed or damaged in the bombing, which government officials blamed on Mafia gangs. In July terrorists set off two bombs in Rome that damaged parts of the Basilica of St. John Lateran and the ancient church of San Giorgio in Velabro. Another bomb in Milan killed five persons and damaged an art gallery.

Political Attacks. Ethnic-religious and nationalist conflicts continued to claim many lives around the world in 1993. In Bosnia an estimated 150,000 people were believed to have been killed or reported missing since war broke out in the former Yugoslav republic in 1992.

In Sri Lanka more than 30,000 people have died since Tamil rebels began fighting for a separate state in 1983. Among the major terrorist events in that country in 1993 were two assassinations. On May 1, President Ranasinghe Premadasa and some of his aides were killed by a suicide terrorist, who detonated explosives that were strapped to his body. Only one week before the assassination, the leading opposition leader, Lalith Athulathmudali, also was assassinated.

In Spain the Basque separatist group ETA was suspected of exploding two bombs in downtown Madrid in June. The blasts killed seven persons and wounded more than 20 others.

The death sentence, or *fatwa*, against Salman Rushdie, author of the novel *The Satanic Verses*, was renewed in February by Iran's spiritual leader, the Ayatollah Ali Khamenei. The *fatwa* originally was pronounced in 1989 by Iran's revolutionary leader, the late Ayatollah Ruhollah Khomeini, who called the book blasphemous for its depiction of the prophet Mohammed. A reward created by Iran for carrying out the death sentence has varied between $1 million and $3 million. In October 1992 the book's Norwegian publisher was shot and seriously wounded, marking the third attack on individuals associated with the book. In 1991 the Japanese translator was murdered, while that same year the Italian translator was stabbed but survived. For the most part, Rushdie has been hiding in England since 1989.

An alleged Iraqi plot to assassinate former President George Bush on a visit to Kuwait in April led to a U.S. retaliatory raid. In an air strike in June, the United States launched 23 Tomahawk missiles at Iraq's intelligence headquarters compound in Baghdad. Sixteen missiles hit their intended targets—Iraqi intelligence offices—while four others landed elsewhere in the compound. Three of the cruise missiles went astray and struck residential neighborhoods, killing several civilians.

Libya continued to defy a UN Security Council order to hand over two suspects, Lamen Khalifa Fhimah and Abdel Basset Ali al-Megrahi, wanted for the 1988 midair bombing of Pan Am Flight 103 over Lockerbie, Scotland. The bombing killed 270 persons, including 11 on the ground.

The signing of a peace accord in September between Israel and the Palestine Liberation Organization (PLO) did not halt terrorism in the Middle East. Several terrorist attacks followed the historic agreement, including a suicide car bombing in October of an Israeli commuter bus outside the Israeli army headquarters in the West Bank. The driver, believed to be a member of the militant Islamic movement Hamas, blew himself up in the attack, which injured 30 Israelis. There also were numerous assassinations of PLO officials in the Gaza Strip by rival factions.

Letter Bomb. Among the terrorist tactics that persisted in 1993 was the use of letter bombs. In June one bomb injured a geneticist at the University of California at San Francisco when he opened a package sent to his home, while another wounded a computer scientist at Yale University when he opened a package mailed to his office. The bombs—disguised as books or manuscripts—were made from match heads, nails, screws, metal, pipes, gunpowder, and batteries. The same person, who was not apprehended, was believed responsible for the two attacks and 12 other letter bombings that date back to 1978.

JEFFREY D. SIMON
Freelance Writer

TEXAS

Texas had an exciting political year in 1993. Attention also was focused on the state early in the year during the 51-day standoff between the Branch Davidians, led by David Koresh, and law-enforcement officials in Waco (*see* page 64).

Politics. When U.S. President Bill Clinton appointed Lloyd M. Bentsen, Jr. (D-TX) as treasury secretary, he unwittingly set the stage for a political disaster for his fellow Democrat, Texas Gov. Ann Richards. As Bentsen's interim successor, Richards selected Democrat Robert Krueger, a member of the Texas Railroad Commission and former congressman who in 1978 and 1984 had made unsuccessful races for the U.S. Senate. Krueger's detractors blamed those two losses in part on his unpopularity with the liberal wing of the Texas Democratic Party. Even so, with the advantage of the incumbency in a mainly Democratic state, Krueger at first seemed likely to win the special election to fill the Senate position for the one and one half years remaining in Bentsen's term.

During his interim term, however, Krueger eroded his already weak standing with the liberals by opposing Clinton's budget. He also drew a formidable opponent in Republican Kay Bailey Hutchison of Dallas, who in 1992 had been elected state treasurer. In the first ballot of the May special election, Hutchison led the field of 24 candidates by fewer than 1,000 votes out of nearly 2 million cast. In the runoff, she swamped Krueger with 67% of the vote. Her feat made history: She became the first woman ever to serve in the U.S. Senate from Texas. Her victory also gave the Republican Party control of both the state's Senate seats for the first time since Reconstruction.

After her election, trouble loomed for Hutchison. A Travis county (Austin) grand jury indicted her on felony and misdemeanor charges stemming from allegations that she conducted political business during state office hours while treasurer. She also was charged with tampering with physical evidence and government records. The indictments later were dropped due to a technicality. It was expected that new indictments would be sought.

Another Texas politician, former U.S. Rep. Albert Bustamante, a 58-year-old Democrat from San Antonio, was sentenced to three and one half years in prison after being convicted on two counts of a ten-count indictment charging him with racketeering and accepting an illegal fee in an influence-peddling scheme.

In off-year elections in November, Texas voters approved a bond issue calling for the state to borrow money to build additional prisons; authorized the denial of bail to suspects charged with certain violent or sexual offenses while on probation or parole for prior felonies; overwhelmingly approved a proposition to remove the legislature's power to enact a state income tax without the electorate's approval; and rejected a plan to

allow the state to borrow $50 million to assist in the establishment of new minority- and women-owned businesses. Houston Mayor Robert Lanier was reelected to a second two-year term.

Economy. Texas began 1993 with an unemployment rate of 7.8%, only slightly less than the 1992 high of 7.9%. The figure fluctuated throughout 1993, reaching a low point of 6.5% in May. The U.S. Bureau of Labor Statistics reported that during the 12 months ending in May 1993, Texas added jobs at a 2.1% rate, compared with a national rate of 1.5%. And the index of economic indicators was 2.6% higher in late summer that it had been a year earlier.

In April monthly oil production in the state—which had been declining steadily since 1972—sank to its lowest point in more than 20 years. April production was down by nearly 6% from the same time in 1992.

Although the U.S. House of Representatives had voted for a second time in 1993 to kill the $11 billion Superconducting Super Collider (SSC) near Dallas, the Senate later rescued the controversial project. In an October vote, however, it was killed. The SSC's defeat left some 2,100 employees of the project without jobs.

Education. Texas lawmakers wrestled with the task of producing a means of financing public schools that would satisfy constitutional requirements. The most recent attempt prohibited school districts from holding more than $280,000 per student in taxable property. Districts that had more were given options for reducing it. More than 40 property-poor school districts were challenging the law, claiming it did not erase differences in money available to property-rich and property-poor districts.

New Historic Landmark. On the 30th anniversary of the death of John F. Kennedy, Dallas' Dealy Plaza, the site of his assassination, was dedicated as a National Historic Landmark.

LYNWOOD ABRAM, *Freelance Writer, El Paso*

TEXAS • Information Highlights

Area: 266,807 sq mi (691 030 km²).
Population (July 1, 1992 est.): 17,656,000.
Chief Cities (1990 census): Austin, the capital, 465,622; Houston, 1,630,553; Dallas, 1,006,877; San Antonio, 935,933; El Paso, 515,342; Fort Worth, 447,619; Corpus Christi, 257,453.
Government (1993): *Chief Officers*—governor, Ann Richards (D); lt. gov., Bob Bullock (D). *Legislature*—Senate, 31 members; House of Representatives, 150 members.
State Finances (fiscal year 1991): *Revenue*, $33,773,000,000; *expenditure*, $29,532,000,000.
Personal Income (1992): $323,687,000,000; per capita, $18,333.
Labor Force (August 1993): *Civilian labor force*, 8,927,900; *unemployed*, 643,900 (7.2% of total force).
Education: *Enrollment* (fall 1991)—public elementary schools, 2,574,983; public secondary, 889,388; colleges and universities, 917,443. *Public school expenditures* (1990-91), $13,695,327,000.

THAILAND

During 1993, Thailand's democratic government led by Prime Minister Chuan Leekpai weathered a no-confidence vote and a reshuffling of coalition partners in its first year in power.

Politics. Although judged short on policy accomplishments, Chuan's fragile coalition government survived blistering opposition attacks and internal bickering among coalition partners. The charges that Chuan was indecisive and colorless were offset by the public's belief in his honesty and commitment to democracy.

The normal turbulence of Thai coalition internal politics was exaggerated during the year. After the September 1992 elections, Chuan, leader of the Democracy Party—the largest parliamentary party, with 79 seats—included the formerly pro-military Social Action Party (SAP) in his coalition to ensure a stable majority. The SAP constantly undermined the government's position on issues. SAP's leader, Montri Pongpanich, publicly ridiculed the prime minister. In September, SAP's open opposition led Chuan to dismiss it from the coalition. To offset the loss of SAP's 21 seats to the opposition, Chuan brought the Seritham Party into the government, giving his coalition a 26-vote majority in the 360-member National Assembly.

The precariousness of what was dubbed the Chuan II government was underlined quickly when an opposition walkout on a critical vote on a copyright-protection bill left the government without a legislative quorum to conduct business. The government later installed new whip mechanisms to ensure future quorums, but the instability inherent in the slim parliamentary majority fostered some calls for a dissolution of the National Assembly and a new national election, which Chuan resisted.

The opposition failed to capitalize on the opportunities presented by policy delay and disarray in the coalition. This inability to promote coherent policy alternatives was clear in the debate on the opposition's no-confidence motion in June. The opposition resorted to savage personal attack, which strongly contrasted with Chuan's dignified demeanor and his reassuring outline of his government's program. Chuan's government easily won the confidence vote.

Economy. Although economists outside the government felt that the official forecast of 7.8% gross-domestic-product (GDP) growth in 1993 was unrealistic, there was little doubt that Thailand was sustaining its drive to become the next "newly industrialized economy." The business climate was buoyed after the defeat of the no-confidence debate.

Thailand's rapid economic growth has not been accomplished without social cost. For example, there has been laxity in regulating or enforcing basic codes. The tragic consequences of violation of the most rudimentary building and safety standards were evident in a fire in May at a Bangkok toy factory that killed more than 200 workers, and in a hotel collapse in northeast Thailand that left 102 dead.

Foreign investors in Thailand's greatly needed infrastructure were shocked in September when the Interior Ministry-controlled Expressway and Rapid Transit Authority forced the opening of a new Bangkok toll expressway in a dispute with its private, Japanese-majority investors and operators. The Minister of Interior led the coalition's New Aspiration Party and the action was taken while the prime minister was out of the country. The matter was in litigation but doubts were raised about the government's manipulation of the legal system against a foreign investor for domestic political reasons.

Foreign Policy. Thailand continued to be preoccupied by its neighbors. The success of the United Nations Transitional Authority (UNTAC) mission in Cambodia and the installation of a freely elected Cambodian government focused attention on the Thai military's continued cross-border connections to the Khmer Rouge and Thai exploitation of the resources of western Cambodia. In April the Chuan government showed greater sensitivity than its predecessors to the human-rights situation in Myanmar by allowing a meeting in Bangkok of seven Nobel Peace Prize laureates seeking to gain the freedom of imprisoned laureate Daw Aung San Suu Kyi. The government quickly hastened to reassure the Myanmar junta that this did not change its policy of friendly "constructive engagement."

Thailand's relations with the United States continued to be irritated by U.S. complaints of Thai infringement of trade law. The United States also put great pressure on Bangkok to force the withdrawal of three Thai companies believed to be developing Libyan chemical-weapons facilities. The strain in Thai-U.S. relations was illustrated by Thailand's application to join the Nonaligned Movement.

DONALD E. WEATHERBEE
University of South Carolina

THAILAND • Information Highlights

Official Name: Kingdom of Thailand (conventional); Prathet Thai (Thai).

Location: Southeast Asia.

Area: 198,456 sq mi (514 000 km²).

Population (mid-1993 est.): 57,200,000.

Chief City (1990 census prelim.): Bangkok, the capital, 5,876,000.

Government: *Head of state,* Bhumibol Adulyadej, king (acceded June 1946). *Head of government,* Chuan Leekpai, prime minister (took power September 1992).

Monetary Unit: Baht (25.30 baht equal U.S.$1, Nov. 16, 1993).

Gross National Product (1991 est. U.S.$): $92,600,000,000.

Economic Index (Bangkok, 1992): *Consumer Prices* (1980 = 100), all items, 172.3; food, 166.0.

Foreign Trade (1992 U.S.$): *Imports,* $40,883,000,000; *exports,* $32,437,000,000.

THEATER

As threadbare as the 1992-93 Broadway season was of good new productions, it was not uneventful. The event was *Angels in America, Part 1: Millennium Approaches*, a comedy-drama by relative newcomer Tony Kushner that was awarded the 1993 Pulitzer Prize for drama and instantly recognized as an American classic with its opening on Broadway (after initial stagings in London and Los Angeles).

Angels was a dreamlike epic weaving together many crises of U.S. society—from AIDS to spiritual malaise—in a portrait of the nation hurtling toward a dark, mysterious reckoning in the 1980s. Even as it redeemed Broadway as a home for new works of literary merit, this self-styled "Gay Fantasia on National Themes" (as it was subtitled) marked a critical, risky turning point in the visibility of the theater's homosexual artists. In that sense it built upon the breakthroughs of 1992's *Falsettos*, which still was running when *Angels* opened. With the spring of 1993 also witnessing the opening of the musical *Kiss of the Spider Woman*, featuring a gay hero, a *Time* magazine headline dubbed Broadway "The Gay White Way."

But with more openly gay artists than ever before appearing on the network television broadcast of the Tony Awards ceremony in June, it remained to be seen how the heartland audience—the heart of the Broadway tourist trade—would respond to this "coming out."

Angels won the Tony for best play, overshadowing all other plays at the awards except perhaps *The Sisters Rosensweig*, Wendy Wasserstein's warm and literate comedy of a trio of Jewish-American sisters and their search for fulfillment, professional and romantic.

Ron Leibman, whose volcanic Roy Cohn was the hysterical villain of *Angels*, won the Tony for best actor in a play—with some competition from red-hot Irishman Stephen Rea (fresh from the hit film *The Crying Game*), whose brooding performance redeemed the otherwise static hostage drama *Someone to Watch Over Me*. Madeline Kahn won for best actress in a play for her utterly delightful performance as the wise-ditsy Gorgeous Rosensweig.

To compensate for the flatness of competition among the plays, there was a classic showdown in the musicals: *Kiss of the Spider Woman* versus *The Who's Tommy*. Both shows were original—dramatically charged, with spectacular scenic innovations. And yet on a symbolic level they represented the Old Guard of *Spider Woman* (director Hal Prince and the songwriting team of John Kander and Fred Ebb) versus The Young Turks of *Tommy* (director Des McAnuff of La Jolla [CA] Playhouse, who coadapted the 1969 rock opera of Pete Townshend and The Who). McAnuff won for best director, and Townshend shared the award for best score with Kander and Ebb, but *Spider Woman* took the Tony for best musical—a reflection, certainly, of the age of the 600 Tony voters, most of whom are retired theater artists or critics.

"Angels in America, Part I: Millennium Approaches," a three-and-one-half-hour apocalyptic epic by Tony Kushner, was Broadway's dramatic highlight of 1993. It captured a Pulitzer Prize for drama and four Tony Awards, including best play.

Chita Rivera dances with Jeff Hyslop in "Kiss of the Spider Woman." For her highly praised performance, Rivera was voted a Tony Award as best actress in a musical.

© Martha Swope

The season's big human-interest story was dancer-actress Chita Rivera, who at 60 came back not only from a long career drought but also a devastating leg injury to win the best actress/musical as the sinuous dream figure, the Spider Woman. Canadian newcomer Brent Carver won best actor/musical as Molina, the gay Latin American political prisoner whom she jauntily tempts toward death.

Still, it was the success of *Tommy,* with its thrillingly dreamlike collage of projections by set designer John Arnone, that had hopeful ramifications for Broadway's future. It represented a long-overdue breakthrough for rock musicals on Broadway, which in years past (*Hair, Jesus Christ Superstar*) had been corny recyclings of rock material. Some rock purists complained that the new Townshend-McAnuff version of the story—about a deaf, dumb, and blind boy who becomes a "pinball wizard"—had lost its edge and its mystery in its transfer to the commercial stage. But few could argue that the sleek, eye-filling show had a sure sense of hipness and style, appealing to both nostalgic baby-boomer parents and their preteen kids. Also, its poignant portrait of a traumatized child struck an even more sensitized chord in 1993 audiences.

The Resident Theaters. The New York Shakespeare Festival (NYSF), which for many years under the late Joseph Papp had been the inspirational flagship of resident nonprofit U.S. theaters, had become the reverse by 1993: a showcase of these theaters' troubles. Papp successor JoAnne Akalaitis, after less than two years as artistic director, was dismissed in March by the NYSF board. (A factor was an analysis by *The New York Times* citing her low rate of productivity as well as the chilly intellectualism of her work.)

The appointment of George C. Wolfe in her place (making him the highest-ranking African American in the U.S. theater) was hailed widely, since he had been one of the institution's most successful playwright-directors of recent years (*Spunk*). But since Wolfe was already in such intense demand, booked for almost all of 1993 (primarily to mount *Angels in America, Part 2: Perestroika*), the Shakespeare Festival continued to drift virtually directorless for the remainder of the year.

In *Twilight: Los Angeles 1992,* playwright/solo performer Anna Deavere Smith explored the riots surrounding the Rodney King verdict, much as she had explored the Crown Heights race riots in her earlier *Fires in the Mirror,* by interviewing scores of people who were participants or observers in the incidents, and who were on both sides of the racial barricade, and then embodying them in a kind of dramatized oral history. The work was acclaimed in its world premiere at Los Angeles' Mark Taper Forum and later at its East Coast debut at the McCarter Theatre in Princeton, NJ.

The mysterious and pseudonymous playwright Jane Martin leapt into the abortion debate with *Keely and Du*—the tale of a pregnant young woman who is held hostage by right-to-life zealots to keep her from having a desired abortion. Described as a complex (though ultimately pro-choice) exploration of the issue, the suspenseful play was the hit of Jon Jory's Humana Festival of New American Plays at Actors Theatre of Louisville and later was restaged (to acclaim by *Time* magazine) at Hartford Stage Company. (Martin managed to maintain the secret of "her" identity, although the playwright was believed widely to be Jory.)

Lincoln Center, under new artistic director Andre Bishop, instituted its own Festival of New American Plays in its intimate Mitzi Newhouse Theatre and launched it impressively with Howard Korder's *The Lights*. It was a searing and darkly funny exposé of an urban problem center very much like New York, harrowingly evoked by director Mark Wing-Davey with assault-weapon bursts of movement, light, and sound (but lacking in the script any redemptive glimpse of how things might change). However, Lincoln Center's big gambit of 1993 was a rare revival of Robert Sherwood's historical epic, *Abe Lincoln in Illinois*. Despite a solid Sam Waterston in the title role, the huge production generally was deemed an honorable attempt of a dated, creaky work.

Actor-comedian Steve Martin, who had received respectful reviews for a New York *Waiting for Godot* a few seasons earlier, made his playwriting debut with the playfully philosophic *Einstein and Picasso at the Lapin Agile* at Chicago's Steppenwolf Theatre. The Old Globe Theatre of San Diego mounted an acclaimed revival of the popular 1950s musical *Damn Yankees* that at year's end was being prepared for a 1994 transfer to Broadway.

In San Francisco, where the theater scene had lost much of its pace-setting excitement of the 1970s, Carey Perloff was seen as a welcome new provocateur. As artistic director of the American Conservatory Theatre, Perloff outraged some patrons with Dario Fo's Vatican farce, *The Pope and the Witch,* but she likewise was acclaimed for bold new slants on the classics.

The most popular new drama on subscription lists at the major resident theaters was *Dancing at Lughnasa* (pronounced LOO-na-sa), the haunting memory play by Ireland's Brian Friel that had come out of the Abbey Theatre of Dublin to become a surprise Broadway hit in 1991. Set in a remote Irish village in the 1930s and told through the author's boyhood eyes, it sets the poignantly thwarted lives of his mother and her four unmarried sisters against the lusty and mysterious Celtic harvest festival of Lughnasa. During the 1993-94 season, *Lughnasa* was performed at the Goodman Theatre of Chicago; the Arena Stage of Washington, DC; the Alliance Theatre of Atlanta, GA; Berkeley (CA) Repertory Theatre; the Alley Theatre of Houston, TX; and a host of smaller companies across the country.

The Road. Two big musicals drawn from blockbuster movies—*Sunset Boulevard* and *Beauty and the Beast*—enjoyed splashy "out-of-town" openings in December 1993 and began the tryout road to Broadway.

Andrew Lloyd Webber's *Sunset Boulevard* was a retelling of the classic suspense film about a down-and-out writer's relationship with the strange and reclusive former Hollywood diva, Norma Desmond—played by Glenn Close in the U.S. premiere in Los Angeles. Two songs for the Desmond character already had been recorded by Barbra Streisand on her album, *Back to Broadway*. Word from the musical's summer world premiere in London was that it featured the most spectacular set yet for producer-composer Lloyd Webber (*Cats, Phantom of the Opera*), but that leading lady Patti LuPone lacked the regal stature for the role. *Time* magazine generally preferred the Los Angeles production over London's, including the more patrician Close over LuPone.

Beauty and the Beast, the smash animated film for the Disney Company, featured a marvelous Alan Menken score that seemed ready-made for a projected Broadway opening in the spring of 1994. The stage version of the beloved family tale (whose central romantic relationship

© Joan Marcus

"The Who's Tommy," the stage adaptation of the 1969 rock opera by the rock band The Who, also was a Broadway musical hit of 1993. Pete Townshend was the musical's composer and lyricist; Des McAnuff cowrote the book with Townshend and directed; and Michael Cerveris (right) portrayed the adult Tommy.

BROADWAY OPENINGS | 1993

MUSICALS

Ain't Broadway Grand, music by Mitch Leigh; lyrics by Lee Adams; book by Thomas Meehan; directed by Scott Harris; with Mike Burstyn, Maureen McNamara, Debbie Shapiro Gravitte; April 18–May 9.

Blood Brothers, music, book, and lyrics by Willy Russell; directed by Bill Kenwright and Bob Tomson; with Con O'Neill, Mark Michael Hutchison, Stephanie Lawrence (April 25–Aug. 25); with David Cassidy, Shaun Cassidy, Petula Clark (Aug. 25–); April 25–.

Camelot, by Alan Jay Lerner and Frederick Loewe; based on a novel by T. H. White; directed by Norb Joerder; with Robert Goulet; June 21–Aug. 7.

Cyrano—The Musical, music by Ad Van Dijk; book and lyrics by Koen Van Dijk; English lyrics by Peter Reeves; directed by Eddy Habbema; with Bill Van Dijk, Anne Runolfsson, Paul Anthony Stewart; Nov. 21–.

The Goodbye Girl, music by Marvin Hamlisch; lyrics by David Zippel; book by Neil Simon; directed by Michael Kidd; with Bernadette Peters, Martin Short; March 4–Aug. 15.

A Grand Night for Singing, music by Richard Rodgers; lyrics by Oscar Hammerstein II; conceived and directed by Walter Bobbie; with Victoria Clark, Jason Graae, Alyson Reed, Martin Vidnovic, Lynne Wintersteller; Nov. 17–.

Joseph and the Amazing Technicolor Dreamcoat, music by Andrew Lloyd Webber; lyrics by Tim Rice; directed by Steven Pimlott; with Michael Damian; Nov. 10–.

Kiss of the Spider Woman, music by John Kander; lyrics by Fred Ebb; book by Terrence McNally; directed by Harold Prince; with Chita Rivera, Brent Carver, Anthony Crivello; May 3–.

My Fair Lady, music by Frederick Loewe; book and lyrics by Alan Jay Lerner; directed by Howard Davies; with Richard Chamberlain, Paxton Whitehead, Julian Holloway, Melissa Errico; Dec. 9–.

The Red Shoes, music by Jule Styne; lyrics by Marsha Norman and Paul Stryker; book by Norman; directed by Stanley Donen; with Roger Rees, Margaret Illmann; Dec. 16–Dec. 19.

She Loves Me, music by Jerry Bock; lyrics by Sheldon Harnick; book by Joe Masteroff; directed by Scott Ellis; with Boyd Gaines, Judy Kuhn, Sally Mayes, Howard McGillin; June 10–Aug. 1; Oct. 7–.

Tango Pasiòn, conceived by Mel Howard; arrangements and musical direction by Jose Libertella and Luis Stazo; choreographed by Héctor Zaraspe; April 28–May 2.

The Who's Tommy, music and lyrics by Pete Townshend; book by Townshend and Des McAnuff; additional music and lyrics by John Entwistle and Keith Moon; directed by McAnuff; with Michael Cerveris; April 22–.

PLAYS

Abe Lincoln in Illinois, by Robert E. Sherwood; directed by Gerald Gutierrez; with Sam Waterston; Nov. 29–.

Angels in America: Millennium Approaches, by Tony Kushner; directed by George C. Wolfe; with Ron Leibman; May 4–.

Angels in America: Perestroika, by Tony Kushner; directed by George C. Wolfe; with Ron Leibman; Nov. 23–.

Anna Christie, by Eugene O'Neill; directed by David Leveaux; with Natasha Richardson, Liam Neeson, Anne Meara, Rip Torn; Jan. 14–Feb. 28.

Any Given Day, by Frank Gilroy; directed by Paul Benedict; with Sada Thompson, Peter Frechette, Andrea Marcovicci; Nov. 16–Dec. 12.

Black Comedy/White Liars, by Peter Shaffer; directed by Gerald Gutierrez; with Nancy Marchand, Anne Bobby, Keene Curtis, Peter MacNicol, Kate Mulgrew, Brian Murray; Sept. 1–Oct. 3.

Candida, by George Bernard Shaw; directed by Gloria Muzio; with Robert Foxworth, Robert Sean Leonard, Mary Steenburgen; March 25–April 25.

Fool Moon, by Bill Irwin and David Shiner; with Bill Irwin, David Shiner, The Red Clay Ramblers; Feb. 25–Sept. 5.

In the Summer House, by Jane Bowles; directed by JoAnne Akalaitis; with Dianne Wiest, Jaime Tirelli, Frances Conroy; Aug. 1–22.

The Kentucky Cycle, by Robert Schenkkan; directed by Warner Shook; with Stacy Keach; Nov. 14–Dec. 12.

Laughter on the 23rd Floor, by Neil Simon; directed by Jerry Zaks; with Nathan Lane, Paul Provenza, Mark Linn-Baker, Randy Graff; Nov. 22–.

Mixed Emotions, by Richard Baer; directed by Tony Giordano; with Katherine Helmond, Harold Gould; Oct. 12–Nov. 28.

Redwood Curtain, by Lanford Wilson; directed by Marshall W. Mason; with Jeff Daniels, Debra Monk, Sung Yun Cho; March 30–May 2.

Saint Joan, by Bernard Shaw; directed by Michael Langham; with Maryann Plunkett, John Neville, Remak Ramsay, Edmund C. Davys; Jan. 31–March 14.

Shakespeare for My Father, conceived and written by Lynn Redgrave; directed by John Clark; with Lynn Redgrave; April 26–.

The Sisters Rosensweig, by Wendy Wasserstein; directed by Daniel Sullivan; with Jane Alexander, Madeline Kahn, Robert Klein (March 18–Aug. 15); Michael Learned, Linda Lavin, Hal Linden (Aug. 15–); March 18–.

The Song of Jacob Zulu, by Tug Yourgrau; lyrics by Yourgrau and Ladysmith Black Mambazo; music by Ladysmith Black Mambazo; directed by Eric Simonson; with K. Todd Freeman, Zakes Mokae; March 24–May 9.

Three Men on a Horse, by John Cecil Holm and George Abbott; directed by John Tillinger; with Ellen Greene, Julie Hagerty, Jack Klugman, Tony Randall, Jerry Stiller; April 13–May 16.

Timon of Athens, by William Shakespeare; directed by Michael Langham; with Brian Bedford; Nov. 4–Dec. 5.

Twilight of the Golds, by Jonathan Tolins; directed by Arvin Brown; with Jennifer Grey, David Groh, Judith Scarpone, Michael Spound; Oct. 21–Nov. 14.

Wilder, Wilder, Wilder: Three by Thornton, by Thornton Wilder; directed by Edward Berkeley; with Michael Rispoli, Cynthia Besteman; April 21–May 16.

Wonderful Tennessee, by Brian Friel; directed by Patrick Mason; with Donal McCann, John Kavanagh; Oct. 24–Oct. 31.

---

was not unlike that of *Phantom of the Opera*) premiered at Houston's Theater Under the Stars to begin a tryout tour. More than 10,000 tickets were sold on the first day of sales, the second-highest total (after Broadway's *Phantom*) in the history of the U.S. theater.

One of the most popular tours of 1993 was *My Fair Lady,* starring Richard Chamberlain as Professor Henry Higgins. Capitalizing on the actor's three decades of television fame—from *Dr. Kildare* to *Shogun* to *The Thorn Birds*—the tour did brisk business all across the country. The irony of the show's success was that its biggest marketing boon (Chamberlain) was not its main

artistic asset. Never known as a comic actor, Chamberlain lacked the avuncular warmth that the late Rex Harrison so memorably brought to the role, so that his put-downs of Eliza Doolittle came across with an arrogant, antifeminist meanness that brought an unwanted chill to the Lerner and Loewe musical classic. On the other hand, Chamberlain's costars, especially newcomer Melissa Errico as Eliza, were excellent. British director Howard Davies (*Les Liaisons Dangereuses*) sparked the evening with stylish production concepts, including an "Ascot Races" scene where snooty spectators were suspended on wires at heights corresponding to their social

Anna Deavere Smith, a 42-year-old Stanford University professor, concluded her series of one-person shows, "On the Road: A Search for American Character," with "Twilight: Los Angeles 1992." Her account of the 1992 upheaval in Los Angeles was seen at the Mark Taper Forum in Los Angeles and later at the McCarter Theatre in Princeton, NJ.

© Jim McHugh/Outline

rank. The seven-month tour culminated on Broadway in December.

The Fall 1993 Broadway Season. No recent season began with so many promising openings that seemed destined to break Broadway out of the lopsided, silent-fall/hectic-spring cycle that it had adopted in the late 1980s than the 1993 fall season. And no fall season seemed to collapse as quickly as in 1993, due to disappointing productions—or good productions that received disappointing responses.

With warm memories of his *Dancing at Lughnasa* still fresh, audiences awaited Brian Friel's *Wonderful Tennessee,* a portrait of three Irish couples comparing seriocomic notes on their midlife awareness of mortality. More experimental than *Lughnasa,* it was deemed intelligent but under-energized, and closed quickly.

An even more highly touted work, *The Kentucky Cycle,* lasted only 34 performances. In 1992 it had won acclaim for productions in Seattle and Los Angeles and had become the first play to win a Pulitzer Prize without having been seen in New York (where its vast size and cost—not to mention reservations about the script—scared off investors). On Broadway, Robert Schenkkan's two-part, six-hour-plus epic proved to be a good, old-fashioned, plot-driven, historical melodrama. It featured a renewed Stacy Keach as patriarch over several generations of an Irish-American family suffering frontier hardships, the treachery of coal-mine operators, and their own misguided collaboration with the exploiters. It was a strong, if unsubtle, parable of a lovely land sacrificed to greed, although *The New York Times* panned it as simplistic. But even if it had won the *Times'* blessing, the drama's length and ticket prices (mostly in the $100 range) made it unworkable for the stage in any case. Cable television's Home Box Office purchased the rights to convert it into a miniseries format.

Another large-scale disappointment was the musical version of *The Red Shoes.* Lovely dance sequences and shimmering Heidi Landesman

sets evoked a bit of the magic of the classic, backstage-at-the-ballet film upon which it was based. But the leads were unexceptional, and several of the songs by Marsha Norman (lyrics) and 89-year-old *Gypsy* legend Jule Styne (music) were boringly flat-footed.

A glitz-drenched revival of Andrew Lloyd Webber's first musical, *Joseph and the Amazing Technicolor Dreamcoat,* was deemed unspiritual at best (vulgar at worst) by most critics. But a healthy run seemed assured by its popularity with kids and the often shirtless presence of soap-opera star Michael Damian.

Two blasts from the past—1963 to be exact—boosted Broadway's fall box office. The first was Neil Simon—celebrating the 30th anniversary of his first major hit, *Barefoot in the Park*—who showed no signs of slowing down in his current hilarious *Laughter on the 23rd Floor.* This affectionate (but laced with acid) portrait of his days on the legendary television writing staff of Sid Caesar's *Your Show of Shows* in the 1950s was graced with an all-pro squad of comic actors, led by Nathan Lane in the Caesar role, and director Jerry Zaks—both returning from their triumphs in *Guys and Dolls.*

The other 1963-vintage item was *She Loves Me,* a sparkling romantic musical with a likable young cast and a rediscovered golden score by Jerry Bock and Sheldon Harnick (*Fiddler on the Roof*). It marked the second recent coup for the resurgent Roundabout Theatre. (Its *Anna Christie* won the 1993 Tony for best revival.)

As one critic noted, *Angels in America* was on one level a "terrific cliffhanger" that kept fans in suspense for more than six months. Its conclusion, *Part 2: Perestroika,* reasserted the entirety of Tony Kushner's epic as a contemporary masterpiece. The play (produced in repertory with *Part 1,* with the same superb cast) was a letdown only in its theatricality, no doubt unavoidable following the astonishing *Part 1* of the drama.

DAN HULBERT
"The Atlanta Journal and Constitution"

TRANSPORTATION

The transportation industry was challenged in 1993 by economic conditions, tough weather in the United States, and safety-related events.

Airlines. Preliminary data indicated that major U.S. airlines earned a total operating profit of roughly $1.7 billion. However, this failed to cover interest payments, taxes, and charges against income for special expenses, and made 1993 the fourth consecutive year in which the industry suffered a net loss. Although serious, 1993's loss fell some $2.7 billion below the 1992 deficit due to lower fuel prices, reductions in service and personnel, and other cost-cutting actions. Also contributing to the improved results was a 1.6% increase in revenue passenger-kilometers during January-July over the same period in 1992 for the nine major U.S. airlines. Cargo traffic showed greater strength, with a 6.4% rise in freight-ton kilometers for the major carriers handling freight. Revenue passenger-kilometers on international routes of the Association of European Airlines jumped 8.3% between January-August 1993 from the same period in 1992, while freight-ton kilometers rose 6.0%.

The unprecedented severity of the industry's financial plight prompted the federal government to create the National Airline Commission to investigate conditions affecting airline performance. After four months of deliberations ended in August, the commission issued a report recommending fewer restrictions on foreign ownership of U.S. air carriers, revised laws governing airline bankruptcies, a panel to assess the fitness of troubled airlines, the transfer of air-traffic-control functions from the Federal Aviation Administration (FAA) to an independent organization, and the cutting of ticket and cargo taxes. Observers felt that the report would have little impact on policy. Neither President Bill Clinton nor Secretary of Transportation Federico Peña endorsed any of the report's recommendations, and these was no visible enthusiasm for the report among congressional leaders.

Carriers pursued their own efforts to restore profitability. Most dramatic was American Airlines' quest to reduce labor costs, which triggered a strike by flight attendants just days before the Thanksgiving travel rush. The strike ended after direct communication with company and union officials by President Clinton.

In March the Clinton administration approved a $300 million investment in USAir by British Airways. This marked a reversal in policy from the Bush administration. In December 1992, British Airways had withdrawn a proposal to invest $750 million in USAir when the Department of Transportation indicated that the proposal would be rejected. In the new agreement, British Airways obtained permission to implement a code-sharing agreement with USAir, tying together separate flights of the two carriers in their computer-reservation systems to enable them to act as one company with interline reservations and ticketing functions. The agreement also gave British Airways limited permission to lease USAir planes and fly them with its own crews on transatlantic flights. British Airways also acquired a 49.7% equity stake in TAT European Airlines, a French company. Terms of the agreement call for British Airways to acquire the remaining 51.1% of TAT by April 1997. The USAir and TAT investments represented an important advance in British Airways' ongoing drive to improve its market position in an increasingly multinational industry.

Continental Airlines and Trans World Airlines (TWA) emerged from bankruptcy by completing changes in their financial capital structures successfully under Chapter 11 of the federal bankruptcy code. Continental's reorganization included a $450 million cash infusion by Air Canada and Air Partners, an investment group in Texas. Continental announced the elimination of 2,500 jobs; the retirement of 30 planes; the termination of all service to Australia, New Zealand, and Vancouver, B.C.; and the reduction of operations at its Denver hub. Labor savings were a key part of TWA's reorganization, as

Some 21,000 American Airlines flight attendants went on strike for five days in November 1993 after a major salary dispute could not be resolved. The walkout created havoc for early Thanksgiving-holiday travelers in the United States and overseas.

workers received 45% of common shares in the restructured company in exchange for $660 million in concessions.

Other airlines also issued stock to employees in return for cost-saving labor contracts. Northwest Airlines personnel gave $886 million in concessions for a new class of stock, convertible for up to 37.5% of the company's common stock. In December, United Airlines and two of its unions—the Air Line Pilots Association and the International Association of Machinists—inked a tentative pact in which the UAL Corporation (the parent of United) would exchange up to 63% of its common shares for $5 billion in labor savings. The deal was subject to approval by shareholders and members of the unions.

The quest by established airlines to reduce operating costs significantly became more urgent as competition mounted from carriers with lower operating costs. In September, Southwest Airlines, a low-cost and profitable carrier which previously did not operate east of Cleveland, initiated service to Baltimore, causing a fare war. Southwest sparked more fear among higher-cost airlines on December 13, when it agreed to buy Salt Lake City-based Morris Air for $129 million in stock. Morris' 22-city system in the West joined Southwest's 37-city territory—the Midwest, Southwest, and West Coast.

The new competitive thrust by Southwest struck at the heart of USAir's eastern-route network. Faced with this threat to its revenue base along with five consecutive years of losses and wage and other labor-related costs among the highest in the airline industry, USAir announced on September 30 that it would cut 5.4% of its workforce, totaling 2,500 jobs, by mid-1994.

European airlines also continued to cut costs. Efforts by Air France to cut 4,000 jobs resulted in a bitter strike in October and the resignation of the company's chairman. His successor sought to deal with the company's massive losses, estimated at $1.27 billion for 1993, through increases in productivity and reductions in personnel costs. Personnel-cost reductions would be achieved by distributing company shares to employees in exchange for wage reductions.

Negotiations about a merger of Swissair, Scandinavian Airlines System (SAS), KLM Royal Dutch Airlines, and Austrian Airlines broke off in November after the companies could not agree on a U.S. air carrier with which to form a transatlantic alliance. SAS wanted Northwest Airlines while the others preferred Delta Airlines. After the breakdown, Delta announced that it would begin code-sharing on the New York-Brussels route with Sabena Belgian World Airlines. The flights were to be operated with Sabena aircraft and flight crews, and Delta cabin crews.

Business conditions were brighter in the all-cargo airline sector. Burlington Air Express' operating profit of $15.1 million for July-September 1993 was almost triple that for the same period in 1992. Emery Worldwide, long a loser for parent Consolidated Freightways, generated a $3.7 million operating profit during the first nine months of 1993. Federal Express reported continuing profits for its domestic operations and its first profit for its international services. In a surprise May announcement, Roadway Express, a major motor freight carrier, revealed plans to enter the heavyweight air-freight industry with a $100 million investment in a new subsidiary, Roadway Global Air.

Bus. Harsh business conditions confronted intercity bus operators. In the first half of 1993, revenue passengers carried by the ten largest regional Class I motor carriers of passengers increased 1.9%, from 4.28 million to 4.36 million over the same period in 1992. However, the additional revenue from this rise in traffic failed to offset increased operating expenses, as aggregate net operating income dropped 33%, from $2.56 million to $1.69 million. After deducting fixed charges, income taxes, and unusual expenses from net operating income, and adding nonoperating income, the carriers' aggregate net loss rose to $865,000 from $711,000.

At Greyhound Lines, Inc., the only nationwide carrier, ridership fell 2.5% during January-August 1993 compared with the same period in 1992. However, Greyhound's net operating income was expected to increase by roughly 45% due to various actions to cut costs and increase productivity. On July 27, Greyhound issued the first automated ticket using its new TRIPS computerized reservations system. The system was operational in about 100 of the company's top 200 stations before year's end. Strain continued between Greyhound and the regional carriers on matters such as interline ticketing and terminal sharing.

Rail. Total carload shipments (excluding intermodal traffic) on major U.S. freight railways during the 49 weeks beginning January 1 declined 0.1% from the same period in 1992. Intermodal traffic moved in containers and railers increased 7.6%, reflecting continuing shifts of freight away from all-highway movement and a stronger economy. Revenue ton-miles rose 1.6%.

The 2,500-mi (4 000-km) Kansas City Southern completed acquisition of the 1,200-mi (1 900-km)-long Mid-South Corp. On August 27, after eight months of sparring with rail unions, Wisconsin Central completed its takeover of the 227-mi (365-km) Green Bay & Western and the 208-mi (335-km) Fox River Valley Corp., consolidating them under a new subsidiary, Fox Valley & Western. Wisconsin Central also invested in the privatization of New Zealand's rail system and initiated efforts to acquire the 322-mi (518-km) Algoma Central Railway in Ontario.

Canada's two major freight railways—Canadian National (CN) and Canadian Pacific (CP) Rail System—began exploring joint use of track in areas where they possessed underutilized parallel lines. CN put up for sale its Central Vermont line, from the Quebec border to New London,

CT, and announced elimination of 30,000 jobs in Canada and the United States within three years. CP obtained Canadian government permission to abandon its line between Sherbrooke, Que., and St. John, N.B.

Other carriers sought to relieve bottlenecks caused by surges in coal and intermodal traffic. Union Pacific initiated programs to increase mainline track capacity at several locations on its system. Consolidated Rail Corporation (Conrail) and CP's Delaware & Hudson subsidiary, in partnership with the Commonwealth of Pennsylvania, moved forward with tunnel-enlargement projects to accommodate double-stack intermodal equipment, and CN began construction of a new underwater tunnel between Sarnia, Ont., and Port Huron, MI, for the same purpose.

The alternating-current (AC) traction motor, a high-powered technology new to U.S. diesel-electric freight locomotives, debuted in March when Burlington Northern ordered 350 AC locomotives from General Motors' Electro-Motive Division for $675 million. In December, CSX ordered 250 AC locomotives from General Electric.

The floods in the Midwest had major operational and financial impacts on the railroads. Key mainline yards and other installations were disrupted by high waters. Strenuous efforts by operating and maintenance personnel kept much freight traffic moving over improvised detours and restored washed-out trackage, bridges, and signal systems. Overall costs from the floods in terms of repairs, detours, overtime pay, and lost revenues were estimated at $300 million.

In the rail-passenger sector, low federal funding forced cuts in maintenance and service for the National Railroad Passenger Corporation (Amtrak). But Amtrak gained a 3.3% increase in passengers carried in 1993 over 1992, covering 80% of operating costs from fares and other user revenues—a rise from the 48% that these revenues covered in 1981. New bilevel Superliner passenger cars and 4,000-horsepower AMD-103 Genesis locomotives began arriving from builders, and a German Inter-City Express (ICE) high-speed train set on loan from its owner was tested in revenue service.

Tragedies struck U.S. passenger trains twice. On January 18 seven persons died when two South Shore Line trains collided on a gauntlet at a bridge in Gary, IN. Primary responsibility for the crash was placed on the motorman of the eastbound train for failing to obey a signal at the gauntlet's entrance. On September 22 three locomotives and four cars in Amtrak's eastbound Sunset Limited plunged off a low bridge into a bayou of the Mobile River delta near Mobile, AL, killing 47 persons. The rails apparently were pushed out of alignment shortly before the train's arrival by a barge tow which had strayed from its navigation channel in the dark fog.

Truck. Summer Midwest floods tested trucking as well as railways. Although most interstate-

© Reuters/Bettmann

A German-built Inter-City Express (ICE) train—tested at speeds exceeding 250 mph (402 km/h)—began limited service for Amtrak between Washington and New York in October 1993.

system links remained open, numerous other primary and secondary roads were blocked, along with several key Mississippi River bridges. Additional freight was thrust on truckers by disruptions in rail intermodal service.

Competition remained intense. By June price discounting had offset most of the 4.6% rate increase implemented in January by less-than-truckload (LTL) carriers. In October profit margins were squeezed further by higher diesel-fuel prices due to a 4.3% increase in the federal fuel tax and an Environment Protection Agency-mandated switch to low-sulfur diesel fuel. Closure befell several well-known carriers, including St. Johnsbury Trucking Company, the largest general-freight carrier in the Northeast, and Friedman's Express, the oldest continuously family-operated U.S. trucking company.

Truck-rail intermodal-service agreements continued to grow. Greater use of rail or long-haul movements also was being eyed by LTL carriers as they prepared to negotiate a new contract with the Teamsters' Union. The old contract, set to expire on March 31, 1994, limited substitution of rail for over-the-road movements.

Water. Barge lines on the Mississippi and Missouri rivers suffered severe losses as flooding closed long stretches during the summer.

Controversy raged about collective pricing by ocean carriers within so-called shipping conferences. Sen. Howard Metzenbaum (D-OH) introduced a bill to end the antitrust immunity allowing ocean carriers to set rates and manage capacity collectively via the conference system, contending that the immunity imposed a huge cost burden on U.S. consumers. The future of subsidized U.S.-flag ship operations seemed to hang in the balance. Although the House of Representatives approved a ten-year, $1.2 billion measure to replace the existing program, the Senate withheld action pending procurement of funding sources for the proposed new program.

JOHN C. SPYCHALSKI
The Pennsylvania State University

TRAVEL

U.S. travel in 1993 reflected a sluggish domestic economy and a continuing global recession. Both domestic and international travel by U.S. residents posted modest gains, but leisure travel was up only 5% and the business market remained flat, with corporate spending levels on a par with 1992. The dollar was stronger against several European currencies than it had been in over a year, but high summer airfares and consumer skittishness helped keep visitor arrivals below the record numbers expected by the European Travel Commission. Altogether, U.S. tourists made some 478.3 million trips of at least 100 mi (161 km), according to the U.S. Travel & Tourism Administration—a gain of 2% over 1992. A record 46.5 million foreign visitors flocked to the United States to spend an estimated $77 billion.

Safaris, jungle treks, and river trips were up significantly in 1993, making adventure travel and ecotourism popular packages in leisure travel. In this market, the most popular international destinations were Africa, Costa Rica, India, and Mexico, while Yellowstone National Park and Alaska led domestic venues.

Domestic Travel. Determined U.S. travelers took shorter vacations, ferreted out bargain rates, and used advance purchases for discounted fares. The American Automobile Association reported a 4% increase in motor-vehicle travel during the summer. Amtrak—thanks in part to successful high-speed-equipment trials on short runs and the popularity of the transcontinental Sunset Limited—saw a similar growth in leisure ridership for the first 11 months. The motorcoach tour industry, which depends on senior volume, registered only modest gains because of declining interest rates on savings.

Even with disastrous flooding in the Midwest and downtrends in summer travel to California and Hawaii, U.S. hotels had their best occupancy rates in more than a decade. Publicity surrounding violent crimes against foreign tourists hurt Florida's international tourism, but it still ranked as the top destination for American travelers. National, state, and theme parks also ranked high in visitor numbers. Colorado's escalating tourism had led to the construction of a new airport in Denver—which was nearing completion late in 1993—as the nation's first major new airfield in 20 years.

International Travel. Canada and Mexico remained popular with U.S. vacationers. In 1993 a record number of Americans from the East Coast were drawn to the Canadian Rockies. Also, more than 65 million Americans made excursions south of the border.

While new Buckingham Palace summer tours helped Great Britain's inbound-visitor levels climb 9% over 1992, the bombing of Florence's Uffizi art museum made Americans jittery, leaving Italy with only minor gains. Demand for air transportation in the Asia/Pacific area grew faster than for any other region in the world. Australia's appeal continued steady, while Orient tourism jumped—with Hong Kong and China registering large gains. Travel to Israel soared 12% over record highs in 1992. Conversely, Egypt saw an 18% drop in overnight stays by U.S. visitors during the first half of 1993 due to terrorist attacks on tourist sites, mainly in Cairo. But new Middle East peace accords raised hopes for tourism in the beleaguered region.

Cruising. The most steady performer in the travel market was the cruise-line industry, which chalked up a 5% growth in 1993. Caribbean cruises attracted more than 50% of the 4.4 million passengers, followed by Mediterranean and Alaska sailings. More than 20 new ships were scheduled to come on-line in the next few years, ranging from an upscale 300-passenger liner to a 2,600-passenger megacruiser. The United States and Canada composed 80% of the cruise market. To tap this potential, 159 cruise ships from more than 50 lines are marketed to U.S. passengers. Surveys in the cruising industry still showed passenger ages and income levels declining and interest in exotic locations increasing.

BARBARA J. BRAASCH
Freelance Travel Writer

TUNISIA

Events in Tunisia in 1993 were marked by preparations for general and presidential elections in March 1994 and by continued human-rights controversy.

Politics. President Ben Ali confirmed his position as head of the ruling Constitutional Democratic Rally (RCD) at an extraordinary congress in July. Ben Ali, who had gained power in 1987 when he overthrew lifetime president Habib Bourguiba in a bloodless coup, was reelected

---

TUNISIA • Information Highlights

Official Name: Republic of Tunisia.
Location: North Africa.
Area: 63,170 sq mi (163 610 km²).
Population (mid-1993 est.): 8,600,000.
Chief City (1987 est.): Tunis, the capital, 1,600,000, district population.
Government: *Head of state,* Zine El Abidine Ben Ali, president (took office Nov. 7, 1987). *Head of government,* Hamed Karoui, prime minister (took office Sept. 27, 1989). *Legislature* (unicameral)—National Assembly.
Monetary Unit: Dinar (0.967 dinar equals U.S.$1, April 1993).
Gross Domestic Product (1991 U.S.$): $10,900,000,000.
Economic Index (1992): *Consumer Prices* (1980 = 100), all items, 249.2; food, 255.1.
Foreign Trade (1992 U.S.$): *Imports,* $6,415,000,000; *exports,* $4,042,000,000.

unanimously as RCD president, and his support-ers were elected to the party's key decision-making bodies. The RCD held all the parliament seats, but was preparing to relinquish a handful to the opposition in the March 1994 elections.

As the RCD rallied to face the elections, the largest opposition party, the Movement of Democratic Socialists (MDS), was torn with internal divisions. At a party congress in March, MDS leader Mohammed Moada expelled dissidents who accused him of being too close to authorities. He was elected party president and eliminated the posts of vice-president and secretary-general.

After successfully repressing the banned Islamic fundamentalist Al-Nahda movement in 1992, the government turned to the illegal Communist Workers Party of Tunisia (POCT). In the past the party had been tolerated because it countered the influence of Islamic fundamentalists, especially on the university campuses. Early in 1993, POCT leaders and members were arrested and convicted on charges of belonging to an illegal organization. Despite eliminating the fundamentalists and the Communists, the government faced a series of university strikes against reforms to the higher-education system led by the powerful student union. Shortly after the strikes, the union's leader was jailed on drug charges in what was seen widely as a political trial.

Human Rights. The issue of human rights continued to be prominent during 1993. In April more than 200 Tunisian intellectuals signed a petition calling for an end to one-party rule. They said human rights were being violated in the name of security. Two months later, Amnesty International accused Tunisia of detaining and mistreating hundreds of women as part of its campaign against Islamic fundamentalists and other government opponents. Tunisia reacted with indignation, accusing Amnesty of unquestioningly reproducing tracts by extremist groups.

Foreign Relations. The government's foreign policy was marked by a diplomatic offensive against fundamentalists and other opponents of the regime—whom the authorities accused of being terrorists—living in exile in Europe. The campaign suffered a severe setback in August when Britain granted political asylum to Al-Nahda's exiled leader, Rachid Ghannouchi.

Tunisia had more success with France's newly elected right-wing government. During a June visit to Tunis, France's Interior Minister Charles Pasqua said that his nation would not allow anyone to use the country as a base to oppose the Tunisian government. He also reassured Tunisia that new French immigration controls were not aimed at the 300,000-strong Tunisian immigrant community.

Relations with Algeria improved considerably, with both sides committed to fighting Islamic fundamentalists. The relations were sealed by the February visit of the Algerian head of state, Ali Kafi, during which the countries signed an agreement defining their common border.

Tunisia became one of the few Arab countries to receive an Israeli government delegational Middle East peace talks on refugees in mid-October.

ALFRED HERMIDA
BBC's North Africa Correspondent

TURKEY

Two important changes in Turkey's highest governmental ranks—president and prime minister—dominated Turkish public affairs in 1993. Meanwhile problems with the Kurds and Islamic fundamentalists continued.

Politics. President Turgut Özal died of a heart attack on April 17. His death ended a period of increasing internecine strife that was caused to no small extent by his domineering personality, which also was a major factor in the 1991 electoral defeat of his Motherland Party. Veteran politician Suleyman Demirel was elected to succeed Özal as president. Demirel had held the office of head of government seven times since 1961, leading a succession of moderate conservative political parties. For the 18 months preceding the presidential election, Demirel had served as prime minister, representing the True Path Party (TPP).

In June the TPP chose a new leader, economics professor Tansu Ciller, who became Turkey's first woman prime minister. She had entered politics in 1990 and rose rapidly in the TPP hierarchy and the National Assembly—to which she had been elected in 1991. Her defeat of several other strong, more experienced candidates indicated the desire of Turkey's leaders to give renewed high priority to new approaches to economic problems, most particularly to try once again to reduce the inflation rate, which continued to hover around 60%.

Another important change in political personnel was the resignation of Erdal Inonu as head of the Social Democratic Populist Party—

TURKEY • Information Highlights

Official Name: Republic of Turkey.
Location: Southeastern Europe and southwestern Asia.
Area: 301,382 sq mi (780 580 km²).
Population (mid-1993 est.): 60,700,000.
Chief Cities (1990 census): Ankara, the capital, 2,559,471; Istanbul, 6,620,241; Izmir, 1,757,414.
Government: *Head of state,* Suleyman Demirel, president (took office May 16, 1993). *Head of government,* Tansu Ciller, prime minister (took office July 5, 1993). *Legislature*—Grand National Assembly.
Monetary Unit: Lira (13,136.00 liras equal U.S. $1, Nov. 10, 1993).
Gross Domestic Product (1991 est. U.S.$): $198,000,000,000.
Economic Index (1992): *Consumer Prices* (1987 = 100), all items, 1,283.1; food, 1,459.2.
Foreign Trade (1992 U.S.$): *Imports,* $22,507,000,000; *exports,* $14,883,000,000.

After only three years in politics, Tansu Ciller (right, with microphone) became the first woman to be elected prime minister of Turkey in June 1993. The 47-year-old American-educated economist vowed to reform Turkey's centralized economy and to tackle high inflation and the national debt.

© ABC Ajansi/Gamma-Liaison

the TPP's coalition partner. He was succeeded by Murat Karayalcin, the mayor of Ankara.

Economy. Excluding inflation, the remainder of Turkey's economic record in 1993 was strong. Turkey's 1992 rate of economic growth was the highest of the 24 members of the Organization for Economic Cooperation and Development (OECD), and during the first half of 1993 the economy grew at an annual rate of nearly 10%. Major increases in production of motor vehicles and continued growth of hydroelectric-power production in the southeast were among the cornerstones of growth. The economy also benefited from a rise of about 12% in tourist revenues. But there was no progress in Turkey's efforts to be admitted to the European Community (EC).

Domestic Crises. Turkey continued to be troubled by Islamic fundamentalism and the Kurdish problem. In January, Ugur Mumcu, a prominent journalist, became the latest victim in a series of assassinations of liberals and secularists. Shortly thereafter, Jak Kamhi, leader of the Turkish Jewish community, barely escaped an attempt on his life. And in July, Islamic militants set fire to a hotel in Sivas, where a conference of leftist intellectuals was in progress, killing 40.

The Kurdish problem seemed to grow worse in 1993. Several major battles were fought between the Turkish armed forces and Kurdish separatists, with heavy casualties on both sides. In May more than 30 soldiers were killed in a serious clash near Bingöl that ended a cease-fire that the rebels had declared. While the cease-fire had not been accepted formally by the Turkish government, it had issued an amnesty decree for members of the Kurdish Workers' Party (PKK) who had not been involved in military actions, but this program also was suspended after the battle. There also was continued controversy about the abilities of the rebels to flee across the Iraqi and Iranian borders, while the Turkish army refrained from pursuing them there.

Incidents outside southeastern Turkey also were attributed to Kurdish separatists, including injury to tourists in a shoot-out in the Mediterranean city of Antalya. Bitter reaction from the Turkish government and public was stirred in June when several Turkish workers were murdered by Kurdish nationalists in Germany as part of a campaign against foreigners there. One government estimate reported that some 7,400 persons had died in nine years of fighting. Political measures designed to reduce support for the rebels among the Kurdish public included continued investment for economic development in southeast Turkey and the symbolic convening of a session of the National Assembly in the southeastern province of Hakkari.

To improve a dubious world image, Turkey adopted a major judicial reform that included a broad widening of the rights of accused persons and guarantees of other aspects of due process of law. Turkey continued to be troubled, however, by reports that it mistreated political prisoners.

Foreign Affairs. Turkey continued to show interest in the Turkic republics of the former Soviet Union. Investment by Turkish entrepreneurs in the Central Asian republics approached $6.5 billion during the first half of 1993 and the government continued to extend credits and expand cultural relations. In March agreement was reached on a plan to build an oil pipeline from the city of Baku, in the Russian republic of Azerbaijan, through Iran, to the Turkish port of Ceyhan, to replace the pipeline through Iraq that had been closed since the Persian Gulf war.

Turkey continued to watch other Balkan trouble spots carefully, but acted with increasing caution to avoid becoming involved directly in any of these disputes. Turkey frequently expressed outrage at the attacks by Serbs and Croatians against Bosnian Muslims, but joined other European nations in refraining from direct action beyond air-dropping food and medicine to Bosnian Muslims. Turkey also issued warnings to Armenian forces at war with Muslim Azerbaijan, but refrained from giving the latter aid.

WALTER F. WEIKER, *Rutgers University*

UGANDA

In 1993, President Yoweri Museveni continued to pursue a rigorous program of liberal economic reform, while proposing political reforms that continued to ban activities by political parties.

Political Affairs. On Dec. 31, 1992, the Constitutional Commission presented a draft constitution to Museveni that called for direct presidential elections, scheduled for 1994. In order to avoid the divisions of the past, the draft continued the suspension of party politics for another seven years. The newly created Constituent Assembly was to draw up the final draft constitution, which then would be presented to the National Resistance Council for ratification.

Museveni, in office since 1986, remained very popular but had yet to create a power base independent of the military, large segments of which had been demobilized. Large-scale layoffs also were planned for the civil service. Thus, the reinstatement of political parties could draw significant support away from the president. Moreover, the extent to which Museveni's popularity would pass to his lieutenants was questionable.

Existing political structures included the Resistance Committees operating at the local and regional levels. In recent elections, several advocates of multiparty elections were defeated, but not all those elected were staunch supporters of the president.

In an attempt to create alternative political institutions, Museveni began to reestablish traditional kingdoms. In July, Ronald Mutebi, the son of the former *kabaka* (king) of Buganda, Edward Mutesa, succeeded his father to the throne. The new *kabaka* is the cultural head of the Baganda people, though he has no official political role.

Economic Affairs. The government continued to broaden its tax base during the year in an effort to reduce an anticipated 60-billion-shilling ($50 million) deficit. Access to foreign exchange was liberalized, and the Uganda shilling was made fully convertible. In an effort to increase production, the government also proposed the privatization of cotton marketing. Economic

indicators for 1992 were impressive: Inflation declined from 66% to -1.3%, and the gross domestic product (GDP) grew by 7% in 1992.

Uganda's $2.6 billion debt continued to be a major drain. In February, Uganda concluded an agreement with the International Development Association of the World Bank through which it "bought back" $153 million, or nearly 75% of its commercial debt, at the rate of 12 cents per dollar. The agreement removed much of Uganda's debt to its suppliers and was expected to facilitate the country's access to imports.

In separate moves, Germany canceled about $2 million of Uganda's $16 million debt to the former East Germany and rescheduled the rest, while Shell Oil exchanged $10 million in debt for 50% equity in Shell (Uganda), which had been nationalized by Idi Amin in 1970.

International trade was vital to Uganda's continued growth. In April, Uganda and Tanzania signed a communiqué in which they agreed to expand and upgrade rail and sea links between their two countries. At the regional level, Museveni was serving as the chair of the Preferential Trade Area of East, Central, and Southern Africa, to which Egypt and South Africa currently were applying for membership.

WILLIAM CYRUS REED
The American University in Cairo

USSR. *See* BALTIC REPUBLICS; GEORGIA, REPUBLIC OF; RUSSIA AND THE COMMONWEALTH OF INDEPENDENT STATES.

UNITED NATIONS

The Security Council expanded United Nations (UN) peacekeeping missions to a record 18 early in 1993, increasing the number of blue-helmeted soldiers deployed to about 75,000 on four continents. However, confronted with the world organization's huge financial problems and embarrassing setbacks to its most prominent operations, the Council later in the year became reluctant to approve new missions.

The Somalia Debacle. In November the UN Operation in Somalia II (UNOSOM II) reported the end of the famine that in 1992 had brought U.S. troops to that war-scarred nation on a humanitarian rescue mission, but this was a rare piece of good news from a once-ambitious operation nearing collapse. UNOSOM II's 30,000 peacekeepers from 32 nations took over from the United States on May 4, with orders from UN Secretary-General Boutros Boutros-Ghali to prepare Somalia for civil rule by disarming its warlords, of which the most powerful was Gen. Mohammed Farah Aidid. However, Aidid refused to cooperate, and in battles in the summer and fall, his fierce and well-disciplined forces inflicted heavy losses on the UN army. Thousands of Somalis were killed in the fighting.

UGANDA • Information Highlights
Official Name: Republic of Uganda.
Location: Interior of East Africa.
Area: 91,135 sq mi (236 040 km²).
Population: (mid-1993 est.): 18,100,000.
Chief Cities (1991 census): Kampala, the capital, 773,463; Jinja, 60,979.
Government: *Head of state*, Yoweri Museveni, president (took office Jan. 29, 1986). *Head of government*, George Cosmas Adyebo, prime minister (took office Jan. 22, 1991). *Legislature* (unicameral)—National Resistance Council.
Monetary Unit: Uganda shilling (1,191.5 shillings equal U.S. $1, Aug. 1993).
Foreign Trade (1992 U.S.$): *Imports*, $516,000,000; *exports*, $143,000,000.

© Martin Simon/Saba

UN Secretary-General Boutros Boutros-Ghali focused much attention on Somalia in 1993 as he sought to disarm that nation's warlords. He also visited North and South Korea at year's end.

The Council, with strong U.S. support, ordered a manhunt for Aidid after his forces killed 24 Pakistani peacekeepers in an ambush on June 5. But public outrage in the United States forced President Bill Clinton to abandon his support of the UN's strategy after Aidid forces killed 18 U.S. soldiers in one battle.

Clinton drastically reduced U.S. troops' role in Somalia and set a March 31, 1994, deadline for a U.S. withdrawal. Most Western nations and many developing nations in the operation said they also would pull out, which forced the UN to abandon its hunt for Aidid and to seek a political solution to Somalia's problems. At year's end, Aidid was refusing to participate in UN-mediated negotiations among the warlords.

Haiti. UN efforts to restore Haiti's exiled president, Rev. Jean-Bertrand Aristide, to power stalled after that nation's military leaders refused to step down in October, violating the UN-brokered agreement they had signed in July on Governor's Island in New York. Under that accord, Lt. Gen. Raoul Cedras—who led the September 1991 coup that ousted Aristide—was to have resigned, clearing the way for the reinstatement of the president by October 30.

The pact also provided for a force of 1,300 UN peacekeepers to retrain Haiti's military and police. But on October 11 a small group of armed protesters, plainly supported by the military, prevented a U.S. ship carrying 194 U.S. and 25 Canadian soldiers—the first contingent of UN peacekeepers—from docking in Port-au-Prince. On October 19 the Security Council reimposed the oil and arms embargo on Haiti that it had established originally in June and suspended in August following the Governor's Island pact.

The Former Yugoslavia. The UN and the European Community's diplomatic efforts to end the carnage in the former Yugoslav republic of Bosnia-Herzegovina were futile in 1993. The leaders of Bosnia's warring Serbs, Muslims,

and Croats signed a November agreement to stop, by force if necessary, attacks on UN relief convoys by "uncontrolled elements" in their armies; but the attacks, mainly by Bosnian Serbs, continued. The UN mediator for Yugoslavia, Thorvald Stoltenberg, a Norwegian who earlier in the year replaced former U.S. Secretary of State Cyrus Vance, vowed that UN soldiers would use force to get supplies to the millions of Bosnians facing starvation and exposure over the winter.

In June the United States along with Muslim countries tried without success to convince the Council to lift partially the ban on arms sales to the former Yugoslavia, to allow sales to Bosnian Muslims.

As of December the UN Protection Force in Yugoslavia (UNPROFOR) had about 26,000 peacekeepers from 36 countries. Some 13,000 were in Croatia as a shaky buffer between Croatian and Serbian forces; some 12,000 were in Bosnia; and another 1,000 were in Macedonia.

On November 17 the UN Yugoslavia war-crimes tribunal held its first session in The Hague, Netherlands. The Security Council set up the tribunal of 11 judges—the first such body since the Nuremberg and Tokyo trials judged World War II criminals—to try people accused of rape, torture, ethnic cleansing, and other human-rights violations.

Qualified Success in Cambodia. The UN declared its Cambodia operation complete after UN-supervised parliamentary elections in May brought in nearly 90% of eligible voters, despite Khmer Rouge threats to attack polling stations, a Khmer Rouge boycott, and violent attacks by the Communist regime in Phnom Penh against its principal opponent, the Royalist Party. However, the victorious Royalists were forced to share power with the Communists, who had threatened to destroy the country rather than step down. The UN Transitional Authority in Cambodia (UNTAC) withdrew most of its 22,000 peacekeepers from Cambodia by November 15, despite continued violence.

New Caution on Peacekeeping. U.S. President Bill Clinton, addressing the General Assembly in September, asserted that "the UN simply cannot become engaged in every one of the world's conflicts. If the American people are to say yes to peacekeeping, the UN must know when to say no." In November the Council, under U.S. pressure, said no to a peacekeeping mission for Burundi, where a military coup on October 21 was followed by tribal battles that sparked an exodus of more than 800,000 refugees.

In October the Council did approve a peacekeeping force of 2,500 soldiers and 331 military observers for Rwanda, to supervise a cease-fire signed in August by the Rwandan army and rebel forces and to help to prepare for new elections. However, it set strict deadlines for completion of the force's assignments and for pulling out eventually.

ORGANIZATION OF THE UNITED NATIONS

THE SECRETARIAT *Secretary-General:* Boutros Boutros-Ghali (until Dec. 31, 1996)

THE GENERAL ASSEMBLY (1993) *President:* Samuel Insanally, Guyana

The 184 member nations were as follows:

Afghanistan	Cape Verde	Germany	Lebanon	Norway	Spain
Albania	Central African	Ghana	Lesotho	Oman	Sri Lanka
Algeria	Republic	Greece	Liberia	Pakistan	Sudan
Andorra	Chad	Grenada	Libya	Panama	Suriname
Angola	Chile	Guatemala	Liechtenstein	Papua New Guinea	Swaziland
Antigua and	China, People's	Guinea	Lithuania	Paraguay	Sweden
Barbuda	Republic of	Guinea-Bissau	Luxembourg	Peru	Syria
Argentina	Colombia	Guyana	Macedonia	Philippines	Tajikistan
Armenia	Comoros	Haiti	Madagascar	Poland	Tanzania
Australia	Congo	Honduras	Malawi	Portugal	Thailand
Austria	Costa Rica	Hungary	Malaysia	Qatar	Togo
Azerbaijan	Croatia	Iceland	Maldives	Romania	Trinidad and
Bahamas	Cuba	India	Mali	Russia	Tobago
Bahrain	Cyprus	Indonesia	Malta	Rwanda	Tunisia
Bangladesh	Czech Republic	Iran	Marshall Islands	Saint Kitts and Nevis	Turkey
Barbados	Denmark	Iraq	Mauritania	Saint Lucia	Turkmenistan
Belarus	Djibouti	Ireland	Mauritius	Saint Vincent and	Uganda
Belgium	Dominica	Israel	Mexico	The Grenadines	Ukraine
Belize	Dominican Republic	Italy	Micronesia	Samoa	United Arab
Benin	Ecuador	Ivory Coast	Moldova	San Marino	Emirates
Bhutan	Egypt	Jamaica	Monaco	São Tomé and	United Kingdom
Bolivia	El Salvador	Japan	Mongolia	Príncipe	United States
Bosnia-Herzegovina	Equatorial Guinea	Jordan	Morocco	Saudi Arabia	Uruguay
Botswana	Eritrea	Kazakhstan	Mozambique	Senegal	Uzbekistan
Brazil	Estonia	Kenya	Myanmar	Seychelles	Vanuatu
Brunei Darussalam	Ethiopia	Korea, Democratic	Namibia	Sierra Leone	Venezuela
Bulgaria	Fiji	People's Republic of	Nepal	Singapore	Vietnam
Burkina Faso	Finland	Korea, Republic of	Netherlands	Slovak Republic	Yemen
Burundi	France	Kuwait	New Zealand	Slovenia	Yugoslavia
Cambodia	Gabon	Kyrgyz Republic	Nicaragua	Solomon Islands	Zaire
Cameroon	Gambia	Laos	Niger	Somalia	Zambia
Canada	Georgia	Latvia	Nigeria	South Africa	Zimbabwe

COMMITTEES

General. Composed of 28 members as follows: The General Assembly president; the 21 General Assembly vice-presidents (heads of delegations or their deputies of Bangladesh, Burkina Faso, Canada, China, Egypt, France, Grenada, Guatemala, India, Iran, Liberia, Liechtenstein, Pakistan, Poland, Republic of Korea, Russian Federation, Tanzania, United Kingdom, United States, Zaire, and Zambia); and the chairmen of the main committees below, which are composed of all 184 member countries.

First (Disarmament and International Security): Adolf Ritter von Wagner (Germany)
Second (Economic and Financial): René Valéry Mongbé (Benin)
Third Committee (Social, Humanitarian and Cultural): Eduard Kukan (Slovakia)
Fourth Committee (Special Political and Decolonization): Stanley Kalpagé (Sri Lanka)
Fifth Committee (Administrative and Budgetary): Rabah Hadid (Algeria)
Sixth Committee (Legal): María del Luján Flores (Uruguay)

THE ECONOMIC AND SOCIAL COUNCIL

President: Robert Mroziewicz (Poland)
Membership ends on December 31 of the year noted.

Angola (1994)	France (1996)	Pakistan (1996)
Australia (1994)	Gabon (1995)	Paraguay (1996)
Bahamas (1995)	Germany (1996)	Philippines (1994)
Bangladesh (1994)	Ghana (1996)	Poland (1994)
Belarus (1994)	Greece (1996)	Portugal (1996)
Belgium (1994)	India (1994)	Romania (1995)
Benin (1994)	Indonesia (1996)	Russia (1995)
Bhutan (1995)	Ireland (1996)	Senegal (1996)
Brazil (1994)	Italy (1994)	Sri Lanka (1995)
Bulgaria (1996)	Japan (1996)	Suriname (1994)
Canada (1995)	Korea, Republic of	Swaziland (1994)
Chile (1996)	(1995)	Tanzania (1996)
China (1995)	Kuwait (1994)	Ukraine (1994)
Colombia (1994)	Libyan Arab	United Kingdom
Costa Rica (1996)	Jamahiriya (1995)	(1995)
Cuba (1995)	Madagascar (1994)	United States (1994)
Denmark (1995)	Mexico (1995)	Venezuela (1996)
Egypt (1996)	Nigeria (1995)	Zaire (1995)
Ethiopia (1994)	Norway (1995)	Zimbabwe (1996)

THE SECURITY COUNCIL

Membership ends on December 31 of the year noted; asterisks indicate permanent membership.

Argentina (1995)	France*	Russia*
Brazil (1994)	New Zealand (1995)	Rwanda (1995)
China*	Nigeria (1995)	Spain (1994)
Czech Republic (1995)	Oman (1995)	United Kingdom*
Djibouti (1994)	Pakistan (1994)	United States*

THE TRUSTEESHIP COUNCIL

President: (to be elected in 1994)

China[2]   France[2]   Russia[2]   United Kingdom[2]   United States[1]
[1]Administers Trust Territory. [2]Permanent member of Security Council not administering Trust Territory.

THE INTERNATIONAL COURT OF JUSTICE

Membership as of February 6, 1994.

President: Sir Robert Y. Jennings (United Kingdom, 2000)
Vice-President: Shigeru Oda (Japan, 2003)

Roberto Ago (Italy, 1997)	Raymond Ranjeva (Madagascar, 2000)
Andrés Aguilar Mawdsley (Venezuela, 2000)	Stephen Schwebel (United States, 1997)
Mohammed Bedjaoui (Algeria, 1997)	Mohamed Shahabuddeen (Guyana, 1997)
Carl-August Fleischhauer (Germany, 2003)	Nikolai Konstantinovich Tarassov (Russia, 1997)
Gilbert Guillaume (France, 2000)	Christopher G. Weeramantry (Sri Lanka, 2000)
Géza Herczegh (Hungary, 2003)	Ni Zhengyu (China, 2003)
Abdul G. Koroma (Sierra Leone, 2003)	

INTERGOVERNMENTAL AGENCIES

Food and Agricultural Organization (FAO); General Agreement on Tariffs and Trade (GATT); International Atomic Energy Agency (IAEA); International Bank for Reconstruction and Development (World Bank); International Civil Aviation Organization (ICAO); International Fund for Agricultural Development (IFAD); International Labor Organization (ILO); International Maritime Organization (IMO); International Monetary Fund (IMF); International Telecommunication Union (ITU); United Nations Educational, Scientific and Cultural Organization (UNESCO); United Nations Industrial Development Organization (UNIDO); Universal Postal Union (UPU); World Health Organization (WHO); World Intellectual Property Organization (WIPO); World Meteorological Organization (WMO).

In September the Council imposed an arms and oil embargo on the National Union for the Total Independence of Angola, the rebel force known as UNITA, which restarted Angola's 18-year civil war after losing to the government in UN-sponsored elections in September 1992. The UN estimated that the war was killing 1,000 persons per day. The UN Angola Verification Mission (UNAVEM II) had only about 75 members at year's end, but the Council was considering expanding the mission pending the signing of a cease-fire agreement at UN-sponsored talks in Lusaka, Zambia.

Other Council Resolutions. On November 11 the Council voted 11-0—with China, Djibouti, Morocco, and Pakistan abstaining—to expand sanctions on Libya, because that country continued to refuse to hand over two suspects in the bombings of Pan American Flight 103 in 1988 and a French UTA flight in 1989, which killed a total of 441 persons.

The resolution froze Libya's assets overseas and banned some sales of its oil equipment. It required members to close all offices of Libya's national airline and to cut the size of Libyan diplomatic missions. Because the Council's European members rely on Libya for fuel imports, the new sanctions let Libya continue oil and gas production. In 1993 the Council banned commercial air links with Libya, as well as sales of arms, aircraft, and spare parts.

On November 18 the Council, asserting that Iraq still had failed to comply with the Persian Gulf war cease-fire resolutions, declined to ease or remove sanctions that it had imposed shortly after Iraq's August 1990 invasion of Kuwait. The Council reviews Iraq's compliance with the resolutions every 60 days.

General Assembly. The General Assembly began its 48th session in September, electing Guyana's Samuel R. Insanally as president. He replaced Stoyvan Ganev, a former Bulgarian foreign minister. In December the Assembly voted to establish a UN High Commissioner for Human Rights, settling an issue hotly argued since the post first was proposed by Uruguay in 1952. Under a compromise worked out between proponents of the post—mostly Western nations—and its opponents—mostly from the developing world—the commissioner would have no power to force governments to end human-rights abuses, but could publicize results of his or her investigations into alleged abuses and report them to the 53-nation Humans Rights Commission in Geneva.

During 1993 the Assembly admitted Andorra, the Czech Republic, Eritrea, the Former Yugoslav Republic of Macedonia, Monaco, and Slovakia, for a total of 184 members.

In October the Assembly elected Argentina, the Czech Republic, Oman, Rwanda, and Nigeria as nonpermanent members of the Council, for two-year terms beginning Jan. 1, 1994, to replace outgoing Japan, Cape Verde, Morocco, Hungary, and Venezuela.

In October and November the Assembly lifted the remaining economic sanctions, including an oil embargo, that it had imposed on South Africa in 1962 to force that nation to end apartheid. A Council-imposed arms embargo was not removed. In 1991 the Assembly had ended prohibitions against academic, scientific, cultural, and sports contacts with South Africa, which has been barred from taking its UN seat since 1974.

UNHCR. The UN High Commissioner for Refugees (UNHCR), Sadako Ogata, reported on November 9 that since the Cold War's end, ethnic conflicts had expanded the world's refugee population to about 44 million, a figure that included some 24 million displaced within their own countries.

Secretary-General. In 1993, the second year of his five-year term, Boutros-Ghali made good on his preelection promise that, because he did not intend to seek a second term, he would be able to be candid and to take unpopular but necessary actions. In one such instance he publicly clashed with the United States over its efforts to scale back the UN's Somalia mission, arguing that political negotiations could not precede disarmament. During his November tour of Africa, Boutros-Ghali traveled to Somalia, where he was extremely unpopular, to visit UN installations, despite U.S. protests that it could not guarantee his safety.

In December, as part of a tour of Asia, Boutros-Ghali traveled to the Korean peninsula to discuss tensions that had arisen over North Korea's suspected development of nuclear weapons, an issue that had led the Council to consider, but not yet impose, economic sanctions. The secretary-general made his trip despite U.S. worries that he would interfere with its efforts to convince Pyongyang to allow nuclear inspections by the International Atomic Energy Commission. Boutros-Ghali, noting that the UN Charter gave him the authority to go where he pleased, said his visit was intended only as a fact-finding and goodwill mission. The North Koreans reportedly told Boutros-Ghali—the first secretary-general to travel from South to North Korea through the demilitarized zone and the first to visit the North since Kurt Waldheim in 1979—that they did not want UN help in the nuclear dispute.

Finance. Boutros-Ghali was hamstrung by the UN's severe financial crisis. As of December, UN members were in arrears more than $1.6 billion on regular and peacekeeping dues, against an assembly-adopted budget of just less than $2.6 billion for the 1994-95 biennium. In particular, the secretary-general criticized the United States—$475 million in arrears—for asking the organization to do more and more while consistently being its biggest deadbeat.

RICK MITCHELL
"UN Observer & International Report"

© Greg Gibson/AP/Wide World

On the Mall in Washington, DC, on Veterans Day 1993, a bronze sculpture in recognition of the women who served in the Vietnam war was dedicated officially. The sculpture depicts three women helping a wounded GI and is intended to be a symbol of healing.

UNITED STATES

In Bill Clinton's first year in the White House he demonstrated the imagination and energy that helped him win the election. But for all his personal strengths, he often had a difficult time contending with the inherent difficulties that go with the job of being president of the United States.

Domestic Affairs

As the first Democrat to sit in the Oval Office in 12 years, Clinton engendered high hopes among his supporters because of his party's tradition of government activism. In his inaugural address on January 20, he tried to temper these expectations. He warned against "the bad habit" of depending too much on government and urged Americans to "take more responsibility not only for ourselves and our families but for our communities and our country." Still, he evoked the memory of Franklin Roosevelt, who 60 years earlier had established a new and more vigorous model for the presidency, by calling for "bold persistent experimentation" to help government solve the nation's problems.

The first problem Clinton attacked was the ailing economy, which had made possible his election and which he had pledged to revive. On February 17, in a televised address to a joint session of Congress, he proposed a combination of spending cuts and tax increases totaling nearly $500 billion that he claimed would fund a range of long- and short-term efforts to spark the economy and still cut the federal deficit by $325 billion over four years. It was the most extensive attempt to overhaul the economy since the massive cuts in taxes and domestic spending implemented by President Ronald Reagan when he took office in 1981.

But Clinton's plan came under heavy attack from Republicans and conservative Democrats, who complained that it depended too much on tax increases and not enough on spending cuts. Clinton suffered a setback on April 21 when his economic-stimulus package died in the Senate because Democrats were unable to break a filibuster against the $15.4 billion proposal mounted by Republicans. The president suffered still another defeat on June 16, when the Senate Finance Committee dropped the broad-based energy tax he had proposed as a key part of his plan and substituted a narrower tax on gasoline and other fuels. As the fierce debate continued, Clinton had to make still more compromises before his budget plan finally cleared Congress in August. The margin of victory was the narrowest possible—a 218-to-216 vote in the House and a 51-to-50 tally in the Senate, where Vice-President Al Gore cast a tiebreaking vote. Not a single Republican voted for the measure in either house. In addition to the gasoline-tax hike, taxes were increased on the wealthy, including upper-income social-security benefi-

ciaries; Medicaid spending was curbed; and small businesses and the working poor were given tax credits.

No sooner was his budget approved than Clinton set out to gain congressional approval of the North American Free Trade Agreement (NAFTA). On this issue, Clinton could count on strong support from Republicans. But he had to face serious opposition from many Democrats, including House Majority Leader Richard Gephardt, and from organized labor, the party's most influential interest group, which charged that adoption of the pact would cost hundreds of thousands of jobs. Critics also contended that the pact would undercut U.S. environmental regulations because of lower standards on air and water pollution in Mexico. To offset the opposition, Clinton arranged for former Presidents Gerald Ford, George Bush, and Jimmy Carter to join him at the White House on September 14 in a bipartisan show of support for the agreement. A forceful performance by Vice-President Gore in a television debate with outspoken NAFTA foe Ross Perot, along with intensive White House lobbying, helped NAFTA gain House approval by a 234-to-200 vote on November 17. The Senate followed suit on November 20 with a 61-to-38 vote.

In the midst of these struggles over economic issues, Clinton pushed ahead with plans to keep another campaign promise to reform the nation's health-care system. His plan, unveiled in a speech to Congress on September 22, would guarantee every American health-insurance coverage, arranged in most cases through large groups of purchasers called "health alliances" to be established in each state. The government would not take over the health-insurance industry, but instead would rely on so-called "managed competition" between groups of private doctors and hospitals to help keep costs down. The president's most controversial idea was requiring all employers to provide coverage for their workers, something that many small companies said they could not afford to do. To win approval in 1994, the plan also would have to overcome opposition from insurance companies, health-care providers, and Republicans, some of whom likened the Clinton proposal to socialism. (*See also* FEATURE ARTICLE, page 36.)

Yet another campaign promise that caused problems for Clinton was his pledge to allow gays to serve in the armed forces. In the face of stiff opposition from some top military commanders, Clinton on July 19 announced a compromise policy, subsequently approved by Congress, termed "don't ask, don't tell." Homosexuals could serve in the military if they did not engage in homosexual acts; commanders were forbidden to investigate individuals for homosexual behavior merely on the basis of suspicion or rumor.

To help live up to his campaign self-description as "a different kind of Democrat," Clinton on September 7 announced a series of proposals developed by Vice-President Gore for "reinventing government." He claimed these would save more than $100 billion over five years, mostly by cutting the federal workforce.

The president's first year was marred by hard luck with some of his appointments. At the Justice Department, in addition to the difficulties he experienced before settling on Janet Reno (*see* BIOGRAPHY) as his attorney general, he was forced to withdraw his first choice as head of the Civil Rights Division, University of Pennsylvania law professor Lani Guinier, amid complaints that her views were too militant and charges that she was a "quota queen." The post remained vacant at year's end. Clinton's defense secretary, former

With the new administration's economic-stimulus package being considered by Congress, President Bill Clinton and Vice-President Al Gore held a bipartisan meeting with congressional leaders at the White House on April 1, 1993.

© Reuters/Bettmann

Although President Clinton was successful in his efforts to get Congress to enact the family-leave bill, the Brady gun-control bill, and his budget as well as to approve the North American Free Trade Agreement (NAFTA) in 1993, final action on health-care reform—a presidential priority—awaited another congressional session.

John Branch/ © 1993 "San Antonio Express-News"

Congressman Les Aspin, resigned December 15 after the president reportedly lost confidence in him. Aspin had drawn criticism due to his role in the controversy over gays in the military and his decision not to reinforce U.S. troops in Somalia. Clinton chose retired Adm. Bobby Ray Inman—former deputy director of the Central Intelligence Agency (CIA)—to replace him, but Inman withdrew from consideration early in 1994. Aspin agreed to remain until a successor was named.

Congress. With the same political party controlling both the White House and Capitol Hill for the first time since 1980, the first session of the 103d Congress marked an end to the gridlock that had been one of the chief complaints against the federal government in recent years. In addition to enacting Clinton's economic plan and approving NAFTA, major accomplishments included:

• *Gun Control.* In the closing hours of the session, the Senate gave its approval to the so-called Brady Bill, named after Reagan's White House press secretary James Brady, who was wounded and permanently disabled in the 1981 assassination attempt on the president. The first major gun-control law since 1981, it established a five-day waiting period for handgun purchases. The waiting period would be phased out within five years and replaced with a computerized system that would provide an immediate check of criminal records to prevent sales to convicted felons.

• *National Service.* Redeeming a Clinton campaign promise and breathing new life into the tradition of volunteerism, the new law establishing national youth service gives young people a chance to earn up to $4,725 per year to help pay the cost of college by performing community service. Also, local service programs can pay recruits up to $7,400 per year, with the federal government picking up 85% of the cost. Maximum federal outlays were set at $300 million in 1994 and would rise to $700 million by 1996. Organizers hoped to enroll 20,000 by fall 1994. (*See* SIDEBAR, page 211.)

• *Family Leave.* One of the earliest achievements of the new Congress, the family-leave bill gives a worker the right to take 12 weeks of unpaid leave per year because of the birth or adoption of a child, to care for an ailing family member, or to recover from a serious illness. Companies employing fewer than 50 people are exempt. This was the same bill as the one enacted in 1992 but vetoed by President Bush.

• *Voter Registration.* Beginning in 1995 states must provide all eligible citizens the chance to register to vote when they apply for or renew a driver's license. The bill requires states to permit registration by mail and to make registration forms available at agencies that distribute welfare checks. Enactment of the so-called "motor-voter" bill climaxed a five-year struggle, mostly by Democrats against Republican opposition. Bush vetoed a similar measure in 1992.

In addition, lawmakers got much of the work done on a number of other proposals, which stood a good chance of enactment in 1994. Among the legislation approved in different forms by both the House and Senate that would go to joint conference committees to be reconciled were measures to reform federal campaign-finance regulations, to make it a crime to obstruct access to abortion clinics, and to increase federal aid to local police in the fight against crime.

For all its accomplishments, however, the overall record of the Congress was clouded by a variety of allegations of misconduct. Probably the most-heralded case was the Senate Ethics Committee's investigation of allegations of sexual misconduct against Republican Sen. Bob Packwood of Oregon. The investigation stalled late in the year when Packwood balked at turning over his diaries to the committee, which then sought a federal court order to obtain the documents. Earlier in the year the committee abandoned a similar investigation of Democratic Sen. Daniel K. Inouye of Hawaii because none of the supposed victims would cooperate.

553

Newly elected Republican Sen. Kay Bailey Hutchison of Texas was indicted by a Texas grand jury on charges of using state personnel and other resources for political and personal gain while she was state treasurer. Although the charge then was dropped on a technicality, she was reindicted promptly. The second indictment later was declared to be too vague. Also dropped was an indictment against Republican Sen. David Durenberger of Minnesota for charging the Senate for paying rent in a building he secretly owned.

At any rate, Durenberger, who in 1992 had been censured by the Senate as a result of this episode, announced he would not seek reelection in 1994. Similarly, retirements were announced by Democratic Senators Dennis DeConcini of Arizona and Don Riegel of Michigan, both of whom had been rebuked in 1991 by the Senate Ethics Committee for intervening with federal regulators on behalf of savings and loan executive Charles H. Keating, Jr. Keating later was convicted of fraud and racketeering.

Politics. After losing the White House for the first time in 12 years, Republicans staged an impressive comeback, taking away from the Democrats two Senate seats, two governorships, and the mayoralties of the nation's two largest cities. Republicans gave much of the credit for their success to Clinton, who they claimed had alienated many of the voters who had supported him in November of 1992 by tilting toward his party's traditional liberalism. After a brief honeymoon, Clinton's standing in public-opinion polls slumped and he had trouble getting an approval rating above 50% until late December, when 58% of those interviewed in a *Washington Post-ABC News* survey approved of his performance.

The Republican string of successes actually started in 1992, right after the election, when GOP challenger Paul Coverdell defeated incumbent Democrat Sen. Wyche Fowler in Georgia. Then on June 5, 1993, Texas Republican Kay

Bailey Hutchison overwhelmed Democrat Sen. Bob Kreuger, who had been appointed to fill the vacancy left by Lloyd Bentsen, whom Clinton named treasury secretary. Hutchison had made Clinton's economic program, particularly his tax policies, a major issue in the campaign.

On June 8, Republican Richard Riordan, a wealthy businessman, became the first Republican elected mayor of Los Angeles since 1961 when he defeated Democratic City Councilman Michael Woo. Riordan, who replaced the city's longtime Democratic chief executive Tom Bradley, made opposition to crime a major issue in a city still shaken by the bloody 1992 riots. Clinton went to the city to campaign for Woo.

On November 2 the Republicans enjoyed a red-letter day. In New Jersey, Republican Christine Todd Whitman became the state's first woman governor, ousting Democrat James Florio. Florio had been hurt at the start of his tenure by pushing through a big increase in sales and income taxes after having pledged as a candidate not to raise taxes. President Clinton and First Lady Hillary Rodham Clinton campaigned for him, and Clinton's top political strategist, James Carville, managed his campaign.

In Virginia former Republican Congressman George F. Allen, son of the late professional football coach, defeated Democratic candidate Attorney General Mary Sue Terry, who once had been favored heavily. Terry, who would have been the state's fourth consecutive Democratic governor since 1981, apparently was hurt by voter weariness with Democratic Party rule and particularly with outgoing Democratic Gov. L. Douglas Wilder and with incumbent Democratic Sen. Charles Robb.

In New York City, Republican Rudolph W. Giuliani, a former U.S. attorney, defeated Mayor David Dinkins in a campaign whose outcome reversed the result of the 1989 election, when the two men first ran against each other. Dinkins, the city's first black mayor, was hurt by charges that he sided with blacks in racially tinged rioting violence in the city. Exit polls showed that whites, who made up 55% of the city's population, provided 85% of Giuliani's support.

Blacks did better in other mayoralty contests. Democratic City Council President Sharon Sayles became the first woman and the first black to be elected mayor of Minneapolis. And Seattle Mayor Norm Rice and Cleveland Mayor Michael White—both black Democrats—were reelected to second terms.

In California voters rejected a ballot proposal that would have given elementary- and secondary-school students $2,600 in state-funded school vouchers each year. In Maine voters approved a measure prohibiting state officials from serving more than four two-year terms, and in New York City voters adopted a limit of two four-year terms on top city officials.

Crime. Eruptions of crime and violence jarred the nation in 1993, spurring demands for

---

UNITED STATES • Information Highlights

Official Name: United States of America.

Location: Central North America.

Area: 3,618,768 sq mi (9 372 610 km²).

Population (Jan. 1, 1993 est.): 256,600,000.

Chief Cities (1990 census): Washington, DC, the capital, 606,900; New York, 7,322,564; Los Angeles, 3,485,398; Chicago, 2,783,726; Houston, 1,630,553; Philadelphia, 1,585,577; San Diego, 1,110,549.

Government: *Head of state and government*, Bill Clinton, president (took office Jan. 20, 1993). *Legislature—* Congress: Senate and House of Representatives.

Monetary Unit: Dollar.

Gross Domestic Product (1993, third quarter est.): $6,396,300,000,000.

Economic Indexes (September 1993): *Consumer Prices* (1982 = 100), all items, 124.5; food, 126.4. *Industrial Production* (1987 = 100), 111.0.

Foreign Trade (1992): *Imports*, $532,665,000,000; *exports*, $448,164,000,000.

tougher law-enforcement measures. The most spectacular incident was a bomb blast in a garage below New York City's World Trade Center on February 26 that killed six persons and forced the evacuation of 50,000 others. An investigation by the Federal Bureau of Investigation (FBI) and New York police led to federal indictments against six men linked to a Muslim extremist group. In a related case, in June the FBI arrested eight more men, also described as Muslim extremists, on charges of plotting terrorist bombings at other sites in New York, including UN headquarters and the Lincoln and Holland tunnels. Then on August 25 a federal grand jury indicted Sheikh Omar Abd al-Rahman, who was accused of masterminding the Trade Center bombing as well as the foiled bomb plots in New York.

Another dramatic incident was the 51-day siege by federal law-enforcement officials of the Branch Davidian cult compound near Waco, TX. The confrontation ended on April 19 with a fire that took the lives of some 75 cult members, including cult leader David Koresh. Later in the year, a Treasury Department report criticized U.S. Bureau of Alcohol, Tobacco, and Firearms officials for their allegedly improper handling of a February raid that led to the siege. (*See* FEATURE ARTICLE, page 64.)

The judicial system grappled with the aftermath of crime linked to racial tension. On April 17, Los Angeles remained calm after a federal jury convicted two police officers, Laurence M. Powell and Stacey C. Koon, of violating the civil rights of Rodney King, a black motorist whose videotaped beating by police in March 1991 stirred national indignation. Two other officers were acquitted. The acquittal of all four officers on all but one charge filed against them in the King case by the state of California in April 1992 had led to one of the worst riots in the nation's history.

In October a Los Angeles jury acquitted two black men of attempted murder in the videotaped beating of a white truck driver, Reginald Denny, during those riots. The defendants, Damian Wilson and Henry Watson, were found guilty of less serious charges of mayhem and assault. Also in October a Detroit judge imposed prison sentences on two white former police officers, Larry Nevers and Walter Budzyn, who had been convicted of second-degree murder in the fatal beating of a black motorist. Nevers was sentenced to 12 to 25 years, and Budzyn to eight to 18 years.

Racial bitterness also was apparently a factor in a shooting spree on a Long Island (NY) Rail Road train on December 7 in which six passengers were wounded fatally and more than a score were injured. The suspected gunman, Colin Ferguson, a 35-year-old Jamaican immigrant, was carrying notes in his pocket in which he expressed outrage at Asians, whites, and "Uncle Tom Negroes."

BOBBY RAY INMAN

On Dec. 16, 1993, President Clinton named Bobby Ray Inman, a retired four-star admiral, to succeed Les Aspin as U.S. secretary of defense. Born on April 4, 1931, in Rhonesboro, TX, Inman was graduated from the University of Texas and the National War College. A longtime naval-intelligence officer, he served as director of the National Security Agency (1977-81) and deputy director of the Central Intelligence Agency (1981-82). Inman surprised many Americans in early 1994 by suddenly withdrawing his nomination.

While the highest crime rates were in big cities, even the suburbs were not safe, as demonstrated by a spate of kidnappings and child molestings. In Los Angeles' San Fernando Valley police counted more than 32 attacks on young children, most on their way to school. In Petaluma, CA, Polly Klaas, age 12, was kidnapped from her bedroom during a slumber party and murdered. On November 18, Angie Housman, age 9, was abducted and murdered in St. Ann, MO, a suburb of St. Louis; two weeks later 10-year-old Cassidy Senter was kidnapped and killed in nearby Hazelwood.

Searching for answers, some analysts blamed television for contributing to crime by its depiction of violence. Testifying before a Senate Commerce Committee hearing on October 20, Attorney General Janet Reno warned the industry to decrease the level of violence in its programs or face federal action. President Clinton announced his tentative support for a proposal to require licensing of all gun owners and called for early congressional action in 1994 on anticrime legislation proposed in 1993.

ROBERT SHOGAN
Washington Bureau, "Los Angeles Times"

Thomas Jefferson's 250th Birthday

Thomas Jefferson, third U.S. president and author of the Declaration of Independence, was hailed as the architect of democracy in 1993 during a yearlong commemoration of the 250th anniversary of his birth—April 13, 1743.

Often called the "Sage of Monticello," Jefferson spent most of his adult life building his "little mountain" home just outside of Charlottesville, VA, while holding numerous public posts—including county administrator, governor, member of Congress, secretary of state, vice-president, and president.

Jefferson died on July 4, 1826, on the 50th anniversary of the approval of the Declaration of Independence. Throughout his life he emphasized that Americans must be educated to fulfill that document's promises of liberty and equality. He spent his retirement designing and building the University of Virginia in Charlottesville, which he called "the hobby of my old age." He handpicked the faculty, organized the curriculum, and saw the first classes begin a year before his death.

© Francis Mayer/Independence National Historical Park

Commemorations and Celebrations. During 1993, Jefferson's face appeared on a new postage stamp, his house underwent restoration, and his life was the subject of a nationwide lecture tour as well as educational programs for elementary- and secondary-school students. The Massachusetts Historical Society, American Philosophical Society, and other organizations sponsored exhibits from their collections of President Jefferson's documents and portraits. Others showcased Jefferson's contributions to architecture.

The Thomas Jefferson Memorial Foundation, which owns and operates Jefferson's Monticello today, brought back to the house more than 150 pieces of art, artifacts, and furniture for the first time since their dispersal after his death on July 4, 1826.

Current U.S. President William Jefferson Clinton honored his namesake by starting his January 1993 inaugural celebration at Monticello. Later in the year, Clinton appointed a committee, created by Congress, which would promote commemorations of Jefferson on the local, national, and international levels.

Notable citizens and scholars, including U.S. Chief Justice William Rehnquist, gathered at the University of Virginia on April 13, 1993, to honor recent achievements in the disciplines of law and architecture. Former Soviet President Mikhail Gorbachev, who oversaw democratic reforms in the former Soviet Union, addressed thousands who gathered at celebrations at Monticello and the university.

In recent years, the words Jefferson penned have been studied with increasing interest abroad, including in China and in the former Soviet-bloc countries of Eastern Europe. The eminent Jefferson scholar Merrill Peterson emphasized these themes when he spoke at daybreak ceremonies April 13 at Jefferson's birthplace in Shadwell, VA. "The power of Jefferson's words created its own monument," Peterson said, "and not only in America, but in the world, for Jefferson formulated the philosophy of freedom in universal terms so that it is accessible to all peoples."

Reevaluation of the Jefferson Legacy. In autumn 1992 the "Jeffersonian Legacies" conference at the University of Virginia highlighted recent attention focused on Jefferson's anomalous position as a Virginia slave owner. Researchers also were studying the lives of the more than 100 African-American slaves who were personal servants at Monticello and who worked Jefferson's plantations. A lifelong critic of slavery, Jefferson did not believe the time had arrived yet for a general abolition but declared that "nothing is more certainly written in the book of fate than that these people are to be free." He did not believe in a multiracial society, however, and thought deportation must go hand in hand with emancipation.

As the scholarly "Legacies" meeting suggested, Thomas Jefferson will continue to hold a central place in any discussion of our society today, as we look to history to help explain racism and inequality in the context of the principles of U.S. democracy.

MITCH WHITTEN
Thomas Jefferson Memorial Foundation

The Economy

After meandering through most of 1993—its brief spurts of growth generally followed by relapses—the U.S. economy gathered momentum in the final quarter. Encouraging reports emerged daily from government agencies and private-sector businesses and research groups, and previously tightfisted consumers used their credit cards heavily. Democratic President Bill Clinton, whose economic and taxing policies created controversy throughout his first year in office, declared the U.S. economic recovery to be on a sustainable course.

Signs of Recovery. As the year ended, consumers were spending heavily for automobiles, new and existing homes, and computers. Manufacturing picked up after having been weak through most of the year. The Federal Reserve Board reported in mid-December that industrial production shot up 0.9% in November, the sixth straight monthly advance and the largest in a year. The annual rate of productivity improvement soared to 4.3% in November, one of the largest gains in three years. The jobless rate dropped to 6.4% in November from 6.8% in October.

Interest rates remained at some of the lowest levels in two decades—the 30-year Treasury bond yield was just more than 6%, a full point below the year-earlier level—and consumer-price inflation into December was at an annual rate of just 2.8%—the lowest since 1986—aided by a surprising fall in energy prices. Under the impact of job cutting, productivity growth was at its highest rate in several years, and business failures were down 11% from a year earlier; in fact, they had decreased more than 40% in terms of total liabilities.

Reflecting the good news, the Conference Board's consumer-confidence index jumped nearly 11 percentage points in one month to a 71.2% reading in November, the highest since January. At the same time, the United States, Canada, and Mexico agreed on the North American Free Trade Agreement (NAFTA). A few weeks later, in December, they achieved an accord with the European Community on tariff cuts; this was one of the last remaining obstacles to completion of the 117-nation General Agreement on Tariffs and Trade (GATT), which would reduce tariffs among the three nations. When finally approved by the individual countries, GATT would lower tariffs on more industries in more countries than any other trade agreement in history.

Emerging Uncertainties. Such news reinforced the views of those who believed the economy finally was poised to move forward again, or actually was doing so. Throughout the year, however, a peculiar quality persisted: Despite high hopes and sometimes similar expectations, wariness prevailed in some of the consumer, business, and academic communities. A growing feeling existed that the traditional economic statistics did not explain conditions fully, at least to the increasingly knowledgeable consumer. What

satisfied professional economists often seemed at variance with the experience of ordinary people. Productivity increases, for example, were hailed as promising for the future, but to a great extent they were a consequence of massive job terminations, and many of those who lost well-paying jobs were forced to take employment in lower-wage service positions, if they could find employment at all.

In addition, almost everyone was aware to some extent of impediments to strong economic growth. Consumer spending, for example, rose 2.2% from April to December, while incomes grew only 1.4%. People who had cut installment debts over the previous two or three years now were allowing them to grow again, and they were saving less. Visa said retail spending on its credit cards rose 28% from a year earlier for the holiday-shopping period from Thanksgiving through mid-December, and the savings rate late in the year dipped to 3.7%, near its all-time low. Besides using credit cards, people were financing their lifestyles by taking tax-deductible loans on their home equity.

The Tax Foundation, a not-for-profit research organization, helped explain why people felt stressed. Its research showed that while the median income of the typical family (two adults, two children) almost doubled to $51,883 in 1993 from $26,879 in 1980, rising costs left only $4,504 to use. Higher costs for medical-care expenses—to 10.3% of income from 7%—contributed, but the major losses were to a 90% jump in taxes and a 73% rise in prices. While ordinary people might not have understood the full implications of federal-budget deficits—about $255 billion for fiscal 1993—and the merchandise-trade deficit—which averaged $10 billion per month and totaled $30 billion more than a year earlier—they observed the negative tone in front-page articles and evening newscasts.

Business doubts continued to exist about the nation's economic policies, as reflected in a poll among the mostly small-business members of the National Federation of Independent Business. Economist William C. Dunkelberg, dean of Temple University's school of business, found in November that only 4% of respondents thought President Clinton was doing a "good" or "excellent" job. Congress fared worse; it failed to win even one full point in the "excellent" category, and only 1% in the "good" designation.

White House Initiatives. Although the Clinton administration got off to a slow start in the economic arena, it gave evidence by the spring of 1993 that it would be among the most economically active administrations in decades, perhaps since the Depression years of Franklin D. Roosevelt. Observing that 37 million Americans had no medical insurance, it promised universal coverage through the introduction of managed competition. And, though Clinton had indicated throughout his campaign for the presidency that he would avoid tax increases, he conceded by February that this would not be so. His "vision

GROSS DOMESTIC PRODUCT
Percent Change from Preceding Quarter

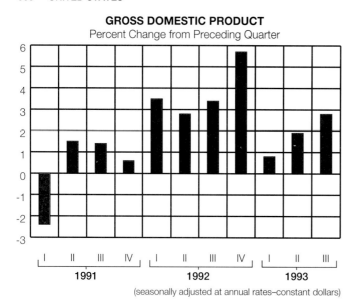

1991   1992   1993

(seasonally adjusted at annual rates–constant dollars)

CONSUMER PRICES
Percent Change

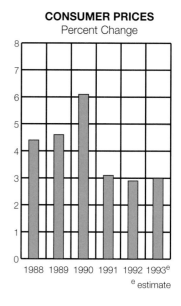

1988 1989 1990 1991 1992 1993^e

^e estimate

SAVINGS
As Percent of Disposable Personal Income

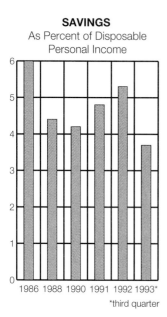

1986 1988 1990 1991 1992 1993*

*third quarter

UNEMPLOYMENT RATE
All Civilian Workers

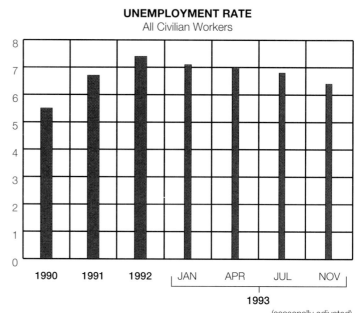

1990   1991   1992   JAN   APR   JUL   NOV

1993

(seasonally adjusted)

of change for America" adopted the slogan "shared sacrifice." His economic plan included promises of $2 in spending cuts for every $1 in new taxes, although critics quickly pointed out that by their analyses it was nearer a $1-to-$1 ratio, and some claimed the ratio was closer to $3 of taxes for every $1 of cuts.

The president said that his proposed Omnibus Budget Reconciliation Act of 1993 (OBRA) would cut the deficit by $325 billion over four years. Total spending would grow but be restrained below what it would have been, rising to $1.677 trillion in 1997 from its current level of about $1.475 trillion. The bill included a multibillion-dollar shot-in-the-arm stimulus for

the 1993 economy, the rationale for this being that such a financial injection would lift the economy out of the doldrums, and that the boost in time would add to revenues.

To finance the plan, the bill would raise personal-income taxes to 36% from 31% for millions of Americans, and to 39.6% on taxable incomes of $250,000 or more. Energy taxes would rise, some corporate taxes would edge higher, and some Medicare recipients also would pay higher tax bills. The president said 98% of households would not see a tax increase, but the claim seemed to collapse under examination. After analyzing the details, the Tax Foundation, for example, claimed that 46% of all taxpayers

would pay higher individual income taxes. The president, however, insisted that it would impact mainly those who, he said, got rich in the 1980s at the expense of others.

Battles with Congress. While many praised the president for what they saw as a firm stand against government growth, some business groups saw his proposals as doing just the opposite. Accustomed to a hands-off attitude during the administration of Ronald Reagan, and a similar philosophy if not practice under George Bush, they viewed Clinton's tax and other proposals as interventionist, overly activist, and uncalled for. Early on, it appeared the budget bill was headed for defeat, but relentlessly the president worked the telephones, cajoling and promising members of Congress. His efforts were matched pro and con by various other groups, public and private. Perhaps never before in U.S. political history was the lobbying effort more intense, and seldom was a vote so close. Although the outcome remained in doubt up to the evening before, the bill passed early in August by a margin of two votes in the House and one vote in the Senate. It was proclaimed a new beginning by supporters, but Republican members of Congress—none of whom voted for it—tagged the bill as just more taxing and spending.

The health-care debate promised to be even more controversial. As outlined in a massive, 1,342-page document called the Health Security Act, the administration's proposal would seek to limit price increases by encouraging large user-bargaining units with sufficient power to contract with hospitals, insurers, and pharmaceutical suppliers. It would seek to make health care universal and a right; the administration emphasized on every occasion the number of Americans without health-care insurance or access to affordable drugs, and asserted that because of this lack, they were being denied the right to good health. The president and his wife, Hillary Rodham Clinton—the chair of the task force on health-care reform—publicly castigated both the pharmaceutical and insurance industries for having allowed health-care costs to rise beyond the pocketbooks of millions of Americans, not to mention those with no access to care at all.

Anticipating the attacks, both industries were well-equipped with data to support their positions. The pharmaceutical companies stressed that steps had been made toward conquering or alleviating the effects of various diseases in recent years because of drugs developed through extremely costly basic research, much of it leading to no commercial product. Always aware of the bottom line, insurers already had begun lining up alliances with smaller service companies specializing in holding down costs through technological advances and strict cost-control accounting.

While nobody could be certain about the final contents of any health-care bill—the administration advertised that it was willing to accommodate suggestions and changes—or even when it might come to a vote, the threat of price and other restraints helped slow the inflation rate for health care to a bit more than 7%, versus the double-digit rates that had become common in recent years. (*See also* FEATURE ARTICLE, page 36.)

Year-end Growth. Amid the controversies, and despite warnings from the business community that the private sector would become too heavily burdened by taxes and mandates, the economy managed to grow. As the statistics showed greater strength during November and December, the president sought to take credit, but his Republican and business critics were loath to agree. As some of them put it, he might lay claim to having written the words, but he did not compose the tune. That, they said, was the result of continued low inflation and a Federal Reserve policy of low interest rates. They said people hardly could not be enticed into the marketplace when conditions were so much in their favor, and they pointed out that consumers still held to the conservative habits they had developed over the past two or three years. Dun & Bradstreet reported that while coupon redemptions were down 10% in the first half of the year, they remained higher than in 1990. There were more than 3.7 billion redemptions worth $2.1 billion in savings. And the experts indicated that the numbers might have been even higher except for the spread among retailers of so-called everyday low-price policies that reduced the need for incentives.

Whatever the reasons, even the die-hards had to concede that the U.S. economy at year's end was moving ahead. Whether or not it was a spurt that would end in another fizzle was almost irrelevant because, in spite of all its ups and downs, the 1993 economy put up some numbers that could not be challenged. Gross domestic product in comparable or real (1987) dollars, grew 2.8% to more than $5.1 trillion from $4.99 trillion a year earlier. The jobless rate was down to an average for the year of 6.8% from 7.4% in 1992. Pretax corporate profits rose to $443 billion from just more than $395 billion a year earlier. Housing starts rose to 1.27 million from less than 1.21 million in the year before, and the rate was rising as the year ended. The 30-year Treasury bond yield, an important long-term indicator, fell more than a percentage point to an average for the year of 6.6%, and the prime lending rate dropped to 6% from 6.25%. Gains in real disposable income edged up to 2.9%, while the Consumer Price Index held steady at around 3%.

It was in all a hectic, controversial economic year, marked by restraint and filled with doubts too, but in the broadest of terms if not in all the specifics it was a good year, even if many people felt otherwise.

JOHN CUNNIFF
Business Analyst, The Associated Press

Foreign Affairs

Much as Bill Clinton might have preferred to concentrate on the U.S. domestic agenda, the new president could not escape the pressures and pitfalls of international relations during his first year in office.

By autumn, the promise of at least a year's bipartisan foreign-policy grace period had evaporated, with loud congressional calls in both parties to limit the president's prerogatives in the use of force, and entrenched opposition, especially among Democrats, to the North American Free Trade Agreement (NAFTA)—a policy which, among others, Clinton adopted rather willingly from his predecessor, George Bush. Some blamed the president as well for failing to carry through with campaign promises of policy changes on issues such as Haiti and Bosnia-Herzegovina.

Among the year's successes, the Clinton administration could point to a remarkable handshake scene on the White House lawn in September between Israeli Prime Minister Yitzhak Rabin and Palestine Liberation Organization (PLO) chairman Yasir Arafat. Although the groundwork for the limited Israeli-PLO autonomy agreement and mutual recognition had been laid in secret talks in Norway without much evident input from Washington, the agreement represented the culmination of arduous Bush and Clinton State Department efforts to keep Middle East dialogue going. Fulfillment of the peace promise, though, would depend partly

Bill Clinton promised U.S. aid to Russia at an April meeting with President Boris Yeltsin (below right) in Vancouver, B.C. The new U.S. president steadfastly supported Yeltsin during 1993.

© Bayne Stanley/Saba

on funding for the Palestinian territories of Gaza and Jericho. The United States immediately took the lead in organizing a multinational aid consortium, pledging $250 million as a start to what by year's end was a $2 billion fund.

Russia. Russia and the United States remained on a generally cooperative course, covering such issues as arms control and the Bosnian crisis. Despite the violent presidential-parliamentary showdown in Moscow in September-October, and the reality that Russia's President Boris Yeltsin had acted outside the constitution, Clinton maintained steadfast support of Yeltsin in his struggles with extreme right- and left-wing opponents. Vice-President Al Gore was dispatched to Moscow immediately after alarming electoral gains for Yeltsin's opponents in December. Yet there was little Washington could do to assure long-term Russian stability. Release of funds in the promised $28 billion international-aid package was gradual and conditional on Moscow's continued progress in restricting government expenditures. The Russian economy, meanwhile, still without a convertible currency or effective central bank, staggered under 240% annual inflation. Assistance for former Soviet republics nevertheless represented $2.5 billion out of a total U.S. foreign-aid budget of $13 billion for 1993-94.

Trade Issues. Limited economic progress was achieved during the midsummer G-7 summit in Tokyo, with Yeltsin in attendance. The framework for agreement was reached on international tariff reductions across a broad range of manufactured goods. Hopes to include agricultural commodities were chilled, however, by farmers' strikes and protest movements, particularly in France. Yet intensive year-end bargaining overcame these obstacles and others to move at last toward fulfillment of the General Agreement on Tariffs and Trade (GATT) Uruguay Trade Round, begun in 1986. Hopes of agreement with Japan on precise targets for U.S. exports also proved unworkable, and the two sides settled instead for general statements of intentions to open the Japanese market. As part of the GATT agreement, in December, Japan's Prime Minister Morihiro Hosokawa announced that Japan reluctantly would open its rice markets to imports. The Clinton administration also mounted a campaign to stimulate U.S. exports and investments in all of Asia, but a full opening to Vietnam was delayed once again.

Criticized by Republicans for supporting NAFTA only lukewarmly, the president by summer's end looked to employ public-relations and congressional-pressure tactics to get the agreement approved by the U.S. Congress. Fulfilling campaign promises, Clinton had added somewhat mild provisions to NAFTA to improve Mexico's environmental and labor conditions. Yet strong opposition by unions, those in industrial states, the sugar lobby, and political opponent H. Ross Perot meant a rough ride for the pact before it was approved.

President Clinton hosted the first large-scale summit meeting of the leaders of the four-year-old Asia-Pacific Economic Cooperation (APEC) group in November in Seattle, WA. Those attending included (l-r): New Zealand's Prime Minister James Bolger, Indonesia's President Suharto, Philippine President Fidel Ramos, Singapore's Prime Minister Goh Chok Tong, the U.S. president, and Taiwan's Chairman for Economic Planning Vincent Siew. Trade was a major subject on the summit's agenda.

© Reuters/Bettmann

Security Areas. The president, as promised during the campaign, acted to restrain the spread of weapons of mass destruction. Some U.S.-Russian and U.S.-Indian friction developed during the summer when Washington successfully induced Moscow to cancel a sale of advanced rocket motors suitable for India's nuclear-delivery missiles. The United States remained intent on supporting Russian scientists in the task of dismantling nuclear weapons, and in pressing Ukraine to return its weapons to Russian control. North Korea was threatened with United Nations (UN) sanctions if it did not permit international inspections of suspected nuclear facilities. While promising cooperation, the North Koreans—who objected to U.S.-South Korean security preparations—still resisted direct on-site visits, thus alarming both Japan and South Korea. Washington continued to express hope of a negotiated solution.

Periodic pressure also was applied to various countries over security issues. Iraq was subjected to occasional bombing and continued economic embargo, both because of reported conspiracies to assassinate former President George Bush and slow cooperation on weapons location and inspection. Pakistani-U.S. relations remained cool over the nuclear issue as well. Economic sanctions, excluding the oil trade, were imposed by the UN Security Council on Libya for failure to turn over suspected terrorists. Washington also hoped to gain support for global bans and inspections on the production of chemical/biological weapons and highly enriched uranium and plutonium, the latter a tricky issue because of production by U.S. European allies. Restrictions were proposed as well on the trade of highly destructive weapons components.

Yet U.S. leadership on arms control was questioned, as the administration launched a vigorous sales-promotion campaign for U.S. weapons exports and proposed to reduce taxes on them. Congress also debated arms-export loan guarantees, as the United States continued as the world's Number 1 arms dealer with key sales to Taiwan and the Middle East. Efforts to control the global proliferation of missiles also conflicted somewhat with the planned release of advanced missile technology to Israel.

In efforts to coordinate security policy, military consultations were renewed with China, despite Clinton's campaign criticism of Beijing's human-rights record. The president ultimately supported continuation of China's "most favored nation" trade status, under conditions of progress in human rights. However, U.S. proposals of an extended nuclear-testing moratorium were shaken by China's refusal to reciprocate, and Washington therefore prepared for new tests of its own. (*See also* MILITARY AFFAIRS.)

Peace Momentum, Haiti, and Somalia. The momentum for peace slowed in some regions, while picking up in others. In Central America reports of the Reagan and Bush administrations' connections with right-wing human-rights violations during the 1980s underscored the possibility of renewed civil strife. Some more positive peacemaking results were reported in Cambodia, where a coalition government appeared feasible with UN and Chinese backing. By October the United States had paid the UN more than half of the $1 billion it owed the organization.

Soon after taking office, the president disappointed many campaign supporters by continuing, with only slight liberalization, the Bush policy of turning back boatloads of Haitian refugees. At the same time, he pressed hard for a negotiated settlement of the Haitian dispute, and appeared on the verge of success during the summer. The agreement, brokered under UN

auspices at New York's Governor's Island, was to have restored President Jean-Bertrand Aristide while granting amnesty to members of the Haitian armed forces which had deposed him. However, strongman Gen. Raul Cedras refused to step down as scheduled, and a show of rebellion in Port-au-Prince caused the United States abruptly to withdraw its military escort force. By early November strict UN and Organization of American States (OAS) economic embargoes were reimposed on Haiti, but Washington also worried that too much pressure would cause the complete collapse of Haitian society.

Some speculated that the Haitian defiance was fueled by the difficulties U.S. forces experienced in Mogadishu, Somalia, during the early fall, as Clinton sought to make good on the Bush administration's prior commitment there. The U.S. peacekeeping force, the first to be put under UN command, had been reduced to only a few hundred and was withdrawn from the streets in hopes of turning over responsibilities to other nations. However, the killing of several Pakistani and Nigerian peacekeepers over the summer led to attempted UN crackdowns on the clan forces of Gen. Mohamed Farah Aidid. Conflicting with its Italian allies, Washington joined in the UN effort, which proved futile and resulted in the deaths of many Somali civilians. Aidid eluded arrest and his forces then retaliated against U.S. units, humiliating Washington by dragging the body of an ambushed soldier through the streets in front of TV cameras.

Amid strong congressional demands for withdrawal, the president announced a Somali pullout deadline of March 1994. In the interim, U.S. units were reinforced and negotiations with Aidid and other clan leaders resumed. Facing vocal domestic and Somali criticism of his foreign-policy skills, Clinton conceded that it had been a mistake to neglect the political for the military process. Unfortunately, hesitant progress in both the Angolan and Liberian civil wars also threatened to unravel during the year, and Sudan remained strife-torn.

Africa. In view of such difficulties, the administration generally placed new emphasis on building democracy and prosperity in Africa. By midyear it had shifted to back the Angolan government's side against the UNITA rebels, former U.S. clients. Similarly, U.S. criticism also was leveled at other authoritarian regimes, such as those of Generals Mobutu Sese Seko of Zaire and Ibrahim Babangida of Nigeria, with the latter finally stepping down. Conspicuously, democratically elected Namibian President Sam Nujoma was the first African head of state invited to the Clinton White House. In light of congressional pressure, an additional $100 million African foreign-aid/debt-relief fund was created, along with efforts to protect the African environment and alleviate drought. Nevertheless, economies continued to sag throughout the continent, human-rights abuses mounted in Burundi, and as U.S. economic sanctions were eased, sporadic violence also marked South Africa's progress toward its first universal-suffrage elections in 1994.

Bosnia. The other major frustration for the new president was the tragic Bosnian war. Here, President Clinton's desires for more-active opposition to Serb attacks on Bosnian Muslims met with both UN and European opposition. In the process, the administration was made to look indecisive, threatening strong action—including the bombing of troop concentrations and strategic points and the lifting of the arms embargo for the Muslims—but ultimately pulling back from such moves in the face of diplomatic opposition. No firm and unified response by the North Atlantic Treaty Organization (NATO) was achieved: The Europeans waited for U.S. leadership, while Washington cited the need for increased European responsibility. Food and supplies were air-dropped to besieged villages; small contingents of additional U.S. forces were sent to bolster potentially endangered zones such as Macedonia; and the United States promised to take direct part in peacekeeping once final stable agreements were achieved.

The Clinton administration had remained skeptical of the UN-sponsored Vance-Owen peace plan, with its provisions for ten separate Bosnian zones. The plan fizzled by midyear, but Washington's military threats indeed seemed to spur Serbian President Slobodan Milosevic to pressure his Bosnian Serb allies for a settlement which would have divided the area into three zones. However, deprived of much territory, the Bosnian Muslims ultimately rejected the proposal, and with winter approaching, the UN was left to attempt only local mediation through its hard-pressed peacekeeping forces. (*See also* FEATURE ARTICLE, page 26.)

Advisers. The Bosnian crisis caused a remarkable series of State Department resignations during the year, as desk officers protested what they considered the U.S. failure to make a resolute stand for the Muslim victims. All of these difficulties took a toll on administration credibility. By November the press was speculating about the future of the president's three top foreign-policy aides—Secretary of State Warren Christopher (*see* BIOGRAPHY), Defense Secretary Les Aspin, and National Security Adviser Anthony Lake. Indeed, Deputy Secretary of State Clifton Wharton, Jr., did resign under pressure from Christopher, and in December, Aspin stepped down as well. After a rocky first year, then, and despite new stature gained from the NAFTA victory, many argued that the president would have to become involved more personally and thoroughly in foreign-policy deliberations or find advisers with a greater sense of vision, especially regarding ethnic conflicts similar to those in the former Yugoslavia which were looming in the former Soviet republics.

FREDERIC S. PEARSON, *Wayne State University*

URUGUAY

Uruguay's President Luis Alberto Lacalle continued to advance his economic programs and political reforms during 1993. The civilian government also surmounted its worst confrontation with the military.

Politics. Lacalle urged congress to reform an almost bankrupt state-pension system, end a state monopoly on fuels and insurance, establish new work rules for government employees, and simplify the budget process. The president intended to assure the cohesiveness of political parties by introducing a new law on party splintering. To strengthen his National Party's chances of retaining the presidency beyond 1994, Lacalle in January tapped Sen. Sergio Abreu to head the foreign ministry and named Manuel Romay as housing minister. President Lacalle gained legislative support for his programs by ordering two of his administrative appointees to reoccupy their legislative seats in September.

Civil-Military Relations. In a major shake-up of the military command in August, Defense Minister Mariano Brito was replaced by Daniel Hugo Martins. The government's distrust of the military was attributed to sporadic bombings—for which mysterious military groups claimed responsibility—and to the discovery in June that the armed forces had maintained clandestine links with the military forces of Chile, Argentina, Paraguay, and Brazil forged during the military rule and accompanying "dirty wars" of the 1970s and 1980s.

The armed service's links to other military forces had been utilized in Uruguay to hide Eugenio Barrios, a Chilean secret-police agent, wanted in connection with a murder trial in his country. His attempt to return to Chile exposed the Uruguayan army, and the military-intelligence chief was removed. Even though President Lacalle—who shortened an official visit in June to Great Britain to rush home and deal with the scandal—confirmed all military commanders in their posts except one general, the armed forces claimed to be victims of "unjustified aggression" by the civilian government.

Economy. As inflation rose above 56% by August, the government was unable to hold pay increases to its 35% ceiling. Officials were confronted with demands from many public employees—including teachers, doctors, and health workers—after allowing hikes of 50% to police and military personnel. Mounting dissatisfaction among wage earners led to the tenth general strike against the Lacalle administration on July 28. A Gallup poll conducted in September revealed that 82% of those responding were dissatisfied with their economic situation. Vice-President Gonzalo Aguirre and Sen. Carlos Julio Pereyra publicly urged the president to formulate social programs to alleviate the impact of his economic measures.

URUGUAY • Information Highlights

Official Name: Oriental Republic of Uruguay.
Location: Southeastern coast of South America.
Area: 68,039 sq mi (176 220 km²).
Population (mid-1993 est.): 3,200,000.
Capital (1985 census): Montevideo, 1,251,647.
Government: *Head of state,* Luis Alberto Lacalle, president (took office March 1, 1990). *Legislature—* National Congress: Senate and House of Deputies.
Monetary Unit: Peso (4.45 pesos equal U.S.$1, financial rate, Dec. 31, 1993).
Gross Domestic Product (1991 est. U.S.$): $9,100,000,000.
Foreign Trade (1992 U.S.$): *Imports,* $2,024,000,000; *exports,* $1,701,000,000.

Uruguay was warned in October by the World Bank that its $7 billion foreign debt was 64% of its gross domestic product (GDP), well above the bank's safety level of 50%. Interest on the debt consumed nearly 17% of export earnings in 1992. Uruguay's failure to comply with spending and inflation targets contained in an economic-performance agreement monitored by the International Monetary Fund necessitated the negotiation of a new accord in June. The following month, Finance Minister Ignacio de Posadas announced spending cuts and higher fees on services provided by the government that would save $300 million.

Trade. Uruguay's exports fell by 19% as imports rose by nearly 13% in the first quarter of 1993. One third of the exports went to Mercosur, the trading bloc that was also the source of 43% of Uruguay's imports. The "irreversibility" of Mercosur was ratified at a summit in Montevideo on Dec. 28, 1992, by the presidents of Argentina, Brazil, Paraguay, and Uruguay. The leaders rejected all pleas to delay freeing up trade among the partners beyond Jan. 1, 1995, and moved ahead to coordinate fiscal, monetary, and exchange policies among the member countries. Labor confederations and industrialists in Uruguay and other states in the Southern Cone protested the timetable for complete integration.

LARRY L. PIPPIN
University of the Pacific

UTAH

Utah experienced an unusually robust economy in 1993 with one of the highest economic-growth rates in the nation. The economy was fueled by higher income for workers, a growing job market, a boom in housing construction, and a banner year for the ski industry.

New Leaders. Following 1992 elections, a historic number of Utahans—including a U.S. senator, a governor, an attorney general, a U.S. congresswoman, and several state legislators—took office for the first time in 1993. Utah's new governor, Mike Leavitt, was sworn into office in early 1993, extending eight years of Republican

UTAH • Information Highlights

Area: 84,899 sq mi (219 889 km²).
Population (July 1, 1992 est.): 1,813,000.
Chief Cities (1990 census): Salt Lake City, the capital, 159,936; West Valley City, 86,976; Provo, 86,835.
Government (1993): *Chief Officers*—governor, Mike Leavitt (R); lt. gov., Olene S. Walker (R). *Legislature*—Senate, 29 members; House of Representatives, 75 members.
State Finances (fiscal year 1991): *Revenue,* $4,344,000,000; *expenditure,* $4,108,000,000.
Personal Income (1992): $28,328,000,000; per capita, $15,624.
Labor Force (August 1993): *Civilian labor force,* 849,700; *unemployed,* 28,300 (3.3% of total force).
Education: *Enrollment* (fall 1991)—public elementary schools, 326,969; public secondary, 129,461; colleges and universities, 130,419. *Public school expenditures* (1990-91), $1,235,916,000.

control. Leavitt replaced the top echelon of the state government, but the new leaders reflected a philosophy much like that of the last administration. However, Leavitt's style was more hands-on than that of previous Gov. Norman Bangerter. Leavitt's interest in health-care reform made him a leader among other governors on the issue.

Politics. The Utah legislature passed few controversial bills in 1993, focusing on school reform, averting a teachers' strike, and working to appropriate money to settle a lawsuit with federal retirees in the state. The legislature passed Governor Leavitt's education-reform bill, which provided for "Centennial Schools," a program designed to identify excellent schools that merited additional appropriations and recognition. A growing economy enabled Utah to raise more money in taxes than was budgeted, and to become one of the few states in the nation with more money to spend on pressing needs.

Utah dropped its abortion-statute litigation in 1993. Following decisions in the U.S. Supreme Court, the governor announced that Utah no longer would defend its abortion law in court. Utah courts also confronted the long-standing issue of separation of church and state. The Utah constitution prohibited using public funds to further religion. A lower court ruled that this clause made prayer in city council and other public meetings unconstitutional, but the state Supreme Court overturned this court decision.

Utah remained concerned with such distinctively "Western" issues as land use, water conservation, and wilderness. Utah ranchers and political leaders challenged Secretary of Interior Bruce Babbitt's proposed increase in grazing fees. Since President Bill Clinton had no Utah citizens in his administration, there was a sense that the needs and circumstances of the state were not understood. Nevertheless, most state leaders appeared to move away from outright opposition to creating more wilderness.

The Economy and Crime. The computer-software industry remained strong but appeared to

have leveled off in its growth. Kennecott Copper, a large mining company and a leading employer, announced a major expansion of its Utah copper operations.

Gang violence became a major concern in Utah. Accordingly, Salt Lake City passed a five-day waiting period for the purchase of handguns; the state legislature appropriated additional money to fight gangs; and civic leaders pressed for earlier intervention to prevent gang violence from occurring.

The Mormons. Six dissidents in the Church of Jesus Christ of Latter-Day Saints were excommunicated in September. Earlier in 1993, Pulitzer Prize-winner Steve Benson, grandson of ailing Mormon president Ezra Taft Benson, raised the question of his grandfather's competence to lead the church.

DAVID B. MAGLEBY
Brigham Young University

VENEZUELA

Venezuelan democracy survived its 35th year in 1993, overcoming challenges posed by a difficult presidential succession, falling oil prices, civil unrest, and rumors of coup conspiracies.

Presidential Suspension. Although presidential elections were scheduled for December, President Carlos Andrés Pérez was so unpopular that some Venezuelans—angered by corruption, the high social costs of the government's economic reforms, and the unresponsiveness of politicians in general—sought to remove him from office ahead of schedule. After two coup attempts failed in 1992, an opposition congressman accused Pérez of corrupt activities and called for his impeachment. An investigation of the charges by Attorney General Ramón Escovar Salom produced allegations that a secret interior-ministry fund, intended for state security, had been used to buy dollars just before a major devaluation of the bolívar in 1989. The dollars were sold after the devaluation for a $17 million profit.

Pérez maintained that no illegal actions were taken, but in March the Supreme Court agreed to consider the charges, and reported on May 21 that sufficient evidence existed to warrant a trial. The Senate immediately authorized a trial, removing Pérez from office. The president of the congress, Octavio Lepage of the governing Acción Democrática (AD) party, automatically became acting president until June 5, when the congress selected respected historian Ramón J. Velásquez to finish Pérez' term, which was to end in February 1994. Pérez argued that the congress had no constitutional authority to elect an interim president as long as the possibility of acquittal in his trial remained, but the congress settled the question on August 31 by voting to make Pérez' removal permanent.

Legislation. The congress cooperated with President Velásquez to pass legislation that had

© Carlos Angel/Gamma-Liaison

After campaigning as an independent, Rafael Caldera was elected president of Venezuela on Dec. 5, 1993. The 77-year-old head of a 17-party coalition had held the office before—from 1969 to 1974.

been delayed by the impeachment struggle. In August he was given special-decree powers to restart the privatization process, while the congress approved a value-added tax to reduce the menacing budget deficit, a banking law, and a statute guaranteeing the independence of the central bank. Velásquez also moved to prevent future coup attempts by announcing a large pay hike for soldiers and low-ranking officers, and moderate increases for senior officers.

Elections. In the meantime an uncharacteristically low-key presidential campaign was under way. Ordinarily the only candidates with a chance to win were those from AD or the opposition Social Christian Party (COPEI). In 1993, however, those candidates were hurt by their endorsement of Pérez' economic policies and by ties to the two "establishment" parties that Venezuelans blamed for corruption.

Instead, one of the strong candidates was Andrés Velásquez, a labor leader and popular governor of the eastern industrial state of Bolívar. But the front-runner was Rafael Caldera, the nation's former president (1969-74) and founder of COPEI, who abandoned his own party to run an independent candidacy with the backing of a 17-party leftist coalition, the Convergencia Nacional. Caldera publicly promised to renegotiate Venezuela's debt agreement (26.5% of the 1994 budget was allocated to debt service) and to increase social spending and subsidies. Behind the scenes, however, Caldera and his advisers assured the international business community that he would continue privatization and maintain free-market reforms. Caldera won a tight December 5 election with roughly 30% of the vote, as three other candidates gained at least a 20% share of the vote.

Economy. The election resolved the succession crisis, but economic problems remained. Reversing the growth of two previous years, the economy contracted 2.3% during the first six months of 1993. The rapid deterioration was attributed, in addition to political uncertainty, to a public-sector deficit of some $3 billion, inflation of nearly 40%, and interest rates of up to 80%. The economic problems were compounded by a continued drop in oil prices. Nontraditional exports grew by 24% during the first six months, but this was offset by a more than 40% drop in foreign investments, leaving the government with a large current-account deficit. Coup rumors ran rampant, and investors worried that Caldera's shallow commitment to neoliberal economic policies and his narrow base of political support would endanger economic recovery, but few groups called for military intervention.

MICHAEL COPPEDGE
Johns Hopkins University

VENEZUELA • Information Highlights

Official Name: Republic of Venezuela.
Location: Northern coast of South America.
Area: 352,143 sq mi (912 050 km²).
Population (mid-1993 est.): 20,700,000.
Chief Cities (June 30, 1990 est., incl. suburbs): Caracas, the capital, 3,435,795; Maracaibo, 1,400,643; Valencia, 1,274,354.
Government: *Head of state and government,* Rafael Caldera, president (elected Dec. 1993). *Legislature—* National Congress: Senate and Chamber of Deputies.
Monetary Unit: Bolívar (106.1 bolívares equal U.S.$1, floating rate, Dec. 31, 1993).
Gross Domestic Product (1991 est. U.S.$): $52,300,000,000.
Economic Index (Caracas, 1992): *Consumer Prices* (1984 = 100), all items, 943.3; food, 1,725.4.
Foreign Trade (1992 U.S.$): *Imports,* $12,946,000,000; *exports,* $13,173,000,000.

VERMONT

Enactment of the toughest no-smoking law in the United States, financial difficulties, and continued debate over development in the state marked 1993 in Vermont.

Legislature. Legislative achievements were minimal, except for the passage of a ban on smoking in public buildings, enclosed indoor areas, restaurants, and bars. Hotels and motels were given until 1995 to comply with the new rules. An economic-progress act aimed at creating jobs through tax credits also was enacted. Democratic Gov. Howard Dean failed for the second straight year to get his conservative welfare-reform package passed.

Budget. After a long deadlock during which legislators went home, the committee of conference negotiated a budget compromise, setting the 1994 budget at $657.8 million. Despite a projected $45 million deficit, the governor and legislature allowed a series of temporary tax increases to expire on July 1, because of a "promise" to the voters. But after the legislature adjourned in May, it became clear that the sluggish economy would cause an even greater deficit—as much as 10% of Vermont's budget—in 1993-94. With the state's AA bond rating in jeopardy, Dean called a special legislative session to raise the sales tax to 5%, effective September 1.

Politics. Governor Dean was elected vice-chair of the National Governor's Association, and took the lead for the governors in health-care reform. However, before the Vermont Health Care Authority, which was created in 1992, could report, the governor came out in support of the multipayer (private-insurance) approach rather than the public, Canadian-style single-payer approach. During the summer, acrimony flared between Governor Dean and Auditor of Accounts Edward Flanagan, an independently elected Democrat. Flanagan began performance auditing and faulted the executive branch's contract-letting procedures. Each side accused the other of misrepresentations and political motives in the controversy.

Burlington's two-term Progressive Coalition Mayor Peter Clavelle was defeated by Republican Peter Brownell. Both Brownell and Clavelle attributed the Progressives' loss of City Hall after 12 years to Clavelle's successful support of health-care benefits for domestic partners of city workers. Brownell, who became Burlington's first Republican mayor since 1965, had opposed the proposal.

Domestic Partners. The domestic-partners issue spread to the University of Vermont when the Vermont Labor Relations Board overruled the university and ordered it to extend health benefits to the same-sex partners of its employees. Three months later the Vermont State Personnel Department denied health-insurance benefits to homosexual partners of state employees.

Endangered History. In June the National Trust for Historic Preservation designated Vermont as one of the nation's 11 most "endangered historic places," the first time an entire state made the list. This symbolic distinction served—along with the economic problems—to fuel the ongoing debate over the extent to which Vermont should be open to development and in what ways Act 250 legislation regulating development might be eased.

Weather and Hunting. March brought record snowfalls and record cold, but also a good skiing season. In April, Lake Champlain crested at a record level of almost 7 ft (2 m) above normal, causing millions of dollars in damage....In an effort to curb the growing moose population, the first moose hunt in 96 years was held in October.

SAMUEL B. HAND and ROBERT V. DANIELS
University of Vermont

VIETNAM

Vietnam continued to normalize its relations with the West during 1993. In February, President François Mitterrand of France paid a state visit to Hanoi—the first Western leader to travel to Vietnam in 18 years. In July, U.S. President Bill Clinton announced that the United States would end its opposition to loans to Vietnam by the International Monetary Fund (IMF). This opened the

Edmund Reilly, president of Digital Equipment, Asia, gives a computer demonstration to Vietnam's Minister of Science, Technology, and Environment Dang Hu (left). With Hanoi opening its economy to international markets, a greater number of U.S. companies sought to do business with Vietnam. A U.S. trade embargo against Vietnam remained in effect, however.

© Claro Cortes IV/ Reuters/Bettmann

way to approximately $500 million worth of aid from the World Bank and Asian Development Bank to upgrade roads, railroads, and utilities.

Politics. While opening its economy to Western capital and market forces, Vietnam's political system remained controlled tightly by the Communist Party, in a dual system similar to China's. Both states often have imprisoned political dissidents, but Vietnam's leaders appeared more vulnerable to economic pressures than the Chinese, as shown by Vietnam's acceptance of a human-rights clause in its economic accord with the European Community (EC).

If Vietnamese leaders were sensitive to the human-rights concerns of Western investors, this concern was not reflected in their treatment of dissident Buddhists. In July police detained Thich Hanh Duc, the abbot of a pagoda near Vung Tau, along with some of his supporters. Buddhists claimed the government used tanks to assault the pagoda, though Hanoi denied the charge. This incident followed an outbreak of political violence in Hue during May that was reminiscent of clashes between Buddhist groups and the pro-U.S. regime of Ngo Dinh Diem during 1963.

Economics. A key 1993 reform was a new land-tenure law that gave farming families a 20-year renewable lease on land used for growing annual crops like rice, and a 50-year lease for long-term crops. The law sparked a hot debate in the National Assembly, where assemblymen from the sparsely settled south wanted tenure without a time limit so they could improve their holdings. Assemblymen from the crowded north wanted shorter term limits so they could reshuffle their holdings after five to ten years.

Another major economic reform strove to create a graduated pay scale for Vietnam's 3.2 million civil servants, including teachers and health workers. Under the old, egalitarian wage scale, all government workers received very low salaries that were supplemented by allowances and benefits. Under the new system, benefits would be cut, but basic pay would rise according to a worker's skills and responsibilities. However, the cost of implementing the new system could threaten the country with bankruptcy.

With the economy already rising, inflation and the budget deficit down, and foreign trade almost in balance, Vietnam seemed poised for rapid economic takeoff after years of war, Communist mismanagement, and a U.S. trade embargo aimed at forcing Vietnam to provide a full accounting for U.S. servicemen missing in action. In July, President Clinton relaxed U.S. opposition to loans to Vietnam by the IMF after it became apparent that the other nations in the IMF might override U.S. objections anyway. Clinton's action opened the way to large-scale aid by the World Bank and the Asian Development Bank.

Those institutions planned to provide capital to rebuild the dilapidated transportation, telecommunications, and electric-power systems, which was expected to attract a greater flow of private investment. But Vietnam still had serious problems that could impede this progress—including government corruption, political repression, a shaky legal system, and rapid population growth.

Foreign Relations. President Clinton's decision to relax U.S. opposition to IMF loans to Vietnam was politically difficult for the president, because the families of missing U.S. servicemen had a powerful lobby that opposed more-open relations with Vietnam. Also, a document had surfaced earlier purporting to show that Hanoi lied to the United States in 1972 about how many U.S. prisoners it was holding. The document was proven to be false, but President Clinton did not end the trade embargo, even though a growing number of U.S. firms were opening offices in Vietnam.

By contrast, the EC signed a new accord with Vietnam that raised its relations to the same level as with Thailand. Hanoi's relations with China remained cool despite a visit by Chinese Premier Li Peng in December 1992.

PETER A. POOLE
Author, "Eight Presidents and Indochina"

VIRGINIA

A gubernatorial election highlighted 1993 events in Virginia.

Politics. In a sharp rebuke to 12 years of Democratic rule, Virginia voters in 1993 overwhelmingly elected George F. Allen as their next governor. Allen, who was born on March 8, 1952, is a Republican who had served in the state and federal legislatures for a decade. He is the son of George Allen, a former professional-football coach. Allen not only won the November election by a stunning 17 percentage points over Democrat Mary Sue Terry, a two-term state attorney general, but he came back from a 20-point deficit in early polls.

Allen's long coattails carried Republican James S. Gilmore III into the office of state attorney general and helped Republicans pick up six seats in the state's House of Delegates, bringing the GOP to near parity with the Democrats. Lt. Gov. Donald S. Beyer, Jr., a Democrat, retained his post, but only after a bitter and hard-fought campaign against Michael P. Farris, a Republican newcomer. Farris heads a nationwide home-schooling movement and was credited with bringing thousands of conservative Christians to the polls.

In June, Gov. L. Douglas Wilder, who was prohibited by law from seeking reelection, announced that he would run for the U.S. Senate in 1994. Earlier a federal grand jury had refused to indict Sen. Charles Robb, Wilder's probable opponent for the Democratic senatorial nomination, on charges that he had conspired with top aides to discredit Wilder by releasing a secretly taped telephone conversation.

Legislature. The biggest issue before the state's General Assembly in 1993 was gun control—a measure restricting handgun purchases to one per month per person. The restriction, which was passed into law, was propelled by a murder rate in the state's capital, Richmond, that was among the top five in the United States. The General Assembly also passed bills requiring proof of residency before a person could receive a driver's license and strengthening regulations for private day-care centers. For what may be the last time, the Virginia legislature again rejected a requirement that the parents of an unmarried girl under the age of 16 must be notified before she can seek an abortion. The governor-elect favors the passage of such a law.

Courts. In a closely watched court case, the state proposed to create an alternative military-training program for women at Mary Baldwin College, rather than allow women to enter Virginia Military Institute (VMI) in Lexington. In May the U.S. Supreme Court refused to review the constitutionality of the VMI's all-male admissions policy.

VIRGINIA • Information Highlights

Area: 40,767 sq mi (105 586 km²).

Population (July 1, 1992 est.): 6,377,000.

Chief Cities (1990 census): Richmond, the capital, 203,056; Virginia Beach, 393,069; Norfolk, 261,229; Newport News, 170,045; Chesapeake, 151,976.

Government (1993): *Chief Officers*—governor, L. Douglas Wilder (D); lt. gov., Donald S. Beyer, Jr. (D). *General Assembly*—Senate, 40 members; House of Delegates, 100 members.

State Finances (fiscal year 1991): *Revenue*, $14,523,000,000; *expenditure*, $13,352,000,000.

Personal Income (1992): $135,003,000,000; per capita, $21,170.

Labor Force (August 1993): *Civilian labor force*, 3,330,700; *unemployed*, 183,400 (5.5% of total force).

Education: *Enrollment* (fall 1991)—public elementary schools, 741,005; public secondary, 275,199; colleges and universities, 356,325. *Public school expenditures* (1990-91), $4,891,212,000.

George Allen, a former state legislator and member of the U.S. House of Representatives, and his 5-year-old daughter Tyler enjoy his victory in Virginia's 1993 gubernatorial race. The 41-year-old son of a former football coach would be the first Republican in 12 years to hold the office.

As the result of a June ruling by the U.S. Supreme Court, federal pensioners who claimed they are owed almost $500 million in back taxes should get a full court hearing on whether the state should repay them. The case was watched ardently by many Virginians.

Economy and the Weather. With its large number of military installations, Virginia was one of the states hardest hit by the nationwide move to close and realign military bases. More than 15,000 civilian and military jobs were expected to be lost, with Virginia sustaining close to one in every four civilian-job losses. Virginians were clobbered economically by the worst tornadoes and drought in years. The hottest summer since 1900, together with the drought, helped bring the state its second-driest year on record. Farmers' losses on the state's three major crops—corn, soybeans, and peanuts—were expected to top $90 million. Two twisters ripped through the Petersburg area in August, causing $11 million in damage and killing four persons.

ED NEWLAND
"Richmond Times-Dispatch"

WASHINGTON

Tough economic times and higher state spending in Washington in 1993 triggered a tax revolt that resulted in the passage of Initiative 601, which ties spending increases to inflation and population growth. But Washington voters turned down a companion measure, Initiative 602, which would have repealed some taxes.

Government. In local elections, Seattle Mayor Norm Rice won a second term, but incumbent mayors were defeated in Tacoma, Everett, and Spokane. State voters approved a measure to sentence criminals to life in prison after three serious offenses. Accomplishments of the 1993 legislature included a health-care-reform plan designed to provide universal care and control costs, and new legal protection against malicious harassment of homosexuals and women.

Economy. Continuing problems in the airline industry caused a second year of job losses at the Boeing Company; the company's state employment dropped from 98,325 to about 89,000.

While manufacturing declined, agriculture gained: The value of the state's top cash crop, apples, approached $1 billion. Other key crops were milk, cattle, wheat, and potatoes.

In November leaders from the United States, China, Japan, and other nations in the Asia-Pacific Economic Cooperation (APEC) met in Seattle to discuss trade issues.

Timber Dispute. Required to act by a federal-court order, U.S. President Bill Clinton called for significant reductions in the amount of logging allowed in national forests. He also proposed the expenditure of $1.2 billion over five years to retrain timber workers in Washington, Oregon, and northern California. (*See also* ENVIRONMENT/SPECIAL REPORT, page 224.)

Crime. Westley Allan Dodd, 31, who refused to appeal his death sentence for the 1989 sex-related killings of three young boys in Vancouver, WA, became the first person executed in Washington since 1963 and the first hanged in the United States since 1965. Dodd chose hanging over the alternative, lethal injection. Joseph Meling, 31, of Tumwater was sentenced to life in federal prison for killing two strangers by placing cyanide-filled capsules in Sudafed cold-remedy packages in stores. Prosecutors said Meling's intended victim was his wife, who survived. Paul Keller, 27, of Everett, was sentenced to 75 years in prison after he admitted setting more than 70 fires in the Seattle-Everett area.

A Pierce county couple's claim of finding a syringe in a can of Diet Pepsi triggered a rash of more than 50 similar reports in 23 states. Federal officials said none of the cases was confirmed, and many were prosecuted as false reports. The scare cost Pepsi $35 million.

Disasters. Six persons were killed and power was cut to 500,000 western Washington homes and businesses in a January 20 storm carrying winds up to 90 mph (145 km/h). Five railroad workers were killed in a head-on collision of two freight trains near Kelso on November 11.

An outbreak of food poisoning from *E. coli* bacteria linked to undercooked hamburgers at Jack in the Box restaurants caused the illness of 500 state residents and the deaths of three children.

Sports. The University of Washington's football program received major sanctions—including a two-year bowl-game ban and one-year loss of television revenue—when a Pac-10 conference investigation showed violations of NCAA recruiting guidelines and other rules. Don James, Husky coach for 18 years, retired when the sanctions were announced.

JACK BROOM
"The Seattle Times"

WASHINGTON • Information Highlights

Area: 68,139 sq mi (176 479 km²).

Population (July 1, 1992 est.): 5,136,000.

Chief Cities (1990 census): Olympia, the capital, 33,840; Seattle, 516,259; Spokane, 177,196; Tacoma, 176,664.

Government (1993): *Chief Officers*—Governor, Mike Lowry (D); lt. gov., Joel Pritchard (R). *Legislature*—Senate, 49 members; House of Representatives, 98 members.

State Finances (fiscal year 1991): *Revenue,* $16,394,000,000; *expenditure,* $15,666,000,000.

Personal Income (1992): $108,301,000,000; per capita, $21,088.

Labor Force (August 1993): *Civilian labor force,* 2,610,900; *unemployed,* 216,400 (8.3% of total force).

Education: *Enrollment* (fall 1991)—public elementary schools, 632,781; public secondary, 236,546; colleges and universities, 274,760. *Public school expenditures* (1990-91), $3,906,529,000.

WASHINGTON, DC

The year 1993 was one of celebration and demonstration in the nation's capital, as large crowds gathered to inaugurate a president, commemorate a civil-rights leader, and celebrate gay pride. The city continued to battle record-setting crime and violence, and supporters of statehood lost their bid in November.

Celebrations and Demonstrations. William Jefferson Clinton was sworn in as the 42d president of the United States in a ceremony January 20 on the West Front of the Capitol. The ceremony, witnessed by hundreds of thousands of onlookers, was the highlight of two weeks of pomp and partying. The huge crowd on the Mall lined the streets to witness the event and wave to the nation's young president as he and his wife, Hillary Rodham Clinton, walked the inaugural parade route. Thousands more attended two weeks of parties and events staged throughout Washington to celebrate the event.

A large crowd gathered in April to march for gay pride and gay rights, urging passage of antidiscrimination measures. Though event organizers claimed the event drew more than 1 million people, Park Police estimates of more than 300,000 still made the march one of the largest in Washington history.

In August a demonstration to commemorate the 30th anniversary of the civil-rights march on Washington drew about 75,000 people to the Lincoln Memorial, the site of Rev. Martin Luther King's famous 1963 "I Have A Dream" speech. King's widow, Coretta Scott King, led a group of speakers which included civil-rights leader Jesse L. Jackson; New York Mayor David N. Dinkins; National Association for the Advancement of Colored People (NAACP) executive director Benjamin Hooks; and Rosa Parks, who has become a symbol of the civil-rights movement.

Crime. Washington suffered through another record-setting year for murders and juvenile homicides. The community was battered by a series of violent robberies targeting Asian merchants, and the September shooting death of a 4-year-old girl, Launice Smith. Smith's death in particular—she was hit by a stray bullet while watching a football game with her mother in a city schoolyard—enraged already-frustrated residents. In October an exasperated Mayor Sharon Pratt Kelly asked President Clinton for the authority to call in the National Guard to help combat the city's worst year of crime. The president denied her request, but referred the matter to Congress. Late in the year, Kelly unveiled a plan to fight crime which included stiffer penalties for gun possession and the recommendation that legislation be enacted to lower the age at which a juvenile can be prosecuted in adult court.

Government. The City Council was stunned by the May suicide of its chairman, John A. Wil-

© Paul Hosefros/NYT Pictures

In October 1993, Washington Mayor Sharon Pratt Kelly—with Police Chief Fred Thomas at her side—asked for authority to call up the National Guard to help combat crime in the U.S. capital.

son, 49, one of the most volatile yet well-respected members of the city government. Wilson, who had battled depression for several months before his death, was said to have been struggling to reach a decision on whether to run for mayor or retire from politics. A fiercely committed and outspoken member of the council, he was known for his committment to the poor and his pleas for fiscal conservatism. He was a frequent, and very vocal, critic of the handling of the city's budget problems. Wilson had won his first term on the council in 1974. In a special September election, former council member David Clarke succeeded Wilson as chairman.

In November the U.S. House of Representatives, by a vote of 277-153, defeated a bill that would have made Washington, DC, the nation's 51st state. The bill's supporters, including Eleanor Holmes Norton—the district's nonvoting congressional delegate—declared it was a victory simply to get the issue to a vote, and vowed to continue their fight for statehood.

Other. The city's sports scene took a blow when popular Washington Redskins head coach Joe Gibbs abruptly retired after 12 enormously successful years with the team. He had led the Redskins to three Super Bowl championships and eight play-off appearances....The U.S. Holocaust Memorial Museum was dedicated in April (*see* Religion/Special Report, page 456)....National Weather Service warnings urged District of Columbia residents to stay inside during a record-setting heat wave that engulfed the area in July. Thirteen straight days of stifling temperatures and high humidity slowed business and loosened ties throughout the city....On Veteran's Day, November 11, the Vietnam Women's Memorial was dedicated by Vice-President Al Gore to honor the 11,500 women who served in the Vietnam war, and the 265,000 women in the military during that era.

Robert Kaplow, *Freelance Writer*

WEST VIRGINIA

West Virginia's economic difficulties of 1992 blended imperceptibly into 1993 as executive and legislative leaders still faced many of the same problems. Solutions remained elusive and hard to come by.

State Budget. Early in January, Gov. Gaston Caperton announced an all-too-familiar cutback for all state spending agencies—1.5% for higher education, 5% for other agencies. The legislature came up with $100 million in new taxes and $92 million in increases in old ones, but weary taxpayers faced January 1994 with the knowledge that a long-delayed reappraisal of property values would bring even higher tax bills.

Legislature. The legislature enacted a mandatory seat-belt law—after failing to do so for seven straight years; gave teachers in higher education a raise of $5,000 over a three-year period; passed a tough water-quality law aimed at reducing mine drainage and other industrial pollutants in rivers and streams; added 5 cents to the gasoline tax and 25 cents per ton to coal-extraction levies; and approved sweeping workers-compensation reform. But both parties agreed that some of the issues they had seen in January 1993 as their major challenges remained unsolved at the session's end. These included matching funding for Medicaid, major governmental reorganization, and a solution to the problem of funding for school-building construction.

A special legislative session produced no solutions to a ten-item agenda, then a second did hammer out three or four new laws. But as much movement as there was forward, there was just as much backward. The governor signed a health bill into law and then challenged the constitutionality of a section barring the use of its funds for abortions. In another instance, a law was passed which seemed to solve the school-construction bond problem, but the state Supreme Court declared it invalid in July. Another special session of the legislature in October addressed the school-construction bond issue exclusively and authorized the setting aside of a portion of the state's sales tax to finance the sale of bonds. On December 13, however, the state Supreme Court declared this approach unconstitutional, too. Governor Caperton immediately began work on a new proposal, coupling the matter with an anticrime bill as his major legislative targets for 1994.

Economy and Weather. A bituminous coal strike—though much less violent and widespread than earlier ones—began in May and continued until an agreement was signed in mid-December. The strike contributed to the announcement in October that the state had the nation's third-highest percentage of citizens under the poverty level—more than 22%. Unemployment in the state remained near the double-digit figure.

The worst blizzard in 15 years in March and a forced drainage of some of the popular recre-

---

WEST VIRGINIA • Information Highlights

Area: 24,232 sq mi (62 760 km²).
Population (July 1, 1992 est.): 1,812,000.
Chief Cities (1990 census): Charleston, the capital, 57,287; Huntington, 54,844; Wheeling, 34,882.
Government (1993): *Chief Officers—*governor, Gaston Caperton (D); secy. of state, Ken Hechler (D). *Legislature—*Senate, 34 members; House of Delegates, 100 members.
State Finances (fiscal year 1991): *Revenue,* $4,896,000,000; *expenditure,* $4,741,000,000.
Personal Income (1992): $27,784,000,000; per capita, $15,332.
Labor Force (August 1993): *Civilian labor force,* 770,000; *unemployed,* 74,100 (9.6% of total force).
Education: *Enrollment* (fall 1991)—public elementary schools, 221,545; public secondary, 98,704; colleges and universities, 88,602. *Public school expenditures* (1990-91), $1,473,744,000.

ational lakes at the height of a midsummer heat wave were among weather highlights.

Corruption. The dreary procession of corruption in high places found a former head of the state lottery commission convicted of fraud and advertising bid-rigging. Meanwhile, former Republican Gov. Arch A. Moore, Jr., who had been jailed in 1990 following his guilty plea to charges of extortion and election fraud, was released from federal prison in April. He served the last four months of his sentence at home.

DONOVAN H. BOND
West Virginia University

WISCONSIN

A deadly outbreak of illness caused by impure water and another initiative on welfare reform highlighted 1993 in Wisconsin.

Water Illness. The water disease that devastated Milwaukee in 1993 started in the spring with a few schoolchildren complaining of nausea and diarrhea and staying home. By the time it ended, more than 400,000 Milwaukeeans fell ill and six persons had died. The cause of the problem was the little-known parasite *cryptosporidium,* which had infiltrated the city's water supply. It was the world's largest reported outbreak of cryptosporidiosis. The microscopic parasite had gotten into the city's Howard Avenue Purification Plant, resisting chemical disinfectants. Investigators said that insufficient amounts of a substitute chemical early in the water-treatment process likely allowed heavy concentrations of the parasite to reach the water plant's sand filters.

During the crisis, the city urged residents not to drink water out of the tap. Instead they were to boil it or use bottled water. Many Milwaukeeans already were infected, however, and those most vulnerable were the most affected. Of those who died, five were AIDS patients unable to fight off another infection. Beyond that, it was estimated that the outbreak cost the

In Fond du Lac, WI, in 1993, Leslie C. Robins (extreme left), a 30-year-old English teacher, and his fiancée, Colleen De Vries (right), a 24-year-old hospital nurse, won a $111 million lottery jackpot.

© Todd Rosenberg/Sygma

city more than $54 million—much of it in lost wages and productivity, but also in hospitalization and treatment costs and water-utility testing and expenses.

The crisis ended within two months, but the fears remained. In October *cryptosporidium* was found in the city's other purification plant, but officials said that the water supply was safe and a boil advisory was not needed. Nevertheless, an investigation by *The Milwaukee Journal* found that federal agencies had known of the parasite's threat as early as 1974 but had refused repeatedly to recommend tests for it. The Environmental Protection Agency (EPA) was not expected to complete writing rules to cover testing for *cryptosporidium* until 1994. In November, however, Wisconsin began a two-year search of rivers and lakes for the parasite and other microorganisms.

Legislative Action. In another successful move to curb welfare dependency, Gov. Tommy Thompson (R) pushed a "work, not welfare" plan through the legislature, claiming it would make Wisconsin the first state to put a time limit on welfare benefits. The plan, which would require those receiving Aid to Families With Dependent Children (AFDC) payments to sign a pledge to work for their benefits, was to be implemented in two counties on an experimental basis. A few other states have somewhat similar plans, but this was believed to be the first that sets a limit on cash benefits. Federal food-stamp and other programs would continue under the plan. For their part, Democrats added far-reaching proposals that would end the welfare system by 1999.

In the only other major accomplishment of the fall session, legislators approved an omnibus crime bill to cover carjacking, drive-by shootings, and terrorism, as well as increased penalties for drug possession and gang-related crimes. With strong lobbying from the National Rifle Association (NRA), legislators refused to act on a bill to restrict the sale of snub-nosed handguns. The legislature postponed action on other issues, including health-care reform, until the spring session.

Economy. The economic outlook for the state remained modestly upbeat, with continued growth expected over the next three years. Total employment growth for 1993 was expected to be 2%, slightly better than the national average. Jobs continued to be created in manufacturing, with a .9% increase. Most of the gain came in durable goods, especially in electrical machinery. Construction employment registered an 11.4% gain. Total personal income in the state grew by an average of 5.3% and nonfarm proprietors' income was expected to rise by 9.6%.

U.S. House Election. In a special May election for the U.S. House of Representatives seat vacated when Les Aspin joined President Bill Clinton's Cabinet, state Rep. Peter W. Barca (D) defeated Mark W. Neumann, a Republican homebuilder. In an extremely tight race that was dominated by economic issues, Barca won by less than 1,000 votes.

PAUL SALSINI
"The Milwaukee Journal"

WISCONSIN • Information Highlights

Area: 56,153 sq mi (145 436 km²).

Population (July 1, 1992 est.): 5,007,000.

Chief Cities (1990 census): Madison, the capital, 191,262; Milwaukee, 628,088; Green Bay, 96,466.

Government (1993): *Chief Officers*—governor, Tommy G. Thompson (R); lt. gov., Scott McCallum (R). *Legislature*—Senate, 33 members; Assembly, 99 members.

State Finances (fiscal year 1991): *Revenue*, $14,137,000,000; *expenditure*, $12,448,000,000.

Personal Income (1992): $95,936,000,000; per capita, $19,162.

Labor Force (August 1993): *Civilian labor force*, 2,685,500; *unemployed*, 126,200 (4.7% of total force).

Education: *Enrollment* (fall 1991)—public elementary schools, 579,863; public secondary, 234,808; colleges and universities, 308,986. *Public school expenditures* (1990-91), $4,292,434,000.

WOMEN

Women continued to make gains in 1993 in political and other arenas in the United States and around the world.

United States. Following his inauguration, U.S. President Bill Clinton kept a campaign promise to name a cabinet that looks more like the United States. He appointed a record number of women and minorities to the cabinet and to other high-level advisory posts. Among new women cabinet members were Attorney General Janet Reno, Health and Human Services Secretary Donna Shalala, Energy Secretary Hazel O'Leary, Council of Economic Advisers chair Laura D'Andrea Tyson, and UN Ambassador Madeleine Albright. Others gained major sub-cabinet positions, like Environmental Protection Agency Director Carol Browner and Alice Rivlin, deputy director of the Office of Management and Budget.

Clinton also named the second woman ever to sit on the U.S. Supreme Court—Ruth Bader Ginsburg, who said her appointment signaled an end to token appointments of women, and that she expects three, four, or more women to serve on the Supreme Court in her lifetime. (*See also* BIOGRAPHY.)

The year saw a record number of women in other political spheres as well, including the U.S. Congress and state offices nationwide (*see* SPECIAL REPORT).

Also in 1993, women achieved a hard-fought guarantee that they will not lose their jobs when they take leave for family reasons, including maternity leave. Clinton signed into law the Family and Medical Leave Act, which guarantees workers—both men and women—time off to care for a new child or elderly parent.

In other issues affecting women and their place in U.S. society, a November Supreme Court decision made sexual harassment easier to prove and the U.S. Navy continued to deal with the Tailhook scandal. The latter had raised the public's consciousness about sexual harassment in the military and had ended the careers of a number of military officials. A Pentagon report in April 1993 accused 140 fliers of indecent exposure, assault, and lying under oath about the rowdy convention at a Las Vegas hotel in which women were fondled and pinched by male Navy and Marine aviators. The problems of sexual harassment also hit home in the U.S. Senate. Sen. Robert Packwood (R-OR) remained under a cloud due to allegations that he had made unwanted advances to women who worked on his staff and others over a 20-year period.

The U.S. Census Bureau reported major break-throughs in the labor market for women. It said the number of women in executive, administrative, and managerial job categories climbed 95% to nearly 6.2 million between 1980 and 1990. Men, however, continued to dominate U.S. management ranks. Of the 14.6 million workers in those positions in 1990, nearly 58% were men, the bureau said.

A Labor Department report said women were less likely than men to lose their jobs during a recession. Men hold a disproportionate share of jobs in industries like construction that are affected by downturns in the economy, while the concentration of women workers tends to be higher in the more stable service and government sectors of the economy, the report said.

International. In Canada the governing Progressive Conservative Party named Defense Minister Kim Campbell as its leader; she thus became the first woman to serve as Canadian prime minister. Campbell was defeated in October elections, however, by Jean Chrétien. Tansu Ciller, a 47-year-old economist who had been in politics only three years, was elected to be Turkey's first woman prime minister. Women also made political gains in legislative elections in Jordan and Morocco. And in Japan, Takako Doi, a liberal member of the Socialist Party, was named speaker of the house. Japan also saw a modern, Western-educated woman—Masako Owada, a 29-year-old foreign-service official who holds degrees from Harvard and Oxford—become the new wife of Crown Prince Naruhito. (*See* BIOGRAPHY).

JUDI HASSON
"USA Today"

Women's Growing Political Clout

Women politicians gained new power in the U.S. Congress in 1993. As their presence grew, they increasingly were able to work to achieve their own agendas while retaining the respect and support of their colleagues. And at the White House, first lady Hillary Rodham Clinton made history as an unprecedentedly influential and involved U.S. president's wife.

Hillary Rodham Clinton. It was Hillary Rodham Clinton, the wife of President Bill Clinton, who provided the biggest symbol of change for women in Washington in 1993. Named to head the president's task force on health reform, she was a tough advocate and trailblazer for the president's major domestic-policy initiative. As head of the task force, she worked for months with more than 500 health-policy experts to design a proposal to overhaul the health-care system and provide universal coverage to Americans. Clinton proved an effective lobbyist in Congress as well. With her historic appearance to campaign for health-care reform, she became only the third first lady to testify before Congress (the others were Eleanor Roosevelt and Rosalynn Carter).

Women members of the 103d U.S. Congress, right, gathered on the steps of the Capitol, April 27, 1993. As a result of the 1992 elections, a record number of women were serving in both houses of the U.S. legislative branch.

© Jeffrey Markowitz/Sygma

U.S. House and Senate. Record numbers of women took seats in both the U.S. House and Senate, and these new lawmakers quickly staked out their territory, forcing some significant changes almost immediately. In the House, 24 new women were sworn into office in 1993, bringing the total to 48—including nonvoting District of Columbia delegate Eleanor Holmes Norton. And in the Senate, four new Democratic women were sworn into office, joining incumbents Sen. Barbara Mikulski (D-MD) and Sen. Nancy Kassebaum (R-KS).

Republican Kay Bailey Hutchison of Texas was elected to the Senate in June, bringing the number of women senators to seven. Hutchison, the first woman elected to the U.S. Senate from Texas, also became the first Texas senator to be indicted while in office. An Austin grand jury accused her of abusing her former office of state treasurer by using state resources for her Senate campaign. The indictment later was dropped. Chosen by a special election to fill the seat vacated by Lloyd Bentsen, who was named treasury secretary, Hutchison planned to run for a full term in 1994.

Women lawmakers flexed their newly won political muscle throughout the year, often uniting in support of legalized abortion, health-care reform, and economic issues affecting not only their respective constituents, but women in general. They also brought their personal experiences to the issues. Rep. Carrie Meek (D-FL), the granddaughter of sharecroppers, described her experiences as a domestic in backing legislation to protect workers. Rep. Lynn Woolsey (D-CA) spoke of her life as a single mother on welfare when supporting a piece of legislation.

In the wake of President Clinton's reform proposal to overhaul the health-care-delivery system and provide coverage for every American, the Congressional Women's Caucus demanded better medical coverage in the plan for women and specific language guaranteeing abortion coverage. Complaining that women's health is short-changed in the proposal, they urged improvements in coverage for cancer detection and signaled that this would remain a key issue for them throughout the health-reform debate.

Two new women senators—Carol Moseley-Braun (D-IL) and Dianne Feinstein (D-CA)—became members of the Senate Judiciary Committee, the panel which had come under attack for being insensitive to women when Oklahoma University law professor Anita Hill accused Supreme Court nominee Clarence Thomas of sexual harassment in 1991. Moseley-Braun, the first African-American woman elected to the Senate, successfully challenged a routine proposal by Sen. Jesse Helms (R-NC) to renew a patent on the Confederate flag insignia for the United Daughters of the Confederacy. Threatening a filibuster, Moseley-Braun gave a dramatic speech on the Senate floor, directly challenging business as usual in the once male-dominated Senate. Her challenge prompted expressions about racism rarely heard in the Senate. The patent renewal was defeated.

In another sign of change, freshman Rep. Marjorie Margolies-Mezvinsky (D-PA) cast one of two deciding votes that gave President Clinton a victory on a major economic package, putting her own political career at risk by doing so.

State and Local Politics. A record 72 women held 22.2% of statewide elective executive offices in 1993. In five states—Colorado, Delaware, Indiana, Nevada, and Oregon—women held at least half of statewide elected positions. And, in another record figure, women made up one fifth (20.4%) of all state legislators. During 1993, every state (except Nebraska, which has a unicameral legislature) had at least one woman in its Senate and at least five women in its lower House.

In November 1993 elections, New Jersey's Democratic Gov. Jim Florio was defeated by Christine Todd Whitman in a narrow victory for Republicans. Whitman became the first woman ever to be elected New Jersey's governor. In Virginia, Democrat Mary Sue Terry was defeated by Republican candidate George F. Allen.

JUDI HASSON

WYOMING

Wyoming's news for 1993 focused on the legislature, economy, environment, and the sesquicentennial of the Oregon Trail. Former Wyoming Gov. and U.S. Sen. Milward Simpson (R), father of U.S. Sen. Alan Simpson, died in Cody on June 10, 1993.

Legislature. The state's compliance with a federal mandate to reapportion its legislative districts resulted in new members in more than half of the 60-member House and five new members in the 30-member Senate. Dominated by Republicans, the legislature nevertheless passed several bills dealing with issues underscored by Gov. Mike Sullivan (D) in his State of the State address, including a 1% increase in the state sales tax and bills dealing with worker's compensation, welfare reform, and child-support enforcement. The legislature also increased the classroom unit by $1,000, approving a school budget of $507 million for fiscal year 1994.

While the 1993 session displayed greater bipartisanship than the quarrelsome 1992 budget session, many legislators expressed disappointment that the 1993 session was unable to pass "good government" bills. Wyoming remained the only state without lobbyist disclosure laws. Anticipating a $160 million shortfall in revenues for funding state government and schools through 1994 and fiscal years 1995 and 1996, Governor Sullivan predicted that the 1994 budget session would be especially difficult. He continued to call for lessening the state's dependence on the mineral industry.

Economy. The state's troubled economy continued to be driven by the mineral industry, tourism, and agriculture. The mineral industry received good news when the 1993 legislature passed a bill giving the oil industry a tax break. The coal and trona industries were pleased that the legislature refused to extend a 1.5% severance tax on coal and trona that expired on January 1. The oil industry continued to decline, with sporadic fluctuations in rig counts. On the other hand, the coal industry—supported by a continuing demand for low-sulfur coal—remained strong. Wyoming likely would continue as the nation's leading coal producer. Strikes in the trona industry troubled that sector of the economy, but production and demand remained high.

Tourists continued to visit Grand Teton and Yellowstone national parks in record numbers, creating concern that growing numbers of visitors may overload the National Park Service's ability to handle so many people.

Problems in the agricultural sector included increases or threatened increases in grazing fees on public lands, predation losses—especially from coyotes, and impending reforms in management of rangelands. The sheep industry, the third-largest in the nation, was stung by congressional repeal of the 1954 Wool Act, phasing out subsidies for wool producers by 1997.

WYOMING • Information Highlights

Area: 97,809 sq mi (253 326 km²).

Population (July 1, 1992 est.): 466,000.

Chief Cities (1990 census): Cheyenne, the capital, 50,008; Casper, 46,742; Laramie, 26,687.

Government (1993): *Chief Officers*—governor, Michael J. Sullivan (D); secretary of state, Kathy Karpan (D). *Legislature*—Senate, 30 members; House of Representatives, 64 members.

State Finances (fiscal year 1991): *Revenue*, $1,979,000,000; *expenditure*, $1,813,000,000.

Personal Income (1992): $8,545,000,000; per capita, $18,330.

Labor Force (August 1993): *Civilian labor force*, 238,300; *unemployed*, 14,800 (6.2% of total force).

Education: *Enrollment* (fall 1991)—public elementary schools, 73,890; public secondary, 28,184; colleges and universities, 32,118. *Public school expenditures* (1990-91), $529,413,000.

Environment. Environmental issues focused on the bitter debate over government policies on grazing fees, timber harvesting, predator control, snowmobile use, federal roundups of wild horses, grizzly-bear protection, and the reintroduction of wolves into the Yellowstone ecosystem. Of special concern to environmental groups was a proposed gold mine to be operated by a Canadian firm near Cooke City, MT. It was feared that its proximity to Yellowstone Park could create an ecological disaster.

The 150th anniversary of the Oregon Trail was celebrated in the state with a variety of events.

ROBERT A. CAMPBELL
University of Wyoming

YUGOSLAVIA. *See* FEATURE ARTICLE, page 26.

YUKON

In the Yukon during 1993, heavy territorial and municipal tax increases and hydropower-rate hikes followed the shutdown of the territory's only two hard-rock mines. The mines at Faro—250 mi (402 km) north of Whitehorse and just north of Watson Lake—owned by Curragh Resources Inc. were closed down as a result of low lead and zinc prices on the world market. The economic spin-off from the closure of the two mines deepened the recession and brought unemployment to about 17%.

Politics. In early 1993 economic belt-tightening dictated territorial-government policy for the recently elected Yukon Party. The government introduced a wide range of tax increases over two years in such areas as personal income, general corporate, small business, gas, and tobacco. The minority government, elected in October 1992, barely survived a vote of confidence on the budget in June, when the speaker of the legislature broke an 8-8 tie vote in the 17-member

© George Hunter/Miller-Comstock

Low lead and zinc prices on the international market caused the closing of the mines at Faro, above, north of Whitehorse. The closure further dampened Yukon's depressed economy.

House. A defeat on a money bill would have meant an immediate general election. The government also instituted spending cutbacks in the civil service to achieve a balanced budget, the only government in Canada to do so.

In Canada's October federal election, Yukon returned Audrey McLaughlin, leader of the New Democratic Party, to the House of Commons.

Indian Land Claims. The signing of the final umbrella agreement covering all 14 First Nations Indian bands, agreement of individual band claims, and self-government agreements with four of those bands awaited final approval by the Canadian Parliament to end more than two decades of negotiations. The ten other First

Nations bands were in the process of completing their individual agreements, most of which were expected to be signed late in 1993 and in 1994. The overall agreement provides aboriginal ownership of more than 15,830 sq mi (41 000 km²) or 8.6% of the Yukon's total landmass. It also provides $280 million in cash from Ottawa over 15 years and guarantees participation in the management of lands, water, resources, fish, and wildlife.

DON SAWATSKY
Freelance Writer, Whitehorse

ZAIRE

The continuing struggle for power between Zaire's President Mobutu Sese Seko and the transitional parliament, the High Council of the Republic (HCR), resulted in endemic violence and prevented any solution to the nation's catastrophic economic problems during 1993. Mobutu clung to power despite outside pressure, an economy in tatters, and concerted internal opposition. His position was secured by his control of the central bank and, most importantly, continued loyalty from most of the army.

Domestic Affairs. In December 1992 the National Conference—created to pave the way for elections targeted for August 1993—gave way to the HCR. Étienne Tshisekedi was chosen prime minister. According to previous agreements, Mobutu was required to relinquish most of his authority to the new prime minister and the HCR. He refused, creating a stalemate which prevented concrete actions to redress many problems of potentially the richest African state. Confronted with an inflation rate of roughly 6,000%, Mobutu ordered the central bank—against the opposition of the HCR—to issue a new 5-million-zaire (roughly U.S.$2) note. However, most businesses would not accept it.

The impasse flared into violence when soldiers were paid with the new currency. There

Fighting broke out in Zaire early in 1993 after President Mobutu Sese Seko paid soldiers in new banknotes. Issued in denominations of 5 million zaires, they were worth about U.S.$2 each.

© Isopress/Sipa

YUKON • Information Highlights

Area: 186,660 sq mi (483 450 km²).
Population (June 1993): 29,000.
Chief City (1991 census): Whitehorse, the capital, 17,925.
Government (1993): *Chief Officers*—commissioner, J. Kenneth McKinnon; premier, John Ostashek (Yukon Party). *Legislature*—17-member Legislative Assembly.
Public Finance (1993-94 fiscal year budget est.): *Revenues,* $483,000,000; *expenditures,* $483,000,000.
Personal Income (average weekly earnings, June 1993): $755.87.
Education (1993-94): *Enrollment*—elementary and secondary schools, 5,970 pupils; postsecondary—community colleges, 290.
(All monetary figures are in Canadian dollars.)

French troops, left, were sent to Zaire to help evacuate its nationals after several Europeans, including France's ambassador to Zaire, were killed as result of fighting between mutinous troops and those loyal to President Mobutu.

© Reuters/Bettmann

were short-lived mutinies at Kisangani and Lisala. Soldiers in Kinshasa began looting on January 28 and clashed with Mobutu's elite presidential guard for three days. The death toll was estimated at 1,000 persons, including the French ambassador. French paratroops crossed the river from the Congo to protect French nationals and Belgian commandos threatened to intervene.

In the wake of the riots, Mobutu dismissed Tshisekedi as prime minister and troops loyal to Mobutu forced merchants to accept the new currency. Tshisekedi and the HCR—with French, Belgian, and U.S. support—disputed Mobutu's right to remove him. Soldiers loyal to Mobutu surrounded the legislative meeting on February 24 and temporarily forced its capitulation. HCR members were not allowed to use the legislative buildings until late July. Mobutu gained the support of dissident soldiers by announcing in March that they would be paid in banknotes other than the worthless currency.

In March a conference convened by Mobutu sanctioned the appointment of Faustin Birindwa as prime minister. Although this arrangement was not recognized by any major powers, Birindwa formed a government and in May announced that a new constitution would be drafted, a referendum held in July, and a general election in October. Continual opposition from Tshisekedi and the HCR upset this timetable. A new opposition coalition party, the Democratic Force of the Congo (FDC), announced that no further negotiation would be held with Mobutu and Birindwa's government. Mobutu rescheduled the referendum to October and general elections to December.

Economy. The economy continued to unravel due to mass urban unemployment, civil servants going unpaid, and endemic violence hampering the movement of goods. Mineral exports continued to decline. The European Community, France, Belgium, and the United States had cut off economic aid in 1992 and were considering freezing Zaire's assets. The United Nations (UN) Human Rights Commission condemned Zaire for violations in March, but with little visible effect. Ethnic riots erupted in the Shaba and Kivu provinces, as some 3,000 persons were killed and at least 250,000 more displaced. Mobutu's troops were accused of murdering hundreds of Rwandan refugees.

HARRY A. GAILEY, *San Jose State University*

ZAIRE • Information Highlights

Official Name: Republic of Zaire.
Location: Central equatorial Africa.
Area: 905,564 sq mi (2 345 410 km²).
Population (mid-1993 est.): 41,200,000.
Chief City (1987 est.): Kinshasa, the capital, 2,500,000.
Government: *Head of state*, Mobutu Sese Seko, president (took office 1965). *Head of government*, Faustin Birindwa, prime minister (appointed March 1993). *Legislature* (unicameral)—High Council of the Republic (transitional).
Monetary Unit: Zaire (950,000 zaires equal U.S.$1, third quarter, 1992).
Foreign Trade (1991 U.S.$): *Imports*, $872,000,000; *exports*, $886,000,000.

ZIMBABWE

Although Zimbabwe began to recover from a record drought in 1993, the country remained plagued by high inflation, widespread unemployment, and escalating costs for basic commodities. Many blamed these economic woes on the Economic Structural Adjustment Program (ESAP) introduced by the government in 1990. The government delayed its intentions to reform the bureaucracy and public enterprises.

New Opposition. On March 28 the country's two main opposition groups—the Forum for Democratic Reform and the Open Forum—merged into the Forum Party of Zimbabwe with

ZIMBABWE • Information Highlights

Official Name: Republic of Zimbabwe.
Location: Southern Africa.
Area: 150,803 sq mi (390 580 km²).
Population (mid-1993 est.): 10,700,000.
Chief Cities (1983 est.): Harare (formerly Salisbury), the capital, 681,000; Bulawayo, 429,000; Chitungwiza, 202,000.
Government: *Head of state and government*, Robert Mugabe, executive president (sworn in Dec. 31, 1987). *Legislature*—unicameral Parliament.
Monetary Unit: Zimbabwe dollar (6.674 Z dollars equal U.S.$1, July 1993).
Economic Index (1992): *Industrial Production* (1980 = 100), 127.
Foreign Trade (1991 U.S.$): *Imports,* $1,600,000,000; *exports,* $1,800,000,000.

support from church leaders, intellectuals, businesspeople, and white liberal politicians. Its leader, former Chief Justice Enoch Dumbutshena, said that the Forum Party sought to replace the government because it "condones violence and intimidation" and because of economic chaos. He advocated a market economy to increase investment and jobs, and attacked the government's proposed land appropriation.

Whether or not this opposition had the strength to become a threat to the ruling party was unclear, but the ruling Zimbabwe African National Union-Patriotic Front (ZANU-PF) increased publicity for its drought-relief efforts and for its role in bringing peace to Mozambique—in order to counter opposition groups. The government was confident that it could overcome lost urban support with its strength in the populous rural areas gained through its drought-relief efforts and land-redistribution policies. This strong rural support led to speculation that ZANU-PF might call an election before the 1995 deadline.

Land Acquisition Act of 1993. On April 30 the government announced plans to buy 70 large commercial farms with a total area of 470,000 acres (190 000 ha) as the beginning of a plan to redistribute 12.4 million acres (5 million ha) to black farmers. This move unsettled the country's large-scale white commercial farmers, since the target represented half of their holdings. The bill permitted the government to nationalize land at prices it set and prevented landowners from suing the government for better prices. In July, President Robert Mugabe emphasized that the government would not accept Supreme Court decisions which blocked its powers to seize land nor rulings which enabled owners to sue due to unfair compensation. Many commercial farmers nonetheless were prepared to fight the new policy in court because they believed it violated the Zimbabwean constitution.

President Mugabe was critical of foreign objections to his plan to nationalize the white-owned farms. In August he argued: "How can these countries who have stolen land from the Red Indians, the Aborigines, and the Eskimos dare to tell us what to do with our land?" Some observers saw the policy as an effort to deflect attention from Zimbabwe's serious economic problems. General elections had to be held by 1995, and with growing dissatisfaction with government corruption and Zimbabwe's economic policies, some observers thought that Mugabe was using the West as a scapegoat to gain popularity.

Defense Reforms. In May, Minister of Defense Moven Mahachi was quoted as saying that the Zimbabwean army and air force would be merged over five years. The move was designed to build a more mobile and efficient armed services, but would cause a substantial loss of jobs in the army.

The Economy. The economic-reform program launched in 1990 led to the decontrol of prices and greater access to foreign exchange, but inflation, estimated at more than 30%, and high interest rates continued. The country's budget deficit was more than 10% of the gross domestic product (GDP), one of the highest rates in the world, and estimates indicated that it might have soared to 14% before the end of the fiscal year. High government expenditures (55% of GDP) coupled with the budget deficit contributed to the high inflation. In September, Mugabe said that poor economic growth, high population growth, and the large number of school dropouts had sent unemployment to alarming levels. Mugabe said that only one third of the 300,000 people who annually left school to enter the job market found jobs in the formal sector.

The president's hope was that the program of economic structural adjustment ultimately would generate high levels of investment and an expansion of employment opportunities. However, after three years, ESAP generated heated controversy and Finance Minister Bernard Chidzero was blamed for many of the country's economic ills. The government anticipated that the prospects for ESAP would improve with the end of the devastating effects of the drought, which had cut agricultural production by 30% and reduced GDP by 8%.

Despite a record tobacco crop following the drought's end, falling prices for Zimbabwe's major export crop adversely affected commercial farmers and the country's balance of payments. Tobacco earned surprisingly low prices and some growers began plans to diversify.

In September there were demonstrations in Harare and other parts of the country over increases in the price of bread and flour. Demonstrators seized bread and flour stocks, looted and stoned stores, and attacked passing cars. In an ensuing boycott against bread-price hikes, protesters attacked shoppers who were seen carrying bread. Projected future currency devaluations and government retrenchment suggested that hardship would persist.

PATRICK O'MEARA
Indiana University

ZOOS AND ZOOLOGY

North America gained a new zoo in 1993: Cameron Park Zoo in Waco, TX, opened its gates in mid-July. Covering more than 50 acres (20.23 ha), it features Gibbon Island, with waterfalls and a viewing deck from which visitors can see acrobatic gibbons from Asia; and the African Treetops village, which overlooks giraffes, zebras, kudus, rhinos, and elephants.

The former Prospect Park Zoo in Brooklyn, NY, has been renovated into the Prospect Park Wildlife Conservation Center, which opened in October 1993. The center focuses on children and is the last branch to be completed in New York City's network of five wildlife centers, all operated by NYZS/The Wildlife Conservation Society. Its three major exhibits—The World of Animals, Animals in Our Lives, and Animal Lifestyles—are based on the Society's award-winning WIZE (Wildlife Inquiry through Zoo Education) program. A 2.5-acre (1.01-ha) Discovery Trail introduces youngsters to a prairie-dog town, a marsh, an Australian wallaby walkabout, and a woodland inhabited by red pandas and porcupines. Children can sketch animals and also learn about life on the farm.

Exhibits. In March, Moody Gardens in Galveston, TX, unveiled its Rainforest Pyramid. The 40,000-sq-ft (3 716-m^2), 10-story glass building is filled with freshwater fish, butterflies, and birds from the rain forests of Asia, Africa, and South America. An IMAX theater shows 3-D films immersing visitors in these habitats. Moody Gardens is a nonprofit center where disabled people receive animal- and plant-assisted therapy.

Another "jungle under glass" opened during the year at the Cleveland (OH) Metroparks Zoo. On the top floor, the South American River Basin highlights tapirs, capybaras, sloths, and tropical birds, while orangutans are the stars of the Asian Jungle. Reptiles and amphibians rule the lower level.

During the spring an extravaganza of new exhibits opened at Florida's Cypress Gardens and at several Sea World locations, all of which are operated by Anheuser-Busch. At Cypress Gardens more than 50 types of butterflies from around the world fly freely in Wings of Wonder, the Butterfly Conservatory. Orlando's Sea World of Florida unveiled "Manatees: The Last Generation?" A new circular theater and Bi-Vision™ show create a sense of swimming with these critically endangered marine mammals, of which perhaps as few as 2,000 remain in the wild in Florida. At San Diego's Sea World, the new Rocky Point Preserve features dolphins and sea otters; two of the sea otters originally were rescued from the site of the 1989 *Exxon Valdez* oil spill in Alaska. And Shark Encounter at Sea

Together with other rare and exotic wildlife from Asia and Africa, the orangutan (left) took up residence at Jungle Trails, a naturalized rainforest habitat which opened at the Cincinnati Zoo and Botanical Garden in July 1993.

Two Siberian tiger cubs, Khuntami and Nadirzda, were transported to Omaha's Henry Doorly Zoo in 1993 after their mother was killed by poachers in Siberia, Russia. The tiger population has been diminishing in recent years, and the Doorly Zoo was selected as the cubs' new home because of its special interest in the species.

© Henry Doorly Zoo, Omaha

World of Ohio, in Aurora, explains how overfishing and hunting for sport are decimating these important ocean predators.

Sea otters went on exhibit for the first time in the eastern United States in April 1993 at the Aquarium for Wildlife Conservation in Brooklyn, NY. The 300-ft (91.44-m)-long Sea Cliffs display replicates a rocky coast with habitats for harbor, fur, and gray seals; Pacific walruses; California sea lions; and a large colony of more than 100 black-footed penguins, as well as the sea otters.

With the opening of Jungle Trails on July 10, the Cincinnati (OH) Zoo and Botanical Garden became the first U.S. zoo to display the aye-aye, a bizarre-looking native of Madagascar and perhaps the world's most endangered primate. Jungle Trails also features bonobos (pygmy chimpanzees), shoebill storks, orangutans, and many birds.

The star of a new underground complex at the Bronx (NY) Zoo/Wildlife Conservation Park, the naked mole-rat, definitely falls into the category of "a face only a mother could love." Naked mole-rats are blind and have huge incisors strong enough to gnaw through concrete. Computer technology and video "mole-cams" give close-up views of this subterranean species.

After months of planning, the lowland gorillas and chimpanzees at the Oklahoma City Zoo made their Great EscApe on July 31 to new, spacious naturalistic habitats with waterfalls, rocks, termite mounds, and fallen trees for climbing. The Great EscApe includes a research and conservation center that allows zoo staff to monitor the animals' activities closely.

When visitors see the new marsh exhibit at the Greater Baton Rouge (LA) Zoo, they have no idea they are looking at more than a habitat for native wildlife. In reality, the marsh is a highly effective wastewater-treatment facility designed by Harold Moise of Simmons J. Barry and Associates in Baton Rouge. The artificial marsh will save the zoo more than $150,000 per year in sewer-use fees and is expected to pay for itself in just three years. Bacteria growing on an enormous bed of rocks and plants feed on organic matter in the wastewater, which then is oxygenated by aquatic plants and microorganisms. Remaining bacteria are destroyed by underwater ultraviolet lights, and the resulting contaminant-free water can be released into a nearby bayou, run back through the marsh, or used for anything but drinking water.

Endangered Species and New Discoveries. Two wild-born, orphaned Siberian tiger cubs were transferred from the Sikhote-Alin Biosphere Reserve in Russia to the Henry Doorly Zoo in Omaha, NE. The cubs' mother, a study animal being followed in a joint Russian-U.S. project to learn more about tigers and their habitat, was shot by poachers. Researchers reported that more than 20 tigers were poached during 1992 in the area. Because of the bleak Russian economy, antipoaching patrols have been cut by as much as 80%. Tiger skins can fetch 200,000 rubles, equal to four years' salary. Tigers are in serious trouble around the world, and Siberian tigers are thought to number only 300. The orphaned youngsters eventually could make an important genetic contribution to the Siberian Tiger Species Survival Program of the American Association of Zoological Parks and Aquariums, which seeks to breed the cats for possible future release into protected sites in the wild.

Deep in the lush remote forests of Vietnam, a new mammal species was found and another rediscovered. The first new large mammal to be discovered in 50 years was named *Pseudoryx nghetinhensis;* local villagers call it the forest goat. British biologist John MacKinnon and five Vietnamese scientists did not see a live animal, but described the cowlike creature from a series of skulls, hides, teeth, and skins. Meanwhile, there was a confirmed sighting in northern Vietnam of the Tonkin snub-nosed langur, *Rhinopithecus avunculus,* which had not been seen in the wild by zoologists since the late 1960s. Vietnamese scientist Le Xuan Kanh estimated there may be only 150 of the langurs left.

See also AFRICA—THE BLACK RHINO.

DEBORAH A. BEHLER
"Wildlife Conservation" Magazine

Statistical and Tabular Data

NATIONS OF THE WORLD[1]

A Profile and Synopsis of Major 1993 Developments

Nation, Region	Population in millions	Capital	Area Sq mi (km²)	Head of State/Government
Antigua and Barbuda, Caribbean	0.1	St. John's	170 (440)	James B. Carlisle, governor-general Vere C. Bird, prime minister

The U.S. Federal Aviation Administration (FAA) disclosed in April that it had suspended the landing rights for Regal Air of Antigua because of safety deficiencies. At its annual convention in September, the ruling Antigua Labour Party (ALP) elected as its leader Lester Bird, the current foreign-affairs, planning, and trade minister; he was to assume that office in early 1994, although Vere Bird was to remain prime minister until 1994 elections. Gross Domestic Product (GDP) (1989 est.): $418 million. Foreign Trade (1990 est.): Imports, $325.9 million; exports, $33.2 million.

Bahamas, Caribbean	0.3	Nassau	5,382 (13 940)	Clifford Darling, governor-general Hubert A. Ingraham, prime minister

In May the government announced its intention to offer to private investors up to 49% in state-owned telecommunications, electricity, and sewage corporations. An August cabinet reshuffle involved, among others, the naming of Orville Turnquest as deputy prime minister. GDP (1990 est.): $2.5 billion. Foreign Trade (1991): Imports, $1.14 billion; exports, $306 million.

Bahrain, W. Asia	0.5	Manama	239 (620)	Isa bin Salman Al Khalifa, emir Khalifa bin Salman Al Khalifa, prime minister

Bahrain was one of several Middle Eastern countries that agreed in September to support the Israeli-Palestinian peace agreement. GDP (1990): $4.0 billion. Foreign Trade (1991): Imports, $4.0 billion; exports, $3.4 billion.

Barbados, Caribbean	0.3	Bridgetown	166 (430)	Dame Nita Barrow, governor-general L. Erskine Sandiford, prime minister

In a cabinet reshuffle in August, David Thompson took over the finance portfolio from the prime minister; the foreign-affairs portfolio was assumed by Branford Taitt. A protocol on wages and prices signed in August called for a wage freeze from April 1, 1993 to March 31, 1995. GDP (1990 est.): $1.7 billion. Foreign Trade (1991): Imports, $695 million; exports, $202 million.

Benin, W. Africa	5.1	Porto Novo	43,483 (112 620)	Nicephore Soglo, president

President Nicephore Soglo lost his majority in the National Assembly on October 11 when 15 deputies with his Renewal group left to form an independent group. In April the nation was disturbed by violent clashes between Muslims and animists. GDP (1991 est.): $2.0 billion. Foreign Trade (1990 est.): Imports, $428 million; exports, $263.3 million.

Bhutan, S. Asia	0.8	Thimphu	18,147 (47 000)	Jigme Singye Wangchuck, king

King Wangchuck paid a state visit to India in January, and the Indian prime minister returned the visit in August. During the year an agreement was signed in which India agreed to assist Bhutan in the development of a multipurpose hydroelectric project. Bhutan was receiving Indian assistance on other power projects as well. GDP (1991 est.): $320 million. Foreign Trade (1991 est.): Imports, $106.4 million; exports, $74 million.

Botswana, S. Africa	1.4	Gaborone	231,803 (600 370)	Quett Masire, president

With significant funding from France and the United States, a controversial military air base in Molepolole neared completion. The ruling Botswana Democratic Party was weakened by the reemergence of two ministers who had resigned in 1992 due to a land scandal. GDP (1991 est.): $3.6 billion. Foreign Trade (1990): Imports, $1.6 billion; exports, $1.8 billion.

Brunei Darussalam, S.E. Asia	0.3	Bandar Seri Begawan	2,288 (5 770)	Sir Muda Hassanal Bolkiah, sultan and prime minister

Foreign Minister Prince Mohamed Bolkiah visited China in June, the first such visit since China established diplomatic relations in 1991; the month before, Iran's foreign minister had visited Brunei during a tour of Southeast Asia. In June, Sultan Hassanal Bolkiah topped Fortune magazine's list of the world's richest people, with a worth of $37 billion. GDP (1990 est.): $3.5 billion. Foreign Trade (1990): Imports, $1.7 billion; exports, $2.2 billion.

Burkina Faso, W. Africa	10.0	Ouagadougou	105,869 (274 200)	Blaise Compaoré, president

Maurice Yameogo, the first president of Burkina Faso (1959-66), died on September 15 at the age of 71. GDP (1990): $2.9 billion. Foreign Trade (1989): Imports, $619 million; exports, $262 million.

Burundi, E. Africa	5.8	Bujumbura	10,745 (27 830)	Sylvie Kinigi, prime minister

GDP (1990): $1.13 billion. Foreign Trade (1991): Imports, $248 million; exports, $91 million. (See Africa.)

Cameroon, Cen. Africa	12.8	Yaoundé	183,568 (475 440)	Paul Biya, president Simon Achidi Achu, prime minister

In May the government introduced a bill on constitutional reform, which would create an independent judiciary, a senate, and plans for a "grand national debate" on the reforms. The opposition Social Democratic Front criticized the plan and said it would boycott the debate. GDP (1990 est.): $11.5 billion. Foreign Trade (1990 est.): Imports, $2.1 billion; exports, $2.1 billion.

Cape Verde, W. Africa	0.4	Praia	1,556 (4 030)	Antonio Monteiro Mascarenhas, president Carlos Alberto Wahnon de Carvalho Veiga, prime minister

Serving its second and last year on the UN Security Council, Cape Verde voted to support the Bosnian arms embargo. GDP (1990): $310 million. Foreign Trade (1989): Imports, $107.8 million; exports, $10.9 million.

Central African Republic, Cen. Africa	3.1	Bangui	240,533 (622 980)	Ange-Felix Patasse, president Jean-Luc Mandaba, prime minister

Former Prime Minister Ange-Felix Patasse was elected president on September 19. He appointed Jean-Luc Mandaba as prime minister in October. Their party—the Movement for the Liberation of the Central African People—was able to secure a majority in the National Assembly after gaining several coalition partners. GDP (1990 est.): $1.3 billion. Foreign Trade (1990): Imports, $214.5 million; exports, $151.3 million.

---

[1] Independent nations not covered separately in alphabetical section.

Nation, Region	Population in millions	Capital	Area Sq mi (km²)	Head of State/Government
Chad, Cen. Africa	5.4	Ndjamena	495,753 (1 284 000)	Gen. Idriss Déby, president

Violent battles arose in southern Chad as troops of President Idriss Déby fought rebel forces led by former Defense Minister Abbas Koti, with particularly bloody confrontations in August. Peace negotiations were under way late in 1993, but tensions were still high. GDP (1989 est.): $1.02 billion. Foreign Trade (1990 est.): Imports, $264 million; exports, $174 million.

Comoros, E. Africa	0.5	Moroni	838 (2 170)	Said Mohammed Djohar, president

The eighth cabinet of President Said Mohammed Djohar, led by Prime Minister Halidi Abderemane Ibrahiim, was ousted after a no-confidence vote by the Federal Assembly. President Djohar appointed a new prime minister in May, but the assembly brought down the new prime minister and his cabinet within weeks. In June the president dissolved the legislature and scheduled elections for October, but this voting was delayed in September amid widespread opposition. GDP (1991 est.): $260 million. Foreign Trade (1990 est.): Imports, $41 million; exports, $16 million.

Congo, Cen. Africa	2.4	Brazzaville	132,046 (342 000)	Pascal Lissouba, president Jacques-Joachim Yhombi Opango, prime minister

After two rounds of voting in May and October, the Presidential Tendency, a coalition aligned with President Pascal Lissouba, captured 65 of 125 seats in the National Assembly. On June 23, Jacques-Joachim Yhombi Opango was named as Congo's new prime minister. GDP (1990 est.): $2.4 billion. Foreign Trade (1990): Imports, $600 million; exports, $976 million.

Djibouti, E. Africa	0.5	Djibouti	8,494 (22 000)	Hassan Gouled Aptidon, president Barkat Gourad Hamadou, premier

Incumbent President Hassan Gouled Aptidon defeated four other candidates in Djibouti's first multiparty presidential elections on May 7. President Hassan, who has led the nation since 1977, received more than 60% of the votes cast, although only half of the electorate participated in the election. Gross National Product (GNP) (1989): $340 million. Foreign Trade (1990): Imports, $311 million; exports, $190 million.

Dominica, Caribbean	0.1	Roseau	290 (750)	Crispin Anselm Sorhaindo, president Eugenia Charles, prime minister

In August, External Affairs Minister Brian Alleyne was elected as the new leader of the governing Dominica Freedom Party (DFP); however, Eugenia Charles was to continue as prime minister until a general election in 1995. In October the Dominica House of Assembly chose Crispin Sorhaindo as the new president. GDP (1990 est.): $170 million. Foreign Trade (1990): Imports, $103.9 million; exports, $59.9 million.

Dominican Republic, Caribbean	7.6	Santo Domingo	18,815 (48 730)	Joaquín Balaguer Ricardo, president

In January four diplomats were recalled from neighboring Haiti, and military forces were installed along the Dominican-Haitian border. Six months later it was reported that border guards had permitted trucks carrying petroleum to enter Haiti in violation of the United Nations embargo; officials insisted that the government had not authorized the shipments. GDP (1991 est.): $7 billion. Foreign Trade (1991 est.): Imports, $1.8 billion; exports, $775 million.

Equatorial Guinea, Cen. Africa	0.4	Malabo	10,830 (28 050)	Obiang Nguema Mbasogo, president Silvester Siale Bileka, prime minister

Multiparty legislative elections were held in November. Many of the nation's leading opposition parties refused to participate in the election, adding to the political tension. GNP (1988 est.): $144 million. Foreign Trade (1990 est.): Imports, $68.3 million; exports, $37 million.

Fiji, Oceania	0.8	Suva	7,054 (18 270)	Sitiveni Rabuka, prime minister

In January, Cyclone Kina killed at least 13 persons and caused extensive property damage, leaving thousands homeless. GDP (1990 est.) $1.36 billion. Foreign Trade (1991): Imports, $840 million; exports, $646 million.

Gabon, Cen. Africa	1.1	Libreville	103,348 (267 670)	El Hadj Omar Bongo, president Casimir Oye Mba, premier

The first round of Gabon's first multiparty presidential elections was scheduled to be held on December 5, while general elections were scheduled to begin on December 26. President Omar Bongo, who has been in power since 1967, faced at least 13 other candidates. GDP (1990): $3.3 billion. Foreign Trade (1989): Imports, $780 million; exports, $1.16 billion.

Gambia, W. Africa	0.9	Banjul	4,363 (11 300)	Sir Dawda Kairaba Jawara, president

On April 7 parliament adopted a law which officially abolished the death penalty in Gambia. GDP (1991 est.): $207 million. Foreign Trade (1990): Imports, $155.2 million; exports, $122.2 million.

Ghana, W. Africa	16.4	Accra	92,100 (238 540)	Jerry Rawlings, president

President Jerry Rawlings—who previously led Ghana as a military dictator—was sworn in as constitutionally elected president on January 7. As a result of an opposition boycott, his National Democratic Congress won 189 of 200 parliament seats. However, the opposition New Patriotic Party recognized the 1992 election in an August announcement by party leader Joao da Rocha. In September, Ghana was readmitted to the Commonwealth Parliamentary Association after a ten-year suspension. GNP (1991 est.): $6.2 billion. Foreign Trade (1990): Imports, $1.2 billion; exports, $841 million.

Grenada, Caribbean	0.1	St. George's	131 (340)	Reginald Palmer, governor-general Sir Nicholas Brathwaite, prime minister

GDP (1990): $200.7 million. Foreign Trade (1989 est.): Imports, $115.6 million; exports, $27.9 million.

Guinea, W. Africa	6.2	Conakry	94,927 (245 860)	Lansana Conté, president

Presidential elections were scheduled for December 5. President Lansana Conté was accused of using state funds for his campaign. GDP (1990 est.): $3.0 billion. Foreign Trade (1990 est.): Imports, $692 million; exports, $778 million.

Guinea-Bissau, W. Africa	1.0	Bissau	13,946 (36 120)	Joao Bernardo Vieira, president

An alleged coup attempt left a senior military adviser of President Brig. Gen. Joao Bernardo Vieira dead. Joao da Costa, leader of the opposition Party of Renovation, was arrested in connection with the attempt, but was released within a few weeks. GDP (1989): $162 million. Foreign Trade (1989 est): Imports, $68.9 million; exports, $14.2 million.

Guyana, N.E. South America	0.8	Georgetown	83,000 (214 970)	Cheddi Jagan, president Samuel Hinds, prime minister

In January the government suspended its privatization program. Hamilton Green, deputy leader of the main opposition party, was expelled from the party. GDP (1991 est.): $250 million. Foreign Trade (1991 est.): Imports, $246 million; exports, $189 million.

Ivory Coast, W. Africa	13.4	Yamoussoukro	124,502 (322 460)	Henri Konan-Bedie, president Alassane Ouattara, prime minister

Ivory Coast took a leading role in trying to end Angola's long-fought civil war. Meanwhile, the civil war in Liberia reportedly spilled over Ivory Coast's borders in early September. President Félix Houphouët-Boigny died in December at the age of 88. He

Nation, Region	Population in millions	Capital	Area Sq mi (km²)	Head of State/Government

had ruled Ivory Coast since the nation gained independence in 1960. GDP (1990): $10 billion. Foreign Trade (1989): Imports, $1.4 billion; exports, $2.5 billion.

Jamaica, Caribbean	2.4	Kingston	4,243 (10 990)	Howard Cooke, governor general P.J. Patterson, prime minister

In February a rescheduling of $366 million of Jamaica's debt was reported. In August, Pope John Paul II visited Jamaica. GDP (1991): $3.6 billion. Foreign Trade (1991): Imports, $1.8 billion; exports, $1.2 billion. (See CARIBBEAN.)

Kiribati, Oceania	0.07	Tarawa	277 (717)	Teatao Teannaki, president

GDP (1990 est.): $36.8 million. Foreign Trade (1990 est.): Imports, $26.7 million; exports, $5.8 million.

Lesotho, S. Africa	1.9	Maseru	11,718 (30 350)	Letsie III, king Ntsu Mokhehle, prime minister

On March 27, Ntsu Mokhehle, a 74-year-old civilian, was elected as prime minister, ending 23 years of military rule. His party— the Basotholand Congress Party—gained all of the 243 seats in the legislature. GDP (1990 est.): $420 million. Foreign Trade (1990 est.): Imports, $604 million; exports, $59 million.

Liberia, W. Africa	2.8	Monrovia	43,000 (111 370)	Amos Sawyer, president

GDP (1988): $988 million. Foreign Trade (1989 est.): Imports, $394 million; exports, $505 million. (See AFRICA.)

Liechtenstein, Cen. Europe	0.03	Vaduz	62 (160)	Hans Adam II, prince Mario Frick, prime minister

In May, Markus Buechel was elected by parliament as the premier after his Progressive Citizens' Party won one more seat than the Patriotic Union Party in February elections; represented in parliament for the first time was the environmentalist Free List Party. In September, Prince Hans Adam II dissolved the parliament following a motion of no confidence against Buechel. In the October general election that followed, the Patriotic Union Party won 13 seats, the Progressive Citizens' Party won 22 votes, and the Free List Party took one seat. In July, Crown Prince Alois and Bavaria's Duchess Sophie were married in Vaduz. GDP (1990 est.): $630 million.

Luxembourg, W. Europe	0.4	Luxembourg	998 (2 586)	Jean, grand duke Jacques Santer, prime minister

European Community (EC) news that related to Luxembourg included the January appointment of René Steichen, a former agriculture and culture minister, to the European Commission, and the lowering in April of key interest rates by Luxembourg banks. Luxembourg registered 1992 defense spending of $0.1 billion as a member of the North Atlantic Treaty Organization (NATO). GDP (1991 est.): $7.83 billion. (Luxembourg's foreign trade is recorded with Belgium's.)

Madagascar, E. Africa	13.3	Antananarivo	226,656 (587 040)	Albert Zafy, president Francisque Ravony, prime minister

After a second round of voting on February 10, Albert Zafy captured the presidency with 67.5% of the vote. In general elections for the legislature held in June, pro-Zafy groups won a majority of seats. The new parliament elected Francisque Ravony as prime minister on August 11. GDP (1990): $2.4 billion. Foreign Trade (1990): Imports, $436 million; exports, $290 million.

Malawi, E. Africa	10.0	Lilongwe	45,745 (118 480)	Hastings Kamuzu Banda, president

GDP (1991 est.): $1.9 billion. Foreign Trade (1990): Imports, $560 million; exports, $390 million. (See AFRICA.)

Maldives, S. Asia	0.2	Malé	116 (300)	Maumoon Abdul Gayoom, president

President Maumoon Abdul Gayoom was reelected in October for a fourth consecutive term, winning more than 92% of the vote in a national referendum in which he was the only candidate. GDP (1990): $174 million. Foreign Trade (1990 est.): Imports, $128.9 million; exports, $52.0 million.

Mali, W. Africa	8.9	Bamako	478,764 (1 240 000)	Alpha Omar Konare, president Abdoulaye Sekou Sow, prime minister

On April 9, amid violent student protests, President Alpha Omar Konare was forced to announce the resignation of his administration, including Prime Minister Younoussi Toure. Three days later the president appointed Abdoulaye Sekou Sow as the new prime minister, who formed an administration that included several opposition members. GDP (1990 est.): $2.2 billion. Foreign Trade (1989): Imports, $513 million; exports, $285 million.

Malta, S. Europe	0.4	Valletta	124 (320)	Vincent Tabone, president Edward Fenech Adami, prime minister

In February, Palestinian Omar Mohammed Ali Rezaq received amnesty from Maltese authorities after serving seven years of a 25-year sentence for a 1985 airliner hijacking. He later was arrested by the U.S. Federal Bureau of Investigation in Nigeria. GDP (1991): $2.5 billion. Foreign Trade (1990): Imports, $2.0 billion; exports, $1.1 billion.

Mauritania, W. Africa	2.2	Nouakchott	397,954 (1 030 700)	Maaouiya Ould Sid Ahmed Taya, president

Relations between Negro-Africans and the Maures Blanc, who historically have held greater power, grew worse in 1993. Meanwhile, tensions between Mauritania and Senegal grew more hostile. In late September, Mauritania joined the Nuclear Non-Proliferation Treaty. GDP (1991 est.): $1.1 billion. Foreign Trade (1990 est.): Imports, $389 million; exports, $436 million.

Mauritius, E. Africa	1.1	Port Louis	718 (1 860)	Cassam Uteem, president Rabindranath Ghurburren, vice-president

Prime Minister Aneerood Jugnauth dismissed Foreign Minister Paul Bérenger on August 18 for criticizing government policy. The men belonged to two different political parties that maintained a tenuous coalition to lead the country. GDP (1991): $2.5 billion. Foreign Trade (1991): Imports, $1.5 billion; exports, $1.1 billion.

Monaco, S. Europe	0.03	Monaco-Ville	0.7 (1.9)	Rainier III, prince Jacques Dupont, minister of state

In May, Monaco was admitted to membership in the United Nations.

Namibia, W. Africa	1.5	Windhoek	318,259 (824 290)	Sam Nujoma, president

Ending a long territorial dispute, the South African government agreed to relinquish its sovereignty over Walvis Bay, the only deepwater port in Namibia. GNP (1990 est.): $1.8 billion. Foreign Trade (1989): Imports, $894 million; exports, $1.021 billion.

Nation, Region	Population in millions	Capital	Area Sq mi (km²)	Head of State/Government
Nauru, Oceania	0.009	Nauru	8 (21)	Bernard Dowiyogo, president

Settlement of Nauru's compensation claim against Australia for damage inflicted by phosphate mining in the preindependence period was announced in August when Australia agreed to pay about $73 million in compensation; Australia was to approach the United Kingdom and New Zealand for contributions toward this compensation. Foreign Trade (1984): Imports, $73 million; exports, $93 million.

Nepal, S. Asia	20.4	Katmandu	54,363 (140 800)	Birendra Bir Bikram, king Girija Prasad Koirala, prime minister

In February the finance ministry announced the full convertibility of the rupee against foreign currencies, ending a system of partial convertibility begun during 1992. A joint Nepal-Bhutan commission to oversee problems of Bhutan refugees of Nepalese origin was announced in Bhutan in July; in October an agreement with Bhutan was signed in Katmandu, categorizing the bona fide status of more than 100,000 Bhutanese refugees of Nepalese origin. In June antigovernment protests organized by Nepal's Communist Party caused the deaths of 25; the protest was sparked after the government inquiry into two party leaders' deaths found no evidence of foul play. July monsoon rains killed an estimated 3,000 persons. GDP (1991): $3.2 billion. Imports, $545 million; exports, $180 million.

Niger, W. Africa	8.5	Niamey	489,189 (1 267 000)	Mahamane Ousmane, president Mahamadou Issoufou, prime minister

In the second round of presidential elections held on March 27, Mahamane Ousmane was elected head of state and was installed on April 16. He immediately appointed Mahamadou Issoufou—who had come in second in the first round of presidential voting—as prime minister. GDP (1991): $2.4 billion. Foreign Trade (1990 est.): Imports, $439 million; exports, $320 million.

Oman, W. Asia	1.6	Muscat	82,031 (212 460)	Qaboos bin Said, sultan and prime minister

Visiting Oman in January was British Prime Minister John Major on a trip to promote British exports. Other visitors were the vice-president of Yemen, who came in April for the first high-level talks since Oman and Yemen had signed a border agreement in 1992, as well as officials from Lebanon and Iran and the Palestinian leader Yasir Arafat, who sought support for the Israeli-PLO peace agreement signed in Washington in September. GDP (1989 est.): $10.6 billion. Foreign Trade (1990): Imports, $2.5 billion; exports, $5.5 billion.

Papua New Guinea, Oceania	3.9	Port Moresby	178,259 (461 690)	Wiwa Korowi, governor-general Paias Wingti, prime minister

Fighting continued during the year with the secessionist Bougainville Revolutionary Army (BRA), which caused strained relations with the Solomon Islands, on whose territory government troops sometimes incurred. In March the government and three Australian gold-mining companies reached an agreement whereby each party would hold a 25% stake in the Porgera gold mine. In November, Papua New Guinea was admitted to the Asia-Pacific Economic Cooperation group. More than 60 persons were killed by four earthquakes that struck in October. GDP (1991 est.): $3.1 billion. Foreign Trade (1991): Imports, $1.4 billion; exports, $1.3 billion.

Qatar, W. Asia	0.5	Doha	4,247 (11 000)	Khalifa bin Hamad Al Thani, emir and prime minister

In January, Qatar demanded that enforcement of UN resolutions in Iraq be matched to protect Bosnian Muslims and to force Israel to repatriate Arab deportees. In September, Qatar agreed to support the Israeli-Palestinian peace agreement. The emir in December 1992 signed an agreement with the Saudi king, establishing a committee to delineate by 1994 their common disputed border. GDP (1990): $7.4 billion. Foreign Trade (1990 est.): Imports, $1.5 billion; exports, $3.2 billion.

Rwanda, E. Africa	7.4	Kigali	10,170 (26 340)	Juvénal Habyarimana, president

GDP (1989 est.): $2.2 billion. Foreign Trade (1991): Imports, $43.5 billion; exports, $58.7 billion. (See AFRICA.)

Saint Kitts and Nevis, Caribbean	0.04	Basseterre	139 (360)	Clement A. Arrindell, governor-general Kennedy A. Simmonds, prime minister

GDP (1990): $146.6 million. Foreign Trade (1990): Imports, $103.2 million; exports, $24.6 million.

Saint Lucia, Caribbean	0.1	Castries	239 (620)	Sir Stanislaus A. James, governor-general John Compton, prime minister

GDP (1990 est.): $295 million. Foreign Trade (1990): Imports, $270 million; exports, $127 million.

Saint Vincent and the Grenadines, Caribbean	0.1	Kingstown	131 (340)	David Jack, governor-general James F. Mitchell, prime minister

GDP (1989 est.): $146 million. Foreign Trade (1990): Imports, $130 million; exports, $75 million.

San Marino, S. Europe	0.023	San Marino	23 (60)	Coregents appointed semiannually

In general elections in May the Christian Democrat Party won 26 seats in the Grand and General Council, while the Socialist Party took 14 seats. The former Communists, renamed the Progressive Democratic Party in 1990, won 11 seats, and three other smaller parties gained nine seats.

São Tomé and Príncipe, W. Africa	0.1	Sao Tomé	371 (960)	Miguel Trovoada, president Norberto Costa Alegre, prime minister

GDP (1989): $46.0 million. Foreign Trade (1990 est.): Imports, $21.3 million; exports, $4.4 million.

Senegal, W. Africa	7.9	Dakar	75,749 (196 190)	Abdou Diouf, president Habib Thiam, prime minister

GDP (1990 est.): $5.0 billion. Foreign Trade (1990 est.): Imports, $1.05 billion; exports, $814 million. (See AFRICA.)

Seychelles, E. Africa	0.1	Victoria	176 (455)	France Albert René, president

Incumbent President Albert René was reelected for another five-year term on July 23. Members of René's Seychelles People's Progressive Front won 28 of 33 legislative seats. GDP (1991 est.): $350 million. Foreign Trade (1991): Imports, $173 million; exports, $48 million.

Sierra Leone, W. Africa	4.5	Freetown	27,699 (71 740)	Valentine Strasser, president

Head of State Capt. Valentine Strasser promised to return the nation to multiparty democratic civilian rule by April 1996. Throughout the year, government forces clashed with rebels from the Revolution United Front (RUF). By late September the RUF rebellion appeared to be contained. GDP (1991): $1.4 billion. Foreign Trade (1991): Imports, $162 million; exports, $145 million.

Nation, Region	Population in millions	Capital	Area Sq mi (km²)	Head of State/Government
Solomon Islands, Oceania	0.3	Honiara	10,985 (28 450)	Sir George Lepping, governor-general Francis Billy Hilly, prime minister

In May general elections, the Group for National Unity and Reconciliation won 21 of the 47 seats in the parliament; however, an opposition coalition selected a new prime minister, Francis Billy Hilly. GDP (1990 est.): $200 million. Foreign Trade (1990): Imports, $86.0 million; exports, $67.3 million.

Suriname, S. America	0.4	Paramaribo	63,039 (163 270)	Ronald Venetiaan, president

In May, Col. Arthy Gorré, approved by the National Assembly, was sworn in as army commander in chief, despite strong military opposition and the threat of a coup by Lt. Col. Désiré Bouterse, who had resigned the post in 1992; it was reported in February that Bouterse had been elected chairman of the opposition National Democratic Party. GDP (1989 est.): $1.35 billion. Foreign Trade (1989 est.): Imports, $331 million; exports, $549 million.

Swaziland, S. Africa	0.8	Mbabane	6,703 (17 360)	Mswati III, king Andreas Fakudze, interim prime minister

In September and October the Swazi electorate cast votes in the first free elections held in 20 years. In this election much of the ruling group—including Prime Minister Obed Dlamini—failed to win in general elections. King Mswati III appointed Andreas Fakudze as acting prime minister until a new premier and cabinet could be appointed. GNP (1990 est.): $563 million. Foreign Trade (1990): Imports, $632 million; exports, $557 million.

Togo, W. Africa	4.1	Lomé	21,927 (56 790)	Gnassingbé Eyadéma, president Joseph Kokou Koffigoh, prime minister

In an election boycotted by the opposition, incumbent President Gen. Gnassingbé Eyadéma retained his post. Eyadéma captured 96.5% of the vote on August 25. Multiparty legislative elections were scheduled for late in 1993. France sent military observers to monitor the elections. GDP (1990 est.): $1.5 billion. Foreign Trade (1990 est.): Imports, $502 million; exports, $396 million.

Tonga, Oceania	0.1	Nuku'alofa	289 (748)	Taufa'ahau Tupou IV, king Baron Vaea, prime minister

In January, Cyclone Kina passed over the main island of Tongatapu, causing extensive damage to crops. In February pro-democracy candidates won six of the nine seats contested in a general election. Under the constitution only nine of the 30 legislative seats were open to election. GDP (1990 est.): $92 million. Foreign Trade (1991): Imports, $62 million; exports, $14 million.

Trinidad and Tobago, Caribbean	1.3	Port-of-Spain	1,981 (5 130)	Noor Hassanali, president Patrick Manning, prime minister

The ruling People's National Movement (PNM) government placed the army on alert in February due to growing labor unrest that took place as a result of budget cuts, salary arrears, and increased privatization. In April the government floated its dollar in currency markets; the Trinidad-Tobago dollar had been fixed at 4.25 to the U.S. dollar since 1989. In July, PNM Secretary-General Nello Mitchell was expelled from the party. Also in July, the National Development Party was formed. GDP (1990 est.): $4.9 billion. Foreign Trade (1991): Imports, $1.65 billion; exports, $1.96 billion.

Tuvalu, Oceania	0.009	Funafuti	10 (26)	Sir Toaripi Lauti, governor-general Bikenibeu Paeniu, prime minister

In May, Tuvalu was admitted to membership in the World Health Organization. An election held in September was inconclusive in terms of selecting a prime minister. The governor-general later dissolved parliament with the intention of calling new elections. GNP (1989 est.): $4.6 million. Foreign Trade (1983 est.): Imports, $2.8 million; exports, $1 million.

United Arab Emirates, W. Asia	2.1	Abu Dhabi	32,278 (83 600)	Zayid bin Sultan Al Nuhayyan, president Rashid d Al Maktum, prime minister

In a December 1992 meeting of the Gulf Cooperation Council, the Iranian president warned of bloodshed if there were attempts to seize three Gulf islands in dispute between Iran and the United Arab Emirates (UAE). In May the UAE prime minister announced the resumption of diplomatic relations with Ethiopia and pledged aid to Ethiopia. The UAE in September agreed to support the Israeli-Palestinian peace agreement. GDP (1990 est.): $33.7 billion. Foreign Trade (1990 est.): Imports, $11.0 billion; exports, $21.3 billion.

Vanuatu, Oceania	0.2	Port-Vila	5,699 (14 760)	Frederick Timakata, president Maxime Carlot Korman, prime minister

GDP (1990 est.): $142 million. Foreign Trade (1990 est.): Imports, $60.4 million; exports, $15.6 million.

Vatican City, S. Europe	0.001	Vatican City	0.17 (0.438)	John Paul II, pope

Raymond Flynn, the former mayor of Boston, MA, became U.S. ambassador to the Vatican in July. In December the Vatican and Israel formally recognized each other and signed an agreement to establish diplomatic relations.

Western Samoa, Oceania	0.2	Apia	1,104 (2 860)	Tanumafili II Malietoa, head of state

GDP (1990 est.): $115 million. Foreign Trade (1990 est.): Imports, $87 million; exports, $9.4 million.

Yemen, S. Asia	11.3	San'a	203,850 (527 970)	Ali Abdullah Saleh, president

In April, Yemen held its first parliamentary election since the 1990 unification of North and South Yemen. The balloting was the first Arabian election in which women were permitted to vote. North Yemen's former ruling party won the most seats. In late May a coalition government was created by the three main parties. That same month the ruling parties of northern and southern Yemen agreed to govern as a single party; together they controlled 164 of 301 parliamentary seats. In October a political crisis emerged over the election of a new five-member Presidential Council, which in turn had reappointed Saleh as president; the crisis reflected growing tensions between the two main northern and southern political parties. GDP (1990 est.): $5.3 billion. Foreign Trade (North—1988): Imports, $1.3 billion; exports, $606 million; (South—1989 est.): Imports, $553.9 million; exports, $113.8 million.

Zambia, E. Africa	8.6	Lusaka	290,583 (752 610)	Frederick Chiluba, president Levy Mwanawsa, vice president

President Frederick Chiluba declared a state of emergency in March over an alleged coup plot. The declaration was not revoked until late in May. Zambia also ended diplomatic ties with Iran and Iraq in March. Tensions with Zaire grew during 1993 as border areas became increasingly chaotic. GDP (1991): $4.7 billion. Foreign Trade (1991): Imports, $1.3 billion; exports, $1.1 billion.

WORLD MINERAL AND METAL PRODUCTION[f]

ALUMINUM, primary smelter (thousand metric tons)

	1991	1992
United States	4,121	4,042
USSR (former)	3,251	3,115[e]
Canada	1,822	1,950
Australia	1,235	1,216
Brazil[e]	1,140	1,200
China	860	950
Norway[e]	833	813
Germany	690	600
Venezuela	601	600[e]
India[e]	504	500
France	286	417[e]
Spain	355	350[e]
Bahrain	227	290[e]
Yugoslavia (former)	315	275[e]
New Zealand	259	242
United Arab Emirates: Dubai	239	240[e]
United Kingdom	294	240[e]
Netherlands	264	235[e]
Italy	206	180[e]
Ghana	175	178[e]
Other countries	1,851	1,586[e]
Total	19,528	19,219

ANTIMONY, mine (metric tons)[a]

	1991	1992
China[e]	45,000	45,000
USSR (former)[e]	16,000	13,500
Bolivia	7,287	6,500
South Africa	4,485	4,000
Mexico	2,753	1,760
Australia[e]	1,500	1,500
Czechoslovakia[e]	1,000	1,000
Guatemala	609	600
Yugoslavia (former)[e]	350	550
Peru[e]	400	400
Other countries	995	849
Total	80,379	75,659

ASBESTOS (thousand metric tons)[a]

	1991	1992
USSR (former)[e]	2,000	1,700
Canada	689	585[e]
China[e]	230	240
Brazil	233	233[e]
Zimbabwe	142	140[e]
South Africa	149	124
Swaziland	14	35[e]
India	24	25[e]
Other countries	52	39[e]
Total	3,533	3,121

BARITE (thousand metric tons)

	1991	1992
China[e]	1,800	1,800
India	615	620[e]
Morocco	433	433[e]
USSR (former)[e]	450	400
United States	448	316
Turkey	279	280[e]
Iran	191	200[e]
Mexico	204	200[e]
Germany	164	160[e]
Peru	150	130[e]
Thailand	100	100[e]
Italy	88	85[e]
Other countries	763	712[e]
Total	5,685	5,436

BAUXITE (thousand metric tons)[a]

	1991	1992
Australia	40,503	39,950
Guinea[e]	14,899	13,773
Jamaica	11,552	11,302[e]
Brazil	10,414	10,800[e]
USSR (former)[e]	5,000	4,500
India	4,738	4,475[e]
Suriname	3,198	3,250[e]
China[e]	2,600	3,000
Guyana	2,204	2,300[e]
Greece	2,133	2,100[e]
Yugoslavia (former)[e]	2,700	1,950
Hungary	2,037	1,721[e]
Sierra Leone	1,288	1,246[e]
Venezuela	1,992	1,052[e]
Other countries	2,899	2,206
Total	108,157	103,625

CEMENT (thousand metric tons)

	1991	1992
China[e]	248,000	304,000
USSR (former)[e]	127,000	110,431
Japan	89,560	90,700
United States (incl. Puerto Rico)	66,753	71,426
India	51,000	50,000[e]
South Korea	38,335	42,600[e]
Italy	40,717	41,347
Germany	34,396	37,500[e]
Turkey	26,026	28,607
Brazil	27,490	28,100
Mexico	25,100	26,900[e]
Spain (incl. Canary Islands)	27,581	26,000[e]
France	26,507	21,600[e]
Taiwan	19,389	20,700[e]

CEMENT (cont.)

	1991	1992
Iran[e]	15,000	18,000
Thailand[e]	18,054	18,000
Indonesia	16,153	17,280
North Korea[e]	16,000	17,000
Egypt	16,427	16,000[e]
Saudi Arabia	13,000	15,000[e]
Greece	13,580	13,100[e]
Poland[e]	12,031	12,000
United Kingdom[e]	11,662	10,720
Iraq[e]	5,000	10,000
Malaysia	7,451	9,525[e]
Romania[e]	10,000	9,000
Canada	9,396	8,484
Other countries	178,149	178,481
Total	1,189,757	1,252,501

CHROMITE (thousand metric tons)

	1991	1992
USSR (former)	3,800[e]	3,721
South Africa	5,110	3,361
India	995	1,000[e]
Turkey[e]	870	850
Zimbabwe	564	560[e]
Finland[e]	458	480
Brazil	340	340[e]
Albania	800	150[e]
Philippines	184	132[e]
Iran	90	100[e]
Other countries	234	202
Total	13,445	10,896

COPPER, mine (thousand metric tons)

	1991	1992
Chile	1,814	1,910[e]
United States	1,631	1,761[e]
USSR (former)[e]	900	812
Canada[e]	811	764
Zambia	410	440[e]
Poland	320	387[e]
China[e]	300	375
Peru	400	368[e]
Australia	311	326
Mexico	325	320[e]
Indonesia	212	281
Papua New Guinea	205	193
Zaire[e]	251	171
South Africa	185	167
Portugal	165	151[e]
Philippines	148	123
Mongolia	90	105
Other countries	709	636
Total	9,187	9,290

COPPER, refined, primary and secondary (thousand metric tons)

	1991	1992
United States	1,995	2,154
Chile	1,228	1,243
Japan	1,076	1,161
USSR (former)[e]	1,070	925
Germany	522	582[e]
China[e]	560	580
Canada	538	539
Zambia	403	450[e]
Poland	378	387[e]
Australia	287	327
Belgium	297	295[e]
Peru	246[e]	250
Mexico[e]	192	220
South Korea[e]	203	207
Brazil	179	185[e]
Spain	149	179[e]
South Africa	139	130[e]
Yugoslavia (former)	134	130
Philippines	117	122[e]
Sweden	97	101
Other countries	827	750
Total	10,637	10,917

DIAMOND, natural (thousand carats)

	1991	1992
Australia	35,956	42,000[e]
USSR (former)[e]	20,000	18,000
Botswana	16,506	15,000[e]
Zaire	17,814	15,000[e]
South Africa	8,431	10,156
Namibia	1,187	1,549
Brazil[e]	1,500	1,500
Angola	961	1,000[e]
China[e]	1,000	1,000
Ghana[e]	700	700
Other countries	1,800	1,866
Total	105,855	107,771

FLUORSPAR (thousand metric tons)[b]

	1991	1992
China[e]	1,600	1,600
Mexico	370	364[e]
USSR (former)[e]	350	300
Mongolia[e]	370	277
South Africa	270	258
France[e]	170	160
Spain[e]	112	90
United Kingdom	78	85[e]
Other countries	757	712
Total	4,077	3,846

GOLD, mine (kilograms)

	1991	1992
South Africa	601,013	613,900
United States	296,805	329,124
USSR (former)	260,000	252,000[e]
Australia	234,218	240,000[e]
Canada	176,552	158,049
China[e]	120,000	140,000
Papua New Guinea	60,780	80,390
Brazil	75,844	76,000[e]
Indonesia	16,879	37,983
Colombia	34,844	37,000[e]
Chile	28,668	33,300[e]
Ghana	26,310	31,031
Philippines	24,938	24,000[e]
South Korea	20,809	21,000[e]
Zimbabwe	17,800	18,000[e]
Ecuador	12,000	11,000[e]
Mexico	8,937	10,000[e]
Other countries	132,346	135,063
Total	2,148,743	2,247,840

GYPSUM (thousand metric tons)

	1991	1992
United States	14,021	14,759
China[e]	10,523	10,977
Iran	8,050	7,983
Canada	6,830	7,054
Thailand	7,197	6,985
France	5,625	5,715
Mexico	5,534	5,534
Japan[e]	5,443	5,443
Spain[e]	4,990	4,990
Germany	4,211	4,300
USSR (former)	3,992	3,502
United Kingdom[e]	3,538	2,994
Australia[e]	2,000	2,000
Other countries	15,838	15,555
Total	97,792	97,791

IRON ORE, marketable equivalent (thousand metric tons)

	1991	1992
China	175,300	194,000[e]
USSR (former)	199,000	178,200[e]
Brazil	151,500	146,000[e]
Australia	121,820	117,170[e]
United States	56,596	55,593
India	57,638	54,000[e]
Canada	36,383	34,136[e]
South Africa	28,958	28,226
Venezuela	21,222	22,000[e]
Sweden	19,328	19,280
North Korea[e]	10,000	10,500
Mauritania	10,246	10,300[e]
Chile	8,414	8,500[e]
Mexico	7,539	7,380[e]
France	7,472	5,700[e]
Turkey	5,400	5,300[e]
Iran	4,890	5,000[e]
Other countries	34,518	28,469
Total	956,224	929,754

IRON, crude steel (thousand metric tons)

	1991	1992
USSR (former)	132,666	117,365
Japan	109,649	98,131
United States	79,738	84,322
China	70,570	80,000[e]
Germany	42,169	39,768
South Korea	26,001	28,054
Italy	25,046	24,904
Brazil	22,617	24,000[e]
India	17,100	18,000[e]
France	18,437	17,961
United Kingdom	16,511	16,050
Canada	12,987	13,924
Spain	12,933	12,295
Czechoslovakia	12,133	11,140[e]
Taiwan	10,957	11,000[e]
Turkey	9,336	10,343[e]
Belgium	11,334	10,276
Poland	10,439	9,800[e]
South Africa	9,358	9,061
Mexico	7,883	8,435
North Korea[e]	8,000	8,100
Australia	6,018	6,322
Netherlands	5,171	5,438
Romania	7,116	5,372
Other countries	51,838	51,254
Total	736,007	721,315

LEAD, mine (thousand metric tons)

	1991	1992
Australia	571	548
United States	477	408
China[e]	380	385
USSR (former)	380	340
Canada	235	343
Peru	200	193
Mexico	165	174[e]
Sweden	91	106
Yugoslavia (former)[e]	90	82
South Africa	76	75[e]
North Korea[e]	80	75
Other countries	531	513
Total	3,276	3,242

	1991	1992
LEAD, refined, primary and secondary (thousand metric tons)		
United States	1,229	1,221[e]
USSR (former)[e]	630	540
United Kingdom	311	347
Germany	363	345[e]
Japan	332	330[e]
China[e]	330	330
France	294	284[e]
Australia[e]	238	264
Canada	212	255[e]
Italy	208	195[e]
Mexico	160	173
Belgium	111	116[e]
Spain[e]	115	110
Sweden	88	91
South Korea[e]	80	90
Other countries	902	851
Total	5,603	5,542
MAGNESIUM, primary (thousand metric tons)		
United States	131	137
USSR (former)[e]	80	70
Norway	44	30
Canada	36	26[e]
France[e]	14	12
Japan	12	8
Brazil[e]	8	7
Yugoslavia (former)[e]	4	4
Other countries	11	10
Total	340	304
MANGANESE ORE (thousand metric tons)		
USSR (former)	7,240	7,009[e]
China[e]	3,400	3,500
South Africa	3,146	2,464
Brazil	2,000	1,800[e]
Gabon	1,620	1,556
India	1,401	1,400[e]
Australia	1,482	1,200[e]
Mexico	254	407
Ghana	320	279
Morocco	59	59[e]
Iran	48	50[e]
Romania	50	45[e]
Other countries	193	160
Total	21,213	19,929
MERCURY, mine (metric tons)		
China[e]	950	950
USSR (former)[e]	750	700
Mexico	720	700[e]
Algeria	431	425[e]
Czechoslovakia	75	70[e]
Finland	74	70[e]
United States	58	64
Yugoslavia (former)[e]	30	30
Turkey	25	5[e]
Other countries	100	—
Total	3,213	3,014
MOLYBDENUM, mine (metric tons)		
United States	53,364	49,725
China[e]	16,000	16,000
USSR (former)[e]	16,000	15,000
Chile	14,434	14,500[e]
Canada	11,329	9,540[e]
Peru	3,045	3,000[e]
Mexico	1,716	1,582
Other countries	1,844	2,320[e]
Total	117,732	111,667
NICKEL, mine (thousand metric tons)		
USSR (former)[e]	245	220
Canada	192	192
New Caledonia	114[e]	113
Indonesia	72	78
Australia	69	64
China[e]	31	37
Cuba	33	32
South Africa	28	28
Dominican Republic	29	25[e]
Other countries	136	133
Total	949	922

	1991	1992
NITROGEN, content of ammonia (thousand metric tons)		
China[e]	18,000	18,000
USSR (former)[e]	17,100	15,626
United States	12,801	13,404
India	7,044	7,000[e]
Canada	3,016	3,104
Indonesia	2,706	2,700[e]
Netherlands	3,033	2,667
Mexico	2,221	2,222[e]
Germany	2,123	2,160[e]
Japan	1,553	1,602
Trinidad and Tobago	1,524[e]	1,568
Poland	1,669	1,500[e]
France	1,604[e]	1,407
Other countries	19,601	19,572
Total	93,995	92,532
PHOSPHATE ROCK (thousand metric tons)		
United States	48,096	46,965
China[e]	22,000	23,000
USSR (former)[e]	28,400	21,000
Morocco	17,900	19,184
Tunisia	6,400	6,400[e]
Jordan	4,433	4,296
Israel	3,370[e]	3,595
Brazil	3,280	3,300[e]
South Africa	3,050	3,051
Senegal	1,741	2,300[e]
Togo	2,965	2,083
Other countries	8,030	8,579
Total	149,665	143,753
POTASH, K_2O equivalent basis (thousand metric tons)		
Canada	7,406	7,327
USSR (former)[e]	8,560	7,300
Germany	3,902	3,470
United States	1,749	1,705
Israel	1,320	1,300[e]
France	1,129	1,130
Other countries	2,028	2,095
Total	26,094	24,327
SALT (thousand metric tons)		
United States (incl. Puerto Rico)	35,943	34,830
China[e]	24,100	25,000
Germany[e]	16,025	13,125
Canada	11,993	11,154[e]
USSR (former)[e]	14,000	11,000
India[e]	9,503	9,503
Brazil	8,213	8,200[e]
Australia	7,791	8,000[e]
Mexico	7,595	7,600[e]
France[e]	6,500	6,600
United Kingdom	6,828	6,600[e]
Romania[e]	6,500	6,000
Italy[e]	4,000	4,100
Poland[e]	3,900	3,900
Other countries	29,389	29,242
Total	192,280	184,854
SILVER, mine (metric tons)		
Mexico	2,224	2,316[e]
USSR (former)[e]	2,200	1,900
United States	1,855	1,804
Peru	1,770	1,570[e]
Australia	1,180	1,245
Canada	1,339	1,207[e]
Chile	674	1,000[e]
Poland[e]	870	850
Spain[e]	400	400
Morocco	296	295
Bolivia	376	260[e]
South Korea	265	250[e]
Sweden	239	240[e]
Brazil	194	194[e]
South Africa	171	172
Other countries	1,639	1,642
Total	15,692	15,345
SULFUR, all forms[c d] (metric tons)		
United States	10,820	10,663
USSR (former)[e]	8,100	7,250
Canada[e]	7,102	7,246
China[e]	5,670	5,970
Poland[e]	4,105	3,060
Japan[e]	2,680	2,635
Saudi Arabia	2,000	2,000
Mexico[e]	2,074	1,600
Germany[e]	1,744	1,415
France[e]	1,199	1,155

	1991	1992
SULFUR (cont.)		
Spain[e]	910	910
Iran[e]	700	750
Other countries	7,937	7,755
Total	55,041	52,409
TIN, mine (metric tons)[a]		
China[e]	43,000	43,000
Brazil	29,253	30,000[e]
Indonesia	30,061	25,000[e]
Bolivia	16,830	15,300[e]
Thailand	14,937	15,000[e]
Malaysia	20,710	14,339
USSR (former)[e]	13,500	10,500
Portugal	8,333	6,500
Australia	5,700	6,400
Peru	6,559	6,000[e]
Zaire	1,635	1,500[e]
Zimbabwe	1,060	1,060
United Kingdom	2,326	1,000[e]
Other countries	8,819	3,867
Total	202,723	179,466
TITANIUM MINERALS[a] (thousand metric tons)		
ILMENITE AND LEUCOXENE		
Australia	1,381	1,518[e]
Norway	625	718
USSR (former)[e]	400	350
Malaysia	336	338
India	312	300[e]
China[e]	150	150
Brazil	69	70[e]
Other countries	138	137
Total	3,411	3,581
RUTILE		
Australia	201	200[e]
Sierra Leone	155	145[e]
South Africa[e]	75	75
Other countries	27	22
Total	458	442
TITANIFEROUS SLAG[e]		
Canada	701	753
South Africa	808	884
Total	1,509	1,637
TUNGSTEN, mine (metric tons)[a]		
China[e]	25,000	17,000
USSR (former)[e]	8,000	6,500
Portugal[e]	1,400	1,200
Bolivia	1,065	1,100
North Korea[e]	1,000	1,000
Austria	1,314	800
Peru	1,229	600
South Korea	780	400
Other countries	2,092	2,155
Total	41,880	30,755
ZINC, mine (thousand metric tons)		
Canada	1,157	1,312
Australia	1,048	1,028
China[e]	650	670
Peru	628	601
United States	547	552
USSR (former)[e]	475	425
Mexico	301	279
Spain	261	202
North Korea[e]	200	200
Ireland	188	194
Sweden	161	170
Poland	144[e]	151
Other countries	1,410	1,353
Total	7,170	7,137
ZINC, smelter (thousand metric tons)		
Japan	731	730
Canada	661	670[e]
China[e]	612	630
USSR (former)[e]	800	475
United States	376	400
Germany	346	383
Spain	273	356[e]
Australia	327	335
France	300	305[e]
Italy	264	253[e]
South Korea	254	253
Belgium	298	215[e]
Netherlands	211	205[e]
Other countries	1,723	1,665
Total	7,176	6,875

[a]Excludes output in the United States because it is company proprietary information. [b]The USSR was dissolved in December 1991. This commodity is believed to be produced in Kazakhstan, Kyrgyzstan, Russia, Uzbekistan, and possibly other former republics of the USSR; however, information is inadequate to formulate reliable estimates of individual country production. [c]Includes: (1) Frasch recovery; (2) native, comprising all production of elemental sulfur by traditional mining methods; (3) pyrites (whether or not the sulfur is recovered in the elemental form or as acid); (4) by-product recovery, either as elemental sulfur or as sulfur compounds from coal gasification, metallurgical operations including associated coal processing, crude oil and natural gas extraction, petroleum refining, tar sand cleaning, and processing of spent oxide from stack gas scrubbers; (5) recovery from the processing of mined gypsum. Recovery of sulfur in the form of sulfuric acid from artificial gypsum produced as a by-product of phosphatic fertilizer production is excluded. It should be noted that production of Frasch sulfur, other native sulfur, pyrite-derived sulfur, mined gypsum-derived sulfur, by-product sulfur from extraction of crude oil and natural gas, and recovery from tar sands are all credited to the country of origin of the extracted raw material; by-product recovery from metallurgical operations, petroleum refineries, and spent oxides are credited to the nation where the recovery takes place. [d]Excludes output in the United States derived from pyrites because it is company proprietary information. [e]Estimated. [f]Excludes fuel-mineral output.

THE UNITED STATES GOVERNMENT

President: William J. (Bill) Clinton

Vice-President: Albert Gore, Jr.

Executive Office of the President
The White House

Chief of Staff to the President: Thomas F. McLarty III
Senior Policy Adviser to the President: George R. Stephanopoulos
Counselor to the President: David R. Gergen
Assistant to the President and Deputy Chief of Staff: Harold Ickes
Assistant to the President and Director for Intergovernmental Affairs: Marcia Hale
Assistant to the President for Legislative Affairs: Pat Griffin
Assistant to the President for Communications: Mark D. Gearan
Assistant to the President and Senior Adviser: Bruce R. Lindsey
Assistant to the President and Director of Public Liaison: Alexis M. Herman
Assistant to the President for Domestic Policy: Carol Rasco
Assistant to the President for Economic Policy: Robert E. Rubin
Assistant to the President for National Security Affairs: Anthony Lake

Counsel to the President: Bernard W. Nussbaum
Deputy Assistant to the President and Press Secretary: Dee Dee Myers
Senior Adviser for Policy Development: Ira Magaziner
Office of Management and Budget, Director: Leon Panetta
Council of Economic Advisers, Chairman: Laura D'Andrea Tyson
Office of the United States Trade Representative, United States Trade Representative: Michael Kantor
Office of Science and Technology Policy, Assistant to the President for Science and Technology and Director: John H. Gibbons
Office of National Drug Control Policy, Director: Lee Patrick Brown
Office of Administration, Special Assistant to the President for Management and Director: Patsy L. Thomasson

The Cabinet

Secretary of Agriculture: Mike Espy
Secretary of Commerce: Ronald H. Brown
Secretary of Defense: Les Aspin[a]
  Joint Chiefs of Staff, Chairman: John Shalikashvili
Secretary of Education: Richard W. Riley
Secretary of Energy: Hazel R. O'Leary
Secretary of Health and Human Services: Donna E. Shalala
  Surgeon General: Joycelyn Elders
  Commissioner of Food and Drugs: David A. Kessler
  Social Security Administration, Commissioner: Shirley Sears Chater
Secretary of Housing and Urban Development: Henry G. Cisneros

Secretary of Interior: Bruce Babbitt
Department of Justice, Attorney General: Janet Reno
  Federal Bureau of Investigation, Director: Louis Freeh
Secretary of Labor: Robert B. Reich
Secretary of State: Warren Christopher
  United Nations Representative: M. K. Albright
Secretary of Transportation: Federico Peña
Secretary of the Treasury: Lloyd Bentsen
  Internal Revenue Service, Commissioner: Margaret M. Richardson
Secretary of Veterans Affairs: Jesse Brown

Independent Agencies

Central Intelligence Agency, Director: R. James Woolsey
Commission on Civil Rights, Chairman: Mary Frances Berry
Commission on National and Community Service: Thomas Ehrlich
Consumer Product Safety Commission, Chairman: Jacqueline Jones-Smith
Environmental Protection Agency, Administrator: Carol W. Browner
Equal Employment Opportunity Commission, Chairman: Tony E. Gallegos
Export-Import Bank of the United States, President and Chairman: Kenneth D. Brody
Farm Credit Administration, Chairman: Billy Ross Brown
Federal Communications Commission, Chairman: Reed Hundt
Federal Deposit Insurance Corporation, Chairman: Ricki Tigert[b]
Federal Election Commission, Chairman: Trevor Potter
Federal Emergency Management Agency, Director: James Lee Witt
Federal Labor Relations Authority, Chairman: Jean McKee
Federal Maritime Commission, Chairman: W. D. Hathaway
Federal Mediation and Conciliation Service, Director: John Calhoun Wells
Federal Reserve System, Chairman: Alan Greenspan
Federal Trade Commission, Chairman: Janet D. Steiger
General Services Administrator: Roger W. Johnson
Interstate Commerce Commission, Chairman: Gail C. McDonald

National Aeronautics and Space Administration, Administrator: Daniel S. Goldin
National Foundation on the Arts and Humanities
  National Endowment for the Arts, Chairman: Jane Alexander
  National Endowment for the Humanities, Chairman: Sheldon Hackney
National Labor Relations Board, Chairman: James M. Stephens
National Science Foundation, Chairman: Neal F. Lane
National Transportation Safety Board, Chairman: Carl W. Vogt
Nuclear Regulatory Commission, Chairman: Ivan Selin
Office of Government Ethics, Director: Stephen D. Potts
Peace Corps, Director: Carol Bellamy
Postal Rate Commission, Chairman: Edward Gleiman[b]
Securities and Exchange Commission, Chairman: Arthur Levitt
Selective Service System, Director: R. W. Gambino
Small Business Administrator: Erskine B. Bowles
Tennessee Valley Authority, Chairman: Craven Crowell
U.S. Arms Control and Disarmament Agency, Director: John Holum
U.S. Information Agency, Director: Joseph D. Duffey
U.S. Agency for International Development, Administrator: J. Brian Atwood
U.S. International Trade Commission, Chairman: Don E. Newquist
U.S. Postal Service, Postmaster General: Marvin Runyon

The Supreme Court

Chief Justice, William H. Rehnquist

Harry A. Blackmun	Sandra Day O'Connor	Anthony M. Kennedy	Clarence Thomas
John Paul Stevens	Antonin Scalia	David H. Souter	Ruth Bader Ginsburg

[a] Announced plans to resign.
[b] Nominated but not confirmed.

Selected listing as of Dec. 31, 1993.

UNITED STATES: 103d CONGRESS
Second Session

SENATE MEMBERSHIP

(As of January 1994: 56 Democrats, 44 Republicans.) Letters after names refer to party affiliation—D for Democrat, R for Republican, I for Independent. Single asterisk (*) denotes term expiring in January 1995; double asterisk (* *), term expiring in January 1997; triple asterisk (* * *), term expiring in January 1999. [1] Appointed to fill vacancy until special election on Nov. 8, 1994. [2] Elected in 1993 to fill vacancy.

Alabama
* * H. Heflin, D
* * * R. C. Shelby, D

Alaska
* * T. Stevens, R
* * * F. H. Murkowski, R

Arizona
* D. DeConcini, D
* * * J. McCain, R

Arkansas
* * * D. Bumpers, D
* * D. H. Pryor, D

California
* D. Feinstein, D
* * * B. Boxer, D

Colorado
* * H. Brown, R
* * * B. N. Campbell, D

Connecticut
* * * C. J. Dodd, D
* J. I. Lieberman, D

Delaware
* W. V. Roth, Jr., R
* * J. R. Biden, Jr., D

Florida
* * * B. Graham, D
* C. Mack, R

Georgia
* * S. Nunn, D
* * * P. Coverdell, R

Hawaii
* * * D. K. Inouye, D
* D. K. Akaka, D

Idaho
* * L. E. Craig, R
* * * D. Kempthorne, R

Illinois
* * P. Simon, D
* * * C. Moseley-Braun, D

Indiana
* R. G. Lugar, R
* * * D. Coats, R

Iowa
* * * C. E. Grassley, R
* * T. Harkin, D

Kansas
* * * R. Dole, R
* * N. L. Kassebaum, R

Kentucky
* * * W. H. Ford, D
* * M. McConnell, R

Louisiana
* * J. B. Johnston, D
* * * J. B. Breaux, D

Maine
* * W. S. Cohen, R
* G. J. Mitchell, D

Maryland
* P. S. Sarbanes, D
* * * B. A. Mikulski, D

Massachusetts
* E. M. Kennedy, D
* * J. F. Kerry, D

Michigan
* D. W. Riegle, Jr., D
* * C. Levin, D

Minnesota
* D. Durenberger, R
* * P. D. Wellstone, D

Mississippi
* * T. Cochran, R
* T. Lott, R

Missouri
* J. C. Danforth, R
* * * C. S. Bond, R

Montana
* * M. Baucus, D
* C. Burns, R

Nebraska
* * J. J. Exon, Jr., D
* J. R. Kerrey, D

Nevada
* * * H. Reid, D
* R. H. Bryan, D

New Hampshire
* * R. C. Smith, R
* * * J. Gregg, R

New Jersey
* * B. Bradley, D
* F. R. Lautenberg, D

New Mexico
* * P. V. Domenici, R
* J. Bingaman, D

New York
* D. P. Moynihan, D
* * * A. M. D'Amato, R

North Carolina
* * J. Helms, R
* * * L. Faircloth, R

North Dakota
* * * B. L. Dorgan, D
* K. Conrad, D

Ohio
* * * J. H. Glenn, Jr., D
* H. M. Metzenbaum, D

Oklahoma
* * D. L. Boren, D
* * * D. Nickles, R

Oregon
* * M. O. Hatfield, R
* * * B. Packwood, R

Pennsylvania
* * * A. Specter, R
* H. Wofford, D

Rhode Island
* * C. Pell, D
* J. H. Chafee, R

South Carolina
* * S. Thurmond, R
* * * E. F. Hollings, D

South Dakota
* * L. Pressler, R
* * * T. A. Daschle, D

Tennessee
* J. R. Sasser, D
* * Harlan Mathews, D[1]

Texas
* * P. Gramm, R
* K. B. Hutchison, R[2]

Utah
* O. Hatch, R
* * * R. F. Bennett, R

Vermont
* * * P. J. Leahy, D
* J. M. Jeffords, R

Virginia
* * J. W. Warner, R
* C. S. Robb, D

Washington
* S. Gorton, R
* * * P. Murray, D

West Virginia
* R. C. Byrd, D
* * J. D. Rockefeller IV, D

Wisconsin
* H. Kohl, D
* * * R. D. Feingold, D

Wyoming
* M. Wallop, R
* * A. K. Simpson, R

HOUSE MEMBERSHIP

(As of January 1994, 257 Democrats, 176 Republicans, 1 independent, 1 vacancy.) "At-L." in place of congressional district number means "representative at large."[1] Elected in 1993 to fill vacancy.

Alabama
1. S. Callahan, R
2. T. Everett, R
3. G. Browder, D
4. T. Bevill, D
5. B. Cramer, D
6. S. Bachus, R
7. E. F. Hilliard, D

Alaska
At-L. D. Young, R

Arizona
1. S. Coppersmith, D
2. E. Pastor, D
3. B. Stump, R
4. J. Kyl, R
5. J. Kolbe, R
6. K. English, D

Arkansas
1. B. Lambert, D
2. R. Thornton, D
3. T. Hutchinson, R
4. J. Dickey, R

California
1. D. Hamburg, D
2. W. W. Herger, R
3. V. Fazio, D
4. J. Doolittle, R
5. R. T. Matsui, D
6. L. Woolsey, D
7. G. Miller, D

8. N. Pelosi, D
9. R. V. Dellums, D
10. B. Baker, R
11. R. W. Pombo, R
12. T. Lantos, D
13. F. H. Stark, D
14. A. G. Eshoo, D
15. N. Y. Mineta, D
16. D. Edwards, D
17. S. Farr, D[1]
18. G. Condit, D
19. R. H. Lehman, D
20. C. Dooley, D
21. B. Thomas, R
22. M. Huffington, R
23. E. Gallegly, R
24. A. Beilenson, D
25. H. P. McKeon, R
26. H. L. Berman, D
27. C. J. Moorhead, R
28. D. Dreier, R
29. H. A. Waxman, D
30. X. Becerra, D
31. M. G. Martinez, Jr., D
32. J. C. Dixon, D
33. L. Roybal-Allard, D
34. E. E. Torres, D
35. M. Waters, D
36. J. Harman, D
37. W. R. Tucker III, D
38. S. Horn, R
39. E. Royce, R
40. J. Lewis, R
41. J. C. Kim, R
42. G. E. Brown, Jr., D
43. K. Calvert, R

44. A. A. McCandless, R
45. D. Rohrabacher, R
46. R. K. Dornan, R
47. C. C. Cox, R
48. R. Packard, R
49. L. Schenk, D.
50. B. Filner, D
51. R. Cunningham, R
52. D. Hunter, R

Colorado
1. P. Schroeder, D
2. D. Skaggs, D
3. S. McInnis, R
4. W. Allard, R
5. J. Hefley, R
6. D. Schaefer, R

Connecticut
1. B. B. Kennelly, D
2. S. Gejdenson, D
3. R. DeLauro, D
4. C. Shays, R
5. G. Franks, R
6. N. L. Johnson, R

Delaware
At-L. M. N. Castle, R

Florida
1. E. Hutto, D
2. P. Peterson, D
3. C. Brown, D
4. T. Fowler, R

5. K. Thurman, D
6. C. Stearns, R
7. J. L. Mica, R
8. B. McCollum, R
9. M. Bilirakis, R
10. C. W. Young, R
11. S. Gibbons, D
12. C. T. Canady, R
13. D. Miller, R
14. P. J. Goss, R
15. J. Bacchus, D
16. T. Lewis, R
17. C. Meek, D
18. I. Ros-Lehtinen, R
19. H. A. Johnston, D
20. P. Deutsch, D
21. L. Diaz-Balart, R
22. E. C. Shaw, Jr., R
23. A. L. Hastings, D

Georgia
1. J. Kingston, R
2. S. Bishop, D
3. M. Collins, R
4. J. Linder, R
5. J. Lewis, D
6. N. Gingrich, R
7. G. Darden, D
8. J. R. Rowland, D
9. N. Deal, D
10. D. Johnson, D
11. C. McKinney, D

Hawaii
1. N. Abercrombie, D
2. P. Mink, D

589

Idaho
1. L. LaRocco, D
2. M. D. Crapo, R

Illinois
1. B. Rush, D
2. M. Reynolds, D
3. W. O. Lipinski, D
4. L. V. Gutierrez, D
5. D. Rostenkowski, D
6. H. J. Hyde, R
7. C. Collins, D
8. P. M. Crane, R
9. S. R. Yates, D
10. J. E. Porter, R
11. G. E. Sangmeister, D
12. J. F. Costello, D
13. H. W. Fawell, R
14. J. D. Hastert, R
15. T. W. Ewing, R
16. D. Manzullo, R
17. L. Evans, D
18. R. H. Michel, R
19. G. Poshard, D
20. R. J. Durbin, D

Indiana
1. P. J. Visclosky, D
2. P. R. Sharp, D
3. T. Roemer, D
4. J. Long, D
5. S. Buyer, R
6. D. Burton, R
7. J. T. Myers, R
8. F. McCloskey, D
9. L. H. Hamilton, D
10. A. Jacobs, Jr., D

Iowa
1. J. Leach, R
2. J. Nussle, R
3. J. Lightfoot, R
4. N. Smith, D
5. F. Grandy, R

Kansas
1. P. Roberts, R
2. J. Slattery, D
3. J. Meyers, R
4. D. Glickman, D

Kentucky
1. T. Barlow, D
2. W. H. Natcher, D
3. R. L. Mazzoli, D
4. J. Bunning, R
5. H. Rogers, R
6. S. Baesler, D

Louisiana
1. B. Livingston, R
2. W. J. Jefferson, D
3. W. J. Tauzin, D
4. C. Fields, D
5. J. McCrery, R
6. R. H. Baker, R
7. J. A. Hayes, D

Maine
1. T. H. Andrews, D
2. O. J. Snowe, R

Maryland
1. W. T. Gilchrest, R
2. H. D. Bentley, R
3. B. L. Cardin, D
4. A. R. Wynn, D
5. S. H. Hoyer, D
6. R. G. Bartlett, R
7. K. Mfume, D
8. C. A. Morella, R

Massachusetts
1. J. Olver, D
2. R. E. Neal, D
3. P. I. Blute, R
4. B. Frank, D
5. M. T. Meehan, D
6. P. G. Torkildsen, R
7. E. J. Markey, D
8. J. P. Kennedy II, D
9. J. J. Moakley, D
10. G. E. Studds, D

Michigan
1. B. Stupak, D
2. P. Hoekstra, R
3. V. Ehlros, R[1]
4. D. Camp, R
5. J. Barcia, D
6. F. Upton, R
7. N. Smith, R
8. B. Carr, D
9. D. E. Kildee, D

10. D. E. Bonior, D
11. J. Knollenberg, R
12. S. M. Levin, D
13. W. D. Ford, D
14. J. Conyers, Jr., D
15. B. R. Collins, D
16. J. D. Dingell, D

Minnesota
1. T. J. Penny, D
2. D. Minge, D
3. J. Ramstad, R
4. B. F. Vento, D
5. M. O. Sabo, D
6. R. Grams, R
7. C. C. Peterson, D
8. J. L. Oberstar, D

Mississippi
1. J. L. Whitten, D
2. B. Thompson, D[1]
3. G. V. Montgomery, D
4. M. Parker, D
5. G. Taylor, D

Missouri
1. W. Clay, D
2. J. M. Talent, R
3. R. A. Gephardt, D
4. I. Skelton, D
5. A. Wheat, D
6. P. Danner, D
7. M. Hancock, R
8. B. Emerson, R
9. H. L. Volkmer, D

Montana
P. Williams, D

Nebraska
1. D. Bereuter, R
2. P. Hoagland, D
3. B. Barrett, R

Nevada
1. J. H. Bilbray, D
2. B. F. Vucanovich, R

New Hampshire
1. B. Zeliff, Jr., R
2. D. Swett, D

New Jersey
1. R. E. Andrews, D
2. W. J. Hughes, D
3. J. Saxton, R
4. C. H. Smith, R
5. M. Roukema, R
6. F. Pallone, Jr., D
7. B. Franks, R
8. H. C. Klein, D
9. R. G. Torricelli, D
10. D. M. Payne, D
11. D. A. Gallo, R
12. D. Zimmer, R
13. R. Menendez, D

New Mexico
1. S. Schiff, R
2. J. Skeen, R
3. B. Richardson, D

New York
1. G. J. Hochbrueckner, D
2. R. A. Lazio, R
3. P. T. King, R
4. D. A. Levy, R
5. G. L. Ackerman, D
6. F. H. Flake, D
7. T. J. Manton, D
8. J. Nadler, D
9. C. E. Schumer, D
10. E. Towns, D
11. M. R. Owens, D
12. N. M. Velazquez, D
13. S. Molinari, R
14. C. B. Maloney, D
15. C. B. Rangel, D
16. J. Serrano, D
17. E. L. Engel, D
18. N. Lowey, D
19. H. Fish, Jr., R
20. B. A. Gilman, R
21. M. R. McNulty, D
22. G. B. H. Solomon, R
23. S. L. Boehlert, R
24. J. M. McHugh, R
25. J. T. Walsh, R
26. M. D. Hinchey, D
27. B. Paxon, R
28. L. M. Slaughter, D
29. J. J. LaFalce, D

30. J. Quinn, R
31. A. Houghton, R

North Carolina
1. E. Clayton, D
2. T. Valentine, D
3. H. M. Lancaster, D
4. D. E. Price, D
5. S. L. Neal, D
6. H. Coble, R
7. C. Rose, D
8. W. G. Hefner, D
9. J. A. McMillan, R
10. C. Ballenger, R
11. C. H. Taylor, R
12. M. Watt, D

North Dakota
At-L. E. Pomeroy, D

Ohio
1. D. Mann, D
2. R. Portman, R[1]
3. T. P. Hall, D
4. M. G. Oxley, R
5. P. E. Gillmor, R
6. T. Strickland, D
7. D. L. Hobson, R
8. J. A. Boehner, R
9. M. Kaptur, D
10. M. R. Hoke, R
11. L. Stokes, D
12. J. R. Kasich, R
13. S. Brown, D
14. T. C. Sawyer, D
15. D. Pryce, R
16. R. Regula, R
17. J. A. Traficant, Jr., D
18. D. Applegate, D
19. E. Fingerhut, D

Oklahoma
1. J. M. Inhofe, R
2. M. Synar, D
3. B. Brewster, D
4. D. McCurdy, D
5. E. J. Istook, Jr., R
6. vacant

Oregon
1. E. Furse, D
2. R. F. Smith, R
3. R. Wyden, D
4. P. A. DeFazio, D
5. M. Kopetski, D

Pennsylvania
1. T. M. Foglietta, D
2. L. E. Blackwell, D
3. R. A. Borski, Jr., D
4. R. Klink, D
5. W. F. Clinger, Jr., R
6. T. Holden, D
7. C. Weldon, R
8. J. Greenwood, R
9. B. Shuster, R
10. J. M. McDade, R
11. P. E. Kanjorski, D
12. J. P. Murtha, D
13. M. M. Margolies-Mezvinsky, D
14. W. J. Coyne, D
15. P. McHale, D
16. R. S. Walker, R
17. G. Gekas, R
18. R. Santorum, R
19. W. F. Goodling, R
20. A. J. Murphy, D
21. T. J. Ridge, R

Rhode Island
1. R. K. Machtley, R
2. J. F. Reed, D

South Carolina
1. A. Ravenel, Jr., R
2. F. D. Spence, R
3. B. C. Derrick, Jr., D
4. B. Inglis, R
5. J. M. Spratt, Jr., D
6. J. E. Clyburn, D

South Dakota
At-L. T. Johnson, D

Tennessee
1. J. H. Quillen, R
2. J. J. Duncan, Jr., R
3. M. Lloyd, D
4. J. Cooper, D
5. B. Clement, D
6. B. Gordon, D
7. D. K. Sundquist, R
8. J. S. Tanner, D
9. H. E. Ford, D

Texas
1. J. Chapman, D
2. C. Wilson, D
3. S. Johnson, R
4. R. M. Hall, D
5. J. Bryant, D
6. J. Barton, R
7. B. Archer, R
8. J. M. Fields, Jr., R
9. J. Brooks, D
10. J. J. Pickle, D
11. C. Edwards, D
12. P. Geren, D
13. B. Sarpalius, D
14. G. Laughlin, D
15. K. de la Garza, D
16. R. D. Coleman, D
17. C. W. Stenholm, D
18. C. Washington, D
19. L. Combest, D
20. H. B. Gonzalez, D
21. L. Smith, R
22. T. DeLay, R
23. H. Bonilla, R
24. M. Frost, D
25. M. A. Andrews, D
26. R. K. Armey, R
27. S. P. Ortiz, D
28. F. Tejeda, D
29. G. Green, D
30. E. B. Johnson, D

Utah
1. J. V. Hansen, R
2. K. Shepherd, D
3. B. Orton, D

Vermont
At-L. B. Sanders, I

Virginia
1. H. H. Bateman, R
2. O. B. Pickett, D
3. R. C. Scott, D
4. N. Sisisky, D
5. L. F. Payne, Jr., D
6. R. W. Goodlatte, R
7. T. J. Bliley, Jr., R
8. J. P. Moran, D
9. R. Boucher, D
10. F. R. Wolf, R
11. L. L. Byrne, D

Washington
1. M. Cantwell, D
2. A. Swift, D
3. J. Unsoeld, D
4. J. Inslee, D
5. T. S. Foley, D
6. N. D. Dicks, D
7. J. McDermott, D
8. J. Dunn, R
9. M. Kreidler, D

West Virginia
1. A. B. Mollohan, D
2. R. E. Wise, Jr., D
3. N. J. Rahall II, D

Wisconsin
1. P. Barca, D[1]
2. S. Klug, R
3. S. Gunderson, R
4. G. D. Kleczka, D
5. T. M. Barrett, D
6. T. E. Petri, R
7. D. R. Obey, D
8. T. Roth, R
9. F. J. Sensenbrenner, Jr., R

Wyoming
At-L. C. Thomas, R

AMERICAN SAMOA
Delegate, E. F. H. Faleomavaega, D

DISTRICT OF COLUMBIA
Delegate, Eleanor Holmes Norton, D

GUAM
Delegate, R. A. Underwood, D

PUERTO RICO
Resident Commissioner
Carlos Romero-Barcelc, D

VIRGIN ISLANDS
Delegate, Ron de Lugo, D

Contributors

ABRAM, LYNWOOD, Freelance Writer and Newspaper Correspondent, El Paso, TX: CULTS IN AMERICA—DAVID KORESH AND THE BRANCH DAVIDIANS; TEXAS

ADRIAN, CHARLES R., Professor of Political Science, University of California, Riverside; Author, *A History of City Government: The Emergence of the Metropolis 1920-1945;* Coauthor, *State and Local Politics, A History of American City Government: The Formation of Traditions, 1775-1870, Governing Urban America:* BIOGRAPHY—*Richard Riordan;* CALIFORNIA; LOS ANGELES

ARNOLD, ANTHONY, Author, *Afghanistan: The Soviet Invasion in Perspective, Afghanistan's Two-Party Communism: Parcham and Khalq, The Fateful Pebble: Afghanistan's Role in the Fall of the Soviet Empire:* AFGHANISTAN

ATTNER, PAUL, Senior Writer, *The Sporting News:* BIOGRAPHY—*Charles Barkley;* SPORTS—*Basketball, Football, Soccer*

AUSTIN, TERESA, Freelance Writer: ENGINEERING, CIVIL

BATRA, PREM P., Professor of Biochemistry, Wright State University: BIOCHEMISTRY

BEAUCHAMP, LANE, *The Kansas City Star:* THE GREAT FLOOD OF '93; MISSOURI

BECK, KAY, Department of Communications, Georgia State University: GEORGIA

BEHLER, DEBORAH A., Executive Editor, *Wildlife Conservation* magazine: AFRICA—*The Black Rhino;* ZOOS AND ZOOLOGY

BEST, JOHN, Chief, *Canada World News,* Ottawa: NEW BRUNSWICK; PRINCE EDWARD ISLAND; QUEBEC

BOND, DONOVAN H., Professor Emeritus of Journalism, West Virginia University: WEST VIRGINIA

BOULAY, HARVEY, Director of Development, Rogerson House; Author, *The Twilight Cities:* MASSACHUSETTS

BOWER, BRUCE, Behavioral Sciences Editor, *Science News:* ANTHROPOLOGY; ARCHAEOLOGY

BRAASCH, BARBARA, Freelance Travel Writer: TRAVEL

BRAMMER, DANA B., Director, Public Policy Research Center, University of Mississippi: MISSISSIPPI

BRANDHORST, L. CARL, and JoANN C., Department of Geography, Western Oregon State College: OREGON

BROACH, GLENN, Professor of Political Science, Winthrop University: SOUTH CAROLINA

BROOM, JACK, Reporter, *The Seattle Times:* WASHINGTON

BUGAJSKI, JANUSZ, Associate Director of East European Studies, Center for Strategic and International Studies; Author, *Nations in Turmoil: Conflict and Cooperation in Eastern Europe, East European Fault Lines: Dissent, Opposition, and Social Activism:* ALBANIA; BULGARIA; HUNGARY; ROMANIA

BURKS, ARDATH W., Professor Emeritus Asian Studies, Rutgers University; Author, *Third Order of the Rising Sun, Japan: A Postindustrial Power:* BIOGRAPHY—*Morihiro Hosokawa, Crown Prince Naruhito and Masako Owada;* JAPAN

BUSH, GRAHAM W. A., Associate Professor of Political Studies, University of Auckland; Author, *Governing Big Cities, Advance in Order: The Auckland City Council 1971-89:* NEW ZEALAND

CAMP, RODERIC AI, Tulane University; Author, *Generals in the Palacio, Entrepreneurs and Politics in Twentieth Century Mexico:* MEXICO

CAMPBELL, ROBERT, University of Wyoming; Coauthor, *Discovering Wyoming:* WYOMING

CASEY, DAN, Staff Writer, *The (Annapolis) Capital:* MARYLAND

CASSIDY, SUZANNE, Freelance U.S. Journalist, London: GREAT BRITAIN; GREAT BRITAIN—*The Arts*

CHRISTENSEN, WILLIAM E., Professor of History, Midland Lutheran College; Author, *Saga of the Tower: A History of Dana College and Trinity Seminary, New Song to the Lord: A History of First Lutheran Church, Fremont, Nebraska:* NEBRASKA

COLE, JOHN N., Maine Journalist; Founder, *Maine Times;* Author, *Fishing Came First, In Maine, Striper, Salmon:* MAINE

COLLINS, BUD, Sports Columnist, *The Boston Globe;* Author, *My Life With The Pros:* SPORTS—*Tennis*

COLTON, KENT W., Executive Vice-President and Chief Executive Officer, National Association of Home Builders, Washington, DC: HOUSING

CONRADT, DAVID P., Professor of Political Science, East Carolina University; Author, *The German Polity, West European Politics:* GERMANY

COOPER, ILENE, Children's Book Editor, *Booklist Magazine:* LITERATURE—*Children's*

COOPER, MARY H., Staff Writer, *CQ Researcher,* Congressional Quarterly; Author, *The Business of Drugs:* ABORTION; ENERGY; FOREIGN AID; INSURANCE, LIABILITY

COPPEDGE, MICHAEL, Assistant Professor, Latin American Studies Program, Paul H. Nitze School of Advanced International Studies, Johns Hopkins University: ECUADOR; PERU; VENEZUELA

CORLEW, ROBERT E., Dean, Middle Tennessee State University: TENNESSEE

CORNWELL, ELMER E., JR., Professor of Political Science, Brown University: RHODE ISLAND

CRONK, DOUGLAS R., Open University of British Columbia; Author, *Canadian Viewpoint: An Anthology of Canadian Writing;* Editor, *Wacousta, Or The Prophesy. A Tale of the Canadas:* CANADA—*The Arts;* LITERATURE—*Canadian*

CUNNIFF, JOHN, Business News Analyst, The Associated Press; Author, *How to Stretch Your Dollar:* BUSINESS AND CORPORATE AFFAIRS; INDUSTRIAL PRODUCTION; UNITED STATES—*The Economy*

CURRIER, CHET, Financial Writer, The Associated Press; Author, *The Investor's Encyclopedia, The 15-Minute Investor;* Coauthor, *No-Cost/Low-Cost Investing:* STOCKS AND BONDS

CURTIS, L. PERRY, JR., Professor of History, Brown University: IRELAND

CUSHMAN, JOHN H., JR., Washington Bureau, *The New York Times:* BANKING AND FINANCE

DANIELS, ROBERT V., Professor of History, University of Vermont; former Vermont state senator; Author, *Russia: The Roots of Confrontation:* VERMONT

DARBY, JOSEPH W., III, Reporter, *The Times-Picayune,* New Orleans: LOUISIANA

DAVID, LEONARD, Director, Space Data Resources and Information: SPACE EXPLORATION; SPACE EXPLORATION—*The Space Station*

De GREGORIO, GEORGE, Sports Department, *The New York Times;* Author, *Joe DiMaggio, An Informal Biography;* OBITUARIES—*Arthur Ashe;* SPORTS—*Boxing, Swimming, Track and Field, Yachting*

DELZELL, CHARLES F., Professor of History Emeritus and Adjunct Professor, Vanderbilt University; Author, *Italy in the Twentieth Century, Mediterranean Fascism, Mussolini's Enemies:* ITALY

DENNIS, LARRY, Editor, *Senior Golfer* magazine: SPORTS—*Golf*

DUFF, ERNEST A., Professor of Politics, Randolph-Macon Woman's College; Author, *Agrarian Reform in Colombia, Violence and Repression in Latin America, Leader and Party in Latin America:* COLOMBIA

EADINGTON, WILLIAM R., Director, Institute for the Study of Gambling and Commercial Gaming; Professor of Economics, University of Nevada, Reno: GAMBLING

ELKINS, ANN M., Fashion Director, *Good Housekeeping Magazine:* FASHION

ENSTAD, ROBERT H., Writer, *Chicago Tribune:* CHICAGO; ILLINOIS

EWEGEN, ROBERT D., Editorial Writer, *The Denver Post:* COLORADO

FALLESEN, LEIF BECK, Editor-in-Chief, *Boersen,* Copenhagen: DENMARK; FINLAND; NORWAY; SWEDEN

FIERO, ROBERT C., Consultant, Alpha Byte Computer Services: COMMUNICATION TECHNOLOGY; COMMUNICATION TECHNOLOGY—*The Video Phone*

FISHER, JIM, Editorial Writer and Columnist, *Lewiston Morning Tribune:* IDAHO

FRANCIS, DAVID R., Economy Page Editor, *The Christian Science Monitor:* INTERNATIONAL TRADE AND FINANCE; INTERNATIONAL TRADE AND FINANCE—*The North American Free Trade Agreement*

GAILEY, HARRY A., Professor of History, San Jose State University; Author, *History of the Gambia, History of Africa, Road to Aba:* NIGERIA; ZAIRE

GEORGE, PAUL S., Assistant Professor, Miami-Dade Community College; Author, *Florida: Yesterday and Today, A Guide to the History of Florida:* FLORIDA

GIBSON, ROBERT C., Associate Editor, *The Billings Gazette;* Coauthor, *The Big Drive;* Editor, *Yellowstone on Fire, Wagons Across Wyoming:* MONTANA

GOODMAN, DONALD, Associate Professor of Sociology, John Jay College of Criminal Justice, City University of New York: PRISONS

GOODWIN, FREDERICK K., Director, National Institute of Mental Health: MEDICINE AND HEALTH—*Mental Health*

GORDON, MAYNARD M., Detroit Bureau Chief, *Dealer Business* magazine; Author, *The Iacocca Management Technique:* AUTOMOBILES

GOUDINOFF, PETER, Professor, Department of Political Science, University of Arizona; Member, Arizona Senate; Author, *People's Guide to National Defense:* ARIZONA

GRAYSON, GEORGE W., Class of 1938 Professor of Government, College of William and Mary; Author, *The Politics of Mexican Oil, The United States and Mexico: Patterns of Influence, Oil and Mexican Foreign Policy:* BRAZIL; PORTUGAL; SPAIN

GREGORY, BARBARA J., American Numismatic Association: COINS AND COIN COLLECTING

GROSSMAN, LAWRENCE, Director of Publications, The American Jewish Committee: RELIGION—*The U.S. Holocaust Museum;* RELIGION—*Judaism*

GROTH, ALEXANDER J., Professor of Political Science, University of California, Davis; Author, *People's Poland, Contemporary Politics: Europe, Comparative Resource Allocation, Public Policy Across Nations:* POLAND

HALLER, TIMOTHY G., Department of Political Science, Western Nevada Community College: NEVADA

HALSEY, MARGARET BROWN, Professor of Art History, New York City Technical College of the City University of New York: ART

HAND, SAMUEL B., Professor of History, University of Vermont: VERMONT

HARMON, CHARLES, American Library Association: LIBRARIES

HARVEY, ROSS M., Senior Policy Adviser, Department of Education, Culture and Employment, Government of the Northwest Territories: NORTHWEST TERRITORIES

HASSON, JUDITH B. Congressional Reporter, *USA Today:* WOMEN; WOMEN—*Women's Growing Political Clout*

HELMREICH, JONATHAN E., Professor of History, Allegheny College; Author, *Belgium and Europe: A Study in Small Power Diplomacy, Gathering Rare Ores: The Diplomacy of Uranium Acquisition, 1943-54;* Coauthor, *Rebirth: A History of Europe Since World War II:* BELGIUM; NETHERLANDS

HELMREICH, PAUL C., Professor of History, Wheaton College; Author, *Wheaton College: The Seminary Years, 1834-1912, From Paris to Sèvres: The Partition of the Ottoman Empire at the Peace Conference of 1919-1920;* Coauthor, *Rebirth: A History of Europe Since World War II:* SWITZERLAND

HERMIDA, ALFRED, North Africa Correspondent, BBC: MOROCCO; TUNISIA

HOLLOWAY, HARRY, Professor Emeritus, Department of Political Science, University of Oklahoma; Coauthor, *Public Opinion: Coalitions, Elites, and Masses, Party and Factional Division in Texas:* OKLAHOMA

HOOVER, HERBERT T., Professor of History, University of South Dakota; Author, *South Dakota Leaders, The Yankton Sioux, To Be an Indian, The Chitimacha People, Higher Education in South Dakota:* SOUTH DAKOTA

HOPKO, THE REV. THOMAS, Assistant Professor, St. Vladimir's Orthodox Theological Seminary: RELIGION—*Orthodox Eastern*

HOWARD, CARLA BREER, Furnishings and Antiques Editor, *Traditional Home:* INTERIOR DESIGN

HOYT, CHARLES K., Senior Editor, *Architectural Record;* Author, *More Places for People, Building for Commerce and Industry:* ARCHITECTURE

HUFFMAN, GEORGE J., Science Systems and Applications: METEOROLOGY

HULBERT, DAN, *Atlanta Journal & Constitution:* TELEVISION AND RADIO; THEATER

HUSTED, THOMAS A., Assistant Professor, Department of Economics, The American University: TAXATION

JACKSON, PAUL CONRAD, Editor, *The Calgary Sun;* Columnist, *Saskatoon Star-Phoenix;* Author, *Battleground: The Socialist Assault on Grant Devine's Canadian Dream:* ALBERTA; SASKATCHEWAN

JENNERMANN, DONALD, Director, University Honors Program, Indiana State University; Author, *Born of a Cretan Spring, Literature for Living:* LITERATURE—*English*

JOHNSON, LONNIE, Institute for Human Sciences, Vienna, Austria; Author, *Introducing Austria:* AUSTRIA

JONES, H. G., Curator, North Carolina Collection, University of North Carolina at Chapel Hill; Author, *North Carolina Illustrated, 1524-1984:* NORTH CAROLINA

JURGENS, DAVE, *The Forum,* Fargo, ND: NORTH DAKOTA

KAPLOW, ROBERT, Freelance Writer: WASHINGTON, DC

KARNES, THOMAS L., Professor of History Emeritus, Arizona State University; Author, *Latin American Policy of the United States, Failure of Union: Central America 1824-1960:* CENTRAL AMERICA

KERNER, MARY C., Freelance Writer; Author, *Barefoot to Balanchine: How to Watch Dance:* BIOGRAPHY—*Emma Thompson;* OBITUARIES—*Audrey Hepburn, Helen Hayes*

KIM, HAN-KYO, University of Cincinnati; Author, *Korea and the Politics of Imperialism, 1876-1910; Studies on Korea: A Scholar's Guide:* KOREA

KING, PETER J., Professor of History, Carleton University, Ottawa; Author, *Utilitarian Jurisprudence in America:* ONTARIO; OTTAWA

KINNEAR, MICHAEL, Professor of History, University of Manitoba; Author, *The Fall of Lloyd George, The British Voter:* MANITOBA

KISSELGOFF, ANNA, Chief Dance Critic, *The New York Times:* DANCE; OBITUARIES—*Rudolf Nureyev*

KOZINN, ALLAN, Music Critic, *The New York Times;* Author, *Mischa Elman and the Romantic Style, The Guitar: The History, The Music, The Players:* MUSIC—*Classical;* OBITUARIES—*Marian Anderson*

KRONISH, SYD, Stamp Editor, The Associated Press: STAMPS AND STAMP COLLECTING

LaFRANCHI, HOWARD, Staff Correspondent, Paris Bureau, *The Christian Science Monitor:* FRANCE

LaGOW, BETTE, Freelance Writer: PETS: A GROWING PREOCCUPATION

LAI, DAVID CHUENYAN, Professor of Geography, University of Victoria, British Columbia; Author, *The Forbidden City Within Victoria: Myth, Symbol and Streetscape of Canada's Earliest Chinatown:* HONG KONG

LAWRENCE, ROBERT M., Professor of Political Science, Colorado State University; Author, *The Strategic Defense Initiative:* MILITARY AFFAIRS

LEEPSON, MARC, Freelance Writer: DRUGS AND ALCOHOL; SOCIAL WELFARE

LEVINE, LOUIS, Professor, Department of Biology, City College of New York; Author, *Biology of the Gene, Biology for a Modern Society:* BIOTECHNOLOGY; GENETICS; MICROBIOLOGY

LEWIS, ANNE C., Education Policy Writer: EDUCATION; EDUCATION—*National Service Plan*

LEWIS, JEROME R., Director for Public Administration, College of Urban Affairs and Public Policy, University of Delaware: DELAWARE

LOBRON, BARBARA L., Editor, Photographer, Writer: PHOTOGRAPHY

LOESCHER, GIL, Professor of International Relations, University of Notre Dame; Author, *Calculated Kindness: Refugees and America's Half-Open Door, Refugees and International Relations:* REFUGEES AND IMMIGRATION; REFUGEES AND IMMIGRATION—*The Illegal Immigrant*

LOHR, STEVE, Reporter, *The New York Times:* BUSINESS—*The IBM Story*

MAGELBY, DAVID, Chair, Political Science Department, Brigham Young University: UTAH

MARCOPOULOS, GEORGE J., Professor of History, Tufts University: CYPRUS; GREECE

MATHESON, JIM, Sportswriter, *Edmonton Journal:* SPORTS—*Ice Hockey*

MAYERCHAK, PATRICK M., Professor of Political Science, Virginia Military Institute; Author, *Scholar's Guide to Southeast Asia;* Coauthor, *Linkage or Bondage: US-ASEAN Economic Relations:* MALAYSIA; SINGAPORE

McCORQUODALE, SUSAN, Professor of Political Science, Memorial University of Newfoundland: NEWFOUNDLAND

McGILL, DAVID A., Professor of Marine Science, U.S. Coast Guard Academy: OCEANOGRAPHY

McLAURIN, RONALD D., President, Abbott Associates, Inc.; Author, *The Emergence of a New Lebanon: Fantasy or Reality?, Lebanon and the World in the 1980s:* LEBANON

MEDINGER, DANIEL, Editor, *The Catholic Review:* RELIGION—*Roman Catholicism*

MICHAELIS, PATRICIA A., Director, Library and Archives Division, Kansas State Historical Society: KANSAS

MICHIE, ARUNA NAYYAR, Associate Professor of Political Science, Kansas State University: BANGLADESH

MILLER, PENNY M., Professor of Political Science, University of Kentucky; Coauthor, *Political Parties and Primaries in Kentucky, The Kentucky Legislature: Two Decades of Change:* KENTUCKY

MILLER, RANDALL M., Department of History, St. Joseph's University; Author, *Ethnic and Racial Images in American Film and Television, Immigrants and Religion in Urban America, Essays on Race, Ethnicity and the Urban South:* ETHNIC GROUPS, U.S.

MILWARD, JOHN, Freelance Writer and Critic: MUSIC—*Popular and Jazz*

MITCHELL, G. E., Professor of Physics, North Carolina State University: PHYSICS

MITCHELL, RICK, *U.N. Observer and International Report:* UNITED NATIONS

MONASTERSKY, RICHARD, Earth Sciences Editor, *Science News:* GEOLOGY

MORTIMER, ROBERT A., Professor, Department of Political Science, Haverford College; Author, *The Third World Coalition in International Politics;* Coauthor, *Politics and Society in Contemporary Africa:* ALGERIA

MORTON, DESMOND, Professor of History and Principal, Erindale College, University of Toronto; Author, *Working People: An Illustrated History of the Canadian Labour Movement, A Military History of Canada:* BIOGRAPHY—*Kim Campbell, Jean Chrétien;* CANADA; CANADA—*Leadership and the Election*

MURPHY, ROBERT F., Editorial Writer, *The Hartford Courant:* CONNECTICUT

NAFTALIN, ARTHUR, Professor Emeritus of Public Affairs, University of Minnesota: MINNESOTA

NASH, ALANNA, Author, *Dolly (A Biography of Dolly Parton), Behind Closed Doors: Talking with the Legends of Country Music:* THE COUNTRY-MUSIC BOOM

NEWLAND, ED, Assistant City Editor, *Richmond Times Dispatch:* VIRGINIA

OCHSENWALD, WILLIAM, Professor of History, Virginia Polytechnic Institute and State University; Author, *The Middle East: A History, The Hijaz Railroad, Religion, Society, and the State in Arabia:* KUWAIT; SAUDI ARABIA

O'CONNOR, ROBERT E., Associate Professor of Political Science, The Pennsylvania State University; Coauthor, *Politics and Structure: Essentials of American National Government:* PENNSYLVANIA

O'MEARA, PATRICK, Former Director, African Studies Program, Indiana University; Coeditor, *Africa, International Politics in Southern Africa, Southern Africa, The Continuing Crisis:* AFRICA; ANGOLA; MOZAMBIQUE; SOUTH AFRICA; ZIMBABWE

ORTIZ, PETER J., *The San Juan Star:* PUERTO RICO

PALMER, NORMAN D., Professor Emeritus of Political Science and South Asian Studies, University of Pennsylvania; Author, *Westward Watch: The United States and the Changing Western Pacific, The United States and India: The Dimensions of Influence, Elections and Political Development: The South Asian Experience, The New Regionalism in Asia and the Pacific:* INDIA; SRI LANKA

PEARSON, FREDERIC S., Director, Center for Peace and Conflict Studies, Wayne State University, Detroit; Coauthor, *International Relations: The Global Condition, Fuel on the Fire? Effects of Armament During Warfare:* UNITED STATES—*Foreign Affairs*

PERETZ, DON, Professor Emeritus of Political Science, State University of New York at Binghamton; Author, *The West Bank—History, Politics, Society & Economy, Government and Politics of Israel, The Middle East Today:* EGYPT; ISRAEL

PERKINS, KENNETH J., Assistant Professor of History, University of South Carolina: LIBYA; RELIGION—*Islam, Muslims in the United States*

PERRY, DAVID K., Associate Professor, Department of Journalism, The University of Alabama: PUBLISHING; PUBLISHING—*The Newspaper Today*

PIPPIN, LARRY L., Professor of Political Science, University of the Pacific; Author, *The Remón Era:* ARGENTINA; PARAGUAY; URUGUAY

PLATT, HERMANN K., Professor of History, Saint Peter's College: NEW JERSEY

POOLE, PETER A., Author, *The Vietnamese in Thailand, Eight Presidents and Indochina;* Coauthor, *American Diplomacy:* CAMBODIA; LAOS; VIETNAM

PRIESTER, REINHARD, Center for Biomedical Ethics, University of Minnesota: MEDICINE AND HEALTH—*Medical Ethics*

RALOFF, JANET, Senior Editor, *Science News:* ENVIRONMENT

REED, WILLIAM CYRUS, Director of African Studies, The American University in Cairo (Egypt): KENYA; TANZANIA; UGANDA

REMINGTON, ROBIN ALISON, Professor of Political Science, University of Missouri-Columbia: THE YUGOSLAV WARS OF SECESSION

REUNING, WINIFRED, Writer, Polar Program, National Science Foundation: POLAR RESEARCH

RICHTER, LINDA K., Professor of Political Science, Kansas State University; Author, *Land Reform and Tourism Development, Policy-Making in the Philippines, The Politics of Tourism in Asia:* MYANMAR; PHILIPPINES

RICHTER, WILLIAM L., Professor and Head, Department of Political Science, Kansas State University: PAKISTAN

RIGGAN, WILLIAM, Associate Editor, *World Literature Today,* University of Oklahoma; Author, *Pícaros, Madmen, Naïfs, and Clowns, Comparative Literature and Literary Theory:* LITERATURE—*World*

ROBERTS, SAM, Urban Affairs Columnist, *The New York Times:* BIOGRAPHY—*Rudolph Giuliani;* NEW YORK CITY

ROBINSON, LEIF J., Editor, *Sky & Telescope;* Author, *Outdoor Optics:* ASTRONOMY

RODGERS, THOMAS E., University of Southern Indiana: INDIANA

ROSS, RUSSELL M., Professor of Political Science, University of Iowa; Author, *State and Local Government and Administration, Iowa Government and Administration:* IOWA

ROVNER, JULIE, Correspondent, Medical News Network: U.S. HEALTH CARE—*CONFRONTING THE CRISIS*

RUBIN, JIM, Supreme Court Correspondent, The Associated Press: BIOGRAPHY—*Ruth Bader Ginsburg;* CRIME; LAW; OBITUARIES—*Thurgood Marshall*

RUFF, NORMAN J., Assistant Professor, Department of Political Science, University of Victoria, B.C.; Coauthor, *The Reins of Power: Governing British Columbia:* BRITISH COLUMBIA

SALSINI, PAUL, Staff Development Director, *The Milwaukee Journal:* WISCONSIN

SAWATSKY, DON, Freelance Writer/Broadcaster; Author, *Ghost Town Trails of the Yukon:* YUKON

SCHLOSSBERG, DAN, Baseball Writer; Author, *The Baseball IQ Challenge, The Baseball Catalog, The Baseball Book of Why, Cooperstown: Baseball's Hall of Fame Players:* BIOGRAPHY—*Barry Bonds;* SPORTS—*Baseball*

SCHROEDER, RICHARD, Consultant, Organization of American States: BOLIVIA; CARIBBEAN; CHILE; HAITI; LATIN AMERICA

SCHWAB, PETER, Professor of Political Science, State University of New York at Purchase; Author, *Ethiopia: Politics, Economics, and Society, Human Rights: Cultural and Ideological Perspectives:* ETHIOPIA; ETHIOPIA—*Eritrea;* SOMALIA

SEADER, MARY BETH, Vice-President for Policy and Practice, National Council for Adoption: FAMILY—*Adoption*

SENSER, ROBERT A., Freelance Writer, Washington, DC: HUMAN RIGHTS

SETH, R. P., Chairman, Department of Economics, Mount Saint Vincent University, Halifax: CANADA—*The Economy;* NOVA SCOTIA

SEYBOLD, PAUL G., Professor, Department of Chemistry, Wright State University: CHEMISTRY

SHARLET, ROBERT, Professor of Political Science, Union College; Author, *Soviet Constitutional Crisis:* BALTIC REPUBLICS; GEORGIA; RUSSIA AND THE COMMONWEALTH OF INDEPENDENT STATES

SHEPRO, CARL E., Professor of Political Science, University of Alaska-Anchorage: ALASKA

SHOGAN, ROBERT, National Political Correspondent, Washington Bureau, *The Los Angeles Times;* Author, *A Question of Judgment, Promises to Keep:* THE U.S. VICE-PRESIDENCY—AN ANALYSIS OF THE OFFICE; BIOGRAPHY—*Bruce Babbitt, Warren Christopher, David Gergen, Janet Reno;* UNITED STATES—*Domestic Affairs*

SIMON, JEFFREY D., Author, *The Terrorist Trap: America's Experience with Terrorism:* TERRORISM

SIMON, SHELDON W., Professor of Political Science, Arizona State University-Tempe; Author, *The Future of Asian-Pacific Security Collaboration:* ASIA

SMITH, REX, Editor, *The* (Troy, NY) *Record:* NEW YORK

SNODSMITH, RALPH L., Ornamental Horticulturist; Author, *Ralph Snodsmith's Tips from the Garden Hotline:* GARDENING AND HORTICULTURE

SNYDER, BEATRICE M., Manager of Public Affairs, The Norman Rockwell Museum: ART—*The New Norman Rockwell Museum*

SPRINGER, NEIL, Freelance Writer: ENVIRONMENT—*The Timber Industry-Environmentalist Conflict*

SPYCHALSKI, JOHN C., Chairman, Department of Business Logistics, College of Business Administration, The Pennsylvania State University: TRANSPORTATION

STARR, JOHN BRYAN, President, China Institute in America, New York City; Author, *Continuing the Revolution: The Political Thought of Mao;* Editor, *The Future of U.S.-China Relations:* CHINA; TAIWAN

STEIN, LANA, Associate Professor of Political Science, University of Missouri-St. Louis; Author, *Holding Bureaucrats Accountable: Politicians and Professionals in St. Louis:* CITIES AND URBAN AFFAIRS

STERN, JEROME H., Professor of English, Florida State University; Author, *Making Shapely Fiction:* LITERATURE—*American*

STEWART, WILLIAM H., Professor of Political Science, The University of Alabama; Coauthor, *Alabama Government and Politics;* Author, *Leadership in the Public Service, The Alabama Constitution:* ALABAMA

STIEBER, JACK, Professor Emeritus, School of Labor and Industrial Relations and Department of Economics, Michigan State University; Author, *U.S. Industrial Relations: The Next Twenty Years, Governing the UAW, Public Employee Unionism:* LABOR

SUTTON, STAN, Sportswriter, *The Courier-Journal,* Louisville, KY: SPORTS—*Auto Racing, Horse Racing*

TABORSKY, EDWARD, Professor of Government, University of Texas at Austin; Author, *Communism in Czechoslovakia, 1948-1960, Communist Penetration of the Third World:* CZECH REPUBLIC; SLOVAKIA

TAYLOR, WILLIAM L., Professor of History, Plymouth State College: NEW HAMPSHIRE

TESAR, JENNY, Science and Medicine Writer; Author, *Introduction to Animals, Parents as Teachers:* COMPUTERS; MEDICINE AND HEALTH; MEDICINE AND HEALTH—*Electricity and Cancer—A Connection?*

THEISEN, CHARLES W., Assistant News Editor, *The Detroit News:* MICHIGAN

TORRES, IVETTE, Chief, Section of International Data, U.S. Bureau of Mines: STATISTICAL AND TABULAR DATA—*Mineral and Metal Production*

TURNER, ARTHUR CAMPBELL, Professor of Political Science, University of California, Riverside; Coauthor, *Ideology and Power in the Middle East:* BIOGRAPHY—*Yasir Arafat, Yitzhak Rabin;* IRAN; IRAQ; JORDAN; MIDDLE EAST; MIDDLE EAST—*The Israel-PLO Accord;* SYRIA

TURNER, CHARLES H., Freelance Writer, Honolulu: HAWAII

TURNER, DARRELL J., Freelance Religion Writer; Former Associate Editor, Religious News Service, New York, NY: CULTS IN AMERICA; RELIGION—*Far Eastern, Protestantism*

VAN RIPER, PAUL P., Professor Emeritus and Head, Department of Political Science, Texas A&M University; Editor and Coauthor, *The Wilson Influence on Public Administration:* POSTAL SERVICE

VAUGHAN, KRISTI, Freelance Writer: FAMILY

VOLL, JOHN O., Professor of History, University of New Hampshire; Author, *Islam: Continuity and Change in the Modern World;* Coauthor, *Sudan: Unity and Diversity in a Multicultural Society;* Editor, *Sudan: State and Society in Crisis:* SUDAN

VOLSKY, GEORGE, Center for Advanced International Studies, University of Miami: CUBA

WEATHERBEE, DONALD E., Department of Government, University of South Carolina: INDONESIA; THAILAND

WEAVER, JOHN B., Department of History, Sinclair Community College (Dayton, OH): OHIO

WEIKER, WALTER F., Professor of Political Science, Rutgers University: TURKEY

WELLER, MARC, Lecturer, University of Cambridge Research Centre for International Law; Coeditor, *The Kuwait Crisis, Volumes I and III:* LAW—*International*

WHELPLEY, KEITH, Writer, *Las Cruces Sun-News:* NEW MEXICO

WHITTEN, MITCH, Research Assistant, Monticello Research Department, Thomas Jefferson Memorial Foundation: UNITED STATES—*Thomas Jefferson's 250th Birthday*

WILLIAMS, C. FRED, Professor of History, University of Arkansas at Little Rock; Author, *Arkansas: An Illustrated History of the Land of Opportunity, Arkansas: A Documentary History:* ARKANSAS

WILLIS, F. ROY, Professor of History, University of California, Davis; Author, *France, Germany and the New Europe, 1945-1968, Italy Chooses Europe, The French Paradox:* EUROPE

WINCHESTER, BRIAN, Director, African Studies Program, Indiana University: AFRICA; ANGOLA; MOZAMBIQUE: SOUTH AFRICA

WISNER, ROBERT N., Professor, Iowa State University; Coeditor, *Marketing for Farmers;* Author, *World Food Trade and U.S. Agriculture:* AGRICULTURE; FOOD

WOLF, WILLIAM, New York University; Author, *The Marx Brothers, Landmark Films, The Cinema and Our Century:* MOTION PICTURES

WOLFE, JOHN, Freelance Advertising Writer: ADVERTISING

WORSNOP, RICHARD L., Associate Editor, *The CQ Researcher:* LAW—*Gay Rights in the United States*

YATES, ANNE, Freelance Writer and Translator; Author, *Leifur Eiriksson and Vinland the Good:* ICELAND

YOUNG, JUDITH C., Executive Director, National Association for Sports and Physical Education: EDUCATION—*Physical Education Today*

YOUNGER, R. M., Journalist and Author; Author, *Australia and the Australians, Australia! Australia! A Bicentennial Record:* AUSTRALIA

ZELENAK, MEL J., Department of Family/Consumer Economics, University of Missouri-Columbia: CONSUMER AFFAIRS; RETAILING; RETAILING—*Television Home Shopping*

Acknowledgments

We also wish to thank the following for their services: typesetting, color separations, electronic page composition, and file output, Gamma One, Inc.; text stock printed on Champion's 60# Courtland Matte; dust jacket and covers printed by Mid-City Lithographers; cover materials provided by Holliston Mills, Inc., Decorative Specialties International, and Ecological Fibers, Inc.; and printing and binding by R. R. Donnelley & Sons, Co.

Index

Main article headings appear in this index as bold-faced capitals; subjects within articles appear as lower-case entries. Both the general references and the subentries should be consulted for maximum usefulness of this index. Illustrations are indexed herein. Cross references are to the entries in this index.